W0246222

J.UCS

Annual Print and CD-ROM Archive Edition

Volume 1 • 1995

Springer
Berlin
Heidelberg
New York
Barcelona
Budapest
Hong Kong
London
Milan
Paris
Santa Clara
Singapore
Tokyo

Hermann Maurer • Cristian Calude
Arto Salomaa (Eds.)

J.UCS

The Journal of Universal Computer Science

Annual Print and CD-ROM Archive Edition
Volume 1 • 1995

Springer

Editors in Chief

Prof. Dr. Hermann Maurer
Technical University of Graz
Institutes for Information Processing
and Computer Supported Media (IICM)
Schiessstattgasse 4a
A-8010 Graz, Austria

Prof. Dr. Cristian Calude
Auckland University
Department of Computer Science
Auckland, New Zealand

Prof. Dr. Arto Salomaa
Data City
Turku Centre for Computer Studies
FIN-20 520 Turku, Finland

Die Deutsche Bibliothek - CIP Einheitsaufnahme:
The journal of universal computer science : J.UCS. - Berlin ; Heidelberg ; New York : Springer.
Vol. 1. 1995. - (1996)

ISBN-13:978-3-642-80352-9 e-ISBN-13:978-3-642-80350-5
DOI: 10.1007/978-3-642-80350-5

Softcover reprint of the hardcover 1st edition 1996

Cover design: Erich Kirchner, Springer-Verlag Heidelberg
SPIN 10554695 ISSN 0948-695x Printed on acid-free paper 45/3190 - 5 4 3 2 1 0

Editorial

It is a pleasure to present here the first printed volume of J.UCS, the Journal of Universal Computer Science, containing all papers published in 1995. This book complements the publication of the papers in twelve monthly issues during the year 1995 on the Internet, and also their appearance on a CD-ROM in May 1996: indeed, the CD-ROM is still available free of charge (as long as supplies last) by dropping me an email note.

With the first full year of J.UCS successfully behind us, and the second full year of J.UCS going strong, it is time to review some of the ideas behind J.UCS in a critical fashion. This is most easily done from a "historic" perspective.

It all started in late 1993 when Cris Calude from the University of Auckland, Arto Salomaa from the University of Turku, and myself from Graz University of Technology got together to discuss the plans for a journal dealing with computer science topics that would be primarily published via the Internet, or – more properly – via the then emerging WWW.

Although we were not the only ones to think about publishing a high quality journal via the WWW I believe we were the first ones to tackle the issue in a very substantive way based on a number of observations. It is interesting to review them and to see how they have developed.

(1) To achieve the aim of having a high quality electronic journal a reviewing process has to be carried out like that for any other journal with a substantial rejection rate to avoid publishing papers that were rejected elsewhere.
(2) However high the quality of an electronic journal might be, its prestige at critical junctures like appointment, tenure, and promotion procedures would be likely to remain below that of a refereed printed journal for some years to come. Hence the journal needs also to be published in printed form under an ISSN, and be dealt with like ordinary journals as far as abstracting and so on are concerned.
(3) We thus decided to go for a journal that would be published regularly in electronic form on the Internet (at the end of each month to get readers used to a certain rhythm of publication), but one that would also be published as complete volume on CD-ROM and in printed form in the same format and with identical page numbering. Thus, authors can refer to their paper as soon as it has appeared electronically as if the printed version already existed, since the format for referencing a publication including page numbering is fixed.
(4) We decided to involve a well-known scientific publisher in the project to assure visibility, marketing, production and distribution of the printed "archival" version, and general support. Springer-Verlag enthusiastically endorsed the J.UCS project from the very beginning: our thanks go to Springer for this, particulary to Arnoud de Kemp and Hans Wössner: concerning pricing and timing, a pilot issue was to be published as J.UCS 0,0 in fall 1994, followed with regular (monthly) issues starting in 1995. The electronic version of J.UCS would be free for the first two years 1995 and 1996, and would not exceed US$ 100 for single subscriptions from 1997 onward. The pricing for

the CD-ROM and printed version was initially left open. However, the 1995 CD-ROM is free of charge (it comes bundled with a catalogue of all Springer publications) and the price of the printed "archival" version has meanwhile been fixed at DM 298 for the first years.

(5) The ambitious name J.UCS (Journal of Universal Computer Science) was chosen to reflect the fact that unlike ordinary printed journals no page limit for papers or limit on number of papers per issue would have to be imposed since J.UCS was published primarily in electronic form. Thus, a restriction to specific areas would not be necessary, assuming we could recruit a board of professional editors in all areas of computer science for refereeing purposes. We believe that the board of current editors (see p. xv) proves that we have indeed been successful in this respect.

(6) Concerning the refereeing process we initially intended to send each paper to three selected editors for refereeing and to wait for answers for at most six weeks: as soon as two "accept as is" or "accept with minor changes" were obtained we would accept the paper. We had to reconsider this strategy very early for three main reasons:

   (i) Of the three editors selected by me (as managing editor) some or all would often refuse to referee a paper (or worse, not even react for months on end);
   (ii) The discrepancies between the reports obtained were often too substantial to allow acceptance of a paper even with two clear "accept": typically, the third referee who might have voted for a "reject" would be the only one knowing – by coincidence – that for example an almost identical version of the paper had already been accepted elsewhere.
   (iii) The English of some papers was just not acceptable, or papers showed extreme sloppiness. Editors (justifiably so) refused to do the proof-reading and reformulation in cases where this exceeded a certain amount.

   As a consequence, we have changed the refereeing process as follows. All editors obtain the abstracts of all papers submitted. Those editors willing to referee a paper within eight weeks send an email, and the first three obtain the paper for refereeing. If the English of a paper is totally unacceptable or the paper is very sloppy, editors send the paper back without full review: authors are then invited to resubmit their papers after careful polishing (or having a native English speaker help with the English).
   Further, papers with two "accept" are not automatically accepted but are reviewed once more if major points of criticism are voiced.

(7) An electronic journal needs a platform. The use of the WWW was clear, but the choice of system and of necessary features proved to be difficult:

   (i) It was desirable to have the capability to perform both "keyword" and "full text" searches in papers and particularly in defined subsets of all papers, e.g., in papers belonging to a certain subject category or published within a certain time period.
   (ii) WWW uses the text format HTML, which is known to be poor when it comes to the representation of formulas. Hence another or additional format for formula-intensive papers seemed necessary.
   (iii) It seemed important that the electronic and printed versions of J.UCS be as similar as possible, and that the CD-ROM version be easy to produce.

In the end, the logical choice seemed Hyper-G/HyperWave [Maurer 1996]: it supports attribute, keyword, and full-text searching within easily definable subsets of the database as required by (i), allows handling of documents both in HTML and PostScript (even with hyperlink features) in line with (ii), the electronic and printed PostScript versions are identical (and well suited for arbitrary documents), and CD-ROM production is easy.

However, over the past two years a number of weaknesses concerning both (i) and (ii) have become apparent that will be resolved in 1997. Thus, the decision to have a pilot issue J.UCS no. 0, vol. 0 (1994), and two complete volumes J.UCS vol. 1 (1995) and J.UCS vol. 2 (1996) proved to be correct, also for reasons discussed in point (8) below. For the curious reader, the weaknesses mentioned above are that PostScript does not so far allow full-text searches, that PostScript files are large and have to be downloaded even if only a single page of a paper is required; and despite recent improvments HTML is just impractical when it comes to very heavily formula-oriented papers. As a consequence, J.UCS will use PDF [Adobe 1993] as second format for all papers in 1997, and will not hold very formula-intensive papers in HTML format.

(8) It was our belief that a single server offering J.UCS worldwide would not be sufficient for two reasons: first, Internet connectivity is quite good regionally, but can be very bad (i.e., slow) between some locations; and second, if J.UCS proved to be a success, a single J.UCS server would eventually get drowned by requests. Thus, a mirroring scheme involving J.UCS servers in many places worldwide seemed the solution. However, we had to learn an important lesson in this connection: although many colleagues offered to run a J.UCS mirror server it was difficult to run a reliable server 24 hours a day, 7 days a week, as well as update the database once a month with substantial amounts of data. We will return to this point in (9). As a consequence, it turned out to be better to have only a few "official" mirror servers that are 99% reliable than to have many with poor reliability. Thus, although we still encourage universities to run a J.UCS mirror, we only offer four "official" sites at the moment (two each in Europe and in the USA) and only want to extend this moderately, just enough to offer good connectivity to everyone.

(9) Just about when J.UCS started to take on serious forms, and the papers for the pilot issue J.UCS 0,0 (1994) were collected, Odlyzko's famous paper on the demise of printed scientific journal publishing appeared [Odlyzko 1994]. Although we agree with Odlyzko on a number of issues, particularly that electronic publishing will take over more and more as far as scientific journals are concerned, we also disagree on one important issue: contrary to Odlyzko's views we still see the role of publishing companies as that of organizing, advertising, and holding journals on their servers, rather than just leaving this to well motivated scientists or others. Our friendly discussion on this has been going on for two years, and we would like to thank Odlyzko for his continuing support of J.UCS (even as one of the most active editors). The difficulty of running reliable mirror sites (with systems that restart automatically after a power failure, run regular back-ups, don't go down for hours or days when a hard drive crashes, guarantee archival of papers for many years, etc.) might indicate that indeed even just running a reliable server requires a professional organization like a publisher.

The number of electronic journals available on WWW has exploded since the start of J.UCS in 1994. However, few can boast of being as successful as J.UCS (and we are certainly not aware of one in computer science) from various points of view including quality, number of papers submitted and published, underlying technology, etc. Still, much remains to be done: in particular, publishing on the WWW, how to handle hyperlinks, and multimedia are issues that must not be ignored, and are indeed being addressed (see, e.g., [Maurer and Schmaranz 1995]).

At this point it is time to thank all who have helped to make J.UCS a success. Such thanks go to all readers, authors, editors, and the two other Editors-in-Chief Cris Calude and Arto Salomaa, who have guided me yet always left me enough freedom to maneuver and have not complained when I took suboptimal decisions. Thanks go to Springer and Odlyzko as mentioned earlier, but particularly to Klaus Schmaranz in Graz for his wonderful and never-ending technical support, and to his team of helpers including Michaela Gmeindl and Dana Kaiser.

I hope that I will be able to write a similarly positive report in a year's time! Now, please enjoy reading and do let me know of things you think can be improved.

H. Maurer
Managing Editor-in-Chief
Graz University of Technology
hmaurer@iicm.edu
http://www.iicm.edu/jucs

References

[**Adobe 1993**] Adobe Systems Inc.: "Portable Document Format reference manual"; Addison-Wesley (1993).

[**Maurer and Schmaranz 1995**] Maurer, H., Schmaranz, K.: "J.UCS and extensions as paradigms for electronic publishing"; Proc. DAGS '95, Birkhäuser, Boston (1995), 191–196.

[**Maurer 1996**] Maurer, H.: "HyperWave – The next generation Web solution"; Addison-Wesley, UK (1996).

[**Odlyzko 1994**] Odlyzko, A.: "Tragic loss or good riddance? The impending loss of traditional scholarly journals"; J.UCS, 0, 0 (1994), 3–53.

Contents

Editorial Board xv

Instructions for Authors xxiii

ACM Computing Reviews Classification System xxix

Issue 1

Managing Editor's Column 1

High-Radix Division with Approximate Quotient-Digit Estimation 2
P. Fenwick

On Implementing EREW Work-Optimally on Mesh of Trees 23
V. Leppänen

Levels of Anonymity 35
B. Flinn, H. Maurer

What is a Random String 48
C. Calude

Grammars Based on the Shuffle Operation 67
A. Salomaa, G. Rozenberg, G. Păun

Issue 2

Managing Editor's Column 83

A Scalable Architecture for Maintaining Referential Integrity
in Distributed Information Systems 84
F. Kappe

A Variant of Team Cooperation in Grammar Systems 105
R. Freund, G. Păun

On Four Classes of Lindenmayerian Power Series 131
J. Honkala, W. Kuich

The Relationship Between Propagation Characteristics
and Nonlinearity of Cryptographic Functions 136
J. Seberry, X. Zhang, Y. Zheng

On Completeness of Pseudosimple Sets 151
V. Bulitko

Issue 3

Managing Editor's Column 155

Combining Concept Mapping and Adaptive Advice
to Teach Reading Comprehension 156
P. Carlson, V. Larralde

Modular Range Reduction: a New Algorithm
for Fast and Accurate Computation of the Elementary Function 162
M. Daumas, C. Mazenc, X. Merrheim, J.-M. Muller

Special Cases of Division 176
R.W. Doran

Bringing ITS to the Marketplace: a Successful Experiment
in Minimalist Design 195
C. Gutwin, M. Jones, K. Adolphe, P. Brackett

Halting Probability Amplitude of Quantum Computers 201
K. Svozil

Issue 4

Managing Editor's Column 205

The Hyper-G Network Information System 206
K. Andrews, F. Kappe, H. Maurer

About WWW 221
R. Cailliau

Electronic Publishing 232
D. Götze

Evolution of Internet Gopher 235
M.P. McCahill, F.X. Anklesaria

WAIS and Information Retrieval on the Internet 247
H. Mülner

Issue 5

Managing Editor's Column 251

Conditional Tabled Eco-Grammar Systems Versus (E)TOL Systems . . . 252
E. Csuhaj-Varju, G. Păun, A. Salomaa

HOME: an Environment for Hypermedia Objects 269
E. Duval, H. Olivié, P. O'Hanlon, D. Jameson

Lexical Analysis with a Simple Finite-Fuzzy-Automaton Model 292
A. Mateescu, A. Salomaa, K. Salomaa, S. Yu

Software Patents and the Internet 312
J. Shearer, A. Vermeer

GAC – the Criterion for Global Avalanche Characteristics
of Cryptographic Functions 320
X. Zhang, Y. Zheng

Issue 6

Managing Editor's Column 338

A Translation of the Pi-Calculus into MONSTR 339
R. Banach, J. Balázs, G. Papadopoulos

Distributed Caching in Networked File Systems 399
A. Klauser, R. Posch

From Personal Computer to Personal Assistant 410
J. Lennon, A. Vermeer

Microworlds for Teaching Concepts
of Object Oriented Programming 423
I. Tomek

Issue 7

Managing Editor's Column 435

Introduction to the Special Issue "Real Numbers and Computers" 436
J.-C. Bajard, D. Michelucci, J.-M. Moreau., J.-M. Muller

A High Radix On-line Arithmetic
for Credible and Accurate Computing 439
T. Lynch, M. Schulte

Estimation of Round-off Errors on Several Computers Architectures . . . 454
J. Asserrhine, J. Chesneaux, J. Lamotte

Round-off Error Propagation in the Solution
of the Heat Equation by Finite Differences 469
F. Jézéquel

LCF: A Lexicographic Binary Representation of the Rationals 484
P. Kornerup, D. Matula

Exact Statistics and Continued Fractions 504
D. Lester

On Directed Interval Arithmetic and Its Applications 514
S. Markov

MSB-First Digit Serial Arithmetic 527
A. Nielsen, P. Kornerup

Some Algorithms Providing Rigorous Bounds
for the Eigenvalues of a Matrix 548
R. Pavec

On a Formally Correct Implementation
of IEEE Computer Arithmetic 560
E. Popova

Issue 8

Managing Editor's Column 570

BROCA: A Computerized Environment
for Mediating Scientific Reasoning Through Writing 571
P. Carlson

Differential Ziv-Lempel Text Compression 591
P. Fenwick

Bounds for Heights of Integer Polynomial Factors 603
L. Panaitopol, D. Stefănescu

A Robust Affine Matching Algorithm
Using an Exponentially Decreasing Distance Function 614
A. Pinz, M. Prantl, H. Ganster

Issue 9

Managing Editor's Column 632

An Efficient Distributed Algorithm for st-Numbering
the Vertices of a Biconnected Graph 633
R.F.M. Aranha, C. Pandu Rangan

A Decision Method for the Unambiguity of Sets
Defined by Number Systems 652
J. Honkala

A Method for Proving Theorems
in Differential Geometry and Mechanics 658
J. Wang

Issue 10

Managing Editor's Column 674

An Aperiodic Set of Wang Cubes 675
K. Culik II, J. Kari

Contained Hypermedia 687
E. Duval, H. Olivié, N. Scherbakov

Authoring on the Fly 706
T. Ottmann, C. Bacher

Issue 11

Managing Editor's Column 718

Digital Libraries as Learning and Teaching Support 719
H. Maurer, J. Lennon

Testing a High-Speed Data Path.
The Design of the RSAβ Crypto Chip 728
W. Mayerwieser, K.C. Posch, R. Posch, V. Schindler

A Comparison of WWW and Hyper-G 744
A. Pam, A. Vermeer

Issue 12

Managing Editor's Column 751

A Novel Type of Skeleton for Polygons 752
O. Aichholzer, D. Alberts, F. Aurenhammer, B. Gärtner

Constraint Agents for the Information Age 762
J.M. Andreoli, U.M. Borghoff, R. Pareschi, J.H. Schlichter

Parikh Prime Words and GO-like Territories 790
A. Mateescu, G. Păun, G. Rozenberg, A. Salomaa

Exploiting Parallelism in Constraint Satisfaction
for Qualitative Simulation 811
M. Platzner, B. Rinner, R. Weiss

A Markov Process for Sequential Allocation 821
C. Stefănescu

Author Index 829

Editorial Board

Note: Please note that the J.UCS editors listed below are also the main referees for papers submitted to J.UCS.

Instructions for Authors

1 Structure

1.1 Title

The title part of a paper consists of the title itself, capitalized, unnumbered and centered between the margins (by capitalized we mean that all words except for short connectives should start with a capital letter). Use a serif typeface (e.g. Times), 14 point, bold as font for the title. Leave 2 blank lines after it. Next come the authors, capitalized and centered between the margins, in the form First Name Second Name. Multiple authors should be delimited by a single blank line. Use a serif typeface (e.g. Times), 10 point. Every author is followed by his/her location and email address, centered between the margins. Use a serif typeface (e.g. Times), 9 point. Leave at least three blank lines after the last author. Please do not put any acknowledgements or thanks here, but place them in the optional Acknowledgement section at the end of the document.

Example:

The Knowledge of Special Formats

Aladin Claus Wonko
(University of Auckland, New Zealand
awonko@cs.aukuni.ac.nz)

Fojin Tsio
(Graz University of Technology, Austria
ftsio@iicm.tu-graz.ac.at)

1.2 Abstract

Start the abstract with the sequence "Abstract:" (without the quotes) in 9 point bold-face without a line break after "Abstract:". Since readers can just look at the abstract in a "browsing" mode, the Abstract is obligatory and should contain enough information about the text to decide whether accessing further parts of the document makes sense. (Note: we don't have superfast information highways everywhere yet.)

1.3 Key Words and Categories

Either a key words section or a categories section or both is necessary for the volume editor to decide to which categories the article belongs. For this purpose start a new line in the abstract and precede this line with either the sequence "Key Words:" or the sequence "Categories:" in 9 point bold-face. The categories must match the ACM Computing Reviews Classification System. A complete overview of the possible categories can be found in this printed version (p. xxix) and is also available electronically at `http://hyperg.iicm.edu/acm_ccs`. We prefer if you specify categories, since reviewers will be selected on that basis. If you use keywords only, the managing editor of J.UCS may erroneously assign the wrong reviewers, making the reviewing process less reliable and longer, and making it more difficult to locate papers in a certain area.

1.4 Text

The text part of an article contains structured text, divided into numbered sections (chapters), starting usually with "1 Introduction", that may be subdivided. Please use expressive section names.

1.5 Literature References

Start the literature references with the single numbered first level header "References" (see [2.1 Headings] below for a detailed description of the first level header format).

1.6 Acknowledgements

This is an optional section. Put every form of thanks and acknowledgements here. Start the acknowledgements section with the sequence "Acknowledgements" in 10 point bold-face, left justified, followed by a single blank line.

2 Typeface and Size

2.1 Headings

Use a typeface with serifs for all levels of headings. It is recommended to use Times or a similar typeface. Leave sufficient room for the title to stand out clearly. Leave 2 lines blank above and 1 line below the headings. If a heading is directly followed by a lower level heading the 2 blank lines before the lower level heading should be omitted. All headings should be capitalized (i.e. all words except for short connectives should have a capital initial). The title should be centered between the margins, all lower level headings should be left-justified.

Font sizes, numbering and styles for the different types of headings:

Title: unnumbered, centered, 14 point, bold
Example: **Computer Theory** (centered)

1st-level heading: single numbered, left-justified, 12 point, bold
Example: **1 Introduction**

2nd-level heading: double numbered, left-justified, 10 point, bold
Example: **2.2 Flow Charts**

3rd-level heading: triple numbered, left-justified, 10 point, bold
Example: **2.2.1 Nodes**

4th-level heading: quadruple numbered, left-justified, 10 point, italic
Example: *2.2.1.2 Input Nodes*

2.2 Running Text

Use a typeface with serifs for running text. It is recommended to use Times or a similar typeface.
Use 10-point type size and one line spacing for normal text and 9-point type size for small text (abstract, literature references and acknowledgements).
Use italic print to emphasize words. Note: bold type and underlining should be avoided. The text should always be justified to occupy the full line width, so that the right margin is not ragged.

2.3 Computer programs

For Computer programs both sans-serif and serif typefaces are allowed. Use 10-point type size and one line spacing.

3 Special Formats

3.1 Markups

Insert the sequence "[<see> Name <(>year<x><)>]" (without the quotes) into the running text for a markup to a literature reference. Name is the second name of the author and year is the year of printing. Also a markup to several authors is allowed. In this case the single authors must be delimited either by commas or the word "and". The phrase "et al." is also valid. The year can either be written in short form or in long form (i.e. 92 and 1992 are both valid entries) <x> is a possible lower case literal, if you refer to more than one article of an author of the same year. The word "see" and the brackets around the year are optional.

Example: ...this special form [see Wonko and Tsio 1999b] is very...
...as described in [Wonko (99a)]...
...and this algorithm [Tsio et al. 1999c] is used...

Insert the sequence "[<see> Fig. n]" (without the quotes) into the running text for a markup to a figure contained in the current document.

Insert the sequence "[<see> Tab. n]" (without the quotes) into the running text for a markup to a table contained in the current document.

When placing a markup to a chapter of the actual document use either the form [<see> Chapter n] or [<see> Section n] or refer to the section name by using the special sequence [<see><Section> n SectionName] or [<see><Chapter> n ChapterName].

Example: ...we will discuss this later in [Chapter 4].
...see [Section 4] for further details on...
...see [Chapter 4 Publishing] for further details on...
...chapter [4 Publishing] provides more information...

For a markup to a footnote use the form [<see> n], where n is the unique number of the footnote [see 3.4 Footnotes]. Please note that footnotes should only be used when unavoidable.

Please use exactly the format given here to allow us to insert Hypertext links automatically by searching for these special sequences. (Note: everything enclosed in '<' and '>' is optional.)

3.2 Literature References

Every Reference must start with the sequence "[Name <(>year<x><)>]" (without the quotes). Name and year must match the markup in the running text [see 3.1 Markups] to be able to automatically detect the matching markup-reference pairs. The single information fields of a Reference (Author1, Author2, Title...) should be divided by commas or semicolons. The brackets around the year are optional. Four examples for the different main types of documents should serve as a template:

– **referencing Books:**

[**Goll (99)**] Goll, J.: "The Guide to Hyper-G"; Springer, Heidelberg / New York (1999)

– **referencing Journals:**

[**Wonko and Tsio 99b**] Wonko, A. C., Tsio, F.: "Extended Use of Hyperlinks"; J.UCS (Journal for Universal Computer Science), 5, 3 (1999), 225-327.

The form 5, 3 (1999) indicates volume number 5, issue number 3, 1999. 225-327 indicates the page numbering.

– **referencing Proceedings:**

[**Tsio 99a**] Tsio, F.: "Hypermedia Systems"; Proc. Ed-MEDIA'99, AACE Publishing, Vancouver (1999), 115-123.

– **referencing Reports:**

[**Mollester, Goll 99c**] Mollester, K., Goll, J.: "Information Landscapes and their Advantages in Large Hypermedia Systems"; IIG Report 998, Graz, Austria (1999), also appeared as electronic version, anonymous FTP autnet.org, in publications/June-99-online.

3.2.1 Figures

Center the figures between the margins with one blank line above. Insert the text "Figure n: description" (without the quotes) after each Figure (n is a unique number that identifies the figure; description is a short description about the contents of Figure n. Please use an expressive description for your figures to allow finding them in a keyword search). Use a 10 point italic font for this text.

3.3 Tables

Center the tables between the margins with one blank line above. Insert the text "Table n: description" (without the quotes) after the table (n is a unique number that identifies the table; description is a short description about the contents of Table n. Please use an expressive description for your figures to allow finding them in a keyword search). Use a 10 point italic font for this text.

3.4 Footnotes

Separate footnotes from the preceding main text by a line from the left to the center of the page. Start the footnote with the sequence "[n]", where n is the unique number of that footnote (unique means, that this number can only appear once on a page, not throughout the whole document). Use a 9 point font for footnote text.

---

[1] As we mentioned earlier this is how to write footnotes.

4 Accepted File Formats

To provide an interface to a wide variety of wordprocessors we decided to accept PostScript as our main file format. However you can also submit articles as RTF, LaTeX or DVI files. Submitted files can be compressed using the following methods: compress, gzip, zip, arj, arc, pak, zoo, lzh.
You should not have problems generating a file in one of those formats, no matter which wordprocessor you are using. When submitting a file, please follow the rules given below, allowing us to be able to read and convert your article.

4.1 PostScript

You MUST include every font information in the PostScript output file to make sure that all the fonts are available for us when converting the document. Depending on the program you use for generating the PostScript file there is either a commandline switch for this purpose, or in the case you generate the file with a printer device driver there should be an option not to use built in printer fonts, but download all fonts instead.

MS-Windows Users: We tested all PS Printer Drivers available to us, and they all worked. But be careful when configuring your printer driver

- There MUST be a PS Header sent with the printing job.
- You MUST use the substitution table for fonts and and you MUST enter "download font" for every font used in the document.

DVIPS users: No problems were detected, the only thing is that you MUST NOT use the M option.

If you want to make sure that the document you submit is in the correct format, you may try, whether ghostscript (or ghostview) can correctly deal with it, since ghostscript is the kernel of our conversion software. Ghostscript is a PostScript Interpreter available on many ftp servers worldwide for various platforms including most of the UNIX derivates, MS-Windows, OS/2 and Windows NT. You may also submit a testfile (e.g. the first page of the paper) as email to JUCS@iicm.tu-graz.ac.at with the Subject [testfile]. We will test its compatibility to our conversion software and send you an email about the test result.

4.2 RTF

Please use common fonts found on most computers. Please do not use decorative typefaces.

4.3 LaTeX

If you use a special LaTeX style file, please submit it together with your article. We recommend to use our prepared style sheet for J.UCS that you can obtain by sending email to `JUCS@iicm.tu-graz.ac.at`, Subject: [latex].

4.4 DVI

Please use common fonts found on most computers. Please do not use decorative typefaces.

ACM Computing Reviews Classification System[1]

Category A - General Literature

A.0 General
A.1 Introductory and Survey
A.2 Reference
A.m Miscellaneous

Category B - Hardware

B.0 General
B.1 Control Structures and Microprogramming (D.3.2)
- **B.1.0** General
- **B.1.1** Control Design Styles
- **B.1.2** Control Structure Performance Analysis and Design
- **B.1.3** Control Structure Reliability, Testing, and Fault-Tolerance
- **B.1.4** Microprogram Design Aids (D.2.2, D.2.4, D.3.2, D.3.4)
- **B.1.5** Microcode Applications
- **B.1.m** Miscellaneous

B.2 Arithmetic and Logic Structures
- **B.2.0** General
- **B.2.1** Design Styles (C.1.1-2)
- **B.2.2** Performance Analysis and Design Aids
- **B.2.3** Reliability, Testing, and Fault-Tolerance
- **B.2.m** Miscellaneous

B.3 Memory Structures
- **B.3.0** General
- **B.3.1** Unassigned
- **B.3.2** Design Styles (D.4.2)
- **B.3.3** Performance Analysis and Design Aids (C.4)
- **B.3.4** Reliability, Testing, and Fault-Tolerance
- **B.3.m** Miscellaneous

B.4 Input/Output and Data Communications
- **B.4.0** General
- **B.4.1** Data Communications Devices
- **B.4.2** Input/Output Devices
- **B.4.3** Interconnections (subsystems)
- **B.4.4** Performance Analysis and Design Aids
- **B.4.5** Reliability, Testing, and Fault-Tolerance
- **B.4.m** Miscellaneous

---

[1] From Computing Reviews Vol. 36, No. 1, 1995.

B.5 Register-Transfer-Level Implementation
- **B.5.0** General
- **B.5.1** Design
- **B.5.2** Design Aids
- **B.5.3** Reliability and Testing
- **B.5.5** Miscellaneous

B.6 Logic Design
- **B.6.0** General
- **B.6.1** Design Styles
- **B.6.2** Reliability and Testing
- **B.6.3** Design Aids

B.7 Integrated Circuits
- **B.7.0** General
- **B.7.1** Types and Design Aids
- **B.7.2** Design Aids
- **B.7.3** Reliability and Testing
- **B.7.m** Miscellaneous

B.m Miscellaneous

Category C - Computer Systems Organisation

C.0 General

C.1 Processor Architectures
- **C.1.0** General
- **C.1.1** Single Data Stream Architectures
- **C.1.2** Multiple Data Stream Architectures (Multiprocessors)
- **C.1.3** Other Architecture Styles
- **C.1.m** Miscellaneous

C.2 Computer-Communication Networks
- **C.2.0** General
- **C.2.1** Network Architecture and Design
- **C.2.2** Network Protocols
- **C.2.3** Network Operations
- **C.2.4** Distributed Systems
- **C.2.5** Local Networks
- **C.2.m** Miscellaneous

C.3 Special-Purpose and Application-Based Systems (J.7)

C.4 Performance of Systems

C.5 Computer System Implementation
- **C.5.0** General
- **C.5.1** Large and Medium ("Mainframe") Computers
- **C.5.2** Minicomputers
- **C.5.3** Microcomputers
- **C.5.4** VLSI Systems
- **C.5.m** Miscellaneous

Category D - Software

D.0 General

D.1 Programming Techniques (E)

D.1.0 General
D.1.1 Applicative (functional) Programming
D.1.2 Automatic Programming (I.2.2)
D.1.3 Concurrent Programming
D.1.4 Sequential Programming
D.1.5 Object-Oriented Programming
D.1.6 Logic Programming
D.1.7 Visual programming
D.1.m Miscellaneous

D.2 Software Engineering (K.6.3)
D.2.0 General (K.5.1)
D.2.1 Requirements/Specifications (D.3.1)
D.2.2 Tools and Techniques
D.2.3 Coding
D.2.4 Program Verification (F.3.1)
D.2.5 Testing and Debugging
D.2.6 Programming Environments
D.2.7 Distribution and Maintenance
D.2.8 Metrics(D.4.8)
D.2.9 Management (K.6.3, K.6.4)
D.2.10 Design
D.2.m Miscellaneous

D.3 Programming Languages
D.3.0 General
D.3.1 Formal Definitions and Theory (D.2.1,F.3.1-2, F.4.2-3)
D.3.2 Language Classifications
D.3.3 Language Constructs and Features (E.2)
D.3.4 Processors
D.3.m Miscellaneous

D.4 Operating Systems (C)
D.4.0 General
D.4.1 Process Management
D.4.2 Storage Management
D.4.3 File Systems Management
D.4.4 Communications Management
D.4.5 Reliability
D.4.6 Security and protection (K.6.5)
D.4.7 Organization and Design
D.4.8 Performance (C.4, D.2.8,I.6)
D.4.9 Systems programs and Utilities
D.4.m Miscellaneous

Category E - Data

E.0 General
E.1 Data Structures
E.2 Data Storage Representations
E.3 Data Encryption
E.4 Coding and Information Theory (H.1.1)

E.5 Files (D.4.3, F.2.2, H.2)
E.m Miscellaneous

Category F - Theory of Computation

F.0 General
F.1 Computation by Abstract Devices
  F.1.0 General
  F.1.1 Models of Computation (F.4.1)
  F.1.2 Modes of Computation
  F.1.3 Complexity Classes (F.2)
  F.1.m Miscellaneous
F.2 Analysis of Algorithms and Problem Complexity (B.6-7, F.1.3)
  F.2.0 General
  F.2.1 Numerical Algorithms and Problems (G.1,G.4, I.1)
  F.2.2 Nonnumerical Algorithms and Problems (E.2-5, G.2, H.2-3)
  F.2.3 Tradeoffs Among Complexity Measures (F.1.3)
  F.2.m Miscellaneous
F.3 Logics and Meanings of Programs
  F.3.0 General
  F.3.1 Specifying and Verifying and Reasoning About Programs (D.2.1, D.2.4,D.3.1, E.1)
  F.3.2 Semantics of Programming Languages (D.3.1)
  F.3.3 Studies of Program Constructs (D.3.2-3)
  F.3.m Miscellaneous
F.4 Mathematical Logic and Formal Languages
  F.4.0 General
  F.4.1 Mathematical Logic (F.1.1, I.2.2-3)
  F.4.2 Grammars and Other Rewriting Systems (D.3.1)
  F.4.3 Formal Languages (D.3.1)
  F.4.m Miscellaneous
F.m Miscellaneous

Category G - Mathematics of Computing

G.0 General
G.1 Numerical Analysis
  G.1.0 General
  G.1.1 Interpolation
  G.1.2 Approximation
  G.1.3 Numerical Linear Algebra
  G.1.4 Quadrature and Numerical Differentiation
  G.1.5 Roots of Nonlinear Equations
  G.1.6 Optimization
  G.1.7 Ordinary Differential Equations
  G.1.8 Partial Differential Equations
  G.1.9 Integral Equations
  G.1.m Miscellaneous

G.2 Discrete Mathematics
- **G.2.0** General
- **G.2.1** Combinatorics (F.2.2)
- **G.2.2** Graph Theory (F.2.2)
- **G.2.m** Miscellaneous

G.3 Probability and Statistics
G.4 Mathematical Software
G.m Miscellaneous

Category H - Information Systems

H.0 General
H.1 Models and Principles
- **H.1.0** General
- **H.1.1** Systems and Information Theory (E.4)
- **H.1.2** User/Machine Systems
- **H.1.m** Miscellaneous

H.2 Database Management
- **H.2.0** General
- **H.2.1** Logical Design
- **H.2.2** Physical Design
- **H.2.3** Languages (D.3.2)
- **H.2.4** Systems
- **H.2.5** Heterogeneous Databases
- **H.2.6** Database Machines
- **H.2.7** Database Administration
- **H.2.8** Database Applications
- **H.2.m** Miscellaneous

H.3 Information Storage and Retrieval
- **H.3.0** General
- **H.3.1** Content Analysis and Indexing
- **H.3.2** Information Storage
- **H.3.3** Information Search and Retrieval
- **H.3.4** Systems and Software
- **H.3.5** Online Information Services
- **H.3.6** Library Automation
- **H.3.m** Miscellaneous

H.4 Information Systems Applications
- **H.4.0** General
- **H.4.1** Office automation (I.7)
- **H.4.2** Types of Systems
- **H.4.3** Communications Applications
- **H.4.m** Miscellaneous

H.5 Information Interfaces and Presentation (I.7)
- **H.5.0** General
- **H.5.1** Multimedia Information Systems
- **H.5.2** User Interfaces (D.2.2, H.1.2, I.3.6)
- **H.5.3** Group and Organization Interfaces

H.m Miscellaneous

Category I - Computing Methodologies

I.0 General
I.1 Algebraic Manipulation
- **I.1.0** General
- **I.1.1** Expressions and Their Representation (E.1-2)
- **I.1.2** Algorithms (F.2.1-2)
- **I.1.3** Languages and Systems (D.3.2-3, F.2.2)
- **I.1.4** Applications
- **I.1.m** Miscellaneous

I.2 Artificial Intelligence
- **I.2.0** General
- **I.2.1** Applications and Expert Systems (H.4, J)
- **I.2.2** Automatic Programming (D.1.2, F.3.1)
- **I.2.3** Deduction and Theorem Proving
- **I.2.4** Knowledge Representation Formalisms and Methods
- **I.2.5** Programming Languages and Software (D.3.2)
- **I.2.6** Learning (K.3.2)
- **I.2.7** Natural Language Processing
- **I.2.8** Problem Solving, Control Methods, and Search
- **I.2.9** Robotics
- **I.2.10** Vision and Scene Understanding (I.4.8, I.5)
- **I.2.11** Distributed Artificial Intelligence
- **I.2.m** Miscellaneous

I.3 Computer Graphics
- **I.3.0** General
- **I.3.1** Hardware Architecture (B.4.2)
- **I.3.2** Graphics Systems (C.2.1, C.2.4, C.3)
- **I.3.3** Picture/Image Generation
- **I.3.4** Graphics Utilities
- **I.3.5** Computational Geometry and Object Modelling
- **I.3.6** Methodology and Techniques
- **I.3.7** Three-dimensional Graphics and Realism
- **I.3.8** Applications
- **I.3.m** Miscellaneous

I.4 Image Processing
- **I.4.0** General
- **I.4.1** Digitization
- **I.4.2** Compression (Coding) (E.4)
- **I.4.3** Enhancement
- **I.4.4** Restoration
- **I.4.5** Reconstruction
- **I.4.6** Segmentation
- **I.4.7** Feature Measurement
- **I.4.8** Scene Analysis
- **I.4.9** Applications
- **I.4.10** Image Representation
- **I.4.m** Miscellaneous

- **I.5** Pattern Recognition
  - **I.5.0** General
  - **I.5.1** Models
  - **I.5.2** Design Methodology
  - **I.5.3** Clustering
  - **I.5.4** Applications
  - **I.5.5** Implementation (C.3)
  - **I.5.m** Miscellaneous
- **I.6** Simulation and Modeling (G.3)
  - **I.6.0** General
  - **I.6.1** Simulation Theory
  - **I.6.2** Simulation Languages
  - **I.6.3** Applications
  - **I.6.4** Model Validation and Analysis
  - **I.6.5** Model Development
  - **I.6.6** Simulation Output Analysis
  - **I.6.7** Simulation Support Systems
  - **I.6.8** Types of Simulation
  - **I.6.m** Miscellaneous
- **I.7** Text Processing (H.4-5)
  - **I.7.0** General
  - **I.7.1** Text Editing
  - **I.7.2** Document Preparation
  - **I.7.3** Index Generation
  - **I.7.m** Miscellaneous
- **I.m** Miscellaneous

Category J - Computer Applications

- **J.0** General
- **J.1** Administrative Data Processing
- **J.2** Physical Sciences and Engineering
- **J.3** Life and Medical Sciences
- **J.4** Social and Behavioral Sciences
- **J.5** Arts and Humanities
- **J.6** Computer-Aided Engineering
- **J.7** Computers in Other Systems (C.3)
- **J.m** Miscellaneous

Category K - Computing Milieux

- **K.0** General
- **K.1** The Computer Industry
- **K.2** History of Computing
- **K.3** Computers and Education
  - **K.3.0** General
  - **K.3.1** Computer Uses in Education
  - **K.3.2** Computer and Information Science Education
  - **K.3.m** Miscellaneous

K.4 Computers and Society
- **K.4.0** General
- **K.4.1** Public Policy Issues
- **K.4.2** Social Issues
- **K.4.3** Organizational Impacts
- **K.4.m** Miscellaneous

K.5 Legal Aspects of Computing
- **K.5.0** General
- **K.5.1** Software Protection
- **K.5.2** Government Issues
- **K.5.m** Miscellaneous

K.6 Management of Computing and Information Systems
- **K.6.0** General
- **K.6.1** Project and People Management
- **K.6.2** Installation Management
- **K.6.3** Software Management
- **K.6.4** Systems Management
- **K.6.5** Security and Protection (D.4.6, K.4.2)
- **K.6.m** Miscellaneous

K.7 The Computing Profession
- **K.7.0** General
- **K.7.1** Occupations
- **K.7.2** Organizations
- **K.7.3** Testing, Certification, and Licensing
- **K.7.m** Miscellaneous

K.8 Personal Computing
- **K.8.0** General
- **K.8.1** Application packages
- **K.8.2** Hardware
- **K.8.3** Management/Maintenance

K.m Miscellaneous

Managing Editor's Column

Dear Readers:

Here is the first "real" issue of J.UCS, the Journal of Universal Computer Science, J.UCS 1, 1 (1995).

It consists of 5 papers selected from 14 submitted ones on the basis of at least 2 positive referees' reports per paper. I hope you will enjoy the papers. It is good to see that the papers submitted cover a wide range of topics: from computer arithmetic (Fenwick), to algorithms on trees (Leppanen), to the problem of "semi-anonymity" in networks (Flinn et al.), to random strings (Calude), to the importance of shuffle operations (Paun et al.).

If you have any comments concerning J.UCS please let me know! Not that J.UCS is just the first of a number of journals that will appear in the same format, and hence cross-referenceable. Also a number of books will be incorporated in what we have started to call our electronic library.

Yours sincerely

Hermann Maurer, Managing Editor
Graz University of Technology,
Graz / Austria, January 28, 1995.
email: hmaurer@iicm.tu-graz.ac.at

P.S.: J.UCS 1, 2 (1995), the next issue, will appear February 28, 1995 on the server http://iicm.tu-graz.ac.at and will be distributed from there to other servers. Those servers that are both publicly accessible and currently active can be found in the public server list.

Journal of Universal Computer Science, vol. 1, no. 1 (1995), 2-22
submitted: 5/9/94, accepted: 21/12/94, appeared: 28/1/95

High-radix Division with Approximate Quotient-digit Estimation

Peter Fenwick
Department of Computer Science, The University of Auckland,
Private Bag 92019, Auckland, New Zealand
p_fenwick@cs.auckland.ac.nz

Abstract : High-radix division, developing several quotient bits per clock, is usually limited by the difficulty of generating accurate high-radix quotient digits. This paper describes techniques which allow quotient digits to be inaccurate, but then refine the result. We thereby obtain dividers with slightly reduced performance, but with much simplified logic. For example, a nominal radix-64 divider can generate an average of 4.5 to 5.5 quotient bits per cycle with quite simple digit estimation logic. The paper investigates the technique for radices of 8, 16, 64 and 256, including various qualities of digit estimation, and operation with restricted sets of divisor multiples.

Keywords : Division, high radix, approximate digit estimates

Category : B2

1. Introduction

Division has always been one of the more difficult of the fundamental operations in computers. Some very early computers omitted it altogether, even if they included multiplication, relying on one of the "multiplicative algorithms" mentioned later. (Many modern "super-computers" also follow this well-established historical precedent!) Division was often restricted to basic restoring or non-restoring methods which develop only one bit per cycle, even on computers where multiplication handled two or more bits per cycle.

There are several methods for achieving binary division which is faster than the simple non-restoring method.

1. The basic techniques of efficient digit-by-digit binary division, originally using multiples of {−1, 0, +1}, were established by [Robertson 1958] and [Tocher 1956], summarised by [MacSorley 1961] and analysed by [Freiman 1961], who introduced the term "SRT division". Robertson discusses Radix-4 SRT division and [Atkins 1970] extends the analysis to higher radix dividers (radices of 16, 64 and 256). [Wilson and Ledley 1961] describe division with shifting over 0s and 1s. A good discussion of these early methods is also given by [Flores 1963]. [Waser and Flynn 1982] describe these as "subtractive algorithms" because they are based on subtraction as the iterative operator.

2. The development of very fast combinational multipliers [Wallace 1964] renewed interest in the older multiplication-intensive methods based on Newton-Raphson or Taylor series approximations to the reciprocal of the divisor. In most cases these methods provide quadratic convergence to the final value, doubling the number of accurate digits at each iteration. ([Knuth 1969] (p244) presents a cubically convergent method which triples the accuracy at each step, but it requires more, less-convenient, arithmetic and is overall no faster than the simpler quadratic methods.) The repeated multiplications lead Waser and Flynn to describe these as "multiplicative algorithms".

3. Other, very significant, developments are in some sense a melding of the subtractive and multiplicative methods. The basic iteration is still subtractive, but combinational multipliers are included as components to form divisor multiples and, often, quotient digits. For example, "Byte Division", described by Waser and Flynn uses a ROM to estimate the divisor reciprocal which is then combined with the residue in a small combinational multiplier to estimate the quotient digit. With Booth recoding of the quotient digit a 4-input adder can form all 256 divisor multiples. Some improved methods of digit estimation are discussed by [Schwarz and Flynn 1993], and [Wong and Flynn 1992], who achieve speeds of at least 12 or 14 bits per iteration, and up to 53 bits per iteration. Following work by [Svoboda 1963], [Ercegovac, Lang and Montuschi 1993] have recently described a method based on pre-scaling the divisor and dividend which allows the development of 12 or more quotient bits per cycle. They again include multipliers as basic components. Thus while these are still essentially subtractive dividers, they use combinational multipliers to accomplish very high radix operation.

The work of this paper is in many ways a return to the traditional subtractive methods, but emphasises the combination of high-radix division (to minimise the time for a division) with relatively simple logic for quotient digit estimation (to minimise complexity and cost) and a minimal set of divisor multiples (again for complexity and cost). A unique feature is the trade-off between performance and complexity; without changing the basic design it is possible to reduce the available divisor multiples or the accuracy of the quotient digit estimation (or both) at the cost of only slightly slower division operation.

2. The Basic Principles of "Subtractive Division"

All of the subtractive methods depend on the relation below, as stated by [Atkins 1961]

$$p_{j+1} = r\, p_j - q_{j+1}\, d,$$

where $p_j =$ the residue used in the j-th cycle,
$p_0 =$ the initial dividend,
$p_m =$ the remainder, and
$q_j =$ the j-th quotient digit

We also have that
$r =$ the radix, eg 2, 4, 8, 16, ...
$d =$ the divisor, and
$m =$ the number of radix-r digits in the quotient

Verbally, we can note that we subtract a multiple (q_j) of the divisor from the residue and enter the same q_j as the corresponding quotient digit. By convention $0 \leq |q_j| < r$, this ensuring that a properly chosen value q_j will eliminate a digit of p_j and ensure that $|p_{j+1}| < |d|$ and p_{j+1} is in the range to allow the iteration to proceed. The crux of most division methods lies in generating the correct value of q_j so that the residue is properly reduced and the generated digit is accurate. For high radices this may require considerable logic; so much so that Waser and Flynn consider that SRT algorithms are unsuitable for any radix greater than 4.

[Knuth 1969] (p235) shows that for any radix r, estimating the quotient digit by taking the two most-significant residue digits divided by one most-significant divisor digit will give an error of at most 2 in the estimate; he includes a refinement which ensures that the digit is usually exact, may be in error by 1, and never has an error of 2. The refinement is, however relatively expensive to implement and he does not discuss the necessary hardware. (It does however have interesting connections with the more recent techniques for producing very accurate quotient estimates.)

[Atkins 1970] presents an extensive analysis of SRT division and its extension to higher radices. He discusses redundancy of the quotient representation (for example, 3 may be represented as either 2+1 or 4–1) and states that "With redundancy, the quotient digit ... need not be precise." Then from a detailed analysis of digit-estimation logic, he shows that the number of bits to be examined is at least

Residue bits $N_p = 2k+3$ or $2k+4$, and
Divisor bits $N_d = 2k+5$
where the radix r is $r = 2^{2k}$

Radix	Residue bits	Divisor bits
4	5	7
8	6	8
16	7	9
64	9	11
256	11	13

Table 1. Atkins' estimates of bits to be examined

For some typical radices, we find that the number of operand bits to be examined is as shown in [Tab. 1].

These results show that quotient estimation for high radix division is indeed a difficult process; even for radix 16 it is a function of at least 16 inputs. Atkins also discusses the problems of converting the quotient from the redundant code in which it is generated into the external binary form and states that a full-length quotient subtracter may be necessary. (This matter will considered later.)

A recent paper [Montuschi and Ciminiera 1994] considers the use of "over-redundant" digits, where the quotient digits may equal or exceed the division radix. In the present context their most important result is that the quotient-digit estimation logic may be simplified by allowing a wider range of quotient digits. Many of their comments (and the over-redundant digits) are germane to the present work, but here we also allow the quotient digits to be inaccurate.

3. The new approach

Underlying most of this paper is the observation that at any stage of the division with divisor d the "residue" p and "partial quotient" q represent a value $V = dq + p$. The value is unchanged if we put $V = d(q+\mu) + (p-\mu d) = dq' + p'$. In other words we can add *any* quantity μ to the quotient, provided that we also subtract μd from the residue. A quotient digit can be formed as a result of several operations with the same operand alignment; if the estimation logic gives a poor estimate of the quotient digit, we can "hold" that division cycle and correct or refine the estimate until the residue is within range for the next reduction.

The new method involves placing a small low-precision adder at the low-order end of the quotient so that new digits are *added* into the quotient rather than jammed in as is usual. We also allow unshifted arithmetic to refine the quotient digit estimate, effectively holding the division at a particular stage until its result is satisfactory. We can use any multiple which we like, or any convenient combination of multiples, in constructing each quotient digit. In particular we do not insist that the generated quotient digit will immediately reduce the residue to the correct range, but are prepared to accept a poor estimate and then repair the damage from that estimate. There are two consequences –

- The bits entered into the quotient do not have to be exact. Small errors can be corrected by carry propagation within the quotient adder, provided that the carry is absorbed within the length of the adder. The divisor multiple need be accurate enough only to allow the residue to be driven toward zero at each step. The resulting changes to the quotient will be referred to as "quotient adjustment".
- If the chosen multiple estimate leaves the residue too far from zero, it is possible to "hold" the division at a step and subtract another divisor multiple without

shifting. Thus if the logic estimated a multiple of 5 instead of the correct value of 6, a correction with a multiple of 1 will ensure the correct result. Carry propagation within the quotient adder will convert the initial estimate to the correct value. These will be referred to as "correction cycles".

Both aspects allow us to reduce the quality of quotient digit estimation without affecting the accuracy of the final result.

The second aspect is especially interesting. While it is relatively easy to provide logic which gives a good quotient estimate most of the time, it is much more difficult (and expensive) to generate an accurate value all of the time. (This complexity is evident from the results of Atkins, especially when compared with the look-up table sizes used here.) With a correction step available at any stage a bad estimate need not affect the final answer – it just requires a little longer to fix up. We can therefore trade off the complexity of the estimation logic against the overall division speed.

4. Limiting the quotient carry propagation.

An assumption of the present work is that the quotient has a short adder; a full-length quotient adder requires a considerable increase in logic complexity and should be avoided if possible. (This is exactly the situation discussed by Atkins and mentioned above in converting from redundantly-represented quotient digits.)

For a positive divisor, excessive quotient carry arises when the residue becomes negative after a subtraction and remains negative for a while thereafter. With conventional non-restoring division, the negative value will force a 0 quotient bit to be entered (from an "unsuccessful" subtraction). By comparison, the algorithm as described enters the multiple which was used (and was too large) and relies on a later negative digit to correct for the overdraw. If there is only a slight overdraw, the residue stays close to zero for several steps while zero quotient digits are generated and the carry must eventually propagate through all of these zero digits.

To minimise the quotient carry propagation, we monitor the sign of the result and, if it is negative, enter as a quotient digit the (*multiple–1*) and set a "`Qcarry`" flag; this is analogous to the action of simple non-restoring division. `Qcarry` is shifted in parallel with the quotient and added in on the next cycle. Thus we subtract 1 from the quotient, but add it back on the next cycle. The operation is similar during a correction cycle, except that the 1 is added directly into the quotient, without any shift.

To illustrate, consider a radix-8 divider where the residue goes just negative from a multiple of 6 and stays negative with no arithmetic (0 digit) for several cycles before being corrected with a –2 multiple.

Assuming that the simple algorithm generates the quotient digit sequence

{ 6 0 0 -2}, the generated quotient bits are { 110 000 000 } before the last digit and become the correct value { 101 111 111 110 } after the –2 multiple is added, but only after the carry propagates through 8 bits of the previous quotient.

With the Qcarry flag, we recognise the overdraw and enter an initial 5 instead of 6; this digit is now correct. On the next two cycles the generated digit of 0 is converted to –1 because of the negative residue, but the shifted Qcarry corresponds to an addition of 8, so the entered digit is 7 or bit pattern 111. We enter the correct quotient digit at each stage, avoiding lengthy carry propagation.

We may note that the Qcarry is in fact redundant, being identical to the residue sign. It is however convenient to regard it as a separate entity connected with the quotient rather than the residue. The carry from the main adder "wraps-round" into the quotient adder.

5. The complete division algorithm.

The final algorithm is shown in [Fig. 1], written in C but with some conditions in descriptive rather than explicit form. The function estDigit produces a suitable quotient digit estimate by some means (in the tests by a table lookup), including operations such as the limitation to "complex multiples" as described in [Section 11]. This program, and indeed all of the work in the paper, assumes a positive divisor.

```
while (dividing)
  {
  Residue <<= BitsPerDigit;              /* align residue */
  Qdigit = estDigit(Residue, Divisor); /* estimate quot. digit */
  Residue -=  Qdigit * Divisor;          /* adjust residue */
  Quotient =
    ((Quotient + Qcarry) << BitsPerDigit) + Qdigit;
  Qcarry = (Residue < 0);                /* to stop long carries */
  Quotient -= Qcarry;                    /* and adjust quotient */

  while (Residue_out_of_range)           /* correction cycles */
    {
    Qdigit = estDigit(Residue, Divisor);  /* est. quot. digit */
    Residue -= Qdigit * Divisor;          /* adjust residue */
    Quotient += Qdigit + Qcarry;          /* adjust quotient */
    Qcarry = (Residue < 0);
    Quotient -= Qcarry;
    }
  } /* end main divide loop */

if (Qcarry > 0) Quotient++;           /* assimilate quotient carry */
while (Residue < 0)                   /* correction if -ve residue */
  { Residue += Divisor; Quotient--; }
```

Figure 1. The basic division program

The first four lines of the main loop are essentially a standard high-radix division and are followed by two lines to control the quotient carry propagation. An inner loop handles the case of the residue being not reduced correctly, using code which is very similar to the main division code but without operand shifts. Finally, after the main loop is complete, we must assimilate any pending `Qcarry` and correct for a residue of the wrong sign.

A point which is not stated is that digit estimation in the inner, correction, loop must never give a zero digit because this loop must *always* change the residue; the digit must be forced to +1 or –1 depending on the sign of the residue.

6. The Hardware

The basic divider hardware is shown in [Fig. 2]. The differences from conventional division hardware are in the presence of the quotient adder and in the ability to operate in an unshifted mode during division. The quotient is shown with two paths from the quotient register, one shifted and one unshifted; the same applies to the residue register and main adder. Two shifts are wired into the residue and quotient logic; a shift of 3, 4, etc bits which determines the nominal radix of the operation and a zero shift which is used during correction cycles.

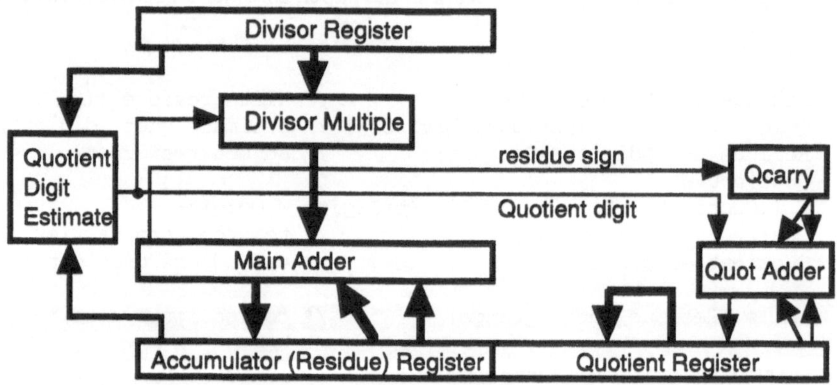

Figure 2. Divider Hardware

In many cases the "divisor multiple" logic is limited to a 2-input adder/subtracter with shifters at each input up to the width of a quotient digit.

7. Simple, radix-8, division

The proposed algorithm was simulated by program using 32-bit integers and 64-bit long integers to provide a basic operand precision of 24 bits (48 bit dividend). In all cases the high-order bits of the divisor and residue are used to index a pre-computed table which yields the estimated multiple. The divisor is assumed normalised with its most-significant bit always 1. The initial tests are with radix-8 division (3 bits per cycle). The test cases were –

- A 7×7 table (7 residue bits and 7 divisor bits), which is similar in size to what Atkins predicts is needed for radix-8 division
- Three smaller sizes (6×6, 5×5, 4×4), the larger two of which are "nearly good enough" for conventional division. The last is intended as a test of an economical estimation table.
- A table which examines only 3 residue bits and 3 divisor bits (just two significant divisor bits). This was tested as a minimal table which is easily implemented in combinational logic.

All cases were tested by a sequence of 100,000 divisions (the same sequence in all cases) counting the total add/subtract operations or cycles, the number of times that an earlier quotient was adjusted, and the number of additional correction cycles needed. With 8 octal digits to be developed for each 24-bit test operand, there are 8 "basic operations" for each test case, or 800,000 operations within each test.

The results are shown in [Tab. 2]. Each column heading shows first the radix and then the residue and divisor bits used to estimate the quotient digit for that test. The same heading convention will be followed for all of the results tables.

	8 : 7x7	8 : 6x6	8 : 5x5	8 : 4x4	8 : 3x3
basic operations	800,000	800,000	800,000	800,000	800,000
quot. adjustments	0	0	0	1,292	9,412
adjustments (%)	0	0	0	0.158	1.085
correction cycles	0	19	699	16,395	66,862
corrections (%)	0	0.002	0.087	2.049	8.357
bits per cycle	3.000	3.000	2.997	2.940	2.769
performance	1.000	1.000	0.999	0.980	0.923
Quotient carry distance	0	1	2	6	6

Table 2. Radix-8 division, with varying look-up table sizes.

Small errors in the digit estimation show up in the "quotient adjustments" which refine the prior quotient, but do not affect the residue or the speed. Larger errors manifest themselves as "correction cycles" which modify the existing quotient and residue, and do slow the operation. In this table, the "quotient adjustments" count only the adjustments which affect more than the least-significant quotient digit; we may expect every correction to alter this digit but count only those which spill into more significant digits. In no case does the quotient carry propagate over more than 2 digits (6 bits).

Whereas the largest, 7×7, table is able to predict a correct digit every time, the 6x6 table is inadequate by normal standards because it gives a few estimates which require correction. Even so it delivers a performance almost identical to the larger table (actually 2.99993 bits per cycle). The 5×5 and 4×4 tables are even less acceptable by normal criteria, with error rates of 0.1% and 2%, but here they still give performance within 0.1% and 2% of the optimal 3 bits per cycle. Even the minimal 3x3 table still yields the correct quotient digit 92% of the time and needs a correction cycle on only 8% of the steps, yielding nearly 2.77 bits per cycle.

Comparative results for different radices are given later in [Fig. 3] (showing bits per cycle) and in [Fig. 4] (showing relative performance). These figures include all of the significant and useful cases to be discussed and should be consulted for quick comparisons.

8. Effect of table aspect ratio

Although Knuth implies that it is better to examine more residue digits than divisor digits, Atkins shows in his analysis that it is desirable to examine about the same number of bits from each value, or perhaps a few more bits from the divisor. We next examine the effect of trading off residue bits against divisor bits, in all cases keeping constant the total number of tested bits. The results of [Tab. 3] are for the "5x5" table of the previous section, but similar results were obtained for other configurations.

For the present situation, where we are concerned only with obtaining a good estimate rather than the accurate value, it seems best to consider about the same number of bits from the two operands. Where the total number of bits is odd, the extra bit should be allocated to the residue. Results for the rest of the paper will mostly assume a "square" table, without further justification.

	8 : 6x4	8 : 5x5	8 : 4x6
basic operations	800,000	800,000	800,000
quot. adjustments	132	0	0
adjustments (%)	0.016	0	0
correction cycles	6,844	699	5,486
corrections (%)	0.856	0.087	0.685
bits per cycle	2.975	2.997	2.980
performance	0.992	0.999	0.993
Quotient carry distance	6	2	3

Table 3. Radix-8 division, varying table aspect ratio.

9. Radix-16 division (4 bits per cycle)

We repeat the above work for radix-16 division. Again, it is not difficult to get close to the ideal performance of 4 quotient bits per cycle. We now show four look-up tables, examining 7, 6, 5 and 4 bits of the residue and divisor. Atkins requires a 7×9 table for radix 16, which is larger than even the largest of the tables used here. The change in radix reduces the number of "basic operations" to 600,000, (6 digits for a 24 bit operand) compared with 800,000 for radix-8 operation (8 digits for 24 bits).

Once again the larger tables give very nearly the maximum performance, with the 5×5 table within 1.5% of the ideal and even the 4×4 table (which considers only a single digit of each operand) only 8% off the possible speed. Quotient adjustments are again needed for the smaller tables, but even the smallest table never modifies more than 8 quotient bits (the current digit and its predecessor).

	16 : 7x7	16 : 6x6	16 : 5x5	16 : 4x4
basic operations	600,000	600,000	600,000	600,000
quot. adjustments	0	0	250	2,854
adjustments (%)	0	0	0.041	0.442
correction cycles	57	615	8,489	46,507
corrections (%)	0.009	0.102	1.415	7.751
bits per cycle	4.000	3.996	3.944	3.712
performance	1.000	0.999	0.986	0.928
Quotient carry distance	1	3	7	8

Table 4. Radix-16 division, with varying look-up table sizes.

10. Radix-64 and radix-256 dividers

For division with higher radices, we initially assume that all multiples are available and observe the effect of only the reduced digit-estimation logic. Actually not much extra hardware is needed to handle radix-64 and even radix-256 division – we certainly do not need an adder input for each possible power of two. By using Booth recoding of the quotient digit we can handle radix-64 with a 3-input adder for the divisor multiples and radix-256 with a 4-input adder. Later we reduce the range of multiples to allow simplified divisor-multiple generation logic. We retain the earlier sizes of look-up table as covering a reasonable range of practical sizes.

Although we assume the full range of divisor multiples for radix-64, we retain estimation logic which is quite small compared with Atkins' predictions (9×11 for radix 64). Particularly in the first two cases, 7×7 and 6×6 tables, we see from [Tab. 5] that the new algorithm largely absorbs any deficiencies of the digit estimation. The performance deteriorates markedly for the 5×5 and 4×4 tables, to the point where these are probably not worth considering, in comparison with the restricted cases later.

	64 : 7x7	64 : 6x6	64 : 5x5	64 : 4x4
basic operations	400,000	400,000	400,000	400,000
quot. adjustments	6	490	1746	0
adjustments (%)	0	0.114	0.330	0
correction cycles	3,492	29,744	128,667	382,634
corrections (%)	0.873	7.436	32.167	95.659
bits per cycle	5.948	5.585	4.540	3.067
performance	0.991	0.931	0.757	0.511
Quotient carry distance	9	12	11	6

Table 5. Radix-64 division – full multiples.

Repeating the exercise for radix-256, we obtain the results of [Tab. 6]. The relatively poor quality of the digit estimates is even more noticeable here, but even so by examining just a single digit (8 bits) of the residue and divisor we achieve nearly 7.5 bits per cycle.

	256 : 8x8	256 : 8x7	256 : 7x7	256 : 6x6	256 : 5x5
basic operations	300,000	300,000	300,000	300,000	300,000
quot. adjustments	64	558	276	0	0
adjustments (%)	0.019	0.157	0.071	0	0
correction cycles	20,247	56,402	90,815	288,049	882,365
corrections (%)	6.749	18.80	30.27	96.02	294.1
bits per cycle	7.494	6.734	6.141	4.081	2.030
performance	0.937	0.842	0.768	0.510	0.254
Quotient carry distance	13	16	14	8	8

Table 6. Radix-256 division – full multiples.

By comparing this table with the previous one, we see that the performance is largely determined by the unexamined bits of the most-significant digit. Thus examining a complete digit (6 or 8 bits respectively for radix-64 and radix-256) gives about 93% of the ideal performance, one bit less (5 or 7 bits) gives 75% and 2 bits less 51%. Nevertheless, it is interesting that reasonable performance is still possible if the estimation logic examines only part of the most-significant digits of the residue and divisor. As a more general observation, the algorithm is robust with respect to changes in the digit prediction logic. A poor prediction does not impair the final result, but may delay achieving that result.

Practically though, it is clear that operation with a radix of 256 is not really satisfactory, at least with the size of look-up table which is used. With a 7×7 table, the performance is very little better than that of a radix-64 divider (6.14 bits, compared with 5.95). The benefit of the higher radix barely offsets the penalty of examining partial digits.

11. Division with few multiples available.

Divisor multiples can be divided into 3 categories –

- "Shifted values", available by just shifting left the raw value (1, 2, 4, 8, ...),
- "Simple multiples", being the sum or difference of pairs of shifted values (3, 5, 6, 7, 9, ...),
- "Complex multiples", which require the combination of 3 or more shifted values (11, 13, ...).

In this section we examine the performance if the only available multiples are the "shifted values" and the "simple multiples". We assume that a "large" shift is available (e g 6 places for radix-64). The initial operation on the shifted residue will be followed in many cases by "corrections" on the unshifted residue as we simulate the more difficult multiples or quotient digits.

	16 7x7	16 6x6	16 5x5	16 4x4
basic operations	600,000	600,000	600,000	600,000
quot. adjustments	0	0	174	4,124
adjustments (%)	0	0	0.027	0.604
correction cycles	22,151	22,725	34,207	82,868
corrections (%)	3.692	3.788	5.701	13.811
bits per cycle	3.858	3.854	3.784	3.515
performance	0.964	0.964	0.946	0.879
Quotient carry distance	2	2	5	8

Table 7. Radix-16 division, with limitation to "simple" multiples.

Initially we examine radix-16, even though a 2-input adder is adequate to form all of the multiples with Booth recoding of the quotient digits. The estimation tables do not use Booth recoding but are just recoded versions of the previous ones with, for example, 11 being rounded to 10 or 12.

As expected, there is some performance degradation as compared with the previous case where all multiples were assumed to be available. However even the simplest case still delivers over 3.5 bits per cycle. The speed is better than we would expect from noting that $^1/_8$ of the multiples are unavailable and must be simulated; about half of these cases are just absorbed into the general operation and do not require explicit correction cycles.

For higher radices it is especially useful to avoid a complete suite of divisor multiples. We still restrict ourselves to simple multiples of the form $2^i \pm 2^j$.

	64 : 7x7	64 : 6x6	64 : 5x5	64 : 4x4
basic operations	400,000	400,000	400,000	400,000
quot. adjustments	10	736	1,482	0
adjustments (%)	0.002	0.143	0.250	0
correction cycles	91,476	116,488	193,466	412,402
corrections (%)	22.87	29.12	48.37	103.1
bits per cycle	4.883	4.647	4.044	2.954
performance	0.814	0.775	0.674	0.492
Quotient carry distance	6	12	11	6
single corrections	91,448	111,560	140,974	147,143
double corrections	14	2,464	26,246	85,618
> double corrections	0	0	0	30,116

Table 8. Radix-64 division, with limitation to "simple" multiples.

	256 : 8x8	256 : 7x7	256 : 6x6
basic operations	300,000	300,000	300,000
quot. adjustments	74	128	0
adjustments (%)	0.015	0.023	0
correction cycles	187,415	245,222	399,179
corrections (%)	62.47	81.74	133.1
bits per cycle	4.924	4.402	3.433
performance	0.616	0.550	0.429
Quotient carry distance	9	9	8
single corrections	173,975	152,214	112,568
double corrections	6,810	46,360	85,170
> double corrections	0	96	36,544

Table 9. Radix-256 division, with limitation to "simple" multiples.

The results in [Tab. 8] and [Tab. 9] are extended to show details of the corrections. Radix-64 division is quite successful, generating an average of nearly 5 bits per cycle with either of the two larger tables. However the smallest table (4×4) is actually inferior to radix-16 with the same table size. The radix-256 results are inferior to the radix-64 results, showing the effect of having relatively fewer multiples available and having to rely much more on correction cycles.

With radix-16, restricted multiples cover $^7/_8$ or 87.5% of the total range of multiples. With radix-64 only 33 multiples are available (51.6% coverage), but only a single correction cycle is ever needed in most cases. Radix-256 uses 58 multiples (22.6%) and the sparse coverage requires many more correction cycles even with the larger tables. (Both radix-64 and radix-256 actually use occasional multiples of 66, 68, 258 and 260, which are available without penalty or extra hardware given that 64 and 256 are provided.) While radix-64 operation is acceptable, there is clearly no benefit in using this method for a radix-256 divider.

12. The effect of using only "shifted values" as multiples

As an extreme restriction on the available multiples, we can restrict them to just powers of 2 (those which are available by shifting). We retain the original style of lookup tables, even though they are clearly inappropriate in this case; we should be able to achieve comparable performance with much simpler quotient estimation.

	64 : 7x7	64 : 6x6	64 : 5x5	256 :7x7
basic operations	400,000	400,000	400,000	300,000
quot. adjustments	0	0	0	0
adjustments (%)	0	0	0	0
corrections	407,228	428,667	484,162	554,306
corrections (%)	101.8	107.2	121.0	184.8
bits per cycle	2.973	2.896	2.714	2.809
performance	0.496	0.483	0.452	0.351
Quotient carry distance	5	5	5	9

Table 10. Radix-64 and radix-256 division, limited to power-of-2 multiples.

The division should tend to be equivalent to a variable shift length algorithm, with multiples of ± 1, shifting over strings of 0s and 1s. Variable shift algorithms are known to have an asymptotic performance of about 3 bits per cycle (2.5 – 3.5, see [Flores 1963]), a performance which is confirmed here in [Tab. 10]. As for the previous high radix operations, the performance is better for a radix of 64 than for 256.

13. Graphical summary of results

In [Fig. 3] and [Fig. 4] we show the performance results for the various radices and sizes of look-up table. Figure 3 shows the average quotient bits delivered per cycle, while Figure 4 shows the performance for each radix, with 100% being N bits/cycle for a radix of 2^N. Results are shown for only the more realistic cases of "full multiples" and "restricted multiples". Results for corrections and quotient adjustments are not presented; they are essentially internal or intermediary phenomena whose consequences are apparent in the final performance.

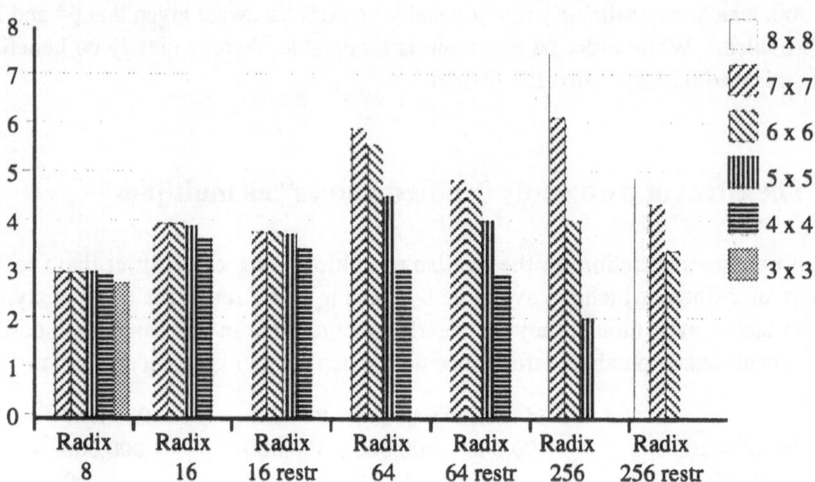

Figure 3. Average bits/cycle, for different radices and table sizes

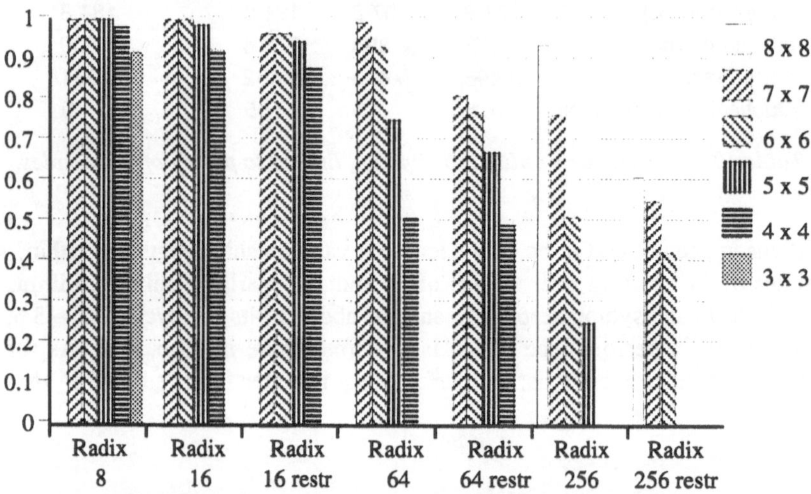

Figure 4. Relative performance, for different radices and table sizes

The graphs show quite clearly that a table should work with about 1 digit for each input; a 6×6 table for example gives negligible benefit on a radix-16 divider, but with radix-256 gives fewer bits per cycle than with radix-64. This will be mentioned again later, in connection with some other recent work.

14. Generation of the quotient digits

The present paper has generated quotient digits only from look up tables addressed by the high order digits of the residue and divisor. This technique might not be the best one and in that regard the current work should be regarded more as a feasibility study of the new technique.

The usual problem in division is that the critical path consists of the generation of the quotient digit, then the generation of the corresponding divisor multiple and finally the addition/subtraction, in other words all of the difficult operations! [Montuschi and Ciminiera 1994] point out indeed that many methods of "improving" division really do little more than move the dominant delay around the critical path! Nevertheless there are several ways of accelerating the digit estimation.

1. The "divisor pre-scaling" methods of [Ercegovac, Lang and Montuschi 1993] and [Svoboda 1963] trivialise the generation of the quotient digit, but at the cost of preliminary arithmetic to get the divisor into a suitable form. With a normalised divisor, they subtract appropriately shifted multiples of the divisor from itself to produce a divisor of the form $1 + \varepsilon$, where $\varepsilon r < 1$. At the same time they apply similar transformations to the dividend; effectively they multiply the divisor and dividend by the same factor, leaving the quotient unchanged. With the divisor of that form, the high order digits of the residue are precisely the desired quotient digit. Without recoding the divisor digits we may expect $(\log_2 r)/2$ iterations to reduce the divisor and the same number of parallel operations to transform the dividend, giving a total of $\log_2 r$ preliminary operations. The cost of these operations would have to be offset against the reduction in the cycle time from the improvement in the time to generate quotient digits. A problem is that it does not yield a remainder.

2. [Wong and Flynn 1992] present quotient digit logic which operates in parallel with the other operations and allows much more overlap and correspondingly higher speed. Their logic does however assume the correctness of the previous quotient digit, using that digit as part of the input for the current estimate. The complexities of handling an approximate previous digit may make their full method unwieldy in this case. However, the essence of the method, which derives the actual logical functions of the quotient bits as explicit functions of the other bits, may still be appropriate.

3. The quotient digit may be estimated from the difference of the logarithms of the divisor and residue (or their high order bits). Although this will still require look-up tables or equivalent logic to produce the logarithms, the table sizes are now $O(r)$, rather than $O(r^2)$. Conversion from the difference back to the actual digit estimate will require logic of similar scale to produce the antilog. Depending upon the logic family, the complex of 3 small tables (or equivalent) will certainly be simpler and may be faster than the single large lookup table. Note that we do not require wholly accurate digit estimates.

   Operation with logarithms has been tested and verified, with similar results to the direct table lookup. The logarithm, if in base 2, needs as many fractional bits as there are bits in the radix, and $\log_2(radix)$ integral bits. Thus radix-16 requires a logarithm of the form *xx.xxxx*, and radix-256 of the form *xxx.xxxxxxxx*. The detailed results are slightly different from those for the direct look-up tables, even though the formulae are nominally equivalent. In some cases there is a slight degradation in performance but many cases improve by 1 – 2%. This demonstrates both the robustness of the algorithm with respect to slight changes in the digit estimates and the possibility of improving the performance in particular cases by fine tuning the digit estimation.

4. An interesting possibility, which has not been investigated, might be to use hybrid analogue/digital techniques in the quotient digit estimation. Similar methods have been used in a recent adder design [Kawahito et al 1994]. The essential point is that the algorithms described here can accommodate poor quotient digit estimates without undue penalty. If hybrid techniques can achieve useful simplification while delivering reasonably good estimates, they could be worth consideration.

It is not easy to predict which is the best method. Most of the table-lookup methods insert extra delay into the division cycle and slow down every cycle; they may be better if there is spare time in each cycle. The prescaling methods however allow faster cycles within the division proper, but require additional steps for the preliminary adjustments and may be better where the system clock matches the critical path delay within the division logic.

15. Other recent work

A very recent paper (published since this paper was submitted) presents some very similar techniques [Cortadella and Lang, 1994]. A comparison of the two methods is conveniently presented as a series of points (with references to "this paper" and "their paper" having the obvious meanings).

- Even though the techniques are similar, the underlying philosophies are different. This paper works in terms of an approximation to the exact quotient digit, with possible refinements to that estimate. Their paper emphasises the speculative nature of the digit estimation, with options such withdrawing the estimation completely or accepting only some of the estimated bits.

- This paper always develops a fixed number of bits, perhaps taking several cycles to achieve an accurate digit. Their paper however allows a "partial advance" to develop fewer bits on some cycles, accepting only as many quotient bits as are known to be accurate. Thus both approaches may develop fewer than the nominal bits per cycle, but in different ways. (Their "basic scheme", without partial advance, is similar to the ideas of this paper.)

- This paper places considerable emphasis on developing the quotient by adding in each new digit. Although perhaps not really apparent from this paper, this was the original idea which led to the work, but had to be supplemented by allowing some digits to require several cycles. Their paper acknowledges a quotient adjustment by ± 1, but does not explore the consequences of possible quotient carry propagation.

- Their paper goes to some trouble to develop a good "speculation function" equivalent to the "estimation tables" used in this paper. This paper (while assuming look-up tables for quotient-digit estimation) provides a much more comprehensive treatment of the effects of varying the table size and therefore the accuracy of the quotient digit.

- One of their optimisation options is to reduce the number of outputs from the speculation function. This parallels exactly the use of the "simple multiples" in this paper.

- Their paper has much more detail concerning the hardware consequences, costs and physical aspects of their design.

- Their results on there being an optimal complexity of the digit-estimation logic are supported by the results here which show, for example, a 6×6 table giving its best performance with radix-64 division.

- Both papers rely very heavily on computer simulations of algorithms which are largely unpredictable in internal details, even though the final result is very well determined.

The two papers present different approaches to the same problem, both illustrating that high-radix division does not require exact high precision quotient-digit estimates.

16. Conclusions

We have shown that it is possible to obtain satisfactory high-radix division, even when the division process is subject to one or two significant restrictions –

1. *Limited precision digit estimation.* By allowing the quotient logic to assimilate corrections from later digits, and by allowing an occasional "hold" of the division process, it is possible to estimate quotient digits to quite low precision. The corrections are needed in relatively few cases and lead to quite small performance degradation except for extremely simple estimation logic. For example, a divider which examines just a single digit of the residue and divisor (i e 3 or 4 bits of each) can average over 2.75 bits per cycle for radix-8 division and 3.7 bits per cycle for radix-16 division.

2. *Limited divisor multiples.* High radix division is expensive in its logic to

estimate quotient digits and its logic to form a complete suite of divisor multiples. We have demonstrated that a radix-64 divider (generating a nominal 6 bits per cycle) can generate an average of more than 4.5 bits per cycle using only those multiples which can be formed with a two input adder-subtracter and considering only a single 6-bit digit of each of the residue and divisor.

The tests indicate that the new techniques are appropriate for radices up to 64, but less satisfactory with a radix of 256, largely because of restrictions on the digit-estimation logic and the number of divisor multiples which are available.

If we have a multiplier which is designed for, say, radix-64 multiplication, its hardware can be used as the basis of a divider with nominal radix-64 operation. This paper shows that, with relatively simple digit estimation logic, it is easy to achieve, if not the full 6 bits per cycle, then certainly 4 or 5 bits.

Appendix: calculation of the quotient digit look-up tables

The lookup tables are generated as a simple function of the high-order residue and divisor bits, assumed to index the rows and columns respectively of the table. The process is parametrised to facilitate the generation of tables of differing sizes and shapes, and for differing radices. The tables are generated for positive residue and divisor (with the most-significant divisor bit always 1) and the negative half then generated as the complement of the positive half. There is evidence that minor improvements might be possible by fine-tuning some table entries in particular cases but that has not been attempted.

The basic parameters are —

`ResBits`	the number of residue bits to examine (excluding the sign)
`DvsBits`	the number of divisor bits to examine, including the normalised bit
`Radix`	the radix of the quotient digit digit

From these are derived several other values —

`DigitBits`	`(Radix = 1 << DigitBits)`	the bits to represent a digit
`maxRow`	`(1 << ResBits)`	the maximum row of the table
`maxCol`	`(1 << DvsBits)`	the maximum column of the table
`minCol`	`(maxCol / 2)`	the minimum column of the table
`beta`	`(2 << DigitBits)*minCol/maxRow`	a scaling factor

Logically, the table rows extend from `-maxRow` to `maxRow-1`, and the columns from `minCol` to `maxCol-1`. We calculate also a scaling factor chosen to give an intermediate result of twice the true estimate. A mapping table then rounds the intermediate value to the correct estimate, or rounds with suppression of complex multiples.

The essential loops for producing the table are then

```
for(col = minCol; col <= maxCol; col++)
      for(row = 0; row <= maxRow; row++)
        Table[row+maxRow][col-minCol] = (beta*row)/col;
```

For operation with less than the full set of divisor multiples the table values are rounded to the nearest available multiple.

References

[Atkins 1970] D.E. Atkins, "Higher-Radix Division Using Estimates of the Divisor and Partial Remainders", *IEEE Trans. Comp.*, August 1970, pp 720–733

[Cortadella and Lang, 1994] J. Cortadella and T Lang, "High-Radix Division and Square Root with Speculation", *IEEE Trans. Comp.*, August 1994, pp 919–931

[Ercegovac, Lang and Montuschi 1993] M.D. Ercegovac, T. Lang, P Montuschi, "Very High Radix Division with Selection by Rounding and Prescaling", *Proc. Eleventh IEEE Symp. Comp. Arithmetic,* 1993, pp 112 - 119

[Freiman 1961] C.V. Freiman, "Statistical Analysis of Certain Binary Division Algorithms", *Proc IRE*, Vol 49, No 1, Jan 1961, pp 91 - 103.

[Hwang 1979] K. Hwang, "Computer Arithmetic: principles, architecture and design", John Wiley and Sons, New York, 1979

[Flores 1963] Ivan Flores, "The Logic of Computer Arithmetic", Prentice-Hall, Englewood Cliffs, 1963

[Kawahito et al 1994] S. Kawahito, M. Ishida, T. Nakamura, M. Kamyama, T. Higuchi, "High-Speed Area-Efficient Multiplier Design Using Multiple-Valued Current-Mode Circuits", *IEEE Trans Comp.*, Vol 43, No 1, Jan 1994, pp 34-42.

[Knuth 1969] D.E. Knuth, "The Art of Computer Programming, Vol 2 Seminumerical Algorithms", Addison Wesley 1969

[MacSorley 1961] O.L. MacSorley, "High Speed Arithmetic in Binary Computers", *Proc IRE*, Vol 49, Jan 1961, pp 67-91

[Montuschi and Ciminiera 1994] P. Montuschi and L. Ciminiera, "Over-Redundant Digit Sets and the Design of Digit-By-Digit Division Units", *IEEE Trans. Comp.*, Vol 43, No 3, March 1994, pp 269 – 277.

[Robertson 1958] J.E. Robertson, "A New Class of Digital Division Methods", *IEEE Trans. Comp.*, Vol C-7, No 8, September 1958, pp 218–222

[Svoboda 1963] A. Svoboda, "An Algorithm for Division", *Information Proc Machines*, Vol 9, pp 25 - 32, 1963.

[Schwarz and Flynn 1993] E.M. Schwarz, M.J. Flynn, "Parallel High-Radix Nonrestoring Division", *IEEE Trans. Comp.*, Vol 42, No 10, Oct 1993, pp 1234 - 1246

[Tocher 1956] K.D. Tocher, "Techniques of Multiplication and Division for Automatic Binary Computers", *Q. J. Mech. Appl. Math.* Vol 11 Pt 3 pp 364–384

[Wallace 1964] C.S. Wallace, "A Suggestion for a Fast Multiplier", *IEEE Trans. Elec. Comp.*, Vol EC-13, Feb 1964, pp 14-17

[Waser and Flynn 1982] S. Waser, M.J. Flynn, "Introduction to Arithmetic for Digital Systems Designers", Holt, Reinhart and Winston New York, 1982

[Wilson and Ledley 1961] J.B. Wilson, R.S. Ledley, "An Algorithm for Rapid Binary Division", *IRE Trans. Elec. Comp.* Vol EC-10, Dec 1961, pp 662-670

[Wong and Flynn 1992] D. Wong, M. Flynn, "Fast Division Using Accurate Quotient Approximations to Reduce the Number of Iterations", *IEEE Trans. Comp.*, Vol 41, No 8, Aug 1992, pp 981 - 995.

Journal of Universal Computer Science, vol. 1, no. 1 (1995), 23-34
submitted: 8/10/94, accepted: 19/12/94, appeared: 28/1/95

On Implementing EREW Work-Optimally on Mesh of Trees

Ville Leppänen
(University of Turku, Finland
Ville.Leppanen@cs.utu.fi)

Abstract: We show how to implement an $\ell_1 \times n \log n$-processor EREW PRAM work-optimally on a 2-dimensional n-sided mesh of trees, consisting of n processors, n memory modules, and $O(n^2)$ nodes. Similarly, we prove that an $\ell_2 \times n^2 \log n$-processor EREW PRAM can be implemented work-optimally on a 3-dimensional n-sided mesh of trees. By the *work-optimality* of implementations we mean that the expected routing time of PRAM memory requests is $O(1)$ per simulated PRAM processor with high probability. Experiments show that on relatively small ℓ_1 and ℓ_2 the cost per simulated PRAM processor is 1.5–2.5 in the 2-dimensional case, and 2–3 in the 3-dimensional case. If at each step at most $\frac{1}{3}$'th of the PRAM processors make a reference to the shared memory, then the simulation cost is approximately 1. We also compare our work-optimal simulations to those proposed for coated meshes.
Key Words: EREW, mesh of trees, shared memory, simulation, work-optimal, randomized, coated mesh.
Category: C.1.2 C.2.1 F.1.2 F.2.2 G.3.

1 Introduction

PRAM is an abstract model of parallel computation. It consists of p processors and a single shared memory of size m. The shared memory concept of the PRAM is generally believed not to be directly implementable as an extension of the conventional memory technique to the p-port memory technique (this does not seem to hold for relatively small p [Forsell 93]). Therefore, the implementation of PRAM is usually considered on distributed memory machines (DMMs), where processor&memory pairs are connected by some interconnection network [Abolhassan et al. 91, Karp et al. 92, Leppänen and Penttonen 94a, Ranade 91, Valiant 90].

Simulation of PRAM on a 2-dimensional Mesh of Trees (MT) based DMM has been considered previously in [Luccio et al. 88, Pucci 93] probabilistically and in [Luccio et al. 90, Pucci 93] deterministically. The probabilistic simulation of an n-processor EREW PRAM on an n-processor ($O(n^2)$-node) MT is proved to work in time $O(\log n)$ with high probability. The deterministic scheme is respectively proved to work in time $O(\frac{\log^2 n}{\log\log n})$. Thus, the work per simulated PRAM processor is $O(\log n)$ and $O(\frac{\log^2 n}{\log\log n})$, respectively.

In this paper, we show how to decrease the work per simulated processor to $O(1)$ with high probability. We prove this result for both 2-dimensional and 3-dimensional MTs. The method is, of course, increasing the multithreading level of each processor so that the cost caused by routing delay decreases – *i.e.*, we make each of the N real processors to simulate p/N EREW processors, and require that the number of PRAM processors p is sufficiently large. In our simulations, we implement each virtual processor as a light-weight thread (= fixed set of registers). For ease of reference, we call the multithreading level of processors simply by *load*, and increasing the load by *overloading*.

The work-optimality of our simulations can be questioned, since the number of MT-nodes is $O(n^2)$ (or $O(n^3)$ in the 3-dimensional case) while the number of real processors is only $O(n)$ (respectively $O(n^2)$). We adopt the approach taken by Valiant in [Valiant 90] for the work-optimal simulation on the butterfly: If the nodes of the routing machinery are very simple (and fast), then it might be fair to ignore their work-complexity. The nodes of MT are required only to do elementary switching operations, and thus we are willing to ignore their work and hardware complexity. We return to this subject [Section 5].

Next, we give some necessary definitions [Section 2], and describe work-optimal EREW PRAM simulation on 2-dimensional and 3-dimensional mesh of trees [Section 3]. Then, we give experimental EREW simulation results [Section 4], and compare [Section 5] the MT results to those obtained for similar work-optimal simulations on coated meshes [Leppänen and Penttonen 94b]. We conclude [Section 6] by proposing some topics for further research.

2 Definitions

2.1 EREW PRAM

Definition 1. EREW (Exclusive-Read-Exclusive-Write) PRAM model consists of p processors and a shared memory M of size m. Each of the processors $P_0, P_1, \ldots, P_{p-1}$ has some local memory and registers. During one step a PRAM processor can either do a local operation, read a shared memory location, or write to a shared memory location. The phases of each step are executed synchronously, and the next step is not started until all processors have finished the current one. The EREW PRAM does not allow concurrent reading or concurrent writing of a shared memory location. However, a shared memory location may be read and written during the same step. A read operation returns the value of the memory location in question *before* the current step.

2.2 Mesh of Trees

Definition 2. An n-sided d-dimensional *Mesh of Trees* (MT) is a graph, which is based on an n-sided d-dimensional mesh of nodes (without grid edges). For each tower of mesh nodes $\{V_{i_1,\ldots i_{j-1},0,i_{j+1},\ldots,i_d}, \ldots, V_{i_1,\ldots i_{j-1},n-1,i_{j+1},\ldots,i_d}\}$, it contains a complete binary tree $T^j_{i_1,\ldots,i_{j-1},i_{j+1},\ldots,i_d}$, whose leaves are the nodes of the tower. The edges of complete binary trees are bi-directional, and have a queue of length q packets for both directions. The MT contains no other edges. The degree of MT is $max(3,d)$, and the number of nodes is $|V| = (d+1)n^d - dn^{d-1}$. Respectively, the diameter is $2d \log n$.

In the 2-dimensional case [see Fig. 1], we call T^1_i the i'th *row tree* RT_i, and T^2_i the i'th *column tree* CT_i. In [Luccio et al. 88, Luccio et al. 90], the roots of RT_i and CT_i are joined for each i, but here we do not assume that to be the case. We assume that processor $\mathcal{P}_{i_2,\ldots,i_d}$ is in the root of $T^1_{i_2,\ldots,i_d}$ for each $i_2, \ldots, i_d \in \{0, \ldots, n-1\}$. Similarly, we assume memory module $\mathcal{M}_{i_1,\ldots,i_{d-1}}$ to reside at the root of $T^d_{i_1,\ldots,i_{d-1}}$. Thus, the n-sided d-dimensional mesh of trees consists of $N = n^{d-1}$ processors and memory modules.

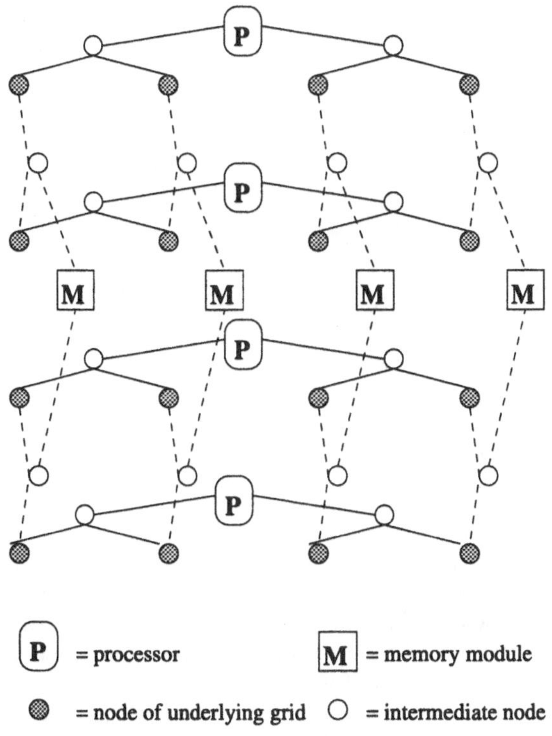

Fig. 1. A 2-dimensional 4-sided mesh of trees.

3 Simulation

Initially, the shared memory is hashed according to some randomly chosen hash function $h \in \mathcal{H}$. Memory references are translated to *read* and *write* packets, which are routed to the memory module on whose custody the referenced shared memory cell is. Each packet is routed along the obvious route as in [Luccio et al. 88, Pucci 93]. The memory modules in turn reply to each read request as they arrive, and route the replies back to the requesting processor. Proper information about the target and the origin are carried in the packets. Before a write packet is "executed", the old value is copied to a backup table (a hash table within each memory module). Those values are used to generate replies to read packets arriving after a write packet with the same target.

For hashing, we use the following family $\mathcal{H}_\varsigma$ of polynomial hash functions.

$$\mathcal{H}_\varsigma = \left\{ h \middle| h(x) = \Big(\sum_{0 \le i < \varsigma} a_i x^i \bmod q \Big) \bmod m; 0 < a_i < q, m \le q = O(m) \right\},$$

where q is a prime and $\zeta \geq 2$. The family $\mathcal{H}_\zeta$ is not the best possible, because we would like to define mappings $owner : \mathbb{Z}_m \longmapsto \{0, \ldots, n-1\}$ and $location : \mathbb{Z}_m \longmapsto \mathbb{Z}_{m'}$ by $owner(x) = (h(x)\ div\ m')\ mod\ n$, and $location(x) = h(x)\ mod\ m'$. This does not work in practice, since a randomly chosen $h \in \mathcal{H}_\zeta$ is not bijective. However, the secondary hashing techniques within memory modules (as in [Ranade 91]) can be used to solve the problem. Notice that the serial evaluation time of $h(x)$ is $O(\zeta)$, but if processors have a certain pipeline of length $O(\zeta)$, then the amortized evaluation time can be pushed down to $O(1)$.

Lemma 3. *[Kruskal et al. 90, Corollary 4.20] If a randomly chosen $h \in \mathcal{H}_\zeta$ is used for hashing a set S of unique memory locations into n modules, for which $|S| = s \geq \zeta n/2$, then for all j $(0 \leq j < n)$:*

$$Pr(b_j > s/n + \epsilon) \leq \frac{\zeta}{2}\left(\frac{e\zeta s}{2n\epsilon^2}\right)^{\frac{\zeta}{2}},$$

where $b_j = |\{x \in S \mid h(x) = j\}|$, and $\ln e = 1$.

3.1 2-dimensional Mesh of Trees

In the 2-dimensional case, the routing is straightforward, since the processors are on the roots of row trees and the memory modules are on the roots of column trees. In fact, the path from $\mathcal{P}_i$ to $\mathcal{M}_j$ via mesh node (i, j) is unique. Moreover, if q is sufficiently large, no collisions can happen, when read and write packets traverse "down" along row trees, or when replies traverse down along column trees. Collision, and thus queuing, happens only, when replies traverse "up" along row trees, or read and write packets traverse up along column trees. If s packets are destined to some memory module $\mathcal{M}_j$, then a packet destined to $\mathcal{M}_j$ is delayed (queued) at most $s-1$ times. Lemma 3 gives a good bound for the number of packets destined to each memory module, and consequently we have Theorem 4.

Theorem 4. *For properly chosen (small) constants k and ℓ, there exists such a constant $\alpha \geq 1$ that a 2-dimensional n-processor MT with $\mathcal{H}_{O(\log n)}$ addressing and $q = O(\ell \log n)$ can simulate an $\ell \times n \log n$-processor EREW PRAM work-optimally in $O(\ell \log n)$ expected routing steps with probability at least $1 - n^{-\alpha}$, if $\zeta = k \log n$ and $\ell \log n \geq \zeta/2$.*

Proof. We assume that each processor simulates $\ell \log n$ EREW processors. For the time being, assume that $q = \infty$. According to Lemma 3 ($s = \ell \times n \log n$; $\epsilon = 2s/n$)

$$\begin{aligned} &Pr(b_j > 3s/n) \\ &\leq \frac{\zeta}{2}\left(\frac{e\zeta s}{2n(2s/n)^2}\right)^{\frac{\zeta}{2}} \\ &= \frac{\zeta}{2}\left(\frac{e\zeta}{8\ell \log n}\right)^{\frac{\zeta}{2}} \end{aligned}$$

$$\leq \frac{\zeta}{2}\left(\frac{e}{4}\right)^{\frac{\zeta}{2}}$$
$$\leq n^{-\alpha'}$$

for some positive constant α', if $\zeta = \Omega(\log n)$. Since b_j tells how many requests memory module $\mathcal{M}_j$ receives at most with high probability, we know that every request reaches its destination in $T_1 = 2\log n + 3\ell \log n$ steps with probability at least $1 - n^{-\alpha'+1}$. Routing the packets back is easier, since each processor receives at most $\ell \log n$ replies. Thus, the last reply is received at most $2\log n + \ell \log n$ steps after some memory module received the last read request.

The queues do not need to be infinite. If $q > 3\ell \log n$, then according to the above reasoning none of the queues becomes full with high probability. Thus, setting $q = 3\ell \log n + 1$ guarantees that the queue length will not affect the routing time with high probability.

How do we know, when to start simulating the next EREW step? We could assume that we first check whether all processors have received all replies. However, we do not actually need such a global control, if we proceed in the following way. Assume that after the last memory reference packet, each processor sends an End-Of-Stream packet. The row tree nodes can spread this EOS-packet to both branches, and respectively the column tree nodes let all other packets go before they combine two EOS-packets, and forward the result upwards. Now, each memory module knows when it has issued the last reply, and can thus send an End-of-Replies packet. Assume that the EOR-packets are transferred in the same way as the EOS-packets. Clearly, each processor can start simulating the next step, when it has received an EOR-packet. In principle, a processor could start simulating the next round right after it has injected its EOS-packet. However, in practice this can cause problems with the coordination of virtual processors. Acting like this, the simulation of at most two consecutive EREW steps are overlapped, but never mixed.

As in [Luccio et al. 88, Pucci 93], we can protect ourselves against some repeatedly occuring bad memory reference patterns, by requiring that the whole shared memory is rehashed, if some memory module receives more than $c \times \ell \log n$ packets for a carefully chosen constant c. Clearly, a memory of size $m = n^{\beta}$ can certainly be redistributed in time $O(n^{\beta} + \log n)$. By now we know that if $c \geq 3$, the redistribution takes place at most with probability $n^{-\alpha''}$. Thus, if $\alpha'' > \beta$, the effect on the expected number of routing steps is negligible. □

3.2 3-dimensional Mesh of Trees

To extend the result of Theorem 4 to the 3-dimensional mesh of trees, we only need to describe how to route the packets, and how to keep the simulation of two consecutive PRAM steps separated. Using Lemma 3, it is again easy to prove that each memory module $\mathcal{M}_{i,j}$ receives at most $3\ell \log n$ packets with high probability.

Let us again call those trees, where the processors and the memory modules are connected, the row and the column trees respectively. Let *depth tree* $DT_{x,y}$ denote tree $T^2_{x,y}$. Now, a packet is sent from processor $\mathcal{P}_{i,j}$ to memory module $\mathcal{M}_{k,l}$ so that the packet goes along $RT_{i,j}$ to mesh node $V_{k,i,j}$, then up along $DT_{k,j}$

and down to mesh node $V_{k,l,j}$, and finally up along $CT_{k,l}$ to $\mathcal{M}_{k,l}$. Similarly, replies go back the same way. Notice that it is not wise to put all the packets to go trough the root of some $DT_{x,y}$.

Can we guarantee that there is no congestion in the depth tree nodes? A read or a write packet entering to a depth tree $DT_{k,j}$ is from one of the n processors $\mathcal{P}_{i,j}$ and is destined to one of the n memory modules $\mathcal{M}_{k,l}$, where $i, l \in \{0, \ldots n-1\}$. By Lemma 3 ($s = \ell \times n \log n$; the number of different banks of n memory modules is $n^2/n = n$; $\epsilon = 2s/n$), we know that at most $c \times \ell \log n$ packets enter to $DT_{k,j}$ with probability at most

$$Pr(b_i > 3s/n) \leq \frac{\zeta}{2}\left(\frac{e\zeta}{8\ell \log n}\right)^{\frac{\zeta}{2}} \leq \frac{\zeta}{2}\left(\frac{e}{4}\right)^{\frac{\zeta}{2}} \leq n^{-\alpha'}$$

for some constant α', if $\zeta = \Omega(\log n)$. Clearly, this also sets a sufficiently large upper bound for q.

As in the 2-dimensional case, we can keep the simulation of consecutive steps separate by sending EOS- and EOR-packets. However, we must require that when they traverse the depth trees, they always go via the root. Based on the above discussion, we have Theorem 5.

Theorem 5. *For properly chosen (small) constants k and ℓ, there exists such a constant $\alpha \geq 1$ that a 3-dimensional n^2-processor MT with $\mathcal{H}_{O(\log n)}$ addressing and $q = O(\ell \log n)$ can simulate an $\ell \times n^2 \log n$-processor EREW PRAM work-optimally in $O(\ell \log n)$ expected routing steps with probability at least $1 - n^{-\alpha}$, if $\zeta = k \log n$ and $\ell \log n \geq \zeta/2$.*

3.3 Practical Remarks

It is straightforward to extend the EREW simulation result to higher dimensional mesh of trees. However, finding an efficient layout for d-dimensional ($d > 3$) mesh of trees is obviously very difficult, if not impossible.

We did not pay much attention to the impracticality of family $\mathcal{H}_\zeta$, since we are mainly interested about the routing cost. We believe that simpler families (*e.g.*, $\mathcal{H}_1$) can be used in practice [Engelmann and Keller 93], since the number of all possible different reference patterns

$$\binom{m}{N}$$

is so huge that it is not necessary to guarantee success with high probability for all of them. After all, what is wanted is that in the long run the average simulation time of one PRAM step is $O(\ell \log n)$.

Although the rehashing method proposed earlier in this paper is sufficiently good for asymptotic complexity results, it is likely to be too "rough" in practice. Undoubtly, it is good to have a rehashing mechanism, but its triggering criteria should be chosen very carefully. We believe that one should make the decision on the basis of a long (bad) simulation sequence.

If we ignore the effect of rehashing on the expected routing cost per PRAM processor, by [Section 3.1] and [Section 3.2], we know that the cost is at most

$$(4+5\ell)/\ell = \frac{\ell \log n + 2\log n + 3\ell \log n + 2\log n + \ell \log n}{\ell \log n}$$

in the 2-dimensional case and $(6+11\ell)/\ell$ in the 3-dimensional case. In practice, we suspect that the cost caused by queuing is not as big as indicated by our naive analysis. Especially, the cost $(2+6\ell)/\ell$ that comes from the depth trees in the 3-dimensional case is too big. In the next section, we confirm this to be the case.

4 Experimental Results

Full details of our routing experiments on the mesh of trees are documented in [Leppänen 94b]. Here, we only give an overview of the test setting and the results.

The integration of processors and the memory modules to the mesh of trees based routing machinery is as described before. We assume that the processors and the routing machinery nodes can send and receive at most one packet in one time unit. We assume that the memory modules can generate a reply in one time unit, and there is a FIFO queue of a fixed length l_q associated to each directed edge. Our experiments indicated that the size of l_q will not significantly affect on the routing time as long as $l_q \geq 2$ [Leppänen 94b]. In the following, $l_q = 2$.

We did not use $\mathcal{H}_\zeta$ to define the destinations of packets, since we did not know how to produce typical access patterns (it makes no sense to apply $\mathcal{H}_\zeta$ to randomly produced access patterns). Instead, we used destinations generated by Unix random function **random**. The packets we perceived as read packets, and thus all the packets were each time routed to their destination and back to their source.

We made about 30 experiments with each chosen parameter combination. Altogether about 2400 routing experiments were conducted on 2-dimensional 64-, 256-, and 512-processor MTs [see Fig. 2], and on 3-dimensional 256-, 1024-, and 4096-processor MTs [see Fig. 3]. We measured only the time to complete a single experiment – as mentioned earlier, overlapping of consecutive steps is likely to decrease the total simulation cost. In each case, the variation of routing times was small. The curves describing our experiments show the dependency of simulation cost c (average simulation time per *Load*) as a function of ℓ ($Load = \ell \times \log n$).

We see that for 2D MT sizes 64, 256 and 512, value $\ell \approx 3$ yields cost $c \approx 5$. When $\ell \approx 8$, then the cost $c \leq 2$. Furthermore, it seems that *the larger the mesh of trees the lower the simulation cost* per processor. Even though our experiments deal only with relatively small MTs, we would like to claim that the simulation cost is very small on large MTs with load $2 \times \log n$.

In the 3-dimensional case, we found out that value $\ell \approx 4$ yields cost $c \approx 4$. When $\ell \approx 7$, then the cost $c \approx 3$. As in the 2-dimensional case, it seems that the larger the mesh of trees the lower the simulation cost.

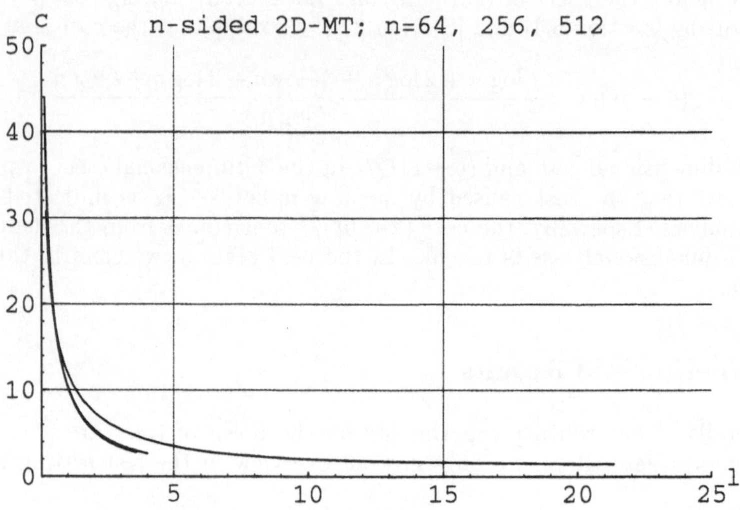

Fig. 2. The simulation cost as a function of ℓ in 2D MT.

The highest and at the same time the longest of the curves represents a 2D MT of size 64. The next highest (and longest) curve corresponds to a 256-processor 2D MT, and the lowest curve represents a 512-processor 2D MT. The Y-axis shows simulation cost c per simulated processor (in terms of routing steps per simulated processor), and the X-axis shows the load as a function of ℓ, where $\ell = Load \div \log n$.

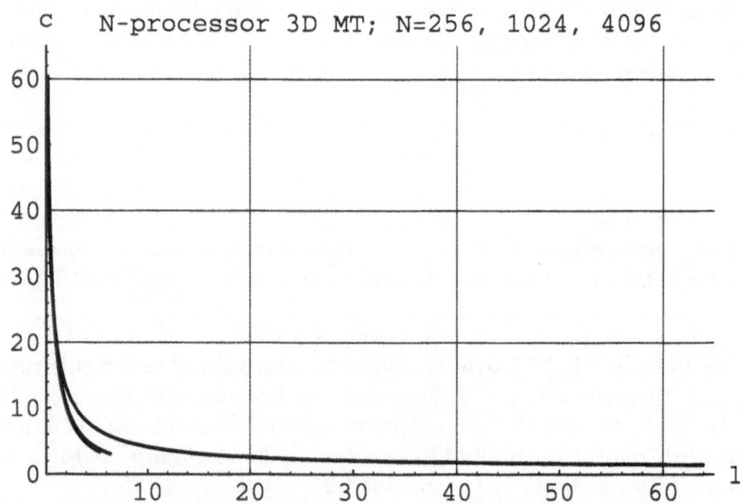

Fig. 3. The simulation cost as a function of ℓ in 3D MT.

The highest and at the same time the longest of the curves represents 3D MT of size 256 processors. The next highest (and longest) curve corresponds to a 1024-processor 3D MT, and the lowest curve represents a 4096-processor 3D MT.

5 Comparison with Coated Mesh

As observed, the simulation cost is very small for the 2-dimensional and 3-dimensional mesh of trees. However, other parameters of EREW PRAM implementations are also important. In the following, we present a comparison with the simulation cost on the coated meshes [Leppänen and Penttonen 94b].

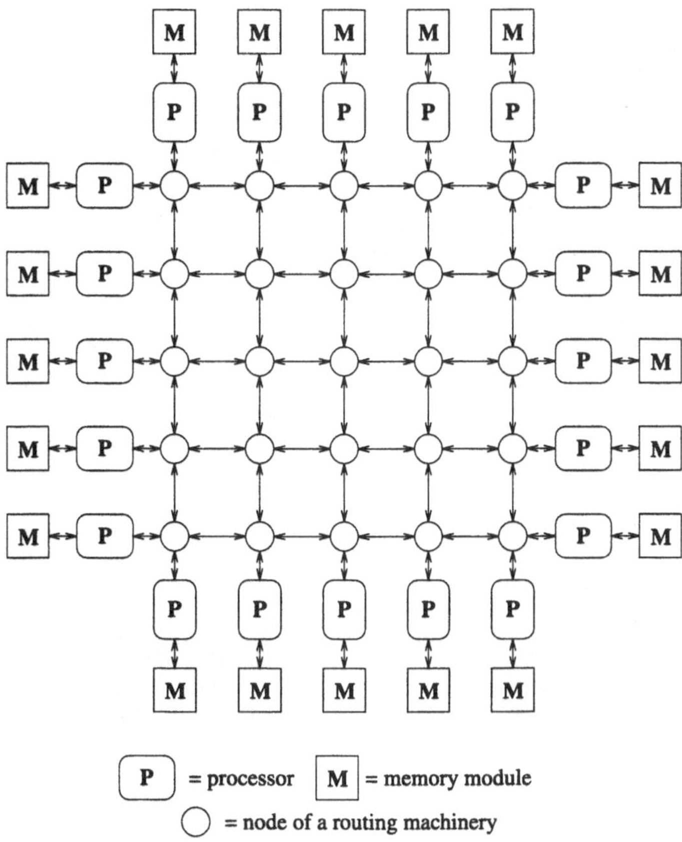

Fig. 4. A 2-dimensional coated mesh with 20 processors.

A coated mesh [see Fig. 4] consists of a mesh connected routing machinery coated with processor&memory pairs. Both the coated mesh and the mesh of trees have a routing machinery of size $O(N^2)$ in the 2-dimensional case, and $O(N^{3/2})$ in the 3-dimensional case. For parameters of our comparison [Tab. 1], we take the routing machinery size with respect to the number of processors and memory modules; simulation cost on a quite moderate load; simulation cost on a heavy load; and the minimum physical distance between logical neighbors. We note that there exist "tricks" to improve efficiency, like integration of the routing machinery nodes; faster clockrate in the routing machinery than in the processors; and delayed memory access operations. All of them can obviously be used to further improve the simulations both cases. We feel that the distance between neighboring nodes is important, since it might limit the clockrate of the routing machinery. So far, increasing the clockrate has been a major source of performance improvements. For the coated mesh structure, we use the experimental results documented in [Leppänen 93, Leppänen 94a].

Property	*MT*	CM	$N = 10^3$	$N = 10^6$
	2-dimensional case			
Cost	2–2.5	9–10	*4*	*4*
Load	5–7log N	$\frac{6-7}{16}N$	*6*	*3100*
Cost	1.5	6	*4*	*4*
Load	20 log N	$\frac{30}{16}N$	*9*	*4700*
Number of nodes	$3N^2 - 4N$	$N^2/16$	48	48
Distance	$\Omega(\lceil\frac{2\sqrt{3N^2-2N-2}}{4\log N}\rceil)$	1	87	43000
	3-dimensional case			
Cost	3–4	13–14	*4*	*4*
Load	3 log N	$0.7\sqrt{N}$	1.4	*12*
Cost	1.5	8	*5*	*5*
Load	60 log N	$3\sqrt{N}$	6	*2.5*
Number of nodes	$4N^{3/2} - 5N$	$(N/6)^{3/2}$	56	59
Distance	$\Omega(\lceil\frac{3\sqrt[3]{4N^{3/2}-3N-3}}{3\log N}\rceil)$	1	5	80

Table 1. Mesh of Trees versus Coated Mesh.

N is the number of real processors in each case. *Distance* tells the lower bound for the minimum (physical) distance between two logical neighbors (measured in routing machinery nodes). To our knowledge, no layout achieving the lower bound is known. *Cost* tells the simulation cost on a given *Load*. The two rightmost columns compare the two PRAM implementations with N processors. An *emphasized* number x means that MT is x times better than CM in this respect. Respectively, plain x means that CM is x times better.

In [Tab. 1], we have chosen two load values for both comparisons. In all cases, the simulation cost depends on the available load in a very similar way. The load values of MT and CM are chosen from similar positions of the load-cost dependency curves [Leppänen 94b, Leppänen and Penttonen 94b]. Especially, we attempted to choose the measure points so that the relative position on the MT curve and on the corresponding CM curve is the same. The first values are chosen from an area, where the load-cost curve begins to show asymptotic behavior, and the second values are chosen from an area were the behavior is asymptotic.

The mesh of trees is clearly better [Tab. 1] in terms of the simulation cost and the load in the 2-dimensional case. In the 3-dimensional case, the mesh of trees is only slightly better in this respect. Moreover, the routing machinery nodes are a little bit simpler in the mesh of trees (less inputs and outputs). However, what is gained in the simulation cost and in the required load, is lost in the size of the routing machinery and in the distance between routing machinery nodes. Especially, in the 3-dimensional case it seems that the coated mesh is actually better than the mesh of trees.

A 10^6-processor 3-dimensional coated mesh has only $\sqrt{N}/6^{1.5} \approx 70$ times more routing machinery nodes than processors. For a corresponding mesh of trees this ratio is about 4000. Remember that this PRAM simulation approach relies on the assumption that the routing machinery nodes are considerably simpler than the processors (and the memory modules). We do not know the actual difference of the routing machinery nodes and the processor&memory pairs in the hardware complexity, but ratio 70 does not seem to be totally unacceptable. Especially, if a bunch of routing machinery nodes (*e.g.*, $8 \times 8 \times 8$) are integrated together to form a building block of a routing machinery.

6 Conclusions and Future Work

We have presented a work-optimal EREW PRAM implementation for the 2-dimensional and 3-dimensional mesh of trees. The simulation uses a novel technique to keep the simulation of consecutive PRAM steps separated. Although the proved simulation costs are small, our experiments show the real simulation costs to be about 2–3 times smaller in practice. We compared the properties of the presented simulations to those proposed for the 2-dimensional and 3-dimensional coated meshes. Neither a mesh of trees nor a coated mesh is strictly better than the other, but our conclusion is that in the 3-dimensional case the coated mesh is better, when all the mentioned properties are considered.

We would like to learn more about the hardware complexity of the routing machinery nodes, and the ability to fast support a large number of virtual processors (how large systolic register set arrays can be built). It would also be interesting to compare these EREW PRAM simulations to those proposed for other logarithmic networks. Extending our work-optimal EREW simulation to an efficient work-optimal CRCW simulation is also an open problem.

References

[Abolhassan et al. 91] Abolhassan, F., Keller, J., Paul, W.J.: "On the Cost-Effectiveness of PRAMs"; Proc. 3rd IEEE Symposium on Parallel and Distributed Computing, ACM Special Interest Group on Computer Architecture, and IEEE Computer Society (1991), 2 – 9.

[Engelmann and Keller 93] Engelmann, C., Keller, J.: "Simulation-Based Comparison of Hash Functions for Emulated Shared Memory"; Proc. PARLE'93 Parallel Architectures and Languages Europe, Springer, LNCS 694 (1993), 1 – 11.

[Forsell 93] Forsell, M.J.: "Are Multiport Memories Physically Feasible?"; Technical Report A-1993-1, University of Joensuu, Department of Computer Science (1993).

[Karp et al. 92] Karp, R.M., Luby, M., Meyer auf der Heide, F.: "Efficient PRAM Simulation on a Distributed Memory Machine"; Proc. 24th Annual ACM Symposium on Theory of Computing (1992), 318 – 326.

[Kruskal et al. 90] Kruskal, C.P., Rudolph, L., Snir, M.: "A Complexity Theory of Efficient Parallel Algorithms"; Theoretical Computer Science, 71 (1990), 95–132.

[Leppänen 93] Leppänen, V.: "PRAM Computation on Mesh Structures"; Technical Report R-93-9, University of Turku, Computer Science Department (1993). Ph.Lic. thesis.

[Leppänen 94a] Leppänen, V.: "Performance of Four Work-Optimal PRAM Simulation Algorithms on Coated Meshes"; Manuscript (1994), submitted for publication.

[Leppänen 94b] Leppänen, V.: "Experimental Results on Simulating EREW PRAM Work-Optimally on Mesh of Trees"; Technical Report R-94-10, University of Turku, Computer Science Department (1994), also appeared as electronic version, anonymous FTP cs.utu.fi, in pub/techreports/1994/R-94-10.ps.Z.

[Leppänen and Penttonen 94a] Leppänen, V., Penttonen, M.: "Simulation of PRAM Models on Meshes"; Proc. PARLE'94 Parallel Architectures and Languages Europe, LNCS 817 (1994), 146 - 158.

[Leppänen and Penttonen 94b] Leppänen, V., Penttonen, M.: "Work-Optimal Simulation of PRAM Models on Meshes"; Technical Report R-94-1, University of Turku, Computer Science Department (1994), submitted for publication.

[Luccio et al. 88] Luccio, F., Pietracaprina, A., Pucci, G.: "A Probabilistic Simulation of PRAMs on a Bounded Degree Networks"; Information Processing Letters, 28 (1988), 141–147.

[Luccio et al. 90] Luccio, F., Pietracaprina, A., Pucci, G.: "A New Scheme for the Deterministic Simulation of PRAMs in VLSI"; Algorithmica, 5, 4 (1990), 529 - 544.

[Pucci 93] Pucci, G.: "Parallel Computational Models and Data Structures"; Technical Report TD-13/93, PhD thesis, Dipartimento di Informatica, Universitá di Pisa - Genova - Udine, Italia (1993).

[Ranade 91] Ranade, A.G.: "How to Emulate Shared Memory"; Journal of Computer and System Sciences, 42 (1991), 307–326.

[Valiant 90] Valiant, L.G.: "General Purpose Parallel Architectures"; Algorithms and Complexity, Handbook of Theoretical Computer Science A (1990), 934–971.

Acknowledgements

The author would like to thank Martti Penttonen for guidance and helpful comments. This work was possible due to a grant provided by the computer science department of the University of Turku.

Journal of Universal Computer Science, vol. 1, no. 1 (1995), 35-47
submitted: 8/10/94, accepted: 20/12/94, appeared: 28/1/95

Levels of Anonymity

Bill Flinn
(Computer Science Department, University of Auckland,
Auckland, New Zealand
b_flinn@cs.aukuni.ac.nz)

Hermann Maurer
(Institute for Information Processing and Computer Supported New Media,
Graz University of Technology, Austria
hmaurer@iicm.tu-graz.ac.at)

Abstract: In this paper we make a first attempt at systematically investigating levels of anonymity required in networked computer systems: we feel it is often overlooked that beyond such obvious cases as identified by means of a password" or "anonymous use" there are many other levels of anonymity, identification and authenticity necessary in various applications.

Key Words: security, anonymous use, access control, authentication, big brother
Category: C.2.0, D.4.6, K.6.5

1 Introduction

At present, most users of computers are usually aware of two modes for operation within a computer system:

- Logging on with user-id and password. (The standard way of operating any networked computer systems.)
- Using the computer anonymously; in this situation the user is unidentified, and does not have to provide a password. (This latter version, maybe first introduced in the Austrian videotex systems [Maurer 84] is becoming increasingly propular with Internet services such as anonymous FTP to download files or with networked multimedia systems such as Gopher, WAIS, WWW or Hyper-G, see [Maurer 92] or [Kappe 93])

However, there exist many alternative modes for interaction with a computer system. In this paper we will identify several such modes and show their appropriateness in the context of particular applications.

2 An overview of possible levels

Level 5. Super-identification. Here the user must be authenticated; i.e. the user has to be identified uniquely to the system in a completely secure way. Ideally, no-one can impersonate a user, and all transactions carried out by each user are associated unambiguously with that user (maybe even a complete audit trail is kept). This might e.g. be necessary in a commercially sensitive environment, particularly where a company is operating large mainframe systems which may be accessed (and modified) by large numbers of users.

In a wider context, and looking more from the point of view of the user, consider the problem of ensuring the authenticity of information acquired from a computer system or network, or determining that a message purporting to be from a particular person really is from that person. More generally, how can a user validate the credentials of an author of an article which is undergoing electronic distribution? These situations require total identification (and therefore zero anonymity). This may be provided directly i.e. suppliers of such information may be required to identify themselves completely, or alternatively the information may be supplied under the auspices of some some third party organisation which could guarantee the authenticity of such information that it provides.

Oberve that with super-identification there are a number of completely different issues involved:

- identification of a user vis-a-vis a system (so that the "system" is assured that this is indeed a duly authorized user; passwords may not be safe enough for such purpose as we will discuss later)
- identification of a user vis-a-vis another user (so that the receiver of an email or reader of a file does indeed know for sure who the originator of the file is; special cryptographic protocols like digital signatures [Salomaa 90] may be useful to achieve this aim)
- objective knowledge about the person or organisation associated with an identification (so that the user knows that person X is indeed "qualified" to write about topic Y; this may require a third party broker as mentioned above).

Level 4. Usual identification. The user is known within the system by a user-name and associated password. The user has to log on with this user-name and use the correct password to be admitted into the system. This is typically the case today for multiple user systems.

Level 3. Latent (potential) identification. Here the user is known as person to the system. Each user may develop a set of pseudonyms. These sets of pseudonyms are mutually disjoint (so two distinct users may not share a given pseudonym). Distinct users cannot directly identify other users using the computer system; however the system has exact knowledge of each user. This mode is used in some computer assisted instruction (CAI) settings and electronic bulletin board discussion forums.

Level 2. Pen-name identification. The user is known within the system by some user-name, but there is no proper identification of the user as person. Users log on with their pen-name, and using a password. Again multiple pseudonyms can be used. Mail may be sent to such a user (pen-name). This mode may also be used for bulletin board systems; some game playing systems operating on networks such as Internet employ this technique, too.

Level 1. Anonymous identification. Here the user is identified by the system, but not as a specific individual and without pen-name, i.e. is not "addressable". Typically, a user logs on anonymously (probably using a password), and the system keeps a log of events engaged in by that particular user. This allows the system to tailor its interactions with the user according to the log - for example in a museum visitor system.

Level 0. No identification of user. This is the usual situation in using a PC; however even here there is the possibility of an application which keeps a log as in Level 1 and tailors its interactions with the user accordingly. Such so-called "intelligent" applications , or more precisely, applications utilising intelligent agents, will certainly proliferate as processing and memory power of PCs increase.

We observe that the existence of a log as in Levels 1 and 0 provides a kind of profile of the (unknown) user, and can be used by a third party to gain information about user behaviour. In this regard, true anonymity would even go beyond that and would correspond to the absence of any personal history within the system or application.

3 Detailed discussion of various levels

3.1 Level 5

Super-identification may be required either by the computer system or the application being accessed, or by a user attempting to access information across a network, or communicate securely with another person across such a network (maybe in a far away location).

With currently applied technology, particularly in regard to Internet, it is impossible to guarantee authenticity of this kind unless cryptographic protocols are used [Salomaa 90]. Generally today, Internet users are identified by their email (electronic mail) address. It is possible to forge the originating address of a message, either by corrupting the mailing software itself, or by connecting via telnet to the sendmail socket of another machine on one's local network, and typing in a mail message which purports to come from someone else. It is also possible, although much more difficult, for a message to be intercepted en route and modified. This requires the interceptor to have access to network nodes en route and to be able to access and modify the system software which is forwarding mail. This would appear to require resources beyond most individuals (although not necessarily beyond government agencies).

In the near future, it will be possible to embellish electronic communications with facial image and voice data. However in itself this will not resolve the authenticity issue, because these can be modified or forged as readily as text! Already forged and reconstructed images are regularly posted in Internet newsgroups.

In order to guarantee authenticity and privacy of electronic communications it is necessary to use cryptographic techniques. There is currently much debate on the use of crytography, particularly in the US, largely because of governmental desire to be able to monitor electronic communications. As stated in [Detweiler 93]:

"To date no feasible system that guarantees both secure communication and government oversight (monitoring) has been proposed (the two goals are largely incompatible) ... Electronic privacy issues, and particularly the proper roles of networks and the Internet, can be foreseen to become highly visible and explosive over the next few years". For an easy to read introduction on the state of the discussion of the "Clipper Affair" see [Time 94].

3.2 Level 4

This kind of identification is currently the most commonly used means of access to a computer system or network. The reasons for this are largely historical; when timesharing systems were originally set up, it was necessary to ensure that only those users who were properly entitled could access the system and use system resources. In particular, a check had to be kept for accounting purposes on the scope of each user's activities. In fact computer users today who work on company or other institution computer systems are largely subject to the same disciplines. However with the advent of large-scale computer networks and ever more powerful personal computers, both in terms of processing power and disk storage space, the situation is changing and it is with these developments in mind that the considerations to follow become relevant.

3.3 Levels 1-3 for partial anonymity

In keeping with the theme above, partial anonymity corresponds to partial identity. There are a number of reasons why an individual might wish to use a computer system in a partially anonymous way.

First, a person may wish to be consistently identified by a certain pseudonym or "handle" and establish a reputation under it in some area. The pseudonym would in some sense 'belong to' that person. In order to ensure that only one particular person could use a particular pseudonym requires a controlling application. This controlling application may or may not require exact identification of its users. These situations give rise to levels 3 and 2 respectively.

Second, a person may wish to be anonymous as person but carry on a conversation with others (with either known or anonymous identities) via an anonymous return address. This is level 2 anonymity.

Third, users may wish to make public certain important and sensitive information, but to do so in a way that makes them untraceable because to do so openly might jeopardise their lives or those of their families in some way. This would require the user to be completely anonymous (Level 1 or even Level 0). However, information publicised without being able to trace the originator is probably only possible for small groups (like in decision room situations) but is not viable for public services such as Videotex in Europe, or Internet: such anonymity tends to lead to personal slander, to the violation of laws (such as on pornography, or on encouragmenet of criminal actions, etc.). In most cases Level 3 anonymity is required here.

Fourth, a user may wish to make use of an electronic service and hide all signs of this usage, for reasons of privacy. See for example [Maurer 84].

Fifth, during the use of a certain application (even across session boundaries) users may want to keep track of their actions: to get an objective evaluation by some CAI package at the end of a number of sessions (yet without anyone having a way to establish a connection between the performance achieved and a particular person), or by visitors of e.g. the Franklin Institute at Philadelphia or the Information Age Exhibit of the Smithonian at Washington who have the option of printing information concerning their visit on exiting.

3.4 Level 0

This basically corresponds to turning on a PC that is not password protected: The default situation for use of PCs is for files etc to be accessible to whoever happens to switch the machine on. The user in this case is completely unidentified. Even if files etc are password protected, there is no real notion of the identity of the user. In the absence of such identity, we have true anonymity, with the proviso that no logs are kept as discussed at the end of Section 2.

3.5 Rationale for anonymity

Allowing users to access a computer system anonymously has a number of possible consequences; we shall discuss these in general here, and consider them in more detail later in this paper, where we consider several specific example applications.

On computer bulletin boards and in other discussion forums such as decision rooms - see later - opinions and ideas can be put forward anonymously. Many people find it easier to put forward ideas in this way, particularly if they are unsure of themselves or of their ideas. One may have an idea which one is not sure about, and by floating it for discussion, very quickly get some useful feedback. Again in a discussion forum, a single individual using two pen-names may put forward two opposing sides of an argument to spark discussion. This doesn't necessarily require anonymity; however there are situations where this anonymity makes it easier to put forward the ideas. The freedom to publicly air one's point of view has a long tradition in several countries. In certain situations citizens are allowed the right to speak their minds on any topic. Speakers Corner in Hyde Park, London is a prime example. Soapbox orators in such a situation are not required to identify themselves to a watching policeman - unless they break the law.

Again in public arenas like computer bulletin boards, there are advantages in being able to converse and get to know people anonymously.

The ability to express a proposal anonymously has definite advantages in an employment situation or heavily politicised arena. Most employees do not feel able to put forward ideas, no matter what their merit, in the presence of a boss who is known to strongly disagree with those ideas. In Parliament, it is not generally possible for members of a particular party to view objectively a proposal coming from "the other side" - or indeed one coming from their own party. Anonymous interactions allow ideas to be argued about and to stand or fall on their own merit, rather than on the status and power of the individuals concerned.

Another benefit of anonymous interactions is the user's privacy. For example, as pointed out in [Maurer 90], why should a user suffering from cancer who is desperately searching the medical pages in a videotex system for help be required to identify him or herself? Such users are unlikely to want their database accesses logged. Again there is the every-day analogy of the public library; it is not usually necessary to identify oneself before going to consult a book on a publicly accessible shelf. Extending the analogy, the Internet itself, viewed as an information resource, may be considered as a huge library. Like many large libraries, it will contain information that may be considered offensive by some users but interesting to others. If we do not believe in censorships in libraries (and the authors of this paper don't), such potentially offensive material should be accessible if someone actively searches for it (and only then!), yet anonymity might well be desirable to avoid embarassement or fear of reprisals.

Of course there is a downside to anonymous usage, particularly with respect to bulletin board systems and indeed any publicly accessible network or computer system: allowing users to voice opinions anonymously means that any and every perverted viewpoint can be expressed - much as currently occurs on a wider scale with graffiti on public lavatory walls. The electronic versions of lavatory graffiti include pornographic images, racist attacks, slander, and incitement to commit criminal acts. It is interesting to observe that the situation is somewhat blurred by the fact that networks are now globally accessible, and as of now, and probably for the forseeable future, there are disparities in law between countries. One immediate example is in the area of cryptography; the RSA public key encryption method is patented in the US, but not elsewhere in the world. There are a number of sites on the Internet which hold copies of an application program called PGP (for Pretty Good Privacy). PGP uses RSA's patented algorithm, and so is legally unable to be used by US citizens, yet perfectly legal outside the US.

It is the fact that anonymous usage of public systems below Level 3 has often led to much misuse that we strongly propagate Level 3 for public discussion and have indeed implemented this version in the E.R.D.E., the electronic discussion corner of the Austrian Videotex system: although users are anonymous with respect to each other, an encrypted record of the real identity of each user is kept, allowing to determine the identity of a penname if a court-order is issued. This limited amount of "non-anonymity" is known to the users and has been successful in preventing serious misuse of the system.

In general we are in a much better position with computer systems and networks to enforce decency and at least local legality than the hapless custodians and users of public lavatories. It is possible to use identification at several levels. For example, akin to what has been described for the E.R.D.E., in order to make use of a particular system or network, a user can be required to identify themselves completely. Then the user can choose one (or several) pen-names and, once the pen-name has been associated with that particular user by the system, users can then make use of the bulletin board or other system using one of their associated pen-names. Other users are not able to identify the user from a particular pen-name in the usual course of events. However if a user were to violate the conventions of the system or institution or the laws of the country in which the server resides, some authority could be invoked to retrieve the connection between the anonymous pen-name and the actual user.

For a network like Internet, which operates internationally, however, the situation has proved rather more problematic. Within the Internet community, many people feel very strongly about the issue of anonymity. At the time of writing, there is at least one anonymous server in operation in Finland, but the future of such servers, and anonymous services in general, is extremely uncertain. Several such servers have been closed down in the recent past, either voluntarily by their operators or forcibly by higher authorities. An anonymous server operates by assigning an anonymous identity (pen-name) to a user who requests such an identity. The user may protect usage of their pen-name via a password. From then on, the user can communicate with other people or newsgroups on the internet, using only their pen-name. Any such message appears to originate from the anonymous server.

Strong opinions in favour of such anonymous services come from people seeking advice or therapy over the net, or advertising in 'Personal' ads. Strong opinions against come from people who have been attacked or slandered anonymously, and from those who feel that no sanctions can be brought to bear against an anonymous user who violates the ethical code of the Internet or indeed acts illegally. Several newsgroups have adopted a policy of filtering out all anonymous messages. This policy is difficult to automate however, because automation relies on detecting certain characteristics of the incoming message, and these can be altered by the anonymous server.

As stated in [Detweiler 93], the future of anonymous services on the Internet is extremely uncertain. There are strong forces for and against anonymity. However, from network traffic statistics, it appears that there is a large demand for anonymous services. Several thousand messages per day pass through the anonymous Finnish server mentioned.

When communicating electronically in a situation where pen-names are being used, it is possible for users to not only conceal their identity, but also to project a completely disguised persona. For example, one can appear to be of a different sex, different profession, etc. Such an ability to disguise oneself may be beneficial but clearly it may also be abused.

In many ways, being able to hide "superficial" features such as looks or some physical handicap encourages communication between persons who would never start to communicate, otherwise. Persons who would never meet otherwise first meet electronically, start to like each other and end up setting up real-life rendezvous.

A celebrated case is the case of a paraplegic girl who made friends via the Austrian Videotex network, giving away her physical problems only after having established quite a "fan club". When that fan-club finally met in person with her (the second author was amoung them) the usual problems of a healthy person confronting a handicapped one, i.e. the usual mixture of pity and not-knowing how to react (stifling any real contact) was completely absent.

How often do persons (men in partiuclar?) react on the basis of looks, rather than on other at least as important values? How often are people intimitated by the position of a person, turn to flattery because of the wealth of someone involved, etc. How many movies are there where a rich guy pretends to be poor just to make sure he is loved for his own sake, not for his money! Well, electronic pen-name based contacts do have exactly this property of disregarding some superficial layers: we like a person electronically because we like the ideas, the wittiness, the softness, the kindness ...and are neither distracted by looks, age or other external features. One of the authors has coined the term "electronic shards" [Maurer 93] to describe the phenomenon of persons inadvertently revealing facets of themselves during extended electronic communications. One can form a partial picture of such a communicant, in the same way that one forms an image of an ancient vase by seeing a broken fragment of the whole. Thus, it is not surprising that pen-name based electronic communication has lead to many deep relationships.

On the other hand, the idea of pen-names can also be misused. An interesting example is detailed in [van Gelder 85]. This concerns a persona known on the CB channel of the Compuserve network as "Joan". Joan supplied an elaborate biography about herself to others on the network, and over a two year period (1983-1985) became a major on-line presence. She presented herself as a severely disabled neuropsychologist who was using the computer network to communicate and make friends with others on-line. She did this so successfully that over this period she served both as a support for other disabled women and as an inspiration to the able-bodied. It was a great shock to her intimate on-line penpals when it transpired that in real life Joan was not disabled at all - and in fact was a prominent male New York psychiatrist. What had apparently begun as an experiment had escalated out of control over an extended period of time. "Joan", despite her supportive friendship to others, had clearly violated their trust.

While this particular case seems clear-cut, there are delicate issues involved here. Perhaps newcomers joining electronic networks should be warned ahead of time that any data presented to one across such a network may not be as it seems. However there is also the situation to consider where a user deliberately misleads others for personal gain. If there are as yet no laws in place to deal with this kind of misrepresentation, there surely will be in the future. Once again there are implications for international law.

At the pen-name level, it is still often the case that users inadvertently reveals their identity, at least to other persons who know their "electronic style" – much as an expert chess player may be able to identify a player from a game record, simply by knowing that person's style of play. Indeed on the chess and go servers on the Internet, where players are not required to make their identity public and may play under several pen-names, there is often discussion between the kibitzers as to whether player "x" is really the same as player "y". (For Chess servers see ics.ucknor.edu 500 or 130.225.16,82 500; for Go servers see flamingo.pasteur.fr or hellspark.wharton.upenn.edu).

In order to remain totally anonymous, it would thus appear that a "style scrambler" is required. It is an open question whether such a scrambler could be automated: we are investigating this further. The idea is to define a set of syntactic parameters which might be used to modify a text message, or sequence of such messages. Such parameters might include: gender of author, use of upper case letters, punctuation devices, ranges of spelling errors (set at one of a number of levels). Each pseudonym would appear consistent, but there would be no relationship between pseudonyms. There are several variations on this idea, for example the user might choose a set of parameters, or alternatively, the system could randomly allocate a set. Thus, we may at some stage be able to establish two different pen-names with sufficiently different "style-parameters" to disguise that the two pen-names belong to the same person!

3.6 Implementation

Ensuring the high degree of identification (and authentification) at Level 5 requires cryptographic techniques as discussed in [Chaum 85] and [Salomaa 90]. Briefly, the ideas are as follows: Each person communicating within the system does so using a digital signature. This term is a little misleading, since it refers to a complete message which is encoded using a pair of keys, one private and one public. One important property of digital signatures is their resistance to forgery. To decode a message in digital signature form without knowledge of the private key using currently available techniques is regarded as an infeasible computing problem. From the standpoint of this article, digital signatures have a further important property; they can be extended to blind digital signatures which as well as being secure are also anonymous. This will be discussed further in the Section below.

As Level 4 is the standard mode we will not consider it further, except to note that in many systems, administrators have power to access all files. As a result, security may be significantly undermined, so the whole rationale for identification with user-id and password becomes weakened. This situation could be improved by requiring at least two people to co-operate to gain access to user files.

Level 3 identification is implemented as follows: In order to be admitted to a system, the user has to log in and be identified in the usual (level 4) way. A first time user then chooses a pseudonym, which the system confirms available or not. Existing users may also add to their set of pseudonyms.If the pseudo is available (not already associated with a user), the system asks the user to choose a password to go with that pseudonym. From then on the user may interact with the system using the pseudonym plus password. The system keeps an encrypted file connecting each user-name with the pseudonyms chosen. If a public and private key encryption mechanism is being used, the keys can be kept separate as an additional security measure. As mentioned above, normally the connection between pseudonyms and user-names remains secret; however in exceptional circumstances the link can be made explicit.

Level 2 identification is maintained by the system maintaining a file which links pen-names to passwords. Messages can be transmitted between pen-names, or stored by the system and made available to users when they next log on using their pen-name with password.

Level 1 identification is maintained by the system independently of the users, whose only knowledge of it is via their log-on character sequence (name or password). See the museum visitor system example below.

4 Applications

4.1 Once more: Level 5

For a number of applications top-notch secure identification is crucial. The first wide-spread application where this became apparent was telebanking via systems such as Videotex in Europe, now used by well over 5 million customers.

Initial ideas of using a sequence of two pass-words were discarded in favor of one-time TAN's (TransAction Numbers). The advantage of TAN's is that even a "spy" observing the log-in process and the TAN cannot make use of the TAN, since it is only good for one transaction.

Modern cryptographic protocols involving so-called zero-knowledge proofs might provide even more elegant solutions: a user can be identified with certainty without ever revealing the password! [Salomaa 90].

4.2 Some example applications

The first example we consider is a system due to David Chaum ([Chaum 85]) for making payments to an organisation for goods or services. In this system a consumer wishing to make a purchase for say \$100 would do the following. First, using digital signatures, users would instruct their bank to deduct \$100 from their account and issue a "certificate" worth \$100. This certificate is in fact just a number which has the properties that

- It is constructed by both the user and the bank.
- (Although the bank is guaranteeing the authenticity of the certificate, it does not know the final number (and therefore to which user it was supplied). This is the concept of the blind digital signature.
- It can be validated by a third party and the bank as being a genuine certificate.

This certificate would then be presented to a third party in payment for goods or services. This third party then presents the certificate to the bank for payment. Such a certificate is like a cash note that has a valid serial number but not the number under which it is circulated from the bank. Although the consumer has to initially identify himself to the bank, the payment process itself is totally anonymous in that the number issued by the bank cannot be linked to the number supplied in payment, which can only be checked for validity (and that it has not been previously presented).

Our second example is a system for anonymous delivery of goods. Following [Maurer 84], the idea is that a user ordering merchandise x from company 'A' chooses two passwords 'p' (public) and 's' (secret) and a post office 'm' for delivery. Company 'A' sends merchandise x to post office m. The merchandise has 'p' visibly marked on the outside and inside has a sealed envelope containing 's'. The user goes to post office 'm', asks for the parcel labelled 'p', and presents his secret password 's'. If this matches with the password inside the sealed envelope the post office releases the merchandise.

Notice that this system, combined with the first example, allows for completely anonymous purchase and delivery of goods, in marked contrast to current systems involving credit or debit cards, which contain complete histories of customer usage, thus allowing detailed profiles of user spending patterns to be constructed.

For our third example we consider electronic discussion and games corners. The E.R.D.E. discussion corner and its Level 3 anonymity has been mentioned already above. Early versions just using Level 2 did not work: there was too much slander, abuse and often shrill arguments.

In a similar fashion a Level 3 server for chess in the Austrian Videotex system is working well, but similar Level 2 servers for Chess and Go seem to be running into problems. The Internet Go-server mentioned earlier is one such example: several anonymity issues arise: many people using the server are upset at others actions, including denigrating other players, antisocial behaviour while playing games etc. There is an interesting clash of cultures also: New York "street language" versus professional go players precisely formal interactions. Several professional players have become so incensed at comments of kibitzers that they regard as intolerably rude that they have refused to play again on the server. Anonymity is a rather peripheral issue here, although some users have felt that bad behaviour was being accentuated by anonymity. All in all though, it seems to prove that Level 3 should be used if a large number of persons is involved, rather than Level 2.

For our fourth example we look at software systems which are known variously as Decision Rooms, Group Support Systems or Electronic Meeting Support Systems. See for example [Nunamaker 91], [Sheffield 93], [Visotschnigg 85]. In particular we consider some findings of the Decision Support Centre established at the University of Auckland in 1990. In the Decision Support Centre, face-to-face meetings are augmented with each participant in a meeting able to converse via a workstation as well as in the normal way. Meetings are guided by a trained facilitator. The actual meeting process is a combination of facilitated group discussion, and the use of a software system to collect and organise ideas from all group members. Participants in the meeting are able to switch between "public" and "private" windows. Comments on a particular topic are entered in private windows and may shortly afterwards be viewed by all participants via their public windows. The public display of messages is anonymous. In [Sheffield 93], the following results for meetings of this type are reported:

1. Because the ideas are presented anonymously, each idea must speak for itself. Unlike a conventional face-to-face meeting, attention is focussed on the content of the message rather than its form (which essentially involves its originator).
2. The sending of an unpopular message may or may not be a personal attack. In a normal face-to-face meeting, social and emotional damage may result as the receiver may feel duty bound to defend him/herself by making remarks to avoid loss of face which may escalate the conflict. The anonymity which ensues when the messages are communicated on screen assists in depersonalising these attacks.
3. All participants can send and receive as they feel like it; consequently there is no need for speakers to play to the gallery, hold the floor or generally over-dominate the group.
4. Participants can report bad news or a state a point of view that they know will be unpopular without fear of being "stamped on" by superiors.

We observe that the software system used at Auckland ensures that the messages are presented completely anonymously. There seems no reason in principle why such a system should not operate with a variety of modes - say from Level 3 down to Level 0.

Our fifth example looks at anonymity in an educational setting, where the facility to have an anonymous electronic discussion removes the authoritarian role from the teacher or lecturer and enables the more diffident students to advance ideas without threat. Perhaps the most useful mode here is level 3. The teacher may wish to review or assess the degree and quality of statements and ideas expressed by participants, and in order to do this needs access to the system records to link pseudonyms to actual student ids. One very useful aspect of being able to use multiple pseudonyms comes into play in this example; the teacher (or any other participant) is able to present several different viewpoints or sides of an argument using different pen-names. We feel that this is particularly valuable in an educational setting : it would appear a useful skill to be able to look at an argument (or scientific theory, or hypothesis) in the round, without being forced to be identified with or even to strongly hold a particular point of view. What is important is being able to marshal the appropriate facts to support or cast doubt on a particular hypothesis. Using the physical world as an analogy, it is generally accepted that in order to fully perceive or appreciate an object such as a mountain, we need to perceive it "in the round". We are advocating a similar approach to understanding ideas and concepts. Students might be encouraged to assume different standpoints and to construct supporting arguments. In [Lennon 94] the case of Level 2 is recommended for certain learning situations.

For our sixth example we consider a museum or exhibition visitor system. In this system, on entry to the museum, visitors acquire a card which they plug into card slots as they move about the museum. The computer system keeps a history of the visitors movements and thereby is able to 'personalise' various interactions such as languages or which parts of a recording are played at which exhibit. In this way visitors are spared needless repetition and can even be assisted with information about additional exhibits related to their interests as the system develops knowledge about them. In order to carry out the above, all the system requires to identify the users is a number on the card, perhaps together with a pseudonym chosen by the user as a form of address (also stored on the card). The visitor's history could be stored on the card (preferably), or centrally in the system's computer. This is an example where Level 1 identification is appropriate.

5 Concluding Remarks

Applications of modern computer networks require a rethinking of how anonymous users should be for various applications. We have made a first attempt to point out some of the issues involved and hope that this will stimulate further work and discussion.

Thanks are due to Bruce Benson who helped us figure out some of the intricacies of e-mail and the Internet.

References

[Chaum 85] D. Chaum: Security without Identification: Transaction Systems to make Big Brother obsolete, Communications of the ACM, October 1985, pp 1030 - 1044.

[Detweiler 93] L. Detweiler: Privacy and Anonymity on the Internet FAQ, sci.crypt newsgroup (Internet).

[van Gelder 85] Lindsy van Gelder: The Strange Case of the Electronic Lover, Ms Magazine, October 1985, pp 364 - 375.

[Kappe 93] F. Kappe, H. Maurer, N. Scherbakov: Hyper-G – A Universal Hypermedia System, J. EMH 2, 1 (1993), 39-66.

[Lennon 94] J. Lennon, H. Maurer: Lecturing Technology – A Future with Hypermedia, to appear in: Educational Technology (1994).

[Maurer 84] H.A. Maurer, N. Rozsenich, and I. Sebestyen : Videotex without "Big Brother", Electronic Publishing Review 1984, Vol. 4, No. 3.

[Maurer 90] H. Maurer: Privacy and security on videotex systems, New Media: Communication Technologies for the 1990s.

[Maurer 92] H. Maurer: Why Hypermedia Systems Are Important, LNCS 6022, Springer Pub.Co. (1992), 1-15.

[Maurer 93] Die Elektronischen Scherben, Maurer's Meinung 153, Austrian Videotex *MAURER###4.

[Nunamaker 91] J. Nunamaker, A. Dennis, J. Valacich, D. Vogel, J. George: Electronic Meeting Systems to Support Group Work, Communications of the ACM, 34, 7 (1991), pp 40 -61.

[Salomaa 90] A. Salomaa : Public Key Cryptography, EATCS Monographs 23, Springer-Verlag 1990.

[Sheffield 93] J. Sheffield: The Impact of Electronic Meeting Systems on New Zealand Organisations, Vol 1 of Proceedings of the 13th New Zealand Computer Society Conference, John Hosking ED., NZCS (1993), pp 21 - 40.

[Time 94] Time Magazine: Who Should Keep The Keys?; Time Magazin March 14 (1994), 38-39.

[Visotschnigg 85] P. Visotschnigg: Verstaendigung im machtfreien Raum; P. Zolnay Pub Co Vienna (1985)

Journal of Universal Computer Science, vol. 1, no. 1 (1995), 48-66
submitted: 21/10/94, accepted: 3/1/95, appeared: 28/1/95 © Springer Pub. Co.

What Is a Random String? [1] [2]

Cristian Calude
(Computer Science Department
The University of Auckland, New Zealand
email: cristian@cs.auckland.ac.nz)

Abstract: Chaitin's algorithmic definition of **random strings**—based on the complexity induced by self-delimiting computers—is critically discussed. One shows that Chaitin's model satisfy many natural requirements related to randomness, so it can be considered as an **adequate model** for finite random objects. It is a better model than the original (Kolmogorov) proposal. Finally, some open problems will be discussed.

Keywords: Blank-endmarker complexity, Chaitin (self-delimiting) complexity, random strings.
Category: G.3

1 Motivation

Suppose that persons A and B give us a sequence of 32 bits each, saying that they were obtained from independent coin flips. If A gives the string

$$u = 01001110100111101001101001110101$$

and B gives the string

$$v = 00000000000000000000000000000000,$$

then we would tend to believe A and would not believe B: the string u *seems* to be random, but the string v does not. Further on, if we change the value of a bit (say, from 1 to 0) in a (non) "random" string, then the result is still a (non) "random" string. If we keep making such changes in a "random" string, then we will eventually complete distroy randomness.

Laplace [21], pp.16-17 was, in a sense, aware of the above paradox, as it may be clear from the following phrase:

> *In the game of heads and tails, if head comes up a hundred times in a row then this appears to us extraordinary, because after dividing the nearly infinite number of combinations that can arise in a hundred throws into regular sequences, or those in which we observe a rule that is easy to grasp, and into irregular sequences, the latter are incomparably more numerous.*

[1] This paper is an expanded version of an invited lecture given to the International Symposium *The Foundational Debate*, Vienna, 15-17 September, 1994.

[2] This work has been partially supported by Auckland University Research Grant A18/XXXXX/62090/F3414022.

In other words: non random strings are strings possessing some kind of regularity, and since the number of all those strings (of a given length) is **small**, the occurrence of such a string is **extraordinary**.

Furthermore, regularity is a good basis for compression. Accordingly, randomness means the absence of any compression possibility; it corresponds to maximum information content (because after dropping any part of the string, there remains no possibility of recovering it). As we shall prove in Section 5, most strings have this property. In opposition, *most strings we deal with do not.*

The information content of a phrase in a natural language (English, for example) can be recovered even some letters (words) are omitted. The reason comes from the redundancy of most spoken languages. As a consequence, there exist many efficient programs to compress texts written in natural languages. It is important to emphasize that all these methods work very well on texts written in some natural language, but they do not work well on average, i.e. on *all* possible combinations of letters of the same length. Redundancy is also a very powerful handle to readers of mathematical books (and, in general, of scientific literature), and also to cryptanalysts (for example, Caesar's ciphers—just permutations of letters—can be broken by frequency analysis; see more on this topic in Salomaa [27]). A hypothetical language in which there are only strings with maximum information content gives no preference to strings (i.e. they have equal frequency); this makes the cipher impossible to break. However, such languages do not exist (and cannot be constructed, even with the help of the best computers, available now and in the future); redundancy is essential and inescapable in a spoken language (and to a large extent in most artificial languages; see Marcus [25]).

Before passing to some the formal treatment it is natural to ask the following question: Are there any random strings? Of course, we do not have yet the necessary tools to properly answer this question, but we may try to approach it informally. Let us call *canonical program* the smallest program generating a string. We claim that *every canonical program should be random*, independently if it generates or not a random output. Indeed, assume that x is a canonical program generating y. If x is not random, then there exists a program z generating x which is substantially smaller than x. Now, consider the program

from z calculate x, then from x calculate y.

This program is only a few letters longer than z, and thus it should be much shorter than x, which was supposed to be canonical. We have reached a contradiction.

Borel [1, 2] was the first author who systematically studied random sequences. The complexity-theoretic approach was independently initiated by Kolmogorov [22] and Chaitin [9]. For more historical facts see Chaitin [17] (A Life in Math), Uspensky [31], Li and Vitányi [23] and Calude [4].

2 Computers and Complexities

Denote by N the set of natural numbers; $N_+ = N \setminus \{0\}$. If S is a finite set, then $\#S$ denotes the cardinality of S. We shall use the following functions: i) $rem(m, i)$, the remainder of the integral division of m by i $(m, i \in N_+)$, ii) $\lfloor \alpha \rfloor$, the integral part of the real α, iii) $\log_Q$, the base Q logarithm, $\log = \lfloor \log_2 \rfloor$.

Fix $A = \{a_1, \ldots, a_Q\}, Q \geq 2$, a finite alphabet. By A^* we denote the free monoid generated by A (under concatenation). The elements of A^* are called *strings*; λ is the empty string. For x in $A^*, |x|$ is the length of $x(|\lambda| = 0)$. For m in N, $A^m = \{x \in A^* \mid |x| = m\}$. For every $x \in A^*$ and natural n put $x^n = xx\ldots x$, (n times); $x^0 = \lambda$.

Every total ordering on A, say $a_1 < a_2 < \cdots < a_Q$, induces a quasi-lexicographical order on $A^* : \lambda < a_1 < \cdots < a_Q < a_1a_1 < \cdots < a_1a_Q < a_Qa_Q < \cdots < a_1a_1a_1 < \cdots$. We denote by $string(n)$ the nth string in A^* according to the quasi-lexicographical order. The induced order on each set A^m coincides with the lexicographical order.

Working with *partial recursive (p.r.) functions* $\varphi : A^* \times A^* \stackrel{o}{\rightarrow} A^*$ (called sometime *blank-endmarker computer*—see Chaitin [15]) we adopt the notations from Calude [3]. If $x \in dom(\varphi)$, that is x is in the domain of φ, then we write $\varphi(x) < \infty$. A *Chaitin computer* is a p.r. function $C : A^* \times A^* \stackrel{o}{\rightarrow} A^*$ with a *prefix-free domain* (i.e. for every string z, there is no pair of distinct strings x, y such that $U(x, z) < \infty$, $U(y, z) < \infty$, and x is a prefix of y). To a Chaitin computer C one associates the *self-delimiting complexity* or *Chaitin complexity*

$$H_C : A^* \stackrel{o}{\rightarrow} N,\ H_C(x/y) = \min\{|z| \mid z \in A^*, C(z, y^*) = x\},$$

with the convention $\min \emptyset = \infty$; here $y^* = \min\{w \in A^* \mid U(w, \lambda) = y\}$, the operator min being taken according to the quasi-lexicographical order.

The basic result obtained by Chaitin [9] (called the *Invariance Theorem*) states the existence of a Chaitin computer U (called *universal Chaitin computer*) such that for every Chaitin computer C there exists a constant c (depending upon U and C) such that

$$H_U(x/y) \leq H_C(x/y) + c,$$

for all $x, y \in A^*$.[3] The complexity induced by a blank-endmarker computer φ, K_φ is defined by $K_\varphi(x/y) = \min\{|z| \mid z \in A^*, \varphi(z, y) = x\}$. A similar Invariance Theorem holds true for blank-endmarker computers. See also Chaitin [9, 10], Kolmogorov [22], Martin-Löf [26], Calude [3].

For this paper we fix a universal Chaitin computer U and denote by H the induced complexity. Also, fix a universal blank-endmarker computer $\psi : A^* \times A^* \stackrel{o}{\rightarrow} A^*$ and denote by K the induced complexity. By $H(x)$, $K(x)$ we denote the complexities $H(x/\lambda)$, $K(x/\lambda)$, respectively.

Let $f, g, h : A^* \rightarrow [0, \infty)$ be three functions. We write $f \leq g + \mathrm{O}(h)$ in case there exists $C > 0$ such that $f(x) \leq g(x) + Ch(x)$, for almost all strings x. We write $f = g + \mathrm{O}(h)$ in case $f \leq g + \mathrm{O}(h)$ and $g \leq f + \mathrm{O}(h)$; $f \asymp g$ means that there exists two positive reals α, β such that

$f(x) \leq \alpha g(x)$ and $g(x) \leq \beta f(x)$, for almost all strings x.

3 Chaitin Random Strings

To motivate our approach we use the analogy between "tallness" and "randomness". To appreciate if a person is or is not tall we proceed as follows. We choose a unity measure (say, centimetre) and we evaluate the height. We get an *absolute*

[3] Exact values for all additive constants discussed in this paper have been recently computed by Chaitin [19]—using a Lisp model of computation.

value. Next, we establish "a set of people of reference". For instance, if we have to appreciate how tall is a little girl we fix an age and we relate her height to the average height of girls of that age. But, if we discuss the same question for a teenager, the situation is completely different. It follows that the adjective tall is *relative*. To correctly appreciate it we need both components: the exact one (height) and the relative one (comparison within a fixed set). It is fortunate that in English we have two words to express this: height and tall.

For randomness we proceed in a similar way, trying to capture, as best as possible, the idea that *a string is random if it cannot be algorithmically compressed*. First we use a measure of complexity for strings (H); this represents the "absolute component". Secondly, we define randomness "relative to a set"—the relative component. In our case we appreciate the degree of randomness of a string with respect to the set of all strings, over a fixed alphabet, having the same length.[4]

Of course, the success or failure of the approach depends upon the measure of complexity we are adopting. The use of self-delimiting programs instead of blank-endmarker programs is motivated by Chaitin [16] as follows:

> *A key point that must be stipulated ... is that an input program must be self-delimited: its total length (in bits) must be given within the program itself. (This seemingly minor point, which paralyzed progress in the field for nearly a decade, is what entailed the redefinition of algorithmic randomness.) Real programming languages are self-delimiting, because they provide constructs for beginning and ending a program. Such constructs allow a program to contain well-defined subprograms nested in them. Because a self-delimiting program is built up by concatenation and nesting self-delimiting subprograms, a program is syntactically complete only when the last open subprogram is closed. In essence the beginning and ending constructs for programs and subprograms function respectively like left and right parentheses in mathematical expressions.*

We first recall the asymptotical behaviour of the complexity H (see Chaitin [12, 14]):

Theorem 3.1. *Let $f : N \to A^*$ be an injective, recursive function. a) One has:*

$$\sum_{n\geq 0} Q^{-H(f(n))} \leq 1.$$

b) Consider a recursive function $g : N_+ \to N_+$.[5]

i) If $\sum_{n\geq 1} Q^{-g(n)} = \infty$, then $H(f(n)) > g(n)$, for infinitely many $n \in N_+$.
ii) If $\sum_{n\geq 1} Q^{-g(n)} < \infty$, then $H(f(n)) \leq g(n) + O(1)$.

Proof. a) It is plain that:

$$\sum_{n\geq 0} Q^{-H(f(n))} \leq \sum_{x\in A^*} Q^{-H(x)} \leq \sum_{x\in A^*} P(x) \leq 1.$$

---

[4] So, the "context" is determined by the length and the size of the alphabet.

[5] Actually, this part is still true in case g is a function semi-computable in the limit from above.

b) i) Assume first that $\sum_{n\geq 1} Q^{-g(n)} = \infty$. If there exists a natural N such that

$$H(f(n)) \leq g(n), \text{ for all } n \geq N,$$

then we get a contradiction:

$$\infty = \sum_{n\geq N} Q^{-g(n)} \leq \sum_{n\geq N} Q^{-H(f(n))} \leq \sum_{n\geq 0} Q^{-H(f(n))} \leq 1.$$

In view of the hypothesis in b) ii), there exists a natural N such that $\sum_{n\geq N} Q^{-g(n)} \leq 1$. We can use Kraft-Chaitin Theorem in order to construct a Chaitin computer $C : A^* \times A^* \xrightarrow{o} A^*$ with the following property: For every $n \geq N$ there exists $x \in A^*$ with $|x| = g(n)$ and $C(x, \lambda) = f(n)$. So, there exists a natural c such that for all $n \geq N$,

$$H(f(n)) \leq H_C(f(n)) + c \leq g(n) + c.$$

□

Example 3.2. $\sum_{n\geq 0} Q^{-H(string(n))} \leq 1.$

Example 3.3. *i) Take $g(n) = \lfloor \log_Q n \rfloor$. It is seen that $\sum_{n\geq 1} Q^{-g(n)} = \infty$, so $H(string(n)) > \lfloor \log_Q n \rfloor$, for infinitely many $n \geq 1$.*
ii) For $g(n) = 2\lfloor \log_Q n \rfloor$, one has:

$$\sum_{n\geq 1} Q^{-g(n)} \leq Q \sum_{n\geq 1} \frac{1}{n^2} < \infty,$$

so $H(string(n)) \leq 2\lfloor \log_Q n \rfloor + O(1)$. For $Q > 2$ and $g(n) = \lfloor \log_{Q-1} n \rfloor$, one has:

$$\sum_{n\geq 1} Q^{-g(n)} \leq Q \sum_{n\geq 1} \frac{1}{n^{\log_{Q-1} Q}} < \infty,$$

so $H(string(n)) \leq \lfloor \log_{Q-1} n \rfloor + O(1)$.

Remark. Chaitin complexity H can be characterized as a minimal function, semi-computable in the limit from above, that lies on the borderline between the convergence and the divergence of the series

$$\sum_{n\geq 0} Q^{-H(string(n))}.$$

Put $H_C(x, y) = H_C(< x, y >)$, where $<, >: A^* \times A^* \to A^*$ is a recursive bijection.

The following three formulae come from Chaitin [12, 13, 14]:

Lemma 3.4. *There exists a natural c such that for all string s $x, y \in A^*$ one has*

$$H(x) \leq H(x, y) + c,$$
$$H(x, y) \leq H(x) + H(y/x) + c,$$
$$H(x, y) \leq H(x) + H(y) + c.$$

We are in the position to evaluate the complexity of the most complex strings of a given length (first obtained in Chaitin [12]).

Theorem 3.5. *For every $n \in N$, one has:*

$$\max_{x \in A^n} H(x) = n + H(string(n)) + O(1).$$

Proof. In view of Lemma 3.4, for every string x of length n,

$$H(x) \leq H(string(n), x) + O(1) \leq H(string(n)) + H(x/string(n)) + O(1).$$

To get the relation

$$\max_{x \in A^n} H(x) \leq n + H(string(n)) + O(1)$$

we shall prove that for every string x of length n,

$$H(x/string(n)) \leq n + O(1).$$

Fix $n \geq 0$ and define the Chaitin computer $C_n : A^n \times A^* \xrightarrow{o} A^*$ by

$$C_n(x, y) = x \text{ if } U(y, \lambda) \neq \infty.$$

Accordingly, $U((string(n))^*, \lambda) = string(n)$ and

$$\begin{aligned} H(x/string(n)) &\leq H_{C_n}(x/string(n)) + O(1) \\ &= \min\{|z| \mid z \in A^*, C_n(z, (string(n))^*) = x\} + O(1) \\ &\leq n + O(1). \end{aligned}$$

To prove the converse relation we need the following
Intermediate Step. For every $n \geq 0$,

$$\#\{x \in A^n \mid H(x) < n + H(string(n)) - t + O(1)\} < Q^{n-t+O(1)}.$$

By Lemma ?? one has:

$$H(x) < n + H(string(n)) - t + O(1) \Longleftrightarrow H(x/string(n)) < n - t + O(1),$$

so

$$\#\{x \in A^n \mid H(x) < n + H(string(n)) - t + O(1)\} =$$
$$\#\{x \in A^n \mid H(x/string(n)) < n - t + O(1)\} < Q^{n-t+O(1)}.$$

Accordingly, not all strings of length n have the complexity less than $n + H(string(n)) + O(1)$, i.e. $\max_{x \in A^n} H(x) \geq n + H(string(n)) + O(1)$. □

The above discussion may be concluded with the following definition. Let $\Sigma : N \rightarrow N$ be the function defined by

$$\Sigma(n) = \max_{x \in A^n} H(x).$$

In view of Theorem 3.5, $\Sigma(n) = n + H(string(n)) + O(1)$. We define the random strings of length n to be the strings with maximal self-delimiting complexity among the strings of length n, i.e. the strings $x \in A^n$ having $H(x) \approx \Sigma(n)$.

Definition 3.6. *A string $x \in A^*$ is **Chaitin m-random** (m is a natural number) if $H(x) \geq \Sigma(|x|) - m$; x is **Chaitin random** if it is 0-random.*

The above definition depends upon the fixed universal computer U; the generality of the approach comes from the Invariance Theorem.

Obviously, for every length n and for every $m \geq 0$ there exists a Chaitin m-random string x of length n. Denote by $RAND_m^C$, $RAND^C$, respectively, the sets of Chaitin m-random strings and random strings.

It is worth to note that the property of Chaitin m-randomness is asymptotic. Indeed, for $x \in RAND_m^C$, the larger is the difference between $|x|$ and m, the more random is x. There is no sharp dividing line between randomness and pattern, but it looks as though all $x \in RAND_m^C$ with $m \leq H(string(|x|))$ have a true random behaviour.

How many strings $x \in A^n$ have maximal complexity, i.e. $H(x) = \Sigma(|x|)$? The answer was given by Chaitin [18]:

Theorem 3.7. *There exists a natural constant $c > 0$ (which depends upon the size of the underlying alphabet, Q) such that*

$$\gamma(n) = \#\{x \in A^n \mid H(x) = \Sigma(|x|)\} > Q^{n-c},$$

for all natural n.

How large is c? Out of Q^n strings of length n, at most $Q + Q^2 + \cdots + Q^{n-m-1} = (Q^{n-m} - 1)/(Q - 1)$ can be described by programs of length less than $n - m$. The ratio between $(Q^{n-m} - 1)/(Q - 1)$ and Q^n is less than 10^{-i} as $Q^m \geq 10^i$, irrespective of the value of n. For instance, this happens in case $Q = 2, m = 20, i = 6$; it says that *less than one in a million among the binary strings of any given length is not Chaitin 20-random.*

So, in a strictly quantitative sense, almost all strings are Chaitin random.

Problem. Denote by $(c_Q)_{Q\geq 2}$ the sequence of constants appearing in Theorem 3.7. Is this sequence bounded?

The rest of this paper will be devoted to the analysis of the adequacy of Chaitin's definition of randomness.

4 A Statistical Analysis Random Strings

In this section we confront Chaitin's definition of randomness with the probability point of view. As we have already said, the present proposal identifies *randomness* with *incompressibility*. In order to justify this option we have to show that the strings that are incompressible justify the various properties of stochasticity identified by the classical Probability Theory. It is not so difficult, although tedious, to check *separately* such a single property. However, we may proceed in a better way, due to the celebrated theory developed by Martin-Löf: We demonstrate that the incompressible strings do possess all conceivable effectively testable properties of stochasticity. Here we include the known properties, but also the possible unknown ones. A general transfer principle will emerge, by virtue of which various results from classical probability theory carry automatically for random strings.

The ideas of Martin-Löf's theory are rooted in the statistical practice. We are given an element x of some sample space (associated to some distribution) and we want to test the hypothesis *x is a typical outcome*. Being typical means "belonging to every reasonable majority". An element x will be "random" just in case x lies in the intersection of all such majorities.

A level of a statistical test is a set of strings which are found relatively non-random (by the test). Each level is a subset of the previous level, containing less and less strings, considered more and more non-random. The number of strings decreases exponentially fast at each level. In the binary case, a test contains at level 0 all possible strings, at level two only at most 1/2 of the strings, at level three only 1/4 of all strings, and so on; accordingly, at level m the test contains at most 2^{n-m} strings of length n.

We give now the formal definition.

Definition 4.1. *An r.e. set $V \subset A^* \times N_+$ is called a* ***Martin-Löf test*** *if the following two properties hold true:*
1) $V_{m+1} \subset V_m$, for all $m \geq 1$ (here $V_m = \{x \in A^* \mid (x, m) \in V\}$ is the m-section of V),
2) $\#(A^n \cap V_m) < Q^{n-m}/(Q-1)$, for all $n \geq m \geq 1$.

By definition, the empty set is a Martin-Löf test.

The set V_m is called the *critical region at level $Q^{-m}/(Q-1)$*. (Getting an outcome string x in V_m means the rejection of the randomness hypothesis for x.) A string x is declared "random" at level m by V in case $x \notin V_m$ and $|x| > m$.

The following example models the following simple idea: If a binary string x has too many ones (zeros), then it cannot be random.

Example 4.2. *The set*

$$V = \{(x, m) \in A^* \times N_+ \mid | \frac{N_i(x)}{|x|} - \frac{1}{Q} | > Q^m \frac{1}{\sqrt{|x|}}\},$$

where $N_i(x)$ is the number of occurrences of the letter a_i in x, is a Martin -Löf test.

Proof. Clearly, V is r.e. and satisfies condition 1). In view of the formula:

$$\#\{x \in A^n \mid | \frac{N_i(x)}{|x|} - \frac{1}{Q} | > \varepsilon\} \leq \frac{Q^{n-2}(Q-1)}{n\varepsilon^2},$$

one gets

$$\#(A^n \cap V_m) = \#\{x \in A^n \mid | \frac{N_i(x)}{|x|} - \frac{1}{Q} | > Q^m \frac{1}{\sqrt{|x|}}\}$$

$$= \frac{Q^{n-2}(Q-1)}{Q^{2m}} = Q^{n-2-2m}(Q-1) \leq \frac{Q^{n-m}}{Q-1}.$$

□

Definition 4.3. *To every Martin-Löf test V we associate the* ***critical level*** $m_V : A^* \to N$,

$$m_V(x) = \begin{cases} \max\{m \geq 1 \mid (x,m) \in V\}, & \text{if } (x,1) \in V, \\ 0, & \text{otherwise.} \end{cases}$$

A string x is declared ***random*** *by a Martin-Löf test V if $x \notin V_q$, for some $q < |x|$, or, equivalently, if $m_V(x) < |x| - 1$.*

Definition 4.4. *A Martin-Löf test $\mathcal{U}$ is called* ***universal*** *in case for every Martin-Löf test V, there exists a constant c (depending upon $\mathcal{U}$ and V) such that*

$$V_{m+c} \subset \mathcal{U}_m, m = 1, 2, \ldots$$

It is easy to see that a *Martin -Löf test $\mathcal{U}$ is universal iff for every Martin-Löf test V there exists a constant c (depending upon $\mathcal{U}$ and V) such that*

$$m_V(x) \leq m_{\mathcal{U}}(x) + c, \text{ for all } x \in A^*.$$

Our aim is to prove that almost all Chaitin random strings pass all conceivable effective tests of stochasticity, i.e. they are declared random by every Martin-Löf test.

Theorem 4.5. *Fix $t \in N$. Almost all strings in $RAND_t^C$ will be declared eventually* random *by every Martin-Löf test.*

Proof. If K is the complexity induced by a fixed universal blank-endmarker computer, then by a result in Calude, Chitescu [7], the set $\mathcal{U} = \{(x,m) \in A^* \times N_+ \mid K(x) < |x| - m\}$ is a universal Martin-Löf test. Every section $\mathcal{U}_t$ is r.e., so when a string x belongs to $\mathcal{U}_t$, then
we can eventually discover this. Moreover, there are less than

$$Q^{n-t}/(Q-1)$$

strings of length n having this property. Thus if we are given $|x| = n$ and t we need to only know $n - t$ digits to pick out any particular string $x \in A^n$ with this property. I.e., as the first x that we discover has this property, the second x that we discover has this property,...,the ith x that we discover has this property, and $i < Q^{n-t}/(Q-1)$. Accordingly, every string $x \in A^n \cap \mathcal{U}_t$ has the property that

$$H(x/ < string(n), string(t) >) < n - t + O(1).$$

So, by Lemma 3.4:

$$\begin{aligned} H(x) &< H(x/ < string(n), string(t) >) + H(< string(n), \\ &\quad string(t) >) + O(1) \\ &< n - t + H(string(n), string(t)) + O(1) \\ &< n - t + H(string(n)) + H(string(t) + O(1) \\ &< n - t + H(string(n)) + O(\log_Q t), \end{aligned}$$

since in general $H(string(m)) < O(\log_Q m)$.

Finally, take $x \in RAND_t^C$, i.e. $H(x) \geq \Sigma(|x|) - t$, and fix an arbitrary Martin-Löf test V. Take a natural T such that $T - O(\log_Q T) \geq t$. It follows that $x \notin \mathcal{U}_T$—otherwise we would have

$$H(x) < \Sigma(|x|) - T - O(\log_Q T),$$

which means $T - O(\log_Q T) < t$. By virtue of the universality of $\mathcal{U}$ we get a constant c such that $V_{m+c} \subset \mathcal{U}_m, m = 1, 2, \ldots$, i.e. $x \notin V_{c+T}$. The constant $c+T$ is *independent* of x. So, for large enough random strings x, one has $x \notin V_m$ and $|x| > m$. □

5 A Computational Analysis Random Strings

We pursue the analysis of the relevance of Chaitin's definition by confronting it with a natural, computational requirement: *there should be no algorithmic way to recognize what strings are random.*

The following result, due to Chaitin [11], Theorem 4.1, was used for deriving the first information-theoretic incompleteness results (see also Chaitin [17]). We use it now to discuss the uncomputability of $RAND_t^C$.

Let $<>: A^* \times N \to A^*$ be a recursive bijective function.

Theorem 5.1. *We can effectively compute a constant d such that if*

$$W_e \subset \{< w, m > \in A^* \times N \mid H(w) > m\},$$

then $n \leq H(e) + d$, *for all* $< u, n > \in W_e$.

Recall that a subset $X \subset A^*$ is immune iff it is infinite and has no infinite r.e. subsets.

Corollary 5.2. *Let* $g : N \to N$ *be a recursive function such that the set* $S = \{w \in A^* | H(w) > g(|w|)\}$ *is infinite. Then, the set S is immune.*

Proof. Let $W_e \subset \{w \in A^* | H(w) > g(|w|)\}$. Put $V_e = \{< w, g(|w|) > | w \in W_e\}$; clearly, V_e is r.e. and $V_e = W_{f(e)}$, for some recursive function $f : A^* \to A^*$. So,

$$V_e = W_{f(e)} \subset \{< w, m > | H(w) > m\}$$

and in view of Theorem 5.1 from $< w, g(|w|) > \in V_e = W_{f(e)}$ we deduce $g(|w|) \leq H(f(e)) + d$, i.e., V_e is finite. This shows that W_e itself is finite. □

Corollary 5.3. *The set* $RAND_t^C$ *is immune for every* $t \geq 0$.

Proof. Fix $t \in N$. It is plain that

$$RAND_t^C \subset \{x \in A^* | H(x) \geq |x| - t\}.$$

The set $\{x \in A^* | H(x) \geq |x| - t\}$ is immune by Corollary 5.2 and every infinite subset of an immune set is itself immune. □

The above theorem can be expressed as:

$$(\forall B \subset A^*)(B \text{ infinite and r.e. } \Rightarrow B \setminus RAND_t^C \neq \emptyset).$$

There are two (classically equivalent) ways to represent the above statement:

1. $(\forall x \in A^*)$ $(W_x$ infinite $\Rightarrow \exists y \in A^* : y \in W_x - etminusRAND_t^C)$,
2. $\forall x \in A^* : (W_x \subset RAND_t^C \Rightarrow (\exists n \in N)\, \#(W_x) \leq n)$.

Based on theses statements we can formulate two constructive versions of immunity:

> The set $R \subset A^*$ is called *constructively immune* (Li [24]) if there exists a p.r. function $\varphi : A^* \stackrel{o}{\rightarrow} A^*$ such that for all $x \in A^*$, if W_x is infinite, then $\varphi(x) \neq \infty$ and $\varphi(x) \in W_x \setminus R$.
>
> The set $R \subset A^*$ is called *effectively immune* (Smullyan [30]) if there exists a p.r. function $\sigma : A^* \stackrel{o}{\rightarrow} N$ such that for all $x \in A^*$, if $W_x \subset R$, then $\sigma(x) \neq \infty$ and $\#(W_x) \leq \sigma(x)$.

It is worth noticing that there exist constructively immune sets which are not effectively immune and vice-ve rsa. Moreover, if the complement of an immune set is r.e., then that set is constructively immune. Hence, we get:

Theorem 5.4. *For every $t \geq 0$, $RAND_t^C$ is constructively immune.*

Proof. Fix $t \in N$. The set $\{x \in A^* | H(x) \geq |x| - t\}$ is constructively immune since its complement is r.e. As $RAND_t^C$ is an infinite subset of a constructive immune set it follows that itself is constructive immune. □

As a scholium of Corollary 5.2 one obtains:

Scholium 5.5. *If $g : N \rightarrow N$ is a recursive function with $\lim_{n\rightarrow\infty} g(n) = \infty$, recursively (i.e. there exists an increasing recursive function $r : N \rightarrow N$, such that if $n \geq r(k)$, then $g(n) \geq k$) and the set $S = \{w \in A^* \mid H(w) > g(|w|)\}$ is infinite, then S is effectively immune.*

Proof. In the context of the proof of
Corollary 5.2, $\#W_e = \#W_{f(e)}$ and if $w \in W_e \subset \{u \in A^* \mid H(u) > g(|u|)\}$, then

$$g(|w|) < H(w) \leq H(f(e)) + d \leq |f(e)| + 2\log|f(e)| + d + c + c'.$$

If $|w| \geq r(|f(e)| + 2\log|f(e)| + d + c + c')$, then $g(|w|) > |f(e)| + 2\log|f(e)| + d + c + c'$, so $w \notin W_e$. Accordingly, if $w \in W_e$, then $|w| < r(|f(e)| + 2\log|f(e)| + d + c + c')$, i.e.

$$\#W_e \leq (Q^{r(|f(e)|+2\log|f(e)|+d+c+c')} - 1)/(Q - 1),$$

and the upper bound is a recursive function of e. □

Corollary 5.6. *For all $t \geq 0$, $RAND_t^C$ is effectively immune.*

Proof. An infinite subset of an effectively immune set is effectively immune. □

6 Random Strings Are Borel Normal

Another important restriction pertaining a good definition of randomness concerns the frequency of letters and blocks of letters. In a "true random" string each letter has to appear with approximately the same frequency, namely Q^{-1}. Moreover, the same property should extend to "reasonably long" substrings.

These ideas have been stated by Borel [1, 2] for sequences. In Chaitin [10] one shows that Chaitin Omega Number representing the halting probability of a universal self-delimiting computer is Borel normal.

Motivated by these facts we formalize the Borel normality property for strings. First, let $N_i(x)$ be the number of occurrences of the letter a_i in the string x, $1 \leq i \leq Q$. Accordingly, the ratio $N_i(x)/|x|$ is the relative frequency of the letter a_i in the string x.

For strings of length $m \geq 1$ we proceed as follows. We consider the alphabet $B = A^m$ and construct the free monoid $B^* = (A^m)^*$. Every $x \in B^*$ belongs to A^*, but the converse is false. For $x \in B^*$ we denote by $|x|_m$ the length of x (according to B) which is exactly $|x|m^{-1}$.

For every $1 \leq i \leq Q^m$ denote by N_i^m the number of occurrences of y_i in the string $x \in B^*, B = \{y_1, \ldots, y_{Q^m}\}$. For example, take $A = \{0,1\}, m = 2, B = A^2 = \{00, 01, 10, 11\} = \{y_1, y_2, y_3, y_4\}, x = y_1y_3y_3y_4y_3 \in B^* (x = 0010101110 \in A^*)$. It is easy to see that $|x|_2 = 5, |x| = 10, N_1^2(x) = 1, N_2^2(x) = 0, N_3^2(x) = 3, N_4^2(x) = 1$. Note that the string $y_2 = 01$ appears three times into x, but not on the right positions.

Not every string $x \in A^*$ belongs to B^*. However, there is a possibility "to approximate" such a string by a string in B^*. We proceed as follows. For $x \in A^*$ and $1 \leq j \leq |x|$ we denote by $[x;j]$ the prefix of x of length $|x| - rem(|x|, j)$ (i.e. $[x;j]$ is the longest prefix of x whose length is divisible by j). Clearly, $[x;1] = x$ and $[x;j] \in (A^j)^*$. We are now in a position to extend the functions N_i^m from B^* to A^*: put $N_i^m(x) = N_i^m([x;m])$, in case $|x|$ is not divisible by m. Similarly, $|x|_m = |[x;m]|_m$.

Definition 6.1. *A non-empty string $x \in A^*$ is called **ε-limiting** (ε is a fixed positive real) if for all $1 \leq i \leq Q$, x satisfies the inequality:*

$$\left| \frac{N_i(x)}{|x|} - Q^{-1} \right| \leq \varepsilon.$$

Definition 6.2. *A string $x \in A^*$ is called **Borel normal** iff for every natural m, $1 \leq m \leq \log_Q \log_Q |x|$,*

$$\left| \frac{N_j^m(x)}{|x|_m} - Q^{-m} \right| \leq \sqrt{\frac{\log_Q |x|}{|x|}},$$

for every $1 \leq j \leq Q^m$.

In Calude [5] one proves the following result:

Theorem 6.3. *For every natural $t \geq 0$ we can effectively compute a natural number M_t (depending upon t) such that every string of length greater than M_t in $RAND_t^C$ is Borel normal.*

Theorem 6.3 can be used to prove the following result (a weaker version was obtained in Calude, Campeanu [6]):

Theorem 6.4. *For every natural t and for every string x we can find two strings u, v such that $uxv \in RAND_t^C$.*

Proof. Fix $t \in N, x \in A^i, i \geq 1$. Almost all strings $z \in RAND_t^C$ are Borel normal by Theorem 6.3, i.e. they satisfy the inequality

$$\left| \frac{N_j^m(z)}{\lfloor n/m \rfloor} - Q^{-m} \right| \leq \sqrt{\frac{\log_Q n}{n}},$$

for every $1 \leq j \leq Q^m, 1 \leq m \leq \log_Q \log_Q n; n = |z|$.
Take $m = i$, x to be the jth string of length i and pick a string $z \in RAND_t^C$ such that $n = |z| = Q^{Q^{2i+1}}$. It follows that

$$\left| \frac{N_j^i(z)}{\lfloor n/i \rfloor} - Q^{-m} \right| \leq \sqrt{\frac{\log_Q n}{n}},$$

in particular,

$$Q^{-i} - \sqrt{\frac{\log_Q n}{n}} \leq \frac{N_j^i(z)}{\lfloor n/i \rfloor}.$$

To prove that $N_j^i(z) > 0$ it is enough to show that

$$Q^{-i} > \sqrt{\frac{\log_Q n}{n}},$$

which is true because

$$\sqrt{\frac{\log_Q n}{n}} = Q^{\frac{2i+1}{2} - \frac{1}{2}Q^{2i+1}},$$

and

$$\frac{1}{2}Q^{2i+1} \geq \frac{1}{2}2^{2i+1} = 4^i > 2i + \frac{1}{2}.$$

□

7 Extensions of Random Strings

In this section we deal with the following problem: To what extent is it possible to extend an arbitrary string to a Chaitin random or no n-random string ?

Theorem 6.4 says that every string x can be embedded into a Chaitin random string. The next results will put some more light on this phenomenon.

Theorem 7.1. *For every natural t and every string $x \in A^*$ there exists a string $u \in A^*$ such that for every string $z \in A^*$, $xuz \notin RAND_t^C$.*

Proof. Fix $t \in N$ and $x \in A^*$. Append to x a string u such that $xu = string(m)$ and $1+T < |string(m)|$, where T is a natural number such that $T - O(\log T) \geq t$. Put

$$y = xua_1^m.$$

Next define the Chaitin computer $C(a_1^m a_2(z)) = yz = xua_1^m z$, where $d(z)$ is a self-delimiting program for z. It is seen that

$$\begin{aligned} H(yz) &\leq m + 1 + H(z) + O(1) \\ &= |yz| + (H(z) - |z|) + m - |y| + O(1) \\ &= |yz| + (H(z) - |z|) - |string(m)| + O(1) \\ &\leq \Sigma(|yz|) - t. \end{aligned}$$

This shows that every extension xuz of x lies in $A^* \setminus RAND_t^C$. □

Corollary 7.2. *For every natural t we can find a string x no extension of which is in $RAND_t^C$.*

The above result shows that in Theorem 6.4 we need both the prefix u and the suffix v, i.e. it is not possible to fix $u = \lambda$ and then find an appropriate w. However, such a possibility is regained—conforming with the probabilistic intuition—as far as we switch from $RAND_t^C$ with a *fixed* t to $RAND_t^C$ with an *appropriate, small* t.

We start first with a preliminary result:

Lemma 7.3. *Let $<$ be a partial order on A^* which is recursive and unbounded. Assume that $<$ satisfies the relation*

$$\sum_{x<w} Q^{-|w| - \lfloor \log_Q |w| \rfloor} = \infty, \text{ for all } x \in A^*.$$

Then, for every string x we can find a string y such that $x < y$ and $H(y) \geq |y| + \lfloor \log_Q |y| \rfloor$.

Proof. Assume, by absurdity, that there exists $x \in A^*$ such that for all $x < u$ one has $H(u) < |u| + \lfloor \log_Q |u| \rfloor$. Put

$$X = \{v \in A^* \mid x < v, H(v) < |v| + \lfloor \log_Q |v| \rfloor\}$$

and notice that

$$\sum_{w \in X} Q^{-H(w)} \leq \sum_{v \in domU_\lambda} Q^{-|v|} < 1.$$

So,

$$1 > \sum_{w \in X} Q^{-H(w)} \geq \sum_{w \in X} Q^{-|w| - \lfloor \log_Q |w| \rfloor} = \sum_{x<w} Q^{-|w| - \lfloor \log_Q |w| \rfloor} = \infty,$$

since

$$\{w \in A^* \mid x < w, H(w) \geq |w| + \lfloor \log_Q |w| \rfloor\} = \emptyset.$$

We have got a contradiction. □

Theorem 7.4. *For every string x and natural n we can find a string u such that: i) $|xu| \geq n$, ii) for some natural t (which is about $\lfloor \log_Q |xu| \rfloor$), $xu \in RAND_t^C$.*

Proof. Let $< = <_p$ be the prefix order ($x <_p y$ in case $y = xz$, for some string z). First it is seen that all conditions in Lemma 7.3 are verified: $<_p$ is recursive, unbounded and

$$\begin{aligned}\sum_{x <_p w} Q^{-|w| - \lfloor \log_Q |w| \rfloor} &= \sum_{y \in A^*} Q^{-|xy| - \lfloor \log_Q |xy| \rfloor} \\ &\geq \sum_{y \in A^*} Q^{-|xy| - \log_Q |xy|} \\ &\geq Q^{-|x| - \log_Q |x|} \sum_{n=1}^{\infty} \sum_{y \in A^n} Q^{-|y| - \log_Q |y|} \\ &\geq Q^{-|x| - \log_Q |x|} \sum_{n=1}^{\infty} \frac{1}{n} \\ &= \infty.\end{aligned}$$

Now take $x \in A^*$ and $n \geq 1$. Let y be an arbitrary string such that $|xy| \geq n$. By virtue of the preceding argument we can find a string w such that $xy <_p w$ and

$$H(w) \geq |w| + \lfloor \log_Q |w| \rfloor = \Sigma(|w|) - t,$$

where $t = H(string(|w|)) - \lfloor \log_Q |w| \rfloor$ is about $\lfloor \log_Q |w| \rfloor$. □

8 Chaitin's Model vs Kolmogorov's Model

The original definition of random strings (see Kolmogorov [22], Chaitin [9, 10, 15]) is motivated by the fact that

$$\max_{|x|=n} K(x) = |x| + O(1);$$

accordingly, x is called *Kolmogorov t-random* if $K(x) \geq |x| - t$; $RAND_t^K$ stands for the set of Kolmogorov t-random strings.[6]

All results proven in this paper concerning the adequacy of Chaitin's definition of random strings actually hold true for Kolmogorov's model of random strings.[7] To the best of our knowledge there are no "natural" properties associated with randomness valid for one model and not valid for the other one. The underlying complexities H and K are "asymptotical equivalent". Indeed, a crude relation between H and K is the following:

$$H(x) \asymp K(x).$$

[6] Martin-Löf [26] used the blank-endmarker complexity of a string relative to its length to measure the degree of randomness of a string "within" the context of all strings having the same length.

[7] See Chaitin [11, 12, 13, 14, 15], Martin-Löf [26], Solovay [28], Calude [3, 4], Li and Vitányi [23] for a more detailed discussion.

A more exact relation was obtained by Solovay [28]. Put:

$$K^1(x) = K(x),\ K^{n+1}(x) = K(string(K^n(x))),$$

$$H^1(x) = H(x),\ H^{n+1}(x) = H(string(H^n(x))).$$

Theorem 8.1. *The following relations hold true:*

$$H(x) = K(x) + K^2(x) + O(K^3(x)),$$

$$K(x) = H(x) - H^2(x) + O(H^3(x)).$$

In view of Theorem 8.1 it might be the case that the set of Kolmogorov random strings actually coincides with the set of Chaitin random strings. **This is not the case!**

Using the proof of Theorem 3.5 one can show that every Chaitin random string is Kolmogorov random. However, the converse is not true as Solovay [28] has shown. Actually, Solovay [29] conjectures that there exists a constant L such that for all sufficiently large n, there are at least $Q^{n/2}$ strings of length n, s, such that:

$$K(s) \geq |x| - L,$$

$$H(s) \leq |s| + H(string(n)) - \frac{1}{2}K^2(string(n)).$$

So, many Kolmogorov random strings only "look" random, but in fact, they are not. It is an **open question** to find out "natural" properties related to the informal notion of randomness which hold true for Chaitin random strings, but fail to be true for Kolmogorov random strings. Martin-Löf analysis, developed in Section 4, is not fine enough for this problem.

9 The Role of the Underlying Alphabet

It seems that there is a wide spread feeling that the binary case encompasses the whole strength and generality of coding phenomena, at least from an algorithmic point of view. The problem is the following: Does there exist a *binary* asymptotical optimal coding of all strings over an alphabet with $q > 2$ elements? Surprisingly, the answer is *negative*. The answer is negative for both complexities K and H. As our main interest is directed to Chaitin complexity we shall outline the results for this complexity measure.

Let $q > p \geq 2$ be naturals, and fix two alphabets, A, X, having q and p elements, respectively. The lengths of $x \in A^*$ and $y \in X^*$ will be denoted by $|x|_A$ and $|y|_X$, respectively. Fix a universal Chaitin computer $U : A^* \times A^* \stackrel{o}{\rightarrow} A^*$ and denote by H its induced complexity.

Does there exist a Chaitin computer $C : X^* \times A^* \stackrel{o}{\rightarrow} A^*$ which is universal for the class of all Chaitin computers acting on A^*?

The upshot is the following result (see Calude [4], Calude, Jürgensen, and Salomaa [8]):

Theorem 9.1. *There is no Chaitin computer $C : X^* \times A^* \stackrel{o}{\rightarrow} A^*$ which is universal for the class of all Chaitin computers acting on A^*.*

The proof is based on the fact that Chaitin complexity cannot be optimized better than linearly, i.e. the Invariance Theorem is the best possible result in this direction: For every fix a real number $0 < \alpha < 1$, there is no Chaitin computer $C : A^* \times A^* \stackrel{o}{\rightarrow} A^*$ such that for all Chaitin computers D one has:

$$H_C(x) \leq \alpha H_D(x) + O(1).$$

Let us study Chaitin complexity acting on alphabets of different size. We need some more notation. For every natural $i \geq 2$ put $A_i = \{0, 1, \ldots, i-1\}$, and let us denote by $string_i(n)$ the nth string in A_i^* (according to the quasi-lexicographical order induced by $0 < 1 < \cdots < i-1$); let $H_i : A_i^* \rightarrow N$ be Chaitin complexity.

Theorem 9.2.
Let $2 \leq q < Q$. Then, there exists a constant α (which depends upon q, Q) such that for all $x \in A_q^*$ we have:

$$|H_q(x) - (\log_q Q) H_q(x)| \leq \alpha.$$

Proposition 9.3. *For every $2 \leq q < Q$ and all $x \in A_q^*$,*

$$H_Q(x) < |x| + O(1).$$

So, no string $x \in A_q^*$ is random over A_Q^*.[8] In the binary case we have only two such strings, namely

$$00\ldots0 \text{ and } 11\ldots1,$$

which are obviously non-random. In the non-binary case we have

$$\sum_{i=2}^{Q-1} i^n \binom{Q}{i}$$

strings over the alphabet A_Q which are non-binary because they do not contain all Q letters. For instance, for $Q = 3$ one has 3×2^n such strings, some of them (in fact, according to Theorem 3.7, more then $3 \times 2^{n-c_2}$, where c_2 is a constant which depends on the size of the alphabet but not on the length n) are random as *binary* strings. So, it is shown once again, that randomness is a contextual property.

10 Conclusion

In view of the above discussion we conclude that Chaitin's model of random strings satisfy many natural requirements related to randomness, so it can be considered as an **adequate model** for finite random objects. It is a better model than the original (Kolmogorov) proposal. The distinction between Chaitin and Kolmogorov models is far from being elucidated, e.g. no property—naturally associated with randomness—holding true for Chaitin random strings and failing to be satisfied by Kolmogorov random strings is actually known. All descriptional complexities in the binary and non-binary cases have crucial differences, so it appears that it is only natural to discuss the complexity and randomness of finite objects in a non-necessarily binary framework.

[8] This result follows also from Theorem 6.3.

Acknowledgment

I wish to warmly thank Greg Chaitin for many stimulating discussions on random strings (by email, in Auckland, New Zealand and Bar Harbor, Maine, US) and for kindly permitting to incorporate his proofs for Theorems 4.5 and 6.4. I express my gratitude to Helmut Jürgensen, Per Martin-Löf, Charles Rackhoff, Arto Salomaa, and Bob Solovay for their illuminating comments.

References

1. É. Borel. Les probabilités dénombrables et leurs applications arithmétiques, *Rend. Circ. Mat. Palermo* 27(1909), 247-271.
2. É. Borel. *Lecons sur la théorie des fonctions*, Gauthier-Villars, Paris, 2nd ed., 1914.
3. C. Calude. *Theories of Computational Complexity*, North-Holland, Amsterdam, New York, Oxford, Tokyo, 1988.
4. C. Calude. *Information and R andomness. An Algorithmic Perspective*, Springer-Verlag, Berlin, 1994. (Forewords by G. J. Chaitin and A. Salomaa)
5. C. Calude. Borel normality and algorithmic randomness, in G. Rozenberg, A. Salomaa (eds.). *Developments in Language Theory*, World Scientific, Singapore, 1994, 113-129. (With a note by G. J. Chaitin)
6. C. Calude, C. Câmpeanu. Note on the topological structure of random strings, *Theoret. Comput. Sci.* 112(1993), 383-390.
7. C. Calude, I. Chitescu. A class of universal P. Martin-Löf tests, *EATCS Bull.* 25 (1984), 14-19.
8. C. Calude, H. Jürgensen, A. Salomaa. *Coding without Tears*, manuscript, February 1994, 15 pp.
9. G. J. Chaitin. On the length of programs for computing finite binary sequences, *J. Assoc. Comput. Mach.*. 13(1966),547-569. (Reprinted in: Chaitin [15], 369-410.)
10. G. J. Chaitin. On the length of programs for computing finite binary sequences: statistical considerations, *J. Assoc. Comput. Mach.* 16(1969), 145-159. (Reprinted in: Chaitin [15], 411-434.)
11. G. J. Chaitin. Information-theoretic limitations of formal systems, *J.Assoc. Comput. Mach.* 21(1974), 403-424. (Reprinted in: Chaitin [15], 291-333.)
12. G. J. Chaitin. A theory of program size formally identical to information theory, *J. Assoc. Comput. Mach.* 22(1975), 329-340. (Reprinted in: Chaitin [15], 197-223.)
13. G. J. Chaitin. Algorithmic information theory, *IBM J. Res. Develop.* 21(1977), 350-359,496. (Reprinted in: Chaitin [15], 83-108.)
14. G. J. Chaitin. *Algorithmic Information Theory*, Cambridge University Press, Cambridge,1987. (third printing 1990)
15. G. J. Chaitin. *Information, Randomness and Incompleteness, Papers on Algorithmic Information Theory*, World Scientific, Singapore, New Jersey, Hong Kong, 1987.(2nd ed., 1990)
16. G. J. Chaitin. Randomness in arithmetic, *Scientific American* 259(1988), 80-85. (Reprinted in: Chaitin [15], 14-19.)
17. G. J. Chaitin. *Information-Theoretic Incompleteness*, World Scientific, Singapore, New Jersey, Hong Kong, 1992.
18. G. J. Chaitin. On the number of N-bit strings with maximum complexity, *Applied Mathematics and Computation* 59(1993), 97-100.
19. G. J. Chaitin. *The Limit s of Mathematics*, IBM Watson Center, Yorktown Heights, Draft July 23, 1994, 219 pp.

20. P. Gács. *Lecture Notes on Descriptional Complexity and Randomness*, Boston University, 1988, manuscript, 62 pp.
21. P. S. Laplace. *A Philosophical Essay on Probability Theories*, Dover, New York, 1951.
22. A. N. Kolmogorov. Three approaches for defining the concept of "information quantity", *Problems Inform. Transmission* 1(1965), 3-11.
23. M. Li, P. M. Vitányi. *An Introduction to Kolmogorov Complexity and Its Applications*, Springer-Verlag, Berlin, 1993.
24. X. Li. Effective immune sets, program index sets and effectively simple sets - generalizations and applications of the recursion theorem, in C. -T. Chong, M. J. Wicks (eds.). *South-East Asian Conference on Logic*, Elsevier, Amsterdam, 1983, 97-106.
25. S. Marcus (ed.). *Contextual Ambiguities in Natural & Artificial Languages*, Vol. 2, Ghent, Belgium, 1983.
26. P. Martin-Löf. The definition of random sequences, *Inform. and Control* 9(1966), 602-619.
27. A. Salomaa. *Public-Key Cryptography*, Springer Verlag, Berlin, 1990.
28. R. M. Solovay. *Draft of a paper (or series of papers) on Chaitin's work ... done for the most part during the period of Sept. - Dec. 1974*, unpublished manuscript, IBM Thomas J. Watson Research Center, Yorktown Heights, New York, May 1975, 215 pp.
29. R. M. Solovay. Email to C. Calude, August 13, 1994.
30. R. M. Smullyan. Effectively simple sets, *Proc. Amer. Math. Soc.* 15(1964), 893-895.
31. V. A. Uspensky. Kolmogorov and mathematical logic, *J . Symbolic Logic* 57(1992), 385-412.

Journal of Universal Computer Science, vol. 1, no. 1 (1995), 67-82
submitted: 8/11/94, accepted: 10/1/95, appeared: 28/1/95

Grammars Based on the Shuffle Operation

Gheorghe PĂUN
Institute of Mathematics of the Romanian Academy of Sciences
PO Box 1 764, Bucureşti, Romania

Grzegorz ROZENBERG
University of Leiden, Department of Computer Science
Niels Bohrweg 1, 2333 CA Leiden, The Netherlands

Arto SALOMAA
Academy of Finland and University of Turku
Department of Mathematics, 20500 Turku, Finland

Abstract: We consider generative mechanisms producing languages by starting from a finite set of words and shuffling the current words with words in given sets, depending on certain conditions. Namely, regular and finite sets are given for controlling the shuffling: strings are shuffled only to strings in associated sets. Six classes of such grammars are considered, with the shuffling being done on a leftmost position, on a prefix, arbitrarily, globally, in parallel, or using a maximal selector. Most of the corresponding six families of languages, obtained for finite, respectively for regular selection, are found to be incomparable. The relations of these families with Chomsky language families are briefly investigated.

Key Words: Shuffle operation, Chomsky grammars, L Systems
Categories: F4.2 [Mathematical Logic and Formal Languages]: Grammars and other Rewriting Systems: *Grammar types*, F4.3 [Mathematical Logic and Formal Languages]: Formal Languages: *Operations on languages*

1 Introduction

In formal language theory, besides the basic two types of grammars, the Chomsky grammars and the Lindenmayer systems, there are many "exotic" classes of generative devices, based not on the process of rewriting symbols (or strings) by strings, but using various operations of adjoining strings. We quote here the string adjunct grammars in [7], the semi-contextual grammars in [3], the ξ-grammars in [10], the pattern grammars in [2], and the contextual grammars [8]. The starting point of the present paper is this last class of grammars, via the paper [9], where a variant of contextual grammars was introduced based on the shuffle operation. Basically, one gives two finite sets of strings, B and C, over some alphabet, and one considers the set of strings obtained by starting from B and iteratively shuffling strings from C, without any restriction. This corresponds to the simple contextual grammars in [8].

We consider here a sort of couterpart of the contextual grammars with choice, where the adjoining is controlled by a selection mapping. In fact, we proceed in a way similar to that used in conditional contextual grammars [12], [13], [14] and in modular contextual grammars [15]: we start with several pairs of the form (R_i, C_i), R_i a language (we consider here only the case when R_i is regular or finite) and C_i a finite set of strings, and allow the strings in C_i to be shuffled only to strings in R_i. Depending on the place of the string in R_i in the current string generated by our grammar, we can distinguish several types of grammars: prefix (the string in R_i appears in the left-hand of the processed string, as a prefix of it), leftmost (we look for the leftmost possible occurrence of a string in R_i), arbitrary (no condition on the place where the string in R_i appears), global (the whole current string is in R_i), and parallel (the current string is portioned into strings in R_i). An interesting variant is to use a substring as base for shuffling only when it is maximal. Twelve families of languages are obtained in this way. Their study is the subject of this paper.

It is worth noting that the shuffle operation appears in various contexts in algebra and in formal language theory; we quote only [1], [4], [5], [6] (and [11], for applications). In [1], [6] the operation is used in a generative-like way, for identifying families of languages of the form $FAM(\cup, \cdot, Shuf; FIN)$, the smallest family of languages containing the finite languages and closed under union, concatenation and shuffle. (From this point of view, the family investigated in [9] is a particular case, $FAM(Shuf; FIN)$.)

The shuffle of the symbols of two words is also related to the concurrent execution of two processes described by these words, hence our models can be interpreted in terms of concurrent processes, too. For instance, the prefix mode of work corresponds to the concurrent execution of a process strictly at the beginning of another process, the "beginning" being defined modulo a regular language; in the global case the elementary actions of the two processes can be freely intercalated.

As it is expected, the languages generated by shuffle grammars are mostly incomparable with Chomsky languages (due to the fact that we do not use nonterminals). Somewhat surprising is the fact that in the regular selection case the five modes of work described above, with only one exception, cannot simulate each other (the corresponding families of languages are incomparable).

2 Classes of shuffle grammars

As usual, V^* denotes the set of all words over the alphabet V, the empty word is denoted by λ, the length of $x \in V^*$ by $|x|$ and the set of non-empty words over V is identified by V^+. The number of occurrences of a symbol a in a string x will be denoted by $|x|_a$. For basic notions in formal language theory (Chomsky grammars and L systems) we refer to [16], [17]. We only mention that $FIN, REG, CF, CS, 0L$ are the families of finite, regular, context-free, context-sensitive, and of 0L languages, respectively.

For $x, y \in V^*$ we define the *shuffle* (product) of x, y, denoted $x \sqcup\!\sqcup y$, as

$$x \sqcup\!\sqcup y = \{x_1y_1x_2y_2 \dots x_ny_n \mid x = x_1x_2\dots x_n, y = y_1y_2\dots y_n, \\ x_i, y_i \in V^*, 1 \leq i \leq n, n \geq 1\}.$$

Various properties of this operation, such as commutativity and associativity, will be implicitely used in the sequel. The operation $\sqcup\!\sqcup$ is extended in the natural way to languages,

$$L_1 \sqcup\!\sqcup L_2 = \{z \mid z \in x \sqcup\!\sqcup y, x \in L_1, y \in L_2\},$$

and iterated,

$$L^{(0)} = \{\lambda\},$$
$$L^{(i+1)} = L^{(i)} \sqcup\!\sqcup L, \ i \geq 0,$$
$$L^{\sqcup\!\sqcup} = \bigcup_{i \geq 0} L^{(i)}.$$

The grammars considered in [9] are triples of the form $G = (V, B, C)$, where V is an alphabet, B and C are finite languages over V. The language generated by G is defined as the smallest language L over V containing B and having the property that if $x \in L$ and $u \in C$, then $x \sqcup\!\sqcup u \subseteq L$. (Therefore, this language is equal to $B \sqcup\!\sqcup C^{\sqcup\!\sqcup}$.)

There is no restriction in [9] about the shuffling of elements of C to current strings. Such a control of the grammar work can be done in various ways of introducing a context-dependency. We use here the following natural idea:

Definition 1. A *shuffle grammar* is a construct

$$G = (V, B, (R_1, C_1), \dots, (R_n, C_n)),$$

where V is an alphabet, B is a finite language over V, R_i are languages over V and C_i are finite languages over V, $1 \leq i \leq n$.

The parameter $n \geq 1$ is called the *degree* of G. If R_i are languages in a given family F, then we say that G is *with F choice*. Here we consider only the cases $F = FIN$ and $F = REG$.

The idea is to allow the strings in C_i to be shuffled only to strings in the corresponding set R_i. The sets R_i are called *selectors*.

Definition 2. For a shuffle grammar G as above, a constant $i, 1 \leq i \leq n$, and two strings x, y in V^*, we define the following derivation relations:

$$\begin{aligned}
x \Longrightarrow_i^{arb} y \quad &\text{iff} \quad x = x_1x_2x_3, x_1, x_3 \in V^*, x_2 \in R_i, y = x_1x_2'x_3, \\
&\text{for some } x_2' \in x_2 ш u, u \in C_i, \\
x \Longrightarrow_i^{pr} y \quad &\text{iff} \quad x = x_1x_2, x_2 \in V^*, x_1 \in R_i, y = x_1'x_2, \\
&\text{for some } x_1' \in x_1 ш u, u \in C_i, \\
x \Longrightarrow_i^{lm} y \quad &\text{iff} \quad x = x_1x_2x_3, x_1, x_3 \in V^*, x_2 \in R_i, y = x_1x_2'x_3, \\
&\text{for some } x_2' \in x_2 ш u, u \in C_i, \text{ and there is no } j, 1 \leq j \leq n, \\
&\text{such that } x = v_1v_2v_3, |v_1| < |x_1|, v_2 \in R_j, \\
x \Longrightarrow_i^{gl} y \quad &\text{iff} \quad x \in R_i, y = x ш u, \text{ for some } u \in C_i.
\end{aligned}$$

These derivation relations are called ***arbitrary, prefix, leftmost, and global*** derivations, respectively. Moreover, we define the *parallel* derivation as

$$\begin{aligned}
x \Longrightarrow^{pl} y \quad &\text{iff} \quad x = x_1x_2 \dots x_k, k \geq 1, y = x_1'x_2' \dots x_k', \\
&\text{for } x_i \in R_{j_i}, x_i' \in x_i ш u_i, u_i \in C_{j_i}, 1 \leq j_i \leq n, 1 \leq i \leq k.
\end{aligned}$$

We denote $M = \{arb, pr, lm, gl, pl\}$.

Definition 3. The *language generated* by a shuffle grammar G in the mode $f \in M - \{pl\}$ is defined as follows:

$$\begin{aligned}
L_f(G) = B \cup \{x \in V^* \quad | \quad &w \Longrightarrow_{i_1}^f w_1 \Longrightarrow_{i_2}^f \dots \Longrightarrow_{i_m}^f w_m = x, \\
&w \in B, 1 \leq i_j \leq n, 1 \leq j \leq m, m \geq 1\}.
\end{aligned}$$

For the parallel mode of derivation we define

$$L_{pl}(G) = B \cup \{x \in V^* \mid w \Longrightarrow^{pl} w_1 \Longrightarrow^{pl} \dots \Longrightarrow^{pl} w_m = x, w \in B, m \geq 1\}.$$

The corresponding families of languages generated by shuffle grammars with F choice, $F \in \{FIN, REG\}$, are denoted by $ARB(F), PR(F), LM(F), GL(F), PL(F)$, respectively; by SL we denote the family of languages generated by grammars as in [9], without choice. Subscripts n can be added to ARB, PR, LM, GL, PL when only languages generated by grammars of degree at most $n, n \geq 1$, are considered.

3 The generative capacity of shuffle grammars

From definition we have the inclusions $X_n(F) \subseteq X_{n+1}(F)$, $X_n(FIN) \subseteq X_n(REG)$, for all $n \geq 1$, $X \in \{ARB, PR, LM, GL, PL\}$ and $F \in \{FIN, REG\}$.

Every family $ARB(FIN), PR(FIN), LM(FIN), GL(FIN), PL(FIN)$ contains each finite language. This is obvious, because for $G = (A, B, (B, \{\lambda\}))$ we have $L_f(G) = B$ for all f. In fact, we have

Theorem 1. (i) *Every family $ARB_1(REG), PR_1(REG), LM_1(REG), GL_1(REG)$, $PL_1(REG)$ includes strictly the family SL.*
(ii) *The family SL is incomparable with each $X_n(FIN), n \geq 1, X \in \{ARB, PR, LM, PL\}$.*
(iii) $GL(FIN) = GL_1(FIN) = FIN$.

Proof. (i) If $G = (V, B, C)$ is a simple shuffle grammar, then $L(G) = L_f(G')$ for each $f \in M$ and

$$G' = (V, B, (V^*, C)).$$

(The only point which needs some discussion is the fact that a parallel derivation $x \Longrightarrow^{pl} y$ in G', with $x = x_1x_2 \dots x_k$ and $y = x_1'x_2' \dots x_k', k \geq 2$, can be simulated by a k-step derivation in G, because the strings shuffled into $x_1, \dots, x_k$ do not overlap each other.) Consequently, $SL \subseteq X_1(REG)$, for all X.

The inclusion is proper in view of the following necessary condition for a language to be in SL (Lemma 10 in [9]): if $L \in SL$ and

$$V_0 = \{a \in V \mid \text{ for every } n \geq 1 \text{ there is } x \in L \text{ with } |x|_a \geq n\},$$

then each string in V_0^* is a subword of a string in L. This condition rejects languages such as $L = a^+ \cup b^+$; this language can be generated by the shuffle grammar with finite choice

$$G = (\{a, b\}, \{a, b\}, (\{a\}, \{\lambda, a\}), (\{b\}, \{\lambda, b\}))$$

in all modes of derivation excepting the global one. For gl we take

$$G' = (\{a, b\}, \{a, b\}, (V^*, \{a\}), (b^*, \{b\})).$$

(ii) We have already seen that $X_1(FIN) - SL \neq \emptyset$ for $X \in \{ARB, PR, LM, PL\}$. Consider now the simple shuffle grammar

$$G = (\{a, b, c\}, \{abc\}, \{abc\}).$$

We have

$$L(G) \cap a^+b^+c^+ = \{a^m b^m c^m \mid m \geq 1\}.$$

Assume that $L(G) = L_f(G')$ for some shuffle grammar $G' = (\{a, b, c\}, B, (R_1, C_1), \dots \dots, (R_n, C_n))$ with finite $R_1, \dots, R_n$ and $f \in \{arb, pr, lm\}$. Take a string $z = a^m b^m c^m$ in $L(G)$ with arbitrarily large m. A derivation $w \Longrightarrow_i^f z$ must be possible in G', with $w = a^p b^p c^p$, $p < m$, for some $1 \leq i \leq n$. We must have $w = w_1 w_2 w_3, w_2 \in R_i$, and $z = w_1 w_2' w_3$ for $w_2' \in w_2 ⧢ u, u \in C_i$. If $u = \lambda$, this derivation step can be omitted, hence we may assume that $u \neq \lambda$.

The sets R_i, C_i are finite. Denote

$$r = \max\{|x| \mid x \in R_i, 1 \leq i \leq n\},$$
$$q = \max\{|x| \mid x \in C_i, 1 \leq i \leq n\}.$$

Therefore $|w_2| \leq r, |u| \leq q$, that is $p \geq m - q$. For $m > r + q$ we have $p \geq m - q > r$, hence either $w_2 \in sub(a^p b^{p-1})$ or $w_2 \in sub(b^{p-1} c^p)$. In both cases, the shuffling with u modifies at most two of the three subwords a^p, b^p, c^p, hence a parasitic string is obtained. (In the prefix derivation case we precisely know that only a^p is modified.)

Consider now the parallel case. Take $G' = (\{a, b, c\}, B, (R_1, C_1), \dots, (R_n, C_n))$ such that $L_{pl}(G') = L(G)$, R_i finite sets. For obtaining a string $a^m b^m c^m$ with large enough m we need a derivation $a^p b^p c^p \Longrightarrow^{pl} a^m b^m c^m, p < m$. This implies we have sets R_i containing strings $a^r, r \geq 1$ and with the corresponding sets C_i containing strings $a^q, q \geq 1$ (similarly for b and c).

Assume that we find in the sets R_i two strings a^{r_1}, a^{r_2} and in the associated sets C_i we find two strings a^{q_1}, a^{q_2}. Similarly, we have pairs (b^{r_3}, b^{q_3}) and (c^{r_4}, c^{q_4}). The string $a^t b^t c^t$ for $t = r_1 r_2 r_3 r_4$ is in $L(G)$ and it can be rewritten using the same pairs of strings containing the symbols b and c and different pairs for a:

$$a^t b^t c^t \Longrightarrow^{pl} a^{(t/r_1)(r_1+q_1)} b^s c^s,$$
$$a^t b^t c^t \Longrightarrow^{pl} a^{(t/r_2)(r_2+q_2)} b^s c^s, \text{ for some } s.$$

Consequently, we must have

$$\frac{t}{r_1}(r_1 + q_1) = \frac{t}{r_2}(r_2 + q_2),$$

which implies

$$\frac{q_1}{r_1} = \frac{q_2}{r_2}.$$

For all such pairs (a^r, a^q) we obtain the same value for $\frac{q}{r}$. Denote it by α. Rewriting some $a^s b^s c^s$ using such pairs we obtain

$$\frac{s}{r}(r + q) = s(1 + \alpha)$$

occurrences of a. Continuing $k \geq 1$ steps, we get $s(1+\alpha)^k$ occurrences of a, hence a geometrical progression, starting at $a^s b^s c^s$.

Symbols a can be also introduced in a derivation $a^p b^p c^p \Longrightarrow^{pl} a^m b^m c^m$ by using pairs $(a^i b^j, z)$ with x containing occurrences of a. At most one such pair can be used in a derivation step. Let h be the largest number of symbols a in strings z as above (the number of such strings is finite). Thus, in a derivation $a^p b^p c^p \Longrightarrow^{pl} a^m b^m c^m$, the number m can be modified by such pairs in an interval $[m_1, m_2]$ with $m_2 - m_1 \leq h$.

We start from at most $g = card(A)$ strings of the form $a^s b^s c^s$, hence we have at most g geometrical progressions $s(1+\alpha)^k, k \geq 1$. The difference $\beta_k = s(1+\alpha)^{k+1} - s(1+\alpha)^k$ can be arbitrarily large. When $\beta_k > gh$, the at most g progressions can have an element between $s(1+\alpha)^{k+1}$ and $s(1+\alpha)^k$; each such element can have at most h values. Consequently, at least one natural number t between $s(1+\alpha)^{k+1}$ and $s(1+\alpha)^k$ is not reached, the corresponding string $a^t b^t c^t$, although in $L(G)$, is not in $L_{pl}(G')$. This contradiction concludes the proof of point (ii).

(iii) As only strings in the sets $R_i, 1 \leq i \leq n$, of a grammar $G = (V, B, (R_1, C_1), \ldots, (R_n, C_n))$ can be derived, we have $GL(FIN) \subseteq FIN$. The inclusion $FIN \subseteq GL_1(FIN)$ has been pointed out at the beginning of this section. ◊

Corollary. *The families $X_n(REG), n \geq 1, X \in \{ARB, LM, PR, PL, GL\}$, contain non-context-free languages.*

For $PL(FIN), PL(REG)$ and $GL(REG)$ this assertion can be strenghtened.

Theorem 2. *Every propagating unary 0L language belongs to the family $PL_1(FIN)$.*

Proof. For a unary 0L system $G = (\{a\}, w, P)$ with $w \in V^*$ and

$$P = \{a \to a^{i_1}, a \to a^{i_2}, \ldots, a \to a^{i_r}\},$$

with $i_j \geq 1, 1 \leq j \leq r$, we construct the shuffle grammar

$$G' = (\{a\}, \{w\}, (\{a\}, \{a^{i_1 - 1}, a^{i_2 - 1}, \ldots, a^{i_r - 1}\})).$$

It is easy to see that $L(G) = L_{pl}(G')$. ◊

This implies that $PL(FIN), PL(REG)$ contain one-letter non-regular languages. This is not true for the other modes of derivation.

Theorem 3. *A one-letter language is in $ARB(F), PR(F), LM(F), F \in \{FIN, REG\}$, or in $GL(REG)$ if and only if it is regular.*

Proof. Take a shuffle grammar $G = (\{a\}, B, (R_1, C_1), \ldots, (R_n, C_n))$ with regular sets $R_i, 1 \leq i \leq n$. Clearly, $L_{arb}(G) = L_{pr}(G) = L_{lm}(G)$. Because we work with one-letter strings, a string x can be derived using a component (R_i, C_i) if (and only if) the shortest string in R_i is contained in x, hence is of length at most $|x|$. Therefore we can replace each R_i by a^{k_i}, where

$$k_i = \min\{|x| \mid x \in R_i\}, 1 \leq i \leq n,$$

without modifying the generated language. Denote

$$K = \max\{k_i \mid 1 \leq i \leq n\}$$

and construct the right-linear grammar $G' = (V_N, \{a\}, S, P)$ with

$$\begin{aligned} V_N &= \{S, X\} \cup \{[p] \mid 0 \leq p \leq K\}, \\ P &= \{S \to a^p[p] \mid a^p \in B, p < K\} \cup \\ &\cup \ \{S \to a^p X \mid a^p \in B, p \geq K\} \cup \\ &\cup \ \{S \to a^p \mid a^p \in B\} \cup \end{aligned}$$

$$\cup \quad \{[p] \to a^s[p+s] \mid p \le K, p+s \le K, p \ge k_i, a^s \in C_i, 1 \le i \le n\} \cup$$
$$\cup \quad \{[p] \to a^s \mid p \le K, p \ge k_i, a^s \in C_i, 1 \le i \le n\} \cup$$
$$\cup \quad \{[p] \to a^s X \mid p \le K, p+s \ge K, p \ge k_i, a^s \in C_i, 1 \le i \le n\} \cup$$
$$\cup \quad \{X \to a^s X \mid a^s \in C_i, \text{ for some } 1 \le i \le n\} \cup$$
$$\cup \quad \{X \to a^s \mid a^s \in C_i, \text{ for some } 1 \le i \le n\}.$$

At the first steps of a derivation in G', the nonterminals $[p]$ count the number of symbols a introduced at that stage, in order to ensure the correct simulation of components of G; when this number exceeds K, then each component can be used, and this is encoded by the nonterminal X. Thus we have the equalities $L(G') = L_f(G), f \in \{arb, pr, lm\}$.

For the global derivation we start from an arbitrary shuffle grammar $G = (\{a\}, B, (R_1, C_1), \ldots, (R_n, C_n))$, with regular sets $R_i, 1 \le i \le n$, take for each R_i a deterministic finite automaton $A_i = (Q_i, \{a\}, s_{0,i}, F_i, \delta_i)$, $1 \le i \le n$, and construct the right-linear grammar $G' = (Q_1 \times Q_2 \times \ldots \times Q_n, \{a\}, (s_{0,1}, \ldots, s_{0,n}), P)$ with P containing the following rules:

$$(s_{0,1}, \ldots, s_{0,n}) \to a^r, a^r \in B,$$
$$(s_{0,1}, \ldots, s_{0,n}) \to a^r(s_1, \ldots, s_n), \text{ for } a^r \in B, s_i = \delta_i(s_{0,i}, a^r), 1 \le i \le n,$$
$$(s_1, \ldots, s_n) \to a^r(s'_1, \ldots, s'_n), \text{ for } s'_j = \delta_j(s_j, a^r), s_j \in Q_j, 1 \le j \le n,$$
$$\text{and } a^r \in C_i, s_i \in F_i, \text{ for some } i \in \{1, \ldots, n\},$$
$$(s_1, \ldots, s_n) \to a^r, \text{ for } s_j \in Q_j, 1 \le j \le n, \text{ and } a^r \in C_i, s_i \in F_i,$$
$$\text{for some } i \in \{1, \ldots, n\}.$$

New occurrences of a, corresponding to sets C_i, are added (it does not matter where) only when the current string belongs to R_i, and this is checked by the simultaneous parsings of the current string in the deterministic automata recognizing $R_1, \ldots, R_n$. Consequently, $L_{gl}(G)$ is a regular language.

Conversely, each one-letter regular language L is known to be equal with the disjoint union of a finite language F and a finite set of languages of the form

$$L_i = \{a^m \mid m = p_i + jq, j \ge 0\}.$$

(The constant p_i is associated to L_i, but q is the same for all L_i.) Assume we have n languages L_i; denote

$$K = \max\{t \mid t = p_i, 1 \le i \le n, \text{ or } a^t \in F\}.$$

Then $L = L_f(G), f \in \{arb, pr, lm\}$, for the grammar

$$G = (\{a\}, \{a^s \in L \mid s \le K + q\}, (\{a^{K+1}\}, \{a^q\})),$$

hence we have the theorem for $ARB(F), PR(F), LM(F), F \in \{FIN, REG\}$.

For the global case, starting from $L \subseteq a^*$ regular, written as above $L = F \cup \bigcup_{i=1}^{n} L_i$, $L_i = \{a^m \mid m = p_i + j \cdot q, j \ge 0\}$, $1 \le i \le n$, we consider the grammar

$$G = (\{a\}, \{a^s \in L \mid s \le K + q\}, (\{a^m \mid a^{m+q} \in L\}, \{a^q\})).$$

The equality $L = L_{gl}(G)$ is obvious and this concludes the proof. ◊

In view of the previous result, it is somewhat surprising to obtain

Theorem 4. *The family GL(REG) contains non-semilinear languages (even on the alphabet with two symbols only).*

Proof. Consider the shuffle grammar $G = (\{a, b, c\}, \{abc\}, (R_1, C_1), \ldots, (R_8, C_8))$, with the following eight components:

$$\begin{array}{ll}
R_1 = (a^2b^2c^2)^*abc(abc)^*, & C_1 = \{a\},\\
R_2 = (a^2b^2c^2)^*a^2bc(abc)^*, & C_2 = \{b\},\\
R_3 = (a^2b^2c^2)^*a^2b^2c(abc)^*, & C_3 = \{c\},\\
R_4 = (abc)^*a^2b^2c^2(a^2b^2c^2)^*, & C_4 = \{b\},\\
R_5 = (abc)^*abab^2c^2(a^2b^2c^2)^*, & C_5 = \{c\},\\
R_6 = (abc)^*abcab^2c^2(a^2b^2c^2)^*, & C_6 = \{c\},\\
R_7 = (abc)^*abcabcbc^2(a^2b^2c^2)^*, & C_7 = \{a\},\\
R_8 = (abc)^*abcabcabcc(a^2b^2c^2)^*, & C_8 = \{ab\}.
\end{array}$$

Examine the derivations in G in the global mode. The whole current string must be in some R_i in order to continue the derivation. Assume we start from a string $w = (abc)^r$ (initially we have $r = 1$). This string is in R_1 only, hence we can add one more occurrence of a. This can be done in all possible positions of w and we obtain a string in $L_{gl}(G)$, but only when we obtain $aabc(abc)^{r-1}$ we can continue the derivation, namely by using the second component of G. Now a symbol b can be added, and again the only case which does not block the derivation leads to $aabbc(abc)^{r-1}$. We can continue with the third component and either we block the derivation, or we get $a^2b^2c^2(abc)^{r-1}$. From a string of the form $(a^2b^2c^2)^+(abc)^*$ we can continue only with the first component, hence the previous operations are iterated. When all symbols a, b, c are doubled, we obtain the string $w' = (a^2b^2c^2)^r$.

Note that $|w'| = 2|w|$ (more precisely, $|w'|_a = 2|w|_a, |w'|_b = 2|w|_b, |w'|_c = |w|_c$), but for each intermediate string z in this derivation at least one of the following inequalities holds: $|z|_a \neq |z|_b, |z|_b \neq |z|_c, |z|_a \neq |z|_c$.

To a string of the form of w' above only the fifth component of G can be applied and again either the derivation must be finished, or it continues only in (R_6, C_6). The derivation proceeds deterministically through $(R_6, C_6), (R_7, C_7), (R_8, C_8)$, inserting step by step new symbols a, b, c between pairs of such symbols in order to obtain again triples abc. In this way we obtain either strings from which we cannot continue or we reach a string of the same form with w, namely $(abc)^{2r}$. The number of a, b, c occurrences has been doubled again, whereas in the intermediate steps we have strings with different numbers of occurrences of at least two of a, b, c.

The process can be iterated. From the previous discussion one can see that for all strings $w \in L_{gl}(G)$ with $|w|_a = |w|_c$ we also have $|w|_a = |w|_b$ and $|w|_a = 2^n, n \geq 0$. Consequently, denoting by $\Psi_{\{a,b,c\}}$ the Parikh mapping with respect to the alphabet $\{a, b, c\}$, we have

$$\Psi_{\{a,b,c\}}(L_{gl}(G)) \cap \{(n, m, n) \mid n, m \geq 1\} = \{(2^n, 2^n, 2^n) \mid n \geq 1\}.$$

This set is not semilinear; the set of semilinear vectors of given dimension is closed under intersection, therefore $L_{gl}(G)$ is not a semilinear language.

Consider now the morphism $h : \{a, b, c\}^* \longrightarrow \{a, b\}^*$ defined by $h(a) = bab, h(b) = baab, h(c) = baaab$. Define the grammar

$$G' = (\{a, b\}, \{h(abc)\}, (h(R_1), h(C_1)), \dots, (h(R_8), h(C_8))).$$

Shuffling a string $h(a), h(b), h(c)$ with a string $h(z), z \in R_i$, in a way different from inserting $h(a), h(b), h(c)$ as a block leads to strings with substrings of the forms bbb or aba. Take, for example, $h(z) = z_1bbabbz_2$ and examine the possibilities to shuffle $h(b) = baab$ after z_1. In order to not get a substring bbb we must insert the first symbol of $h(b)$ after the specified occurrence of a in $h(z)$. If we continue with the symbol b of $h(z)$, this is as starting after this occurrence of b, if we continue with the symbol a of $h(b)$, then we obtain aba. Starting after bab in $h(z)$, after introducing one b from $h(b)$ we either get bbb (if we continue in $h(z)$), or $baba$ (if we alternate in $h(b), h(z), h(b)$), or $baab$ (hence $h(b)$ is inserted as a block). Similarly, take for example $h(z) = z_1bbaaabbz_2$ and shuffle the same $h(b) = baab$. Introducing b after z_1bba we have to continue either with a from $h(z)$ or with a from $h(b)$, in both cases obtaining the subword aba. The same result is obtained in all other cases. After producing a substring bbb or aba, the derivation is blocked. Inserting $h(a), h(b), h(c)$ in $h(z)$ as a compact block corresponds to inserting a, b, c in z. Consequently, the derivations in G' correspond to derivations in G. When a derivation is blocked, it can terminate with a string z with $|z|_a = |z|_b$ only when z contains the same number of substrings bab abd $baaab$, with the possible exception of such substrings destroyed by the last shuffling, that of $baaab$ when using the pair $(h(R_3), h(C_3))$ or of $babbaab$ when using the pair $(h(R_8), h(C_8))$.

Moreover,

$$\Psi_{\{a,b\}}(L_{gl}(G')) \cap \{(n,n) \mid n \geq 1\} = \{(6 \cdot 2^n, 6 \cdot 2^n) \mid n \geq 1\}.$$

Indeed, from a string z containing 2^n occurrences of every symbol a, b, c we get a string $h(z)$ with

$$2^n + 2 \cdot 2^n + 3 \cdot 2^n = 6 \cdot 2^n \text{ occurrences of } a,$$
$$2 \cdot 2^n + 2 \cdot 2^n + 2 \cdot 2^n = 6 \cdot 2^n \text{ occurrences of } b.$$

Conversely, if a string $h(z)$ contains the same number of a and b occurrences, assume that it contains α substrings bab, β substrings $baab$ and γ substrings $baaab$. Then it contains $2\alpha + 2\beta + 2\gamma$ occurrences of b and $\alpha + 2\beta + 2\gamma$ occurrences of b. Consequently,

$$2\alpha + 2\beta + 2\gamma = \alpha + 2\beta + 2\gamma$$

which implies $\alpha = \gamma$. As we have seen in the first part of the proof, when $|w|_a = |w|_c$, then also $|w|_a = |w|_b$, hence $\alpha = \beta$, too. Therefore the obtained string x corresponds to a string z (in the sense $x = h(z)$) such that $|z|_a = |z|_b = |z|_c$. This implies $|x|_a = |x|_b$ and $|x|_a = |x|_b = 6 \cdot 2^n$.

In conclusion, also $L_{gl}(G')$ is not semi-linear. ◊

For the case of finite selection we have

Theorem 5. *$PR(FIN) \subseteq REG$.*

Proof. Let $G = (V, B, (R_1, C_1), \ldots, (R_n, C_n))$ be a shuffle grammar with all sets R_i, $1 \leq i \leq n$, finite. We construct a left-linear grammar $G' = (N, V, S, P)$ as follows.

Let

$$q = \max\{|x| \mid x \in R_i, 1 \leq i \leq n, \text{ or } x \in B\}.$$

Then

$$\begin{aligned}
N = \{[x] \mid x \in V^*, |x| \leq q\} \cup \{S\},\\
P = \{S \to [x] \mid x \in B\} \cup\\
\cup\{[w] \to [z] \mid \text{ if } |w| \leq q, w = w_1w_2, w_1 \in R_i \text{ for some } 1 \leq i \leq n,\\
z = uw_2, \text{ for some } u \in w_1 ⧢ x, x \in C_i \text{ and } |z| \leq q\} \cup\\
\cup\{[w] \to [z]v \mid \text{ if } |w| \leq q, w = w_1w_2, w_1 \in R_i \text{ for some } 1 \leq i \leq n,\\
zv = uw_2 \text{ for some } u \in w_1 ⧢ x, x \in C_i \text{ and } |z| = q\} \cup\\
\cup\{[w] \to w \mid |w| \leq q\}.
\end{aligned}$$

The derivation proceeds from right to left; the nonterminals $[w]$ in the left-hand side of sentential forms memorize the prefix w of large enough length to control the derivation in G in the prefix mode. Therefore, $L_{pr}(G) = L(G')$ and $L_{pr}(G) \in REG$. ◊

Theorem 6. *$ARB_1(FIN)$ contains non-linear languages.*

Proof. Take $G = (\{a, b\}, \{\lambda\}, (\{\lambda\}, \{ab\}))$. We obviously have $L_{arb}(G) =$ the Dyck language over $\{a, b\}$, known to be a (context-free) non-linear language. ◊

Open problems. Are there non-semilinear languages in families $ARB(F), LM(F), F \in \{FIN, REG\}$, or in $PR(REG)$? Are there non-context-free languages in families $ARB(FIN), LM(FIN)$?

We proceed now to investigating the relations among families $ARB(F), PR(F), LM(F), GL(F), PL(F)$ for F as above. We present the results in the next theorem, whose proof will consist of the series of lemmas following it.

Theorem 7. (i) *Each two of the families $ARB(REG), PR(REG), LM(REG), GL(REG), PL(REG)$ are incomparable, excepting the case of $ARB(REG), PL(REG)$ for which we have the proper inclusion $ARB(REG) \subset PL(REG)$.*

(ii) *Each pair* $(PL(FIN), PR(FIN))$, $(PL(FIN), LM(FIN))$, $(PR(FIN), LM(FIN))$, $(ARB(FIN), PR(FIN))$, $(ARB(FIN), LM(FIN))$ *consists of incomparable families; the following inclusions are proper:* $GL(FIN) \subset X(FIN)$ *for all* $X \in \{ARB, PL, PR, LM\}$, *and* $ARB(FIN) \subset PL(FIN)$.

Lemma 1. *For each* $X \in \{ARB, PR, LM, GL\}$ *we have* $PL(FIN) - X(REG) \neq \emptyset$.

Proof. Follows from the fact that $PL(FIN)$ contains one-letter non-regular languages, but the one-letter languages in the other families F are regular (Theorem 3). ◇

Lemma 2. $ARB(F) \subseteq PL(F), F \in \{FIN, REG\}$.

Proof. For a shuffle grammar $G = (V, B, (R_1, C_1), \ldots, (R_n, C_n))$ used in the arbitrary mode of derivation, construct $G' = (V, B, (R_1, C_1), \ldots, (R_n, C_n), (V, \{\lambda\}))$.

For $a_1a_2\ldots a_kx_2b_1b_2\ldots b_j \Longrightarrow_i^{arb} a_1a_2\ldots a_kx_2'b_1b_2\ldots b_j$ in G, with $x_2 \in R_i, x_2' \in x_2 \sqcup\!\sqcup C_i$, for some $1 \leq i \leq n$, we have $a_s = a_s \sqcup\!\sqcup \lambda, 1 \leq s \leq k$, $b_s = b_s \sqcup\!\sqcup \lambda, a \leq s \leq j$, hence $a_1a_2\ldots a_kx_2b_1b_2\ldots b_j \Longrightarrow^{pl} a_1a_2\ldots a_kx_2'b_1b_2\ldots b_j$ in G'.

Conversely, a derivation $x_1\ldots x_k \Longrightarrow^{pl} x_1'\ldots x_k'$ in G' corresponds to a derivation $x_1x_2\ldots x_k \Longrightarrow_{i_1}^{arb} x_1'x_2\ldots x_k \Longrightarrow_{i_2}^{arb} x_1'x_2'x_3\ldots x_k \Longrightarrow_{i_3}^{arb} \ldots \Longrightarrow_{i_k}^{arb} x_1'\ldots x_k'$ in G, with the steps $\Longrightarrow_{i_j}^{arb}$ omitted when $x_j' = x_j$.

In conclusion, $L_{arb}(G) = L_{pl}(G')$. ◇

Lemma 3. *The language* $L_{gl}(G)$, *for* $G = (\{a, b\}, \{ab\}, (a^+b^+, \{ab\}))$ *is not in* $ARB(REG), PR(REG)$, *or* $LM(REG)$.

Proof. We have

$$\begin{aligned} L_{gl}(G) &= \{a^nb^n \mid n \geq 1\} \cup \\ &\cup \{a^naba^mb^{n+m} \mid n, m \geq 0\} \cup \\ &\cup \{a^{n+m}b^nabb^m \mid n, m \geq 0\}. \end{aligned}$$

Assume that this language can be generated in one of the modes arb, pr, lm by a grammar $G' = (\{a, b\}, B, (R_1, C_1), \ldots, (R_n, C_n))$. Each string in $L_{gl}(G)$ contains the same number of occurrences of a and of b, hence for each string in C_i which is used in a derivation we must have the same property. In the mentioned modes f of derivation, if we have a derivation $x_1x_2x_3 \Longrightarrow_i^f x_1x_2'x_3$ (for $f = pr$ we have $x_1 = \lambda$) using a string $u \in C_i$, then we can obtain $x_1x_2x_3 \Longrightarrow_i^f x_1x_2ux_3$, too, hence the use of u can be iterated, thus producing strings $x_1x_2u^nx_3$ with arbitrary n. For $u \neq \lambda$ this is contradictory ($|u|_a = |u|_b$). ◇

Lemma 4. *The language* $L = ab^+a$ *is in* $ARB(FIN) \cap LM(FIN)$ *but not in* $GL(REG) \cup PR(REG)$.

Proof. The language L can be generated by the grammar $G = (\{a, b\}, \{aba\}, (\{b\}, \{b\}))$ in both modes of derivation arb and lm, but it cannot be generated by any shuffle grammar in modes gl or pr: in order to arbitrarily increase the number of b occurrences we have to use a string $b^r, r \geq 1$, which is shuffled to a string containing the leftmost occurrence of the symbol a in the strings in L. In this way, strings beginning with b^ra can be produced, a contradiction. ◇

Lemma 5. *The language* $L = ab^+a \cup bab^+a$ *is in* $PR(FIN)$ *but not in* $GL(REG)$.

Proof. For $G = (\{a, b\}, \{aba\}, (\{ab\}, \{b\}))$ we have $L_{pr}(G) = L$ but L cannot be generated in the gl mode by any grammar: we need a string u which introduces occurrences of b and in the global mode this u can be adjoined in the right hand of the rightmost occurrence of a in the strings of L. ◇

Lemma 6. *The language* $L_{pr}(G)$, *for the grammar* $G = (\{a, b\}, \{ab\}, (\{ab\}, \{ab\}))$, *is not in* $LM(REG)$.

Proof. We have

$$L_{pr}(G) = (ab)^+ \cup aabb(ab)^*.$$

(When the leftmost two symbols are not ab, the derivation is blocked.)

Assume that $L_{pr}(G) = L_{lm}(G')$ for some $G' = (\{a,b\}, B, (R_1, C_1), \ldots, (R_n, C_n))$. For every $z \in L_{pr}(G)$ we have $|z|_a = |z|_b$, hence the same property holds for all strings in sets C_i effectively used in derivations. Take such a nonempty string $u \in C_i$ and examine the form of strings $x \in R_i$. Such strings cannot be prefixes of $aabb(ab)^n, abb(ab)^n, bb(ab)^n$, because otherwise we can obtain parasitic strings by introducing u in the left of the pair bb in strings $aabb(ab)^m$. Suppose that x is a prefix of $b(ab)^n$ different from b. Then we can shuffle the string u in such a way to obtain a pair aa in the right of the pair bb already existing in strings of the form $aabb(ab)^n$. Again a contradiction, hence the strings of the form $aabb(ab)^n$ cannot be derived. This implies that they are obtained by derivations of the form $(ab)^n \Longrightarrow_i^{lm} aabb(ab)^m$. Consequently, also $aabb(ab)^n \Longrightarrow^{lm} aabbaabb(ab)^m$ is possible (we have found that the prefix $aabb$ cannot be rewritten, hence the derivation is leftmost). Such strings are not in $L_{pr}(G)$. ♢

Lemma 7. *The language $L = L_{pr}(G)$ in the previous lemma is not in the family $PL(REG)$.*

Proof. Assume that $L = L_{pl}(G')$ for some $G' = (\{a,b\}, B, (R_1, C_1), \ldots, (R_n, C_n))$.

If a derivation $(ab)^n \Longrightarrow^{pl} aabb(ab)^m$ is possible in G', then also $(ab)^n(ab)^n \Longrightarrow^{pl} aabb(ab)^m aabb(ab)^m$ is possible, a contradiction. Consequently, the strings $aabb(ab)^q$ can be produced only by derivations of the form $aabb(ab)^p \Longrightarrow^{pl} aabb(ab)^q$.

Assume that there is a derivation of the form $(ab)^n \Longrightarrow^{pl} (ab)^m$.

We cannot have pairs (R_i, C_i) with $\lambda \in R_i, C_i \neq \{\lambda\}$. Indeed, if such a pair exists, then from a derivation $aabb(ab)^p \Longrightarrow^{pl} aabb(ab)^q$ we can produce also $uaabb(ab)^q$, for each $u \in C_i$.

Examine the pairs $(x, u), x \in R_i, u \in C_i$, used in the derivation $(ab)^n \Longrightarrow^{pl} (ab)^m$. We know that $x \neq \lambda$. If x contains a symbol a and also u contains an occurrence of a, then we can produce strings having the subword aa; this is forbidden ($(ab)^n$ cannot generate strings of a form different from $(ab)^r$). Similarly, we cannot have occurrences of b both in x and in u. Therefore, $x = a^j, u = b^k$ or $x = b^s, u = a^t$. Clearly, we must have $i = s = 1$ (no other subwords consisting of a or of b only appear in the derived string) and $j = t = 1$ (no other subwords consisting of a or of b only appear in the produced string). Such pairs (x, u) can be clearly used for producing a parasitic string, a contradiction.

In conclusion, the strings $(ab)^n$ cannot be derived, hence such strings with arbitrarily long n must be obtained by derivations $aabb(ab)^p \Longrightarrow^{pl} (ab)^n$. Then the symbols aa and bb in the prefix of $aabb(ab)^p$ must be separated by an occurrence of b, respectively of a. Irrespective whether this a must be introduced *after* the first b or *before* the second b, we can introduce it *before* the first b, respectively *after* the second b, thus preserving the pair bb. If the pair aa in its left-hand has been correctly shuffled with b, then we obtain a string of the form $x_1 bb x_2$ with $|x_1| \geq 3$, which is not in L. The equality $L = L_{pl}(G')$ is impossible. ♢

Lemma 8. *There are languages in $GL(REG) - PL(REG)$.*

Proof. Consider the grammar

$$G = (\{a,b\}, \{ab\}, ((ab)^*, \{ab\})).$$

We have

$$L_{gl}(G) = (ab)^+ \cup (ab)^* a (ab)^+ b (ab)^*,$$

which is not a parallel shuffle language. The argument is similar to that in the previous proof, hence it is left to the reader. ♢

Lemma 9. *There are languages in $ARB(FIN) - LM(REG)$.*

Proof. For the grammar $G = (\{a,b\}, \{abba\}, (\{a\}, \{a\}))$ we have

$$L_{arb}(G) = a^+ bba^+.$$

Assume that $L_{arb}(G) = L_{lm}(G')$ for some $G' = (\{a,b\}, B, (R_1, C_1), \ldots, (R_n, C_n))$. For every $u \in C_i$ effectively used, we must have $u = a^r, r \geq 0$. No derivation can use a pair $(x,u), x \in R_i, u \in C_i$, with x containing a symbol b, otherwise we can produce strings of the form $a^n b a^p b a^m, p \geq 1$. Consequently, all selectors R_i can be supposed to contain only strings in a^*. A pair (R_i, C_i) can be used in a derivation if (and only if) the pair $(\{x_i\}, C_i)$ can be used, for x_i the shortest string in R_i; for two pairs $(\{x_i\}, C_i), (\{x_j\}, C_j)$, only that with the shortest x_i, x_j can be used. Denote

$$k = \min\{|x| \mid x \in R_i, 1 \leq i \leq n\}.$$

From a string $a^n bba^m$ in B with $n < k, m < k$ we can produce no other string; when $n \geq k$, we produce only strings of the form $a^t bba^m$ without modifying the number m; when $n < k$ and $m \geq k$, then we can produce strings of the form $a^n bba^t$. However, $L_{arb}(G)$ contains strings $a^s bba^t$ with simultaneously arbitrarily large s, t, a contradiction. ◊

Lemma 10. *The language generated by $G = (\{a,b\}, \{ab\}, (\{ab\}, \{ab\}))$ in the leftmost mode is not in PL(REG).*

Proof. We have

$$L_{lm}(G) = (ab)^+ \cup \{a^i((ab)^* b)^i (ab)^* \mid i \geq 1\}.$$

Here is a derivation in G in the leftmost mode:

$$\begin{aligned} ab \quad & \Longrightarrow^{lm} abab \Longrightarrow^{lm} ababab \Longrightarrow^{lm} \ldots \Longrightarrow^{lm} (ab)^n \Longrightarrow^{lm} \\ & \Longrightarrow^{lm} aabb(ab)^{n-1} \Longrightarrow^{lm} \ldots \Longrightarrow^{lm} a(ab)^m b(ab)^{n-1} \Longrightarrow^{lm} \\ & \Longrightarrow^{lm} aaabb(ab)^{m-1} b(ab)^{n-1} \Longrightarrow^{lm} \ldots \Longrightarrow^{lm} aa(ab)^p b(ab)^{m-1} b(ab)^{n-1}. \end{aligned}$$

Assume that $L_{lm}(G) = L_{pl}(G')$ for some $G' = (\{a,b\}, B, (R_1, C_1), \ldots, (R_n, C_n))$.

Examine the possibilities to obtain the strings $(ab)^n$ with arbitrarily large n. We cannot have a derivation $w \Longrightarrow^{pl} (ab)^n$ for w a string in $a^i((ab)^* b)^i (ab)^*, 1 \geq 1$, because we must separate both the i left occurrences of a and the i pairs bb appearing in the string; irrespective of the used strings to be shuffled we can do only part of these operations, letting for instance a pair aa unchanged and separating all pairs bb; we obtain a parasitic string. Therefore we must have derivations $(ab)^n \Longrightarrow^{pl} (ab)^m$, $m > n$. If in such a derivation we use a pair $(x,u), x \in R_i, u \in C_i$, such that a occurs both in x and in u, then we can produce strings with substrings aa. Starting from a string $(ab)^n (ab)^n$ we can then produce strings having aa not in the left-hand end, a contradiction. It follows that symbols a are introduced only by pairs (x,u) with $x = b$ (no other subword of $(ab)^n$ consists of only occurrences of b). In order to cover $(ab)^n$ we must use also pairs (y,v) with y containing a and v not containing a. This implies $v = b$ or $v = \lambda$. The use of (b,u) introduces at least one new occurrence of a for each b, hence, in order to keep the number of a and b equal, we must have $v = b$, which implies $y = a$. Using such pairs we can produce again strings containing pairs aa not in the left-hand end, a contradiction which concludes the proof. ◊

Let us note that in all previous lemmas the considered languages are generated by grammars with only one component (R, C). Consequently, we have

Corollary 1. *For all families $X(F), X'(F)$ with $X, X' \in \{ARB, PR, LM, GL, PL\}$, $X \neq X'$, $F \in \{FIN, REG\}$, which are incomparable, all $X_i(F), X'_j(F)$ are incomparable, too, for every $i, j \geq 1$.*

Corollary 2. *Each family F such that $REG \subsetneq F \subsetneq CF$ is incomparable with each family $ARB(REG)$, $PR(REG), LM(REG), GL(REG), PL(REG)$.*

Proof. The fact that $X(REG) - CF \neq \emptyset$, for each $X \in \{ARB, PR, LM, GL, PL\}$, has been already pointed out. On the other hand, the language ab^+a in Lemma 4 is not in $GL(REG)$ or in $PR(REG)$, and the language $(ab)^+ \cup aabb(ab)^*$ in Lemma 6 is not in $LM(REG)$ or on $PL(REG)$, hence it is not in $ARB(REG)$. These languages are regular, which concludes the proof. ◊

By a straightforward simulation in terms of context-sensitive grammars of checking the conditions defining the correct derivation in a shuffle grammar and of performing such a derivation, we get

Theorem 8. *All families $X(F), X \in \{ARB, PR, LM, GL, PL\}, F \in \{FIN, REG\}$, are strictly included in CS.*

The properness of these inclusions follows from the previous Corollary 2.

4 The case of using maximal selectors

For a shuffle grammar $G = (V, B, (R_1, C_1), \ldots, (R_n, C_n))$ as in the previous sections, we can also define the following mode of derivation: for $x, y \in V^*$ and $1 \leq i \leq n$, write

$$\begin{aligned} x \Longrightarrow_i^{max} \quad \text{iff} \quad & x = x_1x_2x_3, x_1, x_2 \in V^*, x_2 \in R_i, \\ & y = x_1x_2'x_3, \text{ for some } x_2' \in x_2 \sqcup\!\sqcup u, u \in C_i, \\ & \text{and} \\ & \text{there is no decomposition of } x \text{ of the form} \\ & x = x_1'x_1''x_2x_3'x_3'', \text{ with } x_1''x_3' \neq \lambda, \\ & x_1''x_2x_3' \in R_j \text{ for some } j, 1 \leq j \leq n. \end{aligned}$$

(We use x_2 for shuffling only if no longer string can be used containing that occurrence of x_2 as a substring.)

We denote by $L_{max}(G)$ the language generated in this way and by $MAX(FIN)$, $MAX(REG)$ the corresponding families of languages.

Lemma 11. $MAX_1(FIN) - X(REG) \neq \emptyset, X \in \{PR, LM, GL\}$, $MAX_2(FIN) - ARB(REG) \neq \emptyset$.

Proof. For $X \in \{PR, GL\}$ the assertion is proved by the language in Lemma 4: in general, if $G = (V, B, (\{x\}, C))$ (one component, with a singleton selector), then the maximality has no effect, the maximal derivations in G are arbitrary derivations. This is the case with the grammar in Lemma 4.

This is also true for the grammar in the proof of Lemma 9: that language covers the case $X = LM$.

Consider now the grammar

$$G = (\{a, b, c\}, \{cab\}, (\{cab\}, \{ab\}), (\{acab, bcab\}, \{\lambda\}).$$

Starting from a string $c(ab)^n$ (initially we have $n = 1$), we can shuffle the string ab in the prefix ab in five essentially different ways:

$$\begin{aligned} (1) \quad & c(ab)^n \Longrightarrow^{max} abc(ab)^n, \\ (2) \quad & c(ab)^n \Longrightarrow^{max} acb(ab)^n, \\ (3) \quad & c(ab)^n \Longrightarrow^{max} acabb(ab)^{n-1}, \\ (4) \quad & c(ab)^n \Longrightarrow^{max} c(ab)^{n+1}, \\ (5) \quad & c(ab)^n \Longrightarrow^{max} caabb(ab)^{n-1}. \end{aligned}$$

In cases (2) and (5) the derivation cannot continue (all selectors contain the subword cab); in cases (1) and (3) we cannot use the selector cab because $acab$ or $bcab$ are present; the latter selectors entail the shuffle of λ, which changes nothing, hence the derivation is blocked. Only case (4) can be continued. Consequently,

$$L_{max}(G) = c(ab)^+ \cup abc(ab)^+ \cup acb(ab)^+ \cup acabb(ab)^* \cup caabb(ab)^*.$$

This language cannot be generated by a shuffle grammar $G' = (\{a, b, c\}, B, (R_1, C_1), \ldots, (R_n, C_n))$ in the arbitrary mode. Assume the contrary. Every string in B, in a grammar G' as above, must contain the symbol c and every string in $C_i, 1 \leq i \leq n$, must contain the same number of occurrences of a and of b. If $\lambda \in C_i$, then this string can be ignored without modifying the language of G'. In order to generate strings $c(ab)^m$ with arbitrarily large m we must have derivation steps $w \Longrightarrow^{arb} c(ab)^m$ with $w = c(ab)^p$

or $w = caabb(ab)^p, p < m$ (the other strings in $L_{max}(G)$ contain symbols a or b in front of c). Starting from $caabb(ab)^p$ we have to introduce one occurrence of b between symbols a in the substring aa and one occurrence of a between symbols b in bb, that is we need a pair (z, u) with $z \in R_i, u \in C_i$, $z = z_1abz_2$ and $u = u_1bu_2au_3$. Then from $caabb(ab)^p$ we can also produce $x_1z_1u_1bu_2au_3abz_2x_2 = x_1z_1u_1bu_2au_3abbx_2'$, a parasitic string. If $c(ab)^p \Longrightarrow^{arb} c(ab)^m$ uses a pair (z, u) with $z \in c\{a, b\}^*$, then $u^sc(ab)^p$ can be produced, for arbitrary $s \geq 1$ (we introduce u in the left of c, thus leaving the occurrence of z in $c(ab)^p$ unchanged). Consequently, we have to use a pair (z, u) with $z \in \{a, b\}^*$. More exactly, z is a substring of $(ab)^p$. As u contains occurrences of both a and b, we can derive $c(ab)^s(ab)^p$ with arbitrary s (all such strings are in $L_{max}(G)$) in such a way to obtain $c(ab)^sy$ with y containing a substring aa or a substring bb. Such a string is not in $L_{max}(G)$, hence the grammar G' cannot generate strings $c(ab)^m$ with arbitrarily large m. The equality $L_{max}(G) = L_{arb}(G')$ is impossible. ◊

Lemma 12. $GL(F) \subseteq MAX(F), F \in \{FIN, REG\}$.

Proof. As $GL(FIN) = FIN$ and, clearly, $FIN \subseteq MAX(FIN)$, the case $F = FIN$ is obvious.

Take now a grammar $G = (V, B, (R_1, C_1), \ldots, (R_n, C_n))$ with regular $R_i, 1 \leq i \leq n$, and construct $G' = (V, B, (R_1, C_1), \ldots, (R_n, C_n), (R_{n+1}, C_{n+1}))$ with

$$R_{n+1} = V^*(\bigcup_{i=1}^{n} R_i)V^*, \quad C_{n+1} = \{\lambda\}.$$

We have $L_{gl}(G) = L_{max}(G')$.

($\subseteq$) If $x \Longrightarrow_i^{gl} y$, that is $x \in R_i, y \in x ⧢ u, u \in C_i$, then the derivation is maximal, we also have $x \Longrightarrow_i^{max} y$. Consequently, if $w \in B$ derives z in G in the global mode, then w derives z in G' in the maximal mode.

($\supseteq$) Take a derivation in G', $x \Longrightarrow_i^{max} y$. If $i = n + 1$, then $x = y$. If $i \leq n$, then we have $x \in R_i$, otherwise the derivation is not allowed: for $x = x_1x_2x_3, x_2 \in R_i, x_1x_2 \neq \lambda$, we have $x_1x_2x_3 \in R_{n+1}$, hence the derivation in (R_i, C_i) is not allowed. By induction on the length of derivations, we can now show that for every maximal derivation in G' there is a global derivation in G producing the same string, hence $L_{max}(G') \subseteq L_{gl}(G)$. ◊

Lemma 13. $PR(FIN) - MAX(REG) \neq \emptyset$.

Proof. Consider the grammar

$$G = (\{a, b\}, \{ab\}, (\{ab\}, \{ab\})).$$

We obtain

$$L_{pr}(G) = (ab)^+ \cup aabb(ab)^*.$$

This language is not in $MAX(REG)$. Assume the contrary, that is $L_{pr}(G) = L_{max}(G')$ for some $G' = (\{a, b\}, B, (R_1, C_1), \ldots, (R_n, C_n))$.

If we have a derivation of the form $aabb(ab)^n \Longrightarrow^{max} (ab)^m$, then we have to separate the symbols in the subwords aa and bb by b or some $bxb, x \in \{a, b\}^*$, and by a or some $aya, y \in \{a, b\}^*$, respectively. To this aim, a string of the form z_1abz_2 must be used as selector and a string $u = u_1bu_2au_3$ must be shuffled. But then also $aabb(ab)^n \Longrightarrow^{max} au_1bu_2au_3abb(ab)^n$ is possible, and this is not the language $L_{pr}(G)$, a contradiction.

Assume that we have a derivation $(ab)^n \Longrightarrow^{max} (ab)^m, m > n \geq 2$. Then we must have $(ab)^n = x_1x_2x_3, x_2 \in R_i$, for some i such that $(ab)^m = x_1x_2'x_3, x_2' \in x_2 ⧢ v, v \in C_i$. Clearly, $|v|_a = |v|_b \geq 1$. Then from $(ab)^{2n}$ we can derive $(ab)^n(ab)^m$. If $x_2 = \lambda$ and v starts by an occurrence of $a, v = av'$, then we can produce $(ab)^nz_1aav'bz_2$, for some $z_1, z_2 \in \{a, b\}^*$; if v starts by $b, v = bv'$, then we can produce $(ab)^nz_1abbv'z_2$, for some $z_1, z_2 \in \{a, b\}^*$. No one of these strings is in $L_{pr}(G)$, a contradiction. Therefore we must have $x_2 \neq \lambda$. If x_2 contains the symbol a, then we can obtain $(ab)^nz_1aaz_2$, for some $z_1, z_2 \in \{a, b\}^*$, by appropriate shuffling of x_2 and v. If x_2 contains the letter b, then we can obtain

$(ab)^n z_1 bb z_2$, for some $z_1, z_2 \in \{a, b\}^*$, by appropriate shuffling. In both cases we have obtained parasitic strings.

Consequently, the strings $(ab)^n$ cannot be generated, they must be introduced as axioms; this is impossible, because the set B is finite, hence $L_{pr}(G) \notin MAX(REG)$. ◊

Lemma 14. *A one-letter language is regular if and only if it is in $MAX(FIN)$.*

Proof. The proof of Theorem 3 shows the fact that every one-letter regular language is in $MAX(FIN)$.

Conversely, take a grammar $G = (\{a\}, B, (R_1, C_1), \ldots, (R_n, C_n))$ and write each R_i, $1 \leq i \leq n$, in the form

$$R_i = H_i \cup \bigcup_{s=1}^{k_i} \{a^m \mid m = p_{i,s} + j \cdot q_i, j \geq 0\},$$

for H_i finite languages, and q_i associated with $R_i, 1 \leq i \leq n$. Denote

$$T = \max\{q_i \mid 1 \leq i \leq n\},$$
$$K = \max\{t \mid a^t \in B \text{ or } a^t \in H_i, \text{ or } t = p_{i,s}, 1 \leq s \leq k_i, 1 \leq i \leq n\}.$$

Take for each R_i a deterministic finite automaton

$$A_i = (Q_i, \{a\}, s_{0,i}, F_i, \delta_i), 1 \leq i \leq n.$$

We construct the right-linear grammar $G' = (N, \{a\}, S, P)$ with

$$N = Q_1^T \times Q_2^T \times \ldots \times Q_n^T \cup \{S\},$$

and P contains the following rules:

(1) $S \to a^r$, for $a^r \in L(G), r \leq K + T$;

(2) $S \to a^r(s_{1,1}s_{2,1} \ldots s_{T,1}, s_{1,2}s_{2,2} \ldots s_{T,2}, \ldots, s_{1,n}s_{2,n} \ldots s_{T,n})$,
for $K + T \leq r < K + 2T, \delta_i(s_{0,i}, a^{r-T+j}) = s_{j,i}, 1 \leq j \leq T, 1 \leq i \leq n$,

(3) $(s_{1,1}s_{2,1} \ldots s_{T,1}, \ldots, s_{1,n}s_{2,n} \ldots s_{T,n}) \to a^r(s'_{1,1}s'_{2,1} \ldots s'_{T,1}, \ldots, s'_{1,n}s'_{2,n} \ldots s'_{T,n})$,
where $a^r \in C_i$ for some $i \in \{1, 2, \ldots, n\}$ such that $s_{T-j,i} \in F_i$ and $s_{m,l} \in Q_l - F_l$ for all $1 \leq l \leq n$ and $T - j + 1 \leq m \leq T$; moreover, $s'_{j,l} = \delta_l(s_{j,l}, a^r), 1 \leq j \leq T, 1 \leq l \leq n$.

(4) $(s_{1,1}s_{2,1} \ldots s_{T,1}, \ldots, s_{1,n}s_{2,n} \ldots s_{T,n}) \to \lambda$ for all $(s_{1,1}s_{2,1} \ldots s_{T,1}, \ldots, s_{1,n}s_{2,n} \ldots s_{T,n}) \in N$.

For every language R_i, the difference between the length of two consecutive strings in R_i is bounded by q_i. Therefore the difference between two strings in any of these languages is bounded by T. In the nonterminals of G' we memorize the last T states used by the automata A_i when recognizing the current string. A prolongation to right is possible (by rules of type (3)) only according to that language R_i which contains the largest subword of the current string (thus we check the maximality). The derivation can stop in any moment by rules of type (4). Consequently, $L_{max}(G) = L(G')$, hence $L_{max}(G) \in REG$, which concludes the proof. ◊

Summarizing these lemmas and the fact that $PL(FIN)$ contains one-letter non-regular languages, we obtain

Theorem 9. *$MAX(F)$ includes strictly $GL(F)$ and is incomparable with $PR(F')$, $F, F' \in \{FIN, REG\}$; $MAX(FIN) - X(REG) \neq \emptyset$ for $X \in \{ARB, PR, GL, LM\}$.*

Open problems. Are the differences $ARB(F) - MAX(F), LM(F) - MAX(F), MAX(F) - PL(F)$, for $F \in \{FIN, REG\}$, non-empty?

The diagram in figure 1 summarizes the results in the previous sections (an arrow from X_1 to X_2 indicates the strict inclusion of the family X_1 in X_2.)

The maximal derivation discussed above can be considered as arbitrary-maximal, since we are not concerned with the place of the selector in the rewritten string, but only with its maximality. Similarly, we can consider prefix-maximal and leftmost-maximal derivations, when a maximal prefix or a substring which is both maximal and leftmost is used for derivation, respectively. We hope to return to these cases. At least the prefix-maximal case looks quite interesting. For instance, if the sets R_i are disjoint, then in every step of a derivation only one of them can be used, which decreases the degree of nondeterminism of the derivations.

5 Final remarks

We have not investigated here a series of issues which are natural for every new considered generative mechanisms, such as closure and decidability problems, syntactic complexity, or the relations with other grammars which do not use the rewriting in generating languages. Another important question is whether or not the degree of shuffle grammars induces an infinite hierarchy of languages. We close this discussion by emphasizing the variety of places where the shuffle operation proves to be useful and interesting, as well as the richness of the area of grammars based on adjoining strings.

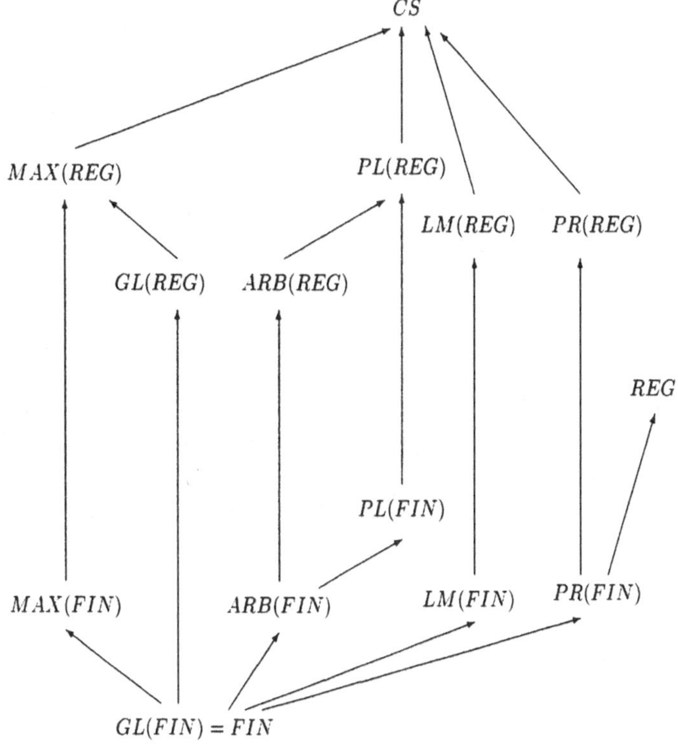

Fig. 1

References

[1] B. Berard, Literal shuffle, *Theoretical Computer Science*, 51 (1987), 281 - 299.

[2] J. Dassow, Gh. Păun, A. Salomaa, Grammars based on patterns, *Intern. J. Found. Computer Sci.*, 4, 1 (1993), 1 - 14.

[3] B. C. Galiukschov, Polukontekstnie gramatiki, *Mat. Logica i Mat. Ling.*, Kalinin Univ, 1981, 38 - 50 (in Russ.).

[4] G. H. Higman, Ordering by divisibility in abstract algebra, *Proc. London Math. Soc.*, 3 (1952), 326 - 336.

[5] M. Ito, G. Thierrin, S. S. Yu, Shuffle-closed languages, submitted, 1993.

[6] M. Jantzen, On shuffle and iterated shuffle, *Actes de l'ecole de printemps de theorie des langages* (M. Blab, Ed.), Murol, 1981, 216 - 235.

[7] A. K. Joshi, S. R. Kosaraju, H. M. Yamada, String adjunct grammars: I. Local and distributed adjunction, *Inform. Control*, 21 (1972), 93 - 116.

[8] S. Marcus, Contextual grammars, *Rev. Roum. Math. Pures Appl.*, 14, 10 (1969), 1525 - 1534.

[9] Al. Mateescu, Marcus contextual grammars with shuffled contexts, in *Mathematical Aspects of Natural and Formal Languages* (Gh. Păun, ed.), World Sci. Publ., Singapore, 1994, 275 - 284.

[10] L. Nebesky, The ξ-grammar, *Prague Studied in Math. Ling.*, 2 (1966), 147 - 154.

[11] Gh. Păun, *Grammars for Economic Processes*, The Technical Publ. House, Bucureşti, 1980 (in Romanian).

[12] Gh. Păun, *Contextual Grammars*, The Publ. House of the Romanian Academy of Sciences, Bucureşti, 1982 (in Romanian).

[13] Gh. Păun, G. Rozenberg, A. Salomaa, Contextual grammars: Erasing, determinism, one-sided contexts, in *Developments in Language Theory* (G. Rozenberg, A. Salomaa, eds.), World Sci. Publ., Singapore, 1994, 370 - 388.

[14] Gh. Păun, G. Rozenberg, A. Salomaa, Contextual grammars: Parallelism and blocking of derivation, *Fundamenta Informaticae*, to appear.

[15] Gh. Păun, G. Rozenberg, A. Salomaa, Marcus contextual grammars: Modularity and leftmost derivation, in *Mathematical Aspects of Natural and Formal Languages* (Gh. Păun, ed.),World Sci. Publ., Singapore, 1994, 375 - 392.

[16] G. Rozenberg, A. Salomaa, *The Mathematical Theory of L Systems*, Academic Press, New York, London, 1980.

[17] A. Salomaa, *Formal Languages*, Academic Press, New York, London, 1973.

Managing Editor's Column

Dear Readers:

It is a pleasure to present number 2 of volume 1 of J.UCS with again 5 substantial contributions with a good mix, maybe a bit loaded towards theory.

To make sure that J.UCS is not seen as a mainly theory journal I would like to encourage all editors and readers to advocate J.UCS as a timely medium for the dissemination of research results and surveys concerning **ALL** fields of Computer Science.

The reaction to the first two issues has been good. I will compile a detailed breakdown of usage after the half-year mark for information. However, one point is clearly emerging: the current hypertext formats such as HTF or HTML are not well suited for formula-rich material, since even simple formulae like x squared, i.e. x^2 have to be inserted as inline images. This is due to the fact that HTML does not handle anything but text and inline images. Thus, the PostScript version of the documents should be prefered, at least for formula-rich material.

The PostScript version can be used in conjunction with the native Hyper-G viewers Amadeus and Harmony but also with other Webviewers such as Mosaic or NetScape if installed properly with a ghostview viewer. For details see the general description how to do this in the general section of J.UCS.

Finally, it is a pleasure to see that more and more J.UCS servers are becoming publicly available. So to read J.UCS, use the one "nearest" to you (in terms of Internet topology!)...or consider installing a server yourself. All software and instructions are available free for all non-profit organisations by just contacting Klaus Schmaranz at kschmar@iicm.tu-graz.ac.at.

If you have any comments on the journal, please do send me an email to hmaurer@iicm.tu-graz.ac.at.

Thanks for your support of J.UCS!

With best wishes

Hermann Maurer, Managing Editor
Graz University of Technology,
Graz / Austria, January 28, 1995.
email: hmaurer@iicm.tu-graz.ac.at

Journal of Universal Computer Science, vol. 1, no. 2 (1995), 84-104
submitted: 10/1/95, accepted: 8/2/95, appeared: 28/2/95,

A Scalable Architecture for Maintaining Referential Integrity in Distributed Information Systems

Frank Kappe
(Institute for Information Processing and Computer Based New Media (IICM), Graz University of Technology,
A-8010 Graz, Austria
fkappe@iicm.tu-graz.ac.at)

Abstract: One of the problems that we experience with today's most widespread Internet Information Systems (like WWW or Gopher) is the lack of support for maintaining referential integrity. Whenever a resource is (re)moved, dangling references from other resources may occur.
This paper presents a scalable architecture for automatic maintenance of referential integrity in large (thousands of servers) distributed information systems. A central feature of the proposed architecture is the *p-flood* algorithm, which is a scalable, robust, prioritizable, probabilistic server-server protocol for efficient distribution of update information to a large collection of servers.
The *p-flood* algorithm is now implemented in the Hyper-G system, but may in principle also be implemented as an add-on for existing WWW and Gopher servers.
Key Words: Hypertext, Link Consistency, Distributed Information System, Internet, Gopher, WWW, Hyper-G, Scalability, p-flood.
Category: H.5.1, C.2.4

1 Introduction

The problem is quite familiar to all net surfers: Every now and then you activate a link (in the case of WWW [Berners-Lee et al. 94]) or menu item (in the case of Gopher [McCahill 94]), but the resource the link or menu item refers to cannot be fetched. This may either be a temporary problem of the network or the server, but it may also indicate that the resource has been permanently removed. Since the systems mentioned above rely on *Uniform Resource Locators* (URLs) [Berners-Lee 93] for accessing information, it may also mean that the resource has only been moved to a new location. It may also happen that a resource is eventually replaced by a different one under the same name (location).

The net effect of this is that a certain percentage of references are invalid. We may expect that this percentage will rise as time goes by, since more and more documents become outdated and are eventually removed, services are shut down or moved to different servers, URLs get re-used, etc. Obviously, it would be desirable to have some support for automatically removing such dangling references to a resource which is deleted, or at least to inform the maintainers of those resources.

For the sake of the following discussion, let us stick to the hypertext terminology of *documents* and *links* instead of the more general terms resource and reference. The techniques described will work for any relationship between any kind of object, but for explanation purposes is is easier to speak only about links and documents.

Let us assume that we would maintain a link database at every server that keeps track of all the links involving this server, i.e. emanate from and/or point to a document that resides on this server. Storing the links outside of the documents in a link database (like it is done in the Intermedia [Haan et al. 92] and Hyper-G [Andrews et al. 95, Kappe et al. 94] systems) will not only give us an efficient solution for the dangling link problem (as we will see); it also enables more advanced user interfaces for navigation in the information space, such as local maps and location feedback [Andrews and Kappe 94], and allows links between arbitrary document types.

2 Scalability

An important issue that needs to be addressed when dealing with distributed algorithms (systems, protocols) is that of *scalability*. Ideally, the behavior of a scalable system should not – or "almost not" – depend on variables like the number of servers, documents, links, or concurrent users of the system. In the Internet environment, scalability is a very important aspect of system design, since the values of these variables are already high and are continuing to grow extremely fast. Looking more closely at the issue, we may distinguish four kinds of scalability:

- **Scalable Performance:** The performance (measured by the response time perceived by the user) should not depend on the number of concurrent users or documents. This requirement cannot be met in a centralized system, and therefore implies the use of a distributed system, where users and documents are more or less evenly distributed over a number of servers which are connected by a network.
  Unfortunately, it may still happen that for some reason a large number of users access a small set of documents residing on a single server. Under such circumstances the distributed system performs like a centralized system, with all the load placed on a single computer and on a certain part of the network. Obviously, one has to avoid such situations, e.g. through the use of *replication* (placing copies of that scarce resource on a number of servers). A good example of a scalable system which relies heavily on replication is the USENET news service [Kantor and Lapsley 86]. When I read news, I am connected to my local news server which holds copies of the news articles that have been posted lately. When accessing a certain article, it does not need to be fetched from the originating site. Therefore, the response time does not depend on how many other Internet users access the same article at the same time (it does depend on the number of users connected to my local news server, though).
  When searching through a number of documents, the response time will increase with the number of documents searched. Good search engines use data structures giving $O(\log n)$ access performance, i.e. there exists a constant c so that the time t it takes to search n documents is smaller than $c \cdot \log n$. Intuitively, this means that for large n a further increase of n will have less effect on t, which is good. Therefore we may say that logarithmic performance is acceptable for an algorithm to qualify as scalable in performance.

- **Scalable Traffic:** Replication may require additional traffic to be sent over the network. Obviously, every news article has to be sent to every news server so that it can be read locally. However, it may well be that most of the articles that have been sent to my local news server are never read by anyone here. Care has to be taken that total traffic increases not more than linearly with the number of servers. For example, solutions where every server periodically sends state information directly to all other servers are not scalable, since it requires $O(n^2)$ messages to be sent (n being the number of servers this time).
- **Scalable Robustness:** By *robustness* we mean that the system should not rely on a single server or a single network connection to work at all times, nor should it assume that all servers of a given set are available at a given time. The *multi-server transaction*, *master-slave* and *distributed update control* systems described in the next section are all examples that do not scale in this respect.
- **Scalable Management:** The functioning of the system should not rely on a single management entity. For example, the Internet's *Domain Name Service* works because its management is distributed. With the current Internet growth rate of about 3 million hosts per year [Network Wizards 94] (about 10,000 per work day) centralized registration is infeasible. This requirement also suggests that configuration and reconfiguration of server-server communication paths should be automatic, as opposed to managed by a central service.

3 Related Work

3.1 Gopher, WWW and Hyper-G

In the World-Wide Web [Berners-Lee et al. 94] data model, documents are connected by links. The links are stored directly inside the documents, which has the advantage of a simple server implementation. On the other hand, the absence of a separate link database not only limits the set of linkable document types and prohibits advanced user interfaces (overview maps, 3D-navigation, etc.), it also makes it hard if not impossible to ensure the integrity of the Web. When a document is removed, it would require parsing all other documents to find the links pointing to that document, so that they could also be removed or at least the owners of the other documents informed. While such a tool would be conceivable for the local server, it is simply impossible to scan all WWW documents on all Web servers in the world, without the aid of pre-indexed link databases. The consequence is that there is no referential integrity in today's World-Wide Web, not even between documents stored on the same server.

Interestingly, the more primitive Gopher [McCahill 94] system does maintain referential integrity in the local case. When a document (which is an ordinary file on the server's file system) is deleted (or moved or modified), the menu item that refers to it (which is a directory entry) is updated as well. This is automatically taken care of by the underlying operating system (unless you try real hard to break it and use the symbolic links of UNIX). References to remote servers remain insecure, however.

While both Gopher and WWW scale quite well with respect to the number of servers, documents, and links, there is a scalability problem with respect to the number of users. When a large number of users for some reason decides to access the same document at the same time, the affected server and the network region around it become overloaded. This phenomenon (Jakob Nielsen calls it a "Flash crowd" [Nielsen 95] after a 1973 science fiction story of Larry Niven) was observed during the 1994 Winter Olympics in Lillehammer, where the Norwegian Oslonett provided the latest results and event photographs over the Web and drowned in information requests. Similar but smaller flash crowds appear when a new service in announced on the NCSA "What's New" page or in relevant newsgroups.

This problem may be alleviated by the use of *cache servers*, which keep local copies of information which has been recently requested, and give users requesting the same information again the local copy instead of fetching it from the originating site. This strategy does not work, however, in two cases:

1. When users access many different documents from a large data set (e.g., an encyclopedia, a reference database). Replication of the whole dataset would help, but this would in general require moving from URLs to URNs (*Uniform Resource Names*), which identify the document by its name (or ID) rather than location.
2. When the information is updated frequently. Some *update protocol* would be required that ensures that caches are updated so that the latest version of the document is delivered.

In the Hyper-G system [Kappe et al. 93] a full-blown database engine is employed to maintain meta-information about documents as well as their relationships to each other (this includes, but is not restricted to, links). Since the links are stored in this database and not in the documents themselves, and since modifications of documents or their relationships are only possible via the Hyper-G server, referential integrity can easily be maintained for local documents. The link database makes links *bidirectional*, i.e. one can find the source from the destination (as well as vice versa). In order to keep this useful property when a link spans physical server boundaries, both servers store the link information as well as replicas of the remote document's meta-information. This means that all updates related to the documents and the link in question have to be performed on both servers in order to keep the web consistent, thus requiring an *update protocol* between servers.

3.2 Multi-Server Transactions

A possible solution for the update problem is the so-called *multi-server transaction* or *collaborating servers* approach [Coulouris and Dollimore 88]. When a document on one server has to be modified (or deleted), the server storing the document acts as *coordinator* and contacts and informs all other servers which are involved. When all other servers have acknowledged the receipt of the update, the coordinator tells them to make the change permanent. A few more details are necessary to make sure that the transaction is committed by all servers – even in the case of a server crash in the middle of the transaction – [Coulouris and Dollimore 88], but in general, this method works and has been implemented in a number of systems (to my knowledge, first in the *Xerox Distributed File System* [Israel et al. 78]). An earlier version of Hyper-G also adopted this method [Kappe 93].

However, the multi-server transaction has scalability problems in certain situations. When for some reason many servers (say, 1000) decide to refer to a specific document (e.g., by pointing a link to it or by replicating it), all of them have to be informed and acknowledge the update before it can be performed. This not only increases network traffic and slows down things considerably, but it also requires that all servers involved have to be up and running, or the transaction cannot be completed. As the number of participating servers increases (and given the unreliability of the Internet), the probability that *all* of them are reachable approaches zero. This means that it becomes practically impossible ever to modify a heavily-referenced object.

3.3 Master/Slave Systems

In a *Master/Slave System* there is one primary server (the *master*) and a number of secondary servers (the *slaves*). The primary server holds a master copy of the replicated object and services all update requests. The slaves are updated by receiving notification of changes from the master or by taking copies from the master copy. Clients may read data from both master and slaves, but write only to the master.

This scheme is well-suited to applications where objects are read frequently and updates happen only infrequently. The Sun Yellow Pages (YP) service (nowadays known as NIS) is an example of a master/slave system.

The central master server also makes it easy to resolve conflicts between update requests and maintain consistency. The obvious disadvantage is that the master server has to be up and running in order to perform updates. Otherwise, this scheme scales very well (provided that we have a good way of propagating updates from master to slaves).

3.4 Distributed Update Control

The *Distributed Update Control* [Coulouris and Dollimore 88] scheme allows any server that holds a copy of an object to perform updates on it, without a single coordinating server, even when some servers are unreachable, and without the possibility for conflicts.

This requires that a server knows about all the other servers that also have copies (let us call this set of servers the *server-set*). In a perfect world, all the copies would be identical, but because of network failures and for performance reasons it may not be possible or desirable to immediately notify all servers of an update. We may instead adopt a looser form of consistency (*weak consistency*), in which all copies eventually converge to the same value at some time interval after the updates have stopped.

However, one still wants to be sure that all read requests are based on up-to-date copies and all updates are performed on the latest version. The trick which ensures this is *majority consensus*: updates are written to a (random) majority of the server-set (more than 50%). Before every read or write operation, the server that is in charge of performing the request contacts some other servers of the server-set and requests the object's version number (or modification time) to identify the current version. When a majority has answered, at least one of it has the current version. This is because in every two majorities there is at least one common member.

The advantage of this algorithm is its robustness: There is no single point of failure and it works even in the face of failure of almost 50% of the server-set. The downside of it is again scalability: The server-set for any object must be known to all members of the server-set, and more than 50% of the set has to be contacted before every write and even read operation. If the set contains, say, 1000 servers, we have to get a response from 501 of them!

This requirement may be relaxed for read operations if we are willing to accept *weak consistency*. Still, it is mandatory for write operations to ensure that no conflicting updates can occur.

3.5 Harvest and *flood-d*

Harvest [Bowman et al. 94] is a new Internet-based resource discovery system which supports an efficient distributed "information gathering" architecture. So-called "Gatherers" collect indexing information from a resource, while the so-called "Brokers" provide an indexed query interface to the gathered information. Brokers retrieve information from one or more Gatherers or other Brokers, and incrementally update their indexes. The idea is that Gatherers should be located close to the resources they index, while Brokers are located close to the users.

Harvest heavily relies on replication to achieve good performance. The indexes created by the Gatherers are periodically replicated to the Brokers. Since the indexes tend to be large, this has to be done efficiently.

Harvest uses a technique called *flooding* for this purpose. Rather than having a Gatherer send its indexes to all Brokers, they are sent to only k of them (e.g., $k = 2$). It is then the responsibility of the k chosen nodes to distribute the indexes to another k each, and so on. While of course the total number of indexes that have to be transferred remains the same, flooding has the nice property of distributing the network and server load over the whole network.

The flood algorithm used by Harvest is called *flood-d* [Danzig et al. 94]. *Flood-d* tries to minimize the network cost and propagation time of the flood by computing a "cheap", k-connected logical update topology based on bandwidth measurements of the underlying physical network. An important requirement was that this topology should not need manual configuration (like for example the Network News [Kantor and Lapsley 86]), but shall be computed and updated automatically. Finding a good approximation of the optimal topology is computationally expensive, however (finding the optimum is even NP-complete), especially when the replication group becomes very large. The paper [Danzig et al. 94] therefore suggests to use a hierarchical scheme of smaller replication groups. However, it is left open how this hierarchy can be found and updated automatically.

4 An Architecture for Referential Integrity

Let us assume that we maintain a link database at every server which keeps track of all the links local to the server as well as those that go in and/or out of the server, i.e. emanate from and/or point to a document residing on another server. Maintaining referential integrity is relatively easy in the case of local links. We will now concentrate on the issue of maintaining integrity in the case of links which span server boundaries.

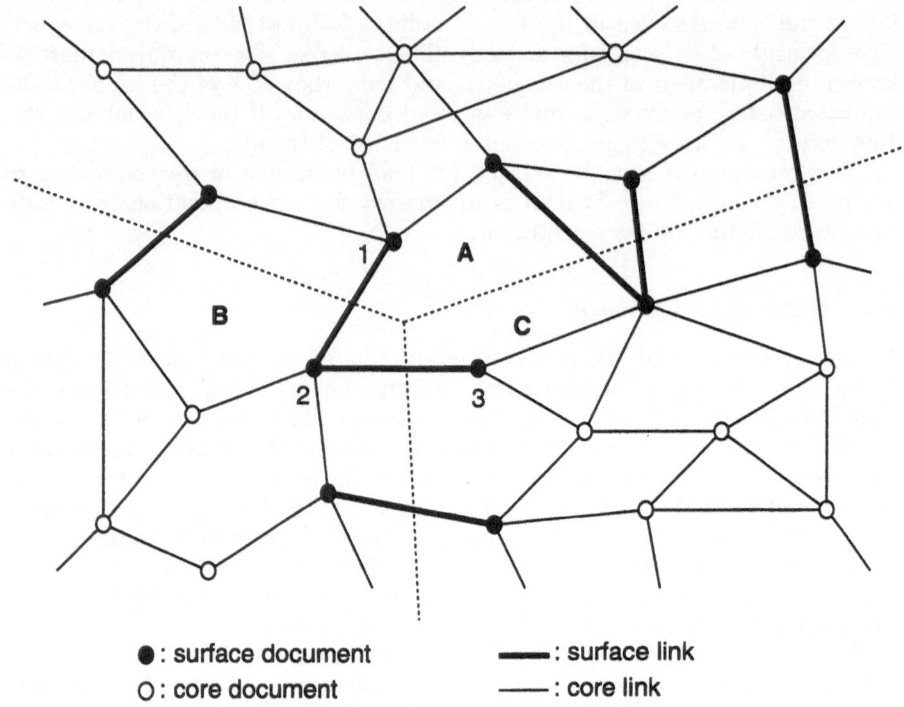

Figure 1: Partitioning the Web among Servers (see text)

Figure 1 illustrates this situation. The hyperweb is partitioned by server boundaries (the servers are labeled A, B, and C in the figure). Links which span server boundaries are shown as thicker edges. We will call these links *surface links*, and documents connected to other servers by such links shall be called *surface documents* (the others are called core links and core documents, respectively). Although not apparent from Figure 1, a server's surface will typically be small compared to its core.

In order to keep the useful property of *bidirectional links*, the link information of surface links must be stored in both affected servers. For increased performance, the servers also keep replicas of the other surface document's meta-information. In figure 1, server A stores document 1 plus a replica of document 2's meta-info and the link between them, while server B stores document 2 plus replicas of documents 1's and 3's meta-info and the links from 1 to 2 and from 2 to 3.

In this setup, documents on different servers are interconnected as tightly as the documents on a single server. The bidirectional links enable more advanced navigation techniques (the link map shown in Figure 1 can actually be computed and shown to the user), but also simplify maintenance of the hyperweb: when I choose to remove document 2, the system can inform me that this will affect document 1 on server A and document 3 on server C (among others on server B). I may either use this information to manually modify the affected documents and links, or let the system ensure automatically that at least the links from 1 to 2 and from 2 to 3 are removed as well.

The problem which remains is how to inform the other servers that document 2 has been removed. As already mentioned, an earlier implementation of Hyper-G used the knowledge about what documents are affected to directly engage the other servers in a multi-server transaction, in order to remove document 2 and all links to and from it. As was also discussed earlier, this approach has problems when many servers must participate in the transaction (because many links point to the document).

Therefore, we decided to adopt a *weak consistency* approach, whereby we accept that the hyperweb may be inconsistent for a certain period of time, but is guaranteed to converge to a consistent state eventually. Of course, we would like to keep the duration of the inconsistency as short as possible.

Like in the master/slave model, updates may only take place at a well-defined server. Unlike the master/slave model, this server is not the same for all operations, but depends on the document or link being modified (or removed or inserted): For documents, it is the server which holds the document; for links, it is the server which holds the document where the link emanates (in our example, server B would be responsible for updates of document 2, while the link from 1 to 2 would be updated by server A). This reduces the problem of overload of the master, while eliminating the problem of conflicting updates (they are handled one after the other). One disadvantage remains: the master server must be available at update time. However, since for security reasons users wishing to update document 2 must have write permission for document 2 (this is checked by server B which holds document 2), this fact is inevitable and we have to live it, anyway.

Updates of core documents or core links require no further action (integrity is maintained by the local link database). However, other servers need to be notified of updates happening at a server's surface (i.e. updates of surface documents or surface links). We chose to use a flood algorithm similar to the one employed by Harvest to propagate updates from the master to the slaves (i.e. all other servers), because of its scalability (the traffic generated does not depend on the number of references to the object in question), because it does not require that the recipients are available at update time, and because it can be used for other purposes as well (like distributing server addresses and statistics, and maintaining the consistency of replicas and caches).

5 The p-flood algorithm

The *flood-d* algorithm described in [Danzig et al. 94] is optimized for minimizing the cost of the flood. This makes sense because it is designed for applications which need to flood large amounts of data. Our application – sending update notifications – sends only small messages ("document 2 removed" can be encoded in a few bytes), and hence has somewhat different requirements:

- **Speed:** Messages should propagate fast in order to minimize the duration of inconsistencies.
- **Robustness:** The protocol should *guarantee* eventual delivery of every message to every server, even when some servers are down. When a server that

has been unavailable comes up again, it should receive all the messages it has missed in between.

- **Scalability:** The time it takes to inform all servers should not depend heavily on the number of servers. Likewise, the amount of traffic generated should not depend heavily on the number of servers. Of course, since every message must be sent to every server at least once, $O(n)$ is a lower bound for the total traffic generated.
- **Automatic:** We do not want to configure flood paths manually (like in the News service).
- **Priority:** Since we intend to use the protocol for other purposes as well, it would be nice to have a priority parameter attached to every message that determines its acceptable propagation delay and bandwidth consumption.

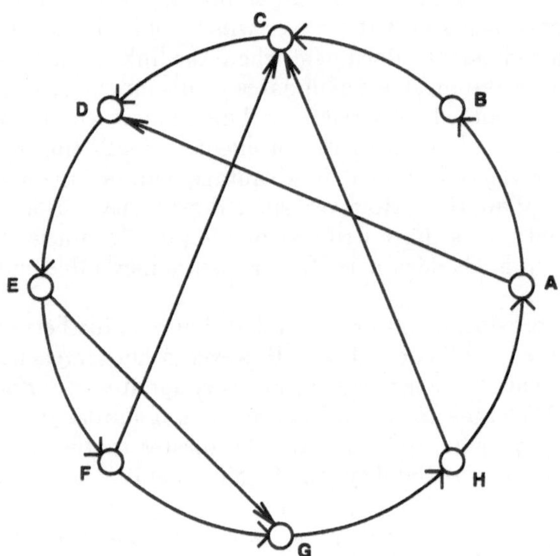

Figure 2: One step of the *p-flood* algorithm ($p = 1.5$)

The *p-flood* algorithm is a probabilistic algorithm which fulfills the above requirements. Figure 2 illustrates its behavior. The servers are arranged in a circle (for example by sorting them according to their Internet address; see section 7.1 for a discussion how this can be done in a better way). Every server knows all other servers (updates of the server list will of course be transported by the algorithm itself).

Servers accumulate *update messages* which are generated either by the server itself (as a result of modification of a surface document or surface link), or are received from other servers, in their *update list*. Once in a while (every few minutes) the update list is sent to p other servers ($p \geq 1$). We will call this time period a *step* of the algorithm. For $p = 1$, updates are sent only to the immediate successor, otherwise they are also sent to $p - 1$ other servers that are chosen at random. If p is fractional, they are sent to other servers only with probability $p - 1$. For example, $p = 1.3$ means that one message is sent to the successor, and another one with probability .3 to a random server; $p = 3.2$ means that it is sent to the successor, two other random servers plus one other random server with probability .2.

Figure 2 shows one step of the p-flood algorithm with $p = 1.5$. Note that at every step the operations described above are performed by all servers in parallel, i.e. within the step time period every server performs one step (the clocks of the servers do not have to be synchronized). We may observe that at every step $p \cdot n$ update lists are sent (n being the number of servers).

The higher the value of p, the shorter the time it takes to reach all servers, but the higher the amount of traffic generated (it happens that the same message is received more than once by some servers). The algorithm in principle allows the assignment of different values of p to individual messages, so we may call p the *priority* of the message.

After a message has successfully been transmitted to a server's immediate successor, it is removed from the sending server's update list and not sent again to any server in future steps. This ensures that messages are removed after they have been received by all servers and keeps the update lists relatively short. Messages are time-stamped using a per-server sequence number, so that duplicates can be discarded and messages can be processed in the correct order by the receiver.

What happens when a server is down or unreachable? Since a message must not be discarded from the update list until it has successfully been sent to the successor (we assume that a reliable transport protocol like TCP is used and that receipt is acknowledged), the message will effectively wait there until the successor comes up again. Almost immediately after that, the accumulated update messages will be sent. In a way, every server is responsible for delivering messages to its successor. The penalty is that when a server is down for a long period of time, its predecessor's update list grows.

Setting the priority $p = 1$ (send messages only to the successor) will effectively block update messages in case of an unreachable server and is therefore not feasible. A higher values of p not only speeds up the propagation of the messages significantly, but also contributes to the robustness of the algorithm. In the example of Figure 2, a crash of server B would not inhibit update messages from server A being propagated to the other servers.

A few extensions of *p-flood* are necessary for real use. They are described later in section 7, in order to not burden the reader with additional complexity at this point.

6 Simulation Results

This section presents data gathered by running extensive simulations of *p-flood*. We will first concentrate on "perfect world" simulations (i.e. all servers are reachable) and then look at the effect of network and server faults.

6.1 The Behavior of *p-flood* in the Perfect World

In this first set of experiments we want to find out how weak exactly our weak consistency is, i.e. how long it takes to arrive at a consistent state after updates have stopped, how this time depends on the number of servers and the priority factor p, and how much traffic is generated over time.

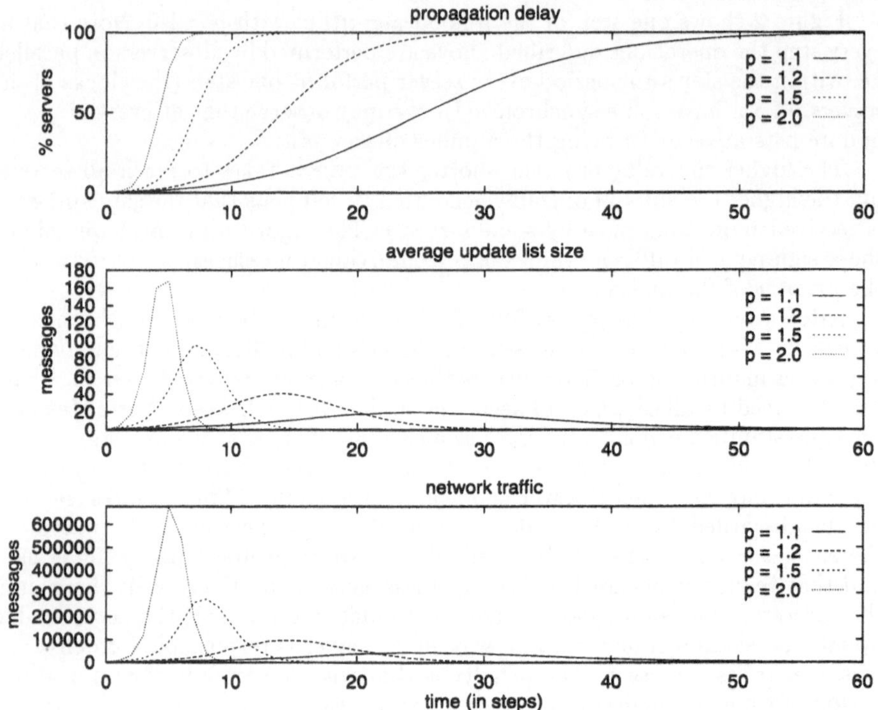

Figure 3: Performance of *p-flood* at different values of p ($n = 1000, m = 1000$)

Figure 3 gives us a feeling of how *p-flood* performs. It is assumed that m update messages have been generated at the n different servers before the simulation starts, and we watch their propagation to the other servers, in particular how long it takes until they arrive there. It turns out that it does not matter whether all m updates are made on a single server or whether they are distributed randomly over the n servers, but the random placements gives smoother curves, so I have chosen this method for producing the graphs.

The top graph shows how the update information is propagated to the 1000 servers, using different values of p. A higher value of p gives faster propagation, e.g. at $p = 2$ and $n = 1000$, 50% of the servers are reached after about 4 steps, 99% after 7 steps, and the last one is typically updated after 10-13 steps. The price for faster propagation is a higher load on the servers and networks: The middle graph shows the average size of the update list held at each server, and the bottom graph shows the traffic in messages that is sent at each step.

Since every message has to be sent to every server at least once, every algorithm that delivers every message to every server will need to transmit at least $m \cdot n$ messages, so we will call this number the *optimum* traffic. Under perfect-world conditions, the total traffic sent by *p-flood* is $p \cdot n \cdot m$ messages, or $p \cdot optimum$. The point is that the flood algorithm distributes this traffic nicely over time and over the whole network, as opposed to the trivial solution where every server simply sends all its updates to all other servers (which requires only *optimum* messages to be sent). The lower the value of p, the more network-friendly the update.

Clearly, there is a tradeoff between fast propagation and peak network load. Figure 3 suggests that a good setting of p is somewhere between 1 and 2.

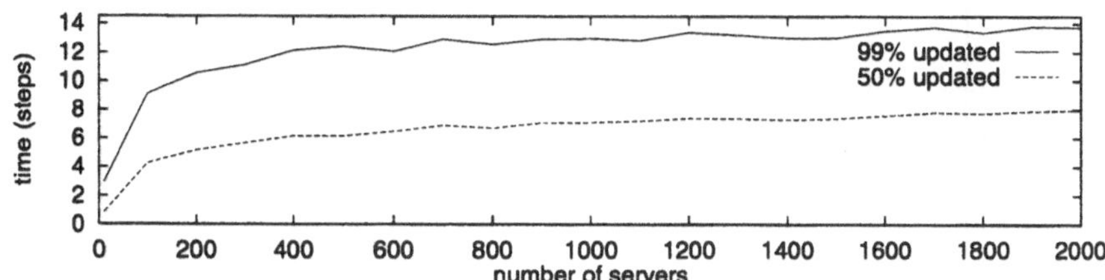

Figure 4: Time to update 50% (99%) of the servers ($p = 1.5$) by n

Figure 4 demonstrates the remarkable scalability of *p-flood* with respect to the number of servers. The time to reach 50% and 99%[1] of the servers is plotted against the number of servers. The logarithmic performance of *p-flood* is clearly visible, meaning that that *p-flood* is well-suited for use in the context of very large server groups.

Figure 5 plots the propagation delay (again, reaching 50% and 99% of the servers) versus the priority p for a constant number of servers ($n = 1000$).

When I first ran the experiments, I was surprised to see that the messages traveled about twice as fast as I had expected. For example, for $p = 1$ it takes about 500 steps (not 1000) to reach all 1000 servers, for $p = 2$ it takes about 4 (not 9; $2^9 = 512$) steps to reach the first 500 servers, etc.

It turns out that this happens because the clocks in the servers which determine the step time are *not* synchronized. When one server's timer expires and the server then sends its update list to another server, the other server's timer will in general not expire a full step time later, but after some random time interval between 0 and the step time. On average, it will expire after half of the step time, which explains the observed effect.

In the simulation, the behavior of the parallel server processes was modeled on a single computer, i.e. for every step the individual servers performed their update operations one after the other. If implemented carelessly, this serialization could lead to wrong results: In the example of figure 2, processing the servers in the order A-B-C-D-E-F-G-H would always propagate all updates to all servers in one single step! Instead, reality was modeled more closely by processing the servers in the order given by a randomly chosen permutation of the servers,

[1] The time to update 100% of the servers is of course always an integer value and subject to a great deal of randomness. The 99% value can be interpolated and is less affected by randomness, so I decided to use this value to get smoother curves in the graphs. The 100% value is about 3-6 steps higher.

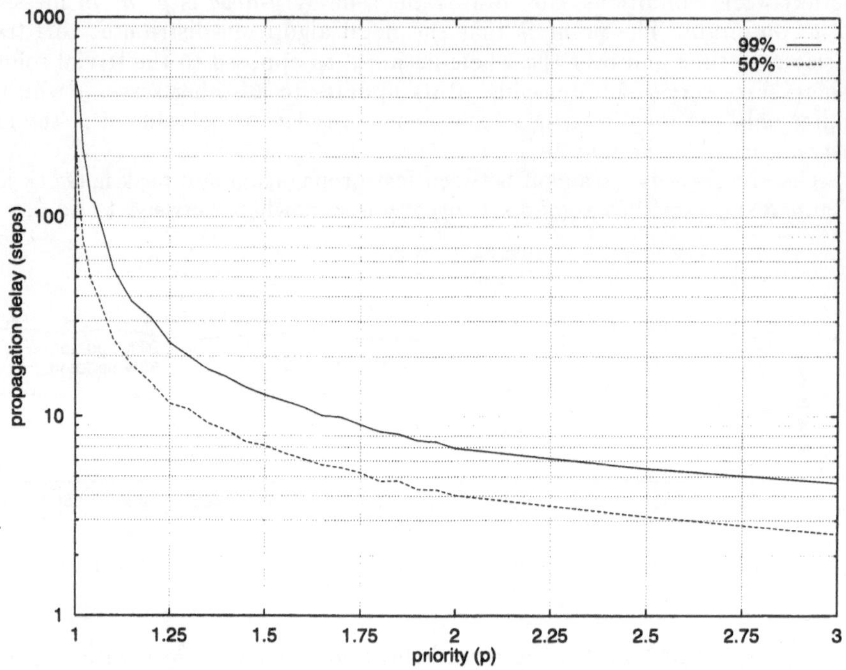

Figure 5: Time to update 50% (99%) of the servers, by p ($n = 1000$)

mimicking the random expiration of the server's timers. Still, messages will travel slightly slower in reality, especially if the step time is not large compared to the average transmission time of updates lists.

6.2 Network and Server Failure

Since one of the major requirements for our flood algorithm was its robustness with respect to network and server failures, we will now take a close look to this issue.

First, let me make the distinction between *soft* or transient errors and *hard* or persistent errors. Soft errors are temporary network errors due to routing problems or network overload. This type of errors occur rather frequently in the Internet, but usually only for a short period of time. Hard errors last longer (e.g, as a result of a hardware failure) but fortunately happen less frequently.

Figure 6 shows the effect of soft errors on the propagation delay and the traffic generated. The propagation delay (i.e. the time to reach 50%/99% of the servers) increases only slowly with increased soft error rate. A soft error rate of 10% means that in every step 10% of the update propagations will fail (10% of the servers are unreachable), which are chosen randomly. In the next step, another random set of 10% fail, but is unlikely that the two sets are identical.

The bottom graph of Figure 6 shows how traffic increases with increased soft error rate. The set of messages that is sent increases, but the number of acknowledged messages (i.e. that are sent successfully) remains constant. Since

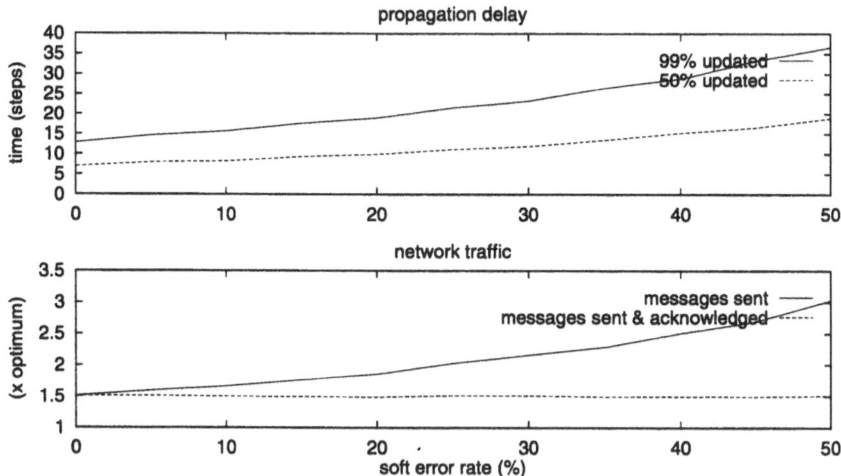

Figure 6: Effect of soft errors on propagation delay and traffic ($p = 1.5, n = 1000$)

p-flood detects duplicate messages and messages that arrive out of order itself, we could in principle use an unreliable protocol like UDP to transmit messages and acknowledgments. However, UDP is very much subject to soft errors (e.g., packets dropped). Using TCP, the transport protocol repairs a large number of soft errors itself. When a server is temporarily unreachable, this will usually already been detected during the opening of the connection, and the messages will never be sent in this case. This means that for TCP the "messages sent" graph is not significant, i.e. the number of messages actually sent is constant with respect to soft errors.

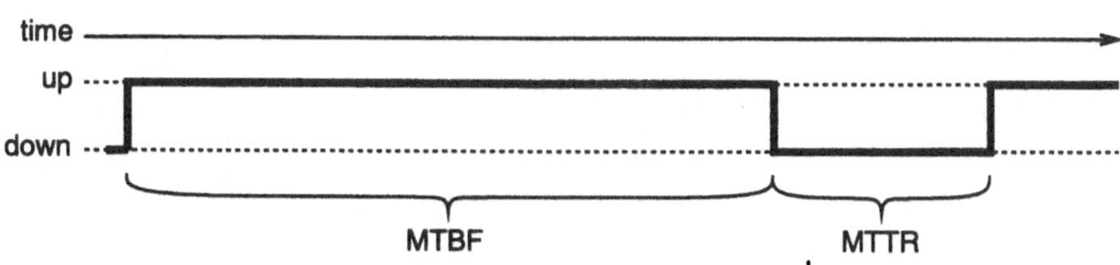

Figure 7: MTBF and MTTR

Hard errors are usually described by the two variables *Mean Time Before Failure (MTBF)* and *Mean Time To Repair (MTTR)* (Figure 7). Then *uptime*, i.e. the fraction of time the server is up, is defined as

$$uptime = \frac{MTBF}{MTBF + MTTR}$$

In our simulations, we will measure MTBF and MTTR in units of steps. For $MTTR = 1$ we have soft (transient) errors, larger values of MTTR mean that a same server is down for a longer period of time. It is expected that server *uptime* will be well over 90% (this is already a bad value; it means that a server will be unreachable for 2.4 hours per day). In the beginning, $MTTR/(MTBF+MTTR)$ servers are marked as down, with the time they remain down chosen randomly between 0 and MTTR. The others are assigned a time they remain up between 0 and MTBF. It is assumed that the servers which are down also carry update messages (they could have been accumulated before they went down; the servers could be only unreachable from the outside but running). During the simulation, servers that come up remain up for MTBF steps, those that go down remain down for MTTR steps.

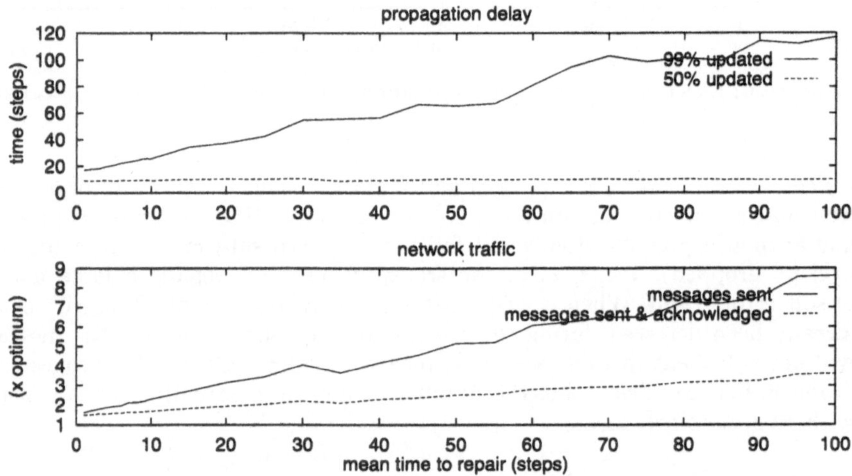

Figure 8: Effect of hard errors ($p = 1.5, n = 1000$, *uptime* $= 90\%$)

In Figure 8, *uptime* is constantly 90%, and MTTR varies between 1 and 100. The top graph shows the effect on the propagation delay. Because of the probabilistic nature of *p-flood* there is almost no effect on the remaining servers, which is why the time to reach 50% of the servers remains almost constant. Of course, there is an impact on the time to reach 99% of the servers (because only 90% are available), which grows linearly with MTTR. The number of messages sent also grows linearly. This time the number of messages which are sent and acknowledged (i.e. the ones that would be sent when we use TCP) also increases, but only slowly.

Figure 9 takes a closer look at the effect of hard errors on the performance of *p-flood*. In order to make the effects clearly visible, 10% of the servers (100) are held down (or unreachable) until step 50, when they all come up simultaneously. The graphs can be divided in three phases:

During the first phase (until about step 17), updates propagate almost as usual (only slightly slower than the $p = 1.5$ curve in Figure 3), but level off when

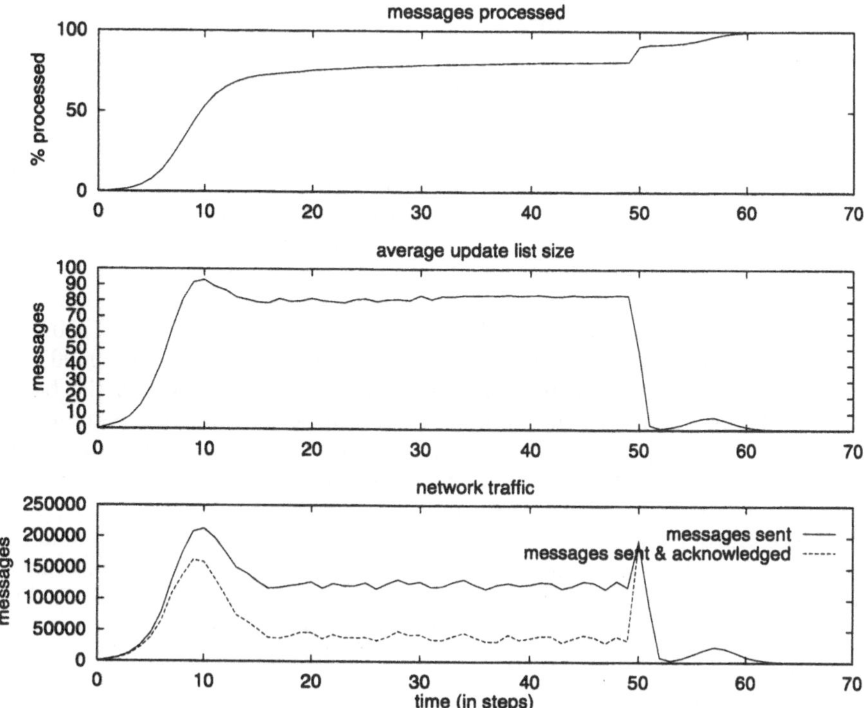

Figure 9: 10% of the servers are down until step 50 ($p = 1.5, n = 1000, m = 1000$)

approximately 81% of the updates are processed (because 90% of the updates are then processed by 90% of the servers; remember that the 10% unreachable servers also generated 10% of the updates).

In the second phase (steps 18 to 49) the system is in a more or less stable state. Since this state may last for a long time (until the servers come up again; in our experiment this is step 50), it is worth analyzing what exactly happens during this phase. We may observe that the set of servers can be partitioned in three disjoint groups:

1. Those that are down. If we call d the fraction of servers that are down, then the number of servers in this group is $d \cdot n$ (in our example: $d = 0.1, n = 1000 \Rightarrow d \cdot n = 100$).
2. The predecessors of the servers that are down. Since a predecessor may also be down (with probability d), in which case it belongs to the previous group, the number of members of this group is $(d - d^2) \cdot n$ (in our example: 90).
3. The others, i.e. those that are up and not predecessors of an unavailable server. The number of such servers is $(1 - d)^2 \cdot n$ (in our example: 810).

The members of group 3 are able to flush their whole update list already during the first phase, i.e. their update list size during phase 2 is zero. Members of group 2 keep messages destined for the group 1 members. The number of such messages is $(1 - d) \cdot m$ at each server. The unavailable servers carry m/n

messages each. The average update list size (as plotted in the middle graph of Figure 9) during phase 2 is therefore

$$\frac{(d-d^2)\cdot n\cdot(1-d)\cdot m+d\cdot n\cdot\frac{m}{n}}{n}=m\cdot(d-2d^2+d^3+\frac{d}{n})\quad(=81.1)$$

The members of group 2 constantly try to send messages to their successors (which are group 3 members) and to other random servers. At $p = 1.5$, every group-2-server sends .5 messages per step to random nodes (which will succeed with probability $(1-d)$), plus one message per step to its successor (which is guaranteed to fail). The members of group 1 and 3 send nothing. The total number of messages sent at each step of phase 2 can therefore be calculated as $p\cdot(d-d^2)\cdot n\cdot(1-d)\cdot m$, in our example $1.5\cdot 90\cdot 900 = 121,500$. Out of these, $(1-p)/p$ are successful (in our example, one third or 40500). The calculation corresponds nicely with the simulated results shown in the bottom graph of Figure 9. Again, the number of messages sent and not acknowledged is insignificant if we use TCP as transport protocol, because the fact that a server is down is discovered already when attempting to open the connection, and nothing will be sent if the open fails.

In the third phase, after the unavailable servers come up at step 50, the members of group 2 immediately succeed in propagating their update lists to their successors, which causes the dramatic effects shown in Figure 9 shown around step 50. After that, it takes a few more steps to propagate the updates that were kept by the unavailable servers to all servers.

6.3 Traffic Estimates

Let us now try to estimate the (additional) amount of network traffic that would be caused by applying the described architecture to a distributed information system. In order to do so, we assume the following values of variables:

- 1,000 servers (n).
- 100 surface objects (documents and links) per server, i.e. we assume a total of 100,000 surface objects. Note that the number of core objects would be much higher but is irrelevant here.
- 10% of the surface objects are updated per day, i.e. a total of 10,000 updates messages (m) have to be propagated every day. Again, updates of core objects are irrelevant.
- Note that while the traffic generated is dependent on the number of servers and documents, it does not depend on the number of users of the system.

Then, the total number of messages sent per day is $p\cdot optimum$, with $optimum = n\cdot m = 10^7$ messages (every message shall be delivered to every server). A message is a few bytes long (say, 10). At $p = 1.5$, we would generate network-wide traffic of 1.5×10^8 bytes (150 MB) per day, or 4.5 GB per month.

On the other hand, the NSFnet currently (Nov. 94) transmits about 22,462 GB per month [Merit Network Information Center 94]. If we assume that 25% of the whole (non-local) Internet traffic pass the NSFnet (i.e. the whole traffic is about 90,000 GB/month), this means that the update messages of our information system would cause an additional 0.005 % of network traffic; in other words, the effect is negligible.

Another nice property of *p-flood* is that the traffic is distributed evenly over the whole set of servers, which means that the amount of traffic seen by a single server does not increase when the number of servers is increased[2]. It only depends on the number of updates of surface objects. Of course, it may is possible to operate servers in an isolated fashion, in order to avoid being molested by any traffic at all.

Since every update message has to be propagated to every server, the nature of *p-flood* can be compared to the USENET news service. However, the messages are much smaller than news articles. The numbers given are for perfect-world performance. Consult Figures 6 and 8 to see the effect of soft and hard errors on network traffic.

7 Extensions of *p-flood*

The description of *p-flood* in section 5 was a bit simplistic for the purpose of understanding the simualtion results. However, the following details have to be addressed when actually implementing *p-flood*:

7.1 Arranging the Servers

A potential weakness of *p-flood* is its random usage of logical Internet connections, without knowledge of the underlying physical network. There is no preference of fast links over slow ones, as in *flood-d*. On the other hand, random selection of flood paths propagates the updates faster than the cost-based selection [Danzig et al. 94], which tends to use the same links again and again.

However, *p-flood* chooses its propagation paths in both non-probabilistic (the immediate successor) and probabilistic (among the other servers) ways. The amount of randomness is controlled by the p parameter. Since for reasonable values of p (see the simulations in section 6) most traffic runs over the static circle of servers (see figure 2), clever arrangement of servers in this circle can vastly reduce network cost and delay, without giving away the advantages of fast propagation and robustness by random choice of some of the flood paths.

Computing the optimal circle using actual bandwidth measurements would be difficult, since it would require gathering a fully connected matrix of bandwidth between servers. Furthermore, the measurements would have to be repeated quite frequently, because global network utilization changes with the time of the day. Hand-configuring is not considered an option. Therefore, we choose a more pragmatic, heuristic approach:

Servers are sorted according to their reversed fully-qualified domain name. Server i then is the successor of server $i-1$, and the first server is the successor of the last one. Sorting by reverse domain name (i.e. by last character first) results in all servers in for example Belgium (domain .be) being neighbors in the circle, followed by the servers in Germany (domain .de) and so forth. Within Germany, the servers located in, e.g., Berlin will be neighbors (domain -berlin.de). Since

[2] As has been shown before, the total Internet traffic generated *does* depend on the number of servers.

in most cases local connectivity is cheaper and faster than international connections, this simple trick will result in better use of the available bandwidth[3]. No computations (other than sorting) and measurements are necessary.

7.2 Adding and Removing Servers

When a server is added to or removed from the server list, *p-flood* itself – with a high priority p – is used to notify all servers. The servers modify their server list accordingly (using the sort order described in section 7.1).

During propagation of server list updates (addition and removal of servers, moving a server to a different host) it is important that a server uses its old server list for flooding, until the message has been acknowledged by the successor. Simple modifications of server attributes (e.g., description, Internet address, e-mail of administrator) do not require such precautions.

7.3 Recovery after Catastrophic Events

When operating a large number of servers it may and will happen (not too often, hopefully) that catastrophic events occur which result in loss of information (for example a head crash on the server's disk). In such cases, operation needs to be resumed from a backup copy of the information base. If the backup copy is i days old, then the restarted server has lost all its updates of the last i days. This is inevitable, though.

However, other servers may also have a now obsolete picture of our server's surface. For example, somebody may have recently (less than i days ago) created a new document in our server, with a link pointing to (or from) another document on another server. The document has now disappeared and of course this link also has to be destroyed in order to keep a consistent state. In other words, the other servers also have to roll back to the situation i days ago.

In such a situation, our server may flood a special message that contains its whole surface (documents and links), thus requesting all other servers to check this picture against their view of our server, and adjust their information about our server accordingly.

7.4 Repairing Inconsistencies

Under certain conditions an inconsistency in the hyperweb may occur. For example, let us assume that a link is made from a document on server A to a document on server B. The document on server B was not previously on the surface. At about the same time (i.e., before the update message reflecting this operation arrives at server B) server B deletes the document the links is going to point to. Since it is not on the surface there is no need to inform other servers about the deletion, so server A will not be notified and will keep its link.

Server B can detect this inconsistency when the update message from server A eventually arrives, since it requests creation of a link to a non-existing object.

[3] Unfortunately, host names in the US domains (.edu, .com, .gov, .mil, .net) in general do not give any hints on the host's geographical location, with the exception of the new .us domain).

It may now flood a "document removed" message for this non-existing object, as if it had been on the surface.

Alternatively, we may choose to live with such (rare) inconsistencies for a while, and have all servers periodically flood their whole surface, like after a catastrophic event (section 7.3). This would serve as a fall-back mechanism that deals with all kinds of inconsistencies and errors, including unforeseeable hardware and software errors in the update server. Since these messages may be rather long, they should be sent infrequently and with low priority. The exact time and priority will have to be determined when we have a feeling of how often such problems occur.

8 Summary

The paper presents a scalable architecure for guaranteeing referential consistency in large, distributed information systems, for example distributed hypermedia systems like Gopher, WWW, and Hyper-G.

Server objects (documents, links) are divided into surface and core objects. We assume that servers are able to maintain referential integrity for core objects (like the Hyper-G server) themselves, so only surface objects need to be treated specially when modified. A fast, robust, prioritizable flood algorithm, *p-flood*, is specified to propagate messages containing update information about surface objects between servers.

Extensive simulations of *p-flood* show that the protocol is scalable, fast, and can cope with spurious errors and persistent failure of servers and networks. The traffic generated is negligable compared to other sources of Internet traffic.

The architecture described and *p-flood* is now being implemented in the Hyper-G system, but can in principle be applied to any kind of distributed information system. 1

References

[Andrews and Kappe 94] Andrews, K., Kappe, F.: "Soaring Through Hyperspace: A Snapshot of Hyper-G and its Harmony Client". In Herzner, W., Kappe, F. (editors), Proc. of Eurographics Symposium on Multimedia/Hypermedia in Open Distributed Environments, Graz, Austria. Springer (1994), 181–191.

[Andrews et al. 95] Andrews, K., Kappe, F., Maurer, H.: "Hyper-G: Towards the Next Generation of Network Information Technology". Information Processing and Management (1995). Special issue: Selected Proceedings of the Workshop on Distributed Multimedia Systems, Graz, Austria, Nov. 1994.

[Berners-Lee 93] Berners-Lee, T.: "Uniform Resource Locators". Available on the WWW at URL `http://info.cern.ch/hypertext/WWW/Addressing/URL/Overview.html` (1993).

[Berners-Lee et al. 94] Berners-Lee, T., Cailliau, R., Luotonen, A., Nielsen, H. F., Secret, A.: "The World-Wide Web". Communications of the ACM, 37, 8 (1994), 76–82.

[Bowman et al. 94] Bowman, C. M., Danzig, P. B., Hardy, D. R., Manber, U., Schwartz, M. F.: "Harvest: A Scalable, Customizable Discovery and Access System". Technical Report CU-CS-732-94, Department of Computer Science, University of Colorado, Boulder (1994). Available by anonymous ftp from `ftp.cs.colorado.edu` in `/pub/cs/techreports/schwartz/Harvest.ps`.

[Coulouris and Dollimore 88] Coulouris, G. F., Dollimore, J.: "Distributed Systems: Concepts and Design". Addison-Wesley (1988).

[Danzig et al. 94] Danzig, P., DeLucia, D., Obraczka, K.: "Massively Replicating Services in Autonomously Managed Wide-Area Internetworks". Technical report, Computer Science Department, University of Southern California (1994). Available by anonymous ftp from `catarina.usc.edu` in `/pub/kobraczk/ToN.ps.Z`.

[Haan et al. 92] Haan, B. J., Kahn, P., Riley, V. A., Coombs, J. H., Meyrowitz, N. K.: "IRIS Hypermedia Services". Communications of the ACM, 35, 1 (1992), 36–51.

[Israel et al. 78] Israel, J. E., Mitchell, J. G., Sturgis, H. E.: "Separating Data from function in a Distributed File System". In Lanciaux, D. (editor), Operating Systems: Theory and Practice, 17–27. North-Holland, Amsterdam (1978).

[Kantor and Lapsley 86] Kantor, D., Lapsley, P.: "Network News Transfer Protocol – A Proposed Standard for the Stream-Based Transmission of News. Internet RFC 977". Available by anonymous ftp from `nic.ddn.mil` in file `rfc/rfc977.txt` (1986).

[Kappe 93] Kappe, F.: "Hyper-G: A Distributed Hypermedia System". In Leiner, B. (editor), Proc. INET '93, San Francisco, California. Internet Society (1993), DCC-1–DCC-9.

[Kappe et al. 93] Kappe, F., Pani, G., Schnabel, F.: "The Architecture of a Massively Distributed Hypermedia System". Internet Research: Electronic Networking Applications and Policy, 3, 1 (1993), 10–24.

[Kappe et al. 94] Kappe, F., Andrews, K., Faschingbauer, J., Gaisbauer, M., Maurer, H., Pichler, M., Schipflinger, J.: "Hyper-G: A New Tool for Distributed Hypermedia". In Proc. Distributed Multimedia Systems and Applications, Honolulu, Hawaii. IASTED/ISSM, ACTA Press, ISBN: 0-88986-194-3 (1994), 209–214.

[McCahill 94] McCahill, M. P., Anklesaria, F. X.: "Evolution of Internet Gopher". Information Processing and Management (1995). Special issue: Selected Proceedings of the Workshop on Distributed Multimedia Systems, Graz, Austria, Nov. 1994.

[Merit Network Information Center 94] Merit Network Information Center: "NSFNET Backbone Statistics". Up-to-date figures are available by anonymous ftp from `nic.merit.edu` in `/nsfnet/statistics` (1994).

[Network Wizards 94] Network Wizards: "Internet Domain Survey". Up-to-date figures are available on the WWW at URL `http://www.nw.com/zone/WWW/top.html` (1994).

[Nielsen 95] Nielsen, J.: "Multimedia & Hypertext: The Internet and Beyond" Academic Press (1995).

Journal of Universal Computer Science, vol. 1, no. 2 (1995), 105-130
submitted: 22/1/95, accepted: 18/2/95, appeared: 28/2/95,

A Variant of Team Cooperation in Grammar Systems

Rudolf Freund
Technical University Wien, Institute for Computer Languages
Resselgasse 3, 1040 Wien, Austria
freund@csdec1.tuwien.ac.at

Gheorghe Păun[1]
Institute of Mathematics of the Romanian Academy of Sciences
PO Box 1-764, 70700 Bucureşti, Romania
gpaun@imar.ro

Abstract: We prove that grammar systems with (prescribed or free) teams (of constant size at least two or arbitrary size) working as long as they can do, characterize the family of languages generated by (context-free) matrix grammars with appearance checking; in this way, the results in [Păun, Rozenberg 1994] are completed and improved.

Keywords: Formal languages, grammar systems, teams
Category: F.4.2, F.4.3

1 Introduction

A cooperating grammar system, as introduced in [Csuhaj-Varjù, Dassow 1990] and [Meersman, Rozenberg 1978], consists of several (usually context-free) grammars, each of them working, by turns, on a common sentential form. A basic protocol of cooperation is the *maximal competence* strategy: a component must rewrite the current sentential form as long as it can do this (and hence never can finish, if it can work forever). In [Csuhaj-Varjù, Dassow 1990] it is proved that in this way exactly the family of $ET0L$-languages can be obtained. In [Meersman, Rozenberg 1978] a variant of this *stop condition* is considered: a component must work until it introduces a non-terminal which cannot be rewritten by the same component.

In [Kari, Mateescu, Păun, Salomaa 1994], a way to increase the power of cooperating grammar systems has been proposed: the cooperation of the components of a grammar system is increased by allowing (or forcing) some of the components of the system to work simultaneously in *teams* on the current sentential form in parallel, i. e. in each step, every member of the currently active team has to apply

[1] Research carried out during the author's visit at the Technical University Wien

a rule. In [Kari, Mateescu, Păun, Salomaa 1994], the condition for a team to stop its work has been the following one: no rule of any member of the team can be used any more. Even with such a strong stop condition, non-$ET0L$-languages can be generated as it is proved in [Kari, Mateescu, Păun, Salomaa 1994] (and moreover, teams of size two are sufficient, as it is shown in [Csuhaj-Varjù, Păun 1993]).

Another stop condition has been considered in [Păun, Rozenberg 1994]: a team stops working if and only if at least one of its members cannot apply one of its rules any more. For this stop condition as well as for that introduced in [Kari, Mateescu, Păun, Salomaa 1994], in [Păun, Rozenberg 1994] it is proved that both using prescribed teams (all of them being of given size or of free size) and using free teams (of given size at least two or of arbitrary size at least two) exactly the family of languages generated by matrix (or programmed) grammars with appearance checking is obtained (thus strenghtening the results proved in [Csuhaj-Varjù, Păun 1993] and [Kari, Mateescu, Păun, Salomaa 1994]).

The stop conditions considered in [Păun, Rozenberg 1994] are not the natural extension of the *maximal competence* strategy from individual components of grammar systems to teams of components: the simplest way for such an extension is to allow a team to become inactive when it is no longer able to rewrite the current sentential form *as a team,* irrespective whether or not some or even all rules of the components can be applied further. For instance, if the current string contains only two occurences of the non-terminal A and we have a team consisting of three components, each consisting of rules of the form $A \rightarrow \alpha$ only, then none of the conditions investigated in [Csuhaj-Varjù, Păun 1993], [Kari, Mateescu, Păun, Salomaa 1994], and [Păun, Rozenberg 1994] is fulfilled, although the team cannot be used any more. Yet the derivation is correctly terminated if we use the natural extension of the maximal competence strategy mentioned above, but not for the variants considered in [Csuhaj-Varjù, Păun 1993], [Kari, Mateescu, Păun, Salomaa 1994], and [Păun, Rozenberg 1994] (the derivation is simply unacceptable for those variants, although it looks quite rationally considered from the point of view of the team).

There is also another reason for considering the new stop condition, namely a mathematical one: grouping sets of rules in teams may remind us of the mode of working of matrix grammars; checking whether rules in a component of a team can be applied may remind us of the appearance checking in matrix grammars. All together, these aspects make the following result somehow non-surprising (although the proof given in [Păun, Rozenberg 1994] is, by no means, obvious): grammar systems with teams (prescribed or free and of given size at least two or of free size at least two) working with the stop conditions considered in [Păun, Rozenberg 1994] characterize the family of languages generated by (context-free) matrix grammars with appearance checking. The new mode of stopping the work of a team is not related to the appearance checking manner of work in such an obvious manner, yet again all languages generated by matrix grammars with appearance checking can be obtained by grammar systems with free teams of given size at least two, but also with free teams of arbitrary size, which is an improvement of the results obtained in [Păun, Rozenberg 1994].

The study of teams, in general the study of classes of grammar systems in which both the sequential and the parallel modes of working are present, requests and deserves further efforts (see also [Csuhaj-Varjù 1994] for motivations of such investigations).

2 Preliminary definitions

We specify only a few notions and notations here; the reader is referred to [Salomaa 1973] for other elements of formal language theory we shall use and to [Dassow, Păun 1989] for the area of regulated rewriting.
For an alphabet V, by V^* we denote the free monoid generated by V under the operation of concatenation; the empty string is denoted by λ, and $V^* - \{\lambda\}$ is denoted by V^+. The length of $x \in V^*$ is denoted by $|x|$, and for any U, $U \subseteq V$, $|x|_U$ denotes the number of occurrences of symbols $a \in U$ in x.
A *matrix grammar (with appearance checking)* is a construct

$$G = (N, T, S, M, F)$$

where N and T are disjoint alphabets (N is the nonterminal alphabet, T is the terminal alphabet), $S \in N$ is the axiom, and M is a finite set of sequences (called *matrices*) of the form $m = (A_1 \to x_1, \ldots, A_s \to x_s)$, $s \geq 1$, $A_i \to x_i$ being a context-free rule over $N \cup T$ with $A_i \in N$ and $x_i \in (N \cup T)^*$, $1 \leq i \leq s$, and F is a subset of the rules occurring in the matrices of M.
For $w, y \in (N \cup T)^*$ we write $w \Longrightarrow y$ if there are strings $w_0, w_1, \ldots, w_s$ in $(N \cup T)^*$ and a matrix $(A_1 \to x_1, \ldots, A_s \to x_s)$ in M such that $w = w_0$, $w_s = y$ and for each i with $1 \leq i \leq s$ either $w_{i-1} = z_i A_i z_i'$ and $w_i = z_i x_i z_i'$ or $w_i = w_{i-1}$, the rule $A_i \to x_i$ is not applicable to w_{i-1}, and $A_i \to x_i$ appears in F. (In words, all the rules in a matrix are applied, one after the other in the given sequence, possibly skipping the rules appearing in F, but only if they cannot rewrite the current string.) If $F = \emptyset$, then the grammar is said to be *without appearance checking* (and the component F can be omitted).
By MAT_{ac}^{λ}, MAT_{ac} we denote the families of languages generated by matrix grammars with arbitrary context-free respectively λ-free context-free rules. The following relations are known ([Dassow, Păun 1989]):

$$ET0L \subset MAT_{ac} \subset CS \subset MAT_{ac}^{\lambda} = RE,$$

where CS and RE denote the families of context-sensitive respectively recursively enumerable languages and $ET0L$ denotes the family of λ-free $ET0L$-languages (i.e. languages generated by extended Lindenmayer systems with tables).
A *cooperating distributed grammar system* (*CD grammar system* for short) is a construct

$$\Gamma = (N, T, S, P_1, \ldots, P_n)$$

where N and T are disjoint alphabets (N is the nonterminal alphabet, T is the terminal alphabet), $S \in N$ is the axiom, and $P_1, \ldots, P_n$, $n \geq 1$, are finite sets of context-free rules over $N \cup T$ and are called the *components* of the system Γ.
For each component P_i, $1 \leq i \leq n$, in the CD grammar system Γ we denote

$$dom(P_i) = \left\{ A \in N \mid A \to x \in P_i \text{ for some } x \in (N \cup T)^* \right\}.$$

Given $w, w' \in (N \cup T)^*$ and i, $1 \leq i \leq n$, we write $w \Longrightarrow_{P_i} w'$ if w' can be derived from w by using a rule in P_i in the usual sense: $w = w_1 A w_2$, $w' = w_1 x w_2$, and $A \to x \in P_i$. By $\Longrightarrow_{P_i}^{+}$ and $\Longrightarrow_{P_i}^{*}$ we denote the transitive respectively the reflexive transitive closure of $\Longrightarrow_{P_i}$.

An important derivation relation for CD grammar systems is the *maximal derivation mode* t (see [Csuhaj-Varjù, Dassow 1990]):

$$w \Longrightarrow_{P_i}^{t} w' \text{ if and only if}$$
$$w \Longrightarrow_{P_i}^{*} w' \text{ and there is no } w'' \in (N \cup T)^* \text{ such that } w' \Longrightarrow_{P_i} w''$$

(such a derivation is *maximal* in the component P_i, i.e. no further step can be done). The language generated by the CD grammar system Γ in the maximal derivation mode t is defined by

$$L_t(\Gamma) = \{x \in T^* \mid S \Longrightarrow_{P_{i_1}}^{t} w_1 ... \Longrightarrow_{P_{i_m}}^{t} w_m = x,$$
$$m \geq 1,\ 1 \leq i_j \leq n \text{ for } 1 \leq j \leq m\}.$$

The family of languages generated in this mode by CD grammar systems with λ-free rules is denoted by $CD(t)$. From [Csuhaj-Varjù, Dassow 1990] we know that $CD(t) = ET0L$.

3 Teams in cooperating grammar systems

In [Kari, Mateescu, Păun, Salomaa 1994] the following extension of CD grammar systems is introduced:

A *CD grammar system with (prescribed) teams (of variable size)* is a construct

$$\Gamma = (N, T, S, P_1, ..., P_n, Q_1, ..., Q_m)$$

where $(N, T, S, P_1, ..., P_n)$ is a usual CD grammar system and $Q_i \subseteq \{P_1, ..., P_n\}$, $1 \leq i \leq m$; the sets $Q_1, ..., Q_m$ are called *teams* and are used in derivations as follows: For $Q_i = \{P_{j_1}, P_{j_2}, ..., P_{j_s}\}$ and $w,\ w' \in (N \cup T)^*$ we write

$$\begin{aligned} w \Longrightarrow_{Q_i} w' \text{ if and only if } & w = w_1 A_1 w_2 A_2 ... w_s A_s w_{s+1}, \\ & w' = w_1 x_1 w_2 x_2 ... w_s x_s w_{s+1}, \\ & \text{where } w_k \in (N \cup T)^*,\ 1 \leq k \leq s+1, \text{ and} \\ & A_r \rightarrow x_r \in P_{j_r},\ 1 \leq r \leq s \end{aligned}$$

(the team is a set, hence no ordering of the components is assumed).

In [Kari, Mateescu, Păun, Salomaa 1994] the following rule of finishing the work of a team $Q_i = \{P_{j_1}, P_{j_2}, ..., P_{j_s}\}$ has been considered:

$$w \Longrightarrow_{Q_i}^{t_1} w' \text{ if and only if}$$
$$w \Longrightarrow_{Q_i}^{+} w' \text{ and } |w'|_{dom(P_{j_r})} = 0 \text{ for all } r \text{ with } 1 \leq r \leq s.$$

(No rule of any component of the team can be applied to w'.)

Another variant is proposed in [Păun, Rozenberg 1994]:

$$w \Longrightarrow_{Q_i}^{t_2} w' \text{ if and only if}$$
$$w \Longrightarrow_{Q_i}^{+} w' \text{ and } |w'|_{dom(P_{j_r})} = 0 \text{ for some } r \text{ with } 1 \leq r \leq s.$$

(There is a component of the team that cannot rewrite any symbol of the current string.)
The language generated by Γ in one of these modes is denoted by $L_{t_1}(\Gamma)$ and $L_{t_2}(\Gamma)$, respectively.
If all teams in Γ have the same size, then we say that Γ is a CD grammar system with *teams of constant size*. If all possible teams are considered, we say that Γ has *free teams*; the teams then need not be specified. If we allow free teams of only one size, we speak of CD systems with *free teams of constant size*. Obviously, if we only have teams of size $s \geq 2$, then we cannot rewrite an axiom consisting of one symbol only, hence we must start from a string or a set of strings as axioms. Therefore, we consider systems of the form

$$\Gamma = (N, T, W, P_1, ..., P_n, Q_1, ..., Q_m),$$

where $W \subseteq (N \cup T)^*$ is a finite set; the terminal strings of W are directly added to the language generated by Γ. The others are used as starting points for derivations. The languages generated by such a system Γ when using free teams of given size s are denoted by $L_{t_1}(\Gamma, s)$ and $L_{t_2}(\Gamma, s)$, respectively; when free teams of arbitrary size are allowed, we write $L_{t_1}(\Gamma, *)$ respectively $L_{t_2}(\Gamma, *)$, and if these free teams must be of size at least two, we write $L_{t_1}(\Gamma, +)$ respectively $L_{t_2}(\Gamma, +)$.
By $PT_sCD(g)$ we denote the family of languages generated in the mode $g \in \{t_1, t_2\}$ by CD grammar systems with prescribed teams of constant size s and λ-free context-free rules; if the size is not constant we replace s by $*$; when the size must be at least 2 (no team consisting of only one component is allowed), then we write $PT_+CD(g)$. If the teams are not prescribed, we remove the letter P, thus obtaining the families $T_sCD(g)$, $T_*CD(g)$, and $T_+CD(g)$, respectively.
As we are interested in the relations with the family MAT_{ac}^{λ}, too, we also consider CD grammar systems with prescribed (arbitrary) teams of constant size s (arbitrary size, of size at least two) and arbitrary context-free rules; the corresponding families of languages generated in the mode $g \in \{t_1, t_2\}$ by such CD grammar systems are denoted by $PT_sCD^{\lambda}(g)$, $PT_*CD^{\lambda}(g)$, $PT_+CD^{\lambda}(g)$, and $T_sCD^{\lambda}(g)$, $T_*CD^{\lambda}(g)$, $T_+CD^{\lambda}(g)$, respectively.

In [Păun, Rozenberg 1994] it is proved that for all $s \geq 2$ and $g \in \{t_1, t_2\}$
$T_sCD(g) = PT_sCD(g) = PT_*CD(g) = T_+CD(g) = MAT_{ac}$ and
$T_sCD^{\lambda}(g) = PT_sCD^{\lambda}(g) = PT_*CD^{\lambda}(g) = T_+CD(g)^{\lambda} = MAT_{ac}^{\lambda}$.

The relations $\Longrightarrow^{t_1}$ and $\Longrightarrow^{t_2}$ as defined in [Csuhaj-Varjù, Păun 1993], [Kari, Mateescu, Păun, Salomaa 1994], and [Păun, Rozenberg 1994] are not the direct extensions of the relation $\Longrightarrow^{t}$ from components to teams. Such an extension looks as follows (where Γ, w, w', Q_i are as above):

$$w \Longrightarrow_{Q_i}^{t_0} w' \text{ if and only if}$$
$$w \Longrightarrow_{Q_i}^{+} w' \text{ and there is no } w'' \in (N \cup T)^* \text{ such that } w' \Longrightarrow_{Q_i} w''.$$

The language generated by the CD grammar system Γ in this mode t_0 is denoted by $L_{t_0}(\Gamma)$, the languages generated by such a system Γ in the mode t_0 when using

free teams of given size s, free teams of arbitrary size, free teams of size at least two are denoted by $L_{t_0}(\Gamma, s)$, $L_{t_0}(\Gamma, *)$, and $L_{t_0}(\Gamma, +)$, respectively.
Obviously, if $w \Longrightarrow_{Q_i}^{t_j} w'$, $j = 1, 2$, then $w \Longrightarrow_{Q_i}^{t_0} w'$, too, but, as we have pointed out in the introduction, the converse is not true; we can have $w \Longrightarrow_{Q_i}^{t_0} w'$ without having $w \Longrightarrow_{Q_i}^{t_j} w'$ for $j = 1, 2$. Consequently, $L_{t_j}(\Gamma) \subseteq L_{t_0}(\Gamma)$, $j = 1, 2$, without necessarily having an equality; the same holds true for the languages $L_{t_j}(\Gamma, s)$, $L_{t_j}(\Gamma, *)$, and $L_{t_j}(\Gamma, +)$. This means that we have no relations directly following from definitions, between families considered above and the corresponding families $PT_sCD(t_0)$, $PT_*CD(t_0)$, $PT_+CD(t_0)$, $T_sCD(t_0)$, $T_*CD(t_0)$, and $T_+CD(t_0)$. However, in the following section we shall prove that again a characterization of the families MAT_{ac} and MAT_{ac}^{λ} is obtained, hence the new termination mode of team work is equally powerful as those considered in [Csuhaj-Varjù, Păun 1993], [Kari, Mateescu, Păun, Salomaa 1994], and [Păun, Rozenberg 1994].

In order to elucidate some of the specific features of the derivation modes t_k, $k \in \{0, 1, 2\}$, we consider some examples. The first example shows that the inclusions, $L_{t_j}(\Gamma) \subseteq L_{t_0}(\Gamma)$, etc., $j \in \{1, 2\}$, can be proper:

Example 1. Let

$$\Gamma_1 = (\{A, B, C\}, \{a\}, \{AB\}, P_1, P_2, P_3, P_4)$$

be a CD grammar system with the sets of rules

$$\begin{aligned} P_1 &= \{A \to B, B \to B\}, \\ P_2 &= \{B \to C, B \to B\}, \\ P_3 &= \{B \to a, B \to B\}, \text{ and} \\ P_4 &= \{C \to a, B \to B\}. \end{aligned}$$

Obviously, $L_t(\Gamma_1) = \emptyset$, because the only way to get rid of the symbol A is to apply the rule $A \to B$ from P_1, but because of the rule $B \to B$ the derivation can never terminate.
If we consider Γ_1 together with the prescribed teams (of size 2)

$$\begin{aligned} Q_1 &= \{P_1, P_2\} \text{ and} \\ Q_2 &= \{P_3, P_4\}, \end{aligned}$$

i.e. if we take the CD grammar system with prescribed teams

$$\Gamma_2 = (\Gamma_1, Q_1, Q_2),$$

then we obtain

$$L_{t_0}(\Gamma_2) = \{aa\}$$

because $AB \Longrightarrow_{Q_1}^{t_0} BC \Longrightarrow_{Q_2}^{t_0} aa$, yet still

$$L_{t_i}(\Gamma_2) = \emptyset$$

for $i \in \{1, 2\}$, because after one derivation step with Q_1, i.e. $AB \Longrightarrow_{Q_1} BC$, Q_1 cannot be applied as a team any more to BC, although the rule $B \to B$, which is in both sets of rules of the team Q_1, is applicable to BC. This means that

the derivation is blocked, although the stop condition for the derivation mode t_i, $i \in \{1,2\}$, is not fulfilled!
As only teams of size at most two can be applied to a string of length two, we also obtain

$$L_{t_j}(\Gamma_1, 2) = L_{t_j}(\Gamma_1, +) = L_{t_j}(\Gamma_1, *) = \emptyset \text{ for } i \in \{1,2\},$$

whereas

$$L_{t_0}(\Gamma_1, 2) = L_{t_0}(\Gamma_1, +) = L_{t_0}(\Gamma_1, *) = \{aa\}.$$

Example 2. Let

$$\Gamma_3 = (\{A, B\}, \{a, b\}, \{AA, BB\}, P_1, P_2, P_3, P_4)$$

be a CD grammar system with the sets of rules

$$\begin{aligned} P_1 &= \{A \to aA, A \to aB, A \to b\}, \\ P_2 &= \{A \to aA, A \to aB, A \to a\}, \\ P_3 &= \{B \to bB, B \to bA, B \to a\}, \text{ and} \\ P_4 &= \{B \to bB, B \to bA, B \to b\}. \end{aligned}$$

If we consider Γ_3 together with the prescribed teams (of size 2)

$$\begin{aligned} Q_1 &= \{P_1, P_2\} \text{ and} \\ Q_2 &= \{P_3, P_4\}, \end{aligned}$$

i.e. if we take the CD grammar system with prescribed teams

$$\Gamma_4 = (\Gamma_3, Q_1, Q_2),$$

then we obtain

$$L_{t_i}(\Gamma_4) = \{wawb, wbwa \mid w \in \{a,b\}^*\}$$

for $i \in \{0,1,2\}$. Although this non-context-free language is obtained in each derivation mode t_i, the intermediate sentential forms (after an application of Q_1 or Q_2) are not the same:
Whereas for $i \in \{1,2\}$ the intermediate sentential forms are $wAwA$ and $wBwB$ with $w \in \{a,b\}^*$, in the derivation mode t_0 we also obtain $wawA$, $wawB$, $wbwA$, $wbwB$, $wAwa$, $wAwb$, $wAwB$, $wBwa$, $wBwb$, and $wBwA$. These strings are somehow ***hidden*** in the other derivation modes t_1 and t_2, because they can be derived from a sentential form $vAvA$ or $vBvB$ with a suitable $v \in \{a,b\}^*$, by using the derivation relation $\Longrightarrow_{Q_1}$ of the team Q_1, but then further derivations with the team Q_1 are blocked, although the stop conditions of the derivation modes t_1 respectively t_2 are not fulfilled. This additional control on the possible sentential forms is not present with the derivation mode t_0, where a derivation using a team stops *if and only if* the team cannot be applied *as a team* any more, which does not say anything about the applicability of the rules in the components of the team on the current sentential form. Nethertheless the same generative power as with the derivation modes t_1 and t_2 can be obtained by teams using the derivation mode t_0, too, which will be shown in the succeeding section.

4 The power of the derivation mode t_0

In this section we shall prove that CD grammar systems with (prescribed or free) teams (of given size at least two respectively of arbitrary size) together with the derivation mode t_0 again yield characterizations of the families MAT_{ac} respectively MAT_{ac}^{λ}.

The following relations are obvious:

Lemma 1. For all $s \geq 1$ we have

$$T_sCD(t_0) \subseteq PT_sCD(t_0) \subseteq PT_*CD(t_0),$$
$$T_sCD^{\lambda}(t_0) \subseteq PT_sCD^{\lambda}(t_0) \subseteq PT_*CD^{\lambda}(t_0),$$
$$T_*CD(t_0) \subseteq PT_*CD(t_0),$$
$$T_*CD^{\lambda}(t_0) \subseteq PT_*CD^{\lambda}(t_0),$$
$$T_+CD(t_0) \subseteq PT_+CD(t_0) \subseteq PT_*CD(t_0),$$
$$T_+CD^{\lambda}(t_0) \subseteq PT_+CD^{\lambda}(t_0) \subseteq PT_*CD^{\lambda}(t_0).$$

Lemma 2. $PT_*CD(t_0) \subseteq MAT_{ac}$ and $PT_*CD^{\lambda}(t_0) \subseteq MAT_{ac}^{\lambda}$.

Proof. Let $\Gamma = (N, T, W, P_1, ..., P_n, Q_1, ..., Q_m)$ be a CD grammar system with prescribed teams and λ-free rules. We construct a matrix grammar

$$G = (N', T \cup \{c\}, S', M, F)$$

with λ-free rules as follows.

For a team

$$Q_i = \{P_{j_1}, ..., P_{j_s}\}$$

consider all sequences of rules of the form

$$\pi = (A_1 \rightarrow x_1, ..., A_s \rightarrow x_s)$$

such that from each set P_{j_r} exactly one rule is present in m. Let

$$\{\pi_{i,1}, \pi_{i,2}, ..., \pi_{i,k_i}\} = R_i$$

be all such sequences associated with the team Q_i.

Then

$$\begin{aligned} N' = {} & N \cup \{A' \mid A \in N\} \cup \{S', \#, X, X'\} \cup \\ & \{[Q_i] \mid 1 \leq i \leq m\} \cup \{R_{i,j}, R'_{i,j} \mid 1 \leq i \leq m, 1 \leq j \leq k_i\} \end{aligned}$$

and

$$\begin{aligned} M = {} & \{(S' \rightarrow wX) \mid w \in W\} \cup \\ & \{(X \rightarrow [Q_i]) \mid 1 \leq i \leq m\} \cup \\ & \{([Q_i] \rightarrow [Q_i], A_1 \rightarrow x'_1, ..., A_s \rightarrow x'_s) \mid 1 \leq i \leq m, \\ & Q_i = \{P_{j_1}, ..., P_{j_s}\}, (A_1 \rightarrow x_1, ..., A_s \rightarrow x_s) \in R_i, \\ & x'_r \text{ is obtained by replacing each nonterminal in } x_r \\ & \text{by its primed version, } 1 \leq r \leq s\} \cup \end{aligned}$$

$\{(A' \to A) \mid A \in N\} \cup \{([Q_i] \to R_{i,1}) \mid 1 \leq i \leq m\} \cup$
$\{(R_{i,j} \to R'_{i,j+1}, A_1 \to \alpha_1, ..., A_s \to \alpha_s) \mid 1 \leq i \leq m, 1 \leq j \leq k_i - 1,$
$\pi_{i,j} = (A_1 \to x_1, ..., A_s \to x_s), \alpha_r \in \{A'_r, \#\}, 1 \leq r \leq s,$
and for at least one $r, 1 \leq r \leq s$, we have $\alpha_r = \#\} \cup$
$\{(R_{i,k_i} \to X', A_1 \to \alpha_1, ..., A_s \to \alpha_s) \mid 1 \leq i \leq m,$
$\pi_{i,k_i} = (A_1 \to \alpha_1, ..., A_s \to \alpha_s), \alpha_r \in \{A'_r, \#\}, 1 \leq r \leq s,$
and for at least one $r, 1 \leq r \leq s$, we have $\alpha_r = \#\} \cup$
$\{(R'_{i,j} \to R_{i,j}, A'_1 \to \#, ..., A'_p \to \#) \mid 1 \leq i \leq m,$
$1 \leq j \leq k_i, \{A_1, ..., A_p\} = N\} \cup$
$\{(X' \to X, A'_1 \to \#, ..., A'_p \to \#) \mid \{A_1, ..., A_p\} = N\} \cup$
$\{(X \to c)\}.$

The set F contains all rules of the form $A \to \#$ in the previous matrices.

The derivation starts form wX, $w \in W$. In general, from a sentential form $wX, w \in (N \cup T)^*$, in a non-deterministic way we can pass to $w[Q_i]$ in order to start the simulation of the team Q_i. Using a matrix

$$([Q_i] \to [Q_i], A_1 \to x'_1, ..., A_s \to x'_s)$$

corresponds to a derivation step in Q_i (the primed symbols in $x'_1, ..., x'_s$ ensure the parallel mode of using the rules $A_1 \to x_1, ..., A_s \to x_s$. The primed symbols can be replaced freely by their originals using the matrices $(A' \to A)$. The symbol $[Q_i]$ can be changed only by passing through $R_{i,1}, ..., R_{i,k_i}$, which checks the correct termination of the derivation in Q_i, in the sense of the mode t_0 of derivation: we can pass from $R_{i,j}$ to $R'_{i,j+1}$, if and only if the corresponding sequence $\pi_{i,j}$ of rules cannot be used (otherwise a symbol # will be introduced, because for each sequence

$$A_1 \to \alpha_1, ..., A_s \to \alpha_s,$$

at least one α_k is #). After obtaining a sequence $\pi_{i,j}$, we introduce the symbol $R'_{i,j+1}$, which is replaced by $R_{i,j+1}$ only after having replaced all primed symbols A' with $A \in N$ by their original A. Then we can pass to checking the sequence $\pi_{i,j+1}$. If none of the sequences $\pi_{i,j}$, $1 \leq j \leq k_i$, can be used, we can introduce the symbol X' and then X; in this way the derivation in Q_i is successfully simulated, and we can pass, in a non-deterministic way, to another team.
When the matrix $(X \to c)$ is used, the string must not contain any further non-terminal, because no matrix can be used any more .
In conclusion, $L(G) = L_{t_0}(\Gamma)\{c\}$. As MAT_{ac} is closed under right derivative, it follows that $L_{t_0}(\Gamma) \in MAT_{ac}$.

A similar construction like that elaborated above shows that for a CD grammar system with prescribed teams and arbitrary context-free rules we can construct a matrix grammar

$$G = (N', T, S', M, F)$$

with arbitrary context-free rules such that $L(G) = L_{t_0}(\Gamma)$; observe that we do not need the additional terminal symbol c, because in the case of arbitrary context-free rules we can simply replace the matrix $(X \to c)$ by the matrix $(X \to \lambda)$. As an immediate consequence, we obtain $L_{t_0}(\Gamma) \in MAT^{\lambda}_{ac}$. □

Lemma 3. $MAT_{ac} \subseteq T_2CD(t_0)$ and $MAT_{ac}^{\lambda} \subseteq T_2CD^{\lambda}(t_0)$.

Proof. Let $L \subseteq V^*$ be a matrix language in MAT_{ac}. We can write

$$L = (L \cap \{\lambda\}) \cup \bigcup_{c \in V} \delta_c^r(L)\{c\},$$

where $\delta_x^r(L)$ denotes the right derivative of L with respect to the string x. The family MAT_{ac} is closed under right derivative, hence $\delta_c^r(L) \in MAT_{ac}$. For each $c \in V$, let $G_c = (N_c, V, S_c, M_c, F_c)$ be a matrix grammar for $\delta_c^r(L)$, and moreover, we suppose that G_c is in the accurrate normal form [Dassow, Păun 1989]:

1. $N_c = N_{c,1} \cup N_{c,2} \cup \{S, \#\}$, where $N_{c,1}, N_{c,2}, \{S, \#\}$ are pairwise disjoint.
2. The matrices in M_c are of one of the following forms:
   a. $(S_c \to w)$, $w \in V^*$;
   b. $(S_c \to AX)$, $A \in N_1$, $X \in N_2$;
   c. $(A \to w, X \to Y)$, $A \in N_1$, $w \in (N_1 \cup V)^+$, $X, Y \in N_2$;
   d. $(A \to \#, X \to Y)$, $A \in N_1$, $X, Y \in N_2$;
   e. $(A \to a, X \to b)$, $A \in N_1$, $X \in N_2$, $a, b \in V$.
3. The set F_c consists of all rules $A \to \#$ appearing in matrices of M_c.

Without loss of generality we may also assume that $|w|_{\{A\}} = 0$ and $X \neq Y$ in matrices of the forms c (if we have a matrix $(A \to w, X \to Y)$ with $|w|_{\{A\}} \neq 0$ or $X = Y$ we can replace it by the sequence of matrices

$$(A \to A_1, X \to X_1),\ (A_k \to w_k, X_k \to X_{k+1}),\ 1 \leq k \leq m-1,$$
$$(A_m \to w_m, X_m \to X),$$

where $w = w_1 ... w_m$, $w_k \in V$, $1 \leq k \leq m$, as well as A_k and X_k with $1 \leq k \leq m$ are new symbols to be added to N_1 and N_2, respectively); in a similar way, we can assume that $X \neq Y$ in a matrix $(A \to \#, X \to Y)$ of form d (a matrix $(A \to \#, X \to X)$ can be replaced by the matrices $(A \to \#, X \to X_1)$ and $(A \to \#, X_1 \to X)$, where X_1 is a new symbol to be added to N_2,).
We take such a matrix grammar G_c for every language $\delta_c^r(L) \neq \emptyset$, $c \in V$; without loss of generality, we may assume that the sets $N_{c,1}$, $N_{c,2}$, $c \in V$, are pairwise disjoint.
Assume all matrices of the forms c, d, e in the sets M_c to be labelled in a one-to-one manner such that the labels used for M_c are different from those used for $M_{c'}$, $c' \neq c$, and let Lab_c, Lab_d, Lab_e, be the set of all the corresponding labels as well as

$$Lab = Lab_c \cup Lab_d \cup Lab_e.$$

Now consider the following sets of symbols

$$N_1 = \bigcup_{c \in V} N_{c,1},$$

$$N_2 = \bigcup_{c \in V} N_{c,2},$$

$$\Pi = \{A_l, A'_l \mid A \in N_1,\ l \in Lab\},$$

$$\Sigma = \{X_l \mid X \in N_2,\ l \in Lab\},$$
$$\Delta = \left\{D^{(c)}, D_l^{(c)}, E_l^{(c)}, F_l^{(c)}, G_l^{(c)} \mid c \in V,\ l \in Lab\right\},$$
$$\Psi = \Pi \cup \Sigma \cup \Delta, \text{ and}$$
$$N = N_1 \cup N_2 \cup \Pi \cup \Sigma \cup \Delta.$$

We construct a CD grammar system Γ with $N \cup \{\#\}$ as the set of non-terminal symbols, V as the set of terminal symbols, the set of axioms

$$W = (L \cap \{\lambda\}) \cup \{wc \mid (S_c \to w) \in M_c,\ w \in V^*,\ c \in V\} \cup \left\{AXD^{(c)} \mid (S_c \to AX) \in M_c,\ c \in V,\ \delta_c^r(L) \neq \emptyset\right\}$$

and the components $P_{l,1}, Q_{l,1}, P_{l,2}, Q_{l,2}$ for $l \in Lab$ constructed as follows:

A. If $l : (A \to w, X \to Y)$ is a matrix of type c with $A \in N_1$, $w \in (N_1 \cup V)^+$, $|w|_{\{A\}} = 0$, and $X, Y \in N_2$, $X \neq Y$, then we take the components

$P_{l,1} = \{X \to X_l, A \to A_l\} \cup \{\beta \to \# \mid \beta \in N\}$,

$Q_{l,1} = \left\{D^{(c)} \to D_l^{(c)}, D_l^{(c)} \to E_l^{(c)}\right\} \cup \left\{\beta \to \# \mid \beta \in (\Psi \cup N_2) - \left\{A_l, X_l, E_l^{(c)}\right\}\right\}$,

$P_{l,2} = \{A_l \to w, X_l \to Y\} \cup \{\beta \to \# \mid \beta \in N\}$,

$Q_{l,2} = \left\{E_l^{(c)} \to F_l^{(c)}, F_l^{(c)} \to D^{(c)}\right\} \cup \{\beta \to \# \mid \beta \in (\Psi \cup N_2) - \{D^{(c)}, Y\}\}$.

B. If $l : (A \to a, X \to b)$ is a matrix of type e, with $A \in N_1$, $a \in V$, $X \in N_2$, $b \in V$, then we take the components

$P_{l,1} = \{X \to X_l, A \to A_l\} \cup \{\beta \to \# \mid \beta \in N\}$,

$Q_{l,1} = \left\{D^{(c)} \to D_l^{(c)}, D_l^{(c)} \to E_l^{(c)}\right\} \cup \left\{\beta \to \# \mid \beta \in (\Psi \cup N_2) - \left\{A_l, X_l, E_l^{(c)}\right\}\right\}$,

$P_{l,2} = \{A_l \to A_l', A_l' \to a, X_l \to b\} \cup \{\beta \to \# \mid \beta \in N\}$,

$Q_{l,2} = \left\{E_l^{(c)} \to F_l^{(c)}, F_l^{(c)} \to G_l^{(c)}, G_l^{(c)} \to c\right\} \cup \{\beta \to \# \mid \beta \in N\}$.

C. If $l : (A \to \#, X \to Y)$ is a matrix of type d (hence with $A \to \# \in F_c$), with $A \in N_1$, $X, Y \in N_2$, $X \neq Y$, then we take the components

$P_{l,1} = \{X \to X_l\} \cup \{\beta \to \# \mid \beta \in N\}$,

$Q_{l,1} = \left\{D^{(c)} \to E_l^{(c)}\right\} \cup \left\{\beta \to \# \mid \beta \in (\Psi \cup N_2 \cup \{A\}) - \left\{E_l^{(c)}, X_l\right\}\right\}$,

$P_{l,2} = \{X_l \to Y\} \cup \{\beta \to \# \mid \beta \in N\}$,

$Q_{l,2} = \left\{E_l^{(c)} \to D^{(c)}\right\} \cup \{\beta \to \# \mid \beta \in (\Psi \cup N_2) - \{D^{(c)}, Y\}\}$.

Let us give some remarks on these constructions:

- The intended *legal teams* of two components are $\{P_{l,1}, Q_{l,1}\}$ and $\{P_{l,2}, Q_{l,2}\}$ for arbitrary labels $l \in Lab$ (which would already solve the problem for prescribed teams of size two); all other pairs of components cannot work in the mode t_0 without introducing the trap-symbol #.
- The symbol # is a trap-symbol and every component contains rules $\beta \to \#$ for "almost all" symbols $\beta \in N$; the termination of a derivation sequence with a legal team is only guaranteed by the "exceptions" in the components of type Q.

– In order to assure the correct pairing of components, we use variants of the control symbol D ($D^{(c)}$, $D_l^{(c)}$, $E_l^{(c)}$, $F_l^{(c)}$, $G_l^{(c)}$), as well as subscripts added to symbols in N_1 (leading to symbols in Π) and to symbols in N_2 (leading to symbols in Σ).

We now show that Γ with free teams of constant size two in the same way as with the prescribed teams of size two described above generates L :
Claim 1. $L \subseteq L_{t_0}(\Gamma, 2)$.
As the "short strings" in L are directly introduced in W, it is enough to prove that every derivation step in a grammar G_c can be simulated by the teams of Γ. More exactly, we shall prove that if $z_1 \Longrightarrow_{G_c} z_2$ is a derivation step in G_c, where z_2 is not a terminal string, then $z_1 D^{(c)} \Longrightarrow_\Gamma^* z_2 D^{(c)}$ in a derivation sequence using teams of size 2 from Γ, and that if z_2 is a terminal string, then $z_1 D^{(c)} \Longrightarrow_\Gamma^* z_2 c$ in a derivation sequence using teams of size 2 from Γ.
If

$$z_1 = x_1 A x_2 X \Longrightarrow_{G_c} x_1 w x_2 Y = z_2$$

by a matrix $l : (A \to w, X \to Y)$ of type c, then

$$x_1 A x_2 X D^{(c)} \Longrightarrow_{\{P_{l,1}, Q_{l,1}\}} x_1 A_l x_2 X D_l^{(c)} \Longrightarrow_{\{P_{l,1}, Q_{l,1}\}} x_1 A_l x_2 X_l E_l^{(c)}$$

and no more step is possible with this team $\{P_{l,1}, Q_{l,1}\}$, hence

$$x_1 A x_2 X D^{(c)} \Longrightarrow_{\{P_{l,1}, Q_{l,1}\}}^{t_0} x_1 A_l x_2 X_l E_l^{(c)}.$$

Now, also in two steps, we obtain

$$x_1 A_l x_2 X_l E_l^{(c)} \Longrightarrow_{\{P_{l,2}, Q_{l,2}\}}^{t_0} x_1 w x_2 Y D^{(c)} = z_2 D^{(c)}.$$

In a similar way, if for a terminal string

$$z_1 = x_1 A x_2 X \Longrightarrow_{G_c} x_1 a x_2 b = z_2$$

by a matrix $l : (A \to a, X \to b)$ of type e, then we obtain

$$x_1 A x_2 X D^{(c)} \Longrightarrow_{\{P_{l,1}, Q_{l,1}\}} x_1 A_l x_2 X D_l^{(c)} \Longrightarrow_{\{P_{l,1}, Q_{l,1}\}} x_1 A_l x_2 X_l E_l^{(c)}$$

and

$$x_1 A_l x_2 X_l E_l^{(c)} \Longrightarrow_{\{P_{l,2}, Q_{l,2}\}} x_1 a x_2 X_l F_l^{(c)} \Longrightarrow_{\{P_{l,2}, Q_{l,2}\}} x_1 a x_2 X_l' G_l^{(c)}$$
$$\Longrightarrow_{\{P_{l,2}, Q_{l,2}\}} x_1 a x_2 bc$$

i.e.

$$x_1 A x_2 X D^{(c)} \Longrightarrow_{\{P_{l,1}, Q_{l,1}\}}^{t_0} x_1 A_l x_2 X_l E_l^{(c)} \Longrightarrow_{\{P_{l,2}, Q_{l,2}\}}^{t_0} x_1 a x_2 bc = z_2 c.$$

If

$$z_1 = xX \Longrightarrow_{G_c} xY = z_2$$

by a matrix $l : (A \to \#, X \to Y)$ of type d, then

$$xXD^{(c)} \Longrightarrow_{\{P_{l,1}, Q_{l,1}\}}^{t_0} xX_l E_l^{(c)} \Longrightarrow_{\{P_{l,2}, Q_{l,2}\}}^{t_0} xYD^{(c)}.$$

Observe that from $xX_lE_l^{(c)}$ no further derivation step with the team $\{P_{l,1}, Q_{l,1}\}$ is possible if and only if $|x|_{\{A\}} = 0$.
In conclusion, every derivation in a grammar G_c can be simulated in Γ by applying a suitable sequence of appropriate teams of pairs of components, which completes the proof of claim 1.

Using *legal teams*, i.e. the teams $\{P_{l,1}, Q_{l,1}\}$ and $\{P_{l,2}, Q_{l,2}\}$, we can only obtain the following sentential forms not containing the trap symbol # (we call them *legal configurations*):

1. $xXD^{(c)}$, with $x \in (N_1 \cup V)^+$, $X \in N_2$, $c \in V$ (initially we have $x \in N_1$).
2. $xA_lx'X_lE_l^{(c)}$, with $x, x' \in (N_1 \cup V)^*$, $A \in N_1$, $X \in N_2$, $c \in V$, $l \in Lab_c \cup Lab_e$, i.e. l being a label of a matrix of type c or ϵ.
3. $xX_lE_l^{(c)}$, with $x \in (N_1 \cup V)^+$, $X \in N_2$, $c \in V$, $l \in Lab_d$, i.e. l being a label of a matrix of type d.

Claim 2. Starting from an arbitrary legal configuration, every illegal team will introduce the symbol #.
First of all we have to notice that in the following we can restrict our attention to components associated with some matrix from M_c, because components associated with some matrix from $M_{c'}$ with $c' \neq c$ already at the first application of a rule force us to introduce the trap symbol #. For the same reasons, we need not take into account teams consisting of two components of type Q : they cannot work together without introducing #, because they can only replace symbols in Δ by symbols different from #.

For the rest of possible illegal teams of size two we consider the following three cases according to the three types of legal configurations:
Case 1: Configuration $xXD^{(c)}$, i.e. of type 1.
Each component being of one of the types $P_{l,2}$ and $Q_{l,2}$ will introduce # at the first application of a rule; therefore it only remains to consider pairs of components of the types $P_{l,1}$ and $Q_{l,1}$ for different labels from Lab associated with matrices from M_c (the labels must be different, because otherwise either the team were legal or else the teams would not be of size two). Hence only the following teams might be possible:

1. $\{P_{l,1}, P_{l',1}\}$, where $l \neq l'$: The intermediate strings coming up during the application of such a team will contain at least one symbol X_l or A_l as well as at least one symbol $X_{l'}$ or $A_{l'}$ for the two different labels l and l', hence before the derivation with the team can terminate, at least one of the rules of the form $\beta \rightarrow \#$ (i.e. $X_l \rightarrow \#$ or $A_l \rightarrow \#$ respectively $X_{l'} \rightarrow \#$ or $A_{l'} \rightarrow \#$) is forced to be applied in at least one of the components.
2. $\{P_{l,1}, Q_{l',1}\}$, where $l \neq l'$: While the component $Q_{l',1}$ works on symbols from Δ, the other component $P_{l,1}$ introduces at least one symbol X_l or A_l. As $P_{l,1}$ contains all rules $\beta \rightarrow \#$ for $\beta \in \Delta$ (and no other rules for $\beta \in \Delta$) and $Q_{l',1}$ contains all rules $\alpha \rightarrow \#$ for $\alpha \in \{X_l, A_l\}$ (and no other rules for X_l, A_l), the derivation with the team $\{P_{l,1}, Q_{l',1}\}$ cannot terminate without a step introducing the symbol # by at least one of the components.

In all cases, further derivations are blocked (they never can lead to terminal strings) because the trap-symbol # has been forced to be introduced.

Case 2: Configuration $xA_lx'X_lE_l^{(c)}$, for $l \in Lab_c \cup Lab_e$.
The only components that may not be forced to introduce # by the first rule they can apply are $P_{l',1}$ for any arbitrary $l' \in Lab_c \cup Lab_e$ as well as $P_{l,2}$ and $Q_{l,2}$. Hence only the following teams might be possible:

1. $\{P_{l',1}, P_{l'',1}\}$, where $l' \neq l''$ (otherwise the team would not be of size two): $P_{l',1}$ will introduce some $A_{l'}$, $A \in N_1$, and $P_{l'',1}$ will introduce some $B_{l''}$, $B \in N_1$, therefore further derivations are blocked by introducing the trap symbol # with $A_{l'} \rightarrow \#$ or $B_{l''} \rightarrow \#$ in $P_{l',1}$ or in $P_{l'',1}$.
2. $\{P_{l',1}, P_{l,2}\}$: $P_{l,2}$ (in two or three steps) can replace A_l and X_l; in the meantime $P_{l',1}$ must introduce some $B_{l'}$, $B \in N_1$.
   (a) If $l' \neq l$, then from $xA_lx'X_lE_l^{(c)}$ in two steps (if a second step in $P_{l',1}$ is possible without introducing #) we obtain $y_1B_{l'}y_2B_{l'}y_3UE_l^{(c)}$, where $U \in N_2$ if $l \in Lab_c$ and $U \in N_2 \cup \{X_l\}$ if $l \in Lab_e$.
      i. If $l \in Lab_c$, then in the third step at least $P_{l,2}$ now must use a rule introducing the trap symbol #, e. g. $B_{l'} \rightarrow \#$, whereas $P_{l',1}$, if not also being forced to use such a trap rule, may be able to use $B \rightarrow B_{l'}$ once again or $U \rightarrow U_{l'}$, if it just happens that U is the right symbol from N_2 that can be handled by $P_{l',1}$.
      ii. If $l \in Lab_e$, then $X_l \rightarrow b$ or $A_l' \rightarrow a$ from $P_{l,2}$ can be applied in the third step, but even if $P_{l',1}$ can replace a third occurrence of B by B_l', at least in the fourth step $P_{l,2}$ now is forced to introduce the trap symbol #, e. g. by $B_l' \rightarrow \#$.
   (b) If $l' = l$, i.e. if we use the team $\{P_{l,1}, P_{l,2}\}$, then again we have to distinguish between two subcases:
      i. If $l \in Lab_c$, then $P_{l,1}$ can replace all occurences of A by A_l, while $P_{l,2}$ can replace X_l by Y and A_l by w. As we have assumed $Y \neq X$, no other rule not introducing # than $A \rightarrow A_l$ can be used in $P_{l,1}$. Moreover we also have assumed the rule $A_l \rightarrow w$ to be non-recursive, i.e. $|w|_{\{A\}} = 0$, hence after a finite number of derivation steps with the team $\{P_{l,1}, P_{l,2}\}$ the occurrences of A will be exhausted, so finally a rule introducing the trap symbol # must be used by $P_{l,1}$ (one possible candidate is $E_l^{(c)} \rightarrow \#$), while $P_{l,2}$ can use $A_l \rightarrow w$ or $X_l \rightarrow Y$ (if this rule has not yet been used before).
      ii. If $l \in Lab_e$, we face a similar situation as above except that from A_l two steps are needed in $P_{l,2}$ in order to obtain a from A_l.
3. $\{P_{l',1}, Q_{l,2}\}$: While $E_l^{(c)} \rightarrow F_l^{(c)}$ is used in $Q_{l,2}$, $P_{l',1}$ must introduce some $A_{l'}$, $A \in N_1$; if no more non-terminal symbol A is available in the current sentential form, when $Q_{l,2}$ uses its rule for replacing $F_l^{(c)}$, $P_{l',1}$ will have to use a trap rule like $A_{l'} \rightarrow \#$; if $P_{l',1}$ can introduce one more $A_{l'}$, then finally a trap rule like $A_{l'} \rightarrow \#$ must be applied by at least one of the components $P_{l',1}$ and $Q_{l,2}$ before the derivation can terminate.

Case 3: Configuration $xX_lE_l^{(c)}$, for $l \in Lab_d$.

The only components that do not introduce # by the first rule they can apply are $P_{l',1}$ for any arbitrary $l' \in Lab_c \cup Lab_e$ (and therefore $l' \neq l$) as well as $P_{l,2}$ and $Q_{l,2}$. Hence only the following teams might be possible:

1. $\{P_{l',1}, P_{l'',1}\}$, where $l' \neq l''$ (otherwise the team would not be of size two): $P_{l',1}$ will introduce some $A_{l'}$, $A \in N_1$, and $P_{l'',1}$ will introduce some $B_{l''}$, $B \in N_1$, therefore further derivations are blocked by introducing the trap symbol # with $A_{l'} \rightarrow \#$ or $B_{l''} \rightarrow \#$ in $P_{l',1}$ or in $P_{l'',1}$.
2. $\{P_{l',1}, P_{l,2}\}$: $P_{l,2}$ can only replace X_l by Y; in the meantime $P_{l',1}$ must introduce some $A_{l'}$, $A \in N_1$. In the second derivation step, in $P_{l,2}$ the trap rule $Y \rightarrow \#$ can be used, whereas from $P_{l',1}$ at least $A_{l'} \rightarrow \#$ can be applied.
3. $\{P_{l',1}, Q_{l,2}\}$: While $E_l^{(c)} \rightarrow D^{(c)}$ is used in $Q_{l,2}$, $P_{l',1}$ must introduce some $A_{l'}$, $A \in N_1$; but then $Q_{l,2}$ has to use a trap rule like $X_l \rightarrow \#$, while $P_{l',1}$ can use $A \rightarrow A_{l'}$ once more or at least $A_{l'} \rightarrow \#$.

In conclusion, only the legal teams can be used without introducing the trap symbol #; they simulate matrices in the sets M_c, $c \in V$, hence also the inclusion $L_{t_0}(\Gamma, 2) \subseteq L$ is true, which completes the proof of $MAT_{ac} \subseteq T_2CD(t_0)$.

Now let $L \subseteq V^*$ be a matrix language in MAT_{ac}^{λ}. As λ-rules are allowed in this case, we need not split up the language L in languages $\delta_c^r(L)$, $c \in V$; hence, for a matrix grammar $G = (N', V, S, M, F)$ with $L(G) = L$ we can directly construct a CD grammar system Γ such that $L_{t_0}(\Gamma, 2) = L$. Again the matrix grammar G can be assumed to be in the accurrate normal form [Dassow, Păun 1989] like in the previous case:

1. $N' = N_1 \cup N_2 \cup \{S, \#\}$, where $N_1, N_2, \{S, \#\}$ are pairwise disjoint.
2. The matrices in M are of one of the following forms:
   a. $(S \rightarrow w)$, $w \in V^*$;
   b. $(S \rightarrow AX)$, $A \in N_1$, $X \in N_2$;
   c. $(A \rightarrow w, X \rightarrow Y)$, $A \in N_1$, $w \in (N_1 \cup V)^*$, $|w|_{\{A\}} = 0$, $X, Y \in N_2$, $X \neq Y$;
   d. $(A \rightarrow \#, X \rightarrow Y)$, $A \in N_1$, $X, Y \in N_2$, $X \neq Y$;
   e. $(A \rightarrow a, X \rightarrow b)$, $A \in N_1$, $X \in N_2$, $a, b \in V \cup \{\lambda\}$.
3. The set F consists of all rules $A \rightarrow \#$ appearing in matrices of M.

In contrast to the λ-free case, matrices of the form c can also be of the form

$$(A \rightarrow \lambda, X \rightarrow Y)$$

and matrices of the form e can also be of the forms

$$(A \rightarrow \lambda, X \rightarrow \lambda),\ (A \rightarrow \lambda, X \rightarrow b),\ (A \rightarrow a, X \rightarrow \lambda), \text{ where } a, b \in V.$$

Assume all matrices of the forms c, d, e in the sets M to be labelled in a one-to-one manner and let Lab_c, Lab_d, Lab_e, be the sets of all the corresponding labels as well as

$$Lab = Lab_c \cup Lab_d \cup Lab_e.$$

Now consider the following sets of symbols

$$\begin{aligned} \Pi &= \{A_l, A'_l \mid A \in N_1,\ l \in Lab\}, \\ \Sigma &= \{X_l \mid X \in N_2,\ l \in Lab\}, \\ \Delta &= \{D, D_l, E_l, F_l, G_l \mid l \in Lab\}, \\ \Psi &= \Pi \cup \Sigma \cup \Delta, \text{ and} \\ N &= N_1 \cup N_2 \cup \Pi \cup \Sigma \cup \Delta. \end{aligned}$$

We construct a CD grammar system Γ with $N \cup \{\#\}$ as the set of non-terminal symbols, V as the set of terminal symbols, the set of axioms

$$W = \{w \mid (S \to w) \in M,\ w \in V^*\} \cup \{AXD \mid (S \to AX) \in M\}$$

and the components $P_{l,1}$, $Q_{l,1}$, $P_{l,2}$, $Q_{l,2}$ for $l \in Lab$ constructed like in the previous case:

A. If $l : (A \to w, X \to Y)$ is a matrix of type c with $A \in N_1$, $w \in (N_1 \cup V)^*$, $|w|_{\{A\}} = 0$, and $X, Y \in N_2$, $X \neq Y$, then we take the components
$P_{l,1} = \{X \to X_l, A \to A_l\} \cup \{\beta \to \# \mid \beta \in N\}$,
$Q_{l,1} = \{D \to D_l, D_l \to E_l\} \cup \{\beta \to \# \mid \beta \in (\Psi \cup N_2) - \{A_l, X_l, E_l\}\}$,
$P_{l,2} = \{A_l \to w, X_l \to Y\} \cup \{\beta \to \# \mid \beta \in N\}$,
$Q_{l,2} = \{E_l \to F_l, F_l \to D\} \cup \{\beta \to \# \mid \beta \in (\Psi \cup N_2) - \{D, Y\}\}$.
B. If $l : (A \to a, X \to b)$ is a matrix of type e, with $A \in N_1$, $X \in N_2$, $a, b \in V \cup \{\lambda\}$, then we take the components
$P_{l,1} = \{X \to X_l, A \to A_l\} \cup \{\beta \to \# \mid \beta \in N\}$,
$Q_{l,1} = \{D \to D_l, D_l \to E_l\} \cup \{\beta \to \# \mid \beta \in (\Psi \cup N_2) - \{A_l, X_l, E_l\}\}$,
$P_{l,2} = \{A_l \to A'_l, A'_l \to a, X_l \to b\} \cup \{\beta \to \# \mid \beta \in N\}$,
$Q_{l,2} = \{E_l \to F_l, F_l \to G_l, G_l \to \lambda\} \cup \{\beta \to \# \mid \beta \in N\}$.
C. If $l : (A \to \#, X \to Y)$ is a matrix of type d (hence with $A \to \# \in F$), with $A \in N_1$, $X, Y \in N_2$, $X \neq Y$, then we take the components
$P_{l,1} = \{X \to X_l\} \cup \{\beta \to \# \mid \beta \in N\}$,
$Q_{l,1} = \{D \to E_l\} \cup \{\beta \to \# \mid \beta \in (\Psi \cup N_2 \cup \{A\}) - \{E_l, X_l\}\}$,
$P_{l,2} = \{X_l \to Y\} \cup \{\beta \to \# \mid \beta \in N\}$,
$Q_{l,2} = \{E_l \to D\} \cup \{\beta \to \# \mid \beta \in (\Psi \cup N_2) - \{D, Y\}\}$.

The intended *legal teams* of two components again are $\{P_{l,1}, Q_{l,1}\}$ and $\{P_{l,2}, Q_{l,2}\}$ for arbitrary labels $l \in Lab$, the *legal configurations* are

1. xXD, with $x \in (N_1 \cup V)^+$, $X \in N_2$ (initially we have $x \in N_1$),
2. $xA_lx'X_lE_l$, for $x, x' \in (N_1 \cup V)^*$, $A \in N_1$, $X \in N_2$, $l \in Lab_c \cup Lab_e$, and
3. xX_lE_l, for $x \in (N_1 \cup V)^+$, $X \in N_2$, $l \in Lab_d$.

In contrast to the λ-free case we can use the λ-rule $G_l \to \lambda$ in the component $Q_{l,2}$ associated with a matrix $l : (A \to a, X \to b)$ of type e, which allows us to avoid the splitting up of the language L into the right derivatives $\delta^r_c(L)$, $c \in V$, yet again we obtain $L \subseteq L_{t_0}(\Gamma, 2)$: If $z_1 \Longrightarrow_G z_2$ is a derivation step in G, where z_2 is not a terminal string, then $z_1D \Longrightarrow^*_\Gamma z_2D$ in a derivation sequence using appropriate teams of size 2 from Γ, and if z_2 is a terminal string, then $z_1D \Longrightarrow_{\Gamma}^{*} z_2$ in a derivation sequence using the appropriate teams of size 2 from Γ.

Similar arguments as in the λ-free case can be used to show that $L_{t_0}(\Gamma, 2) \subseteq L$. Hence again we obtain $L_{t_0}(\Gamma, 2) = L$, which proves $MAT_{ac}^{\lambda} \subseteq T_2CD^{\lambda}(t_0)$, too. □

Lemma 4. $MAT_{ac} \subseteq T_sCD(t_0)$ and $MAT_{ac}^{\lambda} \subseteq T_sCD^{\lambda}(t_0)$ for $s \in \{+, *\}$.

Proof. For a language L in MAT_{ac} respectively MAT_{ac}^{λ} we just take the adequate CD grammar system Γ already constructed in the proof of the previous lemma. As the legal teams of size two still are available, we obviously obtain $L \subseteq L_{t_0}(\Gamma, s)$. On the other hand, we still have $L_{t_0}(\Gamma, s) \subseteq L$, too, although the possibilities for forming teams from the constructed components have increased considerably. Yet we have to adapt our arguments according to this new situation.

As in the previous proof we still have to notice that in the following we can restrict our attention to teams where all components are associated with matrices from only one set M_c, because components associated with some matrix from another set of matrices $M_{c'}$ with $c' \neq c$ already at the first application of a rule force us to introduce the trap symbol #. Hence in the following it is sufficient to consider the case where L in MAT_{ac}^{λ}.

As the *legal teams* of two components again are $\{P_{l,1}, Q_{l,1}\}$ and $\{P_{l,2}, Q_{l,2}\}$ for appropriate labels $l \in Lab$, the *legal configurations* are

1. xXD, with $x \in (N_1 \cup V)^+$, $X \in N_2$ (initially we have $x \in N_1$),
2. $xA_lx'X_lE_l$, for $x, x' \in (N_1 \cup V)^*$, $A \in N_1$, $X \in N_2$, $l \in Lab_c \cup Lab_e$, and
3. xX_lE_l, for $x \in (N_1 \cup V)^+$, $X \in N_2$, $l \in Lab_d$.

As teams of type Q cannot work together without introducing #, because they can only replace symbols in Δ by symbols different from #, we need not take into account teams containing at least two components of type Q. Moreover, every team of size one finally is forced to introduce the trap symbol # when started on a legal configuration (i.e. the result for $s = *$ is the same as for $s = +$). Hence in the following we now take a closer look on every possible combination of components yielding a team with at least three components and allowing at least one derivation step on the legal configurations listed above without introducing the trap symbol # :

Case 1: Configuration $xXD^{(c)}$, i.e. of type 1.
Each component being of one of the types $P_{l,2}$ and $Q_{l,2}$ will introduce # at the first application of a rule; therefore it only remains to consider teams T where each component is of one of the types $P_{l,1}$ and $Q_{l,1}$.

1. T contains only components of the type $P_{l,1}$, where obviously all labels of these components have to be different. Then at most one label can be from Lab_d, because such a component only once can use the rule $X \to X_l$, whereas all the other components $P_{l,1}$ with $l \in Lab_c \cup Lab_e$ can also apply a rule to the symbol X at most once as well as the rule $A \to A_l$ to any occurrence of the corresponding symbol A. Hence, before the derivation with the team can terminate, at least one of the rules of the form $\beta \to \#$ (e.g. $X_l \to \#$ or $A_l \to \#$) is forced to be applied in at least one of the components.

2. T contains exactly one component $Q_{m,1}$, wheras all the other components are of the type $P_{l,1}$, i.e.

$$T = \{Q_{m,1}\} \cup \{P_{l_i,1} \mid 1 \leq i \leq k\},$$

where $k \geq 2$. Denote $Lab_P(T) = \{l_i \mid 1 \leq i \leq k\}$. Again, at most one label in $Lab_P(T)$ can be from Lab_d. In the first derivation step with the team T, $D \rightarrow D_m$ for $m \in Lab_c \cup Lab_e$ respectively $D \rightarrow E_m$ for $m \in Lab_d$ from $Q_{m,1}$ is used, while at most one component P_{l_j} can use the rule $X \rightarrow X_{l_j}$, whereas all the others have to use the rules $A \rightarrow A_{l_i}$ for the corresponding non-terminal symbols $A \in N_1$.

(a) If $m \in Lab_d$, in the next step $Q_{m,1}$ has to use a trap rule.

   i. If the rule $X \rightarrow X_{l_j}$ has been applied in the first step (observe that $l_j \in Lab_d$ if $Lab_P(T) \cap Lab_d \neq \emptyset$), then even if $l_j = m$, every component of T can apply a rule, i.e. for $Q_{m,1}$ we choose $A_{l_{i_0}} \rightarrow \#$ for some $l_{i_0} \in Lab_P(T) - Lab_d$, for $P_{l_j,1}$ we can take $X_{l_j} \rightarrow \#$, from $P_{l_{i_0},1}$ at least $E_m \rightarrow \#$ can be applied, and in the remaining components $P_{l_i,1}$, $l_i \in Lab_P(T) - \{l_j, l_{i_0}\}$ at least $A_{l_i} \rightarrow \#$ is applicable.

   ii. If the rule $X \rightarrow X_{l_j}$ has not been applied in the first step, i.e. for each $l_i \in Lab_P(T)$ the rule $A \rightarrow A_{l_i}$ has been taken from $P_{l_i,1}$ (which implies $Lab_P(T) \cap Lab_d = \emptyset$ and therefore $m \notin Lab_P(T)$, too), again a second step with T is possible: We can choose $X \rightarrow \#$ from $Q_{m,1}$, while at least $A_{l_i} \rightarrow \#$ is applicable in the remaining components P_{l_i}, $l_i \in Lab_P(T)$.

(b) If $m \in Lab_c \cup Lab_e$, then one more derivation step may be possible without $Q_{m,1}$ being forced to use a trap rule, but again in any case the trap symbol $\#$ must be introduced before the derivation can terminate, even if T contains the legal team $\{Q_{m,1}, P_{m,1}\}$:

   i. If $Lab_P(T) \cap Lab_d \neq \emptyset$, i.e. $l_j \in Lab_P(T) \cap Lab_d$, then only one derivation step with T is possible without introducing $\#$, and in this step $P_{l_j,1}$ has used the rule $X \rightarrow X_{l_j}$, whereas all the other $P_{l_i,1}$, $l_i \in Lab_P(T) - \{l_j\}$, had to use $A \rightarrow A_{l_i}$ for the corresponding symbols $A \in N_1$, and $Q_{m,1}$ used $D \rightarrow D_m$. $P_{l_i,1}$ now is forced to use a trap rule like $X_{l_j} \rightarrow \#$ (observe that $m \neq l_j$), whereas $Q_{m,1}$ can use its rule for replacing D_m and the other components $P_{l_i,1}$, $l_i \in Lab_P(T) - \{l_j\}$, at least can apply $A_{l_i} \rightarrow \#$.

   ii. If $Lab_P(T) \cap Lab_d = \emptyset$, then at most two derivation steps with the team T are possible without introducing the trap symbol $\#$, where at most once one component $P_{l_j,1}$ can apply $X \rightarrow X_{l_j}$, whereas otherwise the components $P_{l_i,1}$, have to use the corresponding rules $A \rightarrow A_{l_i}$, while $Q_{m,1}$ can use $D \rightarrow D_m$ and $D_m \rightarrow E_m$.

      A. If two derivation steps without applying a trap rule have been possible, then also a third step with the team T is possible, where $Q_{m,1}$ is forced to apply a trap rule, e.g. for $Q_{m,1}$ we can choose $A_{l_{i_0}} \rightarrow \#$, where $l_{i_0} \in Lab_P(T)$ such that X has not been replaced by $X_{l_{i_0}}$, whereas all the components $P_{l_i,1}$, $l_i \in Lab_P(T)$, can at least apply $A_{l_i} \rightarrow \#$.

B. If only one derivation step without introducing # has been possible, i.e. at least one component $P_{l_{i_0},1}$ cannot apply a rule not introducing # any more, then a second step with T is possible, where $Q_{m,1}$ uses $D_m \rightarrow E_m$ and $P_{l_{i_0},1}$ is forced to apply a trap rule. If X has not been replaced in the first derivation step, $P_{l_{i_0},1}$ can apply $A_{l_{i_0}} \rightarrow \#$, while also the other components $P_{l_i,1}$ with $l_i \in Lab_P(T) - \{l_{i_0}\}$ at least can use $A_{l_i} \rightarrow \#$; if $X \rightarrow X_{l_{i_0}}$ has been applied in the first step, in the second step from $P_{l_{i_0},1}$ we can choose $X_{l_{i_0}} \rightarrow \#$ instead of $A_{l_{i_0}} \rightarrow \#$; if $X \rightarrow X_{l_j}$ has been applied in the first step for some $l_j \neq l_{i_0}$, then we can choose $A_{l_{i_0}} \rightarrow \#$ from $P_{l_{i_0},1}$, from $P_{l_j,1}$ at least $X_{l_j} \rightarrow \#$ can be applied, while from $P_{l_i,1}$ with $l_i \in Lab_P(T) - \{l_{i_0}, l_j\}$ at least $A_{l_i} \rightarrow \#$ is applicable.

In all cases, further derivations are blocked (they never can lead to terminal strings), because the trap-symbol # has been forced to be introduced.

Case 2: Configuration $xA_lx'X_lE_l$, for $l \in Lab_c \cup Lab_e$.
The only components that do not introduce # by the first rule to be applied are $P_{l',1}$ for any arbitrary $l' \in Lab_c \cup Lab_e$ as well as $P_{l,2}$ and $Q_{l,2}$. Hence only the following teams T might be possible:

1. $T = \{P_{l_i,1} \mid 1 \leq i \leq k\}$, where $k \geq 3$ and $\{l_i \mid 1 \leq i \leq k\} \subseteq Lab_c \cup Lab_e$. The components $P_{l_i,1}$ cannot replace the symbols A_l, X_l, E_l without introducing #, hence they will introduce A_{l_i} and therefore finally at least one component will have to use the trap rule $A_{l_i} \rightarrow \#$.
2. $T = \{P_{l,2}\} \cup \{P_{l_i,1} \mid 1 \leq i \leq k\}$, where $k \geq 2$ and $\{l_i \mid 1 \leq i \leq k\} \subseteq Lab_c \cup Lab_e$.
   Denote $Lab_P(T) = \{l_i \mid 1 \leq i \leq k\}$.
   (a) $l \notin Lab_P(T)$. While $P_{l,2}$ can replace A_l or X_l in the first step, the components $P_{l_i,1}$, $l_i \in Lab_P(T)$, can only use the corresponding rules $A \rightarrow A_{l_i}$ in order not to introduce #. If some $P_{l_{i_0},1}$ cannot use a rule not introducing # any more after this first step, at least this component is forced to use a trap rule like $A_{l_{i_0}} \rightarrow \#$, while also the other components $P_{l_i,1}$, $l_i \in Lab_P(T)$, can apply at least $A_{l_i} \rightarrow \#$ (and $P_{l,2}$ can replace the symbol from$\{A_l, X_l\}$ not affected in the first step). If two steps without introducing # are possible with the team T, then all together $2k$ symbols A_{l_i} have been introduced. As $2k > k+1$, these symbols guarantee that a trap rule must be applied, before the derivation with T can terminate.
   (b) $l \in Lab_P(T)$, i.e. $\{P_{l,1}, P_{l,2}\} \subset T$.
      i. If $l \in Lab_c$, then $P_{l,1}$ can replace all occurrences of A by A_l, while $P_{l,2}$ can replace X_l by Y and A_l by w. As we have assumed $Y \neq X$, no other rule not introducing # than $A \rightarrow A_l$ can be used in $P_{l,1}$. Moreover, as we also have assumed the rule $A_l \rightarrow w$ to be non-recursive, i.e. $|w|_{\{A\}} = 0$, the occurrences of the symbol A will be exhausted after a finite number of steps with the team T, so finally at least $P_{l,1}$ will be forced to use a trap rule. The other components $P_{l_i,1}$, $l_i \in Lab_P(T) - \{l\}$, in the first step can only apply the corresponding rules $A \rightarrow A_{l_i}$ and in the succeeding steps one of these components once also might be able to apply a rule to Y.

Now let s be the number of steps that are possible with the team T without introducing $\#$. If $s = 1$, then $P_{l,2}$ has replaced X_l by Y or A_l by w, whereas all the components $P_{l_i,1}$, $l_i \in Lab_P(T)$, have introduced one symbol A_{l_i}. Hence, in the current sentential form $k-1$ symbols A_{l_i} for $l_i \in Lab_P(T) - \{l\}$ are present as well as Y and two symbols A_l respectively X_l and A_l, i.e. at least $k+1$ non-terminal symbols, which guarantees that a second derivation step is possible, where at least one trap symbol $\#$ is introduced. If $s \geq 2$, then at least one symbol from $N_2 \cup \sum$, one symbol from Δ and $s(k-1)+1$ symbols A_m with $m \in Lab_P(T)$ occur in the current sentential form. As $s(k-1)+1+2 \geq 2(k-1)+3 \geq k+1$, again another derivation step introducing $\#$ is possible in any case.

ii. If $l \in Lab_e$, we face a similar situation except that for A_l we need two steps in order to obtain a from A_l by using $A_l \rightarrow A_l'$ and $A_l' \rightarrow a$ in $P_{l,2}$ (i.e. the symbols A_l cannot be "consumed" so fast by $P_{l,2}$ as in the previous case) and moreover, after one step the symbol from $N_2 \cup \sum$ may have vanished, so no other $P_{l_i,1}$ can use a rule on a symbol from $N_2 \cup \sum$. Let s again denote the number of steps possible with T without introducing $\#$; for all s exactly $s(k-1)$ symbols A_{l_i}, $l_i \in Lab_P(T) - \{l\}$, appear in the current sentential form. For $s \geq 3$, $s(k-1) \geq 3k-3 \geq k+1$, which guarantees that after these s steps another derivation step introducing the trap symbol $\#$ can be applied. For $s \leq 2$, we have at least $k-1$ such symbols as well as additional non-terminal symbols appearing in the current sentential form, i.e. one symbol from Δ as well as at least one symbol X_l, A_l' or A_l.

3. $T = \{Q_{l,2}\} \cup \{P_{l_i,1} \mid 1 \leq i \leq k\}$, where $k \geq 2$ and $\{l_i \mid 1 \leq i \leq k\} \subseteq Lab_c \cup Lab_e$.
While $Q_{l,2}$ uses $E_l \rightarrow F_l$ etc. the components $P_{l_i,1}$, $l_i \in Lab_P(T)$, can only apply the corresponding rules $A \rightarrow A_{l_i}$. Even if $l \in Lab_e$, the symbol from Δ can only vanish in the third derivation step with the team T, i.e. in any case, after at most two (for $l \in Lab_c$) respectively at most three (for $l \in Lab_e$) derivation steps without introducing $\#$ we are forced to use a trap rule in a further derivation step, which is always possible, because the number of non-terminal symbols in the current sentential form in all cases is at least $k+1$ (observe that also for $l \in Lab_c$ we can always find a non-terminal symbol $\notin \{D, Y\}$ for $Q_{l,2}$).
4. $T = \{P_{l,2}, Q_{l,2}\} \cup \{P_{l_i,1} \mid 1 \leq i \leq k\}$, where $k \geq 1$ and $\{l_i \mid 1 \leq i \leq k\} \subseteq Lab_c \cup Lab_e$, i.e. T contains the legal team $\{P_{l,2}, Q_{l,2}\}$.
Denote $Lab_P(T) = \{l_i \mid 1 \leq i \leq k\}$.
Because of the presence of $Q_{l,2}$, the legal subteam $\{P_{l,2}, Q_{l,2}\}$ can only make two (for $l \in Lab_c$) respectively three (for $l \in Lab_e$) derivation steps without introducing $\#$.
If at least one derivation step without introducing $\#$ is possible, besides A_l, X_l, and E_l in $xA_lx'X_lE_l$ at least k non-terminal symbols must be present for allowing the components $P_{l_i,1}$, $l_i \in Lab_P(T)$, to use the corresponding rules $B \rightarrow B_{l_i}$. Even after applying $A_l \rightarrow w$ (if $l \in Lab_c$) respectively $X_l \rightarrow b$ (if $l \in Lab_e$) in $P_{l,2}$, at least $k+2$ non-terminal symbols are left to guarantee another derivation step, if at least one component is already forced to apply a trap rule after the first derivation step.

(a) $l \in Lab_c$. Then at most a second derivation step without introducing # is possible. After this second derivation step, again at least $k+2$ non-terminal symbols are left in the current sentential form:

i. $l \in Lab_P(T)$:

A. If we have applied $A_l \to w$ in the first step from $P_{l,2}$, in the second step again we may apply $A_l \to w$, but all together we have $2k-1 \geq k$ non-terminal symbols from Π left in the current sentential form, i.e. together with X_l and D these are $k+2$ non-terminal symbols allowing a third derivation step introducing #.

B. If we have applied $X_l \to Y$ in the first derivation step, the current sentential form contains *two* symbols A_l and k symbols A_{l_i} for the labels $l_i \in Lab_P(T)$ as well as the control symbol F_l. Even if some $l_j \in Lab_P(T)$ can apply the rule $Y \to Y_{l_j}$ in the second step, $Q_{l,2}$ has to use $F_l \to D$, $P_{l,2}$ has to apply $A_l \to w$ (which consumes only one of the two symbols A_l), and all the other components $P_{l_i,1}$, $l_i \in Lab_P(T) - \{l_j\}$, have to use $A \to A_{l_i}$, so that at least $k+3+k-1-1 \geq k+2$ non-terminal symbols are left in the current sentential form after two derivation steps, which again allows a third derivation step introducing #.

ii. $l \notin Lab_P(T)$: The only difference to the previous case is that the components $P_{l_i,1}$, $l_i \in Lab_P(T)$, cannot generate A_l, i.e. similar arguments like those used above show that the derivation with the team T cannot terminate without introducing the trap symbol #.

(b) $l \in Lab_e$. In this case, at most three derivation steps without introducing # are possible.
Like in the case with $l \in Lab_c$, if after the first derivation step at least one component $P_{l_i,1}$, $l_i \in Lab_P(T)$, can only use a trap rule, a further derivation step is possible, because at least $k+2$ non-terminal symbols are available in the current sentential form. Whereas the components $P_{l_i,1}$, $l_i \in Lab_P(T)$, in every step "produce" a non-terminal symbol A_{l_i}, $P_{l,2}$ can use $X_l \to b$, $A_l \to A'_l$ and $A'_l \to a$, and $Q_{l,2}$ uses its rules on the symbols from Δ. After two steps, a symbol from Δ is still occurring in the current sentential form, and $P_{l,2}$ can only have been responsible for the changing of X_l *or* of A_l to a terminal symbol.
In the third step, the symbol from Δ is eliminated by $Q_{l,2}$ and $P_{l,2}$ has the possibility to have eliminated X_l as well as one symbol A_l. Yet in three steps by the components $P_{l_i,1}$, $l_i \in Lab_P(T)$, $3k \geq k+2$ symbols A_{l_i} have been generated, which guarantees a fourth step with introducing # to be possible before the derivation with the team T can terminate.

The special case of a team $\{P_{l,1}, P_{l,2}, Q_{l,2}\}$ for some $l \in Lab_e$ also shows the necessity of delaying the generation of a from A_l by $P_{l,2}$, $l \in Lab_e$ (i.e. l being the label of a terminal matrix $l : (A \to a, X \to b)$), with two rules $A_l \to A'_l$ and $A'_l \to a$ instead of using only one single rule $A_l \to a$.

Case 3: Configuration xX_lE_l, for $l \in Lab_d$.
The only components that do not introduce # by the first rule they can apply are $P_{l',1}$ for any arbitrary $l' \in Lab_c \cup Lab_e$ (and therefore $l' \neq l$) as well as $P_{l,2}$ and $Q_{l,2}$. Hence only the following teams might be possible:

1. $T = \{P_{l_i,1} \mid 1 \leq i \leq k\}$, where $k \geq 3$ and $\{l_i \mid 1 \leq i \leq k\} \subseteq Lab_c \cup Lab_e$. Each component $P_{l_i,1}$ introduces symbols A_{l_i}, until the non-terminal symbols for at least one component are exhausted, therefore finally one rule of the form $A_{l_i} \to \#$ has to be applied in at least one of the components of the team.
2. $T = \{P_{l,2}\} \cup \{P_{l_i,1} \mid 1 \leq i \leq k\}$, where $k \geq 2$ and $\{l_i \mid 1 \leq i \leq k\} \subseteq Lab_c \cup Lab_e$.
   $P_{l,2}$ can only replace X_l by Y; in the meantime, the other components $P_{l_i,1}$, $1 \leq i \leq k$, must introduce symbols A_{l_i}. In the second derivation step, in $P_{l,2}$ the trap rule $Y \to \#$ can be used, whereas all the other components at least can apply $A_{l_i} \to \#$.
3. $T = \{Q_{l,2}\} \cup \{P_{l_i,1} \mid 1 \leq i \leq k\}$, where $k \geq 2$ and $\{l_i \mid 1 \leq i \leq k\} \subseteq Lab_c \cup Lab_e$.
   While $E_l \to D$ is used in $Q_{l,2}$, the other components $P_{l_i,1}$, $1 \leq i \leq k$, introduce symbols A_{l_i}, but in the second derivation step $Q_{l,2}$ has to use a trap rule, e. g. $X_l \to \#$, while the other components $P_{l_i,1}$ at least can apply $A_{l_i} \to \#$.
4. $T = \{P_{l,2}, Q_{l,2}\} \cup \{P_{l_i,1} \mid 1 \leq i \leq k\}$, where $k \geq 1$ and $\{l_i \mid 1 \leq i \leq k\} \subseteq Lab_c \cup Lab_e$, i. e. T contains the legal team $\{P_{l,2}, Q_{l,2}\}$.
   While $P_{l,2}$ uses $X_l \to Y$ and $Q_{l,2}$ uses $E_l \to D$, the other components $P_{l_i,1}$, $1 \leq i \leq k$, introduce symbols A_{l_i}. $Q_{l,2}$ now has to use a trap rule like $A_{l_{i_0}} \to \#$ for some $l_{i_0} \in \{l_i \mid 1 \leq i \leq k\}$, $P_{l,2}$ can use $D \to \#$, $P_{l_{i_0},1}$ can apply at least some rule on Y, and all the other components $P_{l_i,1}$, $l_i \in \{l_i \mid 1 \leq i \leq k\} - \{l_{i_0}\}$ can at least apply $A_{l_i,1} \to \#$.

In conclusion, again we have proved that only the legal teams can be used without introducing the trap symbol #, which completes the proof. □

Lemma 5. $MAT_{ac} \subseteq T_sCD(t_0)$ and $MAT_{ac}^{\lambda} \subseteq T_sCD^{\lambda}(t_0)$ for every $s \geq 3$.

Proof. Let $L \subseteq V^*$ be a matrix language in MAT_{ac}^{λ} and let $G = (N', V, S, M, F)$ be a matrix grammar with $L(G) = L$. Again the matrix grammar G can be assumed to be in the strengthened accurrate normal form described in the preceeding two lemmas:

1. $N' = N_1 \cup N_2 \cup \{S, \#\}$, where $N_1, N_2, \{S, \#\}$ are pairwise disjoint.
2. The matrices in M are of one of the following forms:
   a. $(S \to w)$, $w \in V^*$;
   b. $(S \to AX)$, $A \in N_1$, $X \in N_2$;
   c. $(A \to w, X \to Y)$, $A \in N_1$, $w \in (N_1 \cup V)^*$, $|w|_{\{A\}} = 0$, $X, Y \in N_2$, $X \neq Y$;
   d. $(A \to \#, X \to Y)$, $A \in N_1$, $X, Y \in N_2$, $X \neq Y$;
   e. $(A \to a, X \to b)$, $A \in N_1$, $X \in N_2$, $a, b \in V \cup \{\lambda\}$.
3. The set F consists of all rules $A \to \#$ appearing in matrices of M.

We can construct a CD grammar system Γ such that $L_{t_0}(\Gamma, s) = L$ using the ideas already known from the preceeding proofs for the case $s = 2$, i. e. we add $s - 2$ additional control variables in every legal sentential form as well as $s - 2$ additional control components to every legal team.

Assume all matrices of the forms c, d, e in the sets M to be labelled in a one-to-one manner and let Lab_c, Lab_d, Lab_e, be the set of all the corresponding labels as well as

$$Lab = Lab_c \cup Lab_d \cup Lab_e.$$

Now consider the following sets of symbols

$$\begin{aligned}
\Pi &= \{A_l, A'_l \mid A \in N_1,\ l \in Lab\},\\
\Sigma &= \{X_l \mid X \in N_2,\ l \in Lab\},\\
\Delta &= \{D, D_l, E_l, F_l, G_l \mid l \in Lab\} \cup\\
&\quad \{H_k, H_{k,l,i} \mid 1 \le k \le s-2,\ l \in Lab,\ 1 \le i \le 4\},\\
\Psi &= \Pi \cup \Sigma \cup \Delta, \text{ and}\\
N &= N_1 \cup N_2 \cup \Pi \cup \Sigma \cup \Delta.
\end{aligned}$$

We construct a CD grammar system Γ with $N \cup \{\#\}$ as the set of non-terminal symbols, V as the set of terminal symbols, the set of axioms

$$W = \{w \mid (S \to w) \in M,\ w \in V^*\} \cup \{AXDH_1...H_{s-2} \mid (S \to AX) \in M\}$$

and the components $P_{l,1}, Q_{l,1}, R_{1,l,1}, ..., R_{s-2,l,1}$, and $P_{l,2}, Q_{l,2}, R_{1,l,2}, ..., R_{s-2,l,2}$, for $l \in Lab$:

A. If $l : (A \to w, X \to Y)$ is a matrix of type c with $A \in N_1$, $w \in (N_1 \cup V)^*$, $|w|_{\{A\}} = 0$, and $X, Y \in N_2$, $X \neq Y$, then we take the components

$P_{l,1} = \{X \to X_l, A \to A_l\} \cup \{\beta \to \# \mid \beta \in N\}$,

$Q_{l,1} = \{D \to D_l, D_l \to E_l\} \cup$

$\{\beta \to \# \mid \beta \in (\Psi \cup N_2) - \{A_l, X_l, E_l, H_{1,l,2}, ..., H_{s-2,l,2}\}\}$,

$R_{k,l,1} = \{H_k \to H_{k,l,1}, H_{k,l,1} \to H_{k,l,2}\} \cup \{\beta \to \# \mid \beta \in N\}$, $1 \le k \le s-2$,

$P_{l,2} = \{A_l \to w, X_l \to Y\} \cup \{\beta \to \# \mid \beta \in N\}$,

$Q_{l,2} = \{E_l \to F_l, F_l \to D\} \cup \{\beta \to \# \mid \beta \in (\Psi \cup N_2) - \{D, Y, H_1, ..., H_{s-2}\}\}$,

$R_{k,l,2} = \{H_{k,l,2} \to H_{k,l,3}, H_{k,l,3} \to H_{k,l,4}\} \cup \{\beta \to \# \mid \beta \in N\}$, $1 \le k \le s-2$.

B. If $l : (A \to a, X \to b)$ is a matrix of type e, with $A \in N_1$, $X \in N_2$, $a, b \in V \cup \{\lambda\}$, then we take the components

$P_{l,1} = \{X \to X_l, A \to A_l\} \cup \{\beta \to \# \mid \beta \in N\}$,

$Q_{l,1} = \{D \to D_l, D_l \to E_l\} \cup$

$\{\beta \to \# \mid \beta \in (\Psi \cup N_2) - \{A_l, X_l, E_l, H_{1,l,2}, ..., H_{s-2,l,2}\}\}$,

$R_{k,l,1} = \{H_k \to H_{k,l,1}, H_{k,l,1} \to H_{k,l,2}\} \cup \{\beta \to \# \mid \beta \in N\}$, $1 \le k \le s-2$,

$P_{l,2} = \{A_l \to A'_l, A'_l \to a, X_l \to b\} \cup \{\beta \to \# \mid \beta \in N\}$,

$Q_{l,2} = \{E_l \to F_l, F_l \to G_l, G_l \to \lambda\} \cup \{\beta \to \# \mid \beta \in N\}$,

$R_{k,l,2} = \{H_{k,l,2} \to H_{k,l,3}, H_{k,l,3} \to H_{k,l,4}, H_{k,l,4} \to \lambda\} \cup$

$\{\beta \to \# \mid \beta \in N\}$, $1 \le k \le s-2$.

C. If $l : (A \to \#, X \to Y)$ is a matrix of type d (hence with $A \to \# \in F$), with $A \in N_1$, $X, Y \in N_2$, $X \neq Y$, then we take the components

$P_{l,1} = \{X \to X_l\} \cup \{\beta \to \# \mid \beta \in N\}$,

$Q_{l,1} = \{D \to E_l\} \cup \{\beta \to \# \mid \beta \in (\Psi \cup N_2 \cup \{A\}) - \{E_l, X_l, H_{1,l,2}, ..., H_{s-2,l,2}\}\}$,
$R_{k,l,1} = \{H_k \to H_{k,l,2}\} \cup \{\beta \to \# \mid \beta \in N\}$, $1 \le k \le s-2$,
$P_{l,2} = \{X_l \to Y\} \cup \{\beta \to \# \mid \beta \in N\}$,
$Q_{l,2} = \{E_l \to D\} \cup \{\beta \to \# \mid \beta \in (\Psi \cup N_2) - \{D, Y, H_1, ..., H_{s-2}\}\}$,
$R_{k,l,2} = \{H_{k,l,2} \to H_k\} \cup \{\beta \to \# \mid \beta \in N\}$, $1 \le k \le s-2$.

The intended *legal teams* of two components again are

$\{P_{l,1}, Q_{l,1}, R_{1,l,1}, ..., R_{s-2,l,1}\}$ as well as $\{P_{l,2}, Q_{l,2}, R_{1,l,2}, ..., R_{s-2,l,2},\}$

for arbitrary labels $l \in Lab$, the *legal configurations* are

1. $xXDH_1...H_{s-2}$, with $x \in (N_1 \cup V)^+$, $X \in N_2$ (initially we have $x \in N_1$),
2. $xA_lx'X_lE_lH_{1,l,2}...H_{s-2,l,2}$, for $x, x' \in (N_1 \cup V)^*$, $A \in N_1$, $X \in N_2$, $l \in Lab_c \cup Lab_e$, and
3. $xX_lE_lH_{1,l,2}...H_{s-2,l,2}$, for $x \in (N_1 \cup V)^+$, $X \in N_2$, $l \in Lab_d$.

Again we obtain $L_{t_0} \subseteq L(\Gamma, s)$: If $z_1 \Longrightarrow_G z_2$ is a derivation step in G, where z_2 is not a terminal string, then $z_1DH_1...H_{s-2} \Longrightarrow_\Gamma^* z_2DH_1...H_{s-2}$ in a derivation sequence using appropriate teams of size s from Γ, and if z_2 is a terminal string, then $z_1DH_1...H_{s-2} \Longrightarrow_\Gamma^* z_2$ in a derivation sequence using the appropriate teams of size s from Γ.
As the additional components of type R contain the trap rules $\beta \to \#$ for every $\beta \in N$, these additional components will never be responsible for the termination of a derivation sequence with a team containing such components. Hence, similar arguments as in the previous proofs can be used to show that $L_{t_0}(\Gamma, s) \subseteq L$; thus again we obtain $L_{t_0}(\Gamma, s) = L$, which proves $MAT_{ac}^\lambda \subseteq T_sCD^\lambda(t_0)$.
If $L \subseteq V^*$ is a matrix language in MAT_{ac}, we have to split up L :

$$L = \left(L \cap \left(\bigcup_{0 \le i \le s-2} V^i\right)\right) \cup \bigcup_{c, c_1, ..., c_{s-2} \in V} \delta^r_{cc_1...c_{s-2}}(L)\{cc_1...c_{s-2}\}.$$

The family MAT_{ac} is closed under right derivation, hence $\delta^r_{cc_1...c_{s-2}}(L) \in MAT_{ac}$. For each of these languages $\delta^r_{cc_1...c_{s-2}}(L)$ we consider a matrix grammar $G_{cc_1...c_{s-2}}$ in the strenghtened accurrate normal form in order to construct a CD grammar system Γ with $L_{t_0}(\Gamma, s) = L$ following the ideas described in the first part of this proof and of Lemma 3. The details of this construction for proving $MAT_{ac} \subseteq T_sCD(t_0)$ are obvious and therefore left to the interested reader. □

As it is quite obvious, the proofs of the preceeding lemmas cannot be used for obtaining the results proved in [Păun, Rozenberg 1994] for the derivation mode t_2, e.g. the components $P_{l,1}$ for $l \in Lab_c$ contain the rules $\beta \to \#$ for every $\beta \in N$, which means that $P_{l,1}$ still is applicable to every legal configuration even after the termination of a derivation sequence with the legal team $\{P_{l,1}, Q_{l,1}\}$. On the other hand, the CD grammar systems Γ in the proofs of Lemma 3, Lemma 4 and Lemma 5 were elaborated in such a way that they also work correctly in the dervation mode t_1, which not only allows a new proof of some of the results already obtained in [Păun, Rozenberg 1994] for the derivation mode t_1, but also yields an improvement of these results, because we now can allow teams of arbitrary size without the restriction for these teams to be of size at least two.

Corollary. For every $s \in \{*, +\} \cup \{2, 3, 4, ...\}$,

$$MAT_{ac} \subseteq T_sCD(t_1) \text{ and } MAT_{ac}^{\lambda} \subseteq T_sCD^{\lambda}(t_1).$$

Proof. As we have already pointed out in the previous section, $L_{t_1}(\Gamma, s) \subseteq L_{t_0}(\Gamma, s)$ for every $s \in \{*, +\} \cup \{2, 3, 4, ...\}$ and every CD grammar system Γ. Therefore this relation also holds true for the CD grammar systems Γ constructed in the previous proofs for the matrix languages in MAT_{ac} and MAT_{ac}^{λ}. Moreover, whenever $z_1 \Longrightarrow_T^{t_0} z_2$ with a legal team T from Γ, where z_1 is a legal configuration and z_2 is a legal configuration or a terminal string, then we also have $z_1 \Longrightarrow_T^{t_1} z_2$, because in any case from the component of type Q in the team T no rule can be applied any more when the derivation sequence started from z_1 terminates with z_2 according to the derivation mode t_0, which implies that the derivation sequence terminates in the derivation mode t_1, too. Therefore we conclude $L_{t_0}(\Gamma, s) \subseteq L_{t_1}(\Gamma, s)$, which all together implies $L_{t_1}(\Gamma, s) = L_{t_0}(\Gamma, s)$ and completes the proof of the corollary. □

Combining the main results obtained in this paper we get the following

Theorem. For every $s \in \{*, +\} \cup \{2, 3, 4, ...\}$ and $i \in \{0, 1\}$,

$$MAT_{ac} = PT_sCD(t_i) = T_sCD(t_i) \text{ and}$$

$$MAT_{ac}^{\lambda} = PT_sCD^{\lambda}(t_i) = T_sCD^{\lambda}(t_i).$$

Proof. For the derivation mode t_1 all the results stated in the theorem follow from the results already proved in [Păun, Rozenberg 1994] as well as from the corollary proved above.

For the derivation mode t_0 all the results stated in the theorem follow from the results proved in this section: From Lemma 1 we know that $PT_*CD^{\lambda}(t_0)$ (respectively $PT_*CD(t_0)$) is an upper bound for all the other families of languages generated by CD grammar systems (without λ-rules) with teams in the derivation mode t_0, and in Lemma 2 we have proved $PT_*CD^{\lambda}(t_0) \subseteq MAT_{ac}^{\lambda}$ (respectively $PT_*CD(t_0) \subseteq MAT_{ac}$). On the other hand, in Lemma 3, in Lemma 4 and in Lemma 5 we have proved that $MAT_{ac}^{\lambda} \subseteq T_sCD^{\lambda}(t_0)$ (and $MAT_{ac} \subseteq T_sCD(t_0)$) for every $s \in \{*, +\} \cup \{2, 3, 4, ...\}$, which all together proves the results stated in theorem. □

5 References

[Csuhaj-Varjù 1994] Csuhaj-Varjù, E.: "Cooperating Grammar Systems: Power and Parameters"; in: Results and Trends in Theoretical Computer Science (Karhumäki, J., Maurer, H., Rozenberg, G., eds.), LNCS, 812, 67 - 84; Springer-Verlag, Berlin (1994).

[Csuhaj-Varjù, Dassow 1990] Csuhaj-Varjù, E., Dassow, J.: "On Cooperating/Distributed Grammar Systems"; J. Inform. Proc. Cybern. EIK 26 (1990), 49-63.

[Csuhaj-Varjù, Dassow, Kelemen, Păun 1994] Csuhaj-Varjù, E., Dassow, J., Kelemen, J., Păun, Gh.: "Grammar Systems"; Gordon and Breach, London (1994).

[Csuhaj-Varjù, Păun 1993] Csuhaj-Varjù, E., Păun, Gh.: "Limiting the Size of Teams in Cooperating Grammar Systems"; Bulletin of the EATCS, 51 (1993), 198-202.

[Dassow, Păun 1989] Dassow, J., Păun, Gh.: "Regulated Rewriting in Formal Language Theory"; Springer-Verlag, Berlin (1989).

[Kari, Mateescu, Păun, Salomaa 1994] Kari, L., Mateescu, A., Păun, Gh., Salomaa, A.: "Teams in Cooperating Grammar Systems"; J. Experimental and Theoretical AI, to appear.

[Meersman, Rozenberg 1978] Meersman, R., Rozenberg, G.: "Cooperating Grammar Systems"; Proceedings MFCS'78, LNCS, 64, Springer-Verlag, Berlin (1978), 364-374.

[Păun, Rozenberg 1994] Păun, Gh., Rozenberg, G.: "Prescribed Teams of Grammars"; Acta Informatica, to appear.

[Salomaa 1973] Salomaa, A.: "Formal Languages"; Academic Press, New York (1973).

Journal of Universal Computer Science, vol. 1, no. 2 (1995), 131-135
submitted: 4/1/95, accepted: 9/2/95, appeared: 28/2/95,

On Four Classes of Lindenmayerian Power Series

Juha Honkala
Department of Mathematics
University of Turku
SF-20500 Turku, Finland
juha.honkala@utu.fi

Werner Kuich
Institut für Algebra und Diskrete Mathematik
Technische Universität Wien
Wiedner Hauptstrasse 8-10, A-1040 Wien

Abstract: We show that nonzero axioms add to the generative capacity of Lindenmayerian series generating systems. On the other hand, if nonzero axioms are allowed, nonterminals do not, provided that only quasiregular series are considered.
Category: F.4.2

1 Introduction

To define formal power series generated by L systems, Lindenmayerian series generating systems were introduced in [Honkala 95]. There four classes of morphically generated series were defined. The smallest class $\mathcal{S}(LS_0)$ consists of LS series with the zero axiom. The larger class $\mathcal{S}(LS)$ is obtained if arbitrary axioms are allowed. From these classes the classes $\mathcal{S}(ELS_0)$ and $\mathcal{S}(ELS)$ of ELS series with the zero axiom and ELS series, respectively, are obtained by allowing the use of Hadamard products. In an obvious way this corresponds to the use of nonterminals in language theory.

The inclusions $\mathcal{S}(LS_0) \subseteq \mathcal{S}(LS)$ and $\mathcal{S}(ELS_0) \subseteq \mathcal{S}(ELS)$ are clear by the definitions. It was shown in [Honkala 95] that $\mathcal{S}(LS_0)$ is properly contained in $\mathcal{S}(ELS_0)$. Hence, in the case of the zero axiom nonterminals do add to the generative capacity. The purpose of this note is to prove that $\mathcal{S}(ELS_0)$ is properly contained in $\mathcal{S}(ELS)$ and, furthermore, that the classes $\mathcal{S}(LS)$ and $\mathcal{S}(ELS)$ are equivalent, if only quasiregular power series are considered. Hence, nonzero axioms do add to the generative capacity whereas, if nonzero axioms are allowed, nonterminals do not. However, it will be seen below that in the framework of Lindenmayerian series with nonzero axioms some terminals play the role of nonterminals.

Another approach to define a power series generalization of L systems is given in [Kuich 94]. For the relationship between the two approaches see [Honkala and Kuich 95]. In the case of a complete semiring, power series generalizations of L systems are also discussed in [Honkala 94a] and [Honkala and Kuich 00].

2 Definitions

It is assumed that the reader is familiar with the basics of the theories of semirings and formal power series as developed in [Kuich and Salomaa (86)]. In this paper A will always be a commutative semiring and Σ is a finite alphabet. Suppose $h : \Sigma^* \longrightarrow A < \Sigma^* >$ is a monoid morphism. (Here $A < \Sigma^* >$ is regarded as a multiplicative monoid.) Then we extend h to a semiring morphism

$$h : A < \Sigma^* > \longrightarrow A < \Sigma^* >$$

by

$$h(P) = \sum (P, w)h(w), P \in A < \Sigma^* > .$$

Notice that the assumption of commutativeness is needed in the verification that indeed $h(r_1 r_2) = h(r_1)h(r_2)$ for $r_1, r_2 \in A < \Sigma^* >$. In the sequel we always tacitly extend a morphism $h \in \mathrm{Hom}(\Sigma^*, A < \Sigma^* >)$ to a semiring morphism $h : A < \Sigma^* > \longrightarrow A < \Sigma^* >$ as explained above. Notice that $\mathrm{Hom}(\Sigma^*, A < \Sigma^* >)$, the set of all these semiring morphisms, can be identified with the set

$$\{h : A < \Sigma^* > \longrightarrow A < \Sigma^* > \mid h \text{ is a semiring morphism and } h(a \cdot \lambda) = a \cdot \lambda \text{ for any } a \in A\}.$$

In what follows X is a denumerably infinite alphabet of variables. An *interpretation* φ over (A, Σ) is a mapping from X to $\mathrm{Hom}(\Sigma^*, A < \Sigma^* >)$. A *Lindenmayerian series generating system*, shortly, an LS system, is a 5-tuple $G = (A \ll \Sigma^* \gg, \mathcal{D}, P, \varphi, \omega)$ where A is a commutative semiring, Σ is a finite alphabet, $\mathcal{D}$ is a convergence in $A \ll \Sigma^* \gg$, P is a polynomial in $A < (X \cup \Sigma)^* >$, φ is an interpretation over (A, Σ) and ω is a polynomial in $A < \Sigma^* >$.

The series generated by an LS system is obtained by iteration. Suppose $G = (A \ll \Sigma^* \gg, \mathcal{D}, P(x_1, \ldots, x_n), \varphi, \omega)$ is an LS system and denote $h_i = \varphi(x_i)$ for $1 \leq i \leq n$. Define the sequence $(r^{(j)})$ $(j = 0, 1, \ldots)$ recursively by

$$r^{(0)} = \omega,$$

$$r^{(j+1)} = P(h_1(r^{(j)}), \ldots, h_n(r^{(j)})), j \geq 0.$$

If $\lim r^{(j)}$ exists we denote

$$S(G) = \lim r^{(j)}$$

and say that $S(G)$ is the *series generated* by G. The sequence $(r^{(j)})$ is the *approximation sequence associated to* G. A series r is called an LS *series* if there exists an LS system G such that $r = S(G)$. A series r is an LS *series with the zero axiom* if there exists an LS system $G = (A \ll \Sigma^* \gg, \mathcal{D}, P, \varphi, 0)$ such that $r = S(G)$. ELS series are obtained from LS series by considering only terms over a terminal alphabet. Formally, an ELS system is a construct $G = (A \ll \Sigma^* \gg, \mathcal{D}, P, \varphi, \omega, \Delta)$ consisting of the LS system $U(G) = (A \ll \Sigma^* \gg, \mathcal{D}, P, \varphi, \omega)$ called the *underlying system* of G and a subset Δ of Σ. If $S(U(G))$ exists, G generates the series

$$S(G) = S(U(G)) \odot \mathrm{char}(\Delta^*).$$

A series r is called an ELS *series* if there exists an ELS system G such that $r = S(G)$. A series r is called an ELS *series with the zero axiom* if there exists an ELS system $G = (A \ll \Sigma^* \gg, \mathcal{D}, P, \varphi, 0, \Delta)$ such that $r = S(G)$.

If A and $\mathcal{D}$ are understood, the class of LS series with the zero axiom (resp. LS series, ELS series with the zero axiom, ELS series) is denoted by $\mathcal{S}(LS_0)$ (resp. $\mathcal{S}(LS)$, $\mathcal{S}(ELS_0)$, $\mathcal{S}(ELS)$).

In the sequel we will always use the convergence $\mathcal{D}_d$ obtained by transferring the discrete convergence in A to $A \ll \Sigma^* \gg$ as explained in [Kuich and Salomaa (86)].

3 Results

The purpose of this section is to prove the following result.

Theorem 1. *(i) If A is a commutative semiring and $r \in A \ll \Sigma^* \gg$ is quasiregular, then $r \in \mathcal{S}(LS)$ if and only if $r \in \mathcal{S}(ELS)$.*

(ii) If $A = N$, then $\mathcal{S}(LS_0)$ is properly included in $\mathcal{S}(ELS_0)$ and $\mathcal{S}(ELS_0)$ is properly included in $\mathcal{S}(ELS)$.

Lemma 2. *Suppose $G = (A \ll \Sigma^* \gg, \mathcal{D}_d, P(x_1, \ldots, x_n), \varphi, \omega)$ is an LS system such that $S(G)$ exists and is quasiregular. If $\Delta \subseteq \Sigma$, then there exists an LS system G_1 such that*

$$S(G_1) = S(G) \odot char(\Delta^*).$$

Proof. We assume without loss of generality that each term of the approximation sequence $(r^{(i)})$ of G is quasiregular.

Choose new letters $\#, \$ \notin \Sigma$ and new variables z_1 and z_2. Let $\Sigma^{(1)} = \{\sigma^{(1)} | \sigma \in \Sigma\}$ be an isomorphic copy of Σ and let $\text{copy}_1 : \Sigma \longrightarrow \Sigma^{(1)}$ be the mapping defined by $\text{copy}_1(\sigma) = \sigma^{(1)}$. Denote $P = P_0 + P_1$ where $P_0 \in A < \Sigma^* >$ and each term of P_1 contains a variable. Define $R = \#P_1 + \#z_1 + z_2$. If $x \in \{x_1, \ldots, x_n\}$, define $\varphi_1(x)$ by

$$\varphi_1(x)(\sigma) = \begin{cases} \varphi(x)(\sigma) & \text{if } \sigma \in \Sigma \\ \# & \text{if } \sigma = \# \\ 0 & \text{otherwise} \end{cases}$$

and $\varphi_1(z_1)$ by

$$\varphi_1(z_1)(\sigma) = \begin{cases} \$ + P_0 & \text{if } \sigma = \$ \\ \# & \text{if } \sigma = \# \\ 0 & \text{otherwise} \end{cases}$$

and $\varphi_1(z_2)$ by

$$\varphi_1(z_2)(\sigma) = \begin{cases} \text{copy}_1(\sigma) & \text{if } \sigma \in \Delta \\ \lambda & \text{if } \sigma = \# \\ 0 & \text{otherwise} \end{cases} .$$

Define the LS system G_1 by $G_1 = (A \ll (\Sigma \cup \Sigma^{(1)} \cup \# \cup \$)^* \gg, \mathcal{D}_d, R(x_1, \ldots, x_n, z_1, z_2), \varphi_1, \omega + \$)$. Denote the approximation sequence associated to G_1 by $(s^{(i)})$. It follows inductively that there exists a sequence $(t^{(i)})$ such that

$$s^{(i)} = t^{(i)} + \text{copy}_1(r^{(i-1)} \odot \text{char}(\Delta^*))$$

and

$$\text{proj}_{\Sigma \cup \$}(t^{(i)}) = r^{(i)} + \$$$

for $i \geq 1$. Furthermore, each word in $\text{supp}(t^{(i)})$ contains at least i occurrences of $\#$. (Here the morphism $\text{proj}_{\Sigma \cup \$}$ is defined by $\text{proj}_{\Sigma \cup \$}(\sigma) = \sigma$ if $\sigma \in \Sigma \cup \$$, and $\text{proj}_{\Sigma \cup \$}(\sigma) = \lambda$ if $\sigma \notin \Sigma \cup \$$.) This implies $\lim t^{(i)} = 0$. Therefore $\lim s^{(i)}$ exists and

$$\lim s^{(i)} = \text{copy}_1(S(G) \odot \text{char}(\Delta^*)).$$

Now the claim follows by renaming the letters. □

In the proof of Lemma 2 the letters of $\Sigma \cup \# \cup \$$ play the role of nonterminals. However, because $\lim s^{(i)}$ does not contain any letters of $\Sigma \cup \# \cup \$$, we do not need the Hadamard product.

Next we recall some earlier results.

Lemma 3. *Let $A = N$ and denote $r = \sum_{n\geq 1}(a^n b^n + b^n a^n) \in N \ll \{a,b\}^* \gg$. Then $r \notin \mathcal{S}(LS_0)$ and $r \in \mathcal{S}(ELS_0)$.*

Proof. The claim is shown in Examples 3.6 and 4.3 of [Honkala 95]. □

Lemma 4. *Let $A = N$. Then the series $\sum_{n\geq 1}(a^n b)^n$ does not belong to $\mathcal{S}(ELS_0)$.*

Proof. See [Honkala 94b]. □

For the next lemma we need a definition. A *vector of LS systems* of dimension $k \geq 1$ is a k-tuple $\overline{G} = ((A \ll \Sigma^* \gg, \mathcal{D}, P_i(x_{11}, \ldots, x_{1k}, \ldots, x_{n1}, \ldots, x_{nk}), \varphi_i, \omega_i))_{1\leq i\leq k}$ of LS systems. The *approximation sequence* $((r_{j,1}, \ldots, r_{j,k}))_{j\geq 0}$ *associated to* G is defined recursively by

$$r_{0,s} = \omega_s,$$

$$r_{j+1,s} = P_s(\varphi_s(x_{11})(r_{j,1}), \ldots, \varphi_s(x_{1k})(r_{j,k}), \ldots, \varphi_s(x_{n1})(r_{j,1}), \ldots, \varphi_s(x_{nk})(r_{j,k})), 1 \leq s \leq k.$$

If $\lim_{j\to\infty} r_{j,s}$ exists for every $1 \leq s \leq k$, then we denote

$$S(\overline{G}) = (\lim r_{j,1}, \ldots, \lim r_{j,k})$$

and say that $S(\overline{G})$ is the *(vector of) series generated by* $\overline{G}$.

The next lemma is stated and proved as Theorem 4.5 in [Honkala 95].

Lemma 5. *Suppose $\overline{G} = ((A \ll \Sigma^* \gg, \mathcal{D}_d, P_i(x_{11}, \ldots, x_{1k}, \ldots, x_{n1}, \ldots, x_{nk}), \varphi_i, \omega_i))_{1\leq i\leq k}$ is a vector of LS systems such that $S(\overline{G}) = (r^{(1)}, \ldots, r^{(k)})$ exists and $r^{(1)}, \ldots, r^{(k)}$ are quasiregular. Then $r^{(s)}$ is an ELS series for any s.*

Lemma 6. *Let $A = N$. Then the series $\sum_{n\geq 1}(a^n b)^n$ belongs to $\mathcal{S}(ELS)$.*

Proof. Denote $\Sigma = \{a, b\}$ and define the LS systems G_1, G_2, G_3 by

$$G_1 = (N \ll \Sigma^* \gg, \mathcal{D}_d, x_{11}x_{12}, \varphi_1, ab),$$

$$G_2 = (N \ll \Sigma^* \gg, \mathcal{D}_d, x_{22}, \varphi_2, ab),$$

$$G_3 = (N \ll \Sigma^* \gg, \mathcal{D}_d, x_{31} + x_{33}, \varphi_3, 0)$$

where $\varphi_3(x_{31}) = \varphi_3(x_{33})$ is the identity morphism and $\varphi_1(x_{11}) = \varphi_1(x_{12}) = \varphi_2(x_{22}) = h$ is defined by $h(a) = a, h(b) = ab$. Furthermore, define the 3-dimensional vector $\overline{G}$ of LS systems by $\overline{G} = (G_1, G_2, G_3)$. Denote by $((r_{j,1}, r_{j,2}, r_{j,3}))_{j\geq 0}$ the approximation sequence of $\overline{G}$. Then

$$r_{0,1} = ab, r_{0,2} = ab, r_{0,3} = 0,$$

$$r_{j+1,1} = h(r_{j,1})h(r_{j,2}),$$
$$r_{j+1,2} = h(r_{j,2}),$$
$$r_{j+1,3} = r_{j,1} + r_{j,3}$$

for $j \geq 0$. It follows inductively that

$$r_{j,1} = (a^{j+1}b)^{j+1},$$
$$r_{j,2} = a^{j+1}b,$$
$$r_{j,3} = \sum_{1 \leq n \leq j} (a^n b)^n$$

for $j \geq 0$. Therefore $\lim r_{j,1} = \lim r_{j,2} = 0$ and $\lim r_{j,3} = \sum_{n \geq 1}(a^n b)^n$. Hence $S(\overline{G})$ exists and each component of $S(\overline{G})$ is quasiregular. Therefore the claim follows by Lemma 5. □

Proof of Theorem 1. Claim (i) follows by Lemma 2. Claim (ii) is a consequence of Lemmas 3,4 and 6. □

References

[Honkala 94a] Honkala, J.: "On Lindenmayerian series in complete semirings"; In G. Rozenberg and A. Salomaa, eds., Developments in Language Theory (World Scientific, Singapore, 1994) 179-192.

[Honkala 94b] Honkala, J.: "An iteration property of Lindenmayerian power series"; In J. Karhumäki, H. Maurer and G. Rozenberg, eds., Results and Trends in Theoretical Computer Science (Springer, Berlin, 1994) 159-168.

[Honkala 95] Honkala, J.: "On morphically generated formal power series"; Rairo, Theoretical Inform. and Appl., to appear.

[Honkala and Kuich 95] Honkala, J. and Kuich, W.: "On a power series generalization of ET0L languages"; Fundamenta Informaticae, to appear.

[Honkala and Kuich 00] Honkala, J. and Kuich, W.: "On Lindenmayerian algebraic power series", submitted.

[Kuich 94] Kuich, W.: "Lindenmayer systems generalized to formal power series and their growth functions"; In G. Rozenberg and A. Salomaa, eds., Developments in Language Theory (World Scientific, Singapore, 1994) 171-178.

[Kuich and Salomaa (86)] Kuich, W. and Salomaa, A.: "Semirings, Automata, Languages"; Springer, Berlin (1986).

Journal of Universal Computer Science, vol. 1, no. 2 (1995), 136-150
submitted: 8/10/94, accepted: 18/1/95, appeared: 28/2/95,

The Relationship Between Propagation Characteristics and Nonlinearity of Cryptographic Functions

Jennifer Seberry
(The University of Wollongong, Wollongong, NSW 2522, Australia
jennie@cs.uow.edu.au)

Xian-Mo Zhang
(The University of Wollongong, Wollongong, NSW 2522, Australia
xianmo@cs.uow.edu.au)

Yuliang Zheng
(Monash University, Melbourne, VIC 3199, Australia
yzheng@fcit.monash.edu.au)

Abstract: The connections among the various nonlinearity criteria is currently an important topic in the area of designing and analyzing cryptographic functions. In this paper we show a quantitative relationship between propagation characteristics and nonlinearity, two critical indicators of the cryptographic strength of a Boolean function. We also present a tight lower bound on the nonlinearity of a cryptographic function that has propagation characteristics.

Key Words: Cryptography, Boolean functions, Encryption functions, Nonlinearity, Propagation Characteristics, SAC, S-boxes.
Category: E.3

1 Introduction

Data Encryption Standard or DES is a cryptographic algorithm most widely used by industrial, financial and commercial sectors all over the world [NBS77]. DES is also the root of many other data encryption algorithms proposed in the past decade, including LOKI [BKPS93], FEAL [Miy91] and IDEA [LM91, LaSM91, Lai92]. A core component of these encryption algorithms are the so-called S-boxes or substitution boxes, each essentially a tuple of nonlinear Boolean functions. In most cases, these boxes are the only nonlinear component in an underlying encryption algorithm. The same can be said with one-way hashing algorithms which are commonly employed in the process of signing and authenticating electronic messages [ZPS93, Riv92, NIST93]. These all indicate the vital importance of the design and analysis of nonlinear cryptographic Boolean functions.

Encryption and authentication require cryptographic (Boolean) functions with a number of critical properties that distinguish them from linear (or affine) functions. Among these properties are high nonlinearity, high degree of propagation, few linear structures, high algebraic degree etc. These properties are often called *nonlinearity criteria*. An important topic is to investigate relationships among the various nonlinearity criteria. Progress in this direction has been made in [SZZ94d], where connections have been revealed among the strict avalanche characteristic, differential characteristics, linear structures and nonlinearity, of *quadratic* functions.

In this paper we carry on the investigation initiated in [SZZ94d] and bring together nonlinearity and propagation characteristic of a function (quadratic or non-quadratic). These two cryptographic criteria are seemly quite separate, in the sense that the former indicates the minimum distance between a Boolean function and all the affine functions whereas the latter forecasts the avalanche behavior of the function when some input bits to the function are complemented.

In particular we show that if f, a function on V_n, satisfies the propagation criterion with respect to all but a subset $\Re$ of V_n, then the nonlinearity of f satisfies $N_f \geq 2^{n-1} - 2^{n-\frac{1}{2}\rho-1}$, where ρ is the maximum dimension a linear sub-space contained in $\{0\} \cup (V_n - \Re)$ can achieve.

We also show that 2^{n-2} is the tight lower bound on the nonlinearity of f if f satisfies the propagation criterion with respect to at least one vector in V_n. As an immediate consequence, the nonlinearity of a function that fulfills the SAC or strict avalanche criterion is at least 2^{n-2}.

Two techniques are employed in the proofs of our main results. The first technique is in regard to the structure of $\Re$, the set of vectors where the function f does not satisfy the propagation criterion. By considering a linear sub-space with the maximum dimension contained in $\{0\} \cup (V_n - \Re)$, together with its complementary sub-space, we will be able to identify how the vectors in $\Re$ are distributed. The second technique is based on a novel idea of refining Parseval's equation, a well-known relationship in the theory of orthogonal transforms. A combination of these two techniques together with some careful analyses proves to be a powerful tool in examining the relationship among nonlinearity criteria.

The organization of the rest of the paper is as follows: Section 2 introduces basic notations and conventions, while Section 3 presents background information on the Walsh-Hadamard transform. The distribution of vectors where the propagation criterion is not satisfied is discussed in Section 4. This result is employed in Section 5 where a quantitative relationship between nonlinearity and propagation characteristics is derived. This relationship is further developed in Section 6 to identify a tight lower bound on nonlinearity of functions with propagation characteristics. The paper is closed by some concluding remarks in Section 7.

2 Basic Definitions

We consider Boolean functions from V_n to $GF(2)$ (or simply functions on V_n), V_n is the vector space of n tuples of elements from $GF(2)$. The *truth table* of a function f on V_n is a $(0,1)$-sequence defined by $(f(\alpha_0), f(\alpha_1), \ldots, f(\alpha_{2^n-1}))$, and the *sequence* of f is a $(1,-1)$-sequence defined by $((-1)^{f(\alpha_0)}, (-1)^{f(\alpha_1)}, \ldots, (-1)^{f(\alpha_{2^n-1})})$, where $\alpha_0 = (0,\ldots,0,0)$, $\alpha_1 = (0,\ldots,0,1)$, $\ldots$, $\alpha_{2^{n-1}-1} = (1,\ldots,1,1)$. The *matrix* of f is a $(1,-1)$-matrix of order 2^n defined by $M = ((-1)^{f(\alpha_i \oplus \alpha_j)})$. f is said to be *balanced* if its truth table contains an equal number of ones and zeros.

An *affine* function f on V_n is a function that takes the form of $f(x_1,\ldots,x_n) = a_1x_1 \oplus \cdots \oplus a_nx_n \oplus c$, where $a_j, c \in GF(2)$, $j = 1,2,\ldots,n$. Furthermore f is called a *linear* function if $c = 0$.

Definition 1. The *Hamming weight* of a $(0,1)$-sequence s, denoted by $W(s)$, is the number of ones in the sequence. Given two functions f and g on V_n, the *Hamming distance* $d(f,g)$ between them is defined as the Hamming weight of the truth table of $f(x) \oplus g(x)$, where $x = (x_1, \ldots, x_n)$. The *nonlinearity* of f, denoted by N_f, is the minimal Hamming distance between f and all affine functions on V_n, i.e., $N_f = \min_{i=1,2,\ldots,2^{n+1}} d(f, \varphi_i)$ where $\varphi_1, \varphi_2, \ldots, \varphi_{2^{n+1}}$ are all the affine functions on V_n.

Note that the maximum nonlinearity of functions on V_n coincides with the covering radius of the first order binary Reed-Muller code $RM(1,n)$ of length 2^n, which is bounded from above by $2^{n-1} - 2^{\frac{1}{2}n-1}$ (see for instance [CKHFMS85]). Hence $N_f \le 2^{n-1} - 2^{\frac{1}{2}n-1}$ for any function on V_n. Next we introduce the definition of propagation criterion.

Definition 2. Let f be a function on V_n. We say that f satisfies

1. the *propagation criterion with respect to* α if $f(x) \oplus f(x \oplus \alpha)$ is a balanced function, where $x = (x_1, \ldots, x_n)$ and α is a vector in V_n.
2. the *propagation criterion of degree* k if it satisfies the propagation criterion with respect to all $\alpha \in V_n$ with $1 \le W(\alpha) \le k$.

$f(x) \oplus f(x \oplus \alpha)$ is also called the directional derivative of f in the direction α. The above definition for propagation criterion is from [PLL+91]. Further work on the topic can be found in [PGV91]. Note that the strict avalanche criterion (SAC) introduced by Webster and Tavares [Web85, WT86] is equivalent to the propagation criterion of degree 1 and that the perfect nonlinearity studied by Meier and Staffelbach [MS90] is equivalent to the propagation criterion of degree n where n is the number of the coordinates of the function.

While the propagation characteristic measures the avalanche effect of a function, the linear structure is a concept that in a sense complements the former, namely, it indicates the straightness of a function.

Definition 3. Let f be a function on V_n. A vector $\alpha \in V_n$ is called a *linear structure* of f if $f(x) \oplus f(x \oplus \alpha)$ is a constant.

By definition, the zero vector in V_n is a linear structure of all functions on V_n. It is not hard to see that the linear structures of a function f form a linear sub-space of V_n. The dimension of the sub-space is called the *linearity dimension* of f. We note that it was Evertse who first introduced the notion of linear structure (in a sense broader than ours) and studied its implication on the security of encryption algorithms [Eve88].

A $(1,-1)$-matrix H of order m is called a *Hadamard* matrix if $HH^t = mI_m$, where H^t is the transpose of H and I_m is the identity matrix of order m. A Sylvester-Hadamard matrix of order 2^n, denoted by H_n, is generated by the following recursive relation

$$H_0 = 1, \; H_n = \begin{bmatrix} H_{n-1} & H_{n-1} \\ H_{n-1} & -H_{n-1} \end{bmatrix}, \; n = 1, 2, \ldots. \tag{1}$$

Let ℓ_i, $0 \le i \le 2^n - 1$, be the i row of H_n. By Lemma 2 of [SZZ94a], ℓ_i is the sequence of a linear function $\varphi_i(x)$ defined by the scalar product $\varphi_i(x) = \langle \alpha_i, x \rangle$, where α_i is the ith vector in V_n according to the ascending order.

Definition 4. Let f be a function on V_n. The Walsh-Hadamard transform of f is defined as

$$f(\alpha) = 2^{-\frac{n}{2}} \sum_{x \in V_n} (-1)^{f(x) \oplus \langle \alpha, x \rangle}$$

where $\alpha = (a_1, \ldots, a_n) \in V_n$, $x = (x_1, \ldots, x_n)$, $\langle \alpha, x \rangle$ is the scalar product of α and x, namely, $\langle \alpha, x \rangle = \bigoplus_{i=1}^{n} a_i x_i$, and $f(x) \oplus \langle \alpha, x \rangle$ is regarded as a real-valued function.

The Walsh-Hadamard transform, also called the discrete Fourier transform, has numerous applications in areas ranging from physical science to communications engineering. It appears in several slightly different forms [Rot76, MS77, Dil72]. The above definition follows the line in [Rot76]. It can be equivalently written as

$$(f(\alpha_0), f(\alpha_1), \ldots, f(\alpha_{2^n-1})) = 2^{-\frac{n}{2}} \xi H_n$$

where α_i is the ith vector in V_n according to the ascending order, ξ is the sequence of f and H_n is the Sylvester-Hadamard matrix of order 2^n.

Definition 5. A function f on V_n is called a *bent* function if its Walsh-Hadamard transform satisfies

$$f(\alpha) = \pm 1$$

for all $\alpha \in V_n$.

Bent functions can be characterized in various ways [AT90, Dil72, SZZ94a, YH89]. In particular the following four statements are equivalent:

(i) f is bent.
(ii) $\langle \xi, \ell \rangle = \pm 2^{\frac{1}{2}n}$ for any affine sequence ℓ of length 2^n, where ξ is the sequence of f.
(iii) f satisfies the propagation criterion with respect to all non-zero vectors in V_n.
(iv) M, the matrix of f, is a Hadamard matrix.

Bent functions on V_n exist only when n is even [Rot76]. Another important property of bent functions is that they achieve the highest possible nonlinearity $2^{n-1} - 2^{\frac{1}{2}n-1}$.

3 More on Walsh-Hadamard transform and Nonlinearity

As the Walsh-Hadamard transform plays a key role in the proofs of main results to be described in the following sections, this section provides some background knowledge on the transform. More information regarding the transform can be found in [MS77, Dil72]. In addition, Beauchamp's book [Bea84] is a good source of information on other related orthogonal transforms with their applications.

Given two sequences $a = (a_1, \ldots, a_m)$ and $b = (b_1, \ldots, b_m)$, their componentwise product is defined by $a * b = (a_1 b_1, \ldots, a_m b_m)$. Let f be a function on V_n. For a vector $\alpha \in V_n$, denote by $\xi(\alpha)$ the sequence of $f(x \oplus \alpha)$. Thus $\xi(0)$ is the sequence of f itself and $\xi(0) * \xi(\alpha)$ is the sequence of $f(x) \oplus f(x \oplus \alpha)$.

Set

$$\Delta(\alpha) = \langle\xi(0), \xi(\alpha)\rangle,$$

the scalar product of $\xi(0)$ and $\xi(\alpha)$. $\Delta(\alpha)$ is also called the auto-correlation of f with a shift α. Obviously, $\Delta(\alpha) = 0$ if and only if $f(x) \oplus f(x \oplus \alpha)$ is balanced, i.e., f satisfies the propagation criterion with respect to α. On the other hand, if $|\Delta(\alpha)| = 2^n$, then $f(x) \oplus f(x \oplus \alpha)$ is a constant and hence α is a linear structure of f.

Let $M = ((-1)^{f(\alpha_i \oplus \alpha_j)})$ be the matrix of f and ξ be the sequence of f. Due to a very pretty result by R. L. McFarland (cf. Theorem 3.3 of [Dil72]), M can be decomposed into

$$M = 2^{-n} H_n \operatorname{diag}(\langle\xi, \ell_0\rangle, \cdots, \langle\xi, \ell_{2^n-1}\rangle) H_n \tag{2}$$

where ℓ_i is the ith row of H_n, a Sylvester-Hadamard matrix of order 2^n.

Clearly

$$MM^T = 2^{-n} H_n \operatorname{diag}(\langle\xi, \ell_0\rangle^2, \cdots, \langle\xi, \ell_{2^n-1}\rangle^2) H_n. \tag{3}$$

On the other hand, we always have

$$MM^T = (\Delta(\alpha_i \oplus \alpha_j)),$$

where $i, j = 0, 1, \ldots, 2^n - 1$.

Comparing the two sides of (3), we have

$$(\Delta(\alpha_0), \Delta(\alpha_1), \ldots, \Delta(\alpha_{2^n-1})) = 2^{-n}(\langle\xi, \ell_0\rangle^2, \ldots, \langle\xi, \ell_{2^n-1}\rangle^2) H_n.$$

Equivalently we write

$$(\Delta(\alpha_0), \Delta(\alpha_1), \ldots, \Delta(\alpha_{2^n-1})) H_n = (\langle\xi, \ell_0\rangle^2, \ldots, \langle\xi, \ell_{2^n-1}\rangle^2). \tag{4}$$

In engineering, (4) is better known as (a special form of) the Wiener-Khintchine Theorem [Bea84]. A closely related result is Parseval's equation (Corollary 3, p. 416 of [MS77])

$$\sum_{j=0}^{2^n-1} \langle\xi, \ell_j\rangle^2 = 2^{2n}$$

which also holds for any function f on V_n.

Let S be a set of vectors in V_n. The *rank* of S is the maximum number of linearly independent vectors in S. Note that when S forms a linear sub-space of V_n, its rank coincides with its dimension.

The distance between two functions f_1 and f_2 on V_n can be expressed as $d(f_1, f_2) = 2^{n-1} - \frac{1}{2}\langle\xi_1, \xi_2\rangle$, where ξ_1 and ξ_2 are the sequences of f_1 and f_2 respectively. (For a proof see for instance Lemma 6 of [SZZ94a].) Immediately we have:

Lemma 6. *The nonlinearity of a function f on V_n can be calculated by*

$$N_f = 2^{n-1} - \frac{1}{2}\max\{|\langle\xi, \ell_i\rangle|, 0 \le i \le 2^n - 1\}$$

where ξ is the sequence of f and $\ell_0, \ldots, \ell_{2^n-1}$ are the rows of H_n, namely, the sequences of the linear functions on V_n.

The next lemma regarding splitting the power of 2 can be found in [SZZ94d]

Lemma 7. *Let $n \geq 2$ be a positive integer and $p^2+q^2 = 2^n$ where both $p \geq 0$ and $q \geq 0$ are integers. Then $p = 2^{\frac{1}{2}n}$ and $q = 0$ when n is even, and $p = q = 2^{\frac{1}{2}(n-1)}$ when n is odd.*

In the next section we examine the distribution of the vectors in $\Re$.

4 Distribution of $\Re$

Let f be a function on V_n. Assume that f satisfies the propagation criterion with respect to all but a subset $\Re$ of V_n. Note that $\Re$ always contains the zero vector 0. Write $\Re = \{0, \gamma_1, \ldots, \gamma_s\}$. Thus $|\Re| = s+1$.

Set $\Re^c = V_n - \Re$. Then f satisfies the propagation criterion with respect to all vectors in $\Re^c$.

Consider the set of vectors $\{0\} \cup \Re^c$. Then $\{0\}$ is a linear sub-space contained in $\{0\} \cup \Re^c$. When $|\{0\} \cup \Re^c| > 1$, $\{0, \gamma\}$ is a linear sub-space for any nonzero vector in $\Re^c$. We are particularly interested in linear sub-spaces with the maximum dimension contained in $\{0\} \cup \Re^c$. For convenience, denote by ρ the maximum dimension and by W a linear sub-space in $\{0\} \cup \Re^c$ that achieves the maximum dimension.

Obviously, f is bent if and only if $\rho = n$, and f does not satisfy the propagation criterion with respect to any vector if and only if $\rho = 0$. The case when $1 \leq \rho \leq n-1$ is especially interesting.

Now let U be a complementary sub-space of W, namely $U \oplus W = V_n$. Then each vector $\gamma \in V_n$ can be uniquely expressed as $\gamma = \alpha \oplus \beta$, where $\alpha \in W$ and $\beta \in U$. As the dimension of W is ρ, the dimension of U is equal to $n-\rho$. Write $U = \{0, \beta_1, \ldots, \beta_{2^{n-\rho}-1}\}$.

Proposition 8. *$\Re \cap W = \{0\}$ and $\Re \cap (W \oplus \beta_j) \neq \phi$, where $W \oplus \beta_j = \{\alpha \oplus \beta_j | \alpha \in W\}$, $j = 1, \ldots, 2^{n-\rho}-1$.*

Proof. $\Re \cap W = \{0\}$ follows from the fact that W is a sub-space of $\{0\} \cup \Re^c$. Next we consider $\Re \cap (W \oplus \beta_j)$.

Clearly,

$$V_n = W \cup (W \oplus \beta_1) \cup \cdots \cup (W \oplus \beta_{2^{n-\rho}-1}).$$

In addition,

$$W \cap (W \oplus \beta_j) = \phi$$

for $j = 1, \ldots, 2^{n-\rho}-1$, and

$$(W \oplus \beta_j) \cap (W \oplus \beta_i) = \phi$$

for any $j \neq i$. Assume for contradiction that $\Re \cap (W \oplus \beta_{j_0}) = \phi$ for some j_0, $1 \leq j_0 \leq 2^{n-\rho}-1$. Then we have $W \oplus \beta_{j_0} \subseteq \Re^c$. In this case $W \cup (W \oplus \beta_{j_0})$ must form a sub-space of V_n. This contradicts the definition that W is a linear sub-space with the maximum dimension in $\{0\} \cup \Re^c$. This completes the proof. □

The next corollary follows directly from the above proposition.

Corollary 9. *The size of $\Re$ satisfies $|\Re| \geq 2^{n-\rho}$ and hence the rank of $\Re$ is at least $n-\rho$, where ρ is the maximum dimension a linear sub-space in $\{0\} \cup \Re^c$ can achieve.*

5 Relating Nonlinearity to Propagation Characteristics

We proceed to the discussion of the nonlinearity of f. The main difficulty lies in finding a good approximation of $\langle\xi, \ell_i\rangle$ for each $i = 0, \ldots, 2^n - 1$, where ξ is the sequence of f and ξ_i is a row of H_n.

First we assume that

$$W = \{\gamma | \gamma = (a_1, \ldots, a_\rho, 0, \ldots, 0), a_i \in GF(2)\} \tag{5}$$

$$U = \{\gamma | \gamma = (0, \ldots, 0, a_{\rho+1}, \ldots, a_n), a_i \in GF(2)\} \tag{6}$$

where W is a linear sub-space in $\{0\} \cup \Re^c$ that achieves the maximum dimension ρ and U is a complementary sub-space of W. The more general case where (5) or (6) is not satisfied can be dealt with after employing a nonsingular transform on the input of f. This will be discussed in the later part of this section.

Recall that $\Re = \{0, \gamma_1, \ldots, \gamma_s\}$ and $\Delta(\alpha) = \langle\xi(0), \xi(\alpha)\rangle$, where $\xi(\alpha)$ is the sequence of $f(x \oplus \alpha)$. Since $\Delta(\gamma) \neq 0$ for each $\gamma \in \Re$ while $\Delta(\gamma) = 0$ for each $\gamma \in \Re^c = V_n - \Re$, (4) is specialized as

$$(\Delta(0), \Delta(\gamma_1), \ldots, \Delta(\gamma_s))Q = (\langle\xi, \ell_0\rangle^2, \ldots, \langle\xi, \ell_{2^n-1}\rangle^2). \tag{7}$$

where ξ is the sequence of f, ℓ_i is the ith row of H_n and Q comprises the 0th, γ_1th, ..., γ_sth rows of H_n. Note that Q is an $(s+1) \times 2^n$ matrix.

Let ℓ be the γth row of H_n, where $\gamma \in \Re$. Note that γ can be uniquely expressed as $\gamma = \alpha \oplus \beta$, where $\alpha \in W$ and $\beta \in U$. Let ℓ' be the αth row of H_ρ and ℓ'' be the βth row of $H_{n-\rho}$. As $H_n = H_\rho \times H_{n-\rho}$, ℓ can be represented by $\ell = \ell' \times \ell''$, where $\times$ denotes the Kronecker product.

From the construction of $H_{n-\rho}$, we can see that the βth row of $H_{n-\rho}$ is an all-one sequence of length $2^{n-\rho}$ if $\beta = 0$, and a balanced $(1, -1)$-sequence of length $2^{n-\rho}$ if $\beta \neq 0$.

Recall that $\Re \cap W = \{0\}$ (see also Proposition 8). There are two cases associated with $\gamma = \alpha \oplus \beta \in \Re$: $\gamma = 0$ and $\gamma \neq 0$. In the first case, $\ell = \ell' \times \ell''$ is the all-one sequence of length 2^n, while in the second case, we have $\beta \neq 0$ which implies that ℓ'' is a balanced $(1, -1)$-sequence of length $2^{n-\rho}$ and hence $\ell = \ell' \times \ell''$ is a concatenation of 2^ρ balanced $(1, -1)$-sequences of length $2^{n-\rho}$.

Therefore we can write $Q = (Q_0, Q_1, \ldots, Q_{2^\rho-1})$, where each Q_i is a $(1, -1)$-matrix of order $(s+1) \times 2^{n-\rho}$. It is important to note that the top row of each Q_i is the all-one sequence, while the rest are balanced $(1, -1)$-sequences of length $2^{n-\rho}$.

With Q_0, we have

$$(\Delta(0), \Delta(\gamma_1), \ldots, \Delta(\gamma_s))Q_0 = (\langle\xi, \ell_0\rangle^2, \ldots, \langle\xi, \ell_{2^{n-\rho}-1}\rangle^2).$$

Let σ_0 be the all-one sequence of length $2^{n-\rho}$. Then

$$(\Delta(0), \Delta(\gamma_1), \ldots, \Delta(\gamma_s))Q_0\sigma_0^T = (\langle\xi, \ell_0\rangle^2, \ldots, \langle\xi, \ell_{2^{n-\rho}-1}\rangle^2)\sigma_0^T.$$

This causes

$$(\Delta(0), \Delta(\gamma_1), \ldots, \Delta(\gamma_s)) \begin{bmatrix} 2^{n-\rho} \\ 0 \\ \vdots \\ 0 \end{bmatrix} = \sum_{j=0}^{2^{n-\rho}-1} \langle\xi, \ell_j\rangle^2$$

and

$$\sum_{j=0}^{2^{n-\rho}-1} \langle \xi, \ell_j \rangle^2 = 2^{n-\rho}\Delta(0) = 2^{n-\rho+n} = 2^{2n-\rho}.$$

Similarly, with Q_i, $i = 1, \ldots, 2^\rho - 1$, we have

$$\sum_{j=0}^{2^{n-\rho}-1} \langle \xi, \ell_{j+i2^{n-\rho}} \rangle^2 = 2^{2n-\rho}.$$

Thus we have the following result:

Lemma 10. *Assume that f, a function on V_n, satisfies the propagation criterion with respect to all but a subset $\Re$ of vectors in V_n. Set $\Re^c = V_n - \Re$ and let W be a linear sub-space with the maximum dimension ρ, in $\{0\} \cup \Re^c$, and U be a complementary sub-space of W. Assume that W and U satisfy (5) and (6) respectively. Then*

$$\sum_{j=0}^{2^{n-\rho}-1} \langle \xi, \ell_{j+i2^{n-\rho}} \rangle^2 = 2^{2n-\rho}$$

for all $i = 0, 1, \ldots, 2^\rho - 1$, where ξ is the sequence of f and each ℓ_k is a row of H_n.

Lemma 10 can be viewed as a refinement of Parseval's equation $\sum_{j=0}^{2^n-1} \langle \xi, \ell_j \rangle^2 = 2^{2n}$. It implies that $|\langle \xi, \ell_j \rangle| \leq 2^{n-\frac{1}{2}\rho}$ for all $j = 0, \ldots, 2^n - 1$. Therefore by Lemma 6 we have $N_f \geq 2^{n-1} - 2^{n-\frac{1}{2}\rho-1}$.

So far we have assumed that W and U satisfy (5) and (6) respectively. When this is not the case, we can always find a nonsingular $n \times n$ matrix A whose entries are from $GF(2)$ such that the sub-spaces W' and U' associated with $f'(x) = f(xA)$ have the required forms. f' and f have the same algebraic degree and nonlinearity (see Lemma 10 of [SZZ94b]). This shows that the following theorem is true.

Theorem 11. *For any function on V_n, the nonlinearity of f satisfies $N_f \geq 2^{n-1} - 2^{n-\frac{1}{2}\rho-1}$, where ρ is the maximum dimension of the linear sub-spaces in $\{0\} \cup \Re^c$.*

Theorem 11 indicates that the nonlinearity of a function is determined by the maximum dimension that a linear sub-spaces in $\{0\} \cup \Re^c$ can achieve, but not by the size of $\Re^c$.

In [SZZ94e], we have proved that $N_f \geq 2^{n-1} - 2^{\frac{1}{2}(n+t)-1}$, where t is the rank of $\Re$. By Corollary 9, we have $t \geq n - \rho$. This implies that $2^{n-1} - 2^{n-\frac{1}{2}\rho-1} \geq 2^{n-1} - 2^{\frac{1}{2}(n+t)-1}$. Thus Theorem 11 is an improvement to the result in [SZZ94e]. This improvement can be demonstrated by a concrete example. In [SZZ94e], the following function on V_5

$$f_5(x_1, x_2, x_3, x_4, x_5) = (1 \oplus x_1)(1 \oplus x_2)x_3 \oplus (1 \oplus x_1)x_2x_4 \oplus \\ x_1(1 \oplus x_2)(x_3 \oplus x_4) \oplus x_1x_2(x_4 \oplus x_5)$$

has been shown to satisfy the propagation criterion with respect to all but the following fives vectors in V_5:

$$\Re = \{(0,0,0,0,0), (0,0,0,0,1), (0,0,0,1,0), (0,0,1,0,0), (0,0,1,1,1)\}.$$

The rank t of $\Re$ is equal to 3. By using the result of [SZZ94e], $N_{f_5} \geq 2^{5-1} - 2^{\frac{1}{2}(5+3)-1} = 2^4 - 2^3 = 8$. On the other hand, we can set $W = \{(a_1, a_2, a_3, a_4, a_5) | a_i \in GF(2), a_1 \oplus a_2 \oplus a_3 = 0\}$. W is a four-dimensional sub-space in $\{0\} \cup \Re^c$. Using Theorem 11 with $\rho = 4$, we have $N_{f_5} \geq 2^{5-1} - 2^{5-\frac{1}{2}\rho-1} = 2^4 - 2^2 = 12 > 8$. (Note that according to [CKHFMS85], the maximum nonlinearity a function on V_5 can achieve is 12. Hence we have $N_{f_5} = 12$.)

6 A Tight Lower Bound on Nonlinearity of Functions with Propagation Characteristics

By Theorem 11, $N_f \geq 2^{n-1} - 2^{n-\frac{3}{2}}$ if f, a function on V_n, satisfies the propagation criterion with respect to at least one vector in V_n. This section shows that this lower bound can be significantly improved. Indeed we prove that $N_f \geq 2^{n-2}$ and also show that it is tight.

Theorem 12. *If f, a function on V_n, satisfies the propagation criterion with respect to one or more vectors in V_n, then the nonlinearity of f satisfies $N_f \geq 2^{n-2}$.*

Proof. As in the previous sections, we denote by $\Re$ the set of vectors in V_n with respect to which the propagation criterion is not satisfied by f. We also let $\Re^c = V_n - \Re$, and W be a linear sub-space in $\{0\} \cup \Re^c$ that achieves the maximum dimension ρ.

By Theorem 11, the theorem is trivially true when $\rho > 1$. Next we consider the case when $\rho = 1$. We prove this part by further refining the Parseval's equation.

As in the proof of Lemma 10, without loss of generality, we can assume that

$$W = \{\gamma | \gamma = (a_1, 0, \ldots, 0), a_1 \in GF(2)\} \quad (8)$$
$$U = \{\gamma | \gamma = (0, a_2, \ldots, a_n), a_i \in GF(2)\} \quad (9)$$

Similarly to Lemma 10, we have

$$\sum_{j=0}^{2^{n-1}-1} \langle \xi, \ell_{j+i2^{2^{n-1}}} \rangle^2 = 2^{2n-1}, \ i = 0, 1, \quad (10)$$

where ξ is the sequence of f and ℓ_k is a row of H_n.

Comparing the first row of (2), we have

$$(a_0, a_1, \ldots, a_{2^n-1}) = 2^{-n}(\langle \xi, \ell_0 \rangle, \cdots, \langle \xi, \ell_{2^n-1} \rangle) H_n$$

or equivalently,

$$2^n(a_0, a_1, \ldots, a_{2^n-1}) = (\langle \xi, \ell_0 \rangle, \cdots, \langle \xi, \ell_{2^n-1} \rangle) H_n \quad (11)$$

where each $a_j = \pm 1$ and $(a_0, a_1, \ldots, a_{2^n-1})$ is the first row of the matrix M described in (2).

Rewrite ℓ_i, the ith row of H_n, as $\ell(\alpha_i)$, where α_i is the binary representation of an integer i in the ascending alphabetical order. Set

$$N = (\langle \xi, \ell(\alpha_i \oplus \alpha_j) \rangle), 0 \le i, j \le 2^n - 1.$$

N is a symmetric matrix of order 2^n with integer entries. In [Rot76], Rothaus has shown that $NN = NN^T = 2^{2n} I_{2^n}$. We can split N into four sub-matrices of equal size, namely

$$N = \begin{bmatrix} N_1 & N_2 \\ N_2 & N_1 \end{bmatrix}$$

where each N_j is a matrix of order 2^{n-1}. As $NN = 2^{2n} I_{2^n}$, we have $N_1 N_2 = 0$.

Let $(c(\alpha_0), c(\alpha_1), \ldots, c(\alpha_{2^{n-1}-1}))$ be an arbitrary linear sequence of length 2^{n-1}. Then

$$(c(\alpha_0), c(\alpha_1), \ldots, c(\alpha_{2^{n-1}-1}), c(\alpha_0), c(\alpha_1), \ldots, c(\alpha_{2^{n-1}-1}))$$

is a linear sequence of length 2^n, and hence a row of H_n. Thus from (11), we have

$$\sum_{j=0}^{2^{n-1}-1} c(\alpha_j) \langle \xi, \ell(\alpha_j) \rangle + \sum_{j=0}^{2^{n-1}-1} c(\alpha_j) \langle \xi, \ell(\alpha_j \oplus 2^{n-1}) \rangle = \pm 2^n.$$

Hence

$$(\sum_{j=0}^{2^{n-1}-1} c(\alpha_j) \langle \xi, \ell(\alpha_j) \rangle + \sum_{j=0}^{2^{n-1}-1} c(\alpha_j) \langle \xi, \ell(\alpha_j \oplus \alpha_{2^{n-1}}) \rangle)^2 = 2^{2n}. \quad (12)$$

Rewrite the left hand side of (12) as

$$(\sum_{j=0}^{2^{n-1}-1} c(\alpha_j) \langle \xi, \ell(\alpha_j) \rangle)^2 + (\sum_{j=0}^{2^{n-1}-1} c(\alpha_j) \langle \xi, \ell(\alpha_j \oplus \alpha_{2^{n-1}}) \rangle)^2$$
$$+ 2(\sum_{j=0}^{2^{n-1}-1} c(\alpha_j) \langle \xi, \ell(\alpha_j) \rangle)(\sum_{j=0}^{2^{n-1}-1} c(\alpha_j) \langle \xi, \ell(\alpha_j \oplus \alpha_{2^{n-1}}) \rangle)$$

where

$$(\sum_{j=0}^{2^{n-1}-1} c(\alpha_j) \langle \xi, \ell(\alpha_j) \rangle)(\sum_{j=0}^{2^{n-1}-1} c(\alpha_j) \langle \xi, \ell(\alpha_j \oplus \alpha_{2^{n-1}}) \rangle)$$
$$= \sum_{t=0}^{2^{n-1}-1} \sum_{j=0}^{2^{n-1}-1} c(\alpha_j) \langle \xi, \ell(\alpha_j) \rangle c(\alpha_j \oplus \alpha_t) \langle \xi, \ell(\alpha_j \oplus \alpha_t \oplus \alpha_{2^{n-1}}) \rangle. \quad (13)$$

As $(c(\alpha_0), c(\alpha_1), \ldots, c(\alpha_{2^{n-1}-1}))$ is a linear sequence, $c(\alpha_j) c(\alpha_j \oplus \alpha_t) = c(\alpha_t)$. Hence (13) can be written as

$$\sum_{t=0}^{2^{n-1}-1} c(\alpha_t) \sum_{j=0}^{2^{n-1}-1} \langle \xi, \ell(\alpha_j) \rangle \langle \xi, \ell(\alpha_j \oplus \alpha_t \oplus \alpha_{2^{n-1}}) \rangle.$$

Since $N_1 N_2 = 0$,

$$\sum_{j=0}^{2^{n-1}-1} \langle \xi, \ell(\alpha_j)\rangle \langle \xi, \ell(\alpha_j \oplus \alpha_t \oplus \alpha_{2^{n-1}})\rangle = 0.$$

This proves that (13) is equal to zero and hence

$$(\sum_{j=0}^{2^{n-1}-1} c(\alpha_j)\langle \xi, \ell(\alpha_j)\rangle)^2 + (\sum_{j=0}^{2^{n-1}-1} c(\alpha_j)\langle \xi, \ell(\alpha_j \oplus \alpha_{2^{n-1}})\rangle)^2 = 2^{2n}.$$

By Lemma 7,

$$\sum_{j=0}^{2^{n-1}-1} c(\alpha_j)\langle \xi, \ell(\alpha_j)\rangle = 0 \text{ or } \pm 2^n. \tag{14}$$

Since $(c(\alpha_0), c(\alpha_1), \ldots, c(\alpha_{2^{n-1}-1}))$ is an arbitrary linear sequence of length 2^{n-1} and each linear sequence of length 2^{n-1} is a column of H_{n-1}, from (14) we have

$$(\langle \xi, \ell_0\rangle, \ldots, \langle \xi, \ell_{2^n-1}\rangle)H_{n-1} = 2^n(b_0, \ldots, b_{2^{n-1}-1}) \tag{15}$$

where $b_j = 0$ or ± 1. Therefore

$$(\langle \xi, \ell_0\rangle, \ldots, \langle \xi, \ell_{2^n-1}\rangle)2^{\frac{1}{2}(1-n)}H_{n-1} = 2^{\frac{1}{2}(n+1)}(b_0, \ldots, b_{2^{n-1}-1}).$$

Recall that a matrix A of order s is said to be orthogonal if $AA^T = I_s$. It is easy to verify that $2^{\frac{1}{2}(1-n)}H_{n-1}$ is an orthogonal matrix. Thus

$$\sum_{j=0}^{2^n-1} \langle \xi, \ell_{\alpha_j}\rangle^2 = 2^{n+1} \sum_{j=0}^{2^{n-1}-1} b_j^2.$$

On the other hand, by (10) we have

$$\sum_{j=0}^{2^n-1} \langle \xi, \ell_{\alpha_j}\rangle^2 = 2^{2n-1}.$$

Hence

$$\sum_{j=0}^{2^{n-1}-1} b_j^2 = \sum_{j=0}^{2^{n-1}-1} |b_j| = 2^{n-2}.$$

Now let $\sigma(\alpha_i)$ denote the ith row of H_{n-1}, where $\alpha_i \in V_{n-1}$ is the binary representation of i, $i = 0, 1, \ldots, 2^{n-1} - 1$. From (15),

$$(\langle \xi, \ell_0\rangle, \cdots, \langle \xi, \ell_{2^n-1}\rangle)H_{n-1}\sigma(\alpha_i)^T = 2^n(b_0, \ldots, b_{2^{n-1}-1})\sigma(\alpha_i)^T. \tag{16}$$

Note that

$$\langle \sigma(\alpha_i), \sigma(\alpha_j)\rangle = \begin{cases} 2^{n-1} & \text{if } j = i \\ 0 & \text{if } j \neq i \end{cases}$$

Thus

$$H_{n-1}\sigma(\alpha_i)^T = \begin{bmatrix} 0 \\ \vdots \\ 0 \\ 2^{n-1} \\ 0 \\ \vdots \\ 0 \end{bmatrix} \tag{17}$$

where 2^{n-1} is on the ith position of the column vector.

Write $\sigma(\alpha_i) = (d_0, d_1, \ldots, d_{2^{n-1}-1})$. Then

$$(b_0, \ldots, b_{2^{n-1}-1})\sigma(\alpha_i)^T = \sum_{j=0}^{2^{n-1}-1} d_j b_j.$$

As $d_j = \pm 1$, we have

$$|\sum_{j=0}^{2^{n-1}-1} d_j b_j| \le \sum_{j=0}^{2^{n-1}-1} |b_j| = 2^{n-2}. \tag{18}$$

From (16), (17) and (18)

$$2^{n-1}|\langle \xi, \ell_i \rangle| \le 2^n \sum_{j=0}^{2^{n-1}-1} |b_j| = 2^{2n-2}$$

and hence

$$|\langle \xi, \ell_i \rangle| \le 2^{n-1}$$

where i is an arbitrary integer in $[0, \ldots, 2^{n-1} - 1]$. Similarly,

$$|\langle \xi, \ell_i \rangle| \le 2^{n-1}$$

holds for all $i = 2^{n-1}, 2^{n-1} + 1, \ldots, 2^n - 1$. By Lemma 6, the nonlinearity of f satisfies

$$N_f \ge 2^{n-1} - 2^{n-2} = 2^{n-2}.$$

This completes the proof. □

As an immediate consequence, we have

Corollary 13. *Let f be a function on V_n. Then the following statements hold:*

1. *if the nonlinearity of f satisfies $N_f < 2^{n-2}$, then f does not satisfy the propagation criterion with respect to any vector in V_n.*
2. *if f satisfies the SAC, then the nonlinearity of f satisfies $N_f \ge 2^{n-2}$.*

Finally we show that the lower bound 2^{n-2} is tight. We achieve the goal by demonstrating a function on V_n whose nonlinearity is equal to 2^{n-2}. Let $g(x_1, x_2) = x_1x_2$ be a function on V_2. Then the nonlinearity of g is $N_g = 1$. Now let $f(x_1, \ldots, x_n) = x_1x_2$ be a function on V_n. Then the nonlinearity of f is $N_f = 2^{n-2}N_g = 2^{n-2}$ (see for instance Lemma 8 of [SZZ94c]). f satisfies the propagation criterion with respect to all vectors in V_n whose first two bits are nonzero, which count for three quarters of the vectors in V_n. It is not hard to verify that

$$\{(0,0,0,\ldots,0),(1,0,0,\ldots,0),(0,1,0,\ldots,0),(1,1,0,\ldots,0)\}$$

is the linear sub-space that achieves the maximum dimension $\rho = 2$.

Thus we have a result described as follows:

Lemma 14. *The lower bound 2^{n-2} as stated in Theorem 12 is tight.*

7 Conclusion

We have shown quantitative relationships between nonlinearity, propagation characteristics and the SAC. A tight lower bound on the nonlinearity of a function with propagation characteristics is also presented.

This research has also introduced a number of interesting problems yet to be resolved. One of the problems is regarding the size and distribution of $\Re^c$, the set of vectors where the propagation criterion is satisfied by a function on V_n. For all the functions we know of, $\Re^c$ is either an empty set or a set with at least 2^{n-1} vectors. We believe that any further understanding of this problem will contribute to the research into the design and analysis of cryptographically strong nonlinear functions.

Acknowledgments

We would like to thank the anonymous referees for their helpful comments. The first author was supported in part by the Australian Research Council (ARC) under the reference numbers A49130102, A49131885 and A49232172, and by the Australian Telecommunications and Electronics Research Board (ATERB) under the reference number C010/058, the second author by ARC A49130102 and ATERB C010/058, and the third author by ARC A49232172 and ATERB N069/412. All authors were supported by a University of Wollongong Research Program grant.

This work was done while the third author was with the University of Wollongong.

References

[AT90] C. M. Adams and S. E. Tavares. Generating and counting binary bent sequences. *IEEE Transactions on Information Theory*, IT-36 No. 5:1170-1173, 1990.

[Bea84] K. G. Beauchamp. *Applications of Walsh and Related Functions with an Introduction to Sequency Functions.* Microelectronics and Signal Processing. Academic Press, London, New York, Tokyo, 1984.

[BKPS93] L. Brown, M. Kwan, J. Pieprzyk, and J. Seberry. Improving resistance to differential cryptanalysis and the redesign of LOKI. In *Advances in Cryptology - ASIACRYPT'91*, Lecture Notes in Computer Science, vol. 739, pp. 6-50, Springer-Verlag, Berlin, New York, Tokyo, 1993.

[CKHFMS85] G. D. Cohen, M. G. Karpovsky, Jr. H. F. Mattson, and J. R. Schatz. Covering radius — survey and recent results. *IEEE Transactions on Information Theory*, IT-31(3):328-343, 1985.

[Dil72] J. F. Dillon. A survey of bent functions. *The NSA Technical Journal*, pp. 191-215, 1972. (unclassified).

[Eve88] J.-H. Evertse. Linear structures in blockciphers. In *Advances in Cryptology - EUROCRYPT'87*, Lecture Notes in Computer Science, vol. 304, pp. 249-266, Springer-Verlag, Berlin, Heidelberg, New York, 1988.

[Lai92] X. Lai. *On the Design and Security of Block Ciphers.* ETH Series in Information Processing. Hartung-Gorre Verlag Konstanz, Zürich, 1992.

[LaSM91] X. Lai and J. L. Massey ans S. Murphy. Markov ciphers and differential cryptanalysis. In D. W. Davies, editor, *Advances in Cryptology - EUROCRYPT'91*, Lecture Notes in Computer Science, vol. 547, pp. 17-38, Springer-Verlag, Berlin, New York, Tokyo, 1991.

[LM91] X. Lai and J. L. Massey. A proposal for a new block encryption standard. In I. B. Damgård, editor, *Advances in Cryptology - EUROCRYPT'90*, Lecture Notes in Computer Science, vol. 473, pp. 389-404, Springer-Verlag, Berlin, New York, Tokyo, 1991.

[Miy91] S. Miyaguchi. The FEAL cipher family. In *Advances in Cryptology - CRYPTO'90*, Lecture Notes in Computer Science, vol. 537, pp. 627-638, Springer-Verlag, Berlin, New York, Tokyo, 1991.

[MS77] F. J. MacWilliams and N. J. A. Sloane. *The Theory of Error-Correcting Codes.* North-Holland, Amsterdam, New York, Oxford, 1977.

[MS90] W. Meier and O. Staffelbach. Nonlinearity criteria for cryptographic functions. In *Advances in Cryptology - EUROCRYPT'89*, Lecture Notes in Computer Science, vol. 434, pp. 549-562, Springer-Verlag, Berlin, Heidelberg, New York, 1990.

[NBS77] National Bureau of Standards. Data encryption standard. Federal Information Processing Standards Publication FIPS PUB 46, U.S. Department of Commerce, January 1977.

[NIST93] National Institute of Standards and Technology. Secure hash standard. Federal Information Processing Standards Publication FIPS PUB 180, U.S. Department of Commerce, May 1993.

[PGV91] B. Preneel, R. Govaerts, and J. Vandewalle. Boolean functions satisfying higher order propagation criteria. In *Advances in Cryptology - EUROCRYPT'91*, Lecture Notes in Computer Science, vol. 547, pp. 141-152, Springer-Verlag, Berlin, Heidelberg, New York, 1991.

[PLL+91] B. Preneel, W. V. Leekwijck, L. V. Linden, R. Govaerts, and J. Vandewalle. Propagation characteristics of boolean functions. In *Advances in Cryptology - EUROCRYPT'90*, Lecture Notes in Computer Science, vol. 437, pp. 155-165, Springer-Verlag, Berlin, Heidelberg, New York, 1991.

[Riv92] R. Rivest. The MD5 message digest algorithm, April 1992. Request for Comments (RFC) 1321.

[Rot76] O. S. Rothaus. On "bent" functions. *Journal of Combinatorial Theory*, Ser. A, 20:300-305, 1976.

[SZZ94a] J. Seberry, X. M. Zhang, and Y. Zheng. Nonlinearity and propagation characteristics of balanced boolean functions. To appear in *Information and Computation*, 1994.

[SZZ94b] J. Seberry, X. M. Zhang, and Y. Zheng. Nonlinearly balanced boolean functions and their propagation characteristics. In *Advances in Cryptology - CRYPTO'93*, Lecture Notes in Computer Science, vol. 773, pp. 49-60, Springer-Verlag, Berlin, Heidelberg, New York, 1994.

[SZZ94c] J. Seberry, X. M. Zhang, and Y. Zheng. On constructions and nonlinearity of correlation immune functions. In *Advances in Cryptology - EUROCRYPT'93*, Lecture Notes in Computer Science, vol. 765, pp. 181-199, Springer-Verlag, Berlin, Heidelberg, New York, 1994.

[SZZ94d] J. Seberry, X. M. Zhang, and Y. Zheng. Relationships among nonlinearity criteria. Presented at *EUROCRYPT'94*, 1994.

[SZZ94e] J. Seberry, X. M. Zhang, and Y. Zheng. Structures of cryptographic functions with strong avalanche characteristics. Presented at *ASIACRYPT'94*, 1994.

[Web85] A. F. Webster. Plaintext/ciphertext bit dependencies in cryptographic system. Master's Thesis, Department of Electrical Engineering, Queen's University, Ontario, Cannada, 1985.

[WT86] A. F. Webster and S. E. Tavares. On the design of S-boxes. In *Advances in Cryptology - CRYPTO'85*, Lecture Notes in Computer Science, vol. 219, pp. 523-534, Springer-Verlag, Berlin, Heidelberg, New York, 1986.

[YH89] R. Yarlagadda and J. E. Hershey. Analysis and synthesis of bent sequences. *IEE Proceedings (Part E)*, 136:112-123, 1989.

[ZPS93] Y. Zheng, J. Pieprzyk, and J. Seberry. HAVAL — a one-way hashing algorithm with varialbe length of output. In *Advances in Cryptology - AUSCRYPT'92*, Lecture Notes in Computer Science, vol. 718, pp. 83-104, Springer-Verlag, Berlin, New York, Tokyo, 1993.

Journal of Universal Computer Science, vol. 1, no. 2 (1995), 151-154
submitted: 10/11/94, accepted: 13/1/95, appeared: 28/2/95, © *Springer Pub. Co.*

On Completeness of Pseudosimple Sets

Vadim Bulitko
(Odessa State University, Ukraine
ul. Perekopskoj divizii 67-40
Odessa 270062, UKRAINE
bulitko.odessa@REX.iasnet.com)

Abstract: The paper contains completeness criterions for pseudosimple sets. Those criterions are constructed using effectivization of the definitions as well as extensionally bounded functions.

Key Words: Completeness, Pseudosimple set, Effectivization, Extensionally bounded function
Category: G

A recursively enumerable (r.e.) set is called complete (Turing-complete) if any r.e. set can be reduced to that set using Turing reducibility. Optionally complete sets can have some interesting properties, for instance they can be simple, pseudosimple, etc. Problems of constructing completeness criterions for simple sets by an effectivization of definitions have been investigated by McLaughlin, Smullyan, Lachlan, Arslanov, etc. History and systematical description of that can be found in [Arslanov 87].

Simple sets fall into class $\mathcal{E}_1$ of r.e. set classification by Uspenskij and Dekker-Myhill [Rogers 67]. For creative sets ($\mathcal{E}_4$) the criterions have been constructed even before. However we do not know any specific criterion for pseudosimple ($\mathcal{E}_2$) and pseudocreative ($\mathcal{E}_3$) sets. In this paper we propose some completeness criterions for pseudosimple sets.

Most of our notation follows [Rogers 67] also *r.* means *recursive*, *r.e.* means *recursively enumerable* and *i.r.e.* means *infinite recursively enumerable*. We use $[a, b]$ for $\{x \in N \mid a \leq x \leq b\}$ and $\rightleftharpoons$ as "$\Leftrightarrow$ under definition". Sometimes we use "number of" as "index of". Let us recall the following definitions from [Rogers 67]:

Definition 1. A is *pseudosimple* $\rightleftharpoons$ (1) A is r.e. but not r.; (2) $(\exists i.r.e. C \subset \overline{A})$ $\forall W_z \left[W_z \subset (\overline{A} \backslash C) \Rightarrow |W_z| < \infty\right]$. Such C we will denote C^A.

Definition 2. A is *pseudosimple with center* C $\rightleftharpoons$ (1) A is pseudosimple; (2) $(\exists i.r.e. C \subset \overline{A})\, \forall W_z \left[W_z \subset \overline{A} \Rightarrow |W_z \backslash C| < \infty\right]$.

Above definitions allow the following effectivization:

Definition 1′. A is *weakly effectively pseudosimple* $\rightleftharpoons$ (1) A is pseudosimple; (2) $(\exists$ total $f \leq_T A)\, \forall W_z \left[W_z \subset (\overline{A} \backslash C^A) \Rightarrow |W_z| \leq f(z)\right]$.

Definition 2′. A is *weakly effectively pseudosimple with center* C $\rightleftharpoons$ (1) A is pseudosimple with center C; (2) $(\exists$ total $f \leq_T A)\, \forall W_z [W_z \subset \overline{A} \Rightarrow |W_z \backslash C| \leq f(z)]$.

First prove two complementary lemmas.

Lemma 1. For any complete set A and any r.e. set M the following function is total and recursive in A:

$$f(z) = \begin{cases} 1, W_z \cap M \neq \emptyset, \\ 0, W_z \subset \overline{M}. \end{cases}$$

Proof. $\{x \mid W_x \cap M \neq \emptyset\} \leq_T A$ because $\{x \mid W_x \cap M \neq \emptyset\}$ is an r.e. set. Therefore f is computable with oracle A.□

Lemma 2. Let A be complete and g be partial recursive in A. Then the following function is partial recursive in A:

$$\phi(z) = \begin{cases} |W_{g(z)}|, g(z) \downarrow \ and\ |W_{g(z)}| < \infty, \\ \uparrow, otherwise. \end{cases}$$

Proof. Let us make computation of ϕ as follows. Given z we start computation of $g(z)$ and if it ends, we enumerate numbers of r.e. sets $W_{g(z)} \cap [0, \infty]$, $W_{g(z)} \cap [1, \infty]$, ..., $W_{g(z)} \cap [i, \infty]$, ... until some of them fall into $\{x \mid W_x = \emptyset\}$ which is recursive in A. Let it happen when $i = n$ so we set $\phi(z)$ equal to $|W_{g(z)} \cap [0, n-1]|$. Note we use uniform recursiveness of W_i in respect to complete A.□

Theorem 1. (A is pseudosimple and complete) $\Leftrightarrow$ (A is weakly effectively pseudosimple and $C^A \leq_T A$).

Proof. $\Rightarrow$. Let A be pseudosimple and complete then obviously $C^A \leq_T A$. Define total f as follows:

$$f(z) = \begin{cases} 0, W_z \cap (C^A \cup A) \neq \emptyset, \\ |W_z|, W_z \subset (\overline{A} \backslash C^A). \end{cases}$$

f is computable with oracle A by lemma 1,2, and because $A \cup C^A$ is an r.e. set, and $\overline{A} \backslash C^A$ is immune. Thus A is weakly effectively pseudosimple.

$\Leftarrow$. Using f, which is recursive in A, and possibility to write out elements of $\overline{A} \backslash C^A$ in increasing order with oracle A, construct initial segment $\{\alpha_0, \alpha_1, \ldots, \alpha_{f(z)}\} = X(z)$ of enumeration of $\overline{A} \backslash C^A$ in increasing order. An r.e. index of $X(z)$ can be computed with oracle A because $X(z)$ is finite and recursive in A. Let $g(z)$ be that r.e. index. So $g \leq_T A$ and $\forall z\, [W_z \neq W_{g(z)}]$. Thus A is complete by the Arslanov theorem [Arslanov 87]. (The Arslanov theorem used here and below states that for any r.e.s. A [(A is complete) $\Leftrightarrow$ ($\exists$ total $f \leq_T A$ $\forall z[W_z \neq W_{f(z)}]$)]).□

Another completeness criterion can be obtained introducing concept of special function.

Definition 3. Let A be weakly effectively pseudosimple. We call total and recursive in A function f *special* for A if

$$f(z) = \begin{cases} |W_z| + t, W_z \subset (\overline{A} \backslash C^A), t \geq 1, \\ 0, otherwise. \end{cases}$$

Theorem 2. (A is pseudosimple and complete) $\Leftrightarrow$ (A is weakly effectively pseudosimple and there is f special for A).

Proof. $\Rightarrow$. Define f as follows:

$$f(z) = \begin{cases} 0, W_z \cap (C^A \cup A) \neq \emptyset, \\ |W_z| + 1, W_z \subset (\overline{A} \backslash C^A). \end{cases}$$

f can be computed with oracle A by lemmas 1,2, and because $A \cup C^A$ is an r.e. set, and $\overline{A} \backslash C^A$ is immune. So A is weakly effectively pseudosimple with special function f.

$\Leftarrow$. Let g be defined as follows:

$$W_{g(z)} = \begin{cases} \{a\}, \text{where } a \in (\overline{A} \backslash C^A) \text{ if } f(z) = 0, \\ \{b\}, \text{where } b \in A \text{ if } f(z) \neq 0. \end{cases}$$

g can be computed with oracle A because f is recursive in A. Also g is total and obviously does not have fixed points so we can apply the Arslanov theorem that causes A is complete.□

There is also another approach to effectivization of the definitions. The approach is based on use of functions evaluating complexity characteristics of set other than the number of elements. For instance, Lachlan in [Lachlan 68] used the number of value changes of characteristic function for a given r.e. set on a cohesive set building sufficient conditions for complete maximal sets. Completeness criterion for maximal sets [Bulitko 92] constructed using Kolmogorov complexity of set initial segments is another example. Next step in that direction is use of extensionally bounded functions to construct completeness criterions for special classes of simple sets. That approach has been posed by V.K.Bulitko in [Bulitko 95]. In present paper we use that approach to describe pseudosimple and complete sets.

Definition 4. Total f is *extensionally bounded (e.b.)* $\rightleftharpoons \forall W_x \exists c \forall W_z$ $[W_z = W_x \Rightarrow f(z) \leq c]$.

Theorem 3. (A is pseudosimple and complete) $\Leftrightarrow$ (A is r.e. but not r. & $\exists i.r.e. C^A \subset \overline{A}$ such that the following function f :

$$f(z) = \begin{cases} |W_z \cap [0, z]| + 1, W_z \subset (\overline{A} \backslash C^A), \\ 0, otherwise, \end{cases}$$

is e.b. and recursive in A).

Proof. $\Rightarrow$. Obviously A is r.e. but not r. f is computable with oracle A by lemma 1 and because $\overline{A} \backslash C^A$ is immune. For any number i of r.e. $X \subset (\overline{A} \backslash C^A)$ $f(i)$ is bounded by cardinality of X that is finite because A is pseudosimple. f is equal to 0 for a number of an r.e. set which is not a subset of $\overline{A} \backslash C^A$. Therefore f is e.b.

$\Leftarrow$. Assume $\exists W_z \subset (\overline{A} \backslash C^A)$ $[|W_z| = \infty]$. Then taking in account infiniteness of W_z index set we get f is not bounded on W_z index set. That contradicts with the definition of e.b. function. Therefore our assumption is wrong and A is pseudosimple. Completeness of A can be proved in the same way as in theorem 2.□

Let us consider pseudosimple sets with center.

Theorem 4. (A is pseudosimple with recursive center C and complete) $\Leftrightarrow$ (A is weakly effectively pseudosimple with recursive center C).

Proof. $\Rightarrow$. Define f as follows:

$$f(z) = \begin{cases} 0, (W_z \cap A) \neq \emptyset, \\ |W_z \backslash C|, W_z \subset \overline{A}. \end{cases}$$

f is computable with oracle A by lemmas 1,2 and $(\forall W_z \subset \overline{A})$ $[|W_z \backslash C| < \infty]$. Therefore A is weakly effectively pseudosimple with recursive center.

$\Leftarrow$. We can get total function $g \leq_T A$ that does not have fixed points doing in the same way as in the first theorem. Using the Arslanov theorem we obtain completeness of A.□

Situation regarding case of non-recursive (in general) center is described by the following theorems and remarkable enough. Trying to get the criterion we succeeded in way of using e.b functions *only*.

Theorem 5. (A is weakly effectively pseudosimple with center C recursive in A) $\Rightarrow$ (A is pseudosimple with center C and complete).

Proof. Follows from the first theorem.□

Definition 5. Let A be weakly effectively pseudosimple with center C. Call total and computable with oracle A function f bounding for A if

$$f(z) = \begin{cases} |W_z \backslash C| + t, W_z \subset \overline{A}, t \geq 1, \\ 0, otherwise. \end{cases}$$

Theorem 6. (A is weakly effectively pseudosimple with center C and there is bounding for A function f) $\Rightarrow$ (A is pseudosimple with center C and complete).

Proof. Define g as follows:

$$W_{g(z)} = \begin{cases} \{a\}, \text{where } a \in \overline{A} \text{ if } f(z) = 0, \\ \{b\}, \text{where } b \in A \text{ if } f(z) \neq 0. \end{cases}$$

g can be computed with oracle A because f is recursive in A. Also g is total and does not have fixed points. Thus A is complete by the Arslanov theorem.□

Theorem 7. (A is pseudosimple with center C and complete) $\Leftrightarrow$ (A is r.e. but not r.; $\exists i.r.e. C \subset \overline{A}$; the following f is e.b. and computable with oracle A):

$$f(z) = \begin{cases} |W_z \backslash C \cap [0, z]| + 1, W_z \subset \overline{A}, \\ 0, otherwise. \end{cases}$$

Proof. $\Rightarrow$. Obviously A is r.e. but not r. f is computable with oracle A by lemma 1 and because having oracle A we are able to write out all of W_z elements not belonging to C and situated in $[0, z]$. f is e.b. because f is bounded on numbers of r.e. $X \subset \overline{A}$ by $|X \backslash C|$, which is finite because A is pseudosimple with center, and f is equal to 0 on numbers of an r.e. set which is not a subset of $\overline{A}$.

$\Leftarrow$. A is pseudosimple with center C because f is e.b. and therefore $(\forall W_z \subset \overline{A})$ $[|W_z \backslash C| < \infty]$ (otherwise we would get unbounded f taking in account that any r.e. set has an infinite number of its indexes). Completeness of A can be proved in the same way as in theorem 6.□

References

[Arslanov 87] Arslanov, M.M.: "Local theory of unsolvability degrees and Δ_2^0-sets"; KGU press / Kazan, (1987).(In Russian).

[Rogers 67] Rogers, H. Jr.: "Theory of recursive functions and effective computability"; McGrow-Hill / N.-Y. (1967).

[Lachlan 68] A.H.Lachlan, A. H.: "Complete recursively enumerable sets"; Proc. Amer. Math. Soc., 19, (1968), 99-102.

[Bulitko 92] Bulitko, V. K.: "Subturing reducibilities with bounded complexity"; Izv. VUZov, ser. mat., 1 (1992), 27-37. (In Russian).

[Bulitko 95] Bulitko, V. K.: "On some complexity characteristics of Immune sets"; MLQ, 41, 3 (1995) (in press).

Managing Editor's Column

Vol. 1, No. 3; March 28, 1995

Dear Readers:

This number 3 of volume 1 of J.UCS contains 5 papers that cover an extremly wide range of areas. It is the first time that we have included two award winning papers from a big international conference, something we will continue to do whenever appropriate. Both papers come from the ED-MEDIA '95 conference, the Annual World Conference on Educational Multi- and Hypermedia that takes place in Europe every three years, this time in Graz, Austria, June 17-21, 95. ED-MEDIA is a large conference with some 250 contributions that you may be interested to attend. If you want more information you can just send an email to our mail server edmedia@iicm.tu-graz.ac.at or note the URL http://www.iicm.tu-graz.ac.at/Cedmedia.

The two award winning papers are: "Bringing ITS to the Marketplace: A Successful Experiment in Minimalistic Design" (best student paper) and "Combining Concept Mapping and Adaptive Advice to Teach Reading Comprehension" (best paper). We congratulate the award winning author teams to their very nice papers and look forward to seeing them in Graz!

Of the three remaining papers the one on "Special Cases of Division" is also a novelty: it is the first paper that falls into the category "Survey of a particular special field".

The other two papers on the "Halting Probability Amplitude of Quantum Computers" and "Modular Range Reduction: A New Algorithm for Fast and Accurate Computation of the Elementary Functions" are two technical papers of a more theoretical nature.

I hope you like what you see... and are encouraged to submit papers yourself. Springer is following J.UCS quite closely, is reasonably happy with how things are going and has just agreed to advertise for J.UCS contributions. So, you should see more about J.UCS also in conventional media in the near future.

All the best till April 28, when the next number of J.UCS appears.

Yours sincerely,

Hermann Maurer, Managing Editor
email: hmaurer@iicm.tu-graz.ac.at

Journal of Universal Computer Science, vol. 1, no. 3 (1995), 156-161
submitted: 1/3/95, accepted: 13/3/95, appeared: 28/3/95,

Combining Concept Mapping and Adaptive Advice to Teach Reading Comprehension

Patricia A. Carlson, Ph.D.
U. S. Air Force Armstrong Laboratory
7909 Lindbergh Drive
Brooks Air Force Base, Texas 78235-5352
Email: Carlson@alhrt2.brooks.af.mil

Veronica Larralde
Command Technologies, Inc.
6852 Alamo Downs Parkway
San Antonio, Texas 78238

Abstract: When driven by simple models of information processing, reading instruction focuses on basic decoding skills centering on words and sentences. Factoring in advanced cognitive studies adds at least two more dimensions. First, readers must learn a collection of strategies for constructing meaning from text. Second, and most importantly, readers must develop enough situational awareness to diagnose a text and know which strategy to deploy. Teaching intellectual crafts that involve not only base-line performative skills but also a repertoire of problem-solving heuristics, and the metacognitive maturity to orchestrate multi-leveled activities, works well in a master-apprentice model. However, one-on-one instruction is far too labor-intensive to be commonplace in the teaching of reading. This paper describes a computerized learning environment for teaching the conceptual patterns of critical literacy. While the full implementation of the software treats both reading and writing, this paper covers only the reading aspects of R-WISE (Reading and Writing in a Supportive Environment).

1 Reading Strategies and Metacognition

Research into the cognitive aspects of reading has led to something of a theoretical framework to guide instructional development. For example, awareness that good readers have a repertoire of problem-solving behaviors for various types of tasks and texts launched a new pedagogy for strategy acquisition. The literature for practitioners features a number of techniques for teaching young readers to diagnose levels of understanding and to repair mistakes in comprehension. These routines vary from rather elaborate mnemonics for complicated, multi-stepped procedures (as in the well-known S4R or SQ3R protocols) to thinking frames (graphic representations that support the deconstruction of text into units of meaning).

Unfortunately, strategy training has fairly low durability [Garner, 1987]. Part of the reason for this degradation may be, as suggested by Garner, that the teaching of a specific strategy becomes an end in and of itself, divorcing the skill from the multi-dimensional context of mature reading. For example, the concept diagrams advocated by Armstrong and Armbruster [Armstrong & Armbruster, 1991] require that the learner become comfortable with a sophisticated set of conventions for mapping out ideas. Additionally -- at least until the learner becomes proficient at using this new visual nomenclature -- the teacher must compose the empty maps for each piece of reading. The issue is that such essentially self-contained exercises seem to bear little resemblance to the dynamic, fluid process of comprehending a piece of text in the real world. The adept reader not only has a repertoire of strategies at hand but, more importantly, has the metacognitive ability both to anticipate and to detect abstract problem-types and then to deploy, adapt, combine, or abandon strategic cognitive solutions.

2 Software Components and Instructional Approach

The process model of text comprehension underscores the idea that good readers know that "making meaning" from prose is an interactive process while poor (or immature) readers attempt to slavishly "extract meaning" from the text by decoding word-for-word. Characterizations of these two modes of "reading" are almost diametrical. The poor reader (1) does not vary speed or technique based on text type, (2) does not know how to exploit the "signposts" built into conventional text forms, (3) cannot glean meaning for unfamiliar words and concepts from the context, (4) cannot tell when a statement makes no sense within the confines of its presentation, and (5) has difficulty making "text connecting" inferences as well as reasoning about probable outcomes of information presented in the text. The antithesis, as practiced by good writers, is characterized by (1) guided planning and situational diagnostics, (2) rich mental representations of text possibilities for a wide range of scenarios, and (3) a robust "executive control program" for allocating mental resources and for handling the tremendous cognitive load of deep-processing text.

R-WISE addresses these issues of critical literacy and teaches the use of language as a vehicle for critical thinking. We have developed a battery of "procedural facilitators" staged so as to promote progressively more sophisticated forms of reading comprehension. Specifically, R-WISE promotes three qualitatively different types of activities and models each for the student: (1) identifying concepts and units of meaning in a text, (2) formulating interpretations and making inferences, and (3) metacognitive control over performative skills. Admittedly, these are not definitive categories, and it is impossible to isolate totally the activities of one from those of another. Our purpose is to work with a process-based model that is sensitive to distinctions in knowledge about decoding, inferencing, text structures and text conventions, language, reading purpose, higher-order strategies, and self-monitoring. As described in Sections 2.1 through 2.5, five components make up the R-WISE cognitive architecture.

2.1 Setting Goals

The "decoder" views reading as if it were a straightforward exercise in stripping meaning from the page. For the expert, however, having an explicit, stated set of goals fosters a kind of filtering activity that focuses the task from the outset. In R-WISE, at the beginning of each new lesson, the student is asked to go through a preliminary activity that helps to (1) delineate the requirements of the task, (2) identify features of the text such as level of difficulty, structure, and aim of the discourse, (3) identify strengths (such as prior knowledge) and weaknesses (such as limited experience with the type of discourse) the reader brings to the situation. At this point, the student is working from a paper copy of the text and has read through the materials. A questionnaire helps the student to "preview" the elements of the task that will dynamically interact during the session. Though a truly novice user could spend much time in this preliminary activity, a more seasoned user of the software will work through the interface in a matter of minutes.

Metacognitive awareness has increasingly become an acknowledged component of performance in complex, tasks. In brief, metacognition means the ability to learn about learning. Though a bit fuzzy because such meta (or higher-order) forms of mentation are difficult to observe and measure directly, the explanatory power of this body of research has been championed by a number of researchers in the past decade [Weinert and Kluwe, 1987]. Metacognitive awareness is a kind of calibration among external demands, internal resources, and a desired outcome. Just as an athlete, poised before the beginning of an event, takes a moment to reflect and to visualize a goal and the path toward that outcome, so this introductory, goal-setting workspace for R-WISE encourages the student to formulate a loose plan for the cognitive task about to take place.

Just as importantly, this preliminary work sets the parameters for the software that supply the "intelligence" behind the adaptive advice. The tutor now has a "frame" or backplane of conditions against which further actions can be evaluated during the remainder of the session. (If the student changes goals, the frame is also updated.) Each major area has a number of subsets: Author's Purpose has five; Reader's Purpose has four; and Text Type has six. Clearly, the repertoire of rhetorical situations is rich -- 120 combinations (5x4x6) are tracked at this level. This number becomes even larger and the tutoring capability even richer as these preliminary combinations are conjoined with additional datapoints drawn from the student's subsequent activities.

2.2 Microworld

The second way R-WISE encourages the active construction of meaning during reading fits in with the current emphasis on "visual referents" for teaching abstract concepts, but is actually rooted in comprehension treatments devised as much as two decades ago. The interfaces of R-WISE represent visual organizers for specific intellectual processes. As explained by J. H. Clarke, "[f]rom the standpoint of cognitive theory, graphic frames mimic aspects of semantic memory structures or schemata, that learning theorists believe organize the mind" [Clarke, 1991]. For example, in R-WISE, a concept mapper workspace encourages the deconstruction of linear prose into a more symbolic or semantic network by helping the student tokenize higher-order mental manipulations.

Using standard GUI interface conventions, the student clicks on one of five different buttons located across the top of the concept mapper workspace. Four of these will pop out an icon representing one of four aspects of comprehension: (1) identify the main idea, (2) locate a major support statement, (3) identify a supporting detail, and (4) draw an inference from the text. Multiple occurrences of icons are acceptable and all icons are draggable, meaning that students can use placement of the tokens to construct a visual illustration of a verbal statement. The fifth button on the control panel allows the student to link the icons displayed in the workspace. Implicit in the link is the notion of hierarchical order: a detail attached to a detail is on the same level

(Association); a detail attached to a main idea shows subordination (Elaboration); an inference attached to a main idea shows superordination (Generalization).

Given the premise that most of the clients for R-WISE probably have learning preferences that are concrete/visual rather than abstract/language, we provide "objects" for obscure mental actions. Similar to "webbing" or "schematicizing" -- paper-and-pencil techniques used in the traditional classroom -- this technique encourages the student to formulate a "meta-view" in a simplified, visible language that cuts through much of the complexity of paper text. In addition, working with a malleable, graphical overview helps the student to recognize and to take control of the intellectual processes foundational to reading for comprehension.

2.3 Strategic Elaboration of the Thinking Frame

The process of mapping (clustering and linking) is educationally powerful in that it helps the reader to see things from a higher level or as a synoptic overview. However, even deeper processing of the concepts of the text can be encouraged by having the student elaborate on the meaning for each icon. Clicking on an icon brings up what would be considered a "notecard" screen in a classic implementation of hypertext, but in this context the input screen becomes a "cognition enhancer," helping the student to probe beyond the surface. Instructional statements are generated through a kind of triangulation, based on the rhetorical situation (the several frame conditions set up in the goal-setting phase) and the moves made by the student in the microworld of the concept mapper. Monitoring the combination of rhetorical situation and place in the reading process creates a cognitive task map for firing rules that access instructional statements.

This reading tool captures six hundred unique instructional situations. In writing the attendant advice statements, we addressed each combination of the four strategic elements tracked by the system: (1) Reading Activity, (2) Author's Purpose, (3) Text Type, and (4) Reader's Purpose. Three factors -- Reading Activity (e.g. drawing an inference), Author's Purpose (e.g. attempting to persuade), Text Type (e.g. a poem) -- seemed to be of equal concern in deciding what advice to give to the student. However, Reader's Purpose (e.g. reading for enjoyment versus studying) appeared consistently to carry more weight in determining the exact nature of the instructional statement. Though this started for us as an intuition, the observation is supported in the research [Tierney and Cunningham, 1984]. The basic theoretical framework of metacognition in complex task analysis suggests that having a reason for working a task serves to activate appropriate psychological processes and to provide a basis for effective self-monitoring [Flavell, 1987]. Table 1 serves as an illustration of the advice statements delivered through the active pedagogy.

2.4 Just-in-Time Tutoring

While designing R-WISE, we carefully planned how to integrate the technology into a year-long curriculum. However, the software could be implemented as a classroom resource to be used by identified students while the teacher works with the majority of the class on another activity. As currently planned for group use in a computer laboratory, the tutor takes up about 20% of the course. The production skills necessary for reading (e.g., linear and literal decoding, word recognition and vocabulary, sentence structure and paragraph forms, variable speeds and access features of text, and other fundamentals) are not taught on the computer. This is a deliberate decision. To act as an accelerator or a learning environment, the computer has to support the *process* of literacy. Interrupting the process to teach the enabling skills (1) mixes levels, styles, and purposes of instruction, (2) creates breaks in the train of thought from which the student may not recover, and (3) results in a fairly unexciting electronic workbook.

While production skills and metacognitive skills are not interchangeable, they are correlated in that they must occur simultaneously in expert behaviors. As an extension of this, even though the tutor suggests a strategy in the prompt at the elaboration stage, the student may still be at a loss as to what to do. Recognizing that students may need more explanation, we have embedded short, interactive CAI components that promote focused practice in intellectual activities foundational to critical reading. Drawing from Palincsar and Brown's model of mental activities necessary for critical reading [Palincsar & Brown, 1985], the Just-in-Time Tutoring units (JITTs) offer coordinated instruction in four areas:

Plans and Goals	Node	Adaptive Advice
Author's Purpose: Expository Reader's Purpose: Logic Text Type: Text and Graphics	Detail to Detail ⇨ Association	Which detail comes first and why? For example, if you are reading about a process, are these details linked either in time or in space?
Author's Purpose: Expressive Reader's Purpose: Aesthetic Text Type: Poem	Inference to Detail ⇧ Generalization	How does this detail contribute to the interpretation you have made? Does the detail form part of a pattern or does it call attention to itself because it is different?
Author's Purpose: Persuasion Reader's Purpose: Information Text Type: Newspaper Article	Key Idea to Main Idea ⇩ Specification	How does this key cluster "unpack" the main idea? If the topic were divided into parts, does this cluster deal with a central issue? Does the cluster introduce arguments for and against the claim in the main idea?

Table 1: Examples of Instructional Statements for Linking

- *Predicting:* Somewhat akin to probabilistic reasoning, this activity requires that the student draw a conclusion or forecast an outcome based on interpretation of a pattern of cues within the passage. JITTs in this category tutor two specific areas: (1) activating background knowledge (or schema) as cognitive frameworks for generating likely outcomes, and (2) awareness of textual structures (e.g. transitions, sentence patterns, and other devices of coherence) for bridging informational gaps in prose presentations.

- *Clarifying:* Many studies report that readers -- even mature and accomplished adults -- view text as infallible. Failure either to detect or to acknowledge informational inconsistencies increases with less mature and less sophisticated readers. Therefore, JITTs in this category tutor (1) both the ability and the appropriateness of demanding clarity from texts, and (2) how to generate a useful "fix up" strategy once a misunderstanding has been detected. Instruction is clustered around three types of obstacles to comprehension: lexical difficulties, external inconsistencies, and internal inconsistencies [Garner, 1987].

- *Generating Questions:* In traditional instruction in reading comprehension, students are often asked to answer a set of questions about the targeted passage. Advocates of higher-order instruction in critical reading maintain that reversing the process is more effective. In this cluster of JITTs, students are given a role and a purpose emulating real-world situations and are asked to generate specific types of questions that are instrumental in solving a particular problem. JITTs in this category tutor (1) locating salient information based on a specific frame of reference, and (2) understanding the difference among prompts (e.g. questions that require recall and ones that require interpretation or insight).

- *Summarizing:* Summarizing in traditional instruction can degenerate into a kind of proforma note-taking activity. Used as a self-monitoring strategy, however, guided review becomes a means for the student to check recall of important concepts and integration of the parts into a meaningful whole. JITTs in this category tutor (1) macrorules for constructing a summary (e.g. deleting trivia and redundancy; finding superordinate categories, supplying missing main ideas), and (2) techniques for backgrounding and foregrounding information based on specific situational demands.

The student accesses a JITT from the elaboration prompt interface by clicking on the "Help" button. This action indicates that the reader wants instruction on powerful patterns for reasoning and thinking. Each of the seven reading activity nodes (detail, key idea, main idea, inference, and three types of linking) associates with instruction. A student having difficulty finding a main idea, for example, asks for help. A very brief thinking frame -- demonstrating how to use one of the four reasoning skills to find a main idea -- appears. The choice of

Summary, Clarification, Questioning, Prediction is random. If the student cannot work with the suggested operation, she asks for another and the system moves to the next option in the stack of four.

Palincsar and Brown [Palincsar & Brown, 1983] advocate the teaching of a minimal set of enriched thinking activities, as applied to a variety of text situations. Thus, we constructed 28 separate JITTs. Because of the common thread of the four mental manipulations, however, the JITTs work more like four themes (each with seven variations) than as 28 separate entities.

2.5 Notebook Consolidation

All the elaborations the student makes on icons in the elaboration interface are transferred to a notebook where they are available for review. Each map is associated with a span of paragraphs, whose number might vary from a single unit to all the paragraphs in the text. Notes are then displayed hierarchically, in descending order, starting with inference nodes. Any links made to a node are presented immediately after the target node. The type of relationship (Specification, Association, Generalization) is also indicated. The student may go to the notebook and inspect the contents at any time. These notes are more than glosses or annotations. The computer-mediated prompts emulate powerful teaching concepts and initiate a processing that is deeper and more probing than paraphrase or summary [Bretzing and Kulhavy, 1979 and 1981]. These reworked versions of the text are more than a superficial variation on the original's content and connections; they are new knowledge structures combining both the organization and information of the text with enriched reworkings by an active reader.

3 Conclusions

Pairing "concept mapping" with "node elaboration" provides a loop that (1) partners with the student to reduce the mental load and (2) helps the student to enter into a self-prompting episode. This loop takes a very sophisticated, open-ended problem and pares it down to a manageable set of options for the inexperienced reader. In brief, working in tandem with a synoptic overview and with sponsored elaboration creates a rich learning environment that nurtures the following elements crucial to reading comprehension:

- The elaboration segment encourages students to examine and interlink their previous knowledge with the new knowledge presented in the text. For example, the student may be prompted to compare through analogy a point in the content with something previously known and to come up with a superordinate proposition that encompasses and explains both. Such bridging activities discourage a simple rote incorporation of the text into memory.

- The object-oriented nature of the tutor provides a visualization for obscure mental operations. Through mapping and elaborating, the process becomes sufficiently deliberate so that the student can become both an observer and a participant in these higher-order thinking skills.

- Model building and simulations are popular concepts in today's educational software. Yet, as pointed out by Salomon, et al. [Salomon, Globerson, & Guterman, 1989], merely giving the student the capability to construct a visual representation is not as powerful as combining the manipulations of constructing a model with expert-like guidance. As typical of a computer-mediated learning environment, R-WISE's interactive feedback "[provides] superordinate functions of self-appraisal, [gives] knowledge about one's knowledge, and [initiates] self-management of cognitive activity" [Salomon, Globerson, & Guterman, 1989].

- At first glance the highly segmented nature of the adaptive advice may seem to promote short and choppy episodes of text processing. However, the embedded cueing more accurately represents the "contingency management" process of text processing characteristic of the expert. Additionally, these sprint-like activities facilitate modifying or abandoning a strategy, if necessary. And the opportunistic nature of the prompting keeps any single strategy from expanding into a workbook activity, such as the many check lists, acronymic formulas, and visual templates that seem to become ends rather than means in traditional classroom instruction.

4 References

[Armbruster & Anderson, 1982]. Armbruster, B. B., & Anderson, T. H. (1982). Ideamapping: The technique and its use in the classroom, or simulating the "ups" and "downs" of reading comprehension. (Tech. Rep. No. 36). Urbana: University of Illinois, Center for the Study of Reading.

[Bretzing & Kulhavy, 1981]. Bretzing, B. B., & Kulhavy, R. W. (1981). Note-taking and passage style. *Journal of Educational Psychology, 73*, 242-250.

[Bretzing & Kulhavy, 1979]. Bretzing, B. B., & Kulhavy, R. W. (1979). Note taking and depth of processing. *Contemporary Educational Psychology, 4*,145-153.

[Clark, 1991]. Clarke, J. H. (1991). Using visual organizers to focus on thinking. *Journal of Reading, 34* (7), 526-534.

[Flavell, 1987]. Flavell, J. H. (1987). Speculations about the nature and development of metacognition. In F. E. Weinert, & R.H. Kluwe (Eds.), *Metacognition, motivation, and understanding* (pp. 21-29). Hillsdale, NJ: Lawrence Erlbaum Associates.

[Garner, 1987]. Garner, R. (1987). *Metacognition and reading comprehension*. Norwood, NJ: Ablex.

[Palincsar & Brown, 1985]. Palincsar, A. S., & Brown, A. L. (1985). Reciprocal teaching: Activities to promote 'reading with your mind.'" In T. L. Harris, & I. J. Cooper (Eds.), *Reading, thinking and concept development: Strategies for the classroom* (pp. 147-160). New York: The College Board.

[Palincsar & Brown, 1983]. Palincsar, A. S., & Brown, A. L. (1983). Reciprocal teaching of comprehension-monitoring activities (Tech. Rep. No 269). Urbana: University of Illinois, Center for the Study of Reading.

[Salomon, Globerson, & Guterman, 1989]. Salomon, G., Globerson, T., & Guterman, E. (1989). The computer as a zone of proximal development: Internalizing reading-related metacognitions from a reading partner. *Journal of Educational Psychology, 81* (4), 620-627.

[Tierney & Cunningham, 1984]. Tierney, R. J., & Cunningham, J. W. (1984). Research on teaching reading comprehension. In P. D. Pearson (Ed.), *Handbook of reading research* (pp. 609-655). New York: Longman.

[Weinert & Kluwe, 1987]. Weinert, F. E., & Kluwe, R. H. (Eds.). (1987). *Metacognition, motivation, and understanding*. Hillsdale, NJ: Lawrence Erlbaum Associates.

Acknowledgments

R-WISE is part of a seven-year Air Force effort -- the Fundamental Skills Training project -- to design, build, evaluate, and transition advanced computer-aided instruction to the educational community. This research was done while Patricia Carlson was an associate at the Armstrong Laboratory, on leave from Rose-Hulman Institute of Technology.

Journal of Universal Computer Science, vol. 1, no. 3 (1995), 162-175
submitted: 4/1/95, accepted: 1/3/95, appeared: 28/3/95 © *Springer Pub. Co.*

Modular Range Reduction: a New Algorithm for Fast and Accurate Computation of the Elementary Functions

Marc Daumas
(Lab. LIP, Ecole Normale Supérieure de Lyon
Marc.Daumas@lip.ens-lyon.fr)

Christophe Mazenc
(Lab. LIP, Ecole Normale Supérieure de Lyon
Christophe.Mazenc@lip.ens-lyon.fr)

Xavier Merrheim
(Lab. LIP, Ecole Normale Supérieure de Lyon
Xavier.Merrheim@lip.ens-lyon.fr)

Jean-Michel Muller
(CNRS, Lab. LIP, Ecole Normale Supérieure de Lyon
Jean-Michel.Muller@lip.ens-lyon.fr)

Abstract: A new range reduction algorithm, called *Modular Range Reduction (MRR)*, briefly introduced by the authors in [Daumas et al. 1994] is deeply analyzed. It is used to reduce the arguments to exponential and trigonometric function algorithms to be within the small range for which the algorithms are valid. MRR reduces the arguments quickly and accurately. A fast hardwired implementation of MRR operates in time $O(\log(n))$, where n is the number of bits of the binary input value. For example, with MRR it becomes possible to compute the sine and cosine of a very large number accurately. We propose two possible architectures implementing this algorithm.
Key Words: Computer Arithmetic, Elementary Functions, Range Reduction
Category: B.2, G.1.0

1 Introduction

The algorithms used for evaluating the elementary functions (polynomial or rational approximations [Cody and Waite 1980, Remes 1934], Taylor expansions, shift-and-add algorithms — see [Ercegovac 1973],[DeLugish 1970],[Walther 1971] and [Asada et al. 1987], table lookup methods...) only give a correct result if the argument is within a given bounded interval. In order to evaluate an elementary function $f(x)$ for any x, one must find some "transformation" that makes it possible to deduce $f(x)$ from some value $g(x^*)$, with:

- x^* is deduced from x, x^* is called the *reduced argument*
- x^* belongs to the convergence domain of the algorithm implemented for the evaluation of g.

In practice, there are two different kinds of reduction:

1. *Additive reduction.* x^* is equal to $x - kC$, where k is an integer and C a constant (for instance, for the trigonometric functions, C is a multiple of $\pi/4$).

2. *Multiplicative reduction.* x^* is equal to x/C^k, where k is an integer and C a constant (for instance, for the logarithm function, a convenient choice for C is the radix of the number system).

Example 1 Computation of the cosine function. Assume that we want to evaluate $\cos(x)$, and that the convergence domain of the algorithm used to evaluate the sine and cosine of the reduced argument contains $[-\pi/4, +\pi/4]$. We choose $C = \pi/2$, and the computation of $\cos(x)$ is decomposed in three steps:

- Compute x^* and k such that $x^* \in [-\pi/4, +\pi/4]$ and $x^* = x - k\pi/2$
- Compute $g(x^*, k) =$

$$\begin{cases} \cos(x^*) & \text{if } k \bmod 4 = 0 \\ -\sin(x^*) & \text{if } k \bmod 4 = 1 \\ -\cos(x^*) & \text{if } k \bmod 4 = 2 \\ \sin(x^*) & \text{if } k \bmod 4 = 3 \end{cases} \tag{1}$$

- Obtain $\cos(x) = g(x^*, k)$

The previous reduction mechanism is an *additive reduction*. Let us examine another example of additive reduction.

Example 2 Computation of the exponential function. Assume that we want to evaluate e^x in a radix-2 number system, and that the convergence domain of the algorithm used to evaluate the exponential of the reduced argument contains $[0, \ln(2)]$. We choose $C = \ln(2)$, and the computation of e^x is decomposed in three steps:

- Compute $x^* \in [0, \ln(2)]$ and k such that $x^* = x - k\ln(2)$.
- Compute $g(x^*) = e^{x^*}$
- Compute $e^x = 2^k g(x^*)$

The radix-2 number system makes the final multiplication by 2^k straightforward.

Another way of performing the range reduction for the exponential function (with an algorithm whose convergence domain is $[0, 1]$) is to choose $x^* = x - \lfloor x \rfloor$, $k = \lfloor x \rfloor$, and $g(x^*) = e^{x^*}$. Then, $e^x = g(x^*) \times e^k$, and e^k can either be evaluated by performing a few multiplications — since k is an integer — or by table-lookup. Usually, this latter method is preferable, since there is no loss of accuracy when computing x^*. With the range reduction algorithm we give in the following, the former choices for x^*, g, and k become interesting, for several reasons:

- we will be able to compute x^* very accurately,
- the required convergence interval is smaller, which means that to reach the same accuracy, we need a smaller number of coefficients for a polynomial or rational approximation,
- there will not be any error when deducing e^x from $g(x^*)$.

Anyway, range reduction is more a problem for trigonometric functions than for exponentials, since, in practice, we never have to deal with exponentials of very large numbers: they merely are overflows!

Example 3 Computation of the logarithm function. Assume that we want to evaluate $\ln(x)$, $x > 0$, in a radix-2 number system, and that the convergence domain of the algorithm used to compute the logarithm of the reduced argument contains $[1/2, 1]$. We choose $C = 2$, and the computation of $\ln(x)$is decomposed in three steps:

- Compute $x^* \in [1/2, 1]$ and k such that $x^* = x/2^k$ (if x is a normalized radix-2 floating-point number, x^* is its mantissa, while k is its exponent).
- Compute $g(x^*, k) = \ln(x^*)$
- Compute $\ln(x) = g(x^*, k) + k\ln(2)$

The previous mechanism is a *multiplicative* reduction.

In practice, multiplicative reduction is not a problem: when computing the usual mathematical functions, it only occurs with logarithms and n-th roots. With these functions, as in the example above, C can be chosen equal to a power of the radix of the number system. This makes the computation of x/C^k straightforward. Therefore, in the following, we concentrate on the problem of *additive* range reduction only.

2 The Modular Range Reduction Algorithm

We focus on the following problem: we assume that we have an algorithm able to compute the function g in an interval I of the form $[-C/2 - \epsilon, +C/2 + \epsilon]$ (we call this case *"symmetrical reduction"*) or $[-\epsilon, C + \epsilon]$ (we call this case *"positive reduction"*), with $\epsilon \geq 0$. We want to compute $x^* \in I$ and an integer k such that:

$$x^* = x - kC \tag{2}$$

If $\epsilon > 0$, then x^* and k are not uniquely defined by Eq. 2. In such a case, the problem of deducing these values from x will be called *"redundant range reduction"*. For example, if $C = \frac{\pi}{2}, I = [-1, 1]$ and $x = 2.5$, then $k = 1$ and $x^* = 0.929203\ldots$ or $k = 2$ and $x^* = -0.641592\ldots$ are possible values. If $\epsilon = 0$, this problem is called *"non-redundant range reduction"*. As in many fields of computer arithmetic, redundancy will allow faster algorithms. Table 1 sums-up the different possible cases.

	$I = [-C/2 - \epsilon, C/2 + \epsilon]$	$I = [-\epsilon, C + \epsilon]$
$\epsilon = 0$	symmetrical non-redundant	positive non-redundant
$\epsilon \neq 0$	symmetrical redundant	positive redundant

Table 1. The different cases in additive range-reduction

It is worth noticing that:

1. In some practical cases, it is not necessary to fully compute k. For instance, for the trigonometric functions, if $C = \pi/2$, then one just needs to know $k \bmod 4$. If $C = 2\pi$, there is no need for any information about k.
2. With the usual algorithms for evaluating the elementary functions, one can assume that the length of the convergence domain I is greater than C, i.e. that we can perform a *redundant* range reduction. For instance, with the CORDIC algorithm, when performing rotations (see [Walther 1971]), the convergence domain is $[-1.743\ldots, +1.743\ldots]$, which is much larger than $[-\pi/2, +\pi/2]$. With polynomial or rational approximations, the convergence domain can be enlarged by adding one coefficient to the approximation.

Let us define $\lfloor x \rceil$ as the nearest integer to x. Usually, the range reduction is done by:

- Computing $k = \lfloor x/C \rfloor$ (in the case of a positive reduction), or $k = \lfloor x/C \rceil$ (in the case of a symmetrical reduction) by the means of multiplication or division.
- Computing the reduced argument $x^* = x - kC$ by the means of a multiplication by k or a table-lookup if the values kC are pre computed and stored followed by a subtraction.

The above process may be rather inaccurate (for large values of x, the final subtraction step leads to a catastrophic cancellation — although cunning tricks have been proposed to limit this cancellation [Cody and Waite 1980]). In [Daumas et al. 1994] we briefly proposed a new algorithm, called the *modular reduction algorithm* (MRR), that performs the range reduction quickly and accurately. In the following we deeply analyze that algorithm in terms of speed and accuracy, and we propose architectures implementing it.

2.1 Fixed-point reduction

First of all, we assume that the input operands are *Fixed-point radix-2 numbers*, less than 2^N. These numbers have a N-bit integer part and a p-bit fractional part. So the digit chain:

$$x_{N-1}x_{N-2}x_{N-3}\ldots x_0.x_{-1}x_{-2}\ldots x_{-p}, \quad \text{where } x_i \in \{0,1\}$$

represents the number $\sum_{i=-p}^{N-1} x_i 2^i$.

We assume that we should perform a *redundant* range reduction, and we call ν the integer such that $2^\nu < C \leq 2^{\nu+1}$.

Let us define, for $i \geq \nu$ the number $m_i \in [-C/2, C/2)$ such that $\frac{2^i - m_i}{C}$ is an integer (in the following, we will write "$m_i \equiv 2^i \bmod C$"). The Modular Range Reduction (MRR) algorithm consists in performing the two following steps:

First reduction We compute the number[1]:

$$r = (x_{N-1}m_{N-1}) + (x_{N-2}m_{N-2}) + (x_{N-3}m_{N-3}) + \ldots + (x_\nu m_\nu) \\ + x_{\nu-1}x_{\nu-2}x_{\nu-3}\ldots x_0.x_{-1}x_{-2}\ldots x_{-p} \tag{3}$$

Since the x_i's are equal to 0 or 1, this computation is reduced to the sum of $N-\nu+1$ terms. The result r of this first reduction is between $-(N-\nu+2)C/2$ and $+(N-\nu+2)C/2$. This is a consequence of the fact that all the $x_i m_i$ have an absolute value less than $C/2$, and

$$x_{\nu-1}x_{\nu-2}x_{\nu-3}\ldots x_0.x_{-1}x_{-2}\ldots x_{-p}$$

has an absolute value less than 2^ν, which is less than C.

Second reduction Define the r_i's as the digits of the result of the first reduction:

$$r = r_\ell r_{\ell-1} r_{\ell-2} \cdots r_0.r_{-1}r_{-2}\cdots$$

where $\ell = \lfloor \log_2(N-\nu+2) \rfloor$.
Let us define $\hat{r}$ as the number obtained by truncating the binary representation of r after the $\lceil -\log_2(\epsilon) \rceil$-th bit, that is (using the relation $-\lceil -x \rceil = \lfloor x \rfloor$):

$$\hat{r} = r_\ell r_{\ell-1} r_{\ell-2} \cdots r_0.r_{-1}r_{-2}\cdots r_{\lfloor \log_2(\epsilon) \rfloor}$$

$\hat{r}$ is an m-digit number, where $m = \lfloor \log_2(N-\nu+2) \rfloor + \lceil -\log_2(\epsilon) \rceil$ is a very small number in all practical cases (see the example below). If we define k as $\lfloor \frac{\hat{r}}{C} \rceil$ (resp. $\lfloor \frac{\hat{r}}{C} \rfloor$) then $r - kC$ will belong to $[-C/2-\epsilon, +C/2+\epsilon]$ (resp. $[-\epsilon, C+\epsilon]$), i.e. it will be the correct result of the symmetrical (resp. positive) range reduction.

Proof

1. *In the symmetrical case.* We have $|k - \frac{\hat{r}}{C}| \le \frac{1}{2}$, therefore $|\hat{r} - kC| \le C/2$. From the definition of $\hat{r}$, $|r - \hat{r}| \le 2^{\lfloor \log_2(\epsilon) \rfloor} \le \epsilon$, therefore:
$$|r - kC| \le \frac{C}{2} + \epsilon$$
2. *In the positive case.* We have $k \le \frac{\hat{r}}{C} < k+1$, therefore $0 \le \hat{r} - kC < C$, therefore $-\epsilon \le r - kC < C + \epsilon$.

Since k can be deduced from $\hat{r}$, this second reduction step will be implemented by looking up the value kC in a 2^m-bit entry table at the address constituted by the bits of $\hat{r}$. Fig. 1 Sums up the different steps of MRR.

During this reduction process, we perform the addition of $N-\nu+1$ terms. If these terms (namely the m_i's and the value kC of the second reduction step) are represented in fixed-point with q fractional bits (i.e. the error on each of these term is bounded by 2^{-q-1}), then the difference between the result of the computation and the exact reduced argument is bounded by $2^{-q-1}(N-\nu+1)$. In order to obtain the reduced argument x^* with the same absolute accuracy as the input argument x (i.e. p significant fixed-point fractional digits), one needs to store the m_i's and the values kC with $p + \lceil \log_2(N-\nu+1) \rceil$ fractional bits.

[1] This formula looks correct only for positive values of ν. It would be more correct, although maybe less clear, to write: $r = \sum_{i=\nu}^{N-1} x_i m_i + \sum_{i=-p}^{\nu-1} x_i 2^i$

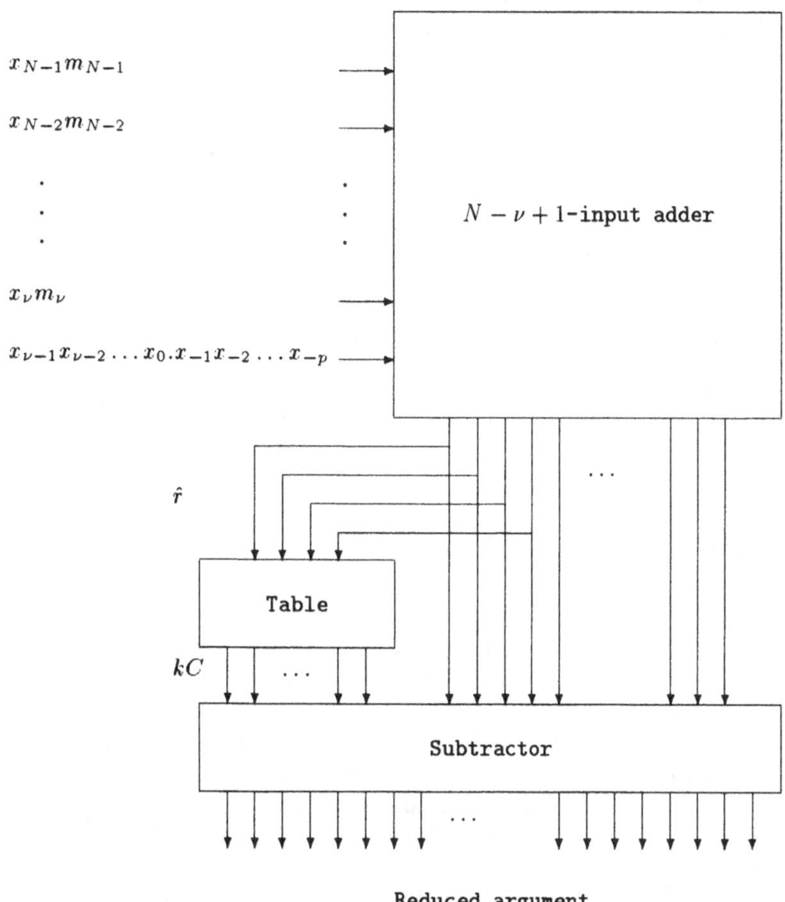

Fig. 1. The Modular Reduction Algorithm

Example 4. Assume we need to compute sines of angles between -2^{20} and 2^{20}, and that the algorithm used with the reduced arguments is CORDIC [Volder 1959], [Walther 1971]. The convergence interval I is $[-1.743\ldots,+1.743\ldots]$, therefore (since $1.743 > \frac{\pi}{2}$) we have to perform a *symmetrical redundant* range reduction, with $C = \pi$ and $\epsilon = +1.743\ldots - \frac{\pi}{2} = 0.172\ldots > 2^{-3}$. We immediately get the following parameters:

- $N = 20$ and $\nu = 2$
- The first range reduction consists of the addition of 19 terms
- $r \in [-10\pi, +10\pi]$, therefore, since $10\pi < 2^5$, the second reduction step requires a table with $5 + \lceil -\log_2 \epsilon \rceil = 8$-address bits.

– To obtain the reduced argument with p significant fractional bits, one needs to store the m_i's and the values kC with $p+5$ bits.

Assume we compute the sine of 355. The binary representation of 355 is 101100011. Therefore during the first reduction, we have to compute $m_8+m_6+m_5+m_1+1$, where:

- $m_8 = 256 - 81 \times \pi = 1.530995059226747684\ldots$
- $m_6 = 64 - 20 \times \pi = 1.1681469282041352307\ldots$
- $m_5 = 32 - 10 \times \pi = 0.5840734641020676153\ldots$
- $m_1 = 2 - \pi = -1.14159265358979323846 2\ldots$

We get $m_8+m_6+m_5+m_1+1 = 3.14162279794315729 21\ldots$ The second reduction consists in subtracting π from that result, which gives $0.00003014435336405372\ldots$, the sine of which is $0.000030144353359488449\ldots$
Therefore, $\sin(355) = -0.000030144353359488449\ldots$

2.2 Floating-point reduction

Now, assume that the input value x is a radix-2 floating-point number:

$$x = 0.x_1x_2x_3\ldots \times x_n 2^{exponent}$$

The range reduction can be performed exactly as in the fixed-point case. During the first reduction, we replace the addition of the terms m_i by the addition of the terms $m_{exponent-i}$. As previously, $m_i \equiv 2^i \bmod C$ is the number belonging to $[-C/2, C/2)$ such that $\frac{2^i - m_i}{C}$ is an integer. The main difference between this reduction method and the other ones is that during the reduction process, we just add numbers (the m_i's) of the same order of magnitude, represented in fixed-point. This makes the reduction very accurate. One can easily show that if the m_i's and the terms kC of the second reduction are represented with q fractional bits then the *absolute* error on the reduced argument is bounded by $(n+1)2^{-q-1}$. Thus, for instance it is possible to compute with good accuracy the sine and cosine of a huge floating-point number. In floating point number systems, one would prefer informations on the *relative* error: this will be discussed later.

3 Architectures for Modular Reduction

The first reduction consists of adding $N - \nu + 1$ numbers. This addition can be performed in a redundant number system (carry-save or signed-digit) in order to benefit from the carry-free ability of such a system, and/or in an arborescent way. This problem is obviously closely related to the problem of multiplying two numbers (multiplying $x = \sum_{i=0}^{q} x_i 2^i$ by $y = \sum_{j=0}^{q} y_i 2^j$ reduces to computing the sum of the $q+1$ terms $y_j 2^j x$). Therefore, almost all the classical architectures proposed in the multiplication literature (see for instance [Braun 1963], [Dadda 1965], [Harata et al. 1987], [Nakamura 1986], [Takagi et al. 1985], [Wallace 1964]), can be slightly modified in order to be used for range reduction. For instance, the architecture shown Fig. 2 is obtained from Braun's cellular array multiplier [Braun 1963], while the logarithmic-time architecture shown in Fig. 4 is a

Wallace tree [Wallace 1964]. In Fig. 3, m_{ij} is the digit of weight 2^{-j} of m_i. This similarity between the Modular Range Reduction algorithm and the multiplication makes it possible to perform both operations with the same hardware, which can save some silicon area on a circuit.

The similarity between the range reduction and the multiplication leads us to another idea: in order to accelerate the first reduction, one can perform a Booth recoding [Booth 1951], or merely a modified booth recoding [Hwang 1979], of x. This would give a signed digit (with digits -1, 0 and 1) representation of x with at least half of the digits equal to zero. Then the number of terms to be added during the first reduction would be halved.

4 Accuracy of MRR with floating-point inputs

As pointed out in section 2.2, if the input value x is a m-mantissa bit radix-2 floating-point number, and if the terms m_i's of the first reduction and the terms kC of the second reduction are represented with q fractional bits then the *absolute* error on the reduced argument is bounded by $(m+1)2^{-q-1}$. This makes it possible to evaluate sines and cosines of huge floating-point numbers with a good *absolute* accuracy. However, in floating-point, one is more concerned with the *relative* accuracy: what could be done if the result of MRR is zero or a number close to zero? This would indicate that the exact reduced argument is very small, but the computed value would only have a few (maybe not at all) significant digits. In the sequel of this paper, we deal with that problem.

4.1 How could MRR results close to zero be avoided ?

As in section 2.2, the input number x is the radix-2 floating-point number:

$$x = 0.x_1x_2x_3 \ldots x_m \times 2^{exponent}$$

Therefore, x is equal to $2^e M$, where:

$$\begin{cases} M = x_1x_2 \ldots x_m \\ e = exponent - m \end{cases}$$

M is an integer. Assume that the result of the range reduction is very small, say less than a very small real number ϵ. This means that there exists an integer k such that:

$$|x - kC| \leq \epsilon$$

This implies:

$$\left| \frac{2^e M}{k} - C \right| \leq \frac{\epsilon}{k} \tag{4}$$

This means that $\frac{2^e M}{k}$ is a very good *rational approximation* of C. To see to what extent relation (4) is likely to happen, we can compare this approximation to the sequence of the "best" possible rational approximations of C, i.e. the sequence of its *continued fraction approximations*. Let us call (P_i/Q_i) the sequence of the continued fraction approximations of C. For instance if $C = \pi$ then:

$$\frac{P_0}{Q_0} = 3 \quad \frac{P_1}{Q_1} = \frac{22}{7} \quad \frac{P_2}{Q_2} = \frac{333}{106} \quad \frac{P_3}{Q_3} = \frac{355}{113} \quad \frac{P_4}{Q_4} = \frac{103993}{33102}$$

Let us define $\mu(k)$ as the integer such that:

$$Q_{\mu(k)-1} < k \leq Q_{\mu(k)}$$

Since (from the theory of continued fractions), for each rational number $\frac{n}{d}$ such that $d \leq Q_i$, we have:

$$\left|\frac{n}{d} - C\right| \geq \left|\frac{P_i}{Q_i} - C\right|$$

we deduce, from (4):

$$\left|\frac{P_{\mu(k)}}{Q_{\mu(k)}} - C\right| \leq \frac{\epsilon}{k}$$

Therefore:

$$\left|\frac{P_{\mu(k)}}{Q_{\mu(k)}} - C\right| Q_{\mu(k)-1} \leq \epsilon \tag{5}$$

So, if one wants to get a relative error ϵ_r for input values lower than x_{max}, the way to proceed is the following one:

- evaluate $k_{max} = \lfloor \frac{x_{max}}{C} \rceil$
- compute $\epsilon = \min_{k \leq k_{max}} \left|\frac{P_{\mu(k)}}{Q_{\mu(k)}} - C\right| Q_{\mu(k)-1}$
- make sure that the number q of fractional digits used for the reduction satisfies $\frac{(m+1)2^{-q-1}}{\epsilon} \leq \epsilon_r$

5 Conclusion

We have proposed a fast and accurate algorithm to perform the range reduction for computing the elementary functions. This algorithm can be implemented using a slightly modified multiplier, so that range reduction and multiplication can be performed using the same hardware, which can save some silicon area on a circuit. Using this algorithm, accurately and quickly computing the sine of a number such as 10^{200} becomes possible.

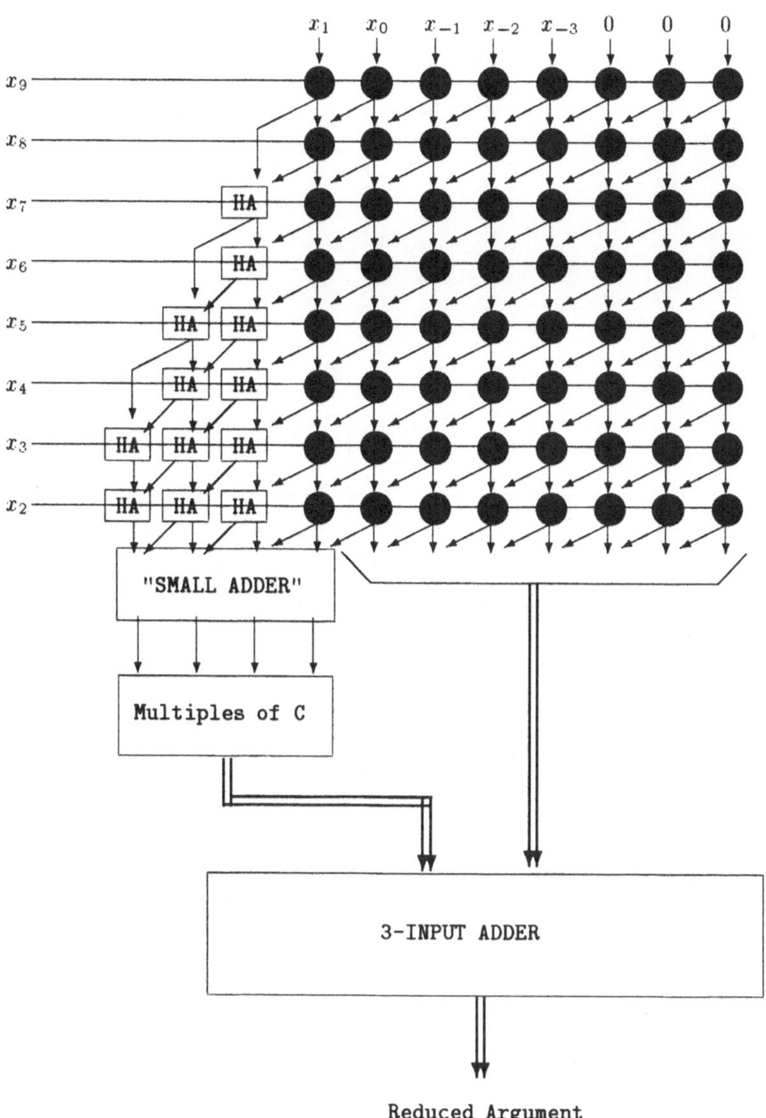

Fig. 2. A cellular array for range reduction

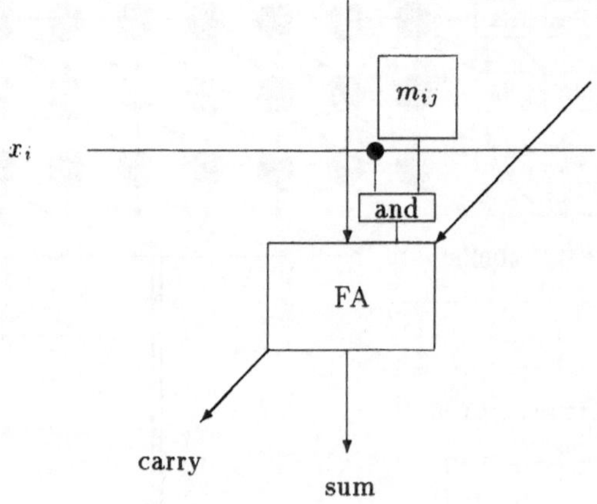

Fig. 3. A black cell of the cellular array

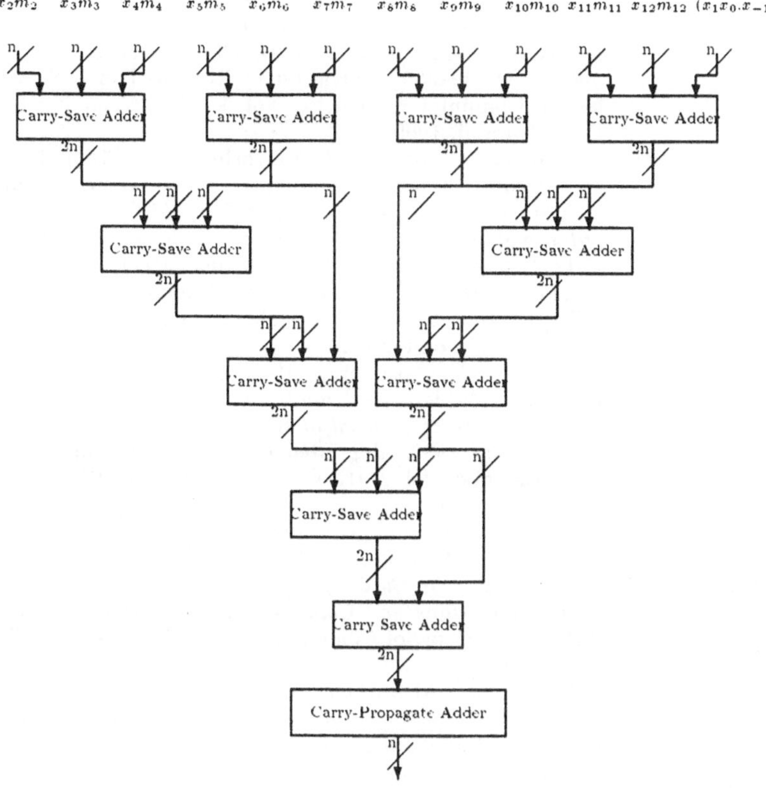

Fig. 4. A logarithmic-time range-reduction tree

References

[Asada et al. 1987] T. Asada, N. Takagi, and S. Yajima. A hardware algorithm for computing sine and cosine using redundant binary representation. *Systems and computers in Japan*, 18(8), 1987.

[Booth 1951] A.D. Booth. A signed binary multiplication technique. *Quarterly journal of mechanics and applied mathematics*, 4(2):236–240, 1951. Reprinted in E.E. Swartzlander, Computer Arithmetic, Vol. 1, IEEE Computer Society Press Tutorial, 1990.

[Braun 1963] E.L. Braun. *Digital computer design*. New York academic, 1963.

[Cody and Waite 1980] W. Cody and W. Waite. *Software Manual for the Elementary Functions*. Prentice-Hall Inc, 1980.

[Dadda 1965] L. Dadda. Some schemes for parallel multipliers. *Alta Frequenza*, 34:349–356, March 1965. Reprinted in E.E. Swartzlander, Computer Arithmetic, Vol. 1, IEEE Computer Society Press Tutorial, 1990.

[Daumas et al. 1994] M. Daumas, C. Mazenc, X. Merrheim, and J.M. Muller. Fast and Accurate Range Reduction for the Computation of Elementary Functions. In *14th IMACS World Congress on Computational and Applied Mathematics*, Atlanta, Georgia, 1994.

[Ercegovac 1973] M.D. Ercegovac. Radix 16 evaluation of certain elementary functions. *IEEE Transactions on Computers*, C-22(6), June 1973. Reprinted in E.E. Swartzlander, Computer Arithmetic, Vol. 1, IEEE Computer Society Press Tutorial, 1990.

[Harata et al. 1987] Y. Harata, Y. Nakamura, H. Nagase, M. Takigawa, and N. Takagi. A high-speed multiplier using a redundant binary adder tree. *IEEE journal of solid-state circuits*, SC-22(1):28–34, February 1987. Reprinted in E.E. Swartzlander, Computer Arithmetic, Vol. 2, IEEE Computer Society Press Tutorial, 1990.

[Hwang 1979] K. Hwang. *Computer Arithmetic Principles, Architecture and design*. Wiley & Sons Inc, 1979.

[DeLugish 1970] B. De Lugish. *A Class of Algorithms for Automatic Evaluation of Functions and Computations in a Digital Computer.* PhD thesis, Dept. of Computer Science, University of Illinois, Urbana, 1970.

[Nakamura 1986] S. Nakamura. Algorithms for iterative array multiplication. *IEEE Transactions on Computers*, C-35(8), August 1986.

[Remes 1934] E. Remes. Sur un procédé convergent d'approximations successives pour déterminer les polynômes d'approximation. *C.R. Acad. Sci. Paris*, 198, 1934.

[Takagi et al. 1985] N. Takagi, H. Yasukura, and S. Yajima. High speed multiplication algorithm with a redundant binary addition tree. *IEEE Transactions on Computers*, C-34(9), September 1985.

[Volder 1959] J. Volder. The cordic computing technique. *IRE Transactions on Electronic Computers*, 1959. Reprinted in E.E. Swartzlander, Computer Arithmetic, Vol. 1, IEEE Computer Society Press Tutorial, 1990.

[Wallace 1964] C.S. Wallace. A suggestion for a fast multiplier. *IEEE Transactions on Electronic Computers*, pages 14–17, February 1964. Reprinted in E.E. Swartzlander, Computer Arithmetic, Vol. 1, IEEE Computer Society Press Tutorial, 1990.

[Walther 1971] J. Walther. A unified algorithm for elementary functions. In *Joint Computer Conference Proceedings*, 1971. Reprinted in

E.E. Swartzlander, Computer Arithmetic, Vol. 1, IEEE Computer Society Press Tutorial, 1990.

Journal of Universal Computer Science, vol. 1, no. 3 (1995), 176-194
submitted: 13/3/95, accepted: 20/3/95, appeared: 28/3/95 © Springer Pub. Co.

Special Cases of Division

R W Doran

(The University of Auckland, New Zealand. bob@cs.auckland.ac.nz)

Abstract: This surveys algorithms and circuits for integer division in special cases. These include division by constants, small divisors, exact divisors, and cases where the divisor and the number base have a special relationship. The related operation of remainder is also covered. Various prior techniques are treated in a common framework. Worked examples are provided together with examples of practical application.
Category: B2.0 Arithmetic and Logic Circuits

1 Introduction

Division, although known in theory to be capable of O(log n) solution [Beame, Cooke and Hoover 1986], is difficult to implement with high performance in practice. However, there are many special cases where division is much easier, so that fast algorithms may be used. Many "tricks" have been discovered over the years. Some of these are not well known and there are others that are familiar to practitioners but have not been described in the literature that is easy to access. The purpose of this paper is to survey the special cases of division and describe them in a uniform manner. We will consider only non-negative integers, extended to fixed-point number representation in some cases.

1.1 Notation

To describe division we will use the notation:

D	dividend	d	divisor
q	quotient	r	remainder

where all the values involved are non-negative integers, with d > 0.

In general, division is the process that, given D and d, finds q and r so that D = q*d + r where $0 \le r < d$. We will sometimes express q as D div d and r as D mod d (r being often referred to as the residue modulo d - remainder and modulo are sometimes defined differently for signed numbers, but are the same for the non-negative integers with which we are concerned here). Usually, the term *division* is restricted to finding q, and the corresponding process of finding r as *remaindering.*

We will assume that integers are presented, using a positive integer base b, as n-digit vectors. In particular we have **D, d, q, r**, where, for example:

$$D = \mathbf{D}_{n-1}\, b^{n-1} + \mathbf{D}_{n-2}\, b^{n-2} + \ldots\ldots + \mathbf{D}_0 b^0$$

The values $\mathbf{D}_i$ are the digits in the base b representation. $0 \le \mathbf{D}_i < b$. The digits are uniquely determined.

We will often use base 10 in examples although most circuits will use binary representation in practice.

1.2 Relationship between div and mod

The operations of division and remaindering are closely related and are reducible to each other. That the remainder can be found after division is obvious, for:

$$r = D \bmod d = D - (D \operatorname{div} d)*d = D - q*d$$

Knowledge of the remainder can reduce division to the special case where the dividend is an exact multiple of the divisor, for D - (D mod d) = q*d. This can simplify the process of division in some circumstances to be covered below. However, the ability to perform remaindering can allow the quotient to be derived without further division, but the process depends on the representation of the numbers and the standard algorithm for division.

Write $D^{(i)} = \mathbf{D}_{n-1}\, b^{n-1-i} + \mathbf{D}_{n-2}\, b^{n-2-i} + \ldots\ldots + \mathbf{D}_i\, b^0$ and $R^{(i)} = D^{(i)} \bmod d$. $D^{(i)}$ is the leading n-i digits of D regarded as an integer. The $R^{(i)}$ are called "partial remainders". The $D^{(i)}$ are each represented as a subrange of the digits **D**. It is possible from **D** to quickly make enough copies of its digits so as to represent all $D^{(i)}$ simultaneously (by *quickly*, we mean logarithmically in terms of time or levels of logic in a circuit). Given the $D^{(i)}$, if remaindering can can be performed quickly then we can apply it to all $D^{(i)}$ in parallel and so obtain all the $R^{(i)}$ quickly.

The standard process of division is to produce the quotient digits $\mathbf{q}_i$ in order, commencing with the high order $\mathbf{q}_{n-1}$. At step i (i from n-1 down to 0) we divide d into the "concatenation" of $R^{(i+1)}$ with the next digit $\mathbf{D}_i$ to find $\mathbf{q}_i$ and $R^{(i)}$. For example, in the following "trace" of standard long division the partial remainders are picked out in bold.

```
       0 2 2 6
2 5 | 5 6 7 3
      0
      5 6
      5 0
        6 7
        5 0
        1 7 3
        1 5 0
          2 3
```

At each step we have to perform the division expressed by $R^{(i+1)}*b+\mathbf{D}_i = d*\mathbf{q}_i + R^{(i)}$ (assume that $R^{(n)} = 0$). As we can find the $R^{(i)}$ in parallel quickly we can then determine the $\mathbf{q}_i$ by dividing each $R^{(i+1)}*b+\mathbf{D}_i$ by d.

Thus the standard process allows us to use remaindering to reduce general division to steps that involve division that produces a small quotient (the $\mathbf{q}_i$ are less than b) - this is the special case that we will cover first, below. However, here the situation is even more special. From above, we have $d*\mathbf{q}_i = R^{(i+1)}*b + \mathbf{D}_i - R^{(i)}$ which can be calculated quickly. ($R^{(i+1)}*b + \mathbf{D}_i$ involves no calculation, it is merely notation for concatenation. The subtraction of $R^{(i)}$ may be performed quickly in a borrow lookahead circuit.)

We now have division that is *exact* and with a *small quotient*. Because $\mathbf{q}_i$ is in the range from 0 to b-1, $\mathbf{q}_i$ may be deduced quickly from knowledge of the constant multiples of d in the range from 0 to b-1.

Example:

D = 5673, d = 25, **D** = (5,6,7,3)
$(D^{(3)},D^{(2)},D^{(1)},D^{(0)})$ = (5,56,567,5673), $(R^{(3)},R^{(2)},R^{(1)},R^{(0)})$ = (5,6,17,23),
d***q** =(0,50,50,150). {calculated as $d*\mathbf{q}_i = R^{(i+1)}*10 + \mathbf{D}_i - R^{(i)}$ }
q = (0,2,2,6) {because 25*0 = 0, 25*1 = 25, 25*2 = 50 etc.)

In even more-special cases the process of finding the quotient digits is further simplified. For example, because $\mathbf{q}_i = 0$ iff $R^{(i+1)}*b+\mathbf{D}_i = R^{(i)}$, in the case of binary division $\mathbf{q}_i$ is fully determined by this comparison.[1]

In summary, if the values $R^{(i)}$ are known it is possible to determine the $\mathbf{q}_i$ quickly in parallel. We will see situations where it is much easier to find the partial remainders than to perform division directly, which is why we are treating special cases of both division and remaindering. The general process of deducing quotient from remainders in parallel is illustrated in [Fig. 1] for n = 8 (this is trivial but it is shown as it will be a component of later circuits, although simplified further - note that the divisor d is an assumed input to all subcircuits).

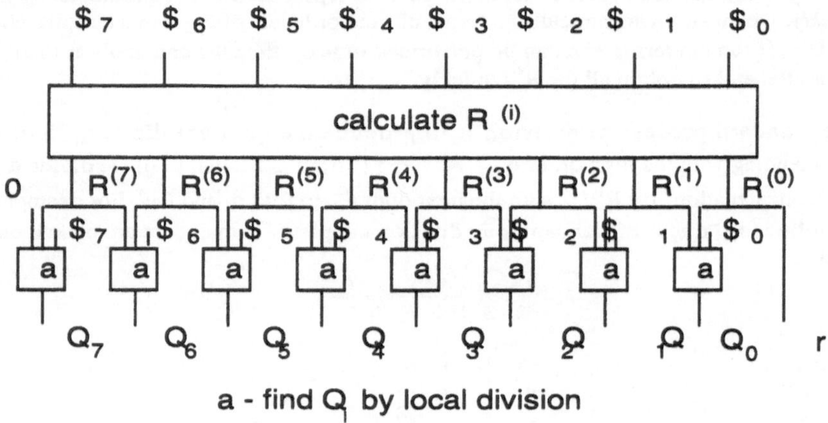

Figure 1: Derivation of quotient from remainders

2 Small quotient

There are sometimes circumstances where it is known that the quotient is small, so that we can find it by using case analysis. Because D = d*q + r, for each possible q' we know that q = q' iff $d*q' \le D < d*(q'+1)$.

One situation arose in the standard division process above where we needed to find each $\mathbf{q}_i$ in turn from $R^{(i+1)} *b+\mathbf{D}_i = d*\mathbf{q}_i + R^{(i)}$, i.e. by dividing d into $R^{(i+1)} *b+\mathbf{D}_i$ to find the quotient $\mathbf{q}_i$ that we know is < b. Using the same data as above:

Example:

> $R^{(i+1)}*b + \mathbf{D}_i$ produces $d*\mathbf{q}_i + R^{(i)}$ as (5,56,67,173), which are, by inspection, in the ranges (0-24,50-74,50-74,150-174), so q = (0,2,2,6).

[1]In [Beame, Cooke and Hoover 1986] this reduction is credited to [Alt and Blum 1983], but it appears to have been well understood by practitioners, and is used in, for example, [Cocke et. al. 1970].

Another situation arises in arithmetic modulo d where $x < d$ and we want to form $(x * y) \bmod d$, where $y < b$, the number base, which is small. Setting $D = x*y$, and $q = D$ div d, we know that $q < b$. Because there are only a limited number of possibilities for the quotient, it can be found first and used to calculate the remainder which has a much wider range of values.

Given that the quotient is small, its value may be estimated in many cases by looking at the first few digits of the values i*d, for the possible values of i, rather than by performing full comparisons.

Example:

> d =567, q < 5.
> From the first digits of d we can make the following definite decisions.
> $D < 0500$ -> $q = 0$,
> $0600\ ^{2}\ D < 1100$ -> $q = 1$,
> $1200\ ^{2}\ D < 1700$ -> $q = 2$,
> $1800\ ^{2}\ D < 2200$ -> $q = 3$,
> $D\ ^{3}2300$ -> $q = 4$.
> So, if D = 1939, we know that, q=3 because D has leading digits 19 and so $r = D - q*d = 238$. However, if D commences with 17 we will have to consider more than two digits of D in order to distinguish between q=2 and q=3.

Full comparisons will be needed to distinguish some cases unless d has other special properties, or unless complete accuracy in determining q is not required.

3 Constant divisor

3.1 Multiplication by the reciprocal of the divisor

Division by d (_0) may always be performed by multiplication by its reciprocal 1/d.

Example:

> to divide D = 99866 by d = 167 find 1/d ~ 0.005988.
> 99866/167 = 99866*0.005988 = 597.99 = 598 rounded.

This is the basis for division in computers such as the Cray 1 series where there is no division instruction. Rather, an instruction is provided that gives an approximation to the reciprocal. Division is performed using software to refine the reciprocal approximation to full precision and to multiply by the dividend [Iliffe 1982]. It is not a popular method for implementing division in hardware because repetitive methods are more facile. However, if there is a need to implement division by a particular constant then the reciprocal may be calculated once and for all in advance.

Perhaps the most common use of division by a constant is in conversion between number bases. There are two approaches, one which generates the least significant digit first as the remainder from division by a small constant - we will encounter that later. The other is to divide by a large constant and generate the most significant digit first. Suppose it is required to convert an n-bit binary number N into a BCD decimal representation providing always the maximum number of digits m, where $10^m\ ^{3}\ 2^n$. Firstly, N can be divided by 10^m (in binary) then the quotient multiplied successively by 10 (in binary, multiplication by a small constant can, of course, be performed by a sequence of additions and shifts), collecting 4-bit decimal BCD digits as they appear to the left of the binary point. Division by 10^m can be performed by multiplying by $1/10^m$ (kept with sufficient precision to convert the largest binary integer).

Example:

Assume n=6 and m=2.
$d=10^2 = 1100100$ and $1/d = 1/10^2 = 0.10100111*2^{-6}$.
To convert N=110001 (49) to BCD, first form:
$N/d = N*(1/d) = 110001*0.10100111*2^{-6} = 0.01111110$
Now, 1. N*(1/d) * 1010 (ten) = 0100.1111, i.e. 0100 (4) + 0.1111
2. 0.1111*1010 (ten) = 1001.0110, i.e. 1001 (9) plus an insignificant remainder. So $((110001 / 10^2)*10)*10 = (4*10^1 + 9)$
i.e. $110001 = 4*10^1 + 9$.

3.2 Direct calculation of the remainder for constant divisor

Calculation of D mod d, where d is a constant, can be performed by calculating D - (D*(1/d))*d, but this requires two multiplications. An alternative method is based on stored constants and properties of the modulus operation.

$$\begin{aligned} D \bmod d &= (\mathbf{D}_{n-1}\, b^{n-1} + \mathbf{D}_{n-2}\, b^{n-2} + ... + \mathbf{D}_0 b^0) \bmod d \\ &= ((\mathbf{D}_{n-1}\, b^{n-1}) \bmod d + (\mathbf{D}_{n-2}\, b^{n-2}) \bmod d + + (\mathbf{D}_0 b^0) \bmod d) \bmod d \\ &= E \bmod d, \end{aligned}$$

where $E = (\mathbf{D}_{n-1}\, b^{n-1}) \bmod d + (\mathbf{D}_{n-2}\, b^{n-2}) \bmod d + ... + (\mathbf{D}_0 b^0) \bmod d$

The constants $(k\, b^i) \bmod d$ $(0 \le k < b)$ can be stored in n tables with b entries of n digits, $(\mathbf{D}_i\, b^i) \bmod d$ selected by table look up, and then E found as the sum. The addition can be performed in software, or, in hardware, in logarithmic time using a tree of adders.

E is in the limited range from 0 to n*d, so we can now use techniques for small quotients to determine k so that $kd \le E < (k+1)d$. D mod d, = E mod d, is then E - kd. This can again be performed in software or, if speed is of essence, in hardware by comparing E in parallel with all the constants i*d.

[Fig. 2] shows an example for the case of n=8. Note that the additions, other than the last, may be carry-save so that the adder tree has similar cost and complexity to a multiplier.

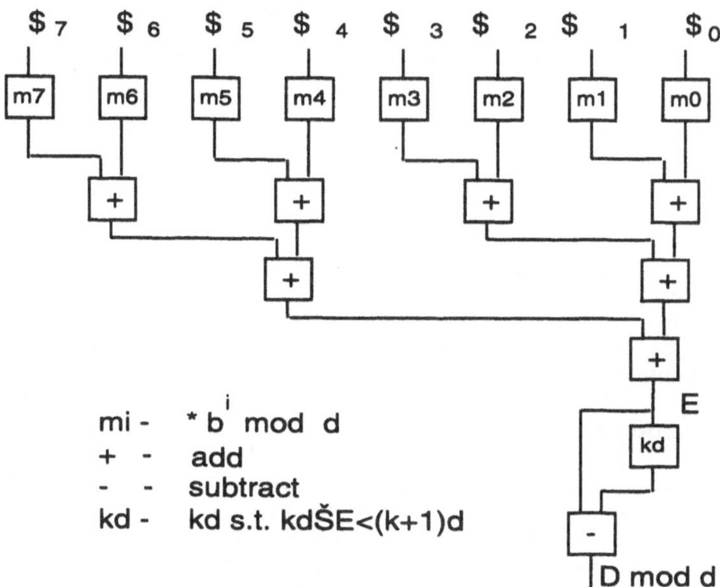

Figure 2: Calculation of D mod d when d is constant

A direct application of remaindering is range scaling for fixed-point numbers. Many processes for calculating elementary functions require that the argument be within a limited range, eg. $[0 : \pi/2]$ for sin. To calculate sin(x) it is necessary to reduce the range of x by determining x mod $\pi/2$. It is possible to make the final "small quotient" step fast, using only a small table look-up, if, as is often the case, the actual range of convergence is somewhat wider than the target range [Daumas et. al. 1994]. That is, we can tolerate an error in finding kd when x is close to a multiple of d as the effect is to slightly increase the range, in this case from $[0 : \pi/2]$ to $[0 : \pi/2 + \text{delta}]$.

4 Small divisor

Small divisors are important in both theory and practice. If small is taken to mean of length O(log n), then there are $O(n^k)$ different numbers representable. Dealing with a variable integer of length O(log n) is thus the same as considering $O(n^k)$ different cases. A hardware selection from $O(n^k)$ results may be made in time O(log n). Hence, operating on small variables is equivalent, in speed, to operating with constants, plus time O(log n) for selection.

One use of small variables is in residue arithmetic [Szabo and Tanaka 1967]. In residue arithmetic, O(n/log n) distinct prime numbers m_i each of length O(log n) are chosen. A number X of length O(n) is then represented by the small numbers x_i where x_i = X mod m_i. The advantage of this system is that (X *op* Y) mod M is performed, for many *op*, as (x_i *op* y_i) mod m_i in parallel. Unfortunately, division is, in general, not in this category. Regardless of the benefit of this approach it leads to interest in operations on numbers of length O(log n).

For example (from [Beame, Cooke and Hoover 1986]), to calculate (D mod d) mod m where D is n digits and m and d are O(log n) digits and d is variable. Tables of the constants $\mathbf{D}_i$ b^i mod d for every possible $\mathbf{D}_i$ and d have size $b{*}n^k$ for each i. Reference to such a table given D_i and d takes time log ($b*n^k$) = O(log n). Thus, the direct calculation approach for determining D mod d given above for constant d may be used with variable small d to also give a O(log n) algorithm.

Under the same conditions, (D div d) mod m may be found using the equivalence between mod and div. For (D^{-1}) mod m (where D^{-1} is defined as the integer < m such that $D*D^{-1}$ = 1 mod m), we may compute y = D mod m and then look up y^{-1} in a table of size n^k.

A related trick is used in practice in ordinary full division or calculation of inverse. To start an iterative process going an approximation to the reciprocal of the divisor is needed. This may be looked up in a table using the first few bits of the divisor itself. This is used, for example, in the reciprocal approximation instruction in the Cray computers mentioned above [Iliffe 1982].

5 Small constant divisor

When the divisor is both constant and small there are further possibilites for simplifying division. This fortuitous combination does occur in practice. A hardware application is with interleaved memory banks. If there are k banks then an address A may be located in bank *A mod k* at address *A div k*. Similar calculations are required at the software level if the size of data items packed into memory differs from the memory word size. Another application is in conversion between number bases.

There are two directions that may be taken, one based on remaindering and the other on multiplication by reciprocals.

5.1 Division following derivation of remainders

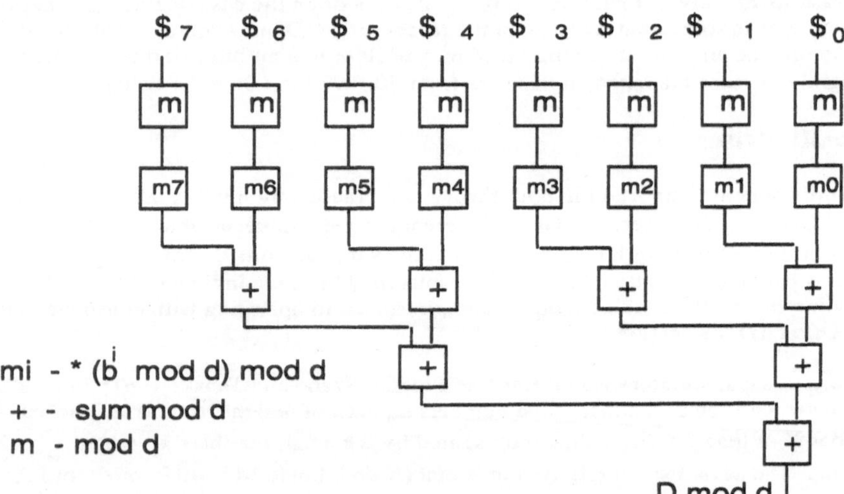

Figure 3. Remainder calculation for small divisor

Here one applies the same technique as before for constant divisors, but, because the divisor is also small, it is possible for all additions to be perfromed modulo the divisor, keeping the intermediate values small. The obvious circuit, [Fig. 3], calculates D_i mod d for each digit, then finds ($\mathbf{D}_i$ mod d)*(2^i mod d) mod d. At each level of the adder tree, addition mod d is performed.

Example:

D=93670341, d = 7, 10^i mod d = (3, 1, 5, 4, 6, 2, 3,1)
$\mathbf{D}_i$ * 10^i mod d = (6, 3, 2, 0, 0, 6, 5, 1)
-> (2, 2, 6, 6)
-> (4, 5)
-> (2)

Because the partial remainders are small, it is now reasonable to calculate all in parallel and hence deduce the complete quotient. The above approach has to be modified because the intermediate steps in calculating D mod d (= $R^{(0)}$) do not help in finding the other partial remainders $R^{(i)}$. A clever procedure [Cocke et. al. 1970] is to omit the *b^i mod d step and do the reduction addition as A*2^j+B mod d steps, thus spreading the "*b^i " operation over multiple stages. This gives the approach shown for n=8 in [Fig. 4] , refining the circuit of [Fig. 1].

Example:

D=93670341, d = 7, m = *mod 7*
p1 = *(A*3+B) mod 7*, p2 = *(A*2+B) mod 7*, p3 = *(A*6 + B) mod 7*,
p4 = *(A*4+B) mod 7*, c = *(A*10+B) div 7*.
(9,3,6,7,0,3,4,1) -> (2,3,6,0,0,3,4,1) -> (2,2,6,4,0,3,4,6) ->
(2,2,5,1,0,3,1,5) -> (2,2,5,1,3,5,5,2)
So $R^{(i)}$ = (0,2,2,5,1,3,5,5,2). $R^{(i+1)}$ *10 + $\mathbf{D}_i$ = (09,23,26,57,10,33,54,51)
q = ($R^{(i+1)}$ *10 + $\mathbf{D}_i$) div 7 = (1,3,3,8,1,4,7,7) with remainder 2.

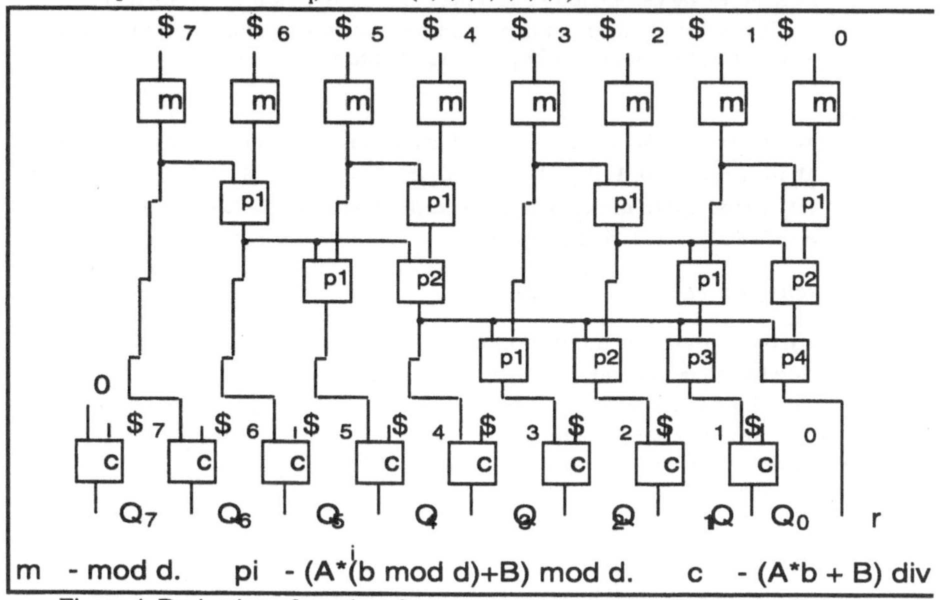

Figure 4: Derivation of quotient from remainders with small constant divisor

5.2 Multiplication by reciprocal

The constant divisor may be factored into two constants as $d = d_1 * d_2$, where d_1 has prime factors that are also factors of the number base b and where d_2 is relatively prime to b. Division by d can be performed by successive division by d_1 and d_2, which need to be treated differently.

Divisor factor of number base

The factor d_1 can be composed into the product of a series of factors c_j such that c_j ² b. Division by d_1 can be performed by successive (or composed) division by c_j. Concentrating on the ith digit:

$$\mathbf{D} = \ldots \mathbf{D}_{i+1}\, b^{i+1} + \mathbf{D}_i\, b^i + \ldots, \text{ so}$$

$$\mathbf{D} \text{ div } c_j = \ldots (\mathbf{D}_{i+1} \text{ div } c_j + (\mathbf{D}_{i+1} \text{ mod } c_j)/c_j) * b^{i+1} + (\mathbf{D}_i \text{ div } c_j + (\mathbf{D}_i \text{ mod } c_j)/c_j) * b^i + \ldots$$

$$= \ldots (\mathbf{D}_{i+1} \text{ div } c_j + (\mathbf{D}_{i+1} \text{ mod } c_j) * (b \text{ div } c_j) * b^{-1}) * b^{i+1}$$
$$+ (\mathbf{D}_i \text{ div } c_j + (\mathbf{D}_i \text{ mod } c_j) * (b \text{ div } c_j) * b^{-1}) * b^i + \ldots$$

$$= \ldots + ((\mathbf{D}_{i+1} \text{ mod } c_j) * (b \text{ div } c_j) + \mathbf{D}_i \text{ div } c_j) * b^i + \ldots$$

The multiplier of b^i in this expression $= (\mathbf{D}_{i+1} \text{ mod } c_j)*(b \text{ div } c_j) + \mathbf{D}_i \text{ div } c_j$. This is non-negative and has maximum value of $((b-1) \text{ mod } c_j)*(b \text{ div } c_j)+ (b-1) \text{ div } c_j = (c_j-1)*(b \text{ div } c_j)+ (b \text{ div } c_j) -1 = c_j*(b \text{ div } c_j)-(b \text{ div } c_j) + (b \text{ div } c_j) -1= c_j*(b \text{ div } c_j) -1 = b-1$. Thus the expression above represents the unique representation base b of D div c_j. The value of each digit is found from the local expressions $(\mathbf{D}_{i+1} \text{ mod } c_j)*(b \text{ div } c_j) + \mathbf{D}_i \text{ div } c_j$ which may be calculated in parallel. That is, division by prime factor of the number base is essentially a trivial operation on digit-size numbers. In particular, of course, if $c_j = b$ then the ith digit is $\mathbf{D}_{i+1}$ - division reduces to shifting.

Example:

$\mathbf{D} = (5, 6, 7, 8, 4, 3, 2, 1)$, $d = c_j = 2$ is a factor of the base 10. b div $c_j = 5$
$\mathbf{D}_i \text{ mod } c_j = (1, 0, 1, 0, 0, 1, 0, 1)$, $\mathbf{D}_i \text{ div } c_j = (2, 3, 3, 4, 2, 1, 1, 0)$.
$(\mathbf{D}_{i+1} \text{ mod } c_j)*(b \text{ div } c_j) + \mathbf{D}_i \text{ div } c_j = (0+2,5+3,0+3,5+4,0+2,0+1,5+1,0+0)$
$= (2, 8, 3, 9, 2, 1, 6, 0)$, remainder 1.

Divisor relatively prime to number base

Division by d_2 is more of a challenge and must, in general, be performed by multiplication by the reciprocal. However, because d_2 is relatively prime to the number base it can be shown that the reciprocal of d_2 is a continued repeating fraction base b. Therefore, multiplication by the reciprocal can be performed by multiplying once by the repeated section, then performing repeated addition. This process is of advantage when the repeated section is tiny (it can be of length up to d_2).

Example:

Divide 240132 by 3 in base 5.
$d_2 = 3$, $d_2^{-1} = 0.13131313.....$
240132*13= 4222321
D = 42223.21 + 422.2321+ 4.222321+ 0.04222321+... = 43210.31....

The additions may be performed in parallel in a tree-like structure but such a circuit is not much more simple than a general multiplier. However, with serial implementation in firmware the technique has certainly been used in practice ([Jacobsohn 1973], [Artzy et. al 1976]) in small computers.

6 Dividend exact multiple of divisor

Having a dividend D ($=D^{(0)}$) that is an exact multiple of the divisor d does not really simplify the division process for standard representations because it is certainly not the case that d divides the other $D^{(i)}$ exactly. However, it can be a help in special cases and with other representations.

In the case of modular representation, if the inverse of X mod M exists and if X = $(....x_i,....)$ then the representation of X^{-1} mod M is $(....x_i^{-1} \bmod m_i....)$. If Y=kX mod M then YX^{-1} mod M is Y div X and is represented by $(....y_i{*}x_i^{-1}...)$. In other words, exact division works precisely as expected in modular representation. Unfortunately, if Y_kX then YX^{-1} mod M has no obvious relationship to Y div X, nor is there an obvious means of calculating quickly (Y div X)mod M.

A situation where prior knowledge of the remainder can be helpful is in calculating the quotient for small constant divisors that are relatively prime to the number base. Suppose that we know the remainder $R^{(0)}$, then $d{*}\mathbf{q}_0 = R^{(1)}{*}b + \mathbf{D}_0 - R^{(0)}$. If d and b are relatively prime there is only one k for which $kb + (\mathbf{D}_0 - R^{(0)})$ is a multiple of d by a factor less than b. We can thus deduce both $\mathbf{q}_0$ and $R^{(1)}$. Having found $R^{(1)}$ we can then deduce $\mathbf{q}_1$ and $R^{(2)}$ from $d{*}\mathbf{q}_1 = R^{(2)}{*}b + \mathbf{D}_1 - R^{(1)}$, and so on. Thus it becomes possible to calculate the quotient, and partial remainders, from least significant digit first.

Example:

d = 7, b = 10

Table for solving $d{*}\mathbf{q}_i = R^{(i+1)}{*}b + (\mathbf{D}_i - R^{(i)})$:

$(\mathbf{D}_i - R^{(i)})$	-6	-5	-4	-3	-2	-1	0	1	2	3	4	5	6	7	8	9
$\mathbf{q}_i$	2	5	8	1	4	7	0	3	6	9	2	5	8	1	4	7
$R^{(i+1)}$	2	4	6	1	3	5	0	2	4	6	0	3	5	0	2	4

D = 93670341, $R^{(0)} = 2$

$\mathbf{D}_0 - R^{(0)} = 1-2 = -1$ so $R^{(1)} = 5$, $\mathbf{q}_0 = 7$

$\mathbf{D}_1 - R^{(1)} = 4-5 = -1$ so $R^{(2)} = 5$, $\mathbf{q}_1 = 7$

....

$\mathbf{D}_7 - R^{(7)} = 9-2 = 7$ so $R^{(8)} = 0$, $\mathbf{q}_7 = 1$

The value $R^{(n)}$ is a check on errors in our calculation because $R^{(n)} = 0$ iff the remainder $R^{(0)}$ was correct. If the remainder $R^{(0)}$ is not known, it is possible to calculate from right to left the supposed quotient for each of the d possible remainders and then select as the correct one that for which $R^{(n)} = 0$.

In [Artzy et. al. 1976] the following elegant version of reciprocal multiplication is given.

Suppose d is relatively prime to the number base then, as before, 1/d is a repeating base-b fraction $0.s_1 s_2 ...s_m s_1 s_2 ...s_m s_1 s_2 ...s_m ......$

If $s = s_1 s_2 ...s_m$ then $1/d = s/(b^m-1)$. Now, suppose that D = qd is an exact multiple of d, then $D{*}s = q{*}d{*}s = q{*}(b^m-1) = q{*}b^m - q$. So, if $q < b^m$, then q is the base-complement of the last m digits of D*s (because $q{*}b^m$ has low-order m digits zero).

Example:

$b = 10$, $d = 27$
$1/d= 0.037037037037.... = 037/(10^3-1)$, $s = 037$
If D=1134 then D*s = 41958, so q = 1000-958 = 42

To convert this into a more practical procedure [Artzy et. al 1976] propose first restricting D to be $< b^m$, in which case $q < b^m$ and it can also be shown that $b^m - (b^m-q)$ ^{2} s only if d divides D exactly, so the error of d not dividing D exactly can be detected. If D^3b^m then the technique is extended to use ss of length 2m, then ssss of length 4m etc., until D is within range, looking at the last 2m, 4m etc digits of D*ss, D*ssss etc. Multiplication by ss, ssss etc. is performed as $*s*(b^m+1)$, $*s*(b^m+1)*(b^{2m}+1)$ etc. (multiplication by $b^{km}+1$, is, of course, shift and add).

Example:

d = 27, D=1466667, length 7 but s = 037 is length 3 so have to use ssss.
D*037 = 54266679
D*037037 = d*037*1001= 54266679*1001 = 54320945679
D*037037037037 = d*037*1001*1000001 = 54320945679*1000001
= 54320999999945679
So q = 1000000000000 - 999999945679 = 54321.
54321< 037037037037, so the division was indeed exact.

A practical use of division where it is known that d divides D exactly is where D is a, for example, byte offset previously constructed by multiplication of an offset q by the element size (in bytes) d.

7 Divisor related to the number base

We have encountered already some simplifying relationships between the divisor and number base. These included cases where the divisor divides the base exactly and where the divisor and the base are mutually prime. Another relationship of interest is when the divisor is close to the base in value.

7.1 Divisor close to number base in value

If the divisor is very close to the base, then it is possible to find the first digit of the quotient very quickly because it is the first digit of the dividend. This process may be continued and used to calculate the next quotient digit at each stage of the division process. The example below has the divisor close to the base but works with fixed point fractions. The same procedure may be applied to integer division where the divisor is close to some power of the base i.e. the same procedure with the point shifted to the right.

Example:

$d = 9.934$, $D = R^{(3)} =$	5678
$q_2 = 5$, $R^{(2)} = 5678 - 993.4*5 =$	711.0
$q_1 = 7$, $R^{(1)} = 711.0 - 99.34*7=$	15.62
$q_0 = 1$, $R^{(0)} = 15.62 - 9.934*1=$	5.686
$5678 = 571*9.934 + 5.686$	

This process is an important one that forms the basis of some of the fastest practical division algorithms [Ercegovac et. al. 1983] .

A case of particular interest is when the divisor is the constant b-1 or b+1. In fact, when the representation is binary many small integer divisors are in this form or are related to it. A binary number may be regarded as being base 4 (each digit of 2 bits), base 8 (each digit of 3 bits) etc. Division by 3 is by 4-1, by 5 4+1, by 7 8-1, by 9 8+1, by 17 16+1 etc

7.2 Division by Base-1

In this case remaindering is very simple. Because b = d+1, b mod d = 1 and so b^k mod d =1. Hence

$$R^{(i)} = D^{(i)} \text{ mod } d = (\mathbf{D}_{n-1}\, b^{n-1-i} + \mathbf{D}_{n-2}\, b^{n-2-i} + \ldots\ldots + \mathbf{D}_i\, b^0) \text{ mod } d$$
$$= (\mathbf{D}_{n-1} + \mathbf{D}_{n-2} + \ldots\ldots + \mathbf{D}_i) \text{ mod } d.$$

The reduction of the sum of digits mod d can be performed serially with the recurrence:

$$R^{(i)} = (R^{(i+1)} + \mathbf{D}_i) \text{ mod } d$$

or can be calculated with parallel tree circuits. If solely $R^{(0)}$ is required then one can use a tree circuits as in [Fig. 2]. If all $R^{(i)}$ are required a circuit as in the top part of [Fig. 5] is appropriate.

The calculation of the remainder mod b-1 is used in checking arithmetic in the classic "casting out nines" procedure. For example, to check the full-sized multiplication A*B=C the relationship ((A mod d) * (B mod d)) mod d = C mod d is tested, where the multiplication is much simpler. In the manual approach the digits are not summed modularly digit by digit but rather they are summed using normal arithmetic and the process reapplied repeatedly until one digit remains:

Example:

D = 93608719, b = 10, d = 9
D mod 9 = (9+3+6+0+8+7+1+9) mod 9 = 43 mod 9 = (4+3) mod 9 = 7

The same approach is used in computers for error checking. Usually, a binary number is regarded as being in base 4 and the remainder found mod 3. The digits 0, 1, 2 are kept in decoded form 100, 010, 001, to simplify the nodes in the tree circuit.

Proceeding further, with the remainders known we can find the quotient as in section 1.2 from $R^{(i+1)}*b+\mathbf{D}_i = d*\mathbf{q}_i + R^{(i)}$. We have:

$$d*\mathbf{q}_i = R^{(i+1)}*b + \mathbf{D}_i - R^{(i)} = R^{(i+1)}*d + R^{(i+1)} + \mathbf{D}_i - R^{(i)}, \text{ so}$$
$$\mathbf{q}_i = R^{(i+1)} + (\mathbf{D}_i + R^{(i+1)} - R^{(i)}) \text{ div } d$$
$$= R^{(i+1)} + (R^{(i+1)} + \mathbf{D}_i - (R^{(i+1)} + \mathbf{D}_i) \text{mod } d) \text{ div } d$$
$$= R^{(i+1)} + (R^{(i+1)} + \mathbf{D}_i) \text{ div } d$$

To summarise:

$$R^{(i)} = (R^{(i+1)} + \mathbf{D}_i) \text{ mod } d$$
$$\mathbf{q}_i = R^{(i+1)} + (R^{(i+1)} + \mathbf{D}_i) \text{ div } d$$

In words, the quotient digit i is the remainder adjusted by 1 if $R^{(i+1)} + \mathbf{D}_i\ ^{3}$ d.This correction may be applied in parallel as a single step as in [Fig. 5] for n=8.

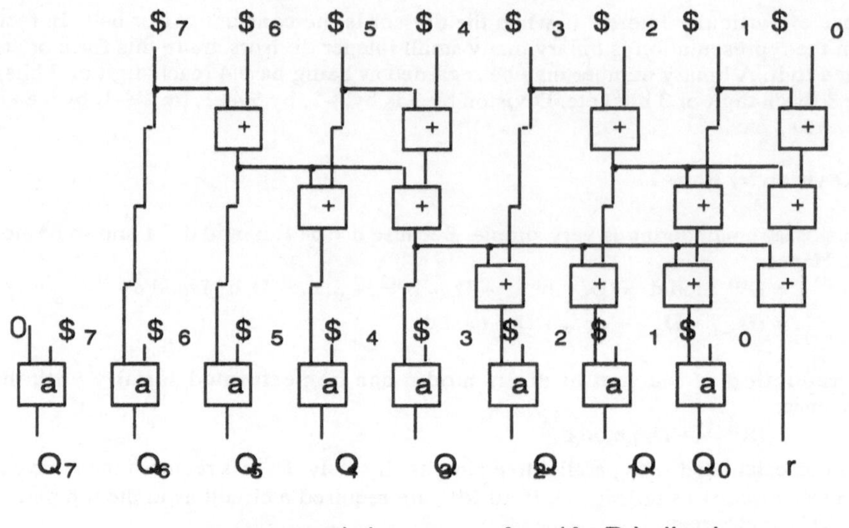

Figure 5: Quotient from remainders for d = b-1

In the circuit of figure 5 there is some duplication of effort in that the calculation of the final adjustment could well be associated with the previous stage.This idea is used in the following serial algorithm where the quotient is calculated as we proceed with determining the partial remainders. This algorithm is particularly nice in that the division is performed entirely by digit addition and comparison ³ d (in the algorithm all arithmetic is standard).

{find **R** := D mod b-1 and **q** the digits of D div b-1}
R := 0
Repeat for i from n-1 down to 0
T := R + $\mathbf{D}_i$
{$\mathbf{q}_i$:= R + T div (b-1), R := T mod (b-1)}
if T ³ b-1 then T := T+1
$\mathbf{q}_i$:= R + T div b {the b^1 digit of T}
R := T mod b {the b^0 digit of T}

Example: Division of a base 10 number by 9.

	9	3	6	0	8	7	1	9	dividend
0	0	3	0	0	8	6	7	7	remainders
	1	0	1	0	0	1	0	1	adjustments
	1	0	4	0	0	9	6	8	quotient

Typical step:
T := 8 + 7 (=15)
if 15 ³ 9 then T := 15+1 = 16
$\mathbf{q}_i$:= 8 + 1
R := 6

Note that it is also possible to calculate the remainders from right to left. From $R^{(i)} = (R^{(i+1)} + \mathbf{D}_i) \bmod d$, we find $R^{(i+1)} = (R^{(i)} - \mathbf{D}_i) \bmod d$. Continuing this expansion we get $R^{(i+1)} = (R^{(0)} - (\mathbf{D}_i + \mathbf{D}_{i-1} \cdots + \mathbf{D}_0)) \bmod d$. Finally, $R^{(n)} = (R^{(0)} - (\mathbf{D}_{n-1} + \mathbf{D}_{n-2} \cdots + \mathbf{D}_0)) \bmod d$.

If we knew $R^{(0)}$ correctly then we would have $R^{(n)} = 0$. However, if we did not know $R^{(n)}$ but assumed it zero then we will have $R^{(n)} = (- R^{(0)}) \bmod d$. The remainders that we have found will be incorrect but they can be restored by now adding $R^{(n)} \bmod d$. This approach is inherent in the circuit of [Duke 1972] , described below.

7.3 Division by Base+1

The above reasoning can be revisited with d = b+1. Noting that (A-B) mod d is the non-negative integer C such that (B+C) mod d = A mod d, in this case we find:

$R^{(i)} = (\mathbf{D}_i - R^{(i+1)}) \bmod d$

$\mathbf{q}_i = R^{(i+1)} + (\mathbf{D}_i - R^{(i+1)}) \operatorname{div} d$

Without going into details, [Fig. 6] is an example circuit.

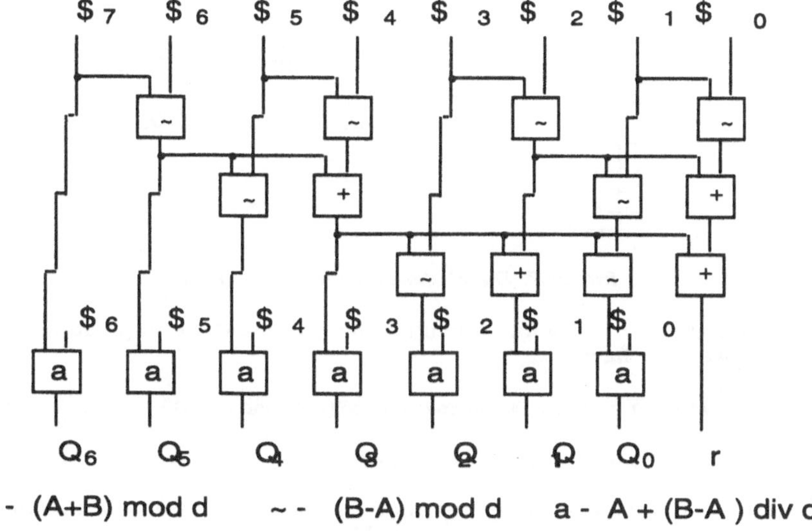

Figure 6: Quotient from remainders for d = b+1

And the serial version is (in standard arithmetic):

{find R := D mod b+1 and **q** the digits of D div b+1}

R := 0

Repeat for i from n-1 down to 0

T := $\mathbf{D}_i$ - R

{$\mathbf{q}_i$:= R + T div (b+1), R := T mod (b+1)}

if T ³ 0 then $\mathbf{q}_i$:= R, R := T

else $\mathbf{q}_i$:= R-1, R := T + b+1

Example: Division of a base 10 number by 11:

```
    9 3 6 0 8 7 1 9      dividend
  0 9 5 1 10 9 9 3 6     remainders
    0 1 0 1 1 1 1 0      adjustments
    0 8 5 0 9 8 8 3      quotient
```

Typical step:
T := 7 - 9 (= -2)
if -2 ³ 0 else q_i := 9 - 1 (=8), R := -2 + 11 (=9)

The above two serial algorithms were described in [Doran 1987] though were presumably known to mental calculators previously. Surprisingly, division and remaindering by b+1 has had at least one practical[2] application in the proposed Burroughs Scientific Processor of the 1970s which had 17 memory banks (b = 16).

7.4 Circuits with feedback

[Duke 1972] describes the circuit illustrated in [Fig. 7].

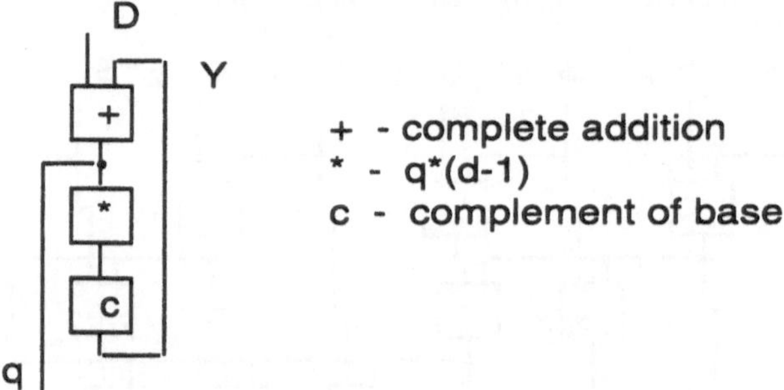

Figure 7: Duke's feedback division circuit

This is unusual in that it is a logic circuit with feedback. If it ever produces a stable output then we must have:

$$q = D+Y,\ Y = -q*(d-1) \text{ and so } q = D-q*(d-1) \text{ and } q*d=D$$

If d divides D exactly then q = D div d.

The question is, when is the output stable? This answer is clearly technology and implementation dependent. In the case of binary representation, the circuit will certainly work when "*(d-1)" introduces a genuine shift. This is when $d-1 = 2^k$, so $d = 2^k+1$. In this case, although at the overall level the circuit has feedback, at the bit level it can be shown that it does not, so is definitely combinational. It is, in fact, a circuit implementation of the algorithm described above for division by b+1 when the remainder is zero but from the right (in a manner analagous to that explained for division by b-1)

The above circuit can be adapted for $d = 2^k + 1$ in the obvious manner. If d does not divide D exactly, then [Duke 1972] showed that the high order carry is non-zero and

---

[2] One could note in passing that in New Zealand the VAT (called GST) had been set at 10% initially then changed to 12.5%. To find the tax included in the purchase price the first rate needed division by 11 and the second by 9 - so these algorithms would have been useful, if we did not have calculators!

provides the correction factor to be added to each digit (also as described above for d = b-1).

[Fenwick 1972] mentions that Boothroyd had proposed a similar circuit with feedback working from the most significant end. In this case, the shift is to the right. Unfortunately, because carry is to the left, this involves real feedback and cannot be guaranteed to stabilise.

7.5 Application to Binary to Decimal Conversion

We can at last see the practical use of division by a small constant for base conversion. The basic idea is that if we wish to convert a number D from a base b to a base d, then, because D = q*d+r, r is the zeroth digit of the representation base d. The process may then be applied to q to get the first digit, etc. If the arithmetic for the division is performed in base b, then the sequence of remainder digits are the representation in base d, with each digit represented in base b.

Example:

To convert N=110001 (49) to BCD:
110001/1010(ten) = 0100, remainder 1001 (nine)
0100/1010(ten) = 0000 remainder 0100 (four)
So, 110001 (base 2) = 0100,1001 (BCD) = 49 (base 10)

The most common case is binary-to-decimal conversion which requires division by 10. This may be performed by dividing the binary number by 5 then by 2. In both divisions the remainders are also found. If the first division is $D = 5*Q+R_5$ and the second is $Q = 2*q + R_2$, the combined effect is $D = 5*(2*q+ R_2) + R_5 = 10*q + (5*R_2 + R_5)$. Thus, as R_2 is 0 or 1, the remainder mod 5 is increased by 5 if the remainder mod 2 is 1, to give the remainder mod 10 which is the next decimal digit. Because $5 = 2^2+1$, we can regard the binary number as being base b=4 and use our circuits for division by b+1, and the division by 2 is, of course, a shift to the right.

If conversion is required to be performed for one particular number then a tree division by b+1 circuit would be appropriate. Another technique, more appropriate for VLSI is to use a *cellular* circuit, where the approach is to use a network of idential components or cells that are connected in a two dimensional grid. Cellular binary-to-decimal circuits are explored in detail in [Schreiber and Stefanelli 1978]. To see an example, we could base a cellular circuit on our repetitive algorithm for b+1 division described above. The circuit consists of multiple levels, each performing a division by 10 and production of the next decimal digit encoded in BCD. The cell corresponds to the inner loop of the algorithm and performs a mod 5 subtraction of the incoming partial remainder (represented in 3 bits as being in range 0 to 4) with the next 2-bit digit of the binary number, followed by correction of the quotient digit based on the subtraction being negative (if it were not modular). Without fully developing the logic, the cell would be as in [Fig. 8].

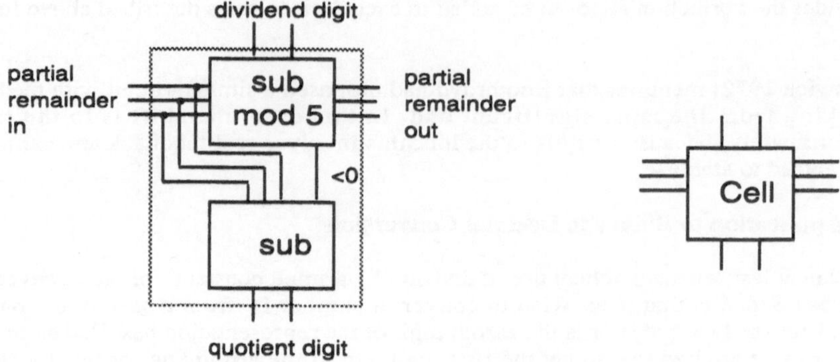

Figure 8: Cell for Binary to Decimal Conversion

The cells are then combined into the grid, with division by 2 being performed by directing the wires to perform a shift. An array of special circuits on the right is needed to conditionally increment the digits by 5. Each level of division needs less circuitry. [Fig. 9] shows the example of 8-bit conversion (maximum value 255).

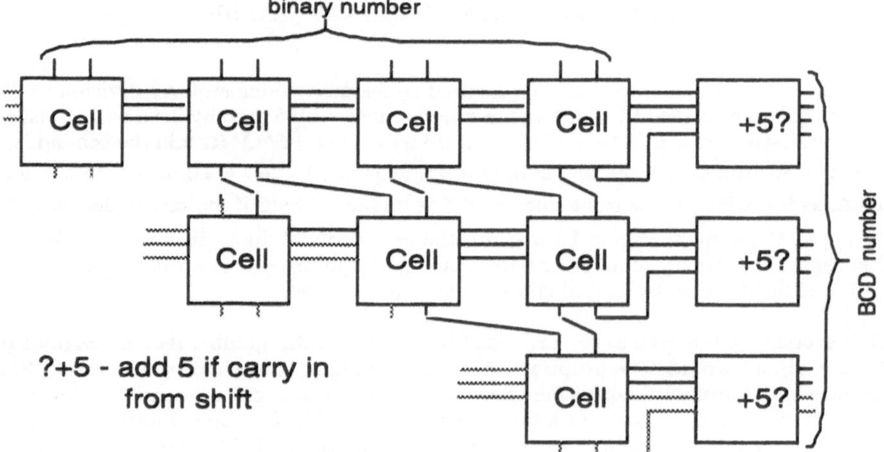

Figure 9: 8-bit cellular binary to decimal converter

The circuit above is somewhat simpler than that presented in [Schreiber and Stefanelli 1978].

8 Conclusion

There have certainly been many interesting procedures proposed for special cases of division. We have seen that these are mainly variations on two themes, division by reciprocal multiplication, or division derived from remaindering.

Of course, for every specific constant divisor there are special tricks that can be brought to bear. These have been developed over the years by mental calculators, see [Aiken 1937] , [Menninger 1964], [Smith 1983], [Yang 1274] . This is a fascinating but endless pursuit that we will leave it to the reader to take further.

Acknowledgments

This work was done while the author was a visitor with the Laboratoire d'Informatique du Parallélisme at the École Normale Supérieure at Lyon, France. Thanks is due to Jean-Michel Muller of LIP ENS and to Elena Calude and Radu Nicolescu of The University of Auckland for helpful suggestions.

References

[Aiken 1937] Aiken, A. C.: "Trial and error and approximation in arithmetic"; The Mathematical Gazette (1937), p. 117.

[Alt and Blum 1983] Alt, H., Blum, N.: "On the Boolean circuit depth of division and related functions"; Dept. of Computer Science, Pennsylvania State University (1983).

[Artzy et. al. 1976] Artzy, E., Hinds, J. A., & Saal, H. J. : "A fast division technique for constant divisors"; CACM, 19, 3 (1976), 98 - 101.

[Beame, Cooke and Hoover 1986] Beame, P. W., Cook, S. A. & Hoover, H.J.:"Log depth circuits for division and related problems"; SIAM Journal on Computing, 15 (1986) 994-1003.

[Cocke et. al. 1970] Cocke, J., Freiman C. V., & Homan M. E.: "High speed division system"; US Patent # 3,527,930 (1970).

[Daumas et. al. 1994] Daumas, M., Mazenc, C., Merrheim, X, and Muller, J-M.: "Fast and Accurate Range reduction for thr computation of elementary functions"; 14th IMACS World Congree on Computational and Applied Mathemaatics, Atalanta, Georgia (1994).

[Doran 1987] Doran, R. W.: "Parallel division circuits for small divisors"; Tech Report No. 38. Department of Computer Science, University of Auckland (1987).

[Duke 1972] Duke, K. A.: "Division by small integers"; IBM Technical Disclosure Bulletin, 14, 9 (1972), 3736-2738.

[Ercegovac et. al. 1993] Ercegovac, M.D., Lang, T., Montuschi, P.: "Very high radix division with selection by rounding and prescaling"; Proceedings of the 11th Symposium on Computer Arithmetic, Windsor, Ontario (1993) 112 - 119.

[Fenwick 1972] Fenwick, P.McA.: "A binary representation for decimal numbers"; The Australian Computer Journal, 4, 4 (1972), 146 - 149.

[Iliffe 1982] Iliffe, J. K.: "Advanced Computer Design"; Prentice Hall. London (1982).

[Jacobsohn 1973] Jacobsohn, D. H.: "A combinatoric algorithm for fixed-integer divisors"; IEEE Transactions on Computers (1973), 608 - 610.

[Menninger 1964] Menninger, K.: "Calculator's Cunning - The Art of Quick Reckoning"; G. Bell and Sons Ltd., London (1964).

[Schreiber and Stefanelli 1978] Schreiber F. A., Stefanelli, R.: "Two methods for fast integer binary-BCD conversion"; Proceedings of 4th Symposium on Computer Arithmetic, Santa Monica, California (1978), 200-207.

[Smith 1983] Smith, S. B.: "The Great Mental Calculators - The Psychology, Methods, and Lives of Calculating Prodigies Past and Present"; Columbia University Press, New York (1983).

[Szabo and Tanaka 1967] Szabo, N. S. & Tanaka, R. I.: "Residue Arithmetic & its Applications to Computer Technology"; McGraw Hill, New York (1967).

[Yang 1274] Yang Hui: "Ch'eng Chu' T'ung Pien Suan Pao (Precious Reckoner for Variations of Multiplication and Division)"; Reprinted, translated with commentary, in Lam Lay Yong, A Critcal Study of the Yang Hui Suan Fa, Singapore University Press (1977).

Journal of Universal Computer Science, vol. 1, no. 3 (1995), 195-200
submitted: 1/3/95, accepted: 13/3/95, appeared: 28/3/95,

Bringing ITS to the Marketplace: A Successful Experiment in Minimalist Design

Carl Gutwin and Marlene Jones
Alberta Research Council, Calgary, Canada
E-Mail: marlene@arc.ab.ca

Patrick Brackett and Kim Massie Adolphe
Gemini Learning Systems Inc., Calgary, Canada
E-Mail: kadolphe@gemini.com

Abstract: Intelligent Tutoring Systems (ITS) have proven to be effective tools for teaching and training. However, ITSs have not become common in industrial and organisational settings, in part because their complexity has proven difficult to manage outside of the research lab. Minimalist ITSs are an attempt to bridge the gap between research and practical application; they simplify research techniques while striving to maintain as much pedagogic intelligence as possible. This paper describes one such system, SWIFT, that is an example of how a minimalist ITS can be delivered as a commercial product. We outline some of the issues facing designers of a minimalist system, and describe the ways that research techniques have been incorporated into four modules of SWIFT: adaptive testing, course planning, guidance, and diagnosis.

1 Introduction

Despite their many successes [see Shute, 1990], intelligent tutoring systems are underemployed in the world's industries and organisations. Complexity, size, and lack of tools to assist course authors have all prevented systems developed in research labs from moving to the commercial world. These limitations point to the need for techniques and strategies that can adapt research results to industrial and commercial systems. The idea of minimalist ITS (e.g. [Brusilovsky et al., 1994], [Winne et al., 1992]) has evolved to fill that need, and SWIFT is an example of a successful attempt to bring a minimalist ITS to the marketplace.

SWIFT, shown in Figure 1, is an adaptive learning environment [Jones, 1992] that has been developed in a joint research venture between the Alberta Research Council and Gemini Learning Systems. Several of SWIFT's

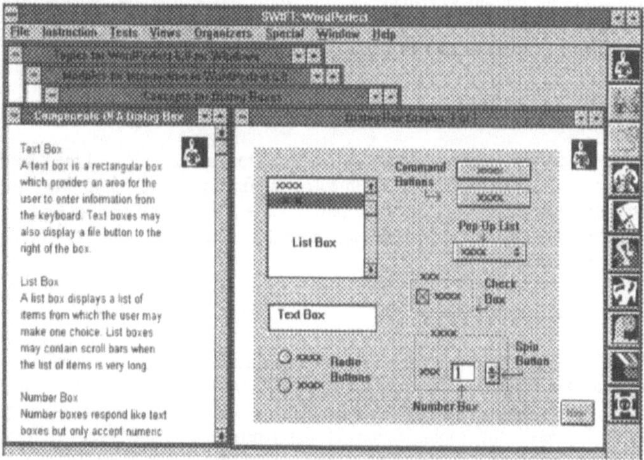

Figure 1. The SWIFT interface.

elements incorporate techniques from ITS research, including an adaptive testing facility, a situation guide, a course planner, and a diagnosis module. SWIFT shows that innovative techniques from research can be successfully modified for use in the real world. The following sections examine more closely what it means to minimise an ITS, and then discuss the design of SWIFT as a minimal system.

2 Minimalist ITS

Many intelligent tutoring systems require computational power that is rare in real-world training situations. The desire to produce training systems that behave intelligently, but that are also feasible on a smaller scale, has led researchers to the idea of minimalist ITS. This area has grown from work on training shells (e.g. [Major & Reichgelt, 1992], [van Marcke, 1990]) and on discovery learning environments (e.g. [Shute & Glaser, 1990], [Elsom-Cook, 1990]). Minimalist ITSs attempt to bridge the gap between research and practical application by simplifying ITS techniques for use in computing environments with limited memory, external storage, and processing speed. Any of the common elements of a typical ITS, such as the domain representation, the learner model, the pedagogic and domain expertise, the instructional and delivery planners, or the diagnosis engines, can be minimised. In addition, minimalist systems often attempt to reduce demands on course designers, since teachers and industrial trainers often do not have the time nor the specialised knowledge necessary to build the knowledge structures used by existing ITSs.

Meeting these needs presents a minimalist designer with several tradeoffs, the most obvious of which is the balance between power and feasibility. To manage this tradeoff effectively, a designer must understand what is lost with each simplification of a technique, and must look for other ways to bolster the system's pedagogic capabilities. In most cases, the minimalist approach implies that a system will gather less information about the student, will have a less-sophisticated domain representation, and will be able to make only relatively straightforward inferences from that information. Additional means must be found to ensure that what is left of the ITS techniques can still be used to advantage, which often means combining the technique with other more robust mechanisms that can make up for reduced intelligence. Our experiences suggest that the minimalist goal involves more than just linear scaling of the techniques–a simplistic approach will result only in a bad approximation of an ITS, not a minimalist one.

One approach that we have taken in SWIFT is to involve the learner in the decision-making processes. Even novices have considerable knowledge about their own learning needs, and they can monitor and alter the system's decisions if given the appropriate support. Other minimalist approaches take strategies from traditional computer-based training (CBT) and enhance them with ITS techniques. For example, CBT is often based upon learning by presentation and questioning. By providing individualised feedback on a learner's answers, an instructional system can add the individualisation of ITS to the simplicity of CBT.

Course designers also play an important part in the successful application of minimalist ITS. Authoring must be made accessible so that domain experts can readily construct new training materials; they must also be able to understand the strengths of the tutoring system in order to maximise its capabilities. KAFITS [Murray & Woolf, 1992] and COCA [Major, 1994] are two examples of systems that concentrate on providing tools for authors; SWIFT also provides extensive support for course design [Massie, 1994].

3 Minimalist Design in SWIFT

The following sections describe the approaches that we have used to make the most of the resources available to our system. In general, our strategies have taken three paths: first, we have found ways to minimise ITS techniques without compromising too much of their power; second, we have found additional mechanisms to make our solutions more robust; and third, we have taken advantage of the abilities of learners and our knowledge of the eventual user population.

3.1 Knowledge Representation

A defining feature of an ITS is a semantic representation of the instructional domain, where concepts are encoded in data structures that allow the system to reason about the course. A minimalist ITS must also employ semantic representation, for an understanding of the concepts in the domain is the basis of much of a system's intelligent behaviour. However, the detail and sophistication of the representation can vary. In SWIFT, we have implemented a representation scheme that allows us to reason about the domain, but does not contain as much detail about specific concepts as might be found in a full ITS. SWIFT courses are stored in a hierarchical structure that divides the instructional material into smaller and smaller pieces, much as a book does with chapters, sections, and subsections. A course has three levels: the first contains a set of *topics*, which are divided at the second level into sets of *modules*, which are divided at the third level into *concepts*. A semantic representation of the course also allows the specification of dependencies between concepts. The current version of SWIFT allows for prerequisite and sequence links between individual concept objects.

3.2 Adaptive Testing

ITSs gather information about a learner's progress by observing them as they interact with the learning environment. Many minimalist systems use exercises, quizzes, and exams as the setting for these observations, since the range of possible inference about the learner can be more easily constrained. Since many organisations (corporate and otherwise) also require that a training system provide concrete records of progress, we have chosen to use formative and summative testing as our means for observing the learner in SWIFT.

One of the problems with traditional exams is that they are of fixed length; a learner must complete a long series of questions in order for the system to determine how well they know a subject. This characteristic can cause frustration for both novices and experts, who may know after a few questions that the subject matter is either bewildering or trivial. Aside from giving the learner greater control over exams–in that they are never forced to take a test–our primary strategy for tackling the problem of fixed-length exams is adaptive testing. Adaptive testing allows exams to be significantly shorter than traditional tests, without losing any predictive power about a learner's mastery of the material. The approach that is implemented in SWIFT is based on the work of [Welch & Frick, 1993]. The algorithm uses Bayes' theorem to estimate the probability that the learner is a master or non-master of the material after each test question is answered. In SWIFT, novices (non-masters) and experts (masters) can be determined in as few as five questions.

3.3 Instructional Planning

Instructional planning in SWIFT is based on two information sources: the results of an adaptive pretest, and the learner's own choice of one or more instructional goals. Each goal specifies which topics and modules of the course are to be included in the learner's path; performance on the pretest then indicates whether concepts within those sections are already known and need not be included. Our approach to instructional planning is effective, but is relatively simple compared to some ITSs (e.g. [Brecht, 1990]) because of SWIFT's less-sophisticated domain representation. Since our simpler approach weakens SWIFT's planning to a degree, we have found other ways of ensuring that appropriate instruction is always available to the learner.

Since we knew that the target population for SWIFT is composed largely of learners that are cooperative and motivated, we were able to view instructional planning as a human-computer problem rather than just a computational one. One of the ways we involve the learner is by providing tools that allow them to monitor their path through the course, and to take control if desired. Figure 2 shows a concept map in SWIFT, one of several displays that explicitly lay out the content and dependencies of a course, and allow the learner to make informed decisions about what to learn next. This approach improves instructional planning by making use of the

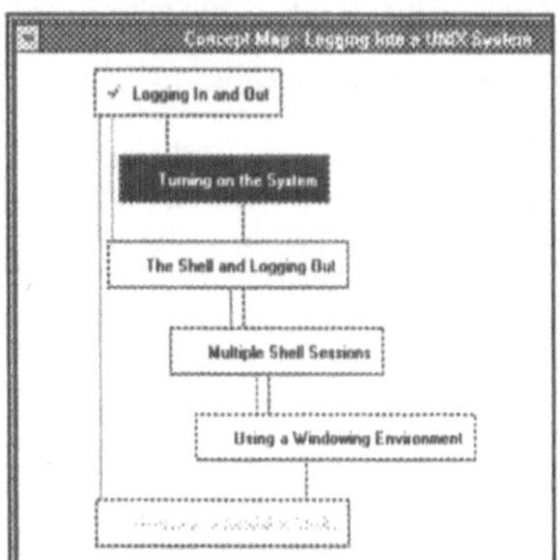

Figure 2. A SWIFT Concept Map.

knowledge of both parties: learners can improve upon or customise the system's course plan if they wish; the recommended path, which is adequate in most cases, provides support for learners who do not wish to venture out on their own.

3.4 Diagnosis

Diagnosis modules attempt to understand problems and misconceptions in a student's knowledge of the domain (e.g. [Johnson & Soloway, 1985], [McCalla & Greer, 1990]). Although any student action may be considered, diagnosis is commonly applied to a learner's answers to test or exercise questions. Diagnosis entails drawing conclusions about the learner's knowledge based on features in their answers; good diagnosis allows systems to provide appropriate feedback and remediation as well as simple indications of whether an answer is right or wrong.

Diagnosis can require significant inferencing power and domain knowledge, which are not the strengths of minimalist systems. An alternative to a fully knowledge-based approach is to detail a number of categories, or cases, of typical errors and misconceptions. Using a case-based approach transforms the inference problem to one of classification, but effective classification can also be difficult to achieve. One problem occurs in specifying the answers that belong to a particular class. The obvious method is to encode every answer. However, this technique implies that any variation of an answer, even those that do not change its essential parts, must also be included. This can be a daunting task for any but the most trivial of exercises.

Our approach to this problem allows a course designer to concentrate on the qualitative differences in the possible answers to a question, rather than on syntactic variations. Our case-based diagnosis subsystem uses regular expressions, constructs that allow a designer to specify a large number of possible variations with a single answer pattern. The system can examine and evaluate any short textual answers for which cases have been designed. The course designer specifies patterns for classes of correct and incorrect answers, and can annotate each class with appropriate feedback and remediation information.

This strategy still requires that the course designer understand the kinds of difficulties that learners can have in a particular area, and how each problem can be manifested in answers to questions. However, we have provided a framework for structuring and using that pedagogic knowledge that is both powerful and efficient enough to be used in a minimal system.

3.5 Situation Recognition and Guidance

SWIFT has more and more become a learner-controlled system, both by design and by necessity. In a self-directed environment, the task of the intelligent tutoring system shifts from tutoring and control to guidance and support. We have been forced to find and implement mechanisms for supporting learners as they explore the system on their own.

We have developed a subsystem within SWIFT that can provide guidance on pedagogic issues according to the specific situation that the learner is in, and can also encourage the learner to initiate certain learning behaviours. Many strategies exist for assisting self-directed learning that promote metacognition and more effective learning behaviour (e.g. [Derry & Murphy, 1986], [Derry, 1992], [Pressley et al., 1989], [Shuell, 1992], [Winne, 1992]). Examples of effective learning behaviour include positive self-talk, note-taking or highlighting, summation, imagery, question-generation, and review of learning objectives.

SWIFT's guide watches system events and monitors a learner's location, history, and current knowledge. When particular kinds of situations occur, the guide can decide to deliver advice to the learner. For example, if a student turned their attention to a new section of course material, the guide might suggest that they test their knowledge of the current section before going on. The guide is implemented as a rule-based system, and the above example would involve a rule such as: "if the learner has not demonstrated mastery in the concepts of the current module, and the learner requests a move to a new module, the system will suggest that the learner take a module test for the current module." The guide's advice is presented in a popup dialogue box, such as the one shown in Figure 3.

The rule-based guidance system provides SWIFT with a generalised architecture for presenting useful information. We are able to give the learner pedagogic guidance in a wide variety of situations, but the

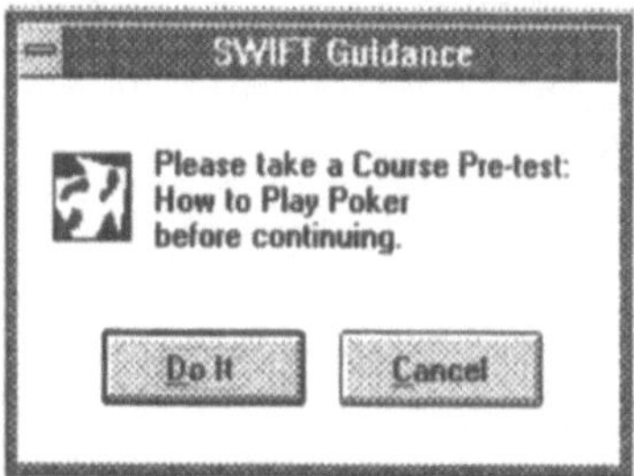

Figure 3: A SWIFT Guidance Window

architecture can also be used to give information about any situation, such as tips on using SWIFT to its full capacity.

4 Current Success and Plans for Further Work

SWIFT has now been released as a commercial product, and a number of organisations are producing courses in domains as varied as air traffic control, Canadian history, high school physics, and football. Designers have so far found course development to be straightforward, but we are planning for a graphical authoring environment to further support the authoring process. SWIFT has been evaluated through formal usability studies involving representative users from industrial settings and from secondary and post-secondary education institutions. The usability testing has validated many of our design decisions, but has also caused us to refine some parts of the system. For example, some users felt that the guide offered advice in too many situations; we have since tuned the guide's rules to reduce repetitive or spurious advice.

We are currently investigating other techniques from ITS research that may be appropriate for implementation in a minimalist system, as well as planning commercial improvements such as more sophisticated multimedia and hypertext support. Some of the possibilities for the next version of SWIFT are:

- Granularity-based diagnosis [McCalla and Greer, 1994];
- Collaborative learning tools, such as support for awareness of other learners (e.g. [Ayala and Yano, 1994]);
- Improved student modeling based on recent techniques of modeling learners based on test results [Shute, 1994].

Our experiences have shown us that minimalist thinking involves more than taking existing techniques and scaling them down, and that additional mechanisms must often be found to ensure robust and rewarding interaction with a minimalist ITS. The examples of our design efforts in SWIFT suggest that minimalist ITS can be successfully constructed within the constraints of the commercial world.

SWIFT is available from Gemini Learning Systems, Inc. and from its distributors.

5 References

[Ayala & Yano, 1994] Ayala, G. and Yano, Y. (1994) Design Issues in a Collaborative Learning Environment for Japanese Language Patterns. *Educational Multimedia and Hypermedia*, AACE, 67-72.

[Brecht, 1990] Brecht (Wasson), B. (1990) Determining the Focus of Instruction: Content Planning for Intelligent Tutoring Systems. Unpublished doctoral dissertation, University of Saskatchewan.

[Brusilovsky et al., 1994] Brusilovsky, P., van Marcke, K., Murray, T., Major, N. and Vassileva, J. (1994) Minimalist ITS. Panel Discussion, *Educational Multimedia and Hypermedia*, AACE.

[Derry & Murphy, 1986] Derry, S., and Murphy, D.A., (1986), Designing Systems that Train Learning Ability: From Theory to Practice. *Review of Educational Research*, 56(1), 1-39.

[Derry, 1992] Derry, S. (1992) Metacognitive Models of Learning and Instructional System Design. In *Adaptive Learning Environments: Foundations and Frontiers*, M. Jones and P. Winne ed. Springer-Verlag. 257-286.

[Elsom-Cook, 1990] Elsom-Cook, M. (1990) *Guided Discovery Tutoring*. London: Paul Chapman Publishing.

[Johnson & Soloway, 1985] Johnson, W. L. and Soloway, E. (1985) PROUST: An Automatic Debugger for Pascal Programs. *Byte*, 10 (4), 179-190.

[Jones, 1992] Jones, M. (1992) Introduction. In *Adaptive Learning Environments: Foundations and Frontiers*, M. Jones and P. Winne ed., Springer-Verlag, 1-10.

[Major, 1994] Major, N. (1994) Evaluating COCA - What do teachers think? *Educational Multimedia and Hypermedia*, AACE, 361-366.

[Major & Reichgelt, 1992] Major, N. and Reichgelt, H. (1992) COCA: A Shell for Intelligent Tutoring Systems. *Intelligent Tutoring Systems*, Springer-Verlag, 523-530.

[Massie, 1994] Massie Adolphe, K. (1994) AI and Education. *Canadian AI Magazine*, 34 (1), 4-8.

[McCalla & Greer, 1990] McCalla, G. I. and Greer, J. E. (1990) SCENT-3: An architecture for intelligent advising in problem-solving domains. In *Intelligent Tutoring Systems: At the Crossroads of Artificial Intelligence and Education*, C. Frasson and G. Gauthier eds. Norwood, NJ:Ablex, 140-161

[McCalla & Greer 1994] McCalla, G.I, and Greer, J.E. (1994), Granularity-Based Reasoning and Belief Revision in Student Models, In *Student Modelling: The Key to Individualized Knowledge-Based Instruction*, J. Greer and G. McCalla eds, Springer-Verlag, 39-62.

[Murray & Woolf, 1992] Murray, T. and Woolf, B. (1992) Tools for Teacher Participation in ITS Design. *Intelligent Tutoring Systems*, Springer-Verlag, 593-600.

[Pressley et al., 1989] Pressley, M., Johnson, C., Symons, S., McGoldrick, J., Kurita, J., (1989), Strategies That Improve Children's Memory and Comprehension of Text. *The Elementary School Journal*, 90(1), 3-32.

[Shuell, 1992] Shuell, T. J. (1992) Designing Instructional Computing Systems for Meaningful Learning. In *Adaptive Learning Environments: Foundations and Frontiers*, M. Jones and P. Winne ed., Berlin:Springer-Verlag, 19-54.

[Shute, 1990] Shute, V. (1990) Rose Garden Promises of Intelligent Tutoring Systems: Blossom or Thorn?, Space Operations, Applications and Research (SOAR) Symposium, June 1990, Albuquerque, NM.

[Shute, 1994] Shute, V. (1994) Regarding the I in ITS: Student Modelling. In *Educational Multimedia and Hypermedia*, AACE, 50-57.

[Shute & Glaser 1994] Shute, V. J. and Glaser, R. (1990) A Large-scale Evaluation of an Intelligent Discovery World: Smithtown. *Interactive Learning Environments*, 1(1), 51-77.

[van Marcke, 1990] van Marcke, K. (1990) "A Generic Tutoring Environment." *The European Conference on Artifical Intelligence*, 655-660.

[Welch & Frick 1993] Welch, R.E., and Frick, T.W. (1993), Computerized-Adaptive Testing in Instructional Settings. *Educational Technology Research and Development*, 41(3), 47-62.

[Winne, 1992] Winne, P. (1992) State-of-the-Art Instructional Computing Systems that Afford Instruction and Bootstrap Research. In *Adaptive Learning Environments: Foundations and Frontiers*, M. Jones and P. Winne ed., Berlin:Springer-Verlag, 349-380.

[Winne et al., 1992] Winne, P., Butler, D., McGinn, M., Sugarman, J., Jones, M., Mark, M., and Field, D. (1992) STUDY: A Tool for Authoring Adaptive Learning Environments and for Advancing Instructional Research. In Appendix to *Proceedings of ITS'92*.

Acknowledgments

Several people have contributed to the design of SWIFT and played a part in the ideas presented here. Thanks to Stuart Williams, Ruby Loo, Joseph Poon, Julia Driver, and Jim Tubman. Special thanks to Jim Tubman and Pam Hirtle for assistance in long-distance preparation of the final draft.

Journal of Universal Computer Science, vol. 1, no. 3 (1995), 201-204
submitted: 20/1/95, accepted: 27/2/95, appeared: 28/3/95, © *Springer Pub. Co.*

Halting probability amplitude of quantum computers*

K. Svozil
Institute for Theoretical Physics, Technische Universät Wien,
Wiedner Hauptstraße 8–10/136, A-1040 Vienna, Austria
e-mail:svozil@tph.tuwien.ac.at

Abstract

The classical halting probability Ω introduced by Chaitin is generalized to quantum computations.

Chaitin's Ω [1, 2, 3] is a magic number. It is a measure for arbitrary programs to take a finite number of execution steps and then halt. It contains the solution for all halting problems, and hence to questions codable into halting problems, such as Fermat's theorem. It contains the solution for the question of whether or not a particular exponential Diophantine equation has infinitely many or a finite number of solutions. And, since Ω is provable "algorithmically incompressible," it is Martin-Löf/Chaitin/Solovay random. Therefore, Ω is both: a mathematicians "fair coin," and a formalist's nightmare.

Here, Ω is generalized to quantum computations.

Consider a (not necessarily universal) quantum computer C and its ith program p_i, which, at time $t \in Z$, can be described by a quantum state [4, 5, 6, 7, 8, 9, 10, 11, 12])

$$|C(t,p_i)\rangle \quad . \tag{1}$$

A typical realisation of C would be by an array of generalized four-port beam splitters [13].

In what follows we shall assume that the program p_i is coded *classically*. That is, we choose a finite code alphabet A and denote by A^* the set of all strings over A. Any program p_i is coded as a classical sequence $\#(p_i) = s_{1i}s_{2i}\cdots s_{ni} \in A^*$, $s_{ji} \in A$. (In what follows, $\#(p_i)$ will be abbreviated by p_i.) We assume prefix coding [14, 1, 15, 3]; i.e., the domain of C is prefix-free such that no admissible program is the prefix of another admissible program. Furthermore, without loss of generality, we consider only empty input strings.

*The quantum omega was invented in a meeting of G. Chaitin, A. Zeilinger and the author (K. S.) in a Viennese coffee house (Café Bräunerhof) in January 1991. Thus, the group should be credited for the original invention, whereas any blame should remain with the author.

In quantum information theory, the state $|C(t,p_i)\rangle$ of the computer C with program p_i is representable by quantum bits (qbits). Every qbit is in a coherent superposition of the classical bit basis $|0\rangle$ and $|1\rangle$. Assume that the states (1) are orthogonal and normalized. The computer C evolves according to a unitary operator U such that (discrete time evolution)

$$|C(t,p_i)\rangle = U|C(t-1,p_i)\rangle \tag{2}$$
$$= U^t|C(0,p_i)\rangle \quad . \tag{3}$$

More specifically, a quantum computer can be in a coherent superposition of the halting and the non-halting state [6, 16]

$$|a,b\rangle = a|HALT\rangle + b|GO\rangle \quad , \qquad |a|^2 + |b|^2 = 1 \tag{4}$$

We shall call this quantum bit $|a,b\rangle$ the *halting bit*. The symbols "$|HALT\rangle$" and "$|GO\rangle$" represent orthonormal vectors [17] in the twodimensional complex Hilbert space spanned by them. Let the halting state $|e^{i\varphi},0\rangle = |HALT\rangle$, $\varphi \in R$ be the physical realization that the computer has "halted;" likewise let $|0,e^{i\varphi}\rangle = |GO\rangle$, $\varphi \in R$ be the physical realization that the computer has not "halted." Note that, since quantum computations are governed by unitary evolution laws which are reversible, the halting state does not mean that the computer does not change as time evolves. It just means that it has set a signal — the halting bit — to indicated that it has finished its task. a and b are complex numbers which are a quantum mechanical measure of the probability amplitude that the computer is in the halting and the non-halting states, respectively. (The corresponding probabilities are $|a|^2$ and $|a|^2$, respectively.) One important feature of the quantum information concept ist that it does not merely allow two-valued states but a coherent superposition thereof.

In the orthonormal halting basis $\{|HALT\rangle, |GO\rangle\}$, the computer C with classical input p_i can be represented by

$$|C(t,p_i)\rangle = |HALT\rangle\langle HALT|C(t,p_i)\rangle + |GO\rangle\langle GO|C(t,p_i)\rangle \quad . \tag{5}$$

In the spirit of quantum recursion theory [16], assume that initially, i.e., at time $t = 0$, the computer is prepared such that its halting bit is in a coherent 50:50-superposition; i.e., in terms of the halting basis,

$$|C(0,p_i)\rangle = \frac{1}{\sqrt{2}}(|HALT\rangle + |GO\rangle) \tag{6}$$

for all $p_i \in A^*$. This corresponds to the fact that initially it is unknown whether or not the computer halts on p_i. When during the time evolution the computer has completed its task, the halting bit value is switched to $|HALT\rangle$ by some internal operation, otherwise it remains in the coherent 50:50-superposition of equation (6). [Alternatively, the computer could be initially prepared in the non-halting state $|GO\rangle$. After completion of the task, the halting bit is again switched to the halting state $|HALT\rangle$. In this case, the subtractions of $\langle GO|C(t,p_i)\rangle$ in equations (7), (8) and (9) below would have to be eliminated.]

In analogy to the fully classical case [1, 18, 3], the quantum halting amplitude Ω can be defined as a weighted expectation over all computations of C with classical input p_i ($|p_i|$ stands for the length of p_i)

$$\Omega \equiv \lim_{t\rightarrow\infty} \sum_{p_i} 2^{-|p_i|} \left[\langle HALT|C(t,p_i)\rangle - \langle GO|C(t,p_i)\rangle \right] \quad . \tag{7}$$

Likewise, for particular output states $|s\rangle$,

$$\Upsilon(|s\rangle) \equiv \lim_{t\rightarrow\infty} \sum_{|C(t,p_i)\rangle = |s\rangle} 2^{-|p_i|} \left[\langle HALT|C(t,p_i)\rangle - \langle GO|C(t,p_i)\rangle \right] \quad . \tag{8}$$

For a set of output states $S = \{|s_1\rangle, |s_2\rangle, |s_3\rangle, \ldots, |s_n\rangle\}$ which correspond to mutually orthogonal vectors in Hilbert space,

$$\Upsilon(S) \equiv \lim_{t\rightarrow\infty} \sum_{|C(t,p_i)\rangle \in S} 2^{-|p_i|} \left[\langle HALT|C(t,p_i)\rangle - \langle GO|C(t,p_i)\rangle \right] \quad . \tag{9}$$

For nontrivial choices of the quantum computer C, several remarks are in order. (In what follows, we mention only Ω, but the comments apply to Υ as well.)

First, note that if the program is also coded in qbits, the above sum becomes an integral over continuously many states per code symbol of the programs. In this case, the Kraft sum needs not converge.

Second, just as for the classical analogue it is possible to "compute" Ω as a limit from below by considering in the t'th computing step (time t) all programs of length t which have already halted. (This "computation" suffers from a radius of convergence which decreases slower than any recursive function.)

Third, the quantum Ω is complex. $|\Omega|^2$ can be interpreted as a measure for the halting probability of C; i.e., the probability that an arbitrary (prefix-free) program halts on C. Both, the relative phases of approximations of Ω, as well as approximations to $|\Omega|^2$ are measurable.

Finally, any measurements of $|\Omega|^2$ causes irreversible state collapses. Since $|C(t,p_i)\rangle$ may not be in a pure state, the series in (7) and (8) will not be uniquely defined even for *finite* times. The *nondeterministic* character of Ω is not only based on classical recursion theoretic arguments [1] but also on the physical proposition that God plays the quantum dice.

References

[1] G. J. Chaitin, *Information, Randomness and Incompleteness, Second edition* (World Scientific, Singapore, 1987, 1990); *Algorithmic Information Theory* (Cambridge University Press, Cambridge, 1987); *Information-Theoretic Incompleteness* (World Scientific, Singapore, 1992).

[2] R. M. Solovay, *unpublished manuscript.*

[3] C. Calude, *Information and Randomness — An Algorithmic Perspective* (Springer, Berlin, 1994).

[4] D. Z. Albert, *Phys. Lett.* **94A**, 249 (1983).

[5] P. Benioff, *J. Stat. Phys.* **29**, 515 (1982); *Phys. Rev. Lett.* **48**, 1581 (1982).

[6] D. Deutsch, *Proc. R. Soc. Lond.* **A 400**, 97 (1985).

[7] R. P. Feynman, *Opt. News* **11**, 11 (1985).

[8] A. Peres, *Phys. Rev.* **A32**, 3266 (1985).

[9] P. Benioff, *Annals New York Akademy of Sciences* **480**, 475 (1986).

[10] N. Margolus, *Annals New York Akademy of Sciences* **480**, 487 (1986).

[11] D. Deutsch, *Proc. R. Soc. Lond.* **A 425**, 73 (1989).

[12] D. Deutsch and R. Jozsa, *Proc. R. Soc. Lond.* **A 439**, 553 (1992).

[13] A. Zeilinger, *Am. J. Phys.* **49**, 882 (1981); M. Reck, A. Zeilinger, H. J. Bernstein and P. Bertani, *Phys. Rev. Lett.* **73**, 58 (1994).

[14] R. W. Hamming, *Coding and Information Theory, Second Edition* (Prentice-Hall, Englewood Cliffs, New Jersey, 1980).

[15] K. Svozil, *Randomness and Undecidability in Physics* (World Scientific, Singapore, 1993).

[16] K. Svozil, *On the computational power of physical systems, undecidability, the consistency of phenomena and the practical uses of paradoxa*, in *International Conference on Fundamental Problems in Quantum Theory*, ed. by D. Greenberger (New York Academy of Sciences, in print); *Quantum recursion theory*, TU Vienna preprint.

[17] Let $d(\cdot,\cdot)$ be the inner product of the Hilbert space. Let further be $\langle x|y\rangle := d(|x\rangle,|y\rangle)$. Orthonormality states that $\langle HALT|HALT\rangle = \langle GO|GO\rangle = 1$ and $\langle HALT|GO\rangle = \langle GO|HALT\rangle = 0$.

[18] R. J. Solomonoff, *Information and Control* **7**, 1 (1964); *IEEE Transactions on Information Theory* **IT-24**, 422 (1978).

Managing Editor's Column

Vol. 1, No. 4; April 28, 1995

Dear Readers:

This number 4 of volume of J.UCS, the Journal of Universal Computer Science contains a selection of 5 papers from a Workshop on Hypermedia Systems held at the Graz University of Technology November 4-5, 1994. The idea to collect some of the most interesting papers into a special issue is due to John Lindsay from Kingston University, UK, who has gone through the trouble of reviewing the papers. Two further papers of this conference: "Applications and Impact of Hypermedia Systems: An Overview" (J.Lennon, H.Maurer) and "On Second Generation Hypermedia Systems" (K.Andrews, F.Kappe, H.Maurer, K.Schmaranz) have already appeared in the pilot issue of J.UCS, J.UCS 0,0 (1994).

Note that the papers present a good survey of information systems that are widespread on the Internet, starting with Gopher (authored by "Mr.Gopher" himself, Mark McCahill from Minnesota), WWW (authored by one of the four originators of WWW at CERN, Robert Cailliau), WAIS (as first full-text search engine that became widely used in connection with a variety of Internet services) to Hyper-G (a paper authored by two of the leading developers, Frank Kappe and Keith Andrews). One paper comes from an expert in the commercial arena: D. Goetze, one of the directors of Springer Pub.Co., a company known for its electronic publishing efforts including the support of this very journal J.UCS!

Hope you find this issue again interesting. Your opinion on the issues that have appeared sofar, or on J.UCS in general and how it compares to other electronic journals are much valued. Please do send me a brief note if you can spare a few moments of your time: I will report on opinions received in a later issue. For the time being, thanks for your continued interest in J.UCS. Due to the fact that we are running a number of servers, some only accessible within a particular organisation, others publicly abvailable we don't know how many readers J.UCS has got. However, our Graz J.UCS homepage has been accessed over 10.000 times by now, so a conservative estimate is that J.UCS has been looked at at least 25.000 times. This is probably quite satisfactory for a start.

With best wishes

Hermann Maurer, Managing Editor
email: hmaurer@iicm.tu-graz.ac.at

Journal of Universal Computer Science, vol. 1, no. 4 (1995), 206-220
submitted: 13/8/94, accepted: 3/10/94, appeared: 28/4/95,

The Hyper-G Network Information System

Keith Andrews, Frank Kappe, and Hermann Maurer
(Institute for Information Processing and Computer Supported New Media (IICM)
Graz University of Technology
A-8010 Graz, Austria.
{kandrews,fkappe,hmaurer}@iicm.tu-graz.ac.at)

Abstract As the Internet continues to experience exponential rates of growth, attention is shifting away from mainstream network services such as electronic mail and file transfer to more interactive information services. Current network information systems, whilst extremely successful, run into problems of fragmentation, consistency, scalability, and loss of orientation.
The development of "second generation" network information systems such as Hyper-G can help overcome these limitations. Of particular note are Hyper-G's tightly-coupled structuring, linking, and search facilities, its projection of a seamless information space across server boundaries with respect to each of these facilities, and its support for multiple languages. The Harmony client for Hyper-G utilises two and three-dimensional visualisations of the information space and couples location feedback to search and link browsing operations, in order to reduce the likelihood of disorientation. This paper presents a comprehensive overview of Hyper-G and Harmony.

Key Words: Hypermedia, information system, information visualisation, graphical interaction, Internet.

Category: H.5

1 Introduction

The Internet, the world-wide computer network, now connects more than 3.8 million individual computers (October 1994) with a growth rate of between 10–15% per month [Network Wizards 1994]. More than 18 terabytes of information traversed the NSFNET, the main US backbone of the Internet, in the month of September 1994 [Merit NIC 1994]. Whilst traditional services such as electronic mail, remote login, and file transfer (FTP) still account for the bulk of Internet traffic, by far the fastest growth is being experienced by network information systems like WAIS, Gopher, and the World-Wide Web.

These three information systems have transformed the way people perceive and interact with information resources on the net. All three are client-server applications using the Internet's underlying TCP/IP protocol: end-users run client software (available for a wide variety of platforms) which communicates over the network with servers managing access to a vast amount of extremely diverse information.

WAIS (Wide Area Information Servers), began in 1989 as a joint development of Thinking Machines, Apple Computer, and Dow Jones to provide on-line access to the Wall Street Journal [Kahle et al. 1992]. WAIS supports powerful content-based search of (previously) indexed databases, including *relevance feedback* by which (parts of) text documents returned by a search and deemed to be particularly relevant by the user are used as input for a subsequent search, in effect refining the search by asking WAIS to look for further similar documents. WAIS is purely a search engine, it supports neither associative browsing (hyperlinks) nor any structuring of its information content.

Gopher was started in 1991 as a campus-wide information system at the University of Minnesota [McCahill and Anklesaria 1995, Anklesaria et al. 1993]. It provides menu-like access to information resources. Although Gopher space is in fact a graph containing many loops, the menu presentation gives the impression of a tree. Typically, users begin navigation at the top of the tree and traverse down to leaf nodes containing actual data. One sub-tree on each server usually contains a menu of other Gopher servers. Gopher has no integrated search facilities of its own, but provides access to optional add-on search engines such as WAIS; it has no provision for hyperlinks.

The World-Wide Web project (WWW, W3, or simply "The Web") was initiated at CERN, Geneva, in 1989, originally as an information system for the particle physics community [Cailliau 1995, Berners-Lee et al. 1994]. W3 is a distributed *hypermedia* system: combining the concept of *hyperlinks* (associative browsing by following links to related information) with *multimedia* (text, image, audio, video, etc.). Through its URL (Universal Resource Locator) mechanism, W3 can represent links to any document on any W3, Gopher, or FTP server worldwide. The CGI script interface allows W3 servers to start arbitrary application programs, for example linking into external databases or implementing complex search algorithms. Simple, intuitive W3 clients such as Mosaic and Netscape have contributed to its tremendous current popularity.

However, W3 has a number of limitations. It does not provide any information structuring facilities beyond hyperlinks; its links are one-way (there is no way of determining which other documents refer to a particular document, leading to inconsistencies when documents are moved or deleted – the frequent "dangling links") and embedded within text documents (there are no links from other kinds of documents). Like Gopher, W3 has no native search facilities, but relies on external search engines such as WAIS, leading to patchy server-by-server provision of search facilities by individual sites and no real-time cross-server searches (searches in previously generated cross-server indices are available). The flexibility provided by CGI is achieved at great cost: the uniformity of the interface disappears, different W3 servers behave differently – resulting in the "Balkanisation" (to quote Ted Nelson) of the Web into independent "W3 Empires". Also, there is little support for the maintenance of large datasets, so it is not uncommon to see several W3 servers within a single organisation, each a fundamentally separate interactive context. The Web today is very much "read-only", in the sense that information providers prepare data sets in which information consumers can generally only browse. Finally, although its URL mechanism endows W3 with scalability in terms of number of servers, it is not scalable in terms of number of users. Extremely popular W3 servers such as Sun Microsystems' World Cup USA '94 [Sun Microsystems] site can often become overwhelmed by tens of thousands of users, necessitating their physical mirroring to many alternative sites.

WAIS, Gopher, and W3 belong to the first generation of information systems on the Internet [Fenn and Maurer 1994]. They work well in particular contexts but run into difficulties when applied to hundreds of thousands of documents distributed over many thousands of servers. They provide no graphical navigation aids, only rudimentary access control, little support for automatic database maintenance, no scalable document replication mechanisms, and little support for multiple languages. In the rest of this paper we describe Hyper-G, a second generation system designed to transcend some of the limitations of existing environments.

2 Hyper-G

Hyper-G is a multi-user, multi-protocol, structured, hypermedia information system, which runs as a client-server application on the Internet [Andrews and Kappe 1994, Andrews et al. 1994, Kappe 1993].

2.1 Design Goals

Based on an analysis of the strengths and weaknesses of existing systems, the following primary design goals were formulated:

1. Provide orientational and navigational aids.
2. Provide automatic structuring and maintenance.
3. Reduce fragmentation across servers.
4. Support user identification and access control.
5. Support multilinguality.
6. Maintain interoperability with existing systems.

To help alleviate the disorientation associated with becoming "lost in hyperspace", Hyper-G provides three closely coupled, orthogonal navigational mechanisms: structuring, hyperlinks, and search. The tight coupling allows clients to correlate search results, link maps, and structure overviews, providing a powerful aid to navigation.

Users of W3 are soon confronted with the "dangling link" syndrome inherent in W3's data model: when a document is moved or deleted, there is no way of automatically updating or deleting links to that document – following such links produces an error message. In Hyper-G, the consistency of links is maintained automatically by the server, as are Hyper-G's aggregate structures.

To counter the Balkanisation of databases, Hyper-G provides much functionality integrated into it (and hence uniform in nature) which has to be implemented on top of W3 or Gopher (and hence potentially differing from site to site), in particular powerful search and retrieval facilities which can be performed simultaneously and seamlessly *across* server borders. Information can also be *structured* both within and across server borders.

In order to differentiate between users and provide tailored views of the available information, support at the system level for user accounts, user groups, access rights, and access modes is essential. They are also a prerequisite for the implementation of charging facilities.

All of the currently popular Internet information systems are more or less implicitly bound to a single language: English. Although the Gopher+ and W3 protocols in theory support multi-language versions of documents, most clients do not use these facilities. Similarly, elements in the user interface are relatively easily translated to other languages, but most clients support only a single interface language; the same applies to full text search in multiple languages. Hyper-G and its clients, on the other hand, were specifically designed for multilingual use.

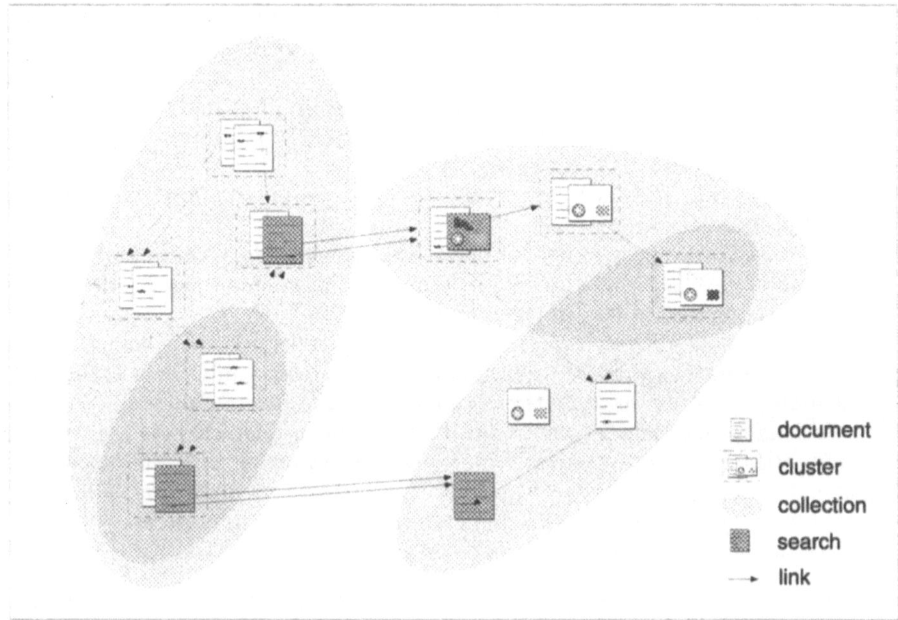

Figure 1: The Hyper-G Data Model

Hyper-G was designed to overcome the limitations of existing tools like WAIS, Gopher, and W3, while at the same time maintaining interoperability with them — interoperability was considered crucial to the acceptance of a system in today's multi-protocol Internet.

2.2 Design Features

The most fundamental design decision was to provide support for orthogonal yet closely coupled structuring, linking, and search facilities at the database level (as shown in Figure 1):

- *Structuring*: Documents may be grouped into aggregate *collections*, which may themselves belong to other collections. Every document must belong to at least one collection. Navigation may be performed down through the collection hierarchy (the collection "hierarchy" is, strictly speaking, a directed acyclic graph), access rights assigned on a collection-by-collection basis, and the scope of searches restricted to particular sets of collections. Collections may span multiple Hyper-G servers, providing a unified view of distributed resources.
- *Linking*: Hyperlinks connect a *source anchor* within one document to either a *destination anchor* within another document, an entire document, or a collection. Links are not stored within documents (as in W3) but in a separate link database (as pioneered by Intermedia [Haan et al. 1992]). This has a number of important advantages:

  - Source and destination anchors are not limited to text documents, but can be attached to any kind of media (image, audio, film, 3D scene, formatted PostScript document, etc.).
  - Links can be attached to otherwise read-only documents (for example documents on CD-ROM or with read-only access rights).
  - Links can be followed backwards.
  - A local map (fish-eye view) can be readily computed and visualised using the link database.
  - Consistency constraints can be met more easily (for example when moving or deleting a document, it is important to know which other documents contain links to it).
- *Attribute and Content Search*: Documents and collections have an associated set of attributes (author, title, keywords, etc.) which may be searched for, including boolean combinations and term truncation. Full text (content) search facilities include vector and fuzzy boolean queries. Every document and collection is automatically indexed upon insertion into the database – no extra indexing steps are required. The scope of a search may be focussed to one or more collections on one or more servers or may be as wide as all collections on all Hyper-G servers worldwide.

Each of these three orthogonal features work *seamlessly* across server boundaries, reducing fragmentation while at the same time promoting consistency. To achieve scalability in terms of number of users, Hyper-G servers replicate and cache remote objects; updates are propagated to other servers using an efficient, scalable flooding algorithm [Kappe 1995].

A special kind of collection, a *cluster*, groups documents into logical entities. Clusters are used both to define multimedia aggregates (for example, a text and an associated image or video clip) which are presented together and multilingual aggregates (for example, English and German translations of a text, audio clip, structure diagram, or any combination of these).

Other design features supported by Hyper-G and not found in comparable systems include:

- Anonymous and identified user identification modes.
- A scheme of user groups and subgroups maintained by the server.
- Access rights for users and user groups on a document or collection basis.
- "Home collections", personal information spaces for identified users (kept on the server) used to organise personal documents and pointers to resources.
- Language preferences, applied both to document retrieval and to the user interface.
- An underlying object-oriented database, which guarantees the consistency and integrity of data (for example the updating of links when a document is moved or deleted).

2.3 Architecture

Figure 2 shows the architecture of Hyper-G. Note the interoperability of Hyper-G with Gopher and W3 clients and servers. When accessed by a Gopher client, the Hyper-G server maps the collection hierarchy into a Gopher menu tree (hyperlinks cannot be represented in Gopher). A synthetic search item is

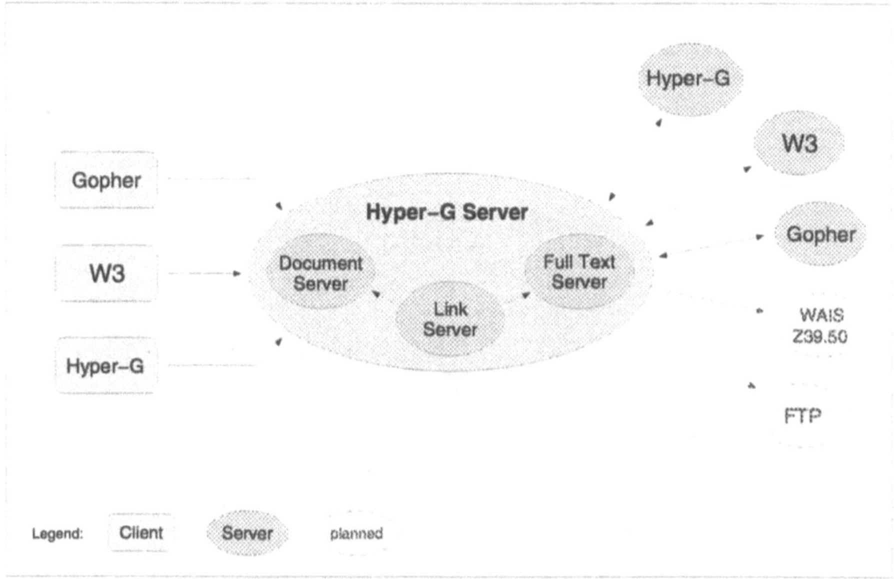

Figure 2: The Architecture of Hyper-G

generated at the foot of each Gopher menu to allow searching the corresponding collection. When accessed by a W3 client, each level of the collection hierarchy is converted to an HTML [Berners-Lee and Conolly 1993] document containing a menu of links to its members. Hyper-G text documents are transformed on-the-fly into HTML documents, including any links they might have. Additional Hyper-G functionality such as user identification, language preference selection, and searching are implemented via HTML forms and are accessible at any time.

The Hyper-G server is able to store pointers to remote objects on Gopher and W3 servers. This allows the incorporation of information on remote non-Hyper-G servers (almost) seamlessly: Gopher menus are transformed into Hyper-G collections and W3 text documents into Hyper-G text documents. Interoperability with WAIS (Z39.50) and FTP servers is planned.

Unlike Gopher or W3 clients which connect to many servers during a typical session, Hyper-G clients talk to a single Hyper-G server for the entire session. Should information from a remote server be needed, the local server acts as a proxy, i.e. it fetches the object and passes it on to the client. This approach has the following advantages:

- Clients are kept simple, the Hyper-G server handles external protocols.
- Remote information can be cached in the local server.
- User accounts and access rights have only to be maintained on the local server (the user has to identify to one server only).
- Statistics and user profile information can be gathered on a per-session basis.

Hyper-G clients connect to a Hyper-G server using the assigned port number 418 by default. Port 418 is used for control information, documents are

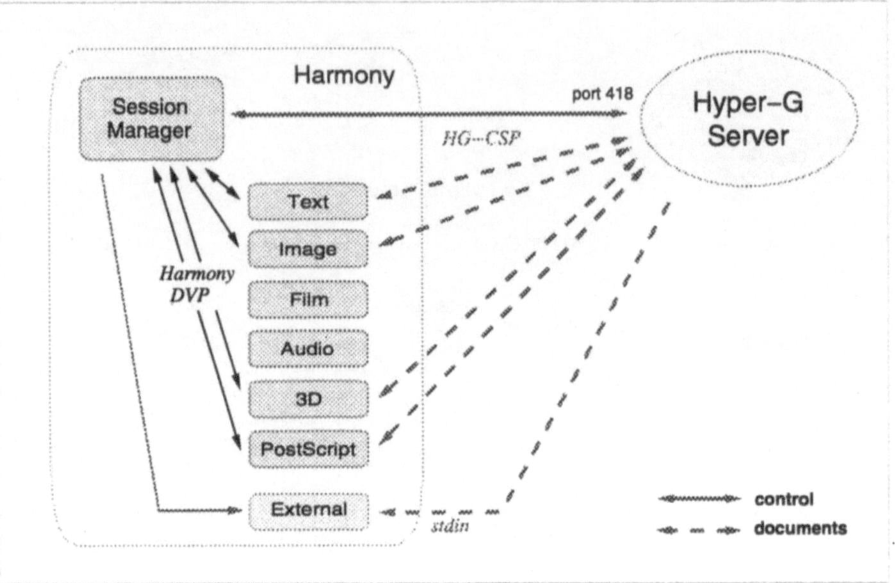

Figure 3: The Architecture of the Harmony Client for Hyper-G

generally sent (simultaneously in the case of multimedia clusters) using dynamically assigned port numbers. The precise mechanism is described in the Hyper-G Client/Server Protocol (HG-CSP) specification [Kappe and Pani 1994].

3 The Harmony Client for Hyper-G

Harmony is the native Hyper-G client for X Windows on Unix platforms. It takes advantage of Hyper-G's underlying facilities to provide intuitive navigational tools and informative feedback about the location of information.

As can be seen in Figure 3, Harmony is a multi-process application: the primary process, the *Session Manager*, communicates with the Hyper-G server, provides navigational facilities, and coordinates all other activities. The session manager starts secondary processes, *document viewers*, as necessary to display particular documents. Native Harmony document viewers conform to the Harmony Document Viewer Protocol (DVP) [Andrews et al. 1995], which defines various browsing, editing, and link functions. There currently exist native document viewers for text, images, MPEG films, audio, 3D scenes, and PostScript. Harmony may be configured to run external programs in place of any native viewer and also for unsupported document types (the document is piped to standard input), however without provision for link activation and editing.

Figure 4 shows a typical Harmony session. The Session Manager (top left) provides navigation through the collection structure, search facilities, and various general functions such as user identification and language selection. Collections

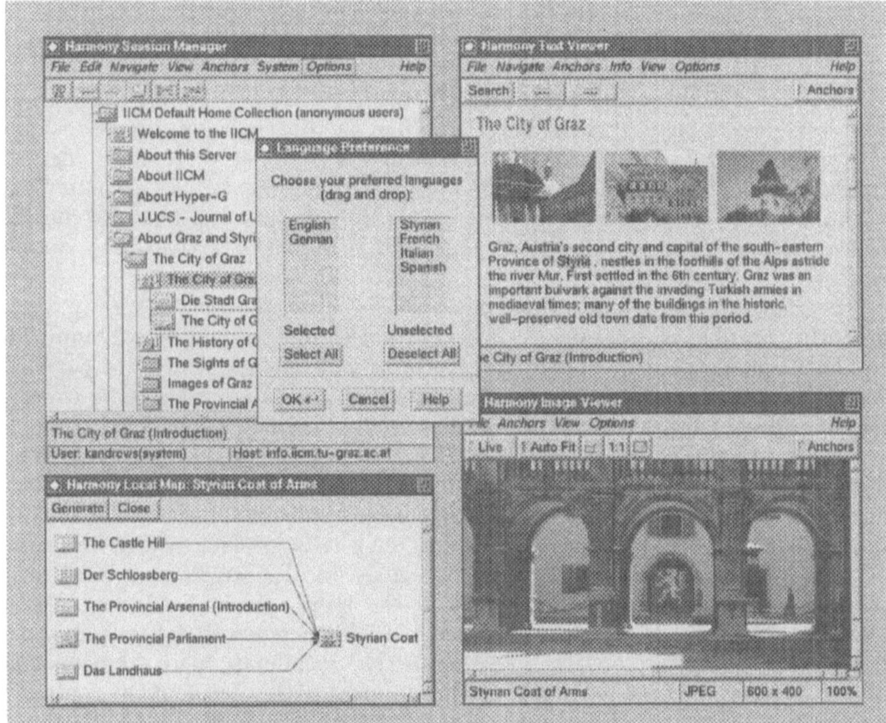

Figure 4: Harmony – The Hyper-G Client for X Windows

may be opened and closed and clusters or individual documents activated within the graphical collection display by double-clicking. Collections, clusters, or documents which have already been visited are marked with a tick. In this example, a descriptive text and an image about the city of Graz have been accessed.

The Harmony Text Viewer (top right) uses a generic SGML parser to display marked-up text documents (both Hyper-G's HTF and W3's HTML formats), and has the usual facilities for scrolling, finding strings, selecting, etc. Hyperlinks within the text can be highlighted in a number of ways. Inline images in TIFF, GIF, and JPEG formats are supported.

The Harmony Image Viewer (bottom right) accepts raster images in a variety of common formats (TIFF, GIF, JPEG, etc.). Operations such as zooming and panning are available. Link anchors are rectangular, circular, or elliptical (soon also polygonal) areas, which are overlaid atop the image. All Harmony document viewers support both interactive link following and definition.

Harmony's Film Player (not shown) displays MPEG (MPEG-1, soon MPEG-2) video streams. It is possible to define a link anchor which follows an object of interest in the video: rectangular and circular anchor regions overlaying the film are simply defined for specific keyframes (they are interpolated in between keyframes). Anchors can be activated both during playback and while playback is paused. The Harmony Audio Player (not shown) can be configured to use either the Network Audio Server [Fulton and Renda 1994] or local audio commands to play audio files in a variety of common formats.

The Local Map facility (bottom left), provides a kind of short-range radar, generating on request (dynamically) a map of the link relationships of a chosen document, similar to the local map of Intermedia [Haan et al. 1992]. By default, two levels of incoming and outgoing hyperlinks are represented. One can navigate within the local map by selecting (single-clicking) another object toward the edge of the map and generating a new display. Objects can be activated by double-clicking.

The language preference dialogue (centre) allows the user to specify an ordered list of preferred languages. Harmony's user interface adjusts dynamically to the language of first choice (English and German interfaces are currently supported), documents available in multiple languages are selected in order of language preference, and searches are optionally language-dependent.

Central to the design of Harmony is the concept of *location feedback*. When a document or collection is visited, its location within the collection structure is automatically displayed in the Session Manager's collection browser (by opening up the path to it), regardless of whether the object was reached as the result of a search, by following a hyperlink, or via the local map. This unique feature of Harmony is a powerful instrument in the fight against becoming "lost in hyperspace" – users can orient themselves with reference to a fixed structural framework. In the case of search results and the local map, mere selection of an object initiates location feedback, providing users with a sense of the context of an object, prior to any decision to view it.

The Harmony search dialogue (not shown) provides an interface to the full range of Hyper-G searches: attribute and content, boolean and fuzzy. The scope of a search may be focussed to a single collection or set of specific collections (possibly spanning server boundaries), or may be as wide as all collections on the local server. Search results are presented as a ranked list. As noted above, Harmony applies the principle of location feedback to search results: selecting an object in the result list causes its location in the collection structure to be displayed, hence users can make informed choices before committing to fetch particular documents.

A further innovative feature of Harmony is its use of three-dimensional visualisations, both hand-crafted and automatically generated [Andrews 1993, Andrews and Pichler 1994]. Model description files representing arbitrarily complex scenes or objects are displayed by the Harmony 3D Scene Viewer. Figure 5 shows the scene viewer displaying a model of the Great Hall of the Austrian National Library (top left) and a staute of Kaiser Karl VI (bottom left). Users typically view a model of a scene by moving themselves (walk, fly, fly to, heads-up) and view a model of an object by moving the model (translate, rotate, zoom). 3D models are fully-fledged hypermedia documents: hyperlinks may be attached to individual objects within a scene or to groups of polygons within an object.

Harmony's Information Landscape, also shown in Figure 5, is an interactive, three-dimensional visualisation of the collection structure, tightly coupled to the Session Manager's two-dimensional collection browser display (changes in one are reflected in the other). The collection hierarchy is mapped out onto a plane, documents within a collection are arranged on top of the corresponding block;

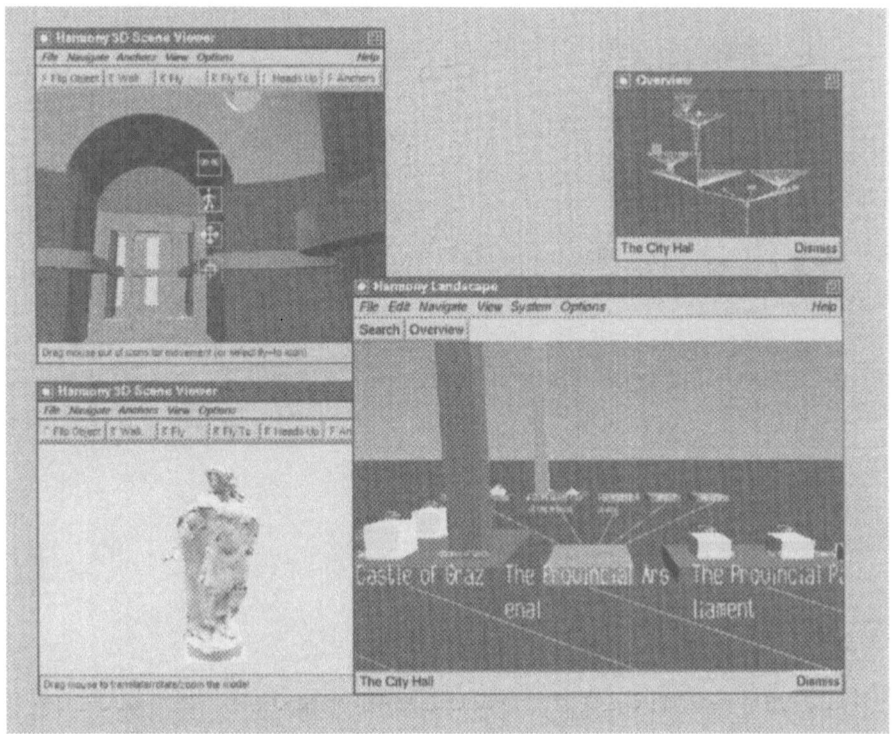

Figure 5: Harmony Landscape and 3D Scene Viewer

colour and height are used to encode document type and size respectively. Users can "fly" over the landscape looking for salient features, like flying over a file system with FSN [Tesler and Strasnick 1992]. A flat overview window (upper right) provides a further aid to orientation. Through their ability to compactly display many thousands of objects, 3D visualisations are perhaps the only effective means of browsing in and judging the extent of large, dynamic information spaces.

The Harmony PostScript Viewer (Figure 6) displays arbitrary documents in PostScript format; the documents are typically stored and transmitted in compressed form and uncompressed locally by the viewer. Rectangular link anchors are supported.

As was mentioned in the opening discussion, Hyper-G clients can be used to *edit* as well as browse the contents of a Hyper-G server, in so far as the user is identified and has appropriate access rights. Figure 7 shows the Harmony Insert Dialogue being used to upload a text document about Graz from the local file system into the user's home collection. Figure 8 shows a link being created from the word Styria in the text about Graz to a multimedia cluster about the Austrian Province of Styria.

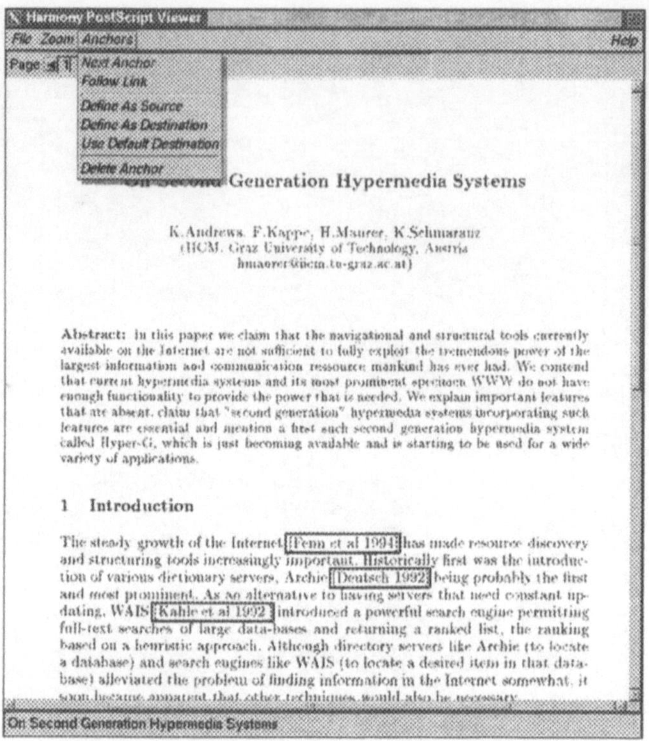

Figure 6: The Harmony PostScript Viewer

Finally, Harmony's History Browser (not shown) offers a timeline of past interactive waypoints, including previous search panels – another means of orienting in hyperspace.

Features to be implemented in Harmony over the coming months include interactive forms, a drag-and-drop interface to the local file system (allowing documents to be simply pulled into collections on the server), integrated electronic mail facilities, semi-automatic link generation, and three-dimensional representations of hyperlink relationships and search results. An immersive (virtual reality) interface is also planned.

4 Concluding Remarks

We have presented the design rationale and the current development status of Hyper-G and its Harmony client for X Windows. Of particular note are Hyper-G's tightly-coupled collection, link, and search facilities, its projection of a seamless information space across server boundaries, and its support for multiple languages. Harmony makes innovative use of location feedback and two

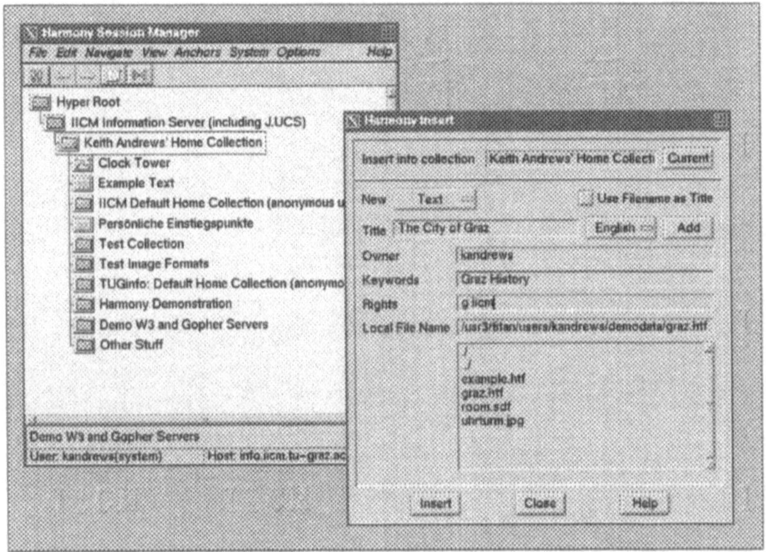

Figure 7: The Harmony Insert Dialogue

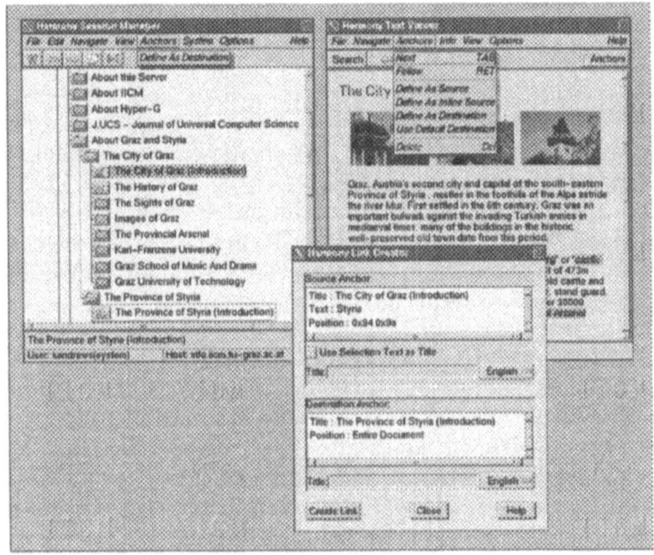

Figure 8: The Harmony Link Creator

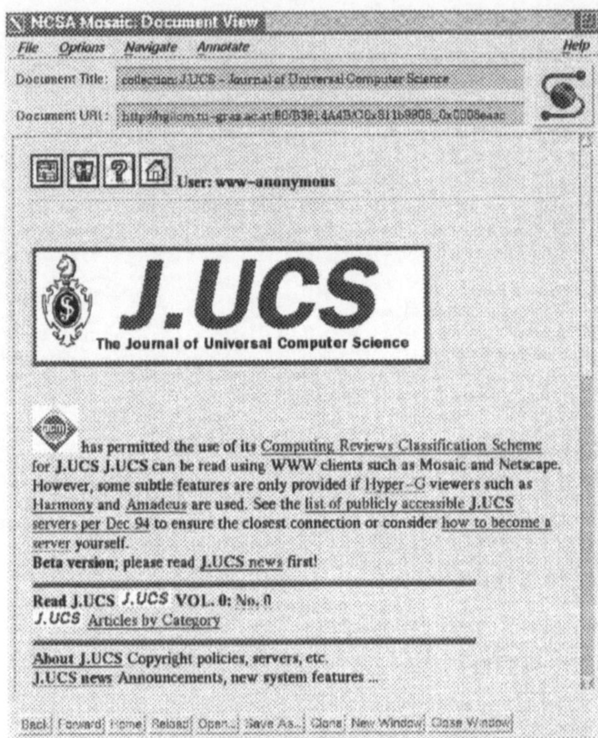

Figure 9: Accessing a Hyper-G Server with Mosaic

and three-dimensional visualisations to help users navigate and orient themselves within large, dynamic information spaces.

A key design goal of Hyper-G was to maintian interoperability with current information systems. The combination of the Hyper-G server's rich structuring and maintenance facilities and its ability to service requests from W3 and Gopher clients in addition to native Hyper-G clients make it ideal for use as a multi-protocol server. Figure 9 shows the Mosaic client for W3 being used to access the J.UCS collection on the IICM's Hyper-G server.

Although still in its infancy, Hyper-G has already gained considerable acceptance. The European Space Agency and the Museum of New Zealand have adopted Hyper-G for their own information systems, the Austrian Ministry of Science has adopted it as its information system of choice for all Austrian universities, and the German Mathematics Association (DMV) is setting up an information system spanning most German universities and colleges, to name just a few examples.

Hyper-G also is being used as the basis for a major new electronic publishing venture. The Journal of Universal Computer Science (J.UCS), supported by Springer Verlag, is among the first high-quality, fully-refereed, fully-citable scientific journals to depend primarily on Internet distribution [Maurer and Schmaranz 1994]. The pilot issue is already available at several sites, the first regular issue will be available world-wide at the end of January 1995.

In addition to the Harmony client described in this paper, native Hyper-G clients are available for Unix VT100-style terminals (hgtv) and MS-Windows (Amadeus), and a client is under development for the Macintosh. Further information about Hyper-G and Harmony and installation details may be retrieved by anonymous ftp from `ftp.iicm.tu-graz.ac.at` in directory `/pub/Hyper-G` or from the IICM Information Server under `http://info.iicm.tu-graz.ac.at/` or `gopher://info.iicm.tu-graz.ac.at/`.

Acknowledgements

Financial support of Hyper-G by the Austrian Ministry of Science, JOANNEUM RESEARCH, and the European Space Agency is gratefully acknowledged.

References

[Andrews 1993] Andrews, K.: "Constructing Cyberspace: Virtual Reality and Hypermedia". Presented at Virtual Reality Vienna '93. Available by anonymous ftp from `iicm.tu-graz.ac.at` in directory `pub/Hyper-G/papers` (1993).

[Andrews et al. 1995] Andrews, K., Faschingbauer, J., Schipflinger, J.: "The Harmony Document Viewer Protocol (DVP)". In preparation (1995).

[Andrews and Kappe 1994] Andrews, K., Kappe, F.: "Soaring Through Hyperspace: A Snapshot of Hyper-G and its Harmony Client". In Herzner, W., Kappe, F. (editors), Proc. of Eurographics Symposium on Multimedia/Hypermedia in Open Distributed Environments, Graz, Austria. Springer (1994), 181–191.

[Andrews et al. 1994] Andrews, K., Kappe, F., Maurer, H., Schmaranz, K.: "On Second Generation Hypermedia Systems". Journal of Universal Computer Science (Pilot Issue), 0, 0 (1994), 127–135. Available at `http://info.iicm.tu-graz.ac.at/Cjucs_root`.

[Andrews and Pichler 1994] Andrews, K., Pichler, M.: "Hooking Up 3-Space: Three-Dimensional Models as Fully-Fledged Hypermedia Documents". In Proc. of East-West International Conference on Multimedia, Hypermedia, and Virtual Reality (MHVR'94), Moscow, Russia (1994), 11–18.

[Anklesaria et al. 1993] Anklesaria, F., McCahill, M., Lindner, P., Johnson, D., Torrey, D., Alberti, B.: "RFC 1436: The Internet Gopher Protocol". Available by anonymous ftp from `ds.internic.net` as `/rfc/rfc1436.txt` (1993).

[Berners-Lee et al. 1994] Berners-Lee, T., Cailliau, R., Luotonen, A., Nielsen, H. F., Secret, A.: "The World-Wide Web". Communications of the ACM, 37, 8 (1994), 76–82.

[Berners-Lee and Conolly 1993] Berners-Lee, T., Conolly, D.: "Hypertext Markup Language (HTML)". Available on the WWW at URL `http://info.cern.ch/hypertext/WWW/Markup/HTML.html` (1993).

[Cailliau 1995] Cailliau, R.: "About WWW". Information Processing and Management (1995). Special Issue: Selected Proc. of Distributed Multimedia Systems '94, Graz, Austria, Nov. 1994.

[Fenn and Maurer 1994] Fenn, B., Maurer, H.: "Harmony on an Expanding Net". Interactions, 1, 4 (1994), 26–38.

[Fulton and Renda 1994] Fulton, J., Renda, G.: "The Network Audio System". Available by anon. ftp from `ftp://ftp.x.org/contrib/audio/nas/xcon94paper.ps.gz` (1994).

[Haan et al. 1992] Haan, B. J., Kahn, P., Riley, V. A., Coombs, J. H., Meyrowitz, N. K.: "IRIS Hypermedia Services". Communications of the ACM, 35, 1 (1992), 36–51.

[Kahle et al. 1992] Kahle, B., Morris, H., Davis, F., Tiene, K., Hart, C., Palmer, R.: "Wide Area Information Servers: An Executive Information System for Unstructured Files". Electronic Networking: Research, Applications and Policy, 2, 1 (1992), 59–68.

[Kappe 1993] Kappe, F.: "Hyper-G: A Distributed Hypermedia System". In Leiner, B. (editor), Proc. INET '93, San Francisco, California. Internet Society (1993), DCC-1–DCC-9.

[Kappe 1995] Kappe, F.: "A Scalable Architecture for Maintaining Referential Integrity in Distributed Information Systems". Available by anonymous ftp from `ftp.iicm.tu-graz.ac.at` as file `/pub/Hyper-G/papers/p-flood.ps`, Graz University of Technology, Austria (1995).

[Kappe and Pani 1994] Kappe, F., Pani, G.: "Hyper-G Client/Server Protocol (HG-CSP)". Technical report, IICM, Graz University of Technology (1994). Available by anonymous ftp from `ftp.iicm.tu-graz.ac.at` in file `/pub/Hyper-G/papers/Protocol.ps.gz`.

[Maurer and Schmaranz 1994] Maurer, H., Schmaranz, K.: "J.UCS – The Next Generation in Electronic Journal Publishing". Computer Networks for Research in Europe, 26 (1994), S63–S69. Supplement to Vol. 26 of Computer Networks and ISDN Systems.

[McCahill and Anklesaria 1995] McCahill, M. P., Anklesaria, F. X.: "Evolution of Internet Gopher". Information Processing and Management (1995). Special Issue: Selected Proc. of Distributed Multimedia Systems '94, Graz, Austria, Nov. 1994.

[Merit NIC 1994] Merit NIC: "NSFNET Backbone Statistics". Available by anonymous ftp from `nic.merit.edu` in `/nsfnet/statistics` (1994).

[Network Wizards 1994] Network Wizards: "Internet Domain Survey". Available on the WWW at URL `http://www.nw.com/zone/WWW/top.html` (1994).

[Sun Microsystems] Sun Microsystems: "World Cup USA '94". Available on the WWW at URL `http://sunsite.doc.ic.ac.uk/wc94/`.

[Tesler and Strasnick 1992] Tesler, J., Strasnick, S.: "FSN: The 3D File System Navigator". Silicon Graphics, Inc., Mountain View, CA (1992). Available by anonymous ftp from `sgi.sgi.com` in directory `sgi/fsn`.

Journal of Universal Computer Science, vol. 1, no. 4 (1995), 221-231
submitted: 22/7/94, accepted: 14/10/94, appeared: 28/4/95,

About WWW

R. Cailliau,
(CERN, cailliau@www.cern.ch)

Abstract: The World-Wide Web is the most talked-about distributed information system today. This paper does not touch on its workings; it tries to give a brief history and outlines the feelings provoked by the explosive adoption in all circles of WWW as the first vehicle on the Global Information Infrastructure.

Keywords: WWW, World-Wide Web, History, SGML, Cultural Aspects, Society.

Category: H.5.1

1. Introduction

Before the World-Wide Web, networked information was difficult to access. With the Web, browsing through distant data bases has become almost a recreational pleasure.

It is fair to say that the Web is now driving the Internet. In fact many recent articles in newspapers and magazines simply make no distinction between the Internet and the World-Wide Web: it is as if the roads had been lying there for some time, waiting for someone to invent the Volkswagen.

I have followed the development of the Web from the days before it had a name. A brief history is therefore in order.

2. Brief History

In 1989, Tim Berners-Lee and I proposed independently a project for studying hypertexts and their possible uses at CERN. We joined efforts quickly, and Tim had already a prototype and a set of ideas to use the hypertext paradigm over the network. In this, he was no doubt influenced by the earlier work of Ted Nelson (Xanadu, [Nelson (88)]).

In 1990, Tim implemented the first browser/editor under the NeXTStep operating system. This was easily possible, since the NeXTStep system came with an object-oriented development kit which included not only a graphical interface builder (itself wysiwyg!) but also a programmable text editing object with paragraph styles. We were off the ground at least as far as we ourselves were concerned: the browser/-editor as a single tool for both navigating and correcting, editing, composing texts and hypertexts was a real dream object. To this date, the easy of use of that program has not been surpassed in the WWW world.

In 1991, Nicola Pellow, a technical student at CERN, wrote the Line Mode Browser. This was a simple, character-grid oriented client which was written in C (not even ANSI, but just flat C!). It could be compiled on just about anything but the kitchen sink. Through its availability, the Web began to spread outside CERN.

In 1992, the first steps were taken to implement format "negotiation", i.e. a mechanism whereby a server and a client could agree on the format of the document to be transmitted. This was also the year of the integration of all the other useful and existing protocols on the Internet: Gopher, ftp, telnet etc.

In 1993, Marc Andreessen, then a graduate student at NCSA, produced an X-window browser. Though I would term it primitive compared to the elegance and functionality of the NeXTStep browser, it had the marketing advantage of permitting colour images to be included. This sudden availability of colour pictures and proportional type fonts to the grey world of Unix gave the Web a boost it had not derived from anything else. Pictures were clearly the means to capture the imagination of the manager of your manager. The Internet programming community went wild. Mosaic became the synonym of WWW.

At the end of 1993, I decided that it was time to have all the early contributors meet each other in a great brainstorming session: I planned the First WWW Conference, which was held at CERN in May 1994.

1994 can truly be called the "Year of the Web". It became clear that CERN could no longer continue core development without external help, and a project was submitted to the European Community to fund a transitional phase of Web development in Europe. This project has a partner in the US. Its major aim is to ensure that there is a single, open standard in the Web mark-up and the Web communications protocol, based on a working reference implementation which is freely available.

The Web is now mentioned in any magazine at any time. Newspapers tell you how to connect to the Internet, URLs are routinely used in scientific journals to refer to information, they proliferate on the teletext pages of MTV, in short, you can no longer get away from it.

3. A successful system

To be a global success, a system must have two basic properties:

- it must have a small learning threshold so many people will join in,
- it must be sufficiently scaleable to stand up after large numbers of users and publishers have in fact joined.

The Web satisfies these conditions because:

- it defines an easy to understand name space for documents which is open-ended and addresses synthetic documents thus allowing interfacing to data bases and systems generating documents.

- it works over the Internet, making it global and accessible to a large community of programmers,
- early HTML was easy to generate, so populating the Web with information from existing data bases could be done through simple server interfaces.
- separation of form and content allows documents to be shipped without worrying about the capabilities of the client, making the web easily portable to all platforms.
- it is also easy to populate the Web because servers can be set up without prior consultation with previous publishers.
- the name space is based on the Internet naming scheme, therefore the Web scales like the Net.
- there are only fleeting connections, so servers can handle requests serially.

But being a success does not mean you are better than others or even merely good. The Web has also well-known disadvantages:

- it is not easy to write browser/editors, which are more difficult to make than word processors.
- it is not easy to find information because indexes do not scale.
- it is easy to get lost.
- it is not possible to control the quality or authenticity of the information, leading to a social problem.
- being open and easy to add to, the danger of divergence into incompatible systems is great.

In any case, to ensure the future, we must:

- maintain interoperability,
- have open standards,
- keep systems mutatable,
- produce interfaces that "can be understanded by them people"

Some of these points will become clear later.

4. Providing Information

4.1 SGML and layout

For the context of the points following, it is necessary to understand something of the SGML philosophy and to remove a number of popular misconceptions.

HTML is not a subset of SGML.

What is today called HTML should in fact have been named "the Web DTD". For the sake of those who do not know all about SGML, I'll briefly describe its most important features.

SGML is not a document format, it is a system for describing structures. It starts from the idea that there are sets of documents that look alike (or should look alike) in structure. For example, all novels are divided into elements called chapters, and each chapter is a sequence of paragraphs.

Elements of a document are marked-up by putting tags at the appropriate places in the text.

The structure of each set of documents can be described by a Document Type Definition (or DTD) which is a formal grammar about its elements.

A DTD defines only the structure, but not the presentation. The presentation of each element is given in a separate object, a so-called style sheet.

SGML then allows for complete separation of structure and presentation.

Now, if a person wants to communicate a document to you, you need in total three objects:

- the document itself, with the mark-up in it (tags),
- the DTD, which tells you what tags mean and how they relate to each other,
- the style sheet, which tells you how to present each element.

The way in which WWW uses SGML is (slightly simplified):

- the Web DTD is agreed beforehand by everyone (and called HTML),
- the presentation is left to the browser (client) so each individual can set it to his/her liking.
- the document only is shipped from server to client.

We are now limited to HTML, since only the document is transferred. However, because there is no objection to ship a complete MIME message from the server, including a DTD and a style sheet, there is room for a complete implementation of distributed SGML systems using the Web.

Keeping presentation separate from contents has enormous advantages:

- automated treatment of information is easy.
- no knowledge is needed of the presentation capabilities of the client.

It is far easier to look for author names when these are tagged properly in simple text documents than when they are embedded in proprietary formats using just text styles.

Thus, HTML tags like <b> for bold and <i> for italic are really meaningless and should be avoided.

The world is alas divided into those who want to supply information and those who want to supply advertising. Information may be given to humans or to their computerised agents. Advertising is normally done by visual impact directly to a receiving human, which requires complete control over layout. The image is omnipresent on the Web, showing that the majority of servers are actually providers of advertising.

4.2 The Paper Metaphor

We are learning how to provide information in the new medium of distributed hypertext. This early phase is dangerous: if we are not bold enough, we may never escape from the paper and book metaphor.

So far, a lot of existing stuff has been made available. This information was destined to be presented on paper. Existing methods and habits for preparing it are all more or less related to text processing for the printed page. The microcomputers in use today are practically all employed for such purposes: printed reports.

The Web does not need printing. It is useless to print a well-conceived hypertext that is kept up-to-date. A paper copy leaves me uneasy: is it still valid? Yet the most frequent question that novice users of the Web ask is "can I print this?". Yes, you can, but why?

For the same reason of attachment to the printed page, we have seen floods of converters from proprietary formats into HTML, but not a serious browser/editor and (to my knowledge) only a single rudimentary tool to assemble a number of Web documents into a larger one for printing.

Everyone seems to see the printed, word-processor document as the original, and the Web document as the derivative. This is bad news.

4.3 Existing Information

Existing information of course has to be published somehow, so converters are not completely undesirable. There are four courses of action to get existing documents published on the Web:

- do nothing at all. This is the easiest method and obviously consumes no resources but also achieves nothing.
- publish references. Here the Web user will find at least that the document exists, and perhaps a way of getting a copy somehow.
- publish as-is. Now some Web users can see the document (if they have an application that is capable of handling the proprietary format after transferring the document file). Others will see only the reference but will not be able to follow the link.
- convert to Web structures. This is best, but consumes most resources, since links have to be put in, redundancies have to be removed, and chunking (dividing the original up into reasonable hypertext portions) is not always obvious.

4.4 New Stuff

For the new stuff, we should think of the far future. The Web is not the ultimate repository of human knowledge. But we want to keep the documents somehow, what they mean and what they have to say. Thus we should think: "how are we going to read this a hundred years from now?" And I'll bet it will not be on an Intel-based PC. So we had better make sure that the semantics are preserved, and that their format is easy to convert from current systems to the next ones. We must make the contents mutatable. For me this is one of the more important reasons to use SGML-like encoding and to encourage authors to use it correctly.

5. Tools

5.1 Collaborative Tools

Currently we have a Read-Only Web. It is not possible to change a displayed document (unless you happen to use a copy of the NeXTStep browser), even if it belongs to you and you have all access rights to the file.

There are projects under way to change this situation, notably the GrifW3 which is based on wysiwyg SGML technology, but we are not there yet. In this respect, the Hyper-G system is far superior to the Web.

Once there is no longer a difference between a browser and a Web editor, people will be able to use the Web as a collaborative tool, developing information and documents together, independently of geographic location or time zones.

Note that an browser/editor gives you these advantages:

- no more problems with starting points, since the construction of my home page (see note at bottom of list) is now easy: it contains the pointers of the places I'm most interested in and perhaps some comments.
- hot lists are a thing of the past, since they are just edited local HTML files, and I can impose any structure on any number of them.
- personal annotations and group annotations and annotation servers and the like are just all unified into sets of HTML files again.
- a lot of converter use goes away.
- pagination, the nightmare of traditional text processing is gone.
- bad HTML is never produced by a proper editor.
- some linking problems disappear (the editor can know about relative links).
- printing diminishes.
- you can organise your own notes in the same hypertext way as anything that you publish, and with drag-and-drop ease on your laptop.

(Note: a "Home page" is where I as an idividual start from when I launch a browser on my computer. Its contents are nobody's business. A "Welcome page" is what I get from a server as the generic page when I specify only the server name in a URL. Currently, the term "home page" is used for what should be called a "welcome page". The confusion comes from the fact that almost everyone gets a local welcome page when they start up a browser: the absence of editors makes it very difficult for non-expert users to build a home page.)

5.2 Rhetoric

Of course, a new rhetoric has to be learned. As today, some people will write badly for the Web, others will be brilliant authors.

5.3 Navigation

Anyone who has seriously tried to work the Web knows that it takes no effort to get lost. Systems like Hyper-G provide you with excellent navigation tools, Gopher is so structured that it is easy to know where you are.

The distributed nature of the Web makes it difficult to show the user a map, unless he/she is prepared to incur a lot of network traffic overhead.

5.4 Construction

Even with collaborative tools and browser/editors we will still need a variety of tools to help us construct the information. In word processors there are items like outliners, style checkers, even tools to help you organise your thoughts. For a distributed system, we need tools like that, but they must concentrate on other aspects: finding existing materials, generic referencing, suggesting which phrases should be linked to explanations, helping cut long parts up and rearranging and merging shorter ones. Plenty of room for research.

6. Social and Cultural aspects

We have in computing seen the negative effects of too many inventors in too many areas. Short-term commercial interests often force us to adopt computing solutions that are frustratingly complicated and that direct us into dead-end streets, holding back real change for decades. Networking has not been an exception.

Too much attention is devoted to backwards compatibility (a term invented by software developers?). Technology should not be worried about the past. I prefer the attitude expressed in this maxim [De Bono (91)]:

Instead of being pushed by our history,

we should be pulled by our vision.

E. De Bono

6.1 Change

Inside the network, we are rebuilding the world we know: we use the book metaphor, we want total layout control (which is a help for visual navigation, but definitely not for computer aided navigation!), we talk about adding a worn-out look to frequently consulted objects (do I want my welcome page to look worn out by complete strangers?).

Is it possible to think about what the networked society should look like or is it only possible to let a thousand weeds grow?

6.2 Isolation

Communication is different from the Gigabit/second number. There is a lot of "communicating" being done, yet I know nobody who is happy receiving 100 e-mail messages a day. You feel obliged to answer (a vestige of the days of personal contact?) but what you get is the stress of having done so badly, hurriedly and tiredly.

Increased isolation of individuals has been the result of increased exteriorisation of information. Books made it possible to know something without having to contact the author. Radio and TV spread news without personal contact. The Walkman effectively shields a person from investing in contact with others on public transport trips and certainly is used in this way. A recent article [? (94)] proclaimed as an advantage of the global network that

> *"Sex, location of a partner, video marriage, ...*
>
> *You can have any kind of interaction without the inconvenience of having someone in your house"*

The key word is "inconvenience". The lack of social contact is perhaps the most negative side of our Western culture, and is so perceived in most other cultures.

6.3 Life, the Universe and Everything

In an article of 1977, describing his graphical user interface, Alan Kay wrote [Kay (77)]:

> *There are three reactions to the introduction of a new medium:*
>
> *illiteracy,*
>
> *literacy*
>
> *and artistic creation*

He goes on to say:

> *After reading material became available the illiterate were those who were left behind by the new medium. It was inevitable that a few creative individuals would use the written word to express inner thoughts and ideas. The most profound changes were brought about in the literate. They did not necessarily become better people or better members of society, but they came to view the world in a way quite different from the way they had viewed it before, with consequences that were difficult to predict or control.*

How will the networked society influence the daily lives of normal people? Below are a number of questions. In the current social structures, I can think of negative answers only:

- will employment go up?
- will people feel better?
- will general education improve?
- will the world be a safer place?
- what will happen to the service sector?
- will power be in the hands of benevolent people?
- is this what we want?

Is it therefore not more urgent to work on structural reforms in our culture rather than on laying down fibre cables or shooting 700 satellites into the sky?

6.4 Work

The argument against Malthus' predictions of overpopulation was that food production could be made to expand faster than the population growth. However, there really is a limit to the number of people that can live on earth, and only the very obstinate now hold that we have no population problem.

Likewise, an old economic argument has been that the introduction of machines will not take away work, just displace it to other activities. So we have seen a massive movement from agriculture to industry and then to services. But the computer is not a machine like any used in the industrial revolution and after: it displaces people.

Consider the distribution of work. Before 1900, there was lots of work, despite mechanisation. Jobs of low and high intellectual content were plenty. There was even a healthy overlap in the middle.

During this century, we have witnessed a constantly growing separation: jobs are either menial or intellectual, and there are fewer of them. They are less gratifying. Menial jobs are done by immigrant workers, intellectual jobs need high qualification which not many can attain. The young generation is acutely aware of the "No Future" syndrome.

With the massive introduction of computing, fewer and fewer real jobs remain. The service sector which absorbed people during the boom years no longer does: those who are unemployed remain so. The recovery of the economy does not result in higher employment.

Networking makes the problem more acute: when you can learn immediately from the best in the world, why go anywhere local?

Will the networked society be able to create more jobs or will it just lead to much more efficient service companies, leading to higher unemployment? Maybe the time has finally come to start working less and less hard.

7. Europe

I was once told that "Europe has a cultural deficit in networking". Brilliantly and concisely expressed. I set out to calculate the value of the deficit. as a simple expression: the number of networks in use per million inhabitants. The Internet statistics give numbers of networks, an encyclopaedia numbers of people. The graph below needs no comment. One could argue whether I now like this situation or not, given what I wrote before.

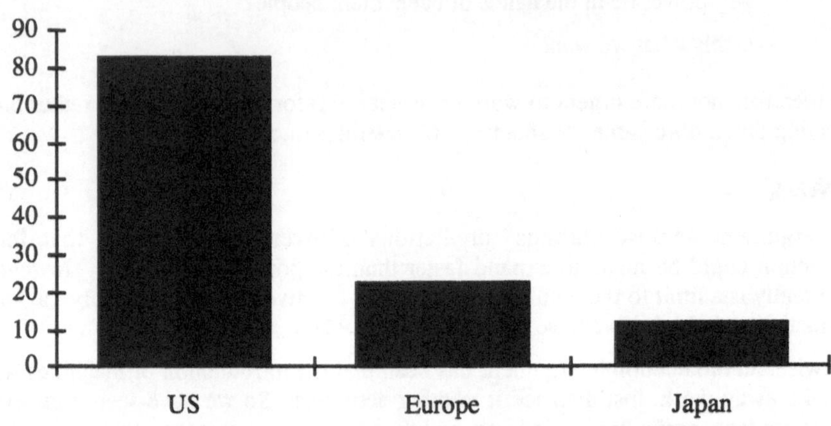

Europe's cultural deficit in networking

Europe has many assets, and I am attached to this strange assemblage of peninsulas. But we have one big problem: reacting speedily and nimbly to situations which need mobilisation of large resources. We seem to be poor at exploiting ideas that we generate here, especially in high-tech. Will Europe play a real role in the global networked society or will we have to buy everything from a US software company, even though we keep generating the important ideas?

Three axes are important for any society that wants to partake of the coming network culture [Abramatic (95)]:

- core technology, (you need to understand the options),
- tools (their use determines your competitive efficiency),
- content published (your visibility in the marketplace).

The content of a network server in WWW is what makes people look at it. We can make a big impact there and remain at level with other parts of the world.

The making of the content is dependent on the tools you use. If Europe makes no good tools to support its diverse cultures, then we will have to wait until someone else supplies us with them. Or doesn't.

Tool construction in turn depends on intimate knowledge of the core technology. It is not only important that the WWW standards remain open. It is even more important for us here that Europe maintains a strong core development effort so that our computer scientists can work locally on projects that will give them the necessary expertise. Our continued presence in the tools and contents areas rests on this expertise.

8. Brief Future & Conclusions

Networks will keep up with the traffic: speed will go up, costs will come down. There will, like on normal motorways, be traffic jams here and there. But on the whole, things will keep pace.

Collaborative work will take off especially in research, where it traditionally has been, but also inside big companies.

A new rhetoric will develop, as compelling as that of advertising. This may distort our perception of reality.

The networked society will probably fall apart not just into rich and poor, but into rich informed and poor information-illiterates.

The Web is fast becoming an entertainment medium. Perhaps Andreessen's ideas of a browser already contained the seeds of the Web entertainment business. But for me, a member of the minority who want to stay in real reality, the questions for humanity are:

- do we want entertainment or collaborative tools?
- do we want to drown in multimedia sense overload or do we want text searches?
- do we want proprietary encryption or trusted carriers?
- ... or ... ?

Maybe I'm just old-fashioned...

9. References

[Nelson (88)] Theodore H. Nelson: "Literary Machines", The Mindful Press, 1988

[De Bono (91)] E. De Bono: "I am right, You are wrong", Penguin, 1991.

[? (94)] Airline in-flight journal, November 1994 (?)

[Abramatic (95)] J.F. Abramatic, INRIA, private communication.

[Kay (77)] Alan C. Kay: Microelectronics and the Personal Computer, Scientific American, September 1977, p.231

Journal of Universal Computer Science, vol. 1, no. 4 (1995), 232-234
submitted: 17/6/94, accepted: 9/10/94, appeared: 28/4/95,

Electronic Publishing

Dietrich Goetze
Springer-Verlag Heidelberg
(email: Goetze@Springer.de)

Table of Contents:

1. General Problems in Scientific Publishing
   - Increasing volume
   - Specialization
   - Dissemination, Acquisition, Archiving because of restricted resources
   - Access
2. Current Options: Transition Print — Electronic
   - Facsimile
   - Electronic Offline Editions of Printed Work
   - Electronic Online Publishing
3. Role of Publishers for Electronic Journals
4. Obstacles to Electronic Publishing Proper

1 General Problems in Scientific Publishing

Publishing the results of scientific research is the basis of the advancement of science, technology and medicine. Over the past decades traditional scientific publishing has been facing ever increasing difficulties because of

- the continuously growing number of publications
- the specialization of science
- the rising cost of
  - distribution
  - acquisition
  - archiving, and with it
- the danger of unavailability and/or inaccessibility

The growing number of publications is the direct result of increased support of education and research all over the world. At the same time, financial resources for purchasing scientific literature are not expanding, thus limiting the dissemination and accessibility of this literature. Solutions for these problems are seen by scientists, publishers and librarians in the development of computer and network (telecommunication) as well as software technology.

Although some circles in science predict the doomsday of traditional publishing arriving within a couple of years, a closer look at the current status rather indicates that we are only in the prenatal phase of electronic publishing in science, technology and medicine. The rapid development and expansion of the science network (INTERNET) all over the world has certainly improved and enhanced communication (most of it even trivial), but we are still far from realizing a true alternative to traditional publishing in this electronic environment. Nevertheless, the electronic technology will eventually also become a publication medium. Many experiments have been initiated to gain experience as well as evaluate and possibly define appropriate methods and conditions for electronic article publishing.

2 Current Options

The initial transition from paper publishing to electronic publishing generates a high diversity of the way publishable or published material is presented, disseminated and made available:

- electrocopying with FAX dissemination of printed articles (document delivery)
- electronic editions of printed works
  - offline: CD-ROM
  - online: RightPages (LAN), INTERNET (WAN)
- electronic publishing proper (i.e. original is provided electronically; secondarily it might be printed) on NETWORKs (f.e. INTERNET)

Electrocopying and electronic offline (CD-ROM) editions of printed journals are not the subject of this discussion, however, publishing on electronic networks (online) is the central issue.

In preparation for setting up electronic publishing, we conducted market research among mathematicians in Europe (and in North America, but the results of the latter are not yet available) on how authors/readers are prepared to use the network and how they view this option.

Of the mathematicians, 90 directly on their desk (66 Of these, 70 services (90 primary use, however, is person-to-person communication.

Even so, close to 40 the last six months and have found relevant literature by searching via the INTERNET; however, regular reading of selected printed journals is still the most important means to keep oneself informed (since almost 100 only available in printed form, this finding is no surprise).

The most important advantage of electronic journals is seen in earlier and more comfortable access to the articles and improved search capabilities. Authors expect publication times to decrease and subscription prices of electronic journals to be lower than for printed journals (5 usage, 65 respondents would like the electronic journal to be delivered directly to the end user, the next preference being the library over the researcher's department or central computer center.

In contrast, authors express fears that their publications may be plagiarized or falsified during the publication process, and that their names will not always be connected to their individual contribution. Furthermore, they are worried about a "publication explosion," in numbers of publications as well as in volume. They also want the refereeing standards to be set as high as for printed journals.

Finally, they are concerned that the state of research at a particular point in time cannot be exactly determined, particularly for older articles, when more and more journals begin to be published electronically. Authors fear that journals may lose their documentation function in this respect if they become "living documents."

3 Role of Publishers for Electronic Journals

The results of the above outlined opinion poll indicate the fields of future activities for publishers:

- selection process, i.e. provision of peer-review organisation and quality control/verification
- editing, styling and formatting as well as fixation (encoding)
- storage, dissemination and documentation of authorized, i.e. "copyrighted" versions (authentication, encryption)
- cataloguing, referencing, indexing
- archiving
- standardizing
- access mode(s) / retrieval mode(s)
- continuous adaptation to new technologies to guarantee access and retrieval for a long period of time
- current awareness services (promotion)
- copyright protection (integrity, security)
- revenue/royalty collection, billing
- secondary or parallel use, e.g. prints of articles, of compilations a.o. more

If members of scientific institutions assume these tasks, they then become publishers.

4 Obstacles to Electronic Publishing Proper

There are still obstacles to the immediate increase in the number of electronic journals (but not necessarily preprint services) and the (at least partial) replacement of printed journals:

- technical
  - computer system (hard- and software) performance
  - network performance
  - accessibility
  - lack of standards
- legal
  - intellectual property protective conventions
  - worldwide (copyright)
- managerial
- economic - security
  - integrity
  - billing
  - tracing usage
- fiscal
  - taxation

Although these obstacles are not considered unsurmountable, it will take some time and concerted effort of all parties involved to reach consensus worldwide on legal and economic issues.

Journal of Universal Computer Science, vol. 1, no. 4 (1995), 235-246
submitted: 3/8/94, accepted: 12/10/94, appeared: 28/4/95,

Evolution of Internet Gopher

Mark P. McCahill
(University of Minnesota, USA
mpm@boombox.micro.umn.edu)

Farhad X. Anklesaria
(University of Minnesota, USA
fxa@boombox.micro.umn.edu)

Abstract: How the Internet Gopher system has evolved since its first released in 1991 and how Internet Gopher relates to other popular Internet information systems. Current problems and future directions for the Internet Gopher system.

Keywords: Distributed Information Systems, Internet Gopher, Gopher+
Category: H.5.1

1 Introduction

This paper considers how the Internet Gopher system has developed since its initial release in the spring of 1991, and some of the problems that are driving further evolution of Gopher and other popular Internet information systems. Although two of the most popular new Internet information systems (Gopher [McCahill (1992)] and World Wide Web [Berners-Lee (1992)]) have become quite widely used, they both have some basic architectural deficiencies that have become apparent as the systems were deployed on a large scale. These deficiencies limit the long term stability of the information stored in these systems. For instance, both Gopher and World Wide Web (WWW) refer to information by location, and so both systems are plagued by references to information that either is stale, has moved, or no longer exists. Beyond the architectural problems, the volume of information being published using Gopher and WWW requires continued evolution of user interfaces and categorization/searching technologies. The imminent arrival of more Internet-aware page description languages must also be accommodated by these systems, and will have a significant impact on how client applications are written.

2 The Original Internet Gopher

Internet Gopher was originally designed to be a simple campus wide information system [Lindner (1994)] to address local needs at one institution (the University of Minnesota). The design philosophy of Gopher was to make it possible for departments and other groups at the University of Minnesota to publish information on their own desktop systems and to hide the distributed nature of the servers from the user using the system [Alberti (1992)].

2.1 A User's View of Gopher

From the user's perspective, Gopher combines browsing a hierarchy of menus, viewing documents selected from menus, and submitting queries to full-text search engines (which return menus of matches for the queries). The structure of the menu hierarchy that the user sees depends on which Gopher server the user first contacts, so there is no notion of central control of the Gopher menu hierarchy. Gopher server administrators run their systems autonomously and are free to organize both the information on their server and references to information on other servers to meet their needs. This architecture makes it possible for the Gopher system to scale up well since there is no central (or "top level") server to get overloaded. On the other hand, because servers are autonomous, it is the responsibility of each server administrator to make sure that references to items on either server are not pointing to stale or nonexistent information. Unfortunately, not all server administrators are vigilant in maintaining the quality of their links to other servers. This is analogous to the problem in WWW of documents containing dangling and stale URLs.

Because of Gopher's distributed architecture, there are many different organizations of the information in the Gopher information space (Gopherspace). It is expected that users will naturally prefer to start their Gopher clients by pointing them to their favorite or home Gopher servers. This distributed architecture encourages the formation of communities of interest which grow up around well-run Gopher servers. If there is no central server and users are expected to naturally gravitate to favorite home servers how does the client software know where to start?

Each user's Gopher client software can be configured with the address and port number of the first gopher server to contact when the client software is launched. When the client software contacts this server, the server returns a list of items (a menu) to the client. Items described in the menu either reside on the server or are references to items residing on other servers. These references to items on other Gopher servers tell the Gopher client the domain name of the server, the port number of the Gopher process, the type of the item (document, directory, search engine, etc.), and the Gopher selector string to be used to retrieve the item. Given the minimal information required to describe the location of an item on a Gopher server, it is easy for server administrators to add references to other servers ("links"), and many servers main value is as subject-matter specific collections of references. Gopher client software also generally provides a facility for saving references ("bookmarks") to items selected by the user.

While the references to items on other servers would seem to be Gopher-specific, this is not strictly true. It is possible to map enough information into a Gopher descriptor to make it possible to describe how to access most popular Internet services, and Gopher descriptors are used to reference items on HTTP servers, finger servers, telnet sessions, CSO/Ph phone books, and via gateways X.500, WAIS, Archie, and anonymous ftp servers.

2.2 Growth of the Gopher System

Although originally designed as a campus wide information system, Gopher was rapidly adopted by a variety of institutions and as of November 1994 it is estimated that there are over 8000 servers on the Internet. Part of the reason for Gopher's widespread adoption as a platform for publishing on the Internet is the ease of setting up and running a server. Server administrators typically run a gopher process and publish a part of their local file system as a gopher hierarchy. By default, the names of the items in the Gopher hierarchy are the filenames of the documents and directories published by the server. Because Gopher accommodates a variety of page description languages there is no need to reformat or markup documents to be published.

Another reason for Gopher's popularity is that server administrators can add links to other Gopher servers and give their users access other collections of information. Since users are not necessarily aware where the information they are accessing resides, server administrators can easily take advantage of each other's efforts.

2.3 Locating Information with Gopher

Part of Gopher's popularity is due to the explicit organization of information in the Gopher system which lends itself to quickly finding information. While hypertext documents are certainly useful as one type of information content, it is not clear that a system consisting of nothing but hypertext documents solves all the problems in an information system. In fact, it is difficult to quickly make sense of a complex, visually rich document. If one goal is to allow users to quickly navigate, it is clear why browsers for file systems always have provisions for a menu-like listing of items: a predictable, consistent user interface (such as a menu) is easy to make sense of quickly, and this is necessary for rapidly traversing an information space. Menu-based system also have advantages in that they can be mapped into a variety of user interface metaphors and browsers and can be compactly represented. Since one of the design points for the Gopher system is to run quickly even over low bandwidth links, a compact representation of a collection (menu) allows users with slow machines to quickly traverse Gopherspace to locate documents of interest.

A good metaphor for current information systems on the Internet to compare them to a book. Books generally are structured into three functional sections: a table of contents, an index, and the pages in the middle of the book (the content). Using this metaphor, Gopher acts something like a book's table of contents since Gopher presents a structured overview of the information and makes it possible to jump directly to the section for a specific topic. Search engines (such as WAIS, Archie, and VERONICA) are similar to the index in the back of the book because they allow users to jump into the content based on one or more words of interest. To complete the metaphor, the pages in the middle of the book are represented in a variety of formats on the Internet; content may be in the form of text, graphics, or page description and markup languages such as postscript, PDF, and HTML. The Gopher protocol can of course provide access to search engines and to document content in different formats.

When an explicit hierarchical organization of information is combined with a searchable index of titles of objects in Gopher (such as the VERONICA index of all Gopher items or a Jughead searchable index of items on a single server) users have the choice of either browsing menus or submitting queries to locate items. The scope of the queries can be either global (VERONICA) or local to a specific server (Jughead), and users can select the scope of their search by traversing the hierarchy to locate an appropriate search engine. Gopher has always been designed to be a hierarchical framework to organize collections of documents and search engines rather than a monomorphic Internet-aware page description language.

2.4 Architectural Limitations

The ease of Gopher server setup goes hand-in-hand with an architectural limitation of Gopher. To run a Gopher server does not require either setting up any sort of replication system or formal agreement with other sites to replicate or mirror information. The lack of a formal system for propagating redundant copies of information stored on Gopher servers means that users may be going to the other side of the world (or across a congested network) to fetch a copy of a document that is also stored locally. Moreover, popular servers are heavily loaded and there is no systematic way of spreading the load to other sites (although ad hoc schemes such as informal mirroring agreements are used to partially address this problem). Note that this architectural limitation is also inherent in WWW. Referring to items on other server by location rather than by name makes it easy to add new servers since there is no registration process required as items are added to (or removed from) servers.

Referring to items by location rather than by name also means that there is no name to location mapping service to be maintained, and clients do not have to go through a name to location resolution before attempting to fetch an item. Unless the name to location mapping service is extremely fast, it has the potential for being a significant performance bottleneck. Given the scale of the Internet, it is clear that any name resolution service will have to be replicated and distributed to scale up properly, but this means that the client will have to first locate the appropriate name mapping server (potentially a slow process) before it can proceed with a name to location lookup.

Clearly, there are significant engineering tradeoffs between a system based on name-to-location resolution and a system that only refers to information by absolute location. The direction the Gopher system is taking to address these architectural problems is to accommodate both reference by location and reference by name. The expectation is that clients will first attempt to resolve the reference by location and if that fails (or the client finds that the server responds slowly), the client will attempt a name to location lookup to find other locations that hold the item of interest. To accommodate multiple references to items by both Uniform Resource Locators (URLs) and Uniform Resource Names (URNs) requires a place to store the references as some sort of meta-information. The original Gopher protocol had no provisions for meta-information, but as we will see later in this paper, Gopher+ solves this problem.

2.5 Gopher Gateways to Other Information Systems

Soon after the initial release of Gopher, a concerted effort was made to develop software gateways to give Gopher clients access to information on servers such as anonymous ftp, X.500, NNTP, and WAIS. These software gateways made information on other systems visible to Gopher users and handling the translation between Gopher requests and the protocol on the target system (for instance: ftp).

The decision to write software gateways was driven by the desire to keep Gopher clients small and simple. Rather than building support for several protocols into the Gopher clients, clients that only understand Gopher protocol can be small, simple, easily written, and run on personal computers that are relatively slow and have limited memory. Gateways for Gopher clients greatly expanded the information Gopher users could access. Not surprisingly, the gateways became quite popular. Unfortunately, excessively popular machines on the Internet tend to be either slow or the machines must throttle back the demand for their services by refusing requests when they are busy.

Since the original Gopher protocol had no provision for expressing meta-information about an item, there was no place in the protocol to tell clever clients which might speak several protocols that the an item could be fetched directly (for instance via an ftp session), so even clients that had the capability for go direct to a non-Gopher service such as ftp had no choice but to go through a Gopher software gateway. Clearly, references to information available via a different protocol ought to enumerate the possible paths to the information (both through the gateway and directly via the other protocol). To take advantage of the work being done to develop URL-aware clients, the enumerated references should be made as URLs. Not surprisingly, the architectural problems and the lack of meta-information in the original Gopher protocol are addressed by the Gopher+ protocol.

3 Gopher+ (the Second Generation Gopher Protocol)

After the first year of Gopher deployment, it had become obvious that Internet Gopher was going to be more widely used than the designers had originally anticipated and that there was a need for an enhanced protocol which retained backward compatibility with the original Gopher protocol. Essentially it was necessary to move beyond a distributed menu system to become a true information system by treating Gopher menu items as objects with extensible collections of attributes (meta-information) associated with each object. A set of upward compatible extensions called Gopher+ were added to the original protocol [Anklesaria (1993)].

3.1 Maintaining Backward Compatibility

To maintain compatibility with the installed base of Gopher servers required finding a way for the new servers to announce their capabilities to Gopher+ clients without breaking old clients. Since old clients parse the item descriptors returned by Gopher servers by looking at the information returned as fields separated by the tab character, it was possible to add another field at the end of the item list. To announce their ability to understand Gopher+ verbs, Gopher+ servers return an extra field (most often a "+") along with Gopher item descriptions. Non-Gopher+ clients ignore the field, while Gopher+ clients use the field to recognize Gopher+ servers.

3.2 Gopher+ Item Attributes

Once a Gopher+ client recognizes a Gopher+ server, it can take advantage of features of the Gopher+ protocol to fetch meta-information about items on the server. The Gopher+ protocol includes verbs that allow clients to request specific types of attributes by name or request all attributes for a Gopher document or directory. For instance, a client may request only the abstract for an item, or it may request all meta-information about an item.

Figure 1 shows a typical Gopher+ item attributes for a document that is available in several languages. The item attributes are defined in labeled blocks. The +INFO block contains the Gopher item descriptor, the +ADMIN block contains information about the owner of the item and the modification date, and the +VIEWS block enumerates the alternate views of the item. Gopher+ alternate views are used to make items available in several data formats (such as text, postscript, PDF, etc.) and describe the language the document in which the document is written. Gopher+ clients typically fetch the alternate views and give the user a choice in which view of the document is to be displayed. Gopher+ clients have built-in support for popular data formats and when necessary can call external helper applications to render data formats not supported inside the Gopher+ client.

```
+INFO:0Welcome 0/Welcome bogus.micro.umn.edu 70 +
+ADMIN:
 Admin: Joe Blow +1 612 625 1300 <joe@bogus.umn.edu>
 Mod-Date: Tue Feb  9 17:06:56 1993 <19930209170656>
+VIEWS:
 Text/plain En_US: <.1k>
 Text/plain De_DE: <.7k>
 Text/plain Es_ES: <1k>
 Text/plain Fr_FR: <.9k>
+ABSTRACT:
 This file tests out the various languages in gopher+
 You should be able to choose your favorite language.
```

Figure 1: Gopher+ attributes for a document available in several languages

Figure 2 shows the item attributes for a Gopher directory. In this example there is a Time To Live (TTL) value for the directory available as an advisory to clients about how long (in seconds) to cache the directory contents. Note that there are alternate views of the directory; this server can provide Gopher, Gopher+ and HTML versions of the directory.

```
+INFO: 1A_Directory 1/dir bogus.umn.edu 70 +
+ADMIN:
 Admin: Joe Blow +1 612 625 1300 <joe@bogus.umn.edu>
 Mod-Date: 12/15/94 12:54:09 <19941215125409>
 TTL: 1800
+VIEWS:
 application/gopher-menu En_US: <1k>
 application/gopher+-menu En_US: <2k>
 text/html En_US: <10k>
```

Figure 2: Gopher+ attributes for a directory

3.3 Item Attributes and Extending Gopher's Capabilities

In addition to the Gopher+ attributes already discussed, there are attributes to hold keywords, the definitions of electronic forms to be displayed and filled out by the user, and authentication/encryption methods to be used for access to the item. Gopher+ item attributes provide an open-ended method for extending Gopher's capabilities, and as schemes for referring to items by name (rather than location) are deployed, the item's name can be stored in a Gopher+ item attribute.

Gopher+ item attributes also provide an obvious container to store references to redundant copies of an item whether the reference is by location (such as a URL) or by name (such as a URN). As discussed later in the paper, we are currently working on extending the Gopher user interface metaphor to encompass 3D scenes. By defining a new Gopher+ attribute block, Gopher is easily extended so that it can hold definitions of 3D polyhedra, textures to be mapped onto the surface of the 3D object, and the location of the object in a scene.

Unlike WWW, Gopher keeps information hierarchy structure and meta-information separate from document contents. Current WWW implementations store all information inside documents. The approach of embedding everything inside the document is much less flexible than storing meta-information separately. Separately stored meta-information makes it is possible to find out how large an item is before starting to fetch it, and to know what sort of authentication methods are required for access before attempting access. Moreover, a server administrator that is referring to a document stored on another server can write and store meta-information without changing the contents of the document. This is important for administrators that maintain references to information published outside the control of the server administrator.

4 Future Directions for Gopher and Related Systems

In the three and a half years since the first version of Gopher was deployed, there have been significant changes in the Internet and computing landscape. The computational capabilities of desktop systems have improved significantly and affordable desktop PC systems that can render simple 3D scenes are now starting to reach the market. In addition, support for component documents is starting to become part of operating systems such as Windows, the Macintosh OS, and Unix as the OpenDoc and OLE document architectures are refined and implemented. The acceptance of Gopher and WWW and the growth of the Internet have demonstrated the utility of distributed information systems designed for use by non-technical users. Where are all these developments leading us?

4.1 More Internet-Aware Page Description Languages

One near-term direction is the development of more widely deployed Internet-aware page description languages. The success of HTML as a vehicle for advertising and marketing is prompting vendors of page description languages to incorporate Internet references into their documents.

For instance, by embedding URLs inside Adobe Acrobat PDF files, it is possible to give PDF documents similar capabilities to HTML documents. A freely available extension named InternetLink (available as part of the TurboGopher version 2.0 release [Anklesaria (1994)]) for use with the Adobe Acrobat Exchange program was recently released by the Gopher software development team at the University of Minnesota. InternetLink allows users to embed URLs into PDF documents by defining hypertext links with the Adobe Acrobat Exchange software. When a user clicks on a link, the InternetLink software looks at the scheme of the URL and calls the appropriate client (Gopher, WWW, NNTP, ftp, etc.) to resolve the URL. Since Internet client writers are now releasing clients that accept "get this URL" messages from other applications, it is not necessary for the software that renders pages to know about Internet protocols. All that is required is the ability to call other applications with a "get this URL" message. Adopting this technique for use in page description languages and component document architectures is straightforward and should become common over the next year.

While some argue that HTML has unstoppable market momentum, HTML is not without problems. The page markup orientation of HTML seriously limits the control the author has over presentation. Unlike HTML, PDF is a page description language, so the author of a PDF document has complete control over the layout, fonts, and look and feel of the document and this is considered to be a key feature by magazine and newspaper publishers and graphic designers.

We expect a proliferation of page description languages and documents that incorporate hypertext links to Internet resources. It is unlikely that HTML will be the only sort of widely deployed Internet-aware document type. Accommodating the proliferation of page languages is easy in the Gopher architecture since Gopher does not try to represent all information in on page markup language; Gopher+ was specifically designed to support a variety of document formats.

4.2 Component Network Applications

With the proliferation of Internet-aware document types, it will be increasingly difficult to write a single application that can render all possible document types. In the same vein, the proliferation of Internet protocols makes it difficult to write Internet clients that fully support a wide range of protocols. While monolithic applications such as Mosaic [Andreesen (1993)] claim to support all popular Internet protocols, close examination of these all-in-one applications reveal that they support subsets of the protocols and require excessive system resources on the user's machine. Given the continued evolution of Internet protocols it is our belief that monolithic applications will always deliver poorer performance than dedicated ftp, WWW, NNTP, WAIS, or Gopher clients. As more sorts of applications (for instance: video conferencing) become popular it will be increasingly impractical to write monolithic applications. Large software developers such as the OpenDoc consortium (Apple

Computer, Word Perfect, Novell, IBM, and others) and Microsoft (OLE) are in the process of building component frameworks, and Internet applications will benefit from these frameworks since they will give users the appearance of an integrated application without requiring development of monolithic applications.

Given standards for representing Internet resource locations (URLs) and names (URNs) it is attractive to write single purpose components that call each other by passing URLs or URNs. This sort of architecture makes it easier to update components as protocols evolve and keeps the Internet tool business from being dominated by a few large code factories that develop and maintain massive monolithic do-it-all applications. This component architecture also works well with developing more Internet-aware document types, since the document rendering application can call the appropriate client application to resolve URLs.

4.3 New User Interface Metaphors

The user interface used in today's Gopher is that of traversing a hierarchy of menus and search engines. WWW's user interface metaphor is to treat everything as a hypertext document. While both these user interface metaphors have obvious strengths, they are also both an artifact of the computational limitations of the systems widely available three or four years ago. Given significantly faster systems available today, we believe that using 3D scenes as a user interface metaphor is worth exploring [McCahill (1994)]. Both Gopher and WWW users complain of feeling "lost in cyberspace" and this problem may be addressed by a user interface that is more similar to navigating through the real world.

Beyond trying to address the "lost in cyberspace" problem, a 3D user interface will give us a more powerful way of representing relationships between documents and the results of searches. The growth in the number of documents available in systems such as Gopher and WWW creates the problem of being able to find and categorize very large collections of documents. Indexes of documents searchable by name (as in Archie or VERONICA) are valuable, but we are rapidly reaching the point where there are so many documents that nearly all queries return a very large number of matches. The same problem can be seen with full-text indexes of large collections of documents; nearly any query returns a very large number of documents. A 3D interface provides more degrees of freedom for representing relative "closeness" of documents than a menu or a document can.

While 3D scenes as a user interface should provide a valuable adjunct to the current user interface metaphors, there is the question of how to apply this interface to existing servers. It is unclear how this could be accomplished for WWW servers since there is no clear structure to the information space other than that embedded inside the documents. Since Gopher keeps the structure of the information space external to the documents it is possible for a 3D client to automatically generate scenes from current gopher directories. For instances, the items in a Gopher directory can be represented as objects in a scene and their names can be written onto the face of the objects. Since Gopher+ supports meta-information, it is also straightforward to add information to override default client-generated scenes for a menu. Development of these sorts of 3D scene generating clients will help drive development of better document classification and clustering schemes by making it easier to visualize the relationships between documents.

5 Concluding Remarks

Gopher has evolved from a simple campus wide information system to a popular, widely deployed information system that makes the Internet appear to be a single large hierarchical collection of documents and search engines. The most serious architectural limitations of the original Gopher protocol were addressed by the Gopher+ extensions to the protocol and we believe that Gopher is well positioned to accommodate a proliferation of Internet-aware document types and new user interface metaphors made possible by faster desktop computers.

6 Acknowledgements

Grateful acknowledgment is made to Hermann Maurer, Frank Kappe, and Kieth Andrews of the Institute for Information Processing and Computer Supported New Media (IICM) at the Graz University of Technology for many enlightening discussions of distributed information systems on the Internet. We also wish to thank Shih-Pau Yen at the University of Minnesota for his encouragement and support of the Gopher development team.

References

[Alberti (1992)] Alberti, B., Anklesaria, F., Lindner, P., McCahill, M., Torrey, D.: "The Internet Gopher Protocol: a distributed document search and retrieval protocol."; University of Minnesota. available by anonymous ftp from boombox.micro.umn.edu in the directory /pub/gopher/gopher_protocol/ <URL:ftp://boombox.micro.umn.edu/pub/gopher/gopher_protocol/>

[Andreesen (1993)] Andreesen, M.: NCSA Mosaic technical summary. Available by anonymous ftp from ftp.ncsa.uiuc.edu as file /Web/mosaic-papers/mosaic.ps.Z <URL:ftp://ftp.ncsa.uiuc.edu/Web/mosaic-papers/mosaic.ps.Z>

[Anklesaria (1993)] Anklesaria, F., Lindner, P., McCahill, M., Torrey, D., Johnson, D., Alberti, B.: "Gopher+: upward compatible enhancements to the

Gopher protocol."; University of Minnesota. Available by anonymous ftp from boombox.micro.umn.edu in the directory /pub/gopher/gopher_protocol/Gopher+ <URL:ftp://boombox.micro.umn.edu/pub/gopher/gopher_protocol/Gopher+/>

[Anklesaria (1994)] Anklesaria, F., Johnson, D., et.al..: University of Minnesota. TurboGopher software version 2.0. Available by anonymous ftp from boombox.micro.umn.edu in the directory /pub/gopher/Macintosh-TurboGopher/ <URL:ftp://boombox.micro.umn.edu/pub/gopher/Macintosh-TurboGopher/>

[Berners-Lee (1992)] Berners-Lee, T., Cailliau, R., Groff, J., Pollermann, B.: "World Wide Web: the information universe"; Electronic Networking: Research, Applications and Policy, 2, 1 (1992) 52-58.

[Lindner (1994)] Lindner, P.: "Internet Gopher user's guide"; University of Minnesota. Available by anonymous ftp from boombox.micro.umn.edu in the directory /pub/gopher/docs/ <URL:ftp://boombox.micro.umn.edu/pub/gopher/docs/Papers/>

[McCahill (1992)] McCahill, M.: "The Internet Gopher: A Distributed Server Information System"; Connexions - The Interoperability Report, 6, 7 (1992) 10-14.

[McCahill (1994)] McCahill, M., Erickson, T.: "A Preliminary Design for a 3-D Spatial User Interface for Internet Gopher"; University of Minnesota. Available by anonymous ftp from boombox.micro.umn.edu in the directory /pub/gopher/Gopher_Conference_94/Papers/ <URL:ftp://boombox.micro.umn.edu/pub/gopher/Gopher_Conference_94/Papers/>

Journal of Universal Computer Science, vol. 1, no. 4 (1995), 247-250
submitted: 22/9/94, accepted: 23/10/94, appeared: 28/4/95,

WAIS and Information Retrieval on the Internet

Helmut Mülner
JOANNEUM Research - IHM, Graz, Austria

1 Abstract

WAIS (Wide Area Information Servers), a development of Thinking Machine Corporation, turned out to be one of the main search engines in connection with the World Wide Web (WWW). This article gives a short overview of WAIS, its history, its basics and some connected developments.

Category: H.5.1

2 Searching on the Internet

The World Wide Web has no inherent facilities to search for informations. All you can do is following links.
But if a beginner browses the WWW (s)he soon will discover that there are lots of pages that mention or offer tools for searching the net.
On close inspection these tools fall into two categories:
Tools to collect information which are usually used to build indexes and tools to query the collected information.
These tools are not integrated in WWW-servers but use a gateway to some other service or program.
Several methods are in use. To name a few of them: grep, perl, archie, netfind, wais, veronica, X.500, whois, finger, ftp to Usenet FAQs and other archives, telnet (hytelnet).
The most important of these services is the interface to WAIS, the Wide Area Information Servers.

3 WAIS

WAIS is is an architecture for a distributed information retrieval system. WAIS is based on the client server model of computation, and allows users of computers to share information using a common computer-to-computer protocol.
It started as a joint effort of Dow Jones News Services ("contents"), Thinking Machine Corporation ("computing power"), Apple Computer ("user interface experience") and KPMG Peat Marwick ("users").
The concept was created in 1989, 1990 the first prototype was ready. 1993 the development leader of WAIS, Brewster Kahle, founded WAIS Inc. to provide commercial WAIS software and services. In Sept. 1994 526 servers were installed worldwide.
WAIS consists of several components: It defines a protocol for communicating queries between clients and servers. It contains an index builder (waisindex) to

collect information. It has a server that ansers queries using the index(es). And there are clients for different platforms.
The WAIS server came in two forms: A commercial server maintained by WAIS Inc., and a free server (freeWAIS) which is now supported by the CNIDR.

4 CNIDR

The Clearinghouse for Networked Information Discovery and Retrieval
Its goals are to

- Promote and Support the implementation and use of networked information discovery and retrieval software applications such as the Wide Area Information Server (WAIS), World Wide Web, the Internet Gopher, freeWAIS, and archie.
- Coordinate to Create Consensus among NIDR applications developers to ensure compatibility and interoperability.
- Disseminate Information about NIDR applications to the network community as well as those active with NIDR applications development.
- Collect or Create Documentation and manuals, Project information, Binaries and source code, Bibliographies and General information.
- Classify Protocol standards and compliance; Identify, classify and integrate noteworthy projects and Identify and cross-reference provider and consumer communities
- Distribute Collected materials and information, Classified materials and information and Educational and research materials

One of the achievements of the CNIDR was the implementation and support of the freeWAIS package. While developing freeWAIS the people at CNIDR concentrated on standard aspects of data exchange protocols which led to better support for the Z39.50 standard. One consequence of this was the renaming of freeWAIS to zdist.

5 Z39.50

Z39.50 - "Information Retrieval Service Definitions and Protocol Specification for Library Applications" - is an American National Standard that was approved in 1988 by the National Information Standards Organization (NISO), an American National Standards Institute- (ANSI) accredited standards writing body that serves the library, information, and publishing communities.
Several companies implemented this standard or variants of this; but it did not develop large scale acceptance.
The WAIS protocol is an approximate implementation of this standard; it includes several extensions and 5 omissions.
Z39.50 is an applications-layer protocol within the OSI reference model developed by the International Standards Organization (ISO). Its purpose is to allow one computer operating in a client mode to perform information retrieval queries against another computer acting as an information server especially in the field

of online library catalogs.
The standard was significantly rewritten for its next version in 1992. One important step in this version of the standard was alignment with ISO 10162/10163, the Search and Retrieval (SR) Service Definition and Protocol Definition. It also incorporated some features of the WAIS protocol.
The next version (Version 3) of the standard was balloted in December 1994.

6 freeWAIS-sf

As the CNIDR concentrated on Z39.50, a group at the University of Dortmund (U. Pfeifer, T. Huynhz) took over the further development of freeWAIS .
They started out in Summer 1993 with bugfixes for freeWAIS-0.202. As they got no feedback from the original developers, they published their own version in September 1994 and name it freeWAIS-sf (sf is for structured fields).
The enhancements included

- field structures (text, date, numeric)
- complex Boolean searches
- stemming
- phonetic coding
- document format specification language
- better installation
- locales
- bug fixes

The package includes detailed instructions for linking to WWW and gopher.

7 Information Retrieval - Basics

One of the achievements of WAIS was that the "general" public of Internet users learned about modern concepts of Information Retrieval (IR).
The classic problem of IR is the balance between recall (defined as number of relevant document that are retrieved by a query divided by the total number of relevant documents), precision (number of retrieved documents that are relevant divided by the total number of retrieved documents) and ease of query formulation.
Boolean queries have many problems, so modern IR very often uses ranked queries with different methods, from simple coordinate matching to vector space and statistical models.
The general idea is that a query is just a (simple) document and the retrieval works by computing the "similarity" of the query document to the database documents resulting in a ranked list of similar documents.

8 Conclusion and Resources

The spreading of the ideas that were the basis of the WAIS retrieval engine can improve the world of the WWW by delivering the means to incorporate sophisticated search engines.
Some resources that should be considered in future developments are:

Managing Gigabytes (mg) a book and freely available software by I.H. Witten, A. Moffat and T.C. Bell.

SMART a system developed by G. Salton and documented in several books and articles.

PAT the commercial system by R.A. Baeza-Yates and G.H. Gonnet that was used in the Oxford English Dictionary project.

Managing Editor's Column

Vol. 1, No. 5; May 28, 1995

Dear Readers:

This fifth regular issue of J.UCS once more contains a wide range of papers: three are more theoretical in nature, one is a nice contribution to hypermedia aspects, and the last is a paper dealing with general and legal problems threatening the spread of Internet. I hope more than one paper will attract your attention.

Note: if you have remarks concerning any of the papers you are welcome to send them to jucs@iicm.tu-graz.ac.at with a note whether I can use parts of them for publication in J.UCS: if so, your remarks will be added as "annotations" to the papers at issue, a feature where an electronic journal really can "shine" in comparison with a printed one: this feature is available in J.UCS yet we have not used it, sofar.

There is one other point worth noting: in all issues to date we have presented all papers in hypertext format and in PostScript. However, since simple hypertext mark-up languages like HTML 2.0 or HTF do not support formulae all formulae have been treated as inline images. In theoretical papers this has lead to the ridiculous situation that some papers contained thousands of tiny inline images! We propose to not use such format for very formula oriented papers in the future until HTML 3.0 will be fully standardized and capable of handling formulae in a reasonable fashion. If you are strongly opposed to our decision we would like to hear about it, and why!

Yours cordially

Hermann Maurer, Managing Editor
email: hmaurer@iicm.tu-graz.ac.at

PS: Have your heard about the new **Web Society**? If not, have a look at http://info.websoc.at and join the society, if you feel you can support its main ideas. Thank you!

Journal of Universal Computer Science, vol. 1, no. 5 (1995), 252-268
submitted: 8/2/95, accepted: 11/5/95, appeared: 28/5/95 © *Springer Pub. Co.*

Conditional Tabled Eco-Grammar Systems versus (E)T0L Systems[1]

Erzsébet Csuhaj-Varjú
Computer and Automation Institute of the Hungarian Academy of Sciences, Kende u. 13 - 19, 1111 Budapest, Hungary
Gheorghe Păun
Institute of Mathematics of the Romanian Academy of Sciences, PO Box 1-764, 70700 Bucureşti, Romania
Arto Salomaa
Academy of Finland and University of Turku, Department of Mathematics, 20500 Turku, Finland

Abstract: We investigate the generative capacity of the so-called conditional tabled eco-grammar systems (CTEG). They are a variant of eco-grammar systems, generative mechanisms recently introduced as models of the interplay between *environment* and *agents* in eco-systems. In particular, we compare the power of CTEG systems with that of programmed and of random context T0L systems and with that of ET0L systems. CTEG systems with one agent only (and without extended symbols) are found to be surprisingly powerful (they can generate non-ET0L languages). Representation theorems for ET0L and for recursively enumerable languages in terms of CTEG languages are also presented.
Categories: F4.2 [Mathematical Logic and Formal Languages]: Grammars and other Rewriting Systems: *Grammar types*, F4.3 [Mathematical Logic and Formal Languages]: Formal Languages
Key Words: Grammar systems, L systems, Artificial Life

1 Introduction

According to [8], one of the most important classes of models already developed in Theoretical Computer Science and useful for Artificial Life are the L systems. The same author emphasizes the fact that of particular interest for Artificial Life is the *pattern of life*, the structure of living organisms and systems, the cooperation between parts of such systems. As an attempt to model such a cooperation at the level of an eco-system, starting with the basic relationship between *environment* and *agents* living/acting in/on that environment, the notion of eco-grammar system has been introduced in [3] (presented first in [4]). Basically, it is a variant of grammar systems, integrating features both of cooperating distributed grammar systems and of parallel cooperating grammar systems – see [2] for details about grammar systems theory. In short, several *agents*, described by 0L systems, and an *environment*, also described by a 0L system, interact as follows: The evolution of agents (the rules used at a given step) depends on the string describing the environment. The agents have also associated some pure rewriting rules, by which they act, locally (one rule only is

[1]Research supported by the Academy of Finland, Project 11281

used in every time unit), on the environment. The action depends on the state of the agent in the current time unit. Schematically, one obtains the picture in figure 1.

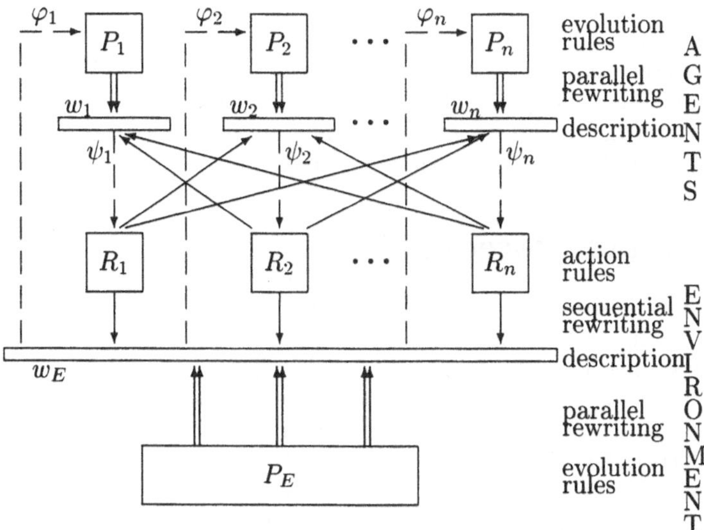

Fig. 1

At every moment, the system is described by a *configuration*, an $(n+1)$-tuple of strings, $(w_E, w_1, \ldots, w_n)$, describing the environment and the agents. Starting from an initial configuration, sequences of configurations will be obtained, describing the evolution of the system. Collecting only the strings w_E, we can associate a language to such a system, the set of environment descriptions. In this way, an eco-grammar system can be viewed as a generative mechanism. Results about the power of such systems can be found in [3], [4], as well as in several contributions to [11] (where also applications of eco-grammar systems are discussed, mainly in questions related to Artificial Intelligence – modelling games strategy, modelling the MIT can-collecting robot Herbert, etc.). In one of these contributions to [11], we have considered a variant of eco-grammar systems, both with practical and theoretical motivation, [5].

On the one hand, the model in [3], [4] assumes that the environment evolves independently of the agents. This does not cover such cases as those when the agents are strongly polluting sources, volcanos, damaged nuclear power plants and so on. Such powerful agents act no longer locally. On the other hand, the model in [3], [4] contains the selection mappings which are only assumed to be computable. It is just natural to consider simplified versions, with particular mappings specifying the active evolution rules in any given time unit.

Following these requests, in the model considered in [5] under the name of *conditional tabled eco-grammar systems* (CTEG systems), we have removed the local action of agents on the environment, but we have introduced a dependence of the environment evolution on the states of agents. More precisely, this dependence is given by condition strings (permitting and forbidding): a prescribed string must be present, another one must be not, in order to apply a given subset of the set of 0L rules (hence a table). We have started the study of the power of such systems in [5], without going into too many details. For instance, we have proved that for certain cases (only permitting condition strings, which must appear as scattered or as permuted scattered subwords of the current strings) CTEG systems with n agents can be simulated by systems with one agent only.

We shall continue here the study of CTEG systems, comparing them with their natural counterparts in L systems theory: regulated T0L systems and ET0L systems. We again find that systems with one agent only are surprisingly powerful (non-ET0L languages can be generated, even with permitting contexts of length one or with forbidding contexts of length two).

2 L systems prerequisites

As usual, we denote by V^* the free monoid generated by an alphabet V; λ is the empty string, $|x|$ is the length of $x \in V^*$, $|x|_a$ is the number of occurrences of the symbol a in the string x, $\Psi_V(x) = (|x|_{a_1}, \ldots, |x|_{a_n})$ is the Parikh vector associated to $x \in V^*$, for $V = \{a_1, \ldots, a_n\}$. The families of finite, regular, context-free, context-sensitive, and recursively enumerable languages are denoted by FIN, REG, CF, CS, RE, respectively. Basic elements of formal language theory which we use here can be found in [13].

A 0L system is a triple $G = (V, w, P)$, where V is an alphabet, $w \in V^*$ and P is a finite set of context-free rewriting rules over V such that for each $a \in V$ there is a rule $a \to x$ in P (we say that P is *complete*). For $z_1, z_2 \in V^*$ we write $z_1 \Longrightarrow z_2$ (with respect to G; if necessary, we specify this by $\Longrightarrow_G$) if $z_1 = a_1 a_2 \ldots a_r$, $z_2 = x_1 x_2 \ldots x_r$, for $a_i \to x_i \in P, 1 \le i \le r$. The language generated by G is $L(G) = \{z \in V^* \mid w \Longrightarrow^* z\}$, where $\Longrightarrow^*$ is the reflexive and transitive closure of $\Longrightarrow$.

An E0L (*extended* 0L) system is a quadruple $G = (V, T, w, P)$, where $G' = (V, w, P)$ is a 0L system and $T \subseteq V$. The language generated by G is defined by $L(G) = L(G') \cap T^*$.

A T0L (*tabled* 0L) system is a construct $G = (V, w, P_1, \ldots, P_n), n \ge 1$, where each $G_i = (V, w, P_i), 1 \le i \le n$, is a 0L system. The generated language is $L(G) = \{z \in V^* \mid w \Longrightarrow_{G_{i_1}} w_1 \Longrightarrow_{G_{i_2}} \cdots \Longrightarrow_{G_{i_m}} w_m = z,\ m \ge 1, 1 \le i_j \le n, 1 \le j \le m\} \cup \{w\}$.

An ET0L (*extended* T0L) system is a construct $G = (V, T, w, P_1, \ldots, P_n), n \ge 1$, where $G' = (V, w, P_1, \ldots, P_n)$ is a T0L system and $T \subseteq V$. We define $L(G) = L(G') \cap T^*$.

The families of languages generated by 0L, E0L, T0L and ET0L systems are denoted by $0L, E0L, T0L, ET0L$, respectively.

Pairs of the form (V, P) (0L systems without axiom) are called 0L *schemes* and $(n+1)$-tuples $(V, P_1, \ldots, P_n)$ (T0L systems without axiom) are called T0L schemes.

The following relations are known (see, for instance, [10], [12]):

1. $0L \subset T0L \subset ET0L$, $0L \subset E0L \subset ET0L$,

2. $CF \subset E0L$,

3. $T0L$ is incomparable with each of the families $FIN, REG, CF, E0L$; $0L$ is incomparable with FIN, REG, CF.

Following the model of regulated context-free grammars, regulated T0L systems were considered (we refer to [6] for details). Because the family of languages generated by *matrix* T0L systems is (strictly) included in the family of languages generated by *programmed* T0L systems, which, in turn, is incomparable with the family of languages generated by *random context* T0L systems (Theorem 8.4 in [6]), we present only these latter classes.

A *programmed* T0L system is a construct $G = (V, w, (b_1 : P_1, E_1), \ldots, (b_n : P_n, E_n))$, where $G' = (V, w, P_1, \ldots, P_n)$ is a T0L system, $b_1, \ldots, b_n$ are *labels* associated to tables and $E_i \subseteq Lab, 1 \leq i \leq n$, for $Lab = \{b_1, \ldots, b_n\}$. For $(b_i, x), (b_j, y) \in Lab \times V^*$ we write $(b_i, x) \Longrightarrow (b_j, y)$ if $x \Longrightarrow y$ using the table P_i and $b_j \in E_i$ (after using the table P_i, with the label b_i, we use a table with the label in the set E_i). The language generated by G is $L(G) = \{x \in V^* \mid (b_{i_0}, w) \Longrightarrow (b_{i_1}, w_1) \Longrightarrow \ldots \Longrightarrow (b_{i_m}, w_m) = (b_{i_m}, x),\ m \geq 0, b_{i_0} \in Lab, b_{i_j} \in E_{i_{j-1}}, 1 \leq j \leq m\}$.

The family of such languages is denoted by $(P)T0L$. (The letter P is parenthesized in order to avoid confusion with the family of propagating T0L languages.)

A *random context* T0L system is a construct $G = (V, w, (Q_1 : P_1), \ldots, (Q_n : P_n))$, where $G' = (V, w, P_1, \ldots, P_n)$ is a T0L system and $Q_i \subseteq V, 1 \leq i \leq n$. A table P_i can be applied to a string $x \in V^*$ only when $|x|_a > 0$ for all $a \in Q_i$.

The family of languages generated in this way is denoted by $(RC)T0L$.

Note that in neither case we have appearance checking features, that is forbidding contexts in random context T0L systems and failure fields in programmed T0L systems.

When the above regulating mechanisms are added to ET0L systems we denote by $E(P)T0L, E(RC)T0L$ the corresponding families.

Proofs of the following results can be found in [6] (Theorems 8.3, 8.4):

1. $T0L \subset (P)T0L \subset ET0L,\ T0L \subset (RC)T0L$,

2. $ET0L = E(P)T0L \subset E(RC)T0L$,

3. $(P)T0L$ and $(RC)T0L$ are incomparable and the same is true for $ET0L$ and $(RC)T0L$.

3 The new class of eco-grammar systems

First, a preliminary definition.

Definition 1. A *conditional T0L scheme* with k-ary context conditions, $k \geq 1$, is a construct

$$G = (V, (c_1, d_1 : P_1), \ldots, (c_n, d_n : P_n)),$$

where V is an alphabet, $P_1, \ldots, P_n$ are (complete) tables of 0L rules over V, and $c_i = (c_{i1}, \ldots, c_{ik}), d_i = (d_{i1}, \ldots, d_{ik}),\ 1 \leq i \leq n$, with $c_{ij}, d_{ij} \in V^*$ for all i, j.

Informally speaking, c_i is used as a *permitting* condition parameter and d_i as a *forbidding* condition parameter, the table P_i being used only when certain predicate *is true* for c_i and certain predicate *is not true* for d_i. The predicates we consider here will be of the following types:

Definition 2. Given an alphabet V, we define the following three predicates over $V^* \times V^*$:

$$\begin{aligned}
\pi_b(x, y) = 1 \quad &\text{iff} \quad y = y_1 x y_2, \\
\pi_s(x, y) = 1 \quad &\text{iff} \quad y = y_1 x_1 y_2 x_2 \dots y_r x_r y_{r+1}, \\
&\qquad x = x_1 x_2 \dots x_r,\ x_i, y_i \in V^* \text{ for all } i, \\
\pi_p(x, y) = 1 \quad &\text{iff} \quad \Psi_V(x) \leq \Psi_V(y), \text{ componentwise.}
\end{aligned}$$

Therefore, $\pi_b(x, y)$ is true when x is a subword of y (a *block* of it), $\pi_s(x, y)$ is true when x is a *scattered* subword of y and $\pi_p(x, y)$ is true when a *permutation* of x is a scattered subword of y.

Using such predicates we can define the derivation relation in a conditional T0L scheme. This corresponds to random context T0L systems, but here the context are given by words, not by symbols.

Definition 3. A *conditional tabled eco-grammar* (CTEG, for short) system of degree $n, n \geq 1$, is a construct

$$\Sigma = (E, A_1, \dots, A_n),$$

where

(i) $E = (V_E, (c_1, d_1 : P_1), \dots, (c_m, d_m : P_m))$ is a conditional T0L scheme with n-ary context conditions, $c_i, d_i \in V_1^* \times \dots \times V_n^*, 1 \leq i \leq m$,

(ii) $A_i = (V_i, (e_{i1}, f_{i1} : P_{i1}), \dots, (e_{ir_i}, f_{ir_i} : P_{ir_i})), 1 \leq i \leq n$, is a conditional T0L scheme with 1-ary context conditions, $e_{ij}, f_{ij} \in V_E^*$ for all i, j.

The component E corresponds to the environment and $A_i, 1 \leq i \leq n$, correspond to the agents.

Therefore, the evolution of the environment (the table to be used) depends on the states of the n agents, whereas the evolution of each agent depends on the state of the environment, in the sense specified by the context condition strings c_i, d_i (in case of the environment) and e_{ij}, f_{ij} (in case of the agents) via predicates as in Definition 2. We shall specify this in a formal way below. One can see that we have a system with the structure as represented in figure 2.

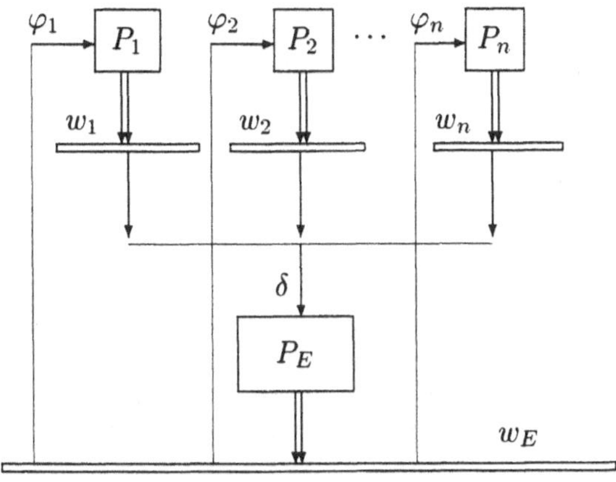

Fig. 2

Definition 4. For a CTEG system as above, a *configuration* is an $(n+1)$-tuple

$$\sigma = (w_E, w_1, \ldots, w_n),$$

with $w_E \in V_E^*, w_i \in V_i^*, 1 \leq i \leq n$.

Definition 5. For a CTEG system Σ as above, $\alpha \in \{b, s, p\}$, and two configurations $\sigma = (w_E, w_1, \ldots, w_n), \sigma' = (w'_E, w'_1, \ldots, w'_n)$, we write $\sigma \Longrightarrow_\alpha \sigma'$ if and only if:

(1) There is a table $(c_j, d_j : P_j)$ in E such that $\pi_\alpha(c_{ji}, w_i) = 1$, $\pi_\alpha(d_{ji}, w_i) = 0$, for all $1 \leq i \leq n$, and $w_E \Longrightarrow_{P_j} w'_E$.

(2) Every $A_i, 1 \leq i \leq n$, has a table $(e_{ij}, f_{ij} : P_{ij}), 1 \leq j \leq r_i$, such that $\pi_\alpha(e_{ij}, w_E) = 1$, $\pi_\alpha(f_{ij}, w_E) = 0$, and $w_i \Longrightarrow_{P_{ij}} w'_i$.

As usual, we denote by $\Longrightarrow_\alpha^*$ the reflexive and transitive closure of $\Longrightarrow_\alpha$, $\alpha \in \{b, s, p\}$.

The *environmental language* associated to a system Σ working in the mode α, when starting from a configuration σ_0, is defined by

$$L_\alpha(\Sigma, \sigma_0) = \{w_E \mid \sigma_0 \Longrightarrow_\alpha^* \sigma = (w_E, w_1, \ldots, w_n)\}.$$

We denote by $CTEG_n(i, j; \alpha), n \geq 1, i, j \geq 0, \alpha \in \{b, s, p\}$, the family of languages $L_\alpha(\Sigma, \sigma_0)$, where Σ is a system of degree at most n, with permitting contexts of length at most i and with forbidding contexts of length at most j. When the number of agents, the length of permitting or of forbidding contexts is not bounded, then we replace the corresponding parameter with ∞.

If in a CTEG system as above we ignore all permitting contexts (for instance, we replace all of them by λ – note that $P_\alpha(\lambda, y) = 1$ for all y and α), then we speak about *forbidding* CTEG systems. The corresponding family of languages is denoted by $CTEG_n(0, j; \alpha)$. Symmetrically, if we ignore the forbidding contexts (for instance, we add a new symbol, c, to all alphabets and replace all forbidding contexts by c, which never appears in the configuration components), then we speak about *permitting* CTEG systems. The associated family of languages is denoted by $CTEG_n(i, 0; \alpha)$. For brevity, we write $\emptyset$ instead of the ignored permitting or forbidding contexts.

A possible generalization is to consider multiple contexts, several permitting and forbidding string contexts. We shall not investigate such a variant here.

It is easy to see that all the introduced above variants of CTEG systems are eco-grammar systems with regular selection of evolution rules, in the sense of [3], [4]: we say that a mapping $\rho : V^* \longrightarrow 2^P$, where V is an alphabet and P is a set of rewriting rules, is *regular* when $\rho^{-1}(R)$ is a regular set for all $R \subseteq P$. Here we deal with tables P_i, and $\rho^{-1}(P_i) = \{w \in V^* \mid \pi_\alpha(c, w) = 1, \pi_\alpha(d, w) = 0\}$ for $(c, d : P_i)$ a table. Clearly, such languages $\rho^{-1}(P_i)$ are regular.

4 Relationships with regulated T0L systems

The following relations directly follow from definitions:

Lemma 1.

(i) $CTEG_n(i, j; \alpha) \subseteq CTEG_m(i', j'; \alpha)$, *for all* $\alpha \in \{b, s, p\}$, *for* $n \leq m$ *and* $i \leq i', j \leq j'$.

(ii) $CTEG_n(i, j; b) = CTEG_n(i, j; s) = CTEG_n(i, j; p)$, for $n \geq 1, i, j \in \{0, 1\}$.

(iii) $CTEG_\infty(0, 0; \alpha) = CTEG_1(0, 0; \alpha) = T0L$, $\alpha \in \{b, s, p\}$.

In view of point (ii) above, when $i, j \in \{0, 1\}$ the specification of α is useless, hence we shall write simply $CTEG_n(i, j)$ instead of $CTEG_n(i, j; \alpha)$.

The following results are proved in [5].

Lemma 2. $CTEG_n(\infty, 0; \alpha) = CTEG_1(\infty, 0; \alpha), n \geq 1$, *for* $\alpha \in \{s, p\}$.

(Therefore, in the case of permitting contexts only, checked in the scattered or in the permuted scattered way, the hierarchy induced by the number of agents collapses to one family.)

Lemma 3. *The languages* $\{a^2, a^3\}, \{a^2, b^3\}$ *do not belong to* $CTEG_\infty(\infty, \infty; \alpha)$, $\alpha \in \{b, s, p\}$.

Combining this with the relation (iii) in Lemma 1, we get the fact that each $CTEG_n(i, j; \alpha)$, for all possible values of i, j, α, is incomparable with each family F such that $FIN \subseteq F \subseteq CF$ (a similar assertion holds true for the family $T0L$). However,

Lemma 4. *For any finite language* L *and any symbol* a, *the language* $\{a\} \cup L$ *belongs to both families* $CTEG_1(1, 0), CTEG_1(0, 1)$.

In order to have an estimation of the size of families $CTEG_n(i, j; \alpha)$ it is just natural to compare them with $(P)T0L$ and $(RC)T0L$.

Theorem 1. $(RC)T0L \subset CTEG_\infty(1, 0)$.

Proof. Consider a random context T0L system, $G = (V, w, (Q_1 : P_1), \ldots, (Q_n : P_n))$, with $Q_i = \{a_{i1}, \ldots, a_{im_i}\}$, where $a_{ij} \in V$ for all $1 \leq j \leq m_i$ and $m_i \geq 0, 1 \leq i \leq n$.

We construct a CTEG system with $M = \sum_{i=1}^{n} m_i$ agents,

$$\Sigma = (E, A_1, \ldots, A_M),$$

where

$$E = (V, (c_1, \emptyset : P_1), \ldots, (c_n, \emptyset : P_n), (c_{n+1}, \emptyset : P_{n+1})),$$

with the context conditions $c_i = (c_{i1}, \ldots, c_{iM}), 1 \leq i \leq n$, such that

$$\begin{aligned} c_{ij} &= \emptyset, && \text{for } 1 \leq j \leq s_{i-1}, \\ c_{i(j-s_{i-1})} &= a_{ij}, && \text{for } s_{i-1}+1 \leq j \leq s_i, \\ c_{ij} &= \emptyset, && \text{for } s_i + 1 \leq j \leq M, \end{aligned}$$

where, for each $1 \leq t \leq n$, $s_t = \sum_{l=1}^{t} m_l$ (when $m_i = 0$, hence $Q_i = \emptyset$, we have $c_i = (\emptyset, \ldots, \emptyset)$), and

$$\begin{aligned} P_{n+1} &= \{a \to a \mid a \in V\}, \\ c_{n+1} &= (d, d, \ldots, d), d \text{ occurs } M \text{ times}, \end{aligned}$$

whereas the agents $A_t, 1 \leq t \leq M$, are defined by

$$\begin{aligned} A_t &= (\{a_{ij}, d, d'\}, (e_{t1}, \emptyset : P_{t1}), (\emptyset, \emptyset : P_{t2})), \ 1 \leq t \leq M, \\ P_{t1} &= \{d \to a_{ij}, \ a_{ij} \to d', \ d' \to d'\}, \ e_{t1} = a_{ij}, \\ P_{t2} &= \{a_{ij} \to d, \ d \to d, \ d' \to d'\}, \end{aligned}$$

where $1 \leq i \leq n, 1 \leq j \leq m_i$ are such that

$$t = \sum_{l=1}^{i-1} m_l + j.$$

For $\sigma_0 = (w, d, d, \ldots, d)$, where d appears M times, we have

$$L(G) = L(\Sigma, \sigma_0).$$

Indeed, in the presence of the symbol d in agents descriptions (this is the case also when starting from σ_0), E can use only tables P_i with $Q_i = \emptyset$ and P_{n+1}, which changes nothing, whereas the agents use either the tables P_{t2} (freely) or P_{t1}, providing that the corresponding symbol a_{ij} is present in the string of E. At the next step, E can use either a table P_i with $Q_i = \emptyset$ or a table P_i whose condition Q_i, although non-empty, is fulfilled. This corresponds to the correct application of the table P_i in the sense of the random context T0L system G. At the same time, all agents will use the tables P_{t2}, returning their strings to d, or the tables P_{t1}. If this table introduces the symbol d', it will never be removed, hence the associated table in E will never be applied from that moment. If P_{t1} introduces a symbol a_{ij}, this again corresponds to fulfilling the condition imposed by the presence of a_{ij} in the string of E. The process can be iterated. Clearly, every derivation in G can be simulated in this way in Σ and, conversely, the evolutions of Σ correspond to correct derivations in G generating the string describing the environment. Consequently, we have the announced equality $L(G) = L(\Sigma, \sigma_0)$, which proves the inclusion $(RC)T0L \subseteq CTEG_\infty(1,0)$.

This inclusion is proper. In [6], page 255, it is proved that the language

$$L = \{a^2, a^4, b^4\}$$

is not in $(RC)T0L$. However, $L \in CTEG_1(1,0)$, because $L = L(\Sigma, \sigma_0)$ for $\Sigma = (E, A_1)$, with

$$E = (\{a,b\}, (c, \emptyset : \{a \to a^2,\ b \to b\}),\ (c', \emptyset : \{a \to b,\ b \to b\})),$$
$$A_1 = (\{c, c'\}, (\emptyset, \emptyset : \{c \to c',\ c' \to c'\})),$$

and $\sigma_0 = (a^2, c)$. □

Corollary. $CTEG_\infty(1,0) - ET0L \neq \emptyset$.

Proof. The assertion follows from the relation $(RC)T0L - ET0L \neq \emptyset$ pointed out in Section 2. □

For the case of programmed T0L systems we obtain a still stronger result.

Theorem 2. $(P)T0L \subset CTEG_1(1,0)$.

Proof. Take a programmed T0L system $G = (V, w, (b_1 : P_1, E_1), \ldots, (b_n : P_n, E_n))$, with $Lab = \{b_1, \ldots, b_n\}$, and construct the CTEG system $\Sigma = (E, A_1)$ with

$$\begin{aligned} E = (V,\quad & (b_0, \emptyset : \{a \to a \mid a \in V\}),\ (b_1, \emptyset : P_1), \ldots, (b_n, \emptyset : P_n)),\\ A_1 = (Lab \cup \{b_0, b_0'\},\quad & (\emptyset, \emptyset : \{b_0 \to b_i,\ b_i \to b_i \mid 1 \le i \le n\} \cup \{b_0' \to b_0'\}),\\ & (\emptyset, \emptyset : \{b_i \to b_j \mid b_j \in E_i \cup \{b_0'\}, 1 \le i \le n\} \cup\\ & \cup \{b_0 \to b_0',\ b_0' \to b_0'\})). \end{aligned}$$

For $\sigma_0 = (w, b_0)$ we have $L(G) = L(\Sigma, \sigma_0)$.

At the first step, we change nothing in E but we can change b_0 either for some $b_i, 1 \le i \le n$ (using the first table of A_1), or for b_0' (using the second table). In the latter case the work of Σ is blocked. This will happen whenever we introduce b_0' and we have to introduce it when $E_i = \emptyset$; this also corresponds to a blocked derivation in G (no continuation is possible). In the presence of b_i as description of A_1 we can apply the table P_i in E, which corresponds to a derivation step in G: the next description of A_1 will be either a label from E_i, if $E_i \neq \emptyset$, or the blocking symbol b_0'. In conclusion, $L(G) = L(\Sigma, \sigma_0)$, that is $(P)T0L \subseteq CTEG_1(1,0)$.

In order to prove the strictness of this inclusion, let us consider the $(RC)T0L$ system

$$G = (\{a,,b,c,d,e,f,g\}, c, (\emptyset : P_1), (\{f\}, P_2)),$$
$$P_1 = \{c \to eca,\ c \to fda\},$$
$$P_2 = \{e \to f,\ f \to g,\ a \to ab\}$$

(the tables contains also all completion rules $q \to q$ for q not appearing in the left-hand member of a rule specified above).

In [6], page 257, it is proved that the language generated by this system is not in $(P)T0L$. According to the proof of Theorem 1, we can construct a CTEG Σ equivalent with G and having only one agent (M in the proof mentioned will be 1). Consequently, $L(G) \in CTEG_1(1,0)$, which completes the proof. □

5 Relationships with ET0L languages

The family $(P)T0L$ is strictly included in $ET0L$. The family $CTEG_1(1,0)$ not only contains strictly the family $(P)T0L$, but contains also non-ET0L languages (which implies again that $(P)T0L \subset CTEG_1(1,0)$ is a proper inclusion and gives a stronger form of the result in the corollary of Theorem 1).

Theorem 3. $CTEG_1(1,0) - ET0L \neq \emptyset$.

Proof. Let us consider the system $\Sigma = (E, A_1)$ with

$$\begin{aligned} E = (\{&s,a,b,c,d,e,f,g,g',g''\},\\ &(a,\emptyset : \{s \to bs\}),\\ &(a,\emptyset : \{s \to bf\}),\\ &(b,\emptyset : \{b \to c,\ f \to g\}),\\ &(c,\emptyset : \{c \to ac,\ c \to ad,\ e \to ae,\ g \to g'\}),\\ &(d,\emptyset : \{d \to e,\ g' \to g''\}),\\ &(e,\emptyset : \{g'' \to g\})),\end{aligned}$$

and

$$\begin{aligned} A_1 = (\{&a,b,c,d,e,f\},\\ &(s,\emptyset : \{a \to a\}),\\ &(s,\emptyset : \{a \to b\}),\\ &(f,\emptyset : \{b \to c\}),\\ &(g,\emptyset : \{c \to d\}),\\ &(d,\emptyset : \{d \to e\}),\\ &(c,\emptyset : \{e \to c,\ c \to f,\ d \to f\})).\end{aligned}$$

(The completion rules $q \to q$, for q not specified above, are not given.)

Then

$$L(\Sigma,(s,a)) \cap (a^+e)^+g'' = \{(a^m e)^n g'' \mid n \geq m \geq 1\},$$

which is not an ET0L language (use Theorem 2.1 in [12]).

Let us examine the work of Σ.

Starting from $\sigma_0 = (s,a)$, using the first two tables of E and of A_1, we generate a configuration $(b^n f, b), n \geq 1$. Only one continuation is possible, $(b^n f, b) \Longrightarrow (c^n g, c)$. Now we have to use the fourth table of E, but for A_1 we can use two tables, the fourth and the sixth ones. Using this latter table we replace c by f and no further step can be taken (no table in E can be used, but the string of E contains the symbol g', hence it is not in $(a^+e)^+g''$). Thus we are led to a configuration of the form $((ah)^n g', d)$, where $h \in \{c, d\}$, depending on its position. Only one table of E is applicable (asked for by d in the string of A_1). The sixth table of A_1 blocks again the system by introducing the symbol f. The only other possibility to continue is by using the table $(d, \emptyset : \{d \to e\})$ of A_1, providing the string of E contains at least one occurrence of d. We obtain $((ah')^n g'', e)$, with $h' \in \{c, e\}$, depending on its position. The only possible continuation is by using the last tables of E and of A_1, but this second table requires the presence of at least one c in the string of E. If the continuation is not possible, then we already have a string in $(a^+e)^+g''$. If we can continue, then we get $((ah')^n g, c)$, and such a configuration, with g present in the string of E and c present in the string of A_1 was already discussed above. Thus, in the presence of the couple (g, c) we can iterate the process, at most a number of times equal to the number of occurrences of c in the initial configuration, that is at most m times. (At every step, at least one c is replaced by d, then by e, and only in the presence of c in the string of E we can continue the work of A_1). In conclusion, the string generated in the first component of configurations, when it is of the form $(a^+e)^+g''$, will be of the form $(a^m e)^n g''$, with $m \leq n$, which completes the proof. □

For the case of CTEG with only forbidding conditions we can obtain a weaker result: conditions of length two are necessary. This, of course, makes relevant the mode of checking the conditions.

Theorem 4. $CTEG_1(0,2;\alpha) - ET0L \neq \emptyset$, $\alpha \in \{s, p\}$.

Proof. Consider the CTEG system $\Sigma = (E, A_1)$, with

$$
\begin{aligned}
E = (&\{s, a, b, c, d, e, f\},\\
&(\emptyset, b : \{s \to bs\}),\\
&(\emptyset, b : \{s \to bf\}),\\
&(\emptyset, b : \{b \to c\}),\\
&(\emptyset, d : \{c \to ac,\ c \to ad,\ e \to ae\}),\\
&(\emptyset, \emptyset : \{d \to e\})),\\
A_1 = (&\{a, b, c, d\},\\
&(\emptyset, f : \{a \to a\}),\\
&(\emptyset, s : \{a \to bc\}),\\
&(\emptyset, dd : \{c \to d\}),\\
&(\emptyset, dd : \{d \to c\})).
\end{aligned}
$$

(Each table also contains all completion rules $q \to q$, for symbols q not specified above.)

Then, for $\alpha \in \{s, p\}$, we have

$$L_\alpha(\Sigma, (s, a)) \cap (a^+e)^+f = \{(a^m e)^n f \mid m \geq n \geq 1\},$$

which is not an ET0L language (see [12], Exercise 2.3, page 260, referring to [7]). As the family $ET0L$ is closed under intersection with regular sets, it follows that $L_\alpha(\Sigma,(s,a)) \notin ET0L$.

Let us examine the work of Σ, starting from $\sigma = (s,a)$. Because of s, A_1 can only use the first table; E can use several times its first table, hence we get $(b^n s, a)$. Eventually, E will use the second table. Assume hence that we have obtained $(b^n f, a)$, for some $n \geq 1$. Now A_1 must use the second table, whereas the only applicable table of E is also the second one. We obtain $(b^n f, a) \Longrightarrow_\alpha (c^n f, bc)$. From now on, b remains present in the description of the agent, hence the only applicable tables of E are the last two; d is not present, hence we have to perform a step $(c^n f, bc) \Longrightarrow_\alpha ((ag)^n f, bd)$, where $g \in \{c,d\}$. Because d is present in the description of the agent, the fourth table of E is not applicable. The last table of E replaces each occurrence of d (if any) by e and leaves all other symbols unchanged. From A_1 we can use one of the last two tables, but only when at most one occurrence of d is present in $(ag)^n f$. If we use $(\emptyset, dd : \{c \to d\})$, then nothing is changed, hence either we use $(\emptyset,\emptyset : \{d \to e\})$ and $(\emptyset, dd : \{d \to c\})$, or we use $(\emptyset,\emptyset : \{d \to e\})$ and $(\emptyset, dd : \{c \to d\})$ for a number of times (only at the first use changing the configuration) and eventually we use the first mentioned pairs of tables. Consequently, we eventually get a configuration of the form $((ah)^n f, bc)$, with $h \in \{c,e\}$, depending on its position, and at most one h is equal to e. The process can continue, at every step the number of a occurrences near each symbol h as above being increased by one and the number of e symbols being increased by at most one. Consequently, when all symbols c are replaced (by d and then) by e, we get a string of the form $(a^m e)^n f$ with $m \geq n$. □

Taking into account that $FIN \subset ET0L$ and $FIN - CTEG_\infty(\infty,\infty;\alpha) \neq \emptyset, \alpha \in \{b,s,p\}$ (Lemma 3), from the previous two theorems we obtain:

Corollary. *$ET0L$ is incomparable with all families $CTEG_\alpha(i,j;\alpha), n \geq 1$, with*

1) $i \geq 1, j \geq 0, \alpha \in \{b,s,p\}$,
2) $i \geq 0, j \geq 2, \alpha \in \{s,p\}$.

The question whether $CTEG_1(0,2;b) - ET0L$ is nonempty or not remains *open.* The next theorem shows that the answer is negative for systems with forbidding contexts of length one, hence Theorem 4 cannot be improved from this point of view.

Theorem 5. $CTEG_\infty(0,1) \subset ET0L$.

Proof. In view of Lemma 3, we have to prove only the inclusion, the strictness is obvious.

Let $\Sigma = (E, A_1, \ldots, A_n)$ be a CTEG system with

$$E = (V_E, (\emptyset, c_1 : P_1), \ldots, (\emptyset, c_m : P_m)),$$
$$A_i = (V_i, (\emptyset, e_{i1} : P_{i1}), \ldots, (\emptyset, e_{ir_i} : P_{ir_i})), 1 \leq i \leq n,$$

with $c_j = (c_{j1}, \ldots, c_{jn}), c_{ji} \in V_i, 1 \leq i \leq n, 1 \leq j \leq m$, and $e_{ij} \in V_E, 1 \leq i \leq n, 1 \leq j \leq r_i$.

Without loss of generality, we may assume that the alphabets V_i are pairwise disjoint and disjoint from V_E (we can easily achieve that by a systematic change of symbols, in tables and conditions).

We construct an ET0L system G as follows.

For every sequence $j_1, j_2, \ldots, j_n, j$ of integers such that $1 \leq j_i \leq r_i, 1 \leq i \leq n$, and $1 \leq j \leq m$, we consider the symbol $[j_1, \ldots, j_n; j]$ and the set $\{e_{1j_1}, e_{2j_2}, \ldots, e_{nj_n}\}$. Denote by $a_1, \ldots, a_k$ the distinct symbols of this set (some symbols e_{ij_i} might be identical, hence $k \leq n$), and construct the tables

$$\begin{aligned} P_{(j_1,\ldots,j_n;j)} &= \{a_1 \to \#, \ldots, a_k \to \#\} \cup \\ &\cup \ \{c_{j1} \to \#, \ldots, c_{jn} \to \#\} \cup \\ &\cup \ \{X \to [j_1, \ldots, j_n; j]\} \cup \\ &\cup \ \{[j'_1, \ldots, j'_n; j'] \to \# \mid \text{for all } [j'_1, \ldots, j'_n; j']\}, \\ P'_{(j_1,\ldots,j_n;j)} &= P_{1j_1} \cup P_{2j_2} \cup \ldots \cup P_{nj_n} \cup P_j \cup \\ &\cup \ \{[j_1, \ldots, j_n; j] \to X\} \cup \\ &\cup \ \{[j'_1, \ldots, j'_n; j'] \to \# \mid (j'_1, \ldots, j'_n; j') \neq (j_1, \ldots, j_n; j)\} \cup \\ &\cup \ \{X \to \#\}. \end{aligned}$$

(These tables contain also all completion rules $q \to q$, for q not specified above.)

Denote by $\mathcal{P}$ the set of all these tables. Then

$$G = (V, T, w_E w_1 \ldots w_n X, \mathcal{P}),$$

where

$$T = V_E \cup \bigcup_{i=1}^{n} V_i \cup \{X\},$$
$$V = T \cup \{\#\} \cup \{[j_1, \ldots, j_n; j] \mid 1 \leq j_i \leq r_i, 1 \leq i \leq n, 1 \leq j \leq m\},$$

and $(w_E, w_1, \ldots, w_n) = \sigma_0$ is a starting configuration for Σ. ¿From the previous construction, it is easy to see that a derivation in G which does not introduce the trap-symbol X consists of alternate use of tables $P_{(j_1,\ldots,j_n;j)}$ and $P'_{(j_1,\ldots,j_n;j)}$, which corresponds to simulating the sequences of tables $P_{1j_1}, P_{2j_2}, \ldots, P_{nj_n}, P_j$, hence to a step in the evolution of Σ ($P_{(j_1,\ldots,j_n;j)}$ checks the non-appearance of the forbidding context both in the agents and in the environment, whereas $P'_{(j_1,\ldots,j_n;j)}$ effectively simulates the sequence of tables in Σ). Consequently,

$$L(G) = \{w'_E w'_1 \ldots w'_n X \mid \sigma_0 \Longrightarrow^*_\alpha (w'_E, w'_1, \ldots, w'_n)\}.$$

Because $ET0L$ is a full AFL (hence it is closed under erasing morphisms), it follows that $L_\alpha(\Sigma, \sigma_0) = \{w'_E \mid w'_E w'_1 \ldots w'_n X \in L(G)\} \in ET0L$. □

Corollary. $CTEG_n(0,1;\alpha) \subset CTEG_n(0,2;\alpha)$, $n \geq 1, \alpha \in \{s, p\}$.

6 Representations in terms of CTEG languages

Based on languages such as those in Lemma 3, in [5] it is proved that the families $CTEG_\infty(\infty, \infty; \alpha), \alpha \in \{b, s, p\}$, are not closed under union, concatenation, λ-free morphisms, inverse morphisms, and intersection with regular sets. Using operations with languages, we can obtain surprising representations of ET0L languages and even of recursively enumerable languages starting from CTEG languages.

Theorem 6. *For every ET0L language L, there are a language $L' \in CTEG_1(1,0)$ (or in $CTEG_1(0,1)$), a T0L language L'' and a regular language R such that $L = L' - L'' = L' \cap R$.*

Proof. We know [10], [11] that each ET0L language is the coding (the image through a length-preserving morphism) of a T0L language. Take $L \in ET0L, L' \in T0L$ with $L \subseteq V_1^*, L' \subseteq V_2^*$, and $h : V_2^* \longrightarrow V_1^*$ such that $L = h(L')$. Consider a T0L system $G = (V_2, w, P_1, \ldots, P_n)$ generating the language L'. We construct the CTEG system $\Sigma = (E, A_1)$ with

$$E = (V_1 \cup V_2', (c, \emptyset : P_1'), \ldots, (c, \emptyset : P_n'), (c', \emptyset : P_{n+1})),$$

for

$$P_{n+1} = \{a' \to h(a) \mid a \in V_2\} \cup \{a \to a \mid a \in V_1\},$$

where $V_2' = \{a' \mid a \in V_2\}$ and $P_i', 1 \leq i \leq n$, are obtained by replacing in rules of P_i each $a \in V_2$ by its primed version a'. (It is assumed that $V_2' \cap V_1 = \emptyset$.) Moreover,

$$A_1 = (\{c, c'\}, (\emptyset, \emptyset : \{c \to c,\ c \to c',\ c' \to c'\})).$$

For $\sigma_0 = (w', c)$, where w' is obtained from w by replacing each symbol with its primed version, we obtain $L = L(\Sigma, \sigma_0) - L(G) = L(\Sigma, \sigma_0) \cap V_1^*$. This can be easily seen: in the presence of c, E simply simulates the T0L system G, with all symbols primed. Then, in the presence of c', E simulates the morphism h. Removing the strings of primed symbols by the intersection with V_1^*, we obtain the set L.

The same language $L(\Sigma, \sigma_0)$ is simulated by the following CTEG $\Sigma' = (E', A_1)$, with

$$E' = (V_1 \cup V_2', (\emptyset, c' : P_1'), \ldots, (\emptyset, c' : P_n'), (\emptyset, c : P_{n+1})),$$

Of course, because $T0L \subset CTEG_1(0,0)$, we can also represent $ET0L$ languages as morphic images of CTEG languages. Similar representations can be obtained also for recursively enumerable languages.

To this aim, we use the following results from [1], [9].

A context-free grammar *with global forbidding context conditions* is a 5-tuple $G = (N, T, S, P, Q)$, where $G' = (N, T, S, P)$ is a context-free grammar and Q is a finite subset of $(N \cup T)^+$. A derivation step $x \Longrightarrow y$ is defined only when x contains no element of Q as a substring, with the exception of the case $S = x$, when no condition is checked. If $Q = \emptyset$, then no checking is made, we have a usual context-free derivation. In [1] it is proved that each context-sensitive language can be generated by a λ-free grammar with global forbidding context conditions of length at most two. When λ-rules are used one obtains a characterization of recursively enumerable languages. A strenghtening of this result can be obtained by using some considerations in [9]: for each context-sensitive language L there is a context-free λ-free grammar G with global forbidding context conditions such that G generates L both in the sequential and in the parallel manner. Using this result we can prove

Theorem 7. *For every recursively enumerable language L there is a propagating $CTEG_1(1,2;b)$ system Σ and a morphism h such that $L = h(L_b(\Sigma, \sigma_0))$, for some σ_0.*

Proof. Let $L \in RE, L \subseteq V_1^*$, and consider a morphism h' such that $L = h'(L'')$ for some $L'' \in CS$. Take a (λ-free) context-free grammar G with global forbidding context conditions, $G = (N, T, S, P, Q), Q = \{w_1, \ldots, w_n\}$, satisfying the conditions in [1], $L(G) = L''$, G working in the parallel or in the sequential manner. We construct a CTEG system $\Sigma = (E, A_1)$ such that $L'' = h(L_b(\Sigma, \sigma_0))$, for a certain configuration σ_0.

Let $V = N \cup T, V_0 = V$, and $V_i = \{A^{(i)} \mid A \in V\}, 1 \leq i \leq n$. Assume $N = \{B_1, \ldots, B_r\}$, and let us consider $H = P \cup \{A \to A \mid A \in V\}$. (Clearly, the E0L system (N, T, S, H) generates the same language as the context-free grammar (N, T, S, P).) Let $c_0, c_1, \ldots, c_n, c_{n+1}$ and $d_0, d_1, \ldots, d_r$ be new symbols.

The construction is based on the following idea: First, by changing its state (symbols $c_i, 1 \leq i \leq n$), the agent checks whether the context conditions are satisfied or not. Meantime, the environment only rewrites its state to the corresponding superscript variant (a string consisting of symbols $A^{(i)}$). If the context conditions are observed, then the environment applies some productions and either a new check of context conditions follows, or the agent checks whether the obtained string corresponds to a superscript version of a word over T, and after that the environment rewrites the string to a word over T. If some conditions are not satisfied, then the process is blocked.

The component E will have the following tables:

$$H_0 = (c_0, \emptyset : \{S \to \alpha^{(1)} \mid S \to \alpha \in P\}),$$
$$H_i = (c_i, \emptyset : \{A^{(i)} \to A^{(i+1)} \mid A \in V\}),\ 1 \leq i \leq n,$$
$$H_{n+1} = (c_{n+1}, \emptyset : \{A^{(n+1)} \to \alpha^{(1)} \mid A \to \alpha \in P\} \cup \{A^{(n+1)} \to A^{(1)} \mid A \in V\}),$$
$$H'_j = (d_j, \emptyset : \{A^{(1)} \to A^{(1)} \mid A \in V\}),\ 0 \leq j \leq r-1,$$
$$H'_r = (d_r, \emptyset : \{A^{(1)} \to A \mid A \in V\}),$$

where $\alpha^{(i)}$ is obtained by replacing in α each symbol $A \in V$ with $A^{(i)}$. Moreover, A_1 has the following tables:

$$P_0 = (\emptyset, \emptyset : \{c_0 \to c_1\}),$$
$$P_j = (\emptyset, w_j^{(j)} : \{c_j \to c_{j+1}\}),\ 1 \leq j \leq n,$$
$$P_{n+1} = (\emptyset, \emptyset : \{c_{n+1} \to d_0,\ c_{n+1} \to c_1\}),$$
$$P'_k = (\emptyset, B_k^{(1)} : \{d_{k-1} \to d_k\}),\ 1 \leq k \leq r.$$

In all cases, completion rules $q \to q$ are assumed, for all q not specified above.

Then for each derivation

$$S \Longrightarrow v_1 \Longrightarrow v_2 \Longrightarrow \ldots \Longrightarrow v_t = v \in T^*$$

in G there is a derivation

$$(S, c_0) \Longrightarrow_b^* (v_1^{(1)}, c_1) \Longrightarrow_b^* (v_2^{(1)}, c_1) \Longrightarrow_b^* \ldots \Longrightarrow_b^* (v_t^{(1)}, d_0) \Longrightarrow_b^* (v_t, d_r),$$

in Σ. Moreover, only derivations in Σ associated in this way to derivations in G produce strings over T.

Let us now define the morphism h'' by $h''(a) = a, a \in T$, and $h''(b) = \lambda$ for any other symbol appearing in the alphabet of E. The equality $L(G) = h''(L_b(\Sigma, \sigma_0))$ follows. Composing with the morphism h', we get a representation of L as a morphic image of $L_b(\Sigma, \sigma_0)$. Note that because G is λ-free, Σ was propagating. □

The above representation is nontrivial, in view of the fact that $CTEG_\infty(\infty, \infty; \alpha)$ does not include the family CS (even when using erasing rules: see again Lemma 3).

7 Final remarks

We want to stress here only two ideas: First, the richness of eco-grammar systems both from the point of view of formal language theory issues and from the point of view of applications. Contributions to [11] might be illustrative in this respect. Second, the surprisingly large power of CTEG with only one agent. Such systems can be depicted as in figure 3.

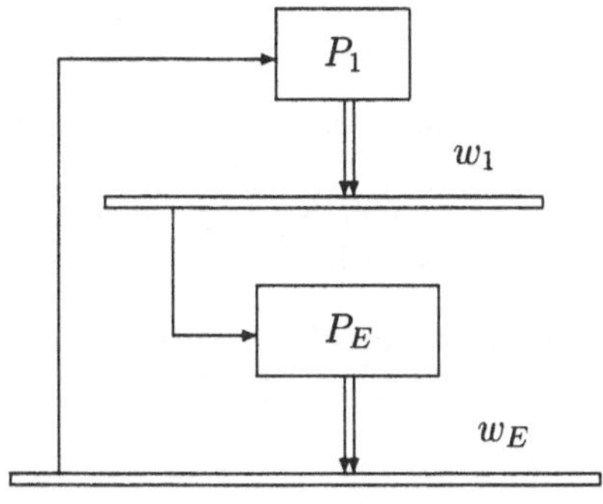

Fig. 3

There is no apparent difference here between the agent and the environment, as in the general case. Systems of this type, consisting of two coupled rewriting devices, each one checking a context condition (in the random context, semi-conditional or conditional sense, in the terminology of [6]) on the string currently generated by the partner device, deserve a deeper investigation (both for Chomsky grammars and L systems). We hope to return to this topic in a forthcoming paper.

8 References

1. E. Csuhaj-Varju, Grammars with local and global context conditions, *Intern. J. Computer Math.*, 47 (1992), 17 - 27.

2. E. Csuhaj-Varju, J. Dassow, J. Kelemen, Gh. Păun, *Grammar Systems: A Grammatical Approach on Distribution and Cooperation*, Gordon and Breach, London, 1994.

3. E. Csuhaj-Varju, J. Kelemen, A. Kelemenova, Gh. Păun, Eco-grammar systems: A language theoretic model for AL (Artificial Life), manuscript, 1993.

4. E. Csuhaj-Varju, J. Kelemen, A. Kelemenova, Gh. Păun, Eco-grammar systems. A preview, in vol. *Cybernetics and Systems '94* (R. Trappl, ed.), World Sci. Publ., Singapore, 1994, 941 - 949.

5. E. Csuhaj-Varju, Gh. Păun, A. Salomaa, Conditional tabled eco-grammar systems, in vol. *Artificial Life. Grammatical Models* (Gh. Păun, ed.), Proc. of the Workshop on Grammatical Models in Artificial Life, Mangalia, 1994, The Black Sea Univ. Press, Bucharest, 1995.

6. J. Dassow, Gh. Păun, *Regulated Rewriting in Formal Language Theory*, Springer-Verlag, Berlin, Heidelberg, 1989.

7. A. Ehrenfeucht, G. Rozenberg, On proving that certain languages are not ET0L, *Acta Informatica*, 6 (1976), 407 - 415.

8. C. G. Langton, Artificial Life, in vol. *Artificial Life, II* (C. G. Langton, C. Taylor, J. D. Farmer, S. Rasmussen, eds.), Proc. of the Workshop on Artificial Life, Santa Fe, 1990, Santa Fe Institute Studies in the Science of Complexity, Proc. vol. X, Addison-Wesley, 1990, 1 - 47.

9. Al. Meduna, A formalization of sequential, parallel and continuous rewriting, *Intern. J. Computer Math.*, 47 (1993), 153 - 161.

10. M. Nielsen, G. Rozenberg, A. Salomaa, S. Skyum, Nonterminals, homomorphisms and codings in different variations of 0L systems, *Acta Informatica*, part I: 4 (1974), 87 - 106, part II: 3 (1974), 357 - 364.

11. Gh. Păun (ed.), *Artificial Life. Grammatical Models*, Proc. of the Workshop on Grammatical Models in Artificial Life, Mangalia, 1994, The Black Sea Univ. Press, Bucharest, 1995.

12. G. Rozenberg, A. Salomaa, *The Mathematical Theory of L Systems*, Academic Press, New York, 1980.

13. A. Salomaa, *Formal Languages*, Academic Press, New York, 1973.

Journal of Universal Computer Science, vol. 1, no. 5 (1995), 269-291
submitted: 31/3/95, accepted: 23/5/95, appeared: 28/5/95,

HOME: an Environment for Hypermedia Objects

Erik Duval
(Departement Computerwetenschappen, Katholieke Universiteit Leuven, Belgium
Erik.Duval@cs.kuleuven.ac.be)

Henk Olivié
(Departement Computerwetenschappen, Katholieke Universiteit Leuven, Belgium
olivie@cs.kuleuven.ac.be)

Piers O'Hanlon,
(Audio-Visual Service, University College London, England
piers@livenet.ac.uk)

David G. Jameson
(Audio-Visual Service, University College London, England
g.jameson@ucl.ac.uk)

Abstract: In this paper, we present HOME, a new environment for distributed hypermedia. We mainly concentrate on the server side, and provide access to World-Wide Web clients through a gateway mechanism. Data and metadata are strictly separated in the distributed HOME server. The architecture is based on a layered approach with separate layers for raw data, multimedia characteristics and hypermedia structure. We briefly present some of the implementation aspects and emphasise distinctive characteristics of HOME. We conclude with a comparison with related research and our plans for the future.
Key Words: HOME, distributed hypermedia, networked multimedia, image store, navigation, query
Category: H.5.1, I.7.2

1 Introduction

The explosion of interest from the general public in Gopher, WAIS the World-Wide Web (W.W.W.) [Berners-Lee, et al. 94] [Cailliau 95] and other Networked Information Discovery and Retrieval (NIDR) systems [Obraczka, et al. 93] indicates that there is a widespread demand for the functionality of such systems. As has been pointed out before [Andrews, et al. 94], the current generation of NIDR systems suffers from a number of problems.

We have been working for some time on a networked hypermedia system, that is in some sense similar in scope to the W.W.W. and Gopher, but that is based on a rather different design and data model. This paper will present our system, called HOME (for Hypermedia Object Management Environment).

2 Background

The authors have collaborated on the development of a networked hypermedia system in a number of European projects, funded within the framework of the DELTA (*D*eveloping *E*uropean *L*earning through *T*echnological *A*dvance) program [Duval, Olivié 94] [Jameson, et al. 93] [Beckwith, et al. 93]:

- The aim of the project CAPTIVE ('*C*ollaborative *A*uthoring, *P*roduction and *T*ransmission of *I*nteractive *V*ideo for *E*ducation', 1989 to 1991) was to develop an infrastructure for collaborative development of multimedia educational resources. An image store and a database *about* such resources were designed, implemented and integrated in a European telecommunication infrastructure, based on Direct Broadcast Satellites (DBS), an analogue video network, Integrated Services Digital Networks (ISDN) and the Internet.
- The MTS project ('*M*ultimedia *T*ele*S*chools', 1992 to 1994) involved large-scale experiments with delivery of interactive sessions, using a combination of DBS transmission from a conventional studio and ISDN feedback from students located throughout Europe. In the ACT project ('*A*dvanced *C*ommunication *T*echnology', also 1992 to 1994) technology was developed for large-scale field experiments in the MTS project.

Underlying most of our efforts in these projects is the fact that educational resources are almost never re-used and that dissemination of these resources is often problematic. In order to promote re-use, authors should be able to find out what is available, where it is located, whether it is suited and how it can be obtained. In order to support re-use, we have developed a general-purpose solution based on database technology, a hypermedia data model and a telecommunication infrastructure, as will be explained in the remainder of this paper.

3 Overview

HOME is based on a client-server architecture, where the server takes care of data management. The client interacts with the end user, initiates requests to the server and displays the result. The HOME server is itself distributed, as will be explained further on.

The next section deals with the reasons for and the consequences of separating data and metadata management. Section 5 and 6 detail the two layers of HOME that are responsible for data and metadata management of multimedia objects respectively. Section 7 presents an additional layer that superimposes a hypermedia structure on the multimedia objects. Section 8 mentions some relevant aspects of our current implementation. Section 9 lists the more distinctive features of HOME, section 10 compares our approach with related work and section 11 briefly mentions some of our plans for the future.

4 Separation of Data and Metadata

A fundamental design decision of our distributed hypermedia system is the separation of 'raw' multimedia data (audio, still images, video, etc., see section 5) and metadata (data describing characteristics of multimedia objects, see section 6). We have taken this decision because 'raw' data and metadata are rather different, so that the tools and techniques used to store and process them differ as well [Little, Venkatesh 94] [Bucci, et al. 94] [Bowman, et al. 94]:

- Compared with metadata that describe e.g. the author of a multimedia object, or its content, the object itself is much *larger* in size.

- Whereas metadata are well structured, this is mostly not the case with 'raw' multimedia data: a bitmap e.g. is (nothing but) a large sequence of bits. Video encoding standards contain little or *no structuring* information (cut points, camera positions), and this information is embedded. Moreover, current image processing and video computing techniques are not able to automatically make this structure explicit, especially in the case of more abstract characteristics [Tonomura, et al. 94] [Jain, Hampapur 94].
- Raw multimedia data are often *time-dependent* [Hardman, et al. 94]. This must be modelled in a multimedia database and affects communication [Little, Venkatesh 94], because the synchronisation between different data streams must be preserved.

Most current database management systems can cope well with metadata of multimedia objects. The raw data themselves must be stored in either external files or so-called Binary Large OBjects ("BLOB's"). In neither of these cases are they integrated very well in the database.

An advantage of separating data and metadata is that a user can examine the contents of the database without having to retrieve the typically very voluminous data objects themselves [Little, Venkatesh 94]. Interaction with a system designed in this way typically proceeds in two phases:

- *location phase*: querying the metadata, the user identifies the relevant data; the end result of this phase is a set of locators of raw data; the locator may also include the protocol to be used to retrieve the data, as in the case of W.W.W. Universal Resource Locators [Berners-Lee, et al. 94] [Cailliau 95];
- *communication phase*: parameters for quality of service are negotiated and delivery of the raw object(s) takes place.

5 Raw Data Layer

5.1 Introduction

The raw data layer contains the *raw data objects*: we use this term to refer to raw multimedia data, i.e. still images, audio clips, video sequences, etc.

In HOME, this layer integrates all raw objects that are accessible through services on the Internet. This is important for interoperability (see section 9) as it enables us to refer to all such objects on the metadata level. For this purpose, we rely on the Universal Resource Locator (U.R.L.) mechanism (see section 6).

The next section presents in some detail a special-purpose data store we have developed for storage of still images and short video sequences. It illustrates the flexibility of our approach that enables us to integrate a wide diversity of multimedia data repositories within our framework.

5.2 Image Store

We have developed an *image store* for storage of still images and video sequences. This store has been integrated in the raw data layer, as will be explained in this section.

5.2.1 Storage

Images and sound are stored in analogue form on laser disc.

- A Write-Once Read Many times (WORM) disc holds up to 36,000 frames per side, of still or moving video.
- A pre-recorded analogue Laservision disc (such as used in the Bristol Biomedical disc, see below) may contain up to 55,000 per side.

These capacities compare well with current digital storage, offering efficient, high quality and reasonably fast accesses, with an average seek time of 0.5 sec.

Once one ventures into the Video On Demand servers [Little, Venkatesh 94], digital systems perform better though the costs are higher. We are currently testing digital storage units and plan to migrate to such systems.

5.2.2 Access

Direct access to the image store is possible over analogue links such as UCL's internal Live Interactive Video Educational Network (LIVE-NET), DBS, and video conference links through the use of Codec's over ISDN or ATM (see figure 1). The Image store is currently being used on the INSURRECT project which is involved with teaching surgery within the UK over the SuperJANET ATM video network.

Frames may be *digitised on-the-fly* and delivered to the network. The server will accept requests in the HyperText Transfer Protocol (HTTP) making it accessible within the W.W.W. (see also section 7). Once a request for digitisation is received, it is parsed by a Common Gateway Interface (CGI) compliant client to retrieve the frame number of the image, its desired size, and encoding [Gleeson, Westaway 95]. The frame number may be checked against an access list so as to provide access to certain sections of the disc. If the request is valid, the frame is accessed on the disc and subsequently digitised. The laser disc is controlled through its serial port which is accessible, along with a digitising card on a networked Sun workstation.

The digital image is converted to the desired size so the user may view 'thumb nail' versions of the images before retrieving an entire image. This also keeps the network load to a minimum whilst users browse the image base. Finally the image is delivered in the requested coding - such as GIF or PPM, which allows the image to be included as an in-lined image in a HTML document.

Further developments are underway to deliver sections of the moving video by conversion into a suitable moving image format such as MPEG or H.261[ITU-T Recommendation 03/93]. Dependent upon network access these may either be delivered in real-time or as one data file. For real-time access the demands on the system are much greater and would require substantial further development. However as interest in Video On Demand services grows, relevant work is being done in both the commercial and academic environments.

By using a hybrid analogue-digital approach we can exploit the benefits of analogue storage media in the digital world. Laser discs offer large storage potential and allow the use of analogue technologies for transfer and manipulation. At UCL we currently utilise our video network LIVE-NET for teaching which is a hybrid of digital and analogue links. All switching is done in the analogue

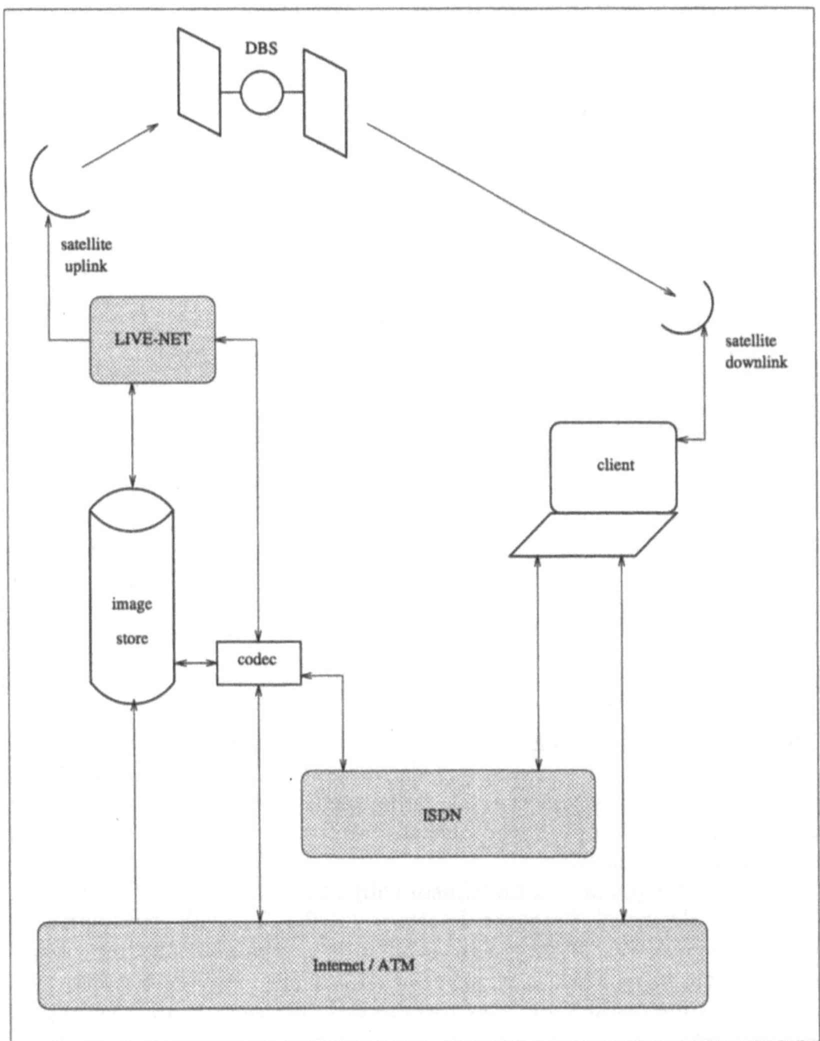

Figure 1: telecommunication between different components

domain on LIVE-NET, though once we go onto the SuperJANET video network digital Multi-point Control Units (MCU) are used to automatically switch video streams dependent upon operational mode.

6 Multimedia Layer

The multimedia layer deals with characteristics of the raw data objects considered in isolation. The data model of this layer is based on an object-oriented approach. Classes can be defined for different kinds of raw data objects. Figure 2 represents the currently implemented class hierarchy:

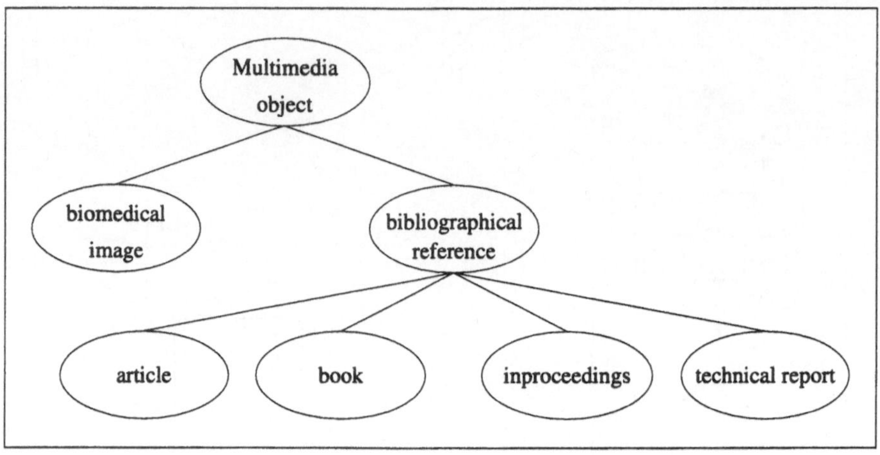

Figure 2: Class hierarchy of the Multimedia Metadata Layer

- The *multimedia object* class groups characteristics common to all raw data objects. An important attribute of this class is the unique name used to refer to an object (see also section 9). Other attributes of this class include the author, the creation date, the person who last modified the object, and the date of last modification.
  The raw data content of a multimedia object is referred to by the mechanism known as Universal Resource Locators (U.R.L.'s). This mechanism stems from the W.W.W. [Berners-Lee, et al. 94] [Cailliau 95] and indicates both the protocol to be used to retrieve the object (e.g. ftp, gopher, http) as well as the location of the object itself (basically the Internet host and a filepath on that host).
  It is important to emphasise the flexibility of the U.R.L. approach: in fact, we believe this is one of the main contributions of the World-Wide Web. Through U.R.L.'s, references can be made to documents accessible over the file transfer protocol, telnet, gopher, etc., on any computer connected to the Internet. These documents can also be generated upon request, using the Common Gateway Interface (CGI [Gleeson, Westaway 95]) mechanism. Moreover, the addressing scheme is easily extensible with new protocols.
  Our terminology is somewhat unusual in that normally the term multimedia object refers to a structured composite of several single media. In fact, HOME uses a black box approach and doesn't address issues such as e.g. synchronisation between different media components of a multimedia object [Buford 94].

- *Biomedical images* constitute a subset of the images on our image store (see section 5.2). Currently, this set includes ca. 5900 images, whose specific characteristics (species, sex, stain, etc.) are modelled by this subclass.
- Another subclass of multimedia objects is the class of *bibliographical references*, with further subclasses for articles in journals, books, papers in conference proceedings and technical reports. Attributes for these classes include e.g. author, title, publisher, etc. This class hierarchy is based on the Bibtex system that is part of the LaTex environment [Lamport 86].

The multimedia layer of our server essentially supports creation, deletion and modification of multimedia objects. Object retrieval based on search criteria is also possible: this facility enables for instance an end user to look for biomedical images donated by a particular person, concerning a particular species, etc. This kind of search facility is very important in a large-scale environment that may include hundreds of thousands of multimedia objects, where simple browsing techniques break down because of the overwhelming amount of available data. (Anyone who ever experienced the frustration of not finding a W.W.W. document he visited some time before will appreciate this point.)

7 The Hypermedia layer

As explained in the previous section and illustrated by figure 3 (where higher layers refer to objects at lower layers), the multimedia layer manages metadata of isolated objects stored at the raw data layer. Metadata concerning interrelationships between different objects are dealt with by the hypermedia layer.

The most simple hypermedia data model is the basic node-link paradigm: information is organised in chunks that are called 'nodes' and that can be interrelated by 'links' [Nielsen 90]. We have developed a new hypermedia data model, based on a set-oriented approach, strongly influenced by the HM data model [Andrews, et al. 95] [Maurer, et al. 94]. The data structuring facilities of our hypermedia data model are presented in section 7.1. Section 7.2 and 7.3 detail navigational and query facilities. Section 7.4 explains how query and navigational access can be combined.

7.1 Data Structuring

The basic data structure of the Sets-Of-Sets (SOS) model is a set, a somewhat modified version of the traditional mathematical concept. A set is identified by its unique *name*. In the SOS model, there are two classes of sets:

- A *singleton* is a set with exactly one element, a multimedia object (see section 6). For every multimedia object created at the multimedia layer, a corresponding singleton (with that object as its single element) is automatically created at the hypermedia layer. In this way, all objects from the multimedia layer are accessible in the hypermedia layer.
  A typical example might be:
  S = {map of the K.U.Leuven campus}.
- A *multiset* is a set with an arbitrary number of elements, that are sets themselves. The elements of a multiset are ordered. A typical multiset is e.g.:

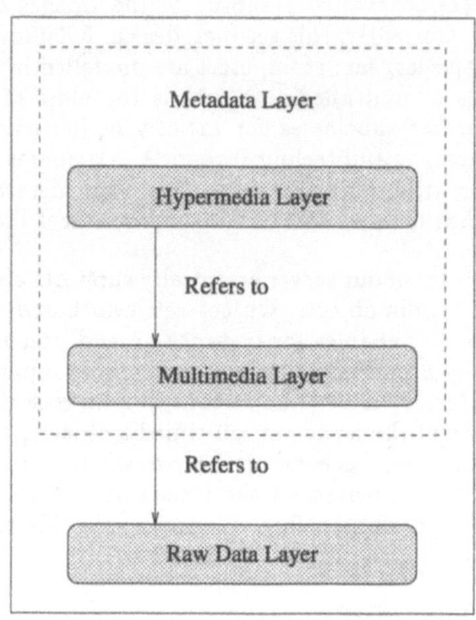

Figure 3: The different layers of HOME

M = { {map of the K.U.Leuven campus},
{ {texts about the history of the K.U.Leuven},
{historical images}},
{administrative information},
{presentation of research at the K.U.Leuven}}.

A multiset can be *extensionally defined*. In that case, membership is defined by manually adding or removing elements to or from the set. Alternatively, a multiset can be *intensionally defined*, when a set of search criteria defines membership to the multiset. In the latter case, the multiset is called a *dynamic multiset* in HOME. This is similar to the notion of a computed composite in [Halasz 88].

It is important to note that set membership does not need to be hierarchical, but can contain loops: recursive relationships are explicitly allowed. Consider e.g. figure 4, where the rounded squares represent sets and the connections indicate membership.

The set on our research unit ('Indigo') contains a set on projects we are involved in and another set with elements for each of the members of our unit. One of the projects is 'HOME', presented in this paper. The multiset on HOME has an element on the people working on HOME. For each of the members of the research unit, there is a set 'Projects' that contains information on all the projects a particular member is involved in. Clearly, there are several cycles in this structure.

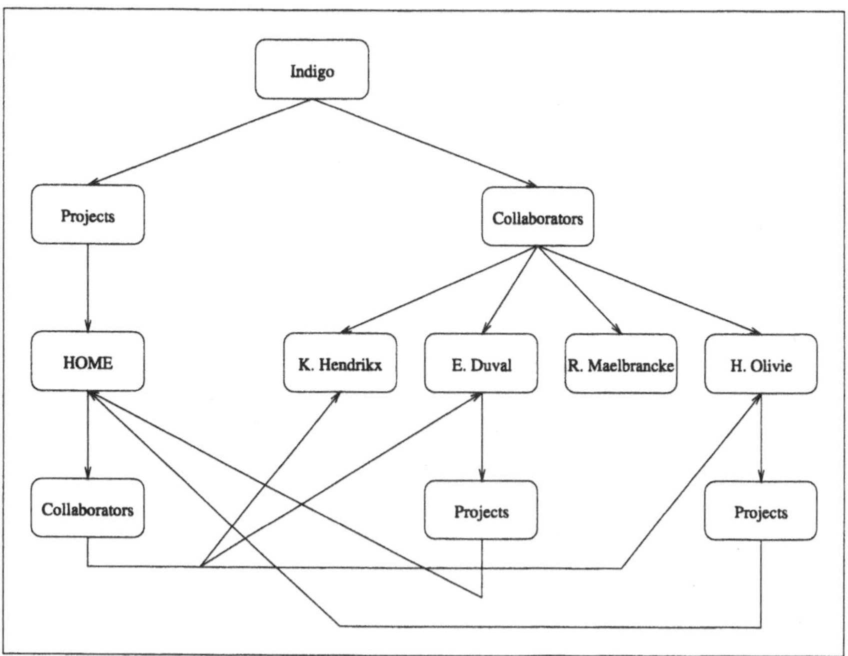

Figure 4: Recursive Membership: an Example

As sketched above, the SOS model is a rather simple hypermedia data model, where information is structured in a (not strictly) hierarchically manner. The net result is rather similar to data structuring in e.g. Hyper-G [Kappe, Maurer 93] [Kappe, et al. 93] or Gopher. We are currently working on a more advanced data model.

7.2 Navigation

In this section, we will present the currently implemented user interface to HOME. When the user first accesses HOME, a list of root sets is presented, as in figure 5. The user can get back to this screen, by clicking on the 'Home' icon, always present in the upper left corner of the screen.

In order to zoom in on a multiset (e.g. 'Hypertext and Hypermedia' in figure 5), the user clicks on the folder icon. The result is shown in figure 6.

The user can now zoom out of the 'Hypertext and Hypermedia' multiset by clicking on the opened folder icon of figure 6. This brings him back to figure 5. If, however, the user zooms further in on 'Hypermedia Systems', again by clicking on the folder icon, then the screen looks like figure 7.

Now, the current set is 'Hypermedia Systems', with a number of multisets as its elements, and a singleton ('On Second Generation Hypermedia Systems (...)'). Clicking on the arrow icon in front of the singleton visualises the multimedia object that is the single element of this singleton, which leads to figure 8.

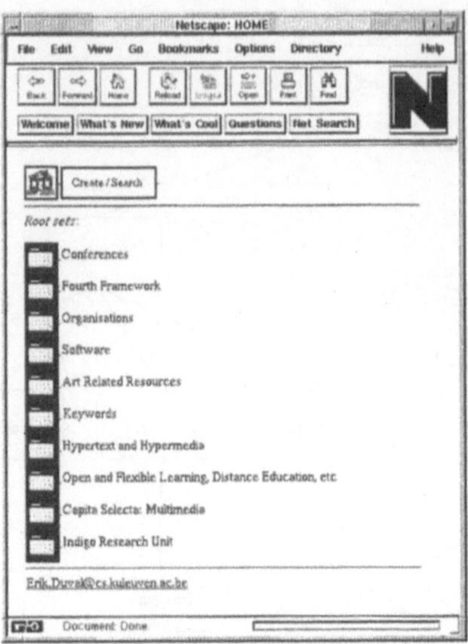

Figure 5: Root Sets

The 'arrow up' icon on figure 8 enables the user to zoom out of the current singleton. This takes him back to the screen of figure 7.

7.3 Query

The 'Create/Search' button at the top of every screen allows an end user to create new sets or to query the HOME system. The screen on figure 9 represents a typical query screen for a multimedia object, in this case a paper in a conference proceedings.

When querying the system, the user can provide a search pattern for any of the attributes. In figure 9, the user searches for all papers in proceedings where the pattern 'Duval' is present in the list of authors. Figure 10 shows the result of the query.

The different singletons that belong to the query result (which is, in fact, a dynamically generated multiset) are listed, with arrow icons to enable the end user to visualise them.

7.4 Combination of Navigation and Query

Navigation and query access can be combined: imagine e.g. that an end user obtains figure 10 as a result of the query in figure 9. When a user visualises, say, 'A Home for Networked Hypermedia (...)' (the third item in the list of figure 10) and then zooms out of that singleton, then the result looks like figure 11.

Navigating from one of the singletons that belong to the result of a query, end users can thus find material related to the query result, but not part of that

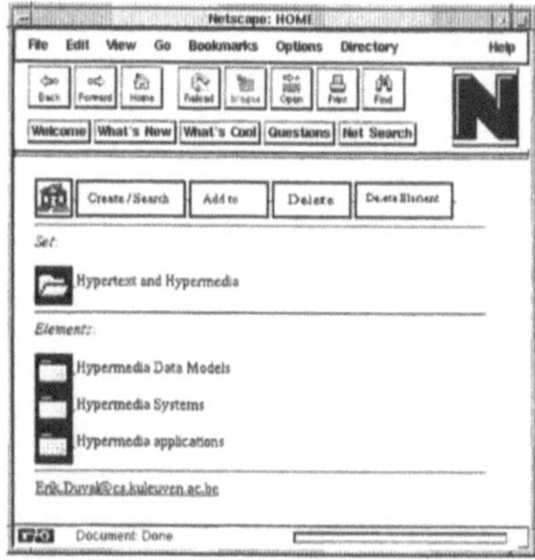

Figure 6: Zooming in on 'Hypertext and Hypermedia'

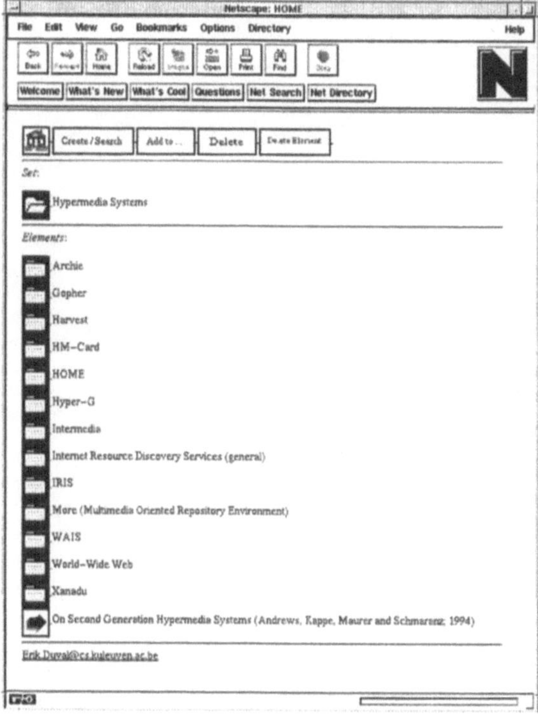

Figure 7: Zooming in on 'Hypermedia Systems'

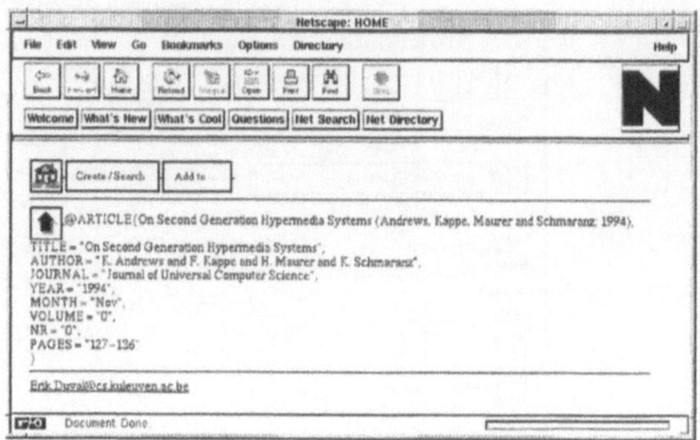

Figure 8: Visualising 'On Second Generation Hypermedia Systems (...)'

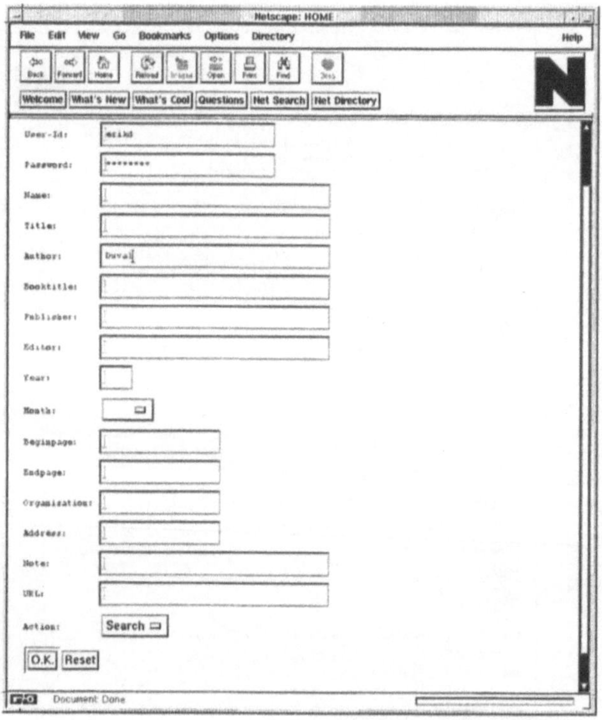

Figure 9: A query screen for proceedings papers

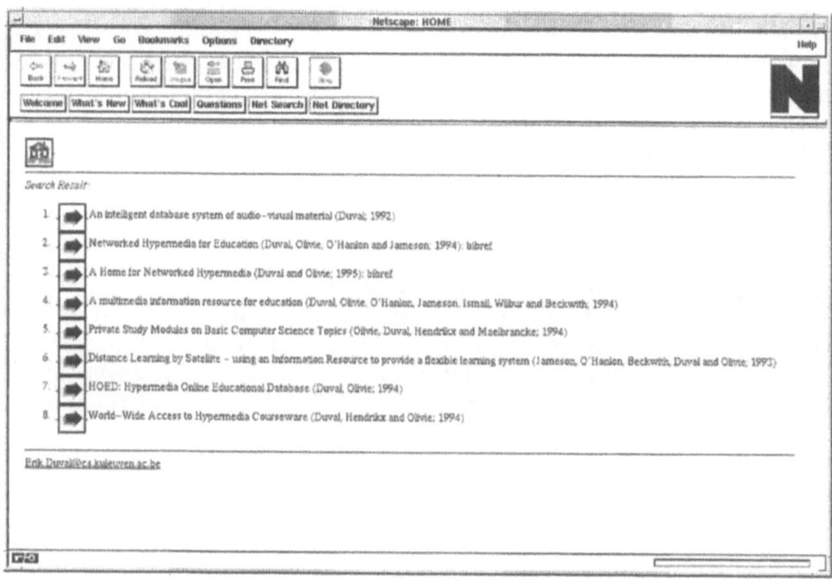

Figure 10: Result from a query

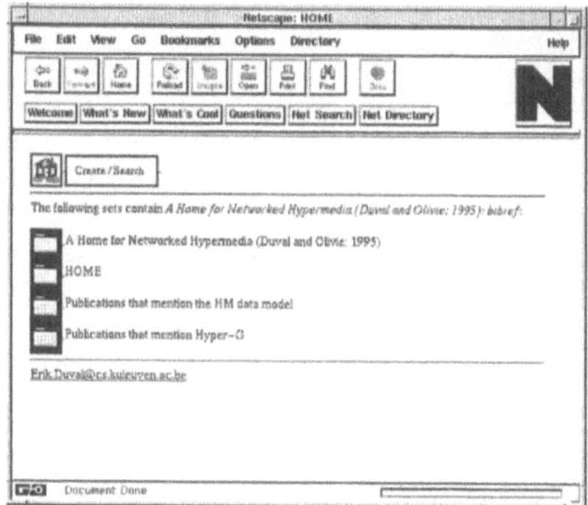

Figure 11: Zooming out of a query result

result itself. Very often, this material will also be of interest to the querying user. This approach can contribute to overcoming a well-known problem in information retrieval: it is often difficult for end users to formulate exact search criteria that identify all and nothing but relevant material. The approach sketched above requires the end user to identify only some of the relevant material. Local navigation (by zooming out of the relevant singletons) enables him to retrieve the other relevant material afterwards, as similar material will normally be linked with the material identified in the query.

8 Some Implementation Aspects

Figure 12 indicates how we have integrated our distributed server in the World-Wide Web. We have set up W.W.W. servers in London and Leuven. W.W.W. clients can access these servers, using the HyperText Transfer Protocol (HTTP). Through the Common Gateway Interface (CGI [Gleeson, Westaway 95]) protocol, the W.W.W. servers interact with the HOME server and the image store. The two latter components deliver the result, package it in the W.W.W. HyperText Mark-up Language (HTML) for document definition and send it to the W.W.W. server, that in turn ships it to the W.W.W. client that originally submitted the request.

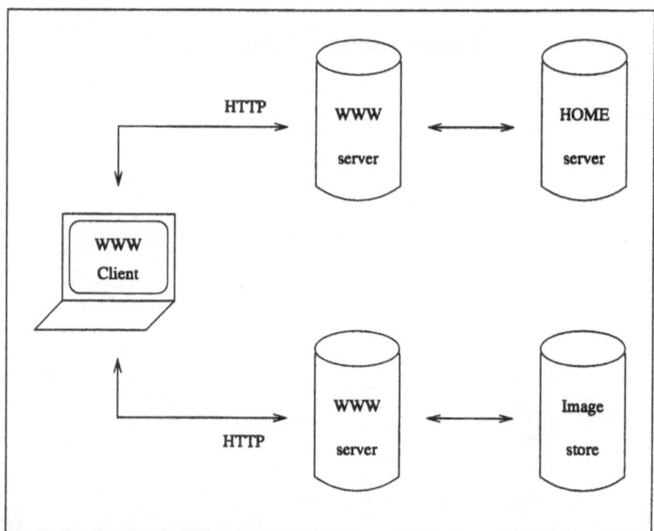

Figure 12: Interaction between W.W.W. client and server components

The main reason why we have integrated our system into the W.W.W., is the availability of client and server software for a wide variety of hard- and software platforms. Section 9 will detail the added value HOME provides when compared with the W.W.W.

The HOME server is implemented in Tcl [Ousterhout 94]. This interpreted scripting language offers considerable functionality, ease of use and flexibility. Tcl is certainly a well suited language for rapid prototyping and early experimentation. Up to now, we have not had any problems with a possible decrease in efficiency, as the connection and transmission times typically far outweigh the time it takes to process requests.

All data describing characteristics of the multimedia objects and their interrelationships are stored in a commercially available Relational DataBase Management System (RDBMS), in our case Oracle, but any full-fledged RDBMS will do, as we only need the typical functionality all comparable products support. Interaction between the Oracle DBMS and the Tcl language is implemented in Oratcl, an extension to the Tcl language.

It is important to note that we have deliberately chosen not to use the SQL language *for client server interaction* [Khoshafian, et al. 93]. (As mentioned at the start of this section, we do rely on SQL for internal server functionality.) There are two reasons for this decision:

- SQL would provide clients with too much flexibility and would enable them to create inconsistent server states.
- Using SQL for client server interaction would make clients more complex as more application logic would need to be replicated in every client.

The Tcl Application Programmer's Interface that we have designed provides a higher level of abstraction and enables us to overcome the difficulties mentioned above.

9 Distinctive Characteristics

In this section, we list some of the more distinctive characteristics of our approach. The next section will compare HOME with related research.

9.1 Separation of Structure and Content

The *separation* of the multimedia and hypermedia layer results in a separation of structure and content, or, in traditional hypermedia terminology, a separation of links and nodes. This is different from the W.W.W. approach, where links are embedded in documents. [Hall, et al. 95] refers to the problem that embedded links cannot be changed without revising the document itself as *link fossilisation.* Separation offers many advantages, especially in a large-scale, networked, multiuser context [Duval, Olivié 94] [Kappe, et al. 93]:

- *Read-only* material can be linked to and from:
  - Documents on e.g. CD-ROM or stored on videodisk (and digitised upon request, as in the case of the image store, see section 5.2) can be linked to and from. In HOME, such material can act as content of a singleton. The latter can in turn be an element of a multiset, etc.

  - In traditional hypertext terminology, users can link to or from any document. In SOS terminology, users can insert sets created by others as elements in their own multisets, without modifying the set originally created by somebody else. This last point is important as it guarantees *document integrity* to the original author, while still allowing anyone to superimpose personal structures on the content.
- Using traditional terminology, ***bi-directional links***, or a ***back-link capability*** [Engelbart 90] can more easily be supported if structure is separated from content, because link information can be queried independently (i.e. without a need to scan all the documents), to identify documents that refer to a particular document. In the SOS context, this corresponds to the fact that one cannot only zoom in on one of the elements of a set, but that it is also possible to zoom out of a set, obtaining a list of sets that contain the current set.
  - This makes it easy to remove ***dangling references*** when a document is deleted. When a set is destroyed, the structure of all multisets it previously belonged to can be updated accordingly. In traditional hypermedia terminology, when a document is destroyed, all links referring to that document can also be deleted.
  - The back-link capability is also important for the generation of local overview maps. Such maps indicate the links to as well as from a particular node. Local maps can help to avoid the disorientation problem known as "lost in hyperspace", although they offer only limited relief for navigation problems in large information spaces. In that case, they can be integrated in a larger overview through so-called "fisheye views" [Sarkar, Brown 94]. In HOME, a graphical overview of the is-an-element-of relationship could be used to provide this sense of context to the user. Such a facility requires the back-link capability.
- *Different structures* can be superimposed *on the same content*: a particular set (e.g. representing an employee) can be linked to some sets (e.g. representing the projects he works on) in the context of one set (e.g. representing the workload of each employee) and to other sets (e.g. the employees he supervises) in the context of another set (e.g. representing the hierarchical structure of the company) - it is difficult to envisage how this could be achieved in e.g. an HTML encoding in the W.W.W.

9.2 Identity rather than Location

As the multimedia layer enforces object identification, the *location* of a multimedia object can easily be modified: this requires only an update of the corresponding attribute. Using identifiers contrasts favourably with the W.W.W. approach of referring to objects by location, because the latter approach implies that all references to a document must be updated as well when the location changes. This is clearly impractical in large-scale hypermedia environments, as daily practice with the W.W.W. illustrates all too well in the form of broken links. The process whereby, in a document, gradually more and more links to locations become invalid, as the destinations change location, is called *link decay* in [Hall, et al. 95].

9.3 Interoperability

Interoperability is an important concept in an open distributed environment. This notion refers to the idea that different information retrieval and discovery [Obraczka, et al. 93] systems should work well together, e.g. that clients of one such system should be able to query servers of another system.

- Our environment interoperates rather well with existing tools and services: any object referred to by a U.R.L. can be incorporated at the multimedia metadata layer and subsequently a structure can be defined over that object at the hypermedia metadata layer. This approach makes our environment interoperable with FTP, WAIS, Gopher and W.W.W. As the U.R.L. mechanism is open and extensible, it can be expected that new services would also fit in this approach.
- As explained above, W.W.W. clients can access our server, through a gateway mechanism that translates W.W.W. requests and packages the result from our server in W.W.W. format (i.e. HTML). This integrates our environment quite seamlessly in the W.W.W. A similar approach could be followed for integrating HOME in other similar environments, e.g. Hyper-G [Kappe, Maurer 93] [Kappe, et al. 93].
- A third form of interoperability results from the fact that documents composed with external application programs can be interlinked with other documents in HOME. Thus we can avoid the problem of *dead ends* which arises in the World-Wide Web because only native HTML documents can have embedded links [Hall, et al. 95].

9.4 Database rather than File Management Systems

We believe it is important to exploit existing *database technology* when designing multimedia or hypermedia databases, rather than directly relying on the file system services offered by the operating system (as in the W.W.W.), because of the extra functionality that comes with databases [Bucci, et al. 94]:

- ACID properties (*a*tomicity, *c*onsistency, *i*solation and *d*urability of transactions): Essentially, these properties guarantee that a transaction, as the atomic unity of client-server interaction either commits in its entirety or not at all, that its effect is the same as if it would have been submitted in a standalone system and that this effect will last over time [Elmasri, Navathe 89].
- *concurrency control, access control, accounting* features: All operations have parameters `userid` and `password`. They will only be executed if the user has sufficient privileges to do so. This will be guaranteed by the DBMS.
- Provisions for *back-up and recovery* are more elaborate in a DBMS than in a traditional file system.
- A *query engine* can be used to:
  - define *dynamic links*: Conventional links are defined in an extensional way, based on the identity of the participating nodes. Dynamic links are defined intensionally: a prescript identifies all nodes the link points to (or from). The prescript is resolved at run-time, when the link is activated [Halasz 88]. Dynamic links are particularly useful if the data involved change frequently over time. Dynamic definition of membership is the HOME concept that corresponds with dynamic links.

- provide *query based access*: As an alternative to navigation, query based access is especially important in a large-scale environment, where the simple browsing paradigm breaks down because of information overload. As explained in section 7.4, it is often quite convenient to issue a query first, in order to locate some of the relevant information. Subsequently, local navigation within or around the search results supports exploration of relevant material either included in or related to the query result.

9.5 Relational Database Technology

Although we had originally anticipated that HOME would benefit from the added value of object oriented database technology, we have completed the implementation phase, using a *relational* DBMS. In retrospect, the choice between a relational and an object oriented DBMS seems to be less important than expected [Bucci, et al. 94]:

- The most important reason is that the DBMS is responsible for management of *meta*-data only: this implies that no novel features for dealing with multimedia content are required.
- An object oriented DBMS would provide more built-in support for the class hierarchy of figure 2. Implementing such support in a language like Tcl [Ousterhout 94] on top of a relational DBMS proved to be a rather moderate effort.
- The core functionality of the SQL query language is sufficiently standardised to allow for a design and implementation that is reasonably independent of the particular RDBMS (Oracle in our case).

9.6 Structured Objects

A rather unique feature of HOME is the *integration of structured objects* (see section 6): subclasses can be defined for objects that share a particular set of characteristics. This feature enables end users to interlink structured data (bibliographical references, co-ordinates of people, etc.) with unstructured multimedia objects (located through the U.R.L. mechanism [Berners-Lee, et al. 94] [Cailliau 95]).

10 Related Work

10.1 Hypermedia Data Models

Our hypermedia data model is strongly influenced by the HM model. In HM [Andrews, et al. 95] [Maurer, et al. 94], the basic unit for structuring information is an S-collection: this is either a primitive node (a name and a multimedia content) or a structure (containing a head, a set of S-collections and a set of links). The most distinctive differences between our SOS model and the HM-model are:

- In HM, a navigable *topology* can be defined between members of an S-collection.

- In HM, when an S-collection is accessed, its content (or the content of its head) is automatically visualised.
- In HM, an S-collection can have an associated multimedia content. The object need not be 'packaged' as a singleton, as in the SOS model.
- [Maurer, et al. 94] mentions that 'extending the functionality of Zoom_Out to give access to any S-collection of which the current collection is a member at first seemed attractive, but on reflection the possibility of users zooming out into a completely different context appeared to promote more confusion than understanding'. This is exactly the opposite of our finding (see e.g. section 7.4, where an elegant combination of navigational and query access is based on the idea rejected in the quote above). Hence, the SOS model defines zooming out as providing access to all sets that the current set is a member of.

A number of other data models are similar to both the SOS and the HM model, because they are also set based [Eichmann, et al. 94] [Garzotto, et al. 94]. As we are currently developing a new data model, we will not further elaborate on this issue here, nor on the relationship between set based and more traditionally oriented data models for hypermedia. These subjects will be dealt with in a forthcoming paper.

10.2 Distributed Hypermedia Systems

- Above, we have repeatedly compared our approach with the *World-Wide Web* [Berners-Lee, et al. 94] [Cailliau 95]. Although we have cited a number of well-known problems with 'the Web', it is appropriate to emphasise here that the Web made at least two important contributions to the development of distributed hypermedia systems - besides, of course, the exposure of the very notion of distributed hypermedia to the public at large:
  - The U.R.L. addressing scheme (see also section 6) accommodates references to documents on any Internet computer, through an extensible set of protocols.
  - The HyperText Transfer Protocol (HTTP) supports requests for documents, referred to by a U.R.L.
- *Hyper-G* is a large-scale hypermedia system under development at the University of Graz [Kappe, Maurer 93] [Kappe, et al. 93]. It is similar in scope to the World-Wide Web, but doesn't suffer from some of W.W.W.'s problems - most notably: links and nodes are stored separately in Hyper-G servers and query based access to documents is supported. Both these characteristics also hold for HOME. The architecture of Hyper-G is different from our layered approach and consists of a full text server, a link server an a document server. The latter two roughly correspond with our hypermedia and multimedia management layer respectively.
- The *Microcosm* design is based on a set of processes. A document viewer can send messages to a chain of filters. These can either block a message, pass it on or change it before passing it on. Finally, the messages arrive at a link dispatcher that displays information to the user (e.g. a list of links that the user can follow) [Hill, Hall 94] [Hall, et al. 95]. In an effort to adhere to the 'open hypertext' approach, third party applications can be used to create, edit and view documents, in a more or less integrated way. Recently, the

Microcosm team has investigated integration of this link service approach in the World-Wide Web [Hall, et al. 95] and started a new project, called *Multicosm*, to investigate large-scale distribution of Microcosm [Mul 94].

- *MORE* (Multimedia Oriented Repository Environment) deals with information for software re-use [Eichmann, et al. 94]. Just like HOME, MORE relies solely on the World-Wide Web for end user access. HTML documents are all generated dynamically, based on data stored in a relational database. It is interesting to note that the MORE team, targeting software re-use, came up with a solution very similar to the one we developed for courseware re-use.

11 Future

- We are currently working on the integration of support for *Computer Supported Collaborative Work* (CSCW) in HOME. More concretely, we are currently concentrating on the functionality required for interaction between student and staff and among students, in a set-up where HOME is used as a Campus-Wide Information System (CWIS). Proper support for CSCW requires:
  - *event notification*: in order to warn users when something happens to shared information;
  - *long transactions*: in traditional database context, a transaction lasts no longer than tenths of seconds; in a collaborative environment, this can be substantially longer (hours or days).

  The hypermedia paradigm lends itself well to asynchronous communication [Andrews, et al. 94]. A real-time component must be integrated within this framework, so that e.g. a student can contact a member of the staff in case of urgent problems. We will therefore elaborate a gateway between electronic mail systems (the Unix mail program in the first place) and HOME. This must enable end users to edit, send and receive email from within HOME.
- As mentioned above, the HOME server is implemented in the Tcl language [Ousterhout 94]. Tcl includes facilities for safe inter-process communication and is integrated with Tk, a user interface toolkit. We are therefore considering to develop specialised HOME client software in Tcl/Tk, bypassing the World-Wide Web environment completely (though some form of interoperability should probably be preserved), which would provide us with a more flexible implementation environment. As newer versions of e.g. the Mosaic W.W.W. client can communicate with Tcl applications, interesting new possibilities arise. These are currently under investigation.
- In Hyper-G [Kappe, Maurer 93] [Kappe, et al. 93], a search can be constrained to a particular (set of) collection(s). This sort of *search scope control* is extremely important in a large-scale networked environment as the number of data objects that satisfy the user's search criteria can be very large. In HOME, a search is currently performed over the largest relevant domain, i.e. the set of all data objects that belong to a particular class (e.g. biomedical images), because the search constraints are expressed in terms of attributes and these are only defined for data objects that belong to the relevant class. On the other hand, HOME is more flexible than Hyper-G in this respect, as it allows arbitrary complex search conditions over an arbitrary large set of attributes defined for a particular data object class.

- The present *user interface* supports creation of hypermedia data. Subsequent modification (apart from deletion) is not supported and should be. User interface issues related to large information spaces should also be elaborated further, based on techniques such as fisheye views [Sarkar, Brown 94], 3D visualisation [Robertson, et al. 93] and treemaps [Shneiderman 92].
- We are currently planning a number of *projects* for development of HOME servers. These include a bibliographical database, a hypermedia server on live art, an annotated slide collection on architecture, a distributed European network of topical courseware databases and an information resource on job opportunities.
- *Active* and *deductive database* technology could be used to model (interaction with) the end user in the server. This would make it possible to design and implement customisation and adaptation of the information presented to the end user.

12 Conclusion

In this paper, we have presented HOME, an environment for hypermedia management. Based upon a rigorous separation of data and metadata, three different layers are discerned in HOME: a storage layer dealing with raw data management, a multimedia layer that takes care of metadata concerning individual objects and a hypermedia layer where interrelationships between objects are defined. The latter layer relies on the 'Sets Of Sets' model that structures data in singletons and multisets. We are currently working on a more advanced data model that will replace the SOS model in a future version of HOME.

Acknowledgements

The financial support of the European Commission, provided within the framework of the DELTA program for the projects CAPTIVE, MTS and ACT is gratefully acknowledged. We are also indebted to the Belgian National Fund for Scientific Research, for its partial funding.

We also wish to thank Richard Beckwith, Jane Williams, Nermin Ismail, Koen Hendrikx, Rudi Maelbrancke and Nick Scherbakov for their helpful comments - they were invaluable to us. Finally, the suggestions and comments by the anonymous reviewers have helped us to improve the overall quality of this paper.

References

[Andrews, et al. 94] K. Andrews, F. Kappe, H. Maurer, and K. Schmaranz. On second generation hypermedia systems. *Journal of Universal Computer Science*, 0:127–136, Nov 1994.

[Andrews, et al. 95] K. Andrews, A. Nedoumov, and N. Scherbakov. Embedding courseware into the internet: Problems and solutions. In *ED-Media 95: World Conference on Educational Multimedia and Hypermedia (June 18-21, 1995, Graz, Austria)*, Jun 1995. To be published.

[Beckwith, et al. 93] R. C. Beckwith, D. G. Jameson, P. O' Hanlon, and E. Duval. Interactive satellite teaching and conferencing using an image server. In *Proceedings of the ESA Olympus Conference, April, 20-22, 1993, Seville*, 1993. To be published.

[Berners-Lee, et al. 94] T. Berners-Lee, R. Cailliau, A. Luotonen, H. F. Nielsen, and A. Secret. The world-wide web. *Communications of the ACM*, 37:76–82, Aug 1994.

[Bowman, et al. 94] C.M. Bowman, P.B. Danzig, D.R. Hardy, U. Manber, and M.F. Schwartz. Harvest: A scalable, customizable discovery and access system. Technical Report CU-CS-732-94, Department of Computer Science, University of Colorado-Boulder, August 1994.

[Bucci, et al. 94] G. Bucci, R. Detti, V. Pasqui, and S. Nativi. Sharing multimedia data over a client-server network. *IEEE Multimedia*, 1(3):44–55, 1994.

[Buford 94] John F. Koegel Buford. *Multimedia Systems*. SIGGRAPH Series. ACM Press, 1994.

[Cailliau 95] R. Cailliau. About www. *Journal of Universal Computer Science*, 1:221–230, Apr 1995.

[Duval, Olivié 94] E. Duval and H. Olivié. HOED: Hypermedia online educational database. In T. Ottman and I. Tomek, editors, *Educational Multimedia and Hypermedia Annual, 1994. Proceedings of ED-MEDIA 94 - World Conference on Educational Multimedia and Hypermedia, Vancouver, BC, Canada; June 25-30, 1994*, pages 178–183, 1994.

[Eichmann, et al. 94] Eichmann, McGregor, and Danley. Integrating structured databases into the web: The more system. In R. Cailliau, O. Nierstrasz, and M. Ruggier, editors, *Proceedings of the First International WWW Conference - Geneva, Switzerland, 25-27 May 1994*, pages 369–378, May 1994. Available at http://rbse.jsc.nasa.gov/eichmann/www94/MORE/MORE.html.

[Elmasri, Navathe 89] R. Elmasri and S. B. Navathe. *Fundamentals of Database Systems*. Benjamin/Cummings, 1989.

[Engelbart 90] D. C. Engelbart. Knowledge-domain interoperability and an open hyperdocument system. In *ACM CSCW 90 Proceedings*, pages 143–156, Oct 1990.

[Garzotto, et al. 94] Franca Garzotto, Luca Mainetti, and Paolo Paolini. Adding multimedia collections to the dexter model. In *Proceedings of ECHT 94: European Conference on Hypermedia technology, Edinburgh, Schotland; September, 18-23, 1994*, pages 70–80, September 1994.

[Gleeson, Westaway 95] Martin Gleeson and Tina Westaway. Beyond hypertext: Using the www for interactive applications. In R. S. Debreceny and A. E. Ellis, editors, *Innovation and Diversity - The World Wide Web in Australia. AusWeb 95 - Proceedings of the First Australian World Wide Web Conference, Ballina, Australia, 30 April - 2 May 1995.* Norsearch Publishing, Apr 1995. Available from http://www.its.unimelb.edu.au:801/papers/AW04-04/.

[Halasz 88] Frank G. Halasz. Reflections on notecards: Seven issues for the next generation of hypermedia systems. *Communications of the ACM*, 31(7):836–852, July 1988.

[Hall, et al. 95] Wendy Hall, Leslie Carr, and David De Roure. Linking the world wide web and microcosm. In *New Directions in Software Development 95: The World-Wide Web (University of Wolverhampton; 8 March 1995)*, Mar 1995. Available from http://scitsc.wlv.ac.uk:80/ndisd/hall.ps.

[Hardman, et al. 94] L. Hardman, D. C. A. Bulterman, and G. van Rossum. The amsterdam hypermedia model - adding time and context to the dexter model. *Communications of the ACM*, 37:50–62, Feb 1994.

[Hill, Hall 94] Gary Hill and Wendy Hall. Extending the microcosm model to a distributed environment. In *Proceedings of ECHT 94: European Conference on*

Hypermedia technology, Edinburgh, Schotland; September, 18-23, 1994, pages 32–40, September 1994.

[Jain, Hampapur 94] Ramesh Jain and Arun Hampapur. Metadata in video databases. *ACM SIGMOD Record*, 23:27–33, Dec 1994.

[Jameson, et al. 93] D. G. Jameson, P. O'Hanlon, R. Beckwith, E. Duval, and H. Olivié. Distance learning by satellite - using an information resource to provi de a flexible learning system. In G. Davies and B. Samways, editors, *Teleteaching, Proceedings of the IFIP TC3 Third Teleteaching Conference, Teleteaching 93, Trondheim, Norway, 20-25 August 1993*, pages 459–467. International Federation for Information Processing, Elsevier Science, 1993.

[Kappe, et al. 93] Frank Kappe, Hermann Maurer, and Nick Scherbakov. Hyper-g. a universal hypermedia system. *Journal of Educational Multimedia and Hypermedia*, 2:39–66, 1993.

[Kappe, Maurer 93] F. Kappe and H. Maurer. Hyper-g: A large universal hypermedia system and some spin-offs. *ACM Computer Graphics*, May 1993.

[Khoshafian, et al. 93] S. Khoshafian, A. Chan, A. Wong, and H. K. T. Wong. *Client/Server SQL Applications*. Morgan Kaufmann Series in Data Management Systems. Morgan Kaufmann, 1993.

[Lamport 86] Leslie Lamport. *Latex: A Document Preparation System*. Addison-Wesley, May 1986.

[Little, Venkatesh 94] Thomas D. C. Little and Dinesh Venkatesh. Prospects for interactive video-on-demand. *IEEE Multimedia*, 1:14–24, 1994.

[Maurer, et al. 94] H. Maurer, N. Scherbakov, K. Andrews, and P. Srinivasan. Object-oriented modelling of hyperstructure: overcoming the static link deficiency. *Information and Software Technology*, 36:315–322, 1994.

[Mul 94] The multicosm project: Towards a scaleable distributed multimedia information environment. Dec 1994. Available at: http://vim.ecs.soton.ac.uk/multicosm.html.

[Nielsen 90] J. Nielsen. *Hypertext and Hypermedia*. Academic Press, 1990.

[Obraczka, et al. 93] K. Obraczka, P. B. Danzig, and S. Li. Internet resource discovery services. *IEEE Computer*, 26(9):8–22, September 1993.

[Ousterhout 94] J. K. Ousterhout. *Tcl and the Tk toolkit*. Addison-Wesley, 1994.

[Robertson, et al. 93] G. G. Robertson, S. K. Stuart, and J. D. Mackinlay. Information visualization using 3d interactive animation. *Communications of the ACM*, 36(4):57–71, April 1993.

[Sarkar, Brown 94] Manojit Sarkar and Marc H. Brown. Graphical fisheye views. *Communications of the ACM*, 37:73–84, Dec 1994.

[Shneiderman 92] Ben Shneiderman. *Designing the User Interface: Srategies for Effective Human-Computer Interaction*. Addison-Wesley, 1992.

[Tonomura, et al. 94] Yoshinobu Tonomura, Akihito Akutsu, Yukinobu Taniguchi, and Gen Suzuki. Structured video computing. *IEEE Multimedia*, 1:34–43, 1994.

Journal of Universal Computer Science, vol. 1, no. 5 (1995), 292-311
submitted: 21/1/95, accepted: 14/5/95, appeared: 28/5/95

Lexical Analysis with a Simple Finite-Fuzzy-Automaton Model [1]

Alexandru Mateescu
Academy of Finland and the Mathematics Department, University of Turku, 20500 Turku, Finland.

Arto Salomaa
Academy of Finland and the Mathematics Department, University of Turku, 20500 Turku, Finland.

Kai Salomaa
Mathematics Department, University of Turku, 20500 Turku, Finland.

Sheng Yu
Department of Computer Science, The University of Western Ontario, London, Ontario, Canada N6A 5B7

Abstract: Many fuzzy automaton models have been introduced in the past. Here, we discuss two basic finite fuzzy automaton models, the Mealy and Moore types, for lexical analysis. We show that there is a remarkable difference between the two types. We consider that the latter is a suitable model for implementing lexical analysers. Various properties of fuzzy regular languages are reviewed and studied. A fuzzy lexical analyzer generator (FLEX) is proposed.
Category: G.2

1 Introduction

In most of the currently available compilers and operating systems, input strings are treated as crisp tokens. A string is either a token or a non-token; there is no middle ground. For example in UNIX, if you enter "yac", it does not mean "yacc" to the system. If you type "spelll" (the key sticks), it will also not be

[1]The work reported here has been supported by the Natural Sciences and Engineering Research Council of Canada grants OGP0041630 and the Project 11281 of the Academy of Finland.

treated as "spell" although there is no confusion. Would it be more friendly if the system would ask you whether you meant "yacc" in the first case and "spell" in the second case, or simply decide for you if there is no confusion ? Sure. There are many different ways available which can be used to implement the above idea. Various models of fuzzy automata have been introduced in, e.g., [7], [10], [6], [2], [11]. However, what is needed here is a model that is so simple, so easy to implement, and so efficient to run that it makes sense to be utilized.

Here we describe a very simple model for this purpose. The fuzzy automaton model we describe in this article follows those described in [7], [4], [5], [10], [2], [11], etc. in principle. Fuzzy languages and grammars were formally defined by Lee and Zadeh in [4]. Maximin automata as a special class of pseudo automata were studied by Santos [9, 10]. A more restricted, Mealy type model was also studied by Mizumoto et al. [5]. Note that many concepts described in this paper are not new. The main purpose of this article is to try to renew an interest in fuzzy automata as language acceptors and, especially, their applications in lexical analysis and parsing.

In the following, we first review the basic concept of fuzzy languages and define regular fuzzy languages. Then we describe two types of finite fuzzy automata, the Mealy and Moore types. We compare them and argue that one is better than the other for the purpose of lexical analysis. We also study other properties of finite fuzzy automata and their relation to fuzzy grammars [4].

2 Regular fuzzy languages

Many of the following basic definitions on fuzzy languages can be found in [4].

Definition 2.1 *Let Σ be a finite alphabet and $f : \Sigma^* \to M$ a function, where M is a set of real numbers in $[0,1]$. Then we call the set*

$$\widetilde{L} = \{(w, f(w)) \mid w \in \Sigma^*\}$$

a fuzzy language over Σ and f the membership function of $\widetilde{L}$.

In the following, we often use $f_{\widetilde{L}}$ to denote the membership function of $\widetilde{L}$.

Let $\widetilde{L}$ be a fuzzy language over Σ and $f_{\widetilde{L}} : \Sigma^* \to M$ the membership function of $\widetilde{L}$. Then, for each $m \in M$, denote by $S_{\widetilde{L}}(m)$ the set

$$S_{\widetilde{L}}(m) = \{w \in \Sigma \mid f_{\widetilde{L}}(w) = m\}.$$

Note that $S_{\widetilde{L}}$ as a function is just $f_{\widetilde{L}}^{-1}$.

Definition 2.2 *Let $\widetilde{L}_1$ and $\widetilde{L}_2$ be two fuzzy languages over Σ. Then the basic operations on $\widetilde{L}_1$ and $\widetilde{L}_2$ are define in the following:*

(1) The membership function $f_{\widetilde{L}}$ of the union $\widetilde{L} = \widetilde{L}_1 \cup \widetilde{L}_2$ is defined by

$$f_{\widetilde{L}}(w) = max\{f_{\widetilde{L}_1}(w), f_{\widetilde{L}_2}(w)\},\ w \in \Sigma^*.$$

(2) The membership function $f_{\widetilde{L}}$ of the intersection $\widetilde{L} = \widetilde{L}_1 \cap \widetilde{L}_2$ is defined by

$$f_{\widetilde{L}}(w) = min\{f_{\widetilde{L}_1}(w), f_{\widetilde{L}_2}(w)\},\ w \in \Sigma^*.$$

(3) The membership function $f_{\widetilde{L}}$ of the complement of $\widetilde{L}_1$ is defined by

$$f_{\widetilde{L}}(w) = 1 - f_{\widetilde{L}_1}(w),\ w \in \Sigma^*.$$

(4) The membership function $f_{\widetilde{L}}$ of the concatenation $\widetilde{L} = \widetilde{L}_1 \cdot \widetilde{L}_2$ is defined by

$$f_{\widetilde{L}}(w) = max\{min(f_{\widetilde{L}_1}(x), f_{\widetilde{L}_2}(y)) \mid w = xy,\ x, y \in \Sigma^*\},\ w \in \Sigma^*.$$

(5) The membership function $f_{\widetilde{L}}$ of the star operation $\widetilde{L} = \widetilde{L}_1^*$ is defined by

$$f_{\widetilde{L}}(w) = max\{min(f_{\widetilde{L}_1}(x_1), \ldots, f_{\widetilde{L}_1}(x_n)) \mid w = x_1 \cdots x_n,$$
$$x_1, \ldots, x_n \in \Sigma^*, n \geq 0\},\ w \in \Sigma^*,$$

assuming that $min\emptyset = 1$.

(6) The membership function $f_{\widetilde{L}}$ of the + operation $\widetilde{L} = \widetilde{L}_1^+$ is defined by

$$f_{\widetilde{L}}(w) = max\{min(f_{\widetilde{L}_1}(x_1), \ldots, f_{\widetilde{L}_1}(x_n)) \mid w = x_1 \cdots x_n,$$
$$x_1, \ldots, x_n \in \Sigma^*, n \geq 1\},\ w \in \Sigma^*.$$

Since fuzzy languages are just a special class of fuzzy sets, the equivalence and inclusion relations between two fuzzy languages are the equivalence and equivalence relations between two fuzzy sets. Let $\widetilde{L}_1$ and $\widetilde{L}_2$ be two fuzzy languages over Σ. Then

$$\widetilde{L}_1 = \widetilde{L}_2 \text{ iff } f_{\widetilde{L}_1}(w) = f_{\widetilde{L}_2}(w) \text{ for all } w \in \Sigma^*,$$

and

$$\widetilde{L}_1 \subseteq \widetilde{L}_2 \text{ iff } f_{\widetilde{L}_1}(w) \leq f_{\widetilde{L}_2}(w) \text{ for all } w \in \Sigma^*.$$

Definition 2.3 *Let $\tilde{L}$ be a fuzzy language over Σ and $f_{\tilde{L}} : \Sigma^* \to M$ the membership function of $\tilde{L}$. We call $\tilde{L}$ a regular fuzzy language if*

(1) the set $\{m \in M \mid S_{\tilde{L}}(m) \neq \emptyset\}$ is finite and

(2) for each $m \in M, S_{\tilde{L}}(m)$ is regular.

It is obvious that the first condition can be replaced by

(1') M is finite.

For convenience, when we write $f_{\tilde{L}} : \Sigma^* \to M$, we mean that $M = \{f_{\tilde{L}}(w) \mid w \in \Sigma^*\}$, i.e., for each $m \in M, S_{\tilde{L}}(m) \neq \emptyset$. Also, the second condition in the above definition can be replaced by

(2') for each $m \in M$, $\{w \in \Sigma^* \mid f_{\tilde{L}}(w) \geq m \}$ is regular.

We choose (2) instead of (2') since it can be used more directly in the subsequent proofs.

Example 2.1 *Let $\tilde{L}_1$ be a fuzzy language over $\Sigma = \{a, b\}$ and $f_{\tilde{L}_1}$:*

$$f_{\tilde{L}_1}(x) = \begin{cases} 1, & \text{if } x \in a^*, \\ 0.7, & \text{if } x \in a^*ba^*, \\ 0.5, & \text{if } x \in a^*ba^*ba^*, \\ 0, & \text{otherwise.} \end{cases}$$

Then $\tilde{L}_1$ is a regular fuzzy language.

Example 2.2 *The membership function $f_{\tilde{L}_2}$ of $\tilde{L}_2$ over $\Sigma = \{a, b\}$ is defined by*

$$f_{\tilde{L}_2}(x) = |x|_a/|x|,$$

where $|x|$ denotes the length of x and $|x|_a$ the number of appearances of a in x. Then $\tilde{L}_2$ is not a regular fuzzy language.

The next theorem can be easily proved.

Theorem 2.1 *Regular fuzzy languages are closed under union, intersection, complement, concatenation, and star operations.*

Proof. Let $\tilde{L}_1$ and $\tilde{L}_2$ be two regular fuzzy languages over Σ and $f_{\tilde{L}_1} : \Sigma^* \to M_1$ and $f_{\tilde{L}_2} : \Sigma^* \to M_2$. Let $\tilde{L}$ be the resulting language after an operation (union, ..., or star) and $f_{\tilde{L}} : \Sigma^* \to M$. Then obviously, $M \subseteq M_1 \cup M_2$ (in the case of a union, an intersection, a concatenation, or a star operation) or $M = \{1 - m \mid m \in M_1\}$ (in the case of a complementation) is finite. Let m be in M. Then $S_{\tilde{L}}(m)$ is defined by:

(1) Union:

$$S_{\tilde{L}}(m) = \begin{cases} S_{\tilde{L_1}}(m) - \bigcup_{m'>m} S_{\tilde{L_2}}(m'), & \text{if } m \in M_1 - M_2, \\ S_{\tilde{L_2}}(m) - \bigcup_{m'>m} S_{\tilde{L_1}}(m'), & \text{if } m \in M_2 - M_1, \\ ((S_{\tilde{L_1}}(m) \bigcup S_{\tilde{L_2}}(m)) - \bigcup_{m'>m} S_{\tilde{L_1}}(m')) - \bigcup_{m''>m} S_{\tilde{L_2}}(m''), & \\ \qquad \text{if } m \in M_1 \cap M_2; \end{cases}$$

(2) Intersection:

$$S_{\tilde{L}}(m) = \begin{cases} S_{\tilde{L_1}}(m) - \bigcup_{m'<m} S_{\tilde{L_2}}(m'), & \text{if } m \in M_1 - M_2, \\ S_{\tilde{L_2}}(m) - \bigcup_{m'<m} S_{\tilde{L_1}}(m'), & \text{if } m \in M_2 - M_1, \\ ((S_{\tilde{L_1}}(m) \bigcup S_{\tilde{L_2}}(m)) - \bigcup_{m'<m} S_{\tilde{L_1}}(m')) - \bigcup_{m''<m} S_{\tilde{L_2}}(m''), & \\ \qquad \text{if } m \in M_1 \cap M_2; \end{cases}$$

(3) Complement: ($M = \{1 - m \mid m \in M_1\}$)

$$S_{\tilde{L}}(m) = S_{\tilde{L_1}}(1 - m),$$

(4) Concatenation:

$$S_{\tilde{L}}(m) = \bigcup_{\substack{min(m_1, m_2) = m \\ m_1 \in M_1 \\ m_2 \in M_2}} S_{\tilde{L_1}}(m_1) S_{\tilde{L_2}}(m_2) - \bigcup_{\substack{min(m'_1, m'_2) > m \\ m_1 \in M_1 \\ m_2 \in M_2}} S_{\tilde{L_1}}(m'_1) S_{\tilde{L_2}}(m'_2).$$

(5) Star: assuming that $M_1 = \{m_1, \ldots, m_n\}$ and $1 \geq m_1 > m_2 > \ldots > m_n \geq 0$,

$$S_{\tilde{L}}(m_1) = (S_{\tilde{L_1}}(m_1))^* \text{ if } m_1 = 1,$$

$$S_{\tilde{L}}(1) = \{\lambda\} \text{ and } S_{\tilde{L}}(m_1) = (S_{\tilde{L_1}}(m_1))^+ - \{\lambda\} \text{ if } m_1 \neq 1,$$

$$S_{\tilde{L}}(m_i) = (\bigcup_{j \leq i} S_{\tilde{L_1}}(m_j))^+ - \bigcup_{k<i} S_{\tilde{L}}(m_k) - \{\lambda\}, \ \ 1 < i \leq n.$$

It is clear that all the sets defined above are regular. So, we have finished this proof. □

3 Finite fuzzy automata

The reader may refer to [8, 3] for basic definitions in automata theory.

Definition 3.1 *A nondeterministic finite automaton with fuzzy transitions (FT-NFA) $\widetilde{A}$ is a 5-tuple $\widetilde{A} = (Q, \Sigma, \tilde{\delta}, s, F)$, where*

Q is the finite set of states;

Σ is the finite set of input symbols;
$\tilde{\delta} : Q \times \Sigma \times Q \to [0,1]$ is the degree function of state transitions;
s is the initial state; and
$F \subseteq Q$ is the set of final states.
For $x \in \Sigma^*$ and $p, q \in Q$, define

$$\tilde{\delta}^*(p,x,q) = \begin{cases} 0, & \text{if } x = \lambda \text{ and } p \neq q, \\ 1, & \text{if } x = \lambda \text{ and } p = q, \\ \max_{r \in Q}\{min\{\tilde{\delta}^*(p,x',r),\ \tilde{\delta}(r,a,q)\} \mid x = x'a,\ x' \in \Sigma^*,\ a \in \Sigma\}, & \\ \quad \text{otherwise.} & \end{cases}$$

Then we say that $x \in \Sigma^*$ is accepted by $\widetilde{A}$ with degree $d_{\widetilde{A}}(x)$, where

$$d_{\widetilde{A}}(x) = max\{\tilde{\delta}^*(s,x,q) \mid q \in F\}.$$

We denote by $\widetilde{L}\,(\widetilde{A})$ the set:

$$\widetilde{L}\,(\widetilde{A}) = \{(x, d_{\widetilde{A}}(x)) \mid x \in \Sigma^*\}.$$

Note that by the above definition, the value of $d_{\widetilde{A}}(\lambda)$ only can be either 1 or 0 for any FT-NFA $\widetilde{A}$. In many discussions, this restriction is easily understood but can be cumbersome to describe. So, if there is no special mentioning when considering problems related to FT-NFA in the sequel, the reader should assume that λ and its degree are not considered.

Example 3.1 *Let $\Sigma = \{a, b\}$ and an FT-NFA $\widetilde{A}_1$ be defined in the following:*

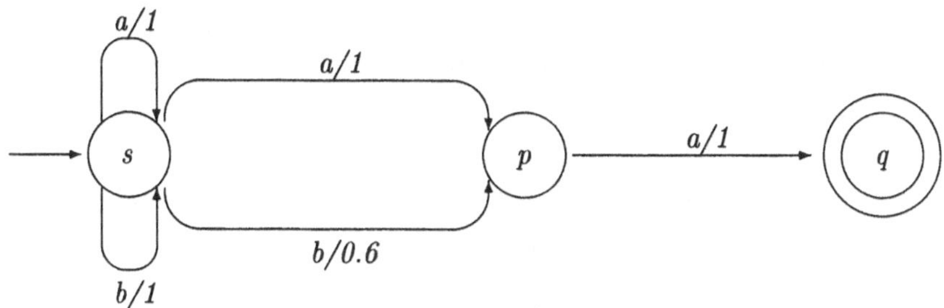

Figure 1

Obviously,

$$\widetilde{L}\,(\widetilde{A}_1) = \{(x,1) \mid x \in \{a,b\}^*aa\} \cup \{(y,0.6) \mid y \in \{a,b\}^*ba\}.$$

We omit the pairs whose second components are 0.

FT-NFA are a special type of Mealy machines, where the output has a special meaning. They are also a special class of the maximin automata introduced by Santos in [9]. In an FT-NFA, the set of final states is a crisp set (which, of course, is a special case of fuzzy sets) and the initial state is crisp, too.

Definition 3.2 *A deterministic finite automaton with fuzzy transitions (FT-DFA)* $\widetilde{A} = (Q, \Sigma, \tilde{\delta}, s, F)$ *is an FT-NFA with the condition that for each* $p \in Q$ *and* $a \in \Sigma$, *if* $\tilde{\delta}(p,a,q) > 0$ *and* $\tilde{\delta}(p,a,q') > 0$, *then* $q = q'$.

Theorem 3.1 $\widetilde{L}$ *is a regular fuzzy language iff* $\widetilde{L}$ *is accepted by an FT-NFA* $\widetilde{A}$ *with the exception of* λ.

Proof. Let $\widetilde{L}$ be a regular fuzzy language and $f_{\widetilde{L}} : \Sigma^* \to M$ be the membership function. Then $M = \{m_1, \ldots, m_n\}$ for some $n \geq 1$ and $S_{\widetilde{L}}(m_i)$ is regular for each $m_i \in M$. Note that $S_{\widetilde{L}}(m_i) \cap S_{\widetilde{L}}(m_j) = \emptyset$ for $i \neq j$ since $f_{\widetilde{L}}$ is a function.

Let $A_i = (Q_i, \Sigma, \delta_i, s_i, F_i)$ be a DFA (or an NFA) such that $S_{\widetilde{L}}(m_i) = L(A_i)$, $1 \leq i \leq n$. We construct $\widetilde{A}_i = (Q_i, \Sigma, \widetilde{\delta}_i, s_i, F_i)$ where

$$\tilde{\delta}_i(p,a,q) = \begin{cases} m_i, & \text{if } (p,a,q) \in \delta_i, \\ 0, & \text{otherwise.} \end{cases}$$

We assume that $Q_i \cap Q_j = \emptyset$ for $i \neq j$. Define $\widetilde{A} = (Q, \Sigma, \tilde{\delta}, s, F)$ such that

$$Q = Q_1 \cup \ldots \cup Q_n \cup \{s\} \quad \text{and} \quad s \notin Q_1 \cup \ldots \cup Q_n,$$

$$F = F_1 \cup \ldots \cup F_n,$$

$$\tilde{\delta}(p,a,q) = \begin{cases} \tilde{\delta}_i(p,a,q) & \text{if } p,q \in Q_i \text{ for some } i \in \{1,\ldots,n\}, \\ \tilde{\delta}_i(s_i,a,q) & \text{if} p = s \text{ and } q \in Q_i \text{ for some } i \in \{1,\ldots,n\}, \\ 0 & \text{otherwise.} \end{cases}$$

Clearly, $\widetilde{A}$ accepts $\widetilde{L}$ with the possible exception of λ .

Let $\widetilde{A} = (Q, \Sigma, \tilde{\delta}, s, F)$ be an FT-NFA. Define a fuzzy language $\widetilde{L}$ with $f_{\widetilde{L}}(w) = d_{\widetilde{A}}(w)$ for each $w \in \Sigma^*$, $(f_{\widetilde{L}}(\lambda) = 0)$. We now show that $\widetilde{L}$ is a regular fuzzy language.

Let $M = \{m \mid \tilde{\delta}(p, a, q) = m$ for some $p, q \in Q, a \in \Sigma\}$. Obviously, M is finite. Assume that $M = \{m_1, \ldots, m_n\}$ with $m_1 > m_2 > \ldots > m_n, n \geq 1$. For each i, $1 \leq i \leq n$, define an NFA

$$A_i = (Q, \Sigma, \delta_i, s, F)$$

where $\delta_i = \{(p, a, q) \mid \tilde{\delta}(p, a, q) \geq m_i\}$. Define the languages L_i, $1 \leq i \leq n$, in the increasing sequence of i as follows:

$$L_1 = L(A_1),$$

$$L_i = L(A_i) - \bigcup_{j=1}^{i-1} L_j.$$

Then $S_{\tilde{L}}(m_i) = L_i$ and L_i is a regular language, for each i, $1 \leq i \leq n$. Therefore, $\tilde{L}$ is a regular fuzzy language. □

Theorem 3.2 *Let $\tilde{L}$ be a regular fuzzy language. Then $\tilde{L}$ is accepted by an FT-DFA iff it satisfies the following condition: For $x, y \in \Sigma^+, u \in \Sigma^*$*

$$(*) \qquad x = yu \text{ and } f_{\tilde{L}}(y) > 0 \text{ implies that } f_{\tilde{L}}(x) \leq f_{\tilde{L}}(y).$$

Proof. Let $\tilde{L}$ be accepted by an FT-DFA $\tilde{A} = (Q, \Sigma, \tilde{\delta}, s, F)$. We show that $\tilde{L}$ satisfies $(*)$. Let $x = yu$, $x, y \in \Sigma^+$ and $a \in \Sigma^*$. If $d_{\tilde{A}}(x) = 0$, then $f_{\tilde{L}}(x) \leq f_{\tilde{L}}(y)$ is true trivially. Otherwise,

$$f_{\tilde{L}}(x) = d_{\tilde{A}}(x) = min\{\tilde{\delta}^*(s, y, q),\ \tilde{\delta}^*(q, u, f)\} \leq \tilde{\delta}^*(s, y, q) = d_{\tilde{A}}(y) = f_{\tilde{L}}(y)$$

where $q, f \in F$.

For the other direction of the proof, let $\tilde{L}$, with $f_{\tilde{L}} : \Sigma^* \to M$, satisfy the condition $(*)$. Assume that $M = \{m_1, \ldots, m_n\}$. It is clear that we can construct a DFA $A_i = (Q_i, \Sigma, \delta_i, s_i, F_i)$ such that $L(A_i) = S_{\tilde{L}}(m_i)$ for each i, $1 \leq i \leq n$. Note that for $1 \leq i, j \leq n$ and $i \neq j$,

$$L(A_i) \cap L(A_j) = S_{\tilde{L}}(m_i) \cap S_{\tilde{L}}(m_j) = \emptyset$$

Now we construct a DFA $A = (Q, \Sigma, \delta, s, F)$ where $Q = Q_1 \times \ldots \times Q_n$, $s = (s_1, \ldots, s_n)$, $\delta : Q \times \Sigma \to Q$ is defined by $\delta((q_1, \ldots, q_n), a) = (\delta_1(q_1, a), \ldots, \delta_n(q_n, a))$, and $F = F'_1 \cup \cdots \cup F'_n$ where $F'_i = \{(q_1, \ldots, q_n) \in Q \mid q_i \in F_i$ and $q_j \notin F_j$ for $j \neq i\}$, $1 \leq i \leq n$. It is clear that $F'_i \cap F'_j = \emptyset$, for $i \neq j$, and

$$S_{\tilde{L}}(m_i) = \{w \in \Sigma^* \mid \delta^*(s, w) \in F'_i\}.$$

Based on the above DFA A, we define an FT-DFA $\widetilde{A} = (Q, \Sigma, \tilde{\delta}, s, F)$ such that

$$\tilde{\delta}(p, a, q) = \begin{cases} m_i & \text{if } \delta(p, a) = q \in F_i', \\ 1 & \text{if } \delta(p, a) = q \notin F, \\ 0 & \text{otherwise.} \end{cases}$$

It remains to show that $d_{\widetilde{A}}(w) = f_{\widetilde{L}}(w)$, for each $w \in \Sigma^+$. But first we show that $\widetilde{A}$ has the following property: For each $w \in \Sigma^+$ with $w = xa$, $x \in \Sigma^*$ and $a \in \Sigma$,

$$(**) \quad d_{\widetilde{A}}(w) = m_i > 0 \textbf{ iff } \delta^*(s, x, p) \geq m_i \text{ and } \delta(p, a, q) = m_i \\ \text{for some } q \in F_i, 1 \leq i \leq n.$$

The *if* part holds obviously. For the *only if* part, it holds trivially when $x = \lambda$. For $x \neq \lambda$, we assume the contrary, i.e., $\delta^*(s, x, p) = m_i$ and $\delta(p, a, q) = m_j > m_i$. Then there exists a decomposition of $x = ybz$, $y, z \in \Sigma^*$ and $b \in \Sigma$, such that $\delta^*(s, y, r) \geq m_i$, $\delta(r, b, t) = m_i$, and $\delta(t, z, p) \geq m_i$. By the definition of $\widetilde{A}$, we know that $t \in F_i$ and $q \in F_j$. Thus, we have $f_{\widetilde{L}}(yb) = m_i$ and $f_{\widetilde{L}}(w) = m_j$. Since we assume that $m_j > m_i$, this is a contradiction to $(*)$. So, $(**)$ holds. Furthermore, the righthand side of $(**)$ implies that $xa \in S_{\widetilde{L}}(m_i)$, i.e., $f_{\widetilde{L}}(w) = m_i$. Therefore, we have finished the proof. □

Indeed, the condition (*) can be interpreted as follows. We have n regular languages $R_1, \ldots, R_n$, associated with the decreasing sequence $m_1 > m_2 > \ldots > m_n$. Whenever a word $y \in R_j$ is a prefix of a word $x \in R_i$, then $i \geq j$. This makes the construction possible. The construction does not work, for instance, for the two regular languages $\{a, aba\}$ and $\{ab\}$.

The condition $(*)$ can be used to show that some regular fuzzy languages are not accepted by any FT-DFA.

Corollary 3.1 *The family of fuzzy languages accepted by FT-DFA is properly included in the family of fuzzy languages accepted by FT-NFA.*

Proof. The inclusion is obvious. We only need to show that the inclusion is proper. Consider

$$\widetilde{L} = \{a/0.5, ab/1\}.$$

Obviously, $\widetilde{L}$ is accepted by an FT-NFA but not by any FT-DFA by Theorem 3.2.

Finite automata with fuzzy transitions are apparently a natural model for regular fuzzy languages. Many similar models have been studied in the past.

However, the difference in accepting power between its deterministic and nondeterministic version and the fact that many very simple regular fuzzy languages are not accepted by its deterministic version make it unfavorable to be used in practice. An FT-NFA can be represented in a matrix form. However, it may be feasible only for FT-NFA with a small number of states.

Naturally, another finite-fuzzy-automaton model is a special class of Moore machines. This model also characterizes the family of regular fuzzy languages. But unlike the fuzzy transition model, its deterministic and nondeterministic versions are equivalent in accepting power. This model is also simpler and easier to implement than the previous model.

Definition 3.3 *A <u>nondeterministic</u> finite automaton with fuzzy (final) states (FS-NFA or FS-FA) $\widetilde{A}$ is a 5-tuple $\widetilde{A}= (Q, \Sigma, \delta, s, \widetilde{F}_{\tilde{A}})$ where Q, Σ, δ, and s are the same as in an NFA, and $\widetilde{F}_{\tilde{A}} : Q \to [0,1]$ is the degree function for the fuzzy final-state set.*

Define

$$d_{\widetilde{A}}(x) = max\{\widetilde{F}_{\tilde{A}}(q) \mid (s, x, q) \in \delta^*\}.$$

Note that δ^* is the transitive and reflexive closure of δ defined as for a normal NFA. Then we say that x is accepted by $\widetilde{A}$ with degree $d_{\widetilde{A}}(x)$. The fuzzy language accepted by $\widetilde{A}$, denoted $\widetilde{L}(\widetilde{A})$, is the set $\{(x, d_{\widetilde{A}}(x)) \mid x \in \Sigma^*\}$.

Example 3.2 *Let $\Sigma = \{a, b\}$. An FS-NFA $\widetilde{A}$ is the following:*

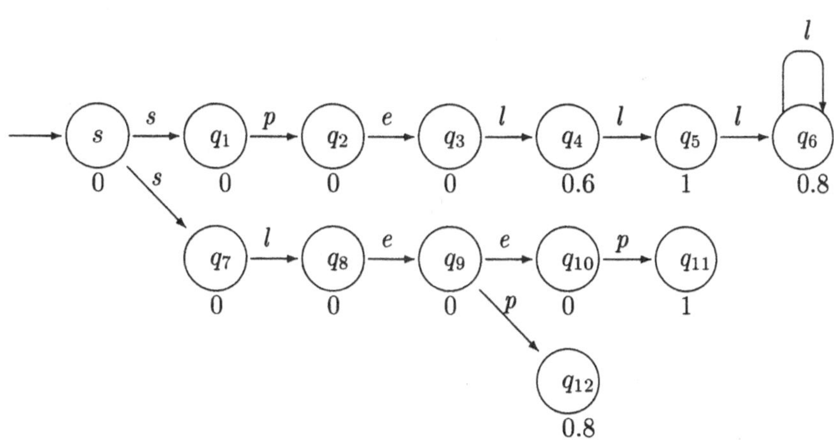

Figure 2

Then $d_{\tilde{A}}(sleep) = 1$, $d_{\tilde{A}}(spellll l) = 0.8$, *and* $d_{\tilde{A}}(sle) = 0$.

Definition 3.4 *A* <u>*deterministic*</u> *finite automaton with fuzzy states (FS-DFA)* $\widetilde{A} = (Q, \Sigma, \delta, s, \widetilde{F}_{\tilde{A}})$ *is an FS-NFA with* δ *being a function* $Q \times \Sigma \to Q$ *instead of a relation. Hence, for each* $x \in \Sigma^*$, $d_{\tilde{A}}(x) = \widetilde{F}_{\tilde{A}}(q)$ *where* $q = \delta^*(s, x)$.

Define $d_{\tilde{A}}(x) = 0$ *if* $\delta^*(s, x)$ *is not defined.*

Theorem 3.3 *Let* $\widetilde{L}$ *be a fuzzy language. Then* $\widetilde{L}$ *is a regular fuzzy language iff it is accepted by an FS-DFA.*

Proof. Let $f_{\tilde{L}} : \Sigma^* \to M$ be the membership function of $\widetilde{L}$. Assume that $\widetilde{L}$ is a regular fuzzy language. Then M is finite and, for each $m \in M$, $S_{\tilde{L}}(m)$ is a regular set. Assume that $M = \{m_1, \ldots, m_n\}$. We construct a DFA $A_i = (Q_i, \Sigma, \delta_i, s_i, F_i)$ for each i, $1 \le i \le n$, such that $L(A_i) = S_{\tilde{L}}(m_i)$. Define an FS-DFA $\widetilde{A} = (Q, \Sigma, \delta, s, \widetilde{F}_{\tilde{A}})$ to be the cross product of $A_1, \ldots, A_n$ with

$$\widetilde{F}_{\tilde{A}}((q^{(1)}, \ldots, q^{(n)})) = \begin{cases} m_i, & q^{(i)} \in F_i \text{ for some } i,\ 1 \le i \le n, \text{ and } q^{(j)} \notin F_j, \\ & \text{for all } j \neq i \\ 0, & \text{otherwise.} \end{cases}$$

Note that if $(q^{(1)}, \ldots, q^{(n)})$ is reachable from $(s_1, \ldots, s_n)$ in $\widetilde{A}$, then it is impossible to have $q^{(i)} \in F_i$ and $q^{(j)} \in F_j$ for $i \neq j$ since $L(A_i) \cap L(A_j) = \emptyset$ for $i \neq j$, $1 \le i, j \le n$. Obviously, $\widetilde{A}$ accepts $\widetilde{L}$.

For the other direction of the proof, let $\widetilde{A} = (Q, \Sigma, \delta, s, \widetilde{F}_{\tilde{A}})$ be an FS-DFA. Define

$$M = \{m \mid \widetilde{F}_{\tilde{A}}(q) = m \text{ for some } q \in Q\}.$$

M is a finite set. For each $m \in M$, define

$$A_m = (Q, \Sigma, \delta, s, F_m)$$

where $F_m = \{q \mid \widetilde{F}_{\tilde{A}}(q) = m\}$. Let $\widetilde{L} = \widetilde{L}(\widetilde{A})$, i.e. $f_{\tilde{L}} = d_{\tilde{A}}$. Then clearly, for each $m \in M$, $S_{\tilde{L}}(m) = L(A_m)$ is regular. $\widetilde{L}$ is a regular fuzzy language. □

Theorem 3.4 *A fuzzy language is accepted by an FS-NFA iff it is accepted by an FS-DFA.*

Proof. It suffices to show that if $\widetilde{L}=\widetilde{L}(\widetilde{A})$ for an FS-NFA $\widetilde{A}$ then $\widetilde{L}=\widetilde{L}(\widetilde{A}')$ for some FS-DFA $\widetilde{A}'$. Let $\widetilde{A}=(Q,\Sigma,\delta,s,\widetilde{F}_{\widetilde{A}})$. The construction of $\widetilde{A}'=(Q',\Sigma,\delta',s',\widetilde{F}'_{\widetilde{A}})$ is straightforward. We can just use the standard subset-construction method and, for each $P\in Q'$ $(P\subseteq Q)$, define

$$\widetilde{F}'_{\widetilde{A}}(P)=max\{m\mid m=\widetilde{F}_{\widetilde{A}}(q),q\in P\}.$$

It is clear that $\widetilde{L}=\widetilde{L}(\widetilde{A}')$. □

Example 3.3 *Let an FS-NFA be defined by:*

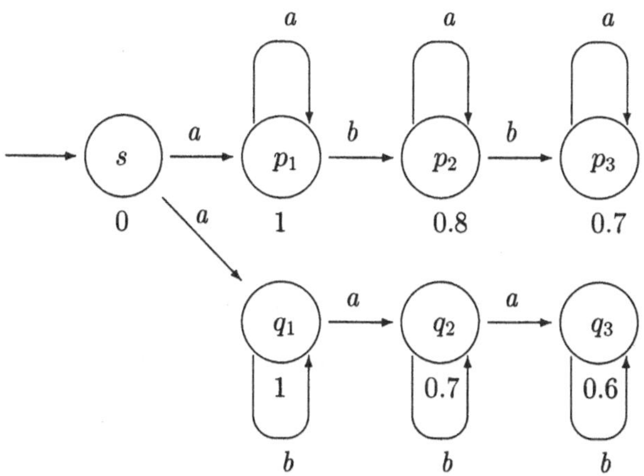

Figure 3

Define $r_1=\{p_1,q_1\}$, $r_2=\{p_1,q_2\}$, $r_3=\{p_2,q_1\}$, $r_4=\{p_1,q_3\}$, $r_5=\{p_2,q_2\}$, $r_6=\{p_3,q_1\}$, $r_7=\{p_2,q_3\}$, $r_8=\{p_3,q_2\}$, *and* $r_9=\{p_3,q_3\}$. *Then an FS-DFA that is equivalent to the above FS-NFA is given in the following:*

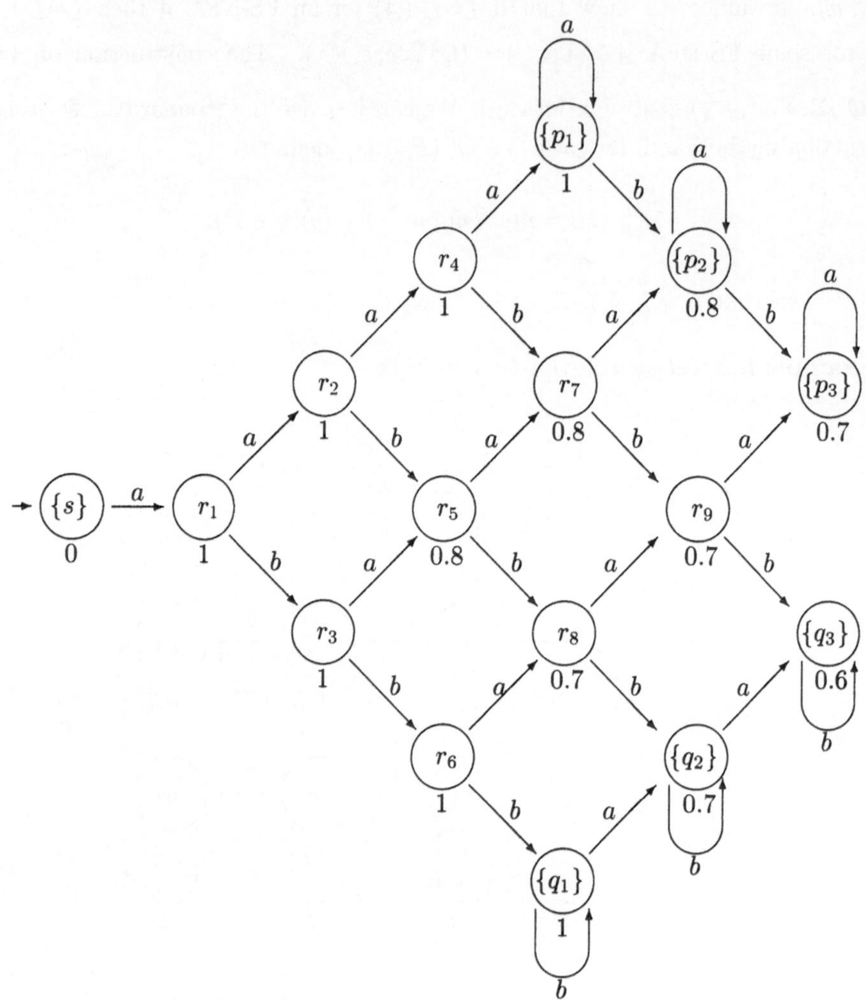

Figure 4

An extension of the Myhill-Nerode Theorem is given below, which can be easily proved.

Theorem 3.5 *(The extended Myhill-Nerode theorem) The following three statements are equivalent:*

(i) $\widetilde{L}$ *is a regular fuzzy language over* Σ .

(ii) $\widetilde{L}$ *is the union of some of the equivalence classes of a right invariant equivalence relation of finite index.*

(iii) Let the relation $R_{\widetilde{L}} \subseteq \Sigma^* \times \Sigma^*$ *be defined by* $xR_{\widetilde{L}}y$ *iff for all* $z \in \Sigma^*$, $f_{\widetilde{L}}(xz) = f_{\widetilde{L}}(yz)$. *Then* $R_{\widetilde{L}}$ *is an equivalence relation of finite index.*

The minimization algorithm for DFA described in [3] can also be extended for FS-DFA as follows:

ALGORITHM 3.1

Let $\widetilde{A}= (Q, \Sigma, \delta, q_0, \widetilde{F}_{\widetilde{A}})$ be an FS-DFA. Assume that $Q = \{q_0, \ldots, q_n\}$, $n \geq 0$, and let $P = \{(q_i, q_j) \mid q_i, q_j \in Q$ and $0 \leq i < j \leq n\}$.

begin

1) **for** each pair $(q_i, q_j) \in P$, and $\widetilde{F}_{\widetilde{A}}\ (q_i) \neq \widetilde{F}_{\widetilde{A}}\ (q_j)$ **do** mark (q_i, q_j);

2) **for** each unmarked pair $(p, q) \in P$ **do**

if for some $a \in \Sigma$, $(\delta(p, a), \delta(q, a))$ is marked then

begin

mark (p, q);

recursively mark all unmarked pairs on the list of (p, q) and

on the lists of other pairs that are marked at this step.

end

else

for all input symbols $a \in \Sigma$ **do**

put (p, q) on the list for $(\delta(p, a), \delta(q, a))$ unless $\delta(p, a) = \delta(q, a)$

end

We omit the proof that the FS-DFA constructed with the above algorithm is minimal in terms of the number of states.

4 Fuzzy regular expressions (FRE)

For each regular fuzzy language, there is a finite number of degrees and the set of all words that are associated with each degree is a regular language. Therefore, we can naturally represent a regular fuzzy language by a modified regular expression like the following:

$$ab^*/0.6 + ab^*a/1 + (bab^* + bbab^*)/0.8$$

The semantics of the expression is clear. We give a formal definition for fuzzy regular expressions (FREs) in the following:

Definition 4.1 *Let Σ be a finite alphabet and M a finite set of real numbers in $[0,1]$.*

1) Let e be a regular expression over Σ and $m \in M$. Then $(e)/m$ is a fuzzy regular expression.

2) Let $\widetilde{e}_1$ and $\widetilde{e}_2$ be fuzzy regular expressions. Then $\widetilde{e}_1 + \widetilde{e}_2$, $(\widetilde{e}_1)\cdot(\widetilde{e}_2)$, and $(\widetilde{e}_1)^*$ are all fuzzy regular expressions.

3) A fuzzy regular expression is formed by applying 1) and 2) a finite number of times.

Definition 4.2 *A fuzzy regular expression over Σ is normalized if it is of the following form*

$$e_1/m_1 + e_2/m_2 + \ldots + e_n/m_n$$

where $e_1, e_2, \ldots, e_n$ are regular expressions over Σ and $m_1, m_2, \ldots, m_n$ are numbers in $[0,1]$, $n \geq 1$.

Note that if $m = 1$ then e/m can simply be written as e. We assume that "$\cdot$" and "$*$" have higher priorities than "/". So, certain pairs of parentheses can be omitted.

Example 4.1 *The following are all valid FRE's:*

(1) $a^*/1 + a^*ba^*/0.8 + a^*ba^*ba^*/0.5$,

(2) $(b^*ab^*/0.7)\cdot(a^*ba^*/0.5) + b^*$,

(3) $abba + baab + (a+b)^*a(a+b)^*b(a+b)^*$,

where both (1) and (3) are normalized. The following are not valid FRE's:

(4) $(a^*/0.5)/0.7 + a^*ba^*/1$,

(5) $(ba^*b/0.2)(a^*)/0.5 + (ab + a)^*/1$,

(6) $(ab/0.9 + b/0.5)^*/0.9 + (aba)^*/1$.

Definition 4.3 *An FRE $\tilde{e}$ is called a strictly normalized FRE if it is normalized, i.e.,*

$$\tilde{e} = e_1/m_1 + e_2/m_2 + \ldots + e_n/m_n,$$

and for any $m_i \neq m_j$, $L(e_i) \cap L(e_j) = \emptyset$.

Definition 4.4 *Let $\tilde{e}$ be an FRE. Then $\tilde{L}(\tilde{e})$ is defined by:*

(1) if $\tilde{e} = e/m$ where e is a regular expression, then $\tilde{L}(\tilde{e}) = \{(x, m) \mid x \in L(e)\}$;

(2) if $\tilde{e} = \tilde{e}_1 + \tilde{e}_2$, $\tilde{e} = (\tilde{e}_1) \cdot (\tilde{e}_2)$, or $\tilde{e} = (\tilde{e}_1)^*$, then $\tilde{L}(\tilde{e}) = \tilde{L}(\tilde{e}_1) \cup \tilde{L}(\tilde{e}_2)$, $\tilde{L}(\tilde{e}) = \tilde{L}(\tilde{e}_1) \cdot \tilde{L}(\tilde{e}_2)$, or $\tilde{L}(\tilde{e}) = (\tilde{L}(\tilde{e}_1))^*$, respectively.

It is easy to show that the families of languages represented by FREs, normalized FREs, and strictly normalized FRE's, respectively, are equivalent, and they all coincide with the family of fuzzy regular languages.

Example 4.2 *The following FREs are equivalent:*

(1) $(b^*/1)(b/0.5) + ((a+b)^*a(a+b)^*/0.5)(b/1) + ((a+b)^*aa(a+b)^*/0.8)(b/1)$,

(2) $b^*b/0.5 + (a+b)^*a(a+b)^*b/0.5 + (a+b)^*aa(a+b)^*b/0.8$,

(3) $(a+\lambda)(b+ba)^*b/0.5 + (a+b)^*aa(a+b)^*b/0.8$,

The reader can verify that (2) and (3) are normalized and (3) is strictly normalized.

5 Marked regular fuzzy languages

In lexical analysis, it is a common practice to construct one automaton for accepting several or many different tokens (i.e., regular languages). In order to distinguish strings belonging to different tokens, final states are marked with token names. Often, there is a linear order of priorities associated with the token names. Strings belonging to two or more tokens are marked with the name that has the highest priority among them. This idea appears to be especially useful when it is applied to fuzzy languages. We formulate this with the following definitions.

Definition 5.1 *Let $\tilde{L}$ be a fuzzy language, T a finite set of names with a linear order $<$, and $\mu : \Sigma^* \to T$ a function. Then we call the set*

$$\{(w, f_{\tilde{L}}(w), \mu(w)) \mid w \in \Sigma^*\}$$

a marked fuzzy language, denoted $(\tilde{L}, \mu)$, and μ the marking function of the language.

Definition 5.2 *Let $(\tilde{L}, \mu)$ with $\mu : \Sigma^* \to T$ be a marked fuzzy language. Then $(\tilde{L}, \mu)$ is called a marked regular fuzzy language if the following two conditions hold:*

1) $\tilde{L}$ is a regular fuzzy language.

2) For each $t \in T$, $\mu^{-1}(t) = \{w \in \Sigma^* \mid \mu(w) = t\}$ is a regular language.

Note that if $f_{\tilde{L}}(w) = 0$ for some $w \in \Sigma^*$, then the value of $\mu(w)$ is unimportant.

Definition 5.3 *Let $(\tilde{L}_1, \mu_1)$ and $(\tilde{L}_2, \mu_2)$ be two marked fuzzy languages over an alphabet Σ. We say that $(\tilde{L}_1, \mu_1)$ and $(\tilde{L}_2, \mu_2)$ are equivalent, denoted $(\tilde{L}_1, \mu_1) = (\tilde{L}_2, \mu_2)$, if*
1) $\tilde{L}_1 = \tilde{L}_2$, and
2) $\mu_1(w) = \mu_2(w)$ for all $w \in \Sigma^*$ such that $f_{\tilde{L}_1}(w) = f_{\tilde{L}_2}(w) \neq 0$.
Similarly, we say that $(\tilde{L}_1, \mu_1)$ is included in $(\tilde{L}_2, \mu_2)$ if
1) $\tilde{L}_1 \subseteq \tilde{L}_2$, and
2) $\mu_1(w) = \mu_2(w)$ for all $w \in \Sigma^*$ such that $f_{\tilde{L}_1}(w) \neq 0$.

Marked union, i.e. union of marked fuzzy languages, is a useful tool in lexical analysis. For example, a string x belongs to token t_1 with 0.9 degree and also to token t_2 with 0.6 degree. Then in the marked union of the two tokens, x is considered to be marked with t_1. If the two degrees are equal, then x is marked with the token that has a higher priority. Formally, we give the following definition.

Definition 5.4 *(Marked union) Let $(\tilde{L}_1, \mu_1)$ and $(\tilde{L}_2, \mu_2)$ be two marked fuzzy languages where $\mu_1, \mu_2 : \Sigma^* \to T$. A marked fuzzy language $(\tilde{L}, \mu)$ is called the marked union of $(\tilde{L}_1, \mu_1)$ and $(\tilde{L}_2, \mu_2)$ if $\tilde{L} = \tilde{L}_1 \cup \tilde{L}_2$ and $\mu : \Sigma^* \to T$ is defined by*

$$\mu(w) = \begin{cases} \mu_1(w), & \text{if } f_{\tilde{L}_1}(w) > f_{\tilde{L}_2}(w) \textit{ or } f_{\tilde{L}_1}(w) = f_{\tilde{L}_2}(w) \text{ and } \mu_2(w) < \mu_1(w), \\ \mu_2(w), & \text{otherwise} \end{cases}$$

for each $w \in \Sigma^*$.

Example 5.1 *Let* $T = \{ID, INT\}$ *with* $INT < ID$, $\Sigma_l = \{a, \ldots, z\}$, $\Sigma_d = \{0, \ldots, 9\}$, *and* $\Sigma = \Sigma_l \cup \Sigma_d$. $\widetilde{L}_1$ *is defined, informally, by*

$$\Sigma_l\Sigma^*/1 + \Sigma_d\Sigma^*\Sigma_l\Sigma^*\Sigma_l\Sigma^*/0.9 + \Sigma_d\Sigma^*\Sigma_l\Sigma^*/0.5$$

and $\widetilde{L}_2$ *by*

$$\Sigma_d\Sigma_d^*/1 + \Sigma_d\Sigma_d^*\Sigma_l\Sigma_d^*/0.7.$$

Let $\mu_1, \mu_2 : \Sigma^* \to T$ *be defined by*

$$\mu_1(x) = ID \text{ and } \mu_2(x) = INT$$

for all $x \in \Sigma^*$. *Let* $(\widetilde{L}, \mu)$ *be the marked union of* $(\widetilde{L}_1, \mu_1)$ *and* $(\widetilde{L}_2, \mu_2)$. *Then* $\mu(32h01) = INT$ *and* $\mu(132n4p) = ID$.

6 A fuzzy lexical analyser

The lexical analyser LEX is available in almost all versions of UNIX. Here we propose a "fuzzy" extension of LEX, named FLEX, in the following.

FLEX is a fuzzy lexical analyser generator. All features of LEX work in FLEX except that the symbol "/" in the expressions should be written as "\/" now.

FLEX has the following two additional features:

(1) Any LEX expression can be followed by a "/" and a number between 0 and 1. For example,

$$[0-9a-zA-Z]+/0.75+[.\,;?!]/1.$$

The "$/n$" part, where n is a number between 0 and 1, is called the degree of the expression. Degrees cannot be nested, i.e., if an expression is specified with a degree, then none of its subexpressions is allowed to be specified with a degree. For example, $\{a/0.6\}bc/0.7$ is an invalid expression. Degrees cannot be specified within a pair of "[" and "]".

(2) Besides the three parts in a LEX program, a fourth part can be used to define actions for different ranges of degrees. For example,

$[0.8, 1]$: ACCEPT ;

$[0.6, 0.8)$: QUESTION ;

$[0, 0.6)$: REJECT ;

where ACCEPT, QUESTION, and REJECT are all key words for FLEX denoting, respectively, that

(a) the string is accepted as the token;

(b) an on-line question is given to the user; the string is accepted if the user answers "yes", rejected if the user answers "no";

(c) the string is rejected,

If the fourth part is not given, the following rules are assumed by default:

$[1, 1]$: ACCEPT;

$[0.9, 1)$: {WARNING; ACCEPT};

$[0.5, 0.9)$: QUESTION;

$[0, 0.5)$: REJECT;

Example 6.1 *An FLEX file for a student-mark handling program is the following:*

```
%%
%{
#include  "type.h"
#include  "yy.tab.h"
%}

%%
list+lis/0.9+(lst+ls)/0.8              { ...... }
enter+(ente+ent)/0.9+(nter+entr)/0.8  { ...... }
print+(prt+prnt)/0.9+rint/0.6          { ...... }
calc+(cal+comp)/0.9+(ca+com)/0.6       { ...... }
./0.0
%%

[0.9 , 1] :   ACCEPT;
[0.8 , 0.9) : {WARNING; ACCEPT};
[0.6 , 0.8) : QUESTION;
[0 , 0.6) :   REJECT;
```

References

[1] D. Dubois and H. Prade, *Fuzzy Sets and Systems: Theory and Applications*, Academic Press, 1980, San Diego.

[2] N. Honda, M. Nasu and S. Hirose, "F-Recognition of Fuzzy Languages", *Fuzzy Automata and Decision Processes, edited by M.M. Gupta, G.N. Saridis and B.R. Gaines*, North-Holland, 1977, 149-168.

[3] J. Hopcroft and J. Ullman, *Introduction to Automata Theory, Languages, and Computation,* Addison-Wesley, 1979.

[4] E.T. Lee and L.A. Zadeh, "Note on Fuzzy Languages ", *Information Sciences*, 1 (1969) 421-434.

[5] M. Mizumoto, J. Toyoda, and K. Tanaka, "Fuzzy Languages", *Systems, Computers, Controls* 1 (1970) 36-43.

[6] M. Mizumoto, J. Toyoda, and K. Tanaka, "Various Kinds of Automata with Weights", *Journal of Computer and System Sciences* 10 (1975) 219-236.

[7] M. Nasu and N. Honda, "Fuzzy events realized by finite probabilistic automata", *Information and Control* 12 (1968) 284-303.

[8] A. Salomaa, *Theory of Automata*, Pergamon Press, New York, 1969.

[9] E.S. Santos, "Maximin Automata", *Information and Control* 13 (1968) 363-377.

[10] E.S. Santos, "Realization of Fuzzy Languages by Probabilistic, Max-Product, and Maximin Automata", *Information Sciences* 8 (1975) 39-53.

[11] E.S. Santos, "Regular Fuzzy Expressions Fuzzy Automata", *Fuzzy Automata and Decision Processes, edited by M.M. Gupta, G.N. Saridis and B.R. Gaines*, North-Holland, 1977, 169-175.

Journal of Universal Computer Science, vol. 1, no. 5 (1995), 312-319
submitted: 18/4/95, accepted: 19/5/95, appeared: 28/5/95,

Software Patents And The Internet: Lessons From The Compuserve/Unisys Graphics Interchange Format Case Study.

Jenny Shearer
(HyperMedia Unit, University of Auckland, New Zealand
jshearer@cs.auckland.ac.nz)

Arnould Vermeer
(Practical ComputerScience 1, University of Hagen, Germany)

Abstract: The attempt by Unisys to obtain royalties from the Lempel Zev Welch Graphics Interchange Format specification through Compuserve has wide implications for the Internet. Increased activity in the US software patents area is likely to result in damage to progress of the software arts and the Internet, and to generate upscaled protest from Internet users. The LZW GIF case highlights the Internet culture in favour of free and unfettered development. Clarification of this important principle will have a major effect on the future of the Internet.

Key Words: Software patents, debate, Internet, Compuserve, Unisys, LZW GIF.

Categories: K.O, K.4.1, K.5.1, K.5.2, K.6.3

1 Introduction

A developing international problem with software patents has been illustrated by the recent Compuserve/Unisys GIF debate on the Internet. A conflict between legal collectors of royalties and makers/ users of software, has signs of escalating in the immediate future. The battle lines are already being drawn. While the United States legislature is preparing to pass laws ensuring patents licences last 20 years, in line with GATT resolutions, members of the Internet community are campaigning on the grounds that software patents are unnecessary, and will damage the Internet and progress in the software arts generally.

In the US, software patents are criticised, but there appears to be little political will to curb them. The well-publicised speech of US Vice-President Al Gore last year on the information superhighway stated a commitment to protection of intellectual property rights. To challenge large and powerful corporations on an issue involving considerable legal complexity is a risky political undertaking. However ACIS (American Committee For Interoperable Systems), which represents large IT companies, has suggested procedural reforms are necessary in the software patents area, and that these reforms should proceed whether or not a process of global harmonisation goes ahead.(1)

Critics of US software patent laws say inventors of software are already protected by copyright and trade secret law, and inappropriate patents are approved, eg "obvious" applications, which may already be well known by programmers or which may be reinvented over and over in the normal course of software development. They claim software developments, whether patented or not, build on prior art, and thus patents are inappropriate. Central to the debate, however, is the charge that large companies are viewing patents as an opportunity to profiteer at the expense of the international software development community.

The wider implications of this perceived threat are important. The proliferation of software patents in the United States may in short order create a heavy international impact, on small businesses and community organisations seeking software to develop their operation.The running of, say, hospitals and schools could be affected in countries inside and outside the US, because of the actions of US patents lawyers. Progress in developing new networks and extending functions of the Internet would also be affected by the cost of extended patents searches and payment of royalties. The international community, as well as factions of the industry in the United States, may move to express their dissatisfaction with protest through the Internet, the primary mode of communication for the computer industry. With little organised political process developed in the Internet, allegations of profiteering and unethical conduct may be freely aired, but the outcome is likely to be messy. Organised large-scale political protest is still some time away.

The Compuserve/Unisys GIF case has underlined a founding principle widely accepted in the Internet, that development should be unfettered and free. But apart from demonstrating an increased politicisation of Internet users, the case has stimulated a lengthy on-line discussion on the software patents issue.

The Compuserve case included a rebellion by customers and Internet users who, acting as individuals, denied royalties should be paid for use of the LZW patent. Compuserve was "flamed" on Internet newsgroups when the decision to pay was announced. Later, a significant objection by users was the perceived time lag of some years between the filing of the patent, and the demand by Unisys that the royalties be paid. In the interim, Compuserve had incorporated the LZW patent into its development programme. The widespread use of the patent appeared to provide a substantial profit opportunity for Unisys. Unisys has denied there was a motive towards large profits, and says it was defending its patent, once its use was discovered, on the principle of protecting the interests of shareholders who have invested in technology development.(2)

Compuserve responded to the criticism by announcing the development of a new GIF standard.

2 Case Study

Compuserve Communications is a company running a large commercial computer communications network in the US. In 1987, CompuServe designed the Graphics Interchange Format (GIF) specification for graphics files. The GIF specification incorporated the Lempel Zev Welch (LZW) compression technology. In early 1993, Unisys Corporation notified Compuserve of patents rights granted to LZW.The patent covers methods and apparatus for lossless compression and decompression of digital data. Unisys holds a U.S patent (number 4,558,302) as well as equivalent patents on the technology in Canada, France, Germany, U.K. and Italy. Equivalent patents are also pending in Japan. Compuserve reached a licensing agreement with Unisys in mid 1994, and on December 29, 1994, announced the GIF Developer Agreement. The agreement meant developers of software and shareware using the LZW technology, intended for use in conjunction with Compuserve, were liable to pay royalties of 1.5 percent.

The result of this attempt to enforce a software patent after the technology had been widely used for some years, caused an outcry from customers and sections of the Internet.

In defending its actions online, Compuserve said when it took up the LZW algorithm, the company had believed it to be in the public domain. In 1993, Unisys had informed Compuserve that it had a patent on the LZW algorithm "that it would enforce". (3) The company assured the community it would not profit from the licensing agreement, and suggested that developers might negotiate independently with Unisys, choose other specifications that did not incorporate LZW, or seek independent counsel on the merit of the Unisys patent claim.

Compuserve then announced it would offer its resources to "develop a follow-on specification to GIF that will offer significant enhancements and be free and open." (4) In an apparent major exercise in damage control, the company solicited input from GIF users such as commercial graphics vendors, the CompuServe Go Graphics Forum community, Internet communities including the World Wide Web, and bulletin board developers and users. In retrospect, Compuserve believes the row showed the effectiveness of computer-based communications in allowing customers' input, with a resulting improvement to services. Spokesperson Pierce Reid (5) said the company chose to ignore "misinformation" and negative comment after the GIF royalties decision was announced.

"Someone compared it to the attack on Pearl Harbour." (the Japanese surprise bombing of US warships, which effectively brought the US into World War II)

"In some ways, you need to have a thick skin, but there is the issue of the greater good, that there are people who can come together. The public brainstorming sessions are of value."

Reid says the row took the issue of a better GIF specification (GIF 24, using a png algorithm) "off the back burner". The outcome is an improved specification which will be copyrighted. However the company plans to have it administered by a third party in order to guarantee it is freely available to the public.

Reid says it is logical to look towards online services such as the Internet undergoing a process of increasing regulation. Whether this would be acceptable would be dependent on whether freedom of discussion was maintained.

"On the other hand, it would make people responsible for such actions as saying "fire" in a crowded theatre."

3 Discussion

The GIF case is an indicator of how software patents are destined to be a growth industry in the United States. For US lawyers and patents examiners, it is simply a matter of extending the realm of existing law into an area which for 20 or so years has seen little patents filing activity. Software engineer Gregory Aharonian warned in the January 1993 issue of "Communications of the ACM (Association for Computing Machinery)" that large numbers of software patents were being wrongly awarded by the US Patents and Trademark Office, and that he foresaw the number of software patents would grow even faster, "despite public comments and any current congressional activities." (6)

Aharonian, who runs an Internet Patent News Service, has calculated the 1995 software patents total will be around 5,400, on the basis of an average of 103 patents awarded a week in the first 16 weeks of 1995. The 1994 total was 4,500 software patents. (7)

3.1 What Is Patentable?

Criticism of the system, of which inconsistency is a major feature, may be made from examination of some of the existing patents. IBM, for example, placed UNIX in the public domain when royalties seemed too difficult to collect (8) However IBM has been active in placing other patents, some of which appear obvious.

Patent number 4,622, 641, filed in 1983, assignee IBM, is described (9) as a "user friendly procedure for the generation and display of geometric figures on a graphics screen (which) uses a cursor placement device such as a joystick to both define the initial position and size of the geometrical figure. Two specific examples are described: the generation of a circle and the generations of a square or rectangle. In the first example, the cursor is first positioned to point to the centre of the circle at which point a small circle is drawn. The circle is expanded in response to the pressing of a designated key by the user until the desired size is attained. In the second example, the pointing by the cursor is to the upper left corner of the square or rectangle., and the square or rectangle is then expanded in response to the user deflecting the joy stick down and to the right."

Patent number 4,648.062, filed in 1985, assignee IBM, is described as a method for providing an on-line help facility for interactive information handling systems. Comment (10) from the MIT files on the patent:

"A pop-up window decribes valid choices for user unput."

Patent number 4, 687, 353, filed in 1986, assignee IBM, is described (11) as follows:
"The patent appears to be on printing a document with different indentation than it is stored with; a suggested implementation is tabbing from from the left margin before beginning to print each line."

3.2 Reactions of the Internet Community

A commentator on a Usenet newsgroup has criticised obvious or "nonsense" patents applications.

"These patents are a weapon (used) by large companies against small ones, a weapon that will grow in time if software patents become widely accepted." (12)

Another Usenet newsgroup commentator claims small companies do not benefit from patents laws:

"We don't need patents to protect Littleguy, Inc. from big companies, such as Microsoft. If it makes more sense for Microsoft to purchase Littleguy's technology than develop it themselves, they'll do so whether it is patented or not. My experience as an in-house lawyer at Computer Associates (CA) which is the second largest software company in the world and an aggressive acquirer of companies, supports this view. CA does not believe in patents. They don't use them to protect their products and don't put much value in them in evaluating potential acquisition candidates. Of the 50 plus acquisitions I completed for CA, none of them had any patented technology to speak of. CA is also living proof that software companies don't need patents to make tons of money ('94 revenues were well over $2 billion).(13)

Software developers are expressing concern about software patents and copyright issues, in ongoing discussions of specialist Usenet newsgroups such as gnu.misc.discuss and comp.software eng. And in 1993, a number of prominent members of the ACM spoke out against a new ACM Code of Ethics which they thought may be read as being incompatible with political activity against patents or extended copyrights.(14)
Clause 1.5 of the Code included an undertaking to "honour property rights including copyrights and patents."
In their statement printed in "Communications of the ACM" the writers commented:
"Surveys suggest that most members disapprove of having patents in software at all; yet the moral imperative calls on members to honour what they may regard as a disaster for their field."
In response, Chair of the ACM Code of Ethics revising committee, Ronald Anderson, defended the code, but encouraged debate on the issues.
"Certainly, most ACM members would like improvement in the socio-technical-legal system to protect intellectual products while promoting exchange of ideas and professional progress. Such improvements require "political advocacy" and legislation." (15)

A spokesperson for Adobe Systems Incorporated, a major company involved in electronic publishing, commented to a public hearing held by the US Commerce Department last year that the constitutional mandate to promote progress in the useful arts is not served by the issuance of patents on software. (16)

"Revenues are being sunk into legal costs instead of into research and development..."

"The case Information International, Inc.v. Adobe, et. al. was filed five years ago. Last year, the trial court ordered for Adobe, finding no infringement. In December, the Appeals Court for the Federal Circuit unanimously affirmed that judgement. Yet, in that time, it has cost Adobe over $4.5 million in legal fees and expenses. I (Douglas Brotz, a scientist) have spent over 3,000 hours of my time and at least another thousand hours was spent by others at Adobe. Our Chairman of the Board spent a month at the trial. This type of company behaviour would not be high on anyone's list of ways to promote progress." (17)

A recent decision by the US Court of Appeals shows how litigation over software issues is now threatening to muddy the waters of copyright law. Lotus Development Corporation has been unsuccessful in its effort to sue Borland International Inc. for creating a Quattro programme which included use of a virtually identical copy of the Lotus 1-2-3 menu tree. (18) Borland did not copy any of Lotus's underlying computer code; it copied only the words and structure of Lotus's menu command hierarchy.The Court of Appeals in March overturned a decision in favour of Lotus made by the District Court. The Court of Appeals found the menu commands are an uncopyrightable "method of operation."

In a"Concurrence" (19) on the Judgement, Circuit Judge Boudin (one of the presiding judges) said:

"Requests for the protection of computer menus present the concern with fencing off access to the commons in an acute form. A new menu may be a creative work, but over time its importance may come to reside more in the investment that has been made by users in learning the menu and in building their own mini-programs-macros- in reliance apon the menu. Better typewriter keyboard layouts may exist, but the familiar QUERTY keyboard dominates the markets because that is what everybody has learned to use...

"Thus, to assume that computer programs are just one more new means of expression, like a filmed play, may be quite wrong... Applying copyright law to computer programs is like assembling a jigsaw puzzle whose pieces do not quite fit."

The problems presented by such cases are numerous. For companies which will bring copyright actions on such grounds as a command menu using terms like "copy" and "print," the field is wide open. With no clear direction from the US Congress on the limits of patent and copyright law as related to software patents, future lawsuits may be expected to be numerous, and the mid-range outcome, at least, alarming to those occupying the "commons" of the Internet.

Building up case law in this area is an unsatisfactory response to the difficulties of US middle-ranked software companies, and will have major international repercussions. The difficulties facing companies in the US is highlighted by the European environment, in which software patents have not been allowed. However, with the acceptance of the GATT package (20) by European countries, litigation and unproductive stalking of software developers over patents and copyright appear inevitable. The largest US companies are protecting themselves with cross-licensing deals, as predicted by the League For Programming Freedom. (LPF) (21) It is unlikely the issue would be taken up substantively by the Internet Society, which concerns itself with governance, rather than political issues. Pressure groups such as the Electronic Frontier Foundation (EFF) are vocal on the issue of freedom of the Internet, but have not settled on a basis for inclusive Internet-wide political process.

The LPF, an organisation opposed to the existence of software patents, has undertaken a campaign to inform the Internet community on the issue, and provides information to assist companies in formulating public policies against patents.

"The clearest way out of the current situation involves companies opposed to software patents formulating and adopting public policies that oppose their continued issuance."(22)

The Compuserve/Unisys GIF case shows that though the Internet has no official political centre, people using it have a certain cultural outlook which enables them to take political action by the accumulated effect of individual (and voluable) protest. This effect of public opinion in the Internet is not moderated by the usual protocols of media representations, protests to government representatives, and so on, operating within the framework of defamation law and standard public procedure.

Rather, the Internet environment is inhabited by a community with a particular loyalty to the Internet environment, who are committed to the principle of freedom and open use of technology relating to the Internet.

Companies (such as Compuserve) attempting to work in this volatile environment must on the one hand, obey the law, while also pleasing the customers, who may have a different, but not stated, agenda. The problems faced by Compuserve were to behave as a company obedient to the law, and to pass on costs incurred by software royalties, while also fielding an angry backlash from customers who said they were not prepared to pay. This backlash included comments which may have proved damaging to the company's standing in the Internet community, with the possibility of accompanying financial repercussions.While in this case Compuserve was able to drop the patented GIF format in response to client dissatisfaction, in other cases the dilemma might prove financially injurious to a company caught in a similar patents dispute.

It may be time for the Internet "community", (the cultural entity discussed in widely read books such as "The Virtual Community" by Howard Rheingold), (23) to reassess itself in terms of its behaviour as a political sector. Though its philosophy works against development of an organised political system, it may be perceived that "kneejerk" mass responses by users to circumstances they see as unfair, may perpetrate further injustice.

On the other hand, to have political activity which is not formalised may be an advantage. The Compuserve/Unisys GIF case shows that the threat of customer boycott drew an immediate response from Compuserve. Given the unique decentralised nature of the Internet, and the intelligent strata of people using it, it might be possible to threaten to conduct, or to actually conduct, boycotts against companies inflicting patents actions seen as damaging by the Internet community. If these events occurred with minimal orchestration, the lawyers could find themselves in the unusual position of having no-one to sue. Given that it is possible to present the community with correct information and full discussion, eg through newsgroups and sites of political pressure groups, political action could be dictated by individual response to violations of principles held by the majority, rather than by traditional policy creation methods.

4 Conclusion

The dispute shows a number of matters remain unresolved. That is, the baseline question of patents royalties and a software using population unwilling to pay them. Unisys, under the GIF LZW license terms, does not require license fees for non-commercial or not-for-profit applications. Presumably, in the future, Unisys or any other company could choose not to make such community-minded decisions. The decision by Unisys to charge royalties indicates that a claim is being staked on the territory. It is unlikely, given the motivation of commercial corporations to make profits, that such claims will be voluntarily withdrawn.

A set of stated ethical principles may work some way towards moderating debates such as the Unisys/Compuserve GIF row. It might also provide a framework for political activity protective of the Internet. For example, if it is accepted that Internet users wish to encourage the best technology towards development of the Internet and global information systems generally, then the argument by large corporations that they have a right to make profits from software patents, (which may incidentally damage development), is seen as a claim with less merit.

Presumably, it would then be the aim of Internet users to facilitate a global harmonisation scheme which would protect intellectual property rights, but not past the point where such rights hinder development of the software arts.

Internet users, who have shown they are not taking their freedom for granted, may need to look towards developing active political pathways to establish and defend their point of view on political issues of major importance, such as the software patents issues. The traditional political process, taking place on a national basis or through international forums, may not serve the interests of Internet users, or the best interests of the progress of information technology.

5 References

1. [Byrne, C 1994] ACIS (American Committee for Interoperable Systems)
submission to a public hearing by the Patent and Trademark Office, US Department of Commerce.
<http://www.uspto.gov/text/pto/hearings/remarks/text>
(February 1995)

2. [Unisys Corporation 1995] LZW Patent Frequently Asked Questions.
<http:// www.unisys.com/Lead Story/lzw terms.html>
(February 1995)

3. [Oren,T 1995] "Key Points on Unisys/Compuserve Licensing Agreement."
On-line announcement from Compuserve Communications,
(Compuserve communications,January 1995)

4. [Oren, T 1995] On-line announcement on GIF issue from Compuserve Communications. (Compuserve Communications, January, 1995)

5. [Reid, P 1995] Compuserve Communications spokesperson, personal communication. (March 3,1995).

6. [Aharonian, G 1993] Forum. Setting the Record Straight on Patents.
Communications of the ACM. January 1993, Volume 36, Number 1. pp.17-18.
(ACM 1515 Broadway, New York)

7. [Aharonian, G. 1995] Software Patenting Chaos Continues.
(Internet Patent News Service. patents@world.std.com)

8. [McIlroy,D.1995] Partial List of Software Patents. Comment.
(ftp mintaka.lcs.mit.edu:/mitlpf/ai/patent-list.)

9. [1995] Partial List of Software Patents.
(ftp.mintaka.lcs.mit.edu:/mitlpf/ai/patent-list.)

10. [1995] Partial List of Software Patents.
(ftp.mintaka.lcs.mit.edu:/mitlpf/ai/patent-list.)

11. [1995] Partial List of Software Patents.
(ftp. mintaka lcs.mit.edu:/mitlpf/ai/patent-list)

12. [Eggert, P 1995] "Why Software Patents Cannot Work".
(Usenet newsgroup misc.int.property, February 1995)

13. [Gracin, H 1995] "Software Patents". (Usenet newsgroup misc.int. property, February 1995)

14. [Steele, Jr. GL. Hillis, D. Stallman, R. Sussman GJ. Minsky, M. McCarthy, J. Backus, J. Corbato, FJ. 1993]
Forum . Code of Ethics Reconsidered.
Communications of the ACM. July 1993 Volume 36, Number 7, pg 17.
(ACM 1515 Broadway, New York)

15. [Anderson, RE 1993] Forum. Response to Code of Ethics Reconsidered.
Communications of the ACM July 1993 Volume 36, Number 7 pg 17.
(ACM 1515 Broadway, New York)

16. [Brotz, D 1994] Submission on behalf of Adobe Systems Incorporated, to a public hearing by the Patent and Trademark Office, US Department of Commerce.
(http://www.uspto.gov/text/pto/hearings/remarks/text)
(January, 1994.)

17. [Brotz, D 1994] Submission on behalf of Adobe Systems Incorporated, to a public hearing by the Patent and Trademark Office, US Department of Commerce.
(http://www.uspto.gov/text/pto/hearings/remarks/text)
(January, 1994)

18. [Lotus Dev. Corp. v.Borland Intl., Inc. 1995] Lotus Development Corporation, Plaintiff, Appellee, v. Borland International, Inc., Defendant, Appellant. No. 93-2214.
(United States Court of Appeals for the First Circuit US App. LEXIS 4618 March 9, 1995, Decided)

19. [Cicuit Judge Boudin, 1995] Lotus Development Corporation , Plaintiff, Appellee, v. Borland International, Inc.,
Defendant, Appellant. No. 932214.
(United States Court of Appeals for the First Circuit US App. LEXIS 4618 March 9, 1995, Decided)

20. [General Agreement on Tariffs and Trade 1991] Agreement on Trade-Related Aspects on Intellectual Property
Rights , Including Trade in Counterfeit Goods (Annex III) Section 5: Patents.

21. [The League for Programming Freedom 1991] Against Software Patents.
(http://www.lpf.org/)

22. [The League for Programming Freedom 1994] Multimedia and Software Patents.
(http://www.lpf.org/)

23. [Rheingold, H 1994] The Virtual Community. Finding Connection in a Computerised World.
Secker & Warburg, London.

Acknowledgements

I would like to thank Barry Fenn, Auckland University HyperMedia Unit, for his helpful discussions.

Journal of Universal Computer Science, vol. 1, no. 5 (1995), 320-337
submitted: 8/10/95, accepted: 10/5/95, appeared: 28/5/95

GAC — the Criterion for Global Avalanche Characteristics of Cryptographic Functions

Xian-Mo Zhang
(The University of Wollongong, Wollongong, NSW 2522, Australia
xianmo@cs.uow.edu.au)

Yuliang Zheng
(Monash University, Melbourne, VIC 3199, Australia
yzheng@fcit.monash.edu.au)

Abstract: We show that some widely accepted criteria for cryptographic functions, including the strict avalanche criterion (SAC) and the propagation criterion, have various limitations in capturing properties of vital importance to cryptographic algorithms, and propose a new criterion called GAC to measure the global avalanche characteristics of cryptographic functions. We also introduce two indicators related to the new criterion, one forecasts the *sum-of-squares* while the other the *absolute* avalanche characteristics of a function. Lower and upper bounds on the two indicators are derived, and two methods are presented to construct cryptographic functions that achieve nearly optimal global avalanche characteristics.
Category: E.3

1 Why the GAC

In 1985, Webster and Tavares introduced the concept of the *strict avalanche criterion (SAC)* when searching for principles for designing DES-like data encryption algorithms [Web85, WT86]. A function is said to satisfy the SAC if complementing a single bit results in the output of the function being complemented with a probability of a half. More formally, let V_n denote the vector space of n tuples of elements from GF(2), a function f on V_n, a mapping from V_n into GF(2), is said to satisfy the SAC if for any n-bit vector α with $W(\alpha) = 1$, where $W(\cdot)$ denotes the Hamming weight, $f(x) \oplus f(x \oplus \alpha)$ assumes the values zero and one an equal number of times, namely $f(x) \oplus f(x \oplus \alpha)$ is a *balanced* function on V_n, where $\oplus$ denotes the addition in GF(2).

The SAC was generalized in one direction by Forré in [For89]. Forré defines that a function f satisfies the SAC of order k if a partial function obtained by keeping any k input bits to f constant still satisfies the SAC. Enumerating functions satisfying the higher order SAC is an interesting combinatorial problem and various results on this topic have been obtained over the past years (see for instance [Llo90, Llo92, Mit90]). In another direction, the SAC has been generalized by Adams and Tavares [AT90] and independently by Preneel et al [PLL+91] to what is now called the *propagation criterion.* A function f on V_n is said to satisfy the propagation criterion with respect to a vector $\alpha \in V_n$ if $f(x) \oplus f(x \oplus \alpha)$ is balanced, and to satisfy the propagation criterion of degree k if it satisfies the propagation criterion with respect to all nonzero vectors whose Hamming weight is at most k. In informal terms, f satisfies the propagation criterion of degree k if complementing k or less bits results in the output of f being complemented with a probability of a half. We note that functions satisfying the propagation criterion of degree n coincide with *bent functions*, an important combinatorial structure discovered by Rothaus [Rot76]. A combination of the two generalizations has also been studied in [PLL+91, PGV91].

The SAC and its various generalizations are very important concepts in designing cryptographic functions employed by data encryption algorithms and one-way hashing functions. As is shown below, however, these concepts all have their limitations in capturing some of the vital characteristics required by a cryptographically strong function. The following concept of *linear structure* will be useful in our discussions. Given a function f on V_n and a vector $\alpha \in V_n$, the vector is said to be a linear structure of f if $f(x) \oplus f(x \oplus \alpha)$ is a constant. An affine function $f(x) = a_1x_1 \oplus \cdots \oplus a_nx_n \oplus c$, where $a_j, c \in GF(2)$, $j = 1, 2, \ldots, n$, has all the vectors in V_n as its linear structures. Hence having linear structures is generally regarded as an unwelcome property in cryptographic practice.

First we can see that the SAC is an indicator with a very strong local flavor, as it guarantees good avalanche characteristics with respect only to the vectors of Hamming weight one. A function that satisfies the SAC can have a large number of vectors of Hamming weight larger than one as its linear structures. Such functions, if employed in certain cryptographic algorithms or systems, can result in a potential security risk.

Next we consider generalizations of the SAC. The higher order SAC suggested by Forré in [For89] has not been widely accepted by the research community as a criterion of cryptographic significance, although the concept itself seems interesting from a combinatorial point of view. In contrast, the other generalization of the SAC, namely the propagation criterion, has well established its position in cryptographic design. This can be seen from work represented by [AT90, PLL+91, PGV91, DT93, SZZ94b, SZZ95]. A function satisfying the propagation criterion of degree k shows the perfect avalanche characteristic with respect to vectors of Hamming weight not larger than k. This property, however, does not rule out the possibility that the function can have vectors of Hamming weight larger than k as its linear structures. For instance, all currently known methods for constructing functions satisfying higher degree propagation criteria, including those presented in [PGV91, DT93, SZZ94b, SZZ95], yield functions having undesirable linear structures. Therefore the propagation criterion, though being an extension of the SAC, is merely another indicator for local properties. On the other hand, the criterion is too strict in the sense that it requires that $f(x) \oplus f(x \oplus \alpha)$ be 100% balanced. This leads to the situation where a function satisfying the propagation criterion of the largest possible degree becomes bent. Although bent functions have nice properties, they are not balanced and hence can hardly be directly employed in practice.

In designing a cryptographic algorithm, we often need functions that satisfy a number of crucial cryptographic requirements such as balance, high nonlinearity, high algebraic degree and good avalanche characteristics. A function can be considered to have good avalanche characteristics if it does not have a nonzero linear structure and satisfies the propagation criterion with respect to the majority of the vectors.

These discussions show a necessity to search for a new criterion for cryptographic functions. The new criterion should overcome the shortcomings of the SAC or its generalizations, and be able to forecast the overall avalanche characteristic of a cryptographic function. The main aim of this paper is to put forward two closely related indicators that forecast the GAC or *global avalanche characteristic* of a cryptographic function. We also present methods for constructing functions that have promising overall avalanche characteristics.

The rest of the paper is organized as follows: The two new indicators, one is called the *sum-of-squares* indicator and the other the *absolute* indicator, are introduced in Section 2, and the lower and upper bounds on the two indicators are discussed in Sections 3 and 4 respectively. Finally, Section 5 presents two methods, one for even and the other for odd dimensional spaces, for constructing cryptographic functions that have excellent nonlinear characteristics, including GACs, nonlinearity and balance.

2 Introducing the GAC

A *function* on V_n is a mapping from V_n into GF(2). The *truth table* of f is a (0,1)-sequence defined by $(f(\alpha_0), f(\alpha_1), \ldots, f(\alpha_{2^n-1}))$, where $\alpha_0 = (0,\ldots,0,0)$, $\alpha_1 = (0,\ldots,0,1)$, ..., $\alpha_{2^{n-1}-1} = (1,\ldots,1,1)$. The *sequence* of f is a $(1,-1)$-sequence defined by $((-1)^{f(\alpha_0)}, (-1)^{f(\alpha_1)}, \ldots, (-1)^{f(\alpha_{2^n-1})})$, where each exponent is regarded as being real-valued.

f is said to show the perfect avalanche effect with respect to a vector $\alpha \in V_n$ if it satisfies the propagation criterion with respect to the vector, namely, $f(x) \oplus f(x \oplus \alpha)$ is balanced. We note that $f(x) \oplus f(x \oplus \alpha)$ is also called the directional derivative of f in the direction α. To broaden our observation, we say that f shows good avalanche effect with respect to α if $f(x) \oplus f(x \oplus \alpha)$ is almost balanced. By imposing certain conditions on α, we have the notion of the SAC as well as that of the propagation criterion. As shown in the previous section, this approach introduces various limitations in capturing the GAC or global avalanche characteristic of a cryptographic function. To get around the problem, we will not impose restrictions on α. Instead, we will let it be a free vector, which allows us to examine the overall avalanche characteristic of a function. The following are a few notations used in further discussions.

Let $\tilde{a} = (a_1, \cdots, a_m)$ and $\tilde{b} = (b_1, \cdots, b_m)$ be two vectors (or sequences), the *scalar product* of $\tilde{a}$ and $\tilde{b}$, denoted by $\langle \tilde{a}, \tilde{b} \rangle$, is defined as the sum of the component-wise multiplications. In particular, when $\tilde{a}$ and $\tilde{b}$ are from V_m, $\langle \tilde{a}, \tilde{b} \rangle = a_1 b_1 \oplus \cdots \oplus a_m b_m$, where the addition and multiplication are over $GF(2)$, and when $\tilde{a}$ and $\tilde{b}$ are $(1,-1)$-sequences, $\langle \tilde{a}, \tilde{b} \rangle = \sum_{i=1}^{m} a_i b_i$, where the addition and multiplication are over the reals.

Given a function f on V_n and a vector $\alpha \in V_n$, we denote by $\xi(\alpha)$ the sequence of $f(x \oplus \alpha)$. Note that $\xi(0)$ is identical to the sequence of f. In addition, $\xi(0) * \xi(\alpha)$, the component-wise multiplication of the two sequences, is the sequence of $f(x) \oplus f(x \oplus \alpha)$. Set $\Delta_f(\alpha) = \langle \xi(0), \xi(\alpha) \rangle$. $\Delta_f(\alpha)$ is called the *auto-correlation* of f with a shift α. To further simplify our discussions, $\Delta_f(\alpha)$ will be written as $\Delta(\alpha)$ if the function under consideration is clear. Obviously, $\Delta(\alpha) = 0$ if and only if $f(x) \oplus f(x \oplus \alpha)$ is balanced, and $|\Delta(\alpha)| = 2^n$ if and only if $f(x) \oplus f(x \oplus \alpha)$ is a constant, namely, α is a linear structure of f. More generally, we have

Lemma 1. *Let f be a function on V_n. Then the Hamming weight of the truth table of $f(x) \oplus f(x \oplus \alpha)$ is equal to $2^{n-1} - \frac{1}{2}\Delta(\alpha)$.*

Let e_+ and e_- denote the number of ones and minus ones in $\xi(0) * \xi(\alpha)$ respectively. Thus $e_+ - e_- = \Delta(\alpha)$, $(2^n - e_-) - e_- = \Delta(\alpha)$ and hence $e_- = 2^{n-1} - \frac{1}{2}\Delta(\alpha)$. As e_- is also the number of ones in the truth table of $f(x) \oplus f(x \oplus \alpha)$, the lemma holds.

The overall avalanche characteristic of a function f can be measured by examining $|\Delta(\alpha)|$ for all nonzero vectors α. We can say that a function has a good GAC or global avalanche characteristic if for most nonzero α, $|\Delta(\alpha)|$ is zero or very close to zero. Again only bent functions that are unbalanced satisfy the criterion perfectly ! In designing cryptographic algorithms, however, we are mainly interested in balanced functions.

Although simple, the concept of GAC introduces a number of problems to be resolved. These include

1. How to measure precisely the GAC of a function.
2. How to compare the GACs of two different functions.
3. What is the best GAC of a *balanced* function and how to construct balanced functions that achieve the best GAC.

To solve the various problems, we propose the following two indicators:

Definition 2. Let f be a function on V_n. Then the *sum-of-squares* indicator for the avalanche characteristic of f is defined by

$$\sigma_f = \sum_{\alpha \in V_n} \Delta^2(\alpha)$$

and the *absolute* indicator for the characteristic is defined by

$$\Delta_f = \max_{\alpha \in V_n, \alpha \neq 0} |\Delta(\alpha)|.$$

The smaller σ_f and Δ_f, the better the GAC of a function. Like many other nonlinearity characteristics of a function including nonlinearity, algebraic degree and the profile of difference distribution tables, the two indicators for the GAC are invariant under nonsingular linear transforms on the input coordinates.

3 The Sum-of-Squares Indicator σ_f

A $(1, -1)$-matrix H of order m is called a *Hadamard* matrix if $HH^t = mI_m$, where H^t is the transpose of H and I_m is the identity matrix of order m. A Sylvester-Hadamard matrix of order 2^n, denoted by H_n, is defined by the following recursive relation

$$H_0 = 1, \; H_n = \begin{bmatrix} H_{n-1} & H_{n-1} \\ H_{n-1} & -H_{n-1} \end{bmatrix}, \; n = 1, 2, \ldots.$$

Let ℓ_i be the ith row of H_n. By Lemma 2 of [SZZ94b], ℓ_i is the sequence of a linear function defined by $\varphi_i(x) = \langle \alpha_i, x \rangle = a_1x_1 \oplus a_2x_2 \oplus \cdots \oplus a_nx_n$, where $x = (x_1, x_2, \ldots, x_n)$ and $\alpha_i = (a_1, a_2, \ldots, a_n)$ is the ith vector in V_n in the ascending alphabetical order.

Definition 3. Let f be a function on V_n. The Walsh-Hadamard transform of f is defined as

$$\hat{f}(\alpha) = 2^{-\frac{n}{2}} \sum_{x \in V_n} (-1)^{f(x) \oplus \langle \alpha, x \rangle}$$

where $\alpha = (a_1, \ldots, a_n) \in V_n$, $x = (x_1, \ldots, x_n)$ and $\langle \alpha, x \rangle = \bigoplus_{i=1}^{n} a_i x_i$, and $f(x) \oplus \langle \alpha, x \rangle$ is regarded as a real-valued function.

The Walsh-Hadamard transform has numerous applications in areas ranging from physical science to communications engineering. It appears in several slightly different forms [Rot76, MS77, Dil72]. The above definition follows the first formula in [Rot76]. It can be equivalently written as

$$(\hat{f}(\alpha_0), \hat{f}(\alpha_1), \ldots, \hat{f}(\alpha_{2^n-1})) = 2^{-\frac{n}{2}} \xi H_n$$

where α_i is the ith vector in V_n according to the ascending order, ξ is the sequence of f and H_n is the Sylvester-Hadamard matrix of order 2^n. More information regarding the transform can be found in [MS77, Dil72]. In addition, Beauchamp's book [Bea84] is a good source of information on other related orthogonal transforms with their applications.

We now introduce the concept of bent functions.

Definition 4. A function f on V_n is called a *bent* function if its Walsh-Hadamard transform satisfies

$$\hat{f}(\alpha) = \pm 1$$

for all $\alpha \in V_n$.

From [Dil72, AT90, SMZ93, YH89] we know that the following four statements are equivalent

(i) f is bent.
(ii) $\langle \xi, \ell \rangle = \pm 2^{\frac{1}{2}n}$ for any affine sequence ℓ of length 2^n, where ξ is the sequence of f.
(iii) $f(x) \oplus f(x \oplus \alpha)$ is balanced for any non-zero vector $\alpha \in V_n$, where $x = (x_1, x_2, \ldots, x_n)$.
(iv) $M = ((-1)^{f(\alpha_i \oplus \alpha_j)})$, $0 \leq i, j \leq 2^n - 1$, which is called the matrix of f is a Hadamard matrix.

3.1 Bounds on σ_f

McFarland, when studying Walsh-Hadamard transform of functions, obtained the following result (see also Theorem 3.3 of [Dil72]):

$$M = 2^{-n} H_n \operatorname{diag}(\langle \xi, \ell_0 \rangle, \cdots, \langle \xi, \ell_{2^n-1} \rangle) H_n,$$

where f is a function on V_n, ξ is the sequence of f, $M = ((-1)^{f(\alpha_i \oplus \alpha_j)})$, $0 \leq i, j \leq 2^n - 1$, and ℓ_i is the ith row of H_n. Thus

$$MM^T = 2^{-n} H_n \operatorname{diag}(\langle \xi, \ell_0 \rangle^2, \cdots, \langle \xi, \ell_{2^n-1} \rangle^2) H_n.$$

The first row of MM^T is

$$(\Delta(\alpha_0), \Delta(\alpha_1), \cdots, \Delta(\alpha_{2^n-1}))$$

while the first row of $2^{-n} H_n \operatorname{diag}(\langle\xi, \ell_0\rangle^2, \cdots, \langle\xi, \ell_{2^n-1}\rangle^2) H_n$ can be expressed as

$$2^{-n}(\langle\xi^*, \ell_0\rangle, \cdots, \langle\xi^*, \ell_{2^n-1}\rangle) = 2^{-n}\xi^* H_n$$

where

$$\xi^* = (\langle\xi, \ell_0\rangle^2, \cdots, \langle\xi, \ell_{2^n-1}\rangle^2).$$

Hence

$$(\Delta(\alpha_0), \Delta(\alpha_1), \cdots, \Delta(\alpha_{2^n-1})) = 2^{-n}(\langle\xi, \ell_0\rangle^2, \cdots, \langle\xi, \ell_{2^n-1}\rangle^2) H_n.$$

Thus we have proved:

Theorem 5. *Let ξ be the sequence of a function f on V_n. Then*

$$(\Delta(\alpha_0), \Delta(\alpha_1), \cdots, \Delta(\alpha_{2^n-1})) H_n = (\langle\xi, \ell_0\rangle^2, \cdots, \langle\xi, \ell_{2^n-1}\rangle^2).$$

This theorem is in fact a special form of a more general result, the Wiener-Khintchine Theorem [Bea84]. Now write $\eta = (\Delta(\alpha_0), \Delta(\alpha_1), \cdots, \Delta(\alpha_{2^n-1}))$. Since

$$\langle\xi^*, \xi^*\rangle = \langle\eta H_n, \eta H_n\rangle = \eta H_n H_n^T \eta^T = 2^n \langle\eta, \eta\rangle,$$

we have

$$\sum_{j=0}^{2^n-1} \langle\xi, \ell_j\rangle^4 = 2^n \sum_{\alpha \in V_n} \Delta^2(\alpha).$$

Thus the following result holds:

$$\sigma_f = \sum_{\alpha \in V_n} \Delta^2(\alpha) = 2^{-n} \sum_{j=0}^{2^n-1} \langle\xi, \ell_j\rangle^4. \tag{1}$$

A closely related equation is

$$\sum_{j=0}^{2^n-1} \langle\xi, \ell_j\rangle^2 = 2^{2n} \tag{2}$$

(See also p.416, [MS77]). Both (1) and (2) are special forms of a general equation attributed to Parseval [Bea84].

The *nonlinearity* of a function f on V_n, commonly denoted by N_f, is defined as the minimum Hamming distance between f and all the affine functions on V_n. On the other hand, the distance between two functions g_1 and g_2 on V_n, namely the number of disagreeing positions in the truth tables or sequences of the two functions, can be calculated by

$$d(g_1, g_2) = 2^{n-1} - \frac{1}{2}\langle\eta_1, \eta_2\rangle$$

where η_i, $i = 1, 2$, are the sequences of g_1 and g_2 (see for instance Lemma 4 of [SZZ94b]). Hence for any f on V_n, we have

$$N_f = 2^{n-1} - \frac{1}{2}\max\{|\langle\xi, \ell_i\rangle|, 0 \le i \le 2^n - 1\}$$

where ξ is the sequence of f and $\ell_0, \ldots, \ell_{2^n-1}$ are the rows of H_n, namely, the sequences of the linear functions on V_n. Now considering Theorem 5, Lemma 1 and in particular, the equation (1), we can see that the nonlinearity of a function is closely related to the sum-of-squares avalanche characteristic of the function. In general, the larger the nonlinearity, the smaller (i.e., better) the sum-of-squares avalanche characteristic.

Theorem 6. *Let f be a function on V_n. Then*

(i) $2^{2n} \le \sigma_f \le 2^{3n}$,
(ii) $\sigma_f = 2^{2n}$ if and only if f is a bent function,
(iii) $\sigma_f = 2^{3n}$ if and only if f is an affine function.

Proof. (i) Note that $\Delta(0) = 2^n$. Hence

$$\sigma_f = \sum_{\alpha \in V_n} \Delta^2(\alpha) \ge \Delta^2(0) = 2^{2n}. \tag{3}$$

On the other hand, by Parseval's equation (2), we have

$$\sum_{j=0}^{2^n-1} \langle\xi, \ell_j\rangle^2 = 2^{2n}.$$

Thus

$$\sigma_f = 2^{-n}\sum_{j=0}^{2^n-1} \langle\xi, \ell_j\rangle^4 \le 2^{-n}(\sum_{j=0}^{2^n-1} \langle\xi, \ell_j\rangle^2)^2 = 2^{-n}2^{4n} = 2^{3n}.$$

(ii) $\sigma_f = 2^{2n}$ if and only if $\Delta(\alpha) = 0$ for all $\alpha \ne 0$, namely, f is bent.

(iii) Set $b_j = \langle\xi, \ell_j\rangle^2$. Again by Parseval's equation (2), $\sum_{j=0}^{2^n-1} b_j = 2^n$. Now we have the following reasoning:
$\sigma_f = 2^{3n}$ if and only if
$2^{-n}\sum_{j=0}^{2^n-1} b_j^2 = 2^{3n}$ if and only if
$\sum_{j=0}^{2^n-1} b_j^2 = 2^{4n}$ if and only if
$\sum_{j=0}^{2^n-1} b_j^2 = (\sum_{j=0}^{2^n-1} b_j)^2$ if and only if
$b_i b_j = 0$ for $j \ne i$ if and only if
there exists a j_0 such that $b_{j_0} = 2^{2n}$ and $b_j = 0$ for $j \ne j_0$ if and only if
there exists a j_0 such that $\langle\xi, \ell_{j_0}\rangle = \pm 2^n$ and $\langle\xi, \ell_j\rangle = 0$ for $j \ne j_0$ if and only if
there exists a j_0 such that $\xi = \pm\ell_{j_0}$, i.e., f is an affine function. □

A more important topic is to find a lower bound on σ_f for balanced functions f. This is left as a problem for future research.

3.2 σ_f of Some Highly Nonlinear Functions

Now we discuss the sum-of-squares avalanche characteristics of some highly nonlinear functions.

The structure of a function f on V_n that satisfies the propagation criterion with respect to all but a subset $\Re$ of vectors in V_n, has been studied in [SZZ94d]. We note that $\Re$ always contains the zero vector in V_n. It has been shown in [SZZ94d] that

1. if $|\Re| = 2$ then n is odd, the nonlinearity of f satisfies $N_f = 2^{n-1} - 2^{\frac{1}{2}(n-1)}$ and in addition, there exists a nonsingular matrix of order n over GF(2), say A, such that $g(x) = f(Ax)$ can be written as

$$g(x) = cx_n \oplus h(x_1, \ldots, x_{n-1})$$

where c is a constant in GF(2) and h is a bent function on V_{n-1};
2. if $|\Re| = 4$ then n must be even, the nonlinearity of f satisfies $N_f = 2^{n-1} - 2^{\frac{1}{2}n}$ and there exists a nonsingular matrix of order n over GF(2), say B, such that $g(x) = f(Bx)$ can be written as

$$g(x) = c_1x_{n-1} \oplus c_2x_n \oplus h(x_1, \ldots, x_{n-2})$$

where c_1 and c_2 are constants in GF(2), and h is a bent function on V_{n-2};
3. in both cases, all vectors in $\Re$ are linear structures of f.

Now the sum-of-squares avalanche characteristics for the two cases can be determined.

1. if $|\Re| = 2$ then $n = 2k + 1$ and

$$\sigma_f = \sum_{\alpha \in V_{2k+1}} \Delta^2(\alpha) = \Delta^2(0) + \Delta^2(\alpha_1) = 2 \cdot 2^{4k+2} = 2^{4k+3},$$

where α_1 is the nonzero vector in $\Re$;
2. if $|\Re| = 4$ then $n = 2k$ and

$$\sigma_f = \sum_{\alpha \in V_{2k}} \Delta^2(\alpha) = \Delta^2(0) + \sum_{j=1}^{3} \Delta^2(\alpha_j) = 4 \cdot 2^{4k} = 2^{4k+2}$$

where α_i, $i = 1, 2, 3$, are the nonzero vectors in $\Re$.

Functions f on V_n with $|\Re| = 5$ are also studied in [SZZ94d], where it is shown that $N_f = 2^{n-1} - 2^{\frac{1}{2}(n-1)}$, n is odd and that $|\Delta(\alpha_i)| = 2^{n-1}$ for all the four nonzero vectors, α_1, α_1, α_3 and α_4, in the set $\Re$. Thus, the sum-of-squares avalanche characteristic of f with $\Re = 5$ is

$$\sigma_f = \sum_{\alpha \in V_{2k+1}} \Delta^2(\alpha) = \Delta^2(0) + \sum_{j=1}^{4} \Delta^2(\alpha_j) = 2^{4k+2} + 4 \cdot 2^{4k} = 2^{4k+3}.$$

This value is the same as that for the case when $|\Re| = 2$.

It is also shown in [SZZ94d] that functions with $|\Re| = 3$ or 6 do not exist.

4 The Absolute Indicator Δ_f

Let f be a function on V_n. Recall that Δ_f is defined as the maximum among all $\Delta(\alpha)$, $\alpha \neq 0$, and that $\Delta(\alpha) = \pm 2^n$ if and only if α is a linear structure of f. Thus the following result is straightforward.

Lemma 7. *Let f be a function on V_n. Then $0 \leq \Delta_f \leq 2^n$. Moreover, $\Delta_f = 0$ if and only if f is bent, and $\Delta_f = 2^n$ if and only if f has a nonzero linear structure.*

In particular, for any quadratic non-bent function f, we have $\Delta_f = 2^n$. Next we focus on functions whose algebraic degrees are at least three.

Now set $g(x) = f(x) \oplus f(x \oplus \alpha)$. Then the algebraic degree of g is one less than that of f. As $g(x) \oplus g(x \oplus \alpha) = 0$, g cannot be bent. Thus we have the following simple yet helpful lemma.

Lemma 8. *Let f be a function on V_n. Then for any nonzero vector $\alpha \in V_n$, $f(x) \oplus f(x \oplus \alpha)$ is not bent and its algebraic degree is one less than that of f.*

Recall that by Lemma 1, $\Delta_f(\alpha)$ and the Hamming weight $W(g)$ of $g(x) = f(x) \oplus f(x \oplus \alpha)$ are related by $W(g) = 2^{n-1} - \frac{1}{2}\Delta_f(\alpha)$, or equivalently, $\Delta_f(\alpha) = 2(2^{n-1} - W(g))$. Therefore, assume that f is a function on V_n of algebraic degree k, the problem of finding Δ_f is reduced to that of finding the minimum Hamming weight of functions on V_n of algebraic degree $k-1$ which are *integrable* in the sense that they can be expressed as $f(x) \oplus f(x \oplus \alpha)$ with α a nonzero vector in V_n.

For a function f on V_n of algebraic degree $k \geq 3$, Δ_f is to some extent connected to the weight distribution of the $(k-1)$st order binary Reed-Muller code RM$(k-1, n)$. Here RM(r, n) is defined as the collection of *all* functions on V_n, whose algebraic degrees are at most r. The minimum Hamming weight of RM(r, n), i.e., the minimum Hamming weight of functions on V_n of algebraic degree r, is known to be 2^{n-r} (see Theorem 3, p.375 of [MS77]). Now the connection between Δ_f of a function f on V_n of algebraic degree k and RM$(k-1, n)$ can be precisely stated as

$$\Delta_f \geq 2(2^{n-1} - 2^{n-k+1}) = 2^n - 2^{n-k+2}$$

where 2^{n-k+1} is the minimum Hamming weight of RM$(k-1, n)$. This lower bound on Δ_f, however, is very rough and not satisfactory. The reason is that 2^{n-k+1} is the minimum Hamming weight of *all* functions on V_n, whose algebraic degrees are $k-1$, including those which are *not integrable.* Hence it is one of our aims to find a lower bound on Δ_f that is smaller (i.e., better) than the value $2^n - 2^{n-k+2}$.

On the other hand, in designing cryptographic algorithms we are more concerned with balanced nonlinear functions than non-balanced ones. Therefore it is an important issue to know how small the absolute indicator Δ_f can be, for a balanced nonlinear function f on V_n. In the rest of the section we report the result we have obtained on the lower bound of Δ_f of cubic functions. This result can be regarded as the first step towards fully answering the question about Δ_f.

The following two results (see for instance Lemma 9 of [SMZ93] and Lemma 5 of [SZZ94c] respectively), will be employed in the discussions of cubic functions.

Lemma 9. *$f(x_1, \ldots, x_n) = \psi(x_1, \ldots, x_r) \oplus h(x_{r+1}, \ldots, x_n)$ is balanced on V_n if ψ is balanced on V_r or h is balanced on V_{n-r}.*

Lemma 10. *If f is a quadratic function and does not have nonzero linear structures, then it is bent.*

According to Lemma 10, a quadratic non-bent function f must have at least one linear structure. Hence the lower bound on Δ_f for such a function is (trivially) equal to 2^n. For cubic functions, we have a result described in the following theorem.

Theorem 11. *Let f be a non-bent cubic function on V_n. Then $\Delta_f \geq 2^{\frac{1}{2}(n+1)}$.*

Proof. Since f is not bent, there exists a nonzero vector in V_n, say α, such that $f(x) \oplus f(x \oplus \alpha)$ is not balanced. We set $g(x) = f(x) \oplus f(x \oplus \alpha)$ and want to find out the Hamming weight of the truth table of g from which we can find out $\Delta(\alpha)$ and hence the lower bound on Δ_f.

By Lemma 8, g is not bent. Note that g is quadratic. By Lemma 10, g has nonzero linear structures. it is easy to see [Nyb93] that all the linear structures of a function on V_n form a linear subspace of V_n. Denote by W the linear subspace formed by the linear structures of g, and by r the dimension of W. From [SZZ94c], there exists a nonsingular matrix A of order n on GF(2) such that $g^*(x) = g(xA)$ can be expressed as

$$g^*(x_1, \ldots, x_n) = \psi(x_1, \ldots, x_r) \oplus h(x_{r+1}, \ldots, x_n)$$

where ψ is a linear function on W while h is a function on V_{n-r} that does not have nonzero linear structures. Note that the truth tables of g^* and g have the same Hamming weight. Now suppose that ψ is a nonzero linear function. Then ψ is balanced. By Lemma 9, g^* is balanced, which contradicts the fact that g is not balanced. Consequently ψ must be equal to zero and hence

$$g(x_1, \ldots, x_n) = h(x_{r+1}, \ldots, x_n). \tag{4}$$

As h does not have nonzero linear structures, by Lemma 10, it is a bent function on V_{n-r} (which implies that $n-r$ must be even). Thus the Hamming weight of the truth table of h is $2^{n-r-1} + c2^{\frac{1}{2}(n-r)-1}$, where $c = \pm 1$, and the Hamming weight of the truth table of g^*, a function on V_n, is $2^r(2^{n-r-1} + c2^{\frac{1}{2}(n-r)-1}) = 2^{n-1} + c2^{\frac{1}{2}(n+r)-1}$. Equivalently, the Hamming weight of the truth table of $f(x) \oplus f(x \oplus \alpha)$ is $2^{n-1} + c2^{\frac{1}{2}(n+r)-1}$. Applying Lemma 1 to the function f, we have $\Delta(\alpha) = c2^{\frac{1}{2}(n+r)}$. Thus we have proved that there exists a nonzero vector $\alpha \in V_n$ such that $|\Delta(\alpha)| = 2^{\frac{1}{2}(n+r)}$. As r, the dimension of W, is at least 1, we have $\Delta_f \geq |\Delta(\alpha)| \geq 2^{\frac{1}{2}(n+1)}$. □

We stress that the bound $2^{\frac{1}{2}(n+1)}$ in Theorem 11 is satisfied by any non-bent cubic function, be it balanced or non-balanced. The bound, however, is clearly not satisfied by functions of algebraic degree larger than three. For instance, complementing a single bit in the truth table of a bent function f on V_n results in a non-bent, non-balanced function g with $\Delta_g(\alpha) = \pm 2$ for all nonzero $\alpha \in V_n$ (hence $\Delta_g = 2$, and by Theorem 11, g can *not* be cubic.) Nevertheless, we believe that the lower bound $2^{\frac{1}{2}(n+1)}$ is also satisfied by *balanced* functions of algebraic degree larger than three. This leads to the following conjecture:

Conjecture 1 *Let f be a balanced function on V_n, whose algebraic degree is at least three. Then $\Delta_f \geq 2^{\frac{1}{2}(n+1)}$.*

5 Constructing Balanced Functions with Good GAC

Having discussed various bounds of the two indicators σ_f and Δ_f, we now turn our attention to constructing cryptographic functions that have good GACs or global avalanche characteristics measured in terms of the two indicators. A remarkable property of the functions to be constructed is that they are balanced and do not have a nonzero linear structure.

5.1 On V_{2k}

For $z \in V_{2k}$, write $z = (y, x)$ where $y \in V_k$ and $x \in V_k$. Let ω be a permutation on the set of nonzero vectors in V_k, i.e., $V_k - \{0\} = \{\alpha_1, \ldots, \alpha_{2^k-1}\}$, where α_j is the ith vector in V_k in the ascending alphabetical order. Set

$$f(z) = f(y,x) = \begin{cases} \langle \alpha_{j_0}, x\rangle & \text{if } y = 0 \\ \langle \omega(y), x\rangle & \text{if } y \neq 0 \end{cases} \tag{5}$$

where $\langle \cdot, \cdot \rangle$ denotes the scalar product and α_{j_0} is a fixed nonzero vector in V_k. Equivalently (5) can be expressed as

$$f(z) = (1 \oplus y_1)(1 \oplus y_2) \cdots (1 \oplus y_k)\langle \alpha_{j_0}, x\rangle \oplus [1 \oplus (1 \oplus y_1)(1 \oplus y_2) \cdots (1 \oplus y_k)]\langle \omega(y), x\rangle$$

where $y = (y_1, y_2, \ldots, y_k)$.

First we examine the sequence of the function f. Given a vector $\alpha_i \in V_k$, denote by ℓ_i the sequence of a linear function on V_k defined by $\langle \alpha_i, x\rangle$. By Lemma 2 of [SMZ93], ℓ_i is the ith row of H_k, $i = 0, 1, \ldots, 2^k - 1$. Since α_j corresponds to the binary representation of integer j, w can be regarded as a permutation on $\{1, \ldots, 2^k - 1\}$. In particular, $\omega(\alpha_j) = \alpha_i$ can be equivalently written as $\omega(j) = i$. By Lemma 1 of [SMZ93], the sequence of f defined by (5) is

$$\xi = (\ell_{j_0}, \ell_{\omega(1)}, \ldots, \ell_{\omega(2^k-1)}).$$

We can view ξ in the following way: Concatenating the rows in H_k together, we have $(\ell_0, \ell_1, \ldots, \ell_{2^k-1})$. Replacing ℓ_0 by ℓ_{j_0} gives us $(\ell_{j_0}, \ell_1, \ell_2, \ldots, \ell_{2^k-1})$. Finally reordering $\ell_1, \ldots, \ell_{2^k-1}$ according to the permutation ω results in the sequence ξ. As each ℓ_i, $1 \leq i \leq 2^k - 1$, contains an equal number of ones and minus ones, their concatenation ξ has the same property. Thus we have

Lemma 12. *f defined by (5) is a balanced function on V_{2k}.*

We proceed to the discussion of the absolute indicator Δ_f. Let $\gamma = (\beta, \alpha)$ be a nonzero vector in V_{2k}, where $\beta, \alpha \in V_k$. By definition,

$$\Delta(\gamma) = \sum_{y \in V_k} \sum_{x \in V_k} (-1)^{f(y,x) \oplus f(y \oplus \beta, x \oplus \alpha)}.$$

We discuss $\Delta(\gamma)$ in two separate cases: $\beta \neq 0$ and $\beta = 0$.

First we consider Case 1 where $\beta \neq 0$. In this case $\Delta(\gamma)$ can be written as

$$\Delta(\gamma) = \sum_{y=0,\beta} \sum_{x \in V_k} (-1)^{f(y,x) \oplus f(y \oplus \beta, x \oplus \alpha)} + \sum_{y \neq 0,\beta} \sum_{x \in V_k} (-1)^{f(y,x) \oplus f(y \oplus \beta, x \oplus \alpha)}.$$

When $y = 0$, the exponent $f(y,x) \oplus f(y \oplus \beta, x \oplus \alpha)$ becomes

$$f(0,x) \oplus f(\beta, x \oplus \alpha) = \langle \alpha_{j_0}, x \rangle \oplus \langle \omega(\beta), x \oplus \alpha \rangle = \langle \alpha_{j_0} \oplus \omega(\beta), x \rangle \oplus \langle \omega(\beta), \alpha \rangle \quad (6)$$

and when $y = \beta$, it becomes

$$f(\beta, x) \oplus f(0, x \oplus \alpha) = \langle \omega(\beta), x \rangle \oplus \langle \alpha_{j_0}, x \oplus \alpha \rangle = \langle \alpha_{j_0} \oplus \omega(\beta), x \rangle \oplus \langle \alpha_{j_0}, \alpha \rangle. \quad (7)$$

Otherwise when $y \neq 0$ or β, the exponent becomes

$$\begin{aligned} f(y,x) \oplus f(y \oplus \beta, x \oplus \alpha) &= \langle \omega(y), x \rangle \oplus \langle \omega(y \oplus \beta), x \oplus \alpha \rangle & (8) \\ &= \langle \omega(y) \oplus \omega(y \oplus \beta), x \rangle \oplus \langle \omega(y \oplus \beta), \alpha \rangle. & (9) \end{aligned}$$

To find out the value of $\Delta(\gamma)$, we distinguish between the cases of $\omega(\beta) = \alpha_{j_0}$ and $\omega(\beta) \neq \alpha_{j_0}$.

When $\omega(\beta) = \alpha_{j_0}$, (6) becomes a constant $\langle \omega(\beta), \alpha \rangle$, (7) also becomes a constant $\langle \alpha_{j_0}, \alpha \rangle$ and (9) is a nonzero linear function of x for any fixed y and hence balanced. Thus we have

$$\Delta(\gamma) = \sum_{x \in V_k} [(-1)^{\langle \alpha_{j_0}, \alpha \rangle} + (-1)^{\langle \alpha_{j_0}, \alpha \rangle}] = 2 \cdot 2^k \cdot c = 2^{k+1} c$$

where $c = (-1)^{\langle \alpha_{j_0}, \alpha \rangle} = \pm 1$.

On the other hand, when $\omega(\beta) \neq \alpha_{j_0}$, (6), (7) and (9) are all nonzero linear functions and hence balanced. This results in $\Delta(\gamma) = 0$.

Next we consider Case 2 where $\beta = 0$. In this case, it is necessary for α to be nonzero. Thus (5) specializes to

$$\Delta(\gamma) = \sum_{x \in V_k} (-1)^{f(0,x) \oplus f(0, x \oplus \alpha)} + \sum_{y \neq 0} \sum_{x \in V_k} (-1)^{f(y,x) \oplus f(y, x \oplus \alpha)}.$$

When $y = 0$, the exponent $f(y,x) \oplus f(y, x \oplus \alpha)$ becomes

$$f(0,x) \oplus f(0, x \oplus \alpha) = \langle \alpha_{j_0}, x \rangle \oplus \langle \alpha_{j_0}, x \oplus \alpha \rangle = \langle \alpha_{j_0}, \alpha \rangle. \quad (10)$$

Otherwise, when $y \neq 0$, it becomes

$$\begin{aligned} f(y,x) \oplus f(y, x \oplus \alpha) &= \langle \omega(y), x \rangle \oplus \langle \omega(y), x \oplus \alpha \rangle & (11) \\ &= \langle \omega(y), \alpha \rangle. & (12) \end{aligned}$$

Now $\Delta(\gamma)$ can be calculated by

$$\begin{aligned} \Delta(\gamma) &= \sum_{x \in V_k} (-1)^{\langle \alpha_{j_0}, \alpha \rangle} + \sum_{y \neq 0} \sum_{x \in V_k} (-1)^{\langle \omega(y), \alpha \rangle} \\ &= \sum_{x \in V_k} (-1)^{\langle \alpha_{j_0}, \alpha \rangle} + \sum_{u \neq 0} \sum_{x \in V_k} (-1)^{\langle u, \alpha \rangle} \end{aligned}$$

where $u = \omega(y)$. Since ω is a permutation on $V_k - \{0\}$, $u = \omega(y) \neq 0$. Thus we can continue our calculation of $\Delta(\gamma)$:

$$\Delta(\gamma) = \sum_{x \in V_k} (-1)^{\langle \alpha_{j_0}, \alpha \rangle} + \sum_{v \in V_k} \sum_{x \in V_k} (-1)^{\langle v, \alpha \rangle} - \sum_{x \in V_k} (-1)^{\langle 0, \alpha \rangle}.$$

Note that $\langle v, \alpha \rangle$ is a nonzero linear function of v and hence balanced. Thus we have

$$\begin{aligned}\Delta(\gamma) &= \sum_{x \in V_k} (-1)^{\langle \alpha_{j_0}, \alpha \rangle} - \sum_{x \in V_k} (-1)^{\langle 0, \alpha \rangle} \\ &= \sum_{x \in V_k} [(-1)^{\langle \alpha_{j_0}, \alpha \rangle} - 1] \\ &= \begin{cases} 0 & \text{if } \langle \alpha_{j_0}, \alpha \rangle = 0 \\ 2^{k+1} & \text{if } \langle \alpha_{j_0}, \alpha \rangle = 1 \end{cases}\end{aligned}$$

Summarizing the above discussions on Cases 1 and 2, we conclude that $|\Delta(\gamma)| \leq 2^{k+1}$ for any nonzero vector $\gamma \in V_{2k}$. This proves the following lemma:

Lemma 13. *Let f be the function on V_{2k} defined by (5). Then $\Delta_f \leq 2^{k+1}$.*

Now we count the vectors with respect to which the function f satisfies the propagation criterion. We have seen in the above discussions that $\Delta(\gamma) = 0$ in two cases: (1) $\Delta(\gamma) = 0$, $\beta \neq 0$, $\omega(\beta) \neq$ or α_{j_0} and α is arbitrary. (2) $\Delta(\gamma) = 0$, $\beta = 0$ and α satisfies $\alpha \neq 0$ and $\langle \alpha_{j_0}, \alpha \rangle = 0$. For the first case there are $(2^k - 2)2^k = 2^{2k} - 2^{k+1}$ choices, while for the second case there are $2^{k-1} - 1$ choices for $\gamma = (\beta, \alpha)$. Hence there exist $2^{2k} - 2^{k+1} + 2^{k-1} - 1$ vectors $\gamma = (\beta, \alpha)$ such that $\Delta(\gamma) = 0$. This proves

Lemma 14. *The function f defined by (5) satisfies the propagation criterion with respect to $2^{2k} - 2^{k+1} + 2^{k-1} - 1$ vectors in V_{2k}.*

Next we examine the sum-of-squares avalanche characteristic of the function f. Recall that the sequence of f is

$$\xi = (\ell_{j_0}, \ell_{\omega(1)}, \ell_{\omega(2)}, \ldots, \ell_{\omega(2^k-1)})$$

where ℓ_i is the sequence of a linear function on V_k defined by $\langle \alpha_i, x \rangle$.

Let L be a row of H_{2k}. By Lemma 2 of [SMZ93], L is a linear sequence of length 2^{2k}. Since $H_{2k} = H_k \times H_k$, L can be rewritten as $L = \ell_p \times \ell_q$ for some p and q satisfying $0 \leq p, q, \leq 2^k - 1$. Write $\ell_p = (c_0, c_1, \ldots, c_{2^k-1})$. Then we have $L = (c_0\ell_q, c_1\ell_q, \ldots, c_{2^k-1}\ell_q)$.

As H_k is a Hadamard matrix, $\langle \ell_i, \ell_j \rangle = 0$ when $j \neq i$. Also note that as ω is a permutation on $V_k - \{0\}$, $\omega(\alpha_j)$ runs through the nonzero vectors in V_k while j runs through $1, 2, \ldots, 2^k - 1$. So there exists a unique j^* such that $\omega(\alpha_{j^*}) = \alpha_{j_0}$. Thus we have

$$\langle \xi, L \rangle = \begin{cases} (c_0 + c_{j^*})\langle \ell_{j_0}, \ell_{j_0} \rangle\rangle = (c_0 + c_{j^*})2^k & \text{if } \alpha_q = \alpha_{j_0} \\ \pm 2^k & \text{if } \alpha_q \neq \alpha_{j_0}, 0 \\ 0 & \text{if } q = 0 \end{cases}$$

Here $c_0 = 1$ and $c_{j^*} = \pm 1$.

There exist 2^{k-1} linear sequences ℓ_p such that $c_1 = 1$. Hence there exist 2^{k-1} linear sequences L such that $L = \ell_p \times \ell_q$ with $c_{j^*} = 1$ and $\alpha_q = \alpha_{j_0}$. For these sequences we have $\langle \xi, L\rangle = 2^{k+1}$.

For $c_{j^*} = -1$, we have $\langle \xi, L\rangle = 0$. It is easy to see that there exits $2^k \cdot (2^k - 2)$ linear sequences L such that $L = \ell_p \times \ell_q$ with $\alpha_q \neq 0$ or α_{j_0}. With these sequences we have $\langle \xi, L\rangle = \pm 2^k$.

In summary, we have

$$\begin{aligned}\sigma_f &= 2^{-2k} \sum_{s=0}^{2^{2k}-1} \langle \xi, L_s\rangle^4 = 2^{k-1} \cdot 2^{4(k+1)} + 2^k \cdot (2^k - 2) \cdot 2^{4k} \\ &= 2^{4k} + 2^{3k+3} - 2^{3k+1}.\end{aligned}$$

This proves the following conclusion:

Lemma 15. *The sum-of-squares avalanche characteristic of f, a function on V_{2k} defined by (5), satisfies $\sigma_f = 2^{4k} + 2^{3k+3} - 2^{3k+1}$.*

Recall that for a function on V_{2k}, its sum-of-squares indicator is bounded between 2^{4k} and 2^{6k}, with the lower bound 2^{4k} being achieved only when the function is bent. We conjecture that the function f defined by (5) with $\sigma_f = 2^{4k} + 2^{3k+3} - 2^{3k+1}$ achieves nearly optimal sum-of-squares avalanche characteristic of balanced functions on V_{2k}.

From the above discussions, it becomes clear that $|\langle \xi, L_s\rangle| \leq 2^{k+1}$ for any L_s that is a linear sequence of length 2^{2k}. By Lemma 3 of [SMZ93], the nonlinearity of f satisfies $N_f \geq 2^{2k-1} - 2^k$.

Putting the above discussions together, we have

Theorem 16. *Let f be the function on V_{2k} defined by (5). Then*

(i) f is balanced,
(ii) the nonlinearity of f satisfies $N_f \geq 2^{2k-1} - 2^{2k}$,
(iii) f satisfies the propagation criterion with respect to $2^{2k} - 2^{k+1} + 2^{k-1} - 1$ nonzero vectors,
(iv) the sum-of-squares avalanche characteristic of f satisfies $\sigma_f = 2^{4k} + 2^{3k+3} - 2^{3k+1}$,
(v) the absolute avalanche characteristic of f satisfies $\Delta_f \leq 2^{k+1}$.

A final remark is about the strict avalanche characteristic of the function f. The number of vectors with respect to which f satisfies the propagation criterion is $2^{2k} - 2^{k+1} + 2^{k-1} - 1$ which is larger than 2^{2k-1}. Hence these vectors contain at least $2k$ linear independent ones. Let A be the matrix with the $2k$ linear independent vectors as its rows. Then A is nonsingular and of order $2k$. By Theorem 3 of [SZZ94a], $f(zA)$ satisfies the SAC. All the properties described in Theorem 16 are affected by the nonsingular transform A.

5.2 On V_{2k+1}

To construct functions on V_{2k+1} with good avalanche characteristics, we need a permutation $m(u)$ on V_k with a special property that $u \oplus m(u)$ is also a permutation on V_k, namely, $u \oplus m(u)$ runs through the vectors in V_k while u runs V_k. As is shown in the following, such functions can be obtained from maximal length shift register sequences or m-sequences [Gol82]. In a different context, Nyberg showed that m-sequences are useful in constructing cryptographic substitution boxes with the maximum nonlinearity [Nyb91]. (It should be noted, however, that such substitution boxes have been identified to be prone to the differential cryptanalytic attack [BS93, BKPS93].)

Let $(s_0, s_1, \ldots, s_{2^k-2})$ be a m-sequence of length $2^k - 1$, where each s_i is from GF(2). A k-gram is one of the $2^k - 1$ subsequences of length k of the form

$$r_t = (s_{t \bmod (2^k-1)}, s_{(t+1) \bmod (2^k-1)}, \ldots, s_{(t+k-1) \bmod (2^k-1)}),$$

where $t = 0, 1, 2, \ldots, 2^k - 2$. Note that a k-gram can also be viewed as a vector in V_k. Thus we have an ordered list of $2^k - 1$ nonzero vectors in V_k $(r_0, r_1, \ldots, r_{2^k-2})$. Adding to the beginning of the list the zero vector 0 in V_k results in an extended ordered list $(0, r_0, r_1, \ldots, r_{2^k-2})$. The extended list contains all vectors in V_k. Rotating cyclically to the left the nonzero vectors in the list by one position we get $(0, r_1, r_2, \ldots, r_{2^k-2}, r_0)$. Now we have two ordered vector lists:

$$(0, r_0, r_1, \ldots, r_{2^k-2})$$

and

$$(0, r_1, r_2, \ldots, r_{2^k-2}, r_0).$$

Define a mapping $m(u)$ that maps the ith vector in the first list to the corresponding vector in the second list, namely, 0 to 0, r_0 to r_1, r_1 to r_2, ..., and r_{2^k-2} to r_0. By properties of m-sequences, the mapping $m(u)$ is a permutation with the special property that $u \oplus m(u)$ is also a permutation.

Now write $W_1 = \{(0, u) | u \in V_k\}$, $W_2 = \{(1, u) | u \in V_k\}$, where $0, 1 \in GF(2)$. Obviously, $V_{k+1} = W_1 \cup W_2$. For any $y \in V_{k+1}$, write $y = (y_1, u)$ where $y_1 \in GF(2)$ and $u \in V_k$. For $z \in V_{2k+1}$, write $z = (y, x)$ where $y \in V_{k+1}$ and $x \in V_k$.

Then the following is our construction for the case of V_{2k+1}:

$$f(z) = f(y, x) = \begin{cases} 1 \oplus \langle u, x \rangle & \text{if } y \in W_1 \\ \langle m(u), x \rangle & \text{if } y \in W_2 \end{cases} \tag{13}$$

where $m(u)$ is a permutation on V_k with the property that $u \oplus m(u)$ is also a permutation on V_k. Note that (13) can be equivalently written as $f(z) = (1 \oplus y_1)\langle u, x \rangle \oplus y_1 \langle m(u), x \rangle$.

Since α_j is the binary representation of integer j, m can be regarded as a permutation on $\{0, 1, \ldots, 2^k - 1\}$ and hence $\omega(\alpha_j) = \alpha_i$ can be equivalently written as $\omega(j) = i$. Let ξ be the sequence of f. Then the first half of ξ is specified by $1 \oplus \langle u, x \rangle$, while the second half by $\langle m(u), x \rangle$. To be more precise, the first half is (the concatenation of) $-\ell_0, -\ell_1, \ldots, -\ell_{2^k-1}$, where each ℓ_i is the ith row in H_k and $-\ell_i$ means multiplying each component of ℓ_i by -1. And the second half is $\ell_{m(0)}, \ell_{m(1)}, \ldots, \ell_{m(2^k-1)}$, a reordered version of $\ell_0, \ell_1, \ldots, \ell_{2^k-1}$

according to the permutation m on V_k. Thus the sequence of f takes the form of

$$\xi = (-\ell_0, -\ell_1, \ldots, -\ell_{2^k-1}, \ell_{m(0)}, \ell_{m(1)}, \ldots, \ell_{m(2^k-1)}).$$

Obviously ξ contains an equal number of ones and minus ones. Hence f is a balanced function on V_{2k+1}. Using very similar arguments to those for the function f on V_{2k} defined by (5) with attention to the fact that both $m(u)$ and $u \oplus m(u)$ are permutations, we can find out other properties of the function f on V_{2k+1} defined by (13). In particular, we have

Theorem 17. *Let f be the function on V_{2k+1} defined in (13). Then*

(i) f is balanced,
(ii) the nonlinearity of f satisfies $N_f \geq 2^{2k} - 2^k$,
(iii) f satisfies the propagation criterion with respect to $2^{2k} - 1$ nonzero vectors,
(iv) the sum-of-squares avalanche characteristic of f satisfies $\sigma_f = 2^{4k+3}$,
(v) the absolute avalanche characteristic of f satisfies $\Delta_f \leq 2^{k+1}$.

An important property of f is that Δ_f matches the lower bound we conjectured at the end of Section 4. Comparing $\sigma_f = 2^{4k+3} = 2 \cdot 2^{4k+2}$ with 2^{4k+2} and 2^{6k+3}, the upper and upper bounds respectively (see also Theorem 6), we can see that the sum-of-squares avalanche characteristic of the function is also extremely good. Again we conjecture that it achieves the lowest possible value for balanced functions on V_{2k+1}.

It should be noted that since the total number of nonzero vectors with respect to which f satisfies the propagation criterion is $2^{2k} - 1$, there are at most $2k$ linearly independent ones among the vectors. Therefore, unlike the case on V_{2k}, the function f on V_{2k+1} constructed by (13) can not be transformed into an SAC-fulfilling one.

Acknowledgments

The authors would like to thank the anonymous referees for their comments that have helped in improving the presentation of this paper. This work was supported in part by the Australian Research Council (ARC) under the reference number A49232172 and by the Australian Telecommunications and Electronics Research Board (ATERB) under the reference numbers C010/058 and N069/412.

References

[AT90] C. M. Adams and S. E. Tavares. Generating and counting binary bent sequences. *IEEE Transactions on Information Theory*, IT-36 No. 5:1170–1173, 1990.

[Bea84] K. G. Beauchamp. *Applications of Walsh and Related Functions with an Introduction to Sequency Functions.* Microelectronics and Signal Processing. Academic Press, London, New York, Tokyo, 1984.

[BKPS93] L. Brown, M. Kwan, J. Pieprzyk, and J. Seberry. Improving resistance to differential cryptanalysis and the redesign of LOKI. In *Advances in Cryptology - ASIACRYPT'91*, volume 739, Lecture Notes in Computer Science, pages 36–50. Springer-Verlag, Berlin, Heidelberg, New York, 1993.

[BS93] E. Biham and A. Shamir. *Differential Cryptanalysis of the Data Encryption Standard.* Springer-Verlag, New York, Heidelberg, Tokyo, 1993.

[Dil72] J. F. Dillon. A survey of bent functions. *The NSA Technical Journal*, pages 191–215, 1972. (unclassified).

[DT93] J. Detombe and S. Tavares. Constructing large cryptographically strong S-boxes. In *Advances in Cryptology - AUSCRYPT'92*, volume 718, Lecture Notes in Computer Science, pages 165–181. Springer-Verlag, Berlin, Heidelberg, New York, 1993.

[For89] R. Forré. The strict avalanche criterion: Special properties of boolean functions and extended definition. In *Advances in Cryptology - CRYPTO'88*, volume 403, Lecture Notes in Computer Science, pages 450–468. Springer-Verlag, Berlin, Heidelberg, New York, 1989.

[Gol82] S. W. Golomb. *Shift Register Sequences.* Laguna Hills, CA: Aegean Park, 1982.

[Llo90] S. Lloyd. Counting functions satisfying a higher order strict avalanche criterion. In *Advances in Cryptology - EUROCRYPT'89*, volume 434, Lecture Notes in Computer Science, pages 64–74. Springer-Verlag, Berlin, Heidelberg, New York, 1990.

[Llo92] S. Lloyd. Counting binary functions with certain cryptographic properties. *Journal of Cryptology*, 5(2):107–132, 1992.

[Mit90] C. Mitchell. Enumerating boolean functions of cryptographic significance. *Journal of Cryptology*, 2(3):155–170, 1990.

[MS77] F. J. MacWilliams and N. J. A. Sloane. *The Theory of Error-Correcting Codes.* North-Holland, Amsterdam, New York, Oxford, 1977.

[Nyb91] K. Nyberg. Perfect nonlinear S-boxes. In *Advances in Cryptology - EUROCRYPT'91*, volume 547, Lecture Notes in Computer Science, pages 378–386. Springer-Verlag, Berlin, Heidelberg, New York, 1991.

[Nyb93] K. Nyberg. On the construction of highly nonlinear permutations. In *Advances in Cryptology - EUROCRYPT'92*, volume 658, Lecture Notes in Computer Science, pages 92–98. Springer-Verlag, Berlin, Heidelberg, New York, 1993.

[PGV91] B. Preneel, R. Govaerts, and J. Vandewalle. Boolean functions satisfying higher order propagation criteria. In *Advances in Cryptology - EUROCRYPT'91*, volume 547, Lecture Notes in Computer Science, pages 141–152. Springer-Verlag, Berlin, Heidelberg, New York, 1991.

[PLL+91] B. Preneel, W. V. Leekwijck, L. V. Linden, R. Govaerts, and J. Vandewalle. Propagation characteristics of boolean functions. In *Advances in Cryptology - EUROCRYPT'90*, volume 437, Lecture Notes in Computer Science, pages 155–165. Springer-Verlag, Berlin, Heidelberg, New York, 1991.

[Rot76] O. S. Rothaus. On "bent" functions. *Journal of Combinatorial Theory*, Ser. A, 20:300–305, 1976.

[SMZ93] J. Seberry, X. M., and Y. Zhang. Highly nonlinear 0-1 balanced functions satisfying strict avalanche criterion. In *Advances in Cryptology - AUSCRYPT'92*, volume 718, Lecture Notes in Computer Science, pages 145–155. Springer-Verlag, Berlin, Heidelberg, New York, 1993.

[SZZ94a] J. Seberry, X. M. Zhang, and Y. Zheng. Improving the strict avalanche characteristics of cryptographic functions. *Information Processing Letters*, 50:37–41, 1994.

[SZZ94b] J. Seberry, X. M. Zhang, and Y. Zheng. Nonlinearly balanced boolean functions and their propagation characteristics. In *Advances in Cryptology - CRYPTO'93*, volume 773, Lecture Notes in Computer Science, pages 49–60. Springer-Verlag, Berlin, Heidelberg, New York, 1994.

[SZZ94c] J. Seberry, X. M. Zhang, and Y. Zheng. Relationships among nonlinearity criteria. Presented at *EUROCRYPT'94*, 1994.

[SZZ94d] J. Seberry, X. M. Zhang, and Y. Zheng. Structures of cryptographic functions with strong avalanche characteristics. Asiacrypt'94, December 1994.

[SZZ95] J. Seberry, X. M. Zhang, and Y. Zheng. Nonlinearity and propagation characteristics of balanced boolean functions. To appear in *Information and Computation*, 1995.

[Web85] A. F. Webster. Plaintext/ciphertext bit dependencies in cryptographic system. Master's Thesis, Department of Electrical Engineering, Queen's University, Ontario, Cannada, 1985.

[WT86] A. F. Webster and S. E. Tavares. On the design of S-boxes. In *Advances in Cryptology - CRYPTO'85*, volume 219, Lecture Notes in Computer Science, pages 523–534. Springer-Verlag, Berlin, Heidelberg, New York, 1986.

[YH89] R. Yarlagadda and J. E. Hershey. Analysis and synthesis of bent sequences. *IEE Proceedings (Part E)*, 136:112–123, 1989.

Managing Editor's Column

Vol. 1, No. 6; June 28, 1995

Dear Readers:

This issue contains 4 papers in four different areas: typical for J.UCS! (If you want to read papers in a special area only please use either the classification of papers by categories from the start page of J.UCS, or use some of the search capabilities built into J.UCS).

All papers in this issue have a twist to them that is typical for J.UCS: the first (by Banach et al) was submitted early this year: through the electronic refereeing process many changes in contents and presentations were made, resulting now in a substantial expose, substantial to an extent that it might not have been able to publish it in an ordinary printed journal. The other three papers stand out due to the very rapid turn-around time. In particular, Tomek's paper (the fourth) was only received in mid- June: yet, using electronic refereeing two "accept that paper" reports were in, still in time for the June issue.

As pleasant as it is that time from submission to publication is sometimes very short, this does not happen that often: unfortunately, the bottle-neck is still the refereeing process: since this is a voluntary job with little recognition, refereeing never receives very high priority. And with the amount of things all of us have to do refereeing takes often longer than it should. I write this paragraph for three reasons: first, as apology to authors who have been waiting for referees' reports for quite a while... I can't do more than send out reminders after some time has elapsed; second, as message to referees and particular the 170 editors of J.UCS: you are not getting that many papers a year, so please be so kind to review those you get as fast as possible; third, since we are trying a novel way of reaching the "right" referees: I intend to report on this as soon as we have the first concrete experiences (probably in the August or September issue).

Enough for now. Have a good summer (or winter, if you are "down under"),

Cheers,

Hermann Maurer
email: hmaurer@iicm.tu-graz.ac.at

Journal of Universal Computer Science, vol. 1, no. 6 (1995), 339-398
submitted: 20/10/94, accepted: 26/6/95, appeared: 28/6/95 © Springer Pub. Co.

A Translation of the Pi-Calculus Into MONSTR

R. Banach
(Computer Science Dept., Manchester University, Manchester, M13 9PL, U.K.
banach@cs.man.ac.uk)

J. Balázs
(Computer Science Dept., P. J. Šafárik University, 041 54 Košice, Slovakia.
balazs@turing.upjs.sk)

G. Papadopoulos
(Computer Science Dept., University of Cyprus, Nicosia, P.O. Box 537, Cyprus.
george@jupiter.cca.ucy.cy)

Abstract: A translation of the π-calculus into the MONSTR graph rewriting language is described and proved correct. The translation illustrates the heavy cost in practice of faithfully implementing the communication primitive of the π-calculus and similar process calculi. It also illustrates the convenience of representing an evolving network of communicating agents directly within a graph manipulation formalism, both because the necessity to use delicate notions of bound variables and of scopes is avoided, and also because the standard model of graphs in set theory automatically yields a useful semantics for the process calculus. The correctness proof illustrates many features typically encountered in reasoning about graph rewriting systems, and particularly how serialisation techniques can be used to reorder an arbitrary execution into one having stated desirable properties.

Key Words: Concurrency, Pi-Calculus, Term Graph Rewriting, MONSTR, Process Networks, Simulation, Serialisability.

Category: D.1.3, D.3.1, F.3.2, F.4.2

1 INTRODUCTION

As [Aczel (1993)] has pointed out, the word "process" has very different connotations in different branches of computer science. For instance, those who study process algebra, those who work on operating systems, and those who construct systems for supporting "the business process", would hardly recognise each others' use of the word. The work in this paper may partly be seen as a comparison of notions of process from the first two of these, since in presenting a translation from the π-calculus to MONSTR, both areas may be brought into contact.

The π-calculus [Milner et al. (1992), Milner (1993a)] arose as a generalisation of CCS [Milner (1989)] to allow networks of processes to evolve dynamically. It is thus a process algebra language. MONSTR by contrast is a generalised term graph rewriting language that was used as the intermediate language for the Flagship machine. See [Banach et al. (1988), Banach and Watson (1989), Banach (1993a), Banach (1993b), Watson and Watson (1987), Watson et al. (1987), Watson et al. (1989)]. Since the machine needed a runtime system, whose implementation centred round MONSTR, the connection with operating systems emerges. (In fact MONSTR evolved as a restriction of a more general term graph rewriting language DACTL, [see Glauert et al. (1988a), Glauert et al. (1988b)], the restrictions being forced by implementation issues.)

MONSTR therefore rejoices in the virtue of having been implemented in anger for a real machine. In particular, the directed arcs of a MONSTR graph are intended to be directly modeled by pointers in a conventional store in the overwhelming majority of instances, (see [Banach (1993a)] for an exposition of exactly how). So translations of process algebra formalisms (or for that matter anything else) into MONSTR can give a reasonable idea of the practicality of the primitive notions inherent in these formalisms. In the present case we find that the atomicity and synchronisation properties inherent in the communication primitive of the π-calculus extract a heavy price in the translation. This aspect is common to all similar process algebra models such as CCS — one reason why we concentrate on the π-calculus in this paper is that the more flexible mechanisms for channel hiding and binding (compared with eg. CCS), pose no problems for a MONSTR implementation. Other features of the syntax, such as the identification of potential communications by complementary occurrences of the same channel name, free in some particular context, give rise to other sources of minor inconvenience when they interact with the rest of the syntax.

At the heart of these issues is the structure of the syntax of process algebra languages, which is patterned after the structure of the syntax of many conventional languages, and produces a strong desire to use syntax directed techniques in the theory of these systems. For stack based languages such as Pascal, this approach to the meaning of the language is particularly successful, as the denotational semantics of such languages bears out. Unfortunately, the structure of process networks is seldom closely related to the structure of the parse tree of the algebraic expression that defines them, which considerably weakens the case for exclusively pursuing syntax directed analyses. Graph theory is much more in sympathy with the structure of the typical process network, which makes a translation into a graph-based formalism even more attractive.

Ironically, presentations of process algebra, having once described the syntax and some operational semantics, are frequently awash with pictures of process networks — which are of course nothing but graphs of one kind or another. Prodigious manipulations of the syntax ensue; often demonstrating some fairly simple property of the network which could have been established on graph theoretic grounds by elementary means. In the translation presented below, many sources of intricacy residing in the standard syntactic presentation of the π-calculus, once properly understood, can be seen to correspond to elementary constructions in an appropriate category of term graphs, (though we hasten to add, we will not need to make any systematic use of categorical techniques in this paper).

Of course graph based languages also need syntax, but this is used merely as a handy notation for the standard semantic model of graphs, which is what we really have in mind all along. (One could of course contemplate non-standard models of languages for graph theory if one really longs for such exotica.) The emphasis is thus different than in process algebra: rather than starting with the syntax and then wondering what it means, we have the semantics *ab initio*.

The syntax of a graph based language tends to be rather flat — it usually does little more than list the nodes and edges of the graph in question. In the case of term graphs, some slight embellishment of this is possible because of the quasi-term structure of individual nodes which allows some nesting, but the underlying "just list 'em all" philosophy remains. The main consequence of this is that sophisticated notions of scope, or of binding, tend to be absent from such languages. This might be thought to be a great deficiency, but in fact it proves not to be so. All the jobs normally done by notions of scope inside the syntax are taken over by graph structure and by suitable notions of graph homomorphism. These are described at the meta-syntactic level and act directly on the semantic objects of interest. Of course for this to work, we need to know what the semantic objects of interest are — but we have already said that we have the semantics *ab initio* so this is not a problem. In the case of the π-calculus, in which the syntax has the familiar hierarchical flavour, distinct subprocess objects residing in remote peripheral areas of the parse tree may share private names despite their syntactic remoteness. Elaborate notions of scope and of binding are needed to manage the syntactic arm-twisting that forestalls the name clashes that are prone to occur due to the fact that the two subprocess objects may only express their relationship via their closest common ancestor in the tree. In a graph based language, this is unnecessary — one simply encodes the required relationship by suitable edges or arcs and that is it.

The present authors are not the only ones to notice that graphs have some utility in process algebras and similar systems. One may cite [Milner (1979), Degano and Montanari (1987), Milner (1993b), Corradini et al. (1994), Parrow (1994)] amongst others. However it is not clear that these other formalisms have the same closeness to direct implementation that MONSTR gains by virtue of its association with the Flagship machine.

The structure of the rest of this paper is as follows. In [Section 2] we give a description of MONSTR, while in [Section 3] we set out the version of π-calculus that we will use. [Section 4] describes the key features behind the translation strategy, and [Section 5] presents the details. [Section 6] establishes the basic properties of translated systems that are needed in proving the translation correct, and the correctness proof itself appears in [Section 7]. [Section 8] contains some discussion of aspects of the π-calculus not directly treated in the version of [Section 3]. [Section 9] concludes, and contains further discussion of the material herein, drawing analogies between the proof of soundness on the one hand, and serialisability theory or forcing techniques on the other.

2 MONSTR

MONSTR arose as a result of the attempt to reconcile the desire for an intermediate language with rewriting-based semantics, with the reality of a parallel machine where the primitive atomic actions were in principle of much smaller granularity than atomic rewrites of arbitrary size. The result was a term graph rewriting language MONSTR, for which the implementation problem did not make excessive demands on the architecture's semantics.

Term Graph Rewriting

The operational semantics of MONSTR deals with the transformation of term graphs. These are graphs in which the nodes are labelled with node symbols from an alphabet $\mathbf{S}$; each node x having an arity $A(x) = \{1 \ldots n\}$, indicating that x has a sequence of n out-arcs. A node x may be the target of an arbitrary number of in-arcs.

The nodes and arcs of MONSTR graphs are further decorated with certain markings which relate to reduction strategy. Specifically, if a node is marked with $*$, then it is active and can serve as the root of a redex. If it is marked with $\#^n$, then it is suspended waiting for n "notifications" (see below), and then (usually) some of its out-arcs are notification arcs, i.e. are marked with the notification mark ^, which is whence the notifications will arrive. The only other possibilities are that nodes and arcs are unmarked (i.e. idle, written visibly as ε where necesary).

Here is the formal definition. In definition 2.1, N^* is the set of sequences over N, similarly for $\{\varepsilon, \wedge\}^*$; the domain of a sequence is the set of its indices; and the arity of a node x, $A(x)$, is defined in clause (3).

Definition 2.1 A term graph (or just graph) G, is a quintuple $(N, \sigma, \alpha, \mu, \nu)$ where

(1) N is a set of nodes,

(2) σ is a map $N \to \mathbf{S}$, the symbol map,

(3) α is a map $N \to N^*$, giving the arcs of x, with for all x, $A(x) = \mathrm{dom}(\alpha(x))$,

(4) μ is a map $N \to \{\varepsilon, *, \#, \#\#, \#\#\#, \ldots \#^n \ (n \geq 1)\}$, the node marking map,

(5) ν is a map $N \to \{\varepsilon, \wedge\}^*$, the arc marking map, with for all x, $\mathrm{dom}(\nu(x)) = A(x)$.

(The nomenclature is meant to be alliterative: σ for symbols, α for arcs, μ for markings, ν for notifications.) We refer to an arc of a graph by writing (p_k, c) where p is the parent and c is its k'th child. Alternatively using α, we write $c = \alpha(p)[k]$ where –[–] is the lookup operator on sequences. [Fig. 1] below shows a term graph, in which each node is depicted by its symbol followed by its sequence of out-arcs in brackets, and only non-idle markings are shown.

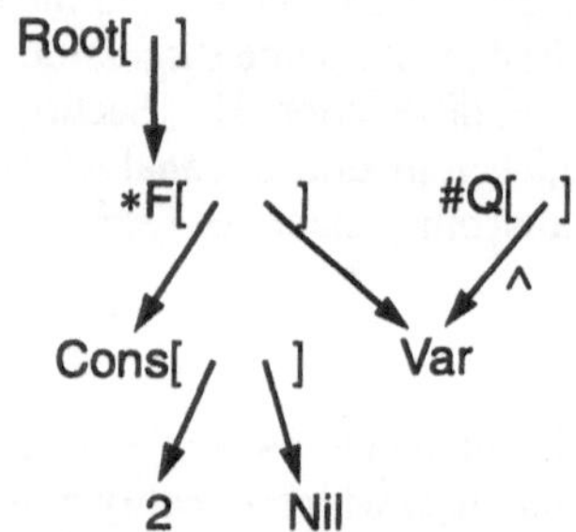

Fig. 1

For rewriting, we need a notion of pattern, and a sufficiently flexible notion of pattern matching. Accordingly a pattern satisfies definition 2.1 except that the signature of σ is $N \to \mathbf{S} \cup \{\mathsf{Any}\}$ where Any is special node symbol not in **S**, the intention being that Any-labelled nodes may match "anything". For later convenience Any-labelled nodes are called implicit whereas other nodes are explicit. We restrict Any-labelled nodes to occur only at leaves of patterns so that

$$\sigma(x) = \mathsf{Any} \Rightarrow A(x) = \varnothing \quad \text{i.e. } \alpha(x) = \nu(x) = \varnothing$$

Evidently a graph is a kind of pattern, but not vice versa.

Definition 2.2 A rule D is a quadruple (P, *root*, *Red*, *Act*) where

(1) P is a pattern, called the full pattern of the rule.

(2) *root* is an explicit node of P called the root, and all implicit nodes of P are accessible from the root. If $\sigma(root) = S$, then D is a rule for S. The subpattern of P accessible from (and including) *root* is called the left pattern L of the rule, and nodes of P not in L are called contractum nodes. L is unmarked, i.e. for all $x \in L$, $\mu(x) = \varepsilon$, and $\nu(x)[k] = \varepsilon$ for all $k \in A(x)$.

(3) *Red* is a set of pairs of nodes, (called redirections) such that $Red \subseteq L \times P$, and if $(x, y) \in Red$, then x is explicit. *Red* is the graph of a function with distinctly labelled nodes in the domain, i.e. if $(x, y), (u, v) \in Red$ then $x = u \Rightarrow y = v$ and $x \neq u \Rightarrow \sigma(x) \neq \sigma(u)$. For $(x, y) \in Red$, x is called the LHS and y the RHS of the redirection.

(4) *Act* is a set of nodes (called activations) of P such that $Act \subseteq L$.

[Fig. 2] is a picture of a rule, with *root* indicated by the short stubby arrow, *Red* indicated by the dotted arrows, and *Act* indicated by adorning the relevant (single in this case) nodes of L with a $*$ (these are unmarked according to definition 2.2.(2)).

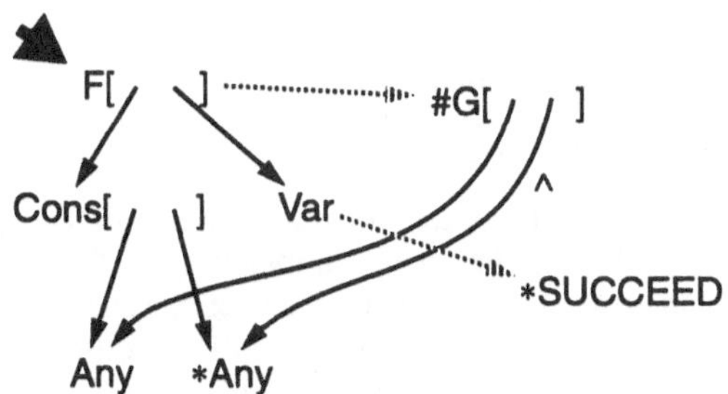

Fig. 2

In concrete syntax this becomes

```
F[Cons[a b] x:Var] => #G[a ^*b] , x := *SUCCEED
```

In this notation, clutter is saved by nesting node definitions where practicable. The *root* node is always the one listed first, and the nesting indicates that it has a Cons first child and a Var second child. The Cons child has two Any children, indicated by just mentioning the node identifiers **a** and **b** (as opposed to node labels which are always capitalised). The left pattern is everything that occurs to the left of the **=>**, and the material to the right describes everything else. Thus the contractum contains a once-suspended G node whose children are those of the left Cons node, (such shared references mean that in general node identifiers are needed as well as node labels). The fact that G's second child is marked with **^*** indicates firstly that the relevant arc is ^-marked, and secondly that that the node is in *Act* (being a *****-marked reference to a left pattern node — in general *any* *****-marked occurrence of a left pattern node on the right of a rule indicates that the node is in *Act*). The other contractum node is an active SUCCEED node. By convention the **=>** indicates that the root node is to be redirected to the node immediately following the **=>**, and the syntax **x := *SUCCEED** indicates that the Var node is to be redirected to the SUCCEED node, in agreement with [Fig. 2]. Note that only the Var node needs to be specified in full (i.e. using both a node identifier and a node label).

A rule system $\mathcal{R}$ is just a set of rules. In outline, given a rule system and some graph, an execution proceeds thus. First choose some active (*-marked) node of the graph; secondly examine the rule system to see which rules will match at that active node; if there are some, choose one of them and rewrite the graph using it; alternatively if there are none, perform notifications from the active node. Continue to repeat the whole process with the new graphs successively generated thereby as long as possible.

Here are the technical definitions, starting with matching or homomorphism.

Definition 2.3 A matching of a pattern P with root r say, to a graph G at a node $t \in G$, is a node map $h : P \to G$ such that

(1) $h(r) = t$

(2) If $x \in P$ is explicit then, $\sigma(x) = \sigma(h(x))$, $A(x) = A(h(x))$, and for all $k \in A(x)$, $h(\alpha(x)[k]) = \alpha(h(x))[k]$.

Omitting mention of roots, the same definition will suffice for matching arbitrary patterns to other patterns or, for matching graphs to other graphs. If $h : P \to G$ is a matching, then we say that $z \in G$ is explicitly matched if it is the h image of an explicit node. Otherwise we say that it is implicitly matched.

Now the definitions pertinent to rewriting.

Definition 2.4 Let X be a graph, $t \in X$ a node of X such that $\mu(t) = *$, and $\mathcal{R}$ a system. Let $Sel = \{D \mid$ there is a $D \in \mathcal{R}$ such that there is a matching $h : L \to X$ of the left pattern L of the full pattern P of the rule D to X at $t\}$. Rule selection is some (otherwise unspecified) process for choosing a member of Sel assuming it is non-empty. The chosen D makes t the root of the redex $h(L)$ and D the selected rule that governs the rewrite.

Assuming we have X, t, $D = (P, root, Red, Act)$ and h given as above, rewriting according to the rule proceeds via three phases (contractum building, redirection, activation), each of which can be viewed as a mini graph transformation. Naturally, our graph and rule given above provide a running example. There is clearly a redex rooted at F.

Definition 2.5 Contractum building adds a copy of each contractum node of P to X. Copies of arcs of P from contractum nodes to their children are added in such a way that there is an extended matching h' from the whole of P to the graph being created, which agrees with h on L. Node and arc markings for the new items are copied from P. Call the resulting graph X' and let $i_{X,X'}$ be the natural injection.

In our running example, doing the above yields [Fig. 3]. We see that copies of exactly the contractum nodes and arcs, suitably marked, have been added, and that this enables the extended matching h' of the whole of P to be constructed.

Definition 2.6 Redirection replaces each arc (p_k, c) of X', such that $c = h'(x)$ for some $(x, y) \in Red$, with $(p_k, h'(y))$. This can be done consistently since the LHSs of two distinct redirections cannot map to the same node of X' since their node symbols are different by definition 2.2.(3). All such redirections are performed simultaneously. Let the resulting graph be called X'' and let $i_{X',X''}$ be the natural injection. Note that $i_{X',X''}$ is just an injective map on nodes rather than a matching as for $i_{X,X'}$. We define the map

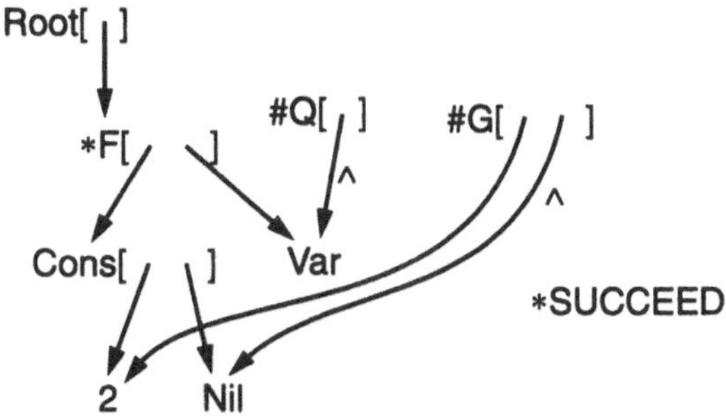

Fig. 3

$r_{X',X''}$ by $r_{X',X''}(c) = i_{X',X''}(c)$ unless $c = h'(x)$ for some $(x, y) \in Red$, in which case $r_{X',X''}(c) = i_{X',X''}(h'(y))$.

Performing the redirections on our example yields [Fig. 4].

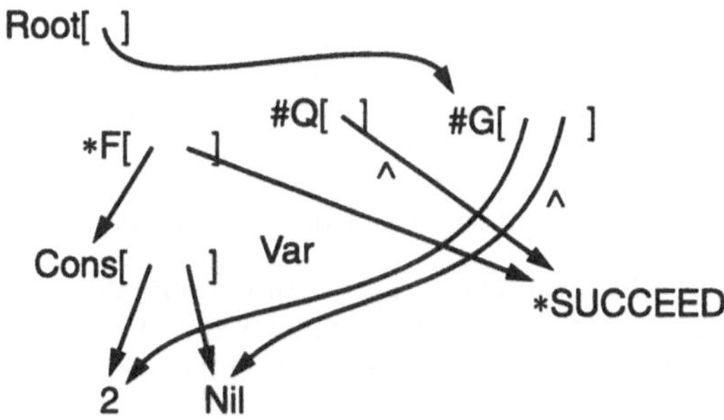

Fig. 4

Definition 2.7 Activation merely alters some node markings. Roughly speaking, *root* is made idle and the nodes in *Act* are made active. More precisely $\mu(i_{X',X''}(h'(root)))$ is changed to ε, and for each $u \in Act$, provided $\mu(i_{X',X''}(h'(u))) = \varepsilon$ beforehand, the marking $\mu(i_{X',X''}(h'(u)))$ is changed to $*$. We call the resulting graph Y, and define $i_{X'',Y}$ as the natural injection.

Doing this for our running example yields [Fig. 5].

The graph Y is taken to be the result of the rewrite, i.e. the result of a single atomic action in the rewriting model. Note that no node of the original graph X is ever removed modulo the identifications of nodes among the various stages. This lack of garbage collection is an issue which will be remedied in due course.

By composing the various maps $i_{X,X'}$, $i_{X',X''}$ or $r_{X',X''}$, etc., we can track the history of a node through an execution of the system. We thus have $i_{X,Y}(x) = (i_{X'',Y} \circ i_{X',X''} \circ i_{X,X'})(x)$ as the node which is the copy in Y of $x \in X$, and $r_{X,Y}(x) = (i_{X'',Y} \circ r_{X',X''} \circ i_{X,X'})(x)$ as the node of Y that x got redirected to. This notation is a little cumbersome, but consider the following. The phrase "adds a copy of each contractum node" is really a euphemism for disjoint union. If one knows in advance which such disjoint unions are needed, one can arrange that all the copies used are distinct, and thus implement disjoint union by

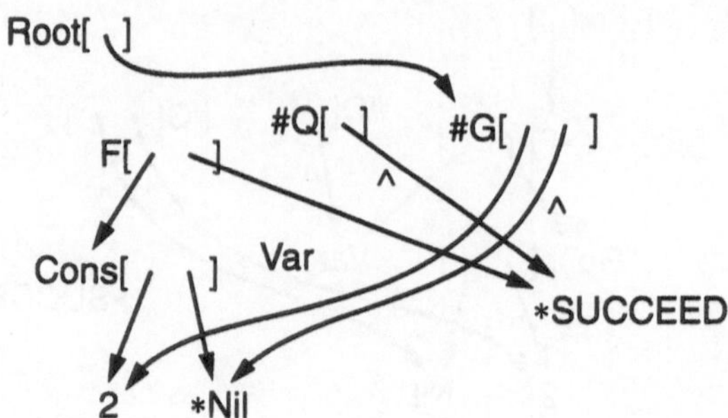

Fig. 5

ordinary union. In more general situations though this is not possible, and one has to take the demands of disjoint union more seriously (such cases arise in the detailed repercussions of the issues we discuss in [Section 8]). In such cases one uses some kind of tagging to make copies distinct, and in these cases the obvious natural injections are no longer identities. In this respect, the more involved notation is more portable. Furthermore, we will need to keep close track of nodes through an execution sequence in [Section 7] and our notation provides a firm foundation for this; also it is useful when we delve into the innards of a rewrite, as we do in lemma 6.10.

Suppose now that *Sel* is empty. Then as we said, instead of a rewrite, notification takes place. Again let X be the graph, and $t \in X$ the chosen node of X such that $\mu(t) = *$.

Definition 2.8 Notification merely alters some node and arc markings. The node marking $\mu(t)$ is changed to ε. Further for all arcs (p_k, t) in X such that the arc making $\nu(p)[k]$ is ^, the marking $\nu(p)[k]$ is changed to ε, and if the node marking $\mu(p)$ is $\#^n$ (for $n \geq 1$), $\mu(p)$ is changed to $\#^{n-1}$, with $\#^0$ being understood as $*$. We call the resulting graph Y and define $i_{X,Y}$ to be the natural injection.

The result of the notification is the graph Y as before.

In [Fig. 5], assuming there are no rules for Nil or SUCCEED, there is scope for two notifications. When they have both been performed, [Fig. 6] results. What might happen subsequently depends on what rules, if any, there might be for Q and G.

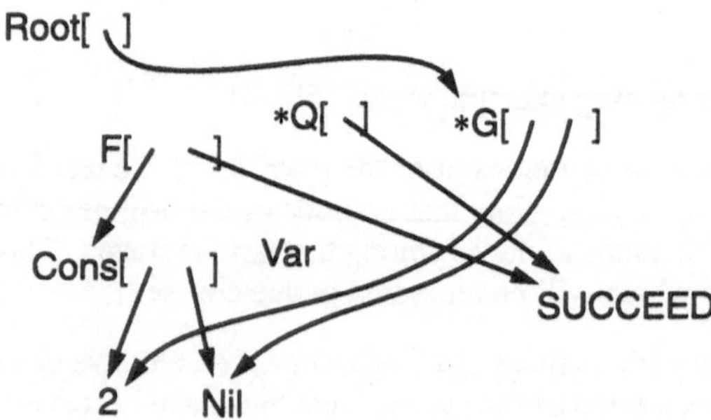

Fig. 6

The remaining technicalities we need in our rewriting model are disposed of in the following couple of definitions.

Definition 2.9 An initial graph is one which consists of an isolated node of empty arity, with the active (*) node marking, and labelled by the symbol Initial.

Definition 2.10 An execution $\mathcal{G}$ of a system $\mathcal{R}$ is a sequence of graphs $[G_0, G_1 \ldots]$ of maximum length such that G_0 is initial and for each $i \geq 0$ such that $i+1$ is an index of $\mathcal{G}$, G_{i+1} results from G_i either by rewriting (in case there is an applicable rule) or by notification (otherwise) at some arbitrarily selected active node t_i of G_i. Graphs occuring in executions are called execution graphs.

The above presents a general framework in which term graph rewriting (with programmed control of strategy) may be developed. To be closer to executable machine semantics, MONSTR imposes a collection of restrictions as follows.

The MONSTR Restrictions

First the symbol alphabet **S** is partitioned into **F** ∪ **C** ∪ **V**, where **F** consists of *functions* which have rules but which cannot occur at subroot positions of patterns of rules; and **C** and **V**, consisting of *constructors* and *variables* (or *stateholders*) respectively, neither of which can occur at root positions of patterns of rules and therefore neither of which have rules; in addition constructors are not permitted to occur as the LHS of a redirection. Compared to the use of term graph rewriting as an implementation vehicle for functional languages, where only functions and constructors are needed, the presence of stateholders within MONSTR considerably increases the flexibility of the language for conveniently modelling imperative notions such as storage cells, synchronisation objects, and the logical variable. They will play a vital role in our translation of the π-calculus below by representing channels and encoding protocol states.

Next we insist that rules are of two kinds, normal rules and default rules. A default rule has a pattern which consists of an active function node and as many distinct implicit children as its arity dictates. Otherwise it is normal. Thus a default rule's pattern will always match at an active execution graph node labelled with the appropriate function symbol.

We insist that there is at least one default rule for every function symbol, and we require a normal rule to be selected in preference to a default rule whenever either will match. In the concrete syntax of MONSTR, we can enforce this rule selection policy using the nondeterministic rule separator | and the sequential rule separator **;**.

Definition 2.11 MONSTR graphs, rules and rule systems must conform to the following list of restrictions.

(1) Symbols have fixed arities, i.e. the map sending a node x to its arity $A(x)$ depends only on $\sigma(x)$, and thus $A(x) = A(\sigma(x))$ (where the second A is a notation for symbol arity).

(2) Functions have fixed matching templates, i.e. for each $F \in \mathbf{F}$ there is a subset $M(F) \subseteq A(F)$ such that for any normal rule for F with root *root*, $k \in M(F)$ iff $\alpha(root)[k]$ is explicit.

(3) Functions may explicitly match a stateholder in at most one position, and must otherwise explicitly match only constructors, i.e. for each $F \in \mathbf{F}$ there is a subset $\Sigma(F) \subseteq M(F) \subseteq A(F)$, at most a singleton, such that for any normal rule for F with root *root*, if $k \in \Sigma(F)$, then $\sigma(\alpha(root)[k]) \in \mathbf{C} \cup \mathbf{V}$; else for explicit $\alpha(root)[l]$, such that $l \neq k$, $\sigma(\alpha(root)[l]) \in \mathbf{C}$.

(4) Left patterns are shallow, i.e. for each rule, any grandchild of the root is implicit.

(5) Any nodes may not be tested for pointer equivalence, i.e. for every rule, no implicit node may have more than one parent in the left pattern.

(6) Every node x in every rule is balanced, i.e. $\mu(x) = \#^n$ for some $n \geq 1$ iff n is the cardinality of $\{k \in A(x) \mid \nu(x)[k] = \wedge\}$.

(7) Every notification arc (p_k, c) in every rule is state saturated or head activated, i.e. if $\nu(p)[k] = \wedge$, then if $\mu(c) = \varepsilon$ then either c is explicit and $\sigma(c) \in \mathbf{V}$, or $c \in Act$.

(8) A redirection to an unactivated idle node is to a stateholder, i.e. for every rule, if $(x, y) \in Red$ with $\mu(y) = \varepsilon$ then either y is explicit and $\sigma(y) \in \mathbf{V}$, or $y \in Act$.

(9) The root is always redirected, i.e. for every rule with root *root*, $(root, t) \in Red$ for some t.

(10) LHSs of redirections must not be activated unless they are also RHSs of redirections, i.e. for every rule, if $(y, z) \in Red$ and $y \in Act$, then $(x, y) \in Red$ for some x.

There isn't the space here to explain all the ramifications of these restrictions, or why they are a good idea (see [Banach (1993a)] for a thorough discussion). Essentially, the restrictions enable one to prove a number of run-time properties of arbitrary MONSTR systems, that are desirable from an implementation's point of view.

It is easy enough to check that our running example above, conforms to all of these restrictions, and that the rewrite we showed is in fact a MONSTR rewrite (up to garbage). We will deal with garbage shortly.

It turns out that the MONSTR systems that result from our translation have a relatively simple run-time structure, and using the general properties provable from the syntactic restrictions will not be necessary in the fairly involved correctness proof which is the main concern of this paper — all the facts we will need will be derived directly from the structure of the rule system. Accordingly, we point out one additional feature of MONSTR rewriting that is important in the general theory but that becomes superfluous in the specific systems we deal with.

The definition 2.3, of pattern matching, is insensitive to the markings on nodes and arcs, and aside from the fact that the root of a redex must be active, this carries through to the term graph rewriting model described above. For MONSTR rewriting, as well as the syntactic restrictions, we demand that the explicitly matched arguments of the root of a redex are idle; and in case an active node attempts to rewrite when this is not the case, the rewrite is suspended until such time as it becomes true. This is a run-time mechanism. Fortunately for us, we will be able to prove directly that in our translated systems, all the explicitly matched arguments in a rewrite are idle, and so we needn't concern ourselves with the details of this mechanism. To achieve this simplification though, one of the rules we will use later (in fact rule [9] of the communication protocol of [Section 5]) violates restriction 2.11.(8) as it performs a redirection to an unactivated implicit node. We will prove directly that in fact this Any node is only ever matched to idle stateholders in any execution of the system. As a consequence, our transgression does not affect any of the desirable run-time properties. Given the complexity of the correctness proof that we tackle below, we regard this avoidance of having to deal with suspensions, as reasonable under the circumstances. (In fact all such run-time suspensions can be eliminated. [Banach (1993b)] discusses in detail how this is done.)

It is time we addressed garbage collection, since the rewriting model described above, which never throws anything away, is rendered somewhat unsatisfactory thereby. The following definition of liveness is sound in the presence of the MONSTR restrictions (and run-time suspensions), in that garbage collection may be done eagerly after every rewrite or notification, or delayed, without changing the live part of any execution graph. (See [Banach (1993a)] for a full discussion.) In the sequel, we will be ambivalent about whether garbage is actually present in the graphs we consider. Obviously, when we do garbage collection, the maps $i_{X,X'}$, $r_{X',X''}$, etc. become partial, as some of the codomain elements disappear.

Definition 2.12 Given a MONSTR graph X, garbage collection removes all non-live nodes and arcs from X, giving a subgraph Live(X). A live node x is one that can be proved so on the basis of the following rules of inference:

(1) If $\sigma(x)$ is a special symbol Root (a constructor), then x is live.

(2) If $\mu(x) = *$, then x is live.

(3) If p is live and (p_k, x) is an idle arc, then x is live.

(4) If c is live and (x_k, c) is a notification arc, then x is live.

A live arc is one for which both head and tail nodes are live; and non-live nodes and arcs are garbage.

Returning to our running example, the original graph in [Fig. 1] clearly contains no garbage. When we perform the rewrite getting [Fig. 5], a certain amount of garbage is generated. Removing this results in [Fig. 7].

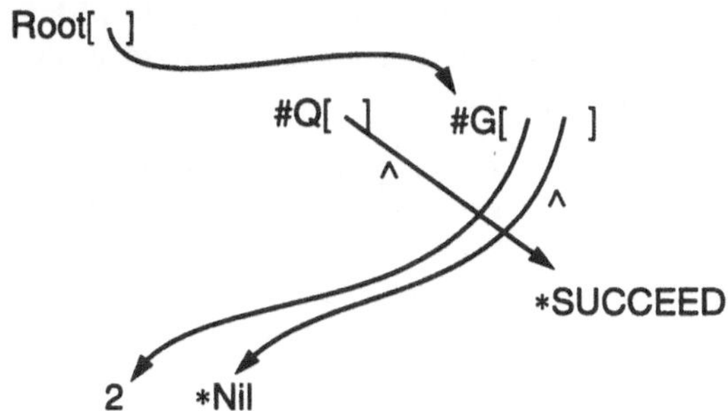

Fig. 7

In general, and despite the soundness result, Live(X) does not satisfy all the conditions for being a MONSTR graph (since eg. a live node may have a garbage child node); however, this possibility will not occur in the systems we consider below. In more general cases, the possibility makes theoretical treatments of MONSTR easier when garbage is retained. Once more, the reader is refered to [Banach (1993a)] for a fuller discussion.

3 THE PI-CALCULUS

The π-calculus first appeared in [Milner et al. (1992)] and since that time has been seen in a number of minor variants. We will fix on a version of the monadic calculus, as presented in the first part of [Milner (1993a)], since it is in many ways the most economic version, and so leads to the most transparent translation. We regard as given a suitable alphabet **CN** of channel names, ranged over by x, y, z etc. Here is the formal syntax.

Definition 3.1 The π-calculus language of process expressions is given by the following syntax where P is a process and the various Q_i are subprocesses (thus corresponding to the same nonterminal in a formal BNF). We will take it for granted that parentheses may be used in the usual way.

$$\begin{aligned} P = \ & \pi_1.Q_1 + \pi_2.Q_2 + \ldots + \pi_n.Q_n \\ | \ & Q_1 \mid Q_2 \mid \ldots \mid Q_n \\ | \ & \nu x Q \\ | \ & !Q \\ | \ & \mathbf{0} \end{aligned}$$

Speaking informally, the first case is guarded summation where each π_i is of the form $x(y)$ or $\bar{x}z$. Here the parentheses and the overbar are constant symbols within the syntax, and as below x, y, z are in **CN**. The input expression $x(y).Q$, means that some channel name q say, is to be read over the channel x which plays the role of a communication link, and then q is bound to all free occurences of y in Q; y is a bound name in $x(y).Q$ and Q is its scope. Conversely the output expression $\bar{x}z.Q$ means that the channel name z (the data) is to be written to the channel x which acts as the communication link. A process which is a sum can evolve into exactly one of the alternatives, the others being discarded. The second case is parallel composition; all the Q_i's are parallel processes and evolve concurrently. The third case is restriction; in νxQ, where the ν is a constant of the syntax, the channel name x is bound, and refers to a channel that is private to νxQ, so νx is a binder and its scope is Q. The fourth case is replication, in which the ! in $!Q$ is another constant of the syntax. $!Q$ is intended to be (syntactically) equivalent to the parallel composition of as many copies of Q as one might wish for, i.e. $!Q \equiv Q \mid Q \mid Q \mid \ldots \mid !Q$. However we will take a different approach to replication as described below. Finally the process **0** does nothing.

Process algebra definitions are normally supplemented by demanding that summation and parallel composition are monoidal operators with **0** as unit. We will simplify our subsequent task a little by not demanding the "**0** as unit" part, so that any top level **0**'s that get exposed during the evolution of a process expression (see below) just end up lying around as inactive parallel subprocesses. (We could overcome this at the price of extra complexity.)

Further, since the subprocesses in our sums are always prefixed, we do not demand that (prefixed) summation is associative, else prefix might in some sense become left distributive, a possibility that is usually regarded as not *a priori* desirable. (In this respect, we must regard a process expression such as $((\pi_1.Q_1 + \pi_2.Q_2) + \pi_3.Q_3)$ as merely a meta-level shorthand for a flattened ternary summation $(\pi_1.Q_1 + \pi_2.Q_2 + \pi_3.Q_3)$ rather than as a true two level summation according to the formal syntax.) Of the monoidal laws, we are thus left with associativity of parallel composition, and commutativity of both summation and parallel composition. More formally:

Definition 3.2 The language of π-calculus expressions is required to conform to the congruences generated by the following equations

$$(Q_1 \mid Q_2) \mid Q_3 \equiv Q_1 \mid (Q_2 \mid Q_3)$$
$$Q_1 \mid Q_2 \equiv Q_2 \mid Q_1$$
$$\pi_1.Q_1 + \pi_2.Q_2 \equiv \pi_2.Q_2 + \pi_1.Q_1$$

The free channel names of π-calculus expressions in particular, will play an important part in the translation of [Section 5]. We give below the free and bound channel names for each of the syntactic constructs. (For the first case, we just give the binary variant to avoid clutter.)

Definition 3.2 The free and bound channel names of a π-calculus expression are given by recursion by the rules:

$$\text{Free}(x(y).Q_1 + \bar{z}w.Q_2) = \{x, z, w\} \cup (\text{Free}(Q_1) - \{y\}) \cup \text{Free}(Q_2)$$
$$\text{Free}(Q_1 \mid Q_2 \mid \ldots \mid Q_n) = \text{Free}(Q_1) \cup \text{Free}(Q_2) \cup \ldots \cup \text{Free}(Q_n)$$
$$\text{Free}(\nu x Q) = \text{Free}(Q) - \{x\}$$
$$\text{Free}(!Q) = \text{Free}(Q)$$
$$\text{Free}(\mathbf{0}) = \varnothing$$

$$\text{Bound}(x(y).Q_1 + \bar{z}w.Q_2) = \{y\} \cup \text{Bound}(Q_1) \cup \text{Bound}(Q_2)$$
$$\text{Bound}(Q_1 \mid Q_2 \mid \ldots \mid Q_n) = \text{Bound}(Q_1) \cup \text{Bound}(Q_2) \cup \ldots \cup \text{Bound}(Q_n)$$
$$\text{Bound}(\nu x Q) = \text{Bound}(Q) \cup \{x\}$$
$$\text{Bound}(!Q) = \text{Bound}(Q)$$
$$\text{Bound}(\mathbf{0}) = \varnothing$$

The above makes clear that the $x(y)$ in $x(y).Q$ and the νx in $\nu x Q$, are binders. We will need to regard the alpha-convertibility of bound variables as fundamental below, so we have the next definition.

Definition 3.3 The language of π-calculus expressions is required to conform to the congruence generated by alpha-convertibility

$$\Phi(x(y).Q) \equiv \Phi(x(y').Q\{y'/y\})$$
$$\Phi(\nu x Q) \equiv \Phi(\nu x' Q\{x'/x\})$$

where in the above, Φ is a π-calculus expression containing eg. $\nu x Q$ as a subexpression, x' and y' are some other names not free in Q, and eg. $Q\{x'/x\}$ refers to Q with all free occurrences of x substituted by x'. In general, when we exploit alpha-convertibility, we will typically assume x' and y' are fresh names not appearing anywhere else in the whole expression, rather than just not appearing free in Q.

We turn now to the dynamics of the π-calculus. For most of the time (until [Section 8] in fact), we will restrict our attention to the behaviour of closed systems.

Definition 3.4 A closed π-calculus system evolves using the replication rewrite rule

$$!P \to_{\mathrm{R}} P \mid !P$$

and the communication rewrite rule

$$(\ldots + x(y).P + \ldots) \mid (\ldots + \bar{x}z.Q + \ldots) \to_{\mathrm{C}} P\{z/y\} \mid Q$$

where in the RHS of the latter, $P\{z/y\}$ again refers to the substituted version of P.

The replication rule shows that rather than regarding replication as a syntactic congruence which is the usual approach in the π-calculus, we will regard the spawning of copies of a replicated subexpression as being done via an explicit rule within the dynamics of a π-calculus system. This is because the translation will also manufacture copies of (the translation of) a replicated subexpression by explicitly rewriting, and consequently the correctness proof will become more managable if we can pick out points in the dynamics of the original π-calculus expression at which replication was needed.

It is to be understood that both of the dynamic rules are applicable only "near the top level" of a π-calculus expression, which brings out an analogy with the Chemical Abstract Machine [Berry and Boudol (1990)]. The top level proviso may be stated in precise terms as follows.

Definition 3.5 The contexts within which the rules of π-calculus dynamics are applicable, are given by the additional rules

$$\frac{P \rightarrow_Y Q}{P \mid R \rightarrow_Y Q \mid R}$$

and

$$\frac{P \rightarrow_Y Q}{\nu x P \rightarrow_Y \nu x Q}$$

where above, $\rightarrow_Y$ stands for either of $\rightarrow_R$ and $\rightarrow_C$ (we will use this notation below where convenient).

Thus dynamic behaviour can only take place under parallel compositions and νx binders. As a result, a communication must be done either entirely inside, or entirely outside the scope of a νx binder. The reason for this is as follows. Consider the input and output subprocesses of a potential communication, $x(y).P$ and $\bar{x}z.Q$. If z is free in the whole expression, then the communication can go ahead, since then if x is bound in a νx binder, both processes will be in the scope of the νx, otherwise it doesn't matter. But if z is bound in a νz binder, then if the $x(y).P$ were to occur outside the scope of the νz, doing the communication would create via substitution an occurrence of z outside its scope, and and such a z would be a different name according to the conventions regarding bound variables. Therefore we canot allow bound names to escape their scopes in this manner and must forbid such communications. However this has the undesirable consequence of forbidding potential communications wherein the sender and recipient have a communication link in common, but the sender is prevented from sending his data because it would escape the scope that that happens to contain that data at the given moment.

The original description of the π-calculus in [Milner et al. (1992)] provided mechanisms to overcome this. We will take a simpler approach that allows us to simply enlarge the scope of a νz binder sufficiently, so that any communication link x over which z might be transmitted using a prefix $\bar{x}z$, has all corresponding input prefixes $x(y)$ which are visible near the top level, within the scope of the νz binder. More precisely we have the following.

Definition 3.6 The syntactic reduction $\Rrightarrow$ is defined as follows.

$$(\nu z Q_1 \mid Q_2 \mid \ldots \mid Q_n) \Rrightarrow \nu z'(Q_1\{z'/z\} \mid Q_2 \mid \ldots \mid Q_n)$$

Above, the $\nu z'$ and $\{z'/z\}$ refer to an alpha-conversion of the binder νz performed to avoid potential capture of free variables in the enlarged scope. We write $\Rrightarrow^+$ and $\Rrightarrow^*$ for the transitive and reflexive transistive closure of $\Rrightarrow$. The contexts in which $\Rrightarrow$ is allowed to apply are given once more by the rules in definition 3.5.

Lemma 3.7 The relation $\Rrightarrow^*$ is a simulation; i.e. if $P \Rrightarrow^* P'$ and $P \rightarrow_Y Q$, then there is a Q' with $Q \Rrightarrow^* Q'$ such that $P' \rightarrow_Y Q'$.

Proof. Immediate from definitions 3.5 and 3.6. ☺

The above result allows us to enlarge the scopes of νz binders until they permit all prospective communications to take place. We will regard the extended potential for communications that arises in this way as part of the operational semantics of a π-calculus expression.

Definition 3.8 Let $E = \Phi(\bar{x}z.P, x(y).Q)$ be a π-calculus expression such that $\bar{x}z.P$ and $x(y).Q$ are at top level, i.e. the syntactic constructs above $\bar{x}z.P$ and $x(y).Q$ in the parse tree of Φ consist of parallel compositions and restrictions. Then E is standard with respect to z, iff any νz binder (for the specific channel name z) in Φ, contains either both $\bar{x}z.P$ and $x(y).Q$, or neither of them, in its scope. E is in standard form iff it is standard with respect to all output prefix data channel names occurring at top level.

For practical purposes therefore, we will enhance the dynamics of π-calculus expressions to include conversion to standard form, by applying $\Rrightarrow^*$ after each $\rightarrow_Y$ step until all output prefix data channel names at top level eg. $\bar{x}z$ which occur within a νz binder, have all corresponding input prefixes eg. $x(y)$ included in the scope of the binder.

The following result will be useful later.

Lemma 3.9 Let $\Phi(\nu xP, Q)$ be a π-calculus expression (containing νxP and Q as subexpressions), and let

$$\Phi(\nu xP, Q) \Rrightarrow^* \Psi(\nu x'\Delta(P\{x'/x\}, Q))$$

i.e. the νx binder has been lifted till its scope has captured Q. Then the free and bound names of Q in both LHS and RHS of the above relation are the same, and such a name is free (resp. bound) in $\Phi(\nu xP, Q)$ iff it is free (resp. bound) in $\Psi(\nu x'\Delta(P\{x'/x\}, Q))$.

Proof. This is because the bound name in the νx binder will have been alpha-converted to x' precisely to ensure this. ☺

Remark 3.10 We point out that lemmas 3.7 and 3.9 remain true if we also include the clauses

$$(\pi_1.\nu zQ_1 + \pi_2.Q_2 + \ldots + \pi_n.Q_n) \Rrightarrow \nu z'(\pi_1.Q_1\{z'/z\} + \pi_2.Q_2 + \ldots + \pi_n.Q_n)$$
$$\nu x\nu yQ \Rrightarrow \nu y\nu xQ$$

in definition 3.6, but we will not need this fact subsequently.

We cannot however extend the lifting of νz binders arbitrarily. Eg. we note that νz binders cannot be lifted past replications. It is clear why: a replication rewrite of $!Q$ creates a copy of any νz-bound scope within Q, and any such copy will refer to its own distinct bound name (regardless of whether this bound name is called z, or alpha-converted). If the νz binder were floated above the !, then the references to z within these scopes would become references to a common name, free in all copies of Q, quite the opposite of what is intended.

Here is a small example of a π-calculus system and one possible evolution. It will provide a running example for the translation later on.

$$
\begin{aligned}
&x(u).u(t).\mathbf{0} \mid (\bar{x}v.\bar{v}s.\mathbf{0} + \bar{x}v.\mathbf{0}) \mid x(y).\mathbf{0} \\
&\quad \rightarrow_C \; v(t).\mathbf{0} \mid \bar{v}s.\mathbf{0} \mid x(y).\mathbf{0} \\
&\quad \rightarrow_C \; \mathbf{0} \mid \mathbf{0} \mid x(y).\mathbf{0}
\end{aligned}
$$

Readers may check that the same system may also evolve to $v(t).\mathbf{0} \mid \mathbf{0} \mid x(y).\mathbf{0}$ or to $x(u).u(t).\mathbf{0} \mid \bar{v}s.\mathbf{0} \mid \mathbf{0}$ or to $x(u).u(t).\mathbf{0} \mid \mathbf{0} \mid \mathbf{0}$.

We emphasise once more that we are dealing with closed π-calculus systems for the moment. This gives us a more easily comprehensible goal for translation. The original formulation of the π-calculus in [Milner et al. (1992)] was presented via a more finegrained transition system suited to the description of open systems (ones with external as well as internal communications), and featuring phenomena such as the opening, closing, and extrusion of the scopes of restriction operators. These latter permit the extension of our syntactic reduction $\Rrightarrow$ above to a congruence, and of our simulation $\Rrightarrow^*$ to a true bisimulation, and legitimise our use of $\Rrightarrow^*$ to enhance the communication capabilities of a π-calculus expression. Once we have the translation of closed systems under control, we will see that it is not hard to understand these more subtle mechanisms using the concepts that arise in the development of the translation. We will discuss this more fully in [Section 8], after we have presented the translation and proved it correct.

4 AN OVERVIEW OF THE TRANSLATION

The general idea of the translation is that π-calculus processes in an evolving system, are represented by active function nodes in a MONSTR execution graph, since in the MONSTR world such nodes represent independent loci of control in a computation. Therefore π-calculus processes which are potentially able to communicate by virtue of not being ancestrally guarded, correspond to active function nodes. Channels are represented by stateholder nodes, and all processes with an interest in a given channel share (i.e. have an out-arc to) the stateholder representing that channel. Two facts make this an appropriate representation strategy. Firstly, MONSTR nodes have fixed arities, so modelling the sharing of a channel by out-arcs from the channel to the community of processes that share it, would be awkward in view of the fact that this community changes as the system evolves; on the other hand, there is no such restriction on the in-arcs of a node. Secondly, the notion of arc redirection, having been designed as the natural directed-graph generalisation of substitution in the term world, is ideally suited to model the substitution operation that takes place when a pair of processes communicate.

Suppose then a pair of active processes P and Q share a channel chan, (we assume that the symbols P and Q encode the potential behaviours of the two processes), and P wishes to send a channel chan_out along chan, and Q wishes in turn to receive a channel along chan to bind to its channel chan_in. We represent this action as the term graph transformation in [Fig. 8].

Note that this achieves the substitution of chan_in by chan_out via the redirection chan_in := chan_out, the channel of communication chan playing an almost incidental role. P′ and Q′ represent the subsequent potential behaviours of P and Q. (We have assumed for the sake of argument that both P′ and Q′ retain an interest in both channels, though this needn't be the case.)

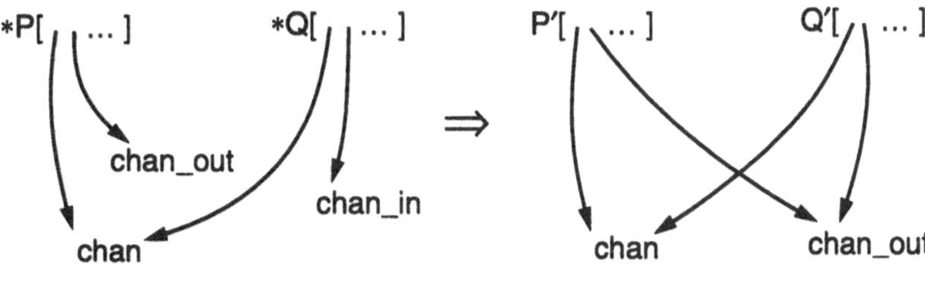

Fig. 8

One thing prevents us from turning this insight directly into a MONSTR rewrite rule, and that is that MONSTR forbids multi-rooted LHSs of rules — our left hand configuration above is double-rooted. The reason for this is purely to do with the efficiency of pattern matching of single-rooted LHSs of rules; they are operationally much easier to test for a successful match than multi-rooted ones. (Nevertheless, given that the formal notion of matching is that of graph homomorphism, there is no obstacle to multi-rooted-LHS rules as far as the abstract semantics of graph rewriting is concerned.) This has a number of consequences. Neither P nor Q can be assumed to know about the other in any rule that initiates communication. The best that they can do is to propose a communication via chan, and hope that a suitable partner process offers to cooperate.

At this point π-calculus semantics enters the fray. Offers of communication by individual processes must be rescindable, otherwise deadlock could occur if a cycle of processes were involved in making offers to others without any of them being reciprocated. Furthermore, the actions that constitute the playing out of the communication protocol for any representation of a π-calculus system must be equivalent to some serial shedule of atomic communication events in the original system.

The easiest way to ensure this is to impose a global synchronisation on the execution. A global semaphore, shared by all processes, is introduced, and processes accede to a mutex discipline in order to enter some offers of communication on some channel, or to rescind or cooperate with an offer already made. Such a protocol can easily be shown to have the correct serialisability properties. Expressing such a protocol in MONSTR is however quite expensive in terms of the number of rewrite rules needed. Further, the concurrency permitted by such a protocol is easily seen to be rather small, which is perhaps rather against the spirit of a formalism specifically designed to express concurrency. Instead, we prefer a much simpler, much more concurrent protocol, synchronised on a per-channel basis. It does however suffer from a busy waiting overhead, because each process proposing an offer to communicate over some channel is responsible for (nondeterministically) rescinding its own offer, since in the end, it may be the only process with an interest in that given channel.

Here is an outline of our preferred protocol. The states of a channel are represented by the three stateholder symbols Empty, Busy_Unlocked, and Busy_Locked. Empty means no reader has recorded an offer on this channel. Busy_Unlocked means that a reader has registered an offer on this channel. At this stage, either the offer may be rescinded by the original reader and the state of the channel reverts to Empty, or a writer completes a rendezvous with the reader, installing its data, and changing the state to

Busy_Locked. In the latter case it becomes the reader's responsibility to extract the data and bind it to the input channel, and to reset the channel state to Empty.

The behaviour of a process $P = (\ldots + chan(chan\_in).Q + \ldots)$ is represented by a collection of rules, one for each summand. The rule for the summand displayed, records a decision, made nondeterministically, for P to attempt to communicate via *chan*, and when successful to evolve to Q. The node for P rewrites to P_Q and spawns a helper process Help_r[chan chan_in] to manage the protocol. If the attempt is unsuccessful, P_Q backtracks to P once more.

5 THE TRANSLATION IN DETAIL

The translation of a π-calculus expression proceeds in a bottom up fashion. First of all we label all nodes of the parse tree of the expression with new (process) names; we do this by introducing a pair of squiggly brackets round each possible subexpression, and labelling each pair with the new name. For example $Q_1 \mid Q_2 \mid \ldots \mid Q_n$ becomes $\{Q_1 \mid Q_2 \mid \ldots \mid Q_n\}_P$ and $\nu x Q$ becomes $\{\nu x Q\}_P$. For later convenience, we permit identical or alpha-convertible subexpressions to be identically labelled provided that all their own corresponding identical or alpha-convertible subexpressions are also identically labelled, but we do not insist on this. Generally at the meta level we will use P for the name of the subexpression and Q, Q_i etc. for the names of the immediate subcomponents. The names are available to serve both as meta-names for the subexpressions themselves and as names for the MONSTR function symbols that encode the behaviour of the relevant subprocess.

Secondly, we will translate each process subexpression P to a pair. The second component of each pair is a set of MONSTR rules for the function symbol **P** that encodes the behaviour of P. The first component of the pair is a mapping $Args_P : \mathrm{Free}(P) \rightarrow \mathbf{args_P}$ from the free channel names of P as given in [Section 3], to the arguments $\mathbf{args_P}$ of the corresponding MONSTR function symbol. Strictly speaking, this is a map from free channel names to positive integers (argument positions); but in the context of a rule, an $\mathbf{args_P}$ sequence will always be a sequence of node identifiers. Equalities between the channel node identifiers occuring in the codomains of $Args$ maps for symbols on the left and right sides of rules, shows how channels migrate through the execution of a MONSTR representation of a π-calculus system.

As in all rule systems, from the rewriting viewpoint, all occurrences of node identifiers in MONSTR rules are bound; they are templates for nodes of execution graphs that are either located during pattern matching, or instantiated during the contractum building phase of the rewrite. As such their identity is fluid in that they can be renamed (alpha-converted) to avoid node identifier clashes. Therefore when we speak of $\mathbf{args_P}$ etc. below, we assume it contains a sequence of distinct node identifiers, all different from any node identifiers that might arise from the translation of channel identifiers occurring visibly in a π-calculus subexpression, eg. x in $\nu x Q$; such explicit channel identifiers are translated "by font change". A consequence of the latter is that we assume that all bound variables occurring in the π-calculus expression that we are translating have been renamed apart from each other and apart from any free names in the expression. This forestalls the need to actually invoke alpha-conversion in the translation. Note that since all occurrences of node identifiers in rules are bound, the relationship between occurrences of node identifiers in $\mathbf{args_P}$ and $\mathbf{args_Q}$ lists in a rule needs to be consistent only on a per-rule basis. Note also that the bound names of the π-calculus do not occur as such in the translation. Only their free instances get translated. This is in line with our comments in the introduction on the absence of scope and binding mechanisms in (the syntax of) graph rewriting. We will make suitable remarks as we go.

Lastly, if the π-calculus expression is to be treated as a module to be combined with others at some future stage, the output of the translation is the set of rules generated, together with the $Args_P$ map for the top level function symbol. If the expression is to stand for a self contained system, the output is the set of generated rules together with a rule for **`Initial`** which instantiates the free channels of the top level function.

The Translation Body

Here is the translation, easiest cases first. We recall that all channels have been suitably renamed apart. The separate cases below generate rules for various MONSTR function symbols, but do not give much of a clue as to what rule selection strategy is to be employed. It is a property of the rules we generate here that all normal (i.e. non-default) rules have non-overlapping patterns. The appropriate rule selection strategy is therefore: "Given an active function node, attempt to match a normal rule; if no normal rule matches, match a default rule". We therefore omit the rule separators **|** and **;** from the text of the translation.

$\{\mathbf{0}\}_P$: Free(P) = ∅ ; $Args_P$ = ∅ ; Rules(P) ≡ { `P => *Root` }

$\{\nu x Q\}_P$: Free(P) = Free(Q) – $\{x\}$;

If $x \notin$ Free(Q) then Set $Args_P = Args_Q$ and $\mathbf{args}_P = \mathbf{args}_Q$;

Rules(P) ≡ { `P[args`$_P$`] => *Q[args`$_Q$`]` }

else ($x \in$ Free(Q)) then assume for simplicity that **x** occurs last in $\mathbf{args}_Q$;

Set $Args_P = Args_Q |_{\text{Free}(P)}$ and $\mathbf{args}_P$ =

all_except_the_last_of($\mathbf{args}_Q$) ;

Rules(P) ≡ { `P[args`$_P$`] => *Q[args`$_P$` x:Empty]` }

Note that there is no trace of x in `P[...]`. Only when **P** evolves to **Q** is **x** created as a fresh **`Empty`** stateholder.

$\{!Q\}_P$: Free(P) = Free(Q) ; Set $Args_P = Args_Q$ and $\mathbf{args}_P = \mathbf{args}_Q$;

Rules(P) ≡ { `P[args`$_P$`] => *Q[args`$_Q$`],*P[args`$_P$`]` }

Note that since $\mathbf{args}_P = \mathbf{args}_Q$, all the correct channels are shared by **P** and **Q** on the RHS.

$\{Q_1 \mid Q_2 \mid \ldots \mid Q_n\}_P$: Free(P) = $\bigcup_{i \in [1 \ldots n]}$ Free(Q_i) ;

Let $blend_P$ be a function that merges a set of sequences into a single sequence without repetitions (so providing an implementation of set union). Set

$\mathbf{args}_P = blend_P(\mathbf{args}_{Q_1}, \mathbf{args}_{Q_2}, \ldots, \mathbf{args}_{Q_n})$;

$\forall i \bullet \forall d \in$ Free(Q_i) $\bullet$ $Args_P(d) = Args_{Q_i}(d)$;

Rules(P) ≡ { `P[args`$_P$`] =>`

`*Q`$_1$`[args`$_{Q_1}$`],*Q`$_2$`[args`$_{Q_2}$`],...,*Q`$_n$`[args`$_{Q_n}$`]` }

$\{\Sigma_{i\in[1...n]}\, x_i(u_i).Q_i^R + \Sigma_{j\in[1...m]}\, \bar{z}_j w_j.Q_j^W\}_P$:

$$\mathrm{Free}(P) = \{x_1,\ldots, x_n, z_1,\ldots, z_m, w_1,\ldots, w_m\}$$
$$\cup \bigcup_{i\in[1...n]} (\mathrm{Free}(Q_i^R) - \{u_i\}) \cup \bigcup_{j\in[1...m]} \mathrm{Free}(Q_j^W) \;;$$

Assume a $blend_P$ function as above. Set

$$\mathbf{args}_P = blend_P\,([x_1,\ldots, x_n, z_1,\ldots, z_m, w_1,\ldots, w_m],\; \mathbf{args}_{Q_1^R},\ldots, \mathbf{args}_{Q_n^R}, \mathbf{args}_{Q_1^W},\ldots, \mathbf{args}_{Q_m^W}) \;;$$

and

$$\forall i \bullet \forall d \in \mathrm{Free}(Q_i^R) - \{u_i\} \bullet Args_P(d) = Args_{Q_i^R}(d) \;;$$

$$\forall j \bullet \forall d \in \mathrm{Free}(Q_j^W) \bullet Args_P(d) = Args_{Q_j^W}(d) \;;$$

Rules(P) is given by firstly $\bigcup_{i\in[1...n]}$ of

```
P[argsP] => #P_Q_i^R [^*Help_r[x_i u_i] argsP
      u_i:Empty]
P_Q_i^R [Yes argsP u_i] => *Q_i^R [args_Q_i^R]
```

(note that if $u_i \in \mathrm{Free}(Q_i^R)$ then $\mathbf{u}_i$ occurs in $\mathbf{args}_{Q_i^R}$)

```
P_Q_i^R [No argsP u_i] => *P[argsP]
P_Q_i^R [a argsP u_i] => *P_Q_i^R [a argsP u_i]
```

and secondly $\bigcup_{j\in[1...m]}$ of

```
P[argsP] => #P_Q_j^W [^*Help_w[z_j w_j] argsP]
P_Q_j^W [Yes argsP] => *Q_j^W [args_Q_j^W]
P_Q_j^W [No argsP] => *P[argsP]
P_Q_j^W [a argsP] => *P_Q_j^W [a argsP]
```

The above constitutes the body of the translation. This must be supplemented by the communication protocol rules described below. To make a component module of a larger system, on the assumption that T is the top level symbol labelling the outermost construct of the original π-calculus expression E, the accumulated set of rules (with the selection strategy mentioned above) is combined with the map $Args_T : \mathrm{Free}(T) \to \mathbf{args}_T$ to form the output of translation called $\mathrm{Tr}^-(E)$. The latter holds the information on how arguments of **T** correspond to the free channels of the module, which is needed for interfacing to other modules. To form a stand alone system, we needn't retain $Args_T$, but we need to form an initial rule. If $\mathbf{args}_T$ has k entries, this rule is

```
Initial => *T[u_1:Empty,...,u_k:Empty]
```

which simply instantiates the top level free channels and sets the system in motion. To prevent confusion, we call this version of the output of translation Tr(E).

Like many translations, the one above is prone to some inefficiencies. Some of the translation steps do not do very much. Nevertheless, it is simple enough to be reasonably transparent for pedagogical purposes. The reader who has grasped the structure of the translation above would have no difficulty in altering it so that it translated a more meaty chunk of syntax such as

$$\{\nu x_1,\ldots, x_n(\Sigma\, \pi_{i_1}.Q_{i_1} \mid \Sigma\, \pi_{i_2}.Q_{i_2} \mid \ldots \mid \Sigma\, \pi_{i_m}.Q_{i_m})\}_P$$

all in one go, saving on both rules and rewrites.

The Communication Protocol

To effect a communication, the helper functions Help_r[x u] and Help_w[z w] must actually make contact and transfer data. A collection of rules is needed to handle various aspects of the protocol. Unlike the body rules above which were mainly default rules as all they had to do was to manage the plumbing, the rules below do a fair amount of pattern matching. The default rules for the symbols in question are forced by the definition of MONSTR and are mainly superfluous. Again the normal rules have non-overlapping patterns (with the exception of `Help_r_test_chan` which has two overlapping rules that implement a nondeterministic busy wait), and so the strategy for rule selection in the complete system is once again "(nondeterministically) select a normal rule if one will match, otherwise a default rule". The rules are numbered for future reference.

Rules for read helper.

`Help_r` initiates an offer; no offers in progress. [1]

```
Help_r[chan:Empty chan_in]
 => *Help_r_test_chan[chan':Busy_Unlocked chan_in],
     chan := chan'
```

`Help_r` default rule; backs off. [2]

```
Help_r[chan chan_in]
 => *No
```

Rules for write helper.

`Help_w` sees a channel containing an offer; starts a rendezvous. Below, this rule will be known as the communication commit rule (or just commit rule); rewrites using this rule will be called commit rewrites. [3]

```
Help_w[chan:Busy_Unlocked chan_out]
 => *Yes , chan := chan':Busy_Locked[chan_out]
```

`Help_w` default rule. [4]

```
Help_w[chan chan_out]
 => *No
```

Rules for `Help_r_test_chan`.

`Help_r_test_chan` waits a bit longer. [5]

```
Help_r_test_chan[chan:Busy_Unlocked chan_in]
 => *Help_r_test_chan[chan chan_in]
```

`Help_r_test_chan` revokes its own offer. [6]

```
Help_r_test_chan[chan:Busy_Unlocked chan_in]
 => *No , chan := chan':Empty
```

`Help_r_test_chan` detects a rendezvous. [7]

```
Help_r_test_chan[chan:Busy_Locked[data] chan_in]
 => *Help_r_assign_data[chan data chan_in]
```

`Help_r_test_chan` default rule. [8]

```
Help_r_test_chan[chan chan_in]
 => *Help_r_test_chan[chan chan_in]
```

Rules for `Help_r_assign_data`.

`Help_r_assign_data` assigns data and prepares to unlock `chan`. [9]

```
Help_r_assign_data[chan data chan_in:Empty]
 => *Help_r_unlock[chan] , chan_in := data
```

`Help_r_assign_data` default rule. [10]

```
Help_r_assign_data[chan data chan_in]
 => *Help_r_assign_data[chan data chan_in]
```

Rules for `Help_r_unlock`.

`Help_r_unlock` unlocks chan and resets protocol. [11]

```
Help_r_unlock[chan:Busy_Locked[data]]
 => *Yes , chan := chan':Empty
```

`Help_r_unlock` default rule. [12]

```
Help_r_unlock[chan]
 => *Help_r_unlock[chan]
```

It is clear from the above structure that the protocol offered is by no means the only one that will do the job. It just seems to us to be the simplest one that makes the points that we wish to make. From the relatively straightforward way in which the protocol rules interface to the body rules, it is obvious that a more hard-nosed protocol could be substituted for ours, if for example one wished to avoid the penalty of busy waiting, (as exemplified by rule [5] for `Help_r_test_chan`). However each such protocol poses its own challenge where correctness is concerned. See below.

An Example

Let us see what our translation scheme does to the small π-calculus example we discussed in [Section 3]. Here it is again in fully bracketed form.

$$\{\ \{x(u).\{u(t).\{\mathbf{0}\}_Z\}_U\}_{X1} \mid \{\bar{x}v.\{\bar{v}s.\{\mathbf{0}\}_Z\}_V + \bar{x}v.\{\mathbf{0}\}_Z\}_S \mid \{x(y).\{\mathbf{0}\}_Z\}_{X4}\ \}_T$$

When translated, as well as the protocol rules, the following rules would be generated. For variety, we write them out with rule separators, but emphasise that these merely embody the rule selection strategy mentioned above.

```
Z => *Root                                              ;

U[u] => #U_Z[^*Help_r[u t] u t:Empty]                   ;

U_Z[Yes u t] => *Z                                      |
U_Z[No u t] => *U[u]                                    ;
U_Z[a u t] => *U_Z[a u t]                               ;

X1[x] => #X1_U[^*Help_r[x u] x u:Empty]                 ;

X1_U[Yes x u] => *U[u]                                  |
X1_U[No x u] => *X1[x]                                  ;
X1_U[a x u] => *X1_U[a x u]                             ;

X4[x] => #X4_Z[^*Help_r[x y] x y:Empty]                 ;

X4_Z[Yes x y] => *Z                                     |
X4_Z[No x y] => *X4[x]                                  ;
X4_Z[a x y] => *X4_Z[a x y]                             ;

V[v s] => #V_Z[^*Help_w[v s] v s]                       ;

V_Z[Yes v s] => *Z                                      |
V_Z[No v s] => *V[v s]                                  ;
V_Z[a v s] => *V_Z[a v s]                               ;

S[x v s] => #S_V[^*Help_w[x v] x v s]                   |
S[x v s] => #S_Z[^*Help_w[x v] x v s]                   ;

S_V[Yes x v s] => *V[v s]                               |
S_V[No x v s] => *S[x v s]                              ;
S_V[a x v s] => *S_V[a x v s]                           ;

S_Z[Yes x v s] => *Z                                    |
S_Z[No x v s] => *S[x v s]                              ;
S_Z[a x v s] => *S_Z[a x v s]                           ;

T[x v s] => *X1[x] , *S[x v s] , *X4[x]                 ;

Initial => *T[x:Empty v:Empty s:Empty]                  ;
```

In [Fig. 9] below we give a picture of the execution graph just after the system has been set in motion; and in [Fig. 10] we show the execution graph just after the first successful data transfer by process S which has synchronised with process X1.

6 PROPERTIES OF TRANSLATED SYSTEMS

In this section we state a number of definitions and establish a number of mostly easy lemmas, which enable us to speak more incisively about the structure of execution graphs of translated systems, and about the transitions between them effected by the rules we have proposed. We assume henceforth that we are dealing with complete systems, i.e. given a π-calculus expression E, the translation of E is Tr(E), which contains a suitable rule for Initial.

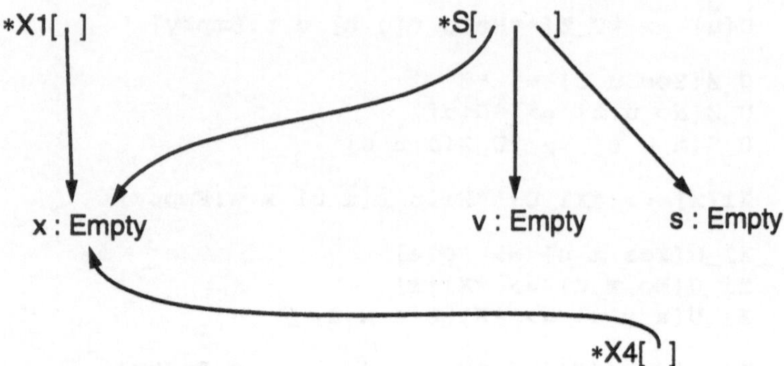

Fig. 9

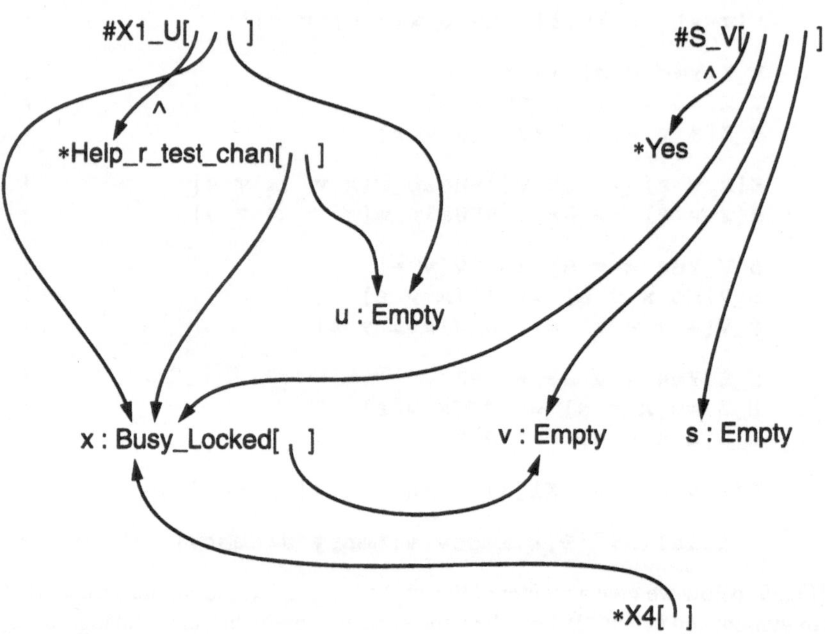

Fig. 10

Definition 6.1 A function symbol F arising from the translation of a construct C will be called a

- proposer function symbol if C is $\{\Sigma_i\, \pi_i.Q_i\}_P$ and F is P,
- proposer-intermediate function symbol if P is a proposer symbol and F is $\mathsf{P\_Q}_i$ for some summand Q_i of $\{\Sigma_i\, \pi_i.Q_i\}_P$,

* auxiliary function symbol if C is $\{\mathbf{0}\}_P$, $\{\nu x Q\}_P$, or $\{Q_1 \mid Q_2 \mid \ldots \mid Q_n\}_P$ and F is P; and more specifically, P is called a zero symbol, ν symbol, or composition symbol respectively,
* replication function symbol if C is $\{!Q\}_P$ and F is P,
* initial function symbol if F is Initial,
* protocol function symbol if F is one of the functions defined in the communication protocol section of the translation, i.e. Help_r, Help_w, Help_r_test_chan etc.

Definition 6.2 The stateholder symbols Empty, Busy_Unlocked, and Busy_Locked will be called channel symbols.

Lemma 6.3 Let E be a π-calculus expression, and Tr(E) its translation. Then the live part of every execution graph of Tr(E) has the following properties.

(1) Each non-protocol function node and each Root constructor has no parent.

(2) Each function node is active unless it is a proposer-intermediate node in which case it is either active or suspended.

(3) Each protocol function node has a unique parent which is a suspended proposer-intermediate node. Each active Yes or No constructor node has a unique parent which is a suspended proposer-intermediate node, and each idle Yes or No constructor node has a unique parent which is an active proposer-intermediate node.

(4) Each function node has only channel nodes as children, except for proposer-intermediate nodes, which in addition have as a child either a protocol function node, or a Yes, or a No constructor.

(5) Each protocol function node has only channel nodes as children, either two or three of them according to arity.

(6) Each channel node is an idle Empty, Busy_Unlocked, or Busy_Locked[data], where data is another channel node.

Proof. We proceed by induction on the structure of executions. The initial graph obviously satisfies the properties. For the induction step suppose all execution graphs up to G_i in some execution have the properties. Then G_{i+1} is given by either a notification or a rewrite.

For a notification, it is easy to see that all the properties are preserved as the only possible notifications in an execution are from Root constructors which by induction hypothesis (1) for G_i notify nobody, and from Yes and No constructors which by induction hypothesis (3) for G_i notify their unique suspended proposer-intermediate node parent. (All stateholders are always idle by induction hypothesis (6) for G_i so never notify.)

For a rewrite there are a large number of cases to check, six for each rule type in the translation. Fortunately all of them are easy and we briefly examine one example rule and leave the diligent or skeptical reader to check as many others as he wishes. Consider a rule of the form

```
Help_r_test_chan[chan:Busy_Locked[data] chan_in]
  => *Help_r_assign_data[chan data chan_in]
```

By hypothesis (6) for G_i, **data** and **chan_in** are (matched in G_i to) idle channel nodes. Therefore the creation of a *Help_r_assign_data[chan data chan_in] node as specified in the rule, creates a new protocol function node satisfying (4). The other conditions are equally easy. ☺

Definition 6.4 Let D be a MONSTR rule, and p a node of the left pattern. We say that p is rewritten to q if

* D specifies a redirection (p, q), or
* p is the root of the left pattern of D and q is a contractum node.

We also say that p is rewritten to q to refer to the fact that there is a graph X, a match h of the left pattern of some rule D to X, and a rewrite governed by D with result graph Y and either

* D specifies a redirection (u, w), and $h(u) = p$ in X is redirected to $r_{X,Y}(h(u)) = q$ in Y where $r_{X,Y}$ is the redirection function from [Section 2], or
* u is the root of the left pattern of D, w is a contractum node, $h(u) = p$ is the root of the redex in X, and $i_{X',Y}(h'(w)) = q$ is w's copy in Y where $i_{X',Y}$ (the composition $i_{X'',Y} \circ i_{X',X''}$), is the injection function from [Section 2].

The use of the same phraseology to refer to both syntactic and semantic phenomena as legitimised in definition 6.4 avoids excruciating circumlocutions in the discussion below, without losing the reader's conviction that we are telling the truth. Further, we will say that p is rewritten to q when (in the semantic sense) the reflexive transitive closure of the above phenomena is intended, i.e. there is a sequence of zero or more rewrites of X to $X1$ to $X2$ ... to Y such that p in X is (in the preceding sense) rewritten to $p1$ in $X1$, which is rewritten to $p2$ in $X2$, ... , which is rewritten to q in Y. Where necessary, we will allow rewrites which do not pattern match any of the p ... , and also notifications, to interrupt the rewriting sequence $[X \dots Y]$.

Lemma 6.5 Let E be a π-calculus expression, and Tr(E) its translation. Let P be an initial, auxiliary or replication function symbol of Tr(E) and let p:P[...] be a node of an execution graph X. Then p can be rewritten to a collection of nodes which are active proposer function nodes, active replication nodes, and idle Root constructors.

Proof. Since P is a function symbol of Tr(E), it arises from a labelled subexpression of E, $\{\dots\}_P$ say. Consider the parse tree of $\{\dots\}_P$. Each node of the tree with its children corresponds to a syntactic construct of the π-calculus, and each leaf corresponds to a zero; each of these having corresponding rules (call them $\{\}_P$-rules) in Tr(E). Consider an execution graph Y formed from X by: (a), allowing p to be rewritten using $\{\}_P$-rules corresponding to Initial, |, v, and **0** as long as there are redexes for such rules; (b) performing all notifications of active Root constructors; (c), allowing a finite number of uses of $\{\}_P$-rules corresponding to replication and applying (a) and (b) to any non-replication nodes generated thereby. Since the parse tree is finite, a finite amount of work is involved. Then Y has the property claimed. ☺

Definition 6.6 The protocol function symbols Help_r_test_chan, Help_r_assign_-data, Help_r_unlock will be called protagonist symbols. All other function symbols will be called non-protagonist symbols. A channel node c is said to be in the chan position of a protocol function node p in a graph X if there is an arc (p_1, c) in X, i.e. c occurs in the position matched to **chan** in rules for $\sigma(p)$. In this case p is called a chan position parent of c.

Lemma 6.7 Let E be a π-calculus expression, and Tr(E) its translation. Then

(I) Every channel node in every execution graph of Tr(E) is in one of the following states.

(α) Empty, and all its chan position parents are non-protagonists.

(β) Busy_Unlocked, with exactly one Help_r_test_chan chan position protagonist parent and zero or more other chan position non-protagonist parents,

(γ1) Busy_Locked[data] with exactly one Help_r_test_chan chan position protagonist parent and zero or more other chan position non-protagonist parents,

(γ2) Busy_Locked[data] with exactly one Help_r_assign_data chan position protagonist parent and zero or more other chan position non-protagonist parents,

(γ3) Busy_Locked[data] with exactly one Help_r_unlock chan position protagonist parent and zero or more other chan position non-protagonist parents.

(II) The state changing transitions for a channel node c in chan position in an execution graph are the following (where the reference numbers of the rules used are noted).

(α) → (β) when c is rewritten by a Help_r chan position parent, [1]

(β) → (α) when c is rewritten by a Help_r_test_chan chan position parent, [6]

(β) → (γ1) when c is rewritten by a Help_w chan position parent, [3]

(γ1) → (γ2) when c is matched by a Help_r_test_chan chan position parent, [7]

(γ2) → (γ3) when c is matched by a Help_r_assign_data chan position parent, [9]

(γ3) → (α) when c is rewritten by a Help_r_unlock chan position parent. [11]

(III) The non state changing transitions for a channel node c in chan position in an execution graph are the following (again including rule numbers).

(α) → (α) when c is matched by a Help_w chan position parent, [4]

(β) → (β) when c is matched by either a Help_r, or a Help_r_test_chan chan position parent, [2, 5]

(*) → (*) when c is matched by either a Help_r or a Help_w chan position parent, where (*) is any of (γ1), (γ2), (γ3), [2, 4]

(*) → (*) when c is matched by any non protocol chan position function parent, where (*) is any of (α), (β), (γ1), (γ2), (γ3).

Proof. Again by induction on the structure of executions. In fact we need to strengthen the induction hypothesis by adding a number of clauses. Rather than present them all at once, we will introduce them only as needed in discussing features of the proof.

The base case is trivial, as is the inductive step for notifications. For rewrites, we need to merely check that the rewrite rules which match in chan position indeed implement the required behaviour. This has two aspects. Firstly that the normal protocol rewrite rules effect the transitions stated; and secondly that any transitions in principle permitted by the rules but unstated above, do not in fact take place. The latter transitions are the ones determined by the default rules for Help_r_test_chan, Help_r_assign_data, and Help_r_unlock, as an inspection of the rules used in parts (II) and (III) shows.

To show that these rules are never used, it is sufficient to strengthen the induction hypothesis to assert that

(IV) (a) the chan position child of every Help_r_test_chan function node is a Busy_Unlocked channel node or a Busy_Locked[data] channel node,

(b) that the third (`chan_in`) child of every Help_r_assign_data function node is an Empty channel node,

(c) the chan position child of every Help_r_unlock function node is a Busy_Locked[data] channel node,

since then Help_r_test_chan, Help_r_assign_data, and Help_r_unlock will always be able to match a normal rule.

To prove (IV).(b), the only part that doesn't follow from a trivial inspection of the rules, we need to strengthen the induction hypothesis yet further to assert that

(V) (a) a read proposal initiated by a proposer node rewriting to a proposer-intermediate node, instantiates the input node as a new Empty channel node whose only parents are the suspended proposer-intermediate node and the corresponding read helper,

(b) a read helper that matches an Empty chan position channel, passes its Empty input node to Help_r_test_chan (in second position), whereupon the Empty input node's only live parents are the suspended proposer-intermediate node and the Help_r_test_chan node,

(c) a Help_r_test_chan that detects a rendezvous, passes its Empty input node to Help_r_assign_data (in third position), whereupon the Empty input node's only live parents are the suspended proposer-intermediate node and the Help_r_assign_data node.

It is easy to see that (V).(a) ⇒ (V).(b) ⇒ (V).(c) ⇒ (IV).(b).

Checking the induction step for rewrites involves showing that the various rules used, preserve the properties of states claimed in part (I), and implement the various transitions described in the remaining parts. Essentially there are two sorts of deductions.

Firstly, if a rule rewrites its chan position node c then it first matches it explicitly, and in such cases it is a feature of the protocol rewrite rules that all redirections of nodes in chan position by protocol functions are also to explicit nodes of the rule, which makes the behaviour immediately evident.

Otherwise the rule just matches c without redirection. This possibility has two cases, the Help_r_test_chan function which implements (γ1) → (γ2) by inspection, and the Help_r_assign_data function which implements (γ2) → (γ3). For the latter we need a final strengthening of the induction hypothesis to assert that

(VI) the chan position child of every Help_r_assign_data function node is a Busy_ Locked[data] channel node,

which is immediate given the form of rule [7] for Help_r_ test_chan.

With the full induction hypothesis laid bare, the induction step for rewrites is mostly trivial, consisting of a large number of rather elementary cases. All that is required is a simple inspection of the information available in the rules, modulo the properties of the set of chan position parents of channel nodes in various states; all subtler properties needed are captured in the various clauses above. We omit the tedious details. ☺

As a corollary to lemma 6.7, we have shown that the communication protocol does not deadlock assuming that every active function node will rewrite eventually, a property that we will formalise as weak fairness in [Section 7]. Part (II) of lemma 6.7 is summarised in the transition diagram of [Fig. 11] below.

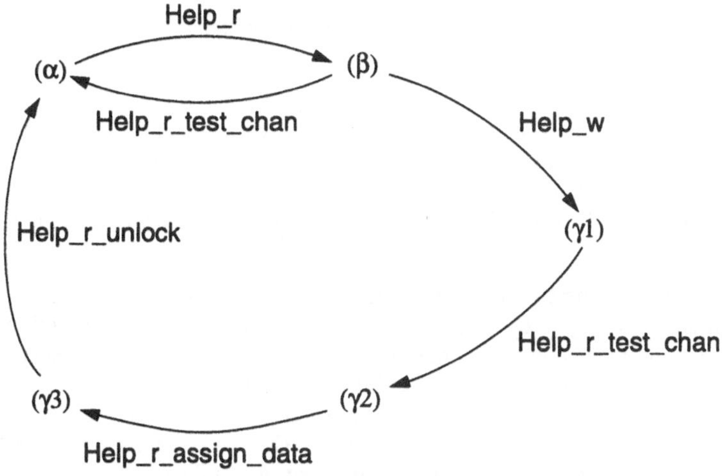

Fig. 11

The final topic we need to consider in this section concerns some subcommutativity lemmas which allow us to permute rewriting steps under suitable circumstances. In the following, for technical simplicity, we assume that we rewrite without removing garbage, so that the injection and redirection functions *i* and *r* are total.

Lemma 6.8 In a MONSTR execution sequence, two adjacent notification steps may be interchanged.

Lemma 6.9 In a MONSTR execution sequence, a notification step adjacent to a rewrite may be interchanged with it.

Given that notifications merely make the notifying constructor or stateholder idle, and alter the non-idle markings on some other nodes and arcs, we regard the above two results as sufficiently obvious to allow us to both omit their proofs and even be a bit vague in their statement. We are rather more careful about the next lemma, which incidentally provides a guide round which lemmas 6.8 and 6.9 may be rephrased more accurately.

Lemma 6.10 Let E be a π-calculus expression, and Tr(E) its translation. Let G be an execution graph of Tr(E). For $i = 1, 2$, let $D_i = (P_i, root_i, Red_i, Act_i)$ be two rules of Tr(E) with left subpatterns L_i, and let $g_i : L_i \to G$ be two redexes. Suppose that $g_1(root_1) \neq g_2(root_2)$, and that if s_i is an explicit stateholder of L_i, then $g_1(s_1) \neq g_2(s_2)$. Let H_i be the graph obtained by rewriting $g_i : L_i \to G$ and let r_{G,H_i} be the corresponding redirection function. For either choice of i, let j denote the alternative choice. Then

(1) D_j has a redex $h_i : L_j \to H_i$ in H_i given by

$$h_i = r_{G,H_i} \circ g_j$$

(2) Let K_i be the graph obtained by rewriting h_i and let r_{H_i,K_i} be the respective redirection functions. Then there is an isomorphism $\theta : K_1 \to K_2$ and for all $x \in G$,

$$\theta(r_{H_1,K_1} \circ r_{G,H_1}(x)) = r_{H_2,K_2} \circ r_{G,H_2}(x)$$

(3) Restricted to Live(K_1), θ provides an isomorphism

$$\theta : \text{Live}(K_1) \to \text{Live}(K_2)$$

Proof. Assume that both L_1 and L_2 explicitly match a stateholder; otherwise we just have a simplified form of what follows. So $g_1(root_1)$, $g_2(root_2)$, $g_1(s_1)$, $g_2(s_2)$ are all distinct nodes of G. Consequently, the arcs of G partition into five classes: those with heads at $g_1(root_1)$, at $g_2(root_2)$, $g_1(s_1)$, $g_2(s_2)$, and fifthly those with head at some other node.

Suppose g_1 rewrites first. Contractum building, forming G_1' does not alter any arc from $g_2(root_2)$ so $i_{G,G_1'} \circ g_2 : L_2 \to G_1'$ is a redex for D_2. Likewise redirection, forming G_1'' does not alter (the copy in G_1' of) the arc $(g_2(root_2)_{m2}, g_2(s_2))$ between the root and single explicitly matched stateholder child of the redex $i_{G,G_1'} \circ g_2$. Other arcs of this redex may be affected by the redirection but since they are all implicitly matched, this does no harm and so $r_{G_1',G_1''} \circ i_{G,G_1'} \circ g_2 : L_2 \to G_1''$ is a redex for D_2. Finally, the activation phase, forming H_1 merely makes the root of g_1 idle, so

$$r_{G_1'',H_1} \circ r_{G_1',G_1''} \circ i_{G,G_1'} \circ g_2 = r_{G,H_1} \circ g_2 \ : L_2 \to H_1$$

is a redex for D_2 and by symmetry we get (1).

To get (2) we note that the contractum building phases of both rewrites independently add copies of contractum nodes of P_i to the execution graph. Since we are refraining from garbage collection, we immediately infer the existence of a node bijection $\theta : K_1 \to K_2$. This obviously extends to a bijection on tails of arcs, and to show that θ extends to a graph isomorphism, we need to examine the effects of the various redirections on the heads of arcs. This is because the remaining phases, the activation phases, are easily seen to be independent of each other and of the rest of the rewriting phases.

As before, arcs partition into those with heads at (a): $g_1(root_1)$, (b): $g_2(root_2)$, (c): $g_1(s_1)$, (d): $g_2(s_2)$, and (e): none of the preceding. We extend θ to the various sets of arcs as follows.

Obviously if a node is not redirected, one can make it the head of an additional collection of arcs by adding these arcs in any order, so θ extends to arcs in (e) immediately. From the form of Tr(E) rules and from lemma 6.3.(1) and 6.3.(3), nodes in (a) and (b) either have no parent or have a unique one, so do not acquire any new parents via contractum building, and independently get redirected to contractum nodes. So θ easily extends to arcs in (a) and (b). This leaves the arcs in (c) and (d).

Now by inspection of the rules in Tr(E), all non-root redirections are of channel nodes to fresh (contractum) channel nodes, apart from in the normal rule [9] for Help_r_assign_data. So if neither D_1 nor D_2 is rule [9], then we can interchange the the order of rewriting with impunity as contractum building and redirection are independent for the two rewrites. If both D_1 and D_2 are this rule, then since s_1 and s_2 are both the matched input nodes of this rule, by clause (V).(c) in the proof of lemma 6.7, neither of them is accessible from the other redex, so neither **data** argument matches s_1 or s_2 and the rewrites may again be swapped.

If say D_1 is rule [9] and D_2 is not, if D_1's **data** argument does not match s_2, then we can obviously swap the rewrites as before. If D_1's **data** argument does match s_2, then if D_1 is done first, we find that the arcs in (c) get redirected to s_2, (from the form of D_1 it is clear that no new arcs are added to (c) during contractum building); and then they and all arcs in (d) (both arcs existing in H_1 and any new ones added during contractum building) get redirected to z_2, the redirection target of s_2. Otherwise the D_2 rewrite is done first, and redirects the arcs in (d) to z_2 (these are arcs existing in H_2, any new ones added during contractum building, and including any arc(s) of the D_1 redex that matched the **data** argument of Help_r_assign_data). The D_1 redex, now $r_{G,H_2} \circ g_1$, redirects the arcs in (c) to z_2 directly. A symmetric argument works if D_2 is rule [9], so the results of either rewriting sequence are equivalent and $\theta : K_1 \rightarrow K_2$ extends to a graph isomorphism as claimed.

To conclude that θ restricts to an isomorphism on live parts, we note that θ preserves graph structure and node symbols, but particularly that it also preserves node and arc markings. Therefore the rules of inference in definition [2.12.(1) – (4)] are invariant under θ, and a proof of liveness of a node or arc in K_1 will map by induction into a proof of liveness of a node or arc in K_2, and vice versa. Likewise for garbage. This gives us (3). ☺

In the above, we have indicated that we can interchange the order of rewriting given some mild conditions. Essentially the same result holds true for quite arbitrary MONSTR systems, though we have to take note of non-trivial activations and dynamic suspensions. However in general, we do not have the wealth of detailed information about the structure of execution graphs that we exploited to make the preceding proof fairly straightforward, and the demonstration in the general case is rather more arduous.

7 CORRECTNESS OF THE TRANSLATION

What can we say about the correctness of the translation? When source and target languages are as far apart as in this case, one has to be careful about what one means by correctness. For instance in the π-calculus itself, there is no possibility that a single communication may thrash without making progress, whereas the busy waiting feature of the MONSTR communication protocol leaves Tr(E) systems open to the possibility of readers and writers perpetually failing to make appropriate contact, and the system as a whole stalling thereby, despite there being a copious quantity of rewrites being performed. Under such circumstances it is reasonable to guard claims of correctness by suitable fairness assumptions. Even with fairness though, an execution of the MON-

STR system will contain quite an amount of fruitless work, as processes make attempts to communicate which are futile for one reason or another; eg. there may be attempts to communicate while offers or rendezvouses are in progress on the same channel, or when there are no available writers on the channel in question.

Our claim for correctness amounts to two facts. The first states that "anything that a π-calculus expression E can do, can be simulated by its translation Tr(E)". It is a completeness statement proved by establishing the existence of a "standard simulation" of any π-calculus expression and appears as theorem 7.9. The second states that "anything that the translation Tr(E) of a π-calculus expression E can do, corresponds in a certain sense to (at least a prefix of) a trace of replication and comunication steps of the original π-calculus expression E". This soundness result is guarded by a fairness assumption, and involves a fairly intricate manipulation of an arbitrary fair execution until it becomes a standard simulation. It appears as theorem 7.16. The details of the manipulation constitute one of the main technical contributions of this paper.

Definition 7.1 Let E be a π-calculus expression. A top-level parallel subexpression (TLPSE) of E is a subexpression of the form $\{\mathbf{0}\}_P$, $\{!Q\}_P$, or $\{\Sigma_i\, \pi_i.Q_i\}_P$, such that there is no subexpression of one of these forms that properly contains it.

So a general π-calculus expression is built up out of TLPSEs by using ν and parallel composition, as one would expect.

Definition 7.2 Let E be a π-calculus expression, and Tr(E) its translation. An execution graph G of Tr(E) represents E if

(1) There is a bijection ρ between TLPSEs of E and live nodes of G such that

- $\rho(\{\mathbf{0}\}_P)$ is an idle Root constructor node,
- $\rho(\{!Q\}_P)$ is an active replication function node *P[...],
- $\rho(\{\Sigma_i\, \pi_i.Q_i\}_P)$ is an active proposer function node *P[...].

(2) ρ extends to a bijection between free channel names of the TLPSEs of E and idle Empty channel nodes of G such that

- if channel x is free in the TLPSEs $E_1 \ldots E_k$ then there is a normal arc from each of the $\rho(E_i)$ to $\rho(x)$.

Note that in a representation of an expression E, the bound names of top-level ν's (those not occurring inside any TLPSE), are "unwrapped" and appear explicitly in the graph. For our example π-calculus expression, [Fig. 9] above represents the original expression, before any communications have taken place.

Definition 7.3 Let E be a π-calculus expression, and Tr(E) its translation. We denote by $\rightarrow_{A(E)}$ the relation on execution graphs of Tr(E) given by rewriting from an active initial or auxiliary function node, or by notifying from an active Root constructor. We denote by $\rightarrow_{R(E)}$ the relation on execution graphs of Tr(E) given by rewriting from an active replication function node. We denote by $\rightarrow_{C(E)}$ the relation on execution graphs of Tr(E) given by rewriting from an active proposer, or proposer-intermediate, or protocol function node, or by notifying from an active Yes or No constructor. We write eg. $\rightarrow_{A(E)}{}^+$ or $\rightarrow_{A(E)}{}^*$ for the transitive, resp. reflexive transitive, closure of these.

Lemma 7.4 Let E be a π-calculus expression, and Tr(E) its translation. Then there is an execution graph G of Tr(E) such that

$$*\mathsf{Initial} \rightarrow_{A(E)}^{+} G$$

and G represents E.

Proof. Essentially this is a byproduct of lemma 6.5. We rewrite ∗Initial using rules for Initial, | , ν, and perform notifications by Root constructors as long as we can do so yielding G. An induction on the structure of the derivation of G using the structure of the "rewrites to" relation of definition 6.4 ensures that the correct function nodes are generated, and the properties of the $Args_P$ and $blend_P$ functions of the translation ensure that suitable channel nodes are linked to the correct function nodes. ☺

Most of the remaining results in this section must be understood as holding up to isomorphism, or up to isomorphism of live subgraphs (as appropriate), as in lemma 6.10. We abuse language somewhat by not mentioning the relevant mappings.

Lemma 7.5 Let E be a π-calculus expression, and Tr(E) its translation. Let execution graph G of Tr(E) represent E. Let $E \Rrightarrow^* F$ be a reduction to standard form of E. Then G represents F, provided TLSEs of E and F are consistently tagged and such tags are consistently translated into function symbols.

Proof. Consider the defining clause of $\Rrightarrow$ in tagged form.

$$\{\ \{\nu z\{Q_1\}_{Q_1}\}_N \mid Q_2 \mid \ldots \mid Q_n\ \}_P \Rrightarrow \{\ \nu z'\{\{Q_1\}_{Q_1} \mid Q_2 \mid \ldots \mid Q_n\ \}_{P'}\ \}_{N'}$$

Here we have tagged the subexpresion Q_1 consistently on both sides (leading to the same function symbol Q_1) and have introduced new tags for the restriction and parallel combinators on the RHS. Consider the rules generated by the translations of the LHS and RHS. On both sides, the rules for Q_1, translating Q_1, would be identical since the free and bound names of Q_1 are the same on both sides. The same applies to the other Q_i by lemma 3.9. On the LHS, P would spawn nodes for Q_2 to Q_n and N, the last of which would create a fresh Empty channel node for z and then spawn Q_1. On the RHS, N′ would create a fresh Empty channel node for z' and then spawn P′, which would spawn nodes for Q_1 to Q_n. Clearly in an execution, the nodes P, N, (resp. P′, N′), would be garbaged, so the live subgraphs containing Q_1 to Q_n and the channel nodes that they refer to would be isomorphic. The same applies if the expressions shown on the LHS and RHS were merely subexpressions at top level of a larger expression, and also if the Q_i merely contained restrictions and and parallel compositions of TLSEs. The rest of the proof is an induction on the length of the derivation $E \Rrightarrow^* F$. ☺

We note that if we had included the first clause of remark 3.10 in our definition of reduction to standard form, then νz-binders in the interior of a summand would have been able to float above such summands making the bound channel names in question free in those summands. This would have destroyed the isomorphism (up to garbage) of lemma 7.5 since the representatives of such summands would now have had extra arguments to these channel nodes. However these would just have been dummy arguments, carried around dormant until they were actually needed, so would not have altered the behaviour of the translation.

Lemma 7.6 Let E_1 be a π-calculus expression, and Tr(E_1) its translation. Let $E_1 \rightarrow_R E_2$ be a replication rewrite of E_1. Then there are execution graphs G_1 and G_2 such that G_1 represents E_1 and G_2 represents E_2 and

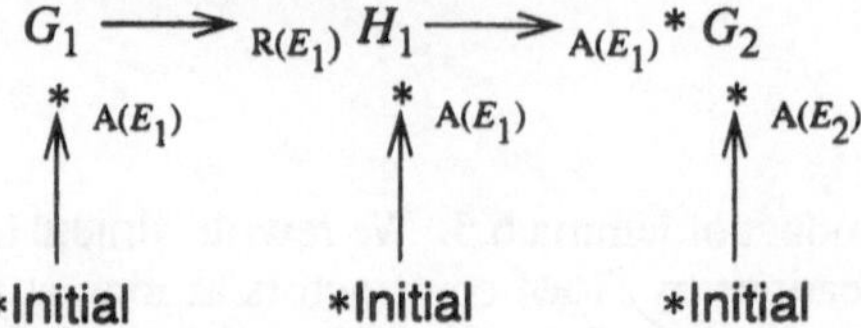

Proof. It is clear that there is an execution graph G_1 that represents E_1 by lemma 7.4. Consider the expression E_1 and its replicated subexpression $\{!Q\}_P$ The latter corresponds to a replication node P of G_1. Assuming "$_Q$" labels the subexpression Q, rewriting *P[...] yields a graph H_1 in which *P[...] is replaced by *P[...], *Q[...]. Now a replication rewrite of $E_1 = \ldots \{!Q\}_P \ldots$ yields $E_2 = \ldots \{\{Q\}_Q \mid \{!Q\}_P\}_R \ldots$. Assuming that R is fresh, that the other subexpressions of E_2 are labelled as in E_1, and assuming that the new instance of Q and its subexpressions are labelled identically to the instance inside $\{!Q\}_P$, it is easy to see by using lemma 6.5 to reduce *Q[...] to proposer nodes, idle Root nodes and replication nodes, that a representation G_2 of E_2 results. ☺

Lemma 7.7 Let E_1 be a π-calculus expression, and Tr(E_1) its translation. Let $E_1 \rightarrow_C E_2$ be a communication rewrite of E_1. Then there are execution graphs G_1 and G_2 such that G_1 represents E_1 and G_2 represents E_2 and

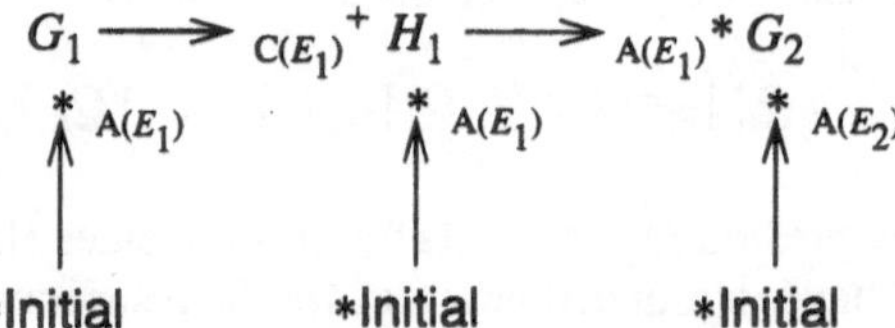

Proof. By lemma 7.4 we obtain a G_1 that represents E_1. Let the communication step $E_1 \rightarrow_C E_2$ involve the summands $\{(\ldots + \pi_r.Q' + \ldots)\}_{P'}$ and $\{(\ldots + \pi_w.Q'' + \ldots)\}_{P''}$ where π_w is a write prefix, and π_r is a suitable read prefix, giving

$$(\ldots \mid \{(\ldots + \pi_r.Q' + \ldots)\}_{P'} \mid \{(\ldots + \pi_w.Q'' + \ldots)\}_{P''} \mid \ldots) \\ \rightarrow_C (\ldots \mid Q'[\chi] \mid Q'' \mid \ldots)$$

where $Q'[\chi]$ is Q' with the appropriate channel substitution applied. The TLPSEs P' and P'' correspond to proposer nodes P′ and P″ in G_1. Running the communication protocol for these nodes for the choices P′ => P′_Q′ and P″ => P″_Q″ we obtain H_1; in which P′ and P″ have been replaced by Q′ and Q″, the input channel node of Q′ has been instantiated and redirected, and perhaps some other channels of P′ and P″ have been garbaged.

The subgraph of H_1 which omits Q′ and Q″ (and their out-arcs, and any garbage that this omission generates), is a representation of the subexpression of E_2 which omits the summands $Q'[\chi]$ and Q'', provided that the other subexpressions of E_2 are labelled consistently with their E_1 counterparts. H_1 itself fails to represent E_2 unless Q′ and Q″ are proposer or replication nodes, but only for this reason. Applying lemma 6.5 to H_1 to reduce Q′ and Q″ to proposer nodes, idle Roots and replicator nodes using auxiliary rules and notifications only, we obtain G_2 which does represent E_2, and which can obviously be obtained from ∗Initial using $\rightarrow_{A(E_2)}{}^*$ only, provided as before, we label the subexpressions of E_1 and E_2 consistently. ☺

Theorem 7.8 Let $E \equiv E_0$ be a π-calculus expression, and Tr(E) its translation. Let $\rightarrow_{A(E)}$, $\rightarrow_{R(E)}$ and $\rightarrow_{C(E)}$ be the corresponding rewrite relations. Then for any trace of communication and replication steps from E, eg.

$$E \equiv E_0 \rightarrow_C E_1 \rightarrow_R E_2 \rightarrow \ldots$$

there is a rewriting sequence

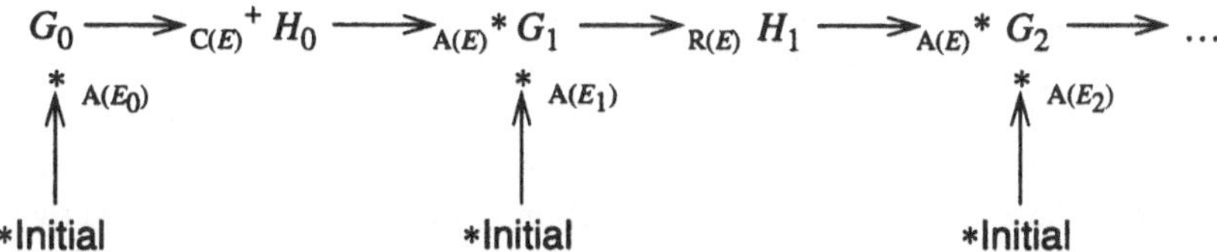

such that for each i, G_i represents E_i.

Proof. We assume that we label all the subexpresions of the E_i consistently as we did in lemmas 7.6, 7.7. Noting that $\rightarrow_{C(E_i)} \subseteq \rightarrow_{C(E)}$, that $\rightarrow_{R(E_i)} \subseteq \rightarrow_{R(E)}$, and that $\rightarrow_{A(E_i)} \subseteq \rightarrow_{A(E)}$, if for no other reason than that E_i is an execution graph of Tr(E_0), we can use induction on the structure of the trace from E, using lemmas 7.6, 7.7 for the induction steps. ☺

Theorem 7.9 Let $E \equiv E_0$ be a π-calculus expression, and Tr(E) its translation. Let $\rightarrow_{A(E)}$, $\rightarrow_{R(E)}$ and $\rightarrow_{C(E)}$ be the corresponding rewrite relations. Then for any trace of communications and replications from E enhanced by reduction to a standard form at each step, eg.

$$E \equiv E_0 \Rrightarrow^* F_0 \rightarrow_C E_1 \Rrightarrow^* F_1 \rightarrow_R E_2 \Rrightarrow^* F_2 \rightarrow \ldots$$

there is a rewriting sequence

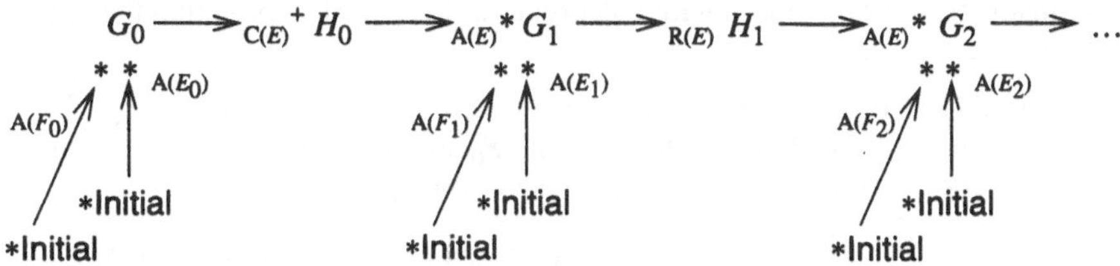

such that for each i, G_i represents both E_i and F_i.

Proof. This is a straightforward enhancement of the induction of theorem 7.8. By lemma 7.5 we note that up to garbage, the same execution graph G_i will do duty for both E_i and F_i, so once we note that a replication can be done in F_i iff it can be done in E_i (and thus can be simulated in G_i), we just need to check that G_i is capable of performing all the communications of F_i which were unavailable to E_i. That this holds, follows once we note that in our translation, sending and receiving are independent activities apart from their need to synchronise. Thus the sender's success in transmitting a ν-bound channel does not depend on knowing that the receiver is in the scope of the ν. Equally, the receiver's success is independent of whether or not the received channel is ν-bound, and if so of what the ν's scope is. ☺

The later remarks in the above proof bring out with some force the fact that our graph based formalism, by directly expressing connectivity in a communication network via connectivity in the graph, handles easily issues that demand some technical pain in the π-calculus.

Definition 7.10 Let E be a π-calculus expression, and Tr(E) its translation. An execution such as the one described in theorem 7.9 is called a standard execution of Tr(E).

Theorem 7.9 says that the translation is complete in providing a standard execution of any possible trace of E. It is clear from the properties of standard executions that they are in fact weak simulations of the traces of E.

Soundness is rather harder. Given an arbitrary execution $\mathcal{H}$ of a system Tr(E), we want to show that there is a trace $\mathcal{T}$ of communications and replications enhanced by reduction to standard form from E, such that $\mathcal{H}$ corresponds to $\mathcal{T}$ in some acceptable way. Given the standard executions furnished by theorem 7.9 for Tr(E) systems, we regard it as sufficient to manufacture from $\mathcal{H}$ a standard execution $\mathcal{G}$ that is equivalent to $\mathcal{H}$ in a convincing sense. This manufacturing process has to accomplish a number of things. The actions corresponding to a successful run of the communications protocol have to be clustered together (the reference points for this are the commit rewrites of the protocol, the rewrites governed by the Help_w normal rule); waste rewrites corresponding to unsuccessful essays of the protocol must be eliminated; and rewrites using auxiliary rules must be suitably clustered to ensure, for each successful commit point or replication point (say the i'th), before the initiation of the communication or replication, that G_i really does represent E_i.

For future notational convenience, if x is a node of an execution graph G_i of an execution $\mathcal{G}$, we presuperscript it, writing ${}^{(i)}x$, to distinguish it from other nodes in other execution graphs of $\mathcal{G}$. So by definition, ${}^{(i)}x \in G_i$. If $j \geq i$ we write ${}^{(j)}x$ for $r_{G_i,G_j}(x) = r_{G_i,G_j}({}^{(i)}x)$ where as in previous sections, r_{G_i,G_j} is the function which maps ${}^{(i)}x$ in G_i to its redirection target in G_j. Also when more than one execution is being discussed, we additionally presubscript nodes with notation to indicate which execution they belong to, eg. ${}^{(i)}_{\mathcal{G}}x \in G_i \in \mathcal{G}$.

Definition 7.11 Let $\mathcal{R}$ be a rule system and $\mathcal{X} = [X_0, X_1, X_2, \ldots]$ and $\mathcal{Y} = [Y_0, Y_1, Y_2, \ldots]$ be two executions of $\mathcal{R}$ where both X_0 and Y_0 are the initial graph. We define the relation Ξ between nodes of execution graphs of $\mathcal{X}$ and $\mathcal{Y}$ as follows.

(1) ${}^{(0)}{}_{X_0}\mathrm{init} \,\Xi\, {}^{(0)}{}_{Y_0}\mathrm{init}$, where ${}^{(0)}{}_{X_0}\mathrm{init}$ and ${}^{(0)}{}_{Y_0}\mathrm{init}$ are the initial nodes of X_0 and Y_0,

(2) If ${}^{(i)}x \,\Xi\, {}^{(j)}y$, $i \leq i'$, $j \leq j'$, then ${}^{(i')}x \,\Xi\, {}^{(j')}y$,

(3) If ${}^{(i)}x \,\Xi\, {}^{(j)}y$, and ${}^{(i)}x$ and ${}^{(j)}y$ are roots of redexes of the same rule D of $\mathcal{R}$, and X_{i+1} and Y_{j+1} are the results of rewriting these redexes, then if ${}^{(i+1)}x' \in X_{i+1}$ and ${}^{(j+1)}y' \in Y_{j+1}$ are copies of the same contractum node p of the full pattern of the rule D introduced during these rewrites, then ${}^{(i+1)}x' \,\Xi\, {}^{(j+1)}y'$.

By clause (1) of the above, any two executions of $\mathcal{R}$ are Ξ-related to some extent. This relationship may easily be a not very useful one if the two executions swiftly diverge from one another, the Ξ-related parts becoming consigned to garbage. However, the more closely the two executions follow one another disregarding inessential detail, the larger the proportion of execution node instances in the first execution, that will be in a useful non-garbage way, Ξ-related to counterparts in the second execution.

We can extend Ξ to arcs, connectivity, and other graph theoretic concepts as required. For example.

Definition 7.12 With the provisions of definition 7.11 understood, let $({}^{(i)}p_k, {}^{(i)}c)$ be an arc of X_i and $({}^{(j)}q_k, {}^{(j)}d)$ be an arc of Y_j. If ${}^{(i)}p \; \Xi \; {}^{(j)}q$, and ${}^{(i)}c \; \Xi \; {}^{(j)}d$ then we say $({}^{(i)}p_k, {}^{(i)}c) \; \Xi \; ({}^{(j)}q_k, {}^{(j)}d)$.

Lemma 7.13 Let E be a π-calculus expression, and Tr(E) its translation. Let $\mathcal{G} = [G_0, G_1, \ldots]$ and $\mathcal{H} = [H_0, H_1, \ldots]$ be two executions of Tr(E) such that

(a) $G_i = H_i$ for $i \in [\, 0 \ldots m, m{+}2 \ldots \,]$.

(b) G_m contains two redexes rooted at ${}^{(m)}{}_{\mathrm{G}}r_1$ and ${}^{(m)}{}_{\mathrm{G}}r_2$ which satisfy the hypotheses of lemma 6.10. Understood as nodes in H_m, these roots are written ${}^{(m)}{}_{\mathrm{H}}r_1$ and ${}^{(m)}{}_{\mathrm{H}}r_2$.

(c) In $\mathcal{G}$, $G_m \to G_{m+1}$ rewrites the redex rooted at ${}^{(m)}{}_{\mathrm{G}}r_1$ and $G_{m+1} \to G_{m+2} = H_{m+2}$ rewrites the redex rooted at ${}^{(m+1)}{}_{\mathrm{G}}r_2$. While in $\mathcal{H}$, $H_m \to H_{m+1}$ rewrites the redex rooted at ${}^{(m)}{}_{\mathrm{H}}r_2$ and $H_{m+1} \to H_{m+2} = G_{m+2}$ rewrites the redex rooted at ${}^{(m+1)}{}_{\mathrm{H}}r_1$.

Then

(1) For every node ${}^{(i)}x \in G_i \in \mathcal{G}$, ${}^{(i)}x \; \Xi \; {}^{(j)}y$ for some ${}^{(j)}y \in H_j \in \mathcal{H}$, and if ${}^{(i)}x$ is live then ${}^{(j)}y$ is live. And conversely.

(2) For every arc $({}^{(i)}p_k, {}^{(i)}c) \in G_i \in \mathcal{G}$, $({}^{(i)}p_k, {}^{(i)}c) \; \Xi \; ({}^{(j)}q_k, {}^{(j)}d)$ for some arc $({}^{(j)}q_k, {}^{(j)}d) \in H_j \in \mathcal{H}$. And conversely.

Proof. For $i \in [\, 0 \ldots m, m{+}2 \ldots \,]$ we can obviously set Ξ to (the closure under the recursive clause of definition 7.11 of) the identity relation on nodes ${}^{(i)}x \in G_i = H_i$ and correspondingly for arcs. For $i = m{+}1$, for non-contractum nodes arising from ${}^{(m)}{}_{\mathrm{G}}x = {}^{(m)}{}_{\mathrm{H}}x$, we set ${}^{(m+1)}{}_{\mathrm{G}}x \; \Xi \; {}^{(m+1)}{}_{\mathrm{H}}x$. For contractum nodes, if p is a contractum node of the rule for the r_1 rewrite, we set ${}^{(m+1)}{}_{\mathrm{G}}p \; \Xi \; {}^{(m+2)}{}_{\mathrm{H}}p$ in an obvious notation for the introduced copies, and likewise ${}^{(m+2)}{}_{\mathrm{G}}q \; \Xi \; {}^{(m+1)}{}_{\mathrm{H}}q$ for a contractum node q of the rule for the r_2 rewrite. The results for arcs follow readily, and the converses are immediate. ☺

Corollary 7.14 The results of Lemma 7.13 hold when one or both of $G_m \to G_{m+1}$ and $G_{m+1} \to G_{m+2}$ are notifications.

Definition 7.15 Let $\mathcal{G}$ be an execution of a rule system $\mathcal{R}$. Let ${}^{(i)}x$ be an active node of G_i in $\mathcal{G}$. Suppose for some $j \geq i$ the next execution step is either a notification by the constructor/stateholder ${}^{(j)}x$ or a rewrite of a redex whose root is ${}^{(j)}x$. If for each i and for each active ${}^{(i)}x$ in G_i there is such a j, then we say the execution is weakly fair.

Note that standard executions as per theorem 7.9 are not necessarily weakly fair unless the trace of E satisfies additional "reasonableness" criteria.

Now for the main theorem.

Theorem 7.16 Let E be a π-calculus expression, and Tr(E) its translation. Let $\mathcal{H} = [H_0, H_1, \ldots]$ be a weakly fair execution of Tr(E). Then there is a trace $\mathcal{T}$ of communications and replications from E, enhanced by reductions to standard form, such that for a standard execution $\mathcal{G} = [G_0, G_1, \ldots]$ of Tr(E) corresponding via theorem 7.9 to $\mathcal{T}$, for some prefix $[G_0, G_1, \ldots, G_N]$ of $\mathcal{G}$, with $0 \le N \le \infty$, if $i \le N$

(1) For every node ${}^{(i)}x \in G_i \in \mathcal{G}$, ${}^{(i)}x \equiv {}^{(j)}y$ for some ${}^{(j)}y \in H_j \in \mathcal{H}$, and if ${}^{(i)}x$ is live then ${}^{(j)}y$ is live.

(2) For every arc $({}^{(i)}p_k, {}^{(i)}c) \in G_i \in \mathcal{G}$, $({}^{(i)}p_k, {}^{(i)}c) \equiv ({}^{(j)}q_k, {}^{(j)}d)$ for some arc $({}^{(j)}q_k, {}^{(j)}d) \in H_j \in \mathcal{H}$.

(3) If $H_j \to H_{j+1} \in \mathcal{H}$ is a rewrite of a redex rooted at ${}^{(j)}y \in H_j$ and governed by either a rule for a replication symbol, or a communication commit rule, there is a corresponding rewrite $G_i \to G_{i+1} \in \mathcal{G}$ of a redex rooted at a node ${}^{(i)}x \in G_i$, which is governed by the same rule, and ${}^{(i)}x \equiv {}^{(j)}y$. Further, if $H_j \to H_{j+1}$ and $H_{j'} \to H_{j'+1}$ are two distinct such rewrites, their corresponding $G_i \to G_{i+1}$ and $G_{i'} \to G_{i'+1}$ are also distinct, and all such rewrites occur in the same order in $\mathcal{H}$ and $\mathcal{G}$.

Thus on the one hand every part of the standard execution $\mathcal{G}$ can be located in $\mathcal{H}$; on the other, every replication or communication step of $\mathcal{H}$ can be found in $\mathcal{G}$ also. On this basis $\mathcal{G}$, which faithfully depicts $\mathcal{T}$, shows that the essence of any execution of Tr(E) corresponds to a trace of E, giving soundness.

Proof. The proof proceeds through a number of phases, gradually transforming $\mathcal{H}$ into the required $\mathcal{G}$, while retaining the properties (1) – (3). Most of the phases are fairly similar so we treat the first in detail, and the others more curtly.

The first few phases eliminate "waste work" of various kinds from the execution $\mathcal{H}$.

Let $\mathcal{X}^{0.0} = [X_0^{0.0}, X_1^{0.0}, \ldots]$ be a working name for the execution $\mathcal{H}$.

PHASE I — Elimination of failed write attempts. These arise from the following sequence of events. (Here and below, the communication protocol rules used in each event are indicated by their reference numbers.)

(a) A proposer node ${}^{(a)}p$ rewrites to a proposer-intermediate node ${}^{(a+1)}p$ with a Help_w child ${}^{(a+1)}h$.

(b) The Help_w child ${}^{(b)}h$ matches a non-Busy_Unlocked channel node ${}^{(b)}c$ and rewrites to a No constructor ${}^{(b+1)}h$ using its default rule. [4]

(c) The No constructor ${}^{(c)}h$ notifies its suspended parent ${}^{(c)}p$.

(d) The parent ${}^{(d)}p$ matches the No constructor ${}^{(d)}h$ and reverts to a proposer node ${}^{(d+1)}p$.

Weak fairness assures us that once such a sequence of events starts within $\mathcal{X}^{0.0}$ it runs to completion. So as indices of graphs of $\mathcal{X}^{0.0}$, a < b < c < d. Suppose further that no a′ < a is the first element of such a subsequence of $\mathcal{X}^{O.0}$, so we are dealing with the first failed write attempt. Let $\mathcal{X}^{O.1}$ be the sequence of graphs obtained from $\mathcal{X}^{O.0}$ by deleting the rewrites/notifications mentioned in (a) – (d). Thus $X_0{}^{O.1} = X_0{}^{O.0}$; $X_1{}^{O.1} = X_1{}^{O.0}$; … ; $X_a{}^{O.1} = X_a{}^{O.0}$; $X_{a+1}{}^{O.1}$ is similar to $X_{a+2}{}^{O.0}$ in that the latter has a Help_w node, and the symbol labelling its parent ${}^{(a+2)}{}_0p \in X_{a+2}{}^{O.0}$ is a proposer-intermediate symbol, while the symbol labelling its counterpart ${}^{(a+1)}{}_1p \in X_{a+1}{}^{O.1}$ is the original proposer symbol; similarly for $X_{a+2}{}^{O.1}$ and $X_{a+3}{}^{O.0}$ etc.; $X_b{}^{O.1}$ is similar to $X_{b+2}{}^{O.0}$ and so on; $X_{c-1}{}^{O.1}$ is similar to $X_{c+2}{}^{O.0}$ etc.; $X_{d-2}{}^{O.1} = X_{d+2}{}^{O.0}$ up to garbage (since we have reached the point where the failed write attempt has aborted) and so on.

We claim that $\mathcal{X}^{O.1}$ is an execution of Tr(E). This is easy to see since no rewrite of $\mathcal{X}^{O.1}$ matches a node whose symbol has been changed compared to $\mathcal{X}^{O.0}$ (the only such node being p mentioned above in (a) – (d), which being a proposer/proposer-intermediate node, has no parents by lemma 6.3.(1)). Therefore all transitions $X_i{}^{O.1} \to X_{i+1}{}^{O.1}$ of $\mathcal{X}^{O.1}$ are legal execution sequence steps: the notifications obviously so, and the rewrites also legally so since no change of rule selection is necessitated by the change of symbol of p.

We can now establish the conclusions (1) – (3) of the theorem for $\mathcal{X}^{O.1}$. To get (1), we see that for each node ${}^{(i)}{}_1x \in X_i{}^{O.1}$ we have

$$ {}^{(i)}{}_1x \equiv {}^{(i+\delta)}{}_0x $$

where ${}^{(i+\delta)}{}_0x \in X_{i+\delta}{}^{O.0}$ and where

$$ \begin{aligned} \delta &= 0 \quad \text{if } 0 \le i \le a, \\ &= 1 \quad \text{if } a{+}1 \le i \le b{-}1, \\ &= 2 \quad \text{if } b \le i \le c{-}2, \\ &= 3 \quad \text{if } c{-}1 \le i \le d{-}3, \\ &= 4 \quad \text{if } d{-}2 \le i. \end{aligned} $$

Clearly if ${}^{(i)}{}_1x$ is live then so is ${}^{(i+\delta)}{}_0x$ given the relatively slight changes made to the execution.

In a similar vein, for (2) we can see that arcs behave well, i.e.

$$ ({}^{(i)}{}_1p_k, {}^{(i)}{}_1c) \equiv ({}^{(i+\delta)}{}_0p_k, {}^{(i+\delta)}{}_0c) $$

for all arcs except those emerging from the affected p node. For those we can see that

$$ ({}^{(i)}{}_1p_k, {}^{(i)}{}_1c) \equiv ({}^{(d+1)}{}_0p_k, {}^{(d+1)}{}_0c) $$

where $a{+}1 \le i \le d{-}3$. And (3) becomes clear once we notice that we have not affected any of the successful communication or replication rewrites.

Thus we have eliminated the first failed write attempt (if there was indeed one at all) from $\mathcal{X}^{O.0}$ giving $\mathcal{X}^{O.1}$. Likewise we can eliminate the first failed write attempt from $\mathcal{X}^{O.1}$ giving $\mathcal{X}^{O.2}$ etc. We get a sequence of executions $\mathcal{X}^{O.i}$ which it is easy to see have a non-decreasing invariant prefix and such that for all relevant i, $\mathcal{X}^{O.i}$ is related to $\mathcal{X}^{O.i+1}$ by conditions (1) – (3).

If $\mathcal{X}^{O.0}$ is finite then this process stops after a finite number of steps. Call the final execution generated $\mathcal{X}^{I.0}$. If $\mathcal{X}^{O.0}$ is infinite then there are two possibilities. Either the non-decreasing invariant prefix is never eventually constant; in which case the $\mathcal{X}^{O.i}$

converge to an infinite execution. Call it $\mathcal{X}^{\mathrm{I.0}}$ as before. (Note that $\mathcal{X}^{\mathrm{I.0}}$ may not be a weakly fair execution. This would arise if some particular proposer node consistently failed to succeed in communicating. In such a case the graphs in $\mathcal{X}^{\mathrm{I.0}}$ would eventually all contain an active node (the said proposer) that was never the root of a rewrite.) Otherwise the the invariant prefix stops increasing after some point say i_0. In this case all active nodes of execution graphs beyond the prefix of $\mathcal{X}^{\mathrm{O}.j}$ for $j \geq i_0$ are involved with failing write attempts. (Such behaviour would be forced if say the expression E contained only writers at the top level, eg. $E = \bar{x}z.\mathbf{0}$.) In this case call the final stable prefix $\mathcal{X}^{\mathrm{I.0}}$. Note that strictly speaking it is not an execution since its final graph will contain active nodes. Nevertheless we will overlook this below. Finally, if there were no failed write attempts at all in $\mathcal{X}^{\mathrm{O.0}}$, we set $\mathcal{X}^{\mathrm{I.0}} = \mathcal{X}^{\mathrm{O.0}}$.

PHASE II — Elimination of clashing read attempts. These arise from the following sequence of events.

(a) A proposer node ${}^{(a)}p$ rewrites to a proposer-intermediate node ${}^{(a+1)}p$ with a Help_r child ${}^{(a+1)}h$, and instantiates the input channel node ${}^{(a+1)}u$.

(b) The Help_r child ${}^{(b)}h$ matches a non-Empty channel node ${}^{(b)}c$ and rewrites to a No constructor ${}^{(b+1)}h$ using its default rule. [2]

(c) The No constructor ${}^{(c)}h$ notifies its suspended parent ${}^{(c)}p$.

(d) The parent ${}^{(d)}p$ matches the No constructor ${}^{(d)}h$ and reverts to a proposer node ${}^{(d+1)}p$.

Since Phase I did not interfere with clashing read attempts, once such a sequence of events starts, it will run to completion by the weak fairness of $\mathcal{X}^{\mathrm{O.0}}$. So we eliminate the first such sequence from $\mathcal{X}^{\mathrm{I.0}}$ giving $\mathcal{X}^{\mathrm{I.1}}$. The technical details are as for Phase I. Again we generate a sequence of executions $\mathcal{X}^{\mathrm{I.0}}, \mathcal{X}^{\mathrm{I.1}}, \mathcal{X}^{\mathrm{I.2}}$ etc. with non-decreasing invariant prefixes. Once more there are three cases depending on whether $\mathcal{X}^{\mathrm{I.0}}$ was finite, and if not, whether the non-decreasing invariant prefix increased indefinitely or not. In all cases we call the resulting execution $\mathcal{X}^{\mathrm{II.0}}$. As previously $\mathcal{X}^{\mathrm{II.0}}$ need not be weakly fair.

PHASE III — Elimination of failed read attempts. These arise from the following sequence of events.

(a) A proposer node ${}^{(a)}p$ rewrites to a proposer-intermediate node ${}^{(a+1)}p$ with a Help_r child ${}^{(a+1)}h$, and instantiates the input channel node ${}^{(a+1)}u$.

(b) The Help_r child ${}^{(b)}h$ matches an Empty channel node ${}^{(b)}c$, and using its normal rule, rewrites to a Help_r_test_chan function ${}^{(b+1)}h$, rewriting the channel ${}^{(b)}c$ to a Busy_Unlocked channel ${}^{(b+1)}c$. [1]

(c_1) The Help_r_test_chan function ${}^{(c_1)}h$ matches the Busy_Unlocked channel ${}^{(c_1)}c$ and rewrites to a Help_r_test_chan function ${}^{(c_1+1)}h$. [5]

(c_2) The Help_r_test_chan function ${}^{(c_2)}h$ matches the Busy_Unlocked channel ${}^{(c_2)}c$ and rewrites to a Help_r_test_chan function ${}^{(c_2+1)}h$. [5]

... ...

(c_m) The Help_r_test_chan function $^{(c_m)}h$ matches the Busy_Unlocked channel $^{(c_m)}c$ and rewrites to a Help_r_test_chan function $^{(c_m+1)}h$. [5]

(d) The Help_r_test_chan function $^{(d)}h$ matches the Busy_Unlocked channel $^{(d)}c$ and rewrites to a No constructor $^{(d+1)}h$, rewriting the Busy_Unlocked channel $^{(d)}c$ to an Empty channel node $^{(d+1)}c$. [6]

(e) The No constructor $^{(e)}h$ notifies its suspended parent $^{(e)}p$.

(f) The parent $^{(f)}p$ matches the No constructor $^{(f)}h$ and reverts to a proposer node $^{(f+1)}p$.

Again once such a sequence of events starts, it will run to completion by the weak fairness of $\mathcal{X}^{\,0.0}$, although this time, it is possible that $m = \infty$ and the events (d) – (f) never take place. Apart from the fact that more events need to be dealt with in eliminating such a sequence, the details are sufficiently similar that we can omit them. One point to note is that unlike the previous phases, elimination of a sequence (a) – (f) changes the state of the channel node *c* from Busy_Unlocked to Empty between stages (b) and (d) inclusive. Since channel nodes are shared, any rewrite explicitly matching *c* in this period would find a different symbol and so would need to use a different rule. However, we can deduce by lemmas 6.3 and 6.7, that any such rewrite must belong to a clashing read attempt, and these have already been eliminated above. So the change of state goes unobserved, and the elimination is safe.

So we generate a sequence of executions as previously, $\mathcal{X}^{\,\mathrm{II.0}}$, $\mathcal{X}^{\,\mathrm{II.1}}$, $\mathcal{X}^{\,\mathrm{II.2}}$ etc. with non-decreasing invariant prefixes. Once more there are three cases depending on whether $\mathcal{X}^{\,\mathrm{II.0}}$ was finite, and if not, whether the non-decreasing invariant prefix increased indefinitely or not. In all cases we call the resulting execution $\mathcal{X}^{\,\mathrm{III.0}}$.

PHASE IV — Elimination of useless work from successful read attempts. These are to be found within sequences of events as follows; where $m > 0$.

(a) A proposer node $^{(a)}p$ rewrites to a proposer-intermediate node $^{(a+1)}p$ with a Help_r child $^{(a+1)}h$, and instantiates the input channel node $^{(a+1)}u$.

(b) The Help_r child $^{(b)}h$ matches an Empty channel node $^{(b)}c$, and using its normal rule, rewrites to a Help_r_test_chan function $^{(b+1)}h$, rewriting the channel $^{(b)}c$ to a Busy_Unlocked channel $^{(b+1)}c$. [1]

(c_1) The Help_r_test_chan function $^{(c_1)}h$ matches the Busy_Unlocked channel $^{(c_1)}c$ and rewrites to a Help_r_test_chan function $^{(c_1+1)}h$. [5]

(c_2) The Help_r_test_chan function $^{(c_2)}h$ matches the Busy_Unlocked channel $^{(c_2)}c$ and rewrites to a Help_r_test_chan function $^{(c_2+1)}h$. [5]

... ...

(c_m) The Help_r_test_chan function $^{(c_m)}h$ matches the Busy_Unlocked channel $^{(c_m)}c$ and rewrites to a Help_r_test_chan function $^{(c_m+1)}h$. [5]

(d) The Help_r_test_chan function $^{(d)}h$ matches the Busy_Locked[data] channel $^{(d)}c$ and rewrites to a Help_r_assign_data function $^{(d+1)}h$. [7]

(e ...) The remaining steps of the communication protocol complete successfully.

In this case all we wish to do is to eliminate the steps (c_1) – (c_m) without affecting the rest of the communication. (This time we can assert that m is finite, regarding all infinite m cases as partially complete failed read attempts.) The elimination can be done without complication, especially when we note that all the eliminated steps are actually null rewrites modulo garbage: none of them changes the live graph at all. The same strategy as before now applies. Once more we generate a sequence of executions, $\mathcal{X}^{\mathrm{III}.0}$, $\mathcal{X}^{\mathrm{III}.1}$, $\mathcal{X}^{\mathrm{III}.2}$ etc. We call the resulting execution $\mathcal{X}^{\mathrm{IV}.0}$.

At this point, we have eliminated all spurious activity from the execution. What remains, is to standardise $\mathcal{X}^{\mathrm{IV}.0}$ by reordering the rewrites in a sensible way. This consists of two subtasks. The first is to cluster the rewrites corresponding to a successful run of the communication protocol at the commit points. The second is to ensure that the rewrites of auxiliary and replication functions occur at suitable places so that we can identify execution graphs that actually represent the expressions E_i of a trace from E. All this must be done in a way that preserves the order of communications and replications so as not to fall foul of causality considerations that would prevent eg. a rewrite (β) from being permuted to a place earlier in the execution than the rewrite (α) which created (β)'s redex root as a contractum node. We start with the communications.

PHASE V — Compression of successful communication sequences. We will standardise on the following sequence of events for a successful communication.

(a) A proposer node $^{(a)}pw$ rewrites to a proposer-intermediate node $^{(a+1)}pw$ with a Help_w child $^{(a+1)}hw$.

(b) A proposer node $^{(b)}pr$ rewrites to a proposer-intermediate node $^{(b+1)}pr$ with a Help_r child $^{(b+1)}hr$, and instantiates the input channel node $^{(b+1)}u$.

(c) The Help_r child $^{(c)}hr$ matches an Empty channel node $^{(c)}c$, and using its normal rule, rewrites to a Help_r_test_chan function $^{(c+1)}hr$, rewriting the channel $^{(b)}c$ to a Busy_Unlocked channel $^{(c+1)}c$. [1]

(d) The Help_w child $^{(d)}hw$ matches the Busy_Unlocked channel node $^{(d)}c$ and rewrites to a Yes constructor $^{(d+1)}hw$, rewriting the channel to a Busy_Locked[-data] channel $^{(d+1)}c$. [3]

(e) The Help_r_test_chan function $^{(e)}hr$ matches the Busy_Locked[data] channel $^{(e)}c$ and rewrites to a Help_r_assign_data function $^{(e+1)}hr$. [7]

(f) The Help_r_assign_data function $^{(f)}hr$ matches the Empty input channel $^{(f)}u$, and rewrites to a Help_r_unlock function $^{(f+1)}hr$, rewriting the input channel to the data channel $^{(f+1)}d$. [9]

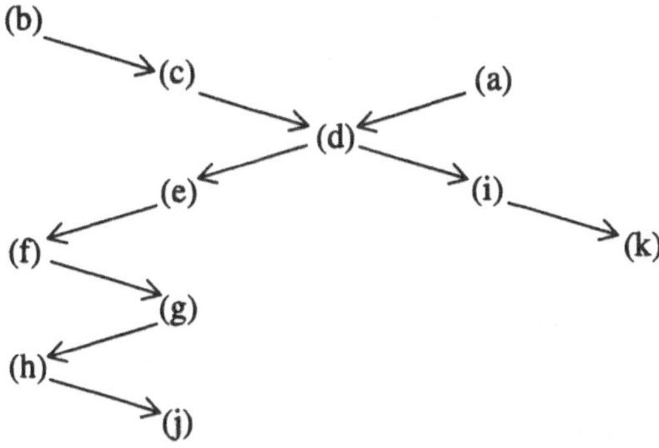

Fig. 12

(g) The Help_r_unlock function $^{(g)}hr$, matches the Busy_Locked[data] channel $^{(g)}c$ and rewrites to a Yes constructor $^{(g+1)}hr$, rewriting the channel to an Empty channel $^{(g+1)}c$. [11]

(h) The Yes constructor $^{(h)}hr$ notifies its suspended proposer-intermediate node parent $^{(h)}pr$.

(i) The Yes constructor $^{(j)}hw$ notifies its suspended proposer-intermediate node parent $^{(j)}pw$.

(j) The active proposer-intermediate parent $^{(i)}pr$ matches the Yes constructor $^{(i)}hr$ and rewrites successfully.

(k) The active proposer-intermediate parent $^{(k)}pw$ matches the Yes constructor $^{(k)}hw$ and rewrites successfully.

The above is one possible ordering compatible with causality. The general situation is illustrated in [Fig. 12] where an arrow indicates that the higher event must causally precede the lower event. That this is indeed the case is easily shown on the basis of lemmas 6.3 and 6.7 and the form of the protocol rules. In fact [Fig. 12], with time flowing down the page, is an elementary event structure for a successful communication according to our protocol [Nielsen et al. (1981), Winskel (1986), Winskel (1988)].

For obvious reasons, the commit events (d) are regarded as pinpointing the position of a communication within an execution. Thus even if the event sequences for two communications overlap, they are still regarded as taking place in the order of their commit events.

Remark 7.16.1 We recall the fact (also pertinent to Phases III and IV above), that between events (c) and (g) inclusive of a communication sequence, no function nodes other than those involved in the communication sequence itself explicitly match the channel c. This is because by lemmas 6.3 and 6.7 such nodes must be participating in a clashing read or failing write attempt, and these have already been eliminated above.

To a communication with events (a) – (k) we apply the following transformation steps.

(1) Interchange event (c) with its succeeding events repeatedly until it becomes the event immediately preceding event (d).

(2) Interchange event (b) with its successors until it immediately precedes event (c).

(3) Interchange event (a) with its successors until it immediately precedes event (b).

(4) Interchange event (e) with its predecessors until it immediately succeeds event (d).

(5) Interchange event (f) with its predecessors until it immediately succeeds event (e).

(6) Interchange event (g) with its predecessors until it immediately succeeds event (f).

(7) Interchange event (h) with its predecessors until it immediately succeeds event (g).

(8) Interchange event (i) with its predecessors until it immediately succeeds event (h).

(9) Interchange event (j) with its predecessors until it immediately succeeds event (i).

(10) Interchange event (k) with its predecessors until it immediately succeeds event (j).

We must be sure that doing the above to a succesful communication sequence transforms an execution of Tr(E) into another execution of Tr(E). For brevity we pretend that all intervening execution steps that we have to consider are rewrites, the case of notifications being simpler by corollary 7.14. To justify step (1) we argue as follows.

If the event following (c) is (d), then we are done and step (1) yields an execution of Tr(E). Otherwise the redex rewritten in rewrite (c+1) $\rightarrow$ (c+2) already existed in execution graph (c), since the only redex that rewrite (c) $\rightarrow$ (c+1) creates is the redex for the corresponding event (d). Consequently, both redexes exist in execution graph (c) and by remark 7.16.1, satisfy the hypotheses of lemma 6.10. Therefore by lemma 6.10 we can do the rewrites in the other order. This yields a new execution which by lemma 7.13 has properties (1) and (2) of the present theorem; while property (3) is obviously preserved since we do not move event (d).

The justifications for the other steps are similar and are omitted.

As in previous phases, we start with the first succesful communication sequence, and the interchanges performed during the compression generate a number of new execution sequences which we resist the temptation of trying to catalogue. Upon completing the compression of the first sequence we proceed to the second. And so on. We will name the end product of this activity $\mathcal{X}^{\text{V.0}}$.

PHASE VI — Compression of auxiliary rewriting sequences. These arise through a sequence of events such as the following.

(a) An active function node ${}^{(a)}f$ rewrites and creates k active composition, ν, or Root nodes ${}^{(a+1)}n_1$, ${}^{(a+1)}n_1$, ... , ${}^{(a+1)}n_k$ as copies of its contractum nodes.

(b_1) One of the active nodes ${}^{(b_1)}n_1$, ${}^{(b_1)}n_1$, … , ${}^{(b_1)}n_k$, ${}^{(b_1)}n_i$ say, rewrites (if it is a composition or ν node), or notifies (if it is a Root node).

(b_2) One of the remaining active nodes of $\{{}^{(b_2)}n_1, {}^{(b_2)}n_1, \ldots, {}^{(b_2)}n_k\} - \{{}^{(b_2)}n_i\}$ rewrites or notifies.

… … … … … … …

(b_k) The last active node ${}^{(b_k)}n_m$ rewrites or notifies.

In such a sequence we call (a) the auxiliary-parent event and the (b_i) the auxiliary-child events. There is a direct correspondence between such auxiliary-parent / auxiliary-children configurations, and fragments of the parse tree of the original π-calculus expression *E*, because the auxiliary rules used, are generated directly from the parse tree in the translation. Rather as in Phase V, such an auxiliary-parent / auxiliary-children configuration, *aka* fragment of parse tree, can be regarded as a mini elementary event structure for the collection of auxiliary rewrites generated, with the parent causally preceding the children.

To such a sequence we can apply the following transformation.

(1) Interchange event (b_1) with its predecessors until it immediately succeeds event (a).

(2) Interchange event (b_2) with its predecessors until it immediately succeeds event (b_1).

… … … … … … …

(*k*) Interchange event (b_k) with its predecessors until it immediately succeeds event (b_{k-1}).

Such a series of interchanges is easily justified by noting that no auxiliary node ever pattern matches to rewrite since its rule is a default rule, so arguments like those used in Phase V apply even more readily.

We apply the transformation above to the first or initial rewrite of $\mathcal{X}^{\text{V.0}}$ if applicable (i.e. if the initial rewrite, interpreted as an auxiliary-parent event, generates any composition, ν, or Root nodes), yielding $\mathcal{X}^{\text{V.1}}$. We then apply the transformation to the second rewrite of $\mathcal{X}^{\text{V.1}}$ if applicable yielding $\mathcal{X}^{\text{V.2}}$. We then apply the transformation to the third rewrite of $\mathcal{X}^{\text{V.2}}$ if applicable yielding $\mathcal{X}^{\text{V.3}}$. And so on. The end product is an execution $\mathcal{X}^{\text{VI.0}}$. It obviously satisfies the properties (1) and (2) of the theorem, also (3) since no replication rewrite (or communication commit rewrite) is moved in Phase VI. An important property of $\mathcal{X}^{\text{VI.0}}$ is that as a result of the order in which the transformations are applied, the only events that can occur between an auxiliary-parent event (a) and any of its auxiliary-child events (b_i), are sibling events of (b_i), their own auxiliary-children etc. In fact following any auxiliary-parent event (a), there is a segment of the execution which is a sequence of auxiliary rewrites corresponding exactly to the rewriting of the root of the auxiliary-parent event redex to a collection of proposer nodes, replication nodes, and idle Root nodes according to lemma 6.5, with no intervening other events. This sequence corresponds to a preorder listing of the sub parse tree rooted at the vertex corresponding to (a), and truncated at summation and replication vertexes.

The order to which "preorder" refers, is constructed by, at each level of the sub parse tree, ordering the child vertexes of a vertex in the same order as the corresponding auxiliary-child events appear in the original execution (this order is obviously preserved by Phase VI). This truncated parse tree in turn corresponds to a larger elementary event structure obtained by gluing together the mini event structures mentioned above. All of this is easy enough to see by induction.

One important consequence of this transformation is that the last two events (j) and (k) of a successful communication, which can both in principle rewrite their roots to auxiliary function nodes, can now both be immediately followed by rewrite sequences that turn these functions into idle Roots, and active proposer or replication functions, i.e. the events (j) and (k) have become separated. This prompts the last Phase.

PHASE VII — Reattachment of communication events (k). We just repeat step (10) of Phase V.

(1) Interchange event (k) with its predecessors until it immediately succeeds event (j).

As before we apply this transformation to each of the successful communications in turn, reattaching their (k) events. This yields the execution $\mathcal{X}^{\text{VII.0}}$.

Execution $\mathcal{X}^{\text{VII.0}}$ which we rename as $\mathcal{G}$, is the execution sought in the theorem. By construction, it satisfies the properties (1) – (3) as required. Further we claim it is (a possibly proper prefix of) a standard execution of Tr(E) corresponding to a trace of communications and replications from E, enhanced by reductions to standard form. The proper prefix property arises since Phases I – III may individually or together dispose of an infinite suffix of $\mathcal{H}$. For the rest we argue as follows.

Let $G_\alpha \to G_{\alpha+1}$ be an execution step of $\mathcal{G}$ which is either a replication rewrite, or a rewrite corresponding to an event (a) of a successful communication. We call the graphs G_α of such steps witness graphs, including also the last graph of $\mathcal{G}$ as a witness graph in case $\mathcal{G}$ is finite. We claim that the sequence of witness graphs represent the expressions in a trace of communications and replications from E, enhanced by reductions to standard form.

We proceed by induction. First the base case. Let $G_{(\alpha 0)}$ be the first witness graph. We claim it represents $E \equiv E_0$. For consider the parse tree of E_0. It will depict how the TLPSEs of E_0 are combined to form E_0. It is clear that:

(1) The initial rewrite and ensuing sequence of auxiliary rewrites (and notifications by Roots) mirrors a preorder listing of this parse tree of the TLPSEs of E_0.

(2) The collection of idle Roots, active replication and proposer nodes of $G_{(\alpha 0)}$ generated, is in a bijective correspondence $\rho_0 : E_0 \to G_{(\alpha 0)}$ with the TLPSEs of E_0, as required by definition 7.2.(1).

(3) ρ_0 extends to an appropriate bijection between free channel names of TLPSEs of E_0 and Empty channel nodes of $G_{(\alpha 0)}$, again as required by definition 7.2.(2).

The above can be verified in detail by a subinduction on the structure of the derivation of $G_{(\alpha 0)}$ from *Initial; using the structure of the "rewrites to" relation of definition 6.4 to ensure that the correct function nodes are generated, and the properties of the $Args_P$ and $blend_P$ functions of the translation to ensure that channel nodes are linked to the correct function nodes. Now let $E_0 \Rrightarrow^* F_0$ be a reduction to standard form, performed in case any of the subsequent communications of $\mathcal{G}$ require top level ν's to have larger scopes than they possess in E_0. By lemma 7.5 we know that $G_{(\alpha 0)}$ represents F_0 too, via a map $\rho'_0 : F_0 \to G_{(\alpha 0)}$.

For the induction step, assume $G_{(\alpha i)}$ represents F_i through the bijection $\rho'_i : F_i \to G_{(\alpha i)}$. There are two cases. Either the next rewrite $G_{(\alpha i)} \to G_{(\alpha i)+1}$ is a replication rewrite of a replication node P of $G_{(\alpha i)}$ or not. If so, then there is a replication TLPSE $\{!\ldots\}_P$ of E_i corresponding to P via ρ_i. Let E_{i+1} be the π-calculus expression obtained by replicating $\{!\ldots\}_P$. In general the replicated subexpression will not be a TLPSE of E_{i+1} but will be a combination of TLPSEs of E_{i+1} using | and ν. The execution steps deriving $G_{(\alpha(i+1))}$ from $G_{(\alpha i)+1}$ mirror a preorder listing of the appropriate sub parse tree. So the next representation $\rho_{i+1} : E_{i+1} \to G_{(\alpha(i+1))}$ can be constructed. This is followed by a reduction to standard form $E_{i+1} \Rrightarrow^* F_{i+1}$ for the usual reason. Using lemma 7.5 again, we find the representation $\rho'_{i+1} : F_{i+1} \to G_{(\alpha(i+1))}$. In detail, this can be established using subinductions on the structure of the derivation $G_{(\alpha i)+1} \to^* G_{(\alpha(i+1))}$, and of the reduction $E_{i+1} \Rrightarrow^* F_{i+1}$.

Otherwise the next rewrite $G_{(\alpha i)} \to G_{(\alpha i)+1}$ is event (a) of a successful communication between proposer nodes P and Q of $G_{(\alpha i)}$, using a channel node x say as transmission link. Then there are two TLPSEs $\{+\ldots+\}_P$ and $\{+\ldots+\}_Q$ of F_i corresponding to P and Q via ρ'_i, and they are able to communicate via channel name x because of the properties of F_i and ρ'_i; specifically the data channel of the communication does not escape any scope it might be contained in because F_i is in standard form. Let E_{i+1} be the π-calculus expression obtained by doing the communication in F_i. In general $\{+\ldots+\}_P$ and $\{+\ldots+\}_Q$ will be replaced by two subexpressions which are not themselves TLPSEs of E_{i+1}, but combinations using | and ν of TLPSEs of E_{i+1}. The execution steps deriving $G_{(\alpha(i+1))}$ from $G_{(\alpha i)+1}$ mirror preorder listings of the two relevant sub parse trees. The execution will be such that the two sub parse tree roots are mirrored first, followed by the two remainders of the preorder listings, one after the other. This is a consequence of the detailed operation of Phases VI and VII. As before, the next representation $\rho_{i+1} : E_{i+1} \to G_{(\alpha(i+1))}$ can now be constructed. This is followed by a reduction to standard form $E_{i+1} \Rrightarrow^* F_{i+1}$ for the usual reason. Using lemma 7.5, we again find the representation $\rho'_{i+1} : F_{i+1} \to G_{(\alpha(i+1))}$. As before, all of the above can be checked in detail using a subinduction on the structure of the derivation $G_{(\alpha i)+1} \to^* G_{(\alpha(i+1))}$, and of the reduction $E_{i+1} \Rrightarrow^* F_{i+1}$.

Evidently $\mathcal{G}$ is a standard execution with the advertised properties, which corresponds via theorem 7.9 to a trace $\mathcal{T}$ of E as required. We are done. ☺

We can modify the theorem in two significant ways. If we drop the fairness assumption, then something like the original conclusion still holds true. The main problem is that for any event in the execution, its logical successor may be absent, which substantially messes up the technical details of the various early phases. Nevertheless, by discarding partially completed event sequences, an analogue of a prefix of a standard execution may be constructed. The main way in which it might fail to be standard, would be if auxiliary rewriting sequences failed to run to completion, leaving auxiliary nodes which did not rewrite to idle Roots, proposers and replicators, blocking the construction of a representation, particulary when reductions to standard form were involved. One could invent a modified notion of representation, or one could impose a more pernickety notion of weak fairness that only applied to auxiliary symbols, in order to cope with this.

In the opposite direction, if we strengthen the fairness assumption by assuming that no proper suffix of an infinite $\mathcal{H}$ consists entirely of useless work, we can drop the caveat about suffixes in the theorem. Viz.

Corollary 7.17 Let E be a π-calculus expression, and Tr(E) its translation. Let $\mathcal{H} = [H_0, H_1, \ldots]$ be a weakly fair execution of Tr(E). Suppose that if $\mathcal{H}$ is infinite, it contains an infinite number of commit rewrites. Then there is a trace $\mathcal{T}$ of communications and replications from E, enhanced by reductions to standard form, such that for a standard execution $\mathcal{G} = [G_0, G_1, \ldots]$ of Tr(E) corresponding via theorem 7.9 to $\mathcal{T}$

(1) For every node ${}^{(i)}x \in G_i \in \mathcal{G}$, ${}^{(i)}x \Xi {}^{(j)}y$ for some ${}^{(j)}y \in H_j \in \mathcal{H}$, and if ${}^{(i)}x$ is live then ${}^{(j)}y$ is live.

(2) For every arc $({}^{(i)}p_k, {}^{(i)}c) \in G_i \in \mathcal{G}$, $({}^{(i)}p_k, {}^{(i)}c) \Xi ({}^{(j)}q_k, {}^{(j)}d)$ for some arc $({}^{(j)}q_k, {}^{(j)}d) \in H_j \in \mathcal{H}$.

(3) If $H_j \to H_{j+1} \in \mathcal{H}$ is a rewrite of a redex rooted at ${}^{(j)}y \in H_j$ and governed by either a rule for a replication symbol, or a communication commit rule, there is a corresponding rewrite $G_i \to G_{i+1} \in \mathcal{G}$ of a redex rooted at a node ${}^{(i)}x \in G_i$, which is governed by the same rule, and ${}^{(i)}x \Xi {}^{(j)}y$. Further, if $H_j \to H_{j+1}$ and $H_{j'} \to H_{j'+1}$ are two distinct such rewrites, their corresponding $G_i \to G_{i+1}$ and $G_{i'} \to G_{i'+1}$ are also distinct, and all such rewrites occur in the same order in $\mathcal{H}$ and $\mathcal{G}$.

Now that we have the preceding results, we remark that we can easily adapt them to the more conventional view of the π-calculus in which replication is viewed as a syntactic congruence. All we need to do is to forget the replication steps in the trace $\mathcal{T}$, concentrating on the witness graphs that represent starting configurations of successful communications. We do not repeat the relevant theorems.

8 OTHER ASPECTS OF THE PI-CALCULUS

Theorem 7.16 is the main objective of this paper. In pursuing it, we omitted mention of a number of aspects of the π-calculus present in the original description [Milner et al. (1992)]. In this section, we return to some of these.

Other Syntactic Features

The original description features zero and parallel composition as before, but summation is *unprefixed*. In a translation such as ours, we can deal with such more general nondeterministic sums in much the same way as we did above. Namely, the symbol representing the sum, nondeterministically rewrites to a symbol representing one of the possibilities, which then attempts to engage in a transition corresponding to that possibility. Enough information must be retained so that backtracking can take place, and the system of choices may need to go (and if necessary to backtrack) several levels deep. The reason for this is that whereas with the prefixed sums of [Section 3], a choice followed by a successful communication commits the system irrevocably, with unprefixed sums, a choice may not yield a possibility capable of committing the system immediately, eg. the chosen summand may be itself an unprefixed sum. Worse, because the prefixes in the original description are not restricted to just the communication primitives, not all of them are committing. All of this offers much scope for optimisations in a real implementation. Let us look through the prefixes now.

The prefixes divide into the committing ones which are $\tau.Q$, $\bar{x}y.Q$, $x(y).Q$, and the non-committing ones namely $[x = y].Q$ and νxQ. We discuss these in a convenient order.

The case of $\tau.Q$ is relatively easy. Since in the π-calculus one has the transition

$$\tau.Q \xrightarrow{\tau} Q$$

one could introduce rules in the translation for symbols that "did nothing for one step" easily enough. In the treatment of correctness, in an augmented theorem 7.16, the rewrites for such rules would simply be left where they were.

The next easiest case is the noncommitting $[x = y].Q$. In standard MONSTR, there is no "pointer equality test". However many systems find such a test extremely useful, so in practice many MONSTR systems admit the additional pair of rules

```
PointersEqual[x x]  => *Yes ;
PointersEqual[x y]  => *No
```

the first being considered a non-default rule. An analysis of the architectural demands of such rules reveals that they are not excessive so their inclusion is permissible, though invevitably they clutter the case analysis of proofs about MONSTR systems, which explains why they are often omitted.

The natural way to incorporate the syntactic construct $\{[x = y].Q\}_P$ into the translation is thus to have symbol P call PointersEqual[x y], and depending on the result, to either proceed to behave as Q if x = y, or to backtrack to P (or an ancestor of P) if not. Here is one sense in which the equality test is noncommitting; if the test fails, it is still perfectly possible that some other process might subsequently make x and y equal, allowing the test to succeed. Furthermore the π-calculus transition rule

$$\frac{Q \xrightarrow{\alpha} Q'}{[x = x].Q \xrightarrow{\alpha} Q'}$$

gives us cause for concern, since it appears to demand the synchronisation of the equality test with the succeeding action α. This is another sense in which the equality test is noncommitting; any committment is contingent on the success of α. The synchronisation poses no problem in a standard execution, but in an arbitrary execution the two subactions may be separated in time. However, an augmented theorem 7.16 may exploit the semantics of substitution and redirection, which both hold that once b has been substituted for / redirected to a, the action cannot be subsequently undone. Thus the rewrites for a successful equality test can be postponed until they occur just before the rewrites for the subsequent α action. In this manner correctness may be extended to include the equality test.

Interestingly, the same does not hold for a hypothetical inequality test, $[x \neq y].Q$, since in the translation of the transition rule

$$\frac{Q \xrightarrow{\alpha} Q'}{[x \neq y].Q \xrightarrow{\alpha} Q'}$$

an arbitrary execution may perform the successful inequality test, and the critical action of α, at distant points of the execution. A priori it is not permissible to move either action to be close enough to the other, so the translated system could exhibit behaviours incommensurate with the original π-calculus expression. Worse, the architectural exigiencies of an inequality test are much more severe than those of an equality test, and thus inequality tests are definitely excluded from the remit of MONSTR. Cf. also remarks on a hypothetical inequality test in [Milner et al. (1991)].

We now briefly mention the prefix form νxQ. This would be implemented very much as in [Section 3], by rules that instantiate the bound channel. As for the equality test, the actions for a νx-prefixed process are not committing eg.

$$\frac{Q \xrightarrow{\alpha} Q'}{\nu xQ \xrightarrow{\alpha} Q'}$$

Therefore, as with the input communication primitive, enough information must be retained to enable backtracking to occur; and when it does occur, the instantiated bound channel is garbaged.

The other prefix forms, $\bar{x}y.Q$ and $x(y).Q$, refer to the communication abilities of a π-calculus expression E. Up to a point we have dealt with these in our translation, insofar as we have translated internal communications faithfully. However, the main reason that the original formulation of the π-calculus is interesting, is the fact that it deals also with external communications, i.e. how a π-calculus expression E communicates with its environment. Once we have understood how environments can be modelled in the context of our translation, we will be able to discuss the analogues of scope extrusion and intrusion within our framework.

Consider the question of environments. If Env is (a π-calculus expression representing) an environment for E, then one places E in the environment Env by forming

$$(E \mid Env).$$

If Tr(E) and Tr(Env) are the corresponding translations, then assuming that subexpression labels have been renamed apart in E and Env to forestall unfortunate name clashes, the analogue of the immersion can be viewed three ways.

One can first consider the ruleset $\mathrm{Tr}(\{E \mid Env\}_T)$ directly, where T is a new top level symbol.

Secondly one can regard it as having arisen from Tr(E) and Tr(Env) by discarding the two initial rules, and introducing a new rule for Initial which causes *Initial to rewrite to a fresh function T, this in turn rewriting as would any other rule for a composition symbol, to active T_1 and T_2 nodes (with suitable channel correspondences), these being the top level symbols for Tr(E) and Tr(Env).

Thirdly one can view the preceding ad-hoc procedure from a more formal perspective, regarding it as a specific example of the modular composition of translated systems alluded to in [Section 5]. If $\mathrm{Tr}^-(E)$ and $\mathrm{Tr}^-(Env)$ are the modular translations of E and Env without initial rules but with $Args$ functions specifically mentioned, then we form

$$\mathrm{Tr}(\{\ [\mathrm{Tr}^-(E)]_{T_1} \mid [\mathrm{Tr}^-(Env)]_{T_2}\ \}_T)$$

where

$$\{ [\ ]_{T_1} \mid [\ ]_{T_2} \}_T$$

is a specific labelled π-calculus context, into the holes of which (the square brackets), we are expected to "place" $\mathrm{Tr}^-(-)$ rulesets, in order to subsequently translate the entire expression to a MONSTR rule system. Depending on exactly how we view the composition of systems as taking place, this "placing" has a number of different interpretations. In the present case, we would just add the rule for T (and then either the rule for ∗Initial, or the $Args_T$: Free(T) $\rightarrow$ **args**$_T$ function, as required).

Let us now examine this process for an arbitrary context, say

$$\{ C([\ ]_{T_1}, [\ ]_{T_2}, \ldots, [\ ]_{T_n}) \}_T$$

where C is a π-calculus context expression, i.e. an expression of π-calculus syntax which is "syntactically non-ground" in that n leaves of its parse tree are π-calculus expression non-terminals. These non-terminals correspond to the n $[\ ]_{T_i}$ holes into which some $\mathrm{Tr}^-(E_i)$ translations of systems are to be "placed". For it to work as it should, we need some restrictions on the behaviour of names and symbols in the different components.

(1) There are no clashes of subexpression labels, either between labels coming from the various E_i, or between labels coming from one of these and labels in the enclosing context C, *except* that the symbols labelling the top-level constructs of the E_i match the symbols labelling the holes into which their $\mathrm{Tr}^-(E_i)$ translations are placed.

(2) The $Args_{T_i}$ functions for the top-level constructs T_i output by the translations of the subcomponents in $\mathrm{Tr}^-(E_i)$, must match the $Args_{T_i}$ functions assumed for these subcomponents by the translation of the context. More specifically, the two versions of the $Args_{T_i}$ functions must agree in their domains i.e. the sets of free channel names involved, and in the argument positions of the various T_i symbols that these free channel names get mapped to. A byproduct of this is that capture of subcomponents' free names by binders in the interior of the context is permitted.

Elaborating a little on the second point, inspection of the translation in [Section 5] shows that the various recursive constructs of a π-calculus expression act as transformers of $Args_P$ functions. The same must be true for "syntactically non-ground" compositions of recursive constructs, i.e. contexts. This leads us to view the translation of an arbitrary context from two complementary perspectives.

Firstly the translation of the context may be "delayed" until the translations of the subcomponents to be inserted into the holes are available, (specifically till the top-level $Args_{T_i}$ functions are available), and then the bottom-up translation may be completed. In this case, the "placing" of the $\mathrm{Tr}^-(-)$ translations we mentioned above, is simply set union of the $\mathrm{Tr}^-(E_i)$ translations with what is generated by the remainder of the translation.

Secondly, the translation may be done eagerly, before the translations of the subcomponents are available, by abstracting away all information obtained from the $Args_{T_i}$ functions within the body of the context's translation. In this case, we obtain the concept of a "standalone" translation of a context C with holes, which as for a closed system, again has two components. The first component is an $Args_T$ function transformer, which takes a collection of $Args_{T_i}$ functions (to be eventually supplied by the $\mathrm{Tr}^-(E_i)$ translations for its holes), and maps them into the $Args_T$ function of the top-level symbol T of the context. Abstracting away from lower level detail, this function constructs the union of the free channel names mentioned in the domains of the $Args_{T_i}$ functions, removes any names that are captured by binders in C, and maps what remains (together with any channel names that are mentioned in C and occur free at the top level) to the argument positions of T. The second component is a partially instantiated set of MONSTR rules for the syntactic structure of T. The uninstantiated features of these rules (eg. their arity) will depend upon which and how many free channels are input from the $\mathrm{Tr}^-(E_i)$ subsystems, which of them are captured by binders in the context, and which of them need to be output in the top-level of the result. Again such a partially instantiated set of rules can be viewed as a function, taking as input a collection of $Args_{T_i}$ functions, and mapping them into the fully instantiated set of rules. In this case, the "placing" of the $\mathrm{Tr}^-(E_i)$ translations corresponds to the composition of a top-level context module $\mathrm{Tr}(C)$ with an appropriate number of input systems $\mathrm{Tr}^-(E_i)$. This is accomplished by the application of the context's $Args_T$ transformer and rule generation function to the $Args_{T_i}$ functions of the input systems, and including the rules of the input systems. This yields an $Args_T$ function for the top-level symbol of the new system, and a fully instantiated set of rules for the system as a whole.

However, in this more general setting, we can contemplate composing a top-level context with an appropriate number of input contexts (with holes). The composition of an $Args_T$ function transformer with a suitable collection of input $Args_{T_i}$ function transformers is another $Args_T$ function transformer. Similarly the composition of a function from a collection of $Args_{T_i}$ functions to a fully instantiated ruleset, with a suitable collection of input $Args_{T_i}$ function transformers, is another function from $Args_{T_i}$ functions to a ruleset. Performing these compositions, and including the input functions from the $Args_{T_i}$ to rulesets in the latter, yields the resulting module

$$\mathrm{Tr}^-(\{\ C([\mathrm{Tr}^-(C_1([\ldots]))]_{T_1}, [\mathrm{Tr}^-(C_2([\ldots]))]_{T_2}, \ldots, [\mathrm{Tr}^-(C_n([\ldots]))]_{T_n})\ \}_T)$$

Pursuing this idea further would lead us to a graph rewriting based fibration semantics for the π-calculus (cf. [Coquand et al. (1989), Asperti and Martini (1992)]). However we will not follow this up here.

We note that a closed system, regarded as a context with no holes, translates to a constant $Args_T$ function transformer (which just yields the top level $Args_T$ function), and a constant function yielding a fully instantiated set of rules, which is as we would expect.

Now that we understand environments, we can make sense of such transitions as

$$\bar{x}y.Q \xrightarrow{\bar{x}y} Q$$

within the translation. Let us consider the more general form

$$E \xrightarrow{\bar{x}y} F$$

which says that (it can be proved within the deduction system of π-calculus that) E is capable of evolving to F by virtue of engaging in a communication in which it ouputs y on x when placed in an environment capable of inputting on x. The natural analogue of this in the MONSTR world is to say that $\mathrm{Tr}^{-}(E)$ is capable of an equivalent communication in a modular composition

$$\mathrm{Tr}(\{\ [\mathrm{Tr}^{-}(E)]_{T_1} \mid [\mathrm{Tr}^{-}(Env)]_{T_2}\ \}_T)$$

in which *Env* has channel name x free at the top level and is capable of inputing on it.

An alternative way of saying this is to consider a graph G which represents E (by rewriting using Tr(E) as in lemma 7.4 for example). The representation $\rho_E : E \to G$ identifies nodes of G which represent the free channels, and channel x in particular. If we have a graph G_{env} which represents a suitable environment *Env*, then the representation $\rho_{Env} : Env \to G_{env}$ picks out a node representing x in G_{env}. If B is a graph consisting exactly of as many Empty channel nodes as E and *Env* have free channel names in common, there are bijections $e : B \to E$ and $env : B \to Env$ identifying nodes in B with the relevant free channel names in E and *Env* respectively. The compositions

$$\rho_E \circ e : B \to G \quad \text{and} \quad \rho_{Env} \circ env : B \to G_{env}$$

are arrows in the category of MONSTR graphs and graph homomorphisms. We can form the pushout $G \boxplus_B G_{env}$ of these two arrows, which just joins the graphs G and G_{env} by identifying nodes representing the common free channel names like x. Pushouts in general are the appropriate analogue in the graph world of modular composition, and it is not hard to see that $G \boxplus_B G_{env}$ represents $(E \mid Env)$.

The significance for the MONSTR world of transitions like

$$E \xrightarrow{\bar{x}y} F$$

should now be clear. Essentially such a piece of notation refers to the possible behaviour of E in a suitable environment, but with the environment abstracted out. Accordingly, we can do the same with the translation and write

$$G \xrightarrow{\bar{x}y} H$$

to mean that G, which represents E, is capable of offering a write of channel y over channel x, and upon successful completion, to perform some auxilliary rewrites in order to get into shape to represent F via graph H. We justify this by an appeal to lemma 7.7 with the role of the environment abstracted away. (Note that it is preferable to have G and H present in such a notation rather than Tr(E) and Tr(F) since the former are the semantic objects which are engaged in any actual communications.)

We can take a similar approach to the input transition of the π-calculus involving the prefix $x(y).Q$.

The main thing from the original description that remains undiscussed is the business of scope extrusion and intrusion. There are no such notions in the system of [Section 3]. In that system, if a private channel y in one part of the π-calculus expression is intended to be communicated to some other part of the expression, the binding νy must have a scope large enough to enclose both parts, for which reason we introduced the syntactic reduction $\Rrightarrow^*$. This means that if one subsystem wishes to send to another subsystem a channel y that it prefers to consider as private, the binding νy must occur in the context into which both subsystems are to be placed. Technically, the the data channel y becomes free in the sending subsystem, and thus there is the risk of unintended name capture unless the channel names in the subsystems and enclosing context are chosen wisely.

Scope extrusion and intrusion delays the necessity of wise name choice, by allowing y to remain bound (and thus alpha-convertible), with scope initially within the sending subsystem. The open rule

$$\frac{Q \xrightarrow{\bar{x}y} Q'}{\nu y Q \xrightarrow{\bar{x}(u)} Q'\{u/y\}}$$

effectively cuts open the scope of the νy binder by transforming the output action $\bar{x}y$ into $\bar{x}(u)$ (where u is a fresh name), which indicates that the data channel name u is bound and is not to be captured by other free names. The wise choice of channel names (implemented now by alpha-converting the bound name u as needed), is thereby postponed until the communication takes place via the close rule

$$\frac{P \xrightarrow{\bar{x}(u)} P' \qquad Q \xrightarrow{x(u)} Q'}{P \mid Q \xrightarrow{\tau} \nu u(P' \mid Q')}$$

which demands that the bound channels in sender and receiver must match (thus forestalling inappropriate name clashes), and binds the result of the communication within a fresh binder whose scope is now large enough to enclose both subsystems, as in the previous discussion.

To achieve this effect in the framework of our translation we need do nothing special. A graph representing the sender subexpression can be generated as usual, but because the data channel u say, is ν-bound, u does not appear in the domain of the $Args_{T_i}$ function of the sender. Because the transmission link channel, x say, must be free in both sender and receiver, x does appear in the domain of the $Args_{T_i}$ functions of both sender and receiver. Now when we perform the pushout to join the sender's and receiver's representing graphs, the two nodes corresponding to x will be identified, though u will remain private to the sender's subgraph. As we said in theorem 7.9, which data channel gets sent in a successful communication is purely the business of the sender and does not depend on the data channel's scope, and the receiver is equally indifferent to this. Thus upon successful completion of the communication, the resulting graph would correspond to a π-calculus expression in which the νu-binder had drifted into the context via a $\Rrightarrow^*$ reduction. This is as we would expect.

Scope extrusion and intrusion are thus superfluous in the translation. This confirms our earlier remarks, that graph connectivity is able to easily accomplish what is achieved (and perhaps a little awkwardly at that) by subtle notions of scope manipulation in the syntax of the π-calculus. In the end, the whole of the theory of the π-calculus can be translated into the world of the MONSTR representatives on the basis of the results in [Section 7], albeit that the precise technical details become more intricate.

Equalities

Much of the theory of the π-calculus and similar systems is concerned with the formulation of equality theories over the expressions of the calculus, formed by considering various bisimulations [see Milner et al. (1992)]. Given that we can translate the π-calculus faithfully into MONSTR, all such theories can be reformulated as properties of the corresponding class of MONSTR graphs as we indicated above. Rather than do this though, we make some comments about equalities that arise naturally in the context of MONSTR rewriting. In general they will be weaker notions than those which arise through the π-calculus bisimulations.

The natural notion of equality in the context of graph rewriting, is that of graph isomorphism (of live subgraphs). Because we are interested in the dynamics of systems, we must ensure that the underlying notion of homomorphism includes equality of the node and arc markings. Isomorphism is quite a weak notion compared to most of the ones studied for the π-calculus, for example it distinguishes between different numbers of copies of replicated processes. But it has some good points. Perhaps its main virtue is that it clearly distinguishes concurrency from interleaving. When x, y, u, v are all different, the two expressions $\bar{x}u \mid y(v)$ and $\bar{x}u.y(v) + y(v).\bar{x}u$, are strongly ground equivalent in [Milner et al. (1992)], but in the MONSTR translation, the representative of $\bar{x}u \mid y(v)$ has two function nodes whereas the representative of $\bar{x}u.y(v) + y(v).\bar{x}u$ has only one (of course this is a consequence of how we chose to do the translation). Opinions differ on whether these expressions ought to be considered equal or not. That they are ground bisimilar rests on the fact that bisimilarity depends on sequential observation. This in turn can be laid at the feet of the inherently sequential rewriting model used to express the transition relation. And that is as true of the MONSTR translation as it is of the π-calculus.

If one goes beyond the sequential rewriting model to a more concurrent one, in which more than one redex may be rewritten simultaneously provided they don't interfere, then a more concurrent environment eg. $x(a) \mid \bar{y}b$ (as opposed to $x(a).\bar{y}b + \bar{y}b.x(a)$) could distinguish between the two expressions. Thus $\bar{x}u \mid y(v)$ might rewrite to $\mathbf{0} \mid \mathbf{0}$ in one step, while $\bar{x}u.y(v) + y(v).\bar{x}u$ would always require two steps to rewrite to $\mathbf{0}$. To explore this in more detail though, would take us far beyond the scope of this paper.

Restricting attention once more to the syntax of [Section 3], another good thing about our translation (up to graph isomorphism) is that it respects the various equivalences of π-calculus systems that we introduced in [Section 3].

Let us mention the semigroup rules for + and |. For the former, we have commutativity since summation of alternatives is translated into set union of rules for distinct function symbols. (And insofar as in [Section 3] we informally permit ourselves to consider summations such as $((\pi_1.Q_1 + \pi_2.Q_2) + \pi_3.Q_3)$, the implied associativity thereof is just a feature of this set union of rules.) For the latter we have commutativity since the parallel composition of a set of subprocesses is translated into the set union of the distinct contractum nodes that represent them in the RHS of a rule for |. Associativity for | arises since the derivation of the representing graph of a compound parallel composition differs from the derivation of the representing graph of its flattened version, by one or more auxiliary rewrites (rather as in lemma 7.5). It is clear that in standard executions, once the garbage is removed, the two resulting representing graphs come out isomorphic, (or even possibly equal if a convenient implementation of a premeditated suite of contractum building operations is adopted).

Another equivalence demanded in [Section 3] is alpha-convertibility. It is clear that this is respected by the translation (up to graph isomorphism), since each bound channel name get translated to an Empty contractum node of some rule, whose instantiations will all be equivalent under graph isomorphism. Finally, our syntactic reduction $\equiv\!>^*$ has been dealt with in lemma 7.5.

A slightly stronger notion of equality for MONSTR systems arises through the "innocent" renaming of symbols. This is worth considering given that the tags that label subexpressions in the translation and ultimately correspond to function symbols in the translated system are arbitrary.

Definition 8.1 Let $\mathcal{R}$ and $\mathcal{S}$ be two MONSTR rule systems. A substitution $\theta : \mathbf{S} \to \mathbf{S}$ on symbols is a system homomorphism iff for all $D = (P, root, Red, Act) \in \mathcal{R}$, θD, interpreted pointwise, is isomorphic to a rule of $\mathcal{S}$. It is a renaming of $\mathcal{R}$ iff $\theta\mathcal{R} = \mathcal{S}$, where $\theta\mathcal{R}$ is interpreted pointwise.

Thus a renaming of a rule system takes rules in $\mathcal{R}$ to rules in $\mathcal{S}$ which "do the same thing" modulo the renaming. Note that renamings automatically respect the constant Initial, and ought to respect the constant Root if garbage collection is to be unchanged.

Definition 8.2 Let $\mathcal{R}$ be a MONSTR rule system and $\mathcal{X} = [X_0, X_1, X_2, \ldots]$ be an execution of $\mathcal{R}$. Likewise for $\mathcal{S}$ and $\mathcal{Y} = [Y_0, Y_1, Y_2, \ldots]$. Let $\theta\mathcal{R} = \mathcal{S}$ be a renaming. Then we write

$$^{(i)}x \in X_i \Xi_\theta \, ^{(j)}y \in Y_j \;\; \text{iff} \;\; ^{(i)}\theta(x) \equiv \, ^{(j)}y$$

where $^{(i)}\theta(x)$ is the node $^{(i)}x$ with its symbol substituted according to θ i.e. $\sigma(^{(i)}\theta(x)) = \theta(\sigma(^{(i)}x))$.

Theorem 8.3 Let $\mathcal{R}$ be a MONSTR system and let $\theta\mathcal{R} = \mathcal{S}$ be a renaming.

(1) For every execution $\mathcal{X} = [X_0, X_1, X_2, \ldots]$ of $\mathcal{R}$ there is an execution of $\mathcal{Y} = [Y_0, Y_1, Y_2, \ldots]$ of $\mathcal{S}$ such that for all i, and all $^{(i)}x \in X_i$,

$$^{(i)}x \, \Xi_\theta \, ^{(j)}y$$

for a suitable $^{(j)}y \in Y_j$.

(2) For any execution $\mathcal{Y} = [Y_0, Y_1, Y_2, \ldots]$ of $\mathcal{S}$, there is an execution $\mathcal{X} = [X_0, X_1, X_2, \ldots]$ of $\mathcal{R}$ such that for all i, and all $^{(j)}y \in Y_j$

$$^{(i)}x \, \Xi_\theta \, ^{(j)}y$$

for a suitable $^{(i)}x \in X_i$.

We regard the above as self-evident and do not bother proving it.

By altering the tags that label subexpressions during translation we end up with a system that is renamed compared to if we had not done so. Theorem 8.3 confirms that we do not alter the intrinsic behaviour thereby. Furthermore, there is one place where we have evaded the necessity of considering renamed systems already. That is when early in [Section 5], we allowed identical subexpressions of a π-calculus expression to be identically labelled. This was exploited in lemma 7.6 when a replicand P was identically tagged to its originating $!P$. Had we been forced to tag the new copy with a fresh label, we would have been forced to consider lemma 7.6 only up to a renaming, an undesirable complication in [Section 7].

Renaming thus provides a natural notion of bisimulation when node symbols are considered as arbitrary "user-supplied" names (as they are for the auxiliary symbols in the translation), rather than universal constants (as applies to symbols such as Initial, Root, and the symbols of the communication protocol). Further, it is clear that renaming is still a weaker bisimulation than the strong ground equivalence of [Milner et al. (1992)].

Being well defined in conventional set theory, both graph isomorphism and renaming provide adequate semantics for the π-calculus via the translation of [Section 5]. Unlike most semantics for process algebras, they are not directly manufactured from the syntactic components that constitute the original expression.

We note finally that [Milner et al. (1992)]'s strong equivalence, which asserts bisimilarity under all substitutions, corresponds in the MONSTR world to a rather unusual relation on graphs given by externally imposed redirections, of channel nodes to other channel nodes. Such a notion does not make any sense for arbitrary MONSTR graphs but can be made to do so for those arising from Tr(E) systems.

9 CONCLUSIONS

The translation of the π-calculus into MONSTR brings out a number of useful points. Firstly it necessitates the clear understanding of the issues of free and bound names and of scoping, as they arise in very different styles of computational system. A good part of the material above can be interpreted as an essay about this. Specifically, we have seen that in a graph based language, where connections between parts of the computational structure are explicitly represented using arcs or edges, the ideas of bound variables and scope as used in the syntax of traditional languages become largely superfluous; the structure of the graph and the notion of graph matching provide an information channel that supercedes the use of the parse tree for this purpose.

Secondly, by targetting our translation to a language designed with a very concrete implementation in mind, the reasonableness in practice of the primitives of the source language may be judged. This is a particularly valuable objective if one is interested in bringing together notions of "process" in use in disparate areas of computer science, as we, by dint of remarks in the introduction, are, at least implicitly. In the case of the π-calculus, we have seen that the amount of synchronisation implicit in the communication rule can make substantial demands of implementations. In MONSTR, in which the capabilities of a single rewrite are rather closely geared to what is cheaply implementable in a single atomic action of a concurrent distributed system, we have seen that it is realistic to have a quantity of state change in such an action, equivalent to the update of the root function and of one other non-root node. Unfortunately, to implement the true dynamic synchronised point to point communication of the π-calculus, in a system featuring maximal concurrency, we need to be able to update at least one further piece of state within a single action. There is nothing to prevent us from doing so within the syntax of graph rewriting (it is easy enough in DACTL, MONSTR's parent), but there are good operational reasons why it is prohibited in MONSTR. Given this state of affairs, to stay within MONSTR, one has to either go for a protocol featuring some degree of wastefulness, or for a much more heavily serialised implementation such as afforded by a global semaphore. In this paper we have chosen the former course.

In the real world, "agents" are normally connected to a set of communication channels of which they are well aware. Generally, the agents are active and the channels are passive. Even if the agents are hazy about which other agents are connected to their channels, little synchronisation hinges on the interactions with channels due to the latters' passivity. The π-calculus communication primitive thus comes across as rather more high level and abstract than might be expected of a basic communication primitive; this particularly so since the collection of channels that an agent may use is a function of the agent's context and the dynamics of the system. In the real world, the closest that we might get to a situation where mutually ignorant agents communicate over a shared medium, is the internet. No one knows precisely who is connected to the internet at any given moment. However, even in this situation, the internet is not used to effect serialised and synchronised point to point communications between an arbitrary mutually ignorant sending/receiving pair of agents. On the contrary side, one cannot argue with the syntactic and algebraic simplicity of the communication rule of the π-calculus, to which its existence is largely attributable. Of course similar remarks apply to many other process calculi, but we have been specific in this paper.

Thirdly, the treatment of correctness deserves comment. Essentially, a suitable weak bisimulation has been set up but the techniques to construct it owe more to rewriting theory and to serialisability theory than to the usual finitistic techniques frequently found in process algebra. A fairly comprehensive and self-contained treatment of the correctness issue has been given, and many of its aspects are to be found in correctness arguments for any MONSTR program. In fact this paper contains the first such MONSTR correctness argument to be written out in reasonable detail, which gives it independent interest.

So in one sense this paper may be viewed as a concrete exercise in MONSTR program verification, the program being the output of translation Tr(E). In another sense, because of the generic nature of the proof, it is also an exercise in compiler correctness, the compiler being the meta-level translation process. The correctness argument is visibly non-trivial, and not formal in the usual sense of the word, but it certainly sets the agenda for what such a formal proof would have to address. A fully formal proof would be a sizeable undertaking, but in reality, given suitable theories for a number of what are well understood but properly higher order concepts such as "graph", "execution" etc., [Section 6] and [Section7] involved nothing other than what could be straightforwardly expressed, in a logic in which the universal quantifiers occur bounded over some well understood set, and the existential quantifiers refered to objects that were explicitly constructed. So a formal proof would not be completely out of the question.

In a third sense, one can see the soundness proof in particular, as an exercise in serialisability theory, another case of a distant area of computer science concerned with notions of process, namely concurrency control theory from the database world, having an impact on a problem in process algebra. In this regard, the recent work on atomicity of [Lynch et al. (1994)] (see also references therein), bears comparison with the contents of this paper. Certainly the complexity of the serialisability proofs there is rather reminiscent of what appears in the present paper. Pursuing the analogy for a moment, we can view the communications of a π-calculus expression as high level transactions (from the viewpoint of the MONSTR system). Nevertheless, unlike normal database systems, individual rewrites themselves have many features of transactions too, in that serialisation is not just a matter of choosing a suitable order for them. The sheduling strategy for rewrites is determined by MONSTR rule selection semantics, and any serialisation performed, must be done within the constraints allowed by this. Up to a point, this makes life harder in our case.

Viewed from yet a different perspective, one can see the serialisability proof of theorem 7.16 (and other serialisability proofs), as a particularly easy example of a forcing or priority or finite injury argument (to use recursion-theoretic jargon), in that the object of interest, the execution $\mathcal{G}$, is constructed as the limit of a number of other executions, all featuring a decreasing proportion of undesirable characteristics. Two things contribute to the easy nature of the argument, the first being the explictly constructible nature of the transformation process, and the second is the vital observation that the process can be neatly split into phases, the earliest of which serve to simplify matters considerably for their successors. A "one pass" version of the theorem would be perfectly feasable, but the technical details would be considerably more intricate, as the reader is invited to imagine.

The translation itself was inspired by other translations into term graph rewriting systems. In particular by those in [Banach and Papadopoulos (1993), Banach and Papadopoulos (1995)], which are concerned with concurrent logic languages. Also [Glauert (1992)] does related work on mapping a process calculus into a term graph rewriting system, however with the crucial ommission of the guarded summation construct. It is precisely that which forces us to adopt a communication protocol and its synchronisation problems, due to the amount of atomic state change implicit in the general case of a single comunication of the π-calculus. It is also that which is the source of most of the fun and games in [Section 6] and [Section 7].

10 References

[Aczel (1993)] Aczel P.H.G., Processes and Final Universes. Seminar, Dept. of Computer Science, Manchester University, (1993).

[Asperti and Martini (1992)] Asperti A., Martini S., Categorical Models of Polymorphism. Information and Computation **99**, (1992), 1-79.

[Banach and Papadopoulos (1993)] Banach R., Papadopoulos G., Parallel Term Graph Rewriting and Concurrent Logic Programs. *in*: Proc. WPDP-93, Bulgarian Acad. of Sci., Boyanov (ed.), (1993), 303-322. (North Holland, to appear.)

[Banach and Papadopoulos (1995)] Banach R., Papadopoulos G., Linear Logic Behaviour of Term Graph Rewriting Programs. *in*: Proc. A.C.M. SAC-95, (1995), 157-163.

[Banach et al. (1988)] Banach R., Sargeant J., Watson I., Watson P., Woods V., The Flagship Project. *in*: Proc. UK-IT-88, (Alvey Technical Conference), 242-245, Information Engineering Directorate, Department of Trade and Industry, IEE Publications, (1988).

[Banach and Watson (1989)] Banach R., Watson P., Dealing with State in Flagship: the MONSTR Computational Model. *in*: Proc. CONPAR-88, Jesshope, Reinhartz (eds.), 595-604, B.C.S. Workshop Series, Cambridge University Press, (1989).

[Banach (1993a)] Banach R., MONSTR I — Fundamental Issues and the Design of MONSTR. *Submitted to* New Generation Computing, (1993).

[Banach (1993b)] Banach R., MONSTR II — Suspending MONSTR Semantics. *Submitted to* New Generation Computing, (1993).

[Banach (1993c)] Banach R., MONSTR: Term Graph Rewriting for Parallel Machines. *in*: Term Graph Rewriting: Theory and Practice, Sleep, Plasmeijer, van Eekelen (eds.), 243-252, John Wiley, (1993).

[Berry and Boudol (1990)] Berry G., Boudol G., The Chemical Abstract Machine. *in*: 17th Annual Symposium on Principles of Programming Languages, A.C.M., (1990). *Also in*: Theoretical Computer Science **96**, (1992), 217-248.

[Coquand et al. (1989)] Coquand T., Gunter C., Winskel G., Domain Theoretic Models of Polymorphism. Information and Computation **81**, (1989), 123-167.

[Corradini et al. (1994)] Corradini A., Montanari U., Rossi F., An Abstract Machine for Concurrent Modular Systems: CHARM. Theoretical Computer Science **122**, (1994), 165-200.

[Degano and Montanari (1987)] Degano P., Montanari U., A Model of Distributed Systems Based on Graph Rewriting. J.A.C.M. **34**, (1987), 411-449.

[Glauert (1992)] Glauert J.R.W., Asynchronous Mobile Processes and Graph Rewriting. *in*: Proc. PARLE-92, Etiemble, Syre (eds.), LNCS **605** 63-78, Springer, (1992).

[Glauert et al. (1988a)] Glauert J.R.W., Kennaway J.R., Sleep M.R., Somner G.W., Final Specification of DACTL. Internal Report SYS-C88-11, School of Information Systems, University of East Anglia, Norwich, U.K, (1988).

[Glauert et al. (1988b)] Glauert J.R.W., Hammond K., Kennaway J.R., Papdopoulos G.A., Sleep M.R., DACTL: Some Introductory Papers. School of Information Systems, University of East Anglia, Norwich, U.K, (1988).

[Lynch et al. (1994)] Lynch N., Merritt M., Weihl W., Fekete A., Atomic Transactions. Morgan Kaufmann, (1994).

[Milner (1979)] Milner R., Flow Graphs and Flow Algebras. J.A.C.M. **26**, (1979), 794-818.

[Milner (1989)] Milner R., Communication and Concurrency. Prentice-Hall, (1989).

[Milner (1993a)] Milner R., The Polyadic Pi-Calculus: A Tutorial. *in*: Logic and Algebra of Specification, Bauer, Brauer, Schwichtenberg (eds.), 203-246, Springer, (1993).

[Milner (1993b)] Milner R., An Action Structure for Synchronous Pi-Calculus. *in*: Proc. FCT-93, Esik (ed.), LNCS **710** 87-105, Springer, (1993).

[Milner et al. (1991)] Milner R., Parrow J., Walker D., Modal Logics for Mobile Processes. *in*: Proc. CONCUR-91, Baeten, Groote (eds.), LNCS **527** 45-60, Springer, (1991).

[Milner et al. (1992)] Milner R., Parrow J., Walker D., A Calculus of Mobile Processes – I / II. Inf. and Comp. **100**, (1992), 1-40, 41-77.

[Nielsen et al. (1981)] Nielsen M., Plotkin G., Winskel G., Petri Nets, Event Structures and Domains, Part I. Theoretical Computer Science **13**, (1981), 85-108.

[Parrow (1994)] Parrow J., Interaction Diagrams. *in*: A Decade of Concurrency, de Bakker, de Roever, Rozenberg (eds.), LNCS **803** 477-508, Springer, (1994). *and* Manuscript, SICS, Kista, Sweden.

[Watson and Watson (1987)] Watson P., Watson I., Evaluating Functional Programs on the Flagship Machine. *in*: Proc. FLCA-87, Kahn (ed.), LNCS **274** 80-97, Springer, (1987).

[Watson et al. (1987)] Watson I., Woods V., Watson P., Banach R., Greenberg M., Sargeant J., Flagship: A Parallel Architecture for Declarative Programming. *in*: Proc. 15th Annual International Symposium on Computer Architecture, Hawaii, ACM, (1987).

[Watson et al. (1989)] Watson I., Sargeant J., Watson P., Woods V., The Flagship Parallel Machine. *in*: Proc. CONPAR-88, Jesshope, Reinhartz (eds.), 125-133, BCS Workshop Series, Cambridge University Press, (1989).

[Winskel (1986)] Winskel G., Event Structures. *in*: Petri Nets, An Advanced Course, LNCS **255**, 325-392, (1986).

[Winskel (1988)] Winskel G., An Introduction to Event Structures. *in*: Linear Time, Branching Time and Partial Order in Logics and Models for Concurrency. de Bakker, de Roever, Rozenberg (eds.), LNCS **354**, 364-397, (1988).

Journal of Universal Computer Science, vol. 1, no. 6 (1995), 399-409
submitted: 31/3/95, accepted: 16/6/95, appeared: 28/6/95

Distributed Caching in Networked File Systems

Artur Klauser
(Institute for Applied Information Processing and Communications,
Graz University of Technology, Austria,
aklauser@iaik.tu-graz.ac.at)

Reinhard Posch
(Institute for Applied Information Processing and Communications,
Graz University of Technology, Austria,
rposch@iaik.tu-graz.ac.at)

Abstract: Changing relative performance of processors, networks, and disks makes it necessary to reconsider algorithms using these three resources. As networks get faster and less congested topologies emerge, it becomes important to use network resources more aggressively to obtain good performance. Substitution of local disk accesses by accesses to remote memory can lead to better balanced resource usage and thus to faster systems. In this work we address the issue of file caching in a networked file system configuration. Distributed block-level in-memory caches are considered. We show that carefully constructed distributed concepts can lead to lower server load and better overall system performance than centralized concepts. Oversimplification, although aimed at gaining performance for single components, may deteriorate overall performance as a result of unbalanced resource usage.

Key Words: networked file systems, distributed file caches, load balancing, file system performance

Category: D.4.2, D.4.3, C.4

1 Introduction

File caching is used as the most important method to overcome the inherent speed difference between processor and disk. In centralized systems file caches form an intermediate storage level between slow disk storage and fast memory. File accesses in distributed systems are based on a client-server computing model [Coulouris, Dollimore 1988] and have to propagate through various instances. These present many opportunities for caching at various levels like the server, the client, or *the network*.

We compare a number of client caching approaches in distributed client-server systems. The performance of a single server cache with cacheless clients is used as a reference point for our comparisons. Our major goal is to find effective approaches for distributed caching which perform at least as well as centralized server caches, while at the same time reducing the load usually put on the server. For this considerations we assume standard Unix file system semantics in the distributed system. Client file caches are maintained in client memory, not on client disks. Caching and cache coherency is based on the file system block level. Clients reading a file see changes to this file immediately after completion of the write operation, not only after close.

To compare the performance of various algorithms we use trace-driven simulations. Traces come from a measured, real workload to prevent biasing the simulation with synthetic workloads that might make inadequate assumptions about the file access and file sharing profile. Simulations also let us lift restrictions typically found in current hardware and allow a prediction of the performance of future systems. Moreover, simulations allow exact repeatability, which is an important advantage for studying algorithms in distributed systems.

Our computing model is a general MIMD type architecture with distributed memory, and a point-to-point interconnection network. This model fits both, networks of workstations (NOWs) with high-performance communication networks (e.g. ATM, HIPPI) and MPP machines. The only means of inter-node communication is by message passing.

An important point of the network structure is its ability to perform multiple network operations concurrently. Distinct pairs of machines can communicate concurrently by means of different communication links. We assume point-to-point networks to be more appropriate for parallel and distributed systems, as they are more scalable than multidrop networks, which are limited to one network operation at a time.

As network speeds evolve rapidly we chose to simulate the internal communication network of an MPP supercomputer, namely an Intel Paragon. Although NOWs do not usually reach this performance yet, they will be able to operate at such speeds in the near future. The model uses a direct network with 2D-mesh topology and wormhole routing with an E-cube routing decision strategy (x-y routing). All message routing is implemented by dedicated hardware. The simulation model comprises of a 4×4 mesh with 16 processing nodes. Basic simulation parameters are 105 μs latency and 26 MBytes/s bandwidth, performance figures measured in Transmittal-8, an early beta release of the Paragon operating system.

[Section 2] gives an overview of the implemented caching policies. The simulator and the file system trace data are introduced in [Section 3]. [Section 4] discusses results of the simulations, [Section 5] presents related work, and the work is concluded in [Section 6].

2 Caching Policies

All caching models have a number of common features. Unless otherwise noted caches are assumed to operate at the file system block level, with a block size of 4-kByte and a write-back policy with server driven invalidations. A cache replacement strategy of least recently used (LRU) is used in all cases. Although this strategy is not optimal, many studies have shown that it is close to optimal ([Maffeis 1992],[Maffeis, Cap 1992]). Moreover, LRU guarantees the inclusion property, i.e. caches of size $i+1$ hold all items of size i caches, plus one additional item. This property is important for variable-size caches, as it guarantees monotony of the cache's hit rate function. Finally, all models use fully associative caches which give good performance and only require minimal additional overhead in the case of file accesses, which are rather expensive operations already.

2.1 Fixed-Size Caches

The following reference models are used in the evaluation process. These models have been chosen to give some upper and lower bounds on specific distribution concepts. They are not intended to be sophisticated implementations of these concepts. The order of presentation is approximately an order of increased complexity. A more detailed description of the models can be found in [Klauser 1994].

Server Cache Only (SCO): Server caching with cacheless clients is used as a reference point for comparing other policies. This model requires every client access to be forwarded to the server, resulting in substantial network and server load. It provides an upper bound on network traffic induced by the file system. The centralized design imposes strong limitations on scalability.

Local Disk (LOD): This model assumes each client to use a local disk for file storage and also assumes a memory cache to be operated by each client. The server's role is only that of a coordination instance, controlling the traffic flow between clients. Our interest is in the cache hit rates. As the client-server traffic does not contribute to this measure it has been omited. This model presents the most optimistic view of a completely distributed file service, where all accesses can be fulfilled locally. Any realistic implementation would also induce some client-server and client-client traffic.

No Coherency (NOC): With this model we assume a configuration with server and client caches. Compared to SCO the traffic on the network is reduced by the introduction of the additional caching level at the clients. Multi-client cache consistency is not modeled in this approach, thus reducing the network load to an absolute minimum. Only misses in the client cache and cache write-back operations generate traffic on the network. This approach presents an unrealistically optimistic network load. Realistic implementations would induce higher network load due to coherency traffic.

Write Through All (WTA): An implementation of the NOC approach with added coherency traffic is presented with this model. WTA uses the easiest way to guarantee consistency in the system, which is a write-through caching scheme. All changed blocks are transferred form client to server as part of the write operation. This guarantees that the server is always in possession of the most recent version of every block and thus can service requests from other clients with up-to-date data. As many files are only used by one client this protocol generates lots of unnecessary operations on the network and on the server. It is intended as a pessimistic model for guaranteeing global consistency on the block level. The amount of write traffic from clients to the server is the same as in the SCO model.

Write Share Sequential (WSS): Whereas WTA writes back blocks which could be kept locally without degrading client cache coherency, WSS seeks to eliminate this additional traffic. Analyzing file access traffic reveals that most of the written files are not actually shared between clients. Only a small fraction of files are actively shared. By using different write policies for shared and non-shared files the excess coherency traffic can be eliminated. WSS uses a write-back policy for non-shared files, which is dynamically changed to write-through as soon as file sharing is detected by the server. This guarantees a consistent view on the server. However, clients may still read old versions of blocks from their local caches. Although this drawback is acceptable for some applications, it might not be desirable in general and can be eliminated by the next algorithm.

Write Share Concurrent (WSC): To overcome the coherency problem inherent in WSS, WSC uses a slight modification of the protocol. Instead of changing the write policy from write-back to write-through when a file is shared, the file caching policy is changed to be non-cachable on the clients. This forces the only version of the file to be kept on the server, which guarantees consistency under any circumstances. This approach loads the server with the burden of handling all shared file accesses. However, as long as the file sharing ratio is not too high this approach is acceptable.

2.2 Remote Memory Variable-Size Client Caches

Besides variations in caching policies as presented in the previous section, another orthogonal direction to explore is the usage of *the network*, i.e. remote memory accesses, to fulfill local cache misses. We investigate the use of remote memory by allowing each client to split its local cache into two distinct regions. One region is used to hold local cache contents, whereas the other region is exported to be used by other clients.

Splitting cache memory into two regions and exporting part of it to other clients reveals two questions. How much memory should be used locally, and which clients are allowed to use the exported regions. Considering the overall performance of the system as the target to be optimized, it can be proven that an optimal solution to this partitioning problem exists [Klauser 1994]. The optimum, i.e. the minimum total number of misses in the whole system, is reached when the derivatives of all clients' miss functions with respect to their cache size are equal.

We have considered this strategy by making two sets of runs over the trace data; during the first set the optimal cache partitioning for various global cache sizes has been collected. The second set of runs uses these optimal cache partitions during its operation. In a production environment this two stage process needs to be replaced by a one stage process that uses an on-line cache partition prediction algorithm.

3 Simulation and Trace Data

Proteus [Brewer, Delloracas, et at. 1991], a public domain parallel architecture simulator has been used to evaluate the presented caching policies. Proteus is an execution-driven simulator for parallel architectures. It handles the simulation of both the processing hardware as well as the communication subsystem and the network. It also provides basic operating system services on processing nodes like multithreading, synchronization and communication. The simulation is performed on a processor clock-cycle basis.

Simulated models are fed with the Sprite File System trace data from the University of California at Berkeley [Baker, Hartman, et al. 1991]. These traces are publically available. They contain a variety of different events like read, write, open, close, delete, lookup and many others. For this simulation only read and write events have been used. The traces come from several different file servers each containing data from several 48-hour and 24-hour sampling periods. For this study, however, we only use traces from the main file server. Traces from secondary servers show such a small amount of traffic that the caches usually did not warm up before the simulation was completed. We use three sets of traces, each representing 48 hours of continuous workload. [Tab. 1] shows the actual workload presented to the simulator after some data reduction to eliminate kernel, backup, and trace gathering references from the traces. The first 24 hours of every trace are used to warm up the caches, and only the second 24 hours are counted towards the results.

Although trace data events are tagged with a time stamp in the traces, it is not used in this case. The events are fed into the simulator as fast as the simulated caching model is able to handle them. There are two restrictions that bound the event flow into the simulator. On one hand obviously serial accesses to each file are serialized in the inbound data stream, i.e. the second request is held back until the first one has completed. On the other hand a static limit of maximal 8 outstanding requests from any node is enforced. This limit simulates the maximum number of processes on a node that will perform I/O requests to the server concurrently. This, however, does not restrict the number of processes that run on any node but is a way to control the mean I/O activity of a client.

Data Set	read				write				read + write	
	count	vol.	c %	v %	count	vol.	c %	v %	count	vol.
1.1	223199	898.2	68.6	54.7	101942	744.6	31.4	45.3	325141	1642.8
1.2	61755	254.6	89.2	89.5	7458	29.8	10.8	10.5	69213	284.4
2.1	185279	746.7	58.7	56.7	130535	570.0	41.3	43.3	315814	1316.7
2.2	42508	165.5	62.4	59.1	25607	114.7	37.6	40.9	68115	280.2
3.1	163955	668.2	70.2	59.5	69646	455.4	29.8	40.5	233601	1123.6
3.2	106741	426.0	67.9	59.9	50395	285.6	32.1	40.1	157136	711.6

Table 1: Results of read/write event data reduction. Split-up of number of read and write events and volume of data (in MByte) actually used for each of the six data sets. The table contains the number of events processed and the volume of traffic transferred for both, read and write events. Also listed is the relative percentage of read and write events for both, event count and traffic volume.

4 Results and Discussion

This section compares hit rates acquired for different caching models throughout the network at the same boundary conditions such as size of the caches, network throughput and latency, disk throughput and seek time.

4.1 Disk Access Traffic

All five client cache models LOD, NOC, WTA, WSS, WSC are simulated with cache sizes ranging from 16 to 8192 blocks per client (i.e. 64 kBytes to 32 MBytes). The hit rate behavior of all five models, though, shows only a difference of some percent from each other, especially as caches get large enough to hold a relevant part of the clients' working sets. Using a server cache as a second-level cache reduces these differences still further. This result gives confidence that neither very sophisticated nor very simple coherency schemes do change much in the access traffic to the server disk. The dominant parameter for this traffic is the size of the caches and not the coherency protocol used. Simple coherency protocols can eventually compensate for disadvantages due to inefficient traffic characteristics, by using less space for the cache state data, thus leaving more space to allocate to actual cache data buffers.

4.2 Network Load

Comparing network traffic shows a completely different situation. Here we see more sophisticated schemes substantially reducing traffic on the network. However, it highly depends on type, topology, and speed of the network whether these effects are of any severity in the perspective of the whole system. Especially on the simulated network model, long term utilization of the communication channels is very low. However, request bursts usually found in file access traffic can lead to significant network loads for short periods of time. As networks get faster more rapidly than disks, the importance of network load will even shrink further. The limiting factor in our simulation was more or less the I/O performance of the disk, which was assumed to be several times lower than the network performance. These observations lead to the insight that, under the aspect of a well balanced system, disks can be off-loaded by putting load on the network. Using remote memory accesses to maintain a system-wide distributed cache can help to increase client cache hit rates and thus off-load both the server and its disks. Additionally, the point-to-point network structure handles request bursts more gracefully as the increased load is distributed over large parts of the system, instead of being concentrated onto a single shared communication link.

4.3 Server Cache vs. Fixed-Size Client Caches

Server caching on its own is a very simple way to approach the situation. Nevertheless, we found that it is by far better than any of the client caching schemes under consideration, even when using the most optimistic assumptions about additional coherency traffic (LOD). This effect even grows drastically with increasing cache sizes in the system. Large client caches, as used sometimes now and certainly used more often in the future, perform several times worse than server caches with the same total number of cache blocks. This behavior is depicted in [Fig. 1] for data set 2.

The reason for this unpleasant behavior can be explained by the access patterns of the trace data. The traces hold requests coming from a large number of different workstations arriving at the server. Although the number of different sources has been reduced in the simulation to fold the traces onto the simulated topology, it still shows an unbalanced static and even more unbalanced dynamic usage pattern. This leads to the effect that some clients user their caches efficiently, while others completely underutilize their caches. Still others are far from optimal in their cache hit rates because they have to handle much larger working sets. [Fig. 2] shows the great variety of client cache behaviors with varying cache size. Adding more memory to all client caches only shows significant effects on overutilized caches, while underutilized ones can not make effective use of additional memory. Hence, from a certain point on, adding more memory is only of marginal benefit for the overall performance of the whole system. Unfortunately it is not predictable in advance how much cache memory each client can use efficiently. Moreover, this cache usage pattern does not stay constant over time.

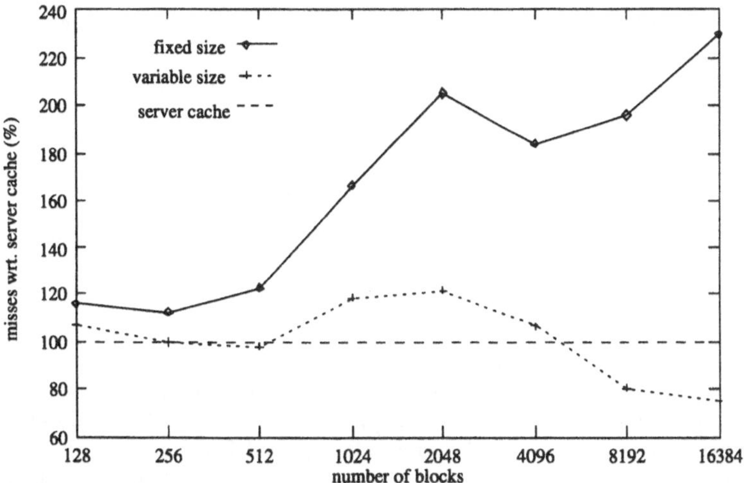

Figure 1: Fixed and variable-size client cache behavior with respect to server cache for data set 2.

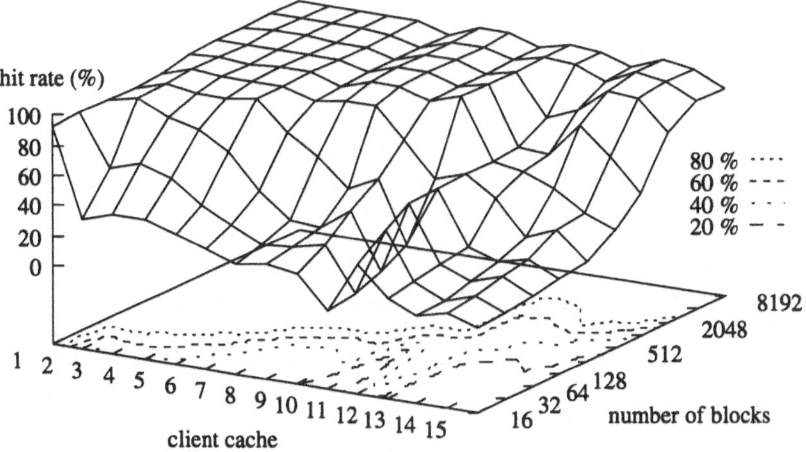

Figure 2: Influence of the cache size on the hit rates of client caches.

4.4 Remote Memory Variable-Size Client Caches

The previous observations lead to the insight that fixed-size caches do not contribute to efficient client caching schemes. Hence, cache memory has to be shared and balanced between clients. By allowing remote memory caches, as described in [Section 2.2], client caching can be made much more efficient.

Simulation studies with varying cache sizes show that a distributed variable-size client cache scheme exhibits almost the same miss rate as a single big server cache. [Fig. 1] shows that distributed variable-size client caches perform very competitively compared to a single big server cache. Due to the increased reference locality in a private client cache compared to a shared server cache, distributed variable-size client caches even perform better than a big server cache for some cache sizes and input data sets.

Although this scheme reintroduces network traffic due to the nonlocal use of memory, it still produces less network traffic than a pure centralized server cache. It frees the server from the burden of processing every single request in the whole system and shows much better hit rates than any of the fixed-size client caching approaches discussed before. Moreover, the additional traffic is distributed throughout the whole system and does not introduce new hot spot communication or processing bottlenecks.

4.5 Network and I/O Speed

To be more confident about the simulated computer model some sets of simulations also have been repeated with varying network and I/O bandwidth parameters. Variations of the network bandwidth ranged from 1 to 200 MBytes/s and variations of the disk throughput ranged from 1 to 10 MBytes/s. All these simulations show that the miss rates reported in the system are fairly independent of these parameters, with variations being in the range of the accuracy of the simulation, which is predicted as $\pm$ 0.5 % by statistical considerations.

5 Related Work

Optimal partitioning of memory for concurrent operations based on multiple unrelated input streams has been investigated by [Thiebaut, Stone, Wolf 1992], [Stone, Turek, Wolf 1992], and [Ghanem 1975]. Our approach of deriving optimal sizes for splitting client cache memory into local and remote parts has some similarities to their work.

[Mohindra, Ramachandran 1991] and [Zhou, Stumm, Li, Wortman 1990] investigate the use of distributed shared memory (DSM) in networks of workstations. Local/remote cache splitting is based on some of these DSM ideas.

[Nelson, Welch, Ousterhout 1988] describe caching approaches taken in the Sprite network file system. Client caches use delayed write-back to reduce server load and vulnerability to crashes.

[Dahlin, Wang, et al. 1994] and [Dahlin, Mather, Wang, et al. 1994] explore the use of remote client memory to improve file system performance in xFS. The approach is based on modifications to the AFS file system to allow direct client-to-client interaction. Their mechanism is based on caching whole files and uses a coherency scheme of write-after-close. Trace driven simulations use the Berkely Sprite and Auspex file system traces.

In the work of [Mann, Birell, et al. 1994] caching strategies in the Echo distributed file system are presented. Client caching with delayed write-back is used to reduce client write traffic to the server. Ordering constraints on write-back allow coherency to be maintained in the case of unreliable clients.

[Biswas et al. 1994] use non-volatile write caches, together with volatile read caches to provide reliability in the case of distributed file systems with client caching. They use synthetic workloads with a commercial production I/O profile.

6 Conclusions

We have compared a number of client caching schemes for high performance networks of workstations and MPPs. Different cache coherency approaches and distribution schemes have been used. Cache hit rates have been compared using centralized server caching as a major reference point.

Variations in miss rate for different coherency schemes used by fixed-size client caches have been found to be negligible compared to the difference between fixed-size schemes and a centralized server cache. To achieve miss rates in the range of a single big server cache it is important to give clients access to remote memory resources. Moreover, clients can adjust their cache sizes among each other for the overall number of misses to reach a minimum. This can be achieved by allowing clients with overutilized caches to use part of the underutilized clients' cache memory.

By increasing networking traffic to access remote parts of client caches, distributed variable-size client caches reduce disk access traffic and thus reach better balanced system resource usage. This approach has advantages over both, centralized server caches and fixed-size client caches.

References

[Baker, Hartman, et al. 1991] Baker, M. G., Hartman, J. H., Kupfer, M. D., Shirriff, K. W., Ousterhout, J. K.: "Measurements of a Distributed File System"; Technical report, University of California at Berkeley, Computer Science Division, July 1991, also appeared in Proceedings of the 13th Symposium on Operating Systems Principles, Oct. 1991.

[Biswas et al. 1994] Biswas, P., Ramakrishnan, K. K., Towsley, D., Krishna, C. M.: "Performance Benefits of Non-Volatile Caches in Distributed File Systems"; Concurrency—Practice and Experience, 6, 4 (1994), 289–323.

[Brewer, Delloracas, et at. 1991] Brewer, E. A., Dellarocas, C. N., Colbrool, A., Weihl, W. E.: "Proteus: A High-Performance Parallel-Architecture Simulator"; Technical report MIT/LCS/TR-516, Massachusetts Institute of Technology, Laboratory for Computer Science, September 1991.

[Coulouris, Dollimore 1988] Coulouris, G. F., Dollimore, J.: "Distributed Systems: Concepts and Design"; Addison-Wessley 1988, ISBN 0-201-18059-6.

[Dahlin, Mather, Wang, et al. 1994] Dahlin, M. D., Mather, C. J., Wang, R. Y., Anderson, T. E., Patterson, D. A.: "A Quantitative Analysis of Cache Policies for Scalable Network File Systems"; Proceedings of the ACM SIGMETRICS Conference on the Measurement and Modeling of Computer Systems, May 1994.

[Dahlin, Wang, et al. 1994] Dahlin, M. D., Wang, R. Y., Anderson, T. E., Patterson, D. A.: "Cooperative Caching: Using Remote Memory to Improve File System Performance"; Proceedings of the Operating Systems: Design and Implementation Conference, November 1994.

[Ghanem 1975] Ghanem, M. Z.: "Dynamic Partitioning of the Main Memory Using the Working Set Concept"; IBM Journal of Research and Development, 19, 9 (1975), 445–450.

[Klauser 1994] Klauser, A. W.: "A Simulation Study for Distributed File Caching in High-Performance Parallel Architectures"; Master's thesis, Graz University of Technology, Austria, Department for Applied Information Processing, January 1994.

[Maffeis 1992] Maffeis, S.: "Cache Management Algorithms for Flexible Filesystems"; Technical report, Institut für Informatik der Universität Zürich (IFI), December 1992.

[Maffeis, Cap 1992] Maffeis, S., Cap, C. H.: "Replication Heuristics and Polling Algorithms for Object Replication and a Replicating File Transfer Protocol"; Technical Report IFI TR 92.06, Institut für Informatik der Universität Zürich (IFI), July 1992.

[Mann, Birell, et al. 1994] Mann, T., Birrell, A., Hisgen, A., Jerian, C., Swart, G.: "A Coherent Distributed File Cache with Directory Write-Behind"; ACM Transactions on Computer Systems, 12, 2 (1994), 123–164.

[Mohindra, Ramachandran 1991] Mohindra, A., Ramachandran, U.: "A Survey of Distributed Shared Memory in Loosely-coupled Systems"; Technical Report GIT-CC-91/01, College of Computing, Georgia Institute of Technology, January 1991.

[Nelson, Welch, Ousterhout 1988] Nelson, M. N., Welch, B. B., Ousterhout, J. K.: "Caching in the Sprite Network File System"; ACM Transactions on Computer Systems, 6, 1 (1988), 134–154.

[Stone, Turek, Wolf 1992] Stone, H. S, Turek, J., Wolf, J. L.: "Optimal Partitioning of Cache Memory"; IEEE Transactions on Computers, 41, 9 (1992), 1054–1068.

[Thiebaut, Stone, Wolf 1992] Thiebaut, D., Stone, H. S., Wolf, J. L.: "Improving Disk Cache Hit-Ratios Through Cache Partitioning"; IEEE Transactions on Computers, 41, 6 (1992), 665–676.

[Zhou, Stumm, Li, Wortman 1990] Zhou, S., Stumm, M., Li, K., Wortman, D.: "Heterogeneous Distributed Shared Memory"; Technical Report CSRI-244, Computer Systems Research Institute, University of Toronto, September 1990.

Appendix A

[Tab. 2] contains hit rates of the various caches for trace data set 2. Abbreviations *CC* and *SC* stand for *client cache* and *server cache* respectively, and *OV* stands for *overall*, which compares the number of misses of the last cache level to the total number of accesses processed in the system. (Entries of * represent the cases where no accesses have been detected, thus no hit rate can be given.)

Data Set 2			SCO	LOD	NOC	WTA	WSS	WSC
32 blocks	CC	read	-	33.4	33.5	33.9	33.5	30.2
		write	-	8.1	8.1	7.5	8.1	8.1
		r+w	-	23.2	23.2	23.2	23.2	21.3
	SC	read	23.2	-	2.1	0.8	2.2	6.5
		write	2.2	-	0.3	2.6	0.5	0.4
		r+w	14.7	-	1.2	1.7	1.4	3.6
	OV	read	23.2	33.4	34.7	34.3	34.8	34.6
		write	2.2	8.1	5.5	2.6	5.6	5.7
		r+w	14.7	23.2	22.9	21.5	22.9	22.9
512 blocks	CC	read	-	73.8	73.8	74.0	73.8	69.3
		write	-	70.5	70.5	70.7	70.4	70.3
		r+w	-	72.4	72.5	72.7	72.4	69.7
	SC	read	45.3	-	14.3	0.6	14.0	26.1
		write	26.6	-	2.2	34.8	2.8	2.6
		r+w	37.7	-	8.1	25.3	8.2	14.9
	OV	read	45.3	73.8	77.5	74.1	77.5	77.3
		write	26.6	70.5	59.5	34.8	60.0	60.0
		r+w	37.7	72.4	70.2	58.2	70.4	70.3
8192 blocks	CC	read	-	98.7	98.7	98.7	98.7	94.4
		write	-	92.2	92.2	92.2	92.2	92.0
		r+w	-	96.1	96.1	96.1	96.1	93.5
	SC	read	85.0	-	32.0	19.2	32.0	84.2
		write	87.4	-	*	78.8	100.0	87.0
		r+w	85.9	-	32.0	77.7	37.2	84.3
	OV	read	85.0	98.7	99.1	98.9	99.1	99.1
		write	87.4	92.2	100.0	78.8	100.0	100.0
		r+w	85.9	96.1	99.5	90.8	99.5	99.5

Table 2: Cache hit rates for data set 2.

Journal of Universal Computer Science, vol. 1, no. 6 (1995), 410-422
submitted: 20/3/95, accepted: 19/6/95, appeared: 28/6/95

From Personal Computer to Personal Assistant

Jennifer Lennon
(Department of Computer Science, University of Auckland, New Zealand)

Arnould Vermeer
(Institute for Applied Computer Science I, University of Hagen, Germany)

Abstract: Much of the confusion that surrounds electronic personal assistants arises from the open-ended complexity of their development. In this paper we categorise some of their more common uses before suggesting several thought-provoking extensions.
Key Words: Electronic assistants, electronic agents, message pads, searches, prediction, programming by example, voice commands.
Category: H.m

1 Introduction

Evolution in human-computer interface design has brought us a long way from the days when computers were all but dictators, when users obeyed enigmatic "rules" or risked ignominious "crashes"! Years of research and many trials involving users (willingly and unwillingly) have steadily improved computer interfaces to the point where today's operators are much more in control. However we believe that the next few years will see another quiet revolution as the computer becomes more of a versatile supportive ally - a true Personal Assistant (PA for short).

The idea of an electronic assistant has already been promoted with much hype by major computer companies. But the impression often given is that computers will eventually dominate our lives, relaying frantic messages between offices and homes, frustrating even our rest and relaxation. This is certainly not our vision: we look to the computer to help us, not discombobulate us.

A PA, as we define it, is not to be confused with the devices that several companies are developing as "personal digital assistants" or "message pads" (see Section 12). Those are still extremely limited in the applications they support. We believe that a PA system should - and can - do a great deal more.

Because application programs are providing constantly better interfaces, the exact nature of an electronic personal assistant is becoming blurred. Some of its functions may be controlled best by a continuous background processor. Others may be delegated to various applications. However, just as there is a move towards "universal documents" that allow text, graphics, spreadsheet and database editing all in the same document, we should also expect a PA to help in activities ranging from simple wordprocessing tasks to scientific research. A PA should support our work in ALL areas of computing.

In this paper we consider the assistance we might expect from a PA in a few everyday activities.

2 Writing Documents

There are probably countless ways in which a PA can aid us in the exacting labour of writing documents. Certainly, as we shall see in Section 7, PAs will relieve us of a large amount of repetitive editing by making predictions based on our personal work patterns. They will do a great deal more than this, however.

2.1 Making Literature Searches

Making a literature search is a frequent necessity, a time-consuming, exacting chore, yet vital whether our need is to find information or to check our work. Additional electronic assistance with literature searches would be a great relief. In particular, we should be able to vet our work much more efficiently than is currently possible. At the very least, a PA will help us set up and manage a filter system so that our searches are as effective as possible. This is particularly important when searching in hypermedial systems (see Section 6.3). The PA will "learn" what filters we prefer to have set under various conditions and apply them, [KM94]. It will provide intelligent cross-links so that better use can be made of huge databases. Obviously everything we write should be open to verification. One such system, "Ways 2", produced by the Swiss researcher Keller, has been marketed by Vobis in Germany with considerable success. In a PA system, data in wordprocessing text will be checked against data in our spreadsheets and databases. Running as a background processor, it can make continuous searches for relevant references, aiding us in the verification of both our own work and the reference material we are reading (see Section 6). Having such checking done automatically, or semi-automatically, is possibly the only way of ensuring that the increasing amount of archived work taken to be authoritative is at least relatively free of errors.

2.2 Improving Spelling Checkers and Grammar Checkers

Spelling and grammar checkers are often inefficient and cumbrous. Most spelling checkers are not even context driven; grammar checkers are clumsy, throwing up too many red herrings. Users should be able to tailor grammar checkers to their personal preferences. An intelligent editor should also be able to "learn" rules of style appropriate to the particular type of document being edited - such as appropriate levels of word difficulty, or suitable sentence length. The system should be flexible enough to allow the user a choice between simultaneous checking and checking only on a File Save or Quit command.

Programs such as these need to be able to "learn" from their "mistakes". For example, in a maths paper the second occurrence of the word "group" probably should not be replaced by "collection"! If a user has to override the "second occurrence", an intelligent editor will query whether it is a technical term and act accordingly.

We need to be able to refer to a whole range of dictionaries - maybe at just the click of a button. Using techniques such as those described in Section 6, we look forward to much better success rates in our searches.

An interesting application applies to natural language translation. Obviously we are not referring to full natural language translation - a complex and subtle specialty still struggling for success. But word-for-word translations are practical and this opens up several rather thought-provoking possibilities. For example, a researcher trying to read foreign journal articles with only a smattering of the language would be greatly helped by a handy translation option. Similarly, if correspondents restrict their sentences to grammatically simple ones, translation programs will have a better success rate. The qualified success of existing style-checking programs suggests that certain types of documents may be amenable to automatic rewriting in simplified words and phrases - a facility of great use to new immigrants, for example.

3 Reading Documents

Browsing electronic text consumes so much of our time that all personalised assistance with it will be valuable. As software systems become daily more complex, the problems associated with training operators in their efficient use multiply exponentially. Since users have neither time nor motivation to wade through extensive manuals, many firms are applying the principle of "just-in-time learning". This will become more effective when employees have their own PA to control the Help systems. The PA will be able to take into account the user's previous experience - or lack of it!

Many people find reading from the screen more tiring than reading print, particularly when windows are densely packed with text. The displayed text is either too small for comfort or too clumsily large. One solution may be to indicate the particular line we are reading by moving the cursor up and down manually (or by methods mentioned in Section 8) so that the editor can enlarge it. It may also be desirable that a line or two above or below the current line be enlarged to some degree as well. This will obviously be dependent on personal preferences, but each user should be able to individually "train" their text windows.

Since reading is so much faster than writing, any reference system that is provided needs to be very efficient for us not to feel unnecessarily held up by it. Hence, though facilities for referencing and checking are just as vital for reading as for writing, they will have to be uninhibiting to be really useful. Perhaps in "Browse mode" a single click on a word could initiate a dictionary look-up or a reference check. Each person will decide which dictionaries or databases are to be filtered and used.

Yet another necessary feature for most applications is the presence of date computation routines. For example, if I read that a colleague is arriving on 18th May, my immediate question will probably be "What day of the week is that?" I should be able to click on the "18" and "May" and have a formula (such as Snell's) calculate the day - given any particular year. Or maybe I need to know what date Easter falls on. Even more important, when making travel arrangements I must know which days are public holidays in the countries I am visiting, so that I can either avoid them or make sure I see any special festivities.

4 E-mail

We all agree that there must be better ways of managing e-mail than keeping our names off mailing lists [Den82]. M.I.T. has made considerable progress with its Information Lens and Object Lens projects [MGT+87] [Rob91]. Certainly we should be able to set up our own preferential filtering systems so that a PA, perhaps working as a background processor, can search all incoming mail for names and keywords. It will search the body of each item, as well as the subject line, and classify the mail according to our own prescriptions, [KAF+94]. Furthermore, we do need additional options such as ranking and grouping by author. Answering mail from your boss may be more urgent than attending to personal matters; and if he has mailed more than one item, it is important that they appear together so that we do not waste time answering the first item only to find that it was superseded by a later item!

As more and more correspondence is sent by e-mail, we are looking forward to additional electronic assistance with all the chores associated with daily avalanches of mail. A personal assistant will serve us by keeping address lists up to date. It will assist us in writing form-letters (see Section 8) and help with addresses. It can manage certain housekeeping tasks such as archiving necessary information before deleting messages. Notices in template format can enable the system to use the advertised dates to generate expiry dates - these may, of course, be overridden by the user. Ideally the user should also be able to define what is to be done with the notice once the expiry date has passed: delete it, or place it in a Past Events list to be maintained by the system. This list will be invaluable for compiling such things as end-of-year reports, although decisions will have to be made on how to maintain it. E-mail must also support structured discussions and systematic collaboration between two or more participants, i.e., conferencing. Furthermore, we should have the option of attaching notes to individual letters in group dispatches. In fact, as information proliferates in all systems, the ability to annotate at all levels of the system becomes increasingly important.

It is intriguing to ponder the consequences of having e-mail answered automatically. For example, we may wish to generate replies that indicate we are unavailable. Of course we would avoid being naive and publicising to all and sundry that a house or office is unattended and hence is a good burglary risk! We could, however, have different responses to different people. Acquaintances could be informed that I am at a meeting or that I am very busy - whereas close friends are told that I am really away at the beach!

5 Intelligent Calendars

Electronic diaries will become much more useful when they are more widely linked into electronic mail systems. Calendars should also be capable of generating mail for us - either mail to ourselves or mail to others. On a personal level, they should be able to send us reminder notices that contain much more than just bald statements of events and dates. Perhaps, when we are prompted that next week is an important anniversary, we also need to be reminded that last year's "bright idea" for a gift wasn't a success!

On a more workaday note, an intelligent PA will be able to set up appointments for us. Incoming e-mail about meetings will be searched, our calendar checked and updated, and outgoing e-mail messages generated. The PA system should be intelligent enough to be capable of adaptive behaviour. Conceivably, it could even "learn" when one person in a group is being unreasonably difficult about the times they are available and it could take a "tough" negotiating line! On the other hand, although I may wish my system to negotiate for me I may also not want all my timetable to be known!

The logical extension of this is, of course, that we shall eventually have networks of PAs communicating with each other and the user will, at best, only be required to approve the final result.

6 Information Retrieval

Electronic journals such as J.UCS (Journal of Universal Computer Science) have significant advantages over traditional and existing electronic journals [CMS94], [JUC94], [MS95]. Since it is based on Hyper-G, [KAF+94], its structure lends itself to user-controlled filtering and automatic notification of new material and updates - all of which are necessary components of any PA.

6.1 Searches

To make the best use of resources such as JUCS [CMS94], [JUC94], researchers need more assistance in searching and checking documents - their own and other people's. This is becoming critically important as daily so much highly questionable data is being quoted as fact.

There are several important requirements to be met by search programs, and we list just a few:

- Appropriate use must be made of filters (see Section 2.1).
- The system should help the user by prompting for alternatives. For example, a search for "kiwi" could well generate the prompt, "Bird, person or fruit?"
- We look to better hit rates in searches. An intelligent search program will tailor its algorithms to fit the type of document being searched, deducing probable error types. For example, when text is entered from the keyboard it will look for transposed characters. Scanned documents on the other hand commonly produce different types of errors. Since scanning produces only a simple bit map, an Optical Character Recognition (OCR) program must be used to convert the bit map into text. Unfortunately, even the best OCR programs introduce new errors into the scanned text such as "g"s being confused with "q"s [COD90]. Here again we look to increasingly intelligent search algorithms to improve translations. We also look forward to a much better hit rate for words with multiple errors by using improvements that fuzzy1 search techniques seem likely to achieve [BYG92], [WM92].
- The system should be able to make fuzzy searches based on semantic nets instead of just lists of synonyms. A search for "air" could lead on to "gas", "oxygen", etc.
- If a search is not successful then the system should be capable of making alternative suggestions - it is frustrating when unsuccessful searches leave us no better off.
- Certainly we would like to have phonetic searches, as well as the option of searching dictionaries that include inflected forms of words, abbreviations, accents - and entire foreign languages.
- Obviously intelligent fuzzy searches should not be restricted to just text files. We should be able to efficiently search file names, directory lists, program names, and so on.

  Above all, such a system must be easy to use. To take a trivial example, if I read that the Sun is 20% helium and 80% hydrogen I will check the figures if and only if it can be quickly done - perhaps with PA assistance, on just the click of a mouse.

6.2 Retrieving Information from Libraries

A big step forward for all researchers will be a PA giving us easier access to library information. We believe that in the foreseeable future it will become standard practice for librarians to insert the table of contents and/or a brief summary into the hypermedia database so that researchers can rapidly access the new information. This much at least can be done without infringing copyright laws. With a system such as this, a PA can constantly check all new books and journals, and using our own categorisation system, notify us of those that are relevant.

The application PC-Bibliothek (PC-Library) is a recent development from Graz University of Technology for PCs running Windows [MMS94]. PC- Library's attractive and easy-to-use graphical interfaces, coupled with powerful search algorithms, highlight the benefits to be enjoyed once complete reference libraries are literally at our fingertips.

6.3 Hypermedia Document Searches

When hypermedia systems were just growing like Topsy, it was not surprising there were problems. In large hypermedia systems users still lose their sense of orientation within the environment. Recent research has seen interesting developments, particularly in the design of hypermedia structures [MKSS93] [MSS93] with links, and even without links [MPS94]. At the very least we should be to be able to signal "Help!" and have the system help us backtrack. However a good PA system will help us avoid disorientation in the first place by indicating our current position on a graphical map of our environment. Furthermore the system will remember from day to day, and week to week, which paths we have used, and how often, so that by making predictions it can help us navigate much more efficiently than we can now.

6.4 Webs and Guided Tours

There is a tremendous amount of work now being done on electronic guided tours such as those in the Hyper-G system [KMS93], [FM94]. The successes and shortcomings of "second generation" hypermedia systems receive a good introductory survey in the paper "Reflections on Notecards: Seven Issues for the Next Generation of Hypermedia Systems" [Hal88]. Interfaces such as those described in "Intermedia: The Concept and the Construction of a Seamless Information Environment" [YHMD88], and "IRIS Hypermedia Services" [HKR+92] help the user navigate hypermedia webs. Intermedia, for example, shows dynamic "tracking maps" that display the user's current position in relation to its predecessor and successor links. In Intermedia, operations "behave identically across all applications" (just one feature of beautiful design). Features such as these will be utilised by an all-embracing electronic assistant.

In an interesting program under development at the University of Auckland [MS94] viewers of a university information system will be given both two and three dimensional guided tours of the campus and buildings. It is hoped that much of the research work will be general enough to apply to other information systems.

Another move in the right direction is the increasing use of the guided task paradigm [TO90] , where users are introduced to new applications by interactively participating in guided demonstrations.

6.5 Sending Electronic Agents Through the Networks

Programs that search for information in wide-area networks are proliferating. Although the trend is being fuelled by commercial interests such as those mentioned briefly in Section 9, obviously all types of archived information are amenable to computer controlled searches. One well known system, WAIS [Ste91], automatically updates "dynamic folders" with relevant information from selected servers.

A PA could be trained to control electronic "agents" sent through Internet, [Com94], so that information relevant to the users' current needs is gathered - and summarised into their own personal newsletter!

A detailed description of collaborative agents in computer conferencing environments is given in "A Framework for Controlling Cooperative Agents" [LMS93].

7 Observing and Predicting: Electronic Assistance

During the past twenty years many papers have been written describing specific applications that incorporate forms of intelligent electronic assistance under various titles: intelligent editors, cooperative agents, programming by example, programming by rehearsal, to list just a few. An exceptionally well presented overview is given in the book *Watch What I Do: Programming by Demonstration* [Cyp93]. In 1985 Zissos and Witten described a "computer coach" that helps users avoid repetitive formatting tasks in a wordprocessing environment [ZW85]. It "unobtrusively monitors interaction with a system and offers individualised advice". The work has been greatly extended and several such systems have now been developed [MW92] [WM93]. A more generalised personal assistant has been proposed by the second author of the present report [Mau93].

Several major computer companies are committed to developing what they are terming "electronic agents". Apple Macintosh recently demonstrated the prototype version of an electronic agent that can learn from simple, mouse-controlled, repetitive actions. For example, as the user steps through each stage of a process, each selection and menu choice may be highlighted with a colour. This indicates to the user that his actions are being shadowed by the agent. If all actions are shadowed correctly, then the user has the option of letting the electronic agent help from then on: for example, selected pieces of text may be copied from one document and tabulated into another automatically.

Producing animated graphical sequences is a very repetitive task and this must surely be one area that will greatly benefit from having an electronic personal assistant or agent to help. In fact some of the earliest work done in the field of programming by example was done using graphics programs. In the paper "Metamouse: Specifying Graphical Procedures by Example" [MWK89] the authors describe a system that "induces picture-editing procedures from execution traces". It incorporates a very likeable icon called Basil - a turtle in the best LOGO tradition [Pap80]. The work has been significantly extended [MW93] [MWKF92].

A unique visual programming environment is described in the paper "Programming by Rehearsal" [FG84], where a "stage" is set and peopled with "performers". In the book Creating User Interfaces by Demonstration [Mye88] the author describes PERIOT (Programming by Example for Real-time Interface

Design Obviating Typing). Graphical menus and windows are created by example. MARQUISE is another interesting example of an interactive tool that creates graphical user interfaces by demonstration [MMK93].

Considered all together, applications such as these suggest that there is a wealth of experience waiting to be pooled into an all-embracing and indispensable interface [PY93] .

8 Making Use of the Computer's Ears, Eyes and Voice

Now that microphones and video cameras are almost standard computer attachments, we shall undoubtably see dramatic innovations stemming from their use. For example, when a significant number of PCs are connected to law enforcement networks then automatic reporting of break-ins will surely result in a proportional reduction in the number of unsolved burglaries!

With the addition of "eyes" and "ears", our PC will be capable of a wide variety of new functions. It will be able to inform us if someone is at the door when our back is turned. As we work it will adjust the screen brightness when the room brightness changes, or boost the volume of our headsets when background noises increase. We shall be able to dictate our e- mail, and have voice prompt and help systems. It is no longer inconceivable that an intelligent PA could even note our mood when we first enter the office in the morning and give appropriate responses - perhaps we might appreciate an occasional joke or even some artificial intelligence doctoring in the style of the Eliza program [Wei66]. Certainly a very practical welcome would be for the machine to open the document we last worked on and have the cursor sitting ready where we left off - surely not too much to ask, considering that there is at least one lap-top already on the market that leaves files open when re-booted.

The ability of the machine to recognise simple gestures such as a nod or shake of the head opens up many possibilities. Work on eye tracking, such as that done by M.I.T.'s Media Lab [SB90] and the Washington Naval Research Laboratory [Jac90], suggests that in the future we shall be able to look at a section of the screen, and, perhaps with only a simple nod, have that particular section enlarge automatically. This will help us in many types of searching tasks - imagine, for example, searching screenfuls of small windows as in applications that use miniaturised photos from CDs or thumbnail pictures as in Hypercard [Hyp89].

If we would like to have lines of text enlarged for working on in a word-processing task, eye movements may prove to give us better control than the cursor method explained in Section 3. Even if eye tracking proves to be too imprecise, then perhaps finger tracking may still be a better alternative. Text scroll bars as well as computer movie options could also be controlled by eye movements. And when presented with choices in a dialogue box we may prefer to focus on an option and then simply nod.

Computers that can carry out a whole range of voice commands are no longer fiction - a fact that has been widely demonstrated recently:

- "Computer open Word file" - the word processing package is opened.
- "Computer write letter to John Jones" - the letter is headed with the sender's and receiver's addresses, plus opening and closing sentences.

– "Computer include thank you message" - a whole paragraph is generated....

And of course this leads us to speculate how widespread computer-generated speech will become and how long it will be before we can actually converse with our personal assistant.

9 Help with Transaction Processing

Electronic shopping is here to stay, and the next question we must address is how we are going to make the best use of yet another barrage of information. Newsgroups have already advertised software that can send electronic agents through the networks to find "best buys" as well as making and changing hotel, restaurant or airline reservations for us. Of course, as with any new technology, we can expect problems both small and large - cases of electronic agents running "amok" in the networks have already been reported too.

In many European countries "telebanking" has become a routine aspect of life due to the continuing spread of Videotex [MS82]. Ideally we could do all our banking and paying of bills via our computer. Gone would be paper invoices, checks and forms. The conversation with the computer might go something like this: Computer please pay 400 dollars to Mike. Mike who? Computer, to Mike Melon of course. PIN no? (I type in my PIN number.) Transaction number? (I type in the correct transaction number from the current block.)

Of course, some security mechanism will be necessary to guard against impersonators. The computer will encrypt messages for security and use a different transaction number with each message to ensure that any electronic eavesdropper cannot simply copy previous messages to repeat transactions.

Although jokes are still made about the "paperless office", with the advent of electronic funds transferral we have made significant steps in that direction and indications are that the current expansion of the home computing market will lead to further advances.

10 The Individualisation Process

There is a rather interesting inference to be made from the current vogue of having personalised emblems put on everything from coffee mugs to designer jeans. With PA assistance in mastering intricacies of design, we shall be design our own emblems, embellishments, and even, if we are so inspired, our own works of art. We can then let our PA scan the networks to find the "best" supplier and have our specifications e-mailed directly to them!

11 Secretary? Tutor? or Even Parent

From all that we have discussed, it is obvious that when we use the term Personal Assistant the emphasis remains on the word "Personal". A good PA system will be "trainable" so that after a few weeks my PA will act in a very different way from yours - even if we purchased identical software to begin with.

Ideally, it will also be desirable to have alternative sets of characteristics built into a PA that modify it for specific tasks. At the office I shall expect my PA to act as my own personal secretary - it will help me with all my correspondence, arrange meetings (see Sectionn 5), help with time management, and so on. Of significant assistance will be a "My archive" program that helps classify and archive all types of information: text, graphics, video and audio clips, important documents and interesting little snippets. All archived material will be amenable to retrieval by powerful search techniques such as those described in Section 7.

At university or school, the PA will become my personal tutor, helping me organise work and make the most of opportunities that are offered. In the paper "Lecturing Technology: A Future With Hypermedia" [LM94], we show what tremendous potential lies in the integration of multimedia lectures with a good database when all students have their own portable PCs. Excellent computer-aided instruction material will be generated. Since students will be able to replay the lecture away from the classroom, important distance learning opportunities will be provided.

However, when I lend my PC to my six-year-old child I hope my PA will not only protect all my work from sabotage but will transact on quite a different level. It could act as a "parent" - even to pulling the plug on games and bringing up some homework!

Thus when designing a PA we shall need to ask ourselves what the characteristics are of a manager's best secretary, a student's favourite lecturer, and even more elusively a "good" parent, to see if we can simulate at least some of their attributes. A challenge indeed!

12 Looking To the Future

As small gets smaller, and more powerful still, we can expect that computers the size of notebooks will support more PA functions than we have described. The initial interest created by pen-based electronic notebooks such as Apple Macintosh's Newton or Casio's Zoomer suggests that users enjoy that environment, limited as it still is. Users particularly enjoy sketching in environments that help them work more efficiently by neatening up their work, letting them work with constraints, and supporting incompleteness [Kim89] [Zha93]. There is even a certain perverse satisfaction in erasing errors by scribbling over them! All this is certainly an indication of things to come.

In the article "To Forecast Information Technology is Impossible Yet Necessary" [ML94] , we argue that future advances in information technology are quite unpredictable. However we go on to surmise: "In ten or fifteen years from now everyone will carry small but powerful Notebook computers around with them. The much heralded Newton is certainly a first step in this direction! You will be able to talk into your notebook and have more commands, programs, and facilities available than we can imagine. For example, if you go to a foreign country and talk into your notebook in English out will come Greek or French. A global positioning system will display maps for you and show you at any time exactly where you are located on the surface of the earth. And of course a mobile telephone will be integrated into your notebook, giving access to all the databases of the world - so you can look up theatre programmes and bus and train connections. It will be your digital photo camera, and it will replace your wallet and credit cards. It will be indispensable."

13 Conclusion

Our definition of a true personal assistant obviously bears little relation to any currently available commercial product. It is not just a glorified Newton. It is part background processor (continuously scanning the networks), part consistent graphical interface (across all applications), and part special routines integrated into application programs. It thus supports the user at all levels of activity. By making predictions from repetitive tasks, it saves us both time and frustration. It manages our e-mail, classifies and archives our work, and employs powerful fuzzy search algorithms to retrieve documents from complex hypermedia systems. It is much more than a generalised help system. It can be a model secretary, tutor and baby-sitter, a police officer who patrols our surroundings while simultaneously ensuring that we do not inadvertently break copyright laws or lose ourselves in hyperspace. It will be our augmented eyes and ears, an alter ego we create for ourselves.

14 Acknowledgement

The authors wish to thank Professor Hermann Maurer for support, encouragement, and many enjoyable discussions during the writing of this paper. Many of the ideas were suggested by him.

References

[BYG92] R. Baeza-Yates and G Gonnet. A new approach to text searching. *Communications of the ACM*, 35(10):74–82, 1992.

[CMS94] C. Calude, H. Maurer, and A. Salomaa. JUCS: The Journal for Universal Computer Science and its applications to science and engineering teaching. Computer Science Report Report 91, University of Auckland, Auckland, NZ, 1994.

[COD90] W. Cushman, P. Ojha, and C. Daniels. Usable OCR: What are the minimum performance requirements? In *Proc. CHI'90: Empowering People*, pages 145–151. ACM, 1990.

[Com94] Special issue on intelligent agents. Communications of the ACM, 37, 7, 1994.

[Cyp93] A. Cypher, editor. *Watch What I Do: Programming by Demonstration.* MIT Press, Cambridge, MA, 1993.

[Den82] P Denning. Electronic junk. *Communications of the ACM*, 25(3):163–165, 1982.

[FG84] W. Finzer and L. Gould. Programming by rehearsal. *Byte*, 9(6):187–210, 1984.

[FM94] B. Fenn and H. Maurer. Harmony on an expanding net. *ACM Interactions*, 1(4):26–38, 1994.

[Hal88] F. Halasz. Reflections on notecards: Seven issues for the next generation of hypermedia systems. *Communications of the ACM*, 31(7):836–852, 1988.

[HKR+92] B. J. Haan, P. Kahn, V. A. Riley, J. H. Coombs, and N. K. Meyrowitz. IRIS hypermedia services. *Communications of the ACM*, 35(1):36–51, 1992.

[Hyp89] Apple Computer Inc., Cupertino, CA. *Hypercard Reference Manual*, 1989.

[Jac90] R. Jacob. What you look at is what you get: Eye movement-based interaction techniques. In *Proc. CHI'90: Empowering People*, pages 11–18. ACM, 1990.

[JUC94] About J.UCS. http://www.iicm.tu-graz.ac.at/Cabout_JUCS, 1994.

[KAF+94] F. Kappe, K. Andrews, J. Faschingbauer, M. Gaisbauer, H. Maurer, M. Pichler, and J. Schipflinger. Hyper-G: A new tool for distributed hypermedia. In *Proc. Distributed Multimedia Systems and Applications Conference*, pages 209–214. ISMM-ACTA Press, 1994.

[Kim89] T. D. Kimura. Pen-based user interface (Panel Session). In *Proc. 1989 IEEE Workshop on Visual Languages*, pages 168–173. IEEE Computer Society Press, 1989.

[KM94] F. Kappe and H. Maurer. From hypertext to active communication/ information systems. *Journal of Micro Computer Applications*, 17:333–344, 1994.

[KMS93] F. Kappe, H. Maurer, and N. Sherbakov. Hyper-G - a universal hypermedia system. *Journal of Educational Multimedia and Hypermedia*, 2(1):39–66, 1993.

[LM94] J. Lennon and H. Maurer. Lecturing technology: A future with hypermedia. *Educational Technology*, 34:5–14, 1994.

[LMS93] K. Lee, W. Mansfield, and A. Sheth. A framework for controlling cooperative agents. *Computer*, 26(7):8–16, 1993.

[Mau93] H. Maurer. *Spekulationen Über die Multimediale Zukunft.* CAP, Debis, 1993.

[MGT+87] T. W. Malone, K. R. Grant, F. A. Turbak, S. A. Brobst, and M. D. Cohen. Intelligent information-sharing systems. *Communications of the ACM*, 30(5):309–402, 1987.

[MKSS93] H. Maurer, F. Kappe, N. Scherbakov, and P. Srinivasan. Structured browsing of hypermedia databases. In *Proc. HCI'93*, pages 51–62, Vienna, 1993. Springer.

[ML94] H. Maurer and J. Lennon. Forecasting: An impossible necessity. *NZ Science Monthly*, 5(1):12–13, 1994.

[MMK93] B. A. Myers, R. G. McDaniel, and D. S. Kosbie. Marquise: Creating complete user interfaces by demonstration. In *Proc. INTERCHI'93: Human Factors in Computing Systems*, pages 293–300, Amsterdam, 1993. ACM.

[MMS94] H. Maurer, H. Muelner, and A. Schneider. An electronic library and its ramifications. Technical Report 382, IIG, Graz, Austria, 1994.

[MPS94] H. Maurer, A. Philpott, and N. Scherbakov. Hypermedia systems without links. *Journal of Microcomputer Applications*, 17:321–332, 1994.

[MS82] H. Maurer and I. Sebestyen. 'Unorthodox' videotex applications: Teleplaying, telegambling, telesoftware and telecomputing. *Information Services & Use*, 2:19–34, 1982.

[MS94] H. Maurer and A. Schneider. New aspects of a hypermedia university representation. In T. Ottmann and I. Tomek, editors, *Proc. ED-MEDIA 94*, pages 504–509. AACE, 1994.

[MS95] H. Maurer and K. Schmaranz. J.UCS and extensions as paradigm for electronic publishing. DAGS'95 Electronic Publishing and the Information Superhighway, 1995.

[MSS93] H. Maurer, N. Scherbakov, and P. Srinivasan. A new hypermedia data model. In *Proc. DEXA '93*, pages 685–696, Prague, Czech Republic, 1993. Springer, LNCS 720.

[MW92] D. Mo and I. Witten. Learning text editing tasks from examples: a procedural approach. *Behaviour and Information Technology*, 11(1):32–45, 1992.

[MW93] D. Maulsby and I. Witten. Metamouse: An instructible agent for programming by demonstration. In A. Cypher, editor, *Watch What I Do: Pro-*

gramming by Demonstration, pages 155–181. MIT Press, Cambridge, MA, 1993.

[MWK89] D. Maulsby, I. Witten, and K. Kittlitz. Metamouse: Specifying graphical procedures by example. *Computer Graphics*, 23(3):127–136, 1989.

[MWKF92] D. L. Maulsby, I. H. Witten, K. A. Kittlitz, and V. G. Franceschin. Inferring graphical procedures: The compleat metamouse. *Human-Computer Interaction*, 7(1):47–89, 1992.

[Mye88] B. Myers. *Creating User Interfaces By Demonstration*. Academic Press, Boston, 1988.

[Pap80] S. Papert. *Mindstorms: Children, Computers, and Powerful Ideas*. Harvester Press, Brighton, 1980.

[PY93] P. P. Piernot and M. P. Yvon. The AIDE project: An application-independent demonstrational environment. In A. Cypher, editor, *Watch What I Do: Programming by Demonstration*, pages 383–401. MIT Press, Cambridge, MA, 1993.

[Rob91] M. Robinson. Through a lens smartly. *Byte*, 16(5):177–187, 1991.

[SB90] I. Starker and R. A. Bolt. A gaze-responsive self-disclosing display. In *Proc. CHI'90: Empowering People*, pages 3–9. ACM, 1990.

[Ste91] R. Stein. Browsing through terabytes - wide-area information servers open a new frontier in personal and corporate information services. *Byte*, 16(5):157–164, 1991.

[TO90] R. Tuck and D. R. Olsen. Help by guided tasks: utilizing UIMS knowledge. In *Proc. CHI'90: Empowering People*, pages 71–78. ACM, 1990.

[Wei66] J. Weizenbaum. Eliza: A computer program for the study of natural language communication between man and machine. *Communications of the ACM*, 9(1):36–45, 1966.

[WM92] S. Wu and U. Manber. Fast text searching allowing errors. *Communications of the ACM*, 35(10):83–91, 1992.

[WM93] I. H. Witten and D. Mo. TELS: Learning text editing tasks from examples. In A. Cypher, editor, *Watch What I Do: Programming by Demonstration*, pages 183–203. MIT Press, Cambridge, MA, 1993.

[YHMD88] N. Yankelovich, B. J. Haan, N. K. Meyrowitz, and S. M. Drucker. Intermedia: The concept and the construction of a seamless information environment. *IEEE Computer*, 21(1):81–96, 1988.

[Zha93] R. Zhao. Incremental recognition in gesture-based and syntax-directed diagram editors. In *Proc. INTERCHI'93: Human Factors in Computing Systems*, pages 95–100, Amsterdam, 1993. ACM.

[ZW85] A. Y. Zissos and I. H. Witten. User modelling for a computer coach: A case study. *International Journal of Man-Machine Studies*, 23:729–750, 1985.

Journal of Universal Computer Science, vol. 1, no. 6 (1995), 423-434
submitted: 5/6/95, accepted: 14/6/95, appeared: 28/6/95

Microworlds for teaching concepts of object oriented programming

Ivan Tomek
(Jodrey School of Computer Science, Acadia University, Canada
ivan.tomek@acadiau.ca)

Abstract: We present two examples of microworlds built into the Smalltalk environment for the purpose of teaching the main concepts of object oriented programming (OOP) and of the Smalltalk programming language. The distinguishing features of our microworlds are that each of them presents the student with a sequence of environments. These environments introduce one OOP concept after another, and disclose the Smalltalk environment and language in a step-by-step fashion. The starting environment does not require any programming and does not encourage the user to use Smalltalk tools, the last environment must be programmed in Smalltalk and discloses the major Smalltalk tools. The intended use of our microworlds is for the introductory part of a course on OOP, to be followed by a detailed presentation of the language. An extension of the presented approach would make the method suitable for teaching basics of computer programming in a computer literacy course.
Key Words: Microworld, object oriented programming, progressive disclosure, Smalltalk, teaching object oriented programming, computer literacy.
Category: D.1.5, D.0, D.2, K.3

1 Introduction

The idea of using microworlds to teach selected aspects of programming is not new. The most prominent reference is probably that of Papert who used this concept in the Logo programming environment [Papert 80]. Others then used it to create environments to teach general programming principles with special programming languages [Pattis 81, Tomek 83], or subsets of full-fledged programming languages such as Pascal [Tomek, Muldner 86] and Smalltalk [Alvarez et al. 95, Borne 91, Leonardi et al. 94]. For a recent survey of the subject see [Brusilovski et al. 94].

The two main justifications for restricted programming environments are:

1. Hiding the richness of the full environment so as not to distract the beginner with too many details, tools, and techniques, and to make learning easier. This is the main motivation for building microworlds for students who want to learn to program.
2. Creating an environment which presents the student with more interesting tasks than commercial programming languages. This is an important motivation for building microworlds for students who want to learn *about* programming.

The motivation for the work presented in this paper belongs mostly into the first category since the immediate use of our microworlds is in a course on object oriented programming (OOP). However, our microworlds are simple and interesting enough that they could be used as a starting point for audiences in the second category as well, for example with students in computer literacy courses.

2 Goals and guiding principles

Our work is guided by two main goals: *First*, to provide a hands-on interactive environment for presenting principles of OOP. At present, all existing textbooks introduce principles of OOP using verbal descriptions of situations that provide OOP motivation and set stage for their abstract presentation. We do not think that this is a necessary or the best approach, and believe that suitable microworlds can illustrate the concepts in a more forceful and convincing way. We also think that by manipulating appropriate microworlds, students will internalize OOP concepts better than if they are only presented with theoretical arguments. *Second*, OOP environments in general, and Smalltalk in particular, are too complex to be presented all at once and their facilities should be disclosed one after another. A series of Smalltalk environments which introduces the environment progressively seems to be a good way to protect the student from the cognitive overload caused by the richness of the language and the tools.

Given this motivation, we propose that the following principles should be used to design the microworlds:

- The student should have access to several *different kinds of microworlds*. This will provide variety for exercises and reinforce the concepts by presenting them in different contexts.
- Each microworld should provide *motivation* for the goal being pursued. In our case, the goal is to introduce OOP concepts and our choice of microworld themes is biased towards situations in which the concepts of objects and messages are as natural as possible.
- Microworlds should be *interesting*. The student should be tempted to use them and explore their possibilities, and thus absorb the concepts that we want to communicate.
- Microworlds should be *simple*. They must engage the student's interest but not lead him away into an exciting virtual reality world in which the learning goal is forgotten and the microworld itself becomes the focus of attention.
- Microworlds should form a *sequence of environments* patterned on the same pedagogical subgoals. As example, version 3 of each of the microworlds designed for a particular goal should be oriented towards presenting the same concepts and use a similar user interface. This makes it easier for the student to move between the different microworlds with ease and explore the same concepts in different contexts.
- The sequence into which the microworlds are divided should start at the most trivial level and proceed in small increments as far as desirable, but not farther.

In the following sections, we will describe how we applied these principles in our microworlds.

3 Types of Microworlds Implemented, Stages of Their Development

Since our goal is to introduce principles of OOP, we attempted to select worlds in which objects and actions performed on them are very natural. Our first choice was a rudimentary variation on Papert's Logo Turtle - a *pen world* containing essentially only two types of objects: a pen for creating bit-mapped drawings, and an eraser for erasing them. As we developed this world into a series of environments and matched them with the concepts that we wanted to introduce, we found that the pen world does not provide enough justification for the concept of polymorphism. We thus added a new microworld called the *geo world* which consists of rectangles and ellipses that can be painted on a drawing pad, and a *collector* object that can be used to select and group rectangles and ellipses previously placed on the pad, and send messages to them. We will explain and illustrate the two microworlds later.

The stages into which we decided to divide our microworld exposition are dictated by the topics which we want to introduce - a combination of general OOP concepts, principles of Smalltalk, and the main tools of the Smalltalk environment. These concepts, the order in which we introduce them, and a brief justification of the order of presentation are as follows:

1. To achieve anything in an object-oriented world, the user must select objects and send them messages. To do this, the user does not have to write programs. Instead, he can click buttons representing *object factories* that create objects, buttons representing previously created objects, and buttons corresponding to messages understood by the selected objects.
2. Object factories are properly called *classes* and when we use them in a programming language such as Smalltalk, their names must follow certain rules. Names of messages must also follow rules. The names of buttons in an environment corresponding to this stage are changed to reflect these conventions, everything else can remain the same.

3. Selecting objects and sending them messages is the principle of OOP. In restricted contexts such as our microworlds, these actions can be accomplished by clicking buttons. In the general Smalltalk environment, however, specification of objects and sending of messages is achieved by writing textual programs. To provide a preliminary taste of what OOP is like in Smalltalk, we extend the user interface of the existing environment by adding a read-only text subview. We use this text view to display a preliminary form of Smalltalk statements that would have the same effect as clicking buttons. As the user clicks buttons, the corresponding statements are automatically created and displayed. The form of the displayed statements follows the rules of Smalltalk but the statements are not executable because they are not complete - we have not yet introduced the concepts of variables, assignment statement, and declaration.
4. Experience with the environment from stage 3 makes it obvious that its preliminary form of programming does not provide enough control. This provides a justification for introducing the concepts of variable, declaration, and assignment statement. Introducing these concepts allows us to create and display executable Smalltalk code fragments as the user clicks buttons to select message receiver objects, and messages. The text view is still a read-only view and the user cannot write programs but the programs are real, a preview of the programs that the student will eventually write when the 'crutch' of buttons is removed in a more advanced version of the world.
5. So far, we concentrated on one aspect of objects - their ability to execute messages. We ignored their *properties*, the fact that objects have internal variables capturing their current state, and that these variables may change during the object's lifetime. The previous worlds provided strong hints that this is so but we have not said this explicitly and we have not provided any means for examining the objects. At this stage of evolution of our microworld, we add a button to display properties of the selected object in an informal style - as English phrases.
6. Up to this point, our environments were artificial grafts on Smalltalk and the student did not have to use any of the standard Smalltalk tools. Eeven though the standard tools were not hidden from the window, we did not encourage the student to use them. All the work was done with buttons, all text was automatically created, the student could not get into problems, there was no possibility to make a mistake and no need to go outside of the pre-defined world. At this stage, we remove all this scaffolding, or most of it, and ask the student to start controlling the microworld by writing and executing Smalltalk programs. This should not be too difficult because the student has already seen what these programs look like and can even go back to a previous environment to generate the required code by clicking the buttons.

   Since control is now via Smalltalk code, the user is exposed to mistakes and we thus introduce principles of dealing with mistakes and the use of the debugger. We also replace the informal presentation of object properties with the formal style used by the Smalltalk 'inspector'.
7. No additional artificial microworlds are needed and we now present the Smalltalk browser to introduce the concept of class hierarchy. We still use the environment from the previous stage but only to demonstrate that the character of some of the objects already present in it quite naturally leads to subclassing, and so on. We also use the browser to create new methods and new classes of objects to demonstrate the use of the browser for creating code.

When the student reaches this point, he has been introduced to all essential OOP concepts and used them actively. He has also seen and used the elements of the language, and used the tools. He is now ready to study the language itself and we proceed to teach it in the usually way starting with basic data types, control of flow of execution, I/O via the built-in user interface builder, and so on.

4 The Microworlds

In this section, we will illustrate the principles outlined in the previous sections on examples of two microworlds implemented in VisualWorks, a popular variet of Smalltalk manufactured by ParcPlace [ParcPlace 94]. Most of the illustrations are taken from the pen world but the last one is from the geo world which was designed specifically to illustrate polymorphism for which we did not consider the pen world sufficient. Our presentation follows the sequence followed in our course. We start by showing how the student opens the microworld and proceed through individual stages of microworld evolution. It should be noted that the seven consecutive stages listed in the previous section are grouped into five stages of microworld evolution; they are illustrated in the following paragraphs.

When the user opens VisualWorks Smalltalk (abbreviated below as VW) the visual launcher shown in Figure 1 appears on the screen. This launcher is identical to that provided by VW except for the new *MicroWorlds* command at the rightmost end of the menu bar. This reflects our belief that microworlds should be a tool helping the student to penetrate into OOP concepts and Smalltalk, but that the student should not be prevented from exploring Smalltalk further if he wishes to do so.

When the student activates the *MicroWorlds* command, two subcommands become available, one providing access to pen worlds, the other to geo worlds. Each of them further expands to allow the user to access one of the sequence of five evolutionary stages of the selected microworld. As we have mentioned before, the two worlds evolve through parallel stages (pen world 1 - geo world 1, pen world 2 - geo world 2, and so on), presenting the same concepts and providing the same user interface, each illustrating the current stage of evolution in a different context.

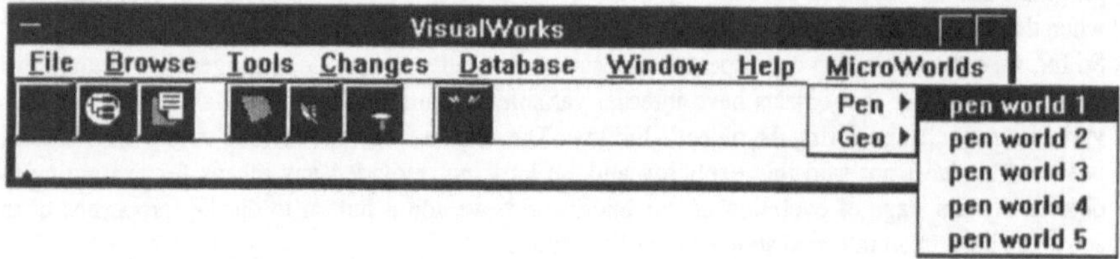

Figure 1: Opening state of Visual Works Smalltalk with MicroWorlds command added.

- If the user selects pen world 1, the window shown in Figure 2 appears on the screen.

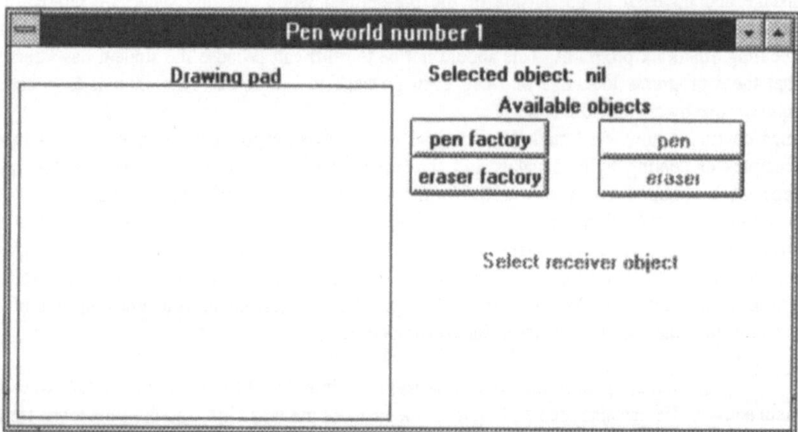

Figure 2: Initial state of pen world window. User must now select a receiver object by clicking its button.

The new window is labeled with the name of the microworld and has the following components:

- A rectangular drawing pad on the left. All actions taken by the student in this and the following microworlds - drawing by pen objects and erasing by eraser objects - are directed towards this pad.
- Buttons for selecting objects. The goal of our interface is to drill the fact that all actions in an object oriented microworld consist of selecting objects (message receivers) and messages. At this stage, only

the *pen factory* and *eraser factory* buttons are enabled; *pen* and *eraser* buttons are disabled because no pen or eraser objects have been created so far.

- A help button is present in all microworld windows.
- A conspicuously colored label advises the student to select a receiver object. A label at the top shows that no object is selected. We use the Smalltalk term nil - again a part of our strategy of introducing the concepts of Smalltalk progressively whenever there is a good opportunity.

Assuming that the student clicked the *pen factory* button, the window now changes to that shown in Figure 3. Object buttons are gone and the label at the top right states that the selected object is a pen factory; buttons showing all messages available for this object are displayed. In this case, only one button labeled *new pen* is shown because this is the only message understood by a pen factory. The user is prompted to select a message for the current receiver.

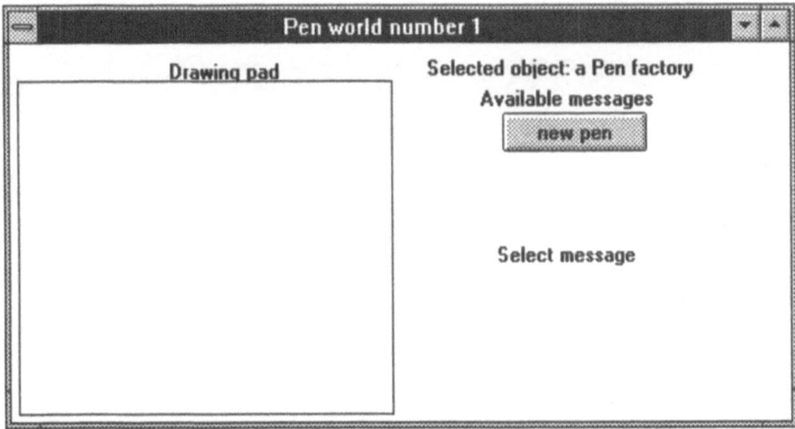

Figure 3: Pen factory has been selected and its messages are displayed. Student will now one by clicking.

After clicking *new pen*, a pen object is created and the window changes to a state similar to that in Figure 2, except that the *pen* button is now enabled; the *eraser* button remains disabled. We do not show this window because it is almost the same as in Figure 2.

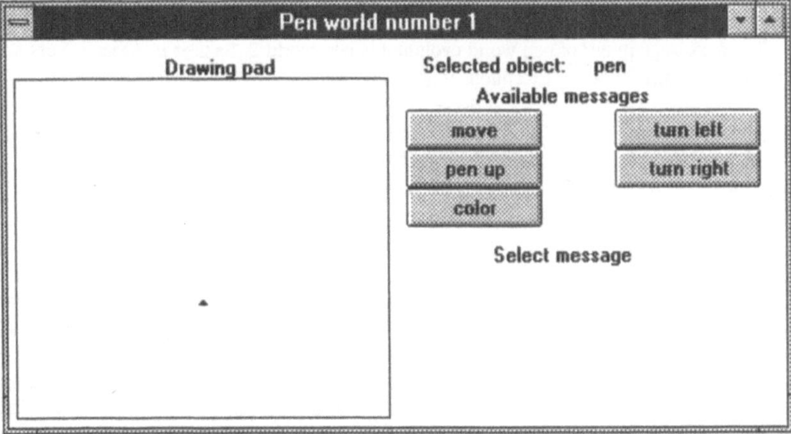

Figure 4: Student selected pen and buttons for all messages understood by pen are displayed.

Assume that student now selects the pen object by clicking the *pen* button. The window changes to the state shown in Figure 4. The label shows that the selected object is a pen, and buttons corresponding to messages understood by pens are displayed. They include *move* to move the pen by a specified number of pixels in the current direction and draw a straight line, *turn left* and *turn right* to turn the pen by +90 or -90 degrees (the pen has orientation), *pen up* (to lift the pen and thus cancel drawing while moving), and *color* to change the color of the line drawn by the pen. The pen is shown in the drawing pad in its default state - at the center of the drawing pad, pointing up, black, and ready to draw.

To further illustrate the interface, assume that the student has created another pen, turned one of the two pens right, and moved each pen by an amount specified via a dialog originated when the *move* button is clicked. The next task is thus to select the receiver of the next message. Assume that the student chooses pen by clicking the *pen* button. Since there are two pens in the pad now, the student must now select one of the two pens shown in the drawing pad by clicking it. The state of the pen world window at this point is as in Figure 5.

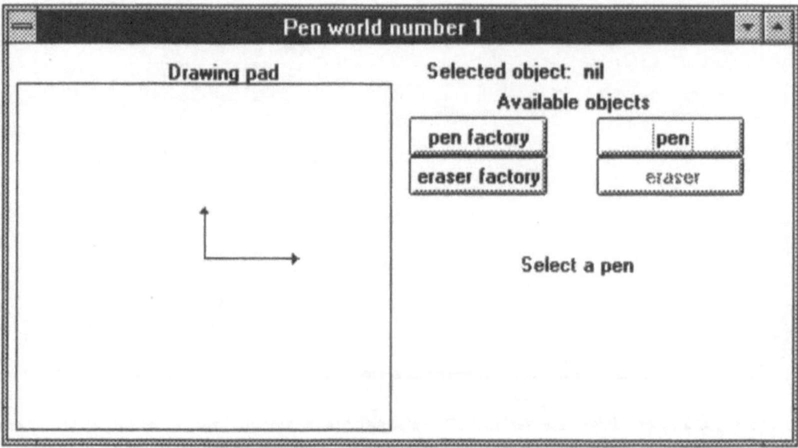

Figure 5: Student clicked the pen button and must select one of the two pens present on the drawing pad.

The operation of pen world 1 should now be obvious and it is clear how it implements the goal of introducing the student to the concepts of objects, messages, message creation, and the fact that all action in object oriented worlds consist of selecting an object, and sending a message to it.

The next stage in our of pen world evolution is pen world 2. Its user interface is very similar to that of world 1 with the following exceptions [Figure 6]:

- Labels on buttons are changed to introduce the terminology and the rules used in Smalltalk. Instead of calling an object button *pen factory*, we now use the term *class Pen*, instead of calling a message button *turn left* we now call it *turnLeft* (not shown), and so on. We use the proper Smalltalk syntax and the actual names of messages as declared in our microworld classes.
- A read-only text view is added at the bottom right. This text view shows a preliminary form of Smalltalk statements equivalent to actions performed by the user by clicking buttons. This view is scrollable and the part displayed in our illustration shows that the students has created a new pen (*unary* message new with no arguments), moved it by 50 pixels (*keyword* message move: with one argument), created another pen and turned it left (using turnLeft - another unary message). The message move: 50 gives us an opportunity to note that everything in Smalltalk is an object, including the argument 50 which is a number object. (The state of the drawing pad in Figure 6 shows that more messages must have been executed to reach this stage - these are hidden in the text view and would be accessed by scrolling it.)

The text view of pen world 2 shows only a preliminary form of Smalltalk statements although the syntax is correct. Situations such as the one shown give us an opportunity to justify the need to refer to objects by names (which of the two pens in our example should turn left?) and this leads to the concept of object identifiers, declaration, and assignment statement. This new feature is introduced in pen world 3.

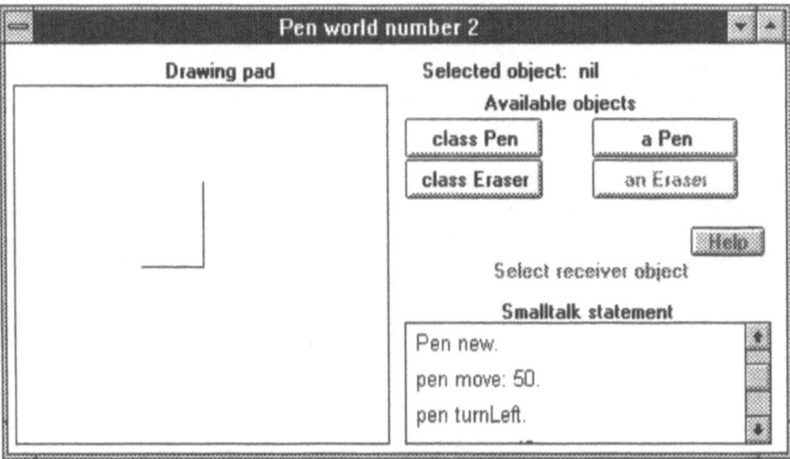

Figure 6: When student selects receiver and message in pen world 2, the text view displays a preliminary form of the Smalltalk equivalent of the button-based operation.

The interface of pen world 3 [Figure 7] is identical to that of pen world 2 but the automatically generated displayed Smalltalk code is now realistic - identical to that which would produce the same effect as button clicks. The text view is still read only and the user thus cannot program the world in Smalltalk, but he can observe the Smalltalk code equivalent to button clicks.

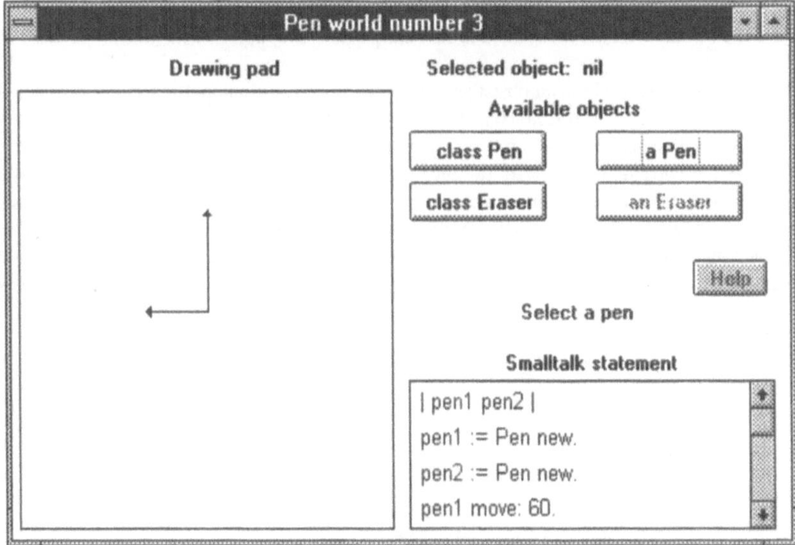

Figure 7: Pen world 3 shows Smalltalk code equivalent to user actions in a read-only view.

The way in which we introduced the concept of an identifier in pen world 3 is very limited - an identifier in our current sense is just a pointer to an object such as a pen or an eraser, and an object is something that understands messages. This is because we have not yet considered the fact that objects have properties which can change and that the nature of objects is thus variable. From our experience it is, however, obvious that at least some of the objects that we use are more than mere message executors. As an example, as the student sends messages to a pen, its position, orientation, color, and drawing state (up or down) must change. This gives us an opportunity to enrich the concept of an identifier and an object, and introduce the concept of a *variable* - an identifier of an object whose internal properties may vary during its lifetime. To introduce these concepts is the role of pen world 4 which adds a *properties* button to the interface of pen world 3 [Figure 8].

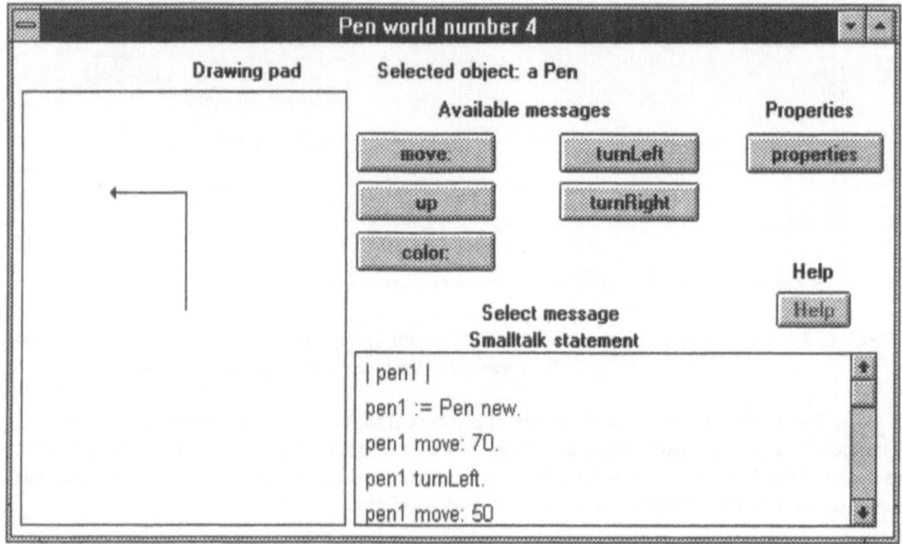

Figure 8: Pen world 4 allows the student to examine properties of objects using the properties button.

When the student selects an object and clicks the *properties* button, the window changes [Figure 9] to show the properties of the selected object. The properties are listed in an informal way.

We think that pen worlds 1 to 4 have introduced enough of the basic concepts for our overall goal, and that the student is now ready to move to Smalltalk and start programming using text. (In a different setting, such as a computer literacy course, this may not be so and we may want to introduce additional environments.) Still, a few concepts and some preliminary practice are desirable before we start teaching the Smalltalk language and we thus present one last stage in which we will expose the student to several more concepts and introduce him to the tools of the Smalltalk environment. This is the role of pen world 5.

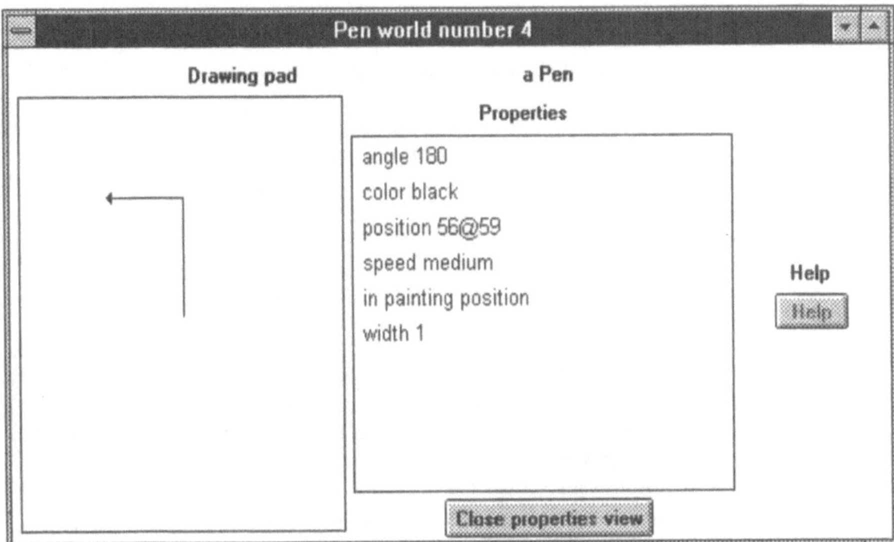

Figure 9: Clicking the properties button in pen world 4 shows properties of the selected object.

In pen world 5, control by clicking buttons is replaced by programming. Object selection buttons and message selection buttons are removed and are replaced by a read-write text view into which the user enters Smalltalk text and executes it in the usual Smalltalk way - by selecting the text [Figure 10] and activating the *do it* command from the pop up menu associated with the mouse button.

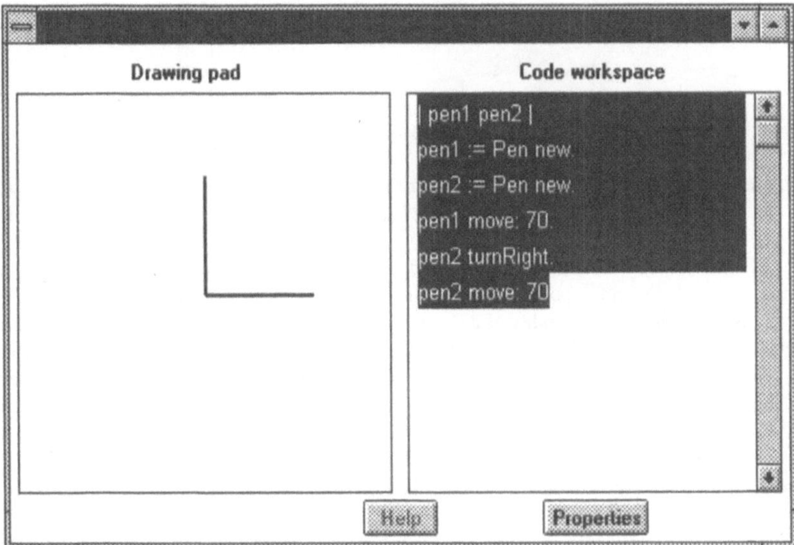

Figure 10: Pen world 5 removes object and message buttons and the student controls it by typing and executing Smalltalk code.

The form of the Smalltalk statements used to program world 5 is identical to that known to the student from worlds 3 and 4, and writing the programs should thus be easy. (Moreover, if the student has problems, he can always return to pen world 4 and have the code generated by clicking the buttons.) Still, even experts make mistakes and students will thus run into problems - both syntax and logic errors. This is a good place to show and explain the most common ones, introduce the concept of the debugger, and use it.

Pen world 5 also introduces the standard *operate* pop up menu with its *do it* command (to execute selected text), text editing commands, and the *inspect* command. The *inspect* command opens the standard Smalltalk which provides access to all properties of the selected object. As an example, if the user inspects a pen object, an inspector as in Figure 11 will open. This gives us an opportunity to introduce further concepts:

- Internal properties of objects are stored in named instance variables.
- Values of instance variables are objects such as numbers, points, and colors.
- Being objects, values of instance variables may themselves have instance variables whose values are other objects, and so on. As an example, by opening an inspector on the *position* object [Figure 11], we find that *position* is a *Point* object which has two instance variables that can again be viewed by the inspector, and so on. This introduces the idea of objects as *aggregates* of other objects and further reinforces the parvasiveness of objects.
- For completeness we must explain that *self* - the first item on the list in each inspector window - is the receiver itself and that it is a very important object in Smalltalk programs.

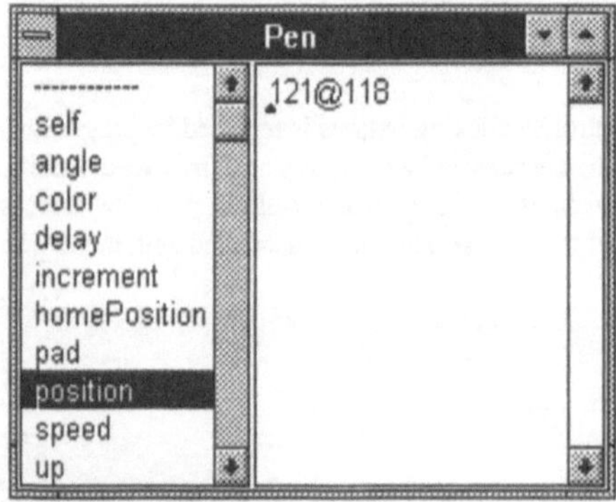

Figure 11: Smalltalk inspector on a pen object shows that pen is an aggregate object with many components..

As we mentioned earlier, we do not find that pen world 5 is sufficient to introduce the one remaining essential concept - polymorphism - in a satisfactory way. In our view, students should understand polymorphism as the ability of different kinds of objects to understand the same message and respond to it in essentially the same way but in a manner appropriate to their nature. In the pen world, erasers and pens are very different objects that don't share any functionality and they are thus unsuitable to introduce polymorphism. A Pen factory and an Eraser factory both understand message new and both respond to it in the same way (create a new object) but each in its own way: A Pen factory create pens whereas an Eraser factory creates erasers. Although this is a good example of polymorphism, it is not sufficient to demonstrate its full implications. For this purpose, we thus created another microworld - the geo world.

The geo world is again a drawing world but it uses pre-defined objects - ellipses and rectangles - drawn in the drawing pad. In addition, the *collector* object allows the user to select objects in the drawing pad and collect them into a collection. Besides the message *collect*, the collector also understands all messages understood by ellipses and rectangles (moving, coloring, stroking and filling) but applies them to all elements of the collection. At this point in the course, we explain that to execute a message such as stroke (changes an object to stroked rather than filled representation), the collector sends message stroke to each element of its collection. Each element of the collection understands this message (the student had an opportunity to test this on individual ellipses and rectangles) and obeys it in the same way (converts itself to a stroked object) but ellipses clearly do this differently than rectangles. This applies to all other messages and shows how powerful polymorphism is - it allows us to deal with a variety of objects in the same way without having to distinguish between their nature, always providing the desired result - if the objects are properly defined, of course.

As we mentioned before, the geo world also allows us to demonstrate the concepts presented in the pen world in a different context and possibly enrich them. As an example, the *move* action in the geo world is implemented by keyword message moveTo:extent: with two arguments [Figure 12], and so on.

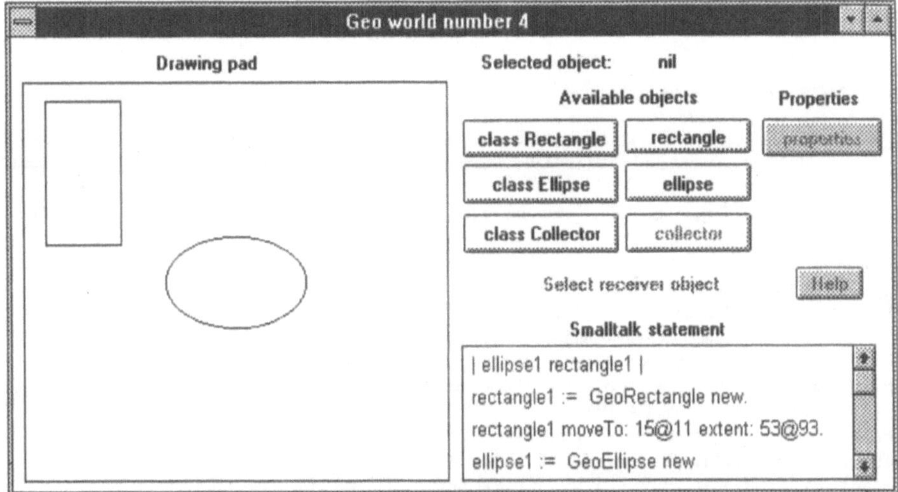

Figure 12: Geo worlds are useful to present concepts from pen worlds in a different context. The Collector object is a good illustration of the power of polymorphism.

5 Conclusion

The concept of microworlds has been used by several authors in the past and we described a variation on the previous implementations. Our microworlds are intended for teaching concepts of object oriented programming and fundamentals of Smalltalk and our approach differs from previously described microworlds in the following ways:

- We use several complementary worlds, each organized into an ordered sequence of stages of development.
- Each sequence begins with an easy to understand intuitive world in which the student achieves the equivalent of programming by clicking buttons.
- From a completely non-programming environment, our sequence evolves to display automatically generated code and eventually leads to an environment in which the user programs actions equivalent to control by buttons.
- The environment progressively introduces OOP concepts, elements of the Smalltalk language, and tools of the Smalltalk environment.

We have developed our microworlds for use in a course on Smalltalk for Computer Science students. Our intention is to use them only for a very short introductory part of the course and then teach the language using the full environment. As a consequence, our microworlds are simple and the amount of language that they introduce very limited. In fact, from the point of view of the language itself, the purpose of our microworlds is mainly to show what Smalltalk looks like rather than try to teach it. In principle, however, there is no reason why our approach could not be used to present much more of the language. We think that this strategy could be useful for other audiences such as students in computer literacy courses. The Smalltalk environment or its restricted subset would be a perfect vehicle for this because it is easy to extend, and because it allows the student to proceed to study Smalltalk itself - a real and increasingly popular programming language.

Our plans for the future include testing our microworlds in the classroom, modifying the user interface if this appears desirable, and creating additional microworlds to provide new demonstrations of the concepts that we want to present. We will also examine whether our division into five stages is appropriate for our purpose.

References

[Alvarez, et al. 95] X. Alvarez, et al.: "Customizing learning environments for teaching object-oriented technology to different communities"; TaTTOO'95, Teaching and Training in the Technology Of Objects), Leicester, UK, 1995.

[Borne 91] I. Borne: "Object-oriented programming in the primary classroom"; Computers and Eductaion 16 (1): 93-98, 1991.

[Brusilovski et al. 94] P. Brusilovski, A. Kouchnirenko, P. Miller, I. Tomek: "Teaching programming to novices: a review of approaches and tools"; Proceedings of ED-MEDIA 94, 103-110, 1994.

[Leonardi et al. 94] C. Leonardi, et al.: "Micro-Worlds: A tool for learning object-oriented modeling and problem solving"; Educators Symposium, OOPSLA'94, 1994.

[Papert 80] S. Papert: "Mindstorms - Children, Computers, and Powerful Ideas", Basic Books, Inc., 1980.

[PP 94] ParcPlace. "User Guide", "Cookbook", "Object Reference" manuals, ParcPlace Systems, Inc., 999 E. Arques Avenue, Sunnyvale, CA, 1994.

[Pattis 81] R. Pattis: "Karel - the robot, a gentle introduction to the art of programming with Pascal"; Wiley, 1981.

[Tomek 83] I. Tomek: "The first book of Josef"; Prentice-Hall, 1983.

[Tomek, Muldner 86] I. Tomek, T. Muldner: "A Pascal primer with PMS"; McGraw-Hill, 1986.

Managing Editor's Column

Vol. 1, No. 7; July 28, 1995

Dear Readers:

This issue is very special: One of the editors of J.UCS, Jean-Michel Muller (Lyon, France) organized a conference dedicated to the manipulation of real numbers at Saint-Etienne (near Lyon) in June 95. The top papers submitted were reviewed once more by Jean-Michel and colleagues. The very best were selected and edited to conform to J.UCS format.

It is those papers that make up this issue of J.UCS. I would like to thank Jean-Michel for his excellent work. He has added some remarks separately below.

All the best,

Hermann Maurer
email: hmaurer@iicm.tu-graz.ac.at

Journal of Universal Computer Science, vol. 1, no. 7 (1995), 436-438
Special Issue, appeared: 28/7/96 © Springer Pub. Co.

Introduction to the Special Issue "Real Numbers and Computers"

This special issue contains a selection of papers presented during the international conference "*Real Numbers and Computers*", Saint-Étienne, France, April 1995.
Efficient handling of real numbers in a computer is not yet solved in a satisfying way, yet. Although the "floating-point" formats most often used in scientific computing usually give sufficient results, some reliability problems may occur. Program portability could imply high rewriting costs: some programs which work well with a machine, may become unreliable with another one. Users (from computer algebra, computational geometry, ...) may need results far more accurate than the ones obtained with usual number systems, if not "exact" results.
Many members of the scientific community are concerned by this problem, they could share their knowledge and come up with new solutions. But they do not have the opportunity to meet, they do not belong to the same scientific fields (computer science, number theory, numerical analysis, computer algebra...) and they have a different vocabulary. The aim of the Saint-Étienne Conference was to bring them together during this meeting, to establish some collaborations.

The very first problem with the manipulation of real numbers in computers is that the set of real numbers is not enumerable. As a consequence, it is not possible to represent each real number by a finite string of symbols taken from a finite alphabet. Depending on the application, one has to choose which finite or enumerable subset of the real numbers will be manipulated.
Even with enumerable subsets of the reals, there remain serious problems: probably the most important is that one cannot determine whether two computable real numbers[1] are equal.
Let us now examine some problems related to the discrete machine approximation of the continuous reals.

- In computational geometry, the main problem is to construct topologically consistent objects using (non-independent) numerical tests (e.g., signs of determinants). For instance, if we try to compute the distance (*a priori* null) between the intersection point of two straight lines and the straight lines separately, using floating-point arithmetic, it is almost certain that the answers will both be different and most likely non-null. For many such situations there is no obvious general treatment known.
- A report of the *United States General Accounting Office* (B-247094, Feb. 1992), explains that on February 1991 (during the war in the Gulf), a Patriot missile defense system failed to intercept an incoming Scud, that killed 28 people, due to an inaccurate tracking calculation.

[1] A real number x is computable if there is a machine that computes, for any given integer n, a rational number r_n that approximates x within error 2^{-n} (for instance, see Ker-I Ko, *Complexity Theory of Real Functions*, Birkhauser, 1991).

- If we try to compute the sequence (u_n) defined as

$$\begin{aligned} u_0 &= 2 \\ u_1 &= -4 \\ u_{n+1} &= 111 - \frac{1130}{u_n} + \frac{3000}{u_n u_{n-1}} \end{aligned}$$

  using any bounded-precision arithmetic (such as floating-point arithmetic) on any computer, then 100 will seem to be the limit value of the sequence, while the correct limit value is 6.
- Define a sequence (x_n) as

$$\begin{aligned} x_0 &= 1.5100050721318 \\ x_{n+1} &= \frac{3x_n^4 - 20x_n^3 + 35x_n^2 - 24}{4x_n^3 - 30x_n^2 + 70x_n - 50} \end{aligned}$$

  depending on your computer, the apparent limit value of x_n will be 1, 2, 3 or 4.

Those are archetypes of problems that happen in real-world computations (maybe especially during iterative calculations).

Many solutions have been proposed to cope with such problems:

- First, one may try to make the usual floating point arithmetic more reliable, and to entirely specify it, in order to be able to elaborate proofs and algorithms that use the specifications. For instance, the IEEE-754 and IEEE-854 standards for floating point computations[2] considerably helped to improve the quality and portability of programs, and to design multiple precision or interval arithmetic programs. The paper by Evgenija Popova (*On a Formally Correct Implementation of IEEE Computer Arithmetic*) is devoted to this topic. The specification of the arithmetic may also help to get *a priori* bounds on numerical errors for various computations. Raymond Pavec (*Some Algorithms Providing Rigorous Bounds for the Eigenvalues of a Matrix*) and Fabienne Jézéquel (*Round-Off Error Propagation in the Solution of the Heath Equation by Finite Differences*) obtained such bounds.
- It is not always possible to get realistic bounds on the numerical errors before the execution of a program, therefore it is most desirable to build tools that dynamically compute such bounds. Two possible ways to do this are the *interval arithmetic*, illustrated by the paper by Svetoslav Markov (*On Directed Interval Arithmetic and its Applications*) and the *perturbation methods*, illustrated by the paper by Jalil Asserhine, Jean-Marie Chesneaux and Jean-Luc Lamotte (*Estimation of Round-Off Errors on Several Computer Architectures*).
- A more drastic solution is to get rid of the usual floating-point arithmetic, and to build systems capable of computing with arbitrary accuracy. One may try to represent real numbers by flows of digits, as in *on-line arithmetic*. This is illustrated by Thomas Lynch and Michael Schulte in their

[2] *IEEE Standard 754-1985 for Binary Floating-Point Arithmetic*, IEEE. Reprinted in *SIGPLAN 22*, 2, pp. 9-25. People interested by this topic should read the paper by David Goldberg, *What Every Computer Scientist Should Know About Computer Arithmetic*, ACM Computing Surveys, Vol. 23 No 1, pp. 5-48

paper (*High-Radix OnLine Arithmetic for Credible and Accurate General Purpose Computing*). OnLine arithmetic was pioneered by one of the invited speakers at the Conference, Milos Ercegovac, professor at the *University of California at Los Angeles*. Another more general scheme is to represent a number by flows of coefficients, such as those of a continued-fraction expansion. This solution is explored by Peter Kornerup and David W. Matula (*LCF: A Lexicographic Binary Representation of the Rationals*, invited paper), by Asger Munk Nielsen and Peter Kornerup (*MSB-First Digit Serial Arithmetic*), and by D. Lester (*Exact Statistics and Continued Fractions*). Peter Kornerup, professor at *Odense University*, Denmark, was our second invited speaker at the Saint-Etienne Conference.

Other approaches, such as symbolic manipulation of numbers, are being explored, but they are not represented in this special issue.

Approximating the continuous real arithmetic as closely as possible with our inevitably discrete tools is attempting the impossible, but it is fascinating. There are still many things to be done in this domain, and we hope that the conference "Real Numbers and Computers No 2", that will be held in Marseille, France, in April 1996, will bring new solutions.

We would like to thank all the authors of submitted papers, including those authors of papers that could not be included in this special issue due to reviewer revision requests that could not be accommodated in our tight time frame for publication. Special thanks are due to the Editor-in-Chief of the *Journal of Universal Computer Science*, Hermann Maurer, for hosting this special issue.

Jean-Claude BAJARD, *Guest Editor*
Laboratoire LMI, Université de Provence
13453 Marseille Cedex 13, FRANCE

Dominique MICHELUCCI, *Guest Editor*
École des Mines de Saint-Étienne, SIMADE, 158 cours Fauriel
42023 Saint-Étienne Cedex 2, FRANCE

Jean-Michel MOREAU, *Guest Editor*
École des Mines de Saint-Étienne, SIMADE, 158 cours Fauriel
42023 Saint-Étienne Cedex 2, FRANCE

Jean-Michel MULLER, *Guest Editor*
CNRS, Laboratoire LIP, ENS Lyon, 46 Allée d'Italie
69364 Lyon Cedex 07, FRANCE

Journal of Universal Computer Science, vol. 1, no. 7 (1995), 439-453
submitted: 15/12/94, accepted: 26/6/95, appeared: 28/7/95

A High Radix On-line Arithmetic for Credible and Accurate Computing

Thomas Lynch
(Advanced Micro Devices, U.S.A
Tom.Lynch@amd.com)

Michael J. Schulte
(University of Texas at Austin, U.S.A
schulte@pine.ece.utexas.edu)

Abstract: The result of a simple floating-point computation can be in great error, even though no error is signaled, no coding mistakes are in the program, and the computer hardware is functioning correctly. This paper proposes a set of instructions appropriate for a general purpose microprocessor that can be used to improve the credibility and accuracy of numerical computations. Such instructions provide direct hardware support for monitoring events which may threaten computational integrity, implementing floating-point data types of arbitrary precision, and repeating calculations with greater precision. These useful features are obtained by the efficient implementation of *high radix on-line arithmetic*. The prevalence of super-scalar and VLIW processors makes this approach especially attractive.
Key Words: High-radix, on-line arithmetic, precision, accurate, reliable, credible, super-scaler, VLIW.

1 Introduction

> *One of the principle problems of numerical analysis is to determine how accurate the results of certain numerical methods will be. A "credibility-gap" problem is involved here: we don't know how much of the computer's answers to believe.*
> - Donald Knuth [Knuth 81]

For a program to be *credible*, the results it produces must not be misleading. Hence, a program that always returns the value 'indeterminate' is credible; although it is not accurate. It is highly desirable to define an arithmetic that can be used to develop credible and accurate programs, and then to support the arithmetic in hardware so that it can be fast and efficient.

The most common approach to the credibility/accuracy problem has been the "use lots of bits" approach. For example, IEEE std. 754 [IEEE 85] implementations often have 64 bit data paths. Although it is unlikely that so much precision is needed at any step in a program, in the rare case that it is needed the precision is available. Still, an IEEE std. 754 conformant program can produce results that are completely inaccurate without warning [Lynch and Swartzlander 92, Bohlender 90].

The IEEE std. 754 rounding specifications facilitate a credible interval arithmetic [Moore 66, Nickel 85, Alefeld 83]. Accordingly, upper and lower bounds of intervals which contain the true results are calculated. This, however, does not guarantee accuracy, since interval boundaries may diverge due to accumulated numerical errors and pessimistic assumptions.

Several software approaches have been developed to produce credible and accurate arithmetic. Some special computer languages such as [Cohen et al. 83, Klatte et al. 92] give the programmer control over precision and cancelation. LeLisp is based on on continued fractions [Vuillemin 90], while the program described in [Boehm et al. 86] is based on a form of on-line arithmetic. In [Wiedmer 80], a method is described by which abstract symbolic manipulations can be used to exactly manipulate values which have infinite representations in conventional form. In [Schwartz 89], a C++ library is presented which allows results to be evaluated to arbitrary precision. Numbers are represented in two parts: a data value, which corresponds to the already known bits of the number, and an expression. When more bits are required, the expression is manipulated to generated the required bits.

A common component of many credible and accurate programs is variable-precision arithmetic. The reason for this is discussed in [Section 2]. Based on this observation, G. Bohlender, W. Walter, P. Kornerup, and D. W. Matula, argue that certain hardware hooks should be added to microprocessors in order to make variable-precision arithmetic more efficient [Bohlender et al. 91]. We take this a step further, and describe a set of microprocessor instructions which implement high radix on-line arithmetic. These instructions can be implemented by simple extensions to conventional microprocessor architectures, and they are well suited for very long instruction word (VLIW) and super-scalar techniques.

On-line arithmetic performs operations serially most significant digit first [Ercegovac 84, Ercegovac 91, Irwin and Owens 87, Muller 94], [Duprat and Muller 93, Bajard et. al 94]. This is possible because of the redundancy in the underlying signed digit representation. On-line operations conceptually operate on arbitrarily long digit streams, and as a consequence changing or mixing precisions is straight forward. Most significant digit first variable-precision techniques were successfully used on the AMD K5(tm) microprocessor for implementing accurate transcendental functions on a processor with a narrow data path [Lynch et al. 95].

This paper presents an efficient method for performing credible and accurate computation through the use of high radix on-line arithmetic. The relationship between credible, accurate arithmetic and variable-precision arithmetic is discussed in [Section 2]. [Section 3] discusses our method for performing high radix on-line arithmetic using sequences of three operand microprocessor instructions. Hardware designs for a significand adder unit and significand multiplier unit are discussed in [Section 4] and [Section 5], respectively. High radix on-line floating-point algorithms are discussed in [Section 6], followed by conclusions in [Section 7]. This paper is an extended version of the research presented in [Lynch 95].

2 Range Expansion and Error

The goal of this section is to establish the relationship between credible, accurate arithmetic and variable-precision calculations. We start by quantifying the limitations of conventional floating-point representations as a function of precision. We then show how these representation limitations interact with the behavior of accurate computer approximations. We conclude the section with an example of how relative error can be controlled by using variable-precision arithmetic.

The distance between neighboring representable values around the point x in a conventional binary floating-point system is:

$$\Delta(x,p) = 2^{\lfloor \log_2|x| \rfloor - (p-1)} \tag{1}$$

where p is the precision of floating-point numbers in the system. This function bounds the minimum worst case error that may be introduced by a computer approximation of any continuous function with a range that spans at least two representable values. If the rounding mode is round-to-nearest, then the worst case absolute representation error in a neighborhood around x is:

$$\frac{1}{2}\Delta(x,p) \tag{2}$$

and the worst case relative error is:

$$\frac{1}{2}\Delta(x,p)/x \tag{3}$$

The distance between neighboring result values of a perfect computer approximation of a continuous function, f, around a point x is closely described as:

$$\delta(f,x,p_{in}) = \Delta(x,p_{in})\frac{df(x)}{dx} \tag{4}$$

where p_{in} is the input precision. The distance between representable result values with a precision of p_{out} around $f(x)$ is $\Delta(f(x),p_{out})$. The ratio of $\delta(f,x,p_{in})$ to $\Delta(f(x),p_{out})$ is:

$$\eta(f,x,p_{in},p_{out}) = \frac{\delta(f,x,p_{in})}{\Delta(f(x),p_{out})} \tag{5}$$

This ratio is a measure of how well round-to-nearest of $f(x)$ maps continuous values of x into a floating-point representation of precision p_{out} without considering the effects of approximation error. We call this ratio the *range expansion* because when this ratio is greater than one (or 1/2 at exponent boundaries), all values belonging to the floating-point representation of precision p_{out} cannot be produced by $f(x)$. Many representable values fall in between neighboring output values and hence there is ambiguity in determining the correct output value.

This point is illustrated further in [Figure 1]. This figure shows that for a perfect approximation of e^x; $e^x \in [1000.000, 1111.111]$, where $p_{in} = 7$ and $p_{out} = 7$, there are multiple representable values between possible output values. In this example, the function was rounded to nearest as though it had been calculated to infinite precision, yet input representation error, which is guaranteed to be present, causes a worst case error of 7 ulps on the output. If equation (5) had been applied to this example to force a small range expansion by raising the input precision, this effect would not occur, as there would not be multiple representable values between output values.

By definition, a credible and accurate computer approximation has a guaranteed output accuracy. The output precision can be set from the output accuracy since it is not helpful for the distance between produced values to be much

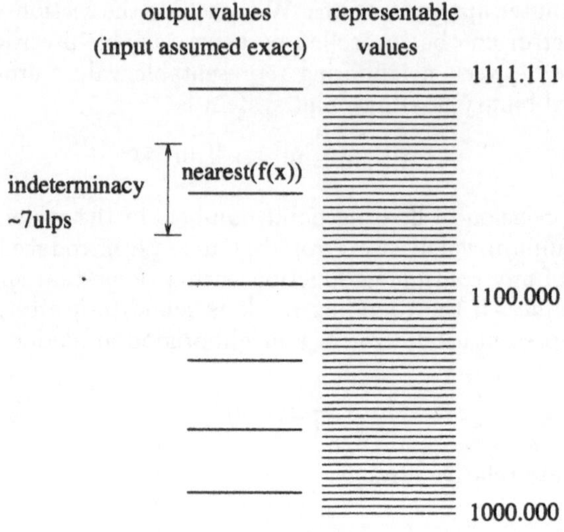

Figure 1: Range Expansion of e^x With a 7 Bit Precise Input

smaller than the dominate output error. By using equation (5), this output precision implies an input precision, which implies an input precision for the next operation back, etc. When precision is set in this way, the accumulation of small rounding errors occur at the end of the word, and therefore are of the order of the representation error, $\Delta(x, p)$. This suggests that error propagates into the values like carries from the bottom of the word, at a rate of $O(log(m))$, where m is the number of floating-point operations.

[Figure 2] shows the range expansion for the function $z-1$ for $z \in [1+2^{-15}, 2]$. The plot on the left shows a worst case factor of 2^{15} more distance between result neighbors than between representable neighbors. The plot on the right shows that the factor can be reduced to a worst case of $\frac{1}{2}$ by adding 16 more bits to the input precision.

The technique of using variable-precision arithmetic to reduce error is illustrated further by coding the function

$$f(z) = \frac{\sqrt{z}+1}{\sqrt{z}-1} \tag{6}$$

in both fixed precision and variable-precision arithmetics. A supplemented version of the language "Mathematica" [Wolfram 91] is used for coding this example. The code segment on the left is a 16 bit fixed precision implementation. The code on the right is a variable precision version with a range expansion of at most one half for each operation. The function *round* rounds the first operand to nearest using the precision specified by the second operand. The accuracy goal for this transformation is a relative error of 2^{-12}. Its domain is $z \in [1+2^{-15}, 2]$.

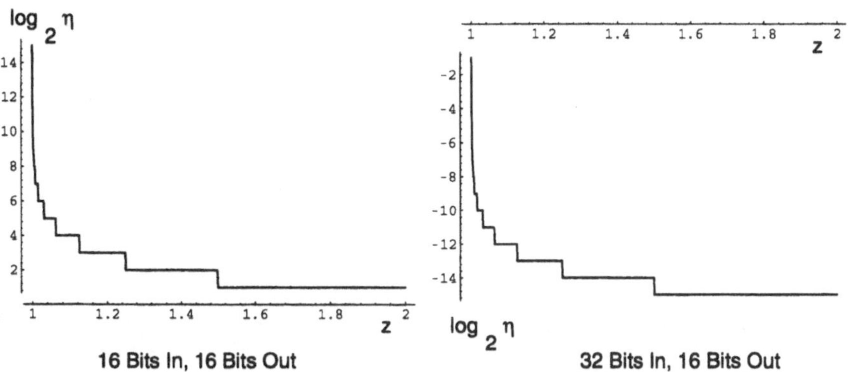

Figure 2: Range Expansion of $z - 1$ for $z \in [1 + 2^{-15}, 2]$

```
f_fixed[z_] := Module[ {},
     zp = round[z,16];
    zsq = round[Sqrt[zp], 16];
      n = round[zsq + 1, 16];
      d = round[zsq - 1, 16];
    nsd = round[ n/d, 16];
    Return [nsd]
]
```

```
f_variable[z_] := Module[ {},
     zp = round[z,31];
    zsq = round[Sqrt[zp], 32];
      n = round[zsq + 1, 16];
      d = round[zsq - 1, 16];
    nsd = round[ n/d, 14];
    Return [nsd]
]
```

In the variable precision code, an output precision of 14 gives two guard bits for roundoff error accumulation. The numerator and denominator sums are computed to an output precision of 16 bits to minimize the roundoff error accumulated in the subsequent divide, and to make up for the small input alignment shifts in the add. The square root is performed with an output precision of 32 bits so that the input precision to the subsequent $zsq - 1$ will be sufficient to ensure a range expansion of at most one half. The input precision to the square root is set to 31 bits to give a satisfactory range expansion.

Here are the results of evaluating each of these code segments for the input value 3072/3071. Values are given in hexadecimal.

$$z = 1.0015571\text{c}97\text{b}74\text{f}469\text{b}3\ldots \tag{7}$$

$$f(z) = 2\text{ffd.fffaaa}71\text{c}42\ldots \tag{8}$$

$$f_{\text{fixed\_precision}}(z) = 3334.0 \tag{9}$$

$$f_{\text{interval}}(z) = [2\text{aab}.4, 4001.8] \tag{10}$$

$$f_{\text{variable\_precision}}(z) = 2\text{ffe}.0 \tag{11}$$

The fixed precision result has only one significant bit. The interval result (16 bit calculation) has less than one significant bit, but it does contain the exact result. Only the variable-precision code produces a result with a small relative error. [Figure 3] shows scatter plots of the relative error in the fixed precision and variable-precision code. The variable-precision code has an even relative error, bounded by about 2^{-13}. The fixed precision code has unbounded error, which becomes large as z approaches 1.

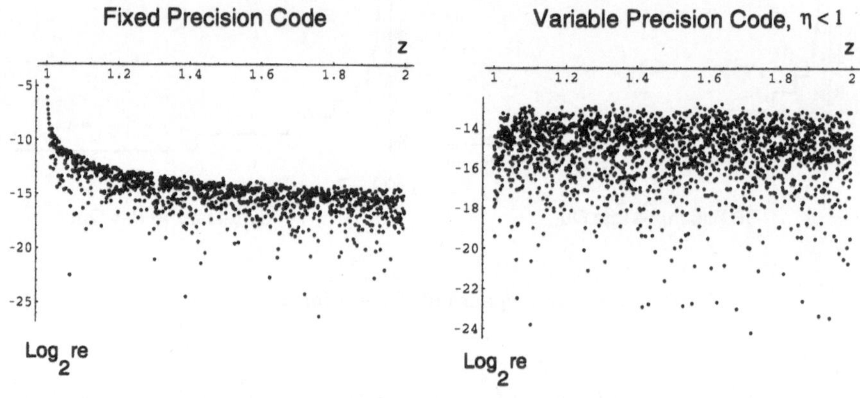

Figure 3: Log Relative Error of $f(z)$ for $z \in [1 + 2^{-15}, 2]$

3 High Radix On-line Arithmetic

In [Bohlender et al. 91], G. Bohlender, W. Walter, P. Kornerup, and D. W. Matula suggest hardware features which make variable-precision arithmetic easier to implement. They suggest that adders should return the rounded sum and the bits shifted off during alignment, that multipliers should return the upper and lower bits of the product, and that dividers should return the quotient and the remainder. The instruction specifications for add, subtract, multiply, and divide using this technique are:

```
add c,d ; a,b
sub c,d ; a,b
mul c,d ; a,b
div c,d ; a,b
```

where a and b are source registers and c and d are destination registers.

There are two main disadvantages of implementing these instructions on a general purpose microprocessor. First, most microprocessors' instruction sets allow at most three operands and would be unable to support these four operand instructions. Second, the internal control of most microprocessors works on the principal of one destination operand per instruction, while these instructions each have two.

To overcome these disadvantages, we propose the use of a high radix on-line arithmetic. The high radix on-line arithmetic is implemented as a sequence of three operand instructions, with two source operands and one destination operand. These instructions require no extraordinary timing, instruction formats, or decoding. Hence they are sufficient primitives for implementing an efficient variable-precision arithmetic congruent with modern architectures. They have the added advantage of being simpler to implement than their conventional fixed-precision, floating-point counter-parts. The sets of instructions for implementing high radix on-line addition and multiplication are:

```
    add_init   spill,  a_0, b_0
  add_extend y_{i-1},  a_i, b_i
add_complete     y_n, null, null

    mul_init    null,  a_0, b_0
  mul_extend y_{i-1},  a_i, b_i
mul_complete     y_n, null, null
```

Sequences of these instructions are combined to perform high radix on-line arithmetic. For example, the instruction sequences for implementing four digit high radix on-line addition and multiplication are:

```
add_init      spill,  a_0,  b_0
add_extend      y_0,  a_1,  b_1
add_extend      y_1,  a_2,  b_2
add_extend      y_2,  a_3,  b_3
add_complete    y_3, null, null

mult_init      null,  a_0,  b_0
mult_init      null,  a_1,  b_1
mult_extend     y_0,  a_2,  b_2
mult_extend     y_1,  a_3,  b_3
mult_complete   y_2, null, null
mult_complete   y_3, null, null
```

An n digit plus n digit high radix on-line addition consists of one *add_init* instruction, $n-1$ *add_extend* instructions, and one *add_complete* instruction. An n digit by n digit high radix on-line multiplication consists of two *mult_init* instructions, $n-2$ *mult_extend* instructions, and two *mult_complete* instructions. For these instructions, each digit is a machine word. Machine integers work naturally as signed digits, and they are supported directly in the processor's data paths, caches, memory busses, etc. Each instruction executes in one machine cycle until the execution unit runs out of some resource such as multiplier width or operand register width, as discussed later.

Since high radix on-line arithmetic produces results most significant digit first, separate code segments may be pipelined. For example, it is not necessary to wait for a series of digit adds to complete before starting a subsequent series of digit multiplies. This can be used to speed up operations on a super-scalar processor where multiple execution units are available simultaneously. In a superscalar design, implementing a number of small units has advantages over using one large unit, because the small units fit in the integer data path, do not limit clock periods, and can also be used for integer instructions. For example, a 64 by 64 bit multiplier may only be partially utilized by programs that perform 32 bit arithmetic, and such programs may even stall for lack of multiplication resources. On the other hand four 32 by 32 bit multipliers require approximately the same total die area, but can be better utilized.

According to this method a floating-point number x is represented as a string of $n_x + 1$ signed integers $(e_x; x_0, x_1, \ldots, x_{n_x-1})$, where e_x is the exponent of x and x_i is the *ith* significand digit. The value of x is:

$$x = \sum_{i=0}^{n_x-1} x_i \cdot r^{e_x-i}$$

where r is the radix of the number system. If each digit is a k-bit signed integer, then $r = 2^{k-1}$. Increasing n_x increases the precision of x, which allows variable-precision computations to be performed. Integer arithmetic can be efficiently performed as single-digit operations on the same hardware.

A signed-digit, floating-point number can have multiple representations. For example, if the digits are decimal, the number 1024 can be represented as $x = (3; 1, 0, 2, 4)$ or equivalently $x = (3; 1, 1, -8, 4)$. Conversion from signed-digit notation to conventional notation is accomplished by subtracting the negative digits from the non-negative digits, as shown below.

```
   (1, 1, 0, 4)
 - (0, 0, 8, 0)
 ---------------
   (1, 0, 2, 4)
```

4 Adder Significand Unit

The functionality of the adder significand unit is described here using C++ classes. These classes can be viewed as hardware behavior models. The declaration for the adder significand unit is:

```
class adder{
public: //three instructions
    int  initial( int a, int b);
    int  extend( int a, int b);
    int  complete();
protected:
    int keepsum;
};
```

Each of the C++ class methods performs the same function that a hardware unit would perform if it received an analogous instruction. For example, calling the method *initial* with two values, a and b is analogous to sending the instruction opcode for *add_init* along with the values a and b on the operand busses to the adder significand unit.

With the proposed method, all digits are streamed through the same functional unit. The signed digit adder carries the sums to the right instead of propagating carries to the left. The sum carried to the right is called *keepsum* in the code. This sum is stored in a register in the add unit.

In the case of a VLIW machine, it is easy to stream instructions through a specific unit, since the instruction sequences may be placed into the correct unit's decode slot. However, for a super-scalar microprocessor there is a problem since the usual dependency checking hardware will not see dependencies between related initial, extend, and complete instructions. A solution to this problem is to code related initial, extend, and complete instructions consecutively in the instruction stream and have the decode unit treat them specially by placing them in an instruction queue in front of the appropriate execution unit.

The *initial* instruction resets the unit's state in preparation for a new sequence of digits. It sets *keepsum* to zero, calculates the most significant sum digit, and returns the value of *spill*. The value of *spill* is zero, unless the most significant sum digit produces a carry. Carry from the most significant digit is a special condition, since the exponent calculation is affected. This event should be fairly rare, since the likelihood of carry when adding full word integers is low.

```
int adder::initial( int a, int b ){ //on-line delay of one
   int spill;
   keepsum = 0;
   return spill = extend(a, b);
}
```

The *extend* instruction outputs a new sum digit by adding a new transfer digit t to the *keepsum* calculated in the previous iteration. It also calculates a new *keepsum* digit to be used in the next iteration.

```
int adder::extend( int a, int b ){
  long long dig_sum;            // this is larger than int
        int adj_sum;
        int t;
        int sum;
        int result_sum;

  dig_sum = (long long)a + (long long)b;//add two digits
  if( dig_sum >= DIG_MAX ){                //check for carry
     t = 1;
     adj_sum = dig_sum - DIG_MAX - 11;  //may go negative
  }else
  if( dig_sum <= -DIG_MAX ){               //check for borrow
     t = -1;
     adj_sum = dig_sum + DIG_MAX + 11;  //may go positive
  }else{
     t = 0;
     adj_sum = dig_sum;
  }
  result_sum = keepsum + t;
  keepsum = adj_sum;
  return result_sum;
}
```

The last sum digit is returned directly by issuing an *add_complete* instruction.

```
int adder::complete(){
```

```
    return keepsum;
  }
```

5 Multiplier Significand Unit

The interface to the multiplier significand unit is similar to the interface to the adder significand unit. The multiplier state consists of two operand registers, a partial product accumulator, and a digit counter which points into the operand registers. The class definition for the multiplier significand unit is shown below.

```
class mul{
 public:
     void initial( int a, int b);
      int extend( int a, int b);
      int complete();
 protected:
      word Xi,Yi; //operand registers:
      word running_product; // a partial product accumulator
      int i; // digit counter
};
```

The used portion of the two operand registers increases as new digits are introduced. This places a limitation on the number of digits that can be multiplied. When the internal state is saturated, a program can scan out the internal partial remainder value by issuing *mult_complete* instructions. This value can then be used to extend the operation.

In order to support internal state manipulations in the multiplier, we introduced maximum word length operations for addition, shifting, and word by digit multiplication. The C++ definition for the *word* class is given below.

```
class word {
 public:
    word( char * d0, ...);
    word();
    word(int);
   ~word();
    void print();
     int & operator[] (unsigned int index);
    word simplify();
    word operator-();
    word operator+( word b);
    word operator-( word b);
    word operator>>( int count );
    word operator<<( int count );
    word word_by_digit( int digit );
 protected:
    int digit[DIGS];  // DIGS is the register width
};
```

The algorithm we use is basically that presented by Trivedi and Ercegovac [Trivedi and Ercegovac 75]. The introduction of new operand digits at each step results in a new row and a new column in the partial product matrix. Carries created by this addition of new rows and columns are limited in duration, and so it is possible to return the leading partial product digit after two new row/column sums are added. The rows and columns are produced with digit by word multiplies. In high radix on-line arithmetic a digit by digit multiplier, or perhaps a digit by a few digits multiplier will be the largest practical unit, so the digit by word operation will become slower as the number of operand digits becomes larger. This causes the result digit latencies to grow as the number of input operands becomes larger.

The *initial* instruction sets the digit counter, i, to zero and computes the most significant partial product digit. The result busses are not driven, since this digit may need to be adjusted in the next iteration.

```
void mul::initial( int xx, int yy){ //on-line delay of two,
   i = 0;
   extend( xx, yy);
}
```

The *extend* instruction produces a new product digit. Initially, it computes a new row and column of the matrix by multiplying the new digit of x by the previous digits of y and the new digit of y by the previous digits of x. The new row and column are added to the running partial product and the leading digit of the running partial product is returned.

```
int mul::extend( int xx, int yy){
  // overflowed our state?
    if( i >= DIGS ){
       fprintf(stderr,"digit overflow\n");
       abort();
    }
  // shift the new digits into the operand registers
    Yi[i+1] = yy;  // Yi is real state
    word Xim1;
    Xim1 = Xi;  // Xi is real state
    Xi[i+1] = xx;
  // add in the new row and the new column to the matrix
    word        trap_row =   Yi.word_by_digit(xx);
    word        trap_col = Xim1.word_by_digit(yy);
    word partial_product = add_nr(trap_row, trap_col);
    running_product = add_nr(running_product, partial_product);
  // extract leading digit of the running product
    word S = add_nr( abs_word(running_product) , half);
    int dj = sign(running_product) * S[0];
  // add cancels the lead digit
    running_product = add_nr(running_product, -dj);
    running_product = running_product << 1;// walks to the left
    i++;
    return dj;
}
```

Two *mult_complete* instructions are used to return the last two product digits.

```
int mul::complete(){
    return extend(0,0);
}
```

6 Floating-point Algorithms

The high radix on-line floating-point algorithms presented in this paper are similar to those given in [Watanuki and Ercegovac 81]. However, these operations have been partitioned into microprocessor instruction sequences. Overflow or cancelation from the leading digit should be fairly rare, because of the large radix. Hence, the exponent and significand operations are somewhat independent. The programmer specifies the steps in the operation explicitly. The following shows the assembly code for a five digit floating-point multiply. The *jnz* instruction should be coded so that it is predicted to be taken by the branch prediction unit. When the branch is found to be not taken, the processor will delete the speculative state. The *jnz* instruction is placed at the end of the sequence so that the decoder gets the multiply instructions to the multiplier as soon as possible. It could be moved up a little to fill delay slots caused by the multiplier getting slower with the introduction of operand digits.

```
add            exp_y, exp_a, exp_b // may get ov trap
mult_init       null,   a_0,   b_0 // perform multiply
mult_init       null,   a_1,   b_1
mult_extend      y_0,   a_2,   b_2
mult_extend      y_1,   a_3,   b_3
mult_extend      y_2,   a_4,   b_4
mult_complete    y_3,   null, null
mult_complete    y_4,   null, null
mult_test       norm,   y_0,  null  // test for normalized result
jnz             done,   norm, null
   // add program personality here;
done: exit
```

The *program personality* code is seldom executed, since it is only looking for three out of 2^k cases, where k is the number of bits per integer. This is a benefit of using a high radix. Hence, we can normally ignore the exponent adjustment, and performance does not suffer. No additional hardware structures beyond those needed for the significand unit are required for performing high radix on-line floating-point multiply.

For addition, the operand alignment step does not require a real shifter, since the operand with the smaller exponent is simply delayed. We decided to perform the exponent subtract and the operand delay inside the significand adder unit. Otherwise floating-point addition code sequences require the declaration of an index variable, and the use of an *if* block and *while* loop. This decision causes the need for an operand register in the unit. The operand register width grows with alignment delay as operand digits are introduced. Operand length limits are already caused by the operand registers in the multiplier, so this situation is tolerable in the adder. The proposed assembly code for a four digit on-line addition is shown below.

```
      add_exponent  exp_y, exp_a, exp_b
      add_init      spill,   a_0,   b_0
      add_extend      y_0,   a_1,   b_1
      add_extend      y_1,   a_2,   b_2
      add_extend      y_2,   a_3,   b_3
      add_complete    y_3,  null,  null
      add_test        spc,  y_0,  spill // test for special cases
      jnz             done, spc,  null
         // add program personality here;
done: exit
```

The **add_exponent** and the **add_init** instruction can be executed in parallel in single cycle. Each **add_extend** instruction the requires another cycle. Finally the **add_test** instruction does not effect performance since it is done after the add is complete – unless the normalization or carry test fails. In which case the fix-up code must be executed. Hence, in the usual case there is an online delay of one cycle followed by one cycle to calculate each digit, for a total of 5 cycles for this add. The adder unit is unavailable for an additional cycle which the test is being performed.

The additional area requirements over that needed for an integer unit is modest. The operand registers and the instruction queue are the largest items. Also these units will fit in an integer data path (unlike most conventional floating-point units). The hardware for the on-line floating-point multiplier unit is:

1. two word width operand registers
2. a word width partial product register
3. a digit counter
4. a digit by word multiplier
5. a word width adder
6. an instruction queue

The hardware needed for the on-line floating-point adder is:

1. a word width operand register
2. a digit width register
3. a digit width adder
4. an instruction queue

The instructions presented can be used to implement various data types by filling in the *personality* sections, and by varying the number of extend instructions. For example, arbitrary width floating-point data types can be easily generated by the compiler by varying the number of extend instructions generated for each type. Language support is as simple as passing a parameter into the type declaration. In C one might imagine a statement such as:

```
rbfloat x(3), y(4);
```

which declares two high radix on line floating-point variables x and y with significand lengths of 3 words and 4 words, respectively.

When performing addition or multiplication, there may be need for normalization, as can be determined by looking at the most significant digit. If normalization is needed, there are a variety of options. The simplest (other than doing nothing) is to adjust the exponent, and then shift the significand digits to the left. The action taken depends on the program's requirements.

We believe that these instructions can also be used with backtracking to produce guaranteed precision results as described by Boehm, et al. [Boehm et al. 86]. When cancelation occurs, the *personality* section would trigger the lazy evaluation of previous operations to fill in the lost significance.

7 Conclusions

The propagation of numerical errors can ameliorated by limiting the disparity between a) the distance between values produced by an operation, and b) the distance between possible representable values. Also, this disparity, *range expansion*, can be controlled through the use of variable precision, multi-precision, arithmetic.

Such an arithmetic is *high radix online* arithmetic. This variation of online arithmetic differs in that the radix is set so that digits are machine integers, and operations are executed on a programmed microprocessor instead of on dedicated hardware.

The proposed high radix on-line execution units have many advantages over conventional floating point execution units: they requires less area than the conventional floating-point hardware; they can perform integer operations; they fit into an integer data path; and they can be used to efficiently implement accurate and credible floating point arithmetic.

References

[Alefeld 83] Alefeld, G.; Herzberger, J.: "An Introduction to Interval Computations"; Academic Press, New York, 1983.

[Bajard et. al 94] J. C. Bajard, J. Duprat, S. Kla, and J. M. Muller.: "Some Operators for On-line Radix 2 Computations"; Journal of Parallel and Distributed Computing, pp 336-345, vol. 22, 2, Aug 1994.

[Boehm et al. 86] Boehm, H., Cartwright, R., Riggle, M., O'Donnell, M.: "Exact Real Arithmetic: A Case Study in Higher Order Programming"; ACM 0-89791-200-4/86/0800-0162.

[Bohlender et al. 91] Bohlender, G., Walter, W., Kornerup, P., Matula, D.: "Semantics for Exact Floating Point Operations"; Proceedings 10th Symposium on Computer Arithmetic, IEEE Computer Society Press, Grenoble, France, 1991, 22-26.

[Bohlender 90] Bohlender, G.: "What Do We Need Beyond IEEE Arithmetic?"; Computer Arithmetic and Self-Validating Numerical Methods Academic Press, New York, 1990, 1-32.

[Cohen et al. 83] Cohen, M., Hull, T., Hamacher, V.: "CADAC: A Controlled Precision Decimal Arithmetic Unit"; IEEE Transactions on Computers, C-32, 4, 1983, 370-377.

[Duprat and Muller 93] J. Duprat and J. M. Muller.: "The Cordic Algorithm: New Results for Fast VLSI Implementation."; IEEE Transactions on Computers, pp 168-178, vol. 42, 2, Feb 1993.

[Ercegovac 84] Ercegovac, M.: "On-line Arithmetic: an Overview"; SPIE, Real Time Signal Processing VII, 1984, 86-93.

[Ercegovac 91] Ercegovac, M.: "On-line Arithmetic for Recurrence Problems"; Advanced Signal Processing Algorithms, Architectures, and Implementations II, SPIE-The International Society for Optical Engineering, 1991.

[IBM 86] IBM: "IBM High-Accuracy Arithmetic Subroutine Library (ACRITH)"; General Information Manual, GC 33-6163-02, IBM Deutschland GmbH (Department 3282, Schönaicher Strasse 220, 7030 Böblingen), 3rd edition, 1986.

[IEEE 85] American National Standards Institute / Institute of Electrical and Electronics Engineers: "A Standard for Binary Floating-Point Arithmetic"; ANSI/IEEE Std. 754-1985, New York, 1985.

[Irwin and Owens 87] Irwin, M. and Owens, R.: "Digit-pipelined Arithmetic as Illustrated by the Paste-Up System: A tutorial"; IEEE Computer, 1987, 61-73.

[Klatte et al. 92] Klatte, R., Kulisch, U., Neaga, M., Ratz, D., Ullrich, Ch.: "PASCAL–XSC - Language Reference with Examples"; Springer-Verlag, Berlin/Heidelberg/New York, 1992.

[Knuth 81] Knuth, D.: "The Art of Computer Programming: Seminumerical Algorithms"; Vol. 2, 2nd ed., Addison-Wesley, Reading, MA, 1981.

[Lynch et al. 95] Lynch, T., Ahmed, A., Schulte, M., Callaway, T., Tisdale, R.: "The K5 Transcendental Functions"; Proceedings of the 12th Symposium on Computer Arithmetic, IEEE Computer Society Press, Bath, England, 1995.

[Lynch 95] Lynch, T.: "High Radix Online Arithmetic for Credible and Accurate General Purpose Computing"; Real Numbers and Computers ... Les Nombre Réels et L'Ordinateur, Ecole des Mines de Saint-Etienne, France, 1995, 78-89.

[Lynch and Swartzlander 92] Lynch, T., Swartzlander E.: "A Formalization for Computer Arithmetic"; Computer Arithmetic and Enclosure Methods, Elsevier Science Publishers, Amsterdam, 1992.

[Moore 66] Moore, R.: "Interval Analysis", Prentice Hall Inc., Englewood Cliffs, NJ, 1966.

[Muller 94] J. M. Muller.: "Some Characterizations of Functions Computable in On-line Arithmetic"; IEEE Transactions on Computers, pp 752-755, vol. 43, 6, June 1994.

[Nickel 85] Nickel, K.(Ed.): "Interval Mathematics 1985: Proceedings of the International Symposium"; Freiburg 1985, Springer-Verlag, Vienna, 1986.

[Schwartz 89] Schwarz, G.: "Implementing Infinite Precision Arithmetic"; Proceedings of the 9th Symposium on Computer Arithmetic, IEEE Computer Society Press, Santa Monica, CA, 1989, 10-17.

[Trivedi and Ercegovac 75] Trivedi, K., Ercegovac, M. "On-line Algorithms for Division and Multiplication"; Proceedings of the IEEE 3rd Symposium on Computer Arithmetic, IEEE Computer Society Press, Dallas, TX, 1975.

[Vuillemin 90] Vuillemin, J: "Exact Real Computer Arithmetic with Continued Fractions"; IEEE Transactions on Computers, C-39, 8, 1990.

[Watanuki and Ercegovac 81] Watanuki, O., Ercegovac M.: "Floating-point On-line Arithmetic Algorithms"; Proceedings of the 5th Symposium on Computer Arithmetic, IEEE Computer Society Press, Ann Arbor, MI, 1981.

[Wiedmer 80] Wiedmer, E.: "Computing with Infinite Objects," Theoretical Computer Science, 10, 1980, 133-155.

[Wolfram 91] Wolfram S., "Mathematica - A System for Doing Mathematics by Computer"; Addison-Wesley, Redwood City, 1991.

Journal of Universal Computer Science, vol. 1, no. 7 (1995), 454-468
submitted: 15/12/94, accepted: 26/6/95, appeared: 28/7/95 © Springer Pub. Co.

ESTIMATION OF ROUND-OFF ERRORS ON SEVERAL COMPUTERS ARCHITECTURES

Jalil Asserrhine
E-mail:asserrhine@masi.ibp.fr

Jean-Marie Chesneaux
E-mail:chesneaux@masi.ibp.fr

Jean-Luc Lamotte
E-mail:lamotte@masi.ibp.fr

Laboratoire MASI-IBP, URA-818 du CNRS
Université Pierre et Marie Curie
4 place Jussieu, 75252 Paris Cedex 05 FRANCE

Abstract: Numerical validation of computed results in scientific computation is always an essential problem as well on sequential architecture as on parallel architecture. The probabilistic approach is the only one that allows to estimate the round-off error propagation of the floating point arithmetic on computers. We begin by recalling the basics of the CESTAC method (*Contrôle et Estimation STochastique des Arrondis de Calculs*). Then, the use of the CADNA software (*Control of Accuracy and Debugging For Numerical Applications*) is presented for numerical validation on sequential architecture. On parallel architecture, we present two solutions for the control of round-off errors. The first one is the combination of CADNA and the PVM library. This solution allows to control round-off errors of parallel codes with the same architecture. It does not need more processors than the classical parallel code. The second solution is represented by the RAPP prototype. In this approach, the CESTAC method is directly parallelized. It works both on sequential and parallel programs. The essential difference is that this solution requires more processors than the classical codes. These different approaches are tested on sequential and parallel programs of multiplication of matrices.

1 Introduction

On computers, using the floating point arithmetic, each elementary operation creates a round-off error because of the limited coding of real numbers. Consequently, every computed result is affected by the round-off error propagation. Then, to validate numerical results on computers we must estimate the number of exact significant digits of every result. Exact significant digits mean the digits in common between the computed result and the mathematical result. The probabilistic approach is the only one which allows to estimate the round-off error of the floating point arithmetic.

On a sequential architecture, the numerical validation of computation can be done by using the CADNA software which is based on the CESTAC method. But, more and more computations are now performed on parallel architectures. A tool for the numerical validation for such kind of computations has become essential.

After recalling the basics of the CESTAC method and explaining the use of the CADNA software for sequential architectures, we present in this note two prototypes for the control of round-off error on parallel architectures.

The first one combines CADNA and the message passing library PVM. In this approach each processor validates its own results using CADNA. The passing of results between processors is performed by adding a specific extension to PVM because of the new stochastic types used by CADNA.

The second one is a direct parallelization of the CESTAC method - the RAPP prototype - available both on sequential and parallel architectures.

2 The CESTAC method

In the probabilistic approach, the round-off errors are modeled by independent identically distributed (iid) random variables [Hamming 70][Hull and Swenson 66]. Therefore, a computed result R is also modeled by a random variable. The number of significant digits of R is estimated from notions like the mean value and the standard deviation of R.

Based on the probabilistic approach, the CESTAC method has been developed by J. Vignes and M. La Porte [Vignes 90][Vignes 93][Vignes and La Porte 74] to estimate the round-off error propagation of the floating point arithmetic. At each step of the computation, the chosen rounding of any intermediate result is the upper or the lower rounding with the probability 0.5 . Practically this is realized by perturbing the lowest bit of the mantissa after each elementary operation. This technique is called the random arithmetic. Then the code is run N times with this new arithmetic. By this way, N different results R_i are obtained.

The computed result is taken as the average of the R_i's :

$$\overline{R} = \frac{1}{N} \cdot \sum_{i=1}^{N} R_i.$$

The number of exact significant digits of $\overline{R}$ is given by the formula :

$$C_{\overline{R}} = Log_{10}\left(\frac{\sqrt{N}.\left|\overline{R}\right|}{s.t_\beta}\right),$$

with $s^2 = \frac{1}{N-1} \cdot \sum_{i=1}^{N} \left(R_i - \overline{R}\right)^2$ and t_β the level of confidence of the t distribution for a probability $(1-\beta)$.

It has been shown [Chesneaux 90] that a computed result obtained with the random arithmetic may be modeled by

$$Z = r + \sum_{i=1}^{n} u_i(d).2^{-p} z_i ,$$

where r is the mathematical result, n is the number of elementary operations, the $u_i(d)$'s are coefficients depending only on the data and the algorithm, p is the length of the mantissa (the hidden bit included) and the z_i's are iid centered random variables.

From the probabilistic point of view, the CESTAC method consists in applying Student's test on a sample of R (which is the R_i's). Then, an estimation of the mean value of R (in the model, it is the mathematical result) is obtained from a confidence interval.

The theoretical study has proved the validity of the CESTAC method on the model [Chesneaux 90]. Then the practical efficiency of the CESTAC method is based on the physical reality of the hypotheses and the approximations which have been assumed during the theoretical study.

Theses hypotheses are :
i) the signs and the exponents of the intermediate results are independent of the random arithmetic,
ii) the model of round-off errors by iid random variables is correct,
iii) the approximation of the R's distribution by the first order terms in 2^{-p} modeled by Z is correct,
iv) the approximation by the first four terms in the Edgeworth's development of the Z's distribution during the study of Student's test is correct,
v) the $u_i(d)$'s coefficients are *regular*, which means that none of them is of a greater order than the sum of the others.

In practice, the hypotheses i), ii), iv), v) are of little importance [Chesneaux 95].

The hypotheses iii) is the only one which may really make the CESTAC method fail. If it is not verified, the mathematical expectation of the terms of order greater than 2^{-2p} is not zero. Then, there could be a bias which is not of a smaller order than the standard deviation of Z. The mean value of R is not yet well modeled by the mathematical expectation of Z which is the mathematical result.

In fact, as the CESTAC method gives an estimation of the mean value of R, it is absolutely necessary that it is closed to the mathematical result according to the standard deviation of R, i.e., that the approximation at the first order is valid. If it is not true, there could be an overestimation of the accuracy of the computed result R.

Only multiplications between two non significant results (called stochastic zeroes) and divisions by non significant results may create preponderant terms of order higher than 2^{-2p} [Chesneaux 95]. Then, such operations must be detected at run-time and the user must be advised. It may also be shown that, for the CESTAC method to work efficently, a control of the accuracy of the operands during tests like $IF\ (A > B)\ THEN$ must be performed. The answer of the test must take the number of exact significant digits of each operand into account [Chesneaux 95].

All of this may be done very easily by using the synchronous implementation of the CESTAC method which allows to estimate the accuracy of any intermediate result at any time. It consists in performing in a complete parallel manner the N runs of a code using the random arithmetic [Vignes 90][Vignes 93]. This implementation allows to have a sample of N values for any variables at each step of the run and so to estimate the accuracy of any result. Then, it is possible to point out the denominators which are non significant, the unstable multiplications and other numerical unstabilities. It leads to a self-validation of the CESTAC method.

All the efficiency of the CADNA software is based on this self-validation.

3 The CADNA software for sequential architectures

CADNA [Chesneaux 92][Vignes 93] means *Control of Accuracy and Debugging for Numerical Applications*. The first goal of this software is the estimation of the round-off error in a scientific code using the floating point arithmetic. CADNA uses the synchronous implementation of the CESTAC method. It also implements and uses the definitions of the order and equality relations of the stochastic arithmetic [Chesneaux 95]. This enables to control the branching, that is, CADNA points out all the tests for which the computed and the real answer have opposite signs. This is the second goal of the software.

The third goal is the numerical debugging. With CADNA, users may detect numerical unstabilities that appear at run-time. We must emphazise that this kind of debugging does not deal with the logical validation of a code but with the ability of the computers to give correct results when the code is performed using the floating point arithmetic.

CADNA also includes all the control tests pointed out by the theoretical study to have an efficient use the CESTAC method. CADNA is copyrighted and marketed, it is the property of the Pierre and Marie Curie University.

CADNA works on codes written in FORTRAN 77 but requires a FORTRAN 90 compiler to generate executable codes. In practice, CADNA is a library which is used during the link. It implements three new numerical types - the stochastic types - and all the arithmetic operators for these new types. The control of round-off error propagation is only performed on variables of a stochastic type.

These types are :
- type (SINGLE_ST) : stochatic single precision;
- type (DOUBLE_ST) : stochastic double precision;
- type (COMPLEX_ST) : stochastic complex single precision.

Declarations of stochastic variables are of the same kind as for the classical numerical types. For instance,

TYPE (DOUBLE_ST) X, Y, Z

The estimation of the number of significant digits is available at any time on any stochastic variable. All the arithmetic operators and order relations have been overloaded for the stochastic types. Intrinsic mathematical functions of the FORTRAN 77 only exist by their generic name. In that way, it is very easy to use CADNA on old FORTRAN 77 codes almost without any modification.

In an arithmetic expression, stochastic types, floating types and integer types may be mixed. The classical rules of prevalence are applied with the prevalence of the stochastic types on the others.

In the writing procedures, only the significant digits are printed for the variables of stochastic types. In this way, it is very easy to see the accuracy of the results.

For the numerical debugging, CADNA detects at any time numerical unstabilities that appear at run-time and let a trace in a special file. With the symbolic debugger, the user may point out the operation which is responsible for the unstability.

The implementation of CADNA on sequential architecture consists in imbedding the computations in $\mathbb{R}^N$. This simple solution perfectly simulates the synchronous implementation of the CESTAC method. Each operation is performed N times. In that way and at any time, there exists a sample of N values for any stochastic variable for the control of accuracy, the branching and the numerical debugging. The use of CADNA multiplies the run time by a factor 3 or 5.

4 Interfacing of CADNA with PVM

Nowadays, parallel computers are more and more used for scientific softwares usually written in FORTRAN. It seems essential to develop a validation tool for numerical softwares on this kind of machine. As the existing parallel machines are very different in structure and programming techniques, we have intentionnally limited our tool to the parallel machine using the IEEE arithmetic for the floating point number and being programmed in MIMD (Multiple Instruction Multiple Data) mode. Then a program may be considered as a set of sequential processes allocated on the different processors of the computer and interacting together by message passing.

To create the numerical validation tool, we have proceeded in the following way : each sequential process uses the sequential CADNA library to locally validate its computations and exchanges by message passing variables of standard type or of stochastic type (to estimate the round-off error).

For the communications between the processors, the message passing library PVM (Parallel Virtual Machine) was chosen for several reasons. First, the concept of Virtual Machine is available on a large number of parallel computers and allows to create easily a parallel virtual machine from a network of sequential and heterogeneous machines. Secondly PVM has been welcome by the scientific community working on parallel computation. Finally it is a freeware software of easy access.

This section is made up of four paragraphs. First, we recall the principle of the foundation of PVM. Then, the different problems encountered to use FORTRAN 90, CADNA and PVM in a same program and the proposed solution are described. Starting with an example of a parallel program (multiplication of two matrices), we explain the modifications we have to perform on a FORTRAN source file to use CADNA library. Finally, the performance obtained on a Connection Machine 5 are presented and commented.

4.1 Presentation de PVM

P.V.M. (Parallel Virtual Machine) [Geist and al. 93] has been developed by the *Heterogeneous Network Project* which embodies research from the Oak Ridge National Laboratory and the universities of Tennessee and of Emory. The aim of this project was to do parallel computations on networks of heterogeneous machines which have different architectures and different representations for floating point numbers.

To interconnect machines, which may be of sequential, parallel or vectorial type, PVM is able to use different types of networks (Ethernet, FDDI, Token Ring, ...). Despite the global view of the computer and of the network, PVM allows the different processes to take the best advantage of the performance of the target machines.

To develop an application, the programmer may use of the C language, the FORTRAN 77 language and a message passing library of high level (synchronous and asynchronous sending and receiving, synchronisation of processes, broadcast of message passing, and concentration and diffusion of values (reduce)). For each message, the user's interface imposes to describe the data type that may be converted in another format for the target machine. This functionalities allow to exchange data between computers with very different architectures.

To create his own virtual machine, the user lists into a file, which is read in the initial phasis of PVM, the accessible machines on the network. Three modes of allocation are available to place the processes on the processors :

1. the transparent mode : each task is automatically located at the most appropriate site.
2. the architecture-dependent mode : the user may indicate the specific architecture on which particular tasks must be executed.
3. the machine-specific mode : a particular machine may be specified

4.2 Extension of PVM

The extensions brought to on PVM have their origin in the use of FORTRAN 90 and the creation of new types in CADNA. We begin by making a demonstration model of feasibility modifying only the main functions of PVM. The first difficulty we have found is due to the interface between FORTRAN 90 and PVM. For example, the subroutines PVMFPACK(type, data, ...) and PVMFUNPACK(type, data, ...) respectively allow to gather the data before sending them or to recover them after receiving them. They use 5 parameters including a pointer on the data and a constant that indicates their type. This technique works very well in FORTRAN 77 and in C because there is no type verification for the parameter of the subroutine and the functions. When these subroutines are used in a same program written in FORTRAN 90 to send or to recover data of different types, the compiler generates errors because it detects variables of different types for the second parameter. So it is necessary to overload PVMFPACK and PVMFUNPACK which leads to write as many subroutines (hidden type in the user's interface) as there are potential types. The problem is the same for the subroutine PVMFSEND (creation and sending of a message with one instruction) and PVMFRECV (receipt and recovering of data with one instruction). The subroutine PVMFREDUCE (concentration and diffusion) has not still been adapted for the new type of CADNA because it needs a development too important in the scope of a demonstration model of feasibility.

The second difficulty consists in integrating the new stochastic types SINGLE_ST , DOUBLE_ST, COMPLEX_ST, defined by CADNA in order to preserve the PVM principle of typed data. We must add the stochastic types to the intrisic types (BYTES, INTEGER2, INTEGER4, REAL4, REAL8, COMPLEX) predefined and used by PVMFPACK and PVMFUNPACK.

4.3 Difference of programmming

To explain in detail how the validation software for parallel computations works, we present an example of matrix multiplication intentionally simple and not optimized not to complicate the problem. The program realizes the multiplication on a computer using 4 processors in the following way : a process named *master* reads 2 matrices a and b. The matrix b is divided into four equal parts. The *master* processor sends to the four *slave* processors the matrix a and one quarter of the elements of b. Each one executes the multiplication between the matrix a and its part of b and sends back its result to the process *master* that builds the matrix solution. The program is written in FORTRAN.

Figure (1) presents in the left column the most interesting part of the source program of the process *slave* without using CADNA and in the right column the same source with the necessary modifications to use CADNA in bold-face. The printing subroutine of the matrix is not detailed. It is necessary to know that CADNA proposes a function $str(var)$ that takes a stochastic variable in parameter and, associated with a *print* or a *write* instruction, only displays the exact significant digits. If the value is no significant, @0 is displayed.

One may note that it is not necessary to do a lot of modifications on the original program to validate the numerical computation.

4.4 Results

To measure the performance of our model, two sequential versions and two parallel versions (each one with and without CADNA) have been written and run. The run times have been measured on a Connection Machine 5 (CM5) manufactured by the society Thinking Machine Corporation on full squared matrices of size 100x100, 200x200, 300x300 and are reported on table (1). For the measure of the run time only 4 processors (or nodes) have been used on a partition of 32. The vector unit associated to each node have been inhibited because it is impossible to change his working mode and therefore to modify their arithmetic. In the sequential versions, the run times represent only the run time of the matrix product subroutine. In the parallel versions, the run times are measured on the *master* processor. It includes the sending of the matrix a and b to the *slave* processors, the run time of the *slave* processors, the receipt of the partial matrix and the rebuilding of solution matrix.

Matrix	Sequential time without CADNA	Sequential time with CADNA	Parallel time without CADNA	parallel time with CADNA
100x100	4.46	16.10	2.26	6.50
200x200	38.20	134.00	14.63	45.23
300x300	153.20	483.00	51.00	147.00

Table 1: Computing time obtained on CM5 using one node for the sequential version and four nodes for the parallel versions.

To estimate the overhead generated by using CADNA, the sequential and parallel times obtained with CADNA are divided by the times obtained in the same conditions but without CADNA (see table (2)). CADNA induces a cost in time near a factor 3 which represents the price of the validation of the numerical results.

To conclude the study of the results, the efficiency of the parallelization is calculated. It is defined by the following ratio :

```
! mtid : address of the master process
integer mtid
double precicion a(100,100)
double precision b(100,25)

! receipt of a and b
call pvmfrecv (mtid,msgtype,info)
call pvmfunpack(REAL8,a,10000,1,info)
call pvmfunpack(REAL8,b,2500,1,info)

call pvmfunpack(REAL8,b,2500,1,info)

! r = a * b
call ProdMat(a,100,100,b,100,25,r,rlig,rcol)

! sending to the master of the result r
call pvmfinitsend(PVMDEFAULT, info)
call pvmfpack(REAL8,r,rlig*rcol,1,info)
call pvmfsend(mtid,msgtype)
end

Subroutine ProdMat(A,alig,acol,B,
        blig,bcol,MatP,rlig,rcol)
implicit none
integer i,j,k,alig,acol,blig,
         bcol,rlig,rcol
double precision A(alig,acol),
        B(blig,bcol),MatP(alig,bcol)
rlig = alig
rcol = bcol
do i=1,alig
    do j=1,bcol
        MatP(i,j)=0.D0
            do k=1,acol
            MatP(i,j)=MatP(i,j)+A(i,k)*B(k,j)
        end do
    end do
end do
return
end
```

```
!mtid : address of the master process
integer mtid
type (double_st) a(100,100)
type (double_st) b(100,25)

! inititialisation of the CADNA librairy
call cadna_init(0)

! receipt of a and b
call pvmfrecv (mtid,msgtype,info)
call pvmfunpack( DOUBLEST,a,10000,1,info)
call pvmfunpack( DOUBLEST,b,2500,1,info)

call pvmfunpack( DOUBLEST,b,2500,1,info)

! r = a * b
call ProdMat(a,100,100,b,100,25,r,rlig,rcol)

! sending to the master of the result r
call pvmfinitsend(PVMDEFAULT, info)
call pvmfpack( DOUBLEST,r,rlig*rcol,1,info)
call pvmfsend(mtid,msgtype)
end

Subroutine ProdMat(A,alig,acol,B,
        blig,bcol,MatP,rlig,rcol)
implicit none
integer i,j,k,alig,acol,blig,
        bcol,rlig,rcol
type (double_st) A(alig,acol),
        B(blig,bcol),MatP(alig,bcol)
rlig = alig
rcol = bcol
do i=1,alig
    do j=1,bcol
        MatP(i,j)=0.D0
            do k=1,acol
            MatP(i,j)=MatP(i,j)+A(i,k)*B(k,j)
        end do
    end do
end do
return
end
```

Figure 1: Source of the slave program. Left column : standard version using PVM, right column : version using PVM and CADNA.

Matrix	Ratio of times with and without CADNA	
	for the sequential program	for the parallel program
100x100	3.61	2.87
200x200	3.50	3.09
300x300	3.15	2.88

Table 2: Overhead due to the use of CADNA

$$eff = \frac{TpsSeq}{NbProc.TpsPara}$$

with :

eff : efficiency of the parallelism,
$NbProc$: number of processors,
$TpsPara$: run time of the parallel program,
$TpsSeq$: run time of the sequential program.

Matrice	efficiency without CADNA	efficiency with CADNA
100x100	49.33	61.92
200x200	65.18	74.06
300x300	75.10	82.14

Table 3: efficiency of the parallel program

The efficiency of 100 % is obtained only in the case where all the processors are independent and do not exchange any data. Table (3) presents the obtained result on the matrix multiplication. Two behaviours must be noticed.

First, the efficiency is less for the small size matrix. When the message is short, the time of initialization of a communication between two processes becomes more predominant. It would be better to send large size messages.

Secondly, with an equivalent matrix size, the efficiency is superior when CADNA is used. This increase is simple to explain : the ratio $\frac{computation}{exchange}$ is more important.

5 Parallelization of the CESTAC method

The previous system (CADNA + PVM) validates the result of a parallel program without modifying the architecture used. Here we present a prototype of direct parallelization of the CESTAC method which brings about an increase of the processors number.

5.1 Extraction of the parallelism of CESTAC

Let us consider an algebraic procedure PA composed of a finite sequence of arithmetical operations. Practically, the CESTAC method consists in executing N ($N = 2$ ou 3) copies of the program of the procedure PA with the random arithmetic in order to be able to estimate the accuracy of all intermediate or final computed results. The N copies constitute N independent tasks of computation. At the time of their execution, it is necessary to know the accuracy of the intermediate computed result in order to carry out certain operations (conditional splitting, division). Then, the tasks communicate their results to a control task that returns the mean of the N representative values with the number of exact significant digits.

The implementation of the CESTAC method on a sequential machine multiplies the run time of a program by a factor depending in the average on the number of image programs. These programs being independent, their implementation on a parallel machine should allow to decrease the run time. Figure (2) presents the scheduling of the tasks in the CESTAC method. A prototype of feasibility named RAPP (Random Arithmetic Parallel Prototype) has been developed on a distributed and reconfigurable machine based on transputers with the OCCAM2 language of INMOS [OCCAM 88].

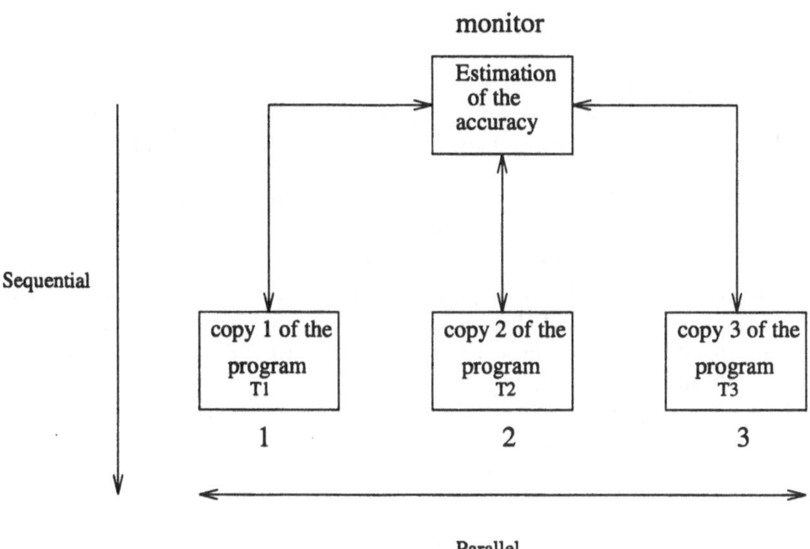

Figure 2: Elementary module of computation for the random arithmetic

5.2 Presentation of RAPP

In the scope of RAPP, we have chosen to use three tasks of computation T_i ($i = 1, 2, 3$) (image program of PA). The T_i are allocated to the processors 1,2 and 3 (see figure (2)) and are run in parallel. The task of accuracy estimation is allocated to a monitor processor which is also used for the communication between the host processor and the rest of the network.

The divisions and the conditionnal splitting synchronize automatically the tasks T_i at the moment of the accuracy estimation. When a division occurs, the values of the denominator are sent to the monitor processor and the trace of a possible unstability is generated into a file and may be consulted after the end of the computation. In the same way, for a conditionnal splitting, a precision control is carried out before the comparison of two variables. The precision estimation is possible for all the other results, but it is not automatically done to preserve the performance of the prototype.

5.3 Communication between the nodes of the RAPP network

The language OCCAM2 gives the possibility to define new protocols of communication between nodes of a network in order to adapt the communication to the type of exchanged data.

The RAPP prototype uses 3 communication protocols to gain in performance and to preserve for the programmer the standard Input/Output, the system call that work according to the standard protocol SP.

The first prototype allows the communications of the tasks $T_i (i = 1, 2, 3)$ towards the task of precision estimation and limits the communication to a table of real numbers coded on 64 bits. The number of elements of this table is variable.

The second protocol allows the task of precision estimation to send back to the task T_i the response to the precision request. A table of real numbers coded on 64 bits and a table of integer numbers form the response. The two tables are of variable size.

Finally, the protocol of standard communication SP is used by the tasks 1,2 and 3 so that every communication (input/output, system call, ...) with the host processor should still be possible for the programmer. It is then necessary to introduce two new processors $mux1$ and $mux2$ (see figure (3)) which are only used for the multiplexing of the communication channel. In the case of a parallel program, the addition of these processors concern only the processor directly linked to the host processors.

On figure (3) the processors $P1$, $P2$, $P3$ and $monitor$ realize the computation of RAPP. The processors $mux1$, $mux2$ and aux are used to solve the problem due to the little number of communication channels of the transputer.

5.4 Application to a sequential program

Let us consider a computer program P giving a single result r and that is executed with the computer's classical arithmetic. For the program to be run with RAPP, it is sufficient :

- to perturb every arithmetic operation and every assignment. (for example to replace $x := y + z$ by $x := p(y + z)$, p being a perturbation function of the tool box of RAPP);
- to use a specific output that takes into account the significant digits of the result r;

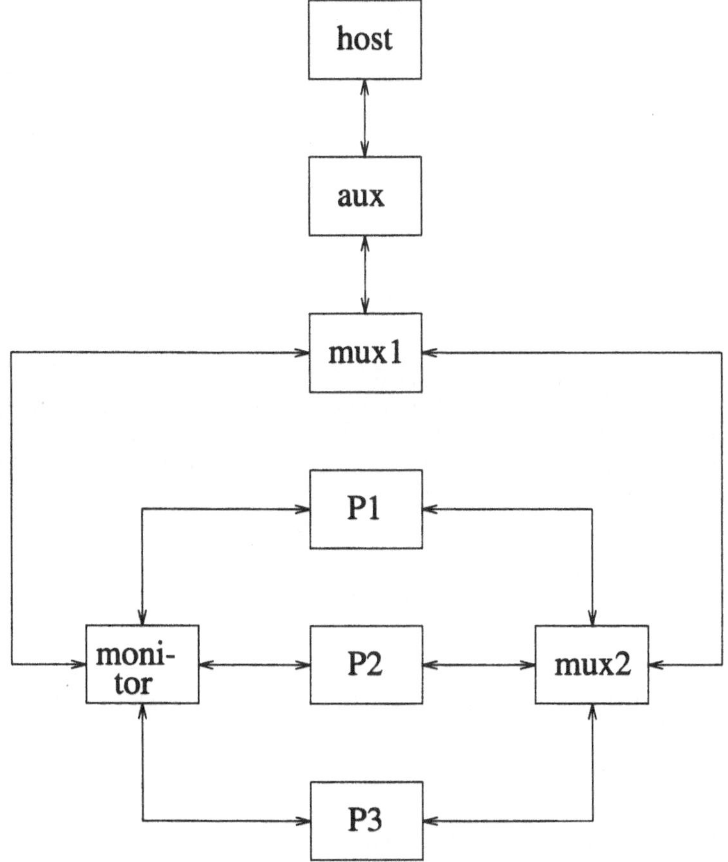

Figure 3: RAPP network for a sequential program

- to add at the beginning of the program P the statement of declaration of the communication channel with the task of precision estimation.

The RAPP user elaborates only a single program but in the reality three identical programs are executed on the RAPP nodes.

By analogy with the synchronous programmation on sequential architectures of the CESTAC method (imbedding in $\mathbb{R}^N$), the RAPP prototype defines a structure. The elements of this structure are distribued on different processors.

To test the performance of RAPP on a sequential program, we considered the example of two square matrices multiplication presented in the previous section. Table (4) shows the results obtained on a machine based on transputer T800.

RAPP use 3 processors for the execution of the image programs and a processor for the precision estimation. So it should be normal to obtain a time ratio with and without near of 1. Therefore according to table (4), this ratio is contained between 4.5 and 5. This increase is principally due to the perturbation of the elementary operation in the image program. Table (5) shows the cost of the perturbation in relation to the arithmetic function.

Matrix	Sequential time without RAPP (in sec.)	Sequential time with RAPP (in sec)	time ratio with and without RAPP
40x40	3.81	19.00	5.09
80x80	30.21	142.00	4.70
100x100	58.81	270.46	4.60
160x160	240.14	1074.75	4.48
200x200	468.37	2091.00	4.46

Table 4: Run time obtained on transputers T800.

operation arithmetic	Cost of the operation without perturbation (μsec)	Cost of the operation with perturbation (μsec)	time ratio
addition	20.30	111.15	5.47
substraction	21.30	105.96	4.97
multiplication	30.59	120.07	3.92
division	35.23	124.7	3.53

Table 5: Perturbation cost in relation to the arithmetic operations

Let us recall that this work deals with a study of feasability. With an optimized perturbation (as in CADNA), we may hope that the time ratio whould be in the order of 1.5.

5.5 Application to a parallel program

Let us consider a computer program P composed of k sequential tasks T_i running in parallel on k processors $Proc_i$. The application of RAPP to the program P consists in replacing each k processors by a subnetwork of figure (2). Thus, each task T_i is replaced with three images plus a task of precision estimation. The interconnection of all the tasks is done in the following way : In the program P, if a task T_i communicates with a task T_j then, in the program working with RAPP, the image tasks $T_{i,1}$, $T_{i,2}$,$T_{i,3}$ communicate respectively with the tasks $T_{j,1}$, $T_{j,2}$,$T_{j,3}$ (see figure (4)).

Here again, we shall use the previous example of matrix multiplication with the same structure of parallel program (see table (6)).

The increase of time that RAPP generates in the case of a parallel program is less important than in the case of a sequential program because RAPP increases only the time corresponding to the computation and not the time corresponding to the communication of the classical parallel program (i.e. without RAPP).

Matrix	Parallel time without RAPP (in s.)	Parallel time with RAPP(in s.)	Parallel time ratio without RAPP and with RAPP
40x40	1.43	5.50	3.85
80x80	11.07	37.98	3.43
100x100	21.45	71.77	3.35
160x160	86.89	278.46	3.20
200x200	169.08	540.62	3.20

Table 6: Run time obtained on transputers T800.

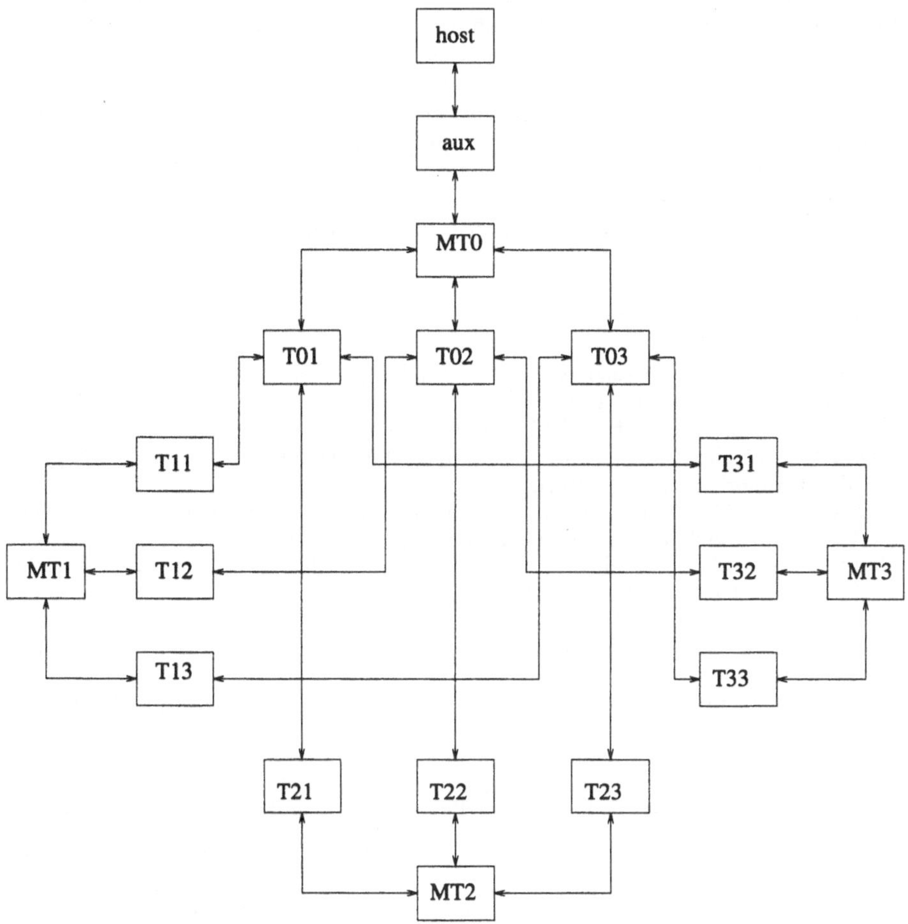

Figure 4: Application of RAPP to the parallel program P. $MT_i(i = 1..4)$: processors monitor

6 Conclusion

This work has shown that it is now possible to study the round-off errors propagation on results provided by sequential or parallel codes written in FORTRAN 77. It is easily done using the CADNA software on sequential architectures and on parallel architectures if the message passing library PVM is used. It was very important to show the feasibility of estimating the accuracy on parallel architectures which play an important role in the scientific computers today. We have seen that the solution CADNA + PVM is very simple and does not modify the number of processors required for running the initial parallel program. But the run time is multiplied in the same way than with the use of CADNA on sequential architecture.

The CESTAC method seems to be well-suited to a direct parallelization. The problem was to find out if the cost of message passing between processors (an absolute necessity) was not too important compared to the running time. The study of the RAPP prototype has shown that it is very satisfactory. Such an approach has a strong future, but there is not a useful FORTRAN tool yet.

We did not mention the numerical validation on vectorial architectures which are very often combined with the parallel architectures. The solution with CADNA or RAPP cut off the vectorisation and the problem is still open.

Aknowledgements : This work has been supported by the team *Arithmétique et précision* of the pool PRC-PRS of the CNRS and by the *Centre National de Calcul Parallèle en Sciences de la Terre.* (CNCPST)

References

[Chesneaux 90] J.-M. Chesneaux, J.-M. : "Study of the computing accuracy by using probabilistic approach"; Contribution to Computer Arithmetic and Self-Validating Numerical Methods, ed. C. Ulrich, (J.C. Baltzer) (1990), 19-30.

[Chesneaux 92] Chesneaux, J.-M. : "Descriptif d'utilisation du logiciel CADNA_ F"; MASI Report, n° 92-32 (1992).

[Chesneaux 95] Chesneaux, J.-M. : "L'arithmétique stochastique et le logiciel CADNA"; Habilitation à diriger des recherches, to appear.

[Hamming 70] R.W. Hamming, R. W. : "On the distribution of numbers"; The Bell System Technical Journal (1970), 1609-1625.

[Hull and Swenson 66] Hull, T.E., Swenson, J. R. : "Test of probabilistic models for propagation of round-off errors"; Communication of A.C.M., vol.9, n° 2 (1966), 108-113.

[Vignes 90] Vignes, J. : "Estimation de la précision des résultats de logiciels nu mé ri ques"; La Vie des Sciences, Comptes Rendus, série générale, 7 (1990), 93-145.

[Vignes 93] Vignes, J. : "A stochastic arithmetic for reliable scientific computation"; Math. Comp. Simul., 35 (1993), 233-261.

[Vignes and La Porte 74] Vignes, J., La Porte, M. : "Error analysis in computing"; Information Processing 74, North-Holland (1974).

[Geist and al. 93] Geist, G. A. and al. : "PVM 3 User's Guide and Reference Manual"; ORNL (Oak Ridge National Laboratory), TM-12187 May (1993)

[OCCAM 88] "OCCAM 2 Reference Manual"; Prentice Hall, International Series in Computer Sciences (1988).

Journal of Universal Computer Science, vol. 1, no. 7 (1995), 469-483
submitted: 15/12/94, accepted: 26/6/95, appeared: 28/7/95 © *Springer Pub. Co.*

Round-off error propagation in the solution of the heat equation by finite differences

Fabienne Jézéquel
(Université Pierre et Marie Curie, France
Fabienne.Jezequel@masi.ibp.fr)

Abstract: The effect of round-off errors on the numerical solution of the heat equation by finite differences can be theoretically determined by computing the mean error at each time step. The floating point error propagation is then theoretically time linear. The experimental simulations agree with this result for the towards zero rounding arithmetic. However the results are not so good for the rounding to the nearest artihmetic. The theoretical formulas provide an approximation of the experimental round-off errors. In these formulas the mean value of the assignment operator is used, and consequently, their reliability depends on the arithmetic used.

Key Words: Floating point arithmetic, numerical error propagation, partial differential equations, finite difference methods
Category: G.1.8

1 Introduction

In the computational solution of partial differential equations, two types of errors are generated : the method error due to approximations inherent in the numerical method and the round-off error due to the floating point arithmetic of the computer used. This paper presents an analysis of the round-off error propagation in the solution of the heat equation by finite differences. For each point of the mesh, the solution is approximated by a scalar product with three terms. Therefore previous studies concerning round-off errors in arithmetical operations and in scalar products are presented. This analysis has been carried out for the towards zero rounding arithmetic and for the rounding to the nearest arithmetic, these two rounding modes respecting the 754-IEEE standard. Different cases have been considered depending on whether initial data and finite difference scheme coefficients are exactly represented or not in the computer. To conclude, the main results obtained are finally represented.

2 Previous results concerning round-off errors

2.1 Assignment error

Let x be a real number and X its floating point representation. The relative assignment error on X is $\alpha = \frac{(X-x)}{X}$. Let **P** be the set of all the possible relative assignment errors α. The mean value $\bar{\alpha}$ and the standard deviation σ^2 of **P** can be computed according to the rounding mode, the base and the number of bits in the mantissa in the floating point representation [see Alt 76, Alt 78, Hamming 70, Knuth 69, La Porte, Vignes, 74a and Vignes 93]. Let b be the base (usually b is 2 or 16) and p the number of digits in the mantissa in the standard floating point representation.

for the towards zero rounding arithmetic :

$$\bar{\alpha} = b^{-p}\frac{(1-b)}{2\log b}$$

$$\sigma^2 = b^{-2p}\left[\frac{(b^2-1)}{6\log b} - \frac{(b-1)^2}{(2\log b)^2}\right]$$

and for the rounding to the nearest arithmetic :

$$\bar{\alpha} = 0$$

$$\sigma^2 = b^{-2p}\frac{(b^2-1)}{24\log b}.$$

2.2 Error due to arithmetical operators

Let $+, -, \times, /$ be the exact operators on real numbers and $\oplus, \ominus, \otimes, \oslash$ the corresponding floating point operators (addition, subtraction, multiplication and division) on **F**, which is the set of all the values representable in the machine. The following formulas have been obtained by considering only first-order approximations in b^{-p} :

Let x and y be real numbers, X and Y their representations in **F** :

$$X \approx x(1+\alpha) \text{ and } Y \approx y(1+\beta)$$

$$X \oplus Y \approx x + y + \alpha x + \beta y + \mu(x+y)$$

$$X \ominus Y \approx x - y + \alpha x - \beta y + \mu(x-y)$$

$$X \otimes Y \approx (x \times y)(1 + \alpha + \beta + \mu')$$

$$X \oslash Y \approx (x/y)(1 + \alpha - \beta + \mu')$$

with α, β, μ , μ' being elements of **P**.

2.3 Error in the computation of scalar products

Let us consider a scalar product $r = \sum_{i=1}^{n} x_i y_i$, with x_i and y_i real numbers. If it is computed using this cumulative method :

$R := 0$; FOR $I = 1$ TO N DO $R := R \oplus X[I] \otimes Y[I]$,

the absolute error ρ on the exact scalar product r is defined by : $\rho = R - r$.

If $X_i = x_i(1+\lambda_i)$ and $Y_i = y_i(1+\mu_i)$ the error ρ can be estimated by the following formula :

$$\begin{aligned}\rho \approx &\sum_{i=1}^{n} x_i y_i(\lambda_i + \mu_i + \beta_i)\\ &+\alpha_1(x_1y_1 + x_2y_2)\\ &+\alpha_2(x_1y_1 + x_2y_2 + x_3y_3)\\ &+\ldots\\ &+\alpha_{n-1}(x_1y_1 + x_2y_2 + \ldots + x_ny_n)\end{aligned}$$

with α_i, β_i, λ_i, μ_i being elements of **P**.

We assume that the errors α_i, β_i, λ_i, μ_i are independent and have the same mean value $\bar{\alpha}$ and the same standard deviation σ^2. Under these hypotheses, the mean values of ρ and ρ^2 are given by :

$$\bar{\rho} = \bar{\alpha}r\frac{(n^2+7n-2)}{2n}$$

$$\bar{\rho^2} = (\bar{\alpha})^2[(\frac{3n^3+41n^2+134n-72}{12n})r^2+(\frac{(n-2)(n^2+3n-6)}{12n})s^2]+\sigma^2[(\frac{n+1}{3})r^2+(\frac{n^2+19n-6}{6n})s^2]$$

with $s^2 = \sum_{i=1}^{n}(x_i y_i)^2$ [see Alt 78 and La Porte, Vignes 74b].

3 Error propagation in the solution of the heat equation

3.1 Finite difference scheme

The one-dimensional heat equation describes the heat propagation in a linear bar. Let $U(x,t)$ be the temperature on this bar at point x and time t. The heat equation in $[a,b] \times [t_0, +\infty[$ is described by the following system :

$$\frac{\partial U(x,t)}{\partial t} - K\frac{\partial^2 U(x,t)}{\partial x^2} = 0 \text{ , with } K > 0$$

$$\forall t \geq t_0 \text{ , } U(a,t) = U_a(t) \text{ and } U(b,t) = U_b(t)$$

$$\forall x \in [a,b] \text{ , } U(x,t_0) = U^0(x)$$

The constant K represents the material thermic diffusivity.

The domain is discretized with space step Δx and time step Δt :

$$x_i = a + i\Delta x, \ i = 0, 1, ...n$$

$$x_0 = a \text{ and } x_n = b$$

$$t_j = t_0 + j\Delta t, j = 0, 1, ...$$

Let U_i^j be the solution at point x_i and time t_j. The explicit finite difference method is used :

$$\frac{U_i^{j+1} - U_i^j}{\Delta t} = K(\frac{U_{i-1}^j - 2U_i^j + U_{i+1}^j}{(\Delta x)^2}) \quad \text{for } i = 1, ..., n-1 \text{ , } j = 0, 1, ...$$

then: $U_i^{j+1} = \frac{K\Delta t}{(\Delta x)^2}U_{i-1}^j + (1 - 2\frac{K\Delta t}{(\Delta x)^2})U_i^j + \frac{K\Delta t}{(\Delta x)^2}U_{i+1}^j$

To ensure the stability of this scheme, the relation $\frac{K\Delta t}{(\Delta x)^2} < \frac{1}{2}$ must be satisfied.

If $c_1 = \frac{K\Delta t}{(\Delta x)^2}$ and $c_2 = 1 - 2c_1$, the finite difference scheme is :

$$U_i^{j+1} = c_1 U_{i-1}^j + c_2 U_i^j + c_1 U_{i+1}^j \quad \text{for } i = 1, ..., n-1 \text{ , } j = 0, 1, ...$$

3.2 Theoretical round-off error

3.2.1 Relative round-off error

To estimate the round-off error in the computation of U_i^j with the finite difference scheme previously proposed, several notations are necessary. Let U_i^j, c_1, c_2 be the algebraic values and $\tilde{U}_i^j$, $\tilde{c_1}$, $\tilde{c_2}$ the computed values.

Then for $i = 1, ..., n-1$, $j = 0, 1, ...,$

$$\tilde{U}_i^{j+1} = ((\tilde{c_1} \otimes \tilde{U}_{i-1}^j) \oplus (\tilde{c_2} \otimes \tilde{U}_i^j)) \oplus (\tilde{c_1} \otimes \tilde{U}_{i+1}^j),$$

this formula being neither commutative nor associative.

Let μ_i^j be the relative error on U_i^j due to the cumulation of assignment errors and round-off errors generated in previous iterations : $\tilde{U}_i^j = U_i^j (1 + \mu_i^j)$.

μ_i^0 merely represents the assignment error on U_i^0 and the mean value $\bar{\mu^0}$ is equal to the mean value of the assignment operator $\bar{\alpha}$.

Let λ_1 and λ_2 be the relative errors on c_1 and c_2 : $\tilde{c_1} = c_1\ (1 + \lambda_1)$ and $\tilde{c_2} = c_2\ (1 + \lambda_2)$.

If c_1 and c_2 are not results of computations or are computed in infinite precision, then λ_1 and λ_2 are merely assignment errors.

U_i^{j+1} is computed by a scalar product with three terms. Therefore the formula providing the round-off error in the computation of scalar products can be applied :

$$\begin{aligned}
\mu_i^{j+1} = \frac{1}{U_i^{j+1}} \Big[& c_1 U_{i-1}^j (\lambda_1 + \mu_{i-1}^j + \beta_1) \\
& + c_2 U_i^j (\lambda_2 + \mu_i^j + \beta_2) \\
& + c_1 U_{i+1}^j (\lambda_1 + \mu_{i+1}^j + \beta_3) \\
& + \alpha_1 (c_1 U_{i-1}^j + c_2 U_i^j) \\
& + \alpha_2 (c_1 U_{i-1}^j + c_2 U_i^j + c_1 U_{i+1}^j) \Big]
\end{aligned}$$

with α_i, β_i being elements of **P**.

The errors α_1 and α_2 are due to additions $\oplus$, β_1, β_2 and β_3 to multiplications $\otimes$. Assignment errors α_i, β_i are assumed to be independent and consequently :

$$\bar{\alpha_i} = \bar{\beta_i} = \bar{\alpha}$$

$$\overline{\alpha_i{}^2} = \overline{\beta_i{}^2} = (\bar{\alpha})^2 + \sigma^2$$

$$\overline{\alpha_i \beta_k} = (\bar{\alpha})^2 \text{ etc ...}$$

3.2.2 First moment

As assignment errors are assumed to be independent and have the same mean value $\bar{\alpha}$, the first moment is, for $j = 0, 1, \ldots$ and $i = 1, \ldots, n-1$:

$$\overline{\mu_i^{j+1}} = \frac{c_1 U_{i-1}^j}{U_i^{j+1}} \left(\overline{\mu_{i-1}^j} + 3\bar{\alpha} + \lambda_1\right) + \frac{c_2 U_i^j}{U_i^{j+1}} \left(\overline{\mu_i^j} + 3\bar{\alpha} + \lambda_2\right) + \frac{c_1 U_{i+1}^j}{U_i^{j+1}} \left(\overline{\mu_{i+1}^j} + 2\bar{\alpha} + \lambda_1\right).$$

The space step and the time step are assumed to be low enough to allow the following approximation :

$$\forall j \geq 0, \quad \forall i = 1, \ldots, n-1, \quad \frac{U_{i-1}^j}{U_i^{j+1}} \approx \frac{U_i^j}{U_i^{j+1}} \approx \frac{U_{i+1}^j}{U_i^{j+1}} \approx 1.$$

Therefore at a fixed iteration, all relative errors μ_i^j have the same mean value :

$$\forall i = 1, \ldots n-1, \quad \overline{\mu_i^j} = \overline{\mu^j}.$$

then

$$\forall j \geq 0, \quad \overline{\mu^{j+1}} = \overline{\mu^j} + (3 - c_1)\bar{\alpha} + 2c_1\lambda_1 + c_2\lambda_2$$

therefore :

$$\forall j \geq 0, \quad \overline{\mu^j} = \overline{\mu^0} + ((3 - c_1)\bar{\alpha} + 2c_1\lambda_1 + c_2\lambda_2)j.$$

The round-off error propagation in the solution of the heat equation by finite differences is theoretically time linear. The general formula above is simplified if the coefficients c_1 and c_2 and the initial data U_i^0 are exactly represented. For the rounding to the nearest arithmetic, the mean value of the assignment errors, $\bar{\alpha}$ is theoretically zero. In this case, if the coefficients c_1 and c_2 and the initial data U_i^0 are exactly represented, $\lambda_1 = \lambda_2 = \overline{\mu^0} = 0$, and the first moment remains theoretically zero. Thus it is necessary to estimate the second moment.

3.2.3 Second moment

The estimation of the second moment has been carried out for the rounding to the nearest arithmetic under the following assumptions :

c_1 and c_2 are exactly represented : $\lambda_1 = \lambda_2 = 0$,

initial data are exactly represented : $\forall i = 1, \ldots, n-1, \; \mu_i^0 = 0$.

As for the estimation of the first moment, it is assumed that :

$$\forall j \geq 1, \quad \forall i = 1, \ldots, n-1, \quad \frac{U_{i-1}^{j-1}}{U_i^j} \approx \frac{U_i^{j-1}}{U_i^j} \approx \frac{U_{i+1}^{j-1}}{U_i^j} \approx 1.$$

The estimation of $\overline{(\mu_i^{j+1})^2}$ induces the emergence of terms $\overline{\gamma\mu_i^j}$, γ being a relative assignment error.

It is assumed that $\overline{\gamma\mu_{i-1}^j} = \overline{\gamma\mu_{i+1}^j} = \overline{\gamma\mu_i^j}$.

Therefore, $\overline{(\mu_i^{j+1})^2} = (2c_1^2 + c_2^2)\ \overline{(\mu_i^j)^2} + (7c_1^2 + 3c_2)\ \sigma^2$

$+2((1-c_1)\overline{\alpha_1\mu_i^j} + \overline{\alpha_2\mu_i^j} + c_1\overline{\beta_1\mu_i^j} + c_2\overline{\beta_2\mu_i^j} + c_1\overline{\beta_3\mu_i^j})$.

As $\forall i = 1, ..., n-1,\ \ \mu_i^0 = 0,\ \ \overline{(\mu^1)^2} = (7c_1^2 + 3c_2)\ \sigma^2$.

$\overline{\gamma\mu_i^j}$ are estimated, γ being a relative assignment error :

$$\overline{\alpha_1\mu_i^j} = (1-c_1)\sigma^2 + \overline{\alpha_1\mu_i^{j-1}}$$
$$\overline{\alpha_2\mu_i^j} = \sigma^2 + \overline{\alpha_2\mu_i^{j-1}}$$
$$\overline{\beta_1\mu_i^j} = c_1\sigma^2 + \overline{\beta_1\mu_i^{j-1}}$$
$$\overline{\beta_2\mu_i^j} = c_2\sigma^2 + \overline{\beta_2\mu_i^{j-1}}$$
$$\overline{\beta_3\mu_i^j} = c_1\sigma^2 + \overline{\beta_3\mu_i^{j-1}}$$

As $\overline{\gamma\mu_i^0} = 0$, finally :

$$\overline{\alpha_1\mu_i^j} = (1-c_1)j\sigma^2$$
$$\overline{\alpha_2\mu_i^j} = j\sigma^2$$
$$\overline{\beta_1\mu_i^j} = \overline{\beta_3\mu_i^j} = c_1 j\sigma^2$$
$$\overline{\beta_2\mu_i^j} = c_2 j\sigma^2.$$

Therefore : $\forall j \geq 1,\ \overline{(\mu_i^{j+1})^2} = (2c_1^2 + c_2^2)\ \overline{(\mu_i^j)^2} + (1+2j)\ (7c_1^2 + 3c_2)\ \sigma^2$.

Then

$$\overline{(\mu^0)^2} = 0$$

and $\forall j \geq 1,\ \overline{(\mu^j)^2} = (7c_1^2 + 3c_2)\ \sigma^2\ \sum_{k=0}^{j-1}(1+2k)\ (2c_1^2 + c_2^2)^{j-k-1}$.

The evolution of the second moment is thus of degree 2. This result remains coherent with the linear evolution of the first moment.

3.3 Experimental round-off error

3.4 First moment

The experimental first moment $\overline{\mu^j}$ is computed according to the following formula :

$$\overline{\mu^j} = \frac{1}{n-1}\sum_{i=1}^{n-1}\left(\frac{\tilde{U_i^j} - U_i^j}{\tilde{U_i^j}}\right)$$

where U_i^j represents the algebraic value and $\tilde{U}_i^j$ the computed value. The number of significant digits lost in computations does not depend on the precision of the floating point arithmetic [see Chesneaux 88 and Chesneaux 90]. Therefore U_i^j, theoretically computed in infinite precision, can be computed in double precision. Then $\tilde{U}_i^j$ is the result of the same computation carried out in single precision [see Hull, Swenson 66].

The theoretical expression of the first moment has been validated for the towards zero rounding arithmetic and the rounding to the nearest arithmetic, on a computer using base 2 with $p = 24$ and respecting the 754-IEEE standard. Four cases can occur depending on whether the coefficients c_1 et c_2 and the initial data U_i^0 are exactly represented or not. Each case has been studied for the rounding to the nearest arithmetic, where the mean value of the assignment errors $\bar{\alpha}$ is zero, and for the towards zero rounding arithmetic, where $\bar{\alpha}$ is not zero. The number of space steps n is set to 100, the number of time steps is set to 1000.

1st case :

If the coefficients c_1, c_2 and the initial data U_i^0 are both not exactly represented, the first moment is :

$$\forall j \geq 0, \quad \overline{\mu^j} = \overline{\mu^0} + ((3 - c_1)\bar{\alpha} + 2c_1\lambda_1 + c_2\lambda_2)j$$

The experimental moment is time linear as well. However the theoretical moment is in absolute value slightly greater than the experimental moment. This difference may be due to an overvaluation of the theoretical mean value $\bar{\alpha}$. Results concerning the following example are presented in the appendix :

$c_1 = \frac{1}{6}, \ c_2 = \frac{2}{3}$

$\forall i = 0, 1, \cdots, n, \ U_i^0 = \sin(\frac{i\pi}{n}) + \log 2$

2nd case :

If the coefficients c_1 and c_2 are exactly represented, but the initial data U_i^0 are not exactly represented, the first moment is :

$$\forall j \geq 0, \quad \overline{\mu^j} = \overline{\mu^0} + (3 - c_1)\bar{\alpha} j$$

In the towards zero rounding arithmetic, the theoretical moment and the experimental one are both linear. The theoretical moment overestimates again slightly in absolute value the experimental moment.
In the rounding to the nearest arithmetic, as the mean value $\bar{\alpha}$ is zero, the first moment remains theoretically equal to the mean error on data $\overline{\mu^0}$. In opposition to the theoretical moment, the experimental moment is not constant. However its order of magnitude (10^{-7}) is very satisfying for single precision results. Graphical results for the following example are presented in the appendix :

$c_1 = \frac{3}{16}, \ c_2 = \frac{5}{8}$

$\forall i = 0, 1, \cdots, n, \ U_i^0 = \sin(\frac{i\pi}{n}) + \log 2$

3rd case :

If the initial data U_i^0 are exactly represented, but the coefficients c_1 and c_2 are not exactly represented, the first moment is :

$$\forall j \geq 0, \quad \overline{\mu^j} = ((3 - c_1)\bar{\alpha} + 2c_1\lambda_1 + c_2\lambda_2)j$$

The choice of initial data which are exactly represented is more problematic than the choice of exactly represented coefficients. For instance, if initial data are of the form :

$$\forall i = 0, 1, \cdots, n, \; U_i^0 = i2^r,$$

with r being a relative integer, the scheme does not perform evolutions in time :

$$\forall j \geq 0, \; U_i^j = U_i^0.$$

The following example is presented in the appendix :

$c_1 = \frac{1}{6}, \; c_2 = \frac{2}{3}$

$$\forall i = 0, 1, \cdots, n, \quad \begin{array}{l} \text{if } i \text{ is odd, } U_i^0 = i/16 \\ \text{if } i \text{ is even,} U_i^0 = i \end{array}$$

The theoretical moment is linear and remains greater than the experimental moment in absolute value. In the towards zero rounding arithmetic, the experimental moment remains linear for all time intervals considered. In the rounding to the nearest arithmetic, the experimental moment is not perfectly linear (see graphical results in the appendix).

4th case :

If the initial data U_i^0 and the coefficients c_1 and c_2 are exactly represented, the first moment is :

$$\forall j \geq 0, \quad \overline{\mu_j} = (3 - c_1)\bar{\alpha}j$$

In this case, the experimental moment is compared with the theoretical moment only in the towards zero rounding arithmetic, because in the rounding to the nearest arithmetic the mean value $\bar{\alpha}$ is theoretically zero.

In the appendix, the following example is presented :

$c_1 = \frac{3}{16}, \; c_2 = \frac{5}{8}$

$$\forall i = 0, 1, \cdots, n, \quad \begin{array}{l} \text{if } i \text{ is odd, } U_i^0 = i/16 \\ \text{if } i \text{ is even,} U_i^0 = i \end{array}$$

The experimental moment, as well as the theoretical one, is linear. The theoretical moment remains slightly greater than the experimental one in absolute value because of the overvaluation of the mean value of the assignment errors $\bar{\alpha}$.

3.4.1 Second moment

The second moment, $\overline{(\mu^j)^2}$, can be experimentally computed according to the following formula :

$$\overline{(\mu^j)^2} = \frac{1}{n-1} \sum_{i=1}^{n-1} \left(\frac{\tilde{U}_i^j - U_i^j}{\tilde{U}_i^j} \right)^2$$

where U_i^j is the algebraic value and $\tilde{U}_i^j$ the computed one. As for the first moment, U_i^j, theoretically computed in infinite precision, is computed in double precision and $\tilde{U}_i^j$ is computed in single precision.

The second moment has been computed using the rounding to the nearest arithmetic, when the initial data U_i^0 and the coefficients c_1 and c_2 are exactly represented. In the appendix, the evolution of the ratio of the experimental moment by the theoretical one $\overline{(\mu^j)^2}^{\frac{1}{2}}{}_{exp}/\overline{(\mu^j)^2}^{\frac{1}{2}}{}_{theo}$ is presented. The example considered is the same as for the study of the first moment, when both initial data and coefficients are exactly represented.

4 Conclusion

In the towards zero rounding arithmetic, the round-off error generated in the solution of the heat equation is correctly modelled for all finite difference scheme coefficients and initial data. The round-off error propagation is then time linear. The theoretical error depends strongly on the mean value of the assignment errors and, while providing the order of magnitude of the experimental error, overestimates it slightly.

In the rounding to the nearest arithmetic, the round-off error generated is always smaller than in the towards zero rounding arithmetic. In the case where neither the coefficients nor the initial data are exactly represented, the round-off error is linear and is correctly described by the theoretical formula. However if the finite difference scheme coefficients or the initial data are exactly represented, theoretical formulas are not verified by the experimental study. The round-off error modelling is rather difficult in the rounding to the nearest arithmetic, where the mean value of the assignment error, which is theoretically zero, is never practically zero.

Theoretical formulas are much more robust in the towards zero rounding arithmetic than in the rounding to the nearest arithmetic. However from this study it seems obvious that the round-off error generated in the solution of the heat equation is usually linear.

Appendix : graphical results

1st case : $c_1 = \frac{1}{6},\ c_2 = \frac{2}{3},\ n = 100,\ \forall i = 0, 1, \cdots, n,\ U_i^0 = \sin(\frac{i\pi}{n}) + \log 2$

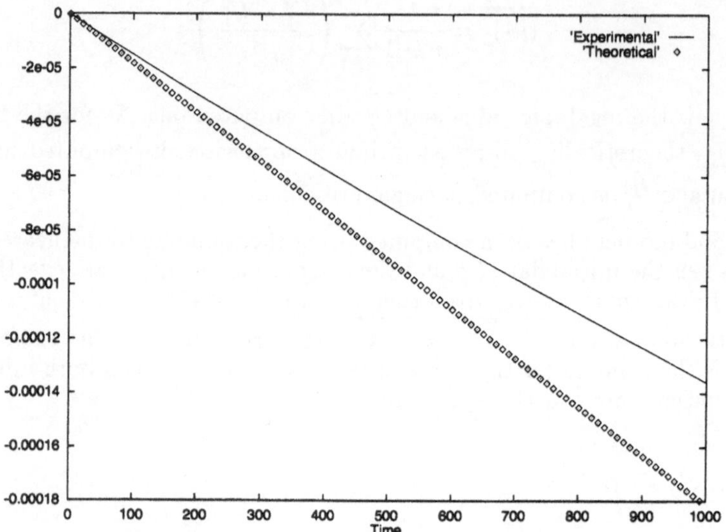

Figure 1: First moment, towards zero rounding arithmetic

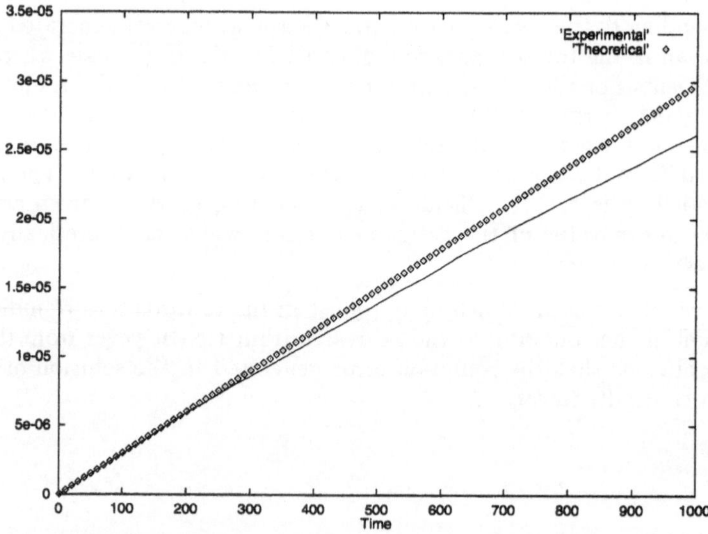

Figure 2: First moment, rounding to the nearest arithmetic

2nd case : $c_1 = \frac{3}{16}$, $c_2 = \frac{5}{8}$, $n = 100$, $\forall i = 0, 1, \cdots, n$, $U_i^0 = \sin(\frac{i\pi}{n}) + \log 2$

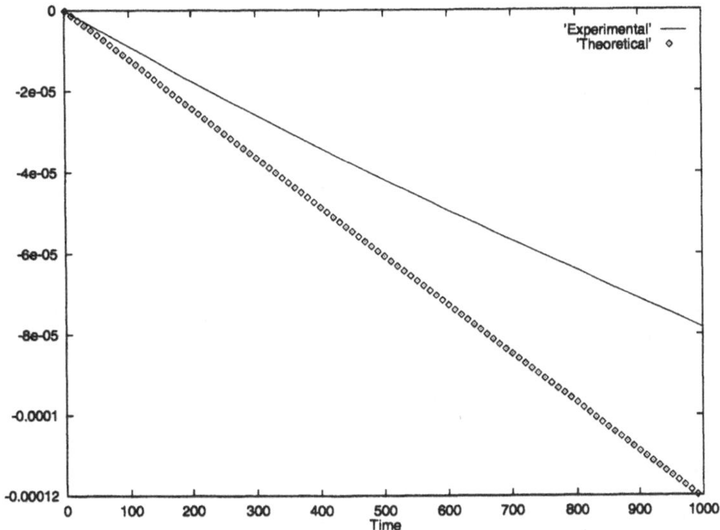

Figure 3: First moment, towards zero rounding arithmetic

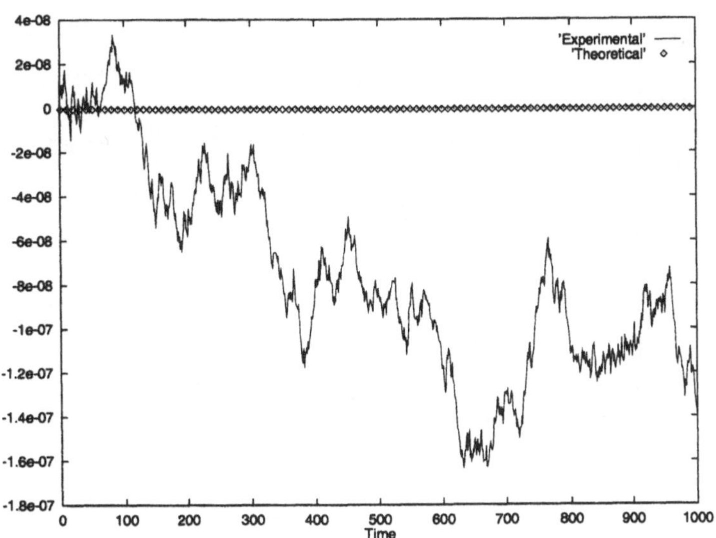

Figure 4: First moment, rounding to the nearest arithmetic

3rd case : $c_1 = \frac{1}{6},\ c_2 = \frac{2}{3},\ n = 100,\ \forall i = 0, 1, \cdots, n,$ if i is odd, $U_i^0 = i/16$
if i is even, $U_i^0 = i$

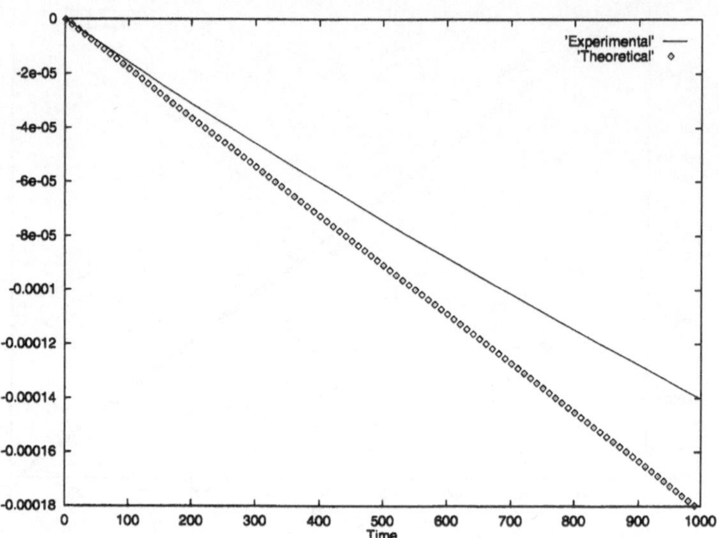

Figure 5: First moment, towards zero rounding arithmetic

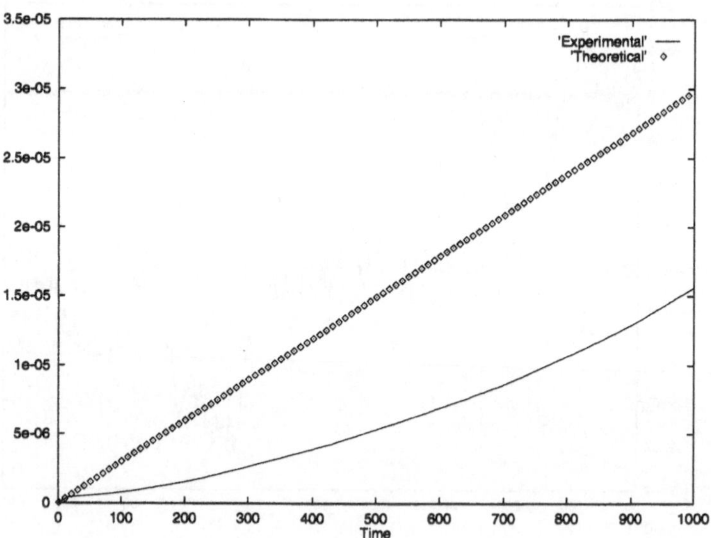

Figure 6: First moment, rounding to the nearest arithmetic

4th case : $c_1 = \frac{3}{16}$, $c_2 = \frac{5}{8}$, $n = 100$, $\forall i = 0, 1, \cdots, n$, if i is odd, $U_i^0 = i/16$
if i is even, $U_i^0 = i$

towards zero rounding arithmetic

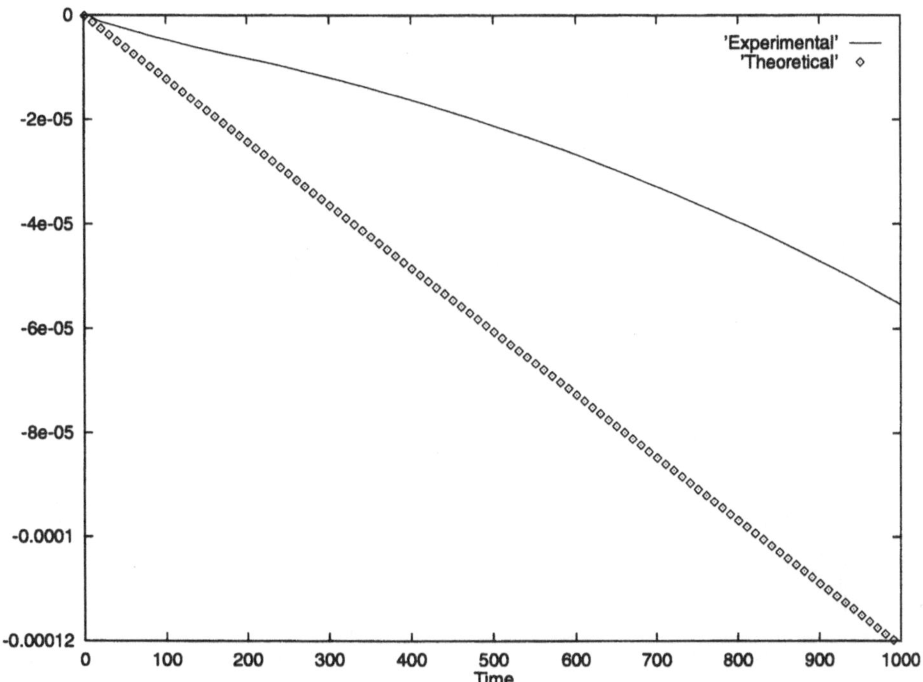

Figure 7: First moment

4th case : $c_1 = \frac{3}{16}$, $c_2 = \frac{5}{8}$, $n = 100$, $\forall i = 0, 1, \cdots, n$, if i is odd, $U_i^0 = i/16$
if i is even, $U_i^0 = i$
rounding to the nearest arithmetic

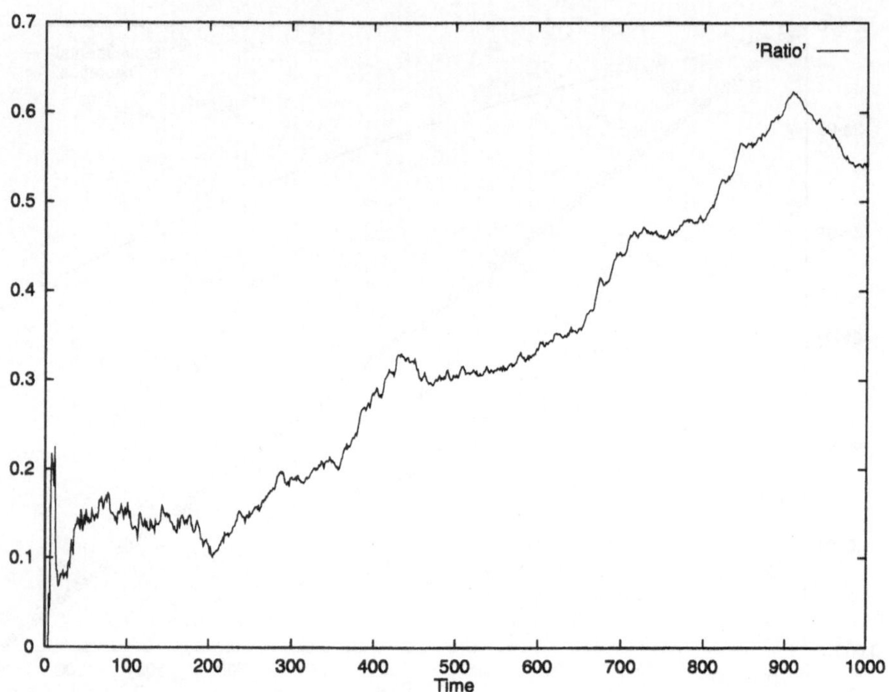

Figure 8: Ratio of the experimental 2nd moment by the theoretical 2nd moment

References

[Alt 76] Alt, R.: "Etude statistique de l'erreur numérique d'affectation sur un ordinateur en base quelconque. Application à l'erreur commise dans le calcul d'une somme de produits de nombres"; IFP Report 76-5 (1976).

[Alt 78] Alt, R.: "Error propagation in Fourier Transforms"; Mathematics and Computers in Simulation, 20 (1978), 37-43.

[Chesneaux 88] Chesneaux, J.-M.: "Etude théorique et implémentation en ADA de la méthode CESTAC"; Doctoral Thesis, Univ. Paris VI, (1988).

[Chesneaux 90] Chesneaux, J.-M.: "Study of the computing accuracy by using probabilistic approach. Contribution to computer arithmetic and self-validating numerical methods"; ed. C. Ulrich, J.C. Baltzer (1990), 19-30.

[Hamming 70] Hamming, R. W.: "On the distribution of numbers"; Bell System Techn. J. 49, 8 (1970), 1609-1625.

[Hull, Swenson 66] Hull, T. E., Swenson, J. R.: "Test of probalistic model for propagation of round-off errors"; A.C.M. 9, 2 (1966) 108-111.

[Knuth 69] Knuth, D. E.: "The art of computer programming"; Add. Wesley. (1969).

[La Porte, Vignes 74a] La Porte, M., Vignes, J.: "Etude statistique des erreurs dans l'arithmétique des ordinateurs; application au contrôle des résultats d'algorithmes numériques"; Numer. Math. 23 (1974) 63-72.

[La Porte, Vignes 74b] La Porte, M., Vignes, J.: "Algorithmes numériques, analyse et mise en œuvre"; Vol. 1, Editions Technip, Paris (1974).

[Vignes 93] Vignes, J.: "A stochastic arithmetic for reliable computation"; Mathematics and Computers in Simulation, 35 (1993), 233-261.

Journal of Universal Computer Science, vol. 1, no. 7 (1995), 484-503
submitted: 14/6/95, accepted: 14/6/95, appeared: 28/7/95

LCF: A Lexicographic Binary Representation of the Rationals

Peter Kornerup
(Dept. of Mathematics and Computer Science
Odense University
DK-5230 Odense, Denmark
kornerup@imada.ou.dk)

David W. Matula
(Dept. of Computer Science and Engineering
Southern Methodist University
Dallas, TX 75275
matula@seas.smu.edu)

Abstract: A binary representation of the rationals derived from their continued fraction expansions is described and analysed. The concepts "adjacency", "mediant" and "convergent" from the literature on Farey fractions and continued fractions are suitably extended to provide a foundation for this new binary representation system. Worst case representation-induced precision loss for any real number by a fixed length representable number of the system is shown to be at most 19% of bit word length, with no precision loss whatsoever induced in the representation of any reasonably sized rational number. The representation is supported by a computer arithmetic system implementing exact rational and approximate real computations in an on-line fashion.
Category: G.1.0 [Numerical Analysis]: Computer Arithmetic. B.5.1 [Register Transfer Level Implementation]: Arithmetic and logic units. E.2 [Data Storage Representations].
Key Words: Computer arithmetic, continued fractions, lexicographic, number systems, number theory, rational numbers.

1 Introduction.

The foundations of a binary representation of the rationals are presented, and many of the representation system's features are described. Evidence is provided indicating that a computer arithmetic system employing this representation would provide a facility for exact rational and approximate real arithmetic not currently available in any single system.

Our proposed binary representation system derives from the continued fraction representation of the rationals. A self delimiting bitstring encoding of the integers is employed to represent each partial quotient. Particular features of the integer encoding and the subsequent concatenation process allow us to obtain bit string representations of the rationals, which are shown lexicographically order preserving over real order. Our bitstring representation is thus termed the lexicographic continued fraction (LCF) representation of a rational number.

The LCF representation can be considered an encoding of the individual steps of the Euclidean algorithm performed in binary, where the determination of the individual remainders are computed using a non-restoring division algorithm. As such, it is derived from algorithms performing arithmetic operations upon rational operands in fraction form, i.e. a numerator/denominator representation, [see Kornerup and Matula 83] where the LCF representation was first described. However, as a number representation it naturally leads to a kind of on-line arithmetic where operands are consumed bit-sequential, and the result is produced bit-sequential, most significant bit first. Such an on-line arithmetic unit has been described in [Kornerup and Matula 88], capable of performing all the basic arithmetic operations in a unified manner as cases of the bihomographic function

$$z(x,y) = \frac{axy + bx + cy + d}{exy + fx + gy + h}$$

specified by eight integer coefficients $a, b, \cdots, h$. By factoring certain transformations (matrices corresponding to the individual partial quotients of a continued fraction) into simple "binary" matrices, the algorithm can be realized by simple shift-and-add operations. However, we shall not further pursue the arithmetic here, but concentrate on properties of the LCF representation.

In [Section 2] we formally define the LCF expansion as a bitstring. We introduce background material from the theory of continued fractions to guide the development of a theory for LCF expansions. In particular we extend the notion of the sequence of convergents (often termed "best rational approximations") of a real number to a super-sequence of biconvergents (binary convergents) determined by the LCF expansion of x. The biconvergents are shown to form a somewhat base dependent sequence of rational approximations to x. The biconvergent sequence is shown to contain, on average, about 3.51 times the number of terms of the subsequence of canonically defined convergents.

In [Section 3] we study the hierarchy of rational numbers as determined bitwise by their LCF expansions through the construct of the LCF binary tree. The LCF tree provides for enumerating biconvergent sequences as paths down the tree, and also provides for enumerating all fixed length LCF expansion values by traversal across the LCF tree truncated at fixed depth. One can visualize in the structure of the tree the order preserving property of LCF expansions, and the fact that LCF representation is one-to-one between finite bit strings and positive rationals. We develop tools for investigating the set Q_k of irreducible fractions in [0,1] whose LCF expansions have order k (equivalently: length $k+1$ bits or depth at most k in the LCF tree). Our principal results are that the fundamental properties from the theory of Farey fractions [Hardy and Wright 79] regarding adjacency, mediant and recursive construction of the tree of Farey fractions, can be extended to comparable concepts of bijacency, binary mediant and recursive construction of the LCF tree. Properties of the LCF tree are then available as tools for both the investigation of the rate of convergence of biconvergent sequences, and for the study of the gap sizes between successive members of the sets Q_k. The latter result dictates the precision obtainable for arithmetic employing such fixed length representations.

Utilizing these tools the extremes of gap size variability over Q_k are then discussed in [Section 4]. The main result is that the maximum gap size in Q_k is of the order 2^{-ak} for $a = 0.814\ldots$. This implies at most a 19% precision loss (storage space loss) in the worst case approximation error by fixed length LCF bit strings, being the price to be able to accommodate the exact representation of a set of simple rationals at a fairly regular spacing, and supporting a rational arithmetic in an on-line fashion. More detailed results of exhaustive and sampled distribution of gap sizes are available in [Kornerup and Matula 85].

2 Continued Fraction and Lexicographic Continued Fraction Expansions.

The lexicographic continued fraction expansion of a rational number is a bitstring whose interpretation will be based on some fundamental properties of continued fraction expansions of rationals. For these purposes our notation should make explicit the particular numerator and denominator components of a fraction, as well as the particular sequence of partial quotient values of a continued fraction expansion, as these terms are not necessarily uniquely determined. For our purposes it is sufficient to treat only representation of finite nonnegative rational numbers, as signs can be appended for the negative values.

Formally, a fraction, denoted p/q or $\frac{p}{q}$, is herein an ordered pair composed of a nonnegative integer ***numerator*** p, and a positive integer ***denominator*** q. The quotient of p/q is the rational number determined by the ratio of p to q. The numerator and denominator of an *irreducible* fraction must have a greatest common divisor (gcd) of unity, other fractions being termed ***reducible***.

Employing the equality symbol between various forms of rational representation will herein denote the weaker interpretation of equality between their rational values with the following exception. Equality between fractions denoted with the horizontal bar format shall imply equal numerator and denominator values. Thus

$$\frac{p}{q} = \frac{r}{s} \text{ iff } p = r \text{ and } q = s,$$

whereas

$$p/q = r/s \text{ iff } qr = ps.$$

Notationally, the symbol $\lessdot$ is used to denote the ***simpler than*** relation between fractions, and is defined over all pairs of fractions by

$$\frac{p}{q} \lessdot \frac{r}{s} \text{ iff } \frac{p}{q} \neq \frac{r}{s} \text{ and both } p \leq r, q \leq s.$$

For example $\frac{0}{1} \lessdot \frac{1}{1}$, and $\frac{1}{2} \lessdot \frac{2}{3} \lessdot \frac{2}{4}$.

We utilize the notation $[a_0/a_1/a_2/\cdots/a_n]$ for the *n-th order* (simple) *continued fraction* expansion

$$a_0 + \cfrac{1}{a_1 + \cfrac{1}{a_2 + \cfrac{1}{\ddots + \cfrac{1}{a_n}}}}$$

where the ***partial quotients*** a_i are assumed to be integral with $a_0 \geq 0$, $a_i \geq 1$ for $1 \leq i \leq n$. It is known from the theory of continued fractions [Khinchin 35, Hardy and Wright 79] that any positive rational number, denoted by the irreducible fraction $\frac{p}{q}$, has exactly two finite expansions herein termed the ***canonical*** and ***long expansions***, as given and related by:

$$\frac{p}{q} = \begin{cases} [a_0/a_1/\cdots/a_{n-1}/a_n] & \textit{canonical} \\ [a_0/a_1/\cdots/a_{n-1}/a_n - 1/1] & \textit{long} \end{cases} \quad \text{where } a_n \geq \begin{cases} 2 \text{ for } n \geq 1 \\ 1 \text{ for } n = 0 \end{cases}$$

with 0 having the unique and canonical expansion $[0]$. It follows that any positive rational number has both a unique *even order* continued fraction expansion $[a_0/a_1/\cdots/a_{2m}]$ together with a unique *odd order* continued fraction expansion $[a_0/a_1/\cdots/a_{2m+1}]$. It is the unique even order expansion $[a_0/a_1/\cdots/a_{2m}]$ that will later be employed for the definition of the lexicographic continued fraction expansion.

The irreducible fractions $\frac{p_i}{q_i} = [a_0/a_1/\cdots/a_i]$ determined for $0 \leq i \leq n$ by truncating the continued fraction $[a_0/a_1/\cdots/a_n]$ constitute a sequence of irreducible fraction approximations to $\frac{p}{q} = \frac{p_n}{q_n} = [a_0/a_1/\cdots/a_n]$ termed *convergents* to $\frac{p}{q}$. The *preconvergent* shall denote the convergent $\frac{p_{n-1}}{q_{n-1}}$ immediately preceding $\frac{p_n}{q_n}$ in the canonical expansion for $\frac{p}{q}$. Note that the long expansion of $\frac{p}{q} \neq 0$ includes one additional convergent termed the *parent* in addition to those for the canonical expansion of $\frac{p}{q}$. For example, the canonical expansion $\frac{277}{642} = \frac{p}{q} = [0/2/3/6/1/3/3]$ has the convergents $\frac{0}{1}, \frac{1}{2}, \frac{3}{7}, \frac{19}{44}, \frac{22}{51}, \frac{85}{197}, \frac{277}{642}$ with preconvergent $\frac{85}{197}$. The parent of $\frac{277}{642}$ is then $\frac{192}{445} = [0/2/3/6/1/3/2]$.

The convergents have many important properties, some of which are cited here for reference from [Hardy and Wright 79, Khinchin 35]:

Theorem 1. *The convergents $\frac{p_i}{q_i} = [a_0/a_1/\cdots/a_i]$ of any (canonical or long) continued fraction $\frac{p}{q} = [a_1/a_2/\cdots/a_n]$ for $i = 0, 1, \cdots, n$ satisfy the following properties:*

i) *Recursive ancestry:*
With $p_{-2} = 0, p_{-1} = 1, q_{-2} = 1$, and $q_{-1} = 0$,

$$p_i = a_i p_{i-1} + p_{i-2},$$
$$q_i = a_i q_{i-1} + q_{i-2},$$

or in matrix form:

$$\begin{Bmatrix} p_{i-2} & p_{i-1} \\ q_{i-2} & q_{i-1} \end{Bmatrix} \begin{Bmatrix} 0 & 1 \\ 1 & a_i \end{Bmatrix} = \begin{Bmatrix} p_{i-1} & p_i \\ q_{i-1} & q_i \end{Bmatrix} \quad \text{and} \quad \begin{Bmatrix} 0 & 1 \\ 1 & 0 \end{Bmatrix} \prod_{j=0}^{i} \begin{Bmatrix} 0 & 1 \\ 1 & a_i \end{Bmatrix} = \begin{Bmatrix} p_{i-1} & p_i \\ q_{i-1} & q_i \end{Bmatrix},$$

ii) *Irreducibility:*

$$gcd(p_i, q_i) = 1,$$

iii) *Adjacency:*

$$q_i p_{i-1} - p_i q_{i-1} = (-1)^i,$$

iv) *Simplicity:*

$$\frac{p_i}{q_i} \lessgtr \frac{p_{i+1}}{q_{i+1}} \quad \text{for } i \leq n-1,$$

v) *Alternating convergence:*

$$\frac{p_0}{q_0} < \frac{p_2}{q_2} < \cdots \frac{p_{2i}}{q_{2i}} < \cdots \leq \frac{p}{q} \leq \cdots < \frac{p_{2i-1}}{q_{2i-1}} < \cdots < \frac{p_1}{q_1},$$

vi) *Best rational approximation:*

$$\frac{r}{s} \lll \frac{p_i}{q_i} \Longrightarrow \left|\frac{r}{s} - \frac{p}{q}\right| > \left|\frac{p_i}{q_i} - \frac{p}{q}\right|,$$

vii) *Quadratic convergence:*

$$\frac{1}{q_i(q_{i+1}+q_i)} < \left|\frac{p_i}{q_i} - \frac{p}{q}\right| \leq \frac{1}{q_i q_{i+1}} \text{ for } i \leq n-1,$$

viii) *Real approximation:*

$\left|x - \frac{p}{q}\right| < \frac{1}{2q^2}$ for irreducible $\frac{p}{q}$ implies that $\frac{p}{q}$ is a convergent of a (possibly infinite) continued fraction expansion of x.

From Theorem 1(v) we see that the even order convergents approach $\frac{p}{q}$ from below and the odd order convergents approach from above, with the interval between any two successive convergents containing $\frac{p}{q}$.

[Tab. 1] illustrates the rate at which the sequence of convergent values for $\frac{277}{642} = [0/2/3/6/1/3/3]$ give better approximations to 277/642. Note from the table that the accuracy attained by successive convergents has a larger incremental improvement when the next partial quotient is large, as anticipated by Theorem 1 (vii).

Continued fraction	*Fraction*	*Decimal representation*	*Relative error*
[0]	0/1	0.0 ···	1
[0/1]	1/2	0.50 ···	0.15
[0/2/3]	3/7	0.428 ···	0.0067
[0/2/3/6]	19/44	0.4318 ···	0.00082
[0/2/3/6/1]	22/51	0.43137 ···	0.00021
[0/2/3/6/1/3]	85/197	0.431472 ···	0.000018
[0/2/3/6/1/3/3]	277/642	0.4314641 ···	0

Table 1: The canonical convergents to $\frac{277}{642}$ in continued fraction, fraction, and decimal form, and the relative errors of these convergents as best rational approximations.

Consider from Theorem 1 and the example of [Tab. 1] that the notion of an i'th order best rational approximation by itself is not useful in finite precision computational practice as the resulting accuracy depends without bound on the size of the particular partial quotients involved. The lexicographic continued fraction expansion we now introduce will be shown quite analogously to identify a sequence of rational approximations termed "biconvergents". The biconvergents contain and supplement the sequence of convergents of the canonical continued fraction suitably granularized at the bit level to allow a measure of accuracy in terms of bit length.

For the purpose of defining a binary based lexicographic continued fraction expansion, we will employ a binary representation of the positive integers which is both "self delimiting", i.e. which implicitly contains an end-marker when read from left to right, and lexicographically order preserving over the integers.

Formally, if the integer $p \geq 1$ has the $(n+1)$-bit binary radix representation $1b_{n-1}\cdots b_1 b_0$, with $n \geq 0$ and $\circ$ denoting string concatenation, the $(2n+1)$-bit bitstring

$$\ell(p) \equiv 1^n \circ 0 \circ b_{n-1}b_{n-2}\cdots b_1 b_0 \tag{1}$$

will be termed the ***lexibinary*** form of p. $\ell(p)$ is thus composed on a (possibly vacuous) ***unary part*** 1^n delimited by the ***switch-bit*** 0, followed by the (possibly vacuous) ***binary part*** $b_{n-1}b_{n-2}\cdots b_0$. The value of the lexibinary integer $1^n 0 b_{n-1}b_{n-2}\cdots b_0$ is then $2^n + \sum_{i=0}^{n-1} b_i 2^i$. This representation is ***order preserving*** in that the lexicographic ordering (leftmost bit first) of lexibinary bitstrings is seen to correspond to the numeric ordering of their values. [Tab. 2] illustrates the lexibinary form of several integers. For a discussion of alternative lexicographic order preserving binary encodings of the integers [see Knuth 82], where similar representations are analysed.

Integer	*Binary*	*Lexibinary*
1	1.	0
2	10.	100
3	11.	101
4	100.	11000
5	101.	11001
6	110.	11010
7	111.	11011
8	1000.	1110000
16	10000.	111100000
32	100000.	11111000000
100	1100100.	1111110100100
200	11001000.	111111101001000
1000	1111101000.	1111111110111101000

Table 2: Right-adjusted standard binary representation and left-adjusted lexibinary bitstring representation of certain integers.

Note from the definition of a continued fraction expansion that $[a_0/a_1/\cdots/a_n]$ is an increasing function of any even order partial quotient, and a decreasing function of any odd order partial quotient. Thus to obtain an order preserving representation of the rationals we simply represent the odd order quotients in complemented lexibinary integer form before concatenation. To be able to compare bit strings lexicographically from left to right it is assumed that any (finite length) representation is extended to the right with an arbitrary number of extra zeroes. This corresponds with the observation that, suitably interpreted and extending the even order continued fraction expansion

$$p/q = [a_0/a_1/\cdots/a_{2m}] = [a_0/a_1/\cdots/a_{2m}/\infty]. \tag{2}$$

If we define $\ell(\infty)$ to be an infinite string of ones, then since ∞ occurs in an odd order position in (2), $\ell(\infty)$ will always appear in complemented form yielding $\overline{\ell(\infty)} = 00\cdots$. This provides a terminal infinite string of zeroes, which may either be denoted by 0^∞ or taken as assumed.

Formally, implicitly handling the case $a_0 = 0$ $(0 \leq p/q < 1)$ by a leading zero bit and $a_0 \geq 1$ $(1 \leq \frac{p}{q})$ by a leading unit bit, the *lexicographic continued fraction* (LCF) expansion of $\frac{p}{q} \geq 0$ is the (infinite) bitstring determined employing (1) and (2) by:

$$LCF\left(\frac{p}{q}\right) = \begin{cases} 1 \circ \ell(a_0) \circ \overline{\ell(a_1)} \circ \cdots \circ \ell(a_{2m}) \circ \overline{\ell(\infty)} & \text{for } 1 \leq \frac{p}{q} \\ 0 \circ \ell(a_1) \circ \cdots \circ \overline{\ell(a_{2m-1})} \circ \ell(a_{2m}) \circ \overline{\ell(\infty)} & \text{for } 0 \leq \frac{p}{q} < 1 \end{cases} \qquad (3)$$

The positive valued LCF expansion $b_0 b_1 \cdots b_{k-1} 1 0^\infty$ is said to have *order* k (the index of the least significant unit), with $\frac{0}{1} = 0^\infty$ having order zero. The LCF expansion denoted with the concatenation symbol $\circ$ at each corresponding partial quotient boundary as in (3) is said to be in *parsed form*. The leading bit b_0 of the LCF expansion $b_0 b_1 \cdots b_{k-1} 1 0^\infty$ is termed the *reciprocal* bit. Note that all subsequent bits may uniquely be identified as members of the unary, switch, or binary portions of the i'th order partial quotient in the even order continued fraction expansion in (3).

The finite bit string $b_0 b_1 \cdots b_n$, with or without trailing zeros, is taken as an alternative finite LCF expansion equivalent to $b_0 b_1 \cdots b_n 0^\infty$. The *minimal* LCF expansion $b_0 b_1 \cdots b_{k-1} 1$ of $\frac{p}{q} > 0$ is truncated at the last unit bit, and thus including the reciprocal bit has length one greater than the order of the LCF expansion. Zero is taken to have its minimal LCF expansion composed of the single 0 reciprocal bit.

Example 1.

$$\begin{aligned} \tfrac{22}{7} &= \tfrac{22}{7} && \text{irreducible fraction form} \\ &= [3/6/1] && \text{even order continued fraction form} \\ &= [3/6/1/\infty] && \text{infinite extension} \\ &= 1 \circ \ell(3) \circ \overline{\ell(6)} \circ \ell(1) \circ \overline{\ell(\infty)} && \\ &= 1 \circ 101 \circ \overline{11010} \circ 0 \circ \overline{1^\infty} && \text{equivalent parsed LCF expansions} \\ &= 1 \circ 101 \circ 00101 \circ 0 \circ 0^\infty && \\ &= 110100101 && \text{minimal LCF expansion (order 8)} \end{aligned}$$

The irreducible fraction $\frac{r_k}{s_k} = b_0 b_1 \cdots b_{k-1} 1$ for $0 \leq k \leq n$ determined by truncating the lexicographic continued fraction $\frac{r}{s} = \frac{r_n}{s_n} = b_0 b_1 \cdots b_{n-1} 1$ at index $k-1$ and appending a unit bit, is termed the k'th order *biconvergent* (*binary convergent*) of $\frac{r}{s}$. Each biconvergent $\frac{r_0}{s_0}, \frac{r_1}{s_1} \cdots \frac{r_n}{s_n}$ in sequence provides then either an improved upper or lower bound on $\frac{r}{s}$ determined by

$$\frac{r_k}{s_k} = b_0 b_1 \cdots b_{k-1} 1 \begin{cases} \geq \frac{r}{s} \text{ if } b_k = 0, \\ \leq \frac{r}{s} \text{ if } b_k = 1. \end{cases}$$

To compare biconvergent approximation with the k-bit binary radix approximation, we can compute the "precision" of the k'th order biconvergent approximation in bits by the negative base two logarithm of the bounding intervals, as illustrated by the following table of biconvergents of $\frac{277}{642}$ through order 12:

k	0	1	2	3	4	5	6	7	8	9	10	11	12
r_k/s_k	1/1	1/2	1/4	1/3	2/5	4/9	3/7	7/16	13/30	25/58	19/44	22/51	41/95
$-\log_2(gap)$	0.00	1.00	2.00	2.58	3.32	4.49	5.97	6.80	7.71	8.76	10.31	11.13	12.24

Some useful facts about biconvergents follow from the definition and certain properties of convergents, and we will summarize these in some observations. Noting that the reciprocal of $\frac{p}{q} = [a_0/a_1/\cdots/a_n] \geq 1$ is $\frac{q}{p} = [0/a_0/a_1/\cdots/a_n]$, so then the convergents to $\frac{p}{q}$ are $\frac{0}{1}$ and the reciprocals of the convergents to $\frac{p}{q}$. From (3) then

Observation 2. *The LCF expansion of the reciprocal of $\frac{p}{q} = b_0 b_1 \cdots b_{k-1}1$ is the 2's complement, $\frac{q}{p} = \overline{b_0 b_1 \cdots b_{k-1}}1$. Thus the reciprocal of a k'th order LCF number is also of k'th order.*

Observation 3. *The biconvergents to the reciprocal $\frac{q}{p} = \overline{b_0 b_1 \cdots b_{k-1}}1$ of $\frac{p}{q} = b_0 b_1 b_{k-1}1$ are the reciprocals of the biconvergents to $\frac{p}{q}$.*

It is immediate from (3) that the even order convergents of the canonical continued fraction for $\frac{p}{q}$ are also biconvergents to $\frac{p}{q}$. The odd order convergents to $\frac{p}{q}$ have reciprocals that are even order convergents to $\frac{q}{p}$ and thus are biconvergents to $\frac{q}{p}$. Using [Observations 2,3] it follows that

Observation 4. *Every convergent of the canonical continued fraction expansion of $\frac{p}{q}$ is also a biconvergent to $\frac{p}{q}$.*

Although the order of the lexicographic continued fraction can be arbitrarily large compared to the order of the ordinary continued fraction for a given rational, on the average the orders can be related. From classical material on continued fractions it is known that the partial quotients in the continued fraction expansion of a randomly chosen $\frac{r}{s} \in [0,1]$ (see [Knuth 81] or [Blachman 84] for details) will have value i with probability essentially given by

$$p_i = \log_2\left(1 + \frac{1}{i(i+2)}\right), \tag{4}$$

where then

$$p_1 = 0.415,\ p_2 = 0.170,\ p_3 = 0.093,\ p_4 = 0.059, \cdots.$$

With the distribution of partial quotient size given by (4), we note that 41.5% of all partial quotients are unity and are encoded by a single bit in the LCF expansion. Another 26.3% of the partial quotients have values two or three and contribute 3 bits each to the LCF expansion, and an average partial quotient from (4) has expected length

$$\sum_i (2\lfloor \log_2 i \rfloor + 1)\log_2\left(1 + \frac{1}{i(i+2)}\right) = 3.51\cdots.$$

Thus in summary,

Observation 5. *From the known distribution (4) of partial quotient size, it follows that the canonical continued fraction expansion and LCF expansion of a rational* $\frac{p}{q} = [a_1/a_2/\cdots/a_n] = b_0 b_1 \cdots b_{k-1}1$ *yield an expected biconvergent to convergent ratio of* $Exp(\frac{k}{n}) = 3.51\cdots$.

Observation 6. *From the known distribution (4) of partial quotient size, it follows that* $1/3.51\cdots = 28.5\%$ *of the biconvergents to* $\frac{p}{q}$ *will also be convergents to* $\frac{p}{q}$, *i.e. the so-called best rational approximations which are characterized without any dependence on the binary representation employed for the LCF expansion.*

LCF expansions and biconvergent approximations have many properties of theoretical interest and/or which find use in employing LCF representation as a basis of computer arithmetic unit design. We shall particularly pursue herein issues related to assessing the accuracy of finite precision computation employing fixed length LCF expansions. A summary of related topics [see Kornerup and Matula 83, 88] that will not be further pursued in this paper are listed here for reference:

Regarding uniqueness of LCF representation of the nonnegative rationals:

- There is a one-to-one correspondence between all minimal LCF expansions and the nonnegative rational numbers.

Regarding arithmetic with LCF represented numbers:

- LCF expansions may be used bit-by-bit in a left-to-right scan as input to on-line algorithms for the direct computation of arithmetic expressions upon LCF operands yielding LCF results [Kornerup and Matula 88]. In this context the LCF bitstring may be interpreted as an encoding of the individual steps (transitions) in a finite automaton performing the Euclidean gcd algorithm (in binary) on p and q.

Regarding the efficiency in bit-length of LCF expansions:

- The minimum redundancy encoding, Huffman encoding, and LCF expansion average bit-length per partial quotient can be computed employing classical results [Knuth 81] on the distribution of the size (4) of partial quotients, yielding:

Average Bits per Partial Quotient	
Minimum redundancy encoding	3.43... ,
Huffman encoding	3.47... ,
LCF expansion	3.51... .

Thus the computationally useful format of the LCF expansion is achieved with an encoding length only about 2% greater than that which could be obtained by any minimal redundancy encoding, and only about 1% greater than that achievable by a Huffman encoding, where the latter two encodings would most likely be of no practical value for arithmetic computation.

Regarding multiplicative and additive inverses:

- LCF representation may be extended with a sign as follows:

$$SLCF\left(\frac{p}{q}\right) = \begin{cases} 1 \circ LCF(\frac{p}{q}) \text{ for } \frac{p}{q} \geq 0, \\ 0 \circ \widetilde{LCF}(\frac{p}{q}) \text{ for } \frac{p}{q} < 0. \end{cases}$$

  where $\widetilde{\text{LCF}}$ denotes the 2's complement of any minimal finite LCF bitstring, and the 1's complement of any infinite bitstring. SLCF representation is then order preserving over the reals. Note then that SLCF representation has leading sign and reciprocal bits that treat both the additive and multiplicative inverses of real numbers in an analogous manner.

3 The LCF Rational Number Hierarchy

A hierarchy is imposed on the rationals by the order (length) of their LCF expansions. The enumeration of this rational hierarchy is conveniently illustrated by associating the positive irreducible fractions with the nodes of an infinite binary tree, termed the LCF tree, where the LCF bitstring denotes the path to the node containing the associated irreducible fraction. The fraction $\frac{p}{q} = b_0 b_1 \cdots b_{k-1} 1$ of order k is assigned to the node at depth k reached by proceeding to the left child when $b_i = 0$ and to the right child when $b_i = 1$ for $i = 0, 1, 2, \cdots, k-1$.

The left half of the LCF tree truncated at depth 5 is illustrated in [Fig. 1], where we note that the values in the nodes of the right half of the LCF tree are simply the reciprocals of those in the left half reached by the complemented bitstring.

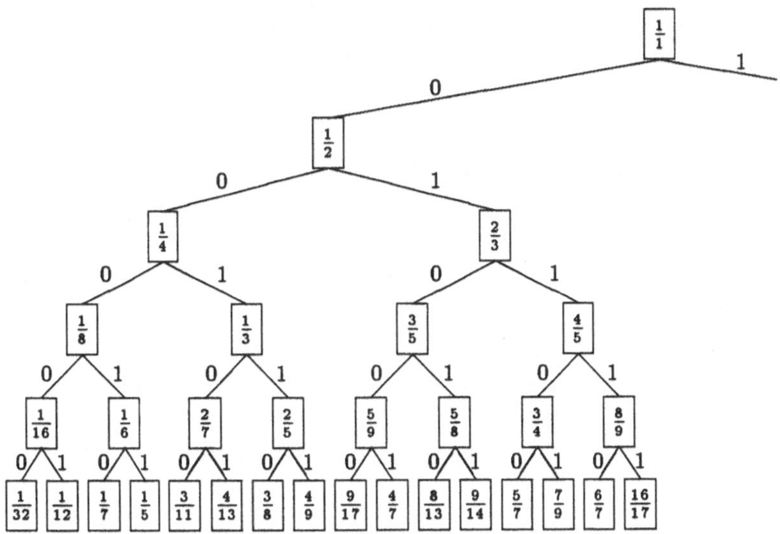

Figure 1: The left half of the LCF tree through depth five.

The LCF tree provides a convenient reference for interpreting the accuracy of finite precision LCF representation both "vertically" and "horizontally":

Vertically: The path from the root down to any node enumerates the biconvergents to the irreducible fraction at that node, e.g. $\frac{1}{1}, \frac{1}{2}, \frac{1}{4}, \frac{1}{3}, \frac{2}{5}, \frac{4}{9}$ is the sequence of biconvergents to $\frac{4}{9}$.

Horizontally: The (nonzero) elements of the set Q_k of irreducible fractions of $[0,1]$ whose LCF expansions have order at most k can be enumerated by an inorder traversal of the left half of the LCF tree truncated at depth k, e.g. including $\frac{0}{1}, \frac{1}{1}$:

$$Q_2 = \left\{ \frac{0}{1}, \frac{1}{4}, \frac{1}{2}, \frac{2}{3}, \frac{1}{1} \right\},$$

and

$$Q_4 = \left\{ \frac{0}{1}, \frac{1}{16}, \frac{1}{8}, \frac{1}{6}, \frac{1}{4}, \frac{2}{7}, \frac{1}{3}, \frac{2}{5}, \frac{1}{2}, \frac{5}{9}, \frac{3}{5}, \frac{5}{8}, \frac{2}{3}, \frac{3}{4}, \frac{4}{5}, \frac{8}{9}, \frac{1}{1}, \right\}.$$

There are then $2^k + 1$ members of Q_k in the interval $[0,1]$ yielding an average gap size of 2^{-k}. The definition of LCF representation provides no immediate clue as to the extent of variation of these gap sizes for fixed k, knowledge of which is essential to assess the precision obtainable by k-bit LCF approximation. In this section we develop tools for investigating gap sizes in Q_k and their relation to gap sizes in Q_{k+1}. For purposes of analysis we shall be particularly concerned with characterizing relations between LCF represented numbers in terms of their more familiar irreducible fraction and continued fraction representations.

For the fractions $p/q < r/s$, the size of the interval $[p/q, r/s]$ is given by the expression $(rq - ps)/qs$ and will be a minimum relative to the size of the denominator qs when $|rq - ps| = 1$. We say the fractions $\frac{p}{q}$ and $\frac{r}{s}$ are *adjacent* whenever $|rq - ps| = 1$. For $\frac{p}{q}$ adjacent to $\frac{r}{s}$ it follows immediately that both $\frac{p}{q}$ and $\frac{r}{s}$ are irreducible, and that either $\frac{p}{q} \lll \frac{r}{s}$ or $\frac{r}{s} \lll \frac{p}{q}$. Note that some, but not all, successive pairs of fractions of Q_k are adjacent.

The notion of adjacency also identifies an important relation among continued fractions that will form a bridge to understanding the neighbor relations for members of Q_k. The following theorem provides alternative characterizations.

Theorem 7. *For the fractions $\frac{p}{q} \lll \frac{r}{s}$ (i.e. $\frac{p}{q} \neq \frac{r}{s}$ and $p \leq r$, $q \leq s$) each of the following four properties implies the other three and serves as an equivalent definition of adjacency.*

i) *Determinant form: $|rq - ps| = 1$,*

ii) *Interval form: $\frac{p}{q}$, $\frac{r}{s}$ are both irreducible and both simpler than any other fraction within the interval bounded by $\frac{p}{q}$ and $\frac{r}{s}$*

iii) *Continued fraction form: $\frac{p}{q}$ and $\frac{r}{s}$ are both irreducible and related by*

$$\frac{r}{s} = [a_0/a_1/\cdots/a_{n-1}/a_n] \qquad \textit{(canonical form of } \tfrac{r}{s})$$

and

$$\frac{p}{q} = \begin{cases} [a_0/a_1/\cdots/a_{n-1}] & \textit{(preconvergent of } \tfrac{r}{s} \textit{ for } n \geq 1) \\ \textit{or} & \\ [a_0/a_1/\cdots/a_{n-1}/a_n - 1] & \textit{(parent of } \tfrac{r}{s} \textit{ for any } n). \end{cases}$$

iv) *Convergent form: $\frac{r}{s}$ is irreducible and $\frac{p}{q}$ is either its preconvergent or parent.*

Proof. The equivalence of (i) and (ii) is known from the classical theory of Farey Fractions, e.g. [Hardy and Wright 79]. The fact that (iii) implies (i) follows from Theorem 1. (iv) is essentially a restatement of (iii). To complete the proof we need only show that the two alternatives given for $\frac{p}{q}$ in (iii) yield the only fractions simpler than and adjacent to $\frac{r}{s}$.

Let $\frac{r_i}{s_i} = [a_0/a_1/\cdots/a_i]$ for $i = 0, 1, \cdots, n$ denote the convergents to the canonical continued fraction for $\frac{r}{s}$. The set of linear equations

$$xr + yp = r_{n-1}$$

$$xs + yq = s_{n-1}$$

will have a unique solution (x, y) since $|ps - qr| = 1$. Note that $|y| = |y||ps - qr| = |r_{n-1}s - s_{n-1}r| = 1$. So $y = \pm 1$, and x must be integral since $\frac{r}{s}$ is irreducible.

For $y = 1$, $0 \leq p = r_{n-1} - xr$, with $r_{n-1} < r$, implies $x = 0$, hence

$$\frac{p}{q} = \frac{r_{n-1}}{s_{n-1}} = [a_0/a_1/\cdots/a_{n-1}].$$

For the case $y = -1$ then $p = xr - r_{n-1}$ implies $x = 1$ since $p \leq r$. Hence $p = x(a_n r_{n-1} + r_{n-2}) - r_{n-1} = (a_n - 1)r_{n-1} + r_{n-2}$ and similarly we find $q = (a_n - 1)s_{n-1} + s_{n-2}$, thus

$$\frac{p}{q} = [a_0/a_1/\cdots/a_n - 1].$$

□

From the LCF tree it is clear that membership of a fraction in Q_k depends in some manner on a truncated binary representation of the final partial quotient of a continued fraction representation of the fraction. This introduces a base dependence phenomenon similar to that obtained in finite length binary radix representation. We seek both to model and understand the ramifications of this base dependency in LCF representation. Importantly, the adjacency relation itself as interpreted on fractions and/or continued fractions suffers no base dependence on the representation of the individual partial quotients. The following extension of adjacency introduces a dependency on the binary representation only in the last partial quotient. This "binary adjacency" relation will be shown sufficient to characterize all neighbor pairs in Q_k.

We first note that two finite bitstrings α, β are termed *lexicographically adjacent* (with α *lexicographically preceding* β) if

$$\alpha = \sigma \circ 0 \circ 1^j$$

$$\beta = \sigma \circ 1 \circ 0^j$$

for some prefix σ and some $j \geq 0$. Lexicographically adjacent bitstrings thus may equivalently be said to differ by a unit in the last place (ulp). This is precisely the relation between neighbors in Q_k we want to express in terms of equivalent relations among rationals in fraction or continued fraction form. However, it turns out to be most convenient to define the relation wanted in terms of continued fraction expansions.

The fractions $\frac{p}{q} \lessdot \frac{r}{s}$ are *bijacent* (of positive, zero or negative degree i) iff $\frac{p}{q}$ and $\frac{r}{s}$ are both irreducible, and

$$\begin{aligned} \frac{p}{q} &= [a_0/a_1/\cdots/a_n] \\ \frac{r}{s} &= [a_0/a_1/\cdots/a_n + 2^i], \end{aligned} \tag{5}$$

where $a_n = k2^i \geq 2$ when $i \geq 1$.

The definition includes situations corresponding to i being positive, zero, or negative which may be separately interpreted as follows:

$i \geq 0$: $\frac{p}{q}$ and $\frac{r}{s}$ have canonical expansions differing only in the last partial quotient

$$\begin{aligned} \frac{p}{q} &= [a_0/a_1/\cdots/a_{n-1}/k2^i] \\ \frac{r}{s} &= [a_0/a_1/\cdots/a_{n-1}/(k+1)2^i]. \end{aligned}$$

$i \leq 0$: In this case we interpret $a_n + 2^i$ as two partial quotients

$$\frac{r}{s} = [a_0/a_1/\cdots/a_n + 2^i] = [a_0/a_1/\cdots/a_n/2^{-i}],$$

and further for i negative, $\frac{r}{s}$ must have a canonical expansion with last partial quotient a positive power of two, i.e. $2^{-i} \geq 2$.

Note that for i being zero both interpretations apply and $\frac{p}{q}$ is the parent of $\frac{r}{s}$. For i being negative, $\frac{p}{q}$ is its preconvergent. When i is positive, $\frac{p}{q}$ is not a convergent to $\frac{r}{s}$, but is a biconvergent to $\frac{r}{s}$.

The notion of bijacency may be equivalently characterized in terms of either LCF bitstrings or irreducible fractions as summarized in the following theorem.

Theorem 8. *Each of the following three properties implies the other two and serves as an equivalent definition of bijacency.*

i) *Continued fraction form: $\frac{p}{q} \lessdot \frac{r}{s}$ are bijacent of degree i as specified in (5),*
ii) *LCF form: The irreducible fractions $\frac{p}{q}$ and $\frac{r}{s}$ have lexicographically adjacent LCF expansions (and thus are neighbors in Q_k for some k),*
iii) *Fraction form: $\frac{p}{q} \lessdot \frac{r}{s}$ are bijacent of degree i iff for*
$i \geq 0$: $|ps - qr| = 2^i = gcd(r-p, s-q)$ and $\frac{r}{s} \lessdot \frac{2p}{2q}$,
$i \leq 0$: $|ps - qr| = 1$ and $\frac{2^{-i}p}{2^{-i}q} \lessdot \frac{r}{s} \lessdot \frac{(2^{-i}+1)p}{(2^{-i}+1)q}$ when $\frac{p}{q} \neq \frac{0}{1}$,
and $\frac{r}{s} = \frac{1}{2^{-i}}$ when $\frac{p}{q} = \frac{0}{1}$.

Proof. It is straightforward to prove ii) and iii) from i). We first prove i) given iii). Let us start with the case where $i \leq -1$ for $p \neq 0$, then there exists $\frac{a}{b} \lessdot \frac{p}{q}$ such that $r = 2^{-i}p + a$ and $s = 2^{-i}q + b$. Since $|\frac{p}{q} - \frac{r}{s}| = \frac{1}{qs} < \frac{1}{2q^2}$ it follows from Theorem 1 (viii) that $\frac{p}{q}$ is a convergent of $\frac{r}{s}$. Since $r \geq 2p$, $\frac{p}{q}$ cannot be the parent of $\frac{r}{s}$, so $\frac{r}{s} = [a_0/a_1/\cdots/a_n/2^{-i}]$ and $\frac{p}{q} = [a_0/a_1/\cdots/a_n]$. For $i = 0$

the same argument applies, except that now $\frac{p}{q} = [a_0/a_1/\cdots/a_n]$ is the parent of $\frac{r}{s} = [a_0/a_1/\cdots/a_n + 2^0]$.

Now, assume $i \geq 1$. Then there exists a and b such that $r - p = 2^i a$ and $s - q = 2^i b$. From

$$2^i|aq - bp| = |(r-p)q - (s-q)p| = |rq - sp| = 2^i$$

we obtain $|aq - bp| = 1$ and similarly $|as - br| = 1$. Hence $\frac{a}{b}$ is irreducible and adjacent to $\frac{p}{q}$ as well as to $\frac{r}{s}$. Now $\frac{r}{s} \lessdot \frac{2p}{2q}$ implies $\frac{r-p}{s-q} = \frac{2^i a}{2^i b} \lessdot \frac{p}{q}$ hence $\frac{a}{b} \lessdot \frac{p}{q}$ and as above we find that $\frac{a}{b}$ is a convergent of $\frac{p}{q}$ as well as of $\frac{r}{s}$. With $\frac{p}{q} = [a_0/a_1/\cdots/a_n]$, $a_n \geq 2$, either $\frac{a}{b}$ is the preconvergent or the parent of $\frac{p}{q}$. Assume $\frac{a}{b}$ is the parent, then

$$\frac{p}{q} = \frac{1 \cdot a + p_{n-2}}{1 \cdot b + q_{n-2}}$$

where $\frac{p_{n-2}}{q_{n-2}}$ is the preconvergent of $\frac{p}{q}$, hence $\frac{p}{q} \lessdot \frac{2a}{2b}$ which contradicts $\frac{2^i a}{2^i b} \lessdot \frac{p}{q}$. Thus we obtain both

$$\frac{a}{b} = [a_0/a_1/\cdots/a_{n-1}],$$
$$\frac{r}{s} = \frac{2^i a + p}{2^i b + q} = [a_0/a_1/\cdots/a_{n-1}/a_n + 2^i],$$

which completes the proof of (iii) $\Rightarrow$ (i).

Finally we have to prove that (ii) implies (i), hence assume for some $j \geq 0$ that $\frac{r}{s} = \sigma \circ 0 \circ 1^j$ and $\frac{p}{q} = \sigma \circ 1 \circ 0^j$. Two automatons decoding the bitstrings $\sigma 0 1^j$ and $\sigma 1 0^j$ after reading the string σ, will both be in the same state, having parsed and decoded an initial sequence of partial quotients $\{a_0, a_1, \cdots, a_{n-1}\}$, being in the state of decoding the n'th partial quotient a_n, when encountering the 0 or 1 following σ. The automatons will be in one of four possible states, depending on n being even or odd (reading in true or complemented form), and either reading the initial (unary including switch bit) part or the trailing (binary) part of $\ell(a_n)$.

We will start with n being even, and let us first assume the automatons are reading the unary part of a_n, having already seen k ones of the unary part. The 10 in the LCF expansion of $\frac{p}{q}$ thus implies that the unary part is completed, and

$$\frac{p}{q} = [a_0/a_1/\cdots/a_{n-1}/2^{k+1}],$$

since a suitable amount of zeroes just completes $a_n = 2^{k+1}$ as the final partial quotient (n is even). The interpretation of LCF($\frac{r}{s}$), however, depends on the relation between k and j, since the zero brings the automaton into the state of decoding the binary part.

If $j \leq k$ we find

$$\frac{r}{s} = [a_0/a_1/\cdots/a_{n-1}/(2^{j+1} - 1)2^{k-j}],$$

whereas when $j > k$ there are more ones than needed to complete the binary part, and the remaining ones then are interpreted as two additional partial quotients:

$$\frac{r}{s} = [a_0/a_1/\cdots/a_{n-1}/2^{k+1} - 1/1/2^{j-k}].$$

so that in both cases, $\frac{p}{q}$ and $\frac{r}{s}$ are found to be bijacent of degree $k - j$.

Now assume the automatons are reading the binary part, still having to read $k \geq 1$ bits to complete a_n, when σ has been read. If $k \geq j + 1$, then for some a we obtain

$$\frac{r}{s} = [a_0/a_1/\cdots/a_{n-1}/a \cdot 2^{k-j-1}] \text{ and } \frac{p}{q} = [a_0/a_1/\cdots/a_{n-1}/(a+1)2^{k-j-1}].$$

If $1 \leq k \leq j$, for some a_n we obtain

$$\frac{p}{q} = [a_0/a_1/\cdots/a_n + 1] \text{ and } \frac{r}{s} = [a_0/a_1/\cdots/a_n/1/2^{j-k}],$$

thus in both cases $\frac{p}{q}$ and $\frac{r}{s}$ are bijacent.

For n odd, the bits have to be inverted when reading a_n, and the continued fractions have to be written in even order expansion form, i.e. an $(n+1)$' partial quotient has to be considered. The results then follow similarly. □

By Theorem 8, the bijacency relation is precisely the relation that holds among neighbors in the inorder traversal of the LCF tree given to any depth k, specifically between consecutive fractions of Q_k. For the purpose of determining the members of Q_{k+1} given Q_k, again intuitively what we want is to characterize, in fraction or continued fraction form, is the rational number from Q_{k+1} whose LCF representation is obtained by one-bit extensions of the LCF representations of members of Q_k. Specifically, given two bijacent neighbors from Q_k with LCF representations $\sigma \circ 0 \circ 1^j$ and $\sigma \circ 1 \circ 0^j$, we want to characterize the unique rational $\sigma \circ 0 \circ 1^{j+1}$ from Q_{k+1}, falling between these.

Let us then for a moment digress to the classical concept of Farey fractions. Recall (e.g. from [Hardy and Wright 79]) that given the *Farey-set*

$$F_n = \left\{ \tfrac{p}{q} \mid 0 \leq p \leq n, 1 \leq q \leq n, gcd(p,q) = 1 \right\}$$

a member of F_{2n} can be constructed as the *mediant* $\frac{p+r}{q+s}$ of two successive rationals $\frac{p}{q} < \frac{r}{s}$ already in F_n, which can always be shown to be adjacent as defined previously. We further obtain $\frac{p}{q} < \frac{p+r}{q+s} < \frac{r}{s}$. However, when say $\frac{p}{q}$ is a "very simple fraction", whereas $\frac{r}{s}$ is not (e.g. $p \ll r$ and $q \ll s$), their mediant will be of numeric value very close to $\frac{r}{s}$, and rather distant from $\frac{p}{q}$. In general, the spacing between consecutive members of F_n is quite erratic, varying between n^{-1} and n^{-2} [Matula and Kornerup 80]. Now if p and q above both were multiplied by some common factor c, chosen such that cp and cq were both of the same order of magnitude as r and s respectively, then the rational value of the expression $\frac{cp+r}{cq+s}$ would split the interval between p/q and r/s in two intervals of more nearly equal widths.

This observation leads us to the introduction of an alternative form of mediant, more nearly bisecting each gap between consecutive members of Q_k, which turns out to be precisely the way we can generate members of Q_{k+1} from Q_k.

The *binary mediant* of the bijacent fractions $\frac{p}{q} \lessdot \frac{r}{s}$ is the irreducible fraction $\frac{u}{v}$ with value

$$u/v = (2^j p + r)/(2^j q + s),$$

where j is the largest integer such that $\frac{2^j p}{2^j q} \lessdot \frac{r}{s}$. The binary mediant $\frac{u}{v}$ is defined to be in reduced form, however $gcd(2^j p + r, 2^j q + s)$ can only have value one or two. The following alternative characterizations and properties of the binary mediant are readily obtained by extending the proof of Theorem 8.

Theorem 9. *The binary mediant of two bijacent fractions $\frac{p}{q}, \frac{r}{s}$ is the irreducible fraction $\frac{u}{v}$ equivalently determined by either of the following three conditions:*

i) *Continued fraction form: If*

$$\frac{p}{q} = [a_0/a_1/\cdots/a_{n-1}/a_n]$$
$$\frac{r}{s} = [a_0/a_1/\cdots/a_{n-1}/a_n + 2^i]$$
$$\textit{with } a_n = k2^i \geq 2 \textit{ when } i \geq 1, \textit{ then}$$
$$\frac{u}{v} = [a_0/a_1/\cdots/an - 1/a_n + 2^{i-1}].$$

ii) *LCF expansion form: If $\frac{p}{q} < \frac{r}{s}$ and for some bit string σ and integer $j \geq 0$,*

$$\frac{p}{q} = \sigma \circ 0 \circ 1^j,$$
$$\frac{r}{s} = \sigma \circ 1 \circ 0^j,$$
$$\textit{then}$$
$$\frac{u}{v} = \sigma \circ 0 \circ 1^{j+1}.$$

iii) *Fraction form: If $\frac{p}{q} \lessdot \frac{r}{s}$ are bijacent of degree i, then*

$$\frac{u}{v} = \begin{cases} \dfrac{2^{-i}p + r}{2^{-i}q + s} & \textit{for } i \leq 0, \\ \dfrac{(p+r)/2}{(q+s)/2} & \textit{for } i > 0. \end{cases}$$

Lemma 10. *The binary mediant $\frac{u}{v}$ of the bijacent fractions $\frac{p}{q}, \frac{r}{s}$ is bijacent to both $\frac{p}{q}$ and $\frac{r}{s}$.*

Theorems 8, 9 and Lemma 10 provide us the computational means of generating sets of bijacent fractions partitioning any interval specified by two bijacent fractions given in either the fraction, continued fraction or lexicographic continued fraction form of representation.

Regarding the LCF tree we then immediately obtain the following "LCF Tree Labelling Lemma", here employing in an obvious way the "infinite" fraction $\frac{1}{0}$.

Lemma 11. *In the LCF tree, the fraction $\frac{1}{1}$ is assigned to the root, and the fraction assigned to any other node is the binary mediant of the fraction assigned to the nearest left ancestor node (or $\frac{0}{1}$ if none exists) and the fraction assigned to the nearest right ancestor node (or $\frac{1}{0}$ if none exists) in the LCF tree. Furthermore, with edges labelled 0 for left branch and 1 for right branch, the bitstring composed from the labels on the edges of the path from the root to a particular node, with a terminal unit appended, provides the minimal LCF expansion of the fraction assigned to that node.*

4 Extremes and Distribution of Gap Sizes over Q_k

Traditional fixed point binary representation with k bits to the right of the radix point $0.b_1b_2\cdots b_k$ allows for the representation of 2^k+1 values over the unit interval $[0,1]$, with all gaps of uniform size 2^{-k}. The LCF expansion $0b_1b_2\cdots b_k$ with k bits beyond the reciprocal zero bit, determine an equal sized 2^k+1 membered set Q_k of representable values over the unit interval. The gap sizes over Q_k necessarily vary about the mean 2^{-k} to accommodate exact representations of the "simple" rational fractions. In this section we shall discuss bounds on the variations on the size of gaps over Q_k for large k. We first confirm the existence of certain relatively large and small gaps in Q_k, that we contend are indicative asymptotically of the maximum and minimum gap sizes in Q_k.

Lemma 12. *Given $\epsilon>0$, then for sufficiently large k, the maximum gap size in Q_k will be at least $2^{-(a+\epsilon)k}$ for*

$$a=\frac{1}{4}\log_2(5+2\sqrt{6})=0.82682\cdots,$$

and the minimum gap size will be no bigger that $2^{-(b-\epsilon)k}$ for

$$b=\log_2\left(\frac{3+\sqrt{5}}{2}\right)=1.38848\cdots.$$

Proof. For the minimum gap result, consider that $z=\frac{\sqrt{5}-1}{2}=[0/1/1/\cdots]=010101\cdots=0.618033\cdots$ has the sequence of convergents $\frac{0}{1},\frac{1}{1},\frac{1}{2},\frac{2}{3},\frac{3}{5},\frac{5}{8},\cdots$ which (deleting $\frac{0}{1}$) are also seen to be the sequence of biconvergents to z. The numerators (and denominators) are the well known Fibonacci numbers and grow asymptotically at the rate $(1+\sqrt{5})/2$. The bounding intervals on z determined by the sequence of biconvergents are then $\frac{1}{1\times2},\frac{1}{2\times3},\frac{1}{3\times5},\frac{1}{5\times8},\cdots$, and decrease at a rate approaching $4/(1+\sqrt{5})^2=2/(3+\sqrt{5})$, verifying the minimum gap size bound.

For the maximum gap size result note that $y=\sqrt{6}-2=[0/2/4/2/4/\cdots]=001111000011110000\cdots=0.449489\cdots$ has a sequence of convergents, where the rate of increase of numerators (and denominators) in two steps, $\frac{p_{i+2}}{p_i}$, approaches $5+2\sqrt{6}=9.898979\cdots$. Note then that after eight bits in the LCF expansion corresponding to encoding another pair of partial quotients 2, 4, the bounding interval only determined by the biconvergents will decrease at a rate approaching $1/(5+2\sqrt{6})^2$, from which the lower bound on the maximum bound follows. □

For the purpose of bounding the approximation error in rounding to a biconvergent in Q_k, we are concerned with determining an upper bound on the maximal gap size in Q_k. By direct computation we first obtain the maximum gap size in Q_k for moderate orders, given in terms of

$$a_k = -\frac{1}{k}\log_2(\text{max gap in } Q_k),$$

the values of which are listed for $k = 1, 2, \cdots, 20$ in the following table:

k	a_k	k	a_k
1	1.000	11	0.812
2	0.792	12	0.816
3	0.774	13	0.819
4	0.792	14	0.820
5	0.817	15	0.816
6	0.812	16	0.819
7	0.804	17	0.821
8	0.810	18	0.822
9	0.815	19	0.818
10	0.818	20	0.821

In these computations we found for the larger k that the maximum size gaps in Q_k always had a boundary point $\frac{p}{q} \in Q_k$ whose LCF representation contains replications of the bit pattern 00001111, consistent with the example of Lemma 12. This lemma further gives us an upper bound on any limiting value for a_k, and we suggest in the following that this is indeed the correct value.

Conjecture 13. $\lim_{k\to\infty} a_k = \frac{1}{4}\log_2(5+2\sqrt{6}) = 0.82682\cdots$, *where furthermore the gaps in* Q_k *containing the real number* $\sqrt{6}-2 = [0/2/4/2/4/\cdots]$ *decrease in size asymptotically in* k *as fast as the maximum size gaps in* Q_k.

The proof of the conjecture at this point appears quite tedious. We quote here without proof from [Kornerup and Matula 85] a somewhat weaker result, which in conjunction with Lemma 12 provides reasonable tight bounds on a_k.

Theorem 14. *Given* $\epsilon > 0$, *then for sufficiently large* k, *the maximum gap size in* Q_k *is no greater than* $2^{-(a-\epsilon)k}$ *for* $a = \frac{1}{4}\log_2(16/153) = 0.814347\cdots$.

Also from [Kornerup and Matula 85] we quote findings on some computations and simulations on the gap size distribution. For values of k up through 24 the distributions were computed exhaustively. In each case it was also found that the minimum gap in Q_k fell between two consecutive rationals of the form $\frac{f_{n-2}}{f_{n-1}}$ and $\frac{f_{n-1}}{f_n}$, where f_n denotes the nth Fibonacci number, in correspondence with the observation about the LCF expansion of $[0/1/1/\cdots/1]$.

The main purpose of the computations was, however, to obtain graphs of the distribution of gap sizes. Exhaustive computations up to $k = 24$ and simulations for $k = 32, 64, 128$ showed the distribution of the negative base 2 logarithm of gaps in Q_k to be bell-shaped between approximately 0.8 and 1.3, and centered around 1.0, the bell-shape getting narrower and higher peaked for increasing values of k.

Overall our study shows that the gaps between LCF representable values are subject to a variation in size corresponding to a worst case 19% precision loss (or equivalently a 19% storage capacity loss), and a best case 38% precision gain, in comparison with an equivalent fixed point binary system with uniform gap size over the unit interval. This appears to be a small price to pay for achieving exact representation of all simple rationals.

5 Conclusions

A binary representation of the rationals has been described and analyzed. It is capable of representing in finite precision a set of rationals fairly regularly spaced on the unit interval. It supports an online arithmetic unit for rational arithmetic, which can alternatively be considered an approximative real arithmetic with embedded exact computations on simple rationals.

The LCF representation is non-redundant, which for an on-line (digit serial, most significant digit first) arithmetic has the implication that the delay between input and output can vary unboundedly. To be able to bound and reduce such delays, it is necessary to introduce redundancy in the representation. It is straightforward to introduce redundancy in the continued fraction representation of rationals (allowing partial quotients suitably restricted to become negative), and furthermore to introduce redundancy in the binary encoding of the individual partial quotients. Arithmetic units supporting such redundant continued fraction representations have also been investigated and reported [see Kornerup and Matula 90], however an analysis of these representations has never been conducted and deserves a similar study.

Acknowledgements

This paper reports some previously unpublished results presented as part of an invited talk entitled "Rational Number Systems and Arithmetic", given by the first author at the symposium "Real Numbers and Computers", in Saint Etienne, April 4-6, 1995. The work has been supported by The Danish Research Councils, grants no. 11-8243 and 8.21.08.02, and by The National Science Fondation under grant DCR-8315289.

References

[Blachman 84] N. M. Blachman. The Continued Fraction as an Information Source. *IEEE Transactions on Information Theory*, IT-30(4):671–674, July 1984.

[Hardy and Wright 79] C. H. Hardy and E. M. Wright. *An Introduction to the Theory of Numbers*. Oxford University Press, London, fifth edition, 1979.

[Khinchin 35] A. Y. Khinchin. *Continued Fractions*. The University of Chicago Press, 1935. Translated from Russian by P. Wynn, P. Noordhoff Ltd., Grooningen, 1963. Also by H. Eagle, The University of Chicago Press, 1964.

[Kornerup and Matula 83] P. Kornerup and D. W. Matula. Finite Precision Rational Arithmetic: An Arithmetic Unit. *IEEE Transactions on Computers*, C-32(4):378–387, April 1983.

[Kornerup and Matula 85] P. Kornerup and D. W. Matula. Finite Precision Lexicographic Continued Fraction Number Systems. In *Proc. 7th IEEE Symposium on Computer Arithmetic*, pages 207–214, 1985. Also reprinted in the collection *Computer Arithmetic, Vol II, E.E. Swartzlander, ed.*, IEEE Computer Society Press, Washington, 1990, pages 341-348.

[Kornerup and Matula 88] P. Kornerup and D. W. Matula. An On-line Arithmetic Unit for Bit-Pipelined Rational Arithmetic. *Journal of Parallel and Distributed Computing*, 5(3):310–330, May 1988.

[Kornerup and Matula 90] P. Kornerup and D. W. Matula. An Algorithm for Redundant Binary Bit-Pipelined Rational Arithmetic. *IEEE Transactions on Computers*, C-39(8):1106–1115, August 1990.

[Knuth 81] D. E. Knuth. *Seminumerical Algorithms*, volume 2 of *The Art of Computer Programming*. Addison Wesley, 2 edition, 1981.

[Knuth 82] D. E. Knuth. Supernatural Numbers. *in Mathematical Gardner, D.A. Klarner, ed.*, 1982.

[Matula and Kornerup 80] D. W. Matula and P. Kornerup. Foundations of Finite Precision Rational Arithmetic. *Computing, Suppl. 2*, pages 88–111, February 1980.

[Matula and Kornerup 83] D. W. Matula and P. Kornerup. An Order Preserving Finite Binary Encoding of the Rationals. *Proc. 6th IEEE Symposium on Computer Arithmetic*, pages 201–209, 1983.

Journal of Universal Computer Science, vol. 1, no. 7 (1995), 504-513
submitted: 15/12/94, accepted: 26/6/95, appeared: 28/7/95

Exact Statistics and Continued Fractions

David Lester
dlester@cs.man.ac.uk
Functional Programming Group,
Department of Computer Science, Manchester University,
Oxford Road, Manchester M13 9PL, UK.

Abstract: In this paper we investigate an extension to Vuillemin's work on continued fraction arithmetic [Vuillemin 87, Vuillemin 88, Vuillemin 90], that permits it to evaluate the standard statistical distribution functions. By this we mean: the normal distribution, the χ^2-distribution, the *t*-distribution, and, in particular, the *F*-distribution. The underlying representation of non-rational computable real numbers is also as continued fractions, in the style of Vuillemin. This permits arbitrary accuracy over a range of values. The number of terms of a continued fraction that are used by the implementation is dynamically controlled by the accuracy demanded of the final answer.
The use of a modern lazy functional language – Haskell – has considerably eased the programming task. Two features are of note. Firstly, the *type-class* structure allows one to augment the varieties of numbers supported by the language. Secondly, the *laziness* inherent in the Haskell's semantics, makes it very straightforward to dynamically control the accuracy of the intermediate evaluations.

1 Introduction

In this paper we investigate the use of continued fractions to evaluate the standard statistical distribution functions, by which is meant: the normal distribution, the χ^2-distribution, the *t*-distribution, and the *F*-distribution. The underlying representation of non-rational computable real numbers themselves is also as continued fractions, in the style of Vuillemin [Vuillemin 87, Vuillemin 88, Vuillemin 90].

The novelty of the work presented in the paper lies in the following areas.

- We use Vuillemin's work in a setting (the calculation of the incomplete beta function) which is highly unstable, and demonstrate that his system is feasible.
- We show that three continued fraction expansions, not discussed by Vuillemin, are nevertheless compatible with his system.
- We show that Gauss' continued fraction may be safely used for a range of values besides those already described by Vuillemin.

The use of Vuillemin's system permits arbitrary accuracy over a range of values. The number of terms of the continued fraction that are used by the implementation is dynamically controlled by the accuracy demanded of the final answer. Here, we exploit the Laziness of mordern functional languages – in this case Haskell [Hudak et al 88].

The use of a modern lazy functional language – Haskell – has considerably reduced the amount of code required; currently amounting to just less than 1000 lines. This includes: an implementation of the rationals, Gosper's continued fraction package, Vuillemin's transcendental function package, and the extra functions for the statistical functions. Two further features are of note. Firstly, the *type-class* structure allows one to augment the varieties of numbers supported by the language. Secondly, the laziness inherent in the Haskell's semantics, makes it very straightforward to dynamically control the accuracy of the intermediate evaluations.

The most interesting problems arise whilst considering the incomplete beta function, which is required to implement Fisher's F-distribution [Fisher 22]. Lackritz [Lackritz 84] has provided a simple method of evaluating this distribution, provided we deal only with small integral degrees of freedom ν_1 and ν_2. The complexity of the evaluation of Lackritz's finite series is $O(N^2)$, where $N = \nu_1 + \nu_2$. We therefore require a method for non-integral ν_1 and ν_2 and for those situations where $\nu_1 + \nu_2$ is large, say 10^5 or more.

As Mardia and Zemroch have observed [Mardia and Zemroch 78], we are mainly concerned with rational-valued degrees of freedom when we consider non-parametric statistical testing. That is, we no longer assume that we are sampling from normally distributed populations. Examples are: the Kruskal-Wallis Test [Kruskal and Wallis 52], and Box's test of Homoscedasticity [Box 49].

We begin by considering the continued fractions that we will be using.

2 Continued Fractions

Continued fractions were much favoured by applied mathematicians of previous centuries, because they provided a relatively straightforward calculating procedure in a pre-computer age (see Gauss and Laplace amongst others) [Gauss 1812, Laplace 1805]. The analytic properties of Gauss' work are well described by Wall [Wall 48]. However, with the development of floating point software and hardware, attention shifted away from them.

A number of researchers are undertaking a reappraisal of algorithms associated with continued fractions. These tend to fall into two categories: firstly those using continued fraction algorithms with floating point implementations of real numbers, and secondly, those using continued fractions to represent real numbers. In this paper I shall be using both techniques to outline some extensions to the Haskell [Hudak et al 88] continued fraction package described in [Lester 92] so that it may perform analysis on standard statistical distributions.

In the field of statistical distribution tabulation – and in particular that of the F-distribution – much use has been made of continued fraction algorithms [Tretter and Walster 79, Tretter and Walster 80]. Unfortunately, it is not possible to make naïve use of these continued fractions for floating point calculations, as cancellation of terms results in a fatal loss of accuracy. To this end, Tretter and Walster use MACSYMA to perform symbolic simplifications on their continued fraction. Brown and Levy [Brown 94] use these simplifications to validate DiDonato and Morris' floating point Algorithm 708 for the incomplete beta function [DiDonato and Morris 92], against a Maple implementation.

The use of continued fractions as a representation of real numbers has been facilitated by two developments. Firstly, Gosper has shown how to manipulate continued fraction representions of real numbers to perform basic arithmetic [Gosper 80, Gosper 81]. His work was subsequently extended to deal with transcendental functions by Vuillemin [Vuillemin 87, Vuillemin 88, Vuillemin 90].

We begin with a review of nineteenth century work on continued fraction algorithms.

3 Gauss' Hypergeometric Function

In the impressively titled paper: "*Disquisitiones Generales Circa Seriem Infinitam*

$$1+\frac{\alpha\beta}{1.\gamma}x+\frac{\alpha(\alpha+1)\beta(\beta+1)}{1.2.\gamma(\gamma+1)}xx+\frac{\alpha(\alpha+1)(\alpha+2)\beta(\beta+1)(\beta+2)}{1.2.3.\gamma(\gamma+1)(\gamma+2)}x^3+\text{ etc.}$$

Pars prior" [Gauss 1812], Gauss outlines the properties of the hypergeometric function. Formally, it can be defined by Equation 1[1].

$$_2F_1(\alpha,\beta,\gamma;z)=1+\sum_{n=1}^{\infty}\left(\prod_{i=1}^{n}\frac{(\alpha+i-1)(\beta+i-1)}{i(\gamma+i-1)}\right)z^n \tag{1}$$

This has a circle of convergence $|z|=1$; and its behaviour on this circle is:

- divergence whenever $\Re(\gamma-\alpha-\beta)\leq -1$;
- absolute convergence whenever $\Re(\gamma-\alpha-\beta)>0$;
- conditional convergence whenever $-1<\Re(\gamma-\alpha-\beta)\leq 0$, the point $z=1$ is excluded.

One of the properties mentioned by Gauss, occurs in the second section of his paper, where a continued fraction is defined for the ratio of a pair of hypergeometric functions.

$$\frac{_2F_1(\alpha,\beta+1,\gamma+1;x)}{_2F_1(\alpha,\beta,\gamma;x)}=\left[\frac{1}{1-}\,\frac{ax}{1-}\,\frac{bx}{1-}\,\frac{cx}{1-}\,\frac{dx}{1-}\cdots\right] \tag{2}$$

Where

$$a=\frac{\alpha(\gamma-\beta)}{\gamma(\gamma+1)}\qquad b=\frac{(\beta+1)(\gamma+1-\alpha)}{(\gamma+1)(\gamma+2)}\quad c=\frac{(\alpha+1)(\gamma+1-\beta)}{(\gamma+2)(\gamma+3)}$$

$$d=\frac{(\beta+2)(\gamma+2-\alpha)}{(\gamma+3)(\gamma+4)}\quad e=\frac{(\alpha+2)(\gamma+2-\beta)}{(\gamma+4)(\gamma+5)}\quad f=\frac{(\beta+3)(\gamma+3-\alpha)}{(\gamma+5)(\gamma+6)}$$

and, as Gauss observes: "*cuius lex progressionis obvia est*".

On its own, Equation 2 is not too useful; what we really require is not a continued fraction for a ratio of hypergeometric functions, but one for an individual function. Observe what happens when we substitute $\beta=0$ into Equation 2: the numerator becomes $_2F_1(\alpha,0,\gamma;x)$, which is 1. Hence Gauss provides a continued fraction expansion for $_2F_1(\alpha,1,\gamma;x)$.

Suitably massaged, this continued fraction can be represented as a potentially infinite sequence of rationals. The sequence will terminate if one of α, γ, or $\gamma-\alpha$ is a negative integer or 0.

$$_2F_1(\alpha,1,\gamma+1;x)=\left[\frac{1}{1-}\,\frac{ax}{1-}\,\frac{bx}{1-}\,\frac{cx}{1-}\,\frac{dx}{1-}\cdots\right] \tag{3}$$

[1] Here, and throughout, we shall refer to the Hypergeometric function as $_2F_1(\alpha,\beta,\gamma;x)$. The leading 2 subscript refers to the two parameters forming the numerator of each coefficient (α and β), and the 1 subscript refers to the one parameter associated with the denominator of each coefficient (γ).

where

$$a = \frac{\alpha\gamma}{\gamma(\gamma+1)} \qquad b = \frac{1(\gamma+1-\alpha)}{(\gamma+1)(\gamma+2)} \; c = \frac{(\alpha+1)(\gamma+1)}{(\gamma+2)(\gamma+3)}$$

$$d = \frac{2(\gamma+2-\alpha)}{(\gamma+3)(\gamma+4)} \; \epsilon = \frac{(\alpha+2)(\gamma+2)}{(\gamma+4)(\gamma+5)} \; f = \frac{3(\gamma+3-\alpha)}{(\gamma+5)(\gamma+6)}$$

In Haskell, we can express Gauss' continued fraction (for rational parameters **a** and **c**) as **gauss1CF a c** which is ${}_2F_1(\mathbf{a}, 1, \mathbf{c}; 1)$.

```
> gauss1CF :: QRational -> QRational -> [QRational]
> gauss1CF a c
>   = 0: 1: c/a: a*(c+1)/ca: cf (ca/(a*(a+1)*c)) 0
>     where cf :: QRational -> Integer -> [QRational]
>           cf p n = (c+(2*n+2)%%1)*p:
>                    (c+(2*n+3)%%1)/(p*(ca+n1)*n2):
>                    cf (p*(ca+n1)*n2/((a+n2)*(c+n1))) (n+1)
>                    where n1 = fromInteger (n+1) :: QRational
>                          n2 = fromInteger (n+2) :: QRational
>           ca = c-a
```

To evaluate ${}_2F_1(a, 1, c; x)$ at a particular value of x we simply divide alternate terms of **gauss1CF** by $-x$, evaluate the resultant continued fraction, and multiply this result by $\frac{-1}{x}$. This can be made to work for real valued x not just rational values.

3.1 Kummer's Confluent Hypergeometric Function

If, in the definition of the hypergeometric function, we let $\beta \to \infty$ as $x \to \frac{x}{\beta}$ we obtain Kummer's Function.

$$ {}_1F_1(\alpha, \gamma; z) = \lim_{\beta\to\infty} {}_2F_1(\alpha, \beta, \gamma; \frac{z}{\beta}) = 1 + \sum_{n=1}^{\infty} \left(\prod_{i=1}^{n} \frac{(\alpha + i - 1)}{i(\gamma + i - 1)} \right) z^n \qquad (4)$$

For our purposes, it suffices to consider ${}_1F_1(\alpha, \gamma; z)$, with $\alpha = 1$ and $\gamma \geq 1$. Given the value of γ we may calculate ${}_1F_1(1, \gamma; 1)$ as **phiCF1** γ.

```
> phiCF1 :: QRational -> [QRational]
> phiCF1 c
>   = 0: 1: cf (-1%%1) 0
>     where cf :: QRational -> Integer -> [QRational]
>           cf p n = (c+fromInteger (2*n)) * p :
>                    ((c+fromInteger (2*n+1)) /
>                              (p*fromInteger n')):
>                    cf p' n'
>                    where p' = -p * (1/c')* fromInteger n'
>                          n' = n+1
>                          c' = c + fromInteger n
```

Once more the calculation of ${}_1F_1(1, \gamma; z)$ involves dividing alternate terms by z and dividing the result by z.

4 The Normal Distribution

This, the simplest of the standard statistical distribution functions we shall consider, is defined as the integral in Equation 5.

$$\Phi(x) = \frac{1}{\sqrt{2\pi}} \int_{-\infty}^{x} e^{-\frac{1}{2}x^2}\, dx \tag{5}$$

To obtain a continued fraction, we need to consider the *Mills' ratio*, of Equation 6.

$$R(x) = \frac{1-\Phi(x)}{\Phi'(x)} = e^{\frac{1}{2}x^2} \int_{x}^{\infty} e^{-\frac{1}{2}x^2}\, dx \tag{6}$$

Laplace was the first to give a continued fraction for this function in [Laplace 1805]. It occurred as a rejected hypothesis for the thermally induced atmospheric distortion that the astronomers of the day were observing.

$$R(x) = \left[\frac{1}{x+}\ \frac{1}{x+}\ \frac{2}{x+}\ \frac{3}{x+}\ \cdots\ \frac{n}{x+}\ \cdots \right] \tag{7}$$

This continued fraction – Equation 7 – suffers from a low rate of convergence for small x. For this reason we use Shenton's continued fraction – Equation 8 – instead [Shenton 54].

$$\bar{R}(x) = \sqrt{\frac{\pi}{2}} e^{\frac{1}{2}x^2} - R(x) = \left[\frac{x}{1-}\ \frac{x^2}{3+}\ \frac{2x^2}{5-}\ \frac{3x^2}{7+}\ \cdots \right] \tag{8}$$

Once more, this algorithm will work for x represented as a continued fraction as well as rational x.

Oddly enough, the most expensive part of the calculation involves the calculation of $\sqrt{\pi}$ = `exp (log pi/2)` rather than that of the Mills' ratio. Since $\Gamma(\frac{1}{2}) = \sqrt{\pi}$, this leads nicely into the next section, where we obtain a more efficient algorithm to perform this calculation.

5 The Gamma Function

The *Gamma function* $\Gamma(\alpha)$ is Euler's generalization of the factorial function on integers. Although we won't be using it at complex values, this function is analytic over the entire complex plane, except at the points $\alpha = 0, -1, -2, \ldots$. It can be defined by the integral given in Equation 9.

$$\Gamma(\alpha) = \int_{0}^{\infty} x^{\alpha-1} e^{-x}\, dx \tag{9}$$

Provided that $|\alpha|$ is reasonably small, *i.e.* less than 10^5, the first part of the implementation uses Equation 10 to adjust the value of α to lie within $0 < \alpha < 2$.

$$\Gamma(\alpha+1) = \alpha\Gamma(\alpha) \tag{10}$$

Clearly, if α is one of $0, -1, -2, \ldots$, then we will be using the formula in reverse and will eventually end by dividing by zero.

Associated with the Gamma function are the pair of *incomplete Gamma functions* : $\gamma(\alpha, x)$ and $\Gamma(\alpha, x)$ defined in Equations 11 and 12.

$$\gamma(\alpha, x) = \int_0^x x^{\alpha-1}\epsilon^{-x}dx \qquad \text{for } 0 \leq x \tag{11}$$

$$\Gamma(\alpha, x) = \int_x^\infty x^{\alpha-1}\epsilon^{-x}dx \qquad \text{for } 0 < x \tag{12}$$

Obviously the following relation holds between the incomplete Gamma functions and the Gamma function proper.

$$\Gamma(\alpha) = \gamma(\alpha, x) + \Gamma(\alpha, x) \qquad \text{for } 0 < x \tag{13}$$

For this to be a viable exact method for the calculation of $\Gamma(x)$ we seek continued fraction expansions for $\gamma(\alpha, x)$ and $\Gamma(\alpha, x)$; these are given in Equations 14 and 15.

$$\gamma(\alpha, x) = \frac{x^\alpha \epsilon^{-x}}{\alpha}\, {}_1F_1(1, \alpha + 1, x) \qquad \text{for } 0 < x \tag{14}$$

Recall that ${}_1F_1$ is the confluent hypergeometric function of Kummer.

$$\Gamma(\alpha, x) = x^\alpha \epsilon^{-x} \left[\frac{1}{x+}\ \frac{1-\alpha}{1+}\ \frac{1}{x+}\ \frac{2-\alpha}{1+}\ \frac{2}{x+}\ \cdots\right] \qquad \text{for } 0 < x \tag{15}$$

In particular, for computational purposes we select $x = 1$. This eliminates the need to calculate x^α – which given that both α and x might, in general, not be integral – leads to a considerable optimization.

$$\Gamma(\alpha) = \epsilon^{-1}\left(\frac{1}{\alpha}\, {}_1F_1(1, \alpha + 1, 1) + \left[\frac{1}{1+}\ \frac{1-\alpha}{1+}\ \frac{1}{1+}\ \frac{2-\alpha}{1+}\ \frac{2}{1+}\ \cdots\right]\right) \tag{16}$$

As a corollary we can compute the *Beta function* $B(p, q)$ which is defined as:

$$B(p, q) = \frac{\Gamma(p)\Gamma(q)}{\Gamma(p+q)} \tag{17}$$

One optimization that is possible in the calculation of $B(p, q)$, is to avoid two of the divisions by ϵ.

The problem with direct use of Equation 17 occurs when p and q are both large – say 10^{50} and 10^{49}. In these circumstances it is no longer practical to use the recurrence relations to simplify the gamma functions. We will explore an alternative at the end of Section 7.

6 The χ^2-Distribution

One direct use that can be made of our work on the Γ functions is that it is now very easy to generate exact values for the χ^2-distribution.

$$Q(\chi^2, \nu) = 1 - \frac{\gamma(\frac{\nu}{2}, \frac{\chi^2}{2})}{\Gamma(\frac{\nu}{2})} \qquad \text{where } 0 \leq \chi^2 \text{ and } 0 < \nu \tag{18}$$

Notice that for small positive integral values of $\frac{\nu}{2}$, we may use the alternative definition of Equation 19.

$$Q(\chi^2, \nu) = \frac{\Gamma(\frac{\nu}{2}, \frac{\chi^2}{2})}{(\frac{\nu}{2} - 1)!} \tag{19}$$

Expanding the continued fraction of Equation 15 results in the finite series of Lackritz [Lackritz 83].

7 The F-distribution

There are some interesting features in the calculation of the F-distribution. For example, Mardia and Zemroch [Mardia and Zemroch 78] show that $F = 8.4872 \times 10^{78}$ to obtain $Q(F, 120, 0.1) = 0.0001$. This value of F is, curiously, close to the limit of the maximum floating point number available on their machine. The points at which Brown and Levy [Brown 94] were able to test DiDonato and Morris' algorithm was also artificially restricted, by floating point limitations in their generation routine.

In [Lackritz 84] Lackritz shows how to obtain exact p values for F and t tests, provided that we are dealing with small integral valued degrees of freedom. The following approach gives exact results for rational valued degrees of freedom.

We begin with a definition: the probability of random variable – F-distributed with ν_1 and ν_2 degrees of freedom – being greater than F is $Q(F|\nu_1, \nu_2)$, defined in Equation 20

$$Q(F|\nu_1, \nu_2) = I_x(\frac{\nu_2}{2}, \frac{\nu_1}{2}) \qquad \text{where } x = \frac{\nu_2}{\nu_2 + \nu_1 F} \text{ and } 0 \leq F,\ 0 < \nu_i \tag{20}$$

The normalized incomplete beta function: $I_x(p, q)$, is given in Equation 21.

$$I_x(p, q) = \frac{B_x(p, q)}{B(p, q)} \tag{21}$$

The incomplete beta function is related to Guass' Hypergeometric in Equation 22.

$$B_x(p, q) = \frac{x^p}{p}\ {}_2F_1(p, 1 - q, p + 1; x) \tag{22}$$

However, using one of Gauss' transformations:

$${}_2F_1(\alpha, \beta, \gamma; x) = (1 - x)^{-\beta}\ {}_2F_1(\beta, \gamma - \beta, \gamma; \frac{x}{x - 1})$$

we obtain:

$$B_x(p,q) = \frac{x^p(1-x)^{q-1}}{p} \, {}_2F_1(1-q,1,p+1;\frac{x}{x-1}) \tag{23}$$

Expanding the hypergeometric function yields Equation 23 which is essentially the continued fraction of Mueller.

The use of this continued fraction is limited to those cases where $-1 \leq \frac{x}{x-1} < 1$ in order that the argument may lie within the radius of convergence of Gauss' Hypergeometric continued fraction. To ensure that this remains the case, whenever $x > \frac{1}{2}$ we use the reflection property of Equation 24.

$$I_x(p,q) = 1 - I_{1-x}(q,p) \tag{24}$$

It is possible – for large values of p and q ($> 10^5$) – for the method of calculating $B(p,q)$ to become too time consuming. For this reason, an alternative exact method for calculating $B(p,q)$ is required.

7.1 Student's *t*-Distribution

This is merely a special case of the *F*-distribution.

$$A(t|\nu) = 1 - I_x(\frac{\nu}{2},\frac{1}{2}) \quad \text{where} x = \frac{\nu}{\nu+t^2} \text{ and } \nu > 0 \tag{25}$$

Once more, care needs to be taken to ensure that the value of x lies in the range $0 \leq x \leq \frac{1}{2}$. If it doesn't we must use the reflection formula of Equation 24.

8 Conclusion and Further Work

In this paper we have shown how to extend Vuillemin's work on continued fraction arithmetic [Vuillemin 87, Vuillemin 88, Vuillemin 90], to the evaluation of the standard statistical distribution functions. The number of terms of a continued fraction that are used is dynamically controlled by the accuracy demanded of the final answer.

Two features of Haskell have proved particularly helpful. Firstly, the *type-class* structure allows one to augment the varieties of numbers supported by the language. Secondly, the *laziness* inherent in the Haskell's semantics, makes it very straightforward to dynamically control the accuracy of the intermediate evaluations.

We have shown how to use Tretter and Walsters' continued fraction to evaluate the incomplete beta function [Tretter and Walster 79, Tretter and Walster 80]. DiDonato and Morris incorporate various improvements in their algorithm, but admit that, for small values of p and q their continued fraction requires many terms of the continued fraction to be evaluated [DiDonato and Morris 92]. Our implementation is capable of handling this problem, albeit at reduced speed.

The principle outstanding problem we have is when p and q are large; then the calculation of $B(p,q)$ becomes inordinately expensive. We are able to work with values of p and q less than 10^5. Improving this requires that we are able to give an *exact* value for the log Gamma function $\ln(\Gamma(1+\alpha))$.

Another avenue of investigation lies with the calculation of the probabilities associated with the non-central χ^2- and *F*-distributions.

References

[Box 49] G.E.P. Box. A general distribution theory for a class of likelihood criteria. *Biometrika*, 36:317–346, 1949.

[Brown 94] B.W. Brown and L.B. Levy. Certification of algorithm 708: Significant digit computation of the incomplete beta function ratios. *ACM Transactions on Mathematical Software*, 20(3):393–397, September 1994.

[DiDonato and Morris 92] A.R. DiDonato and A.H. Morris, Jr. Algorithm 708: Significant digit computation of the incomplete beta function ratios. *ACM Transactions on Mathematical Software*, 18(3):360–373, September 1992.

[Fisher 22] R.A. Fisher. The goodness of fit of regression formulae and distribution of regression coefficients. *Journal of the Royal Statistical Society*, 85:597–612, 1922.

[Gauss 1812] C.F. Gauss. Disquisitiones generales circa serium infinitam $1+\frac{\alpha\beta}{1\,.\,\gamma}x+\frac{\alpha(\alpha+1)\beta(\beta+1)}{1\,.\,2\,.\,\gamma(\gamma+1)}xx+\frac{\alpha(\alpha+1)(\alpha+2)\beta(\beta+1)(\beta+2)}{1\,.\,2\,.\,3\,.\,\gamma(\gamma+1)(\gamma+2)}x^3$ etc. pars prior. In *Werke*, volume 3, pages 123–162. Königlichen Gesellschaft der Wissenschaften, Göttingen, 1812.

[Gosper 80] R.W. Gosper. Continued fraction arithmetic. HAKMEM 101b, MIT, 1980.

[Gosper 81] R.W. Gosper. Continued fraction arithmetic. Unpublished Draft Paper, 1981.

[Gradshteyn and Ryzhik 94] I.S. Gradshteyn and I.M. Ryzhik. *Table of Integrals, Series, and Products.* Academic Press, Inc. (London) Ltd., 24/28 Oval Road, London NW1 7DX, 5th edition, 1994.

[Hudak et al 88] P. Hudak, P. Wadler, Arvind, B. Boutel, J. Fairbairn, J. Fasel, J. Hughes, T. Johnsson, D. Kieburtz, S. Peyton Jones, R. Nikhil, M. Reeve, D. Wise, and J. Young. Report on the functional programming language Haskell. Draft Proposed Standard, 18th December 1988.

[Kruskal and Wallis 52] W.H. Kruskal and W.A. Wallis. The use of ranks in one-criterion variance analysis. *Journal of the American Statistical Society*, 47:583–621, 1952.

[Lackritz 83] J.R. Lackritz. Exact *p*-values for Chi-Squared tests. In *Proceedings of the Section on Statistical Education*, pages 130–132. American Statistical Association, 1983.

[Lackritz 84] J.R. Lackritz. Exact p values for f and t tests. *The American Statistician*, 38(4):312–314, November 1984.

[Laplace 1805] P.S. Laplace. *Traité de Mécanique Céleste*, volume 4. Chez Courcier, Imprimeur-Libraire pour les Mathématiques, 71 Quai des Augustins, Paris, 1805.

[Lester 92] D.R. Lester. Vuillemin's exact real arithmetic. In R. Heldal, C.K. Holst, and P. Wadler, editors, *Functional Programming, Glasgow 1991*, pages 225–238, London, 1992. Springer-Verlag.

[Mardia and Zemroch 78] K.V. Mardia and P.J. Zemroch. *Tables of the F- and related Distributions with Algorithms.* Academic Press Inc. (London) Ltd., 24/28 Oval Road, London NW1 7DX, 1978.

[Shenton 54] L.R. Shenton. Inequalities for the normal integral including a new continued fraction. *Biometrika*, 41:177–189, 1954.

[Tretter and Walster 79] M.J. Tretter and G.W. Walster. Continued fractions for the incomplete beta function: Additions and corrections. *The Annals of Statistics*, 7(2):462–465, 1979.

[Tretter and Walster 80] M.J. Tretter and G.W. Walster. Analytic subtraction applied to the incomplete gamma and beta functions. *SIAM Journal on Scientific Statistical Computing*, 1(3):321–326, September 1980.

[Vuillemin 87] J. Vuillemin. Arithmétic réelle exacte par les fractions continues. Technical Report 760, Instituit National de Recherche en Informatique et en Automatique, Domaine de Voluceau, Roquencourt, BP105, 78153 Le Chesnay Cedex, France, November 1987.

[Vuillemin 88] J. Vuillemin. Exact real computer arithmetic with continued fractions. In *Proceedings of the 1988 ACM Conference on Lisp and Functional Programming*, pages 14–27, Snowbird, Utah, 25–27 July 1988.

[Vuillemin 90] J.E. Vuillemin. Exact Real Computer Arithmetic with Continued Fractions. *IEEE Transactions on Computers*, 39(8):1087–1105, August 1990.

[Wall 48] H.S. Wall. *Analytic Theory of Continued Fractions*. Van Nostrand, Inc., 250 Fourth Avenue, New York 3, 1948.

Journal of Universal Computer Science, vol. 1, no. 7 (1995), 514-526
submitted: 15/12/94, accepted: 26/6/95, appeared: 28/7/95

On directed interval arithmetic and its applications

Svetoslav Markov
(Bulgarian Academy of Sciences, Bulgaria
smarkov@bgearn.acad.bg)

Abstract: We discuss two closely related interval arithmetic systems: i) the system of directed (generalized) intervals studied by E. Kaucher, and ii) the system of normal intervals together with the outer and inner interval operations. A relation between the two systems becomes feasible due to introduction of special notations and a so-called normal form of directed intervals. As an application, it has been shown that both interval systems can be used for the computation of tight inner and outer inclusions of ranges of functions and consequently for the development of software for automatic computation of ranges of functions.

Key Words: computer arithmetic, error analysis, interval algebraic manipulation
Category: G.1.0, I.1.1

1 Introduction

We briefly recall some well-known facts about the interval arithmetic for compact intervals on the real line $\mathbf{R}$. Given $a^{(-)}, a^{(+)} \in \mathbf{R}$, with $a^{(-)} \leq a^{(+)}$, a (proper) interval is defined by $[a^{(-)}, a^{(+)}] = \{x \mid a^{(-)} \leq x \leq a^{(+)}\}$. The set of all intervals is denoted by $I(\mathbf{R})$. Thus $a^{(s)} \in \mathbf{R}$ with $s \in \Lambda = \{+,-\}$ is the left or right endpoint of $A \in I(\mathbf{R})$ depending on the value of s. In what follows the binary variable s will be sometimes expressed as a product of two binary variables from Λ, defined by $++ = -- = +$, $+- = -+ = -$. An interval $A = [a^{(-)}, a^{(+)}]$ with $a^{(-)} = a^{(+)}$ is called degenerate.

Let $A = [a^{(-)}, a^{(+)}]$, $B = [b^{(-)}, b^{(+)}] \in I(\mathbf{R})$. Inclusion in $I(\mathbf{R})$ has the well-known set-theoretic meaning. In terms of the end-points we have

$$A \subseteq B \Longleftrightarrow (b^{(-)} \leq a^{(-)}) \wedge (a^{(+)} \leq b^{(+)}), \quad A, B \in I(\mathbf{R}).$$

Denote $Z = \{A \in I(\mathbf{R}) \mid a^{(-)} \leq 0 \leq a^{(+)}\}$, $Z^* = \{A \in I(\mathbf{R}) \mid a^{(-)} < 0 < a^{(+)}\}$, $I(\mathbf{R})^* = I(\mathbf{R}) \setminus Z^*$. The function "sign" $\sigma : I(\mathbf{R})^* \rightarrow \Lambda$ is defined for $A \in I(\mathbf{R})^* \setminus \{0\}$ with $\sigma(A) = \{+, \text{ if } a^- \geq 0;\ -, \text{ if } a^+ \leq 0\}$, and for zero argument by $\sigma([0,0]) = \sigma(0) = +$. In particular, σ is well defined over $\mathbf{R}$. The sign σ is not defined for intervals from Z^*. Note that the intervals from Z^* comprise both positive and negative numbers.

The operations $+, -, \times, /$ are defined by

$$A * B = \{a * b \mid a \in A, b \in B\},\ * \in \{+, -, \times, /\},\ A, B \in I(\mathbf{R}), \tag{1}$$

assuming in the case "$* = /$" that $B \in I(\mathbf{R}) \setminus Z$ [Moore 1966], [Sunaga 1958]. The following expressions hold true for $A = [a^{(-)}, a^{(+)}]$, $B = [b^{(-)}, b^{(+)}]$

$$A + B = [a^{(-)} + b^{(-)},\ a^{(+)} + b^{(+)}],\ A, B \in I(\mathbf{R}), \tag{2}$$

$$A \times B = \begin{cases} [a^{(-\sigma(B))}b^{(-\sigma(A))},\ a^{(\sigma(B))}b^{(\sigma(A))}], & A, B \in I(\mathbf{R})^*, \\ [a^{(\delta)}b^{(-\delta)},\ a^{(\delta)}b^{(\delta)}], \quad \delta = \sigma(A), & A \in I(\mathbf{R})^*,\ B \in Z^*, \\ [a^{(-\delta)}b^{(\delta)},\ a^{(\delta)}b^{(\delta)}], \quad \delta = \sigma(B), & A \in Z^*,\ B \in I(\mathbf{R})^*, \end{cases} \tag{3}$$

$$A \times B = [\min\{a^{(-)}b^{(+)}, a^{(+)}b^{(-)}\},\ \max\{a^{(-)}b^{(-)}, a^{(+)}b^{(+)}\}],\quad A, B \in Z^*, \tag{4}$$

$$1/B = [1/b^{(+)}, 1/b^{(-)}],\ B \in I(\mathbf{R}) \setminus Z. \tag{5}$$

For a degenerate interval $A = [a, a] = a \in R$, expression (3) gives $a \times B = [ab^{(-\sigma(a))},\ ab^{(\sigma(a))}]$. For $a = -1$ we obtain the operator negation $(-1) \times B = -B = [-b^{(+)}, -b^{(-)}]$. The operations subtraction and division defined by (1) can be expressed as composite operations by $A - B = A + (-B)$, $A/B = A \times (1/B)$. In terms of end-points we have

$$A - B = [a^{(-)} - b^{(+)}, a^{(+)} - b^{(-)}],\ A, B \in I(\mathbf{R}), \tag{6}$$

$$A/B = \begin{cases} [a^{(-\sigma(B))}/b^{(\sigma(A))}, a^{(\sigma(B))}/b^{(-\sigma(A))}], & A \in I(\mathbf{R})^*, B \in I(\mathbf{R}) \setminus Z, \\ [a^{(-\delta)}/b^{(-\delta)}, a^{(\delta)}/b^{(-\delta)}], \quad \delta = \sigma(B), & A \in Z^*, B \in I(\mathbf{R}) \setminus Z. \end{cases} \tag{7}$$

The algebraic properties of $(I(\mathbf{R}), +, \times, /, \subseteq)$ are studied in [Moore 1966], [Ratschek 1969], [Ratschek 1972], [Sunaga 1958]. The subsystems $(I(\mathbf{R}), +)$, $(I(\mathbf{R})^*, \times)$ are commutative semigroups. They are not groups, that is no inverse elements w. r. t. the operations $+$, resp. $\times$ exist in general. The solutions of the equations $A + X = B$, resp. $A \times X = B$ (if existing), cannot be expressed in terms of the interval operations (1). There is no distributivity between $+$ and $\times$, except for very special cases. The interval operations (1) can be used for outer inclusions of functional ranges (which can be rough). They are of little use for the computation of inner inclusions.

The above mentioned "deficiencies" of the system $(I(\mathbf{R}), +)$ are due to our incomplete knowledge of the interval arithmetic system. The algebraic manipulations in the set $I(\mathbf{R})$ of (proper) intervals resamble the algebraic manipulations in the set $\mathbf{R}^+ = \{x \in \mathbf{R}, x \geq 0\}$ of positive numbers. The equality $a + x = b$ possess no solution in $\mathbf{R}^+$ for $a > b$. Similarly, the equality $A + X = B$ has no solution in $I(\mathbf{R})$ if the width of A is greater than the width of B. Similarly to the algebraic completion of the set $\mathbf{R}^+$ by negative numbers (or to the completion of the reals by complex numbers), the set $I(\mathbf{R})$ can be completed by so-called *improper* intervals, having their left "end-points" greater that the right ones. The algebraic completion of $(I(\mathbf{R}), +)$ leads to a set D of *directed* (or *generalized*) intervals, which is suitable for solving interval algebraic problems. An isomorphic extension of the interval operations over D produces the system $\mathcal{K} = (D, +, \times)$, where the operations " $+$ " and " $\times$ " possess group properties [Dimitrova et al. 1991]–[Kaucher 1980], [Markov 1992]–[Markov 1993], [Shary 1993], [Shary 1995]. However, we must learn to solve algebraic problems with directed intervals and to interpret the solutions in case we need realistic solutions, that is, proper intervals, in the same way as mathematicians have learned to solve algebraic problems using real numbers (positive and negative), or later on using complex numbers.

This paper serves for a further development of the algebraic manipulation in the set of directed intervals and the interpretation of the obtained results in the set of proper intervals. We briefly introduce the system $\mathcal{K}$ using two forms of presentation for the elements of D – *component-wise* (already used by other authors) and *normal*. It has been demonstrated that the normal form actually generates two types of operations between normal intervals – the first type are the usual operations (1), which are also called "outer" interval operations and the second type are the "inner" (or "nonstandard") interval operations. The set of normal intervals together with the set of outer and inner operations $\mathcal{M} = (I(\mathbf{R}), +, +^-, \times, \times^-)$ presents an algebraic completion of the familiar interval arithmetic $(I(\mathbf{R}), +)$, which opposite to $\mathcal{K}$ makes no use of improper elements [Markov 1977]–[Markov 1992]. It has been shown that the two systems $\mathcal{K}$ and $\mathcal{M}$ are closely related and that the understanding of the relation between them can greatly increase the scope of applications of interval arithmetic. An efficient relation between the two systems becomes feasible due to the introduction of special ($\pm$)-type notations and a so-called normal form of directed intervals. The new uniform notations make it possible to develop in a consistent way software implementations of all important interval arithmetic systems and to incorporate them in a software environment supporting symbolic computations. Such an unification will be facilitated by the fact that interval algebraic relations become simple with the new notational approach. Both $\mathcal{K}$ and $\mathcal{M}$ can be used for the construction of tight inner and outer inclusions of ranges of functions, which is one of the most important application of interval arithmetic. This is shown in the last section of the paper, where several propositions are formulated that can be directly applied to the development of algorithms for automatic computation of ranges of functions [Corliss and Rall 1991]. Another vast field of applications of the interval systems $\mathcal{K}$ and $\mathcal{M}$ is the solution of algebraic problems involving interval data, where the system $\mathcal{K}$ plays an important role in the formal algebraic manipulations, whereas the system $\mathcal{M}$ can be used for the interpretation of the results in terms of proper intervals (if necessary).

2 Directed intervals and operations over them

We extend the set $I(\mathbf{R})$ up to the set $D = \{[a, b] \mid a, b \in \mathbf{R}\}$ of ordered couples. To avoid confusion with the normal intervals from $I(\mathbf{R})$, we call the elements of D directed or generalized intervals and their "endpoints" will be called components. The first component of $\mathbf{A} \in D$ is denoted by a^-, and the second by a^+, so that $\mathbf{A} = [a^-, a^+]$. The absence of brackets around + and − in this notation suggests that the inequality $a^- \leq a^+$ is not obligatory (as in the case with the endpoints of the proper intervals: $a^{(-)} \leq a^{(+)}$). Every directed interval $\mathbf{A} = [a^-, a^+] \in D$ defines a binary variable "direction" by

$$\tau(\mathbf{A}) = \sigma(a^+ - a^-) = \begin{cases} +, & \text{if } a^- \leq a^+, \\ -, & \text{if } a^- > a^+. \end{cases}$$

The set of all elements of D with positive direction, that is the set of proper intervals, is equivalent to $I(\mathbf{R})$; the set of directed intervals with negative direction, further called improper intervals, will be denoted by $\overline{I(\mathbf{R})}$, so that $D = I(\mathbf{R}) \cup \overline{I(\mathbf{R})}$. To every directed interval $\mathbf{A} = [a^-, a^+] \in D$ we assign a proper interval pro($\mathbf{A}$) with

$$\mathrm{pro}(\mathbf{A}) = \begin{cases} [a^-, a^+], & \text{if } \tau(\mathbf{A}) = +, \\ [a^+, a^-], & \text{if } \tau(\mathbf{A}) = -. \end{cases}$$

We have $\operatorname{pro}(\mathbf{A}) = [a^{-\tau(\mathbf{A})}, a^{\tau(\mathbf{A})}]$. Instead of $\operatorname{pro}(\mathbf{A})$ we shall also write A, if no ambiguity occurs. The interval A will be further called the projection of $\mathbf{A}$ on the set of proper intervals or, briefly, the proper projection of $\mathbf{A}$.

Denote $\overline{Z} = \{\mathbf{A} \in \overline{I(\mathbf{R})} \mid a^+ \leq 0 \leq a^-\}$, $\overline{Z}^* = \{\mathbf{A} \in \overline{I(\mathbf{R})} \mid a^+ < 0 < a^-\}$, $\mathcal{T} = Z \cup \overline{Z} = \{\mathbf{A} \in D \mid 0 \in \operatorname{pro}(\mathbf{A})\}$, $\mathcal{T}^* = Z^* \cup \overline{Z}^* = \{\mathbf{A} \in \mathcal{T} \mid (a^- < 0 < a^+) \vee (a^+ < 0 < a^-)\}$. In $D^* = D \setminus \mathcal{T}^*$ we define the function "sign" of a directed interval $\sigma : D^* \to \Lambda$, by $\sigma(\mathbf{A}) = \sigma(\operatorname{pro}(\mathbf{A}))$ (note that $\operatorname{pro}(\mathbf{A}) \in I(\mathbf{R})^*$ for $\mathbf{A} \in D^*$).

The formal substitution of components for end-points and the replacement of $I(\mathbf{R})^*$ and Z^* by D^* and $\mathcal{T}^*$, resp. in (2)–(3) extends the definitions of the operations $+$, $\times$ from $I(\mathbf{R})$ up to D:

$$\mathbf{A} + \mathbf{B} = [a^- + b^-, a^+ + b^+], \quad \mathbf{A}, \mathbf{B} \in D, \tag{8}$$

$$\mathbf{A} \times \mathbf{B} = \begin{cases} [a^{-\sigma(B)} b^{-\sigma(A)},\ a^{\sigma(B)} b^{\sigma(A)}], & \mathbf{A}, \mathbf{B} \in D^*, \\ [a^{\delta} b^{-\delta},\ a^{\delta} b^{\delta}],\ \ \delta = \sigma(A), & \mathbf{A} \in D^*,\ \mathbf{B} \in \mathcal{T}^*, \\ [a^{-\delta} b^{\delta},\ a^{\delta} b^{\delta}],\ \ \delta = \sigma(B), & \mathbf{A} \in \mathcal{T}^*,\ \mathbf{B} \in D^*. \end{cases} \tag{9}$$

The product $\mathbf{A} \times \mathbf{B}$ is defined for $\mathbf{A}, \mathbf{B} \in \mathcal{T}^*$ by

$$\mathbf{A} \times \mathbf{B} = \begin{cases} [\min\{a^- b^+, a^+ b^-\},\ \max\{a^- b^-, a^+ b^+\}], & \mathbf{A}, \mathbf{B} \in Z^*, \\ [\max\{a^- b^-, a^+ b^+\},\ \min\{a^- b^+, a^+ b^-\}], & \mathbf{A}, \mathbf{B} \in \overline{Z}^*, \\ 0, \quad (\mathbf{A} \in Z^*,\ \mathbf{B} \in \overline{Z}^*) \vee (\mathbf{A} \in \overline{Z}^*,\ \mathbf{B} \in Z^*). \end{cases} \tag{10}$$

It has been shown that the spaces $(I(\mathbf{R}), +)$ and $(I(\mathbf{R}) \setminus Z, \times)$ are isomorphic embeddments in the spaces $(D, +)$, resp. $(D \setminus \mathcal{T}, \times)$ under the operations (8)–(10) [Kaucher 1980]. E. Kaucher gives a table form expression for the multiplication, which is equivalent to (9)–(10).

From (9) for $\mathbf{A} = [a, a] = a$, $\mathbf{B} \in D$ we have $a \times \mathbf{B} = [ab^{-\sigma(a)}, ab^{\sigma(a)}]$. This implies for the operator negation: $\operatorname{neg}(\mathbf{B}) = -\mathbf{B} = (-1) \times \mathbf{B} = [-b^+, -b^-]$. The composite operation $\mathbf{A} + (-1) \times \mathbf{B} = \mathbf{A} + (-\mathbf{B}) = [a^- - b^+, a^+ - b^-]$, for $\mathbf{A}, \mathbf{B} \in D$ is an extension in D of the subtraction $A - B$ and will be further denoted $\mathbf{A} - \mathbf{B}$ as in (6).

The systems $(D, +)$ and $(D \setminus \mathcal{T}, \times)$ are groups [Kaucher 1977], [Kaucher 1980]. Denote by $-_h \mathbf{A}$ the inverse element of $\mathbf{A} \in D$ with respect to "$+$", and by $1/_h \mathbf{A}$ the inverse element of $\mathbf{A} \in D \setminus \mathcal{T}$ with respect to "$\times$". For the inverse elements we have the component-wise presentations $-_h \mathbf{A} = [-a^-, -a^+]$, for $\mathbf{A} \in D$, and $1/_h \mathbf{A} = [1/a^-, 1/a^+]$, for $\mathbf{A} \in D \setminus \mathcal{T}$. The element $-_h \mathbf{A}$ is further called the *opposite* of $\mathbf{A}$ and the element $1/_h \mathbf{A}$ — the *inverse* of $\mathbf{A}$, symbolically $\operatorname{opp}(\mathbf{A}) = -_h \mathbf{A}$, $\operatorname{inv}(\mathbf{A}) = 1/_h \mathbf{A}$.

An important operator in D is the operator *dual element* defined by $\operatorname{dual}(\mathbf{A}) = \operatorname{dual}([a^-, a^+]) = [a^+, a^-]$. The operators negation $-\mathbf{A} = [-a^+, -a^-]$, opposite element $-_h \mathbf{A} = [-a^-, -a^+]$ and dual element $\operatorname{dual}(\mathbf{A} = [a^+, a^-]$ are interrelated by:

$$\operatorname{dual}(\mathbf{A}) = -_h(-\mathbf{A}) = -(-_h \mathbf{A}), \tag{11}$$

that is $\operatorname{dual}(\mathbf{A}) = \operatorname{opp}(\operatorname{neg}(\mathbf{A})) = \operatorname{neg}(\operatorname{opp}(\mathbf{A}))$. The equalities (11) suggest that there might exist an operator $\operatorname{rec}(\mathbf{A})$ in $D \setminus \mathcal{T}$, which (by analogy to the operator $-\mathbf{A}$ in (11)) possibly satisfies:

$$1/_h(\operatorname{rec}(\mathbf{A})) = \operatorname{rec}(1/_h \mathbf{A}) = \operatorname{dual}(\mathbf{A}), \tag{12}$$

that is $\mathrm{dual}(\mathbf{A}) = \mathrm{inv}(\mathrm{rec}(\mathbf{A})) = \mathrm{rec}(\mathrm{inv}(\mathbf{A}))$. The unique such operator is the *reciprocal* operator $\mathrm{rec}(\mathbf{A}) = 1/\mathbf{A} = \mathrm{dual}\ (1/_h\mathbf{A}) = 1/_h(\mathrm{dual}\ (\mathbf{A})) = [1/a^+, 1/a^-]$, for $\mathbf{A} \in D \setminus \mathcal{T}$. Both the opposite and the negative elements play an important role in the substructure $(D, +)$, and so do symmetrically the inverse and the reciprocal elements in the subsystem $(D\setminus\mathcal{T}, \times)$. The composition of these operators with the basic operations (8)–(10) generates a rich set of compound operations.

The operation $\mathbf{A}\times (1/\mathbf{B})$ for $\mathbf{A} \in D$, $\mathbf{B} \in D \setminus \mathcal{T}$ is further denoted by $\mathbf{A}/\mathbf{B}$ (it is an extension in D of the operation A/B, defined by (7)); we have

$$\mathbf{A}/\mathbf{B} = \begin{cases} [a^{-\sigma(B)}/b^{\sigma(A)}, a^{\sigma(B)}/b^{-\sigma(A)}], & \mathbf{A} \in D^*, \mathbf{B} \in D \setminus \mathcal{T}, \\ [a^{-\delta}/b^{-\delta}, a^{\delta}/b^{-\delta}],\ \delta = \sigma(B), & \mathbf{A} \in \mathcal{T}^*,\ \mathbf{B} \in D \setminus \mathcal{T}. \end{cases}$$

From (11) and (12)) we have $-_h\mathbf{A} = -\mathrm{dual}(\mathbf{A})$, $1/_h\mathbf{A} = 1/\mathrm{dual}(\mathbf{A})$. The elements $-_h\mathbf{A}$, $1/_h\mathbf{A}$ generate the operations $\mathbf{A} + (-_h\mathbf{B}) = \mathbf{A} + (-\mathrm{dual}(\mathbf{B})) = \mathbf{A} - \mathrm{dual}(\mathbf{B})$, $\mathbf{A} \times (1/_h\mathbf{B}) = \mathbf{A} \times (1/\mathrm{dual}(\mathbf{B})) = \mathbf{A}/\mathrm{dual}(\mathbf{B})$, which are denoted by $\mathbf{A} -_h \mathbf{B}$, resp. $\mathbf{A}/_h\mathbf{B}$:

$$\mathbf{A} -_h \mathbf{B} = \mathbf{A} - \mathrm{dual}(\mathbf{B}) = [a^- - b^-, a^+ - b^+],\ \mathbf{A}, \mathbf{B} \in D,$$

$$\mathbf{A} /_h \mathbf{B} = \mathbf{A}/\mathrm{dual}(\mathbf{B}) = \begin{cases} [a^{-\sigma(B)}/b^{-\sigma(A)}, a^{\sigma(B)}/b^{\sigma(A)}], & \mathbf{A}, \mathbf{B} \in D \setminus \mathcal{T}, \\ [a^{-\delta}/b^{\delta}, a^{\delta}/b^{\delta}],\ \delta = \sigma(B), & \mathbf{A} \in \mathcal{T},\ \mathbf{B} \in D \setminus \mathcal{T}. \end{cases}$$

From the last equality we obtain $\mathbf{A}/\mathbf{B} = \mathbf{A}/_h(\mathrm{dual}(\mathbf{B})) = \mathbf{A}/_h(-_h((-1) \times \mathbf{B}))$, which shows that division "/" can be expressed by the operations " $\times$ ", " $-_h$ " and "$/_h$". Therefore we may not include division in the list of basic operations of the algebraic system $\mathcal{K} = (D, +, \times)$ thus obtained, as we should do in the case with the familiar system $(I(\mathbb{R}), +, \times, /)$. The system $\mathcal{K}$ involves the compound operations subtraction $\mathbf{A} - \mathbf{B}$ and division $\mathbf{A}/\mathbf{B}$, the operator $\mathrm{dual}(\mathbf{A})$, the operations $\mathbf{A} - \mathrm{dual}(\mathbf{B})$, $\mathbf{A}/\mathrm{dual}(\mathbf{B})$, and their dual operations $\mathrm{dual}(\mathbf{A}) - \mathbf{B}$, $\mathrm{dual}(\mathbf{A})/\mathbf{B}$. Similarly, we can compose $\mathbf{A} + \mathrm{dual}(\mathbf{B})$, $\mathbf{A} \times \mathrm{dual}(\mathbf{B})$, $\mathrm{dual}(\mathbf{A}) + \mathbf{B}$, $\mathrm{dual}(\mathbf{A}) \times \mathbf{B}$, etc.

For the operator dual element we shall further use the notation $\mathbf{A}_- = \mathrm{dual}(\mathbf{A})$. Assuming $\mathbf{A}_+ = \mathbf{A}$, we can introduce the notation $\mathbf{A}_\alpha = \{\mathbf{A}, \text{if } \alpha = +; \mathbf{A}_-, \text{if } \alpha = -\}$. Using this notation we can formulate a simple distributive relation in D^*, which is more convenient than the one formulated in table form in [Kaucher 1980].

Proposition 1. *Conditionally Distributive Law for directed intervals. For* $\mathbf{A} \in D^*, \mathbf{B} \in D^*, \mathbf{C} \in D^*, \mathbf{A} + \mathbf{B} \in D^*$ *we have*

$$(\mathbf{A} + \mathbf{B}) \times \mathbf{C}_{\sigma(A+B)} = (\mathbf{A} \times \mathbf{C}_{\sigma(A)}) + (\mathbf{B} \times \mathbf{C}_{\sigma(B)}).$$

Note that in the above expression we take $\mathbf{C}$ or $\mathrm{dual}(\mathbf{C})$ dependent on the signs of the intervals A, B and $A + B$.

3 Directed intervals in normal form

We introduce another form of presentation for the directed intervals $\mathbf{A} = [a^-, a^+] \in D$, which we call normal form. The set D is equivalent to the direct product $I(\mathbb{R}) \otimes \Lambda$, $\Lambda = \{+, -\}$. Note that the space $I(\mathbb{R}) \otimes \Lambda$ involves degenerate intervals with negative direction, which have not been defined yet. We shall stipulate that such elements coincide with the (same) degenerate intervals with positive direction. Hence a directed interval $\mathbf{A}$ can be presented as a couple consisting of a normal (proper) interval and a sign showing its direction, that is $\mathbf{A} = [A; \alpha] = [a^{(-)}, a^{(+)}; \alpha]$ with $A = [a^{(-)}, a^{(+)}] \in I(\mathbb{R})$ and $\alpha = \tau(\mathbf{A}) \in \Lambda$. For $A = a \in \mathbb{R}$ we have by definition $[a; \alpha] = [a; -\alpha]$.

We may use the following formulae for transition from the component-wise form $[a^-, a^+]$ to normal form $[a^{(-)}, a^{(+)}; \alpha]$ and vice verse

$$\alpha = \sigma(a^+ - a^-),\ a^{(-)} = a^{-\alpha}, \quad a^{(+)} = a^{\alpha},\ a^- = a^{(-\alpha)}, \quad a^+ = a^{(\alpha)}.$$

We can write, of course, other equivalent expressions like $a^{(-)} = \min\{a^-, a^+\}$, $a^{(+)} = \max\{a^-, a^+\}$, but such formulae are not suitable for algebraic manipulations. We shall next find an expression for the sum $\mathbf{C} = \mathbf{A} + \mathbf{B}$ of two directed intervals $\mathbf{A}$, $\mathbf{B}$ involving normal form presentation. Denoting the length of the interval by $\omega(A) = a^{(+)} - a^{(-)}$, we obtain for the direction $\tau(\mathbf{C})$ of the sum $\mathbf{C} = [c^-, c^+] = [a^- + b^-, a^+ + b^+]$

$$\begin{aligned}\tau(\mathbf{C}) &= \sigma(a^+ + b^+ - a^- - b^-) = \sigma((a^{(\alpha)} - a^{(-\alpha)}) + (b^{(\beta)} - b^{(-\beta)}))\\ &= \sigma\left(\alpha\omega(A) + \beta\omega(B)\right)\\ &= \begin{cases}\alpha,\ \alpha = \beta,\\ \alpha,\ \alpha = -\beta,\ \omega(A) > \omega(B),\\ \beta,\ \alpha = -\beta,\ \omega(A) < \omega(B),\\ +,\ \alpha = -\beta,\ \omega(A) = \omega(B).\end{cases}\end{aligned} \tag{13}$$

In the expression $\sigma\left(\alpha\omega(A) + \beta\omega(B)\right)$ the symbols $\alpha, \beta \in \Lambda$ preceding the real positive numbers $\omega(A)$, resp. $\omega(B)$, should be interpreted as signs of these numbers, that is as $\alpha, \beta = \pm 1$.

Denoting for brevity $\gamma = \tau(\mathbf{C}) = \tau(\mathbf{A} + \mathbf{B})$, as given by (13), we have $c^{(-)} = c^{-\gamma} = a^{-\gamma} + b^{-\gamma} = a^{(-\alpha\gamma)} + b^{(-\beta\gamma)}$, $c^{(+)} = c^{\gamma} = a^{\gamma} + b^{\gamma} = a^{(\alpha\gamma)} + b^{(\beta\gamma)}$, so that

$$\begin{aligned}\mathbf{A} + \mathbf{B} &= [a^{(-)}, a^{(+)}; \alpha] + [b^{(-)}, b^{(+)}; \beta]\\ &= [a^{(-\alpha\gamma)} + b^{(-\beta\gamma)}, a^{(\alpha\gamma)} + b^{(\beta\gamma)}; \gamma].\end{aligned} \tag{14}$$

Expression (14) implies that for $\alpha = \beta\ (= \gamma)$ the normal part $\mathrm{pro}(\mathbf{A} + \mathbf{B}) = [a^{(-\alpha\gamma)} + b^{(-\beta\gamma)}, a^{(\alpha\gamma)} + b^{(\beta\gamma)}]$ of the sum $\mathbf{A} + \mathbf{B}$ is equal to $[a^{(-)} + b^{(-)}, a^{(+)} + b^{(+)}] = A + B = \mathrm{pro}(\mathbf{A}) + \mathrm{pro}(\mathbf{B})$. For $\alpha \neq \beta$ the normal part of $\mathbf{A} + \mathbf{B}$ is

$$\begin{aligned}\mathrm{pro}(\mathbf{A} + \mathbf{B})|_{\alpha\neq\beta} &= \begin{cases}[a^{(-)} + b^{(+)}, a^{(+)} + b^{(-)}],\ \text{if}\ \ a^{(-)} + b^{(+)} \leq a^{(+)} + b^{(-)},\\ [a^{(+)} + b^{(-)}, a^{(-)} + b^{(+)}],\ \text{if}\ \ a^{(-)} + b^{(+)} > a^{(+)} + b^{(-)},\end{cases}\\ &= \begin{cases}[a^{(-)} + b^{(+)}, a^{(+)} + b^{(-)}],\ \omega(A) \geq \omega(B),\\ [a^{(+)} + b^{(-)}, a^{(-)} + b^{(+)}],\ \omega(A) < \omega(B),\end{cases}\end{aligned} \tag{15}$$

which is the proper interval with end-points $a^{(-)} + b^{(+)}$ and $a^{(+)} + b^{(-)}$. The interval (15) is called inner (or nonstandard) sum of the proper intervals A, B

and is denoted by $A+^{-}B$ [Markov 1980]. In contrast, the sum $A+B$ is sometimes called *outer sum* of A, B. We have

$$\mathrm{pro}(\mathbf{A}+\mathbf{B}) = \begin{cases} A+B, & \tau(\mathbf{A}) = \tau(\mathbf{B}), \\ A+^{-} B, & \tau(\mathbf{A}) \neq \tau(\mathbf{B}). \end{cases}$$

We thus see that for the presentation of the proper projection of a sum of two directed intervals by means of the proper projections of these intervals we need two types of summation of (proper) intervals: an outer summation ("+") and an inner summation ("$+^{-}$"). For $A, B \in I(\mathbb{R})$ we have $A +^{-} B \subseteq A + B$. We can characterize the sum $A+^{-} B$ in the case when A, B are nondegenerate, resp. the four numbers $c_{\alpha\beta} = a^{(\alpha)} + b^{(\beta)}$, $\alpha, \beta \in \Lambda$, are all different, as follows. Arranging the numbers $c_{\alpha\beta}$ in increasing order and renaming them by $c_i, i = 1, 2, 3, 4$, so that $c_1 < c_2 < c_3 < c_4$, we have $A + B = [c_1, c_4]$, $A +^{-} B = [c_2, c_3]$.

Introducing the notation $+^{+} = +$, we can summarize both cases $\alpha = \beta$, $\alpha \neq \beta$ by writing $C = A +^{\alpha\beta} B$, showing that C is either an outer or an inner sum of A and B. We thus obtain the simple expressions

$$\begin{aligned} [A;\alpha] + [B;\beta] &= [A +^{\alpha\beta} B; \tau([A;\alpha] + [B;\beta])], \quad A, B \in I(\mathbb{R}), \alpha, \beta \in \Lambda, \\ \mathbf{A} + \mathbf{B} &= [A +^{\tau(\mathbf{A})\tau(\mathbf{B})} B; \tau(\mathbf{A}+\mathbf{B})], \quad \mathbf{A}, \mathbf{B} \in D, \end{aligned} \tag{16}$$

wherein the direction $\tau(\mathbf{A}+\mathbf{B}) = \gamma$ is given by (13).

To present a difference $\mathbf{C} = \mathbf{A} - \mathbf{B} = \mathbf{A} + (-\mathbf{B}) = [a^{-} - b^{+}, a^{+} - b^{-}]$ in normal form we first compute $\tau(\mathbf{C}) = \tau(\mathbf{A}-\mathbf{B}) = \tau(\mathbf{A}+(-\mathbf{B})) = \sigma(\alpha\omega(A) + \beta\omega(-B)) = \sigma(\alpha\omega(A) + \beta\omega(B)) = \tau(\mathbf{A}+\mathbf{B})$. Note that $\omega(-(B)) = \omega(B)$ and $\tau(\mathbf{B}) = \tau(-\mathbf{B}) = \beta$. Further, using the transition formulae, we compute $c^{(-)} = c^{-\gamma} = a^{-\gamma} - b^{\gamma} = a^{(-\alpha\gamma)} - b^{(\beta\gamma)}$, $c^{(+)} = c^{\gamma} = a^{\gamma} - b^{-\gamma} = a^{(\alpha\gamma)} - b^{(-\beta\gamma)}$, so that

$$\begin{aligned} \mathbf{A} - \mathbf{B} &= [a^{(-)}, a^{(+)}; \alpha] - [b^{(-)}, b^{(+)}; \beta] \\ &= [a^{(-\alpha\gamma)} - b^{(\beta\gamma)}, a^{(\alpha\gamma)} - b^{(-\beta\gamma)}; \tau(\mathbf{A}-\mathbf{B})], \end{aligned} \tag{17}$$

where $\tau(\mathbf{A}-\mathbf{B}) = \tau(\mathbf{A}+\mathbf{B}) = \gamma$ is given by (13).

Expression (17) implies that for $\alpha = \beta$ $(= \gamma)$ the normal part $\mathrm{pro}(\mathbf{A}-\mathbf{B})$ of the difference $\mathbf{A}-\mathbf{B}$ is equal to $[a^{(-)} - b^{(+)}, a^{(+)} - b^{(-)}] = A - B = \mathrm{pro}(\mathbf{A}) - \mathrm{pro}(\mathbf{B})$. For $\alpha \neq \beta$ the proper projection $\mathrm{pro}(\mathbf{A}-\mathbf{B})$ is given by

$$\mathrm{pro}(\mathbf{A}-\mathbf{B})|_{\alpha\neq\beta} = \begin{cases} [a^{(-)} - b^{(-)}, a^{(+)} - b^{(+)}], & \omega(A) \geq \omega(B), \\ [a^{(+)} - b^{(+)}, a^{(-)} - b^{(-)}], & \omega(A) < \omega(B), \end{cases}$$

which is the proper interval with end-points $a^{(-)} - b^{(-)}$ and $a^{(+)} - b^{(+)}$. The latter interval is called *inner* (or *nonstandard*) difference of $\mathbf{A}$ and $\mathbf{B}$ and is denoted by $A -^{-} B$. We may now write

$$\mathrm{pro}(\mathbf{A}-\mathbf{B}) = \begin{cases} A - B, & \tau(\mathbf{A}) = \tau(\mathbf{B}), \\ A -^{-} B, & \tau(\mathbf{A}) \neq \tau(\mathbf{B}). \end{cases}$$

This shows that for the presentation of the proper projection of the difference of two directed intervals we need two types of subtraction: the familiar (outer) subtraction ("$-$") and the inner subtraction ("$-^{-}$"). For $A, B \in I(\mathbb{R})$ we have $A -^{-} B \subseteq A - B$.

In order to obtain an uniform expression for the difference of two directed intervals we introduce the notation $-^{+} = -$; we then summarize

$$[A;\alpha] - [B;\beta] = [A -^{\alpha\beta} B; \tau([A;\alpha] - [B;\beta])],\ A, B \in I(\mathbf{R}), \alpha, \beta \in \Lambda,$$
$$\mathbf{A} - \mathbf{B} = [A -^{\tau(\mathbf{A})\tau(\mathbf{B})} B; \tau(\mathbf{A} - \mathbf{B})],\ \mathbf{A}, \mathbf{B} \in D,$$

wherein $\tau(\mathbf{A} - \mathbf{B}) = \tau(\mathbf{A} + \mathbf{B}) = \sigma(\alpha\omega(A) + \beta\omega(B)) = \gamma$ is given by (13).

Similarly we obtain $[A;\alpha] \times [B;\beta] = [A \times^{\alpha\beta} B; \tau([A;\alpha] \times [B;\beta])]$ for any $A, B \in I(\mathbf{R})^*$, $\alpha, \beta \in \Lambda$, or

$$\mathbf{A} \times \mathbf{B} = [A \times^{\tau(\mathbf{A})\tau(\mathbf{B})} B; \tau(\mathbf{A} \times \mathbf{B})],\ \mathbf{A}, \mathbf{B} \in D^*,$$
$$\tau(\mathbf{A} \times \mathbf{B}) = \tau([A;\alpha] \times [B;\beta]) = \sigma(\alpha\chi(B) + \beta\chi(A)), \tag{18}$$

where $\chi(A) = a^{(-\sigma(A))}/a^{(\sigma(A))}$, $\times^{+} = \times$, and the inner multiplication "$\times^{-}$" is defined by

$$A \times^{-} B = \begin{cases} [a^{(-\sigma(B))}b^{(\sigma(A))}, a^{(\sigma(B))}b^{(-\sigma(A))}], & \chi(B) \geq \chi(A), \\ [a^{(\sigma(B))}b^{(-\sigma(A))}, a^{(-\sigma(B))}b^{(\sigma(A))}], & \chi(B) < \chi(A). \end{cases}$$

In order to present the proper projection of $\mathbf{A}/\mathbf{B} = \mathbf{A} \times (1/\mathbf{B})$ we need two types of interval division for proper intervals — the (outer) division "/" defined by (7) and an "inner" division "$/^{-}$" defined by

$$A/^{-} B = \begin{cases} [a^{(-\sigma(B))}/b^{(-\sigma(A))}, a^{(\sigma(B))}/b^{(\sigma(A))}], & \chi(B) \geq \chi(A), \\ [a^{(\sigma(B))}/b^{(\sigma(A))}, a^{(-\sigma(B))}/b^{(-\sigma(A))}], & \chi(B) < \chi(A). \end{cases}$$

Using the inner and outer divisions for normal intervals we can write

$$\mathbf{A}/\mathbf{B} = [A/^{\tau(\mathbf{A})\tau(\mathbf{B})} B; \tau(\mathbf{A} \times \mathbf{B})],\ \mathbf{A}, \mathbf{B} \in D^*,$$
$$\tau(\mathbf{A}/\mathbf{B}) = \tau([A;\alpha]/[B;\beta]) = \sigma(\alpha\chi(B) + \beta\chi(A)) = \tau(\mathbf{A} \times \mathbf{B}).$$

Let us make two remarks with respect to the inner operations. First, for $A, B \in I(\mathbf{R})$ we have $A *^{-} B \subseteq A * B$ for $* \in \{+, -, \times, /\}$. Second, we can interpret the result of any inner operation $A *^{-} B$, $* \in \{+, -, \times, /\}$, whenever the four numbers $c_{\alpha\beta} = a^{(\alpha)} * b^{(\beta)}$, $\alpha, \beta \in \Lambda$, are different, as follows (for multiplication and division the case when the intervals contain zero should be excluded). Rearrange these four numbers in increasing order and rename them by $c_i, i = 1, 2, 3, 4$, so that: $c_1 < c_2 < c_3 < c_4$. Then we have $A * B = [c_1, c_4]$, $A *^{-} B = [c_2, c_3]$.

We can perform all computations in $\mathcal{K}$ using normal form presentation. Let us give some examples. Multiplication by a degenerate interval a is expressed by $a \times [B;\beta] = a \times [b^{(-)}, b^{(+)}; \beta] = [ab^{(-\sigma(a))}, ab^{(\sigma(a))}; \beta]$. If $a = -1$ then $(-1) \times [b^{(-)}, b^{(+)}; \beta] = -[b^{(-)}, b^{(+)}; \beta] = [-b^{(+)}, -b^{(-)}; \beta] = -[B;\beta] = [-B;\beta]$. The opposite of $\mathbf{A} = [A;\alpha] = [a^{(-)}, a^{(+)}; \alpha]$ is the directed interval $-\mathbf{A}_{-} = [-A; -\alpha] = [-a^{(+)}, -a^{(-)}; -\alpha]$. Indeed from (14) we have $[a^{(-)}, a^{(+)}; \alpha] + [-a^{(+)}, -a^{(-)}; -\alpha] = [0, 0; \pm] = 0$. The inverse to a negative interval is the dual interval $[A;\alpha]_{-} = [A; -\alpha]$. More generally, for $\lambda \in \Lambda$ we have $\mathbf{A}_{\lambda} = [A;\alpha]_{\lambda} = [A; \lambda\alpha]$. Here the binary variable λ is an indicator for a presence/absence of the operator dual element. Similarly, the inversion of $[A;\alpha] = [a^{(-)}, a^{(+)}; \alpha]$ is the directed interval $1/\mathbf{A}_{-} = [1/A;\alpha]_{-} = [1/A; -\alpha] = [1/a^{(+)}, 1/a^{(-)}; -\alpha]$.

4 Relations for normal intervals derived from directed interval arithmetic

We now make the following observation: **Every proposition from the directed interval arithmetic can be reformulated in terms of normal form presentation of the directed intervals involved. It then implies a corresponding proposition for the proper projections of the participating directed intervals, that is a proposition for normal intervals using outer and inner arithmetic operations.** For directed intervals we have simple expressions and relations, due to the fact that the directed intervals form a nice algebraic structure. As we have shown the arithmetic operations between directed intervals generate both outer and inner operations for normal intervals. The set of (proper) intervals together with the set of outer and inner operations $\mathcal{M} = (I(\mathbf{R}), +, +^-, \times, \times^-, \subseteq)$ has been studied in [Dimitrova 1980]–[Dimitrova et al. 1991], [Markov 1977]–[Markov 1992]. We recall that the operations $-, -^-, /, /^-$ can be expressed via the basic operations $+, +^-, \times, \times^-$. The inner interval operations find application in the analysis of interval functions [Markov 1979], [Markov 1980], [Schröder 1981]. Inner operations are useful for the computation of inclusions (both inner and outer) of functional ranges [Bartholomew-Biggs and Zakovich 1994], [Markov 1993], [Nesterov 1993] (see the last section). We next show how some basic arithmetic relations for directed intervals generate corresponding relations between proper intervals. We consequently obtain simple arithmetic relations for the outer and inner operations.

Proposition 2. *Conditionally-associative laws for proper intervals.*
i) For $A, B, C \in I(\mathbf{R})$, and $\alpha, \beta, \gamma \in \Lambda$ we have

$$(A +^{\alpha\beta} B) +^{\gamma\tau(\mathbf{A}+\mathbf{B})} C = A +^{\alpha\tau(\mathbf{B}+\mathbf{C})} (B +^{\beta\gamma} C),$$

ii) For $A, B, C, D \in I(\mathbf{R})$, and $\alpha, \beta, \gamma, \delta \in \Lambda$ we have

$$(A +^{\alpha\beta} B) +^{\tau(\mathbf{A}+\mathbf{B})\tau(\mathbf{C}+\mathbf{D})} (C +^{\gamma\delta} D) = (A +^{\alpha\gamma} C) +^{\tau(\mathbf{A}+\mathbf{C})\tau(\mathbf{B}+\mathbf{D})} (B +^{\beta\gamma} D),$$

iii) For $A, B, C \in I(\mathbf{R})^*$ and $\alpha, \beta, \gamma \in \Lambda$ we have

$$(A \times^{\alpha\beta} B) \times^{\gamma\tau(\mathbf{A}\times\mathbf{B})} C = A \times^{\alpha\tau(\mathbf{B}\times\mathbf{C})} (B \times^{\beta\gamma} C),$$

iv) For $A, B, C, D \in I(\mathbf{R})^*$, and $\alpha, \beta, \gamma, \delta \in \Lambda$ we have

$$(A \times^{\alpha\beta} B) \times^{\tau(\mathbf{A}\times\mathbf{B})\tau(\mathbf{C}\times\mathbf{D})} (C \times^{\gamma\delta} D) = (A \times^{\alpha\gamma} C) \times^{\tau(\mathbf{A}\times\mathbf{C})\tau(\mathbf{B}\times\mathbf{D})} (B \times^{\beta\gamma} D),$$

wherein the τ-functionals are given by (13), (18).

Proof of i). Substituting $\mathbf{A} = [A;\alpha]$, $\mathbf{B} = [B;\beta]$, $\mathbf{C} = [C;\gamma]$ in $(\mathbf{A}+\mathbf{B})+\mathbf{C} = \mathbf{A}+(\mathbf{B}+\mathbf{C})$ and using (16), we obtain $[A +^{\alpha\beta} B; \tau(\mathbf{A}+\mathbf{B})] + [C;\gamma] = [A;\alpha] + [B +^{\beta\gamma} C; \tau(\mathbf{B}+\mathbf{C})]$. Comparing the proper projection of both sides of this equality, we obtain i). □

Using i) we can change the order of execution of the operations in any expression involving additions (outer or inner) of normal intervals. The relation ii) is obtained in a similar way — this relation plays important role in the analysis for interval functions [Markov 1979], [Schröder 1981]. The relations iii), iv) are obtained in a similar way.

Proposition 3. *Conditionally-distributive law for proper intervals. For arbitrary $A, B, C \in I(\mathbf{R})^*$, such that $A + B \in I(\mathbf{R})^*$ and for any $\alpha, \beta, \gamma \in \Lambda$ we have*

$$(A +^{\alpha\beta} B) \times^{\gamma\tau(\mathbf{A}+\mathbf{B})} C$$
$$= (A \times^{\alpha\gamma\sigma(A)\sigma(A+B)} C) +^{\tau(\mathbf{A}\times\mathbf{C})\tau(\mathbf{B}\times\mathbf{C})} (B \times^{\beta\gamma\sigma(B)\sigma(A+B)} C).$$

Proof. Setting $\mathbf{A} = [A;\alpha]$, $\mathbf{B} = [B;\beta]$, ; $\mathbf{C} = [C;\gamma]$ in the conditionally-distributive law for directed intervals and using (16), we obtain

$$[A +^{\alpha\beta} B; \tau(\mathbf{A}+\mathbf{B})] \times [C;\gamma]$$
$$= [A \times^{\alpha\gamma\sigma(A)\sigma(A+B)} C; \tau(\mathbf{A}\times\mathbf{C})] + [B \times^{\beta\gamma\sigma(B)\sigma(A+B)} C; \tau(\mathbf{B}\times\mathbf{C})].$$

Using again (18) for the left hand-side and (16) for the right hand-side and comparing the proper projections in both sides we obtain the proof. □

The generated above basic relations for normal intervals are suitable for automatic processing, especially in computer algebra systems. The corresponding relations known by now (see e. g. [Markov 1992]) have rather complex form and are not convenient for symbolic manipulations.

5 Applications to functional ranges

Let $CM(T)$ be the set of all continuous and monotone functions f defined in $T = [t^{(-)}, t^{(+)}] \in I(\mathbf{R})$. The image $f(T) = \{f(t) \mid t \in T\} \in I(\mathbf{R})$ of the set T by the function f is called the range of f (over T). If $f \in CM(T)$, then for the range of f we have either $f(T) = [f(t^{(-)}), f(t^{(+)})]$ or $f(T) = [f(t^{(+)}), f(t^{(-)})]$ depending on the type of monotonicity. To every $f \in CM(T)$ corresponds a binary variable $\tau_f = \tau(f;T) \in \Lambda$, which determines the type of monotonicity of f by

$$\tau(f;T) = \begin{cases} +, & f(t^-) \le f(t^+); \\ -, & f(t^-) > f(t^+). \end{cases}$$

For $f, g \in CM(T)$, the equality $\tau_f = \tau_g$ means that the functions f, g are both isotone (nondecreasing) or are both antitone (nonincreasing) in T; $\tau_f = -\tau_g$ means that one of the functions is antitone and the other is isotone. Let $CM(T)^*$ be the set of all functions from $CM(T)$ which do not change sign in T. Obviously, if $f \in CM(T)^*$, then $|f| \in CM(T)^*$ as well and the notation $\tau_{|f|} = \tau(|f|;T)$ makes sense. Since the ranges are proper intervals, we may perform interval arithmetic manipulations over them.

Proposition 4. *Let $f, g \in CM(T)$. For $X \subseteq T$ we have*
i) if $f + g \in CM(T)$, then $(f+g)(X) = f(X) +^{\tau_f \tau_g} g(X)$.
ii) if $f - g \in CM(T)$, then $(f-g)(X) = f(X) -^{-\tau_f \tau_g} g(X)$.
Let $f, g \in CM(T)^*$. For $X \subseteq T$:
iii) if $fg \in CM(T)$, then $(fg)(X) = f(X) \times^{\tau_{|f|}\tau_{|g|}} g(X)$.
iv) if $f/g \in CM(T)$, $g(x) \neq 0$, $\forall x \in T$, then $(f/g)(X) = f(X) /^{-\tau_{|f|}\tau_{|g|}} g(X)$.

If f is continuous in $X \in I(\mathbf{R})$, then $\min_{x \in X} f(x)$, $\max_{x \in X} f(x)$ do exist. Assuming further that the interval X is fixed, we shall shortly write $\min f$, resp. $\max f$. Let f, g be continuous in X. We have:
i) $\min f + \min g \leq \min(f+g)$, $\max(f+g) \leq \max f + \max g$;
ii) $\min(f+g) \leq \min f + \max g \leq \max(f+g)$, $\min(f+g) \leq \max f + \min g \leq \max(f+g)$.

This implies that the interval $(f+g)(X) = [\min(f+g), \max(f+g)]$:
i) is contained in the interval with endpoints $\min f + \min g$, $\max f + \max g$, that is in the interval $f(X) + g(X)$;
ii) contains the interval with endpoints $\min f + \max g$, $\max f + \min g$, that is the interval $f(X) +^- g(X)$.

Symbolically, we obtain $f(X) +^- g(X) \subseteq (f+g)(X) \subseteq f(X) + g(X)$. Using similar arguments for the rest of operations we obtain:

Proposition 5. *Let the functions f, g be continuous in $T \in I(\mathbf{R})$. For $* \in \{+, -, \times, /\}$ and for every $X \subseteq T, X \in I(\mathbf{R})$ we have $f(X) *^- g(X) \subseteq (f * g)(X) \subseteq f(X) * g(X)$. (For "/" we additionally assume that g does not vanish in T.)*

The above proposition shows that the outer operations are convenient for the computation of outer inclusions, whereas the inner interval operations may serve for the computation of inner inclusions. Examples for the use of inner interval operations can be found in [Bartholomew-Biggs and Zakovich 1994], [Dimitrova and Markov 1994], [Markov 1979], [Markov 1980], [Markov 1993], [Nesterov 1993], [Schröder 1981], [Stetter 1990].

We shall now formulate an analogue of Proposition 4 for directed intervals. We first define directed range by admitting improper intervals as arguments:

Definition. Let $T \in I(\mathbf{R})$, $f \in CM(T)$. Let $\mathbf{X} = [x^-, x^+] \in D$, $\mathrm{pro}(\mathbf{X}) \subseteq T$. The *directed range* of f over $\mathbf{X}$ is the directed interval $f(\mathbf{X}) = [f(x^-), f(x^+)]$.

Proposition 6. *Let $f, g \in CM(T)$. For $\mathbf{X} \in D$, pro$(\mathbf{X}) \subseteq T$, we have*
i) if $f + g \in CM(T)$, then $(f+g)(\mathbf{X}) = f(\mathbf{X}) + g(\mathbf{X})$;
ii) if $f - g \in CM(T)$, then $(f-g)(\mathbf{X}) = f(\mathbf{X}) - g(\mathbf{X})_-$.
Let $f, g \in CM(T)^*$. For $\mathbf{X} \in D$, pro$(\mathbf{X}) \subseteq T$
iii) if $fg \in CM(T)$, then $(fg)(\mathbf{X}) = f(\mathbf{X})_{\sigma(g(X))} \times g(\mathbf{X})_{\sigma(f(X))}$;
iv) if $f/g \in CM(T)$, $0 \notin g(X)$, then $(f/g)(\mathbf{X}) = f(\mathbf{X})_{\sigma(g(X))} / g(\mathbf{X})_{-\sigma(f(X))}$.

In the last two expressions $\sigma(f(X))$ means the sign of the interval $f(X) \in I(\mathbf{R})^*$ (we can equally well write either $\sigma(f(\mathbf{X}))$ or $\sigma(f(X))$). For example, we have $g(\mathbf{X})_{\sigma(f(X))} = \{g(\mathbf{X}), \text{ if } f \geq 0;\ (g(\mathbf{X}))_-, \text{ if } f \leq 0\}$.

Proposition 6 gives the direction of the resulting intervals, and therefore supplies additional information (compared to Proposition 4) for the type of monotonicity (isotonicity or antitonicity) of the result $f * g$, $* \in \{+, -, \times, /\}$.

The propositions in this section can be incorporated in algorithms for automatic computation of inner and outer inclusions of ranges of functions and their derivatives. Such algorithms should use a suitable environment supporting the interval arithmetic system $\mathcal{K}$, resp. its subsystem $\mathcal{M}$.

6 Conclusion

We have shown that the set $I(\mathbf{R}) \bigcirc \{+,-\}$ of directed intervals can be used to establish a practical relation between the interval arithmetic $I(\mathbf{R})$ and its algebraic completion D, considered by E. Kaucher. Moreover, this relation generates the inner arithmetic operations in the set of proper intervals $I(\mathbf{R})$, which have proved to be useful for the computation of functional ranges and for the interpretation of algebraic results obtained in D by means of proper intervals, which are proper projections of directed intervals.

Acknowledgements

This work is part of a contracted project of the Institute of Informatics, University of Basel, supported by the Swiss National Science Foundation. I am grateful to Dr. V. Nesterov, Dr. S. Shary, Dr. M. C. Bartholomew-Biggs and Dr. S. Zakovic for reading the manuscript and sending me useful comments and critical remarks. I am also thankful to Dr. R. Alt for presenting the paper at the conference "Real numbers and computers" in Saint-Etienne, 4–6 April 1995.

References

[Bartholomew-Biggs and Zakovich 1994] Bartholomew-Biggs, M., S. Zakovic, "Using Markov's Interval Arithmetic to Evaluate Bessel-Ricatti Functions"; NOC Technical Report 297, University of Hertfordshire, April 1994 (to appear in Numerical Algorithms).

[Corliss and Rall 1991] Corliss, G., Rall, L.: "Computing the Range of Derivatives"; In: Computer arithmetic, scientific computation and mathematical modelling (Eds. E. Kaucher, S. Markov, G. Mayer), Baltzer, Basel (1991), 195–212.

[Dimitrova 1980] Dimitrova, N., "Über die Distributivgesetze der erweiterten Intervallarithmetik"; Computing *24* (1980), 33–49.

[Dimitrova and Markov 1994] Dimitrova, N., Markov, S., "On Validated Newton Type Method for Nonlinear Equations"; Interval Computations, 2 (1994), 27–51.

[Dimitrova et al. 1991] Dimitrova, N., Markov, S.M., Popova, E.: "Extended Interval Arithmetics: New Results and Applications"; In: Computer arithmetic and enclosure methods (Eds. L. Atanassova, J. Herzberger), North-Holland, Amsterdam (1992), 225–232.

[Gardenes and Trepat 1980] Gardeñes, E.; Trepat, A.: "Fundamentals of SIGLA, an Interval Computing System over the Completed Set of Intervals"; Computing, *24* (1980), 161–179.

[Kaucher 1977] Kaucher, E.: "Über Eigenschaften und Anwendungsmöglichkeiten der erweiterten Intervallrechnung und des hyperbolischen Fastkörpers über R"; Computing Suppl. *1* (1977), 81–94.

[Kaucher 1980] Kaucher, E.: "Interval Analysis in the Extended Interval Space IR"; Computing Suppl. *2* (1980), 33–49.

[Markov 1977] Markov, S.M.: "Extended Interval Arithmetic"; Compt. rend. Acad. bulg. Sci., *30*, 9 (1977), 1239–1242.

[Markov 1979] Markov, S.M.: "Calculus for Interval Functions of a Real Variable"; Computing, *22* (1979), 325–337.

[Markov 1980] Markov, S.M.: "Some Applications of the Extended Interval Arithmetic to Interval Iterations"; Computing Suppl. *2* (1980), 69–84.

[Markov 1992] Markov, S.M.: "Extended Interval Arithmetic Involving Infinite Intervals"; Mathematica Balkanica, New Series, *6*, 3 (1992), 269–304.

[Markov 1992a] Markov, S.M.: "On the Presentation of Ranges of Monotone Functions Using Interval Arithmetic"; Interval Computations, 4(6) (1992), 19–31.

[Markov 1993] Markov, S.M.: "Some Interpolation Problems Involving Interval Data"; Interval Computations, 3 (1993), 164–182.

[Moore 1966] Moore, R.: "Interval Analysis"; Prentice-Hall, Englewood Cliffs, (1966).

[Nesterov 1993] Nesterov V. "How to Use Monotonicity Type Information to Get Better Estimates of The Range of Real-Valued Functions"; Interval Computations, 4 (1993), 3–12.

[Ratschek 1969] Ratschek, H.: "Über einige intervallarithmetische Grundbegriffe"; Computing, *4* (1969), 43–55.

[Ratschek 1972] Ratschek, H.: "Teilbarkeitskriterien der Intervallarithmetik"; J. Reine Angew. Math. *252* (1972), 128–138.

[Ratschek and Rokne 1984] Ratschek, H., Rokne, J.: "Computer Methods for the Ranges of Functions"; Ellis Horwood, Chichester (1984).

[Shary 1993] Shary, S. P.: "On controlled solution set of interval algebraic systems"; Interval Computations, 6 (1992), 66–75.

[Shary 1995] Shary, S. P.: "Solving the tolerance problem for interval linear equations"; Interval Computations, 1 (1994), 4–22.

[Schröder 1981] Schröder G., "Bemerkung zur Differentiation von intervallwertigen Funktionen"; Computing 26 (1981), 271–274.

[Stetter 1990] Stetter, H. J., "Validated Solution of Initial Value Problems for ODE"; In: Computer Arithmetic and Self-Validating Numerical Methods (Ed. Ch. Ullrich), Academic Press (1990).

[Sunaga 1958] Sunaga, T.: "Theory of an Interval Algebra and its Applications to Numerical Analysis"; RAAG Memoirs, *2* (1958), 29–46.

Journal of Universal Computer Science, vol. 1, no. 7 (1995), 527-547
submitted: 15/12/94, accepted: 26/6/95, appeared: 28/7/95 © *Springer Pub. Co.*

MSB-First Digit Serial Arithmetic[1]

Asger Munk Nielsen
(Dept. of Mathematics and Computer Science
Odense University, Denmark
asger@imada.ou.dk)

Peter Kornerup
(Dept. of Mathematics and Computer Science
Odense University, Denmark
kornerup@imada.ou.dk)

Abstract: We develop a formal account of digit serial number representations by describing them as strings from a language. A prefix of a string represents an interval approximating a number by enclosure. Standard on-line representations are shown to be a special case of the general digit serial representations. Matrices are introduced as representations of intervals and a finite-state transducer is used for mapping strings into intervals. Homographic and bi-homographic functions are used for representing basic arithmetic operations on digit serial numbers, and finally a digit serial representation of floating point numbers is introduced.

Key Words: Computer Arithmetic, On-line Computation, Number Representations, Redundant Digit sets, Continued Fractions, Intervals.
Category: B.2

1 Introduction

A number is usually represented as a string of digits belonging to some digit set Σ. The number representation specifies a function that maps the string to its value. In the context of this paper a *digit serial number representation* will be a representation, that will allow us to gradually calculate the value of a number, by starting with an empty string and then iteratively calculate better approximations of the number, from increasingly longer prefixes of the string. A prefix of a string represents an approximation of the number, with an associated variance. The variance is determined by the possible extensions of the prefix, and the prefix can be thought of as a representation of an interval that includes the number being approximated. Concatenating the next digit of the string to the prefix, yields a more precise representation of the number, and will effectively narrow down the variance interval. When the whole string has been constructed by successive concatenation (if the string is finite and terminated), the interval will have been narrowed down to a degenerate interval of length zero, i.e. the value of the number. Infinite strings represent computable reals as limits of contracting intervals. A prefix of zero length is a prefix of any number, and has an associated variance interval, with endpoints determined by the largest and

[1] This work has been supported by The Danish Research Councils under the grant no. 5.21.08.02.

smallest representable numbers, this interval will be denoted as *the total variance interval.*

In this paper we will take a formal language approach to describing digit serial operands (e.g. operands are taken to be strings over some alphabet), with this approach the mapping from strings to intervals can be described by means of a finite-state transducer. In [Section 2] we develop a formal account of digit serial number representations, digit serial computable functions and the relation to the equivalent on-line definitions. In [Section 3] a computational model for a function of one variable, based on a matrix representation is developed. In [Section 4], this model is generalized to a cube structure, capable of modelling a function of two variables. In [Section 5] we introduce a representation of digit serial floating point numbers, thereby expanding the set of representable numbers, and discuss normalization problems in on-line and digit serial computation.

2 Digit Serial Representations of Numbers

We will now develop a formal account of digit serial number representations.

Definition 1. Digit Serial Number Representation
Let Σ be a digit set (finite or infinite), τ a terminal symbol, $\mathbb{I}$ the set of intervals with endpoints in $\mathbb{R}$, and $\varphi : \mathbb{S} \rightarrow \mathbb{I}$ is a function mapping a string from $\mathbb{S} = \Sigma^* \cup \Sigma^+ \cdot \{\tau\}$ to its associated interval. Then the tuple (Σ, τ, φ) is called a **digit serial number representation** if it obeys the following axioms:

(Contraction axiom)

$$\forall s \in \mathbb{S} : (x \sqsubset s) \wedge (y \sqsubset s) \wedge (||x|| < ||y||) : \varphi(x) \supset \varphi(y) \supseteq \varphi(s)$$

(Limit axiom)

$$\forall s \in \Sigma^* : \lim_{||x|| \rightarrow \infty, x \sqsubset s} \Delta(\varphi(x)) = 0$$

(Extensibility axiom)

$$\text{If } y \in \Sigma^* \text{ and } a \in \varphi(y) \text{ then } \exists d \in \Sigma : a \in \varphi(y \cdot d)$$

(Termination axiom)

$$\forall s \in \Sigma^+ : \Delta(\varphi(s \cdot \tau)) = 0$$

Here $x \sqsubset s$ denotes that x is a prefix of the string s, ϵ symbolizes the empty string, $\varphi(\epsilon)$ is the total variance interval, $||x||$ denotes the length of the string x, and the interval norm function $\Delta : \mathbb{I} \rightarrow \mathbb{R}$ is defined below.

We will allow intervals of the form $[p_1, p_2]$ where $p_1 > p_2$ specifies an interval that include both plus and minus infinity. If $p_1 = p_2$ the interval is a degenerate interval representing a point. An ordinary interval will be designated by the symbol I_{normal}, and the type that includes plus and minus infinity by the symbol I_∞. In order to treat ∞ as any other number, we use the stereographic

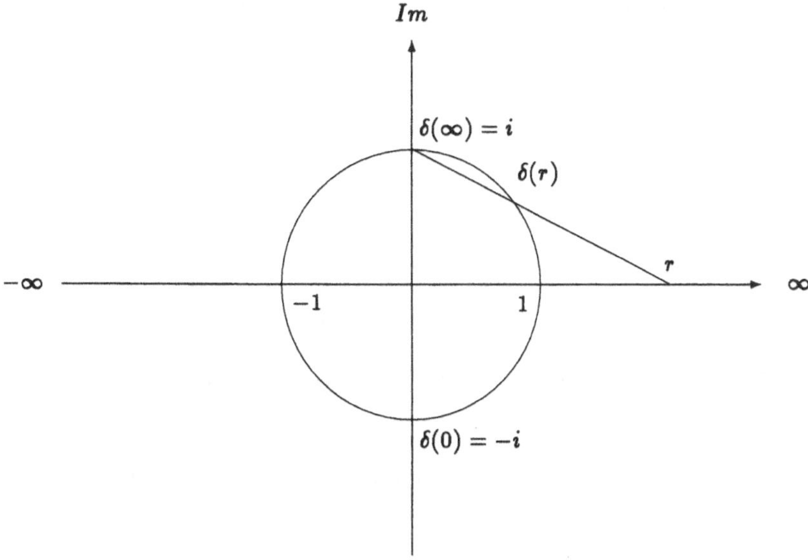

Figure 1: Stereographic representation of IR.

representation of the real line as defined in [Vuillemin 90] [see Fig. 1]. With this representation minus and plus infinity are treated as one point, and the interval $| x |> 1$ is the upper part of the circle, and the reciprocal of this interval (e.g. $| x |< 1$) is the lower part. We will adopt an alternative definition of the width of an interval $[x, y]$ by taking $\Delta : \mathbb{I} \rightarrow \mathbb{R}$ to be the length of the cord joining $\delta(x)$ and $\delta(y)$. With this definition it is possible for an interval including infinity to have finite length, making the limit axiom attainable in such special cases. Notice also that with this distance function it is possible to extend the concept of continuity for functions defined on intervals of the form I_∞.

Many well known number representations can indeed be placed within the digit serial number representation framework.

Example 1. Redundant Binary Fixed-Point Numbers.
Let $\Sigma = \{-1, 0, 1\}$, and define φ as:

$$\varphi(d_1 \cdot d_2 \cdots d_k) = [-2^{-k} + \sum_{i=1}^{k} d_i 2^{-i}, 2^{-k} + \sum_{i=1}^{k} d_i 2^{-i}]$$
$$\varphi(d_1 \cdot d_2 \cdots d_n \cdot \tau) = [\sum_{i=1}^{n} d_i 2^{-i}, \sum_{i=1}^{n} d_i 2^{-i}]$$
$$\varphi(\epsilon) = [-1, 1]$$

Notice that the termination symbol could alternatively be defined as an infinite string of zeros.

Example 2. Continued Fractions.
Let $\Sigma = \mathbb{N}^+$. The continued fraction $\frac{p_k}{q_k} = a_1 + \frac{1}{a_2 + \cdots \frac{1}{a_k}}$ can be calculated by the convergent recurrence defined by: $p_0 = q_{-1} = 1$, $p_{-1} = q_0 = 0$, $p_k = a_k p_{k-1} + p_{k-2}$ and $q_k = a_k q_{k-1} + q_{k-2}$, where $c_k = \frac{p_k}{q_k}$ is the k'th *convergent.* From

the theory of continued fractions it is known that odd numbered convergents are smaller than even numbered convergents, thus we can define φ as:

$$\varphi(a_1 \cdot a_2 \cdots a_{2k}) = \left[\frac{p_{2k}+p_{2k-1}}{q_{2k}+q_{2k-1}}, \frac{p_{2k}}{q_{2k}}\right[$$
$$\varphi(a_1 \cdot a_2 \cdots a_{2k+1}) = \left]\frac{p_{2k+1}}{q_{2k+1}}, \frac{p_{2k+1}+p_{2k}}{q_{2k+1}+q_{2k}}\right]$$
$$\varphi(\epsilon) = [1, \infty[.$$

The endpoints of the interval are calculated by letting the next digit to be seen take on its smallest and largest possible value, i.e. one and infinity. The termination symbol could be defined as an infinite string of infinity symbols. Notice that since only positive terms are allowed, this number system is not redundant, if negative terms are allowed ($\Sigma = \mathbb{Z}$) we will have redundant continued fractions, as is easily seen from the following example: The rational number $\frac{2}{7}$ can be expressed as $\frac{1}{3+\frac{1}{2}}$ or $\frac{1}{4+\frac{1}{-2}}$.

Some functions will enable us to compute the value of the function in a digit serial manner.

Definition 2. Digit Serially Computable Function.
A function $f : \mathbb{R} \to \mathbb{R}$ is *Digit Serially Computable* on the interval $I \subseteq \varphi(\epsilon)$, for a digit serial number representation (Σ, τ, φ) if

$$\forall x \in I : f(x) \subseteq \varphi(\epsilon),$$

and for all infinite strings $x \in \Sigma^*$, with $\varphi(x) \subseteq I$, there exists an infinite string $y = y_1y_2y_3 \cdots \in \Sigma^*$ such that

$$f(\varphi(x)) = \varphi(y), \text{ and}$$
$$\forall p > 0 : \exists u : u \sqsubset x : f(\varphi(u)) \subseteq \varphi(y_1y_2 \cdots y_p)$$

Notice that with this definition, we may have to read an arbitrary number of input digits between the generation of two output digits, thus the output delay can be arbitrarily large, that is the output is not synchronized with the input. It is well known that for special number representations, we can for certain functions compute the output digits with a constant output delay of one, once the first output digit has been computed, i.e. the output is synchronized with the input.

Definition 3. On-Line Computable Function.
A function $f : \mathbb{R} \to \mathbb{R}$ is *On-Line Computable* on the interval $I \subseteq \varphi(\epsilon)$, for a digit serial number representation (Σ, τ, φ) iff there exists an integer δ such that:

$$\forall x \in I : f(x) \subseteq \varphi(\epsilon)$$

and $\forall x = x_1x_2x_3 \cdots \in \Sigma^*$, with $\varphi(x) \in I$, then for all $p \geq 1$ we have:

$$f(\varphi(x_1x_2 \cdots x_{p+\delta-1})) \subseteq \varphi(y_1y_2 \cdots y_{p-1})$$
$$\Downarrow$$
$$\exists y_p \in \Sigma : f(\varphi(x_1x_2 \cdots x_{p+\delta})) \subseteq \varphi(y_1y_2 \cdots y_p)$$

The integer δ is defined as the *On-Line Delay*.

Theorem 4. *Any function that is Digit Serially Computable on an interval I, is continuous*[2] *on this interval.*

Proof. Let $x = \varphi(r) \in I$ and $y = f(x) = \varphi(s)$, with $r = x_1x_2\cdots \in \Sigma^*$ and $s = y_1y_2\cdots \in \Sigma^*$. Given any $\alpha > 0$, we can by the limit axiom, chose a p such that

$$\Delta(\varphi(y_1y_2\cdots y_p)) < \alpha$$

then by the definition of digit serial computability we have

$$\exists u \sqsubset r : f(\varphi(u)) \subseteq \varphi(y_1y_2\cdots y_p).$$

Now take $v \in \varphi(u)$ and since $x \in \varphi(u)$ we conclude:

$$\Delta([x,v]) \leq \Delta(\varphi(u)) = \beta$$

for some $\beta > 0$. Since $f(v), f(x) \in f(\varphi(u))$ we likewise conclude:

$$\Delta([f(x), f(v)]) \leq \Delta(f(\varphi(u)) \leq \Delta(\varphi(y_1y_2\cdots y_p) < \alpha.$$

Thus

$$\forall\alpha > 0 : \exists\beta > 0 : \Delta([x,v]) < \beta \Rightarrow \Delta([f(x), f(v)]) < \alpha$$

hence f is continuous on I.

Note that the class of On-Line computable functions is a subclass of the digit serially computable functions, thus an On-Line computable function is also continuous, as stated in [Duprat, Herreros and Muller 89]. It is straightforward to generalize the definition of digit serial and on-line computability to functions of two variables. Such functions are of paramount importance, since these functions include dyadic operations like addition and multiplication. When generalizing the definitions to two variables, we have the choice of requiring synchronization between the input variables, as is the case with on-line computable functions, or not to require synchronization. Thus there are three basic classes of MSB-first digit serial algorithms, the most general being the class where no synchronization is enforced, a less general subclass where the input is synchronized and the third subclass containing algorithms with both input and output synchronized. The following theorem proves the converse statement, of that formulated in [Theorem 4], but for a function of two variables.

Theorem 5. *If the function $f : \mathbb{R}^2 \to \mathbb{R}$ is continuous on the domain $I_x \times I_y$, and if for all $x \in I_x$ and $y \in I_y$ we have $f(x,y) \in \varphi(\epsilon)$, then f is digit serially computable for any Digit Serial Number Representation.*

Proof. Let $x, y \in \Sigma^*$ be two infinite strings, with $\varphi(x) \in I_x$ and $\varphi(y) \in I_y$. By extensibility we conclude that there exists an infinite string $z = z_1z_2z_3\cdots \in \Sigma^*$ such that $f(\varphi(x), \varphi(y)) = \varphi(z)$. Because of the contraction axiom, we must have:

$$\varphi(z_1) \supseteq \varphi(z_1z_2) \supseteq \cdots \supseteq \varphi(z_1z_2\cdots z_p) \supseteq \cdots \supseteq \varphi(z)$$

and since $x \sqsubset x$ and $y \sqsubset y$ we get by the continuity of f:

$$\forall p > 0 : \exists u \sqsubset x \wedge \exists v \sqsubset y : f(\varphi(u), \varphi(v)) \subseteq \varphi(z_1z_2\cdots z_p).$$

Thus f is digit serially computable.

[2] Continuity is here defined in terms of the stereographic distance measure Δ.

The following algorithm describes how to compute the output of a function in a digit serial manner. The notation: $BooleanExpr1 : ExprSeq1 [] BooleanExpr2 : ExprSeq2$; means if only one of the boolean expressions are true then execute the corresponding statement sequence. If both expressions are true, then according to some rule execute one or both statement sequences. Such a rule might be: Select one of the sequences nondeterministically, or alternatively: Execute both in parallel.

Algorithm 1. *Basic Digit Serial Function Evaluation.*

Stimulus: $f : \mathbb{R}^2 \to \mathbb{R}$, $x, y \in \Sigma^* \cdot \{\tau\}$, $n \in \mathbb{N}$.
Response: $z \in \Sigma^n \cup \Sigma^* \cdot \{\tau\}$.
Method:

$p \leftarrow 1;$
$i, j \leftarrow 0;$
while $p \leq n$ *and* $f(\varphi(x_1 \cdots x_i), \varphi(y_1 \cdots y_j)) \neq \varphi(z_1 \cdots z_{p-1} \cdot \tau)$ *do*
  if $\exists z_p \in \Sigma : f(\varphi(x_1 \cdots x_i), \varphi(y_1 \cdots y_j)) \subseteq \varphi(z_1 \cdots z_p)$ *then*
    output z_p*;*
    $p \leftarrow p + 1;$
  else
    $x_i \neq \tau : i \leftarrow i + 1;\ x_i \leftarrow$ *input from* x
     []
    $y_j \neq \tau : j \leftarrow j + 1;\ y_j \leftarrow$ *input from* y
  end;
end;
if $f(\varphi(x_1 x_2 \cdots x_i), \varphi(y_1 y_2 \cdots y_j)) = \varphi(z_1 z_2 \cdots z_{p-1} \cdot t)$ *then*
  output τ*;*
end;

□

It is well known that a redundant representation is necessary for a function in general to be on-line computable. The following theorem formalizes the on-line property for the signed-digit radix two representation, and can easily be generalized to other redundant radix representations.

Theorem 6. *If the function* $f : \mathbb{R}^2 \to \mathbb{R}$ *is digit serially computable for the signed-digit radix two representation with* $\Sigma = \{-1, 0, 1\}$ *on the domain* $I = I_x \times I_y$*, where* I_x *and* I_y *are of the interval type* I_{normal}*, and if the partial derivatives of* f *are bounded on this domain, then there exists a finite integer constant:* δ *such that* f *is on-line computable with on-line delay* δ*.*

Proof. Suppose that the $p-1$ most significant digits of $z = f(x, y)$ have been calculated from $x_1, x_2, \ldots, x_{p-1+\delta}$ and $y_1, y_2, \ldots, y_{p-1+\delta}$ such that

$$f(\varphi(x_1 x_2 \cdots x_{p-1+\delta}), \varphi(y_1 y_2 \cdots y_{p-1+\delta})) \subseteq \varphi(z_1 z_2 \cdots z_{p-1})$$

Define the domain $D = [a, b] \times [c, d] \subseteq I$ by:

$$a = 0.x_1 x_2 \cdots x_{p-1+\delta} x_{p+\delta} \bar{1}\bar{1}\bar{1} \ldots = -2^{-p-\delta} + \sum_{i=1}^{p+\delta} x_i 2^{-i}$$

$$b = 0.x_1x_2\cdots x_{p-1+\delta}x_{p+\delta}111\ldots = 2^{-p-\delta} + \sum_{i=1}^{p+\delta} x_i 2^{-i}$$

$$c = 0.y_1y_2\cdots y_{p-1+\delta}y_{p+\delta}\bar{1}\bar{1}\bar{1}\ldots = -2^{-p-\delta} + \sum_{i=1}^{p+\delta} y_i 2^{-i}$$

$$d = 0.y_1y_2\cdots y_{p-1+\delta}y_{p+\delta}111\ldots = 2^{-p-\delta} + \sum_{i=1}^{p+\delta} y_i 2^{-i}.$$

The possible variation of $f(x,y)$ within D is easily estimated by:

$$\begin{aligned}|f_{max} - f_{min}| &= \left|\max_{(x,y)\in D}\{f(x,y)\} - \min_{(x,y)\in D}\{f(x,y)\}\right| \\ &\leq |b-a| \max_{(x,y)\in I}\left\{\left|\frac{\partial f(x,y)}{\partial x}\right|\right\} + |d-c| \max_{(x,y)\in I}\left\{\left|\frac{\partial f(x,y)}{\partial y}\right|\right\} \\ &= 2^{-p-\delta+1}\left(\max_{(x,y)\in I}\left\{\left|\frac{\partial f(x,y)}{\partial x}\right|\right\} + \max_{(x,y)\in I}\left\{\left|\frac{\partial f(x,y)}{\partial y}\right|\right\}\right)\end{aligned}$$

Take $\delta \geq \left\lceil log_2\left(\max_{(x,y)\in I}\left\{\left|\frac{\partial f}{\partial x}\right|\right\} + \max_{(x,y)\in I}\left\{\left|\frac{\partial f}{\partial y}\right|\right\}\right)\right\rceil + C$, where C is a positive integer constant. Since δ is an integer we get:

$$2^{\delta-C} \geq \left(\max_{(x,y)\in I}\left\{\left|\frac{\partial f}{\partial x}\right|\right\} + \max_{(x,y)\in I}\left\{\left|\frac{\partial f}{\partial y}\right|\right\}\right)$$

and if $C \geq 1$ we get $|f_{max} - f_{min}| \leq 2^{-p}$. Now

$$\begin{aligned}f(\varphi(x_1\cdots x_{p+\delta}), \varphi(y_1\cdots y_{p+\delta})) &\subseteq f(\varphi(x_1\cdots x_{p-1+\delta}), \varphi(y_1\cdots y_{p-1+\delta})) \\ &\subseteq \varphi(z_1\cdots z_{p-1}) \\ &= \left[-2^{-p+1} + \sum_{i=1}^{p-1} z_i 2^{-i}, 2^{-p+1} + \sum_{i=1}^{p-1} z_i 2^{-i}\right]\end{aligned}$$

Consulting [Fig.2] immediately leads to the conclusion that no matter where the interval $f(\varphi(x_1\cdots x_{p+\delta}), \varphi(y_1\cdots y_{p+\delta}))$ is placed within $\varphi(z_1\cdots z_{p-1})$ there exists a $z_p \in \Sigma$ such that

$$f(\varphi(x_1\cdots x_{p+\delta}), \varphi(y_1\cdots y_{p+\delta})) \subseteq \varphi(z_1\cdots z_p).$$

Since the function is digit serially computable, for $p = 1$ we have that

$$\begin{aligned}f(\varphi(x_1\cdots x_{p+\delta}), \varphi(y_1\cdots y_{p+\delta})) &\subseteq \varphi(\epsilon) = [-1, 1] \\ &= \left[-2^{-p+1} + \sum_{i=1}^{p-1} z_i 2^{-i}, 2^{-p+1} + \sum_{i=1}^{p-1} z_i 2^{-i}\right]\end{aligned}$$

with a similar argument as the one used above, we may conclude that in the base case $p = 1$ we can find a z_1 such that $f(\varphi(x_1\cdots x_{\delta+1}), (y_1\cdots y_{\delta+1}) \subseteq \varphi(z_1)$. Thus if $\delta+1$ input digits have been consumed from input x and y, an output digit can be derived in each subsequent iteration, that is $f(x,y)$ is on-line computable.

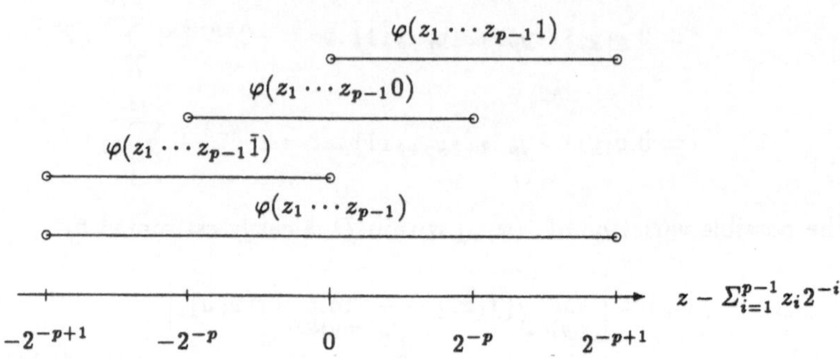

Figure 2: The variation of the output ($z = f(x, y)$).

[Theorem 6] tells us, that for radix two with $\Sigma = \{-1, 0, 1\}$ we can modify [Algorithm 1] to withhold production of output digits until $\delta + 1$ input digits have been read from inputs x and y, and in the subsequent iterations one output digit is generated whenever one input digit is consumed from both operands, this modified algorithm will be an on-line algorithm. This basic algorithm can intuitively be brought to compute the output of an on-line computable function, with an on-line delay that is equal to the theoretical lower bound.

3 Homographic Matrix Coding

As discussed, digit serial numbers can effectively be described with the aid of intervals. In this section we will show, that the intervals corresponding to a digit string can be represented by matrices.

Notation 7. Interval-matrix and Matrix-interval Homomorphism.
An *interval matrix* $A = \begin{bmatrix} p & s \\ q & t \end{bmatrix}$ $p, q, r, s \in \mathbb{Z}$, is a matrix representing an interval: $\Phi(A)$, with endpoints $\frac{p}{q}$ and $\frac{s}{t}$, where the homomorphism $\Phi : \mathbb{M}_{2\times 2} \rightarrow \mathbb{I}$ is dependent on the representation. In some cases it is sufficient to define Φ as

$$\Phi(A) = \left[\frac{p}{q}, \frac{s}{t}\right]$$

Notation 8. Digit-set Isomorphism.
Let $\eta : \Sigma \cup \{\tau, \epsilon\} \rightarrow \Sigma_M \cup \{T, E\}$ be an isomorphism that maps digits, an empty string or the termination symbol into 2×2 matrices. $T = \eta(\tau)$ is denoted as the *termination matrix* and $E = \eta(\epsilon)$ as *the total variance matrix.*

For a specific digit serial representation, it is now possible to construct a matrix product representation of a digit serial number.

Definition 9. Homographic Matrix-coding.
If (Σ, τ, φ) is a digit serial number representation, η a digit-set isomorphism, and Φ a matrix-interval homomorphism, then $C = (\Sigma, \eta, \Phi)$ is a *homographic matrix coding* if the following is obeyed:

$\Phi(E) = \varphi(\epsilon)$, and
If $\Phi(EX_1X_2\cdots X_p) = \varphi(x_1x_2\cdots x_p)$, $x_i \in \Sigma$ and $X_i = \eta(x_i)$ for $i = 1, 2, \ldots, p$, then

$$\Phi(EX_1X_2\cdots X_pD) = \varphi(x_1x_2\cdots x_pd)$$

and

$$\Phi(EX_1X_2\cdots X_pT) = \varphi(x_1x_2\cdots x_p\tau)$$

where $d \in \Sigma$, $D = \eta(d)$.

The termination matrix acts in the same way as the termination symbol, in the sense that it turns some interval matrix into an interval matrix representing a degenerate interval.

Example 3. Continued Fractions ($\Sigma = \mathbb{N}^+, \varphi(\epsilon) = [1, \infty[$)

$$\begin{aligned}\begin{bmatrix} p_k + p_{k-1} & p_k \\ q_k + q_{k-1} & q_k \end{bmatrix} &= \begin{bmatrix} a_kp_{k-1} + p_{k-2} + p_{k-1} & a_kp_{k-1} + p_{k-2} \\ a_kq_{k-1} + q_{k-2} + q_{k-1} & a_kq_{k-1} + q_{k-2} \end{bmatrix} \\ &= \begin{bmatrix} p_{k-1} + p_{k-2} & p_{k-1} \\ q_{k-1} + q_{n-2} & q_{k-1} \end{bmatrix} \begin{bmatrix} 1 & 1 \\ a_k & a_k - 1 \end{bmatrix} \\ &= \begin{bmatrix} p_0 + p_{-1} & p_0 \\ q_0 + q_{-1} & q_0 \end{bmatrix} \begin{bmatrix} 1 & 1 \\ a_1 & a_1 - 1 \end{bmatrix} \cdots \begin{bmatrix} 1 & 1 \\ a_k & a_k - 1 \end{bmatrix} \\ &= \begin{bmatrix} 1 & 1 \\ 1 & 0 \end{bmatrix} \begin{bmatrix} 1 & 1 \\ a_1 & a_1 - 1 \end{bmatrix} \cdots \begin{bmatrix} 1 & 1 \\ a_k & a_k - 1 \end{bmatrix} \\ &= EA_1A_2\cdots A_k.\end{aligned}$$

Now taking the termination matrix as: $T = \begin{bmatrix} 0 & 0 \\ 1 & 1 \end{bmatrix}$ we see that $C_{cf} = (\Sigma, \eta, \Phi)$ is a homographic matrix coding, where $\eta(a_i) = E^{-1} \begin{bmatrix} a_i & 1 \\ 1 & 1 \end{bmatrix} E = \begin{bmatrix} 1 & 1 \\ a_i & a_i - 1 \end{bmatrix}$. The matrix-interval homomorphism Φ, is as defined previously, but with the end-points interchanged when k is odd. Note that the convergents can be computed as:

$$\begin{bmatrix} p_n & p_{n-1} \\ q_n & q_{n-1} \end{bmatrix} = \begin{bmatrix} p_{n-1} & p_{n-2} \\ q_{n-1} & q_{n-2} \end{bmatrix} \begin{bmatrix} a_n & 1 \\ 1 & 0 \end{bmatrix} = \begin{bmatrix} a_1 & 1 \\ 1 & 1 \end{bmatrix} \begin{bmatrix} a_2 & 1 \\ 1 & 1 \end{bmatrix} \cdots \begin{bmatrix} a_n & 1 \\ 1 & 1 \end{bmatrix}.$$

Example 4. Redundant Binary Fixed-Point Numbers. ($\Sigma = \{-1, 0, 1\}, \varphi(\epsilon) =]-1, 1[$)
It is easily verified that choosing η in the following way makes $C_{fp} = (\Sigma, \eta, \Phi)$ a homo-graphic matrix coding:

$$\eta(\epsilon) = E = \begin{bmatrix} -1 & 1 \\ 1 & 1 \end{bmatrix}$$

$$\eta(b) = 2E^{-1}\begin{bmatrix}1 & b\\ 0 & 2\end{bmatrix}E = \begin{bmatrix}-b+3 & -b+1\\ b+1 & b+3\end{bmatrix} \text{ for all } b \in \Sigma$$
$$\eta(t) = T = \begin{bmatrix}1 & 1\\ 1 & 1\end{bmatrix}.$$

Note that the sum $\frac{p_n}{q_n} = \sum_{i=1}^{n} b_i 2^{-i}$ can be computed as:

$$\begin{bmatrix}1 & p_n\\ 0 & q_n\end{bmatrix} = \begin{bmatrix}1 & b_n + 2p_{n-1}\\ 0 & 2q_{n-1}\end{bmatrix} = \begin{bmatrix}1 & p_{n-1}\\ 0 & 2q_{n-1}\end{bmatrix}\begin{bmatrix}1 & b_n\\ 0 & 2\end{bmatrix} = \begin{bmatrix}1 & b_1\\ 0 & 2\end{bmatrix}\cdots\begin{bmatrix}1 & b_n\\ 0 & 2\end{bmatrix}.$$

In this paper we have taken a formal language approach, when describing the behaviour of digit serial arithmetic, it therefore falls natural to implement the generation of the appropriate transformations as a finite-state transducer. The automaton acts as a translator in the sense, that it translates input symbols into matrices, in such a way that when these matrices are multiplied in the order they are received, the product will be an interval matrix representing the interval corresponding to the input string. From the transformations and the knowledge of how one symbol can proceed another symbol, a state table can be constructed.

Example 5. Finite-state Transducer for Redundant Base 2 Fixed-Point Digit-Serial Numbers.
A table [see Tab. 1] can be constructed from the previously developed transformations, based on this table a finite-state transducer can be devised [see Fig. 3].

State	Symbol	Next-state	$(\alpha,\beta,\gamma,\delta)$	Interval Type
Start	–	Fraction	$(-1,1,1,1)$	I_{normal}
Fraction	$\bar{1}$	Fraction	$(4,2,0,2)$	I_{normal}
	0	Fraction	$(3,1,1,3)$	I_{normal}
	1	Fraction	$(2,0,2,4)$	I_{normal}
	τ	Terminated	$(1,1,1,1)$	*point*
Terminated	–	Terminated	$(1,0,0,1)$	*point*

Table 1: Transition/output table for redundant base 2 fixed-point digit-serial numbers.

The table describes the translation of an operand in the form of a digit string into a sequence of matrices. The operand has a state variable, initially assigned the state labeled ***start***, associated with it. Digits are read one by one from the operand, upon reading the symbol s, produce the transformation matrix corresponding to the symbol s in the present state. When the matrix multiplication has been completed move to the state designated by ***next-state***. The column labeled ***interval type*** conveys information about how the interval matrix generated by the subsequent matrix multiplications is to be interpreted, I_{normal} designates an ordinary interval that does not include both plus and minus infinity, *point* designates a degenerate interval representing a point.

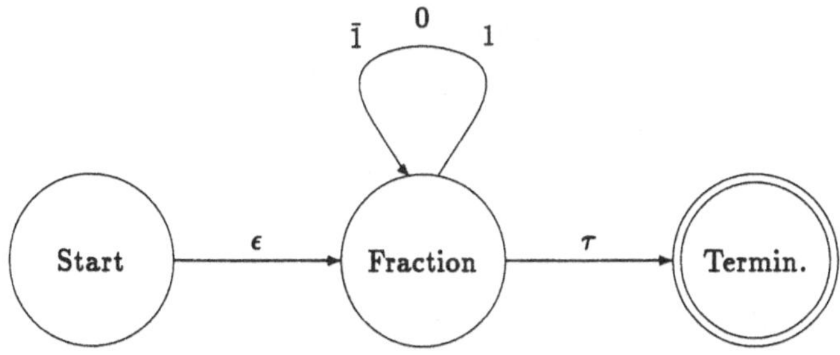

Figure 3: State machine for radix 2 fixed-point numbers.

We now investigate how to compute the output of a function of the form: $f(x) = \frac{ax+b}{cx+d}$ in a digit serial manner. The parameters $a, b, c, d \in \mathbb{Z}$ are chosen such that f is digit serially computable. Evaluating the function at a point $x = \frac{p}{q}$ yields $f(\frac{p}{q}) = \frac{a\frac{p}{q}+b}{c\frac{p}{q}+d} = \frac{ap+bq}{cp+dq}$, and equivalently for $x = \frac{s}{t}$ we get $f(\frac{s}{t}) = \frac{as+bt}{cs+dt}$. Now since the function is monotonic (assumed increasing), when evaluating the function on the interval $[\frac{p}{q}, \frac{s}{t}]$ we get a new interval $[\frac{ap+bq}{cp+dq}, \frac{as+bt}{cs+dt}]$. This computation can effectively be modeled by matrix multiplication.

Definition 10. Homographic Function Matrix
The matrix $F = \begin{bmatrix} a\, b \\ c\, d \end{bmatrix}$ $a, b, c, d \in \mathbb{Z}$, is defined as a matrix representation of the digit serially computable function $f(x) = \frac{ax+b}{cx+d}$, in the sense that if $\Phi(EX_1X_2\cdots X_p) = \varphi(x_1x_2\cdots x_p)$ then $\Phi(FEX_1X_2\cdots X_p) = f(\varphi(x_1x_2\cdots x_p))$

Notice that F is defined in such a way that multiplying from the right with an interval matrix yields a new interval matrix. That is

$$FA = \begin{bmatrix} a\, b \\ c\, d \end{bmatrix} \begin{bmatrix} p\, s \\ q\, t \end{bmatrix} = \begin{bmatrix} ap + bq\;\, as + bt \\ cp + dq\;\, cs + dt \end{bmatrix}. \tag{1}$$

Furthermore if F, G are matrices representing the functions f and g, then FG represents $f \circ g$ and F^{-1} represents f^{-1}.

Since the two different ways of representing digit serial numbers are equivalent, it is straightforward to state analogous definitions and proofs to those of [Section 2] in terms of a homographic matrix coding. For instance the condition $f(\varphi(x_1x_2\cdots x_i)) \subseteq \varphi(y_1y_2\cdots y_p)$ can be stated as:

$$\Phi(FEX_1X_2\cdots X_i) \subseteq \Phi(EY_1Y_2\cdots Y_p) \tag{2}$$

Observation 11. Let F be a function matrix representing a function that is continuous and monotone on an interval represented by the matrix B, then $\Phi(A) \subseteq \Phi(B) \Longleftrightarrow \Phi(FA) \subseteq \Phi(FB)$

Assuming [3] that for all $Y_j \in \Sigma_M$ we have that Y_j^{-1} represents a function that is continuous and monotone on the interval represented by $\Phi(Y_j \cdots Y_p)$, and similarly assume that E^{-1} represents a continuous monotone function on the interval $\Phi(E)$. From (2) and [Observation 11] we arrive at:

$$\Phi(Y_{p-1}^{-1} \cdots Y_2^{-1} Y_1^{-1} E^{-1} F E X_1 X_2 \cdots X_i) \subseteq \Phi(Y_p). \tag{3}$$

Similarly the termination test: $f(\varphi(x_1 x_2 \cdots x_i) = \varphi(y_1 y_2 \cdots y_{p-1} \cdot t)$ can be stated as:

$$\Phi(Y_{p-1}^{-1} \cdots Y_2^{-1} Y_1^{-1} E^{-1} F E X_1 X_2 \cdots X_i) = \Phi(T). \tag{4}$$

Thus an algorithm for computing $f(x)$ in some point $x = \varphi(x_1 x_2 \cdots x_n t)$, could proceed as follows: Let F be the function on matrix form. Transform the function matrix as: $F \leftarrow E^{-1} F E$. Consume input by setting: $F \leftarrow F X_i$, and when possible produce output by $F \leftarrow Y_p^{-1} F$. Where $X_i = \eta(x_i)$ and $Y_i = \eta(y_i)$.

An algorithm based on an automaton could alternatively be used, by assigning a state variable to both the input and output variable. In the case of ***input***, upon receiving the symbol s do the multiplication $F \begin{bmatrix} \alpha & \beta \\ \gamma & \delta \end{bmatrix}$ with the matrix corresponding to the symbol s in the present state, then move to the next state. When performing ***output***, we first need to check if output can be generated. This is done by checking if for any of the symbols in the present state we have:

$$\left[\frac{\alpha}{\gamma}, \frac{\beta}{\delta}\right] \supseteq \Phi(F).$$

If this holds for some symbol then the symbol is output, and the multiplication

$$\begin{bmatrix} \delta & -\beta \\ -\gamma & \alpha \end{bmatrix} F$$

is performed. The range of the function evaluated on the interval corresponding to the prefix of the operand that has been seen so far (specified by $\Phi(F)$), can be computed by knowing the interval type of the operand, and by the knowledge of whether the function is monotonically increasing or decreasing, which is computable from the sign of the determinant of F.

4 The Cube

In this section we consider how to evaluate a function of two variables. The collective variance associated with two variables is a Cartesian product of two intervals. The variance of the function amounting from evaluating the function in all points of the domain will be characterized by a surface in $\mathbb{R}^3$. In the following we will consider a generalization of the homographic function $f(x) = \frac{ax+b}{cx+d}$ to a similar function of two variables (a bi-homographic function):

$$f(x_2, x_1) = \frac{a_{111} x_2 x_1 + a_{101} x_2 + a_{011} x_1 + a_{001}}{a_{110} x_2 x_1 + a_{100} x_2 + a_{010} x_1 + a_{000}}, \; a_i \in \mathbb{Z} \tag{5}$$

[3] This is indeed not an unrealistic assumption, as readily verified from the previous examples.

With an appropriate choice of coefficients in (5), the function can compute the standard arithmetic operations $x + y$, $x - y$, $x \cdot y$ and x/y.

A matrix representation will not suffice for a function of two variables, but as we will show, such a function can be represented by a *cube* [see Fig. 4]. This type of computational unit, has been examined for non-redundant as well as redundant continued fraction representations in [Kornerup and Matula 85, Kornerup and Matula 88, Kornerup and Matula 89, Kornerup and Matula 90], based on an algorithm developed by Gosper in [Gosper 72].

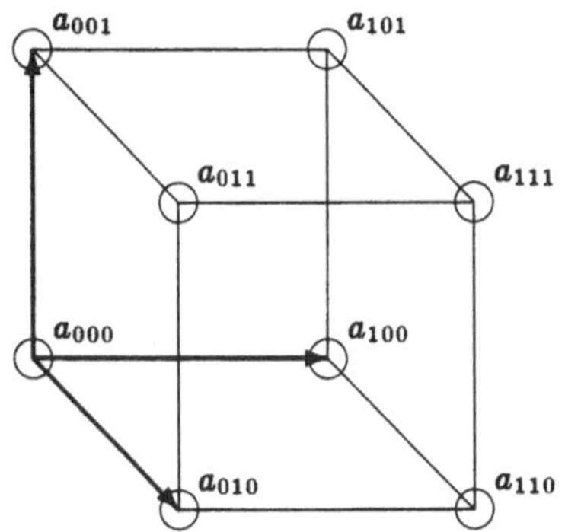

Figure 4: Cube modelling a function of two variables.

If we evaluate $f(x_2, x_1)$ on the endpoints of an interval defined by $x_1 \in [\frac{p_{1,1}}{q_{1,1}}, \frac{p_{1,0}}{q_{1,0}}]$ (respectively $x_2 \in [\frac{p_{2,1}}{q_{2,1}}, \frac{p_{2,0}}{q_{2,0}}]$) we get:

$$f(x_2, x_1 = \frac{p_{1,b_1}}{q_{1,b_1}}) = \frac{(a_{111}p_{1,b_1} + a_{101}q_{1,b_1})x_2 + (a_{011}p_{1,b_1} + a_{001}q_{1,b_1})}{(a_{110}p_{1,b_1} + a_{100}q_{1,b_1})x_2 + (a_{010}p_{1,b_1} + a_{000}q_{1,b_1})}, \; b_1 \in \mathbb{B} \tag{6}$$

respectively

$$f(x_2 = \frac{p_{2,b_2}}{q_{2,b_2}}, x_1) = \frac{(a_{111}p_{2,b_2} + a_{011}q_{2,b_2})x_1 + (a_{101}p_{2,b_2} + a_{001}q_{2,b_2})}{(a_{110}p_{2,b_2} + a_{010}q_{2,b_2})x_1 + (a_{100}p_{2,b_2} + a_{000}q_{2,b_2})}, \; b_2 \in \mathbb{B}. \tag{7}$$

The updating taking place in equations (6) (respectively (7)) can be described by the following matrix multiplications:

$$F_{1xx}X_1 = \begin{bmatrix} a_{111} & a_{101} \\ a_{110} & a_{100} \end{bmatrix} \begin{bmatrix} p_{1,1} & p_{1,0} \\ q_{1,1} & q_{1,0} \end{bmatrix} = \begin{bmatrix} a'_{111} & a'_{101} \\ a'_{110} & a'_{100} \end{bmatrix} = F'_{1xx}. \tag{8}$$

$$F_{0xx}X_1 = \begin{bmatrix} a_{011} & a_{001} \\ a_{010} & a_{000} \end{bmatrix} \begin{bmatrix} p_{1,1} & p_{1,0} \\ q_{1,1} & q_{1,0} \end{bmatrix} = \begin{bmatrix} a'_{011} & a'_{001} \\ a'_{010} & a'_{000} \end{bmatrix} = F'_{0xx} \tag{9}$$

respectively:

$$F_{x1x}X_2 = \begin{bmatrix} a_{111} & a_{011} \\ a_{110} & a_{010} \end{bmatrix} \begin{bmatrix} p_{2,1} & p_{2,0} \\ q_{2,1} & q_{2,0} \end{bmatrix} = \begin{bmatrix} a'_{111} & a'_{011} \\ a'_{110} & a'_{010} \end{bmatrix} = F'_{x1x} \quad (10)$$

$$F_{x0x}X_2 = \begin{bmatrix} a_{101} & a_{001} \\ a_{100} & a_{000} \end{bmatrix} \begin{bmatrix} p_{2,1} & p_{2,0} \\ q_{2,1} & q_{2,0} \end{bmatrix} = \begin{bmatrix} a'_{101} & a'_{001} \\ a'_{100} & a'_{000} \end{bmatrix} = F'_{x0x} \quad (11)$$

The matrices F_{1xx} and F_{0xx} (respectively F_{x1x} and F_{x0x}) can be found as faces of the cube [see Fig. 5]. With this computation model it is now straight forward to expand the interval matrices X_1 (respectively X_2) in terms of the homographic matrix coding developed in [Section 3]. For instance we can expand X_1 as $EX_{1,1}X_{2,1}\cdots X_{n,1}$, with $X_{i,1} \in \Sigma_M$. Thus the process of consuming input from an operand, corresponds to performing two matrix multiplications in parallel.

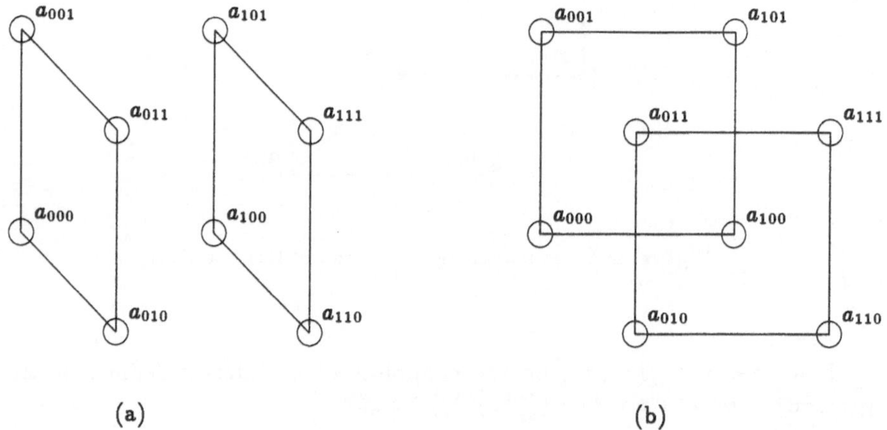

Figure 5: Input transformation. (a) Input from variable x_1. By decomposing the cube we get 2 matrices F_{1xx} and F_{0xx}. (b) Input from variable x_2. Decomposition yields the matrices F_{x1x} and F_{x0x}

Observation 12. If the function $f(x_2, x_1)$, modeled by the cube F, is evaluated on the domain: $]\frac{p_{1,1}}{q_{1,1}}, \frac{p_{1,0}}{q_{1,0}}[\times]\frac{p_{2,1}}{q_{2,1}}, \frac{p_{2,0}}{q_{2,0}}[$, then the value of the function evaluated on a corner of the domain, can be found from F as:

$$f(x_2 = \frac{p_{2,b_2}}{q_{2,b_2}}, x_1 = \frac{p_{1,b_1}}{q_{1,b_1}}) = \frac{a_{b_2b_11}}{a_{b_2b_10}}, \ b_1, b_2 \in \mathbb{B}$$

In the process of transforming the cube during input, we perform two matrix multiplications, and we are thus faced with a notational problem when we want to state a matrix equivalent output equation. To overcome this problem we will use the symbols $\otimes_1$ (respectively $\otimes_2$) to denote the infix operator that performs two matrix multiplications: $F_{1xx}X_1$ and $F_{0xx}X_1$ (respectively $F_{x1x}X_2$ and $F_{x0x}X_2$), when consuming input from x_1 (respectively x_2). We will use a braced notation to denote input transformation from both variables according to some order. In order to compare the cube, evaluated on a domain, against an interval, we introduce a function $\Phi_C : cube \rightarrow \mathbb{I}$ that maps a cube into an interval, as defined by:

$$\Phi_C\left(F\left\{\begin{matrix}\otimes_1 EX_1X_2\cdots X_i\\ \otimes_2 EY_1Y_2\cdots Y_j\end{matrix}\right\}\right) = f(\varphi(x_1x_2\cdots x_i), \varphi(y_1y_2\cdots y_j)). \qquad (12)$$

Thus the condition $f(\varphi(x_1x_2\cdots x_i), \varphi(y_1y_2\cdots y_j)) \subseteq \varphi(z_1z_2\cdots z_p)$ can be stated as:

$$\Phi_C\left(F\left\{\begin{matrix}\otimes_1 EX_1X_2\cdots X_i\\ \otimes_2 EY_1Y_2\cdots Y_j\end{matrix}\right\}\right) \subseteq \Phi(EZ_1Z_2\cdots Z_P). \qquad (13)$$

In [Section 3], output generation for the one-dimensional case was established as multiplying with the inverse of a matrix from Σ_M. This process was equivalent to function composition, as it will be in the case of two variables. Let F be a cube modeling the function $f : \mathbb{R}^2 \rightarrow \mathbb{R}$, and let $G = \begin{bmatrix}\alpha & \beta\\ \gamma & \delta\end{bmatrix}$ be a matrix that represents a function $g : \mathbb{R} \rightarrow \mathbb{R}$. The composition $g \circ f : \mathbb{R}^2 \rightarrow \mathbb{R}$ is:

$$\begin{aligned}
&(g \circ f)(x_2, x_1)\\
&= \frac{\alpha f(x_2,x_1)+\beta}{\gamma f(x_2,x_1)+\delta}\\
&= \frac{(\alpha a_{111}+\beta a_{110})x_2x_1+(\alpha a_{101}+\beta a_{100})x_2+(\alpha a_{011}+\beta a_{010})x_1+(\alpha a_{001}+\beta a_{000})}{(\gamma a_{111}+\delta a_{110})x_2x_1+(\gamma a_{101}+\delta a_{100})x_2+(\gamma a_{011}+\delta a_{010})x_1+(\gamma a_{001}+\delta a_{000})}\\
&= \frac{a'_{111}x_2x_1+a'_{101}x_2+a'_{011}x_1+a'_{001}}{a'_{110}x_2x_1+a'_{100}x_2+a'_{010}x_1+a'_{000}}
\end{aligned}$$

The transformation is clearly equivalent to the matrix multiplications GF_{1xx} and GF_{0xx} or GF_{x1x} and GF_{x0x}, thus in the case of output we have a choice between two possible ways of expressing the output transformation.

Assuming as in [Section 3], that X_l^{-1}, Y_m^{-1} and E^{-1} represents continuous monotone functions, we may transform (13) into:

$$\Phi_C\left(Z_{p-1}^{-1}\cdots Z_2^{-1}Z_1^{-1}E^{-1}\otimes_1 F\left\{\begin{matrix}\otimes_1 EX_1X_2\cdots X_i\\ \otimes_2 EY_1Y_2\cdots Y_j\end{matrix}\right\}\right) \subseteq \Phi(Z_P). \qquad (14)$$

Similarly by replacing Z_p with T, and inclusion by equality in (14) we get the cube equivalent equation of the termination test: $f(\varphi(x_1x_2\cdots x_i), \varphi(y_1y_2\cdots y_j) = \varphi(z_1z_2\cdots z_{p-1}\tau)$.

Thus an algorithm for computing $f(x,y)$ at some point $(\varphi(x_1x_2\cdots x_n\tau), \varphi(y_1y_2\cdots y_m\tau))$, could proceed as follows: Let F be the cube representation of the function f. Transform the function matrix as: $F \leftarrow E^{-1}\otimes_1 F$, $F \leftarrow F\otimes_1 E$ and finally $F \leftarrow F\otimes_2 E$. Consume input from x by setting: $F \leftarrow F\otimes_1 X_i$, similarly from y by $F \leftarrow F\otimes_2 Y_j$. When possible produce output by $F \leftarrow Z_p^{-1}\otimes_1 F$.

As described in [Section 3], an algorithm based on a finite-state transducer can be devised, with the difference that we will have to perform cube transformations rather that simple matrix multiplications, and that we now have two input variables instead of one, each having an associated state variable. In the case of ***input consumption*** from variable i, the table is to be interpreted as: Upon receiving a symbol s, perform the cube transformation

$$F \otimes_i \begin{bmatrix} \alpha & \beta \\ \gamma & \delta \end{bmatrix}$$

with the matrix corresponding to the symbol s in the present state, when the transformation has been completed move to the state designated by ***next-state***. When performing ***output***, we first need to check if output can be generated. This is done by checking if for any of the symbols in the present state we have:

$$\left[\frac{\alpha}{\gamma}, \frac{\beta}{\delta}\right] \supseteq \Phi_C(F)$$

if this holds for some symbol then the symbol is send to the output, and the cube transformation

$$\begin{bmatrix} \delta & -\beta \\ -\gamma & \alpha \end{bmatrix} \otimes_1 F$$

is performed. The range of the function on some domain (specified by $\Phi_C(F)$), can be found by examination of the function evaluated on the boundary of the domain if the function is monotone with respect to each variable on this domain. The domain has 4 edges that can be treated independently. The function values at the endpoints of these 4 intervals can be found in the cube, and the interval type can be resolved by knowing the interval type of the operand that is not constant along the edge under consideration, and by examining whether or not a sign change in the denominator occurs along the edge, this is again computable from the cube.

5 Digit Serial Floating Point Operands

If the operand of some function has a fixed point format, the set of representable number will be very limited, if a larger set is needed we can tag information about the position of the radix point onto the operands. In traditional on-line algorithms this is done by coupling exponent information to the first digit of the mantissa part, where the mantissa part is to be kept quasi-normalized, in the sense that the two first digits should have the same sign, and the first digit can not take on the value zero [Watanuki and Ercegovac 81, Watanuki and Ercegovac 83, Owens 83]. A problem with this type of normalization is that in certain computations cancellation might occur (e.g. if two almost equal numbers are subtracted), requiring extensive normalisation. If this computation is feeding another computation unit, the other units delivering input to the same computation unit will have to delay their output, in order to keep the input to the unit synchronized [see Fig. 6]. Thus the set of representable numbers have been enlarged, at the expense of a variable output delay, due to possible normalization requirements.

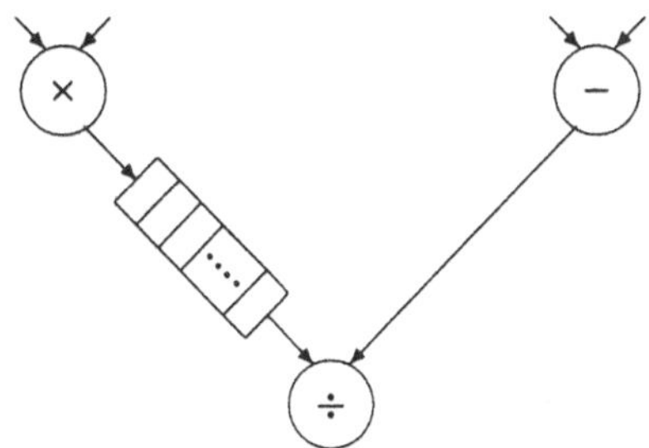

Figure 6: Computation requiring buffering.

We will now show how a floating point can be introduced in the redundant binary fixed point number representation considered in [Section 3] and [Section 4]. We will require normalization of the form:

$$b_0 b_1 \geq 0 \wedge b_0 \neq 0, \tag{15}$$

such that the mantissa part can represent any number in the intervals defined by:

$$\varphi(1) = [1.0\bar{1}\bar{1}\bar{1}\ldots, 1.1111\ldots] = [\frac{1}{2}, 2] \tag{16}$$
$$\varphi(\bar{1}) = [\bar{1}.\bar{1}\bar{1}\bar{1}\ldots, \bar{1}.0111\ldots] = [-2, -\frac{1}{2}]$$

We introduce two new symbols l and u in order to specify negative, respectively positive valued exponents. If the mantissa part is preceded by n symbols of the u type respectively the l type, then the value of the whole string is to be interpreted as 2^n respectively 2^{-n} times the mantissa part. The strings are given the following interpretation:

$$\varphi(u) = [1, -1] \;\; \varphi(l) = [-1, 1] \tag{17}$$
$$\varphi(u^n) = [2^{n-1}, -2^{n-1}] \;\; \varphi(l^n) = [-2^{-n+1}, 2^{-n+1}]\ ,\ n \geq 1 \tag{18}$$

$$\varphi(u^n b_0 \cdots b_{-k}) = [(-2^{-k} + \sum_{i=0}^{k} b_{-i} 2^{-i}) 2^n, (2^{-k} + \sum_{i=0}^{k} b_{-i} 2^{-i}) 2^n], k > 0 \tag{19}$$

$$\varphi(l^n b_0 \cdots b_{-k}) = [(-2^{-k} + \sum_{i=0}^{k} b_{-i} 2^{-i}) 2^{-n}, (2^{-k} + \sum_{i=0}^{k} b_{-i} 2^{-i}) 2^{-n}], k > 0. \tag{20}$$

In the case $k = 0$ in (19) respectively (20) we get one of the intervals (17) multiplied by 2^n respectively 2^{-n}. We take $\varphi(l^+\tau) = [0, 0]$ to represent zero, and $\varphi(u^+\tau) = [+\infty, -\infty]$ to represent infinity ∞. With this coding it is possible to represent any number in the interval $]-\infty, +\infty[$ as well as ∞. As seen from [Fig. 7] the first symbol of a digit string corresponds to a wide interval, with the four intervals collectively covering $\mathbb{R} \cup \{\infty\}$. Furthermore the intervals are overlapping

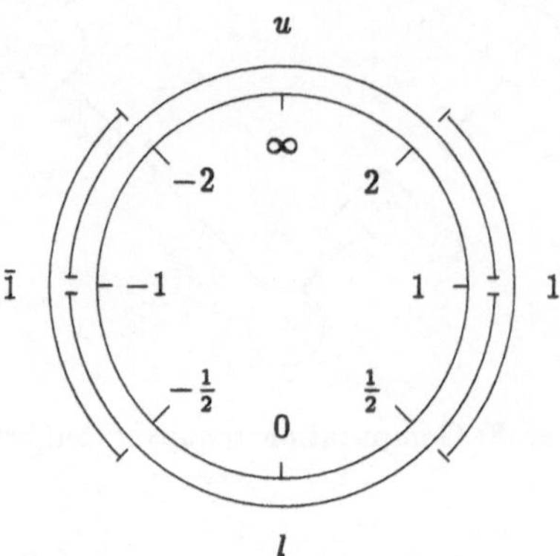

Figure 7: Intervals corresponding to the possible first symbols of a string.

indicating that there is redundancy in the exponent notation, which in turn will speed up the processing of output digits. It is easily seen that this representation satisfies [Definition 1] of a Digit Serial Number Representation. The state table [Tab. 2] describes a transducer that translates symbols into matrices, that when multiplied together will result in an interval matrix representing the interval corresponding to the input string. Notice that the automaton automatically enforces normalization of the mantissa part. The interpretation of the state table is equivalent to that of the state machine in [Section 3]. Notice that in any state there are at most four possible symbols, making a two bit encoding of the symbols feasible.

A floating point unit operating on such a digit serial representation, will accept asynchronous operands, thus buffering due to normalization problems is no longer an issue. Moreover since the exponent bits have been given an interval representation much like the mantissa bits, the exponent bits can be consumed and generated in a digit serial manner, making the unit fully data driven. Another advantage is that the length of the exponent is unlimited, enabling representation of arbitrarily large or small numbers. However, since the encoding of the exponent is unary the representation is most useful if operands are scaled into a range with small absolute values of exponents.

6 Conclusion

Traditional on-line algorithms are based on a recursive formulation of a residual. The residual can to some extent be thought of as a scaled approximation of the midpoint of the interval corresponding to the variation of the function evaluated on some domain, i.e. $f(\varphi(x_1x_2\cdots x_{p+\delta}),\varphi(y_1y_2\cdots y_{p+\delta}))$. Fixing the on-line delay δ to some constant, gives an upper bound on the approximation error and hence the width of the interval. If the on-line delay is chosen sufficiently large, the output digits can be found by a round to nearest operation

State	Symbol	Next-state	$(\alpha, \beta, \gamma, \delta)$	Interval Type
Start	u	Upper	$(1, -1, 1, 1)$	I_∞
	l	Lower	$(-1, 1, 1, 1)$	I_{normal}
	$\bar{1}$	Negative	$(-2, -1, 1, 2)$	I_{normal}
	1	Positive	$(1, 2, 2, 1)$	I_{normal}
Upper	u	Upper	$(3, -1, -1, 3)$	I_∞
	$\bar{1}$	Negative	$(-3, 0, 5, 4)$	I_{normal}
	1	Positive	$(4, 5, 0, -3)$	I_{normal}
	τ	Terminated	$(1, -1, -1, 1)$	$infinity$
Lower	l	Lower	$(3, 1, 1, 3)$	I_{normal}
	$\bar{1}$	Negative	$(4, 5, 0, 3)$	I_{normal}
	1	Positive	$(3, 0, 5, 4)$	I_{normal}
	τ	Terminated	$(1, 1, 1, 1)$	$zero$
Positive	0	Mantissa	$(3, 1, 0, 4)$	I_{normal}
	1	Mantissa	$(1, 0, 1, 3)$	I_{normal}
	τ	Terminated	$(1, 1, 1, 1)$	$point$
Negative	$\bar{1}$	Mantissa	$(3, 1, 0, 1)$	I_{normal}
	0	Mantissa	$(4, 0, 1, 3)$	I_{normal}
	τ	Terminated	$(1, 1, 1, 1)$	$point$
Mantissa	$\bar{1}$	Mantissa	$(4, 2, 0, 2)$	I_{normal}
	0	Mantissa	$(3, 1, 1, 3)$	I_{normal}
	1	Mantissa	$(2, 0, 2, 4)$	I_{normal}
	τ	Terminated	$(1, 1, 1, 1)$	$point$
Terminated	–	Terminated	$(1, 0, 0, 1)$	$previous$

Table 2: Transition/output table for finite state transducer, translating abstract symbols into intervals.

performed on the residual. Thus an on-line algorithm implicitly keeps a center-radius representation of an interval that includes the actual variation interval of the function.

The Cube F can be thought of as a residual as well, but in contrast to ordinary on-line algorithms the interval $f(\varphi(x_1x_2\cdots x_{p+\delta}), \varphi(y_1y_2\cdots y_{p+\delta}))$ is represented by its actual endpoints, thus all information needed when determining output digits is represented as explicit variables in the model. This in turn gives a more powerful algorithm, since we can perform actual interval inclusion tests. An on-line algorithm with *optimal* on-line delay can easily be devised, where the digit selection function could be implemented as a test for interval inclusion, or since the actual midpoint of the function variation interval can be computed, a round to nearest could be performed as in traditional on-line algorithms. The optimal on-line delay for certain functions has been examined in [Duprat, Herreros and Muller 89]. A less obvious consequence of the explicit representation, is that we no longer need to keep input and output synchronous, thus by imposing synchronization restrictions on the cube algorithm for radix number systems , we can realize algorithms in the three different synchronization classes as depicted in figure [Fig. 8].

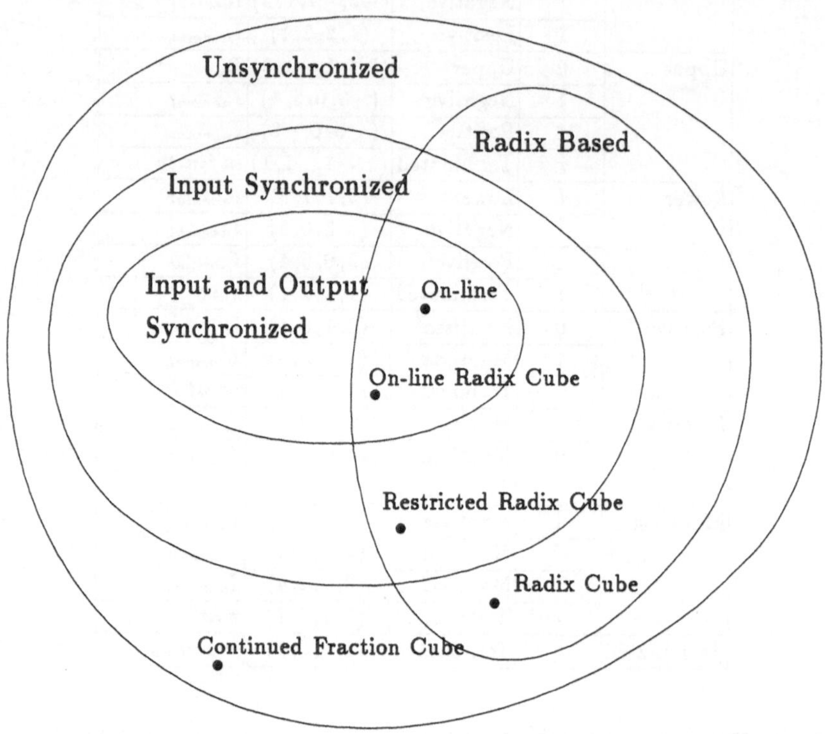

Figure 8: Topological classification of MSB-first digit serial algorithms.

A cube algorithm with no synchronization for continued fractions has been examined in [Gosper 72, Kornerup and Matula 88, Kornerup and Matula 89, Kornerup and Matula 90], it is an open problem whether synchronized algorithms exists for this number system. The continued fractions prove to be an elegant way of representing real valued operands with arbitrary precision, one problem with this number representation is, however, that the individual terms of a continued fractions can be any natural number, or integer number if negative numbers are allowed. This problem can be solved by expanding each term into simpler terms as demonstrated in [Kornerup and Matula 88, Kornerup and Matula 89, Kornerup and Matula 90]. One advantage of this representation is that the range of representable numbers is inherently unbounded. The floating point, digit serial representations introduced in the previous section provides the same unbounded range for radix representations. Digit serial computation on such operands can be performed using homographic or bi-homographic functions as described, however the state information in the matrix - and cube-representations is in simple cases (like addition) inherently large. It will be interesting to see if simpler, digit serial algorithms can be derived in special cases.

A combined way of handling infinite and finite precision arithmetic, can be constructed from the examples shown in this paper. By introducing an extra termination symbol, which signals that an operand was merely terminated due to its length exceeding some bound, operands can be kept as intervals, representing an imprecise operand. Operands terminated in the ordinary way can be taken to represent exact numbers.

References

[Vuillemin 90] Vuillemin, Jean: "Exact Real Computer Arithmetic with Continued Fractions"; IEEE Transactions on Computers, C-39, 8 (1990), 1087–1105.

[Duprat, Herreros and Muller 89] Duprat, J., Herreros, Y., Muller, J.M.: "Some Results about On-Line Computation of Functions"; Proc. 9th IEEE Symposium on Computer Arithmetic, IEEE Computer Society Press, Santa Monica (1989), 112-118.

[Kornerup and Matula 85] Kornerup, P., Matula, D. W.: "Finite Precision Lexicographic Continued Fraction Number Systems"; Proc. 7th IEEE Symposium on Computer Arithmetic, IEEE Computer Society Press, Urbana (1985), 207-214.

[Kornerup and Matula 88] Kornerup, P., Matula, D. W.: "An On-line Arithmetic Unit for Bit-Pipelined Rational Arithmetic"; Journal of Parallel and Distributed Computing, 5, 3 (1988), 310–330.

[Kornerup and Matula 89] Kornerup, P., Matula, D. W.: "Exploiting Redundancy in Bit-Pipelined Rational Arithmetic"; Proc. 9th IEEE Symposium on Computer Arithmetic, IEEE Computer Society Press, Santa Monica (1989), 119-126.

[Kornerup and Matula 90] Kornerup, P., Matula, D. W.: "An Algorithm for Redundant Binary Bit-Pipelined Rational Arithmetic"; IEEE Transactions on Computers, C-39, 8 (1990), 1106–1115.

[Gosper 72] Gosper, R. W.: "Item 101 in Hakmem"; AIM239, MIT, USA (1972), 37-44.

[Watanuki and Ercegovac 81] Watanuki, O., Ercegovac, M. D.: "Floating-Point On-Line Arithmetic: Algorithms"; Proc. 5th IEEE Symposium on Computer Arithmetic, IEEE Computer Society Press, Ann Arbor (1981) 81-86.

[Watanuki and Ercegovac 83] Watanuki, O., Ercegovac, M. D.: "Error Analysis of Certain Floating-Point Algorithms"; IEEE Transactions on Computers, C-32, 4 (1983), 352–358.

[Owens 83] Owens, R. M.: "Techniques to Reduce the Inherent Limitations of Fully Digit On-Line Arithmetic"; IEEE Transactions on Computers, C-32, 4 (1983), 406–411.

Journal of Universal Computer Science, vol. 1, no. 7 (1995), 548-559
submitted: 15/12/94, accepted: 26/6/95, appeared: 28/7/95

Some Algorithms Providing Rigourous Bounds for the Eigenvalues of a Matrix

Raymond Pavec
LIMI, Université de Bretagne Occidentale
Brest,France
pavec@univ-brest.fr

Abstract: Three algorithms providing rigourous bounds for the eigenvalues of a real matrix are presented. The first is an implementation of the bisection algorithm for a symmetric tridiagonal matrix using IEEE floating-point arithmetic. The two others use interval arithmetic with directed rounding and are deduced from the Jacobi method for a symmetric matrix and the Jacobi-like method of Eberlein for an unsymmetric matrix.

1 Bisection Algorithm for a Symmetric Tridiagonal Matrix

Let A be a symmetric tridiagonal matrix of order n:

$$A = A_n = \begin{pmatrix} a_1 & b_2 & & \\ b_2 & a_2 & \ddots & \\ & \ddots & \ddots & b_n \\ & & b_n & a_n \end{pmatrix}$$

Set $b_1 = 0$, and suppose $b_k \neq 0, k = 2, \ldots, n$. The bisection method is based on the fact that the sequence $d_k(x)$ of principal minors of $A - xI$ is a Sturm sequence:

$$d_k(x) = \det(A_k - xI_k), k = 1, \ldots, n, \quad d_0 = 1$$

In floating point arithmetic, as pointed out in [Barth, Martin, Wilkinson 1971], the direct use of this sequence is quite impossible: even for small n underflow and overflow are unavoidable. So they consider (the hypothesis $b_k \neq 0, k = 2, \ldots, n$ can then be removed):

$$p_k = \frac{d_k}{d_{k-1}}, k = 1, \ldots, n$$

This new sequence satisfies the recurrence relations:

$$(\mathcal{S}_x) \quad p_k := \begin{cases} a_k - x \quad \text{if} \quad b_k = 0 \quad \text{or} \quad p_{k-1} = -\infty \\ -\infty \quad \text{if} \quad p_{k-1} = 0 \\ a_k - x - \dfrac{b_k^2}{p_{k-1}} \quad \text{otherwise} \end{cases} \qquad \text{for } k = 1, \ldots, n$$

From the Sturm property and the choice of $p_k = -\infty$ when $p_{k-1} = 0$, it comes that the number of negative terms in (S_x) is equal to the number of eigenvalues of A smaller than x.
Beginning with an interval containing all the eigenvalues of A, the method of bisection provides intervals as small as desired, containing the eigenvalues of A.

1.1 Setting it to work in floating point arithmetic

In floating point arithmetic there are two problems:

- to perform the calculations *without overflow*,
- to give *bounds for the error.*

[Barth, Martin, Wilkinson 1971] give bounds for all the eigenvalues. Godunov [Godunov et al. 1993], page 315, gives a similar result but uses a different sequence and guarantees no overflow.
The method presented here (using the sequence (S_x)) guarantees the absence of overflow and provides bounds separately *for each eigenvalue.*

The set of machine-numbers (IEEE standard, available on Macintosh [Apple 1988] or PC compatible [Crawford, Gelsinger 1988]), provides representations for:

$$\begin{cases} 0, -\infty, +\infty \\ \pm 1{,}a_2 \ldots a_t 2^e, a_i = 0 \text{ or } 1, -min \leq e \leq max, \text{(normalized numbers)} \\ \pm 0{,}a_2 \ldots a_t 2^{-min}, \text{(denormalized numbers)} \end{cases}$$

t is the number of significative digits used. We suppose $min \leq max$.
The positive normalized numbers lie in the interval $[\epsilon_0, M]$:

$$\epsilon_0 = 2^{-min}, \quad M = 1.1\ldots1 \times 2^{max} \approx 2 \times 2^{max}$$

Notice that $min \leq max \Rightarrow 1/\epsilon_0 \leq 2^{max} \approx M/2$.
With *rounding to nearest* the relative error in usual operations is less than $eps = 2^{-t}$, (machine precision). For the machine-operations $\tilde{\top}$ ($\top \rightarrow +, -, \times, /$) we have:

$$x \tilde{\top} y = (x \top y)(1 + \varepsilon), |\varepsilon| \leq eps$$

for normalized numbers x, y, and $x \top y$. Notice that the presence of denormalized numbers insures that an addition or substraction that gives 0 is exact.

1.1.1 Calculation without overflow

In the calculation of (S_x) the critical term is b_k^2/p_{k-1}. To avoid overflow:

- A scaling of the matrix is performed by multiplying it by 2^p, p being chosen so that all elements become less than 1.
- The denormalized numbers occuring during the calculation of (S_x) are replaced by 0. This induces an absolute error $\leq \epsilon_0$.

Thus, the *operations used* ($\hat{\top}$) are:

$$x \hat{\top} y = \begin{cases} 0 & \text{if } x \tilde{\top} y \text{ is denormalized} \\ x \tilde{\top} y & \text{otherwise} \end{cases}$$

and the calculated sequence is (remember that $b_1 = 0$):

$$(\hat{S}_x) \quad \hat{p}_k := \begin{cases} a_k \hat{-} x & \text{if} \quad b_k = 0 \quad \text{or} \quad \hat{p}_{k-1} = -\infty \\ -\infty & \text{if} \quad \hat{p}_{k-1} = 0 \\ a_k \hat{-} x \hat{-} b_k \hat{\times} b_k \hat{/} \hat{p}_{k-1} & \text{otherwise} \end{cases} \qquad \text{for } k = 1, \ldots, n$$

The eigenvalues of A are therefore in $[-3, 3]$, and x also.
If $\hat{p}_{k-1}$ is 0 or infinite there is no problem.
Otherwise $|\hat{p}_{k-1}|$ is a normalized number $\geq \epsilon_0$:

$$|a_k - x - b_k \times b_k / \hat{p}_{k-1}| \leq |a_k| + |x| + 1/\epsilon_0 \leq 4 + 2^{min} < M$$

and this is also true for machine operations.

1.1.2 Error estimation

The scaling of the matrix does not cause any error, except for the elements that become less than ϵ_0 in absolute value and are replaced by 0. The elements b_k^2 that become less than ϵ_0 are also replaced by 0. Thus the matrix becomes $2^p A + E'$. E' is a tridiagonal symmetric matrix which elements are equal to 0 or bounded by ϵ_0 or $\sqrt{\epsilon_0}$.
A is now the scaled matrix. The classical error analysis ($\tilde{\top}$ operations) shows that the calculation of $(\hat{S}_x)$ is identical to the calculation of the sequence (S_x) associated with a matrix $A + E''$. This remains true for the $\hat{\top}$ operations. A symmetric tridiagonal matrix E:

$$E = \begin{pmatrix} e_1 & f_2 & & \\ f_2 & e_2 & \ddots & \\ & \ddots & \ddots & f_n \\ & & f_n & e_n \end{pmatrix}$$

such that $|E''| \leq E$ will be calculated.

It will be shown that there exist small integers $na, da, nb \leq 3$, depending on k such that:

$$e_k = |a_k - x| \left((1 + eps)^{na} - 1\right) + da \times \epsilon_0$$
$$f_k = |b_k| \left((1 + eps)^{\frac{nb}{2}} - 1\right)$$

The term $da \times \epsilon_0$ comes from the operations that give 0 or a denormalized result. Let us examine the different cases that occur in the calculation of $\hat{p}_k$ and determine the values of the integers na, da and nb:

- **Case A**: $b_k = 0$ or $\hat{p}_{k-1} = -\hat{\infty}$.

Then $\hat{p}_k = a_k \hat{-} x$. Let $y = a_k \tilde{-} x$. If y is a normalized number we may write:

$$y = (a_k - x)(1 + \varepsilon_1) = a_k + (a_k - x)\varepsilon_1 - x, |\varepsilon_1| \leq eps$$

So we have: $\hat{p}_k = y, e_k = |a_k - x|\, eps, f_k = 0$. $(na = 1, da = 0, nb = 0)$.

If y is a denormalized number then $|a_k - x| \leq \epsilon_0$ and:

$$\hat{p}_k = 0 = a_k - (a_k - x) - x$$

Thus $e_k = \epsilon_0, f_k = 0$. $(na = 0, da = 1, nb = 0)$.
Lastly if $y = 0$, there is no error and $\hat{p}_k = 0, e_k = f_k = 0.(na = da = nb = 0)$.

• **Case B**: $\hat{p}_{k-1} = 0$.
Then $\hat{p}_k = -\infty$, and $e_k = f_k = 0$. $(na = da = nb = 0)$.

• **Case C**: $\hat{p}_{k-1}$ is a normalized number.
For each operation three cases (at the most) are to be considered according to the result: 0, denormalized (replaced by 0), normalized.

∘ *Usual case C0:* In the usual case all operations give a normalized result and we get:

$$\hat{p}_k = \left((a_k - x)(1 + \varepsilon_1) - \frac{b_k^2 (1 + \varepsilon_2)}{\hat{p}_{k-1}} (1 + \varepsilon_3)\right)(1 + \varepsilon_4), |\varepsilon_i| \leq eps$$

The ε_i are the relative errors occurring in the operations. Thus:

$$\hat{p}_k = a_k + (a_k - x)(\varepsilon_1 + \varepsilon_4 + \varepsilon_1\varepsilon_4) - x - \frac{b_k^2(1 + \varepsilon_2)(1 + \varepsilon_3)(1 + \varepsilon_4)}{\hat{p}_{k-1}}$$

This is the exact result corresponding to:

$$a_k + (a_k - x)(\varepsilon_1 + \varepsilon_4 + \varepsilon_1\varepsilon_4) \quad \text{and} \quad b_k^2 (1 + \varepsilon_2)(1 + \varepsilon_3)(1 + \varepsilon_4)$$

Thus in this case:

$$e_k = |a_k - x| \left(2eps + eps^2\right), (na = 2, da = 0)$$

$$f_k = |b_k| \left(\sqrt{(1 + eps)^3} - 1\right), (nb = 3)$$

∘ *Case C1:* $b_k \tilde{\times} b_k \tilde{/} \hat{p}_{k-1}$ gives 0 or a denormalized result (and thus replaced by 0). In this case:

$$\hat{p}_k = a_k \hat{-} x$$

So we may write:

$$\hat{p}_k = a_k \hat{-} x + \left[\frac{b_k \tilde{\times} b_k}{\hat{p}_{k-1}}\right] - \frac{b_k^2(1 + \varepsilon_2)}{\hat{p}_{k-1}}$$

and in this case we have to add ϵ_0 to the e_k obtained in case **A** (add 1 to da) and $nb = 1$.

∘ *Case C2:* $a_k - x = 0$. Excluding case *C1* we have:

$$\hat{p}_k = -\frac{b_k^2(1 + \varepsilon_2)(1 + \varepsilon_3)}{\hat{p}_{k-1}}$$

and thus: $e_k = 0, (na = 0, da = 0), \quad f_k = |b_k| eps, (nb = 2)$.

∘ *Case C3:* $a_k \tilde{-} x$ is denormalized. This case is the same as *C2*, except that $e_k = \epsilon_0, (na = 0, da = 1, nb = 2)$.

∘ *Case C4:* All operations give a normalized result, except the last substraction. If the result is 0, then consider the usual case and set ε_4 to 0. It comes:

$$e_k = |a_k - x| eps, f_k = |b_k| eps, (na = 1, da = 0, nb = 2)$$

If the result is denormalized add ϵ_0 to e_k, $(na = 1, da = 1, nb = 2)$.

1.2 Bounds for the eigenvalues

Naming $\lambda_i(X), i = 1, \ldots, n$, the eigenvalues of a symmetric matrix X of order n, in increasing order, we have [Wilkinson 1965], page 101:

$$\lambda_i(A) + \lambda_1(E'') \leq \lambda_i(A + E'') \leq \lambda_i(A) + \lambda_n(E'')$$

Let ρ be the spectral radius of E''. We get:

$$\lambda_i(A) - \rho \leq \lambda_i(A + E'') \leq \lambda_i(A) + \rho$$

and also:

$$\lambda_i(A + E'') - \rho \leq \lambda_i(A) \leq \lambda_i(A + E'') + \rho$$

ρ is bounded by $\|E''\|_\infty$, and by $\|E\|_\infty$.
Let m_x be the number of negative terms in $(\hat{S}_x)$. We have:

$$\lambda_i(A + E'') < x, i = 1, \ldots, m_x$$
$$\lambda_i(A + E'') \geq x, i = m_x + 1, \ldots, n$$

Naming δ_x the infinite norm of E, it comes:

$$\lambda_i(A) < x + \delta_x, i = 1, \ldots, m_x$$
$$\lambda_i(A) \geq x - \delta_x, i = m_x + 1, \ldots, n$$

If the interval $[x, y]$ is such that $k = m_y - m_x > 0$, we may say that:

$$\lambda_i(A) \in [x - \delta_x, y + \delta_y[, i = m_x + 1, \ldots, m_y$$

It remains to take into account the scaling of the matrix and the initial rounding errors.
The bisection algorithm gives intervals such that $m_x < m_y$: to determine $\lambda_k(A)$ for a given k first choose $[x, y]$ such that $m_x < k \leq m_y$ and calculate $z = (x \hat{+} y) \hat{/} 2$ and m_z:

- if $m_z \geq k$ the new interval will be $[x, z]$,
- if $m_z < k$ the new interval will be $[z, y]$.

1.3 Algorithm and example

The general structure of the algorithm is the same as in [Barth, Martin, Wilkinson 1971], except the final test: for each eigenvalue the bisection process is continued until the interval $[x, y]$ is such that x and y are two consecutive machine-numbers (denormalized numbers excluded), or until a fixed maximum number of steps is reached.
The machine precision used is $eps = 2^{-64} \approx 5{,}5 \times 10^{-20}$. This precision is available on micro-computers [Apple 1988], [Crawford, Gelsinger 1988]. The results have been obtained using the software [Pavec 1994].
Consider the matrix of order $n = 30$ from [Barth, Martin, Wilkinson 1971]:

$$a_i = i^4, b_i = i - 1, \quad i = 1, \dots, 30$$

The eigenvalues lie in the interval $[0.933.., 8.100.. \times 10^5]$. A few results are shown in the table below:

- the bounds for the absolute error '$\Delta\lambda_i$' and relative error '$\Delta\lambda_i/\lambda_i$' take in account the final rounding from base 2 to base 10,
- 'Steps' is the number of bisection steps performed and is less than the fixed maximum (= 100).

i	λ_i	$\Delta\lambda_i$	$\Delta\lambda_i/\lambda_i$	Steps
30	$8.10000\,00818\,73846\,690 \times 10^5$	2.3×10^{-13}	2.9×10^{-19}	64
20	$1.60000\,00056\,28909\,621 \times 10^5$	1.4×10^{-13}	8.8×10^{-19}	62
10	$1.00000\,02006\,27702\,490 \times 10^4$	9.3×10^{-14}	9.3×10^{-18}	64
1	$0.93340\,70848\,65963$	8.8×10^{-14}	9.5×10^{-14}	68

2 Symmetric Matrices and Jacobi's Algorithm

Jacobi's method [Rutishauser 1991] applied to a symmetric matrix A constructs a sequence of symmetric matrices A_k, similar to A, and converging to a diagonal matrix:

$$A_{k+1} = R_k^T A_k R_k$$

where R_k is a rotation (angle θ_k) matrix calculated to annihilate a non diagonal element (i, j) of A_k. $t_k = \tan\theta_k$ is obtained from $a_{ii}^{(k)}, a_{ij}^{(k)}, a_{jj}^{(k)}$.

2.1 Setting it to work on matrices of intervals

In order to obtain rigourous bounds for the eigenvalues, we work on *matrices of intervals.*
The elementary operations $(+, -, \times, /, \sqrt{})$ on intervals [Moore 1979] are performed using directed rounding provided by the IEEE standard, without using the extensions developped in [Kulisch, Miranker 1981].

A number or a matrix x represented by an interval is written $[x]$.

Let $[A]$ be the initial symmetric matrix of intervals. Starting with $[A]_1 = [A]$, we generate a sequence of symmetric matrices $[A]_k$ such that all symmetric matrix B belonging to $[A]$ is similar to a symmetric matrix B_k belonging to $[A]_k$.
Thus the eigenvalues of B are the eigenvalues of a symmetric matrix B_k belonging to $[A]_k$.
For an interval matrix $[A]_k$, in order to restrict the growth of the intervals, a machine-number t_k is calculated on the *midpoint* of the intervals $[a]_{ii}^{(k)}$, $[a]_{ij}^{(k)}$ and $[a]_{jj}^{(k)}$, using ordinary floating point arithmetic.
The corresponding rotation is:

$$R_k = \begin{pmatrix} c & -s \\ s & c \end{pmatrix} \quad c = 1/\sqrt{1+t_k^2}, s = t_k c$$

Using interval arithmetic to evaluate c and s, we get an interval matrix $[R]_k$ containing R_k and we set:

$$[A]_{k+1} = [R]_k^T \, [A]_k \, [R]_k$$

If B is a symmetric matrix belonging to $[A]$ then

$$B_k = R_{k-1}^T \ldots R_1^T B R_1 \ldots R_{k-1}$$

is similar to B and belongs to $[A]_k$.
Notice that the sequence $[A]_k$ does not necessarily contain the sequence generated by Jacobi's method, and that the element $[a]_{ij}^{(k)}$ is not annihilated but replaced by a *small* interval.
These rotations are performed in a cyclic way, among the elements that do not contain 0.

2.2 Bounds for the eigenvalues

Let D_k be the diagonal matrix which diagonal elements are the midpoint of the elements of $[A]_k$, and $[C]_k$ a matrix such that:

$$[A]_k \subseteq D_k + [C]_k$$

The theorem of Gershgorin [Wilkinson 1965] shows that the eigenvalues of a symmetric matrix belonging to $[A]$ are in the union of the closed intervals:

$$[d_i - r_i, d_i + r_i], \quad r_i = \sum_{j=1}^{n} \left| [c]_{ij} \right|$$

where $\left|[c]_{ij}\right|$ is:

$$\left| [c]_{ij} \right| = \max_{t \in [c]_{ij}} |t|$$

2.3 Examples

- Condider the matrix [Wilkinson, Reinsch, 1991], page 223:

$$A = \begin{pmatrix} 10 & 1 & 2 & 3 & 4 \\ 1 & 9 & -1 & 2 & -3 \\ 2 & -1 & 7 & 3 & -5 \\ 3 & 2 & 3 & 12 & -1 \\ 4 & -3 & -5 & -1 & 15 \end{pmatrix}$$

This matrix is stored as zero-length intervals. After a sweep of the lower triangle the Gershgorin's disks are (radius ≤ 2.1):

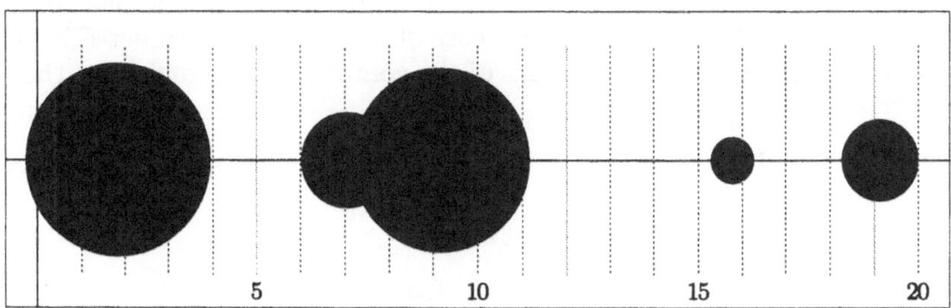

Figure 1: Gershgorin disks after a sweep

Going on with the sweeps until all non-diagonal elements contain 0, the radii of all the disks (*Machine precision*: 2^{-64}) become successively less than:

$$0.073, \quad 1.67 \times 10^{-5}, \quad 2.25 \times 10^{-16}$$

- The matrix $B = 8J - 5J^2 + J^3$ of order 44 [Rutishauser 1991], page 209, where J denotes the tridiagonal matrix with $J_{ii} = 2, J_{i,i+1} = 1$, has eleven eigenvalues in the interval $[4, 4.163]$, the length of which is $1/100$ of the total length of the spectrum.

After 7 sweeps all the eigenvalues are separated, except two that lie in the interval $[4.0032, 4.0065]$.

3 Eberlein's Jacobi-like Method for Unsymmetric Real Matrices

For an unsymmetric real matrix A Eberlein gives a Jacobi-like method [Eberlein 1962]:

$$A_{k+1} = T_k^{-1} A_k T_k$$

A_k generally converges to a block-diagonal matrix, with blocks of order 1 or 2. The blocks of order two have complex conjugate eigenvalues $a \pm ib$:

$$\begin{pmatrix} a & -b \\ b & a \end{pmatrix}$$

T_k is the product of a rotation R_k and of a matrix S_k:

$$S_k = \begin{pmatrix} \cosh y & -\sinh y \\ -\sinh y & \cosh y \end{pmatrix}$$

working in a coordinate plane (i, j).

3.1 Bounds for the eigenvalues

After some sweeps of Eberlein's method we expect a matrix of the form:

$$\Delta + E$$

where Δ is a block-diagonal matrix, and E a matrix with small elements. The following theorem, that is a particular case of the theorem of Bauer-Fike [Golub, Van Loan 1983], page 342, gives disks of the complex plane containing the eigenvalues of $\Delta + E$:

Theorem. *Let $A = \Delta + E$, where Δ is a block-diagonal with blocks of order 1 or 2.*

$$\Delta = diag(\Delta_1, \Delta_2, \ldots, \Delta_p)$$

$$\Delta_r = \alpha_r \quad \text{or} \quad \begin{pmatrix} \alpha_r & -\beta_r \\ \beta_r & \alpha_r \end{pmatrix}$$

Δ can be diagonalised with a unitary block-diagonal matrix X which has the same structure as Δ. Let $F = X^{-1}EX$. Then the eigenvalues of A are in the disks of the complex plane, which centers are the eigenvalues of Δ and the radii:

$$r_i = \sum_{j=1}^{n} |f_{ij}|$$

If the union U of k of these disks is isolated from the others then U contains exactly k eigenvalues of A.

Proof. The blocks of order 1 of X are equal to 1 and the blocks of order 2 to:

$$X_r = \frac{1}{\sqrt{2}} \begin{pmatrix} i & -i \\ 1 & 1 \end{pmatrix}, \quad X_r^{-1} = \frac{1}{\sqrt{2}} \begin{pmatrix} -i & 1 \\ i & 1 \end{pmatrix}$$

Let $\lambda_1, \ldots, \lambda_n$ be the eigenvalues of Δ and

$$\Delta' = X^{-1}\Delta X = diag(\lambda_1, \ldots, \lambda_n)$$

If λ is an eigenvalue of A, then $A - \lambda I$ is singular, and

$$X^{-1}(A - \lambda I)X = \Delta' - \lambda I + F$$

also. There exists a complex vector x, $||x||_\infty = 1$, such that:

$$(\Delta' - \lambda I)x = -Fx$$

Thus

$$(\lambda_i - \lambda)\, x_i = -\sum_{j=1}^{n} f_{ij} x_j, i = 1, \ldots, n$$

Choosing i such that $|x_i| = 1$ we get:

$$|\lambda_i - \lambda| \leq \sum_{j=1}^{n} |f_{ij}| = r_i$$

r_i is easily expressed in terms of E.

If the union U of k of these disks is isolated from the union V of the others, the disks associated with $A(t) = \Delta + tE$ have the same property for all $t \in [0,1]$: the centers do not change and the radii are tr_i.
The result comes then from the fact that U contains exactly k eigenvalues of $A(0)$, and V exactly $n-k$. The eigenvalues of $A(t)$ are continuous functions of t, so they cannot jump from U to V.

3.2 Setting it to work on matrices of intervals

A sequence of matrices $[A]_k$ is generated from the initial matrix $[A]$, such that each matrix $B \in [A]$ is similar to $B_k \in [A]_k$.
At each stage of the method $T_k = RS$ is calculated using ordinary floating point arithmetic and the midpoints of the elements of $[A]_k$.
Then

$$\left[T_k^{-1}\right] \text{ and } [A]_{k+1} = \left[T_k^{-1}\right] [A]_k \, T_k$$

are calculated using interval arithmetic.
It remains then to decompose $[A]_k$ under the form:

$$[A]_k \subseteq \Delta_k + [C]_k$$

where Δ_k is a block-diagonal matrix and to calculate disks containing the eigenvalues. Bounds for the radii of these disks are deduced from the theorem of the preceding section.

3.3 Examples

- Consider the matrix A [Eberlein, Boothroyd 1971], page 334:

$$A = \begin{pmatrix} 6 & -3 & 4 & 1 \\ 4 & 2 & 4 & 0 \\ 4 & -2 & 3 & 1 \\ 4 & 2 & 3 & 1 \end{pmatrix}$$

A has two double eigenvalues equal to $3 \pm \sqrt{5}$ and is defective.

The three first sweeps give:

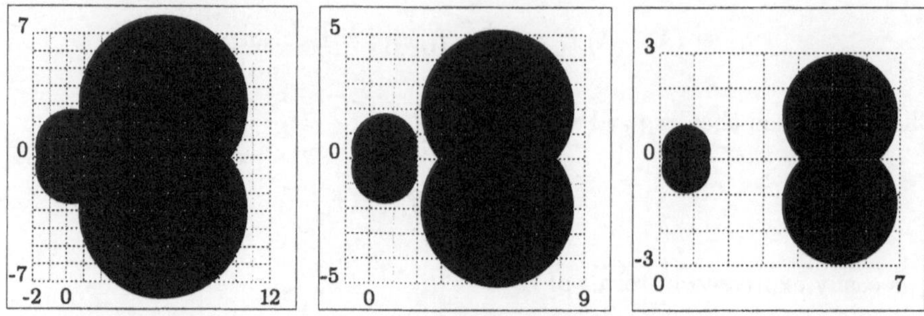

Figure 2: The three first sweeps

After 2 sweeps the disks are included within to disjoint regions.
Finally we get disks whith radii bounded by $3{,}98 \times 10^{-8}$ and $2{,}2 \times 10^{-8}$.

• For the matrix $B = (b_{ij})$ of order 12 [Eberlein, Boothroyd 1971], page 334, defined by:

$$\begin{cases} b_{ij} = 13 - j, \text{ if } i \leq j \\ b_{i,j} = 12 - j, \text{ if } i = j + 1 \\ b_{ij} = 0, \text{ if } i > j + 1 \end{cases}$$

after 33 sweeps the 12 disks are disjoint and the radii are < 0.001.

4 Conclusion

These algorithms are implemented in an interactive software [Pavec 1994] working on the Apple Macintosh series of micro-computers. This software is devoted to:

• teaching of mathematics [Pavec 1993]: a very simple Pascal style language lets you create interactively changeable figures containing curves, text, numerical values ...

• and teaching of elementary numerical analysis: interpolation, approximation, ordinary differential equations, numerical integration, systems of equations, eigenvalues.

A commented Pascal version of the algorithm of bisection is available by e-mail(*pavec@univ-brest.fr*).

References

[Apple 1988] "Apple Numerics manual"; Addison-Wesley (1988).

[Barth, Martin, Wilkinson, 1971] Barth, W., Martin, R.S., Wilkinson, J.H.: "Calculation of the eigenvalues of a symmetric tridiagonal matrix by the method of bisection"; in [Wilkinson, Reinsch, 1991], 249-256.

[Crawford, Gelsinger 1988] Crawford, J.H., Gelsinger, P.P.: "Programmation du 80386"; Sybex (1988).

[Eberlein 1962] Eberlein, P.J.: "A Jacobi-like method for the automatic computation of eigenvalues and eigenvectors of an arbitrary matrix"; J. Soc. Indus. Appl. Math., 10, 74-88 (1962).

[Eberlein, Boothroyd 1971] Eberlein, P.J., Boothroyd, J.: "Solution to the eigenproblem by a norm reducing Jacobi type method"; in [Wilkinson, Reinsch, 1971], 327-338.

[Godunov et al., 1993] Godunov, S.K., Antonov, A.G., Kiriljuk, O.P., Kostin, V.I.: "Guaranteed accuracy in numerical linear algebra"; Kluwer Academic Publishers (1993).

[Golub, Van Loan 1983] Golub, G.H., Van Loan, C.F.: "Matrix Computations"; The Johns Hopkins University Press (1983).

[Kulisch, Miranker 1981] Kulisch, U.W., Miranker, W.L.: "Computer Arithmetic in Theory and Practice"; Academic Press (1981).

[Moore 1979] Moore, R.E.: "Methods and applications of interval analysis"; S.I.A.M. (1979).

[Pavec 1993] Pavec, R.: "Maths&Calculs-io, a software for teaching, combining graphic representations and numerical methods"; Proc. French-Norwegian Symposium on Computer-Aided Mathematics, (1993).

[Pavec 1994] Pavec, R.: "Logiciel Maths&Calculs-io"; Editions JoliCiel, Noisiel, France (1994).

[Rutishauser 1971] Rutishauser, H.: "The Jacobi method for real symmetric matrices" in [Wilkinson, Reinsch, 1991], 201-211.

[Wilkinson 1965] Wilkinson, J.H.: "The algebraic eigenvalue problem"; Clarendon Press. Oxford (1965).

[Wilkinson, Reinsch, 1971] Wilkinson, J.H., Reinsch, C.: "Handbook for Automatic Computation, Volume II: Linear Algebra"; Springer Verlag. Berlin, Heidelberg, New York (1971).

Journal of Universal Computer Science, vol. 1, no. 7 (1995), 560-569
submitted: 15/12/94, accepted: 26/6/95, appeared: 28/7/95

On a Formally Correct Implementation of IEEE Computer Arithmetic

Evgenija D. Popova
(Bulgarian Academy of Science, Bulgaria
epopova@bgearn.acad.bg)

Abstract: IEEE floating-point arithmetic standards 754 and 854 reflect the present state of the art in designing and implementing floating-point arithmetic units. A formalism applied to a standard non-trapping mode floating-point system shows incorrectness of some numeric and non-numeric results. A software emulation of decimal floating-point computer arithmetic supporting an enhanced set of exception symbols is reported. Some implementation details, discussion of some open questions about utility and consistency of the implemented arithmetic with the IEEE Standards are provided. The potential benefit for computations with infinite symbolic elements is outlined.
Key Words: computer arithmetic, implementation, IEEE standards, exception handling
Category: G.1.0

1 Introduction

At the beginning of the computer age arithmetic was defined and implemented by computer manufacturers. The main interest at that time was to optimize the speed of the operations and minimize the circuitry needed to implement them. Accuracy was only considered as a side effect. Numerical scientists suffered from these deficiencies and had to spend much effort to overcome the difficulties. Furthermore many existing floating-point units exhibit machine-dependent irregularities in behaviour which complicate the problem of writing floating-point programs that are portable, in the sense of offering equivalent numerical behaviour on different machines. Upcoming in the early eighties, the IEEE arithmetic standard 754 [ANSI/IEEE 1985], further generalized by the IEEE Std. 854 [ANSI/IEEE 1987] to remove the dependencies on radix and wordlength, changed the situation. The IEEE standards provide direct support of:

- uniform floating-point formats including constrains on parameters defining values of basic and extended floating-point numbers,
- well-defined computer arithmetic operations performed with maximum accuracy,
- four different rounding modes including directed roundings,
- execution-time diagnostics of anomalies and smoother handling of exceptions.

The IEEE arithmetic standards enhance the capabilities and safety available to programmers and facilitate the movement of programs between the diverse computers adhering these standards. Between the main achievements of the standards is the provision of arithmetic operations with directed roundings which allows implementation of numerical algorithms with automatic result verification (see e. g. [Kaucher et al. 1992], [Kulisch and Miranker 1983] for such algorithms).

The IEEE standard has been widely adopted to most hardware platforms (chips: Intel 8087, Motorola 6839, etc.) and software implementations ([Falcó Korn et al. 1992], [Klatte et al. 1992], [Klatte et al. 1993], [Metzger and Walter 1990], etc.). So the IEEE floating-point arithmetic, as intended, is rapidly becoming a *de facto* computer industry standard for the design of floating-point arithmetic units.

The IEEE standards reflect the present state of the art and they are subject to comments, revision, reaffirmation or change. A surprising number of details and variety of different reasons for their selection must be settled in the design of a practical floating-point unit. Any proposal concerning the Standard should be judged by its consistency, utility and ease of implementation. Amongst the other comments on the standards Lynch and Swartzlander [Lynch and Swartzlander 1992] applied a formalism for specifying the number systems to the IEEE Std. 754 and showed that the standard conforming systems exhibit an inconsistency. Having the opportunity to develop a software emulation of decimal floating-point arithmetic according to IEEE Std. 854 [ANSI/IEEE 1987], which was intended to replace the binary arithmetic in the programming language PASCAL-XSC [Klatte et al. 1992], we designed and implemented another version of the decimal arithmetic routines which support an enhanced set of exception symbols as proposed in [Lynch and Swartzlander 1992].

Section [2 IEEE Standard and its error algebra] outlines the formalization of the IEEE non-trapping floating-point system considered in [Lynch and Swartzlander 1992] and the proposed modified system. In [Section 3] we report some implementation details and discuss the cost and the consistency with the IEEE floating-point Standards of this implementation. All considerations below are valid for both standards 754 and 854, so we shall not refer to the standard number except whenever it is especially necessary.

2 IEEE Standard and its error algebra

The IEEE floating-point scheme uses its formats to represent valid floating-point numbers (normalized or denormalized), called also representable numbers; some specially distinguished values as zero and infinity; and a set of special values called NaNs (Not a Number). A formalism considered in [Lynch and Swartzlander 1992] attaches a logical proposition to each element in the operation domain which defines its meaning and specifies the accuracy of the numeric results and the scope of symbolic results. In accordance with the supported floating-point formats the real numbers can be divided into six categories: (1) zero; (2) numbers too small to represent, called underflow numbers; (3) numbers which are too small to be approximated in the normalized format, called denormalized numbers; (4) numbers which may be approximated in the normalized format, called normal numbers; (5) numbers which are too large to represent, called overflow numbers; and (6) infinity. An input real value or the exact result of a floating-point arithmetic operation are approximated by some floating-point number in the supported format. Addition, multiplication and division are defined to include operation on numeric, non-numeric or mixed operands. Four rounding modes corresponding to different type of approximation are supplied by the Standard: rounding to the nearest representable floating-point number as a default mode, rounding to zero, to minus infinity and to plus infinity.

A number of exceptional situations such as *Invalid Operation*, *Overflow*, *Underflow*, *Division by Zero* and *Inexact Result* may arise during numerical computations in a floating-point environment conforming IEEE standards. Every exception, when it occurs must raise a flag that a program may subsequently sense and/or take a trap engineered to pass control to some code to handle the detected exceptional condition. The set of special values called NaNs are used for communicating results of *Invalid Operation* exceptions, attempt to extract the square root of a negative number etc. There are two types of NaNs: *quiet* NaN which propagate through the arithmetic operations without precipitating exceptions and *signaling* NaN which precipitate an *Invalid Operation* exception whenever an attempt is made to use one as arithmetic operand. The IEEE standards require that the default response to the exceptional situations is not to trap on them, but to compute and deliver to the destination a default result, specified in a reasonable way if not universally acceptable, for each possible exception. [Tab. 1] gives the error algebra defined by the IEEE standard for calculations performed in non-trapping mode and positive sign of the operands (valid floating-point numbers are denoted by R).

A	B	$A+B$	$A*B$	A/B
0	0	0	0	NaN
0	R	R	0	0
0	∞	∞	NaN	0
R	0	R	0	∞
R	R	$0, R$ or ∞	$0, R$ or ∞	$0, R$ or ∞
R	∞	∞	∞	0
∞	0	∞	NaN	∞
∞	R	∞	∞	∞
∞	∞	∞	∞	NaN
∞	$-\infty$	NaN	$-\infty$	NaN
NaN	0	NaN	NaN	NaN
NaN	R	NaN	NaN	NaN
NaN	∞	NaN	NaN	NaN

Table 1: The IEEE Std Non-Trapping Mode Substitutions.

As it was mentioned above a standard conforming computer can represent the fact that a result is indeterminate or not real with the symbol NaN. But there is no representation for prerounded results known to be in the underflow region (category 2) or the overflow region (category 5). By the following example Lynch and Swartzlander [Lynch and Swartzlander 1992] showed that the IEEE standard conforming system exhibits an inconsistency. [Fig. 1] shows an example program, the theoretically correct and the computed result in the default rounding mode.

1. A = LNN		
2. B = A+A	B = LNN + LNN = 2 LNN	B = LNN + LNN = ∞
3. C = B/A	C = 2 LNN/LNN = 2	C = ∞/LNN = ∞
4. D = 1/C	D = 1/2 = 0.5	D = 1/∞ = 0
5. E = 1/(D−0.5)	E = 1/(0.5 − 0.5) = ∞	E = 1/(0 − 0.5) = −2

Figure 1: Example Program, its Theoretical and Computer Execution. (LNN stands for the largest normalized number)

Execution of this example is according to the rules of IEEE Standard. Each result satisfies the statement of the Standard "every operation is performed as if it first produced an intermediate result correct to infinite precision and with unbounded range and then rounded accordingly". But incorrect results are evident in lines 3 and 5. In line 3 the IEEE result is infinity, which corresponds to the proposition "the rounded theoretically correct value is greater than the maximum representable, LNN", although the theoretically correct result is 2. In line 5 the standard result is −2, but the theoretically correct result is infinity. This result is especially dangerous, because it appears to be reasonable.

In [Lynch and Swartzlander 1992] the following enhanced set of elements is proposed to be used in IEEE floating-point computations to circumvent the difficulties arising in the above example:

INF:	the theoretically correct value is infinite
OV:	the theoretically correct value is greater than the maximum representable
x$\in$ representables:	the theoretically correct value is approximately x
UN:	the theoretically correct result is smaller than the minimum representable
0:	the theoretically correct result is zero
INDET:	the theoretically correct result is indeterminable.

The repeated calculations of the example based on this alternative set of exception symbols and the corresponding rules [Lynch and Swartzlander 1992] give INDET as the most specific correct result (B = OV, C = INDET since an OV divided by LNN may be an OV or normal number).

The point is how to implement a floating-point arithmetic system in order to take the advantage of the above enhanced set of exception symbols.

3 Implementation and consistency

An unfortunate weakness of the Standard is that so far no common programming language neither allows access to the IEEE floating-point operations with directed roundings nor provide suitable interface for testing and handling the exceptions. Only a few prototype languages [Falcó Korn et al. 1992], [Klatte et al. 1992], [Klatte et al. 1993], [Metzger and Walter 1990] provide software emulated floating-point arithmetic conforming IEEE Std 754.

For the developed floating-point arithmetic supporting an enhanced set of exception symbols the compliance with the PASCAL-XSC design is determined by the use of the following language features:

- Both PASCAL-XSC compiler [Alendörfer and Shiriaev 1992] and the runtime system [Cordes 1991] are written in ANSI C, which ensures running PASCAL-XSC on nearly every computer.
- The runtime routines simulate the decimal IEEE "double" format and the IEEE operations in software and, thus, are independent of the actually used hardware and the floating-point formats of the C compiler in use.
- The PASCAL-XSC runtime system provides a set of routines which allow a flexible monitoring and handling of the exceptions. An individual condition code and a default exception routine is defined for each exception. An unique interface is given by the trap handler for all exception routines.

The IEEE Standard require for each format representation of "at least one signaling NaN" and "at least one quiet NaN". The Standard "does not specify the ... interpretation of the sign and significand fields of NaNs". Representation of a decimal IEEE "double" format number r is given on [Fig. 2] [Bohlender et al. 1991]. According to this representation $2^{53} - 2$ encodings are used for the NaNs. By default the PASCAL-XSC runtime system assumes that a *signaling* NaN is identified by bit 51 of this representation being set. A *quiet* NaN is identified by bit 51 of the representation of the floating-point number being not set. We take advantage of the freedom given by the Standard and use part of the encodings of the quiet NaNs for the representation of the additional exception symbols UN and OV. The INDET value is carried by the qNaN itself. Thus the structure of a quiet NaN in the corresponding floating-point system supporting the extended set of exception symbols becomes as that presented on [Fig. 3]. To be more specific an INDET value is represented by $d = 7$, OV by $d = 3$ and UN by $d = 1$ [see Fig. 2].

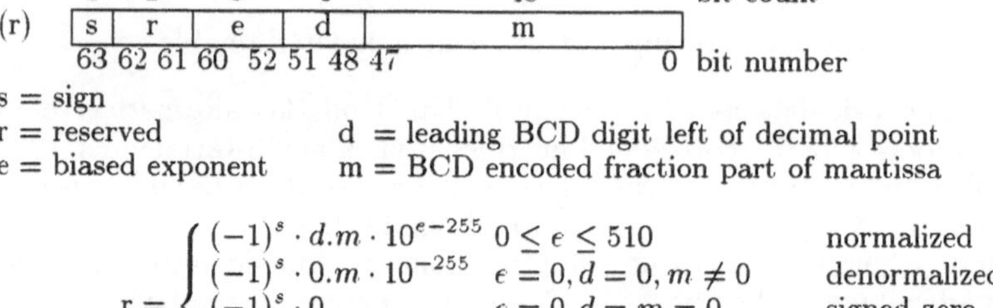

$$r = \begin{cases} (-1)^s \cdot d.m \cdot 10^{e-255} & 0 \le e \le 510 & \text{normalized} \\ (-1)^s \cdot 0.m \cdot 10^{-255} & e = 0, d = 0, m \neq 0 & \text{denormalized} \\ (-1)^s \cdot 0 & e = 0, d = m = 0 & \text{signed zero} \\ (-1)^s \cdot \infty & e = 511, d = m = 0 & \text{signed infinity} \\ \text{NaN} & e = 511, d \neq 0 \text{ or } m \neq 0 & \text{not a number} \end{cases}$$

Figure 2: Representation of a double precision decimal number

In [Tab. 2] we give the detailed non-trapping mode substitutions for addition according to the sign of the operands and according to the rounding modes.

The Standard does not interpret the sign of a NaN but says that "an implementation may find it helpful to provide additional information about a variable that is a NaN through an algebraic sign". For the realization of a correct addition operation involving UN or/and OV arguments their signs have to be properly determined. So the rules of the Standard concerning the algebraic sign of a result have to be applied even when operands or results are zero, infinite, UN or OV. The signs of the other NaNs remain not interpretable.

s	= 0 or 1	(sign)
ϵ	= 511	(all bits are set)
bit 51	= 0	(identifies quiet NaN)
bits 48 – 50		(identify an UN, OV or INDET)
bits 32 – 48	= 0	(reserved)
bits 0 – 31		(exception code)

Figure 3: Structure of a quiet NaN

+	$-\infty$	-OV	-R	-UN	0	UN	R	OV	$+\infty$
$-\infty$	$-\infty$	$-\infty$	$-\infty$	$-\infty$	$-\infty$	$-\infty$	$-\infty$	$-\infty$	qNaN
-OV	$-\infty$	-OV	-OV	-OV	-OV	qNaN	qNaN	qNaN	$+\infty$
-R	$-\infty$	-OV	-R, -OV	$-\mathcal{A}$, -OV	-R	-UN, $-\mathcal{B}$	$\pm$R	qNaN	$+\infty$
-UN	$-\infty$	-OV	-OV, $-\mathcal{A}$	qNaN	-UN	qNaN	UN, $\mathcal{B}$	qNaN	$+\infty$
0	$-\infty$	-OV	-R	-UN	0	UN	R	OV	$+\infty$
UN	$-\infty$	qNaN	-UN, $-\mathcal{B}$	qNaN	UN	qNaN	$\mathcal{A}$, OV	OV	$+\infty$
R	$-\infty$	qNaN	0, $\pm$R	UN, $\mathcal{B}$	R	$\mathcal{A}$, OV	R, OV	OV	$+\infty$
OV	$-\infty$	qNaN	qNaN	qNaN	OV	OV	OV	OV	$+\infty$
∞	qNaN	∞	∞	∞	∞	∞	∞	∞	∞

Table 2: Non-Trapping Mode Substitutions for Addition where $\mathcal{A}$: R + UN $\in$ [R, R + ulp(R)] and $\mathcal{B}$: R – UN $\in$ [R – ulp(R), R].

The following Proposition shows that a valid floating-point number results an addition/subtraction operation on any representable number and an underflow value in any rounding mode.

Proposition *For any nonzero normal or subnormal number R of the supported floating-point format and a positive underflow value UN, $[R, R + ulp(R)]$ is the smallest machine interval containing $R + UN$ and $[R - ulp(R), R]$ is the smallest machine interval containing $R - UN$.*

Proof follows from the inequalities $0 < UN < \text{ulp}(R)$ valid for any positive representable number R.

A result $R + \text{ulp}(R)$ will signal an *Overflow* floating-point exception when R is the largest normal number and a result $R - \text{ulp}(R)$ will signal an *Underflow* floating-point exception when R is the smallest denormalized number of the supported floating-point format.

[Tab. 3] and [Tab. 4] give the non-trapping mode substitutions for multiplication and division operations of positive operands. For negative or mixed sign operands the corresponding IEEE Standard rules for the algebraic sign of the result have to be additionally applied.

×	∞	OV	R	UN	0
∞	∞	∞	∞	∞	qNaN
OV	∞	OV	OV if exp(R) ≥ 0 else qNaN	qNaN	0
R	∞	OV if exp(R) ≥ 0 else qNaN	R UN , OV	UN if exp(R) ≤ 0 else qNaN	0
UN	∞	qNaN	UN if exp(R) ≤ 0 else qNaN	UN	0
0	qNaN	0	0	0	0

Table 3: Non-Trapping Mode Substitutions for Multiplication

All operations involving UN or OV argument will signal no exceptions, except for the special cases of addition mentioned above after the Proposition. Trapped overflow on decimal string to floating-point conversion when the result lies too far outside the range of the exponent to be adjusted will deliver to the trap handler an appropriately signed OV. Similar rule is applied to the trapped underflow.

In order to preserve the main purpose of the directed roundings to provide an enclosure of the theoretically correct result we have implemented the non-trapping substitutions given in [Tab. 2]–[Tab. 4] only for the arithmetic operations in round to nearest mode. The enhanced exception set requires the following modification of the IEEE definition of default result on *Overflow/Underflow*. Round to nearest carries all overflows to OV with the sign of the intermediate result. The delivered default result in round to nearest mode when *Underflow* have been detected and the corresponding trap is not enabled shall be UN with

b / a	∞	OV	R	UN	0
∞	qNaN	∞	∞	∞	∞
OV	0	qNaN	OV if exp(R)≤ 0 else qNaN	OV	∞
R	0	UN if exp(R)≤ 0 else qNaN	R UN , OV	OV if exp(R)≥ 0 else qNaN	∞
UN	0	UN	UN if exp(R)≥ 0 else qNaN	qNaN	∞
0	0	0	0	0	qNaN

Table 4: Non-Trapping Mode Substitutions for Division

the sign of the intermediate result.

Remarkably, the proposed implementation scheme for a floating-point arithmetic supporting an enhanced set of exception symbols fits quite well in the frames prescribed by the IEEE floating-point Standard. This is ensured by the decision UN and OV elements to be implemented as belonging to the set of *quiet* NaNs and except for the substitutions from [Tab. 2]–[Tab. 4] to apply the corresponding rules for quiet NaNs prescribed by the Standard. Non-trapping substitutions from [Tab. 2]–[Tab. 4] do not contradict the Standard. Some minor inconsistencies of no practical importance can be met. The new implementation does not conform the IEEE requirement "Every operation involving one or two input NaNs, none of them signaling, shall signal no exception but, if a floating-point result is to be delivered, shall deliver as its result a quiet NaN, *which should be one of the inputs NaNs*". For example, $R/UN = \begin{cases} \text{OV}, & \text{if } \exp(R) \geq 0, \\ \text{qNaN otherwise} \end{cases}$ and neither OV nor qNaN is "one of the input NaNs" (UN). According to the substitution tables the result of the example of [Fig. 1] will be qNaN and the execution of line 3: C=OV/LNN=qNaN will show the same inconsistency.

It should be mentioned that the difficulties connected with overflowed results in IEEE non-trapping mode computations, as those of the example of [Fig. 1], can be overcomed also at an user level by the following substitutions:

$$\begin{aligned} \pm(\infty - R) &= \text{qNaN} \\ \pm\infty \cdot R &= \begin{cases} \pm\infty, & \text{if } \exp(R) \geq 0 \\ \text{qNaN}, & \text{otherwise} \end{cases} \\ \pm\infty / R &= \begin{cases} \pm\infty, & \text{if } \exp(R) \leq 0 \\ \text{qNaN}, & \text{otherwise} \end{cases} \end{aligned} \tag{1}$$

In order to ensure correct behaviour of the non-trapping floating-point computations, always when *Overflow* exception arises one can switch to predefined arithmetic operations which will check for the special cases (1) and will provide more correct results. This can be done for all rounding modes. Of course, checking special cases (1) will be much more time consuming than using a floating-point arithmetic supporting the enhanced exception set.

The major advantage of the enhanced set of exception symbols proposed in [Lynch and Swartzlander 1992] concerns those applications dealing with infinite input elements. According to the proposed substitutions infinity as a result of a floating-point operation can be obtained only when at least one of the operands is infinity or when a nonzero number is divided by zero. Thus infinite large or infinite small in magnitude values obtained as a result of roundoff errors can be clearly distinguished from the operations involving infinities. Thus the implemented floating-point system provides more functionality and safety for only a small additional implementation cost.

4 Conclusion

A considerable amount of manpower is required for the practical implementation of any proposal concerning IEEE floating-point arithmetic. The presented implementation of floating-point arithmetic supporting an enhanced set of exception symbols comes to answer some open questions about its utility and consistency with the IEEE floating-point Standards. The new expanded computational capability is gained at no additional cost. This implementation does not implicate performance penalty. Moreover, with the enhanced capability, the computer can be used to appraise the quality and the reliability of the computed results over a wide range of applications.

Acknowledgements

This work was made possible due to the contract "Decimal Arithmetic" between the Bulgarian Academy of Sciences and the University of Karlsruhe, Germany.

References

[Alendörfer and Shiriaev 1992] Alendörfer, U., Shiriaev, D.: "PASCAL-XSC to C, A Portable PASCAL-XSC Compiler"; In [Kaucher et al. 1992], 91-104.

[ANSI/IEEE 1985] American National Standards Institute/Institute of Electrical and Electronics Engineers: "IEEE Standard for Binary Floating-Point Arithmetic"; ANSI/IEEE Std 754–1985, New York (1985).

[ANSI/IEEE 1987] American National Standards Institute/Institute of Electrical and Electronics Engineers: "IEEE Standard for Radix-Independent Floating-Point Arithmetic"; ANSI/IEEE Std 854–1987, New York (1987).

[Bohlender et al. 1991] Bohlender, G., Cordes, D., Klatte, R., Krämer, W.: "Technical Specifications for a Decimal Arithmetic"; Institut für Angewandte Mathematik, Universität Karlsruhe, Karlsruhe (1991).

[Cordes 1991] Cordes, D.: "Runtime System for a PASCAL-SC Compiler"; In [Kaucher et al. 1992], 151-160.

[Falcó Korn et al. 1992] Falcó Korn, C., Gutzwiller, S., König, S., Ullrich, Ch.: "Modula-SC. Motivation, Language Definition and Implementation"; In [Kaucher et al. 1992], 161-181.

[Kaucher et al. 1992] Kaucher, E., Markov, S. M., Mayer, G. (Eds.): "Computer Arithmetic, Scientific Computation and Mathematical Modelling"; IMACS Annals on Computing and Appl. Math., 12, J. C. Balzer, Basel (1992).

[Klatte et al. 1993] Klatte, R., Kulisch, U., Lawo, C., Rauch, M., Wiethoff, A.: "C-XSC A C++ Class Library for Extended Scientific Computation"; Springer, Berlin (1993).

[Klatte et al. 1992] Klatte, R., Kulisch, U., Neaga, M., Ratz, D., Ullrich, Ch.: "PASCAL-XSC Language Reference with Examples"; Springer, Berlin (1992).

[Kulisch and Miranker 1981] Kulisch, U., Miranker, W. L.: "Computer Arithmetic in Theory and Practice"; Academic Press, New York (1981).

[Kulisch and Miranker 1983] Kulisch, U., Miranker, W. L. (Eds.): "A New Approach to Scientific Computation"; Academic Press, New York (1983).

[Lynch and Swartzlander 1992] Lynch, T. W., Swartzlander E. E.: "A Formalization for Computer Arithmetic"; In Atanassova, L., Herzberger, J. (Eds.): "Computer Arithmetic and Enclosure Methods" Elsevier Sci. Publishers B. V. (1992), 137-145.

[Metzger and Walter 1990] Metzger, M., Walter, W. V.: "FORTRAN-SC: A Programming Language for Engineering/Scientific Computation" In Ullrich, Ch. (Ed.): "Contribution to Computer Arithmetic and Self-Validating Numerical Methods"; IMACS Annals on Computing and Appl. Math., 7, J. C. Balzer, Basel (1990), 427-441.

Managing Editor's Column

Vol. 1, No. 8; August 28, 1995

Dear Readers:

Summer is usually a quiet time. However, J.UCS seems to be fairly well established by now, since papers keep coming in at about the same rate.

This issue contains four papers from four very different areas: I hope you will enjoy reading them! Don't forget to encourage colleagues to submit papers to J.UCS once in a while. Springer has just printed new brochures about J.UCS, so if you need some for yourself or for friends just drop me a note and I can send you a few.

Best wishes for the rest of the summer,

cordially

Hermann Maurer
email: hmaurer@iicm.tu-graz.ac.at

Journal of Universal Computer Science, vol. 1, no. 8 (1995), 571-590
submitted: 7/6/95, accepted: 7/8/95, appeared: 28/8/95

BROCA: A Computerized Environment for Mediating Scientific Reasoning through Writing

Patricia A. Carlson
Rose-Hulman Institute of Technology
5500 Wabash Avenue
Terre Haute, Indiana 47803
Email: Patricia.Carlson@Rose-Hulman.edu

Abstract: This paper describes a work-in-progress: a computerized learning environment for teaching the conceptual patterns of scientific reasoning. BROCA (Basic Research, Observations, Critical Analysis) is theory-driven, combining two very powerful conceptual models of thinking. The first -- drawn from cognitive psychology and information theory -- focuses on the mental manipulations by which data becomes information and information becomes knowledge. The second theoretical construct comes from rhetoric and describes the intellectual activities carried out in prewriting, drafting, and revision by an expert writing. As an interactive "cognitive tool," BROCA provides scaffolding (through visual algorithms and adaptive prompting) to help a fledgling thinker practice the robust patterns of scientific reasoning.

Categories: Computers and Education; Computer Uses in Education

1. Introduction

The written word is crucial to science for at least two compelling reasonings. First, the texts of science --publications that report findings -- are the life blood of progress for a community of researchers. Framing a question of interest, designing an experiment, collecting data and observations, analyzing the raw findings, and interpreting results in light of theory -- all these demanding tasks are the process of science, but the written work provides the vehicle for dissemination of the product.

Second, writing is important to science because the act of placing ideas into language mediates higher-order intellectual activities that are foundational to scientific thinking [Kuhn, Amsel, & O'Loughlin, 1988]. Though other symbol systems play a major role in scientific reasoning, language fosters mental manipulations such as synthesis, analysis, classification, inferencing, definition, hierarchical order, comparison/contrast, elaboration/extension. Some of the most respected of twentieth-century educational theorists have endorsed this notion of writing as a heuristic for learning and for understanding. Vygotsky [Vygotsky, 1962], Luria [Luria & Yudovich, 1971], and Bruner [Bruner, 1971], to name only a few, have pointed out that higher cognitive functions seem to develop most fully only with the support of verbal language -- particularly, of written language.

In broad terms, the process of scientific inquiry mirrors the writing process. Both the scientist and the writer go through an initial gathering and sorting out of ideas, from which tenuous though testable explanatory notions are made (hypotheses for the scientist and thesis statements for the writer). After considerable trials, sound relationships between entities are found (experimentation for the scientist and drafting for the writer) and a supportable belief structure emerges. Continued scrutiny (replication in science and revision in writing) results in knowledge -- an artifact that can take its place in the body of received opinion. Because of this similarity of intellectual activities, writing can be used as an analog for scientific thinking.

Much of today's educational reform in the United States focuses on declining competency in mathematics and science. Of particular concern is the drop in abilities labeled "scientific reasoning" and "scientific literacy." A national consensus has emerged that education in these subjects must be renewed and improved. In particular, advocates for change call for innovations that:

- Incorporate findings from basic cognitive research to build a "modern" pedagogy.
- Integrate the various performative skills foundational to science, rather than isolating them in artificial subsets.
- Teach the process as much as the product of science.
- Include advanced computer-mediated educational technologies for instruction.
- Accommodate individual differences in learning styles, gender, and background.
- Make the concepts of science accessible through a naturalistic curriculum and authentic exercises, guided-inductive learning, and cognitive apprenticeship models of instruction.

We propose a multimedia, interactive learning environment that weds forms of scientific inquiry to forms of scientific discourse. BROCA (Basic Research, Observation, and Critical Analysis) is an end-to-end knowledge development environment that mediates the intellectual activities implicit in scientific thinking. Our claims are that BROCA will:

- Increase competence, creativity, and confidence in formal reasoning.
- Promote and sustain interest in scientific investigation.

- Engage the user and transfer powerful strategies for problem-solving.
- Bridge the gap between process (thinking) and product (writing).
- Improve quality of writing by improving quality of thinking.

As currently conceived, the system is intended for professionals-in-training in disciplines concerned with brain research and clinical outcomes. An immediate market consists of colleges, universities, and research laboratories/institutes where BROCA could be fielded as stand-alone training technology. With some re-engineering, an "empty engine" version of BROCA could be marketed as a productivity tool to all segments where knowledgeworkers require concept processors as replacements for word processors.

2. Background and Technical Approach

Until recently, philosophers provided much of the explanatory theory for what constitutes scientific thinking. Within the past few decades, however, increasing research by both psychologists and science educators has given us a more distinct working model of the processes and mechanisms by which scientific reasoning take place. Inhelder and Piaget [Inhelder & Piaget, 1958] characterize scientific thinking as "combinatorial cognition." In other words, scientific thinking consists of second order mentations, or "operations on operations" in the sense that the scientist uses reflection (second order mentation) to extract additional meaning from the products of first order mentation such as classification and relation. Newell and Simon [Newell & Simon, 1972] propose that scientific thinking be characterized as a process of search through a problem space, whose complexity is managed by the setting of goals and by invoking a collection of heuristics for partitioning the task into sub-"spaces" which can then be examined through powerful and productive strategies. Holland, Holyoak, Nisbett, and Thagard [Holland, Holyoak, Nisbett, & Thagard, 1986] explain the making of meaning in science as a process of induction. The model these authors describe is essentially a production system made up of condition-action rules. They account for contextuality in their model of inductive reasoning as follows: associations, patterns, regularities are observed, and on the basis of expectations or concepts about organization in the domain, a new, potentially superordinate concept is formed. Additionally, these researchers admit the importance of self-consciousness or metacognition by including a discussion of the "model of the model." Such robust theories have been extended into a new pedagogy which insists that science educators ought to be teaching methods of scientific thinking rather than merely scientific knowledge or concepts [Lawson, 1983].

2.1 Foundations in Theory

We base the design of BROCA on two explanatory models: one from information science and one from cognitive science's finding on discourse strategies. We do not intend our resultant hybrid model to be reductive or prescriptive. Rather, we see this "cognitive tool" [Salomon, 1993], [Salomon, 1988], [Salomon, Perkins, & Globerson, 1991] as an enabling prosthetic to help scientists-in-training recognize and take control of demanding intellectual processes.

Our first model comes from the general premise that there is a qualitative difference between **data**, **information**, and **knowledge**. Data are discrete entities, such as facts. While a body of **data** assembled for a specific purpose undoubtedly has relationships among the elements, these patterns of meaning must be extracted through an examination of the set and a filtering out of extraneous pieces. The systematic processing of data produces **information**, or statements about the associations in the data. Information is a codification and a clarification of the connections in data that produces more compact and easily remembered interpretative statements. A synthesis of information builds belief structures more comprehensive and more resilient than those contained in information.

Thus, **knowledge** is more powerful than information in that it has predictive or explanatory value. In other words, knowledge structures become both the product and the continuing impetus for such intellectual activities as exercising judgment and making rational decisions. These differences -- and more importantly, the transformations that take place when moving up the ladder of abstraction -- are the foundations of human memory and thinking. Moreover, this hierarchical model of knowledge evolution is central to many of the emerging applied fields coming out of the cognitive sciences.

Our second model comes from the cognitive science research into the importance of strategy acquisition for thinking and writing. Generalized models of good thinking include an array of techniques (strategies) for accomplishing goals, knowledge about when and how these techniques should be used (metacognition), and an extensive, task-specific knowledge base that is used in conjunction with the strategic and metacognitive processes [McCormick, Miller, & Pressley, 1989]. Realization that good thinkers have a repertoire of problem-solving behaviors for various types of tasks launched a new pedagogy for strategy acquisition.

Strategies are powerful manipulations by which the problem-solver (1) defines the task and makes analogs to other similar situations, (2) prunes away extraneous elements or eliminates "noise" from the problem space, (3) mediates state transformations, such as clustering specifics and making superordinate categories, and (4) links new knowledge with prior knowledge.

Figure 1 illustrates how we have conjoined the two models and used the process of scientific reasoning merged with the strategies of discourse to create a cognitive architecture by which BROCA melds scientific reasoning with the rhetoric of science. Basically, we specify the problem spaces (data, information, knowledge) as arenas for exercising scientific thinking and the state transitions as discourse manipulations necessary to create a tangible, codified "belief structure" which will be passed up the ladder of abstraction as a value-added artifact to be operated upon in the next higher-level workspace.

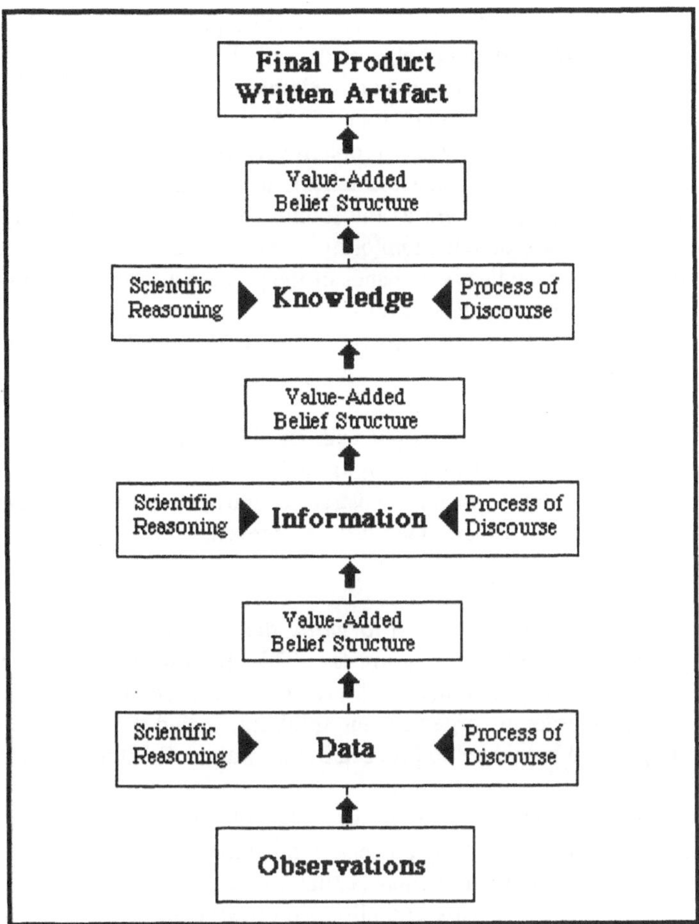

Figure 1: Theoretical Foundations of BROCA

We have modeled the process as three problem-spaces (data, information, knowledge) and three state transitions (prewriting, writing, revision). Manipulations within each of the problem-spaces requires its own specific set of heuristics. For example, within the data workspace, the thinker is basically examining evidence against a set of goals or expectations. This guided exploration involves a set of procedures or rules-of-thumb by which the thinker sorts out the noise from the data.

Methods guiding the exploration are an established set of principles that the thinker has learned, either formally or informally.

2.2 Extending Theory into Instructional Design

Extending a psychological theory into an effective pedagogical enactment usually proves difficult. Though models help to identify the components of thinking, the process is not linear and teaching is not as simple as providing instruction for each component and then putting the parts together. At the heart of the matter seems to be a kind of paradox. Accomplished problem-solvers in any domain demonstrate considerable finesse in higher-order intellectual activities: critical thinking as a precursor to knowledge; judgment as the foundation for decision making; and self-confidence as the initiator of self-monitoring. Unfortunately, novice problem-solvers are so overwhelmed by the heavy demands of the process that they seldom are able to exhibit -- even on a rudimentary level -- these higher-order activities. Thus, they are precluded from working with the very same cognition that would make them better at their task.

How can powerful strategies be taught without divorcing them from the context in which they naturally appear? David N. Perkins [Perkins, 1986] extracts the notion of the "thinking frames" from the more abstract cognitive construct of schema-driven strategy development [Norman, Gentner, & Stevens, 1976]. Perkins offers the following definition:

> . . . [A] *representation intended to guide the process of thought, supporting, organizing, and catalyzing that process.* This representation may be verbal, imagistic, even kinesthetic. When well-practiced, it need not be conscious. A thinking frame, in order to organize our thinking, includes information not only about how to proceed but when to proceed in that way (p. 7, italics in the original).

In practice, thinking frames occur in a number of different domains. Their form spans a gamut from simple (but powerful) mnemonic devices for extending the working memory to rich mental models that foster expert behaviors by invoking appropriate strategies, conserving and allocating mental energies, and orchestrating steps in staged problem-solving techniques. In the realm of problem representation, John Hayes [Hayes, 1981] notes the utility of simple visualizations (such as matrices) to delimit the problem space and to facilitate "search" in a complex situation. For example, Jones, Amiran, and Katims [Jones, Amiran, & Katims, 1985] found that using a grid to encourage name-and-attribute clustering aided in recall and systematically produced effective compare-and-contrast type essays in a study of young adults. The rich body of research into mental models and instructional design [Gentner & Stevens, 1983] [Kieras, 1988] suggests that highly-complex, multi-dimensional intellectual activities can be represented so as to help the novice activate and amplify specific expert strategies. For example, Gentner and Gentner found that the types of thinking people could do about electrical circuits depended on what kind of analogy (teeming crowds or flowing water) was used to represent the system and -- consequently -- the inferences these metaphors enabled [Gentner & Gentner, 1983].

Research indicates that teaching strategies isolated from their context does not produce enduring results [Garner, 1987]. What is needed is an instructional system that serves as a procedural facilitator. This term is used by Vygotsky [Vygotsky, 1962] to explain the cognitive mentoring and developmental dynamics that occur between master and apprentice and between peers during collaboration. Salomon, Globerson, and Guterman [Salomon, Globerson, & Guterman, 1989] and Zellermayer, Salomon, Globerson, Givon [Zellermayer, Salomon, Globerson, & Givon, 1991] use the term to suggest that computer technology can serve as a partner for the fledgling student and provide the scaffolding that allows the novice to practice the more robust problem-solving behaviors of an expert. In brief, such a procedural facilitator for scientific reasoning would:

- Ease demands on short-term memory and help to focus attention on strategically important aspects of the task.
- Guide the inculcation and self-initiation of higher-order processes (metacognition) which the novice is unlikely to activate without prompting.
- Explicitly model strategic intellectual processes so that the learner avoids what Collins & Gentner [Collins & Gentner, 1980] have termed "downsliding," or becoming increasingly entangled in lower and lower levels of mental actions, finally concentrating all attention on surface features and trivial aspects of the task to the exclusion of larger concerns in the process.
- Mediate transitions from abstract thoughts to symbolic representations. For example, in the domain of writing, Smith & Lansman [Smith & Lansman, 1989] conceptualize composition as an activity that takes place in three modes: thinking, organizing, and adapting. Each mode has its own set of goals, processes, and constraints. What is needed, according to these researchers, is a set of visual workspaces that help the novice writer to move gracefully through the various state-transitions inherent in moving from thoughts to finished text.
- Provide embedded strategic models for higher-order cognitive activities (such as discerning patterns in bodies of information, decision-making, staged problem solving, analysis, synthesis, and inferencing).

Pea [Pea, 1985], Perkins [Perkins, 1985], and Salomon, *et al.* [Salomon, 1993], [Salomon, Perkins, & Globerson, 1991], [Salomon, 1988] make a compelling case that some types of computer applications not only facilitate a task's accomplishment but also help the user to internalize profound strategies for later performance of the same or similar tasks.

Pea [Pea, 1985] makes a distinction between "amplification" and "reorganization" in examining the effects of cognitive technologies. Defining "cognitive technology" as " . . . any medium that helps transcend the limitations of the mind, such as memory, in activities of thinking, learning, and problem solving" (p.168), Pea notes that a child can extend her short-term memory with paper and pencil by writing down a long list of words. The short-term memory is amplified in this single instance, but the child's mental capacity has not been improved or altered -- unless the paper and pencil somehow prompt the child to "chunk" the words in more easily processed clusters. In short, cognitive tools that have been carefully designed to move beyond mere conveniences teach strategies for mental activities and -- rather than deskilling -- leave their users better off for having engaged the tool.

Pea uses the electronic spreadsheet as " . . . an illustration of computer technologies that can reorganize, and not merely amplify, mental functioning . . ." (p. 170); therefore, examining the cognitive design features provides us with a point of departure. First, this electronic representation recaptures all the features and functionality of the paper ledger sheet. A two-dimensional array displays categories and attributes, creating individual cells for the placement of data. Even this static ordering enables various forms of complex intellectual activity -- such as inferencing and categorical reasoning.

Placing this representation in electronic form adds new dimensions: now the user can dynamically manipulate data in each cell and watch the impact of change on other elements of the system. This, contends Pea, changes the level of engagement between the material and the user. Instead of merely entering data, the user is empowered to perform financial modeling, forecasting, and other forms of systemic thinking. Recent empirical studies support Pea's claims that using the tool elevates the user's understanding of domain constructs in ways that both endure and generalize, even without the presence of the tool.

Our second example, the abacus, demonstrates how a non-western, non-computerized device can mediate cognitive reorganization. Miller and Stigler [Miller & Stigler, 1991] studied abacus use as a example of research questions inherent in a whole category of representational systems. The abacus has utility in that one uses it to complete specific, well-defined mathematical manipulations. However, in mastering the device, one also gains insights into the conceptual dimensions of the domain. In one study, students who had reached a level of proficiency with the abacus are also better able to answer sophisticated questions about number theory than a set of matched controls who had no exposure to the abacus. Within a wider context, the abacus as cognition reorganizer could lead to questions of minimalism: How small and simple can a device be and still leave a "cognitive residue" by reorganizing mental abilities? Abacus studies show that even within the non-computer examples, cases exist of a simple but eloquent teaching device not only having a pragmatic result but also a conceptual effect.

As a cognitive tool, BROCA encourages its users to move from exploration to final report in a multimedia environment where scaffolding and visual algorithms gently guide the thinker through multi-staged intellectual activities. The software encourages the user to engage in powerful strategies that foster guided-inductive thinking and ensure mindful engagement in the task.

2.3 Extending Instructional Design into Software

The rhetoric task modeled by BROCA involves a type of writing familiar to managers, investigative reporters, engineers, and researchers. In issue-based writing, source inputs (text, graphics, numbers) become the raw materials in composing a position paper, an evaluative summary, an interpretive response. BROCA is a comprehensive, integrated environment providing cognitive support for professionals or professionals-in-training who create complex documents as part of their job. It differs from many other computer-aided writing tools in that it is an end-to-end development tool. It assists the writer throughout the process, from generation of ideas to production of connected prose.

As indicated by Figure 2, BROCA uses Bereiter & Scardamalia's [Bereiter & Scardamalia, 1987] notion of a dual problem-space model for writing: a content space (essentially, summarizing, analyzing, and synthesizing information about the topic) and a rhetoric space (essentially, planning and organizing the domain information into a logically and stylistically appropriate formal text artifact). Six distinct cognition enhancers work in tandem to mediate the multi-staged process.

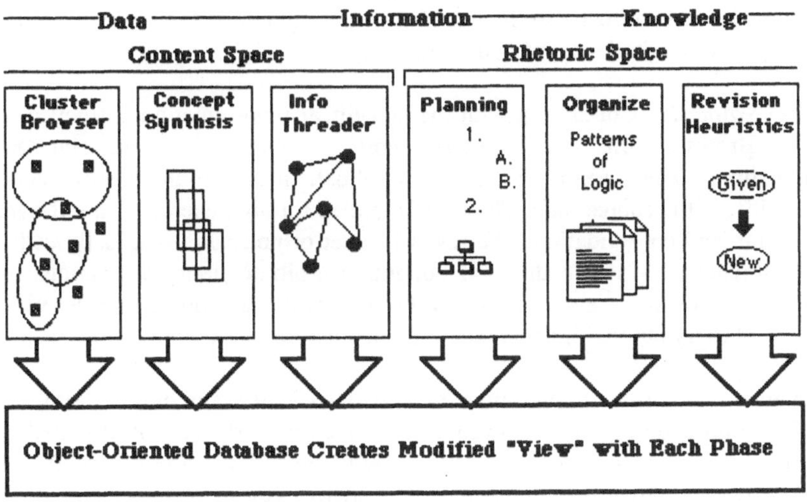

Figure 2: Six Cognition Facilitators of BROCA

The tools vary in their nature and can be roughly classified by placing them on a continuum showing how they mediate the knowledge development process. In general, the six tools operate in a fashion analogous to a database management system (DBMS). Each of the six environments permits the user to call up materials from the object-oriented, multimedia database and manipulate, extend, or connect entities in response to the adaptive instruction and cognition facilitators embedded in the workspace. The movement is sequential through the six tools; thus, gains made in one environment are consolidated and enriched in the next workspace. The following segments briefly describe the types of intellectual activities and the visual representations contained in each tool.

Cluster Browser: Based on a hypertext platform, this tool encourages the early exploration of a body of data. The user examines the evidence and constructs preliminary evaluations or carries out additional analysis and calculation. Thinking frames and adaptive instruction mediate two powerful categories of intellectual activities: (1) transforming data structures (converting verbal structures to numerical; numerical to graphic, and the like) and (2) working with semantic networks (constructing a rudimentary set of relationships among the various data in the workspace).

The resultant "belief structure" is a hyperweb, consisting of links between various segments of the data, annotations for preliminary interpretations, and link-types to indicate the nature of the relationship. Analogous to the convention of "view" in DBMS, this component helps the writer to sort out specific concepts in a collection of elemental inputs. At the resultant concept browser map, the user can click on any button and be taken directly to the linked statement in situ at the source materials or can navigate through the set of nodes and links.

Concept Synthesis: Continuing with the non-linear representation developed in the Cluster Browser, this tool fosters more comprehensive and interpretive manipulations. This exercise aims to consolidate ideas around central concepts extracted from the source data. The user is guided through exercises in observation, elaboration, and consolidation. The result is a set of notecards -- actually cells in a relational database -- that codify, extend, and/or arbitrate among the various source inputs. This workspace also serves as a brainstorming session in that the writer is encouraged to try out various permutations and elaborations on the core concepts.

While these aids foster exploration, they also focus the author's thinking. It is especially important to note that even at this relatively early stage in the "making of meaning," the writer can perform two powerful operations. She can return to the cluster browser at any given time and review existing concept maps or construct new ones -- thus viewing the problem space from a high level of abstraction. Or, she can move down to a more specific level to manipulate a set of notecards. Not only can the writer sort and filter the cards, she can try out different orderings and save each "trial run" as a separate file.

Information Threader: After a reasonable period of working with the Cluster Browser and its complement, the Concept Synthesizer, the writer may start to feel overwhelmed by the sheer amount of "views" (concept maps) and elaborations (files of notecards) generated. The Information Threader begins the sculpting process for the final knowledge structure by coaching the writer to see potential patterns of meaning and to draw inferences from them.

The writer selects a categorical concept that seems to be of major importance in the belief structure constructed in the two previous phases. Prompts aid the writer to perform mental operations such as "comparison" and "contrast" or "inclusion" and "exclusion" in order to formulate an "issues" statement reflecting the concerns of these information clusters. Modeling the notion of basic inquiry, this exercise leads the writer to conflate -- using the dimensions of similarity and difference (comparison and contrast) as pruning criteria. The result is a collection of possible hypotheses, explanatory statements, implications, and/or inferences (which will -- in turn -- become thesis and/or topic statements for the text presentation).

Hierarchical Planning: The Hierarchical Planner marks a major transition in the process modeled in the BROCA. It is a nexus at which the information structures woven in the "thinking and threading" segment must be reconceptualized to meet the requisites of linear text. Smith, Weiss, & Ferguson [Smith, Weiss, & Ferguson, 1987] discuss this change as a transition from a semantic net (essentially 3-D abstract structure) to a hierarchical outline (essentially 2-D concrete representation). This segment helps the writer to make this all-important transition from an implicit mental model to an explicit cultural artifact for a community of scientific scholars.

Though algorithms exist for transferring semantic nets into tree structures, a formalism which simply collapses the content and divests the context from the many complex judgments and intricate decisions may be too "ham-handed" for this application. BROCA uses a pruning algorithm to interpret the predicate expressions of the web. For example, if, in weaving the hypertext web of interconnections, the user has posted a "position" (a working interpretation) and has attached two arguments against the interpretation, linked by "refutes," the entity "_refutes (A1, A2) might indicate a pro / con rhetoric strategy is emerging in this linked cluster. The resultant "outline" is therefore richer in meaning than simply conflating the web into a topical outline.

Organization Mapping: After exploring the subject domain (the source data) and working out a richly interconnected belief structure drawn from these explorations, the writer must shift her attention to constructing a textual artifact that meets a set of external constraints and social expectations. Kopperschmidt [Kopperschmidt, 1985] characterizes this transition as a switch from cognitive macro structures to rhetoric micro structures. Similar to the drafting stage of writing, Organization Mapping helps the writer to focus more intensely on the requisites of the logical form and the conventions of scientific discourse.

Rhetoric and discourse studies have produced fairly detailed descriptions of the logical forms used in blocks of text (e.g., causal analysis, classification, comparison, definition, description, narration, and the like). The writer works not only with organizational features and with expression and stylistics but also with such situation-specific concerns as audience analysis and purpose.

Revision Heuristics: The difference between copy-editing and revision is easily characterized. Revision usually refers to more substantial changes, such as improving style, adding to or subtracting from the content, rearranging parts, or completely writing. These more global, deep-structured revision activities are associated with higher-order cognitive skills (discerning patterns in bodies of information, exercising judgment, analysis, synthesis, and other metacognitive activities). Heuristic Revision comprises a suite of thinking frames for improving both coherence and expression. These heuristics are strategic (encouraging a re-thinking of high-level issues, such as purpose, point-of-view, audience analysis, voice, focus, and form) and tactical (including techniques of elaboration, such as level of detail, examples, support, flow, and balance).

BROCA uses a hybrid paradigm for interactive guidance. Part of the advice comes from adaptive tutoring using traditional AI formalisms and part of the mediating comes from the powers of reification (or representing complex processes as manipulable objects on the computer screen). Each of the six "tools" (1) accommodates deficiencies and thereby reduces frustration for the novice, (2) emulates some of the crucial functionality of traditional data structures and information forms, (3) enhances the environment and thereby sustains motivation, and (4) models robust expert behaviors.

2.4 Instructional Design and Cognitive Architecture

While each of the six "tools" concentrates on a specific cluster of mental activities, all six have a unified method for delivering this layered instruction and a canonical architecture for the software and for the interfaces. Figure 3 gives an overview of the instructional framework and sequence of actions that structures each of the six tools.

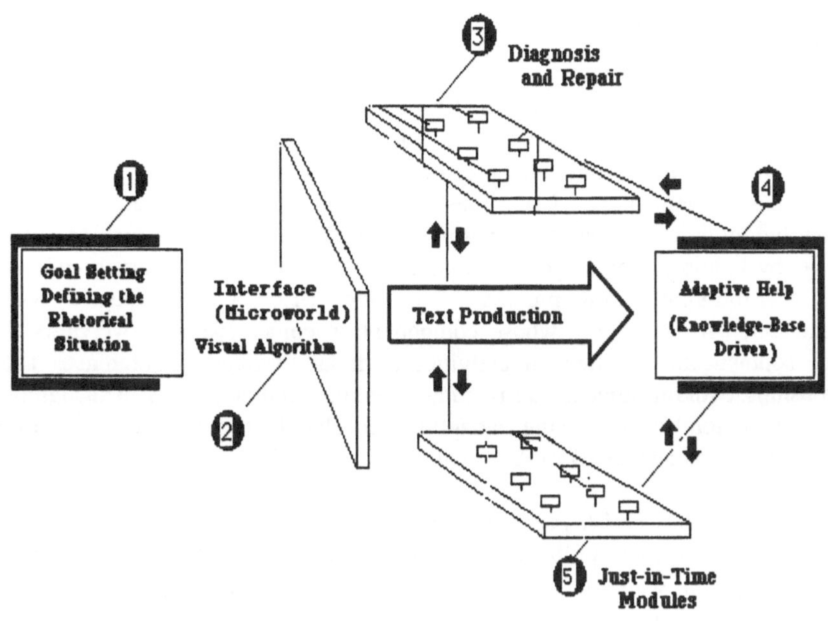

Figure 3: System Overview of Hybrid Tutoring Capabilities

Area 1 -- Goal Setting and Planning: Good thinking is mediated by having both a goal (desired outcome) and a plan (means of accomplishment). In multi-dimensional thinking, having an explicit, stable set of expectations fosters a kind of filtering activity that focuses the task from the outset. Each of the cognition facilitators handles the concretizing of goals in a slightly different manner; presentation and manipulation is appropriate to the phase of the process. Not only does this exercise help the novice focus on problem representation and sequence definition, this preliminary work "sets" the parameters of the adaptive tutor. Each tool now has a "frame" or backplane of conditions against which further actions can be evaluated during the remainder of the session on the tool. At this point, each tool tracks approximately 50 conditions. Clearly, the repertoire is rich, and becomes even richer as these preliminary combinations are supplemented with additional datapoints drawn from the user's subsequent activities in the microworld.

Area 2 -- Microworlds and Visual Algorithms: The second way in which BROCA teaches is similar to the cognitive "ecologies" advocated by Seymour Papert [Papert, 1980] and his LOGO worlds, where the child learner can practice profound concepts in familiar, manageable forms. (For example, Papert's "turtle logic" enables the child to learn the conventions of programming by moving a cursor-turtle as an analog for such relatively sophisticated manipulations as inclusion and exclusion.) Where possible, the interfaces of BROCA represent visual organizers for specific intellectual processes.

Like an adult version of "turtle logic," BROCA tokenizes mental manipulations and places the resultant visualizations in a constrained context so as to model the elaborations, state transitions, and reconfigurations of knowledge structures taking place in the problem spaces. Users interact with the computerized environment in rich but highly defined ways. The microworld mediates thinking by making choices explicit, by helping to manage the cognitive load, and by encouraging reflection during the thinking/writing process. In short, BROCA instantiates a "visual nomenclature" for reasoning whose components becomes synoptic overviews that trigger sophisticated intellectual activities such as formulating inferences about relationships, evoking strategies to facilitate thinking, and prompting metacognition, or self-regulation for deploying, adapting, or abandoning sets and subsets of strategies based on awareness of the situation.

Area 3 -- Diagnosis and Repair: Reasoning is a complex activity analogous to a contingency management problem. Even in scientific reasoning, for some "fuzzy" problems, only in working through candidate solutions does the nature of the problem become fixed, or even definable [Kuhn, Amsel, & O'Loughlin, 1988]. Rather than working in a linear fashion, good thinkers use an opportunistic approach. They constantly measure the emerging knowledge structure against a set of expectations, while at the same time recognizing and capitalizing on serendipitous gains, weaving these "discovered" possibilities into a new rendition of the overall plan and product [Hayes-Roth & Hayes-Roth, 1979].

Unfortunately, reasoning for novices is usually frail and one-dimensional; such impoverished capabilities do not lend themselves to interruptions or re-assessments. As evidenced by Bereiter and Scardamalia's research into the writing process for novices, little evidence can be found that weak writers can participate in self-cueing or self-monitoring activities while engaged in a production of text [Bereiter and Scardamalia, 1987]. In fact, the very act of breaking out of their one-dimensional, stream-of-consciousness mode jeopardizes the continued production of text.

Diagnosis-and-Repair is an evaluation loop that partners with the thinker to reduce the cognitive load and that encourages the student to enter into an strategy-driven assessment episode. This loop takes a very sophisticated, open-ended problem and pares it down to a manageable set of options for the inexperienced user. Succinctly, this facilitator operates in the following sequence. First, the user detects a mismatch between the goals (her intentions) and the on-going process of creating knowledge. As a response to this dissonance, the user requests help. Second, the system brings up a list of potential strategies applicable to the specific subtask the thinker is working on. Third, selecting any one of the suggested strategies brings up a focused workspace -- usually, a thinking frame that mediates the subtask. By presenting a limited set of options and by making suggestions (rather than dictating) about ways to improve, the system both engages and challenges the thinker at the appropriate level.

Area 4 -- Adaptive Advice: In the metacognitive stage (diagnosis and repair), the machine partners with the user to develop the sensitivity and awareness necessary to know what strategy would work best in a given set of circumstances. Yet, because the diagnostic is performed by the user, there is a potential for a misjudgment. Additionally, if the system is to serve as an intelligent "guide" or "coach," the tools should have a feedback loop to indicate the "reasonableness" of the course of action the thinker is pursuing, basedlined against some known set of criteria.

Adaptive advice adjusts its statements based on an "intelligent" assessment of the situation -- meaning that the software compares the manipulation the user is working on with the conditions of the frame and determines how "correct" these actions are given the circumstances. The resultant prompting helps the user to learn the more subtle aspects of adapting to the requirements of the task. They also help the student to stay on the right track and avoid the frustration of pursuing a strategy whose results are later deemed to be inadequate to the task.

For all the intelligent tools of BROCA, adaptive help is generated through a kind of triangulation, based on the task situation (the conditions set in the frame) and the moves made by the problem-solver in the microworld or visual workspace. Monitoring the combination of specific task and place in the problem-solving process creates a lookup table for accessing instructional statements.

Area 5 -- Just-in-Time-Tutoring: While production skills and metacognitive skills are not interchangeable, they are correlated in that they must occur simultaneously in expert behaviors. After diagnosing a problem and getting a repair strategy, the student may still be at a loss as to whether the result measures up to professional expectations. Recognizing that users may need reminders of what a professional "end-result" looks like, we have embedded a set of models (extracts from publications deemed examples of excellence). Relevant portions of these models appear (appropriately correlated with the task the user is working on) with commentary pointing out the specific strengths of the presentation. This instruction (similar to a high-end form of context-sensitive help) is analogous to a job aid in that it gives a synoptic overview of the end-result the user is aiming for. Its purpose is to serve as a reminder or a refocusing prompt for the user rather than a full-blown instructional component. Though imitation, the user can incorporate the methods of the model into her own particular context and content.

2.5 System Overview

Commercial packages offering the writer a collection of tools (such as the analysis routines in the Writer's Workbench) have been around for some time now. Nevertheless, it is important to recognize that these tools are separate entities. While the writer is free to pick and choose among them, the tools are not integrated nor are they supported by AI interpreters. In other words, work done with one tool does not translate seamlessly to the "world" of another tool. At a minimum, this is inconvenient. More telling for a worker or a learner, gains in one stage of composing are not easily consolidated and carried forward to the next stage. In fact, the welter of detail generated by some tools or heuristic routines may constitute a step backwards because the writer has to deal with (1) the cognitive overload of multiple versions or even contradictory instances of the same thoughts and (2) a potentially recurrent dis-integration of thoughts constructed while working with different tools or heuristic devices.

Figure 4 illustrates the "layered" nature of BROCA and shows how gains made in one workspace are passed on to the next. The complete system offers several "knowledge-weaving" paradigms, each designed to meet the requisites of a particular category of cognitive task and to exploit the talents represented by the particular user. Because the system is designed on a database paradigm, with each new "view" representing a value-added re-configuration of the data, it is possible to trace (via the links) higher-level propositions and inferences back to their inception or foundation in the source data.

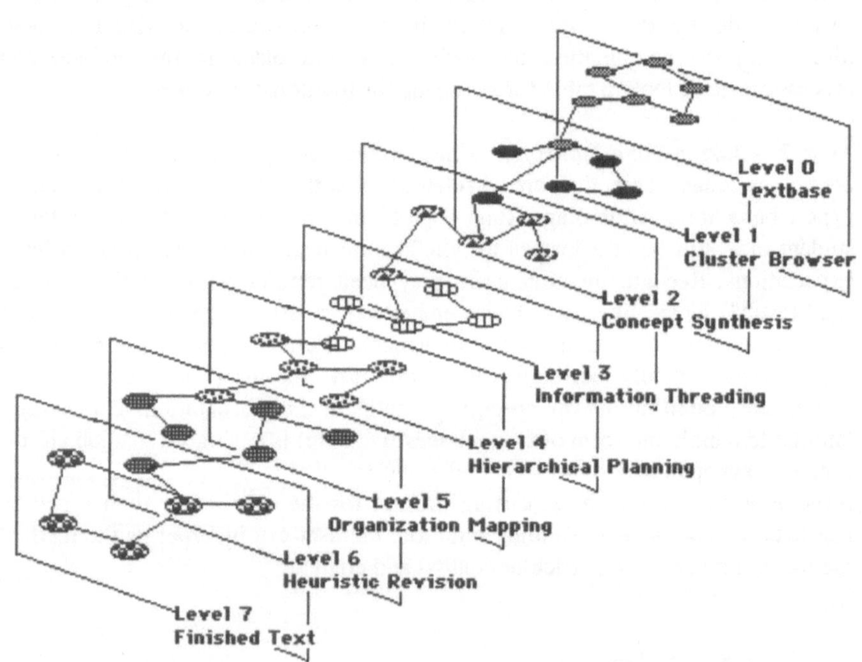

Figure 4: Composite of BROCA's End-to-End Knowledge Development

3. Teaching Scientific Thinking Skills

Scientific reasoning requires that the thinker observe phenomena, perform elemental mental processing (e.g., detecting and classifying recurrent patterns), and then draw conclusions or explanations through higher-order cognition (e.g. inferencing and interpretation and application of enumerative generalizations). Evidence accumulating from the empirical study of scientific reasoning suggests that this ability to interpret does not map one-for-one on to discovery learning or native curiosity. While these facets are surely part of the motivational dimensions of human reasoning, the romantic version of the scientist making serendipitous "discoveries" is hardly the norm for this type of intellectual activity. Rather, scientific reasoning -- as practiced by an experienced professional -- involves a significant degree of awareness and control of the interactions between old knowledge (awareness of theory and expectations) with new information (situational observations). In short, the expert has both experientially derived mental models and metacognitive self-regulation to invoke, abandon, or creatively combine these problem-solving strategies. This expert level of insight has been built up over time and is a direct result of guided practice and painstaking mentoring.

BROCA performs the role of a mentor by mediating the process of scientific reasoning from beginning (data collection) to end (written report). Using visualizations of what might otherwise be opaque mental operations, the software guides the user through (1) collection/evaluation of evidence, (2) comparing data with theory, (3) formulating and testing hypotheses, (4) interpretation of results, (5) validation through replication. These complex mental activities take place within the framework of a second multi-dimensional, staged cognitive task -- that is, producing an acceptable piece of scientific prose (journal article, lab report, scientific journalism). Embedded within this authentic task are the profound acts of understanding necessary to transform observations into prose, or to move from data to knowledge.

4. Summary and Conclusions

This paper describes the conceptual design of BROCA, a computerized environment to merge the "language" of science with the manipulations, observations, and calculations foundational to scientific reasoning. Inherent in the discussion are three overarching assumptions about the design and development of advanced educational technologies. First, the design of automated systems should be rooted in cognitive science and educational theory. Advanced instructional technology holds great promise; however, to truly move beyond pale imitations of existing educational media, designers must harvest the rich insights on how humans think and learn already established by cognitive psychology. Second, complex, multi-staged problem solving (in this case, scientific thinking) is an amalgam of visual and verbal symbol usage. By concurrently performing the manipulative/observational tasks along with the consolidative/interpretive tasks, the learner integrates both lower and higher level intellectual processes, as well as concrete and abstract forms of mentation. Third, highly sophisticated, interactive learning environments are possible without using the typical intelligent tutoring system (ITS) approach of constructing a student model, a domain knowledgebase, and an interpretive expert system. By employing cognitive task analysis, the system designer can model the process of the domain and embed adaptive help within the user's performance of the task. Such "cognitive tools" are just emerging as serious competitors to the more traditional approaches to adaptive pedagogy in interactive systems. We look forward to completing the development, running field evaluations, and reporting on the effectiveness of BROCA.

5. References

[Bereiter & Scardamalia, 1987]. Bereiter, C. & Scardamalia, M. (1987). The psychology of written composition. Hillsdale, NJ: Lawrence Erlbaum Associates.

[Bruner, 1971]. Bruner, J. S. (1971). The relevance of education. New York: W. W. Norton.

[Collins & Gentner, 1980]. Collins, A.M., & Gentner, D. (1980). A framework for a cognitive theory of writing. In L. W. Gregg & E. Steinberg (Eds.), Cognitive processes in writing (pp. 51-72). Hillsdale, NJ: Lawrence Erlbaum Associates.

[Garner, 1987]. Garner, R. (1987). Metacognition and reading comprehension. Norwood., NJ: Ablex.

[Gentner & Gentner, 1983]. Gentner, D., & Gentner, D. (1983). Flowing waters or teeming crowds: Mental models of electricity. In D. Gentner & A. L. Stevens (Eds.), Mental models (pp. 99-129). Hillsdale, NJ: Lawrence Erlbaum Associates.

[Gentner & Stevens, 1983]. Gentner, D., & Stevens, A. L. (1983). Mental models. Hillsdale, NJ: Lawrence Erlbaum Associates.

[Hayes, 1981]. Hayes, J. R. (1981). The complete problem solver. Philadelphia, PA: The Franklin Institute.

[Hayes-Roth & Hayes-Roth, 1979]. Hayes-Roth, B., & Hayes-Roth, F. (1979). A cognitive model of planning. Cognitive Science, 3, 275-310.

[Holland, Holyoak, Nesbett, & Thagard, 1986]. Holland, J., Holyoak, K., Nisbett, R., & Thagard, P. (1986). Induction: Processes of inference, learning, and discovery. Cambridge, MA: MIT Press.

[Inhelder & Piaget, 1958]. Inhelder, B., & Piaget, J. (1958). The growth of logical thinking from childhood to adolescence. New York: Basic Books.

[Jones, Amiran, & Katims, 1985]. Jones, B.F., Amiran, M. R., & Katims, M. (1985). Teaching cognitive strategies and text structures within language arts programs. In J. Segal, S. F. Chipman, and R. Glaser (Eds.), Thinking and learning skills. Vol 1: Relating instruction to research (pp. 259- 295). Hillsdale, NJ: Lawrence Erlbaum Associates.

[Kieras, 1988]. Kieras, D. E. (1988). What mental models should be taught: Choosing instructional content for complex engineered systems. In J. Psotka, L. D. Massey, & S. A. Mutter (Eds.), Intelligent systems: Lessons learned (pp. 85-118). Hillsdale, NJ: Lawrence Erlbaum Associates.

[Kopperschmidt, 1985]. Kopperschmidt, J. (1985). An analysis of argumentation. In T. A. van Dijk (Eds.), Handbook of discourse analysis, Vol 2: Dimensions of discourse (pp. 159- 168). London, UK: Academic Press.

[Kuhn, Amsel, & O'Loughlin, 1988]. Kuhn, D., Amsel, E., & O'Loughlin, M. (1988). The development of scientific thinking skills. New York: Academic Press.

[Lawson, 1983]. Lawson, A. (1983). Investigating and applying developmental psychology in the science classroom. In S. Paris, G. Olson, & H. Stevenson (Eds.), Learning and motivation in the classroom (pp. 113-135). Hillsdale, NJ: Erlbaum Associates.

[Luria & Yudovich, 1971]. Luria, A. R., & Yudovich, F. Ia. (1971). Speech and the development of mental processes in the child. J. Simon (Ed.), Baltimore: Penguin.

[McCormick, Miller, & Pressley, 1989]. McCormick, C. G., Miller, G., & Pressley, M. (1989). Cognitive strategy research: From basic research to educational applications. New York: Springer-Verlag.

[Miller & Stigler, 1991]. Miller, K. F. & Stigler, J. W. (1991). Meanings of skill: Effects of abacus expertise on number representation. Cognition and Instruction, 8(1), 29-67.

[Newell & Simon, 1972]. Newell, A., & Simon, H. (1972). Human problem solving. Englewood Cliffs, NJ: Prentice Hall.

[Norman, Gentner, & Stevens, 1976]. Norman, D. A., Gentner, S., & Stevens, A. L. (1976). Comments on learning schemata and memory representation. In D. Klahr (Ed.), Cognition and instruction. Hillsdale, NJ: Lawrence Erlbaum Associates.

[Papert, 1980]. Papert, S. (1980). Mind-Storms: children, computers, and powerful ideas. New York: Basic Books.

[Pea, 1985]. Pea, R. D. (1985). Beyond amplification: Using the computer to reorganize mental functioning. Educational Psychologist, 20(4), 167-182.

[Perkins, 1986]. Perkins, D. N. (1986). Thinking frames. Educational Leadership, 43, 4 - 10.

[Perkins, 1985]. Perkins, D. N. (1985). The fingertip effect: How information-processing technology shapes thinking. Educational Researcher, (August/September), 11-17.

[Salomon, 1993]. Salomon, G. (1993). On the nature of pedagogic computer tools: The case of the writing partner. In S. P. Lajoie & S.J. Derry (Eds.), Computers as cognitive tools (pp. 179-196). Hillsdale, NJ: Lawrence Erlbaum Associates.

[Salomon, Perkins, & Globerson, 1991]. Salomon, G., Perkins, D. N., & Globerson, T. (1991). Partners in cognition: Extending human intelligence with intelligent technologies. Educational Researcher, 20(3), 2-9.

[Salomon, Globerson, & Guterman, 1989]. Salomon, G., Globerson, T., & Guterman, E. (1989). The computer as a zone of proximal development: Internalizing reading-related metacognition from a reading partner. Journal of Educational Psychology, 81(4), 620-627.

[Salomon, 1988]. Salomon, G. (1988). AI in reverse: Computer tools that turn cognitive. Journal of Educational Computing Research, 4(2), 123-139.

[Smith & Lansman, 1989]. Smith, J. B., & Lansman, M.C. (1989). A Cognitive basis for a computer writing environment. In B. K. Britton & S. M. Glynn. Computer writing environments: Theory, research, and design (pp. 17-56). Hillsdale, NJ: Lawrence Erlbaum Associates.

[Smith, Weiss, & Ferguson, 1987]. Smith J. B., Weiss, S. F., & Ferguson, G. J. (1987). A hypertext writing environment and its cognitive basis. Proceedings, Hypertext '87 Conference (pp. 195-214). Chapel Hill, NC: Association for Computing Machinery.

[Vygotsky, 1962]. Vygotsky, L. (1962). Thought and language. Eugenia Hanfmann & Gertrude Vakar (Trans.) Cambridge, MA: MIT Press.

[Zellermayer, Salomon, Globerson, & Givon, 1991]. Zellermayer, M., Salomon, G., Globerson, T., & Givon, H. (1991). Enhancing writing-related metacognitions through a computerized writing partner. American Educational Research Journal, 28(2), 372-391.

Journal of Universal Computer Science, vol. 1, no. 8 (1995), 591-602
submitted: 8/2/95, accepted: 9/8/95, appeared: 28/8/95

Differential Ziv-Lempel Text Compression

Peter Fenwick,
Department of Computer Science, The University of Auckland,
Private Bag 92019, Auckland, New Zealand
p_fenwick@cs.auckland.ac.nz

Abstract We describe a novel text compressor which combines Ziv-Lempel compression and arithmetic coding with a form of vector quantisation. The resulting compressor resembles an LZ-77 compressor, but with no explicit phrase lengths or coding for literals. An examination of the limitations on its performance leads to some predictions of the limits of LZ-77 compression in general, showing that the LZ-77 text compression technique is already very close to the limits of its performance.

Keywords text compression, LZ-77, arithmetic coding, vector quantisation

Category H.3.3

1. Introduction

It is well known that there are two main approaches to text compression, or "lossless compression". On the one hand we have the dictionary compressors, generally of the Ziv-Lempel type, which replace a later occurrence of a string or phrase by a reference to an earlier occurrence of the same phrase. On the other hand we have the statistical compressors, usually with Huffman or arithmetic coding, which exploit the uneven frequency distribution of symbols and especially the dependence of symbols upon their neighbouring contexts. More powerful compressors may use an initial dictionary compressor and following statistical compressor in cascade.

There are also well-established techniques for "lossy compression", where the recovered information does not have to be an exact replica of the original. These include discrete cosine transforms, wavelets, and vector quantisation. The present work arose out of the question as to whether any of the lossy techniques might be applicable to lossless compression. It is difficult to see the relevance of cosine transforms or wavelets, which depend upon inherent regularities, or near-regularities, in the input data (and are preprocessors rather than compressors). Vector quantisation did however seem to be a useful possibility.

2. Text compression with vector quantisation; principles

In conventional vector quantisation we establish a pool of fixed length "vectors" which resemble portions of the input. We examine the next portion of the input and determine the best matching vector. The compressed output is simply the identification of this vector, together with perhaps a highly compressible approximation to the error. In text compression terms, it resembles LZ-78 compression, but with fixed-length vectors and near-matches, whereas LZ-78 uses variable-length phrases and exact matches.

To combine dictionary compression and vector quantisation we start with a standard LZ-77 scan (with the usual "sliding window", etc) to determine the longest earlier phrase which matches the text to come. This earlier phrase then becomes a reference phrase for the phrase to be emitted. The current phrase is introduced with the displacement to the reference phrase. Then, for each byte, we emit the difference (exclusive-OR) between the known byte in the reference phrase and the corresponding byte in the current phrase. This difference is of course zero for as long as the two phrases match until the phrase is terminated by the non-zero code for the first non-matching byte. The term "differential Ziv-Lempel" will be used to describe the new technique.

A phrase then consists of the initial position code, a sequence of zero symbols and a terminating non-zero symbol. The whole is processed through a set of arithmetic coders, one or more for the displacement, and one for the data. The prevalence of identical zero symbols in the data means that they are encoded very compactly and, for reasonable phrase lengths, we can achieve good compression. The presence of the terminal byte means that it resembles the original LZ-77 compressor, rather than the later variants such as LZSS.

3. Implementation

From the above discussion it is clear that a phrase is defined only by its position and requires no explicit length. Once started, coding for a phrase proceeds until an unexpected character is encoded. Neither is there is any explicit coding for a literal. As a single literal symbol can be based on any byte whatsoever, it is simplest to just emit a displacement of 1. This bases the literal on the immediately preceding byte, forcing some non-zero code and a phrase length of 1. As an optimisation detail, we keep track of the last occurrence of each byte value and point to that occurrence if it is sufficiently close (within 128 bytes), so defining a 2-byte phrase for a literal.

Displacement coding contributes the major part of the compressed output bit stream. With arithmetic coding used for the phrase bodies, the displacements too must go through the arithmetic coder. The displacement encoding finally chosen consists of one or two components, each with its own coding model. The first component is the least-significant 7 bits of the value. If the value exceeds 127, the first component has its high-order bit set and is followed by the more-significant bits as the second component.

The Ziv-Lempel parser is based on a recently-developed string matching algorithm [Fenwick and Gutmann, 1994], a description of which is included in an Appendix to this paper.

For some files it is better to omit the "over-run" byte and allow the non-zero byte of the next displacement to terminate the current phrase. Literals are handled by allowing the first byte of a phrase to be non-zero. This version actually resembles a conventional LZ-77 compressor with {displacement, length} coding, but transmitting the length as a unary code. As we will see later the length coding requires only about 0.2 bits per byte and most lengths can be represented in less than 1.5 bits. The two versions will be compared later, but for now it should be noted that they are used independently, with no attempt to combine in a single compressor.

4. Performance

The actual performance on the files of the "Calgary Corpus" [Bell, Cleary and Witten, 1990] is shown [Table 1], and compared with two of the better LZ-77 style compressors, LZB[Bell, Cleary and Witten, 1990] and LZ3VL[Fenwick, 1993]. The second version, without the phrase over-runs, compares quite well with the reference LZ-77 compressors, while the first version, with over-runs, is particularly good on the binary files.

The "over-run" coding is especially useful if the phrase terminates with a quite unusual byte, which would otherwise have to be emitted as a literal; many of the literals are just absorbed into the phrases and are emitted quite efficiently. GEO in particular benefits from this effect. Interestingly, PIC also benefits for the same reason. Although much of PIC is highly compressible runs of zeros, it contains some much less-compressible regions where phrases terminate on almost random bytes and the over-runs are of considerable benefit. Text files on the other hand tend to have sequences of phrases with few intervening literals and for these the more efficient phrase termination of the "no-overrun" coding is better. PIC also gains considerable benefit from its very long phrases (7 phrases for the first 50,000 bytes, and one of over 36,000 bytes at the end). Several other files (NEWS, OBJ1, PROGP, TRANS) also have phrases exceeding 1000 bytes.

File	diffLZ overrun	diffLZ n-ovrn	LZB	LZ3VL
BIB	3.22	3.22	3.17	3.00
BOOK1	4.13	3.88	3.86	3.65
BOOK2	3.47	3.27	3.28	3.07
GEO	5.34	6.36	6.17	5.93
NEWS	3.83	3.78	3.55	3.47
OBJ1	4.48	4.83	4.26	4.08
OBJ2	2.92	3.17	3.14	2.96
PAPER1	3.47	3.29	3.22	3.08
PAPER2	3.67	3.42	3.43	3.23
PIC	1.02	1.16	1.01	1.04
PROGC	3.34	3.19	3.08	2.97
PROGL	2.23	2.15	2.11	2.03
PROGP	2.31	2.15	2.08	2.01
TRANS	2.14	2.13	2.12	1.96
Average	**3.26**	**3.26**	**3.18**	**3.03**

Table 1. Performance, compared with other good LZ-77 compressors

Attempts to combine the two versions, switching according to data statistics, were totally unsuccessful. It is easy to separate GEO as a special case, but much much harder to detect that PIC needs the overrun coding. The two sets of results are therefore just presented separately, with no attempt at a combined version.

The version described so far was only an initial attempt at incorporating vector quantisation techniques; full quantisation allows for longer strings with continuation after mismatches. A "fuller VQ" version was attempted, allowing multiple mismatches and with phrases stopping on a sequence of fewer than about 5 matched bytes. It gave an improvement of about 3% on the file GEO, but was 3–20% worse for other files and will not be considered further. It is useful only where long phrases differ only in one or two internal bytes, and few real files are like that.

5. Analysis of the differential LZ compression performance

Analysis of the performance of the differential Ziv-Lempel compressor, and in particular the reasons for its slightly inferior performance compared with standard compressors, led to some useful insights concerning the basic limits of LZ-77 compression. Initially we deal only with the new technique, and specifically the version with phrase overruns, but the analysis is later extended to more-conventional LZ-77 compression.

We start with [Table 2] containing some general statistics from the compression of the file PAPER1 of the Calgary Corpus, using the diffLZ compressor. (The "output bits" includes the End-of-File coding, which are not included in the displacement and data values.)

Input bytes	53,161
Output bits	184,527
Displacement bits	98,590
Data bits	85,921
Total phrases	8,224
Avg. phrase length	6.46
Longest phrase	91

Frequencies of displacement lengths —

Length	1	2	3	4	5	6	7	8	9	10	11	12	13	14
Frequ.	429	161	278	341	430	407	512	464	579	701	856	990	1061	1015

Table 2. Compression statistics, PAPER1

The average phrase length is 6.46 bytes, consisting of 1 terminal byte and 5.46 zero bytes.

- The probability of a zero data byte is $^{5.46}/_{6.46} = 0.845$, with an entropy of 0.205 bits per byte.
- If we assume that there are 127 possible terminators for a text file (there are no 8-bit symbols in the file), any given code can occur with a probability of $^{1}/_{(127\times6.46)} = {}^{1}/_{820} = 0.00121$, requiring 9.68 bits to encode.
- From the actual distribution of significant bits (161 2-bit values, 278 3-bit values, and so on), the best possible displacement coding appears to require 76,357 bits.

Encoding the whole file should then require —

phrase terminators	8224 at 9.68 bits	79,608 bits
phrase body	(53161-8224) at 0.205 bits	9,212 bits
	sub-total (Phrases)	**88,820 bits**
displacement		76,357 bits
	TOTAL	**165,177 bits**

The phrases themselves actually need 85,921 data bits, which is 3.5% less than the predicted 88,820. The difference arises because the terminating symbols are not evenly distributed over the possible 127 values; some can be encoded more efficiently, so reducing the overall number of code bits.

The displacement coding however requires 98,590 bits, which is 29% greater than the apparent best coding; the average displacement length is 11.99 bits, compared with the "ideal" of 9.28. The difference arises from the need to specify the displacement length, as well as the value. In practice, the models absorb the statistics on the component lengths and include it implicitly within the coding.

The displacements could be coded as the couple {length, value} with the most-significant 1-bit omitted, giving an average displacement value of 8.28 bits. The entropy of the lengths (using the frequencies of Table 2) is 3.64 bits, giving an average displacement encoding length of 3.64+8.28 = 11.92 bits. The displacement coding achieves 11.99 bits average length, which is within 0.6% of the ideal. It is obvious that little improvement is possible.

6. The relevance of variable length codes

It is useful to consider the general relevance of variable-length integer codings, as given in [Bell, Cleary and Witten, 1990]. These usually use some form of variable-size overhead to allow small values to be coded compactly, but at the cost of less efficient coding for large values which often need a larger overhead. This is precisely the opposite effect of what we want for displacements! Most of the displacements are large, and should be encoded with low overhead. The short displacements, being infrequent, can be coded with larger overheads. Thus the conventional variable-length codes are quite inappropriate for displacements. Very long displacements predominate and even transmitting the raw 14-bit binary value is relatively efficient in comparison with a compact coding of the displacement.

Precisely the opposite situation applies for encoding the phrase lengths in conventional LZ-77 compression. The shorter phrases are much more frequent with relatively little compression gain and must be coded as compactly as possible. The longer phrases are less frequent, give much more benefit, and can be coded inefficiently with little penalty.

7. Interpretation as an arithmetic code

Although the technique has been introduced as a derivative of LZ-77 compression, it can be viewed as high context arithmetic compressor. An LZ-77 parse is used to find the best following context including the next byte and the coder then emits from this context, with 100% certainty, for as long as possible. This is in contrast to conventional high-order arithmetic compression where we establish a preceding context for each byte, and emit probabilistically from this context.

The output from any high order arithmetic compressor consists of two intermingled data streams, one conveying data and one information on the contexts. Thus in a compressor which allows escapes to lower order contexts, the code for every byte must include the information "this is a symbol with some probability" (i.e. data) and "this is not an escape" (context). Explicit escape codes will reverse these meanings. While data in a high context arithmetic coder can be emitted at about 1 bit per byte for many files, we often find that more information is required for context control. Thus context management is more expensive than data encoding proper.

Exactly the same situation applies here. Because the LZ-77 parse establishes a precise context, data can be emitted with zero cost – all of the coding is concerned with context management. The normal "data encoding" uses about 0.2 bit/byte to signal "continue in this context". With some expense it notes the end of the phrase and then requires a dozen or more bits to establish a new context, in all about 20 bits to switch between contexts. The context management, rather than the data, sets the compression performance.

8. Performance limits of standard LZ-77 compression

We can extend the above analysis to conventional LZ-77 compression. The comparisons are somewhat "apples and oranges", because the differential (or vector quantising) compressor alters the definition of an LZ-77 phrase by always overrunning by one byte. We may also note the well-known effects of buffer size on LZ-77 performance, which means that we might not always compare like with like. There are also various subtle differences in details of the encoding, such as the LZ3VL compressor coding displacements to the end of the phrase rather than to its start, and considerable variations within files, so that the overall statistics might not be completely representative. However, the calculations do appear to give a reasonable indication of the possible performance of LZ-77 compression.

	input bytes	literals	phrases	predicted displ bits	displ avg	disp len entropy	phr len entropy
BIB	111,261	7,928	14,279	165,132	11.565	2.898	3.247
BOOK1	768,771	38,179	142,028	1,656,514	11.663	2.874	2.951
BOOK2	610,856	31,167	89,544	1,005,560	11.230	3.076	3.347
GEO	102,400	24,829	23,316	239,324	10.264	3.228	1.383
NEWS	377,109	41,541	53,589	584,734	10.911	3.189	2.780
OBJ1	21,504	6,017	2,238	18,633	8.326	3.498	1.639
OBJ2	246,814	29,110	26,237	247,772	9.444	3.503	2.760
PAPER1	53,161	3,611	7,460	80,716	10.820	3.185	3.251
PAPER2	82,199	4,295	12,952	145,911	11.266	3.022	3.251
PIC	513,216	22,761	16,655	162,731	9.771	3.130	2.990
PROGC	39,611	3,226	5,081	51,914	10.217	3.343	3.304
PROGL	71,646	3,158	6,483	65,374	10.084	3.357	3.726
PROGP	49,379	2,629	4,290	41,079	9.576	3.436	3.525
TRANS	93,695	5,713	7,256	74,326	10.243	3.375	3.378

Table 3. Observed parameters from LZ-77 compression

An LZ-77 compressor (with greedy parsing, 2-byte minimum phrase length and 16 K buffer) was instrumented to report various statistics on compressing the files of the Calgary Corpus, producing the results in [Table 3], with consequent predictions given in [Table 4]. The two basic assumptions are –

1. The phrase is located by an actual displacement, rather than a position in some complex data structure, and
2. A phrase is encoded as the triple { length, displ_precision, displ_value}, where the phrase length and displ_precision are entropy encoded and displ_value is the actual bits following the most-significant 1 of the displacement.

This phrase encoding should be very close to the optimal coding of the phrase definition. Conventional LZ77 encoding (more correctly LZ-SS) uses a flag bit to indicate a literal or phrase; here we use a reserved length, most sensibly 1, and encode a literal as {1, literal}. This coding is slightly less efficient for literals, but saves one bit when encoding the usually more frequent phrases.

Much of the calculation parallels that given earlier for PAPER1. In more detail, consider the file BIB which produced 7,928 literals and 14,279 phrases. The weighted sum of the minimum displacement lengths gives a "*predicted displ bits*" and the average displacement length. The entropy of the displacement lengths gives the minimum cost of specifying the displacement lengths. The phrase length entropy is similarly calculated from the distribution of phrase lengths.

The average length of a phrase is then 10.56+2.90+3.25=16.71 (omitting the most-significant 1-bit of the displacement reduces the displacement length by 1, from 11.56 to 10.56). A literal is encoded as 8 bits plus information to specify one of 7,928 literals out of a total of 22,207 cases, or $8+\log_2(^{22,207}/_{7,928}) = 9.49$ bits, giving 75,205 bits for literals over the whole file. We predict a total of $16.71 \times 14{,}279$ phrase bits, giving a total of 313,807 bits and 2.82 bits per byte. The best available compressor delivers 3.00 bits/byte, or 94% of the predicted limit. Entropy-encoding literals might allow some more compression, but it is unlikely to be significant because it is only the less-probable values which appear as literals — the more-frequent ones, which would benefit from statistical coding, tend to appear within phrases anyway.

Two points are apparent from this study. The first is that for most files one or other of the LZ-77 compressors is within 10% of the apparent limit, with some being within 5%. There appears to be little possible gain beyond what has been achieved already in LZ-77 compressors. The new diffLZ compressor attains the predicted limit for GEO.

The second point is that the phrase length is nearly constant. The average over the whole corpus is 15.6 bits, with a standard deviation of 1.2 bits. Ignoring the binary files gives a length of 16.0±0.6 bits. This gives a useful rule of thumb for LZ77 compression, that

an LZ77 phrase usually needs about 16 bits to encode.

What really varies between files is the average phrase length. Those with more long phrases are more compressible and with more short phrases less compressible; the cost of encoding a phrase is approximately constant. The main limitation is in the coding of the displacement. This is essentially a large random number and not very much can be done to optimise its coding.

	pred avg phrase bits	pred total literal bits	pred total phrase bits	pred limit bit per byte	best of LZB, LZ3VL, diffLZ	perf. rel to limit
BIB	16.71	75,205	238,602	2.80	3.00	94%
BOOK1	16.49	390,907	2,341,758	3.56	3.65	97%
BOOK2	16.66	310,220	1,491,176	2.95	3.07	96%
GEO	13.88	222,353	323,510	5.33	5.34	100%
NEWS	15.88	381,985	850,993	3.27	3.47	94%
OBJ1	12.46	50,881	27,892	3.60	4.08	90%
OBJ2	14.71	259,865	385,868	2.62	2.92	89%
PAPER1	16.27	34,725	121,270	2.94	3.08	95%
PAPER2	16.54	42,974	214,213	3.13	3.23	97%
PIC	14.89	200,120	248,010	0.88	1.02	86%
PROGC	15.86	30,210	80,605	2.80	2.97	94%
PROGL	16.17	30,349	104,811	1.89	2.03	93%
PROGP	15.54	24,702	66,654	1.86	2.01	92%
TRANS	15.99	52,461	116,067	1.80	1.96	92%

Table 4. Predictions of best LZ-77 compression

An interesting observation is that the incompressible files tend to require fewer bits to encode a phrase. Not only are their phrases shorter, requiring fewer length bits to encode, but the shorter phrases are more likely to be matched closer to the current position and with shorter displacements as well.

The deficiencies in the new compressor are, as might be expected, almost entirely in the definition of the phrase length, although the data over-runs do reduce the number of phrases and allow more efficient coding of infrequent literals.

9. Conclusions

We have described a novel combination of Ziv-Lempel, arithmetic and vector quantisation to produce a text compressor of good general performance, and excellent performance on some files. It is unique in that while based on LZ77 parsing, it has no explicit phrase length or literal encoding.

Investigations of the performance of this compressor led to a wider study of LZ77 compression and firm indications that text files cannot be compressed to better than about 3.0 bits/byte with LZ77 compression. The best extant LZ77 compressors are already very close to this predicted limit.

References

[Bell, Cleary and Witten, 1990]. T.C. Bell, J.G. Cleary, and I.H. Witten, *Text Compression*, Prentice-Hall, Englewood Cliffs, NJ 1990

[Fenwick, 1993]. P. M. Fenwick, "Ziv-Lempel coding with multi-bit flags", *Proc Data Compression Conference, DCC-93*, Snowbird, Utah, Mar 1993

[Fenwick and Gutmann, 1994]. P.M. Fenwick and P.C. Gutmann, "Fast LZ77 String Matching", Dept of Computer Science, The University of Auckland, Tech Report 102, Sep 1994

APPENDIX. The Gutmann fast string matching algorithm

A recent study by Gutmann has examined the performance of many string-matching algorithms, from the very simple to very complex. He found that while it is easy to devise extensive data structures to minimise the number of comparisons, it is only too easy to lose out from the overheads of maintaining and traversing the data structure. It may be better to use a simple structure with frequent, but inexpensive, comparisons. His preferred algorithm is described here.

We maintain a conventional LZ buffer as a simple byte array. Pairs of adjacent bytes are hashed and used to index a table which defines links through the array, connecting byte pairs of like hash values. When looking for a string we hash the first bytes of the string and then trace along the chain corresponding to that hash value. The chain *must* include all occurrences of those first bytes (plus any others which collide in the hash table). So far it is a standard simple LZ buffer.

Assume that at some stage we have a longest match of length λ, and are looking for a string of length $\lambda+1$. As there is no benefit in considering any string with *length* $\leq \lambda$, we first look at the "*mismatch*" byte in position $\lambda+1$, one beyond the known best length. If that byte does not match, the position cannot possibly give a better match. If that byte matches, we then compare "*half-match*" bytes at about the midpoint of the known best string. This byte is simply a representative candidate of the strings. Only if the *mismatch* and *half-match* comparisons succeed do we do a full byte-by-byte comparison of the two strings. If the match succeeds to length

$\lambda+1$, we then extend the match as far as possible.

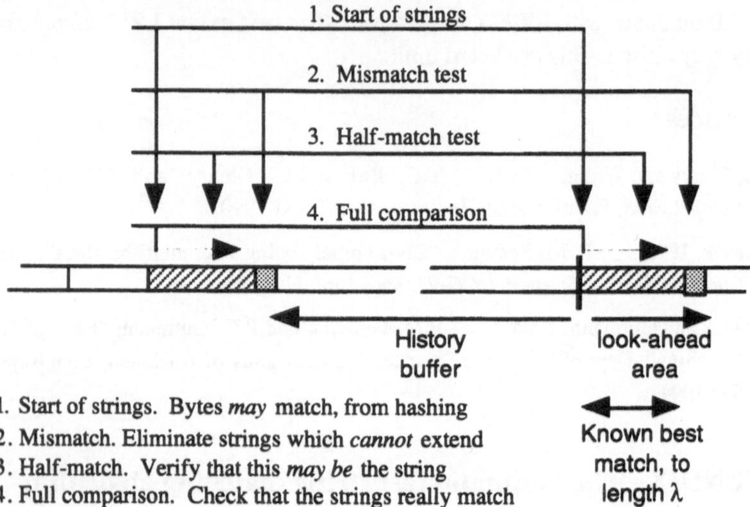
1. Start of strings
2. Mismatch test
3. Half-match test
4. Full comparison
History buffer
look-ahead area
1. Start of strings. Bytes may match, from hashing
2. Mismatch. Eliminate strings which cannot extend
3. Half-match. Verify that this may be the string
4. Full comparison. Check that the strings really match
Known best match, to length λ

Gutmann's experiments show that about 50% of possible phrases are eliminated on the mismatch test and that fewer than 10% survive the half-match as well and need a full comparison. Testing a given candidate string then requires only the following steps, most of which are simple and fast —

1. Check that this position is still valid (not beyond the end of the hash chain)
2. Compare the mismatch bytes
3. Compare the half-match bytes
4. Do a full comparison of the two strings
5. Step to the next position in the hash chain

A further refinement, which is not used here, is to select as the half-match byte one with a low probability. This approximately halves the number of full comparisons for files such as PIC and GEO.

Journal of Universal Computer Science, vol. 1, no. 8 (1995), 603-613
submitted: 4/5/95, accepted: 16/8/95, appeared: 28/8/95 © Springer Pub. Co.

BOUNDS FOR HEIGHTS OF INTEGER POLYNOMIAL FACTORS

Laurenţiu Panaitopol
University of Bucharest, Faculty of Mathematics,
79543 Bucarest, Romania.
Email: pan@math.math.unibuc.ro.

Doru Ştefănescu
University of Bucharest, Faculty of Physics, Department of Mathematics,
P. O. Box 39-95, Bucharest 39, Romania.
Email: stef@imar.ro.

Abstract: We describe new methods for the estimation of the bounds of the coefficients of proper divisors of integer polynomials in one variable. There exist classes of polynomials for which our estimates are better than those obtained using the polynomial measure or the 2-weighted norm.

1 Introduction

A main step in the process of factorization of integer polynomials in one variable is the estimation of the moduli of the coefficients of all possible divisors. Powerful methods are the consideration of estimations using the measure of a polynomial (cf. Mignotte [9]) and the use of weighted norms (cf. Beauzamy [3]).
We shall prove that there exist real polynomials for which sharper results may be obtained working directly with the upper bound of the roots instead of the measure. Such are, the polynomials with roots having moduli greater than one, for example Hurwitz polynomials. Alternative results are obtained for the lower bound.

We use the following standard notations:

$\mathbb{N}$ = the natural numbers,
$\mathbb{Z}$ = the integers,
$\mathbb{Q}$ = the rational numbers,
$\mathbb{R}$ = the real numbers
$\mathbb{C}$ = the complex numbers,
$R[X]$ = the univariate polynomials on the domain R,
$\mathbb{N}^*$ = the nonzero natural numbers,
$\mathbb{R}_+^*$ = the nonzero positive real numbers.

Let us suppose that

$$P(X) = \sum_{i=0}^{n} a_i X^i \in \mathbb{C}[X] \setminus \mathbb{C},$$

and let $z_1, \ldots, z_n \in \mathbb{C}$ be the roots of P.

There are several sizes associated with a polynomial $P \in \mathbb{C}[X]$. Among them we mention

$$\text{the } measure \qquad M(P) = |a_n| \prod_{j=1}^{n} \max(1, |z_j|),$$

$$\text{the } height \qquad H(P) = \max_{0 \le i \le n} |a_i|,$$

$$\text{the } norm \qquad ||P|| = \sqrt{\sum_{i=0}^{n} a_i^2},$$

$$\text{the weighted } \quad l_2 - norm \qquad [P]_2 = \sqrt{\sum_{i=0}^{n} \frac{a_i^2}{\binom{n}{i}}}.$$

The measure was introduced by K. Mahler [8] (cf. also E. Landau [7]), the height was known to Cauchy [4], the norm corresponds to the euclidean norm of the vector given by the coefficients and the weighted norm was considered by Bombieri [2].

If $P \in \mathbb{Z}[X] \setminus \mathbb{Z}$ these sizes proved to be usefull for finding bounds for the coefficients of the divisors. Let Q be a divisor of P from $\mathbb{Z}[X]$ and let $T \in \mathbb{R}_+^*$ be an upper bound for the coefficients of all possible divisors Q, i.e. T is a bound of the height of Q. A key step in factorization devices is the choice of a prime $p > T$ (or of a power of a prime $p^s > T$), which allows us to consider first the factorization of the image of P in a finite field. (See, for example ch. 7 from [10]).

Other sizes associated with P are

$$B = B(P) = \max\{|z_j|; 1 \le j \le n\}$$

and

$$A = A(P) = \min\{|z_j|; 1 \le j \le n\}$$

If Q is a proper divisor of P in $\mathbb{Z}[X]$, then the coefficients of Q are bounded by

$$\max_{0 \le j \le h} |a_n| \binom{h}{j} B^j, \tag{1}$$

where $h = deg(Q) \in \{1, 2, \ldots, n-1\}$. (See a proof, for example, in the monograph of A. G. Akritas [1].) We shall invoke this inequality for obtaining sharper estimates for the moduli of the coefficients of Q. For some classes of polynomials they are better than those obtained using the measure or the l_2 weighted norm. We also obtain other related evaluations of $H(Q)$ which depend on the size of a_0 and of an auxiliary parameter $\alpha > 0$.

2 Evaluation of the height of Q vs upper bounds of the roots

We first prove two results about binomial coefficients involved in the estimation of the moduli of the coefficients of Q.

Proposition 2.1 *Let $h \in \mathbb{N}^*$ and $B \in \mathbb{R}_+^*$, $B \geq 1$. Then*

$$\max_{0\leq i\leq h} \binom{h}{i} B^i = \begin{cases} B^h & \text{if } h < B, \\ \max(B^h, \binom{h}{u} B^u), & \text{if } h \geq B, \end{cases}$$

where $u = \left\lfloor \frac{B(h+1)}{B+1} \right\rfloor$.

Proof. Because $B \geq 1$ one has

$$\binom{h}{0} B^0 = 1 \leq B^h = \binom{h}{h} B^h. \tag{2}$$

Therefore the maximum is equal to B^h or there exists $u \in \{1, 2, \ldots, h-1\}$ such that

$$\max_{0\leq i\leq h} \binom{h}{i} B^i = \binom{h}{u} B^u.$$

In this case we note that

$$\binom{h}{u} B^u \geq \binom{h}{u-1} B^{u-1} \tag{3}$$

and

$$\binom{h}{u+1} B^{u+1} \leq \binom{h}{u} B^u. \tag{4}$$

¿From (3) it follows that

$$\frac{B}{u} \geq \frac{1}{h-u+1},$$

therefore

$$u \leq \frac{(h+1)B}{B+1}. \tag{5}$$

On the other hand, from (4) it follows that

$$\frac{B}{u+1} \leq \frac{1}{h-u},$$

therefore

$$u \geq \frac{Bh-1}{B+1}. \tag{6}$$

From (5) and (6) it follows that

$$\frac{Bh-1}{B+1} \leq u \leq \frac{B(h+1)}{B+1}.$$

But $\frac{B(h+1)}{B+1} - 1 = \frac{Bh-1}{B+1}$. It follows that

$$\frac{B(h+1)}{B+1} - 1 \le u \le \frac{B(h+1)}{B+1}. \tag{7}$$

From (5) and (7) it follows that

$$u = \lfloor \frac{B(h+1)}{B+1} \rfloor. \tag{8}$$

From relations (2) and (8) it follows that

$$\max_{0\le i\le h} \binom{h}{i} B^i = \max(B^h, \binom{h}{u} B^u).$$

We now observe that $h \ge \lfloor \frac{B(h+1)}{B+1} \rfloor$ if and only if $h \ge B$. Indeed

$$h - \frac{B(h+1)}{B+1} = \frac{h-B}{B+1} \ge 0 \iff h \ge B.$$

Now deal with case $H \ge B$.

If $h < B$, then $B^h > \binom{h}{s} B^s$ for all $s < h$. Actually, for $B > h$ and $s < h$ we have

$$B^h - \binom{h}{s} B^s = B^s (B^{h-s} - \prod_{i=0}^{h-s-1} \frac{h-i}{i+1}). \tag{9}$$

But $\frac{h-i}{i+1} < h - i < h < B$. Therefore

$$\prod_{i=0}^{h-s-1} \frac{h-i}{i+1} < B^{h-s}$$

and from (9) it follows that

$$B^h > \binom{h}{s} B^s.$$

Therefore if $h < B$, then

$$\max_{0\le i\le h} \binom{h}{i} B^i = B^h.$$

∎

Theorem 2.2 *Let $n \in \mathbb{N}$, $n \ge 2$ and $B \in \mathbb{R}_+^*$, $B \ge 1$. Then*

$$\max_{1\le h\le n-1} (\max_{0\le i\le h} \binom{h}{i} B^i) = \begin{cases} B^{n-1} & \text{if} \quad n < B+1, \\ \binom{n-1}{\lfloor \frac{Bn}{B+1} \rfloor} B^{\lfloor \frac{Bn}{B+1} \rfloor} & \text{if} \quad n \ge B+1. \end{cases}$$

Proof. For fixed $h \in \{1, 2, \ldots, n-1\}$ let

$$C(h) = \max_{0 \le i \le h} \binom{h}{i} B^i.$$

We have to evaluate

$$\max_{1 \le h \le n-1} C(h).$$

From Proposition 2.1 we know that

$$C(h) = \begin{cases} B^h & \text{if} \quad h < B, \\ \max(B^h, \binom{h}{u} B^u), & \text{if} \quad h \ge B, \end{cases} \tag{10}$$

where $u = \lfloor \frac{B(h+1)}{B+1} \rfloor$.

We first observe that that $B^{n-1} = \max_{1 \le i \le n} B^i$ because $B \ge 1$.

On the other hand we compare $C(h)$ and $C(h-1)$ and we consider

$$u = \left\lfloor \frac{B(h+1)}{B+1} \right\rfloor \quad \text{and} \quad v = \left\lfloor \frac{Bh}{B+1} \right\rfloor.$$

to show that

$$\binom{h}{u} B^u \ge \binom{h-1}{v} B^v. \tag{11}$$

Indeed, we have

$$\frac{B(h+1)}{B+1} - \frac{Bh}{B+1} = \frac{B}{B+1} < 1,$$

so that

$$u - v \le 1.$$

It follows that $u = v$ or $u = v + 1$.

First case: $u = v$.

We observe that $u \ne 0$ because $\frac{B(h+1)}{B+1} \ge 1$.

We have

$$\frac{\binom{h}{u}}{\binom{h-1}{u}} = \frac{h}{h-u} > 1$$

and therefore strict inequality in (11).

Second case: $u = v + 1$.
In this case

$$\frac{\binom{h}{u}}{\binom{h-1}{u-1}} = \frac{h}{u} \geq 1,$$

and again (11) holds.

Now we note that

$$\frac{B(h+1)}{B+1} = h + \frac{B-h}{B+1} \leq h \qquad \text{if} \qquad h \geq B.$$

Hence

$$h \geq \left\lfloor \frac{B(h+1)}{B+1} \right\rfloor \qquad \text{for} \qquad h \geq B. \tag{12}$$

It now follows from relation (11) that $\max_{1 \leq h \leq n-1} C(h)$ is realized for $h = n - 1$.

If $n - 1 < B$, then

$$\max_h C(h) = B^{n-1}$$

by Proposition 2.1.

If $n - 1 \geq B$, then

$$\max_h C(h) = \binom{n-1}{\left\lfloor \frac{Bn}{B+1} \right\rfloor} B^{\left\lfloor \frac{Bn}{B+1} \right\rfloor}$$

again by Proposition 2.1. ∎

In Proposition 2.1 and Theorem 2.2 we considered $B \geq 1$. But with slight modifications the same results hold for $0 < B < 1$.

Proposition 2.3 *Let $h \in \mathbb{N}^*$ and $B \in \mathbb{R}^*_+$, $0 < B < 1$. Then*

$$\max_{0 \leq i \leq h} \binom{h}{i} B^i = \begin{cases} 1 & \text{if } h < \frac{1}{B}, \\ \max(1, \binom{h}{u} B^u), & \text{if } h \geq \frac{1}{B}, \end{cases}$$

where $u = \left\lfloor \frac{B(h+1)}{B+1} \right\rfloor$.

Theorem 2.4 *Let $n \in \mathbb{N}$, $n \geq 2$ and $B \in \mathbb{R}^*_+$, $0 < B < 1$. Then*

$$\max_{1 \leq h \leq n-1} \left(\max_{0 \leq i \leq h} \binom{h}{i} B^i \right) = \begin{cases} 1 & \text{if} \quad n < \frac{1}{B} + 1, \\ \binom{n-1}{\left\lfloor \frac{Bn}{B+1} \right\rfloor} B^{\left\lfloor \frac{Bn}{B+1} \right\rfloor} & \text{if} \quad n \geq \frac{1}{B} + 1. \end{cases}$$

Now we consider an application of Theorems 2.2 and 2.4 to the estimation of the height of a proper divisor Q of P. Let $K > 0$ be a bound for $B(P)$.

Corollary 2.5 *If* $1 \le K \le n-1$ *or* $\frac{1}{n-1} < K < 1$ *then*

$$H(Q) \le |a_n| \binom{n-1}{\left\lfloor \frac{Kn}{K+1} \right\rfloor} K^{\left\lfloor \frac{Kn}{K+1} \right\rfloor}.$$

Proof. If $1 \le K \le n-1$, we apply Theorem 2.2. For $\frac{1}{n-1} < K < 1$ the estimate follows from Theorem 2.4. ∎

3 Limits for roots of polynomials with positive coefficients

We next show that knowledge of upper bounds for the sizes associated with a complex polynomial allows the determination of bounds of the coefficients of the divisors.

If we consider the bound (1) for the coefficients of a divisor of degree h of P, then we are interested in obtaining sharper estimates of B. The usual estimates relative to complex polynomials give evaluations that are too far from the best bound.

But for real polynomials with all the coefficients strictly positive the bound B can be evaluated in a more convenient way, thanks to a result of Eneström [5].

Theorem 3.1 *Let* $P(X) = \sum_{i=0}^{n} a_i X^i \in \mathbb{R}_+^*[X]$. *If* $x_1, x_2, \ldots, x_n \in \mathbb{C}$ *are the roots of* P *then*

$$\min_{1\le i\le n} \frac{a_{i-1}}{a_i} \le |x_j| \le \max_{1\le i\le n} \frac{a_{i-1}}{a_i}, \ \forall j = 1, 2, \ldots, n.$$

Proof. We first recall the key result of Eneström about polynomials with positive real coefficients.

Let $Q(X) = \sum_{i=0}^{n} b_i X^i \in \mathbb{R}_+^*[X]$ *and let* $z_1, \ldots, z_n \in \mathbb{C}$ *be the roots of* Q. *Then*
i) If $b_0 \ge b_1 \ge \ldots \ge b_n > 0$, *then* $|z_j| \ge 1 \ \forall j = 1, \ldots, n$.
ii) If $0 < b_0 \le b_1 \le \ldots \le b_n$, *then* $|z_j| \le 1 \ \forall j = 1, \ldots, n$.

Next, note that the coefficients of the polynomial

$$P_\beta(Y) = P(\beta Y) = \sum_{i=0}^{n} a_i \beta^i Y^i \in \mathbb{R}_+^*[Y],$$

where $\beta > 0$, satisfy

$$a_0 \ge a_1\beta \ge a_2\beta^2 \ge \ldots \ge a_{i-1}\beta^{i-1} \ge a_i\beta^i \ge \ldots \ge a_n\beta^n > 0$$

if and only if

$$\beta \leq \frac{a_{i-1}}{a_i} \forall i.$$

Taking

$$\beta = \min_{1 \leq i \leq n} \frac{a_{i-1}}{a_i}$$

and letting $y_1, \ldots, y_n \in \mathbb{C}$ be the roots of P_β, we therefore have

$$|y_j| \geq 1, \qquad (j = 1, \ldots, n).$$

But $y_j = \frac{x_j}{\beta}$ and therefore

$$|x_j| \geq \min_{1 \leq i \leq n} \frac{a_{i-1}}{a_i}, \ \forall j = 1, \ldots, n.$$

A similar argument, based on ii), shows that

$$|x_j| \leq \max_{1 \leq i \leq n} \frac{a_{i-1}}{a_i}, \ \forall j = 1, \ldots, n$$

which ends the proof. ∎

Remark: Let $P(X) = (-1)^n a_n X^n + \ldots + a_2 x^2 - a_1 X + a_0 \in \mathbb{R}[X]$, where $a_0, a_1, \ldots, a_n > 0$. If $x_1, \ldots, x_n$ are the roots of P then

$$\min_{1 \leq i \leq n} \left|\frac{a_{i-1}}{a_i}\right| \leq |x_j| \leq \max_{1 \leq i \leq n} \left|\frac{a_{i-1}}{a_i}\right|, \ \forall j = 1, 2, \ldots, n.$$

Indeed, the polynomial $P(-X)$ satisfies the hypotheses of Theorem 3.1 and $|x_j| = |-x_j|$ for all j.

4 Height estimates vs lower bounds of the roots

Eliminating X from the relations $P(X) = 0$, $Y = \alpha X$ (where $\alpha > 0$), one obtains a new polynomial $P_\alpha(Y)$. From the study of factors of P_α it is possible to derive new evaluations for the heights of factors of P.

Proposition 4.1 *Let $P \in \mathbb{Z}[X] \setminus \mathbb{Z}$, $P(0) \neq 0$, $x_1, \ldots, x_n \in \mathbb{C}$ the roots of P, and $\alpha \geq \frac{1}{\min_{1 \leq j \leq n} |x_j|}$. If $Q(X) = \sum_{i=0}^{h} b_i X^i \in \mathbb{Z}[X] \setminus \mathbb{Z}$ is a proper divisor of P then*

$$|b_i| \leq |a_0| \binom{h}{i} \alpha^i \quad \textit{for all } i = 0, 1, \ldots, h-1.$$

Proof. Let $Y = \alpha X$. We notice that $y_j = \alpha x_j$ $(j = 1, \ldots, n)$ are the roots of the polynomial

$$P_\alpha(Y) = \alpha^n P(\frac{Y}{\alpha}) = a_n Y^n + a_{n-1}\alpha Y^{n-1} + a_{n-2}\alpha^2 Y^{n-2} + \ldots + a_0\alpha^n \in \mathbb{C}[Y]$$

and $|y_j| \geq 1$ for all j.

We may suppose that $x_1, x_2, \ldots, x_h$ are the roots of the divisor Q. Therefore $y_1, y_2, \ldots, y_h$ are the roots of the polynomial

$$Q_\alpha(Y) = \alpha^h Q(\frac{Y}{\alpha}) = \sum_{i=0}^{h} b_i' Y^i = b_h Y^h + \sum_{i=0}^{h-1} b_i \alpha^{h-i} Y^i \in \mathbb{C}[Y].$$

As each $|y_j| \geq 1$ it follows that

$$|\frac{b_i'}{b_h}| = |\sum y_{u_1} y_{u_2} \ldots y_{u_i}| \leq \binom{h}{i} |y_1 y_2 \ldots y_h| = \binom{h}{i} |\frac{b_0}{b_h}| \alpha^h. \tag{13}$$

But $b_i' = \alpha^{h-i} b_i$. Therefore from (13) it follows that

$$|b_i| \leq \binom{h}{i} |a_0| \alpha^i, \tag{14}$$

which ends the proof. ∎

Corollary 4.2 *If all the roots of P are outside the unit disk then*

$$|b_i| \leq \binom{h}{i} |a_0|, \quad \textit{for all} \quad i.$$

Proof. Let

$$\alpha = \frac{1}{\min |x_j|},$$

where $x_1, \ldots, x_n \in \mathbb{C}$ are the roots of P. But $|x_j| \geq 1$ for all j, therefore $\alpha \leq 1$. The previous result gives now the desired estimate. ∎

Remark: We obtained in [11] necessary and sufficient conditions for a polynomial over the integers to have all roots outside the unit disk. Therefore it is possible to know to which polynomials our corollary 4.2 may be applied.

Now we are able to evaluate the height of a proper divisor Q of P. Let $L > 0$ be a lower bound for $A(P)$.

Corollary 4.3 *If* $\frac{1}{n-1} \leq L \leq 1$ *or* $1 < L \leq n - 1$, *then*

$$H(Q) \leq |a_0| \binom{n-1}{\lfloor \frac{n}{L+1} \rfloor} L^{-\lfloor \frac{n}{L+1} \rfloor}.$$

Proof. This follows from Proposition 4.1, with reference to Theorem 2.2, Theorem 2.4, and the proof of Corollary 2.5. ∎

5 Applications

Let $P \in \mathbb{Z}[X] \setminus \mathbb{Z}$, $P(0) \neq 0$. Let m_1, m_2, m_3, m_4 be the following estimates of bounds heights of a proper polynomial divisor of P:

$$m_1 = \binom{n}{\lfloor \frac{n}{2} \rfloor} M \qquad \text{(Specht, 1949)}$$

$$m_2 = \frac{3^{3/4} \cdot 3^{\frac{n}{2}}}{2\sqrt{\pi n}} [P]_2 \qquad \text{(Beauzamy, 1992)}$$

$$m_3 = |a_n| \binom{n-1}{\left\lfloor \frac{Kn}{K+1} \right\rfloor} K^{\left\lfloor \frac{Kn}{K+1} \right\rfloor} \qquad \text{(Corollary 2.5 of this paper)}$$

$$m_4 = |a_0| \binom{n-1}{\left\lfloor \frac{n}{L+1} \right\rfloor} L^{-\left\lfloor \frac{n}{L+1} \right\rfloor} \qquad \text{(Corollary 4.3 of this paper),}$$

where M is the measure, $[P]_2$ the weighted l_2-norm, K is un upper bound for the maxima of the moduli of the roots and L a lower bound for the minima of the moduli of the roots.

We consider the polynomials

$$P_1 = 2X^7 - 2X^6 + 3X^5 - 4X^4 + 5X^3 - 7X^2 + 9X - 12,$$
$$P_2 = 28X^7 + 19X^6 + 13X^5 + 9X^4 + 6X^3 + 4X^2 + 3X + 2,$$
$$P_3 = X^6 + 2X^5 + 4X^4 + 5X^3 + 6X^2 + 7X + 9,$$
$$P_4 = 3X^7 + 4X^6 + 6X^5 + 9X^4 + 13X^3 + 19X^2 + 13X + 19.$$

We notice that, for these polynomials, the estimates given by Corollary 2.5 (respectively Corollary 4.3) are given by m_3, respectively m_4.

In the following table we compare the upper bounds of $H(Q)$ obtained from the four previous estimates, where Q is a possible proper divisor of P. The first four columns contain the sizes involved in the estimates, and the other four give the values of the estimates.

P	M	$[P]_2$	K	L	m_1	m_2	m_3	m_4
P_1	6	11.369	1.5	1	420	145.627	151.875	420
P_2	1	20.534	0.75	0.666	980	233.680	236.25	151.875
P_3	9	9.775	2	1.666	180	69.302	80	66.122
P_4	≥ 19	29.206	1.5	0.684	≥ 1995	332.046	227.812	1300.426

We note that the estimate m_1 gives better results for polynomials with small measure and small leading coefficients. The estimate m_2 gives good results for broader classes of polynomials. The estimates m_3 and m_4 apply to polynomials with strictly positive or non-zero alternate coefficients. They are useful, for example, in the study of polynomials with 'small distances' between consecutive coefficients.

Remark: In the original problem of factorization of a non-constant polynomial P from $\mathbb{Z}[X]$ it is necessary to find a bound which exceeds not only $H(Q)$, with Q a proper divisor of P, but also $|a_n|$.

Acknowledgment

We are grateful to Professors Douglas Bridges and Cris Calude who read and criticised previous versions of this paper.

References

1. A. G. AKRITAS: *Elements of Computer Algebra with Applications*, Wiley& Sons (1989).
2. B. BEAUZAMY, E. BOMBIERI, P. ENFLO, H. MONTGOMERY: Products of polynomials in many variables, *J. Number Theory*, **36**, 219-245 (1990).
3. B. BEAUZAMY: Products of polynomials and a priori estimates for coefficients in polynomial decompositions: A sharp result, *J. Symb. Comp.* **13**, 463-472 (1992).
4. A.-L. CAUCHY: *Exercices de Mathématiques*, 4ème année, De Bure Frères, Paris (1829).
5. G. ENESTRÖM: Händelning af en allmän formel för antalet pensionärer, som vid en tidpunkt förefinns inom en sluten pension kassa, *Öfversigt af velinskaps-akademiens förhandlinger* (Stockholm) **50**, 405-415 (1893).
6. D. E. KNUTH: *The Art of Computer Programming*, vol. 2, *Seminumerical Algorithms*, Addison-Wesley (1981).
7. E. LANDAU: Sur quelques théorèmes de M. Petrovitch relatifs aux zéros des fonctions algébriques, *Bull. Soc. Math. France*, **33**, 251-261 (1905).
8. K. MAHLER: An application of Jensen's formulæ to polynomials. *Mathematica*, **7**, 98-100 (1960).
9. M. MIGNOTTE: An inequality about factors of polynomials, *Math. Comp.*, **28**, 1153 - 1157 (1974).
10. M. MIGNOTTE: *Mathematics for Computer Algebra*, Springer Verlag (1991).
11. L. PANAITOPOL, D. ŞTEFĂNESCU: Some polynomial factorizations over the integers, *Bull. Math. Soc. Sc. Math. Roumanie*, **37** (**85**), n. 3-4 (1993). [to appear]
12. W. SPECHT: Abschätzungen der Wurzeln algebraischer Gleichungen, *Math. Z.* **52**, 310-321 (1949).

Journal of Universal Computer Science, vol. 1, no. 8 (1995), 614-631
submitted: 31/3/95, accepted: 2/8/95, appeared: 28/8/95 © Springer Pub. Co.

A Robust Affine Matching Algorithm Using an Exponentially Decreasing Distance Function

Axel Pinz, Manfred Prantl, Harald Ganster
Institute for Computer Graphics
Technical University of Graz
Münzgrabenstr. 11
A-8010 Graz, AUSTRIA
email: pinz@icg.tu-graz.ac.at

Abstract: We describe a robust method for spatial registration, which relies on the coarse correspondence of structures extracted from images, avoiding the establishment of point correspondences. These structures (tokens) are points, chains, polygons and regions at the level of intermediate symbolic representation (ISR). The algorithm recovers conformal transformations (4 affine parameters), so that 2-dimensional scenes as well as planar structures in 3D scenes can be handled. The affine transformation between two different tokensets is found by minimization of an exponentially decreasing distance function. As long as the tokensets are kept sparse, the method is very robust against a broad variety of common disturbances (e.g. incomplete segmentations, missing tokens, partial overlap). The performance of the algorithm is demonstrated using simple 2D shapes, medical, and remote sensing satellite images. The complexity of the algorithm is quadratic on the number of affine parameters.
Categories: I.2.10, I.5, I.4
Keywords: Affine Matching, Spatial Registration, Information Fusion, Image Understanding

1 Introduction

In Computer Vision, the establishment of correspondence between different sources of visual information is an important issue. Affine matching has mainly been used for image to model matching (e.g. [Beveridge et al., 1990], [Collins and Beveridge, 1993], see Fig. 1.a) and for image to image matching (e.g. [Zabih and Woodfill, 1994, Collins and Beveridge, 1993, Flusser and Suk, 1994], see Fig. 1.b), often with the purpose of spatial registration of images [Brown, 1992]. Our motivation for this work is driven by the idea of a general framework of *'Information Fusion in Image Understanding'* [Pinz and Bartl, 1992a, Pinz and Bartl, 1992b, Bartl et al., 1993]. In order to be able to deal with multiple visual information on all levels of abstraction, proper transformations of three different kinds are required:

1. spatial (coordinate) transformations,
2. radiometric transformations, and
3. transformations between different levels of abstraction (signal, pixel, feature, and symbol level [Luo and Kay, 1992]).

Information that can be compared with respect to the above transformations is said to be *in registration.* While recent relevant work on fusion simply assumes prior registration of the source images (e.g. [Maître, 1995, Clément et al., 1993, Burt and Kolczynski, 1993, Toet, 1989]), we want to fuse visual information without the requirement of prior manual registration. In this paper we concentrate on the following case:

- different source *images*,
- different coordinate systems. Spatial registration can be achieved by a *conformal transformation* (4 affine parameters),
- the match is established at the *ISR level* (intermediate symbolic representation [Brolio et al., 1989]), see Fig. 1.c.

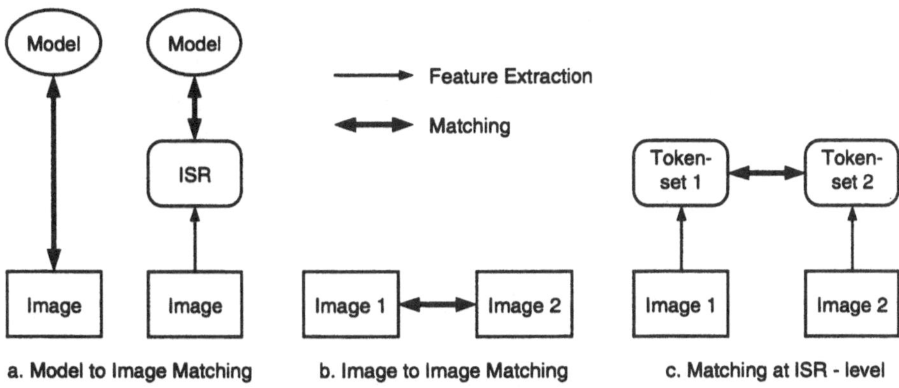

Figure 1: Different types of matching

ISR supports associative retrieval, spatial relations, and multi-level representations and is well suited for many image understanding applications [Draper et al., 1993]. A so-called *token* ('image event') represents one of the following 'location' features: a point, a line, a chain of points, a polygon, and a bitmap representing a region. For each token, an arbitrary number of additional features can be calculated (e.g. shape, spectral and texture parameters). Related tokens are collected in a *'tokenset'*. Figure 2 gives a simple example for an image of a purely 2-dimensional scene with 2D shapes ('shapes' image Fig. 2.a). A region-based segmentation of this image results in a tokenset of 11 bitmaps visualized in Fig. 2.b. The process of segmenting an image into a tokenset is covered in detail in [Pinz, 1994]. In the context of this paper we want to emphasize that the intelligent use of ISR (e.g. application of constraints, perceptual grouping, elimination of irrelevant tokens) often leads to relatively *sparse tokensets*, thus reducing the amount of data dramatically (as compared to the pixels of the original image). This results in a substantial reduction of computational complexity for the subsequent process of matching of two different tokensets (e.g. 11 tokens versus 258000 pixels for Fig. 2).

Consider the situation sketched in Fig. 1.c: Starting from two different images of the same scene, segmentation and feature extraction processes are used to create two tokensets. Under certain assumptions, the spatial relationship between the tokensets (and the images) can be modeled by an *affine transformation.*

(a) Original image

(b) Resulting tokenset

Figure 2: Region based segmentation of a 2D 'shapes' image

This holds for 2-dimensional scenes, as well as for planar structures in 3D scenes (see [Collins and Beveridge, 1993, Grimson et al., 1994, Flusser and Suk, 1994] for more detail):

$$\begin{pmatrix} x_1 \\ y_1 \end{pmatrix} = \begin{pmatrix} a & b \\ c & d \end{pmatrix} \begin{pmatrix} x_2 \\ y_2 \end{pmatrix} + \begin{pmatrix} e \\ f \end{pmatrix},$$

with $\begin{pmatrix} x_1 \\ y_1 \end{pmatrix}$ and $\begin{pmatrix} x_2 \\ y_2 \end{pmatrix}$ denoting locations in image 1 and image 2, respectively. A general affine transformation is defined by six independent parameters $(a \dots f)$. However, a special case of the general affine transformation, the *conformal transformation* with four affine parameters is often sufficient for the given application, or the general affine problem can be converted to a conformal one [Collins and Beveridge, 1993]. The conformal transformation can be written as

$$\begin{pmatrix} x_1 \\ y_1 \end{pmatrix} = s \begin{pmatrix} cos\alpha & -sin\alpha \\ sin\alpha & cos\alpha \end{pmatrix} \begin{pmatrix} x_2 \\ y_2 \end{pmatrix} + \begin{pmatrix} t_x \\ t_y \end{pmatrix},$$

consisting of a translation vector $\mathbf{t} = \begin{pmatrix} t_x \\ t_y \end{pmatrix}$, a rotation angle α, and a scaling factor s.

While Grimson et.al. [Grimson et al., 1994] distinguish between two different types of affine matching algorithms (*hypothesize and test* and *geometric hashing*), Collins and Beveridge [Collins and Beveridge, 1993] find four categories (*key-feature algorithms, generalized Hough transformations, geometric hashing*, and *constraint-based tree search*). Our algorithm could be categorized as a hypothesize and test approach which allows for many-to-many mappings between features.

A review of similar and related work in the area of object recognition, where the task is to determine the transformation between a model and an image, reveals many recent publications (e.g. [Basri and Jacobs, 1995, Rucklidge, 1995]), as well as fundamental work dating back to the mid 80s (e.g. [Ayache and Faugeras, 1986, Borgefors, 1988]). The general approach of performing a search in transformation space for the best matching transformation, which is also followed in this paper, has been explored in the past, e.g. for the purpose of locating images of rigid 3D objects. The algorithm proposed by Cass [Cass, 1992] takes into account the inherent geometric uncertainty of data features when matching a model to image data. By assigning an uncertainty region to each data feature he restricts the space of possible transformations and arrives at an algorithm of polynomial complexity. However, his algorithm seems less suited for the matching of rather dissimilar patterns (like Fig. 11 or Fig. 14). Lowe [Lowe, 1987] also matches 3D rigid model data with 2D images, exclusively using edges as primary features, which are subsequently segmented, perceptually grouped, and matched. His algorithm applies Newton's method and requires partial first order derivatives. Perhaps closest to our work we found the 'Hierarchical Chamfer Matching' algorithm by Borgefors [Borgefors, 1988] using a quadratic distance function to measure the goodness of match. While she briefly mentions the general applicability of the method to many different kinds of features, she only reports on the matching of edges. In this context we want to point out that our approach concentrates on the capability of using any type of tokens (points, edges, lines, regions, as well as quite specialized and application oriented types, e.g. the blood vessels described in section 3.1.2, which are modeled as tubes), and thus could best be described as *'affine matching of intermediate symbolic representations'* or *'affine matching at ISR level'* (see Fig. 1.c).

The paper is organized as follows: We start with a detailed description of the affine matching algorithm, proceed with several experiments on the recovery of simulated transformations and 'real' transformations between data sets originating from different sources, and finally discuss the performance of the algorithm.

2 The Affine Matching Algorithm

We are given two sets of tokens. One is the source and the other the target tokenset for the affine matching algorithm. The aim now is to find the conformal transformation to bring the source tokenset into spatial registration with the target tokenset. The way we chose to tackle this problem is to formulate it as the maximization of an objective function as defined below.

2.1 The Objective Function

The target tokenset is first transformed into a binary image with the resolution of the image depending on the required accuracy. Region tokens are not drawn with all their pixels set but just the border pixels, as the border determines the position, scale and rotation.

Now for each background pixel we calculate an inverse distance function (see section 2.2) to its closest foreground pixel (i.e. to the pixel belonging to the tokenset). In order to keep the computational burden low, we do not transform the whole source tokenset with the transformation in question, but just a number of extracted sample points (described in section 2.4). The objective function to be maximized is then defined as

$$f(\mathbf{p}) = \sum_{i=1}^{N} Dist(x_i(\mathbf{p}), y_i(\mathbf{p})) \tag{1}$$

with N being the number of sample points, $\mathbf{p} = (t_x, t_y, s, \alpha)$ the parameter vector for the conformal transformation and $x_i(\mathbf{p})$, $y_i(\mathbf{p})$ the coordinates of the transformed sample points. $Dist(x_i, y_i)$ denotes the pixel value at position (x_i, y_i) of the distance image.

There are, of course, some limitations on the allowable range for the translation, scale and rotation parameters. Otherwise a scale of zero would always be optimal in the sense that it would transform all sample points onto one position and would result in a maximum value for the objective function if that position is on the target tokenset. The limitations on the parameter range are a first coarse guess on the expected transformation values provided by the user and are implemented as strong penalty terms in the evaluation of the objective function.

2.2 The Inverse Distance Function

The first distance function that might come into one's mind is the Euclidean distance between a background pixel and its nearest foreground pixel (or to be more precise: an inverse Euclidean distance having a maximum at the location of the foreground pixels and then falling off like a 45 degree ramp towards the background). However, this will in general lead to an objective function which is not very robust and which can easily be fooled by points resulting from an incorrect transformation which do not hit the target tokenset but are just somewhat nearby. Fig. 3 depicts such an example.

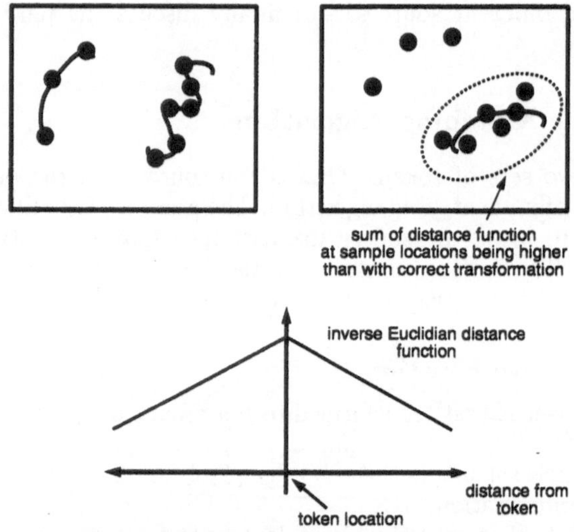

Figure 3: Due to a segmentation error a feature is missing in the target tokenset. Even though the sample points from the wrong feature do not match the target feature exactly, they achieve a higher score in the matching process simply because they are more numerous.

We want to have those points which hit the target tokenset exactly (within the accuracy of the image resolution) to obtain a higher weight than those which

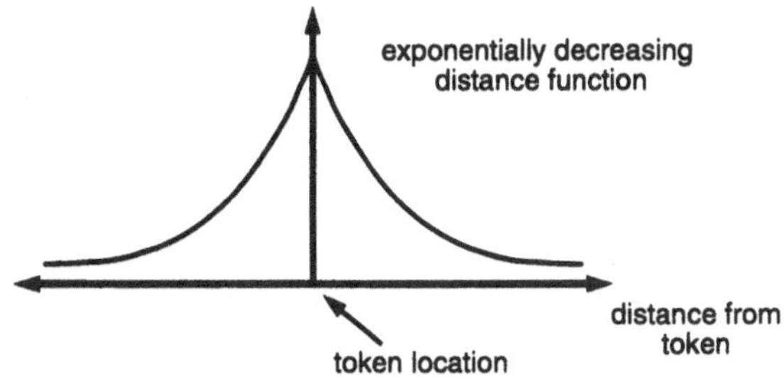

Figure 4: An exponentially decreasing distance function gives stronger weights to points very close to the true location and thus makes the matching more robust.

are just close to the true position. One can achieve such an effect by choosing an inverse distance function that falls off exponentially with the distance from the foreground pixels (see Fig. 4). In such a case the number of transformed points arising from an incorrect transformation and being close to the true position must be much higher to result in a value for the objective function that is larger than what we would have computed by using the correct transformation. Hence, such a choice of the distance function will make the whole matching procedure more robust against outliers. Figures 5.b-d show an intensity coded distance function corresponding to the tokens of Fig. 2.b.

2.3 Optimization Procedure

Now that we are able to compute an objective function for every parameter vector of the conformal transformation, we have formulated the problem of spatial registration as that of finding the global optimum of a function. There exist many different methods for finding such an extremum in the literature. Most of them deal with cases where the global optimum is hid among many local extrema and considerable effort is spent to overcome the problem of getting stuck in one of those local extrema. However, in general, these methods require a long time to converge and still do not guarantee to arrive at the global optimum.

Provided we are dealing with tokensets that are not too dense (a requirement we can often fulfill by choosing the proper parameters for the low-level segmentation tasks that produce the tokensets), we can, however, assume that the chosen objective function will not have that many local extrema. It will exhibit a structure that varies smoothly over large portions of the parameter space. These considerations lead us to an optimization procedure where we simply start local optimization from a couple of different seed points and take the extremum with the highest score. Even though this procedure does not assure to arrive at the global optimum, it performed well in practice. Furthermore, it has the advantage that we can use fast and reliable local optimization procedures like Powell's method (see [Press et al., 1992]).

2.4 Extraction of Sample Points

A tokenset can contain various types of tokens, including points, lines and regions. Generally, the sample points are distributed randomly over the tokenset.

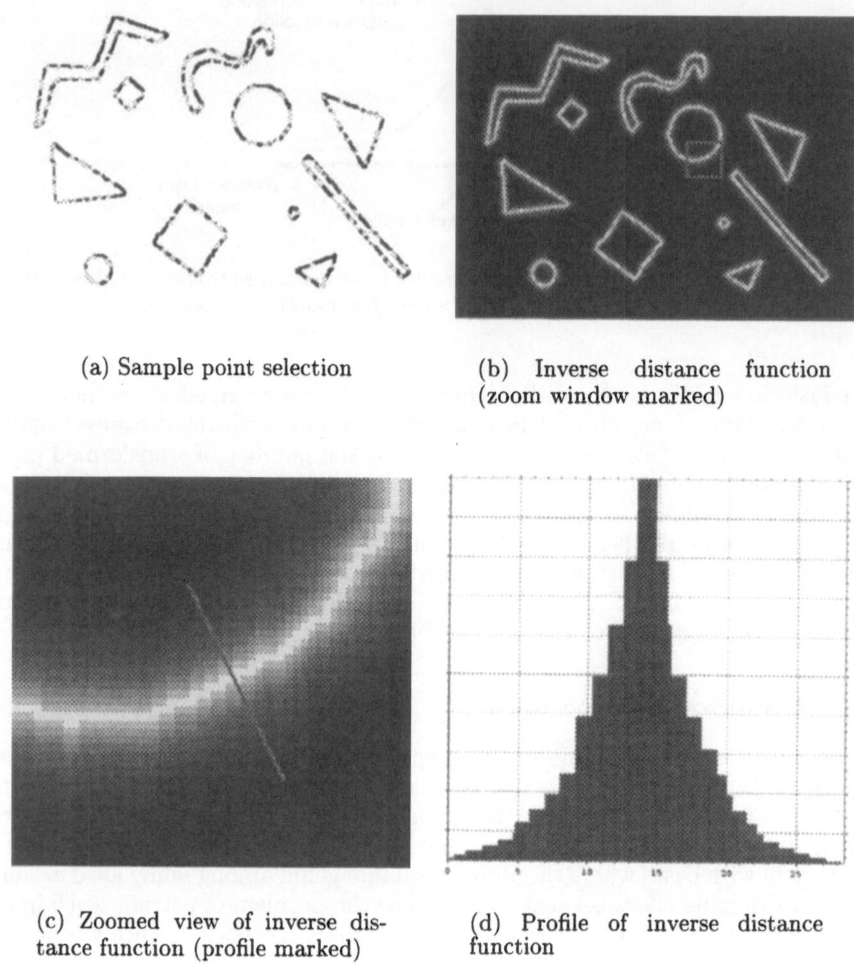

(a) Sample point selection

(b) Inverse distance function (zoom window marked)

(c) Zoomed view of inverse distance function (profile marked)

(d) Profile of inverse distance function

Figure 5: Sample point selection and intensity coded inverse distance function

In some cases there are substructures within the tokenset that are of higher significance than others and should, therefore, get a higher share of the total number of sample points. An example for such a structure are the vessels of Fig. 9.b. There are many short vessels but just a few long and significant ones.

In order to achieve a selective distribution of sample points a weight (belief value) can be assigned to substructures of the tokenset. The actual attachment of the weight to individual tokens is up to the module generating the tokensets and is not the concern of the matching process. Tokens having a higher weight will be treated with preference when the selection of sample points takes place. This causes the matching algorithm to give priority to such substructures in finding the correct match. Figure 5.a shows an example for the sample point selection.

2.5 General Outline of the Algorithm

The general outline of the algorithm is depicted in Fig. 6. The structure is simple and easy to implement. One can use any local optimization technique often available from standard libraries.

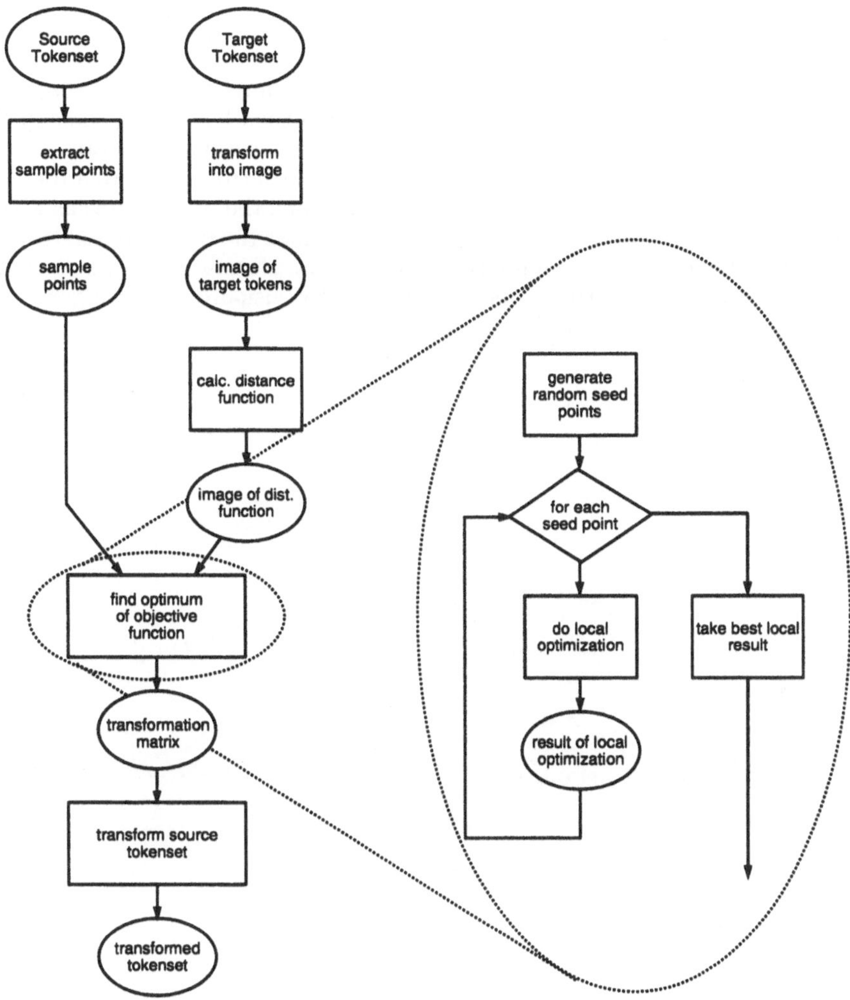

Figure 6: Schematic overview of the affine matching algorithm.

3 Experimental Results

We tested the algorithm on a variety of different image examples. Some of them were generated by simulating a conformal transformation, whereas others stem from real multisource applications of medical imaging and remote sensing.

3.1 Simulated Transformations

Simulated test data was used in order to provide the exact ground truth for evaluating the accuracy of the algorithm and to incorporate some of the common disturbances generally found in many applications (like fragile segmentation, only partial overlap, etc.).

3.1.1 Shapes Image

The first experiment was performed on a simple shapes image (Fig. 2.a). The extracted tokenset (depicted by Fig. 2.b) was disturbed by erasing some of the tokens and adding artifacts corresponding to a noisy feature extraction process (Fig. 7.a). The resulting tokenset was matched by our algorithm onto a tokenset (Fig. 7.b) which in turn was obtained by transforming the original tokens with a known conformal transformation. Figure 8.a illustrates the initial spatial relation of the two sets and Table 1 summarizes the used transformation parameters and the result computed by the proposed method. By visually inspecting Fig. 8.b one can confirm that the algorithm performed well.

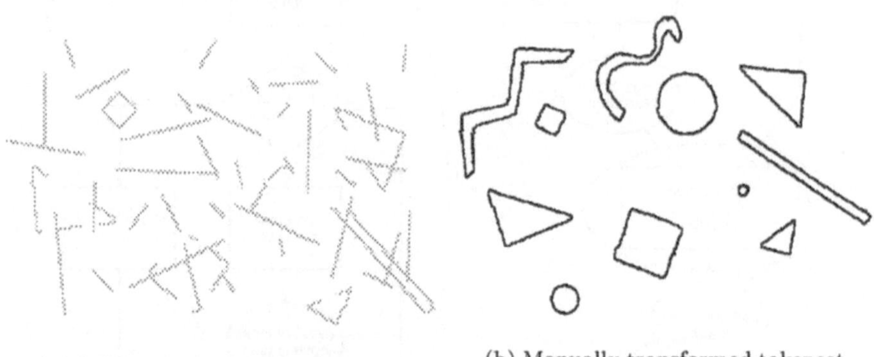

(a) Disturbed original tokenset (b) Manually transformed tokenset

Figure 7: Shape tokensets

3.1.2 Medical Image

Our second experiment with known transformations was performed on an image from a medical application. In contrast to the shape experiment, the image itself and not the extracted tokenset was transformed. An algorithm for the extraction of vessel structures modeling vessels as tubes of varying radius [Huang and Stockman, 1993] was applied onto both images to provide the tokensets. The vessel extraction was done with slightly varying input parameters in order to simulate the fragility of low level segmentation procedures. Figure 9 and 10 illustrate the initial data set, the vessel segmentation results and the matched tokensets. Again visual inspection and comparison of the data in Table 2 reveals good performance of the affine matching algorithm.

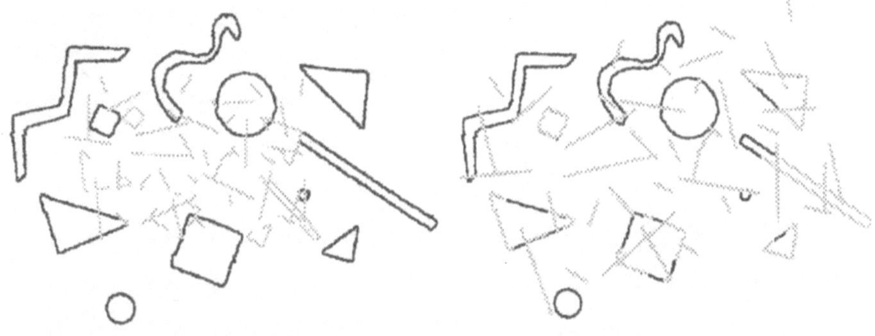

(a) Initial spatial relation (b) Recovered transformation

Figure 8: Matching of shape tokensets

initial parameter range	$t_x \in [-50, 50]$
	$t_y \in [-50, 50]$
	$s \in [0.8, 2.0]$
	$\alpha \in [-30^\circ, 10^\circ]$
resulting transformation	$t_x = 28.9$
	$t_y = -4.59$
	$s = 1.5006$
	$\alpha = 14.95^\circ$
known transformation	$t_x = 27$
	$t_y = -5$
	$s = 1.5$
	$\alpha = 15^\circ$
total computing time	36 sec

Table 1: Results for the shapes tokenset

initial parameter range	$t_x \in [-100, 250]$
	$t_y \in [-100, 250]$
	$s \in [0.8, 1.5]$
	$\alpha \in [-30^\circ, 40^\circ]$
resulting transformation	$t_x = 195.94$
	$t_y = 205.24$
	$s = 1.3499$
	$\alpha = 15.026^\circ$
known transformation	$t_x = 196$
	$t_y = 205$
	$s = 1.35$
	$\alpha = 15^\circ$
total computing time	48 sec

Table 2: Results for the simulated medical data set

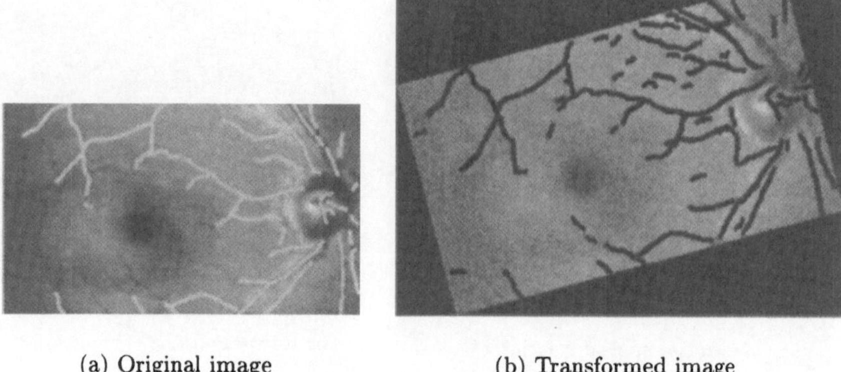

(a) Original image (b) Transformed image

Figure 9: Retinal images with superimposed vessel tokensets

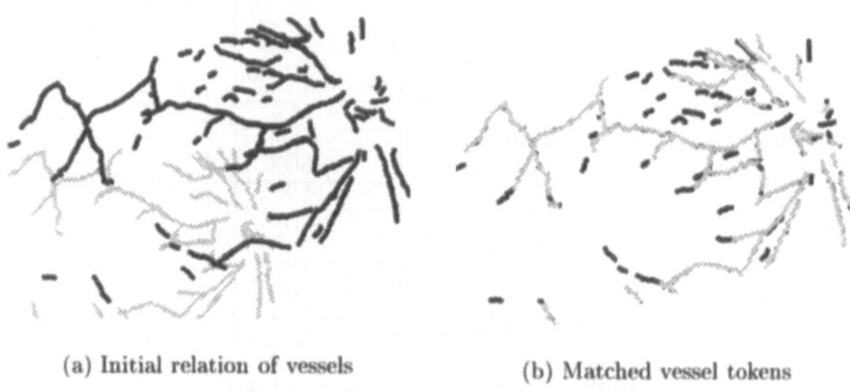

(a) Initial relation of vessels (b) Matched vessel tokens

Figure 10: Matching of vessel tokens

3.2 Real Data Sets

The real data sets consist of images that exhibit a mutual transformation closely resembling (but not exactly matching) a conformal transformation. Since the 'correct' conformal transformation is unknown, we compare the result of our algorithm to 'measured' transformations. They are obtained by manual selection of corresponding points in the two images and calculating the affine parameters by least-squares adjustment.

3.2.1 Medical Data Set

The medical data set shows images of the human retina acquired by a Scanning Laser Ophthalmoscope (SLO)[Webb et al., 1987]. The images were generated using different laser sources and examination methods (e.g. argon-blue laser, fluorescein angiography). In order to detect pathological changes and to perform the appropriate treatment [Pinz et al., 1995a, Pinz et al., 1995b] they have to be spatially registered.

Similar to our experiment using a simulated transformation (section 3.1.2), the features used for registration are again the vessels on the eye background. The reason for using them is that they are the only retinal features visible in all images acquired by the SLO.

As with our previous experiments, Figure 11 and Fig. 12 show the initial data, the tokensets and the result of the matching process. Table 3 shows that the results of the affine matching are very close to the manually 'measured' transformation.

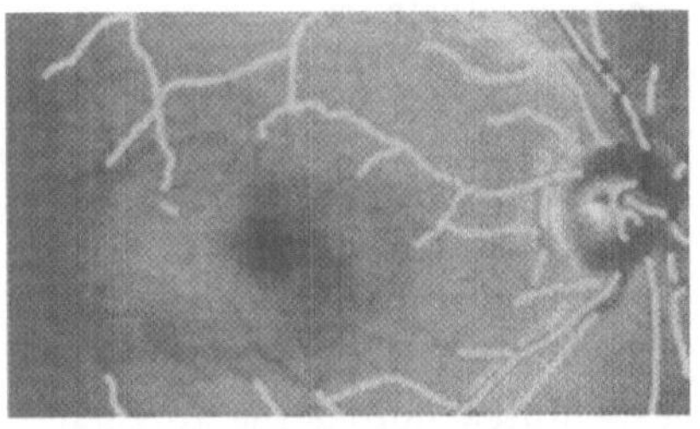

(a) Argon-blue

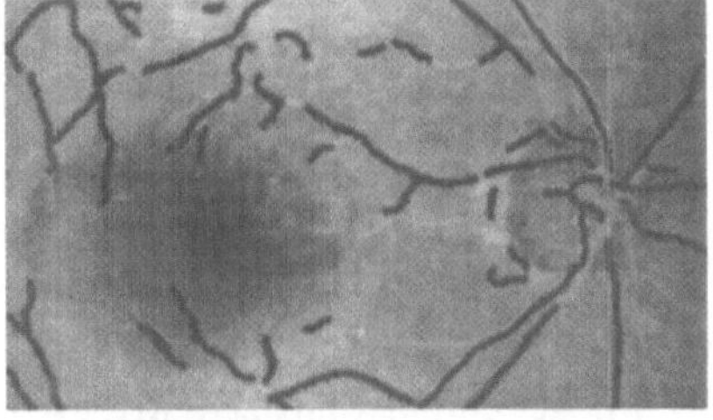

(b) Fluorescein angiography

Figure 11: Retinal images with superimposed vessels

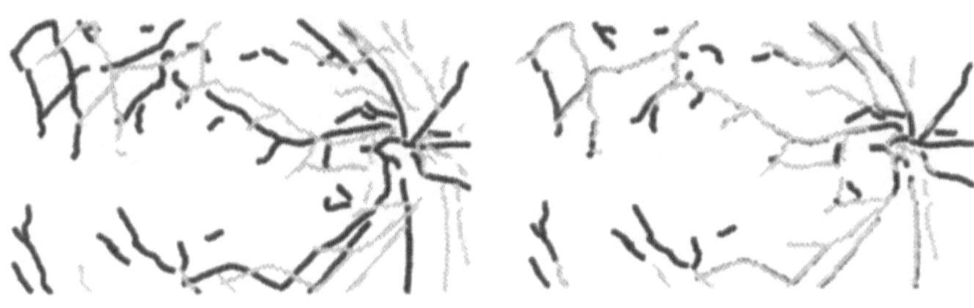

(a) Initial relation between vessels (b) Registered vessel tokensets

Figure 12: Conformal matching of vessel tokensets

initial parameter range	$t_x \in [-100, 250]$
	$t_y \in [-100, 250]$
	$s \in [0.8, 1.5]$
	$\alpha \in [-30^\circ, 40^\circ]$
resulting transformation	$t_x = -65.614$
	$t_y = -0.5633$
	$s = 1.0047$
	$\alpha = -0.1097^\circ$
measured transformation	$t_x = -63.754$
	$t_y = 0.0798$
	$s = 0.99312$
	$\alpha = -0.3313^\circ$
total computing time	40 sec

Table 3: Results for the medical data set

3.2.2 Remote Sensing Data Set

Finally, we want to give an application example from satellite image remote sensing. Figure 13 shows the near infrared (approx. 0.8 μm) channels of a Landsat TM image and a digitized MKF6 image captured during the Russian AUSTROMIR mission. A land use classification of these images was performed. We concentrate on the *forest regions* represented as tokensets shown by Fig. 14. As in the 'shapes' example described above, we use the borders of the forest regions for affine matching. The original images as well as the land use classifications were supplied by the University for Bodenkultur and are described in more detail in [Bartl and Pinz, 1992].

(a) Landsat TM image

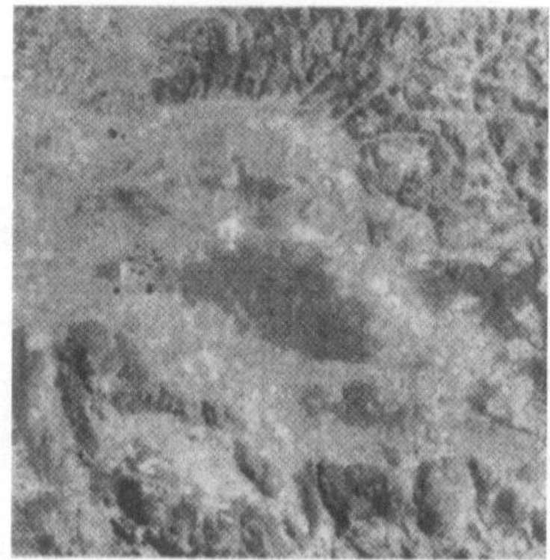

(b) MKF6 image

Figure 13: Two remote sensing images of an area in Lower Austria (Wr. Neustadt)

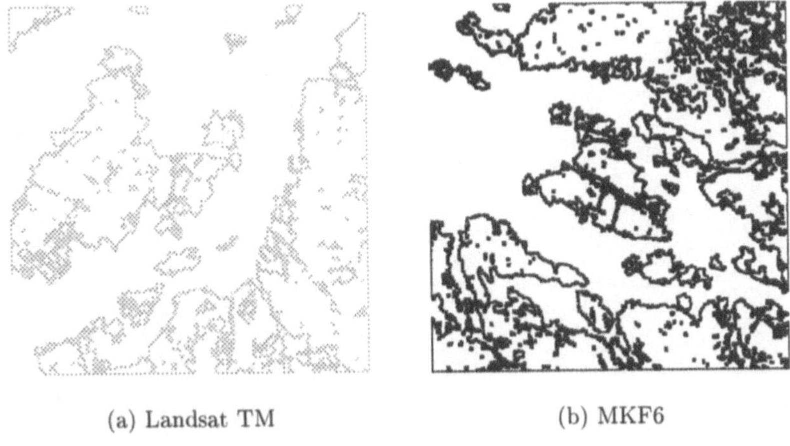

(a) Landsat TM (b) MKF6

Figure 14: Forest regions resulting from land use classification

	correct match	wrong match
initial parameter range	$t_x \in [-100, 100]$	$t_x \in [-200, 200]$
	$t_y \in [-100, 100]$	$t_y \in [-200, 200]$
	$s \in [0.4, 0.8]$	$s \in [0.4, 0.8]$
	$\alpha \in [35^\circ, 150^\circ]$	$\alpha \in [35^\circ, 150^\circ]$
resulting transformation	$t_x = -13.28$	$t_x = 116.35$
	$t_y = 78.86$	$t_y = 141.76$
	$s = 0.61069$	$s = 0.43049$
	$\alpha = 100.11^\circ$	$\alpha = 84.516^\circ$
measured transformation	$t_x = -12.879$	
	$t_y = 78.061$	
	$s = 0.609765$	
	$\alpha = 100.41^\circ$	
total computing time	2 min 15 sec	

Table 4: Results for the remote sensing data set

Figure 15 shows the results for two different runs of the affine matching algorithm, the corresponding parameter settings are given in Table 4. The Landsat tokenset is transformed to the geometry of the MKF6 tokenset. In the case of the correctly recovered conformal transformation (Fig. 15.a) we show an overlay of both images and tokensets, while Fig. 15.b shows an overlay of the correctly transformed Landsat image and the incorrectly recovered Landsat tokenset over MKF6 image and tokenset.

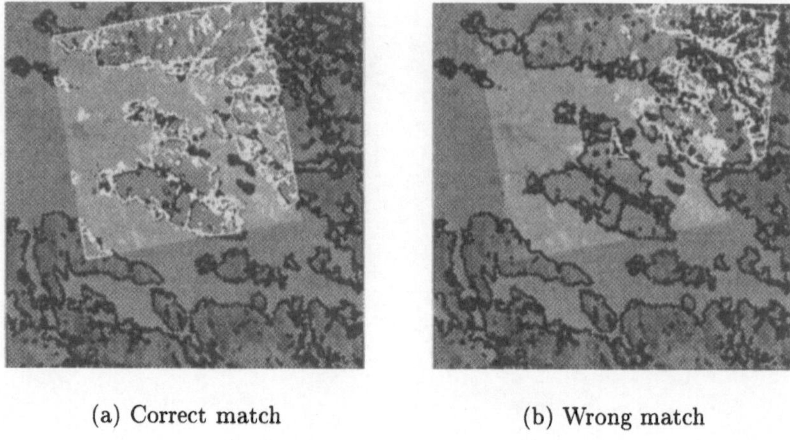

(a) Correct match (b) Wrong match

Figure 15: Affine matching results

4 Discussion

The incorrect result shown by Fig. 15.b directly leads us to a discussion of the performance of our affine matching algorithm. There are several preconditions on the data which are required for the algorithm to work reliably:

- Rough estimates for the scaling s should be given. It is much better to select source and target tokenset in a way that $s < 1$ (i.e. the source tokenset is scaled down), so that the majority of selected sample points will be transformed to the interior area covered by the target tokenset.
- A reasonable amount of overlap of the two tokensets is required, otherwise the algorithm will only work in cases of very sparse tokensets with very dissimilar shapes.
- Both tokensets have to be sparse. In the example shown by Fig. 15.b, the information in the upper right corner of the target tokenset (Fig. 14.b) is too dense. If we allow for a wide range of translations and scalings, the algorithm will be 'attracted' by this dense area, trying to map most of the source tokenset onto it.
- Up to a certain level of complexity, dense tokensets can still be handled, if the number of sample points is increased accordingly. In the experiments shown here, we used 300 sample points for the shapes and for the medical images, and 1500 sample points for the remote sensing data set.
- As with any other affine matching approach, the algorithm will have difficulties with regular periodical structures (parallel lines, grids, etc.).

If these conditions are fulfilled, the algorithm has already shown to perform well for a wide variety of visual data.

Concerning the complexity of the proposed matching algorithm, it goes linear with the number of sample points and seed points, and quadratically with the number of parameters of the affine transformation.

The concept of *'Affine Matching at the ISR-level'* introduced in this paper seems to be a general and promising approach for many correspondence problems encountered in Computer Vision.

5 Implementation Details

The computing times given for the experiments were obtained on a *Silicon Graphics Power Challenge L* (2 x R8000 75MHz processors) running *IRIX 6.01*. The code was implemented using the KBVision image processing package and no effort was spent on optimizing the procedure for speed. As mentioned above the number of sample points was 300 for the shapes and medical images and 1500 for the remote sensing data set. We used 50 seed points for the optimization procedure for all the experiments.

6 Conclusion and Outlook

In this paper, a general method for affine matching at the level of intermediate symbolic representation (ISR) was introduced. The method is easy to implement and to parallelize. Since most applications have to deal with the extraction of *some* kind of significant features, which can conveniently be represented at the ISR level, the method should be of common interest. It could be used in many industrial, medical and remote sensing applications.

Our algorithm relies on the coarse correspondence of tokens extracted from images. It does not require the establishment of point correspondences. If the tokensets are kept sufficiently sparse, low level features (e.g. edge elements) can directly be used without the necessity of further processing (e.g. grouping edge elements into straight lines, ribbons or corners). Since belief values guide the probability that a certain token is selected for correspondence, and many-to-many correspondences are possible, the method is very robust against a broad variety of common disturbances (e.g. incomplete segmentations, missing tokens, partial overlap). An extension of the algorithm to recover a general 6 parameter affine transformation is straightforward and computationally feasible. Multisource visual information fusion (data fusion [Abidi and Gonzalez, 1992], consensus vision [Meer et al., 1990]) is a field of growing interest and importance. The comparison and integration of information from several sources without the necessity of prior (manual) spatial registration is still an issue of ongoing research. In this context, the affine matching algorithm constitutes just one module for spatial reasoning in a complex framework for Information Fusion in Image Understanding (proposed in [Pinz and Bartl, 1992a]).

Acknowledgments

This work was supported by the Austrian 'Fonds zur Förderung der wissenschaftlichen Forschung' under grant S7003. We thank Renate Bartl and Werner Schneider (Univ.f. Bodenkultur Vienna) for putting the original Landsat and MKF6 images and the classifications of these images at our disposal. Several constructive comments by the anonymous referees helped to improve this paper and are gratefully acknowledged.

References

[Abidi and Gonzalez, 1992] Abidi, M. and Gonzalez, R., editors (1992). *Data Fusion in Robotics and Machine Intelligence.* Academic Press.

[Ayache and Faugeras, 1986] Ayache, N. and Faugeras, O. (1986). HYPER: A new approach for the recognition and positioning of two-dimensional objects. *IEEE Transactions on Pattern Analysis and Machine Intelligence*, 8(1):44–54.

[Bartl and Pinz, 1992] Bartl, R. and Pinz, A. (1992). Information fusion in remote sensing: Land use classification. In *Multisource Data Integration in Remote Sensing for Land Inventory Applications, Proc Int.IAPR TC7 Workshop*, pages 9–17.

[Bartl et al., 1993] Bartl, R., Pinz, A., and Schneider, W. (1993). A framework for information fusion and an application to remote sensing data. In Pöppl, S. and Handels, H., editors, *Mustererkennung 1993*, Informatik aktuell, pages 313–320. Springer.

[Basri and Jacobs, 1995] Basri, R. and Jacobs, D. (1995). Recognition using region correspondences. In *Proc. 5.ICCV, International Conference on Computer Vision*, pages 8–15.

[Beveridge et al., 1990] Beveridge, J., Weiss, R., and Riseman, E. (1990). Combinatorial optimization applied to variable scale model matching. In *Proc. of the 10th ICPR*, volume I, pages 18–23.

[Borgefors, 1988] Borgefors, G. (1988). Hierarchical chamfer matching: A parametric edge matching algorithm. *IEEE Transactions on Pattern Analysis and Machine Intelligence*, 10(6):849–865.

[Brolio et al., 1989] Brolio, J., Draper, B., Beveridge, J., and Hanson, A. (1989). ISR: A database for symbolic processing in computer vision. *IEEE Computer*, pages 22–30.

[Brown, 1992] Brown, L. (1992). A survey of image registration techniques. *ACM Computing Surveys*, 24(4):325–376.

[Burt and Kolczynski, 1993] Burt, P. and Kolczynski, R. (1993). Enhanced image capture through fusion. In *Proc. 4.ICCV*, pages 173–182.

[Cass, 1992] Cass, T. A. (1992). Polynomial-Time Object Recognition in the Prescence of Clutter, Occlusion, and Uncertainty. In Sandini, G., editor, *Computer Vision - ECCV'92*, pages 834–842. Springer-Verlag.

[Clément et al., 1993] Clément, V., Giraudon, G., Houzelle, S., and Sandakly, F. (1993). Interpretation of remotely sensed images in a context of multisensor fusion using a multispecialist architecture. *IEEE Transactions on Geoscience and Remote Sensing*, 31(4):779–791.

[Collins and Beveridge, 1993] Collins, R. and Beveridge, J. (1993). Matching perspective views of coplanar structures using projective unwarping and similarity matching. In *Proc.Int.Conf. of Computer Vision and Pattern Recognition, CVPR*, pages 240–245.

[Draper et al., 1993] Draper, B. A., Hanson, A. R., and Riseman, E. M. (1993). Learning blackboard-based scheduling algorithms for computer vision. *International Journal on Pattern Recognition and Artificial Intelligence*, 7(2):309–328.

[Flusser and Suk, 1994] Flusser, J. and Suk, T. (1994). A moment-based approach to registration of images with affine geometric distortions. *IEEE Transactions on Geoscience and Remote Sensing*, 32(2):382–387.

[Grimson et al., 1994] Grimson, W., Huttenlocher, D., and Jacobs, D. (1994). A study of affine matching with bounded sensor error. *International Journal of Computer Vision*, 13(1):7–32.

[Huang and Stockman, 1993] Huang, Q. and Stockman, G. (1993). Generalized tube model: Recognizing 3D elongated objects from 2D intensity images. In *Proceedings CVPR*, pages 104–109.

[Lowe, 1987] Lowe, D. G. (1987). Three-Dimensional Object Recognition from Single Two-Dimensional Images. *Artificial Intelligence*, 31:355–395.

[Luo and Kay, 1992] Luo, R. and Kay, M. (1992). Data fusion and sensor integration: State-of-the-art 1990s. In Abidi, M. and Gonzalez, R., editors, *Data Fusion in Robotics and Machine Intelligence*, chapter 2, pages 7–135. Academic Press.

[Maître, 1995] Maître, H. (1995). Image fusion and decision in a context of multisource images. In Borgefors, G., editor, *Proceedings of the 9th SCIA, Scandinavian Conference on Image Analysis*, volume I, pages 139–153.

[Meer et al., 1990] Meer, P., Mintz, D., Montanvert, A., and Rosenfeld, A. (1990). Consensus vision. In *Proceedings of the AAAI-90 Workshop on Qualitative Vision*, pages 111–115.

[Pinz, 1994] Pinz, A. (1994). *Bildverstehen.* Springers Lehrbücher der Informatik. Springer.

[Pinz and Bartl, 1992a] Pinz, A. and Bartl, R. (1992a). Information fusion in image understanding. In *Proceedings of the 11.ICPR*, volume I, pages 366–370. IEEE Computer Society.

[Pinz and Bartl, 1992b] Pinz, A. and Bartl, R. (1992b). Information fusion in image understanding: Landsat classification and ocular fundus images. In *SPIE Sensor Fusion V, Boston 92*, volume 1828, pages 276–287. SPIE.

[Pinz et al., 1995a] Pinz, A., Ganster, H., Prantl, M., and Datlinger, P. (1995a). Mapping the retina by information fusion of multiple medical datasets. In *Human Vision, Visual Processing, and Digital Display VI*, volume 2411 of *IS&T/SPIE Proceedings*, pages 321–332.

[Pinz et al., 1995b] Pinz, A., Prantl, M., and Datlinger, P. (1995b). Mapping the human retina. In *Proceedings 9th SCIA, Scandinavian Conference on Image Analysis, Uppsala*, volume 1, pages 189–198.

[Press et al., 1992] Press, W., Teukolsky, S., Vetterling, W., and Flannery, B. (1992). *Numerical Recipes in C.* Cambridge University Press, 2nd edition.

[Rucklidge, 1995] Rucklidge, W. (1995). Locating objects using the hausdorff distance. In *Proc. 5.ICCV, International Conference on Computer Vision*, pages 457–464.

[Toet, 1989] Toet, A. (1989). Image fusion by a ratio of low-pass pyramid. *Pattern Recognition Letters*, 9:245–253.

[Webb et al., 1987] Webb, R., Hughes, G., and Delori, F. (1987). Confocal scanning laser ophthalmoscope. *Appl Opt*, 26:1492–1499.

[Zabih and Woodfill, 1994] Zabih, R. and Woodfill, J. (1994). Non-parametric local transforms for computing visual correspondence. In Eklundh, J.-O., editor, *Computer Vision - ECCV'94*, volume 801 of *LNCS*, pages 151–158. Springer.

Managing Editor's Column

Vol. 1, No. 9; September 28, 1995

Dear Readers:

The September issue of J.UCS consists of three papers that have mainly a theoretical flavor. Thus it is appropriate to solicit also, once more, more applied papers: help to spread the information that J.UCS is a medium suitable for all kinds of computer science papers: research and survey, broad or narrow.

It is the last point that I have to particularly emphasize: I have heard a number of times statements to the extent "this is a good paper for a specialized journal, but not for J.UCS". Such statements show a misunderstanding of the aims of J.UCS: J.UCS is NOT intended for just "general" papers that would not fit some specialized journal: it is intended as a kind of union of all possible journals in computer science....hence the title "universal". By selecting a special category a "specialized journal" can be obtained!

Happy reading, and don't forget to submit papers and encourage colleagues to read J.UCS.

Cordially

Hermann Maurer
email: hmaurer@iicm.tu-graz.ac.at

PS: The printed version of volume 1 of J.UCS will appear in February 1996. Since it will be an exact copy of the PostScript form of the electronic version of J.UCS authors can quote their papers, complete with page numbers, already in the correct form in 1995, despite the fact that the printed version will appear in 1996.

Journal of Universal Computer Science, vol. 1, no. 9 (1995), 633-650
submitted: 22/12/94, accepted: 21/9/95, appeared: 28/9/95

An Efficient Distributed Algorithm For st-numbering The Vertices Of A Biconnected Graph

R.F.M. Aranha
(Indian Institute of Technology, Madras, India)

C. Pandu Rangan
(Indian Institute of Technology, Madras, India
rangan@iitm.ernet.in)

Abstract: Given a biconnected network G with n nodes and a specific edge (r, s) of G, the st-numbering problem asks for an assignment of integers to the nodes satisfying the following condition: r is assigned the number 1 and s is assigned the number n and all other nodes are assigned numbers in such a way that every node (other than r and s) has a neighbour with smaller st-number and a neighbour with larger st-number. Since st-numbering exists iff G is biconnected, it serves as a powerful "local characterization" of the "global" property of the network. We present an efficient $O(e)$ message complexity and $O(n)$ time complexity algorithm for st-numbering a biconnected graph.

Key Words: Distributed graph algorithms, st-numbering, biconnected graph

1 Introduction

In almost every application implemented in a distributed system, we often find it necessary to use certain network functions such as traversal through the network, learning of global information not initially known by the sites and determination of optimal routes between the sites. Such network functions, if available at each site, will spare the application programs the pain of handling directly information transfers and the associated controlling tasks. The algorithms for such network functions are known as network algorithms or *distributed graph algorithms*. Distributed graph algorithms are known for a wide variety of graph problems. See [Raynal 1987][Leeuwen 1990] for a comprehensive discussion on this topic.

In this paper we are concerned with the computation of *st-numbering* (to be defined later) for a *biconnected network*. Informally, st-numbering is a numbering scheme in which we number the vertices in such a way that every vertex has at least one neighbour with a larger number and one neighbour with a smaller number associated with it. Such a numbering scheme not only gives a structural characterization of the network but also enables one to identify internally vertex disjoint routes between a pair of sites. In another paper, we have discussed the application of st-numbers to construct the centered spanning tree studied in [Cheston et al. 1989][Easwarakumar et al. 1994].

2 Model

Consider a distributed computing system consisting of a number of autonomous processors interconnected through a network of communication links. The processors do not share common memory, have no global clock and communicate with each other only by passing messages. The interconnection network can be modeled by an undirected communication graph $G = (V, E)$ where nodes correspond to the processors and the edges correspond to the bidirectional communication links. When we look at G as a graph, we refer to elements of V as vertices and when we look at G as a network, we refer to them as nodes. The exchange of messages between two neighbouring processors is asynchronous. The communication subsystem, we assume will deliver the message at its destination without loss after a finite but unbounded delay. The messages sent over any link follow a FIFO rule. The messages received at any processor are transferred to a common queue before being processed. Messages arriving at a node simultaneously from several neighbours may be placed in any arbitrary order in the queue.

The following complexity measures are used to evaluate performances of distributed algorithms operating in the above network. The *communication or message complexity* is the total number of messages sent during execution of the algorithm. The *time complexity* is the maximum time passed from its start to its termination, assuming that the time of delivering a message over each link is at most one unit of time and the computation complexity at each node is negligible. No time out of any sort is assumed and the bounded delay is assumed only for evaluating the time complexity. The algorithm operates correctly with any finite arbitrary message-delivery time.

3 Definitions and Properties

Let $G(V, E)$ be a biconnected graph. The *degree* of a vertex v is the number of vertices adjacent to v in G. An undirected edge from u to v is denoted by (u, v).

Let n denote the number of vertices in the graph.

Definition 2.1 For an edge (r, s) of a biconnected graph G, a one-to-one function $g : V \rightarrow \{1, 2, ..., n\}$ is called an st-numbering with respect to (r, s) if the following conditions are satisfied.

1. $g(r) = 1$
2. $g(s) = n$
3. for every $v \in V - \{r, s\}$ there are adjacent vertices u and w such that $g(u) < g(v) < g(w)$.

It is well known that a graph is biconnected iff it admits an st-numbering with respect to every edge[Even and Tarjan 1976][Ebert and Koblenz 1983].

Definition 2.2 Let T be a DFS (Depth First Search) tree rooted at r. Define

$$level(v) = \begin{cases} 0 & \text{if v is the root of T} \\ \text{level(father(v))+1} & \text{otherwise} \end{cases}$$

Definition 2.3 The height $HEIGHT(T)$ of a rooted tree is $max\{level(v)|v \in V\}$.

The Depth First Search (DFS) tree of a graph G, splits the edge set of G into two disjoint sets, the set of *tree edges* and the set of *back edges*. Denote a tree edge (v, w) by $v \longrightarrow w$ and a back edge by $v \sim\!\rightarrow w$. A path from v to w consisting of zero or more edges is denoted by $v \stackrel{*}{\rightarrow} w$.

Remark: We usually imagine that the edges of the DFS tree are oriented "away" or "downwards" from the root. Also, a non-tree edge can exist only between a pair of vertices with one of them an ancestor of the other. That is why, the non-tree edges are called back edges and we always assume that back edges are oriented "upwards" or "towards" the root.

Definition 2.4 Define $DFS(v)$, where $v \in V$, to be k if v is the k-th vertex to be processed in the formation of the DFS tree. Clearly $DFS(v)$ is the preorder number of v in the DFS tree, T.

Definition 2.5[Tarjan 1972] For all $v \in V$,
$low(v) = \min(\{DFS(v)\} \cup \{low(w)|v \longrightarrow w\} \cup \{DFS(w)|v \sim\!\rightarrow w\})$.

Definition 2.6[Ebert and Koblenz 1983] For all $v \in V$ define

$$low\_child(v) = \begin{cases} w \text{ if } v \longrightarrow w \text{ and } low(v) = low(w) \\ 0 \text{ otherwise} \end{cases}$$

For a given node, there may be more than one node which satisfies this definition. In such cases any arbitrary assignment is made. For example, in [Fig. 2], both G and D are candidates for the low_child(F).

Definition 2.7 For all $v \in V$ define $desc(v)$ to be the number of descendants of v in the DFS tree, including v.

Definition 2.8 For all $v \in V$ define $parent(v)$ to be the parent of v in the DFS tree.

We now state some properties of DFS trees. Henceforth, we denote the DFS tree by T and assume that T is rooted at the vertex r.

Lemma 1 [Tarjan 1972]: *G is biconnected, iff*

1. there is exactly one tree edge $r \longrightarrow u$ *in the DFS tree* T.

2. $low(u) = DFS(r)$, *and*

3. $low(w) < DFS(v)$ *for all other tree edges* $v \longrightarrow w$.

Lemma 2 [Tarjan 1974]: *There is a path* $v \xrightarrow{\star} w$ *in the DFS tree T iff* $DFS(v) \leq DFS(w) < DFS(v) + desc(v)$.

Note, that in order to find an st-numbering with respect to (r, s), s should not be the child of r in T. Therefore by lemma 1, (s, r) will be a back edge. This is clear from the DFS tree in [Fig. 2], for the sample graph in [Fig. 1].

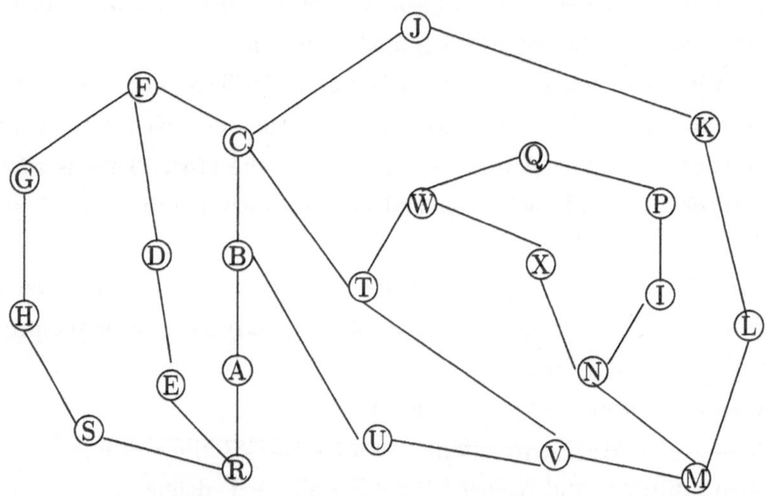

Figure 1: A sample graph G

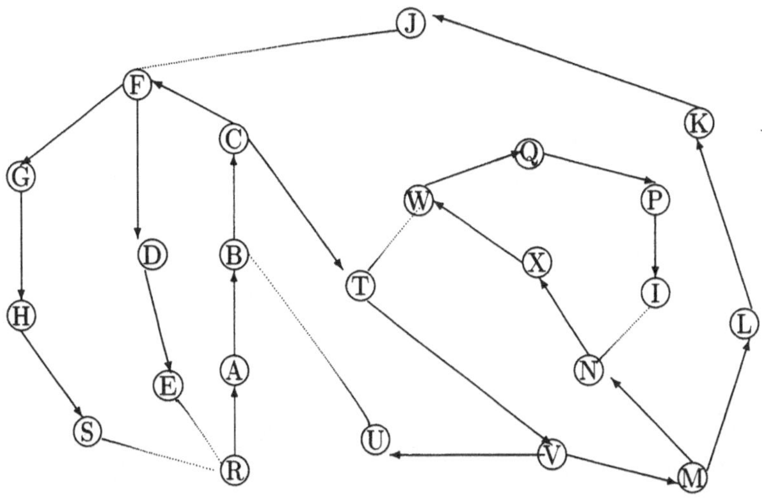

Figure 2: The DFS tree T

Definition 2.9 For all $v \in V$ define

$$next1(v) = \begin{cases} w & \text{if } low\_child(v) = w \neq 0 \\ nil & \text{otherwise} \end{cases}$$

Definition 2.10 The graph defined by $(V, \{(v, next1(v)) : v \in V\})$ is denoted by G_1 and it is clear that

- G_1 is a subgraph of DFS tree T.
- G_1 consists of paths called component paths.

Let $x \overset{\star}{\rightarrow} y$ be a component path. Then x is referred to as the *head vertex* and y as the *tail vertex*. Note that, a vertex x is a head vertex iff the parent z of x in the DFS tree satisfies the condition that $next1(z) \neq x$. That is, x is not the low_child(z). Clearly, a node y is a tail vertex if $next1(y) = nil$.

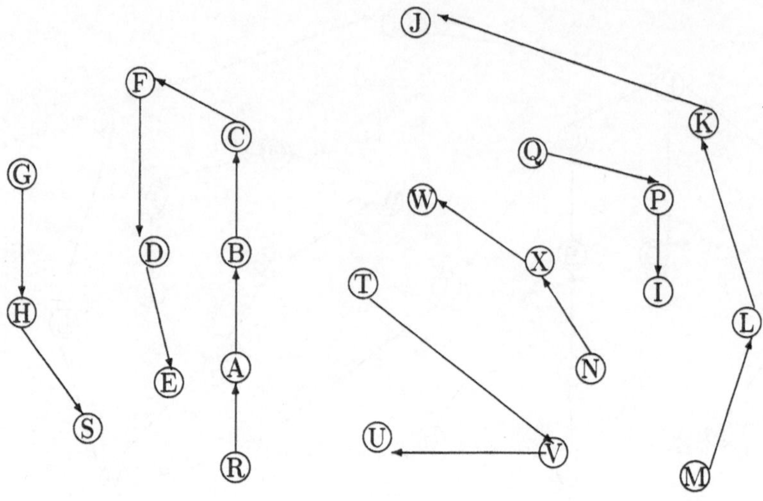

Figure 3: The graph G_1

Lemma 3[Ebert and Koblenz 1983]: *If* $x \overset{\star}{\to} y$, *is a component path in* G_1 *the following assertions hold:*

1. $DFS(x) < DFS(v)$ *for all* $v \neq x$ *on* $x \overset{\star}{\to} y$.
2. $low(x) = low(v)$ *for all* v *on* $x \overset{\star}{\to} y$.
3. $DFS(parent(x)) \neq low(x)$.

Proof: The proof follows from the definition [Section 2.9] of next1. □

Definition 2.11 Let P denote the path $r = v_0, v_1, ...v_t = s$ from r to s in the DFS tree T. By an abuse of notation let P also denote the set of vertices in the path P. Now define for all $v \in V$

$$next2(v) = \begin{cases} nil & \text{if } v \in P \text{ and } v = v_t \\ v_{i+1} & \text{if } v \in P \text{ and } v \neq v_t \\ next1(v) & \text{otherwise} \end{cases}$$

Definition 2.12 Again, consider the auxiliary graph G_2 formed as follows.
$G_2 = (V, \{(v, next2(v)) : v \in V\})$

Clearly G_2 is also a subgraph of the DFS tree T and G_2 consists of one or more paths which we refer to as maximal paths. As in the case of G_1 we can define head and tail vertex for the graph G_2. Note that, P will appear as a maximal path in G_2 and we refer the same as the *trunk path.*

See [Fig. 2][Fig. 3][Fig. 4] for a clear description of the above definitions.

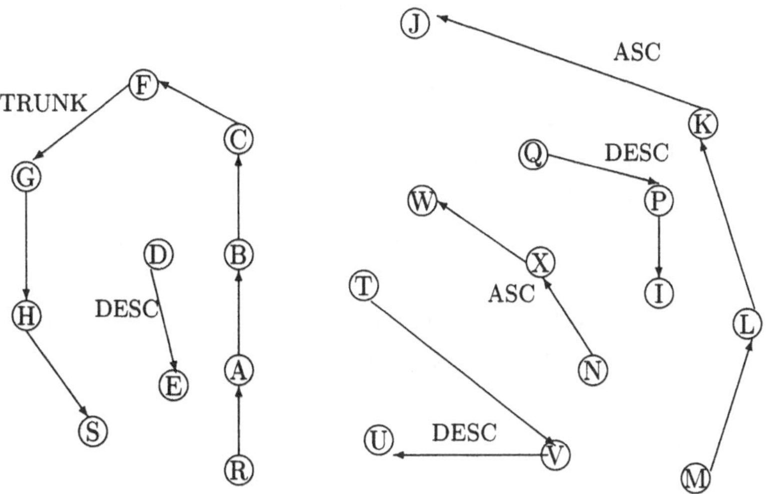

Figure 4: The graph G_2

Lemma 4[Ebert and Koblenz 1983]: *If $x \xrightarrow{\star} y$, is a non-trunk maximal path in G_2 that is, $x \xrightarrow{\star} y \neq r \xrightarrow{\star} s$ then the following assertions hold:*
1. $DFS(x) < DFS(v)$ for all $v \neq x$ on $x \xrightarrow{\star} y$.
2. $low(x) = low(v)$ for all v on $x \xrightarrow{\star} y$.
3. $DFS(parent(x)) \neq low(x)$.

Definition 2.13 For any node $v \in V$, let dfs_ch(v) denote the set of all children of v in T , that is dfs_ch(v) = $\{y|v \longrightarrow y\}$. Define,
$ch\_set(v) = dfs\_ch(v) - next2(v)$.

We have already noted that G_2 is a subgraph of the DFS tree T.The following lemma characterizes the edges of T that are not in G_2.

Lemma 5: *An edge $(z, x) \in T - G_2$ iff x is a head vertex of a maximal path and z is its parent in the DFS tree T.*

Proof: The result follows by the definition of next1 and next2. □

Definition 2.14 For every tail vertex v of G_2 except s, there exists a back edge of the form $v \leadsto z$, where $low(v) = DFS(z)$. Let t be that child of z, which is an ancestor of v in the DFS tree T. Then t, is called the *sign_vertex* of v and z is the *par_sign_vertex* of v.

For example, in [Fig. 4], J is a tail vertex and $low(J)$ is C. Therefore C is the par_sign_vertex of J. T is that child of C which is an ancestor of J. Therefore sign_vertex of J is T.

Lemma 6: *Every tail vertex except s has a sign_vertex.*

Proof: Let $y \neq s$ be a tail vertex such that $low(y) = DFS(z)$. Then, there exists a back edge $y \sim\!\!\rightarrow z$. Clearly, z is an ancestor of y. Therefore there exists a path $z \stackrel{*}{\rightarrow} y$. Let x be the head node of the maximal path on which y lies. By lemma 4, $low(x) = DFS(Z)$. Thus by lemma 1, there exists a vertex $w \neq x$ such that, $z \longrightarrow w \stackrel{*}{\rightarrow} x \stackrel{*}{\rightarrow} y$ is a path in T since $y \neq s$. Thus w is the sign_vertex and the lemma follows. □

Definition 2.15 Define $head\_sum(u)$ for any $u \in V$ to be the sum of $desc(x)$ where x is a child of u and x is a head vertex.

By lemma 5, $head\_sum(u) = \sum desc(x)$, where $x \in ch\_set(u)$.

4 Algorithm

4.1 Stage 1

The first stage of our algorithm is fully devoted to finding the Depth first Search numbers and other tree functions we introduced in the previous section. Specifically, we compute DFS(v), low(v), low_child(v), next1(v), parent(v), dfs_ch(v) and desc(v) for every node v. The DFS starts at the node r and chooses a node other than s as the son of r. Thus r is the root of the DFS tree and the edge (r, s) will be a back edge.

Our computation closely follows the DDFS algorithm presented in [Lakshmanan et al. 1987][Cidon 1988]. The DDFS algorithms in [Lakshmanan et al. 1987][Cidon 1988] use the message TOKEN or DISCOVER to effect a forward phase and a backward phase. Informally, the forward phase carries the message from *root to leaves* and the backward phase does just the opposite.

In the forward phase, DFS(v) and parent(v) are computed by piggybacking the DFS number of the sending node onto the TOKEN or DISCOVER message while in the backward phase $desc(v)$ and $low(v)$ where v is the node sending the message are piggybacked and low(v), low_child(v), next1(v), dfs_ch(v) and desc(v) are computed. Also, the DFS number is piggybacked onto the VISITED message.

Stage 1 terminates at the root node r upon receiving the message DISCOVER or TOKEN in the backward phase.

Basically, both next1 and next2 decompose the DFS tree into maximal paths. The major (and only) difference is that next2 has the trunk path as one of its maximal paths while the definition of next1 is independent of s. Thus, next1 may be constructed explicitly while the DFS tree is built but next2 is (dynamically and implicitly) constructed while the st-numbering is done.

4.2 Stage 2

In this phase, we label each maximal path as either ASC or DESC and the trunk path as TRUNK. The intuitive idea behind such a task is to allocate the st-numbers for the vertices in a maximal path in the increasing or decreasing order (from head to tail) depending on its label (ASC, DESC or TRUNK). The st-numbers for vertices in the TRUNK path will always be in the increasing order.

In order to label the maximal paths in a meaningful way, we put the nodes into one of the following 4 states

TRUNK
DESC
ASC
NORMAL

All the nodes will initially be in the NORMAL state. They will then move into one of the three states (TRUNK, ASC, DESC).

The following messages are used in this stage:

$TRUNK(l, m)$
$PROBE(c)$
$BEGIN$
$SIGN(c)$
$ECHO(c)$
$STN(p, q)$

We also use the following state transition function called *change* which is defined as follows

$change(TRUNK) = DESC$
$change(DESC) = ASC$
$change(ASC) = DESC$

Stage 1 terminates at r and after the termination of stage 1, the root r will initiate stage 2, by sending a message $TRUNK(n, 0)$ to s via the back edge (s, r). Then the node s sends BEGIN message to all its children in the DFS tree and sends TRUNK(n - desc(s), desc(s)) to parent(s). Thus the second stage begins with identifying the trunk path. The node s, which is the tail of the trunk path initiates the task of identifying the trunk. We identify the nodes in the trunk path by passing the TRUNK messages. In the message $TRUNK(l, m)$ sent by a node in the trunk path, l denotes the st-number assigned to the node receiving the message and m denotes the number of descendants of the node sending the message.

When a node $u \neq s$ receives the $TRUNK(l, m)$ message it will assign itself the st-number l and move into the TRUNK state. It will then send $TRUNK(l + m - desc(u), desc(u))$ to parent(u). Thereafter it sends a BEGIN message to every child except next2(u). Thus we note that the TRUNK messages, propagated from s *moves up* and marks all the nodes of the trunk path and changes their states to TRUNK and ends at the root. On its way up, it assigns the st-number for each node and initiates the computation of head_sum and propagates BEGIN messages to all other non-trunk nodes. When a node receives the BEGIN message from its parent it will pass on the BEGIN message to all its children in the DFS tree. The receipt of the TRUNK or BEGIN message initiates the algorithm at each node. When the root r receives the TRUNK message it simply changes its state to TRUNK and does nothing.

Observe that, TRUNK messages, pass through only the trunk path while BEGIN messages travel along other maximal paths. Also, once a node receives the TRUNK or BEGIN message it knows whether it is on the trunk path or not and can compute next2 and ch_st. Thereafter it can compute head_sum.

Our goal now, is to determine if a non-trunk maximal path is an ASC or DESC path. Let $x \overset{*}{\rightarrow} y$ be a maximal path. We stipulate that this path is an ASC path if the state of sign_vertex(y) is DESC and it is a DESC path if the state of sign_vertex is ASC or TRUNK. The justification for such a labeling will be given later.

Hence the tail_vertex does the following

Step 1 Send messages to get the information on the state of sign_vertex(y).

Step 2 Propagate using the state transition function "change", the new state of all nodes on the maximal path along the maximal path to x and then to *parent*(x).

Step 1 is carried out as follows

When a tail node t receives the message BEGIN, it sends PROBE(1) to par_sign_vertex(t) along the edge $(t, par\_sign\_vertex(t))$. Note that, by lemma 3, par_sign_vertex(t) can determine the sign_vertex(t). After receiving PROBE(1), par_sign_vertex(t) sends the message PROBE(2) to sign_vertex(t). Recall that the sign_vertex(t) was initiated to NORMAL state. If it is in the NORMAL state it does not respond to PROBE(2). If sign_vertex(t) has changed to some other state (one of TRUNK, ASC, DESC), it is ready to respond. Now sign_vertex(t) sends the message ECHO(c) to par_sign_vertex(t), which in turn sends the message to t. Here c denotes the current state of sign_vertex(t). In summary, t sends PROBE message via par_sign_vertex(t) to x and x sends ECHO(c) message to t via par_sign_vertex(t).

Step 2 is carried out as follows

When t receives the ECHO(c) message it sends SIGN(change(c)) to parent(t). It also changes its state from NORMAL to change(c). The SIGN(change(c)) travels all the way up in the maximal path for which t is a tail and reaches the head say h of the maximal path. From h, the message SIGN(change(c)) goes one step further along the edge (h,parent(h)), and reaches the node parent(h). As the SIGN(change(c)) message travels up from t to h, we keep updating the state to change(c) for every node including h. This completes the description of stage 2.

Thus, at the end of stage 2, the parent(h) where h is the head node of a maximal path, knows the state of h.

Lemma 7 *A finite time after r sends the $TRUNK(n,0)$ message nodes on the path $r \overset{\star}{\rightarrow} s$ will receive the TRUNK message and all the other nodes will receive the BEGIN message.*

Proof: Obvious. □

Lemma 8 *A finite time after r sends the $TRUNK(n,0)$ message every tail node will change its state, and by that every node on the maximal path of that tail node will change state.*

Proof: By lemma 7, every tail node will receive the BEGIN message and all trunk nodes would have received TRUNK message. Therefore, the state of the trunk nodes would have changed to TRUNK. By lemma 6, every tail node has a sign_vertex. Thus, all the maximal paths $x \overset{\star}{\rightarrow} y$ where $sign\_vertex(y) \in TRUNK$ will change their state. Extending, all other maximal paths will also change their state. □

Lemma 9 *The state of all nodes on a maximal path changes according to the state transition function "change" depending on the state of the sign_vertex of the tail vertex.*

Proof: Obvious. □

Lemma 10 *A finite time after r sends the $TRUNK(n, 0)$ message, every node which has child vertices which are head nodes will have received a SIGN message from each of these nodes.*

Proof: By lemma 7 and lemma 8, the result is easily proved. □

4.3 Stage 3

For this stage of the algorithm each node computes two values i.e. ST_LOW and ST_HIGH. The st-number assignment of nodes on the trunk is done when the TRUNK message arrives while at all other nodes it will be done by STN messages.

The new state that the nodes of a maximal path reach, indicates the direction of assignment of the st-numbering along the maximal path. If the state of the nodes are DESC then the st-number will be in descending order from head vertex to tail vertex and in the other way for the nodes in ASC state. This stage proceeds concurrently with stage 2.

4.3.1 Algorithm at trunk nodes

When a trunk node u receives the $TRUNK(l, m)$ message it assigns itself the st-number l. It then initialises st_high to $l-1$ and st_low to $l+m-desc(u)+1$. It also sends $TRUNK(l+m-desc(u), desc(u))$ to parent(u). Whenever u receives a SIGN message from a child v (which ought to be a head node of a maximal path), u assigns v a chunk of st-numbers in the range $[st\_high - desc(v) + 1 ... st\_high]$ by sending the $STN(st\_high - desc(v) + 1, st\_high)$ message to v. It updates st_high to $st\_high - desc(v)$. It repeats this procedure until it has received a SIGN message from every child except the one on the trunk. At this point the algorithm at this node terminates. For example, node F receives $TRUNK(20, 3)$ from G and sends $TRUNK(17, 6)$ to C. F receives the SIGN(DESC) message from D and sends D $STN(18, 19)$.

Lemma 11 *The algorithm at a trunk node u terminates.*

Proof: The trunk node u receives a SIGN message after it receives the TRUNK message, since for any non-trunk child v, of u, $low(v) < DFS(u)$. Also $low(v)$

points to an ancestor of u(lemma 1) and therefore the sign_vertex does not change state before u receives the TRUNK message. Thus, once u changes its state it will receive SIGN messages from all its children which are head nodes. As these messages are received u responds with an STN message. By lemma 10 u receives SIGN messages from all its children which are head nodes. □

Lemma 12 *When a trunk node assigns an interval of st-numbers to its non-trunk (head node) child v in the DFS tree, the numbers are sufficient and granted exclusively for all the nodes which are descendants of v*

Proof: Observe that v receives an interval consisting of $desc(v)$ numbers. □

Lemma 13 *The st-numbers assigned to the nodes on the trunk path will be in increasing order with $g(r) = 1$ and $g(s) = n$.*

Proof: Clearly, by the movement of the message $TRUNK(n, 0)$ along the edge (r, s) the st-number assigned to s will be n. Now, the st-number assigned to the parent of a node u where u is on the trunk is $n - desc(u)$. This can easily be proved by induction on the nodes of the trunk. Thus, the st-number assignment will be in decreasing order from s to r. By, lemma 1, r has exactly one child v in the DFS tree which is on the trunk. Therefore $desc(v) = n - 1$. Thus $g(r) = 1$. Hence the lemma. □

4.3.2 Algorithm at other nodes

In general every non-trunk node will receive an interval or a continuous chunk of numbers to be assigned to itself and to its descendants, so that the numbers assigned satisfy the st-numbering properties. Thus, every node u will receive an interval of the form $[a, a + desc(u) - 1]$ via the message $STN(a, a + desc(u) - 1)$ from its parent in the DFS tree.

Now, let ch_set(v) $= \{u_1 ... u_k, u_1^{'} ... u_l^{'}\}$ where state of u_i $1 \leq i \leq k$ is ASC and state of $u_j^{'}$ $1 \leq j \leq l$ is DESC.

When u receives the message $STN(p, q)$, it initialises two variables st_high to q and st_low to p. If u is in the state ASC it sends the interval $[st\_low + head\_sum(u) + 1 ... st\_high]$ to $next2(u)$ if $next2(u)$ exists by sending the message $STN(st\_low + head\_sum(u) + 1, st\_high)$ along the edge $(u, next2(u))$. After sending the interval, it updates st_high to $st\_low + head\_sum(u)$. If however, u is in the state DESC it sends the interval $[st\_low ... st\_high - head\_sum(u) - 1]$ to $next2(u)$ if $next2(u)$ exists by sending the message $STN(st\_low, st\_high - head\_sum(u) - 1)$ along the edge $(u, next2(u))$ and updates st_low to $st\_high -$

$head\_sum(u)$.

Note that if u is a tail node then $next2(u)$ will be nil and hence no interval will be sent and no update will take place in this case.

Having sent the STN message to $next2(u)$, u is ready to send intervals to the members of $ch\_set(u)$ once it receives SIGN messages from these nodes. After u receives the $SIGN(ASC)$ message from u_i, it sends the interval $[st\_high - desc(u_i) + 1...st\_high]$ to u_i by sending the message $STN(st\_high - desc(u_i) + 1, st\_high)$ along the edge (u, u_i) and updates st_high to $st\_high - desc(u_i)$. After u receives the $SIGN(DESC)$ message from $u_j^{'}$ it sends the interval $[st\_low...st\_low + desc(u_j^{'}) - 1]$ by sending $STN(st\_low, st\_low + desc(u_j^{'}) - 1)$ to $u_j^{'}$ along $(u, u_j^{'})$ and updates st_low to $st\_low + desc(u_j^{'})$.

After sending st-number intervals in the above fashion to all the members of $ch\_set(u)$, u will be left with an interval of unit size, that is $st\_low = st\_high$. Now, u takes st_low as its st-number and terminates.

For example, in [Fig. 5], the maximal paths with M and N as head nodes will be in ASC state while the maximal paths with Q and T will be in DESC state. We shall consider the algorithm at V. It receives $STN(4, 15)$ from T. It also receives SIGN(ASC) from its only child which is a head node, M. It sends U the node which is on the same maximal path as V $STN(4, 4)$. It sends M $STN(6, 15)$ and will be finally left with the interval $[5, 5]$ and assigns itself the st-number 5.

The final st-numbering for the sample graph is in [Fig. 5].

Lemma 14 *When a non-trunk node assigns an interval of st-numbers to its (head node) child v in the DFS tree, the numbers are sufficient and granted exclusively for all the nodes which are descendants of v*

Proof: Obvious. □

Lemma 15 *The st-number of nodes in a maximal path $x \overset{*}{\rightarrow} y$ will be in descending order from x to y, if the state of the nodes in the maximal path is DESC.*

Proof: If the state of the node u is DESC, then the interval of st-numbers allotted to its child node v in the maximal path is $(st\_high - head\_sum - 1, st\_low)$ where u and v lie on the maximal path. The interval retained for the node u itself is $(st\_high, st\_high - head\_sum)$ which is clearly larger than that allotted to v. Since, the st-number allotted for u is from this interval, the result follows. □

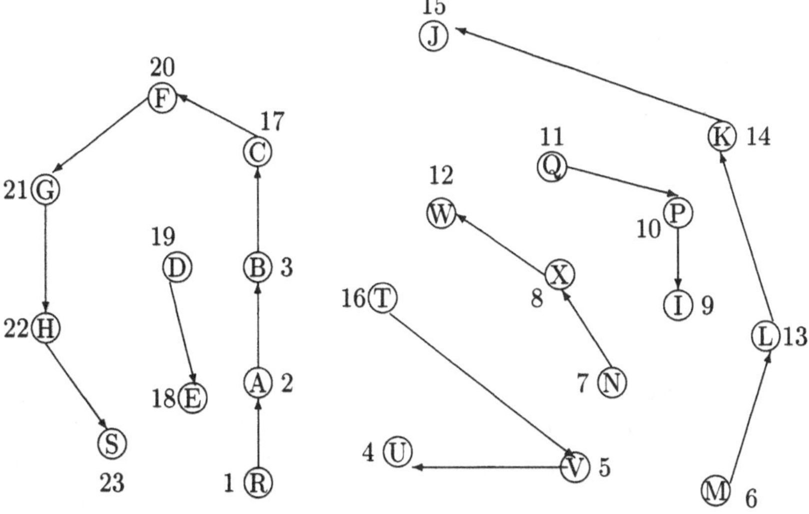

Figure 5: The graph G_2 with st-numbers assigned

Lemma 16 *The st-number of nodes in a maximal path* $x \stackrel{*}{\rightarrow} y$ *will be in ascending order from* x *to* y, *if the state of the nodes in the maximal path is ASC.*

Proof: Similar to lemma 15. □

Lemma 17 *The algorithm at non-trunk nodes terminates*

Proof: By lemma 10, the node would have received all the required SIGN messages. Thus a non-trunk node which has received a STN message would have sent a STN message to all its children in the DFS tree. Thus, it is easily proved that the STN message reaches all the non-trunk nodes. □

Lemma 18 *The st-number interval assigned by a non-trunk node* x *to a child* u *which is a head node, is greater than the st-number assigned to itself if the state of* u *is ASC.*

Proof: x sends the interval $[st\_high...st\_high - desc(u) + 1]$ and reduces its range to $[st\_high - desc(u), st\_low]$ from which its own st-number is assigned. Also, by lemma 12 the range of st-numbers available to x is sufficient. Thus the result follows. □

Lemma 19 *The st-number interval assigned by a non-trunk node* x *to a child* u *which is a head node, is lesser than the st-number assigned to itself if the state of* u *is DESC.*

Proof: By an argument similar to lemma 18 the result follows. □

Theorem 1

The algorithm correctly assigns st-numbers to the entire network.

Proof: By lemma 13, $g(r) = 1$ and $g(s) = n$ and property 3 (def. 2.1) is satisfied by all internal nodes of the trunk path. By lemma 12, 14, 15 and 16 property 3 is satisfied by all the internal nodes of non-trunk maximal paths and the st-number range assigned is sufficient. It remains to show that every head and tail node has a smaller and a larger neighbour. Consider a maximal path $x \overset{\star}{\rightarrow} y$. Let z denote the parent of x i.e. $z = parent(x)$. Let p be the node such that $DFS(p) = low(x) = low(y)$ that is, p is the par_sign_vertex(y).

case 1: z is a trunk node.

By lemma 1 and 4 p should be an ancestor of z. Thus the state of all nodes on the maximal path should be DESC(lemma 9). Clearly, the st-number range allotted to x by z is less than the st-number assigned to z. Therefore st-number assigned to x is less than that assigned to z. Also, the st-number range allotted to any of z's ancestors on the trunk path is smaller than the st-number range allotted to x. To be specific, st-number assigned to p is smaller than the st-number assigned to y. Thus property 3 [see Section 2.1] is also satisfied for x and y.

For example, in [Fig. 4], for the maximal path with T as head node, $parent(T)$ C lies on the trunk path and B is the par_sign_vertex while C is the sign_vertex of U.

case 2: z is not a trunk node.

By lemma 18 and 19 property 3 [Section 2.1] is satisfied for x. It remains to show that it is satisfied for y, the tail node.

Assume y is in the state ASC.

We shall prove that st-number of p is larger than y. Let u be the sign_vertex of y. By lemma 9, the state of u is DESC. Now, consider two cases

case a: *p is on the same maximal path as u.*

Clearly, the st-number range sent by p to u is smaller than the range retained for itself. Since, (lemma 1 and 4) x and y are descendants of u, the result follows.

For example, in [Fig. 4], for the maximal path with Q as head node, W is the $parent(Q)$ and N is the par_sign_vertex while X is the sign_vertex of I. Both N and X lie on the same maximal path.

case b: *p is not on the same maximal path as u*

This implies that u is the head vertex of a maximal path with state DESC. p is the parent of u and by lemma 19 the range of st-numbers assigned to u is less than the st-number assigned to p. Thus by lemma 1 and 4 the result follows.

For example, in [Fig. 4], for the maximal path with M as head node, V is the $parent(M)$ and C is the par_sign_vertex while T is the sign_vertex of J.

If y is in state DESC, u maybe in ASC or TRUNK. The proof for the case u is ASC is similar to the proof given above. If u is in state TRUNK, then p also must be on the trunk and clearly st-number of p is less than that of all vertices in the maximal path, which all have u as an ancestor.
Therefore, by lemmas 11 and 17, the algorithm terminates correctly. □

5 Complexity

The message and time complexity of stage 1 is $3*e$ and $2*n-2$ respectively[Cidon 1988].

Let the number of trunk nodes i.e. nodes in the path $r \overset{\star}{\rightarrow} s$ be p. Let the number of maximal paths $x \overset{\star}{\rightarrow} y \neq r \overset{\star}{\rightarrow} s$ be q. Each trunk node will send a TRUNK message and the total number of TRUNK messages will thus be p. On every other edge of the DFS tree a BEGIN message is transmitted and therefore the message complexity of this part of the algorithm is n. At every unit of time, at least one more message is sent and therefore the time complexity is atmost n.

The probe/echo interaction will require 4 messages per tail vertex and the total probe/echo message complexity is therefore $4 * q$. Each non-trunk node sends a SIGN message and this complexity is $n - p$. By an argument similar to the above, the time complexity will in this case also be bounded by the message complexity.

Each non-trunk node receives one STN message and therefore the total number of STN messages are $n - p$. The time complexity here also is bounded by $n - p$.

The above complexity details are summarised in the following table.

	message complexity	time complexity
DFS tree	$3 * e$	$2 * n - 2$
TRUNK/BEGIN	n	n
PROBE/ECHO	$4 * q$	4
SIGN	$n - p$	$n - p$
STN	$n - p$	$n - p$

Table 1: Complexity

Clearly the message bit complexity at any stage of the algorithm is $O(\log n)$. Hence, we state the following theorem.

Theorem 2

The message complexity of the algorithm is $O(e)$, the time complexity $O(n)$ and the message bit complexity $O(log(n))$. □

6 Conclusions

This paper presents the first distributed algorithm for st-numbering a biconnected graph. st-numbers are among the non-trivial node functions and is extensively used in a variety of graph problems including the planarity test[Even 1979]. Since a graph is biconnected iff it admits an st-numbering of its vertices, we see that this function is a powerful characterization of the entire structure of the network in terms of extremely simple *local information.* Such characterizations are very critical in the context of distributed computing where the fundamental assumption is that every node *knows* only its neighbours and not the entire network. Since every node has a smaller and a larger neighbour, it is easy to see how one can construct internally vertex disjoint paths between a pair of given vertices. Elsewhere, we show an interesting application of the st-numbers for the centering of a spanning tree in a biconnected network[Easwarakumar et al. 1994][Aranha and Rangan 1994].

7 References

[Cheston et al. 1989] Cheston, G.A., Farley, A., Hedetniemi, S.T., Proskurowski, A.: "Centering a spanning tree of a biconnected graph"; Information Processing Letters 32, (1989), 247-250.

[Even and Tarjan 1976] Even, S., Tarjan, R.E.: "Computing an st-numbering"; Theoretical Computer Science (1976), 339-344.

[Even 1979] Even, S.: "Graph Algorithms"; Computer Science press, USA (1979).

[Lakshmanan et al. 1987] Lakshmanan, K.B., Meenakshi, N., Thulasiraman, K.: "A time optimal message-efficient distributed algorithm for dept-first-search"; Information Processing Letters 25, (1987), 103-109.

[Cidon 1988] Cidon, I.: "Yet another distributed depth-first-search algorithm"; Information Processing Letters 26, (1988), 301-305.

[Ebert and Koblenz 1983] Ebert, J., Koblenz,: "st-ordering the vertices of biconnected graphs"; Computing 30, (1983), 19-33.

[Tarjan 1972] Tarjan, R.E.: "Depth-first search and linear graph algorithms"; SIAM J. of Computing 1, (1972), 146 - 160.

[Tarjan 1974] Tarjan, R.E.: "Finding dominators in directed graphs"; SIAM J. of Computing 3, (1974), 62 - 89.

[Raynal 1987] Raynal, M.: "Networks and distributed computation"; North Oxford Academic Press (1987).

[Leeuwen 1990] Leeuwen, J.V.: "Formal models and semantics"; Handbook of theoretical computer science, vol. B. Elsevier Publishers (1990).

[Easwarakumar et al. 1994] Easwarakumar, E.S., Rangan, C.P., Cheston, G.A.: "A linear algorithm for centering a spanning tree of a biconnected graph"; Information Processing Letters 51, (1994), 121-124.

[Aranha and Rangan 1994] Aranha, R.F.M., Rangan, C.P.: "An efficient distributed algorithm for centering a spanning tree of a biconnected graph"; (submitted) (1994).

Journal of Universal Computer Science, vol. 1, no. 9 (1995), 652-657
submitted: 8/2/95, accepted: 29/8/95, appeared: 28/9/95, © *Springer Pub. Co.*

A Decision Method for the Unambiguity of Sets Defined by Number Systems

Juha Honkala
Department of Mathematics
University of Turku
SF-20500 Turku, Finland
juha.honkala@utu.fi

Abstract: We show that it is decidable, given a number system N, whether or not there is an unambiguous number system equivalent to N.
Category: F.4.3

1 Introduction

We study representation of integers in arbitrary number systems. Here "arbitrary" means that the digits may be larger than the base and that completeness is not required, i.e., every integer need not have a representation in the system. Also the number of digits is arbitrary. These number systems were defined and studied in [Maurer, Salomaa and Wood 83]. The work was continued in [Culik II and Salomaa 83] and [Honkala 82]. These references discuss the connections to the theory of L systems and cryptography. Further results on number systems have been obtained in [Honkala 84, 86, 89, 92]. For closely related work see [Berstel 86], [Frougny 88, 92], [de Luca and Restivo 86] and [Shallit 94].

The study of number systems is closely connected with the study of sets of integers recognizable by finite automata. By definition, a set A of nonnegative integers is k-recognizable if and only if there exists a finite automaton which recognizes the representations of the integers of A written at base k. Here $k \geq 2$ is a positive integer. Now, if A is represented by a number system N, the representations of the integers of A can be recognized by an automaton with a single state if the digit set $\{0, 1, \ldots, k-1\}$ is replaced by the digit set of N. Thus, representability by a number system implies simplicity of recognition when the choice of the base and the digits is optimal.

In this paper we give a decision method for the unambiguity problem of sets defined by number systems. More specifically, given a number system N, it is decidable whether or not there is an unambiguous number system equivalent to N. This problem was posed in [Culik II and Salomaa 83]. A solution is previously known only in the case where the base of N is a prime power or the set $S(N)$ is recognizable, i.e., a finite union of arithmetic progressions [Honkala 92]. Our solution is based on automata-theoretic considerations.

2 Definitions and results

By a *number system* we mean a $(v+1)$-tuple $N = (n, m_1, \ldots, m_v)$ of positive integers such that $v \geq 1$, $n \geq 2$ and $1 \leq m_1 < m_2 < \ldots < m_v$. The number n

is referred to as the *base* and the numbers m_i as the *digits* of the number system N. A nonempty word

$$m_{i_k} m_{i_{k-1}} \dots m_{i_1} m_{i_0}, 1 \leq i_j \leq v \tag{1}$$

over the alphabet $\{m_1, \dots, m_v\}$ is said to *represent* the integer

$$m_{i_k} n^k + m_{i_{k-1}} n^{k-1} + \dots + m_{i_1} n + m_{i_0}. \tag{2}$$

The word (1) is said to be a *representation* of the integer (2). The set of all represented integers is denoted by $S(N)$. A set A of positive integers is called *representable by a number system*, shortly RNS, if there exists a number system N such that $A = S(N)$. An integer n is called a *base of an RNS set A* if there is a number system with the base n representing A. By definition, a number system is *unambiguous* if no integer has more than one representation.

Suppose $k \geq 2$ and denote $\mathbf{k} = \{0, 1, \dots, k-1\}$. Define the mapping ν_k from $\mathbf{k}^*$ to the set $\mathbf{N}$ of natural numbers by

$$\nu_k(a_0 a_1 \dots a_m) = \sum_{i=0}^{m} a_i k^i \ (a_i \in \mathbf{k}).$$

Note that we use the reversed interpretation; the most significant digit is the rightmost one. The mapping ν_k is extended in the natural way to concern languages $L \subseteq \mathbf{k}^*$. Hence $\nu_k(L) = \{\nu_k(x) \mid x \in L\}$. By definition, a set A of nonnegative integers is *k-recognizable* if there exists a regular language $L \subseteq \mathbf{k}^*$ such that $A = \nu_k(L)$. By definition, a set A of nonnegative integers is *recognizable* if A is a finite union of arithmetic progressions. For the basic properties of k-recognizable sets see [Eilenberg 74] and [Perrin 90]. Culik II and Salomaa showed an important connection between k-recognizable sets and sets defined by number systems: if $N = (n, m_1, \dots, m_v)$ is a number system then $S(N)$ is n-recognizable. For a proof see also [Honkala 84]. By Cobham's well known result (see [Cobham 69] and [Bruyere, Hansel, Michaux and Villemaire 94]) this implies that if N_1 and N_2 are number systems such that $S(N_1) = S(N_2)$ and $S(N_1)$ is not recognizable, then the bases of N_1 and N_2 are powers of the same integer [Honkala 84].

Suppose $A \subseteq \mathbf{N}$. We say that A has *arbitrarily long gaps* if for every $y \in \mathbf{N}$ there exists an $x \in \mathbf{N}$ such that none of the integers $x+1, x+2, \dots, x+y$ belongs to A. Below we need the result that if $N = (n, m_1, \dots, m_v)$ is a number system such that $S(N)$ has arbitrarily long gaps, then $S(N)$ has no bases other than n [Honkala 84].

The purpose of this paper is to prove the following result.

Theorem 1 *It is decidable, given a number system N, whether or not there exists an unambiguous number system N_1 such that $S(N) = S(N_1)$.*

In the proof of Theorem 1 we need a decision method for the recognizability of k-recognizable sets. For two different methods see [Muchnik 91], [Bruyere, Hansel, Michaux and Villemaire 94] and [Honkala 86]. For the notation concerning finite automata used below see [Eilenberg 74] and [Salomaa 85].

3 Proofs

Suppose N is a number system with base n^r where $r \geq 1$ and $n \in \mathbf{N}$ is not a nontrivial power. Denote $A = S(N)$ and $A^0 = A \cup \{0\}$. Define $L \subseteq \mathbf{n}^*$ by $L = \nu_n^{-1}(A)$. By Lemma 3.1 in [Honkala 84] the set A is n^r-recognizable. Hence A is n-recognizable and there exists a finite deterministic automaton $\mathcal{A} = (Q, \mathbf{n}, q_0)$ with state set Q, input alphabet $\mathbf{n}$ and initial state $q_0 \in Q$ such that $L = L(\mathcal{A})$. By definition, the state $q \in Q$ is *additive* if there exist nonnegative integers m and $c_1, \ldots, c_m$ such that

$$\nu_n(L(\mathcal{A}_q)) = c_1 + A^0 \cup \ldots \cup c_m + A^0 \tag{3}$$

where the union is disjoint. Here $\mathcal{A}_q = (Q, \mathbf{n}, q)$ is the automaton obtained from $\mathcal{A}$ by replacing the initial state q_0 by q. Denote the set of the additive states of $\mathcal{A}$ by $Add(\mathcal{A})$. If $q \in Add(\mathcal{A})$, the nonnegative integers m and $c_1, \ldots, c_m$ in (3) are unique.

Denote

$$UB(\mathcal{A}) = \{k \geq 1 \mid \text{ for each } w \in \mathbf{n}^* \text{ of length } k, \text{ the state } q_0 w \text{ is additive } \}.$$

Now we are ready for the key lemma.

Lemma 1. *There is an unambiguous number system N_1 with base n^k such that $S(N_1) = A$ if and only if $k \in UB(\mathcal{A})$ $(k \geq 1)$.*

Proof. First, suppose N_1 is an unambiguous number system with base n^k such that $S(N_1) = A$. Consider a word $w \in \mathbf{n}^*$ of length k. Let $\nu_n(w) + c_1 n^k, \ldots, \nu_n(w) + c_m n^k$ be the digits of N_1 which are congruent to $\nu_n(w)$ modulo n^k. (If there are no such digits, $\nu_n(L(\mathcal{A}_{q_0 w})) = \emptyset$ and $q_0 w$ is trivially additive.) We claim that

$$\nu_n(L(\mathcal{A}_{q_0 w})) = c_1 + A^0 \cup \ldots \cup c_m + A^0$$

where the union is disjoint. First, suppose $w_1 \in L(\mathcal{A}_{q_0 w})$ where $w_1 \in \mathbf{n}^*$. Because then

$$\nu_n(ww_1) = \nu_n(w) + n^k \nu_n(w_1) \in A,$$

there are nonnegative integers $a \in A^0$ and i, $1 \leq i \leq m$, such that

$$\nu_n(w) + n^k \nu_n(w_1) = \nu_n(w) + c_i n^k + n^k a.$$

Hence $\nu_n(w_1) = c_i + a \in c_i + A^0$. Conversely, if $\nu_n(w_1) = c_i + a$ where $w_1 \in \mathbf{n}^*$, $1 \leq i \leq m$ and $a \in A^0$, then

$$\nu_n(ww_1) = \nu_n(w) + n^k \nu_n(w_1) = \nu_n(w) + c_i n^k + n^k a \in A.$$

Therefore $w_1 \in L(\mathcal{A}_{q_0 w})$ and $\nu_n(w_1) \in \nu_n(L(\mathcal{A}_{q_0 w}))$. Finally, suppose that $x = c_i + a = c_j + b$ where $1 \leq i, j \leq m$ and $a, b \in A^0$. Then

$$\nu_n(w) + n^k x = \nu_n(w) + c_i n^k + n^k a = \nu_n(w) + c_j n^k + n^k b.$$

Because the representation of $\nu_n(w) + n^k x$ according to N_1 is unique, we have $i = j$ and $a = b$. Therefore the sets $c_i + A^0$ are pairwise disjoint $(1 \leq i \leq m)$. This proves the claim and shows that $q_0 w$ is additive. Consequently $k \in UB(\mathcal{A})$.

Conversely, suppose that $k \in UB(\mathcal{A})$. Hence, for each word $w \in \mathbf{n}^*$ of length k there exist nonnegative integers $m(w), c(w)_1, \ldots, c(w)_{m(w)}$ such that

$$\nu_n(L(\mathcal{A}_{q_0 w})) = c(w)_1 + A^0 \cup \ldots \cup c(w)_{m(w)} + A^0$$

where the union is disjoint. Define the number system N_1 as follows. The base of N_1 is n^k and the digits are $\nu_n(w) + c(w)_j n^k$ for $w \in \mathbf{n}^k$ and $1 \leq j \leq m(w)$. Clearly, each digit is positive. Indeed, if $w \neq 0^k$ then $\nu_n(w)$ is positive, and if $w = 0^k$ then $c(w)_j \neq 0$ for $1 \leq j \leq m(w)$ because zero does not belong to A. We claim that N_1 is unambiguous and $S(N_1) = A$.

We show first that $S(N_1) \subseteq A$. Suppose $a \in A^0$. Then $c(w)_i + a \in \nu_n(L(\mathcal{A}_{q_0 w}))$ if $w \in \mathbf{n}^k$ and $1 \leq i \leq m(w)$. Therefore there exists $w_1 \in \mathbf{n}^*$ such that $c(w)_i + a = \nu_n(w_1)$ and $\nu_n(ww_1) \in A$. It follows that

$$\nu_n(w) + c(w)_i n^k + n^k a \in A.$$

Therefore, if d is a digit of N_1, then $d + n^k A^0 \subseteq A$. This implies that $S(N_1) \subseteq A$.

Next, we show that $A \subseteq S(N_1)$. Assume on the contrary that this is not true and denote by x the smallest element in $A - S(N_1)$. Choose the word $w \in \mathbf{n}^k$ such that x is congruent to $\nu_n(w)$ modulo n^k and choose a word $w_1 \in \mathbf{n}^*$ such that $x = \nu_n(ww_1)$. Because $x \in A$, we have $w_1 \in L(\mathcal{A}_{q_0 w})$. Hence $\nu_n(w_1) = c(w)_i + a$ for some $1 \leq i \leq m(w)$, $a \in A^0$. By the choice of x, the integer a, if nonzero, belongs to $S(N_1)$. Consequently

$$x = \nu_n(ww_1) = \nu_n(w) + n^k \nu_n(w_1) = \nu_n(w) + c(w)_i n^k + n^k a \in S(N_1).$$

This contradiction shows that indeed $A \subseteq S(N_1)$. Therefore $A = S(N_1)$.

Finally, suppose that

$$b_0 + b_1 n^k + \ldots + b_s n^{ks} = c_0 + c_1 n^k + \ldots + c_t n^{kt}$$

where $s, t \geq 0$ and $b_0, \ldots, b_s, c_0, \ldots, c_t$ are digits of N_1 such that $b_0 \neq c_0$. Choose the word $w \in \mathbf{n}^k$ such that $\nu_n(w)$ is congruent to b_0 (and c_0) modulo n^k. Then there exist $i \neq j$, $1 \leq i, j \leq m(w)$ such that $b_0 = \nu_n(w) + c(w)_i n^k$ and $c_0 = \nu_n(w) + c(w)_j n^k$. Hence

$$c(w)_i + b_1 + b_2 n^k + \ldots + b_s n^{k(s-1)} = c(w)_j + c_1 + c_2 n^k + \ldots + c_t n^{k(t-1)}$$

$$\in c(w)_i + A^0 \cap c(w)_j + A^0.$$

This contradiction shows that N_1 is unambiguous. □

In the next two lemmas we show that the set $UB(\mathcal{A})$ can be computed effectively if A does not have arbitrarily long gaps.

Lemma 2. *Suppose A does not have arbitrarily long gaps. Given a state $q \in Q$ it is decidable whether or not q is additive. If q is additive one can effectively find the numbers $c_1, \ldots, c_m \in \mathbf{N}$ such that*

$$\nu_n(L(\mathcal{A}_q)) = c_1 + A^0 \cup \ldots \cup c_m + A^0.$$

Proof. Denote $y = d(n^r - 1)^{-1}$ where d is the greatest digit of the given number system N. By Lemma 4.6 in [Honkala 84], for any positive integer $x > d$, the set A contains at least one of the integers $x+1, x+2, \ldots, x+y$. Hence

$$\liminf_{t\to\infty} t^{-1} N(A,t) \geq y^{-1}$$

where $N(A,t)$ is the number of the elements of A less than or equal to t. This implies that for any nonnegative integers $c_1, \ldots, c_{y+1}$, the sets $c_i + A^0$, $1 \leq i \leq y+1$, are not pairwise disjoint.

Now, find the smallest element c_1 of $\nu_n(L(\mathcal{A}_q))$ and check whether or not $c_1 + A^0 \subseteq \nu_n(L(\mathcal{A}_q))$. This decision is possible because $c_1 + A^0$ is n-recognizable. If the inclusion does not hold, q is not additive. If the inclusion holds, check whether $\nu_n(L(\mathcal{A}_q)) = c_1 + A^0$. If not, find the smallest element c_2 in $\nu_n(L(\mathcal{A}_q)) - (c_1 + A^0)$ and check whether $c_2 + A^0$ and $c_1 + A^0$ are disjoint and whether $c_2 + A^0 \subseteq \nu_n(L(\mathcal{A}_q))$. If not, q is not additive. Otherwise, check whether $\nu_n(L(\mathcal{A}_q)) = c_1 + A^0 \cup c_2 + A^0$. If not, find the smallest element in $\nu_n(L(\mathcal{A}_q)) - (c_1 + A^0 \cup c_2 + A^0)$ and proceed similarly.

By the first paragraph of the proof, the procedure stops after at most y steps. This proves the lemma. □

Lemma 3. *Suppose A does not have arbitrarily long gaps. Then the set $UB(\mathcal{A})$ can be computed effectively.*

Proof. Denote $Q_j = q_0\mathbf{n}^j$ for $j \geq 1$. Because the sequence (Q_j) is effectively ultimately periodic, the claim follows by Lemma 2. □

If $S(N)$ is recognizable, it is possible that $S(N)$ has bases which are not powers of n (see [Culik and Salomaa 83]). Therefore, Lemma 1 is not enough to find out the unambiguous bases of $S(N)$. However, the following result has been proved in [Honkala 92].

Lemma 4. *Suppose $S(N)$ is recognizable. Then it is decidable whether or not there exists an unambiguous number system N_1 such that $S(N) = S(N_1)$.*

Proof of Theorem 1. First, decide whether or not $S(N)$ is recognizable. If it is, Theorem 1 follows from Lemma 4. Suppose it is not. Then every base of N is a power of n.

Next, decide whether or not $S(N)$ has arbitrarily long gaps. If it has, n is the only base of $S(N)$, and it suffices to decide whether or not there is an unambiguous number system N_1 with base n such that $S(N) = S(N_1)$. This decision is possible by Theorem 6.3 in [Culik and Salomaa 83]. Finally, if $S(N)$ does not have arbitrarily long gaps, Theorem 1 follows by Lemmas 1 and 3. □

References

[Berstel 86] Berstel, J.: "Fibonacci words - a survey"; In G. Rozenberg and A. Salomaa, eds., The Book of L (Springer, Berlin, 1986) 13-27.

[Bruyere, Hansel, Michaux and Villemaire 94] Bruyere, V., Hansel, G., Michaux, C. and Villemaire, R.: "Logic and p-recognizable sets of integers"; Bulletin of the Belgian Mathematical Society 1 (1994) 191-238.

[Cobham 69] Cobham, A.: "On the base-dependence of sets of numbers recognizable by finite automata"; Math. Systems Theory 3 (1969) 186-192.

[Culik II and Salomaa 83] Culik II, K. and Salomaa, A.: "Ambiguity and decision problems concerning number systems"; Inform. and Control 56 (1983) 139-153.

[Eilenberg 74] Eilenberg, S.: Automata, Languages and Machines, Vol. A; Academic Press, New York (1974).

[Frougny 88] Frougny, C.: "Linear numeration systems of order two"; Inform. and Computation 77 (1988) 233-259.

[Frougny 92] Frougny, C.: "Representations of numbers and finite automata"; Math. Systems Theory 25 (1992) 37-60.

[Honkala 82] Honkala, J.: "Unique representation in number systems and L codes"; Discrete Appl. Math. 4 (1982) 229-232.

[Honkala 84] Honkala, J.: "Bases and ambiguity of number systems"; Theoret. Comput. Sci. 31 (1984) 61-71.

[Honkala 86] Honkala, J.: "A decision method for the recognizability of sets defined by number systems"; RAIRO, Theoret. Informatics and Appl. 20 (1986) 395-403.

[Honkala 89] Honkala, J.: "On number systems with negative digits"; Annales Academiae Scientiarum Fennicae, Series A.I. Mathematica, Vol. 14 (1989) 149-156.

[Honkala 92] Honkala, J.: "On unambiguous number systems with a prime power base"; Acta Cybern. 10 (1992) 155-163.

[de Luca and Restivo 86] de Luca, A. and Restivo, A.: "Star-free sets of integers"; Theoret. Comput. Sci. 43 (1986) 265-275.

[Maurer, Salomaa and Wood 83] Maurer, H., Salomaa, A. and Wood, D.: "L codes and number systems"; Theoret. Comput. Sci. 22 (1983) 331-346.

[Muchnik 91] Muchnik, A.: "Definable criterion for definability in Presburger Arithmetic and its applications"; (preprint in Russian), Institut of new technologies, 1991.

[Perrin 90] Perrin, D.: "Finite automata"; In: J. van Leeuwen, ed., Handbook of Theoretical Computer Science, Vol. B (Elsevier, Amsterdam, 1990) 1-57.

[Salomaa 85] Salomaa, A.: "Computation and Automata"; Cambridge University Press, Cambridge (1985).

[Shallit 94] Shallit, J.: "Numeration systems, linear recurrences and regular sets"; Inform. and Computation 113 (1994) 331-347.

Journal of Universal Computer Science, vol. 1, no. 9 (1995), 658-673
submitted: 10/4/95, accepted: 18/8/95, appeared: 28/9/95, © *Springer Pub. Co.*

A Method for Proving Theorems in Differential Geometry and Mechanics

Dongming Wang
(Institut National Polytechnique de Grenoble, France
wang@lifia.imag.fr)

Abstract: A zero decomposition algorithm is presented and used to devise a method for proving theorems automatically in differential geometry and mechanics. The method has been implemented and its practical efficiency is demonstrated by several non-trivial examples including Bertrand's theorem, Schell's theorem and Kepler-Newton's laws.
Key Words: Differential geometry, mechanics, polynomial elimination, theorem proving, triangular system, zero decomposition
Category: I.1.2, I.2.3

1 Introduction

We consider theorems in elementary differential geometry and plane mechanics which can be expressed algebraically in the form

$$(\forall x_1 \cdots \forall x_n)\,[H_1 = 0 \wedge \cdots \wedge H_h = 0 \wedge D_1 \neq 0 \wedge \cdots \wedge D_d \neq 0 \Longrightarrow C = 0], \quad (1)$$

where H_i, D_j and C are differential polynomials in the variables $x_1, \ldots, x_n$ and any number of their derivatives with respect to (abbr. wrt) a variable t with coefficients in $\boldsymbol{K}$, an ordinary differential field of characteristic 0 consisting of functions of t. That the curvature of a circle is constant and that the orbit described by a particle under a central attractive force is an ellipse if the force varies directly as the distance are examples of such theorems. This paper presents a method that decides the validity of any theorem of this type. The decision problem is solved as determining whether the formula (1) is valid, and if not, finding certain subsidiary (non-degeneracy) condition under which it becomes valid.

Proving theorems in differential geometry and mechanics mechanically was initiated in [Wu 79, Wu 82, Wu 87a], followed up in [Carrà Ferro and Gallo 90, Chou and Gao 93a, Li 91]. In particular, several remarkable theorems have been proved or even "discovered" automatically in [Wu 87b, Wu 87c, Wu 91], and many more later in [Chou and Gao 91, Chou and Gao 92, Chou and Gao 93b], using Wu's method with improvements. An approach based on the evaluation of differential dimension (polynomials) has been proposed in [Carrà Ferro 94, Carrà Ferro and Gallo 90]. The method presented in this paper follows similar algebraic approaches of Wu and others, but employs a different algorithm for the involved zero decomposition. This new decomposition algorithm is developed by the author using ideas from Seidenberg's elimination theory [Seidenberg 56]. The method has been implemented in the Maple system and its practical efficiency is demonstrated by several notable examples including theorems named after Bertrand, Mannheim and Schell, and Kepler-Newton's laws. Experiments with these and other theorems indicate that our method is likely to have better performance [see Remark 4]. Yet complexity analysis and more comparisons between this and other relevant methods remain to be carried.

2 Notations

Write the prefix *d-* for the modifier *differential*, *pol* for *polynomial* and *tri* for *triangular*. A *d-pol* is a pol in $x_1, \ldots, x_n$ and any number of their derivatives wrt t with coefficients in $\boldsymbol{K}$. The set of all such d-pols is denoted by $\boldsymbol{K}\{x_1, \ldots, x_n\}$ or $\boldsymbol{K}\{x\}$ for short. Differentiation of functions x_i will be indicated by means of a second subscript as

$$x_{ij} = \frac{d^j x_i}{dt^j},$$

with $x_{i0} = x_i$. Let $P \in \boldsymbol{K}\{x\}$ be a d-pol. The *jth derivative* of P is obtained by differentiating P j times wrt t, regarding $x_1, \ldots, x_n$ as functions of t. For any x_{ij}, denote the degree of P in x_{ij} by $\deg(P, x_{ij})$. The greatest j, if exists, such that $\deg(P, x_{ij}) > 0$ is called the *order* of P wrt x_i, denoted by $\mathrm{ord}(P, x_i)$. If $\deg(P, x_{ij}) = 0$ for any $j \geq 0$, then define $\mathrm{ord}(P, x_i) = -1$. Let

$$q = \mathrm{ord}(P, x_i), \quad d = \deg(P, x_{iq});$$

the pair $\langle q, d\rangle$ is called the *rank* of P wrt x_i, denoted by $\mathrm{rank}(P, x_i)$. We place $\langle q, d\rangle \prec \langle q', d'\rangle$ if $q < q'$ or $q = q'$, and $d < d'$. Fix the variable ordering as

$$t \prec x_1 \prec \cdots \prec x_n,$$

and order $x_{ij} \prec x_{ik}$ if $j < k$. The leading variable of P, denoted by $\mathrm{lvar}(P)$, is defined to be x_l with l the biggest index such that $\deg(P, x_{lj}) > 0$ for some j if $P \notin \boldsymbol{K}$, and t otherwise.

Let P be a d-pol with

$$\mathrm{lvar}(P) = x_p \succ t, \quad \mathrm{rank}(P, x_p) = \langle q, d\rangle,$$

written as

$$P = P_0 x_{pq}^d + P_1 x_{pq}^{d-1} + \cdots + P_d, \quad P_0 \neq 0,$$

where $\mathrm{ord}(P_i, x_p) < q$ for each i. We call x_{pq} the *lead* of P, denoted by $\mathrm{lead}(P)$, P_0 the *initial* of P, denoted by $\mathrm{ini}(P)$, and $P_1 x_{pq}^{d-1} + \cdots + P_d$ the *reductum* of P, denoted by $\mathrm{red}(P)$. The d-pol $\partial P/\partial x_{pq}$ is called the *separant* of P, denoted by $\mathrm{sep}(P)$.

Pseudo-dividing a d-pol Q by P and its derivatives in x_p, one can get a remainder formula of the form

$$\mathrm{sep}(P)^\alpha \mathrm{ini}(P)^\beta Q = A_1 \frac{d^{k_1} P}{dt^{k_1}} + \cdots + A_s \frac{d^{k_s} P}{dt^{k_s}} + R, \tag{2}$$

where α, β, k_j are non-negative integers and R is a d-pol with $\mathrm{rank}(R, x_p) \prec \langle q, d\rangle$ (cf. [Ritt (50), Wu 89]). We call R the (*pseudo-*) *remainder* of Q wrt P and denote it by $\mathrm{prem}(Q, P)$ (which is not necessarily unique).

Throughout the paper, $\tilde{\boldsymbol{K}}$ denotes an algebraic d-closure of $\boldsymbol{K}\{x\}$, the elements of an ordered set are enclosed in square brackets, and $|S|$ stands for the number of elements of a set S.

A *d-pol set* is a finite set of non-zero d-pols in $\boldsymbol{K}\{x\}$. Let $\mathbb{P}$ and $\mathbb{Q}$ be two d-pol sets. Denote, by $\text{Zero}(\mathbb{P}/\mathbb{Q})$, the set of all common d-zeros (in $\tilde{\boldsymbol{K}}$) of the d-pols in $\mathbb{P}$ which are not d-zero of any d-pol in $\mathbb{Q}$. Namely,

$$\text{Zero}(\mathbb{P}/\mathbb{Q}) = \{x \in \tilde{\boldsymbol{K}}^n \mid P(x) = 0, Q(x) \neq 0, \forall P \in \mathbb{P}, Q \in \mathbb{Q}\}.$$

We write $\text{Zero}(P/\mathbb{Q})$ for $\text{Zero}(\{P\}/\mathbb{Q})$ and $\text{Zero}(\mathbb{P}/Q)$ for $\text{Zero}(\mathbb{P}/\{Q\})$, and write $\text{Zero}(\mathbb{P})$ for $\text{Zero}(\mathbb{P}/\mathbb{Q})$ when $\mathbb{Q} = \emptyset$ or $\mathbb{Q} \subset \boldsymbol{K}$, etc.

By a *d-pol system* we mean a pair $[\mathbb{P}, \mathbb{Q}]$ of d-pol sets, with which $\text{Zero}(\mathbb{P}/\mathbb{Q})$ is of concern. An element of $\text{Zero}(\mathbb{P}/\mathbb{Q})$ is also called a d-zero of $[\mathbb{P}, \mathbb{Q}]$, and

$$\text{Zero}([\mathbb{P}, \mathbb{Q}]) = \text{Zero}(\mathbb{P}/\mathbb{Q}).$$

Definition 1. A finite non-empty ordered set

$$\mathbb{T} = [T_1, T_2, \ldots, T_r]$$

of d-pols is called a *d-tri form* (or *d-tri set*) if

$$t \prec \text{lvar}(T_1) \prec \text{lvar}(T_2) \prec \cdots \prec \text{lvar}(T_r).$$

A pair $[\mathbb{T}, \mathbb{U}]$ is called a *d-tri system* if $\mathbb{T}$ is a d-tri form and $\mathbb{U}$ a d-pol set, possibly empty, such that $\text{ini}(T)$ and $\text{sep}(T)$ do not vanish on $\text{Zero}(\mathbb{T}/\mathbb{U})$ for all $T \in \mathbb{T}$.

Let $\mathbb{T}$ be as above and

$$\text{prem}(Q, \mathbb{T}) = \text{prem}(\cdots \text{prem}(Q, T_r), \ldots, T_1),$$

called the *(pseudo-) remainder* of Q wrt $\mathbb{T}$. A d-tri system $[\mathbb{T}, \mathbb{U}]$ is said to be *fine* if $\text{prem}(U, \mathbb{T}) \neq 0$ for any $U \in \mathbb{U}$. $\mathbb{T}$ is said to be *fine* if

$$[\mathbb{T}, \{\text{ini}(T_i), \text{sep}(T_i) | \ 1 \leq i \leq r\}]$$

is fine.

For any d-pol set $\mathbb{P}$, d-pol T and d-tri form $\mathbb{T}$, we define

$$\text{prem}(\mathbb{P}, T) = \{\text{prem}(P, T) | \ P \in \mathbb{P}\}, \ \ \text{prem}(\mathbb{P}, \mathbb{T}) = \{\text{prem}(P, \mathbb{T}) | \ P \in \mathbb{P}\}.$$

Moreover, let

$$\mathbb{P}^{(k)} = \mathbb{P} \cap \boldsymbol{K}\{x_1, \ldots, x_k\}, \ \ \mathbb{P}^{\langle k \rangle} = \mathbb{P}^{(k)} \setminus \mathbb{P}^{(k-1)}, \ \ \mathbb{P}^{[k]} = \mathbb{P} \setminus \mathbb{P}^{(k)}.$$

$\mathbb{P}$ is said to be of *level* k, denoted as $\text{level}(\mathbb{P}) = k$, if

$$\mathbb{P}^{[k-1]} = \mathbb{P}^{\langle k \rangle} \neq \emptyset.$$

3 Decomposition Algorithm

Let $[\mathbb{P}, \mathbb{Q}]$ be a d-pol system. The algorithm **DECOM** described below decomposes $[\mathbb{P}, \mathbb{Q}]$ into fine d-tri systems. More precisely, it computes a set Ψ which is either empty, that means $\text{Zero}(\mathbb{P}/\mathbb{Q}) = \emptyset$, or of the form $\{[\mathbb{T}_1, \mathbb{U}_1], \ldots, [\mathbb{T}_e, \mathbb{U}_e]\}$ such that

$$\text{Zero}(\mathbb{P}/\mathbb{Q}) = \bigcup_{i=1}^{e} \text{Zero}(\mathbb{T}_i/\mathbb{U}_i), \tag{3}$$

where each $[\mathbb{T}_i, \mathbb{U}_i]$ is a fine d-tri system.

The algorithm employs an elimination top-down from x_n to x_1 (steps D3–D5) with splitting (whenever pseudo-division is performed – according as the initial and separant of the dividing d-pol vanish or not – step D4). For each x_i a single d-pol T with $\text{lvar}(T) = x_i$ is produced from $\mathbb{S}^{\langle i \rangle}$ when it is non-empty. This is done recursively among the d-pols in $\mathbb{S}^{\langle i \rangle}$ by pseudo-dividing those of higher rank with one of minimal rank wrt x_i.

Algorithm DECOM (Input: $\mathbb{P}, \mathbb{Q}$; Output: Ψ).

D1. Set $\Psi \leftarrow \emptyset$ and $\Phi \leftarrow \{[\mathbb{P}, \mathbb{Q}, \emptyset]\}$. Repeat steps D2–D6 until $\Phi = \emptyset$.

D2. Let $[\mathbb{S}, \mathbb{U}, \mathbb{T}]$ be an element of Φ and set

$$\Phi \leftarrow \Phi \setminus \{[\mathbb{S}, \mathbb{U}, \mathbb{T}]\}, \quad m \leftarrow \text{level}(\mathbb{S}).$$

Do steps D3–D5 for $i = m, \ldots, 1$.

D3. If $\mathbb{S} \cap \boldsymbol{K} \neq \emptyset$ then go to D2. If $|\mathbb{S}^{\langle i \rangle}| > 0$ then repeat step D4.

D4. Select from $\mathbb{S}^{\langle i \rangle}$ a T having minimal rank wrt x_i. If $\text{ini}(T)$ does not occur in $\prod_{U \in \mathbb{U}} U$ as factor then set

$$\Phi \leftarrow \Phi \cup \{[\mathbb{S} \setminus \{T\} \cup \{\text{ini}(T), \text{red}(T)\}, \mathbb{U}, \mathbb{T}]\}, \quad \mathbb{U} \leftarrow \mathbb{U} \cup \{\text{ini}(T)\}.$$

If $\text{sep}(T) \neq \text{ini}(T)$ then set

$$\Phi \leftarrow \Phi \cup \{[\mathbb{S} \setminus \{T\} \cup \{\text{prem}(T, \text{sep}(T)), \text{sep}(T)\}, \mathbb{U}, \mathbb{T}]\}, \quad \mathbb{U} \leftarrow \mathbb{U} \cup \{\text{sep}(T)\}.$$

If $|\mathbb{S}^{\langle i \rangle}| = 1$ then go to D5. Otherwise, compute

$$\mathbb{S} \leftarrow \mathbb{S}^{(i-1)} \cup \{T\} \cup \text{prem}(\mathbb{S}^{\langle i \rangle}, T) \setminus \{0\}.$$

D5. Compute $\mathbb{U} \leftarrow \text{prem}(\mathbb{U}, T)$. If $0 \in \mathbb{U}$ then go to D2. Otherwise, set

$$\mathbb{S} \leftarrow \mathbb{S} \setminus \{T\}, \quad \mathbb{T} \leftarrow [T] \cup \mathbb{T}.$$

D6. Set $\Psi \leftarrow \Psi \cup \{[\mathbb{T}, \mathbb{U}]\}$.

Proof. Termination: As step D4 repeats, $\mathrm{rank}(T, x_i)$ steadily decreases. Hence, after finitely many repetitions all the non-zero remainders of the d-pols in $\mathbb{S}^{(i)}$ wrt T will have leading variables $\prec x_i$. Then $|\mathbb{S}^{(i)}|$ becomes 1 and D4 terminates.

Observe that DECOM computes a multi-branch tree on which associated with every node is a triplet $[\mathbb{S}_\alpha, \mathbb{U}_\alpha, \mathbb{T}_\alpha]$. Let $\mathbb{P} = \mathbb{S}_1, \mathbb{S}_2, \ldots, \mathbb{S}_\alpha, \ldots$ be the first components of the triplets associated with one branch of the tree. We want to show that the sequence of d-pol sets $\mathbb{S}_\alpha$ is finite. For this purpose, let us assume that the sequence is infinite and proceed to derive a contradiction.

Any two d-pols F and F' are ordered as $F \prec F'$ if $\mathrm{lvar}(F) \prec \mathrm{lvar}(F')$, or $\mathrm{lvar}(F) = \mathrm{lvar}(F')$ and $\mathrm{rank}(F, \mathrm{lvar}(F)) \prec \mathrm{rank}(F', \mathrm{lvar}(F))$. If neither $F \prec F'$ nor $F' \prec F$, we write $F \sim F'$. Then, any finite set of d-pols can be partially ordered by "$\precsim$" and every steadily decreasing sequence of d-pols is finite.

Let $\mathbb{S}_\alpha$ contain δ_α d-pols, ordered as

$$P_{\alpha 1} \succsim P_{\alpha 2} \succsim \cdots \succsim P_{\alpha \delta_\alpha}, \quad \delta_\alpha \geq 1,$$

for each α. From the enlargement of Φ in DECOM, one sees that each $\mathbb{S}_{\alpha+1}$ is obtained from $\mathbb{S}_\alpha$ by performing some of the following actions:

1. Replace a d-pol T by $\mathrm{ini}(T)$ and $\mathrm{red}(T)$;
2. Replace a d-pol T by $\mathrm{sep}(T)$ and $\mathrm{prem}(T, \mathrm{sep}(T))$;
3. Replace a d-pol by its non-zero remainder (wrt another d-pol of lower rank wrt their common leading variable);
4. Delete a d-pol T (when it has remainder 0 wrt another d-pol of lower rank, or no other d-pol in the set has $\mathrm{lvar}(T)$ as leading variable).

Clearly, the d-pols used to replace T are all $\prec T$. It follows that

$$P_{11} \succsim P_{21} \succsim \cdots \succsim P_{\alpha 1} \succsim \cdots.$$

Thus, there exists an integer β_1 (> 1) such that $P_{\alpha 1} \sim P_{\beta_1 1}$ for all $\alpha \geq \beta_1$.

From the four actions above, it is easy to see that $\delta_\alpha \geq 2$ for any $\alpha \geq \beta_1$. Hence, we are allowed to consider the sequence

$$P_{12} \succsim P_{22} \succsim \cdots \succsim P_{\alpha 2} \succsim \cdots :$$

there exists a β_2 ($\geq \beta_1$) such that $P_{\alpha 2} \sim P_{\beta_2 2}$ for all $\alpha \geq \beta_2$. Now one has $\delta_\alpha \geq 3$ for any $\alpha \geq \beta_2$.

Continuing this argument, we know that there exists a β_{δ_1} ($\geq \beta_{\delta_1 - 1} \geq \cdots \geq \beta_1$), renamed α_1, such that $P_{\alpha k} \sim P_{\alpha_1 k}$ for all $\alpha \geq \alpha_1$ and $k = 1, \ldots, \delta_1$.

On the other hand, $\mathbb{S}_{\alpha_1}$ is obtained from $\mathbb{S}_1$ by performing some of the actions 1–4 as well. Hence, there exists an integer γ_1 ($1 \leq \gamma_1 < \delta_1$) such that

$$P_{11} \sim P_{\alpha_1 1}, \ldots, P_{1\gamma_1 - 1} \sim P_{\alpha_1 \gamma_1 - 1}, \quad \text{while } P_{1\gamma_1} \succ P_{\alpha_1 \gamma_1}.$$

Similarly, there exists an α_2 ($> \alpha_1$) such that $P_{\alpha k} \sim P_{\alpha_2 k}$ for all $\alpha \geq \alpha_2$ and $k = \gamma_1, \ldots, \delta_{\alpha_1}$, and a γ_2 ($\gamma_1 < \gamma_2 < \delta_{\alpha_1}$) such that

$$P_{\alpha_1 \gamma_1} \sim P_{\alpha_2 \gamma_1}, \ldots, P_{\alpha_1 \gamma_2 - 1} \sim P_{\alpha_2 \gamma_2 - 1}, \quad \text{while } P_{\alpha_1 \gamma_2} \succ P_{\alpha_2 \gamma_2}.$$

In this way, we shall construct an infinite sequence of d-pols as follows

$$P_{1\gamma_1} \succ P_{\alpha_1 \gamma_1} \succ \cdots \succ P_{\alpha_k \gamma_k} \succ \cdots.$$

This leads to a contradiction. Therefore, the sequence of d-pol sets $\mathbb{S}_\alpha$ is finite, and thus any branch of the decomposition tree is finite. According to König's infinity lemma, the tree is finite. This proves that steps D2–D6 only have finitely many iterations.

Correctness: Let the state variables be indexed by b and a respectively for their values *before* and *after* the execution of an iteration of D4. We first prove that

$$\begin{aligned}\text{Zero}(\mathbb{S}_b/\mathbb{U}_b) = \text{Zero}(\mathbb{S}_a/\mathbb{U}_a) \cup \text{Zero}(\mathbb{S}_b \setminus \{T\} \cup \{R, S\}/\mathbb{U}_b \cup \{I\}) \\ \cup \text{Zero}(\mathbb{S}_b \setminus \{T\} \cup \{I, \text{red}(T)\}/\mathbb{U}_b),\end{aligned} \tag{4}$$

where

$$\mathbb{S}_a = \mathbb{S}_b^{(i-1)} \cup \{T\} \cup \text{prem}(\mathbb{S}_b^{(i)}, T) \setminus \{0\}, \quad \mathbb{U}_a = \mathbb{U}_b \cup \{I, S\},$$
$$R = \text{prem}(T, S), \quad I = \text{ini}(T), \quad S = \text{sep}(T), \quad T \in \mathbb{S}_b^{(i)}.$$

Let $\bar{x} \in \text{Zero}(\mathbb{S}_b/\mathbb{U}_b)$; then $d^jT/dt^j(\bar{x}) = 0$ for $j \geq 0$ and $P(\bar{x}) = 0$ for $P \in \mathbb{S}_b$. So by the remainder formula (2) we have $H(\bar{x}) = 0$ for all $H \in \mathbb{S}_a$. Clearly, $U(\bar{x}) \neq 0$ for any $U \in \mathbb{U}_b$. If $I(\bar{x}) = 0$ and thus $\text{red}(I)(\bar{x}) = 0$, then

$$\bar{x} \in \text{Zero}(\mathbb{S}_b \setminus \{T\} \cup \{I, \text{red}(T)\}/\mathbb{U}_b). \tag{5}$$

If $I(\bar{x}) \neq 0$ and $S(\bar{x}) \neq 0$, then $\bar{x} \in \text{Zero}(\mathbb{S}_a/\mathbb{U}_a)$. Otherwise, $I(\bar{x}) \neq 0$ but $S(\bar{x}) = 0$. In this case, let $x_{pq} = \text{lead}(T)$ and $d = \deg(T, x_{pq})$; then $\text{lead}(S) = x_{pq}$, $\deg(S, x_{pq}) = d - 1 > 0$, $\text{ini}(S)(\bar{x}) = dI(\bar{x}) \neq 0$, and the remainder formula for $R = \text{prem}(T, S)$ corresponding to (2) is specialized with $\alpha = 0, s = 1$ and $k_1 = 0$. Hence, $T(\bar{x}) = 0$ if and only if $R(\bar{x}) = 0$. It follows that

$$\bar{x} \in \text{Zero}(\mathbb{S}_b \setminus \{T\} \cup \{R, S\}/\mathbb{U}_b \cup \{I\}). \tag{6}$$

Therefore, the left-hand side of (4) is contained in the right-hand side. To show the opposite, we see that if (5) holds then $T(\bar{x}) = 0$ and thus $\bar{x} \in \text{Zero}(\mathbb{S}_b/\mathbb{U}_b)$. If $\bar{x} \in \text{Zero}(\mathbb{S}_a/\mathbb{U}_a)$, then by the remainder formula we have $P(\bar{x}) = 0$ for all $P \in \mathbb{S}_b$, so $\bar{x} \in \text{Zero}(\mathbb{S}_b/\mathbb{U}_b)$ as well. If (6) holds, then $S(\bar{x}) = 0$ and $I(\bar{x}) \neq 0$. In this case, $R(\bar{x}) = 0$ implies that $T(\bar{x}) = 0$ (as demonstrated above), so $\bar{x} \in \text{Zero}(\mathbb{S}_b/\mathbb{U}_b)$, too. By now (4) is proved.

Let the triplets associated with the nodes of the decomposition tree be $[\mathbb{S}_\alpha, \mathbb{U}_\alpha, \mathbb{T}_\alpha]$. Then

$$\text{Zero}(\mathbb{P}/\mathbb{Q}) = \bigcup_\alpha \text{Zero}(\mathbb{S}_\alpha \cup \mathbb{T}_\alpha/\mathbb{U}_\alpha)$$

holds at any time according to (4), where the set union runs over all leaves of the tree. Eventually, the zero decomposition (3) is established.

As the initial and separant of every d-pol $T \in \mathbb{T}_i$ are adjoined in step D4 to the corresponding $\mathbb{U}$ and subsequently replaced by their (non-zero) remainders wrt other d-pols in $\mathbb{T}_i$, we know that

$$\text{prem}(\text{ini}(T), \mathbb{T}_i), \ \text{prem}(\text{sep}(T), \mathbb{T}_i) \in \mathbb{U}_i.$$

By the remainder formula (2), $\text{ini}(T)$ and $\text{sep}(T)$ do not vanish on $\text{Zero}(\mathbb{T}_i/\mathbb{U}_i)$ for all $T \in \mathbb{T}_i$, so $[\mathbb{T}_i, \mathbb{U}_i]$ is a d-tri system.

Since all the d-pols in $\mathbb{U}_i$ are actually the non-zero remainders of some d-pols wrt $\mathbb{T}_i$, $0 \notin \mathrm{prem}(\mathbb{U}_i, \mathbb{T}_i)$ for every i. Hence, each $[\mathbb{T}_i, \mathbb{U}_i]$ is fine and the proof is complete. □

The key step of DECOM is to produce a d-tri system $[\mathbb{T}, \mathbb{U}]$ from an arbitrary d-pol system $[\mathbb{P}, \mathbb{Q}]$ by successively eliminating the variables (from x_n down to x_1) for the d-pols in $\mathbb{P}$ and meanwhile reducing the d-pols in $\mathbb{Q}$. During the computation of $[\mathbb{T}, \mathbb{U}]$, called the *principal d-tri system* of $[\mathbb{P}, \mathbb{Q}]$, other d-pol systems are generated and collected, and to each of them the same procedure is applied recursively.

Remark 1. DECOM has similarities to Seidenberg's original algorithm, Ritt-Wu's and others (e.g., [Chou and Gao 93a, Carrà Ferro 94]). However, it differs from each of them. For any given d-pol system $\mathfrak{P} = [\mathbb{P}, \mathbb{Q}]$, Seidenberg's algorithm can compute d-pol systems involving fewer variables and equivalent to $\mathfrak{P}$ (wrt solvability), but it does not compute any zero decomposition for $\mathfrak{P}$. In his algorithm, heavy *projection* is always carried out (see below). Compared with Ritt-Wu's, the zero decomposition (3) computed by DECOM looks similar, but in (3) whether $\mathrm{prem}(\mathbb{P}, \mathbb{T}_i) = \{0\}$ is not verified. DECOM also has different algorithmic structure and steps: in it desired strategies such as top-down elimination and splitting along with pseudo-division are incorporated; some redundant verification and repeated computation are avoided. In our approach, there is no concept analogous to the *d-characteristic set* of a d-pol system.

A d-tri system $[\mathbb{T}, \mathbb{U}]$ is called *perfect* if $\mathrm{Zero}(\mathbb{T}/\mathbb{U}) \neq \emptyset$. The d-tri systems computed by DECOM are fine but not necessarily perfect. The perfectness may be ensured when projection is embedded. In other words, one can compute a decomposition of the form (3) with all d-tri systems $[\mathbb{T}_i, \mathbb{U}_i]$ perfect. Moreover, for any $1 \leq k < n$ and $\bar{x}_1, \ldots, \bar{x}_k \in \tilde{\boldsymbol{K}}$, there exist $\bar{x}_{k+1}, \ldots, \bar{x}_n \in \tilde{\boldsymbol{K}}$ such that

$$(\bar{x}_1, \ldots, \bar{x}_n) \in \mathrm{Zero}(\mathbb{P}/\mathbb{Q})$$

if and only if

$$(\bar{x}_1, \ldots, \bar{x}_k) \in \mathrm{Zero}(\mathbb{T}_i^{(k)}/\mathbb{U}_i^{(k)})$$

for some i (see [Wang 94a] for details). This provides a quantifier elimination procedure and thus a decision procedure for the existential theory of algebraically closed d-fields. Since the practical efficiency of projection is not high enough and the approach based on it is not very appropriate for geometry theorem proving (GTP) due to the occurrence of non-degeneracy conditions (cf. [Wang 95]), we decide not to go further in this direction. Instead, we shall consider the irreducibility of d-tri forms.

A d-tri form $\mathbb{T}$ as well as a d-tri system $[\mathbb{T}, \mathbb{U}]$ is said to be *quasi-irreducible* if every d-pol in $\mathbb{T}$ is irreducible over $\boldsymbol{K}$. Using pol factorization over $\boldsymbol{K}$, one can replace the computation of $\mathrm{prem}(\mathbb{U}, T)$ in step D5 of DECOM by the following as to compute a zero decomposition of the form (3) with each $[\mathbb{T}_i, \mathbb{U}_i]$ quasi-irreducible:

Compute the irreducible factors $F_1, \ldots, F_s$ of T over $\boldsymbol{K}$, set $\bar{\mathbb{Q}} \leftarrow \mathbb{U}$ and do step D5′ for $j = 1, \ldots, s$.

D5′. Compute $\bar{\mathbb{U}} \leftarrow \mathrm{prem}(\bar{\mathbb{Q}}, F_j)$. If $j = 1$ then set $\mathbb{U} \leftarrow \bar{\mathbb{U}}$ and $T \leftarrow F_j$. Otherwise, if $0 \notin \bar{\mathbb{U}}$ then set

$$\Phi \leftarrow \Phi \cup \{[\mathbb{S}, \bar{\mathbb{U}}, [F_j] \cup \mathbb{T}]\}.$$

It is easy to see the termination and correctness of the algorithm obtained with this simple modification.

Let

$$\mathbb{T} = [T_1, T_2, \ldots, T_r]$$

be a fine d-tri form and

$$\mathbb{T}^{\{i\}} = [T_1, T_2, \ldots, T_i], \quad i = 1, \ldots, r.$$

Definition 2. $\mathbb{T}$ is said to be *irreducible* if for every $1 \le i \le r$ there do not exist D_i and T_i', T_i'' with

$$\begin{aligned} &\text{lead}(D_i) \prec \text{lead}(T_i), \quad \text{lead}(T_i') = \text{lead}(T_i'') = \text{lead}(T_i), \\ &0 \notin \text{prem}(\{D_i, \text{ini}(T_i'), \text{ini}(T_i'')\}, \mathbb{T}^{\{i-1\}}) \end{aligned}$$

such that

$$\text{prem}(D_i T_i - T_i' T_i'', \mathbb{T}^{\{i-1\}}) = 0.$$

A fine d-tri system $[\mathbb{T}, \mathbb{U}]$ is said to be *irreducible* if $\mathbb{T}$ is irreducible.

In fact, $\mathbb{T}$ is irreducible when it is so, considered as a pol tri form (cf. [Ritt (50), p. 107] and [Wu 89]). If $\mathbb{T}$ is reducible, then there exist a k and d-pols D_k and $G_1, \ldots, G_s$ with

$$\begin{aligned} &\text{lead}(D_k) \prec \text{lead}(T_k), \quad \text{lead}(G_1) = \cdots = \text{lead}(G_s) = \text{lead}(T_k), \\ &0 \notin \text{prem}(\{D_k, \text{ini}(G_1), \ldots, \text{ini}(G_s)\}, \mathbb{T}^{\{i-1\}}) \end{aligned}$$

such that $\mathbb{T}^{\{k-1\}}$ and

$$\mathbb{T}^{\{k-1\}} \cup [G_j], \quad j = 1, \ldots, s,$$

are all irreducible and

$$\text{prem}(D_k T_k - G_1 \cdots G_s, \mathbb{T}^{\{k-1\}}) = 0.$$

Here the irreducibility and the d-pols $G_1, \ldots, G_s$ can be determined with usual pol factorization (of T_k over the successive algebraic extension field defined by $T_1, T_2, \ldots, T_{k-1}$ – see [Wang 94b]).

Using the factorization of T_k into $G_1, \ldots, G_s$, one can further decompose $\mathbb{T}$ into d-tri forms, and finally into irreducible ones. We omit the involved details of the decomposition procedure and state the result in the form of the following theorem.

Theorem 1. *There is an algorithm which computes, for any given d-pol system* $[\mathbb{P}, \mathbb{Q}]$, *a set which either is empty, that means* $\text{Zero}(\mathbb{P}/\mathbb{Q}) = \emptyset$, *or consists of finitely many irreducible d-tri systems* $[\mathbb{T}_1, \mathbb{U}_1], \ldots, [\mathbb{T}_e, \mathbb{U}_e]$ *such that the zero decomposition* (3) *holds.*

The proof of this theorem will be given in the sequel of [Wang 94a].

4 Decision Algorithm

On the basis of the zero decomposition method described in the preceding section, we can devise several algorithms for proving theorems and deriving unknown relations automatically in elementary differential geometry and mechanics, which can be formulated in terms of d-pol equations and inequations. In this section we present one of the algorithms for automated theorem proving. Let us first prove two fundamental theorems.

Theorem 2. *Let* $[\mathbb{T}, \mathbb{U}]$ *be a d-tri system and* G *a d-pol. If* $\operatorname{prem}(G, \mathbb{T}) = 0$, *then* $\operatorname{Zero}(\mathbb{T}/\mathbb{U}) \subset \operatorname{Zero}(G)$. *If* $\operatorname{Zero}(\mathbb{T}/\mathbb{U}) \subset \operatorname{Zero}(G)$ *and* $\mathbb{T}$ *is irreducible, then* $\operatorname{prem}(G, \mathbb{T}) = 0$.

Proof. According to the definition of d-tri systems and the remainder formula (2), the first half of the theorem is obvious. To prove the second half, let

$$\Omega = \{P \in \boldsymbol{K}\{x\} \mid \operatorname{prem}(P, \mathbb{T}) = 0\}.$$

Since $\mathbb{T}$ is irreducible, Ω is a non-trivial prime ideal (cf. [Ritt (50), p. 107]). Clearly,

$$\mathbb{U} \cap \Omega = \emptyset, \quad \operatorname{Zero}(\Omega) \subset \operatorname{Zero}(\mathbb{T}).$$

Let η be a generic zero of Ω; then $U(\eta) \neq 0$ for any $U \in \mathbb{U}$ (cf. [Ritt (50), pp. 25–27] and [Wu 89]). It follows that

$$\eta \in \operatorname{Zero}(\mathbb{T}/\mathbb{U}) \subset \operatorname{Zero}(G).$$

That is, $G(\eta) = 0$, so $G \in \Omega$. Hence, $\operatorname{prem}(G, \mathbb{T}) = 0$ and the theorem is proved. □

Theorem 3. *Let a d-pol system* $[\mathbb{P}, \mathbb{Q}]$ *have zero decomposition of the form* (3) *with each* $[\mathbb{T}_i, \mathbb{U}_i]$ *irreducible. Then*

$$\operatorname{Zero}(\mathbb{P}/\mathbb{Q}) = \bigcup_{i=1}^{e} \operatorname{Zero}(\mathbb{T}_i/\mathbb{I}_i \cup \mathbb{Q}), \tag{7}$$

where $\mathbb{I}_i = \{\operatorname{ini}(T), \operatorname{sep}(T) \mid T \in \mathbb{T}_i\}$ *for each* i.

Proof. As

$$\operatorname{Zero}(\mathbb{T}_i/\mathbb{U}_i) \subset \operatorname{Zero}(\mathbb{P}/\mathbb{Q}),$$

by Theorem 2 we have

$$\operatorname{prem}(\mathbb{P}, \mathbb{T}_i) = \{0\}, \quad 0 \notin \operatorname{prem}(\mathbb{Q}, \mathbb{T}_i)$$

for every i. Thus, according to (2), the right-hand side of (7) is contained in the left-hand side. On the contrary, let $\bar{x} \in \operatorname{Zero}(\mathbb{P}/\mathbb{Q})$. By (3) there is an i such that $\bar{x} \in \operatorname{Zero}(\mathbb{T}_i/\mathbb{U}_i)$. Since $[\mathbb{T}_i, \mathbb{U}_i]$ is a d-tri system, $\bar{x}$ is not a zero of any d-pol in $\mathbb{I}$. Hence,

$$\bar{x} \in \operatorname{Zero}(\mathbb{T}_i/\mathbb{I}_i \cup \mathbb{Q})$$

and thus is contained in the right-hand side of (7). □

Return to (1) and observe that many theorems in differential geometry (space curve theory) and mechanics (cf. [Chou and Gao 91]) can be algebraically formulated in that form. Let

$$\mathbb{H} = \{H_1, \ldots, H_h\}, \quad \mathbb{D} = \{D_1, \ldots, D_d\}.$$

A theorem of the form (1) will be denoted by $\mathfrak{T}(\mathbb{H}, \mathbb{D}, C)$. We call

$$\bigwedge_{i=1}^{h} H_i = 0 \wedge \bigwedge_{j=1}^{d} D_j \neq 0$$

the hypothesis and $C = 0$ the conclusion of the theorem.

Algorithm PROVE. Given a theorem

$$\mathfrak{T} = \mathfrak{T}(\mathbb{H}, \mathbb{D}, C),$$

this algorithm decides whether $\mathfrak{T}$ is universally true, and if not, determines a subsidiary condition under which it is true.

P1. Compute $\Psi \leftarrow$DECOM$(\mathbb{H}, \mathbb{D})$. If $\Psi = \emptyset$, then the hypothesis of the theorem $\mathfrak{T}$ is self-contradictory and the algorithm terminates.

P2. Compute

$$R_i \leftarrow \mathrm{prem}(C, \mathbb{T}_i) \quad \text{for} \quad [\mathbb{T}_i, \mathbb{U}_i] \in \Psi.$$

If $R_i = 0$ for all i, then $\mathfrak{T}$ is universally true and the algorithm terminates.

P3. Let Δ be the set of all i for which $R_i \neq 0$. Decompose $[\mathbb{T}_i, \mathbb{U}_i]$ into a finite set Ψ_i of irreducible d-tri systems for each $i \in \Delta$.

P4. Compute

$$R_{ij} \leftarrow \mathrm{prem}(C, \mathbb{T}_{ij}) \quad \text{for} \quad [\mathbb{T}_{ij}, \mathbb{U}_{ij}] \in \Psi_i, i \in \Delta.$$

If $R_{ij} = 0$ for all j and i, then $\mathfrak{T}$ is universally true and the algorithm terminates. Otherwise, $\mathfrak{T}$ is not universally true. It is conditionally true, with the *subsidiary* condition determined in step P5.

P5. For each $i \in \Delta$, let Δ_i be the set of all j for which $R_{ij} \neq 0$. Set

$$\mathcal{D} \leftarrow \bigwedge_{j \in \Delta_i, i \in \Delta} (\bigvee_{T \in \mathbb{T}_{ij}} T \neq 0 \vee \bigvee_{U \in \mathbb{U}_{ij}} U = 0).$$

Then $\mathcal{D}$ is the subsidiary condition under which $\mathfrak{T}$ is true. If $\mathcal{D}$ can be identified either geometrically or algebraically as *non-degeneracy* conditions, then $\mathfrak{T}$ is *generically* true.

This algorithm terminates obviously. As formula (1) is valid if and only if

$$\mathrm{Zero}(\mathbb{H}/\mathbb{D}) \subset \mathrm{Zero}(C),$$

the correctness follows from Theorem 2. Possible variants of the algorithm and its modification for formula derivation are left out. Some other important issues are also omitted. One of them is to simplify the formula $\mathcal{D}$ algebraically (which is not an easy task) and to identify $\mathcal{D}$ to non-degeneracy conditions. In fact, no definition for "non-degeneracy" and "generically true" is given here. The concepts are due to Wu and may be defined when the variables are separated into parameters and geometric dependents and the notions of dimension and order are introduced. The interested reader is referred to [Carrà Ferro 94, Chou and Gao 93a, Wu 79, Wu 82, Wu 87a] for details.

Remark 2. Step P3 requires algebraic pol factorization which is expensive in general. Nonetheless, the author has implemented rather efficient factoring routines, which work well for pols from GTP, as demonstrated in [Wang 94b]. The factoring times for the pols we have encountered in GTP so far are in the matter of seconds.

5 Examples

To illustrate the method explained in the previous sections and its performance, we now present two examples, using a draft implementation of the algorithms in Maple. The timings mentioned below were obtained from Maple V running on a SUN SparcServer 690/51 and are given in CPU seconds. The examples were studied in detail first in [Wu 87b, Wu 87c, Wu 91] and then in [Chou and Gao 92, Chou and Gao 93a, Chou and Gao 93b] and are among the interesting and difficult ones in differential geometry and mechanics considered so far. Experiments on these and other examples show that our method based on d-tri systems is computationally efficient. Systematic comparisons for the examples will be made later when our implementation of the other methods is completed.

Example 1 (Bertrand curves [Chou and Gao 93b, Wu 87b, Wu 91]). Let C and $\bar{C}$ be a Bertrand pair of curves in one-to-one correspondence with arc lengths $s, \bar{s}$ as parameters in the ordinary metric space. Attach the trihedrals (X, e_1, e_2, e_3) and $(\bar{X}, \bar{e}_1, \bar{e}_2, \bar{e}_3)$ to C and $\bar{C}$ at the corresponding points X and $\bar{X}$, and denote the curvature and torsion of C and $\bar{C}$ by κ, τ and by $\bar{\kappa}, \bar{\tau}$ respectively. We have the following theorems.

Schell's Theorem. The product of τ and $\bar{\tau}$ is a constant.

Bertrand's Theorem. There exists a linear relation between κ and τ with constant coefficients.

Mannheim's Theorem. The cross-ratio of $X, \bar{X}$ and the centers of $\kappa, \bar{\kappa}$ is a constant.

To prove the theorems, let

$$\bar{X} = X + a_1 e_1 + a_2 e_2 + a_3 e_3,$$
$$\bar{e}_i = \sum_{j=1}^{3} u_{ij} e_j, \ i = 1, 2, 3.$$

From the Frenet formulae of C and $\bar{C}$, one can easily deduce a set of 12 d-pols (see [Wu 91]). In the classical Bertrand case, $\bar{e}_2 = \pm e_2$. Let us take the positive sign, and similarly for the orthogonality relations between the u_{ij}'s, so that we have

$$a_1 = 0, \ a_3 = 0, \ u_{12} = u_{21} = u_{23} = u_{32} = 0,$$
$$u_{22} = 1, \ u_{11} = u_{33}, \ u_{13} = -u_{31}, \ u_{11}^2 + u_{13}^2 = 1.$$

Combining these relations with the 12 d-pols, one obtains the following set of 14 d-pols (the primes denoting the derivatives wrt s)

$$
\begin{aligned}
H_1 &= \bar{s}'u_{11} + a_2\kappa - 1, & H_2 &= -a_2', \\
H_3 &= \bar{s}'u_{13} - a_2\tau, & H_4 &= -u_{11}', \\
H_5 &= \bar{s}'\bar{\kappa} - \kappa u_{12} + \tau u_{13}, & H_6 &= -u_{13}', \\
H_7 &= \bar{s}'\bar{\kappa}u_{11} - \bar{s}'\bar{\tau}u_{31} - \kappa, & H_8 &= \bar{s}'\bar{\kappa}u_{13} - \bar{s}'\bar{\tau}u_{33} + \tau, \\
H_9 &= -u_{31}', & H_{10} &= -\bar{s}'\bar{\tau} - \kappa u_{31} + \tau u_{33}, \\
H_{11} &= -u_{33}', & H_{12} &= u_{11} - u_{33}, \\
H_{13} &= u_{13} + u_{31}, & H_{14} &= u_{11}^2 + u_{13}^2 - 1.
\end{aligned}
$$

With respect to the ordering

$$
\begin{aligned}
&\bar{s} \prec a_1 \prec a_2 \prec a_3 \prec u_{11} \prec u_{12} \prec u_{13} \prec u_{21} \prec u_{22} \prec u_{23} \prec u_{31} \prec u_{32} \prec u_{33} \\
&\prec \kappa \prec \tau \prec \bar{\kappa} \prec \bar{\tau},
\end{aligned}
$$

$\mathbb{P} = \{H_1, \ldots, H_{14}\}$ can be decomposed (in 91.4 seconds) into 10 irreducible d-tri systems, with the corresponding d-tri forms given as

$$
\begin{aligned}
\mathbb{T}_1 = [&a_2', u_{11}', u_{12} - u_{11}, u_{13}^2 + u_{11}^2 - 1, u_{31} + u_{13}, u_{33} - u_{11}, a_2\kappa + \bar{s}'u_{11} - 1, \\
&a_2\tau - \bar{s}'u_{13}, \bar{s}'\bar{\kappa} + u_{13}\tau - u_{11}\kappa, \bar{s}'\bar{\tau} - u_{11}\tau - u_{13}\kappa], \\
\mathbb{T}_2 = [&\bar{s}'', a_2', \bar{s}'u_{11} - 1, \bar{s}'^2u_{13}^2 - \bar{s}'^2 + 1, u_{31} + u_{13}, u_{33} - u_{11}, \kappa, a_2\tau - \bar{s}'u_{13}, \\
&\bar{s}'\bar{\kappa} + u_{13}\tau, \bar{s}'\bar{\tau} - u_{11}\tau], \\
\mathbb{T}_3 = [&a_2', u_{11} - 1, u_{12} - 1, u_{13}, u_{31}, u_{33} - 1, a_2\kappa + \bar{s}' - 1, \tau, \bar{s}'\bar{\kappa} - \kappa, \bar{\tau}], \\
\mathbb{T}_4 = [&a_2', u_{11} + 1, u_{12} + 1, u_{13}, u_{31}, u_{33} + 1, a_2\kappa - \bar{s}' - 1, \tau, \bar{s}'\bar{\kappa} + \kappa, \bar{\tau}], \\
\mathbb{T}_5 = [&\bar{s}' + 1, a_2', u_{11} + 1, u_{13}, u_{31}, u_{33} + 1, \kappa, \tau, \bar{\kappa}, \bar{\tau}], \\
\mathbb{T}_6 = [&\bar{s}' - 1, a_2', u_{11} - 1, u_{13}, u_{31}, u_{33} - 1, \kappa, \tau, \bar{\kappa}, \bar{\tau}], \\
\mathbb{T}_7 = [&\bar{s}' - 1, a_2, u_{11} - 1, u_{13}, u_{31}, u_{33} - 1, \kappa, \bar{\kappa}, \bar{\tau} - \tau], \\
\mathbb{T}_8 = [&\bar{s}' + 1, a_2, u_{11} + 1, u_{13}, u_{31}, u_{33} + 1, \kappa, \bar{\kappa}, \bar{\tau} - \tau], \\
\mathbb{T}_9 = [&\bar{s}' - 1, a_2, u_{11} - 1, u_{12} - 1, u_{13}, u_{31}, u_{33} - 1, \bar{\kappa} - \kappa, \bar{\tau} - \tau], \\
\mathbb{T}_{10} = [&\bar{s}' + 1, a_2, u_{11} + 1, u_{12} + 1, u_{13}, u_{31}, u_{33} + 1, \bar{\kappa} - \kappa, \bar{\tau} - \tau]
\end{aligned}
$$

such that

$$
\mathrm{Zero}(\mathbb{P}) = \bigcup_{i=1}^{2} \mathrm{Zero}(\mathbb{T}_i/\bar{s}'a_2u_{13}) \cup \bigcup_{i=3}^{4} \mathrm{Zero}(\mathbb{T}_i/\bar{s}'a_2) \cup \bigcup_{i=5}^{10} \mathrm{Zero}(\mathbb{T}_i).
$$

The conclusions of Schell, Bertrand, and Mannheim's theorems to be proved are

$$
\begin{aligned}
C_S &= (\tau\bar{\tau})' = 0, \\
C_B &= \kappa'\tau'' - \kappa''\tau' = 0, \\
C_M &= [(1 + a_2\bar{\kappa})(1 - a_2\kappa)]' = 0
\end{aligned}
$$

respectively. It is easy to verify that

$$
\mathrm{prem}(C_S, \mathbb{T}_i) \begin{cases} = 0, & i = 1, \ldots, 6, \\ \neq 0, & i = 7, \ldots, 10; \end{cases}
$$

$$
\mathrm{prem}(C_B, \mathbb{T}_i) \begin{cases} = 0, & i = 1, \ldots, 8, \\ \neq 0, & i = 9, 10; \end{cases}
$$

$$
\mathrm{prem}(C_M, \mathbb{T}_i) = 0, \quad i = 1, \ldots, 10.
$$

Therefore, the algebraic form of Schell's theorem and of Bertrand's are both conditionally true and of Mannheim's is universally true. The subsidiary conditions for the former may be provided as $\bar{s}' \neq 0$ and $a_2 \neq 0$ (i.e., $C \neq \bar{C}$). The total times of computing the pseudo-remainders for the three theorems are 1.4, 1.7 and 1.9 seconds, respectively.

Note that Bertrand's theorem is also true when $a_2 = 0$ and $\kappa = \bar{\kappa} = 0$ (i.e., $C = \bar{C}$ is a straight line). Mannheim's theorem is considered usually under the condition $\kappa\bar{\kappa} \neq 0$. However, the algebraic form of the theorem is true as well in the degenerate case $\kappa = \bar{\kappa} = 0$.

Remark 3. A relatively large amount of the decomposition time indicated above was spent for verification so that two redundant d-tri systems are removed. The removal of redundancy here is merely to make the list of d-tri systems short. It is not necessary for proving the theorem because the pseudo-remainders of the conclusion d-pols wrt the removed d-tri forms are very easy to compute. This is also true for the following example. Without the verification, the decomposition time can be reduced to 25.7 seconds. The total time needed for proving the three theorems is 31 seconds only.

Example 2 (Kepler-Newton's Laws [Chou and Gao 93a, Wu 87c, Wu 91]). Newton's gravitational laws and Kepler's observational laws play an important role in celestial mechanics. The first two of them may be stated as follows.

K1. Each planet describes an ellipse with the sun at one focus.
K2. The radius vector drawn from the sun to a planet sweeps out equal areas in equal times.
N1. The acceleration of any planet is inversely proportional to the square of the distance from the sun to the planet.
N2. The acceleration vector of any planet is directed to the sun.

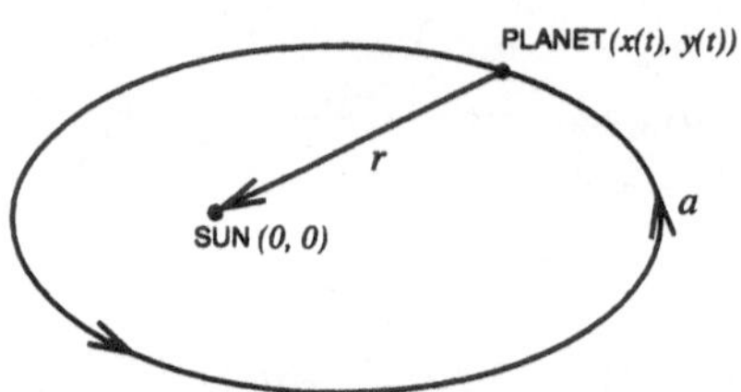

There are inference relations between the two groups of laws. For example, K2 is equivalent to N2. We consider two non-trivial relations as illustration for our method: (i) N1 and N2 imply K1 and (ii) K1 and K2 imply N1.

Let the coordinates of the planet be (x, y), depending on the time variable t. Assume that the sun is located at the origin $(0, 0)$. Then the d-pol equations for Newton's two laws are

$$N_1 = (r^2 a)' = 0, \quad N_2 = xy'' - x''y = 0$$

respectively, where a is the acceleration of the planet and r the length of the radius vector from the sun to the planet. Clearly, we have

$$H_1 = r^2 - x^2 - y^2 = 0, \quad H_2 = a^2 - x''^2 - y''^2 = 0.$$

We assume $a \neq 0$; the problem becomes trivial when $a = 0$. Then,

$$\mathfrak{P} = [\{N_1, N_2, H_1, H_2\}, \{a\}]$$

constitutes the hypothesis d-pol system. Kepler's first law to be proved is equivalent to (cf. [Chou and Gao 93a, part II])

$$K_1 = r'''(x'y'' - x''y') - r''(x'y''' - x'''y') + r'(x''y''' - x'''y'') = 0.$$

With the ordering $x \prec y \prec r \prec a$, $\mathfrak{P}$ can be decomposed (in 17.5 CPU seconds) into 6 quasi-irreducible d-tri systems with the corresponding $\mathbb{T}_i, \mathbb{U}_i$ shown below

$$\begin{aligned}
&\mathbb{T}_1 = [T_1, T_2, H_1, H_2], \qquad \mathbb{T}_2 = [xx''' + 2x'x'', xy' - x'y, H_1, H_2],\\
&\mathbb{T}_3 = [x, yy''' + 2y'y'', r - y, a - y''], \quad \mathbb{T}_4 = [x, yy''' + 2y'y'', r - y, a + y''],\\
&\mathbb{T}_5 = [x, yy''' + 2y'y'', r + y, a - y''], \quad \mathbb{T}_6 = [x, yy''' + 2y'y'', r + y, a + y''],\\
&\mathbb{U}_1 = \{x'', xx''' + 2x'x'', y, r, a, S_2,\\
&\qquad 3x^2x''x'''' - 5x^2x'''^2 - 2xx'x''x''' + 6xx''^3 - 2x'^2x''^2\},\\
&\mathbb{U}_2 = \{x'', r, a\}, \quad \mathbb{U}_3 = \cdots = \mathbb{U}_6 = \{y''\},\\
&T_1 = 9x^3x''^2x''''' - 45x^3x''x'''x'''' + 18x^2x'x''^2x'''' + 40x^3x'''^3 - 30x^2x'x''x'''^2\\
&\qquad -6xx'^2x''^2x''' + 18xx'x''^4 - 4x'^3x''^3,\\
&T_2 = 3x^2x''x''''y^2 - 4x^2x'''^2y^2 + 2xx'x''x'''y^2 + 6xx''^3y^2 + 2x'^2x''^2y^2 + x^4x'''^2\\
&\qquad +4x^3x'x''x''' + 4x^2x'^2x''^2,\\
&S_2 = \mathsf{sep}(T_2)/y = 3x^2x''x'''' - 4x^2x'''^2 + 2xx'x''x''' + 6xx''^3 + 2x'^2x''^2.
\end{aligned}$$

It can be verified (in 95.4 seconds) that $\mathsf{prem}(K_1, \mathbb{T}_i) = 0$ for $i = 1, \ldots, 6$, so that Kepler's first law follows from Newton's two laws. The total proving time is 106.5 CPU seconds [see Remark 3].

In fact, the d-tri forms $\mathbb{T}_1$ and $\mathbb{T}_2$ are both reducible. Using our factoring methods (cf. [Wang 94b]), it is easy to verify that $[T_1, T_2, H_1]$ is irreducible and H_2 in both $\mathbb{T}_1$ and $\mathbb{T}_2$ can be factorized algebraically as

$$H_2 \doteq (xa + x''r)(xa - x''r)/x^2. \tag{8}$$

Therefore, $\mathbb{T}_1$ can be further decomposed into two irreducible d-tri forms

$$\mathbb{T}_{11} = [T_1, T_2, H_1, xa + x''r], \quad \mathbb{T}_{12} = [T_1, T_2, H_1, xa - x''r],$$

and $\mathbb{T}_2$ into

$$\begin{aligned}
\mathbb{T}_{21} &= [xx''' + 2x'x'', xy' - x'y, H_1, xa + x''r],\\
\mathbb{T}_{22} &= [xx''' + 2x'x'', xy' - x'y, H_1, xa - x''r]
\end{aligned}$$

such that

$$\mathsf{Zero}(\mathfrak{P}) = \bigcup_{j=1}^{2} \mathsf{Zero}(\mathbb{T}_{1j}/x''yrS_2) \cup \mathsf{Zero}(\mathbb{T}_{2j}/x''r) \cup \bigcup_{i=3}^{6} \mathsf{Zero}(\mathbb{T}_i/y'').$$

The algebraic factorization (8) can be explained as follows. From $H_1 = 0$ and $H_2 = 0$, one knows that the ratio of the length of the radius vector compared with that of the acceleration vector is r/a. Hence, when $N_2 = 0$ is assumed, the ratio of the corresponding vector components may differ from r/a only by sign, i.e.,

$$x/x'' = y/y'' = \pm r/a.$$

This relation is just reflected by (8).

For (ii), consider

$$\mathfrak{P}^* = [\{K_1, K_2, H_1, H_2\}, \{a\}]$$

as the hypothesis d-pol system, where $K_2 = H_2$. We found that $\mathfrak{P}^*$ can also be decomposed (in 28.5 seconds) into 6 quasi-irreducible d-tri systems $[\mathbb{T}_i^*, \mathbb{U}_i^*]$ with

$$\begin{aligned} &\mathbb{T}_1^* = \mathbb{T}_1, && \mathbb{T}_2^* = [xy' - x'y, H_1, H_2],\\ &\mathbb{T}_3^* = [x, r - y, a - y''], && \mathbb{T}_4^* = [x, r - y, a + y''],\\ &\mathbb{T}_5^* = [x, r + y, a - y''], && \mathbb{T}_6^* = [x, r + y, a + y''],\\ &\mathbb{U}_i^* = \mathbb{U}_i,\ i = 1, \ldots, 6 \end{aligned}$$

(under the same ordering above). The pseudo-remainder of N_1 wrt $\mathbb{T}_i^*$ (computed in 118.7 seconds) is 0 for $i = 1$ and non-zero for $i = 2, \ldots, 6$. Hence, the theorem is conditionally true with the subsidiary condition provided as

$$x(xy' - x'y) \neq 0.$$

Therefore, Kepler's two laws imply Newton's first law under the condition that the ellipse does not degenerate to two lines or points.

If the major axis of the ellipse is taken as the x-axis, then K_1 is simplified to

$$\bar{K}_1 = x'r'' - x''r'.$$

It is somewhat easier to compute a zero decomposition for $[\{\bar{K}_1, K_2, H_1, H_2\}, \{a\}]$, which is the same as that for $\mathfrak{P}^*$, excepting that T_1 and T_2 are replaced by two simpler d-pols – let the first d-tri form so obtained be $\bar{\mathbb{T}}_1$. Then, verifying the 0 remainder of N_1 wrt $\bar{\mathbb{T}}_1$ takes much less time (3.6 seconds). It is also easy to check that the following d-pol

$$N_3 = [x'(xy' - x'y)^2]^2 - [r^2 a(xr' - x'r)]^2$$

has 0 remainder wrt $\bar{\mathbb{T}}_1$. $N_3 = 0$ corresponds to the relation

$$r^2 a = \pm h^2/p$$

given in [Wu 91]. Thus, one can conclude that, under the assumption of K1 and K2, the third law K3 of Kepler and N3 of Newton are equivalent.

Remark 4. The computing times for this example may demonstrate one aspect about the efficiency of our zero decomposition algorithm in comparison with Ritt-Wu's [Chou and Gao 93a, Ritt (50), Wu 89, Wu 91]. Ritt-Wu's algorithm computes a zero decomposition of the form (7) with prem$(\mathbb{P}, \mathbb{T}_i) = \{0\}$ verified for each i. The verification is very time-consuming in most cases. $\mathbb{T}_1$ above is actually a (quasi-) d-characteristic set of $\mathbb{P}$, and verifying prem$(N_1, \mathbb{T}_1) = 0$ takes 110.1 seconds, which are more than six times the total decomposition time (and eleven times when redundant d-tri systems are not removed) for our algorithm. In the case (ii), the verification of prem$(K_1, \mathbb{T}_1) = 0$ takes 90.3 CPU seconds.

Using the same method, one can investigate other relations among Kepler's and Newton's laws. As shown by Wu, Chou and Gao that some of the laws can be derived or discovered automatically from the others, our method with modification may be used to formula derivation as well, following a general device introduced in [Wu 87c, Wu 91] and the techniques developed in [Chou and Gao 92].

Acknowledgements

This work has been supported by FWF and CEC under ESPRIT Basic Research Project 6471 (MEDLAR II) and CNRS-MRE under project inter-PRC "Mécanisation de la Déduction."

References

[Carrà Ferro 94] Carrà Ferro, G. An extension of a procedure to prove statements in differential geometry. *J. Automated Reasoning* **12** (1994), 351–358.

[Carrà Ferro and Gallo 90] Carrà Ferro, G. and Gallo, G. A procedure to prove statements in differential geometry. *J. Automated Reasoning* **6** (1990), 203–209.

[Chou and Gao 91] Chou, S. C. and Gao, X. S. Theorems proved automatically using Wu's method – Part on differential geometry (space curves) and mechanics. *MM Research Preprints* 6 (1991), 37–55.

[Chou and Gao 92] Chou, S. C. and Gao, X. S. Automated reasoning in differential geometry and mechanics using characteristic method – III. In: *Automated Reasoning* (Z. Shi, ed.), pp. 1–12. North-Holland: Elsevier Science Publ. (1992).

[Chou and Gao 93a] Chou, S. C. and Gao, X. S. Automated reasoning in differential geometry and mechanics using the characteristic set method – I, II. *J. Automated Reasoning* **10** (1993), 161–189.

[Chou and Gao 93b] Chou, S. C. and Gao, X. S. Automated reasoning in differential geometry and mechanics using the characteristic method – IV. *Syst. Sci. Math. Sci.* **6** (1993), 186–192.

[Li 91] Li, Z. M. Mechanical theorem proving of the local theory of surfaces. *MM Research Preprints* 6 (1991), 102–120.

[Ritt (50)] Ritt, J. F. *Differential Algebra*. New York: Amer. Math. Soc. (1950).

[Seidenberg 56] Seidenberg, A. An elimination theory for differential algebra. *Univ. California Publ. Math.* (N.S.) **3**(2) (1956), 31–66.

[Wang 94a] Wang, D. M. An elimination method for differential polynomial systems I. Preprint, LIFIA-Institut IMAG (1994).

[Wang 94b] Wang, D. M. Algebraic factoring and geometry theorem proving. In: *Proc. CADE-12, Lecture Notes in Comput. Sci.* **814** (1994), pp. 386–400.

[Wang 95] Wang, D. M. Elimination procedures for mechanical theorem proving in geometry. *Ann. Math. Artif. Intell.* (in press).

[Wu 79] Wu, W.-T. On the mechanization of theorem-proving in elementary differential geometry (in Chinese). *Sci. Sinica* Special Issue on Math. (I) (1979), 94–102.

[Wu 82] Wu, W.-T. Mechanical theorem proving in elementary geometry and elementary differential geometry. In: *Proc. 1980 Beijing DD-Symp.*, Vol. 2, pp. 1073–1092. Beijing: Science Press (1982).

[Wu 87a] Wu, W.-T. A constructive theory of differential algebraic geometry. In: *Proc. 1985 Shanghai DD-Symp., Lecture Notes in Math.* **1255** (1987), pp. 173–189.

[Wu 87b] Wu, W.-T. A mechanization method of geometry and its applications – II. curve pairs of Bertrand type. *Kexue Tongbao* **32** (1987), 585–588.

[Wu 87c] Wu, W.-T. Mechanical derivation of Newton's gravitational laws from Kepler's laws. *MM Research Preprints* 2 (1987), 53–61.

[Wu 89] Wu, W.-T. On the foundation of algebraic differential geometry. *Syst. Sci. Math. Sci.* **2** (1989), 289–312.

[Wu 91] Wu, W.-T. Mechanical theorem proving of differential geometries and some of its applications in mechanics. *J. Automated Reasoning* **7** (1991), 171–191.

Managing Editor's Column

Vol. 1, No. 10; October 28, 1995

Dear Readers:

Volume 1, No.10. of J.UCS contains two papers on multimedia and hypermedia systems, and one of a more theoretical nature. Hope you will enjoy them!

As some of you know, the refereeing process in J.UCS works as follows: abstracts of submited papers go to all editors (over 170), and editors interested in refereeing the paper at issue then receive the full paper. This works better than sending papers to referees for review for obvious reasons. It also produces surprises: the paper on "Authoring on the Fly" evidently was very intriguing from both title and abstract so that over 20 editors asked to review it! We thus expect that the paper will also be extremely popular with readers.

Here is another bit of news, and a bit of good news, indeed: the whole volume 1 of J.UCS including all necessary tools to peruse it will be pressed on a CD-ROM by Springer by February 96...together with titles and information on Springer publications: for this reason 30.000 (!!!) CD's will be pressed, giving J.UCS and all the papers in J.UCS much visibility. Thus, if you still want to make sure that one of your papers is widely distributed (more widely than with most other publications) hurry up and submit your manuscript for the December issue.

Cordially

Hermann Maurer
email: hmaurer@iicm.tu-graz.ac.at

Journal of Universal Computer Science, vol. 1, no. 10 (1995), 675-686
submitted: 31/05/95, accepted: 7/10/95, appeared: 28/10/95

An aperiodic set of Wang cubes [1]

Karel Culik II [2]
Department of Computer Science
University of South Carolina
Columbia, S.C. 29208
Jarkko Kari
Iterated Systems, Inc.
3525 Piedmont Road, Seven Piedmont Center, Suite 600
Atlanta, G.A. 30305-1530

Abstract: We introduce Wang cubes with colored faces that are a generalization of Wang tiles with colored edges. We show that there exists an aperiodic set of 21 Wang cubes, that is, a set for which there exists a tiling of the whole space with matching unit cubes but there exists no periodic tiling. We use the aperiodic set of 13 Wang tiles recently obtained by the first author using the new method developed by the second. Our method can be used to construct an aperiodic set of n-dimensional cubes for any $n \geq 3$.

Key Words: discrete mathematics, automata theory, aperiodic tilings, Wang tiles, Wang cubes, sequential machines
Categories: G.2, F.1.1

1 Introduction

Wang tiles are unit square tiles with colored edges. The tile whose left, right, top and bottom edges have colors l, r, t and b, respectively, is denoted by the 4-tuple (l, r, t, b). A *tile set* is a finite set of Wang tiles. *Tilings* of the infinite Euclidean plane are considered using arbitrarily many copies of the tiles in the given tile set. The tiles are placed on the integer lattice points of the plane with their edges oriented horizontally and vertically. The tiles may not be rotated. A tiling is *valid* if everywhere the contiguous edges have the same color.

Let T be a finite tile set, and $f : \mathbb{Z}^2 \to T$ a tiling. Tiling f is *periodic* with period $(a, b) \in \mathbb{Z}^2 - \{(0,0)\}$ iff $f(x, y) = f(x + a, y + b)$ for every $(x, y) \in \mathbb{Z}^2$. If there exists a periodic valid tiling with tiles of T, then there exists a *doubly periodic* valid tiling, i.e. a tiling f such that, for some $a, b > 0$, $f(x, y) = f(x + a, y) = f(x, y + b)$ for all $(x, y) \in \mathbb{Z}^2$. A tile set T is called *aperiodic* iff (i) there exists a valid tiling, and (ii) there does not exist any valid periodic tiling.

R. Berger in his well known proof of the undecidability of the tiling problem [2] refuted Wang's conjecture that no aperiodic set exists, and constructed the first aperiodic set containing 20426 tiles. He shortly reduced it to 104 tiles. Between 1966 and 1978 progressively smaller aperiodic sets were found by Knuth, Läuchli, Robinson, Penerose and finally a set of 16 tiles by R. Ammann. A discussion of these and related results is in chapters 10 and 11 of [6]. Recently, the second author developed a new method for constructing aperiodic sets that is not based on geometry, as are the earlier ones, but on sequential machines that multiply real numbers by rational constants. This approach makes short and precise correctness arguments possible. He used it to construct a new aperiodic set containing only 14 tiles over 6 colors in [8]. The first author added an additional trick in [3] and obtained an aperiodic set consisting of 13 tiles over 5 colors which we will use here to construct an aperiodic set of Wang cubes.

General 3-D tilings have been extensively studied as applied to crystallography and theoretical physics, see [7]. We introduce Wang cubes, the obvious generalization of Wang tiles to three dimensions. A *Wang cube* is a unit cube with colored faces. The cube with colors l, r, f, g, t, b at the left, right, front, back, top, bottom faces, respectively, will be denoted by the six-tuple (l, r, f, g, t, b). A cube set is a finite set of Wang cubes. We consider 3-D tilings of the infinite Euclidean 3-D space using arbitrarily many copies of the Wang cubes from the given cube set. The cubes are placed on the integer lattice points of the space with their sides oriented parallel to the xy, xz and yz coordinate planes. The cubes may not be rotated. A tiling is valid if everywhere the contiguous faces have the same color.

Let S be a cube set and $f : \mathbb{Z}^3 \to S$ a 3-D tiling. Tiling f is *periodic* with period $(a, b, c) \in \mathbb{Z}^3 - \{(0,0,0)\}$ if $f(x,y,z) = f(x+a, y+b, z+c)$ for every $(x,y,z) \in \mathbb{Z}^3$. A cube set S is called *aperiodic* if

(i) there exists a valid 3-D tiling, and
(ii) there does not exist any valid periodic 3-D tiling.

Clearly, we can extend our definition to n-dimensional Wang cubes and n-dimensional tilings.

A 3-D tiling $f : \mathbb{Z}^3 \to S$ is called *triply periodic* if for some $a, b, c > 0$, and for all $x, y, z \in \mathbb{Z}$ we have $f(x,y,z) = f(x+a,y,z) = f(x,y+b,z) = f(x,y,z+c)$.

Note that in a plane every set of tiles that admits a periodic tiling also admits a doubly periodic tiling. Similarly, in space the existence of a doubly periodic 3-D tiling implies the existence of a triply periodic tiling. However, there are sets of cubes that admit a periodic tiling but not any triply periodic tiling, for example, sets W_1 and W_2 in Section 4.

In Section 2 we review the relation between sets of Wang tiles and sequential machines, introduce the balanced representation of reals, and show how to construct a sequential machine that implements the multiplication of a number in balanced representation by a constant. These techniques are then used in Section 3 to construct tile set T_{13} and prove its aperiodicity. We include Sections 2 and 3 not only to make this paper self-contained but because we need to use some properties of the computations of the sequential machine corresponding to T_{13} in the proof of our main result in Section 4. In the last Section we construct three sets of cubes which are progressively less and less periodic. The first, W_1, admits tilings which are periodic in every non-horizontal direction. The second set, W_2, admits tilings that could be periodic in the vertical direction only. Finally, we present our main result, an aperiodic set of 21 cubes over 7 colors.

2 Balanced representation of numbers, sequential machines and tile sets

For an arbitrary real number r we denote by $\lfloor r \rfloor$ the integer part of r, i.e. the largest integer that is not greater than r, and by $\{r\}$ the fractional part $r - \lfloor r \rfloor$.

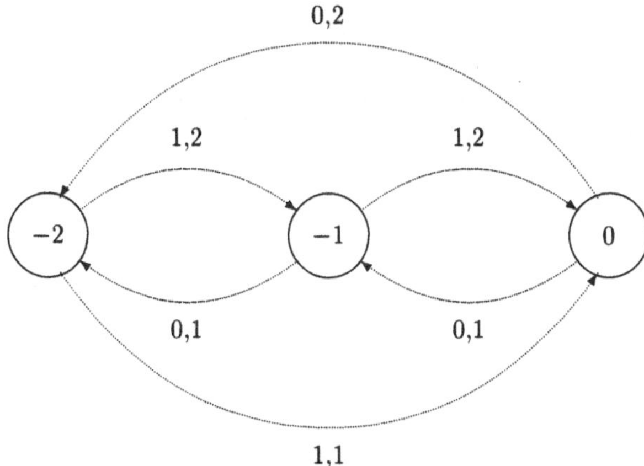

Figure 1: Sequential machine M_3.

In proving that our tile set can be used to tile the plane we use *Beatty sequences* of numbers. Given a real number α its bi-infinite Beatty sequence is the integer sequence $A(\alpha)$ consisting of the integral parts of the multiples of α. In other words, for all $i \in \mathbb{Z}$,

$$A(\alpha)_i = \lfloor i \cdot \alpha \rfloor.$$

Beatty sequences were introduced by S.Beatty [1] in 1926.

We use sequences obtained by computing the differences of consecutive elements of Beatty sequences. Define, for every $i \in \mathbb{Z}$,

$$B(\alpha)_i = A(\alpha)_i - A(\alpha)_{i-1}.$$

The bi-infinite sequence $B(\alpha)_i$ will be called the *balanced* representation of α. The balanced representations consist of at most two different numbers: If $k \leq \alpha \leq k+1$ then $B(\alpha)$ is a sequence of k's and $(k+1)$'s. Moreover, the averages over finite subsequences approach α as the lengths of the subsequences increase. In fact, the averages are as close to α as they can be: The difference between $l \cdot \alpha$ and the sum of any l consecutive elements of $B(\alpha)$ is always smaller than one.

For example,

$$B(1.5) = \ldots 121212\ldots,\ B(\tfrac{1}{3}) = \ldots 001001\ldots \text{ and } B(\tfrac{8}{3}) = \ldots 233233\ldots.$$

Now, we introduce sequential machines which define mappings on bi-infinite strings. We will use them to implement multiplication of numbers in balanced representation and later shown that they are isomorphic to set of tiles.

A *sequential machine* is a 4-tuple $M = (K, \Sigma, \Delta, \gamma)$ where K is the set of states, Σ is the input alphabet, Δ is the output alphabet, and $\gamma \subseteq K \times \Sigma \times \Delta \times K$ is the transition set. Sequential machine M can be represented by a labeled directed graph with nodes K and an edge from node q to node p labeled a, b for each transition (q, a, b, p) in γ.

Machine M computes a relation $\rho(M)$ between bi-infinite sequences of letters. A bi-infinite sequence x over set S is a function $x : \mathbb{Z} \to S$. We will abbreviate $x(i)$ by x_i. Bi-infinite sequences x and y over input and output alphabets, respectively, are in relation $\rho(M)$ if and only if there is a bi-infinite sequence s

of states of M such that, for every $i \in \mathbb{Z}$, there is a transition from s_{i-1} to s_i labeled by x_i, y_i.

For a given positive rational number $q = \frac{n}{m}$, let us construct a sequential machine (nondeterministic Mealy machine) M_q that multiplies a real number in balanced representation $B(\alpha)$ by q. The states of M_q will represent all possible values of $q\lfloor r \rfloor - \lfloor qr \rfloor$ for $r \in \mathbb{R}$. Because

$$q\lfloor r \rfloor - 1 \leq qr - 1 < \lfloor qr \rfloor \leq qr < q(\lfloor r \rfloor + 1),$$

we have

$$-q < q\lfloor r \rfloor - \lfloor qr \rfloor < 1.$$

Because the possible values of $q\lfloor r \rfloor - \lfloor qr \rfloor$ are multiples of $\frac{1}{m}$, they are among the $n + m - 1$ elements of

$$S = \{-\frac{n-1}{m}, -\frac{n-2}{m}, \ldots, \frac{m-2}{m}, \frac{m-1}{m}\}.$$

S is the state set of M_q.

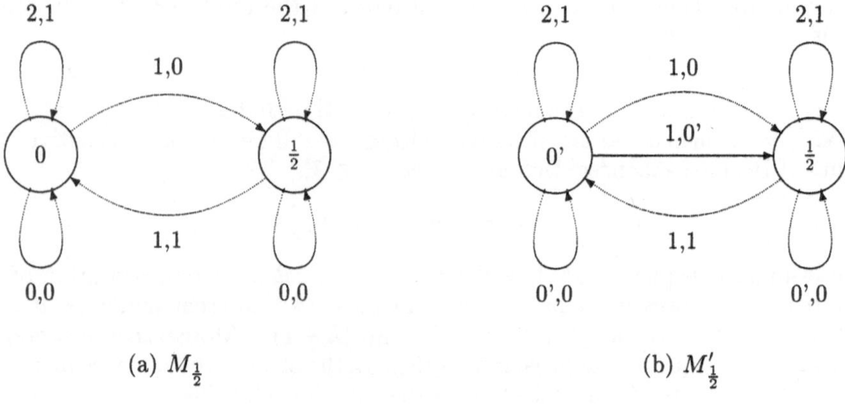

Figure 2: Sequential machines $M_{\frac{1}{2}}$ and $M'_{\frac{1}{2}}$.

The transitions of M_q are constructed as follows: There is a transition from state $s \in S$ with input symbol a and output symbol b into state $s + qa - b$, if such a state exists. If there is no state $s + qa - b$ in S then no transition from s with label a, b is needed. After reading input $\ldots\ B(\alpha)_{i-2}\ B(\alpha)_{i-1}$ and producing output $\ldots\ B(q\alpha)_{i-2}\ B(q\alpha)_{i-1}$, the machine is in state

$$s_{i-1} = qA(\alpha)_{i-1} - A(q\alpha)_{i-1} \in S.$$

On the next input symbol $B(\alpha)_i$ the machine outputs $B(q\alpha)_i$ and moves to state

$$\begin{aligned} s_{i-1} + qB(\alpha)_i - B(q\alpha)_i &= qA(\alpha)_{i-1} + qB(\alpha)_i - (A(q\alpha)_{i-1} + B(q\alpha)_i) \\ &= qA(\alpha)_i - A(q\alpha)_i \\ &= s_i \in S \end{aligned}$$

The sequential machine was constructed in such a way that the transition is possible. This shows that if the balanced representation $B(\alpha)$ is a sequence of input letters and $B(q\alpha)$ is over output letters, then $B(\alpha)$ and $B(q\alpha)$ are in relation $\rho(M_q)$.

Sequential machine M_3 in Fig. 1 is constructed in this fashion for multiplying by 3, using input symbols $\{0,1\}$ and output symbols $\{1,2\}$. This means that $B(\alpha)$ and $B(3\alpha)$ are in relation $\rho(M_3)$ for all real numbers α satisfying $0 \leq \alpha \leq 1$ and $1 \leq 3\alpha \leq 2$, that is, for all $\alpha \in \left[\frac{1}{3}, \frac{2}{3}\right]$. Similarly, $M_{1/2}$, shown in Fig. 2(a), is constructed for input symbols $\{0,1,2\}$ and output symbols $\{0,1\}$, so that $B(\alpha)$ and $B(\frac{1}{2}\alpha)$ are in relation $\rho(M_{1/2})$ for all $\alpha \in [0,2]$.

Our intention is to iterate sequential machines M_3 and $M_{\frac{1}{2}}$ without allowing $M_{\frac{1}{2}}$ to be used more than twice in a row. To assure that we modify $M_{\frac{1}{2}}$ by introducing new input/output symbol $0'$ and changing its diagram to $M'_{\frac{1}{2}}$ as shown in Fig. 2(b). We also change the state 0 to $0'$ to make the sets of states of M_3 and $M'_{\frac{1}{2}}$ disjoint. That allows us to view the union of M_3 and $M'_{\frac{1}{2}}$ as one sequential machine M.

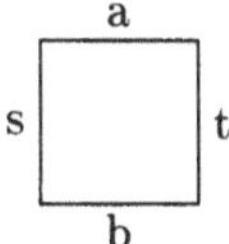

Figure 3: The tile (s,a,b,t) corresponding to the transition $s \xrightarrow{a,b} t$

There is a one-to-one correspondence between the tile sets and sequential machines which translates the properties of tile sets to properties of computations of sequential machines.

A finite tile set T over set of colors C_{EW} on east-west edges and set of colors C_{NS} on north-south edges is represented by sequential machine $M = (C_{EW}, C_{NS}, C_{NS}, \gamma)$ where $(s,a,b,t) \in \gamma$ iff there is a tile (s,a,b,t) in T , see Fig. 3.

Obviously, bi-infinite sequences x and y are in the relation $\rho(M)$ iff there exists a row of tiles, with matching vertical edges, whose upper edges form sequence x and lower edges sequence y. So there is a one-to-one correspondence between valid tilings of the plane, and bi-infinite iterations of the sequential machine on bi-infinite sequences.

Clearly, the two conditions for T being aperiodic can be translated to conditions on computations of M. Clearly, set T is aperiodic if (i) there exists a bi-infinite computation of M, and (ii) there is no bi-infinite word w over C_{NS} such that $(w,w) \in [\rho(M)\ ]^+$, where ρ^+ denotes the transitive closure of ρ.

3 An aperiodic set of tiles

We say that the tile in Fig. 3 multiplies by q if $aq + s = b + t$.

Let denote by T_3 and by $T_{\frac{1}{2}}$ the tile sets representing the sequential machines M_3 and $M'_{\frac{1}{2}}$, respectively. Therefore, T_3 and $T_{\frac{1}{2}}$ multiply by 3 or by 1/2, respectively. The tile set $T_{13} = T_3 \cup T_{\frac{1}{2}}$, consisting of 13 tiles, is shown in Fig. 4.

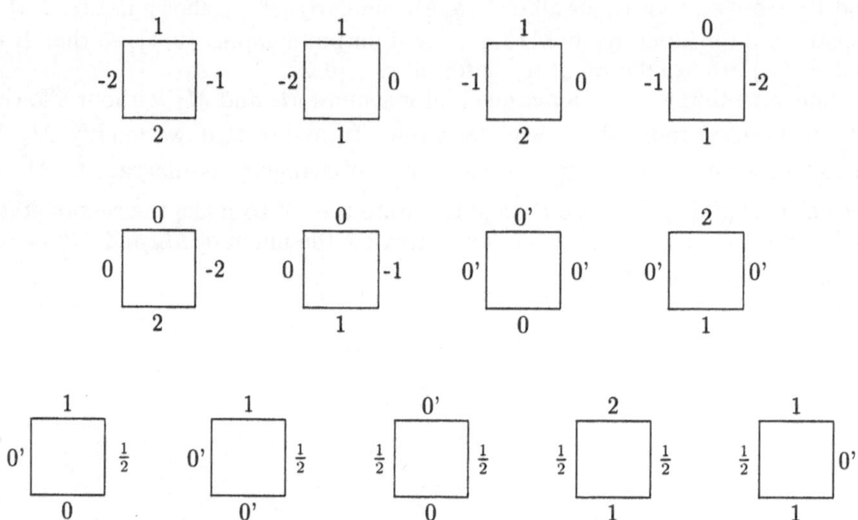

Figure 4: T_{13} — an aperiodic set of 13 Wang tiles

Now, we proceed to prove that T_{13} is an aperiodic set of tiles.

Theorem 1. *The tile set T_{13} is aperiodic.*

1. We show that set T admits uncountably many valid tilings of the plane. For any $\alpha \in [\frac{1}{3}, 2]$, from the input sequence $B(\alpha)$ the sequential machine M computes output $B(3\alpha)$ if $\alpha \in [\frac{1}{3}, \frac{2}{3}]$ and output $B[\frac{\alpha}{2}]$ if $\alpha \in [\frac{2}{3}, 2]$. In the latter case, if $\alpha \in [1, 2]$ then output $\frac{\alpha}{2} \in [\frac{1}{2}, 1]$ can be encoded in alphabet $\{0, 1'\}$ and if $B\frac{\alpha}{2} \geq \frac{2}{3}$ the second application of M computes $\frac{\alpha}{4} \in [\frac{1}{3}, \frac{1}{2}]$ represented in alphabet $\{0, 1\}$. In any case, the machine M can be applied again using the previous output as input, and this may be repeated arbitrary many times.

On the other hand, if $\alpha \in [\frac{1}{3}, 2]$ there is input $B(\frac{\alpha}{3})$ or $B(2\alpha)$, that is in relation $\rho(M)$ with $B(\alpha)$. Input sequence $B(\frac{\alpha}{3})$ is used for $\alpha \geq 1$, and $B(2\alpha)$ for $\alpha \leq 1$. This can be repeated many times so M can be iterated also backwards. Hence, for every bi-infinite $B(\alpha), \alpha \in [\frac{1}{3}, 2]$, there is a bi-infinite iteration yielding a tiling of the plane.

2. Now, we show that the tile set T does not admit a periodic tiling. Assume that $f : \mathbb{Z}^2 \to T$ is a doubly periodic tiling with horizontal period a and vertical period b. We can inspect that there is no tiling for $b = 1$ or 2 so we can assume that $b \geq 3$. Since no more than two consecutive rows of tiles can consist of tiles from subset $T_{1/2}$, we can assume without loss of generality that in row zero the

tiles are from T_3. Let n_i denote the sum of colors on the upper edges of tiles $f(1,i), f(2,i), \ldots, f(a,i)$. Because the tiling is horizontally periodic with period a, the "carries" on the left edge of $f(1,i)$ and the right edge of $f(a,i)$ are equal.

Therefore $n_{i+1} = q_i n_i$, where $q_i = 3$ if tiles from T_3 are used in row i and $q_i = \frac{1}{2}$ if tiles from $T_{1/2}$ are used. Because the vertical period of tiling is b,

$$n_1 = n_{b+1} = q_1 q_2 \ldots q_b . n_1 .$$

Since tiles from T_3 are used for $i = 0$, there are no 0's on the upper edges of the first row and thus $n_1 \neq 0$. Hence, $q_1 q_2 \ldots q_b = 1$. This contradicts the fact that no nonempty product of 3's and $\frac{1}{2}$'s can be 1.

We now show a property of valid tilings by $T_1 3$ which we will need in the next section.

Lemma 2. *On every valid tiling of the plane by T_{13} there exists arbitrarily long horizontal sequences of tiles with 2 on the upper edge.*

Proof. Let $f : \mathbb{Z}^2 \longrightarrow T_{13}$ be a valid tiling. For every $i \in \mathbb{Z}$ let $q_i = 3$ ($q_i = \frac{1}{2}$) iff T_3 ($T_{\frac{1}{2}}$, respectively) is used on row i. Let $n_{N,i}$ denote the sum of the upper edges of tiles $f(1,i), f(2,i), \ldots f(N,i)$, for every $N > 0$ and $i \in \mathbb{Z}$. Because the tiles on the i'th row multiply by q_i, and because the difference between available carries is at most 2, we have for every $i \in \mathbb{Z}$ and $N > 0$,

$$|n_{N,i+1} - q_i \cdot n_{N,i}| \leq 2.$$

Therefore, for every $N, m > 0$,

$$|n_{N,m} - q_0 q_1 \ldots q_{m-1} \cdot n_{N,0}| \leq 2(1 + q_0 + q_0 q_1 + \ldots + q_0 \cdot \ldots \cdot q_{m-2}) \leq 12m.$$

The last inequality follows from the fact that $q_i q_{i+1} \cdot \ldots \cdot q_{i+j}$ is always at most 6.

Let ε be an arbitrarily small positive number. In the following we show that for every large enough N there exists m such that $\frac{n_{N,m}}{N} > 2 - 14\varepsilon$. Consequently the upper edges of tiles $f(1,m), \ldots, f(N,m)$ must contain a long sequence of 2's. (On the average, only every $1/(14\varepsilon)$'th symbol may be 1.)

Because $\log_2 3$ is an irrational number, the set $\{m \log_2 3 \bmod 1 | m \in \mathbb{Z}_+\}$ is dense in $[0,1]$. This means that for any subinterval $I \subset [0,1]$ there exists a number M such that $\forall x \, \exists m < M$, m positive, such that $x + m \log_2 3 \bmod 1 \in I$. Let us choose $I = [\log_2(2 - 13\varepsilon), \log_2(2 - 12\varepsilon)]$, and let M be as above.

Let $N > 12M(1 + \log_2 3)/\varepsilon$ be so large that for every $i \in \mathbb{Z}$, $\frac{n_{N,i}}{N}$ is at least $1/3 - \varepsilon$. This is possible because there cannot be three consecutive 0's on the upper edges of the tiles on the valid tiling f. Now, choose $x = \log_2(\frac{n_{N,0}}{N})$. There exists a positive integer $m < M$ such that $x + m \log_2 3 - k \in I$, where k is a positive integer not greater than $M \log_2 3$. This means that

$$2 - 13\varepsilon \leq \frac{n_{N,0}}{N} \frac{3^m}{2^k} \leq 2 - 12\varepsilon.$$

Necessarily $q_0 q_1 \ldots q_{m+k-1} = \frac{3^m}{2^k}$. Otherwise the product would be either at most $\frac{3^{m-1}}{2^{k+1}}$ or at least $\frac{3^{m+1}}{2^{k-1}}$. This would mean that $\frac{n_{N,0}}{N} q_0 q_1 \ldots q_{m+k-1} \leq 1/3 - 2\varepsilon$ or $\geq 12 - 78\varepsilon$. Because $m + k < M(1 + \log_2 3)$ we know that

$$\left| \frac{n_{N,m+k}}{N} - q_0 q_1 \ldots q_{m+k-1} \cdot \frac{n_{N,0}}{N} \right| \leq 12(m+k)/N < \varepsilon.$$

So we would have either $\frac{n_{N,m+k}}{N} < 1/3-\varepsilon$ (a contradiction), or $\frac{n_{N,m+k}}{N} > 12-79\varepsilon$ (a contradiction, if ε is small). We conclude that $q_0q_1\ldots q_{m+k-1} = \frac{3^m}{2^k}$, and consequently

$$2-14\varepsilon \leq \frac{n_{N,m+k}}{N} \leq 2-11\varepsilon.$$

4 Wang cube sets

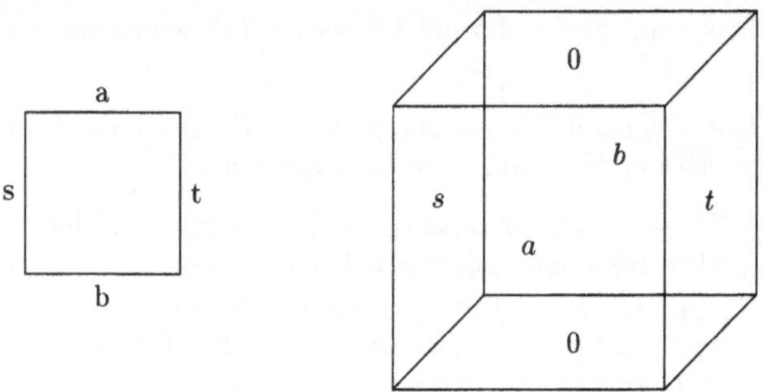

Figure 5: Corresponding Wang tile and Wang cube in Example 1.

Example 1. We convert each tile from tile set T_{13} into a Wang cube by using the edge colors at the corresponding vertical faces, and a uniform color on all horizontal faces, see Fig. 5. Formally,

$$W_1 = \{(s,a,b,t,0,0) \mid (s,a,b,t) \in T_{13}\}.$$

Given any period $(a,b,c) \in \mathbb{Z}^3, c \neq 0$, set W_1 admits a 3-D tiling with period (a,b,c). Indeed, we can choose any 2-D tiling $f : \mathbb{Z}^2 \to T_{13}$ and define 3-D tiling $g : \mathbb{Z}^3 \to W_1$ by $g(x,y,z) = f(x - \lfloor\frac{az}{c}\rfloor, y - \lfloor\frac{bz}{c}\rfloor)$. Clearly, $g(x+a,y+b,z+c) = g(x,y,c)$ for all $x,y,z \in \mathbb{Z}$.

Example 2. Now we construct Wang cube set W_2 that admits tilings periodic at most in one direction. We modify the construction from Example 1. to force identical tilings at all horizontal levels, see Fig. 6. Formally, we define

$$W_2 = \{(s,a,b,t,s,s) \mid (s,s,b,t) \in T_{13}\}$$

In every bi-infinite computation of sequential machine M (corresponding to set T_{13}) a bi-infinite sequence of bi-infinite strings of states uniquely determines the bi-infinite sequence of bi-infinite strings of inputs. Therefore in every valid 3-D tiling $g : \mathbb{Z}^3 \to W_2$ all horizontal levels are identical, i.e. $g(x,y,z) = g(x,y,0)$ for all $x,y,z \in \mathbb{Z}$. Since every horizontal level simulates a 2-D tiling valid for T_{13} and therefore is aperiodic, clearly, g is periodic with period $(0,0,1)$, and its multiples, but with no other period.

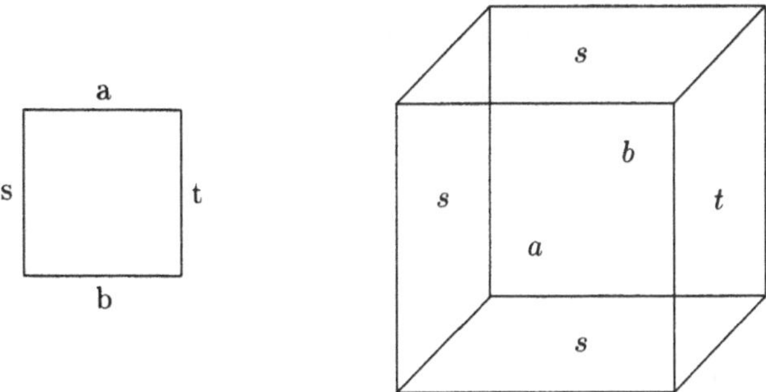

Figure 6: Corresponding Wang tile and Wang cube in Example 2.

Finally, we construct a cube set that does not admit any aperiodic 3-D tiling.

Theorem 3. *There exists an aperiodic set of 21 Wang cubes over 7 colors.*

Proof. We will modify a simplified version of the cube set W_2 from the previous example to prevent the periodicity of its tilings in the vertical direction. According to Lemma 2, on any valid tiling by T_{13} there are arbitrarily long horizontal blocks of tiles $(0', 2, 1, 0')$ or $(\frac{1}{2}, 2, 1, \frac{1}{2})$. We will prevent the periodicity by simulating a simple cellular automaton (trellis automaton, see [4]) on blocks of cubes corresponding to blocks of $(0', 2, 1, 0')$ -tiles or blocks of $(\frac{1}{2}, 2, 1, \frac{1}{2})$ -tiles. We choose this cellular automaton so that its computations will have a period at least as big as the size of its input, i.e. the size of the block of identical tiles. Now, we proceed with technical details, $\oplus$ denotes the operation exclusive-or (addition mod 2).

Let $T_9 = T_{13} - \{(0', 2, 1, 0'), (\frac{1}{2}, 1, 1, 0'), (\frac{1}{2}, 2, 1, \frac{1}{2}), (0', 1, 1, \frac{1}{2})\}$, and define $W_{21} = A \cup B \cup C$, where

$$A = \{((s, 1), a, b, (t, 1), (1, 1), (1, 1)) \mid (s, a, b, t) \in T_9\},$$

$$B = \{((s, x), 2, 1, (s, y), (1, x), (1, x \oplus y)) \mid s \in \{0', \frac{1}{2}\}, x, y \in \{0, 1\}\},$$

$$C = \{((\frac{1}{2}, 1), 1, 1, (0', x), (0, 1), (0, 1)), ((0', 1)1, 1, (\frac{1}{2}, x), (0, 1), (0, 1)) \mid x \in \{0, 1\}\}.$$

First, we have simplified the colors on the horizontal faces of cubes from W_2 by coloring by 0 the faces of the cube that simulates the tiles $(0', 2, 1, 0')$ and $(\frac{1}{2}, 2, 1, \frac{1}{2})$, and coloring by 1 all the other horizontal faces. Then we added a second bit to the colors of all the faces except front and back. For 9 of the cubes, simulating the tiles of T_9, we have made the second bit always 1 so there are no new cubes. The four cubes corresponding to the tiles $(\frac{1}{2}, 1, 1, 0')$ and $(0', 1, 1, \frac{1}{2})$ differ in the second bit in the right face which is the only one that can be either 0 or 1. Finally, for the tiles $(0', 2, 1, 0')$ and $(\frac{1}{2}, 2, 1, \frac{1}{2})$ we created 8 new cubes (4 for each tile) so that the second bits at the top and at the right face are arbitrary, the second bit at the left face is the same as at the top, and the second bit at the bottom is equal to the exclusive-or of the second bits at the top and at the right face. The values of the second bits in the four new cubes (vertical cuts) from B, corresponding to each of the tiles, are shown in Fig. 7.

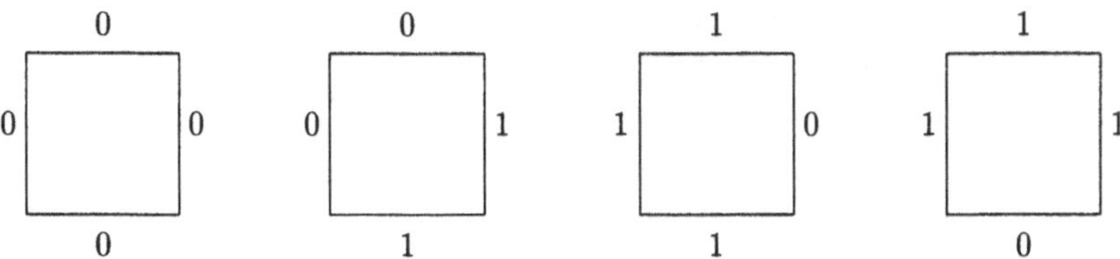

Figure 7: The second bits in each four-tuple of the cubes from B

Since there must be large blocks of either $(0', 2, 1, 0')$ or $(\frac{1}{2}, 2, 1, \frac{1}{2})$ in each 2-D tiling valid for T_{13}, which must match at all horizontal levels, there must be arbitrary wide vertical bi-infinite strips consisting entirely of cubes from B bordered on left in each row by one cube from C. Our choice of bit values guarantees that each row of the cubes in these strips simulates one step of the computation of the trellis type cellular automaton each cell of which computes the logical operation exclusive-or (or equivalently addition mod 2). Indeed, the values of the "second bits" at each cube are first copied, half step to the left (identity) and then the bottom bit is set to the exclusive-or of the left and right bit (same as the left bit of the right neighbor). The whole cellular automaton is deterministic (in the top-down direction) since the first right neighbor out of the block has always new bit 1 in the left face. The neighbor on the left side is always a cube from C and the value of the second bit in its right face is uniquely determined.

Since it is well known (see e.g. [4]) that the exclusive-or cellular automaton always repeats its initial value (string from $\{0,1\}^*$) in no less steps than the size of input we conclude that every strip itself is periodic with a period not shorter than its width. Since there are arbitrary wide strips no tiling admitted by W_{21} is periodic.

Clearly, every 3-D tiling admitted by W_2 can be converted into a tiling admitted by W_{21}, hence W_{21} is an aperiodic set of Wang cubes.

Set T_{13} requires 4 different colors on the horizontal edges, and 5 different colors (states) on the vertical edges. Since we "split" two of the states (colors of vertical edges) and use two bits for the colors of the horizontal faces the set W_{21}, requires 7, 4, and 4 distinct colors at faces parallel to yz, xz, and xy, respectively. Since no rotation of the cubes is allowed max(7,4,4) = 7 distinct colors is sufficient.

References

[1] Beatty,S.: "Problem 3173"; Am. Math. Monthly 33 (1926) 159; solutions in 34 (1927) 159.

[2] Berger,R.: "The Undecidability of the Domino Problem"; Mem. Amer. Math. Soc. 66 (1966).

[3] Culik II,K.: "An aperiodic set of 13 Wang tiles"; Discrete Math., to appear.

[4] Culik II,K. and Dube,S.: " Fractal and Recurrent Behavior of Cellular Automata"; Complex Systems 3, 253-267 (1989).

[5] Culik II,K. and Kari,J.: "Sequential Machines and aperiodic sets of Wang tiles"; manuscript.

[6] Grünbaum,B. and Shephard,G.C.: "Tilings and Patterns"; W.H.Freeman and Company, New York (1987).
[7] Jaric,M.V.: "Introduction to the Mathematics of Quasicrystals"; Academic Press, Inc., San Diego (1989).
[8] Kari,J.: "A small aperiodic set of Wang tiles"; Discrete Math., to appear.

Acknowledgements

The authors are grateful to V. Valenta for implementing several algorithms for testing 2-D tile sets and composing 3-D tile sets, and for comments to the draft of this paper.

Journal of Universal Computer Science, vol. 1, no. 10 (1995), 687-705
submitted: 11/7/95, accepted: 14/11/95, appeared: 28/10/95 © *Springer Pub. Co.*

Contained Hypermedia

Erik Duval
(Departement Computerwetenschappen, Katholieke Universiteit Leuven, Belgium
Erik.Duval@cs.kuleuven.ac.be)

Henk Olivié
(Departement Computerwetenschappen, Katholieke Universiteit Leuven, Belgium
olivie@cs.kuleuven.ac.be)

Nick Scherbakov,
(Institute for Information Processing and Computer Supported New Media (IICM),
Graz University of Technology, Austria
nsherbak@iicm.tu-graz.ac.at)

Abstract: We propose a new hypermedia data model, called CHM for Contained HyperMedia. Our model is based on set-oriented data structuring, with a strong emphasis on automatic maintenance of link integrity. In this paper, the CHM model is presented in detail: both data structuring, navigational facilities and authoring support are presented. We will also explain how we have integrated support for the CHM model in Home, our Hypermedia Object Management Environment, publicly accessible through the World-Wide Web.

Key Words: hypermedia data modeling, automatic link maintenance
Category: H.2.1,H.5.1, I.7.2

1 Introduction

The most simple hypermedia data model is the *basic node-link paradigm:* information is organized in chunks, usually called 'nodes' and interrelated by 'links' [Conklin 1987, Nielsen 1990]. As has been reported before [Andrews, et al. 1995b, Duval, Olivié 1995, Maurer, et al. 1994, Srinivasan, Scherbakov 1995], the simplicity of the basic node-link paradigm leads to a number of problems:

- navigating the links between nodes, users quickly become disoriented (the so-called *"lost in hyperspace"* problem);
- manual *link maintenance* is a tedious burden in large-scale hypermedia systems: whenever e.g. a node is deleted, all references to it must be updated or dangling references will arise;
- most hypermedia systems based on the basic node-link paradigm (notably the World-Wide Web [Berners-Lee, et al. 1994, Cailliau 1995], hereafter referred to as WWW) emphasize *retrieval rather than modification* of information and *individual rather than cooperative* creation and use of the information.

The basic challenge in any attempt to overcome these problems is to propose additional or alternative data structuring facilities, while retaining as much as possible the simplicity and flexibility of the basic node-link paradigm.

For this purpose, we have developed a new hypermedia data model, based on set-oriented data structuring, with a strong emphasis on automatic maintenance of link integrity. Our model is strongly influenced by early work in this area [Parunak 1991], the HM data model [Andrews, et al. 1995c, Maurer, et al. 1994, Srinivasan, Scherbakov 1995] and the SOS model [Duval, et al. 1995].

Our hypermedia model is supported in Home, our Hypermedia Object Management Environment [Duval, et al. 1995, Duval, Olivié 1995]. Home can be considered as a second-generation WWW server [Andrews, et al. 1995b]. In fact, we rely on an ordinary WWW server and use the Common Gateway Interface (CGI) mechanism to add functionality to the server. Home supports:

- more sophisticated data structuring and navigation facilities, so that a *more structured view on the server content* is presented to end users;
- *automatic support of link integrity*, using a set based hypermedia model with automatically maintained navigational topologies, as will be explained further on;
- navigational and query based *access* to the server contents, as well as *authoring* facilities, all through ordinary WWW clients.

The remainder of this text is structured as follows: section 2 introduces the CHM data model. Section 3 deals with navigational facilities in the CHM model. The authoring process is described in section 4. In section 5, we present the concept of "slots". Some implementation aspects are dealt with in section 6. Section 7 compares the results described here with some of our previous work and with related work in general. Before the final conclusion, we mention some of our plans for the future in section 8.

2 Contained Hypermedia Model

2.1 Informal Overview

In the CHM model, content is encapsulated in *multimedia objects*. These are not specified in detail; their only property relevant here is that they can be 'visualized'. This may for instance correspond to showing an image, a video clip or a computer animation. Visualisation of multimedia objects should be understood in a very loose sense here: it can refer to a non-visual action like playing a sound sequence or a more complex series of events, such as for instance an interactive question/answer application.

The basic data structure of the CHM model is a *container*. As will be explained further on, containers are used to structure information in a hypermedia fashion.

To each container is associated a set of zero or more *members*. Each member consists of:

- a *label*: This is a multimedia object. The label defines the content of the member and indicates how the member should be visualized.
- a *container*: This component models the substructure defined by the member, as it consists in turn of a set of members.
- a *ranking*: this is a non-negative integer number, used to determine which members are accessible when a particular member of the container is current.

If a member consists of a label only, then it represents content without further structure: although the multimedia object that acts as a label may possess internal structure, this is not considered in the CHM model, where multimedia objects are 'black boxes'. In this sense, labels are similar to for instance non-HTML documents in the WWW: such documents cannot contain substructure either.

If the member consists of a container only, then its visualisation is not elaborated, but it does define a navigable substructure. This is similar to the status of a menu in Gopher, which can only contain references to submenus or documents and does not contain any multimedia content itself.

If neither the label nor the container are empty, then the label defines the content and the container defines the internal structure of the member.

One of the members is called the *head.* It has a special status as will be further elaborated below.

The function of a member is similar to that of a node in the basic node link paradigm: it acts as the unit of data. The concept of membership replaces that of traditional links, as will be elaborated in the next section.

Membership of containers does not need to be hierarchical: containers can be shared when they belong to members of different containers. Loops, representing recursive relationships, are also allowed.)

2.2 An Example

Consider for instance figure 1: this could be part of a CHM data structure for a Campus-Wide Information System (CWIS). The squares represent containers, the ovals labels. The rankings are indicated between brackets.

In this structure, a professor is modeled by a container with three members:

- two with
  - a label, and
  - a container

  for the courses he teaches and his publications, and
- one with an empty container for his curriculum vitae.

Labels A and B are multimedia objects that visualize the member they belong to in the context of the container *Professor*. Label A could for instance be a video clip of the professor, explaining what his courses are about. Label B can be a list of the more recent of his publications.

Suppose this particular professor teaches two courses, one on databases and another on the Pascal programming language. The container on the database course contains course schedules (label E can for instance be the current schedule, or can indicate where and when the next three lectures take place), reference material for the students, lecture notes, grades (a member probably not freely accessible to everybody, see below) and the practicals submitted by the students (e.g. database schemas they have designed with a CASE tool). The reference material includes a textbook the professor has co-authored with another expert, two standard textbooks and the most influential papers in the field.

One important point is that the container that models the book on databases is *shared* by:

- the container with reference material for the database course, and

– the container with all publications of the professor.

In order to visualize the container *Book on Databases* differently in the two contexts it belongs to, different labels are associated to it in the two containers it belongs to. The label N for instance can adhere to a common format for all publications of this professor, whereas the label J can indicate why this book is relevant as reference material for the course on databases, or for instance which parts of the book are obligatory reading and which parts aren't, etc.

Moreover, there is a *loop* in the data structure: the container on the professor contains a member on his publications, which contains a member on the book, which contains a member on the authors, which contains a member on the professor, etc. (ad infinitum).

Sharing and loops are also illustrated by figure 2, another representation of the CHM data schema of figure 1. Here, a container is linked to his members by directed links from the container to the ranking of the member, from the ranking to its label, and from the label to the container that is part of the member. The loop *Professor – Publications – Book on Databases – Authors – Professor* is evident, as is the fact that the container *Book on Databases* is shared by *Reference Material* and *Publications*. This figure should not give the wrong impression though that the CHM model is equivalent to a hypermedia model based on nodes and labeled links: the arrows in figure 2 do *not* represent links, but rather which members belong to which containers.

3 Navigation

3.1 Introduction

In the CHM model, there is always a *current container* that defines the navigational context. The current container always contains a *current member*. (A container with zero members can never become the current container, see also below.) When a new container becomes current, the head of that container becomes the current member.

3.2 Accessible Members

The CHM model relies on the ranking of members to determine which members are accessible, based on the following rule: *if a member with ranking k is current, then all members with ranking $k-1$, k or $k+1$ are accessible.*

That is why there is a requirement that, for each two rankings k_1 and k_2 with $k_1 \neq k_2$, there must be a member with ranking k for all $k_1 < k < k_2$. This property guarantees that, eventually, all members from a container can be accessed.

As an illustration, consider a container $c = \{(l_1, c_1, k_1), ..., (l_n, c_n, k_n)\}$. In figure 3, different topologies for c are represented, based on different rankings of the members (l_i, c_i, k_i) in c, using the same notation as in figure 1. The arrows point from a member m to all members that are accessible when m is the current member.

In case (a) of figure 3, all members have the same ranking. The result is that, whatever the current member, all members are always accessible. In case (b), the ranking of the members results in a linear sequence: if the current member is not the first (last), then the previous (next) member is accessible. In case (c), all other members are accessible when (l_2, c_2) or (l_3, c_3) is current. When (l_1, c_1) or (l_4, c_4) is current, then only (l_2, c_2) and (l_3, c_3) are accessible. Case (d) can be interpreted along similar lines.

An important consequence of this approach is that *link integrity can be maintained automatically* at all times: in terms of the CHM model, links correspond to membership. Now, if a new member m is added to a container c, then the ranking of m automatically determines when m is accessible. The member m must not be linked manually to the other members of c. Conversely, when m is removed from c, it doesn't need to be explicitly un-linked from the other members of c.

3.3 Access

When Access is applied to a member, then that member becomes the current one, and its label (if non-empty) is visualized: this will typically involve the display of multimedia information on the screen, but it might also be a more complex event, e.g. an interactive question and answer application. The function of a label is to carry information about the member, as appropriate within the container that the member belongs to.

Consider e.g. the following container with seven members:

'Multimedia, Hypertext and Hypermedia' =
{ ('A','General Literature on Hypermedia and Multimedia',1),
('B','Hypermedia Data Models',1)
('C','Hypermedia Systems',1)
('D','Hypermedia Concepts',1)
('E','Hypermedia Applications',1)
('F','Multimedia and Hypermedia Standards',1)
('G','Multimedia',1) }

If a user accesses the second member, then multimedia object 'B' is visualized: this could e.g. be an introduction on hypermedia data models and their role in hypertext and hypermedia systems. The label enables a reader to get information about a member, in terms that are relevant within the navigational context of the current container and without leaving that context.

An important point is that the label associated with a destination is *context-dependent.* Consider e.g. the following container:

'Data Modeling' = { ('X','Database Data Models',1),
('Y','Hypermedia Data Models',1)
('Z','Knowledge Representation',1) }

In this container, another label (multimedia document 'Y') is associated to the same container 'Hypermedia Data Models'. This document 'Y' can explain what hypermedia is all about, rather than label 'B' that deals with the relevance of data modeling in the context of hypermedia.

3.4 Zooming In, Out and Up

The navigational context can be changed by applying the Zoom_In operation on the current member. (This is only possible if the current member is non-empty.) The effect of this operation is that the container of the current member becomes the current container. Its head becomes the current member. If the label of that head is non-empty, then it is visualized.

The opposite effect can be achieved by applying the Zoom_Out operation: basically, the situation before the last Zoom_In is reinstated. By zooming in and out, users can focus more or less on the information presented in a particular container.

An important point is that the navigational context of the container is retained when members are accessed. Only when the user zooms in on a member does a new navigational paradigm become active.

Operations Container_Up and Label_Up identify all containers that contain the current container or label in their members. The user can then zoom in on one of those members. This enables a user to explore all contexts a particular container or label participates in.

In the hypermedia data models the authors developed before (the HM model [Andrews, et al. 1995c, Maurer, et al. 1994, Srinivasan, Scherbakov 1995] and the SOS model [Duval, et al. 1995, Duval, Olivié 1995]), similar operations are defined.

3.5 An Example

In order to make the above more concrete, let us consider the following example, an implementation in Home of the two containers mentioned above. If the container Multimedia, Hypertext and Hypermedia is the current container, and (B,Hypermedia Data Models,1) is the current member, then a screen like figure 4 is presented.

The lower part of the screen displays the label B (an introduction on data modeling within a hypermedia context). The middle and upper part display the navigational context: it indicates the current container, the current member (in italics, in the list of accessible members) and the accessible members.

The current member (Hypermedia Data Models) can be zoomed in upon and the accessible members of the current container can be accessed. (The differences between the icons in front of the names are not very clear on figure 4). Suppose for instance the end user zooms in on the current member (Hypermedia Data Models), by clicking on the icon in front of that member in the list of members of the current container. Figure 5 shows the resulting screen.

In figure 5, the container of the current member is Basic Node Link Paradigm because the author of the container Hypermedia Data Models defined this member as the head. Following the same approach as before, the end user can now zoom in on the current member or access another one.

3.6 Search

As an alternative access paradigm, both labels and containers can be searched for as well, by imposing search constraints on their attributes. Figure 6 e.g. shows the search screen for articles. (These can act as labels.) Search patterns can be defined for any number of attributes and -if the user has the appropriate access rights- the result is a dynamically generated container with a member for each object that satisfies the search criteria. If the object searched for is a multimedia object, then this object will act as a label of a member with an empty container. Otherwise, if containers are searched for, the members of the dynamically generated container will have empty labels.

4 Authoring

4.1 Creation

In this section, we will concentrate on the authoring process in CHM. It is important to note first that content creation, i.e. the design and implementation of multimedia objects, is beyond the scope of this discussion. Multimedia content can be created using a special-purpose authoring system. The result can then act as a label in the CHM model.

The process we discuss here deals with data structuring. This process typically starts with the creation of a container, that will act as a framework for a unit of information. The author then inserts members that include already defined multimedia documents as labels and other containers. In case the latter already exist, they are re-used, possibly in a context different from the one they were originally intended for - as mentioned above, the purpose of the label is exactly to allow integration of existing resources in the context of a new container.

Containers that are part of members can be further elaborated afterwards. In that case, the authoring process proceeds in a top-down way. A bottom-up authoring approach is also possible: in that case, containers are defined and gathered as members of other containers, that can in turn become part of yet other members, etc.

4.2 Deletion

It is important to note that, when a member $M = (A, B, k)$ is removed from a container C, the label A (a multimedia object) and the container B both survive as independent entities. It is only the relationship between A and B, within the context of C, and the relationship between M and the other members of C that are destroyed.

The navigational paradigm of C, as defined by the rankings of its members, is not corrupted when M is removed. This mechanism ensures *link integrity*, as no dangling references can arise. This is very important, especially in a large-scale environment where manual link maintenance is no longer feasible.

When a container C is deleted, all links encapsulated in C cease to exist as well. However, the labels and containers of the members of C survive as independent entities; only their interrelationships in the context of C are destroyed. If C itself belongs to a member $M = (L, C)$ of another container X, then C is replaced in M by a *slot*, i.e. a placeholder for a container (see section 5).

An important point is that *all operations are addressed to one particular container and do not affect other containers.* This leads to self-containment of containers (the more so as navigation is also contained is also encapsulated within a container, as explained in the previous section). Thus, a container is a self-containing module that can be edited and browsed independently of others. This is especially important when a container is re-used as a member of (and therefore in the context of) another container.

4.3 Example

Authoring along the lines discussed above can be carried out with ordinary WWW clients. Note that this is not so when WWW clients access ordinary WWW servers or the Hyper-G gateway [Cailliau 1995]. When the user activates the 'Create/Search' option, then he can define the relevant attribute values (e.g. name, author, etc.), using electronic forms similar to the one of figure 6.

Activation of the 'Add Member' option leads to a number of screens, in order to select the label (out of all available multimedia objects) the container to associate with the label, the container that the member will belong to and the ranking of the member.

5 Slots

The final fundamental notion of the CHM model is a *slot*, which is a placeholder for a container in a member. Slots are useful when an author wants to refer to a container that doesn't exist yet or anymore.

As an example of the first case, consider e.g. an author who wants to create information about database management systems. He can create different containers for such systems based on the hierarchical, network, relational and object-oriented data models. Following a top-down approach, he can first create the general container DBMS, with four members that have slots where the yet-to-be-authored containers for the four different models will fit:

```
DBMS = {(H,slot,1),(N,slot,1),(R,slot,1),(O,slot,1)}
```

where H, N, R and O represent labels that carry information about the hierarchical, network, relational and object-oriented models respectively.

As an example of the case where a slot is a placeholder for a container that doesn't exist any more, consider the case where the author re-uses a container on relational databases that has been elaborated by another author. Suppose that, for whatever reason, the latter author destroys his container. In that case, a slot will remain in the member that the now destroyed container belonged to. The author of the DBMS container can fit another container on relational databases in the slot, if and when such a container becomes available.

It is important to understand how slots and labels interrelate: when a member contains a slot, the label carries information about the sort of information that will be presented in the container that fits in the slot, and about the reason why this container can be a member of the encompassing container.

Another important point is the difference between a member

- with a label and no container, used to include multimedia information only (the label), and no further hypermedia structure;
- with a label and a slot, for the case where the container that will fit in the slot doesn't exist yet or any more;

– with a label and an empty container, in which case the container just happens to be empty (but members can be inserted into it at any time).

6 Some implementation details

As mentioned above, we have implemented the CHM model in the Home environment for management of distributed hypermedia objects [Duval, et al. 1995, Duval, Olivié 1995], although, currently, slots are not fully implemented.

Home includes a layer for multimedia data management. The content of multimedia objects is referred to by Universal Resource Locators, as defined in the WWW [Berners-Lee, et al. 1994, Cailliau 1995]. These multimedia objects can act as labels in the CHM implementation of Home. So, any document accessible over the WWW can act as a label in Home. It doesn't need to be stored in the Home server.

On the lowest relevant layer of Home, data are managed using a commercially available Relational DataBase Mangement System (RDBMS), in casu Oracle. As explained in [Duval, Olivié 1995, Duval, et al. 1995], using a DBMS for data management, rather than directly relying on the file system (as in regular WWW servers), results in extra functionality (ACID properties of transactions, access rights and user groups, query engine, etc.).

The software that implements functionality on top of the Oracle RDBMS has been developed in Tcl [Ousterhout 1994], using the OraTcl extension for interaction with the Oracle database.

Home is accessible to WWW clients through our WWW server, using the Common Gateway Interface (CGI) mechanism of the latter server to gateway requests from the WWW client to the Home server. The same mechanism is used to deliver the results, packaged in the form of dynamically generated HyperText Mark-up Language (HTML) documents.

The Home server can also be accessed in a more direct way, without passing through the WWW gateway. As an example, we have developed an authorinhg client in Tk [Ousterhout 1994].

As a partial summary of the previous section, three key points indicate the main added value of our server when compared to a regular WWW server:

– *link maintenance* is an automatic process, as a member will no longer be accessible when it is removed from a container; compare this situation with the frequent phenomenon of dangling references in the WWW;
– *search facilities* are fully integrated and offer a complementary access paradigm to navigation over hyperlinks;
– *update facilities* are available through any WWW client that supports electronic forms, whereas the standard WWW mode is read-only [Cailliau 1995].

For the above reasons, Home can be considered as a second-generation WWW server [Andrews, et al. 1995b].

7 Previous and Related Work

7.1 Previous Work

As explained in [Duval, et al. 1995], hypermedia facilities in Home used to be based on a very simple data model, called SOS, for "Sets Of Sets". This model is similar to the data model supported by the Gopher system [Obraczka, et al. 1993]. In fact, the SOS model corresponds to a CHM model without labels or slots. The result is a hierarchy of containers (possibly with sharing), which is probably quite appropriate in many database-like applications, but not when more advanced facilities are required (like e.g. in Computer-Aided Learning applications [Andrews, et al. 1995c, Hendrikx, et al. 1995, Srinivasan, Scherbakov 1995]).

The main difference with the HM model [Srinivasan, Scherbakov 1995] is the introduction in CHM of labels that describe the member they belong to in terms appropriate for the context of the current container. In the HM model, when a member is accessed, its head [Srinivasan, Scherbakov 1995] or label [Andrews, et al. 1995c] (a multimedia object associated to the member, whatever container it belongs to) is visualized. This means that the visualization of a member is fixed and cannot be adapted to the contexts of the different containers it belongs to. As mentioned before, labels should facilitate re-use of existing resources in new contexts.

7.2 Related work

A number of other data models are similar to ours, particularly because they are also set based. These models only define data structuring facilities though, without the behavioural component that must be addressed in an object oriented approach.

- In *Hyper-G* [Andrews, et al. 1995a, Kappe, et al. 1993], documents can be grouped into collections. The latter can in turn belong to other collections. One of the members of a collection can be designed as head and will then be displayed automatically when the collection is accessed or zoomed in upon. A Hyper-G collection is somewhat similar to our container concept, but there is no construct in Hyper-G that corresponds to our notion of a context-dependent label. Moreover, hyperlinks can refer to other documents across collection boundaries, so that there is no self-containment of collections. This makes re-use of resources more difficult.
- In [Garzotto, et al. 1994], 'collections' (sets with an inner navigable structure) are added as a fundamental structuring unit to the Dexter model (see also below). Atomic values, called 'slots', are grouped in 'nodes'. The latter act as units of navigation, and can in turn be grouped into a collection. Roughly speaking, a slot in this model corresponds with a multimedia object in CHM. Nodes and collections both correspond with our notion of containers. In fact, we believe the distinction between slot (or rather, a node with one slot automatically created for each atomic value) and node is unnecessary and results in conceptual complications.
  The node associated to a collection in [Garzotto, et al. 1994] is similar to our notion of label, but the latter is context dependent, whereas the former is fixed for a collection. Also, [Garzotto, et al. 1994] defines no `Access`, but only a `Zoom_In` operation. Therefore, when a new collection becomes current, the existing navigational context is lost.

Other, non set based, approaches for advanced hypermedia modeling include e.g.:

- The *Dexter* model [Halasz, Schwartz 1994] is a formalized representant of the basic node link paradigm. The *storage layer* manages persistent components, that include a content, a set of attributes, a presentation specification an a set of anchors. Composite components reflect 'is part of' relationships. In the Dexter model, composites can only contain base components, which correspond to data objects, and cannot contain other composites.
- [Gronbaek 1994] generalizes the Dexter composite mechanism, in the context of the Dexter based *DEVISE Hypermedia* framework (DHM). An important difference with our notion of containers is that components 'do not know about which and how many composites they are members of'; hence, no equivalent to the `Zoom_out` operation in DHM. Moreover, the idea of local containment, both with regard to navigation and authoring, so important for re-use, is not addressed in DHM.
- *Microcosm* is based on an approach radically different from ours: navigation is controlled by a filtering mechanism [Hill, Hall 1994]. User made selections of documents (comparable to the traditional notion of anchors) can be sent to linkbases that deliver the corresponding destination documents.

8 Future

We have a number of ideas for further developments and applications of the Home system. Some of our more concrete plans for the future include:

- As explained above, membership of containers is extensionally defined, by manually inserting members, or by filling in slots. An alternative mechanism can rely on *intensional* membership, when a set of search criteria defines the members of a container. This mechanism is currently supported, but definition of intensional memberships cannot be achieved through ordinary WWW clients yet. Instead, the search criteria must be defined through a Tcl script that accesses the Oracle DBMS through an embedded SQL query.
- The data structuring facilities of our model can be used to define *data schemas*, that are an instantiation of the CHM model for a particular application domain, as is customary in the field of database design. On the one hand, a data schema based approach can be contradictory to the often much appreciated flexibility of the hypermedia approach; on the other hand, it can help to guarantee consistency of data structuring in large scale environments, such as e.g. a Campus-Wide Information System (CWIS). Although some research into this area has been carried out, we believe that this issue certainly deserves further investigation.
- We are currently developing some applications on top of Home. These include a self study course on basic computer science [Hendrikx, et al. 1995] and a project for European collaboration on courseware re-use. We are also investigating the possible use of Home in an information system on architecture and a Campus-Wide Information System.

9 Conclusion

Above, we have presented a new data model for hypermedia. Our model, called CHM, for Contained HyperMedia, follows a set based approach and supports self-containment of data units, both with regards to navigation and authoring. We believe our approach lends itself well for re-use of existing resources in a new context. The discussion of our model not only dealt with data structures, but also presented in some detail the operations for authoring and navigation. We have designed and implemented this model in the context of the Home system for distributed hypermedia management. Because the latter system is accessible to WWW clients, it can be considered a WWW server of the next generation, offering improved support for authoring and automatic link maintenance.

Acknowledgements

We wish to name explicitly Koen Hendrikx and Rudi Maelbrancke, both colleagues working at the computer science department of the K.U.Leuven, for the numerous discussions and their continued support. We also gratefully acknowledge the partial financial support provided by the Belgian National Fund for Scientific Research.

References

[Andrews, et al. 1995a] K. Andrews, F. Kappe, and H. Maurer. Serving information to the web with hyper-g. In *WWW95: Third International World-Wide Web Conference*, April 1995. Available from http://www.igd.fhg.de/www/www95/papers/105/hgw3.html.

[Andrews, et al. 1995b] K. Andrews, F. Kappe, H. Maurer, and K. Schmaranz. On second generation network hypermedia systems. In H. Maurer, editor, *Educational Multimedia and Hypermedia, 1995. Proceedings of ED-Media 95, World Conference on Educational Multimedia and Hypermedia*, pages 75–80, June 1995. Available from http://www.iicm.tu-graz.ac.at/Cedmedia.

[Andrews, et al. 1995c] K. Andrews, A. Nedoumov, and N. Scherbakov. Embedding courseware into the internet: Problems and solutions. In H. Maurer, editor, *Educational Multimedia and Hypermedia, 1995. Proceedings of ED-Media 95, World Conference on Educational Multimedia and Hypermedia*, pages 69–74, June 1995. Available from http://www.iicm.tu-graz.ac.at/Cedmedia.

[Berners-Lee, et al. 1994] T. Berners-Lee, R. Cailliau, A. Luotonen, H. F. Nielsen, and A. Secret. The world-wide web. *Communications of the ACM*, 37:76–82, Aug 1994.

[Cailliau 1995] R. Cailliau. About www. *Journal of Universal Computer Science*, 1:221–230, Apr 1995. Available from http://www.iicm.tu-graz.ac.at/Cjucs_root.

[Conklin 1987] J. Conklin. Hypertext: An introduction and survey. *IEEE Computer*, 2(9):17–41, September 1987.

[Duval, et al. 1995] E. Duval, H. Olivié, P. O'Hanlon, and D. G. Jameson. Home: an environment for hypermedia objects. *Journal of Universal Computer Science*, 1:265–287, May 1995. Available from http://www.iicm.tu-graz.ac.at/Cjucs_root.

[Duval, Olivié 1995] E. Duval and H. Olivié. A home for networked hypermedia. In H. Maurer, editor, *Educational Multimedia and Hypermedia, 1995. Proceedings of ED-Media 95, World Conference on Educational Multimedia and Hypermedia*, pages 193–198, June 1995. Available from http://www.iicm.tu-graz.ac.at/Cedmedia.

[Garzotto, et al. 1994] F. Garzotto, L. Mainetti, and P. Paolini. Adding multimedia collections to the dexter model. In *Proceedings of ECHT 94: European Conference on Hypermedia Technology*, pages 70–80, September 1994.

[Gronbaek 1994] K. Gronbaek. Composites in a dexter-based hypermedia framework. In *Proceedings of ECHT 94: European Conference on Hypermedia Technology*, pages 59–69, September 1994.

[Halasz, Schwartz 1994] F. Halasz and M. Schwartz. The dexter hypertext reference model. *Communications of the ACM*, 37:30–39, Feb 1994.

[Hendrikx, et al. 1995] K. Hendrikx, E. Duval, and H. Olivié. Hypermedia for open and flexible learning. In *WCCE95: Sixth IFIP World Conference on Computers in Education*, July 1995.

[Hill, Hall 1994] G. Hill and W. Hall. Extending the microcosm model to a distributed environment. In *ECHT94: ACM European Conference on Hypermedia Technology*, pages 32–40, September 1994.

[Kappe, et al. 1993] F. Kappe, H. Maurer, and N. Scherbakov. Hyper-g. a universal hypermedia system. *Journal of Educational Multimedia and Hypermedia*, 2:39–66, 1993.

[Maurer, et al. 1994] H. Maurer, N. Scherbakov, K. Andrews, and P. Srinivasan. Object-oriented modelling of hyperstructure: overcoming the static link deficiency. *Information and Software Technology*, 36:315–322, 1994.

[Nielsen 1990] J. Nielsen. *Hypertext and Hypermedia*. Academic Press, 1990.

[Obraczka, et al. 1993] K. Obraczka, P. B. Danzig, and S. Li. Internet resource discovery services. *IEEE Computer*, 26(9):8–22, September 1993.

[Ousterhout 1994] J. K. Ousterhout. *Tcl and the Tk toolkit*. Addison-Wesley, 1994.

[Parunak 1991] H. Van Dyke Parunak. Don't link me in: Set based hypermedia for taxonomic reasoning. In *Hypertext'91 Proceedings*, pages 233–242. ACM, December 1991.

[Srinivasan, Scherbakov 1995] P. Srinivasan and N. Scherbakov. Embedding infer engines into educational hypermedia. In H. Maurer, editor, *Educational Multimedia and Hypermedia, 1995. Proceedings of ED-Media 95, World Conference on Educational Multimedia and Hypermedia*, pages 603–608, June 1995. Available from http://www.iicm.tu-graz.ac.at/Cedmedia.

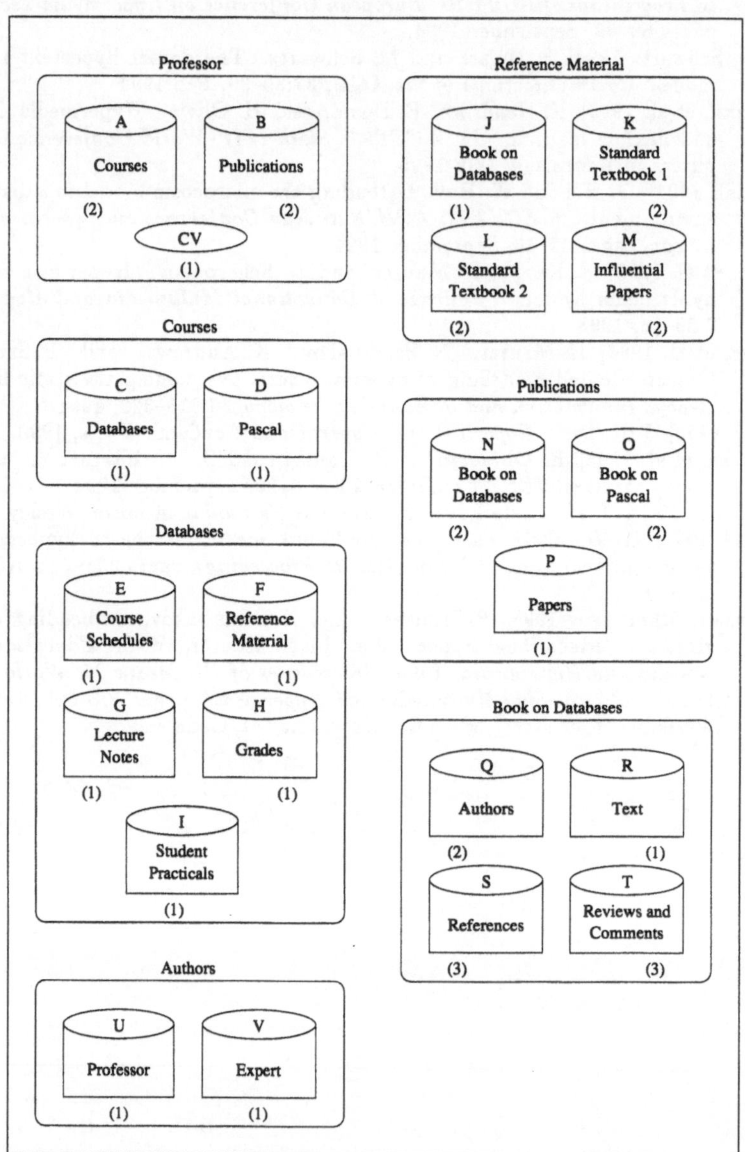

Figure 1: A CHM hypermedia corpus for a CWIS

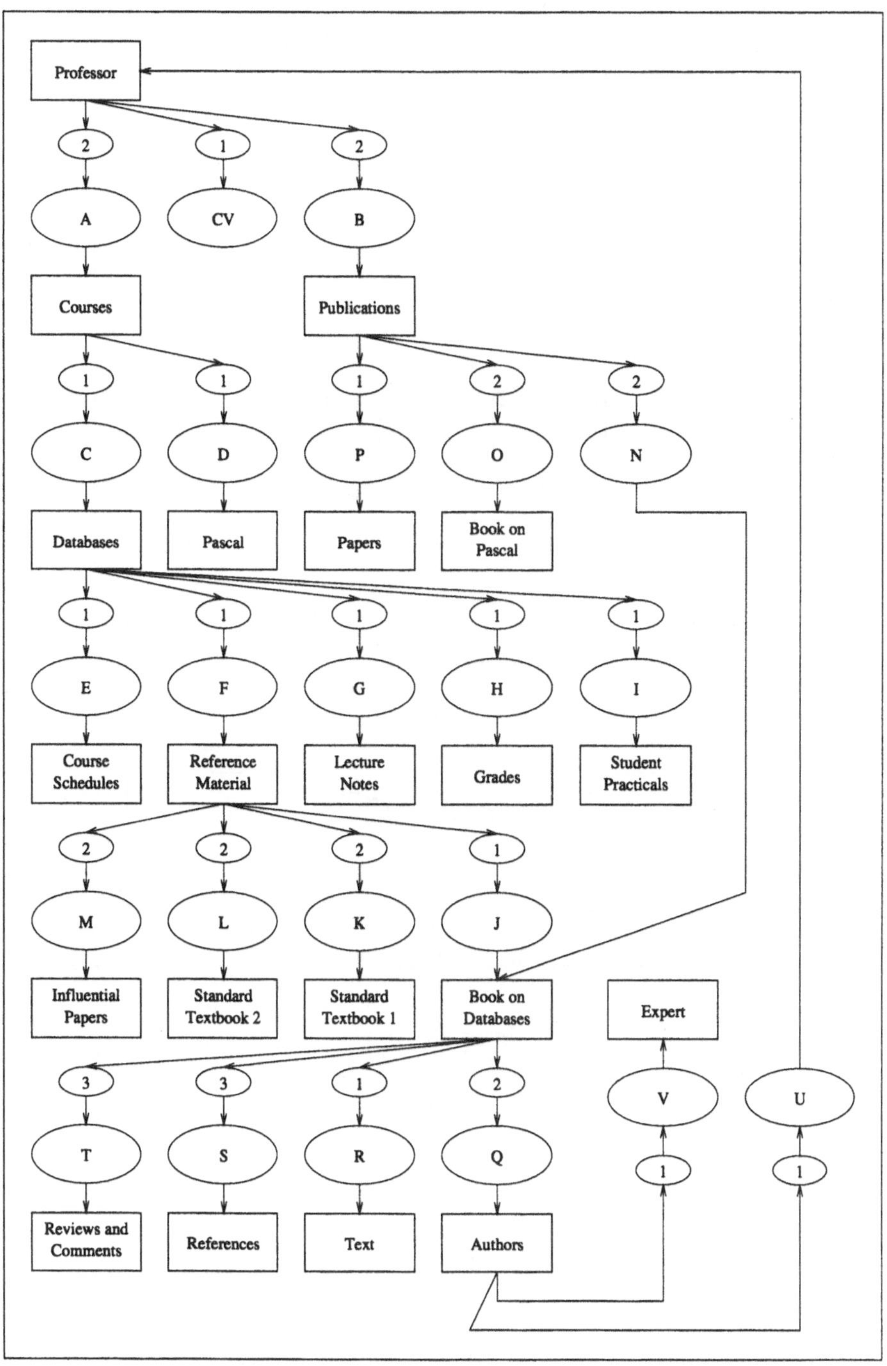

Figure 2: An alternative representation of the data schema

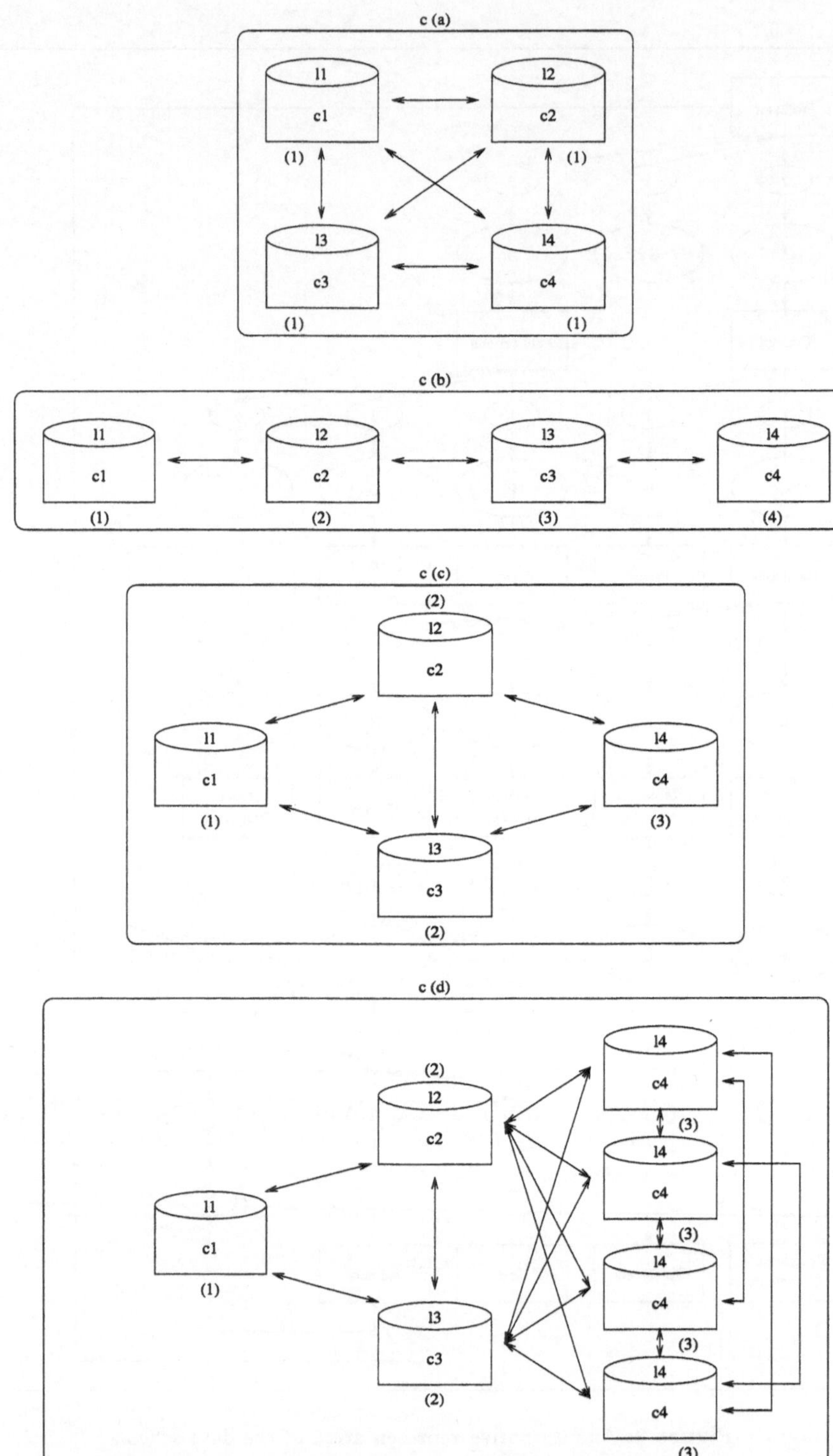

Figure 3: Accessible Members

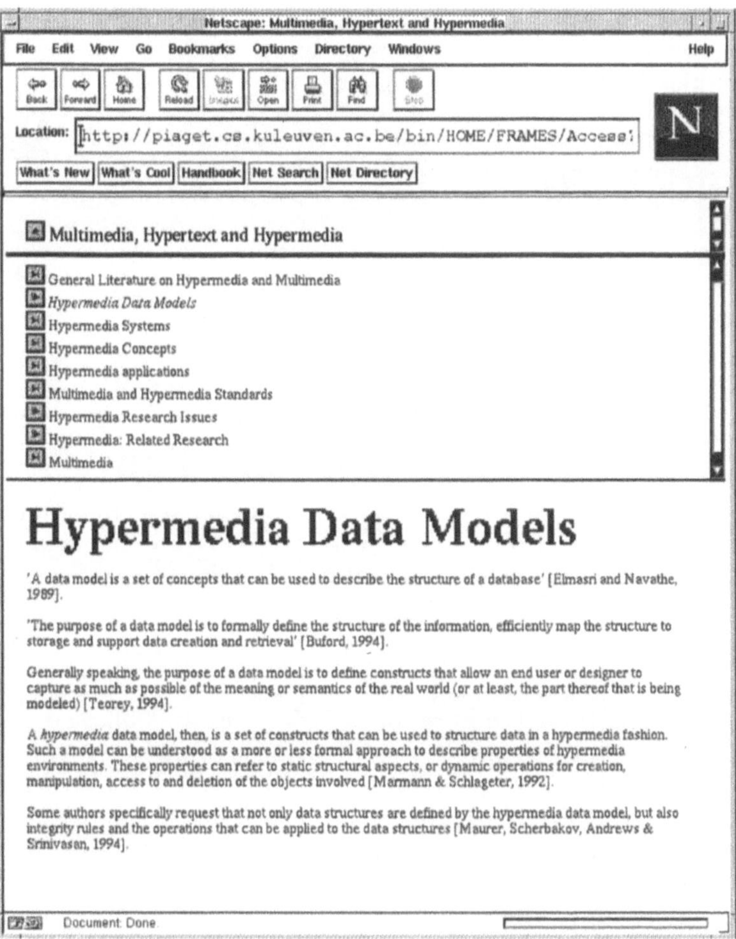

Figure 4: Current container is Multimedia, Hypertext and Hypermedia

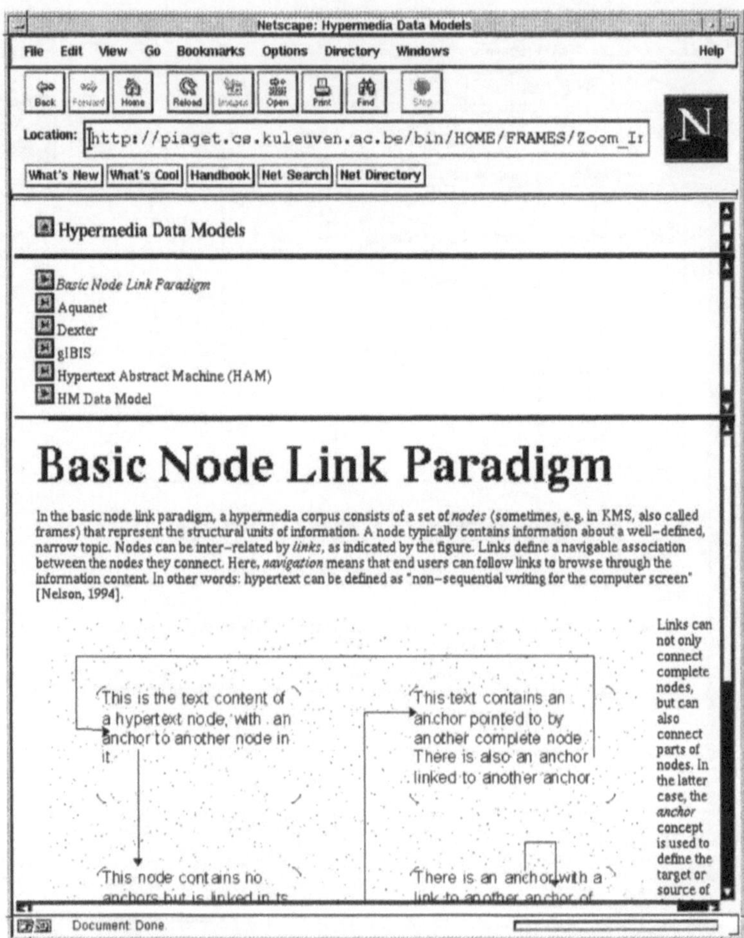

Figure 5: Current container is Hypermedia Data Models

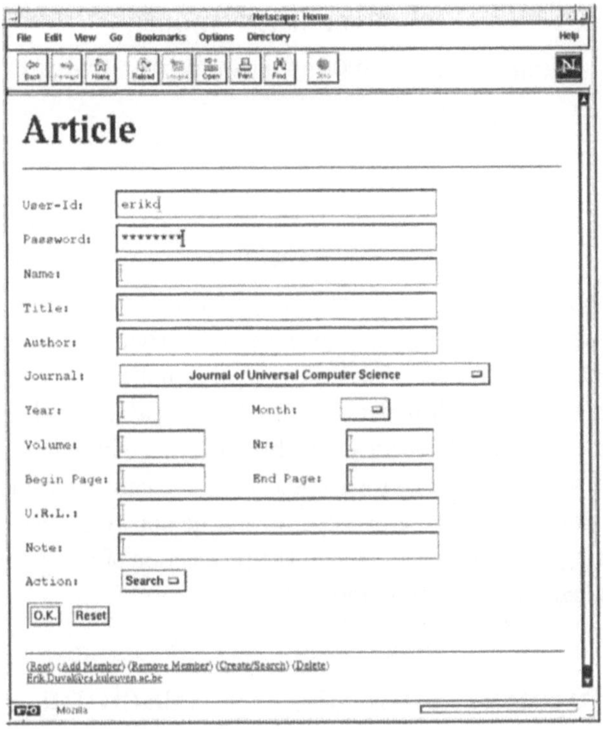

Figure 6: Client screen for searching

Journal of Universal Computer Science, vol. 1, no. 10 (1995), 706-717
submitted: 9/10/95, accepted: 16/10/95, appeared: 28/10/95

Authoring on the fly

Th. Ottmann, Ch. Bacher
Institut für Informatik
Universität Freiburg
bacher/ottmann@informatik.uni-freiburg.de

Abstract

We report about a new way of producing hypermedia documents for supporting teaching at universities. A computer held lecture is automatically converted into the core of a multimedia document and linked together with papers, textbooks, animations and simulations. As an electronic substitute of the blackboard we have used the whiteboard wb of the Mbone toolset and have transmitted the lecture also to remote locations. Our experiments demonstrate that classroom lecturing, distance teaching, and the production of educational hypermedia can be successfully integrated.

1 Computer support for teaching at university level

Today personal computers and workstations have spread over offices and laboratories not only in departments for computer science in universities all over the world. Teachers, students and even the administrative personnel have access to a wide variety of computer supported services inclusive access to the Internet.

This ubiquitous access to computers has resulted in a drastic change in the working behavior of instructors and students. The use of textprocessing, spreadsheeds, and database software has replaced traditional ways of writing, calculation and filing. Communication over the Internet by using electronic mail, news groups, conferences, and data exchange, are taken for granted today. The inclusion of computers in college lessons is becoming more attractive since hardware and software have reached a level at which a multimedia presentation of nontrivial content has become feasible. There are already many examples of successful use of new media in college teaching. These examples include computer support for displaying dynamic processes, visualisation of complex phenomena and simulations, as well as the access to full-text- and image- databases.

Nevertheless, college teaching is still dominated by the traditional style of lecturing, meaning teaching in the front of the classroom using the chalkboard and overhead projector. And students write their own notes on the professor's lecture. In addition, the students sometimes obtain copies of the transparencies used by the instructor in class. If they are lucky, they may read the lecture material in an accompanying textbook.

Especially mathematicians have developed a culture of not using any technology for lecturing at all. By using chalk and chalkboard (and almost no manuscript) they write down all essential parts and slowly develop definitions and proofs. Students go to the lectures because this developmental style of lecturing supports their understanding; reading the same material from a textbook requires more effort.

Computer science instructors have learned to use transparencies and the overhead projector in order to explain and comment long programs. A few of them may even use computer animation and visualization in order to explain a complicated algorithm. But the use of multimedia technology for teaching at university level is still an exception.

There are various reasons for the loyalty to traditional methods, such as the considerable amount of work and energy associated with the preparation of lectures as multimedia or even as linked hypermedia documents, lacking standards, rapidly changing technology, insufficient experience, and — last but not least — no clear perception of what the right form for passing knowledge is.

2 Possible ways out of the dilemma

Because instructors, as experts for a subject, would likely be little interested in the existing problems with the production and distribution of prepared multimedia for college teaching, it is necessary to search for ways to alleviate their burden while using their specific knowledge optimally. There are at least three possible ways to accomplish this:

2.1 The team approach

Teams are formed of instructors responsible for the content, experts for media technique (computer, network technique, design, distribution) and pedagogues (educators, cognitive scientists, psychologists). Together they prepare a theme for employment into college teaching as a multimedia teaching packet. The considerable time-consumption and financial burden with this form of multimedia preparation of content used for teaching results in confinement to content that is stable in the long term and which is standardized and useful in many locations. However, this form also offers the possibility of producing high-quality teaching material. There are already a few convincing examples on various subjects (for example, the CD ROM from Time Life "How Computers Work" [Med93], the CD ROM version of the book from Cormen Leiserson Rivest [CLR90], the physics program Albert [Wue94]).

2.2 Seperating form and content

The tools to be used when preparing courseware or multimedia material for teaching purpose still dominate today which were conceptualized according to the WYSIWYG principle. Their ever increasing functionality makes it very difficult for the unexperienced and casual user to produce high-quality material. Therefore, we suggested [AOS91], a new way of authoring multimedia courseware and implemented a prototype authoring system, called TRAIN (type and rule directed authoring). The TRAIN-system allows a strict separation of the logical content-structure of a course from its layout-structure. This is achieved by following well established principles underlying modern document preparation systems like LaTeX. With the help of LaTeX a scientist can bring an article on his research result or even a whole textbook into a form in accordance with the professional quality requirements traditionally guaranteed by printers and publishers and completed by specialists. Unfortunately there is no comparable tool available on the market to produce multimedia documents in a similar way.

2.3 Combining current and future lecturing technologies

Here the goal is to capture as much as possible the various advantages of the traditional form of preparation of college teaching material and to combine them with the advantages of multimedia computer systems.

That is, utilize the extensive experience of instructors to structure and present nontrivial content in lectures, but use the computer as an electronic substitute for a chalkboard or an overhead projector. Furthermore, convert a recorded computer lecture into the core of a hypermedia document for offline use and access.

The aim is that instructors do not become too much dependent on sophisticated technology but are still able to contribute considerably to the creation of a highly useful hypermedia document for teaching purposes.

There are already a few examples (such as the CD-ROM produced as the multimedia proceedings of a scientific conference [Glo94]) which show that high-quality material can result when lectures from conferences, which are held in a significantly traditional manner, are converted into a multimedia document and distributed on a CD-ROM.

In the rest of this paper we will report about first steps into this direction, an approach which we have called *authoring on the fly* in order to express that the process of creating a multimedia document is more a byproduct of a traditionally held lecture and highly automated rather than the result of using a specialized authoring tool. We have transmitted a number of lectures over the Internet using the MBone tools [Eri94], recorded the lectures using a novel program for recording whiteboard sessions, and, finally, converted the lectures into hypermedia documents which can be accessed from a Hyper-G [KMS93] server.

The message that we want to communicate by this paper is that on the one hand producing a useful hypermedia document is easier than you think, because we have all the tools available to make it going; on the other hand, if one wants to take the third path of multimedia preparation of teaching material for the university, then one does not only have to gather information on the use of existing tools but, at least to some degree, also develop new tools.

3 The lecture scenario

We now describe the scenario which we have used in order to deliver a lecture on the computer and to convert it into a hypermedia document.

The instructor first decides on the topic to be presented. In our case we have chosen the area of algorithms and data structures, among them backtracking and the Towers-of-Hanoi problem as our first topics. Next he prepares slides as usual using a standard tool like Showcase on Silicon Graphics machines, or Framemaker, or LaTeX. The result are colored slides in postscript format. Note that *good* transparencies should contain less text than a scholarly paper. Just the essential keywords are enough, and, furthermore slides should be used as templates to be filled in by the hand of the instructor while lecturing! The lecture itself is delivered using the computer (we have used a SGI workstation).

We used the MBone whiteboard to deliver a computer lecture. The slides were loaded into the whiteboard wb, orally commented by the instructor, marked and illustrated with on-line drawings carried out using the tools which wb offers. Several other people at distant hosts "attended" the lecture via the MBone. They used the MBone tools sd, nv, vat and wb to get the video (about 3 frames per second), audio and also the explanation of the slides using the wb.

Students could follow the lectures both locally in Freiburg on student workstations and on remote hosts at different universities in Germany (Mannheim and Munich). There was also the possibility for the audience to ask questions and to carry out actions on the (shared) whiteboard. But, as in most lectures at least at German universities, students do not ask many questions, if the instructor presents a well prepared lecture.

The transmission rate and the synchronization of the different data streams (audio, video, and whiteboard actions, in particular slide changes) was completely acceptable both on the local and at the remote sites.

Feedback from the audience revealed that the video of the lecturer is not as important as the sound and the action on the wb. So even a frozen picture of the lecturer, combined with sound and wb movements would be a possible way of teleteaching.

4 Converting a computer held lecture into a multimedia document

The lecture was recorded on a S-VHS video tape, which was later digitized (audio and video) with the SGI capture tools. The capturing of the audio and video stream in a sufficient quality needs a powerful hardware and some experience in a proper use of the software tools. The wb output was recorded with MCASTREC [1] , a novel program to record a whiteboard session, and then converted into a format which is readable for an external Hyper-G viewer SYNCVIEW[2]. Then a textfile with the paths of the postcript slides and titles was edited.

As a result you get a multimedia document consisting of sound and video of the lecturer's talk, but also the demonstrations on the wb. The program SYNCVIEW presents this multimedia document by synchronizing the wb actions with video and sound. It is also possible to scroll back and forward in the document by using a slider. Figure 1 shows a screenshot of the movie and the accumulated whiteboard. The embedding of the multimedia document into Hyper-G is achieved by making use of other specialized tools.

Though the MBone wb does not match all requirements which are desired by a lecturer, it was just adequate for the topics which we have chosen so far. It allows paging up slides in postscript format, writing, drawing, and marking actions, including the deletion of such actions, on the current page.

We decided to restrict ourselves to the area of algorithms and data structures in order to deliver a series of computer lectures which are then converted into multimedia documents automatically by our software. Our specific aim is to produce a series of lectures on topics which are normally difficult to understand for 2nd year students; among them are the major algorithmic paradigms like divide-and-conquer, backtracking, exhaustive and heuristic search, randomization, and others.

[1] available under ftp://ftp.informatik.uni-freiburg.de/AOF
[2] see 1.

5 Integration of distance teaching and CAI authoring

Note that the production of the hypermedia document as described above is a byproduct of teleteaching. The technology which we have used for *authoring on the fly* integrates various technologies which are still separate today: computer presentation software, CAI, and distance teaching. Though this is an attractive aspect, it is not essential for our approach of converting a computer held lecture almost automatically into a hypermedia document.

We have used the MBone tools, in particular wb, simply because there was not available any other reasonable electronic substitute for a chalkboard or overhead projector.

At various locations so-called *MBone recorders* have been developed ([Kle94, Hol95]) which allow to record and replay a broadcasted MBone session. At first glance it appears simple to use such a recorder for the production of a multimedia document: an Mbone recorder tracks the flow of data during a session. An Mbone player sends the recorded data once more through the network. Were one to start Mbone tools, one could visually follow the recorded Mbone session.

However, a multimedia document especially suited for offline use is not obtained in this way. In this case it would have to be possible to page up and down in the recorded data and to combine the data with other documents such as a scholarly paper, a glossary, an application program, or a training and testing segment. The simple recording of session data does not however suffice in all cases in which a particular point of the lecture held at the computer is dependent upon the history of actions. We explain this in the example of MBone tool wb as a presentation medium. A lecture held with the help of the whiteboard wb cannot simply be rewinded, in contrast to CD-ROM [PFJ+94]. The whiteboard runs namely only sequentially. If one wanted to rewind the lecture, say 23 seconds, for example, one would have to both start wb and carry out anew all of the operations up to the desired point in time in order to display the situation up until that point in the lecture. Similar problems occur when the instructor runs a simulation of his lecture at the computer, launches an application program, consults an image data base, etc.

The main achievement of the software which we have developed is, therefore, that it provides a true synchronization of the audio- and video streams and the accumulated situation on the whiteboard at any instance of time.

6 Conclusion

As already mentioned we are preparing a whole series of computer lectures on algorithmic paradigms as computer held lectures and convert them "on the fly" into multimedia documents. For the first two topics, backtracking and the Towers-of-Hanoi problem (as an example of a recursive algorithm), this has been successfully completed already. The facilities, which the wb of the Mbone toolset offered, were just sufficient for these two topics. Instead of launching an application showing a simulation or animation of an algorithm we have drawn simple figures on the screen and moved them just as on an overhead projector. In this way the usual examples for illustrativity the backtrack principle (4-queens problem) and the Towers-of-Hanoi problem (with 3 or 4 disks) could be presented dynamically (cf. Figures 2 and 3).

The lack of a grouping facility for graphical objects in wb was already considered harmful. Hence, it is obvious, that enhanced whiteboards are necessary in order to present other topics optimally. In [LH94] one can find a large number of desirable features of an ideal electronic whiteboard. Of course, every enhancement of the whiteboard implies that the recording software and the Hyper-G viewer have to adopted appropriately. Furthermore, specialized editors for postprocessing a recorded lecture are necessary if an other wants to change his lecture for off-line use.

This shows that there is still a lot of work to be done. But, nevertheless, we have shown that authoring on the fly is a way of producing high quality hypermedia documents for educational purposes using currently available technology.

References

[AOS91] F. Augenstein, Th. Ottmann, and J. Schöning. Ein typ- und regelgesteuertes Autorensystem. In H. Maurer, editor, *Hypertext/Hypermedia 91*, pages 25–33, Graz, Austria, 1991. Springer-Verlag, Informatik-Fachbericht Nr. 276.

[CLR90] T. Cormen, C. Leiserson, and R. Rivest. *Introduction to Algorithms.* MIT Press, 1990.

[Eri94] H. Eriksson. Mbone: The multicast backbone. *ACM Communications*, 37:54–60, 8 1994.

[Hol95] W. Holfelder. An MBone VCR Tool. http://www.icsi.berkeley.edu/mbone-vcr/, 1995.

[Kle94] A. Klemets. The design and implementation of a media on demand system for www. http://www.it.kth.se/ klemets/www.html, 1994.

[KMS93] F. Kappe, H. Maurer, and N. Scherbakov. Hyper-G – a universal hypermedia system. *Journal of Educational Multimedia and Hypermedia*, 2:39–66, 1 1993.

[LH94] J. Lennon and Maurer H. Lecturing technology, a future with hypergmedia. *Educational Technology*, pages 5–14, 4 1994.

[Med93] Warner New Media. How computers work. CD-ROM, 1993.

[PFJ+94] P.Gloor, F.Makedon, J.Matthews, D. Johnson, and P. Metaxas, editors. *Parallel Computation: Practical Implementations of Algorithms and Machines.* Dartmouth Institute for Advanced Graduate Studies (DAGS) & TELOS/Springer Verlag, New York, 1994.

[Wue94] M. Wuellenweber. *Albert (CD-ROM).* Springer-Verlag (electronic media), 1994.

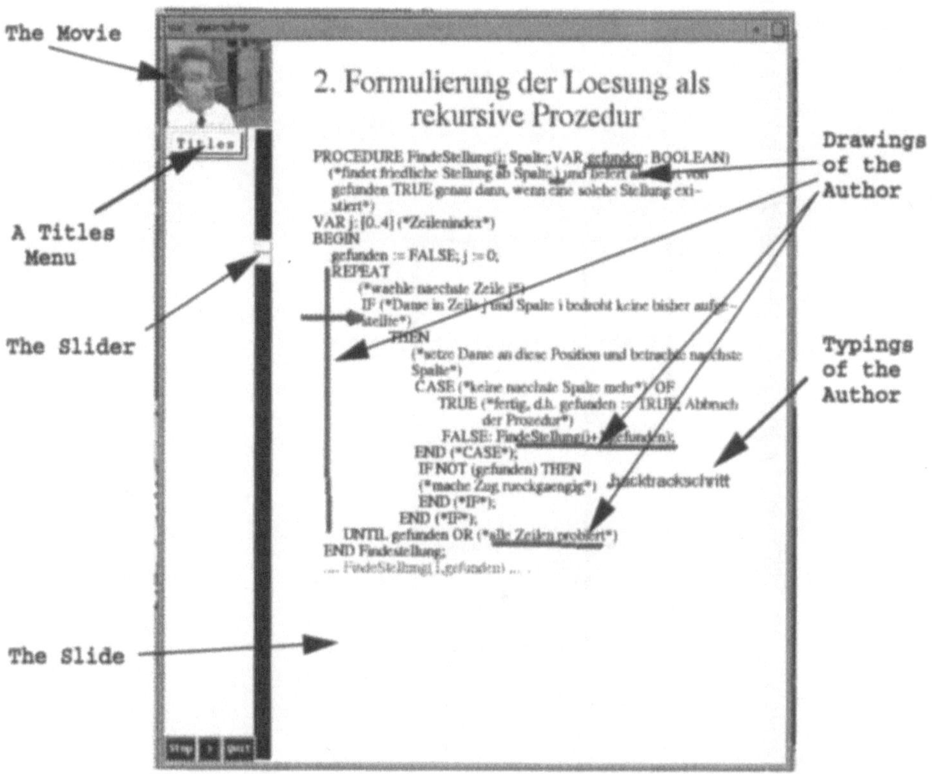

Figure 1: A screenshot of SYNCVIEW

Figure 2: The presentation of the 4-queens problem

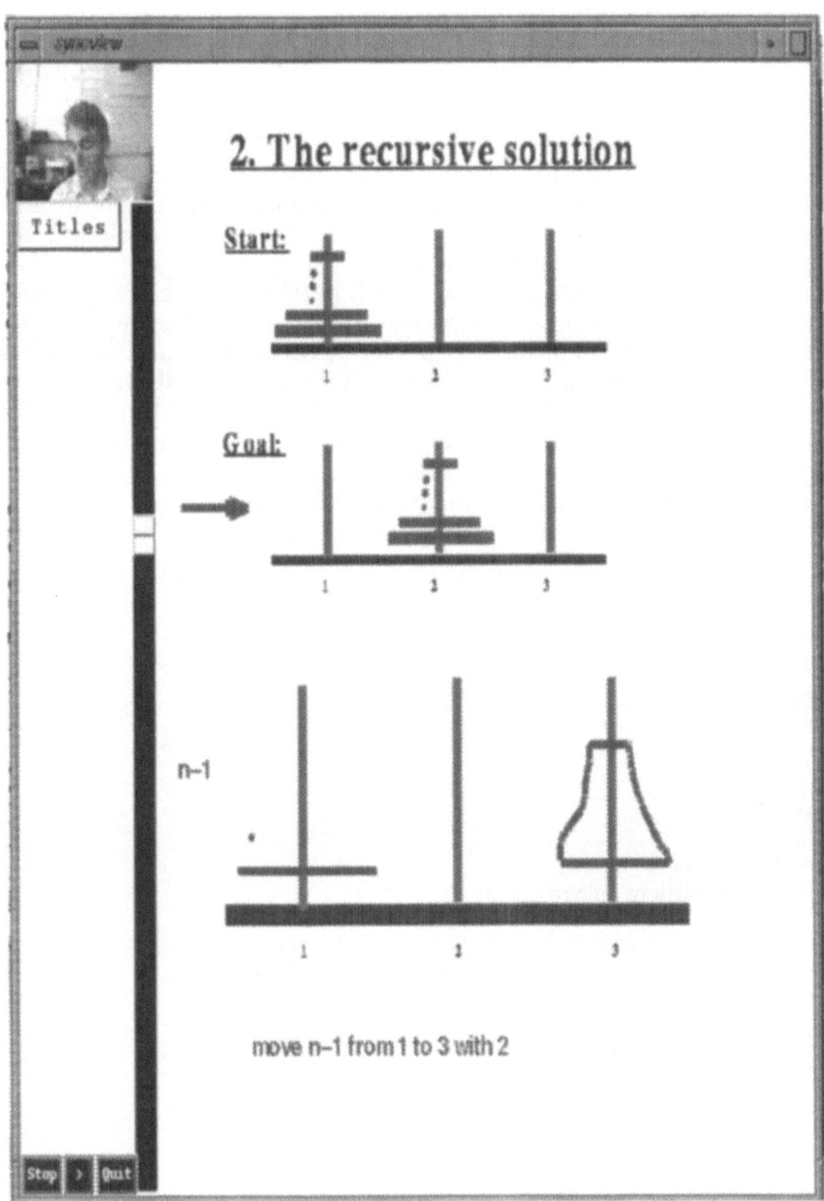

Figure 3: The presentation of the Towers-of-Hanoi problem

Managing Editor's Column

Vol. 1, No. 11; November 28, 1995

Dear Readers:

here is the last-but-one number of J.UCS of 1995: and with it a pleasant surprise. Springer Publ. Co. will press 30.000 CD ROM's that will contain the first volume (1995) of J.UCS (all papers!) together with information on all material available from Springer. This CD ROM will be distributed free of charge, and will thus bring J.UCS to thousands of users.

Thus, all papers that have appeared in J.UCS in 1995 will receive much more publicity than any author could ever have expected! Because of this we encourage everyone to still consider submitting a paper for the December issue: we will try to review some of them within 2 weeks so they still can go into the first volume of J.UCS and hence onto the CD ROM mentioned. This will only be possible for those papers where we manage to find superfast referees, where no changes are necessary and the format is exactly as required for J.UCS.

The printed version of volume 1 will appear in March 96.

Hope you enjoy this issue of J.UCS...which is more applied than most previous ones!

Cheers,

Hermann Maurer
email: hmaurer@iicm.tu-graz.ac.at

Journal of Universal Computer Science, vol. 1, no. 11 (1995), 719-727
submitted: 7/11/95, accepted: 23/11/95, appeared: 28/11/95,

Digital Libraries as Learning and Teaching Support

Hermann Maurer
(Graz University of Technology, Graz/Austria
and The University of Auckland, Auckland/NZ
email: hmaurer@iicm.tu-graz.ac.at)

Jennifer Lennon
(The University of Auckland, Auckland/NZ
email:J_Lennon@cs.auckland.ac.nz)

Abstract: For 30 years repeated attempts have been made to use computers to support the teaching and learning process, albeit with only moderate success. Whenever major attempts failed, some seemingly convincing reasons were presented the for less than satisfactory results. In the early days cost or even lack of suitable equipment was blamed; after colour graphics computers started to be widespread, production costs of interactive and graphically appealing material were considered the main culprits; when modern multimedia authoring techniques did not change the situation either, the lack of personalized feed-back, of network support and the difficulty of producing high quality simulations were seen as main obstacles. With networks now offering excellent multimedia presentation and communication facilities the final breakthrough of computers as ultimate teaching and learning tool is (once more) predicted. And once more results will be disappointing if one crucial component is again overlooked: good courseware must give both guidance to students but also provide a rich variety of background material whenever such is needed. It is the main claim of this paper that the advent of sizeable digital libraries provides one of the most significant chances for computer based training ever. We will argue that such libraries not only allow the efficient production of courseware but also provide the extensive background reservoir of material needed in many situations.

Key Words: Digital libraries, electronic libraries, learning support, teaching support, instructional technology, CAI, CBT

Category: H.3, H.4, H.5, K.3

1 Introduction

The saga of trying to use computers for education and training goes back well over thirty years. Rather than repeating all that has been said over and over we refer to one of the last major "presentation type" efforts in computer assisted instruction, COSTOC, and the arguments presented there, see (Makedon et al 1987) and (Huber et al 1989). The essence is, however, that even large scale projects involving fairly high quality animated colour graphics and sophisticated question-answer mechanisms did not succeed as replacement or even support for teaching on a large scale: although some successes due to better production tools ranging from Hyper-Card and Toolbook to Authorware and particularly HM-Card (Maurer et al 1995) have been attained, supported by the integration of advanced media such as digital audio and video segments a decisive change has not occured mainly due to three facts: (a) courseware has been always difficult to customize; (b) students did not have sufficient background material available in electronic form when getting stuck; and (c) no direct feedback from students to teachers has been provided in most cases in the past.

We believe that the proper use of digital libraries imbedded in modern "second generation" hypermedia systems is about to offer the best chance ever to succeed in using computers for educational purposes.

This paper is structured as follows. In Section 2 we explain the need for second generation hypermedia systems and how they relate to digital libraries. In Section 3 we describe how such digital libraries can address the points (a) - (c) mentioned above. And we will argue in Section 4 that the always mentioned problem of copyrights and payments for electronic books can indeed be solved easily using existing techniques. The paper concludes with references in section 5.

For a general look on hypermedia see (Nielsen 1995). For a survey of applications (Lennon et al 1994b).

2 Second generation systems and digital libraries

In this section we explain some of the properties of first generation hypermedia systems, using WWW as the most prominent example. We contrast them with those of Hyper-G, the first second generation model. We confine attention to networked hypermedia systems with a client/server architecture. For completeness' sake we refer to papers describing important attempts such as Gopher (Alberti 1992 et al), WWW (Berners-Lee et al 1992), IRIS (Haan et al 1992), WAIS (Kahle et al 1992). For papers on Hyper-G see (Andrews et al 1995a), (Andrews et al 1995b), (Kappe et al 1994), (Maurer 1994), and the book (Maurer 1996b).

Information in a hypermedia system is usually stored in "chunks". Chunks consist of individual documents which may themselves consist of various types of "media". Typically, a document may be a piece of text containing a picture. Each document may contain links leading to (parts of) other documents in the same or in different chunks. Typical hypertext navigation through the information space is based on these links: the user follows a sequence of links until all relevant information has hopefully been encountered.

In WWW, a chunk consists of a single document. Documents consist of textual information and may include pictures and the (source) anchors of links. Pictures and links are an integral part of the document. Pictures are thus placed in fixed locations within the text ("inline images"). Anchors can be attached to textual information and inline images, but not to parts of images. Links may lead to audio or video clips which can be activated. The textual component of a document is stored in so-called HTML format, a derivative of SGML.

In Hyper-G the setting is considerably more general: chunks, called "clusters" in Hyper-G terminology consist of a number of documents. A typical cluster may, for example, consist of five documents: a piece of text (potentially with inline images), a second piece of text (for example in another language, or a different version of the same text, or an entirely different text), a third piece of text (the same text in a third language perhaps), an image and a film clip. Anchors can be attached to textual information, to parts of images, and even to regions in a film clip. Links are not part of the document but are stored in a separate database. They are both typed and bidirectional: they can be followed forward (as in WWW) but also backwards.

Hyper-G allows multiple pieces of text within a cluster to handle e.g., multiple languages in a natural way. This also elegantly solves the case where a document comes in two versions: a more technical (or advanced) one and one more suitable for the novice reader. As indicated, pictures can be treated as inline images or as separate documents. Often, inline images are convenient, since the "author" can define where the user will find a picture in relation to the text. On the other hand, with screen resolution varying tremendously, the rescaling of inline images may pose a problem: if a picture is treated as separate document, however, it appears in a separate window, can be manipulated (shifted, put in the background, kept on-screen while continuing with other information, etc.) independent of the textual portion (which in itself can be manipulated by for example narrowing or widening its window). Thus, the potential to deal with textual and pictorial information separately provides more flexibility when required. Text can be stored in Hyper-G in a number of formats, clearly important for digital library purposes.

In addition to the "usual" types of documents found in any modern hypermedia system, Hyper-G also supports 3D objects and scenes.

Let us now turn to the discussion of the philosophy of links in WWW versus Hyper-G. The ability to attach links to parts of a picture is clearly desirable, when additional information is to be associated with certain sub-areas of an image. That links are bidirectional and not embedded in the document has a number of very important consequences: first, links relating to a document can be modified without necessarily having access rights to the document itself. Thus, private links and a certain amount of customisation are possible; second, when viewing a document it is possible to find all documents refering to the current one. This is not only a desirable feature as such, but is of crucial importance for being able to maintain the database. After all, when a document is deleted or modified, all documents refering to it may have to be modified to avoid the "dangling link syndrome", or to avoid being directed to completely irrelevant documents. Hyper-G offers the possibilty of automatically notifying the owner of a document that some of the documents that are being refered to have been changed or deleted, an important step towards "automatic link maintainance". Thirdly, the bidirectionality of the links allows the graphic display of a "local map" showing the current document and all documents pointing to it and being pointed at, an arbitrary number of levels deep. Harmony makes full use of this fact and provides local maps as an invaluable navigational aid that cannot be made available for WWW databases (Fenn et al 1994). Finally, the fact that links can have types can be used to show to the user that a link just leads to a footnote, or to a picture, or to a film clip, or is a counter- or supporting argument of some claim at issue: typed links enhance the perception of how things are related and can be used as tool for discussions and collaborative work.

Navigation in WWW is performed solely using the hypertext paradigm of anchors and links. It has become a well accepted fact that structuring large amounts of data using only hyperlinks such that users don't get "lost in hyperspace" is difficult to say the least. WWW databases are large, flat networks of chunks of data and resemble more an impenetrable maze than well-structured information. Indeed every WWW database acknowledges this fact tacitly, by preparing pages that look like menus in a hierarchically structured database: items are listed in an orderly fashion, each with an anchor leading to a subchapter (subdirectory). If links in WWW had types, such links could be distinguished from others. But as it is, all links look the same: whether they are "continue" links, "hierarchical" links, "referential" links, "footnote links", or whatever else.

In Hyper-G not only can have links a type, links are by no means the only way to access information. Clusters of documents can be grouped into collections, and collections again into collections in a pseudo-hierachical fashion. We use the term "pseudo-hierarchical" since, technically speaking, the collection structure is not a tree, but a DAG. I.e., one collection can have more than one parent: an impressionist picture X may belong to the collection "Impressionist Art", as well as to the collection "Pictures by Manet", as well as to the collection "Museum of Modern Art". The collection "hierarchy" is a powerful way of introducing structure into the database. Indeed many links can be avoided this way (Maurer et al 1994), making the system much more transparent for the user and allowing a more modular approach to systems creation and maintainance. Collections, clusters and documents have titles and attributes. These may be used in Boolean queries to find documents of current interest. Finally, Hyper-G provides sophistacted full-text search facilities. Most importantly, the scope of any of such searches can be defined to be the union of arbitrary collections, even if the collections reside on different servers.

Note that some WWW applications also permit full-text searches. However, no full-text search engine is built into WWW. Thus, the functionality of full text search is bolted "on top" of WWW: adding functionality on top of WWW leads to the "Balkanisation", the fragmentation of WWW, since different sites will implement missing functionality in different ways. Thus, to stick to the example of the full text search engine, the fuzzy search employed by organisation X may yield entirley different results from the fuzzy search employed by organisation Y, much to the bewilderment of users. Actually, the situation concerning searches in WWW is even more serious: since documents in WWW do not have attributes, no search is possible on such attributes; even if such a search or a full text search is artificially implemented, it is not possible to allow users to define the scope for the search, due to the lack of structure in the WWW database. Hence full-text searches in WWW always work in a fixed, designated part of the WWW database residing on one particular server.

The acceptance of a hypermedia system is certainly not only dependent on deep technical features, but above all on the information content and the ease of use. Due to the fact that large hypermedia systems tend to lead to disorientation, second generation hypermedia systems have to try very hard, both at the server and at the client end, to help users with navigational tools. Some navigational tools, like the structuring and search facilities have already been described; others, such as maps, history lists, specific and personal collections can also be of great help and are available in Hyper-G; a particular speciality of the Harmony client (assuming an OpenGL environment) is a 3D browser: the "information landscape" depicts collections and documents (according to their size) as blocks of varying size spread out across a three-dimensional landscape, over which the user is able to fly.

The architecture of Hyper-G is clearly well suited for handling the material one would want to put into an electronic library. Such material includes tradititional journals in electronic form, see e.g., (Calude et al 1994) and (Maurer et al 1994), books in electronic form, see e.g., the Internet guide found under http://iicm.tu-graz.ac.at/Cinternet_guide, courseware such as found under http://iicm.tu-graz.ac.at/Chmcard, diverse pictures, audio- and video-clips, etc. The structuring and search facilities of Hyper-G allow easy access to information, the variety of navigational tools help to prevent the "lost in hyperspace" phenomenon, and the fact that links can be added to documents even if one is not allowed to change the contents of the document allow a high degree of customisation and personalisation. Finally, the multimedia capabilities available supported by the animation and question-answer facilities of HM-Card (Maurer et al 1996a) provide the possibility to prepare modern instructional material and integrate it into the digital library.

3 How to use a digital library

¿From the student's point of view a digital library is used by "activating" certain material as "relevant background material" to define the scope of future searches (in Hyper-G this is done by defining suitable collections) and then by starting an instructional unit. While working through such a unit students can perform all kinds of searches within the background material as it becomes necessary. Indeed they can create their own links, thus being able to personalize and customize as they find it appropriate. Students cannot only read documents, they can prepare their own documents by integrating into passages they have written (using links) sections of books, journals or other works as may be pertinent.

¿From the teacher's point of view the availability of the digital library and the possibility to prepare instructional material by combining existing ressources with those made up by the teachers for a particular purpose is especially important. This reduces the amount of work to prepare courseware and allows to change courseware at will by adding, deleting or changing sections. Note that this is done by using the flexible link concept of Hyper-G to combine components rather than "copying and pasting" components together. Using the link structure for this purpose has two significant advantages: first, link consistency is much easier to maintain; second, copying and pasting results is usually violating copyrights and royalties to be payed for material being used. We will see in the next section that this problem does not occur when proper linking mechanisms are used as already proposed by Ted Nelson's "transclusions" (Nelson 1987). Indeed preparation of courseware can be done "on the fly", i.e., as part of presenting lectures as we have first pointed out in (Lennon et al 1994a). For a more complete description of digital libraries see (Marchionini et al 1995).

4 Commercial aspects of a digital library

When electronic material is sold over networks some charging mechanisms are necessary. Assuming that users identify themselves with some username/password combination, charging mechnisms typically are:
(1) by time,
(2) by volume,
(3) by number of accesses,
(4) by subscription.

Note that in cases (1) – (3) there is some potential danger to the user (if others manage to get access to the username/password – something fairly easy to do on the Internet), and that (4) is dangerous to the publisher: persons may allow friends to use their username/password, resulting in many more readers than paid subscribers. Thus, (1) – (3) requires sophisticated security mechanisms (see e.g., (Posch 1995)) to protect users, (4) requires additional mechanisms to protect publishers.

An alternative is to use pre-paid accounts that e.g. allow a fairly liberal yet limited number of accesses. This is a mix of essentiallly (3) and (4) that offers a number of advantages: Even if the username/password is dedected by others it is only of limited use and can cause only limited damage (by illegally "exhausting" the pre-paid sum). Thus, the consumer is better protected in this mode, hence complicated security measures are not that essential. The publisher is also protected: users who pass on their username/password are welcome to do so. After all, whatever use they or friends make of the material offered has been pre-paid. This latter technique has e.g. been used with the electronic version of the ED-MEDIA'95 proceedings, see http://hyperg.iicm.tu-graz.ac.at/Cedmedia or http://hyperg.iicm.tu-graz.ac.at/Celectronic_library.

All of the above assumes that the information resides on one (or a few) servers in the Internet and users access that server. We consider such assumptions unrealistic for two reasons. First, world-wide access to Internet nodes is often painfully slow; second, if large numbers of users access a server, it and Internet connections leading to it will be overloaded unless complex counter-measures are taken.

For this reason we have been propagating for some time that electronic material should reside in local servers, with Internet used to update the material, but users accessing the local (library) servers. This approach taken in J.UCS (see (Maurer et al 1994), (Calude et al 1994)) improves performance for users and also allows publishers a new way of selling information: they sell for each server a license for "at most n simultaneous users", where n can be arbitrary. Typically, a university library could start with $n=1$ and increase n as necessary (i.e. if the material is popular enough that often more than a single user wants to access it at the same time). Note that "same time" is really a parameter that can be adjusted by publishing companies: it means "an electronic book accessed by a person is blocked for other persons for m minutes" (values of m that we have actually experimented with are between 3 and 10 minutes); observe in passing that connection - less protocols such as http in WWW are not well suited for this approach since persons accessing a book block themselves from accessing it again shortly thereafter; this is one of the many reasons why a connection-oriented protocol is built into Hyper-G. The above charging regime is easy to administer for publishers, and allows to install electronic material on a network for all users of the network at low cost (a single license), yet upgrading is easy. Note that the upgrades can even be system supported: Suppose the license is set to "20 users at a time" and the system monitors that usage is increasing steadily and peaks of 19 simultaneous users become more and more frequent; then the system can alert the librarian to buy additional licenses. Indeed variants are possible: no limit to the number of simultaneous users is fixed, but the charges for some electronic material are made to depend on the "average number of simultaneous users".

We now come to the main point: using second generation systems like Hyper-G and a version of above charging regime it is possible to customize material from various sources without violating copyright restrictions. This is so since customisation in systems such as Hyper-G is done by linking not by copying, very much in the spirit of Nelson's Xanadu proposal.

To be concrete, suppose on a server a number of books from various publishers have been installed, each licensed for some number of simultaneous users.

An instructor wanting to customise information by taking material from various books and combining it (potentially integrating own material) can do so in Hyper-G by not copying the material but by adding links that are only visible to a specific group, e.g. the group of intended students. This is depicted in a small example in Fig.1 .

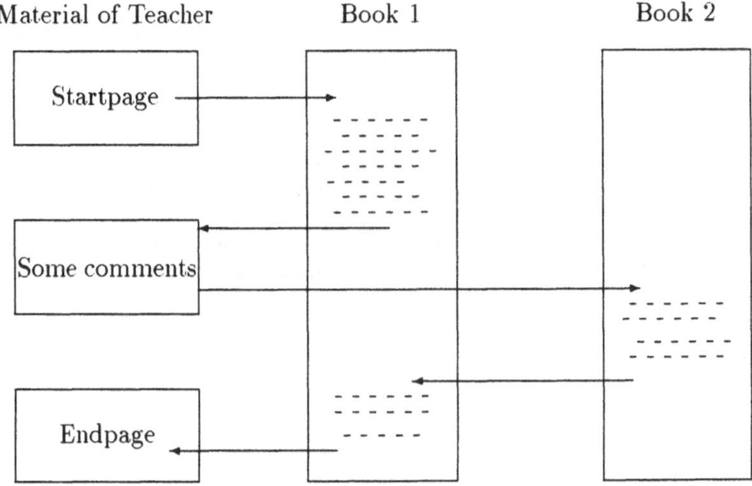

Fig.1

The arrows in Fig. 1 present links created by the teacher and are only visible to the intended usergroup.

Note that the teacher has thus combined the information on the "Startpage" with a section of Book 1, followed by "Some comments", a section in Book 2, a further section in Book 1 and some material on the "Endpage". Even if Book 1 and Book 2 are from different publishers no copyright violation accurs: if many students use the material as customised, Book 1 will be accessed more often then Book 2, hence the number of licenses for Book 1 may have to be increased, as should be the case.

Thus, holding electronic material in LAN's and using systems such as Hyper-G customisation is not only possible but can be done without any infringements on copyrights. In a way what the proposed set-up does is to implement Nelson's vision of "world-wide publishing using transclusion" (Nelson 1987) in a local environment.

5 References

References

[Alberti et al 1992] Alberti, B., Anklesaria, F., Lindnder, P., McCahill, M., & Torrey, D.(1995). Internet Gopher Protocol: A Distributed Document

Search and Retrieval Protocol; FTP from boombox.micro.umn.edu, directory pub/gopher/gopher_protocol.

[Andrews et al 1995a] Andrews, K., Kappe, F., Maurer, H., & Schmaranz, K. (1995). On Second Generation Hypermedia Systems. *Proc.ED-MEDIA'95*, Graz (June 1995), 75-80. See also J.UCS 0,0 (1994),127-136 at http:///www.iicm.tu-graz.ac.at /Cjucs_root.

[Andrews et al 1995b] Andrews, K., Kappe, F., & Maurer, H. (1995). Serving Information to the Web with Hyper-G; *Computer Networks and ISDN Systems 27 (1995)*, 919-926.

[Berners-Lee et al 1992] Berners-Lee, T., Cailliau, R., Groff, J., & Pollermann, B. (1992) WorldWideWeb: The Information Universe. *Electronic Networking: Research, Applications and Policy 1,2 (1992)*, 52-58.

[Calude et al 1994] Calude, C., Maurer, H., & Salomaa, A. (1994). J.UCS: The Journal of Universal Computer Science. *J.UCS 0,0 (1994)*, 109-117 at http://www.iicm. tu-graz.ac.at/Cjucs_root.

[Fenn et al 1994] Fenn, B.& Maurer, H. (1994). Harmony on an Expanding Net; *ACM Interactions 1,3 (1994)*, 26-38.

[Haan et al 1992] Haan, B.J., Kahn, P., Riley, V.A., Coombs, J.H. & Meyrowitz, N.K. (1992). IRIS Hypermedia Services; *Communications of the ACM 35,1 (1992)*, 36-51.

[Huber et al 1989] Huber, F., Makedon, F., & Maurer, H. (1989). HyperCOSTOC: a Comprehensive Computer-Based Teaching Support System. *J.MCA 12 (1989)*, 293-317.

[Kahle et al 1992] Kahle, B., Morris, H., Davis, F., Tiene, K., Hart, C., & Palmer, R. (1992). Wide Area Information Servers: An Executive Information System for Unstructured Files; *Electronic Networking: Research, Applications and Policy 1,2 (1992)*, 59-68.

[Kappe et al 1994] Kappe, F., Andrews, K., Faschingbauer, J., Gaisbauer, M., Maurer, H., Pichler, M., & Schipflinger, J. (1994). Hyper-G: A New Tool for Distributed Multimedia; *Proc.Conf.on Open Hypermedia Systems, Honolulu (1994)*, 209-214.

[Lennon et al 1994a] Lennon, J., & Maurer, H. (1994). Lecturing Technology: A Future With Hypermedia; *Educational Technology 34,4 (1994)*,5-14.

[Lennon et al 1994b] Lennon, & Maurer, H. (1994). Applications and Impact of Hypermedia Systems: An Overview. *J.UCS 0,0 (1994)*, 54-108 at http://www.iicm.tu-graz.ac.at/Cjucs_root.

[Makedon et al 1987] Makedon, F., Maurer, H., & Ottmann, Th. (1987). Presentation Type CAI in Computer Science Education at University Level. *J.MCA 10 (1987)*, 283-295.

[Marchionini et al 1995] Marchionini, G. & Maurer, H. (1995). The Role of Digital Libraries in Teaching and Learning. *Communications of the ACM 38,4 (1995)*, 67-75.

[Maurer 1994] Maurer, H. (1994). Advancing the ideas of WorldWideWeb. *Proc. Conf. on Open Hypermedia Systems, Honolulu (1994)*, 201-203.

[Maurer et al 1994] Maurer, H. & Schmaranz, K.(1994). J.UCS – The Next Generation in Electronic Journal Publishing. Proc. Electronic Publ. Conference, London (November 1994) in: *Computer Networks for Research in Europe 26, Supplement 2-3 (1994)*, 63-69.

[Maurer et al 1995] Maurer, H., Schneider A., & Scherbakov, N. (1995). HM-Care: A New Hypermedia Authoring System. To appear in: *Multimedia Tools and Applications.*

[Maurer et al 1996a] Maurer, H., & Scherbakov, N. (1996). *HM-Card.* Addison Wesley Pub.Co. Germany (1996).

[Maurer et al 1996b] Maurer, H. (1996). *Power to the Web! The Official Guide to Hyper-G.* Addison Wesley Pub.Co., UK (1996).

[Nelson 1987] Nelson, T.H. (1987). *Literary machines.* Edition 87.1, 702 South Michigan, South Bend,IN 46618, USA (1987)

[Nielsen 1995] Nielsen, J. (1995). Hypertext and Hypermedia; Academic Press (1995)

[Posch 1995] Posch, R. (1995). Information Security in Educational Networks. *Proc.ED-MEDIA'95*, Graz (June 1995), 45-50.

Journal of Universal Computer Science, vol. 1, no. 11 (1995), 728-743
submitted: 28/6/95, accepted: 18/11/95, appeared: 28/11/95,

Testing a High–Speed Data Path

The Design of the RSAβ Crypto Chip

Wolfgang Mayerwieser
(Graz University of Technology, Austria
wmayer@iaik.tu-graz.ac.at)

Karl C. Posch
(Graz University of Technology, Austria
kposch@iaik.tu-graz.ac.at)

Reinhard Posch
(Graz University of Technology, Austria
rposch@iaik.tu-graz.ac.at)

Volker Schindler
(Graz University of Technology, Austria
vschindl@iaik.tu-graz.ac.at)

Abstract High speed devices for public key cryptography are of emerging interest. For this reason, the RSAα crypto chip was designed. It is an architecture capable of performing fast RSA encryption and other cryptographic algorithms based on modulo multiplication. Besides the modulo multiplication algorithm called *FastMM*, the reasons for its high computation speed are the *As Parallel As Possible* (APAP) architecture, as well as the high operation frequency. The RSAα crypto chip also contains on–chip RAM and a special–purpose control logic, enabling special features like encrypted key loading. However, this control mechanism influences to some extend testability of the MM data path which is the heart of the chip. For this reason, the RSAβ crypto chip has been designed to be able to evaluate the behaviour of the pure MM data path.
In the following, we describe the strategies used with the RSAβ crypto chip for testing the MM data path under realistical conditions. In this context, analyzing control signal flow turns out to be the key action.
This work has been sponsored as part of the project Nr. P9384PHY "Sichere Kommunikation bei hohen Geschwindigkeiten" by the Austrian Science Foundation.
Key Words: high speed multipliers, hardware algorithms, design for testability, public key cryptography

1 Introduction

Simulating a CMOS VLSI design and testing the prototype of a newly designed chip is a sophisticated and time consuming task. This is in particular true in the special case of the RSAβ Crypto Chip, which has as its core a data path of rather high complexity for performing modulo multiplications (MM), organized as a bitslice SIMD architecture [Lippitsch et al (1992)]. Several reasons are responsible for the need of detailed testing:

- The modulo multiplier is built in modified domino logic [Weste et al (1993)], which results in smaller area and higher speed, but requires a very careful design process.

- The necessity for handling very large integers for a secure RSA implementation causes a width of the MM data path of about 700 bits. Designing CMOS circuits of this size leads to specific problems not present when designing much smaller systems.

Therefore, it is quite advisable to spend very much effort on simulating the chip's function, and to provide built-in testing features. Furthermore, stand-alone testing of the MM data path without control logic driving it would be a preferable strategy.

We will concentrate on the last item. Real stand-alone testing of the MM data path in a separate package results in feeding its control signals directly via the chip's pads. At this point, a problem arises: The maximum clock rate allowed by the pads is lower than the clock rate we would need at the MM data path to reach the desired processing speed by a factor of about 5. It makes no sense (and even might be impossible for dynamic logic) to test the MM data path at a much lower speed than it was designed for. Therefore we cannot avoid adding some kind of control logic between the pads and the MM data path.
Test results should not be influenced by that control structure. It should not cause any changes to the layout of the MM data path, and it must be of very high reliability. Both requirements call for an "as simple as possible" control structure. The key for finding such a minimum version of the control structure is to analyze the control signal flow, which allows for reducing redundancy, and even leads to the use of a modified version of the original modulo multiplication algorithm for optimizing control signal flow.

In this paper, we will take a closer look at the modulo multiplication algorithm (which is the heart of the RSA implementation), as well as at the MM data path designed for performing this operation efficiently. After analyzing the control signal flow, enough information is available to introduce a simple mechanism for compensating the clock rate difference without loss of overall performance. Finally, we will show an outline of a possible hardware implementation.

2 The FastMM Algorithm

The RSA algorithm [Rivest et al (1978)] performs both, encryption and decryption, by calculating

$$c = C^x \pmod N,$$

with c, C the cipher text and plain text or vice versa, and x the encryption or decryption key. To meet security demands, the modulus N must be of a length of approximately 700 bits. Exponentiation can be performed by the well known Square-and-Multiply algorithm [Knuth (1981)]. Therefore, for our purpose it is sufficient to consider the RSA implementation as a sequence of continued modulo multiplications with very long integers, separated by simple register transfer operations.

With the RSAβ Crypto Chip, modulo multiplication is done by the FastMM algorithm [Posch et al (1990)]. This algorithm performs

$$y = a \cdot b \bmod N + e \cdot N, \qquad e \in \{0, 1, 2\},$$

which is much easier to compute than the exact modulo multiplication

$$z = a \cdot b \bmod N,$$

as it avoids division and uses multiplication only like the Montgomery approach [Montgomery (1985)]. We will refer to y as *relaxed residuum*, since it is possibly not fully reduced.

The efficiency of FastMM is based on a fast and good approximation Q of the quotient $q = \lfloor \frac{a \cdot b}{N} \rfloor$, which is used to calculate the relaxed residuum

$$y = a \cdot b - Q \cdot N.$$

Q is calculated as follows:

$$Q = \left\lfloor \left\lfloor a \cdot b \cdot 2^{-(k-1)} \right\rfloor \left\lfloor \frac{1}{N} \cdot 2^{2k+4} \right\rfloor \cdot 2^{-(k+5)} \right\rfloor$$

k is the length of the modulus N in bits. For convenience, we introduce

$$NegN = -N$$

$$N1 = \left\lfloor \frac{1}{N} \cdot 2^{2k+4} \right\rfloor$$

Note that both, $NegN$ as well as $N1$ can be precomputed.
Now, FastMM can be represented using the following symbolic instructions ($w[i]$ denotes the i rightmost bits of w, $[i]w$ denotes the i leftmost bits of w):

$$X[2k+4] \leftarrow a[k+2] \cdot b[k+2] \qquad \text{(A)}$$

$$Q[2k+10] \leftarrow N1[k+5] \cdot [k+5]X \qquad \text{(B)}$$

$$y[k+2] \leftarrow NegN[k+2] \cdot [k+5]Q + X[k+2] \qquad \text{(C)}$$

In [Posch et al (1990)] it is shown that the results of continued relaxed modulo multiplications never exceed the limit given by e. Therefore, only after the last multiplication a final modulus reduction might be necessary. Obviously, this reduction step does not decrease throughput, compared to the hundreds of modulo multiplications which are to be performed for getting the relaxed result. This final modulus reduction can be done by adding $NegN$ to the result. Note that $NegN$ and the possibility to perform an addition are needed by the FastMM algorithm, anyway. Therefore, the final modulus reduction requires no additional hardware effort or constants.

3 The MM Data Path

3.1 The Structure of the MM Data Path

The design of the MM data path, shown in [Figure 1], meets the special requirements of the FastMM algorithm. It consists of several main registers with length 696 bits (**IO, Cph, Mkd, NegN, N1, Low, High**), an APAP–structure [Lippitsch et al (1991)] (described in [Section 3.2]) and a few auxiliary registers of length eight bits. **Adder-1** and **Adder-2** are needed for converting the redundant number representation — used by register **High** and the APAP–adder — into binary numbers. **Adder-3** performs the addition of multiplication step (C). The purpose of the transmission gates as well as the overall function of the MM

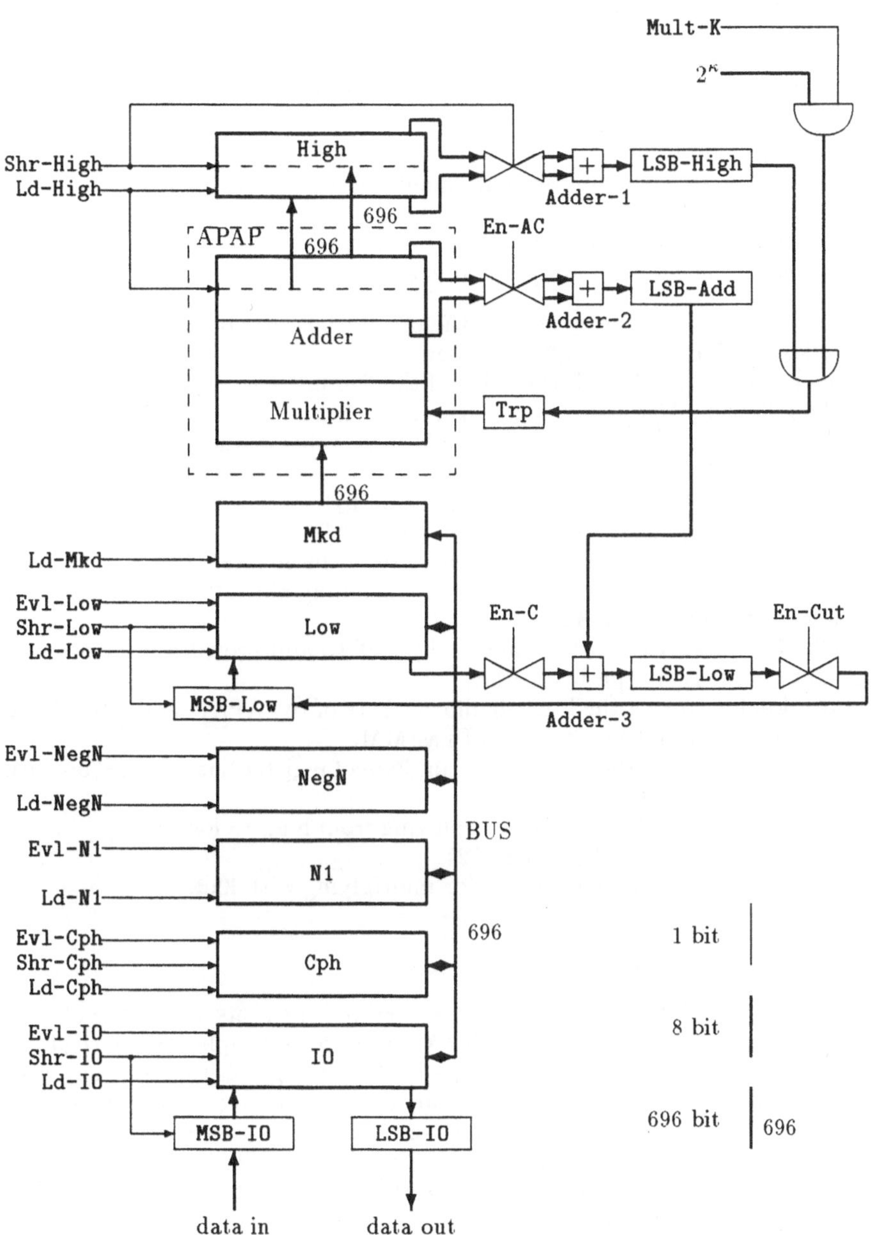

Figure 1: The MM data path

data path will become clear in [Section 3.3].
We will use the main registers in the following way: The **IO** register is needed for input/ouput operations, **Cph** (for *cipher text*) is commonly used for storing the last result while the next modulo multiplication is running. **NegN** and **N1** hold the corresponding constants mentioned in [Section 2], **Mkd** must contain the actual multiplicand. **Low** receives the lower part of the result of a multiplication in binary number representation, while **High** gets the higher part in redundant number representation.

The MM data path requires quite many control signals, denoted as a *control word*.
We present a complete list of the control signals which shows the actions in each clock cycle if the corresponding signal is active:

Evl-X: Write value of register X to the 696 bit bus, where X can be one of the following: **IO, Cph, NegN, N1, Low**.
Ld-Y: Load register Y with the value of the 696 bit bus, where Y can be one of the following: **IO, Cph, NegN, N1, Low, Mkd**.
Ld-High: Load register **High** with the current value of the APAP–adder, then clear the APAP–adder.
Shr-High: Enable storing the least significant byte of register **High** to **LSB-High**, then shift **High** to the right by one byte.
Shr-Low: Shift **Low** to the right by one byte, including **MSB-Low**.
Shr-IO: Shift **IO** to the right by one byte including **MSB-IO**, thus loading a new byte from outside via **MSB-IO**.
LSB-IO buffers the least significant byte of **IO** and provides it for output.
Shr-Cph: Shift right **Cph** by one bit.
En-AC: Enable storing the least significant byte of the APAP–adder to **LSB-Add** during operation (A) resp. (C) of FastMM.
En-C: Enable storing the least significant byte of register **Low** to **LSB-Low** during operation (C) of FastMM.
En-Cut: Cut off the bit stream on changing from high to low.
2^{κ}: Eight bits, holding the value of 2^{κ}.
Mult-K: Load register **Trp** with 2^{κ} for multiplying with **Mkd**.

3.2 The APAP–Structure

The APAP (**As** **P**arallel **As** **P**ossible)–structure represents a mixture of a serial/parallel multiplier and a full parallel Wallace tree multiplier [Wallace (1964)]. This approach has been chosen because for long integer arithmetic conventional serial/parallel multipliers would be far too slow, whereas a full Wallace tree multiplier cannot be implemented on reasonable chip area with current technology. The degree of parallelism (i.e., the number p of new partial products that can be processed each cycle) may vary between certain boundaries, which allows for scaling the APAP design. To avoid carry delays, redundant number representation is used.

For our purpose, we hide these implementation details, since we are only interested in the overall understanding of control signal handling. Therefore, we consider the APAP–structure together with **Adder-2**, as well as **High** together with **Adder-1** to be "black boxes", thus hiding the internal function of the APAP–adder and the redundant number representation. (However, for understanding the timing of the control signal sequence, the number of cycles consumed by the APAP–adder and **Adder-1** resp. **Adder-2** would have to be known.) Multiplication can now simply be described as a serial/parallel multiplication, where p bits of the multiplier are processed each cycle. For the RSAβ Crypto Chip, $p = 8$ has been chosen.

The following example [Figure 2] provides such a pure behavioural description

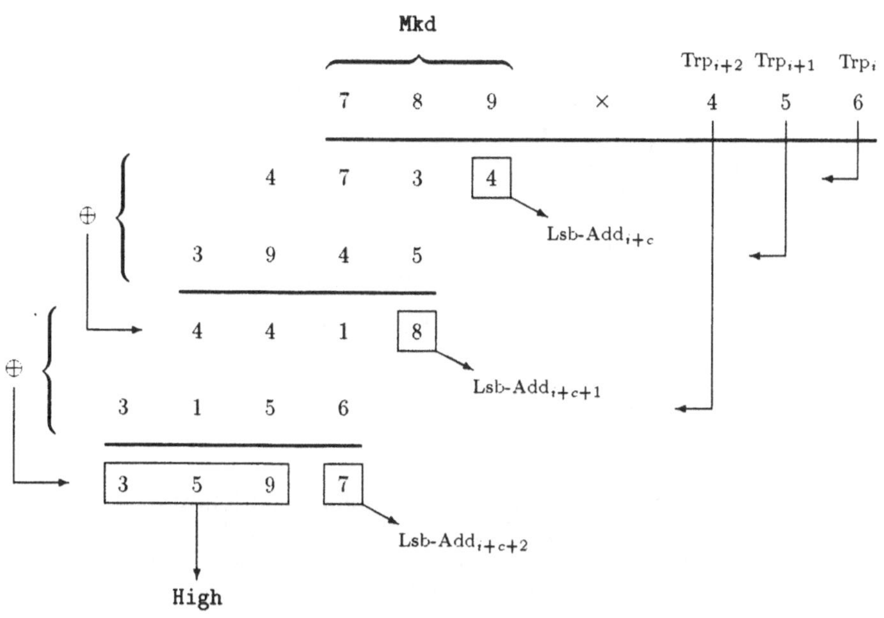

Figure 2: Multiplication scheme

of the multiplication procedure. It uses decimal digits instead of bytes, showing the principle of calculating the product of the multiplicand 789 and the multiplier 456. Reg_n denotes the content of Reg at the nth cycle; c is a positive constant depending on the APAP–structure and the adders.

The APAP–adder gets the first partial product (PP) by multiplying the multiplicand (held in **Mkd**) with the least significant digit of the multiplier. Note that the least significant digit of this PP represents the least significant digit of the the final result and can be loaded into **Lsb-Add**. Therefore, this PP is shifted to the right by one digit, being aligned for the addition with the PP of the next multiplication cycle as well. The least significant digit of the result of that addition represents the next digit of the result, and so forth. After the multiplicand has been multiplied with the most significant digit of the multiplier, the APAP–adder contains the higher part of the result, which can be loaded into **High**.

Note that the APAP–adder always shifts its content to the right by one byte each cycle, while `Low` resp. `High` can be forced by the corresponding control signals to do so. It is important to understand that the MM data path is able to perform these actions in parallel: For example, while the APAP–multiplier is fed from `High` via `Trp` with a sequence of bytes to multiply, former multiplication results may be shiftet into register `Low`. There are concurrent data streams, and their flow is controlled by a few control signals.

3.3 Performing a Modulo Multiplication with the MM Data Path

operation	action	Mkd	High	Low
Mult-2^κ	b — High		$b[k+2]$	
	a — Mkd	$a[k+2]$		
Mod-Mul	Mult. step (A)	$a[k+2]$	$[k+5]X$	$X[k+2]$
	$N1$ — Mkd	$N1[k+5]$	$[k+5]X$	$X[k+2]$
	Mult. step (B)	$N1[k+5]$	$[k+5]Q$	$X[k+2]$
	$NegN$ — Mkd	$NegN[k+2]$	$[k+5]Q$	$X[k+2]$
	Mult. step (C)	$NegN[k+2]$		$y[k+2]$

Table 1: The FastMM scheme with the MM data path

Table 1 shows the overall scheme of the modulo multiplication with the MM data path. Once registers `NegN` and `N1` are loaded with the corresponding constants, the multiplier b must get into `High`. Figure 1 shows that this can only be done by loading it into `Mkd` first, followed by a multiplication by one. We will call this operation `Mult-2`$^\kappa$, because we assign the correct value to κ (in this context we consider $\kappa = 0$) and set `Mult-K` to high for one cycle. This way, the content of `Mkd` gets multiplied with one (i.e., 2^κ), and must be loaded from the APAP–adder into `High` at the very right moment, since the APAP–adder is shifting its content permanently.

After loading `Mkd` with the multiplicand a, we can start with operation `Mod-Mul`, the modulo multiplication using the FastMM algorithm. Figure 3 — which shows the control signal waveforms of a 664–bit modulo multiplication simulation — can now be understood:
We start multiplication step (A) with setting high `Shr-High` to feed the APAP–structure with the multiplier byte by byte. `En-AC`, `En-Cut` and `Shr-Low` are also set to high for shifting the lower part of the intermediate result into `Low`; it will be needed in step (C). When the higher part of the result is ready, it is loaded into `High` by activating `Ld-High`. At the same time, `N1` can be loaded into `Mkd`, starting multiplication step (B). This step is similar to step (A) except that shifting the result into `Low` is omitted. Step (C) starts with loading `NegN` into `Mkd` and is equal to step (A), but additionally sets `En-C` to high, thus adding the lower part of the multiplication result with the previous content of `Low`. After this procedure, the final result can be fetched from `Low`.

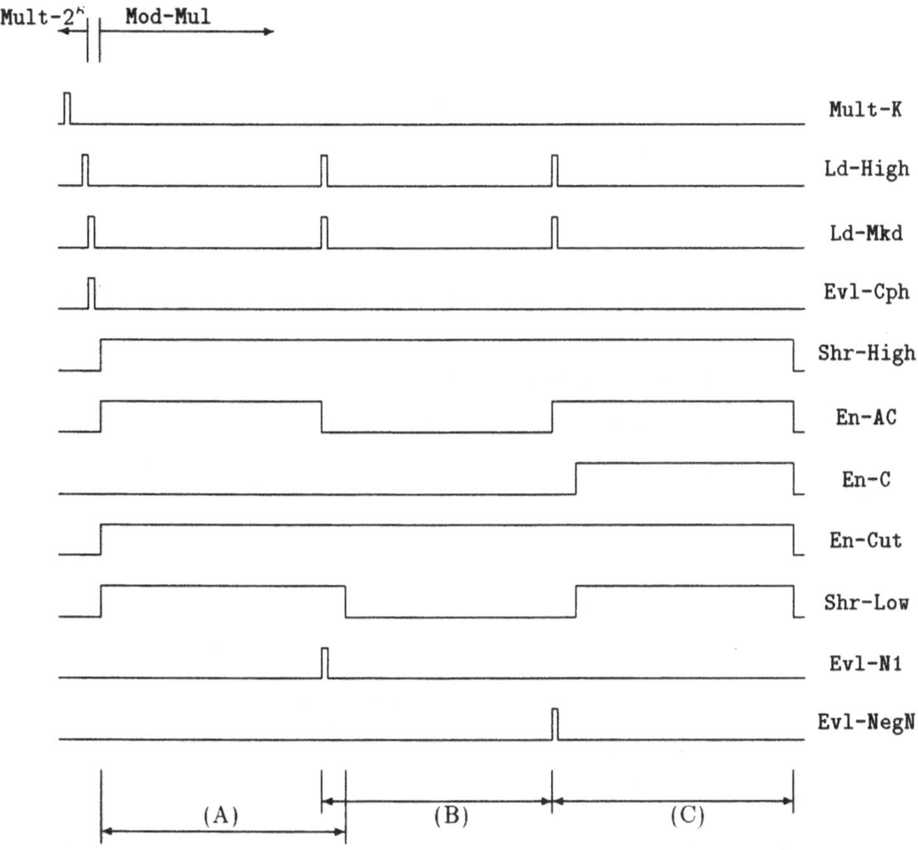

Figure 3: Timing diagram of the control signals during **Mult-2$^{\kappa}$** and **Mod-Mul**

3.4 Observations about the Control Words

We note that the two operations **Mult-2$^{\kappa}$** and **Mod-Mul** work correctly if and only if their related sequences of control words appear in a given order with a given timing; in particular, the control words within these two operations must not be separated by any additional control word, not even by a NOP (that is, a control word which performs no operation onto the MM data path). That is because the flow of the different data streams will proceed with the internal clock, and synchronization with external feeding of control words is to be assumed at given cycles. Obviously, a wrong product would be calculated otherwise. We will refer to such a non–interruptable sequence of control words as an *atomic sequence*.
We further note that throughout the algorithm some control words are repeated several times. These sections will be referred to as *stable sections*.

With respect to [Section 5] it is useful to consider an atomic sequence as a sequence of stable sections, where the number of the stable sections is called the

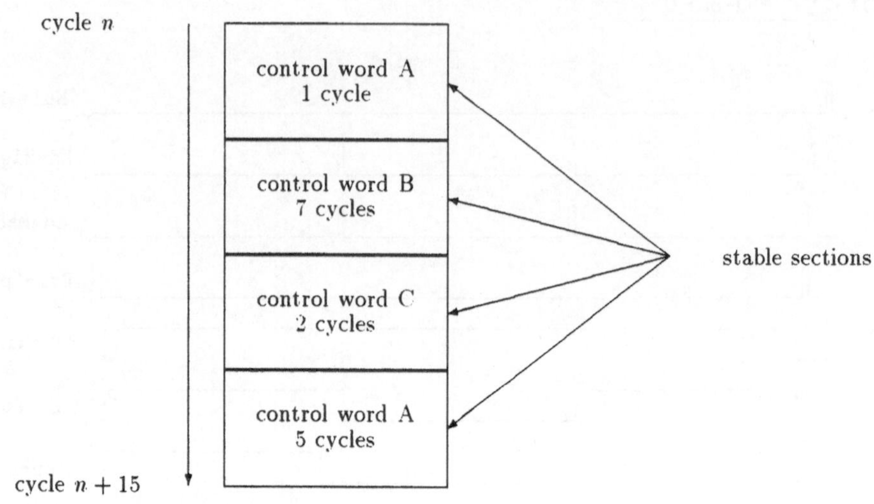

Figure 4: An atomic sequence, consisting of several stable sections

depth of the atomic sequence. Figure 4 shows an atomic sequence of a length of 15 cycles and depth 4.

4 A Modification of the FastMM Algorithm: FastMM*

A closer look at the FastMM algorithm shows that truncation of intermediate results is necessary. For reasons of regularity it would be easier to implement truncation only at multiples of i bits rather than at arbitrary positions. With FastMM, values would generally be cut off at positions $\neq i \cdot n$.

To facilitate implementation, a solution of this problem is given by a method called *preshifting*. With this method, constants $NegN$ and $N1$ as well as a and b are preshifted to the left by certain values. Loading the multiplier into **`High`** is done by using a $\kappa \neq 0$ when performing operation **`Mult-2`**$^{\kappa}$, thus shifting the multiplier to the left by κ bits for aligning at a desired border. After the modulo multiplication is finished, a final alignment is necessary to get the correct result. Furthermore, **`En-Cut`** must be able to truncate at arbitrary bit borders rather than at a position $i \cdot n$.

It is needless to mention that these additional procedures make the handling of the control signals more complicated. Therefore, the lengths of stable sections within the atomic sequence of operation **`Mod-Mul`** are shortened, increasing the depth of the atomic sequence — this is disadvantageous, as we will see in [Section 5]. For that reason, we would prefer an algorithm which avoids these difficulties.

The obvious goal in algorithm design is to minimize depth for a given algorithm by control word rearranging. A solution is given by a modified version of FastMM, called FastMM*.
FastMM* consists of the following steps:

$$X \leftarrow a \cdot b$$

$$Z \leftarrow M1 \cdot \frac{X}{2^{shift_1}}$$

$$y \leftarrow NegN \cdot \frac{Z}{2^{shift_2}} + X$$

The basic idea is to apply shifts only to constants which can be performed in advance. This algorithm has the same structure as FastMM, but uses a different constant $M1$ instead of $N1$. Preshifting will not be necessary because $shift_1$ and $shift_2$ can be determined to meet the conditions $shift_1 \equiv 0 \pmod{i}$ and $shift_2 \equiv 0 \pmod{i}$. Typically, one chooses $i = \log_2 r$, where r is the radix on which the long integer hardware is operating. The goals defined above can be achieved by calculating $M1$, $shift1$ and $shift2$ in the following way:

$$adj2 = (k-1) \bmod i$$

$$adj1 = i - ((k + 5 + adj2) \bmod i)$$

$$shift1 = k - 1 - adj2$$

$$shift2 = k + 5 + adj1 + adj2$$

$$M1 = 2^{2k+4+adj1} \cdot \frac{1}{N}$$

k is the length of the modulus N in bits.

A further benefit of FastMM* is that it allows optimization in terms of the possibility to change more control signals at the same time (i.e., a higher degree of parallelism) than with FastMM. This results in a significant reduction of the depth of the atomic sequence associated with `Mod-Mul`. Additionally, for FastMM* κ is always 0, therefore control signals associated with 2^{κ} may be omitted.

5 Managing the Clock Rate Difference Using a FIFO

In this section, a method for compensating the difference between the maximum clock rate allowed by the pads and the clock rate of the MM data path is presented.

First, data flow at the control signal interface will be reduced. This can easily be done because the MM data path doesn't need to be fed with one control word each cycle if we use stable sections instead. Each stable section is described by the corresponding control word and the numer of cycles it is "stable" [see figure 4]. The control structure between the pads and the MM data path now consists of a buffer for the control word, and a down counter to decide when to fetch the control word of the next stable section. That would be sufficient if each stable section consisted of enough cycles, ensuring that continuous fetching of control words never exceeds the maximum clock rate allowed by the pads.

Unfortunately, there are a lot of stable sections consisting only of a few cycles. Therefore, a mechanism has to be added which feeds internally generated NOPs into the MM data path until the next control word is available. Otherwise, control words could influence the MM data path in a wrong way.
However, this will still not work because atomic sequences must not be interrupted by NOPs. (The problem arises because of the existence of atomic sequences which contain stable sections of length one, as we will see in [Section 5.1].) The

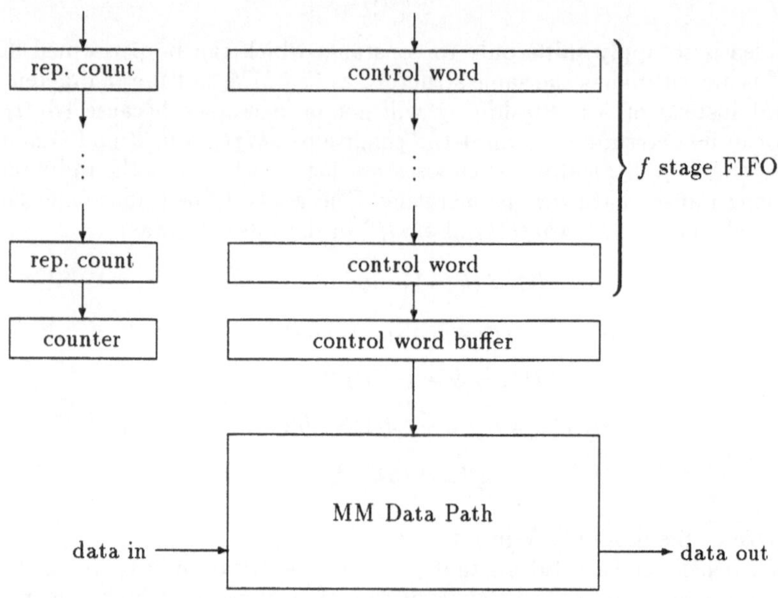

Figure 5: A FIFO for compensating the clock rate difference

solution is to add a FIFO between the pads and the control word buffer [see figure 5]. Inserting NOPs in between an atomic sequence can be prevented by preceding each atomic sequence with an externally inserted NOP as the control word, and a repeat count big enough to fill the FIFO with the stable sections of the entire atomic sequence. When the down counter expires, the stages of the FIFO are shifted, and the counter gets the next repeat count as start value. Internally generated NOPs will only reach the MM data path if the FIFO is cleared before the next external control word could reach the control word buffer. Therefore, the depth of the FIFO must not be lower than the depth of the longest atomic sequence.
As will be shown in [Section 5.2], analyzing atomic sequences of FastMM* allows for reducing this depth.

5.1 Atomic Instruction Sequences of FastMM*

For observing the control word flow at the MM data path, a simulation environment has been developed. This environment uses *GENIE*[1] for controlling the simulation of an RSA encryption with *Lsim*[2]. The simulation is based on an functional M^3–model of the MM data path.
The use of the procedural simulation interface provided by *GENIE* has several advantages:

- Simulation runs of high complexity can be controlled and evaluated by using a C–like language, thus allowing a higher level of abstraction than with conventional methods.
- Straightforward observation of the 696 bit wide MM data path becomes enabled.
- One can get the sequence of stable sections (that is, the control words and the associated number of cycles) for a modulo multiplication totally automatic.
- Flexibility in controlling the simulation simplifies extracting the atomic sequences.
- Once the simulation environment is "debugged", the occurance of errors when analyzing the interface is minimized.

Using this environment, the control signal interface of the MM data path can easily be analyzed for different algorithms as well as for different implementations of the same algorithm. Additionally, it supplies the control words needed for controlling a test chip which uses the proposed FIFO.

	Control Word	Repetitions
1	0180000_h	0
2	0100000_h	1
3	0104000_h	0

Table 2: Stable sections of **`Mult-2`**$^\kappa$

In [Table 2] and [Table 3], the atomic sequences for **`Mult-2`**$^\kappa$ and **`Mod-Mul`** of a full 664 bit modulo multiplication are shown. For each stable section the first value represents the control word, the second value the required repeat count. We observe that **`Mod-Mul`** calls for a FIFO of at least depth 9. This result is only valid for the FastMM* algorithm; as mentioned in [Section 4], the FastMM algorithm would increase depth significantly.

[1] $GENIE^{TM}$ (**G**eneral **I**nterpreted **E**nvironment) is a general–purpose interpreted language well–suited for use as a control language attached to application programs like *Lsim*.

[2] $Lsim^{TM}$ is a $MentorGraphics^R$ design automation tool that allows to analyze the behaviour of electronic designs ranging from high–level, abstract system models through full–custom integrated designs.

[3] *M* is a hardware description language for describing the behaviour of circuits in functional models, for use with the *Lsim* simulator.

	Control Word	Repetitions
1	0158020_h	88
2	$014E420_h$	0
3	0148020_h	6
4	0148000_h	81
5	$015F000_h$	0
6	0158000_h	5
7	0178020_h	85
8	0124020_h	0
9	0120020_h	1

Table 3: Stable sections of `Mod-Mul`

5.2 Reducing Depth of the Instruction FIFO

Having in mind [Table 3], we are able to introduce some optimizations. Since `Mod-Mul` starts with a control word which is repeated many times, this atomic sequence doesn't need to be preceded by an externally inserted NOP; the FIFO will be filled, anyway. Thus, waste of execution cycles can be reduced. That is true because we made the implicit assumption $T_e/T_i \leq r$, where T_e is the external cycle time (the maximum cycle time allowed by the pads), and T_i is the internal cycle time the MM data path uses. It seems to be adequate to assume $r = 5$.
A closer look at [Table 3] shows that for $r = 5$ a FIFO of depth 3 is sufficient because within `Mod-Mul` there are stable sections long enough to prevent clearing out the FIFO. This depth also satisfies `Mult-2`$^\kappa$.

A second possible method to reduce the depth of the FIFO is to split the atomic sequence associated with `Mod-Mul` into three shorter atomic sequences associated with the multiplication steps (A), (B) and (C). This method adds extra cycles to the entire modulo multiplication, but does not lead to a smaller FIFO than the first method does. Because speed of the modulo multiplication is the bottleneck of an RSA implementation, that method is not of prime interest.

6 An Outline of the Hardware Implementation

Using a FIFO for controlling the MM data path meets the goal of having an "as simple as possible" control structure for testing purposes. It would be quite consistent to avoid extremely complex design methods when implementing the FIFO in hardware. For the same reason, shifting the contents of the FIFO stages is chosen to be done synchronously rather than asynchronously.
The clock of the MM data path is used, since the FIFO must operate at the same (high) speed. This high speed seems to be the only substantial difficulty when designing the FIFO circuit layout.

As we have seen in [Section 5], a down counter will be needed. It has to fulfil the given timing constraints: decrementing, detecting underflow, setting up load signals for the stages and shifting the stages must work within a single cycle. Therefore, the down counter is replaced by a shifter, as shown in [Figure 6]. This

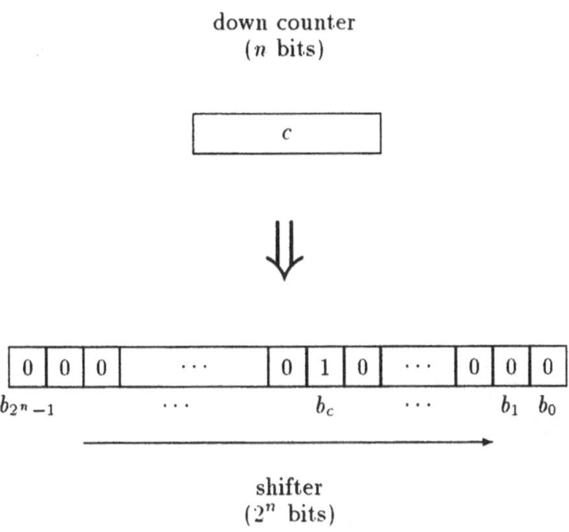

Figure 6: Replacing the down counter by a shifter

way, much of time is saved because shifting a single bit works a lot faster than decrementing a counter, and no decoder is necessary for detecting whether the next control word has to be loaded; this can be done by inspecting the single bit b_0. To avoid an excessively long shifter, its length can be decreased by limiting the repeat count to a certain power of two, thus splitting long stable sections. On the increasing FIFO depth resulting thereof and the length of the shifter a good compromise has to be evaluated.

Figure 7 shows a schematic diagram with a FIFO of depth 4. Precise timing issues are omitted; in particular, the circuit for the handshake signal timing has to be designed carefully. Special attention has to be paid to the asynchronous **`Strobe`** input to avoid metastable states and synchronization failure.

The handshake procedure works in the following way: If the top FIFO stage is empty, **`Busy`** is set to low, indicating a request for the next control word. The positive edge of **`Strobe`** signals that the next control word is available from outside, and sets **`Busy`** to high. For the time **`Busy`** is low, internal NOPs with repeat count 0 are to be inserted. This is done by "anding" the input signals with **`Busy`**. Additionally, the **`Ext`** bit is cleared, indicating an internally generated NOP. If **`Busy`** is high and the load signal for the top stage is set, there must have been a rising edge of **`Strobe`** (because the load signal resets **`Busy`**). In that case, the top stage is loaded from outside.

Load signals are generated as follows: Expiration of the shifter means to load all stages. If any stage is marked as an internally generated NOP, it should be overwritten at the next cycle, and all stages above have to move down; with other words, the decision for shifting an upper stage depends on the state of all underlying stages. This results in cascaded **`OR`** gates, shown in [Figure 7]. Remember there is only one cycle for setting up all load signals, therefore serious

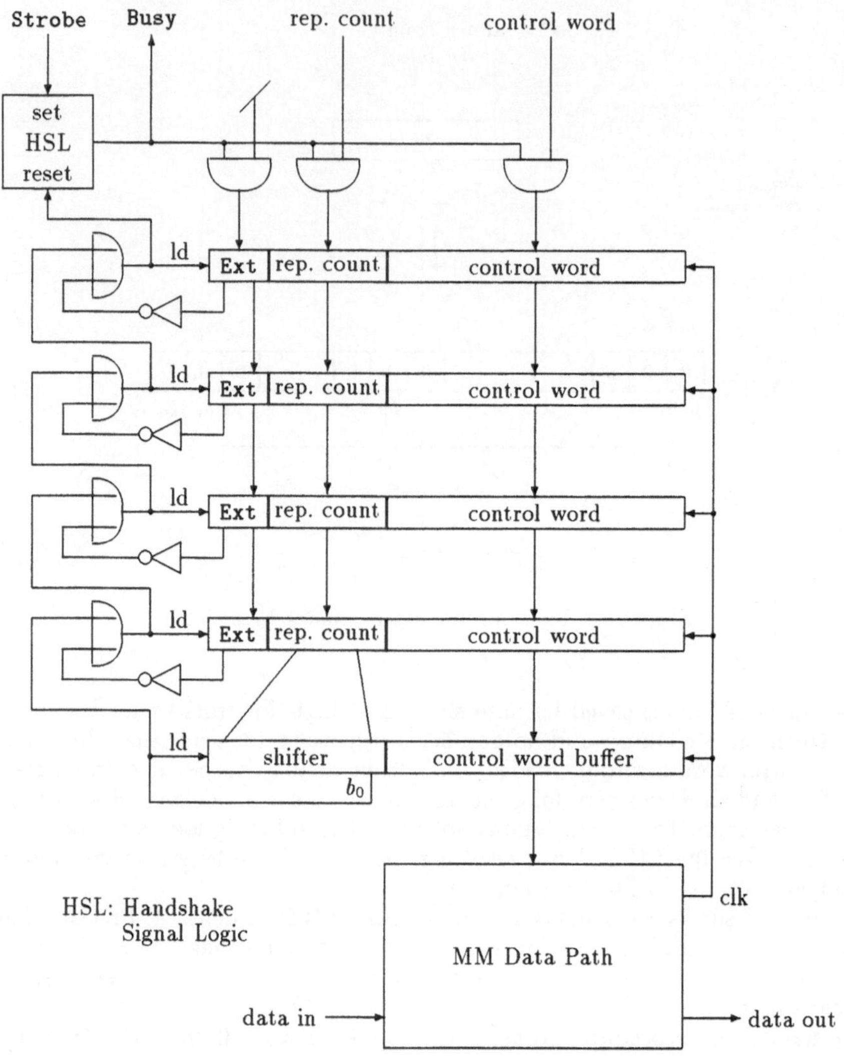

Figure 7: Schematic diagram of the FIFO

delays caused by cascaded gates must be avoided.

7 Conclusion

In order to design a chip for testing the MM data path, we searched a minimum version of the control structure. After analyzing the data flow at the control interface, we introduced a FIFO for compensating the difference of the maximum clock rate allowed by the chip's pads, and the clock rate the MM data path requires to reach the desired encryption rate.

Simulation results for a complete 664 bit RSA run based on M–models of the FIFO and the MM data path showed that it is sufficient to precede the whole sequence of multiplications with only a few NOPs, if we use the FastMM* algorithm and do not reduce the depth of the FIFO as described in [Section 5.2]. In this case, not even a single additional NOP needs to be inserted in between that sequence of multiplications. Because almost all cycles of a complete RSA run are needed for that sequence of multiplications, overall performance is not significantly affected by a slow clock rate at the pads. Therefore, if there is no need to reduce the depth of the FIFO (e.g. for shrinking down its size to save chip area), an RSA chip using the proposed control stucture might be appropriate even beyond testing purposes.

References

[Knuth (1981)] , D.E. Knuth: *The Art of Computer Programming.* Second Edition, Volume 2 / Seminumerical Algorithms, Addison–Wesley (1981), pp 441–442.

[Lippitsch et al (1991)] P. Lippitsch, K.C. Posch, R. Posch: *Multiplication As Parallel As Possible.* First International Conference of the Austrian Center for Parallel Computation, (Sep. 1991).

[Lippitsch et al (1992)] P. Lippitsch, K.C. Posch, R. Posch, V. Schindler: *A scalable design with encryption rates from 200 kBit/s to 1.5 MBit/s.* 32nd International Science Week, Damascus, (Dec. 1992).

[Montgomery (1985)] P.L. Montgomery: *Modulo Multiplication without Trial Division.* Mathematics of Computation, Volume 44, Number 170, (Apr. 1985). pp 519–521.

[Posch et al (1990)] K.C. Posch, R. Posch: *Approaching encryption at ISDN speed using partial parallel modulus multiplication.* Microprocessing and Microprogramming 29, (1990), pp 177–184.

[Rivest et al (1978)] R. Rivest, A. Shamir, L. Adleman: *A method for obtaining digital signatures and public–key cryptosystems.* Comm. ACM (1978), pp 120–126.

[Wallace (1964)] C.S. Wallace: *A suggestion for a fast multiplier.* IEEE Transactions on Electronic Computers, Vol. EC–13, (Feb. 1964), pp 14–17.

[Weste et al (1993)] N.H.E. Weste, K. Eshraghian: *Principles of CMOS VLSI Design. A Systems Perspective.* Second Edition, Addison–Wesley (1993).

Journal of Universal Computer Science, vol. 1, no. 11 (1995), 744-750
submitted: 12/11/95, accepted: 24/11/95, appeared: 28/11/95,

A Comparison of WWW and Hyper-G

Andrew Pam,
Xanadu Australia

Arnould Vermeer
University of Hagen, Germany

Abstract: In this paper we attempt to compare features of WWW and Hyper-G, the first fully operable networked multimedia system that goes much beyond WWW and incorporates many features first proposed in Xanadu and later partially tested in systems such as Intermedia.
Key Words: Hypermedia, Hyper-G, WWW, Xanadu, networked information systems, Internet
Categories: H.5.1

1 Introduction

Although WWW has become a major buzz word in connection with the Information Superhighway it was originally designed for limited size information system applications. As it is being used for more and more diverse and large efforts it is become increasingly clear that more powerful tools are necessary.

Although not yet as widely known, one such tool has emerged in 1995 that deserves attention: its compatibility with WWW combined with a more sophisticated architecture and many desperately needed features is making Hyper-G one of the obvious candidates to take over where WWW reaches its limits.

This paper is an attempt to present a comparison between the two systems and indicate why we believe WWW is less suitable for large or complex applications.

2 Data Representation

2.1 Text

a) The native text representation format for WWW is HTML, which is evolving through a series of official versions (1.0, 2.0 and now 3.0) 3and a range of of proprietary extensions implemented in browsers from companies such as IBM, Microsoft and Netscape. Hyper-G uses HTF (Hyper Text Format) and HTML. Both HTML and HTF are applications of SGML.
HTML and HTF have many similarities, although HTF has more powerful hyperlinks which may overlap while HTML has forms for user interaction and is being extended with a variety of interesting presentation facilities. Neither is suitable for scientific publishing, as they do not support the advanced type control necessary to present formulae, resulting in many authors currently resorting to inline images of the desired typography! HTML 3.0 will support mathematical notation.

b) Other text formats: both WWW and Hyper-G servers can support a variety of other text formats which can then be presented by viewing software either integrated into the browser or externally invoked as a "helper application". The existing native Hyper-G browsers already support Postscript (and can support hyperlinks on the Postscript documents). Internal support for Adobe PDF (Portable Document Format) and HTML in the Hyper-G browsers is in development.
c) The future: WWW is firmly committed to HTML, with gradual adoption of HTML 3.0 as the standard begins to coalesce although additional proprietary tags will no doubt continue to complicate the issue, perhaps to be included in later revisions of the HTML standard.
   Hyper-G will add HTML 3.0 support by the end of 1995, including tables, forms and CGI (Common Gateway Interface) scripts, thus providing full compatibility with WWW.

2.2 Other Data

a) Both WWW and Hyper-G servers and viewers support images in GIF and JPEG format, both inline and as documents in their own right.
b) Both WWW and Hyper-G servers and viewers support audio and video clips. There is no mechanism to support hyperlinks within audio and video objects in WWW. Only the entire media object can be a link destination. Hyper-G permits links to and from sections of audio and video objects.
c) 3D scenes are supported in both WWW and Hyper-G using the VRML standard.

3 Data Structures

3.1 Basic Units

WWW: documents; Hyper-G: clusters of documents which are intended to be presented simultaneously or represent the same information in different forms, for example in different languages. The WWW concept is a special case of the Hyper-G version when a cluster contains only one document.

3.2 Structuring of Documents

WWW: no structuring beyond (uni)directional links; thus, a WWW database has no well-defined document groupings other than the server filesystem directory structure, which is therefore often used to define the scope for searches and access authorisation. This requires considerable planning and maintenance of the server filesystem layout.

Hyper-G: bi-directional links; clusters have attributes (that can be searched on) and are grouped into collections. Collections can themselves be members of other collections, and may belong to more than one parent collection; thus, Hyper-G provides two orthogonal structuring paradigms, elements of a relational database and hence a variety of access techniques.

4 Link Philosophy

4.1 Basic Links

WWW: links are uni-directional and embedded into documents. They can be attatched to text or images, but not to other media. The destination is generally an entire document but may also be a position within the document or (with some servers) a byte range within a document.

Hyper-G: links are bi-visible and bi-followable, stored in a separate link database, can be associated with any part of text, image, audio and video material and can have as destination a collection, a document or part of a document.

Hyper-G is more flexible in its link concept: the bi-visibility makes it possible to determine all documents pointing to any given document (particularly important for database maintenance!); keeping links in a separate server database from the documents allows users to add their own private links even to documents they do not own ("construction of private views and customization"); links to no longer existing documents can be easily removed; source and destination anchors in Hyper-G are generalisations of the WWW concept.

4.2 Forms and Clickable Imagemaps

WWW supports forms that can be filled out and "clickable imagemaps". In clickable imagemaps a cursor position can be returned and used in an arbitrary program. Since Hyper-G inherently supports source anchors for links on regions of an image, it can provide the same functionality without additional programming at the server. This is similar to the new "USEMAP" HTML tag which defines the image regions for the browser. Hyper-G will also support HTML forms.

5 Server Philosophy

5.1 Network of Servers vs. Distributed Database

WWW: Users access one server at a time and switch from server to server using a "stateless" protocol. Each document request generates a separate connection to the server where that document is stored, possibly via a proxy server.

Hyper-G: Users access one server and through that server all others, unless explicitly overruled. This makes it much easier to generate statistics on user navigation through the server.

The Hyper-G approach allows extensive caching: when 100 persons access, through a local Hyper-G server X, a picture from a remote server Y that picture will be transfered from Y to X only a single time; in WWW the picture will be transmitted from Y to each of the 100 persons unless those persons all point their clients to a proxy server with caching running. The Hyper-G server-server protocol also ensures cache consistency, which is a difficult issue with WWW proxy caches.

The fixed connection approach of Hyper-G has one potential drawback: suppose a New Yorker accesses a Hyper-G server in Paris and finds a link there to another New York server. In WWW selecting this link by-passes Paris immediately; in Hyper-G the user has to explicitly disconnect with the Paris server if the "detour" is considered undesirable. It may, however, be desirable since billing services and disciplined use of the Internet become easier using this Hyper-G approach.

5.2 Integration of Other Servers

WWW provides a common Gateway Interface (CGI) to integrate external applications; a similar interface has been announced for Hyper-G. SQL gateways (Oracle, Sybase, etc.) have also been implemented for Hyper-G.

5.3 Searching

WWW has no built-in search facility. Some WWW servers such as WN do have built in searching, and most allow third-party search engines such as WAIS or GLIMPSE to be added. However, this requires additional configuration and is implemented differently (if at all) on each site.

There are also various search engines that index documents from as many WWW servers as possible, such as Lycos, Webcrawler and Excite. However, these indexes are built by programs which laboriously "crawl" around the WWW following links to discover documents, and thus often contain many documents which no longer exist or have been moved. Many documents are not indexed because they have not been discovered by the program.

Hyper-G has a built-in search facility: as search scope a union of collections (even distributed over geographically distant servers) can be specified. Attribute, title and full-text searches are supported.

5.4 Platforms

WWW servers are available from CERN, NCSA, NetScape, and others. Most platforms are supported.

Hyper-G servers are available under UNIX (including Linux) and have been announced for Windows NT. Hyper-G is freely available, and maintenance contracts for commercial users are provided. Sources are available but have to be licensed for commercial usage.

5.5 Security

"Secure" servers are available from NCSA (S-HTTP) and Netscape (SSL and S-HTTP). Hyper-G has pledged to follow the NCSA approach to provide authentication, security and privacy, and to have additonal billing possibilities.

Hyper-G offers two ways for billing information right now: a "subscription" approach based on passwords and a "limited number of users at a time" licensing technique.

5.6 Annotations

In Hyper-G users can "annotate" documents (by adding their own linked documents), and annotations can themselves be annotated. Since viewers support the annotation process this provides for an asynchronous computer conferencing feature not available in WWW (where the embedded link concept does not allow this kind of annotation).

5.7 "Local" Database

A "local" server that allows previously downloaded documents to be viewed is available in rudimentary form for Netscape. A powerful version has been announced for Hyper-G. Thus, parts of Hyper-G databases can be directly transferred to CD-ROM. The ED-MEDIA'95 proceedings available under <http://hyperg.iicm.tu-graz.ac.at/electronic_library> is one example: it is available in exactly the same form also on a CD.

6 Clients and Interoperability

6.1 Clients

A host of WWW clients are available on the PC, Mac and Unix platforms. The best known are NCSA Mosaic and Netscape. The latter has achieved some 70% market share within the last six months. Netscape is easy to install and to use, fast, and offers a number of features like access to Newsgroups and FTP that other viewers (including Hyper-G viewers) are still lacking.

For Hyper-G there is the "Terminal Viewer" HGTV, a simple text-based viewer and editor for all platforms, the fancy X-Windows viewer Harmony and the MS-Windows viewer Amadeus. Both Harmony and Amadeus have navigational features going beyond WWW clients (see 6.2. below) and can be used as powerful structure-editing tools. A particularly easy to use "one-window" viewer for Hyper-G under MS-Windows is in preparation. A Mac viewer is also under development.

6.2 Navigational Features

All clients (WWW and Hyper-G) provide basic navigational facilities like "back", "history", "bookmark", clicking on a link, etc. The extent of navigational facilities depends also on the server. Hence, Hyper-G viewers give "location feedback" (showing where users are within the collections of Hyper-G), a "local map" (showing in- and outgoing links, currently only supported by Harmony) and "3D Information landscapes" (Harmony only). Navigational features for Hyper-G even with WWW clients include search facilities and "go to parents of current collection": these features are provided to non-Hyper-G clients in the Hyper-G WWW gateway.

6.3 Interoperability

All WWW viewers allow access to Hyper-G servers (and profit in this case from some of Hyper-G's functionality). Conversely, all Hyper-G viewers allow access to all WWW servers. Note that 100% compatibility even between WWW clients is impossible as long as HTML 3.0 is not universally accepted as standard.

However, it is important to understand that the choice of viewer is independent of the choice of server.

7 Penetration and Developments

WWW has literally exploded during the last 2 years. Numbers vary, but some 20,000 servers are installed, albeit the vast majority containing not more then a few pages. Hyper-G (server and Harmony viewer) was released in January 95, causing some ripples. By mid 1995, over 100 Hyper-G servers are installed with remarkable growth. WWW is better suited for small applications, but Hyper-G is the only viable alternative for large databases when WWW (without much "propping up") tends to break down.

Some main players at the moment are:

(1) NCSA working on server and client (Mosaic) development.

(2) IICM/IHM Graz working on Hyper-G.

(3) Netscape working on Netscape servers and clients.

(4) University of Minnesota working on the next generation Gopher system.

(5) CERN, the original home of WWW, working on standardisation, particularly of HTML 3.0.

(6) INRIA, which just has entered the arena to take over some of the work CERN has previously been doing.

The W3 Consortium, headed by MIT with INRIA its European partner, is trying to channel new developments; and so is the recently formed Web Society (see <http://info.websoc.at/>), where members of IICM/IHM Graz, UMN, CERN and INRIA have become directors, with NCSA potentially to follow. The directors of the Web Society (in contrast to W3C) must come from non-profit organisations.

NCSA, IICM/IHM Graz, UMN, and CERN are in close coordination to assure interoperability on the viewer level now and in the future; they will also try to join forces with INRIA.

As a first cooperative venture a VRML Viewer has recently been jointly announced by NCSA, IICM/IHM Graz and UMN. These organisations have also agreed on further joint development work on future integrated Internet tools combining the best of Gopher, WWW, and Hyper-G.

The IICM/IHM Graz and UMN are cooperating closely on the client side and on providing Gopher users an upgrade path to Hyper-G.

A Hyper-G consortium has been formed. Details can be found at <hyperg://hyperg.hgc.org/> or <http://www.hgc.org/>.

References

[Alberti 1992 et al] Alberti, B., Anklesaria, F., Lindnder, P., McCahill, M., Torrey, D.: Internet Gopher Protocol: A Distributed Document Search and Retrieval Protocol; <ftp://boombox.micro.umn.edu/pub/gopher/gopher_protocol/>.

[Andrews et al 1995a] Andrews, K., Kappe, F.,Maurer, H., Schmaranz, K.: On Second Generation Hypermedia Systems; Proc.ED-MEDIA'95, Graz (June 1995). See also J.UCS 0.0 (1994), 127-136 at <http://hyperg.iicm.tu-graz.ac.at/jucs>.

[Andrews et al 1995b] Andrews, K., Kappe, F., Maurer, H.: Serving Information to the Web with Hyper-G; Computer Networks and ISDN Systems 27 (1995), 919-926.

[Berners-Lee et al 1992] Berners-Lee, T., Cailliau, R., Groff, J., Poll WorldWideWeb: The Information Universe; Electronic Networking: Research, Applications and Policy 1,2 (1992), 52-58.

[Calude et al 1994] Calude, C., Maurer, H., Salomaa, A.: J.UCS: The Journal of Universal Computer Science; J.UCS 0.0 (1994) 109-117 at <http://hyperg.iicm.tu-graz.ac.at/jucs>.

[Conklin 1987] Conklin, E.J.: Hypertext: an Introduction and Survey; IEEE Computer 20 (1987), 17-41.

[Deutsch 1992] Deutsch, P.: Resource Discovery in an Internet Environment - the Archie Approach; Electronic Networking: Research, Applications and Policy 1.2 (1992), 45-51.

[Fenn et all 1994] Fenn, B., Maurer, H.: Harmony on an Expanding Net; ACM Interactions 1.3 (1994), 26-38.

[Haan et al 1992] Haan, B.J., Kahn, P., Riley, V.A., Coombs, J.H., Meyrowitz, N.K.: IRIS Hypermedia Services; Communications of the ACM 35.1 (1992), 36-51.

[Kahle et al 1992] Kahle, B., Morris, H., Davis, F., Tiene, K., Hart, C., Palmer, R.: Wide Area Information Servers: An Executive Information System for Unstructured Files; Electronic Networking: Research, Applications and Policy 1.2 (1992), 59-68.

[Kappe et al 1993] Kappe, F., Maurer, H., Scherbakov, N.: Hyper-G - a Universal Hypermedia System; Journal of Educational Multimedia and Hypermedia 2.1 (1993), 39-66.

[Kappe et al 1994] Kappe, F., Andrews, K., Faschingbauer, J., Gaisbauer, M., Maurer, H., Pichler, M., Schipflinger, J.: Hyper-G: A New Tool for Distributed Multimedia; Proc. Conf. on Open Hypermedia Systems, Honolulu (1994), 209-214.

[Lennon et al 1994a] Lennon, J., Maurer, H.: Lecturing Technology: A Future With Hypermedia; Educational Technology 34.4 (1994), 5-14.

[Lennon et al 1994b] Lennon, J., Maurer, H.: Applications and Impact of Hypermedia Systems: An Overview; J.UCS 0.0 (1994), 54-108 at <http://hyperg.iicm.tu-graz.ac.at/jucs>.

[Marchionini et al 1995] Marchionini, G.,Maurer, H.: The Role of Digital Libraries in Teaching and Learning; Communications of the ACM 38.4 (April 1995)

[Maurer 1994a] Maurer, H.: Advancing the ideas of WorldWideWeb; Proc. Conf. on Open Hypermedia Systems, Honolulu (1994), 201-203.

[Maurer et al 1994] Maurer, H., Schmaranz, K.: J.UCS - The Next Generation in Electronic Journal Publishing; Proc. Electronic Publ. Conference, London (November 1994), in: Computer Networks for Research in Europe 26, Supplement 2-3 (1994), 63-69.

[Maurer 1994 a] Maurer, H.: Hypermedia in a Gambling Casino Setting; Proc. HIM, Konstanz (April 1995)

[Maurer 1994b] Maurer, H.: The A.E.I.O.U. Hypermedia Project; Proc. Computer Animation '94, Geneva (May 1994), 192-196.

[Nelson 1987] Nelson, T.H.: Literary machines; Edition 87.1, 702 South Michigan, South Bend, IN 46618, USA (1987)

[Nielsen 1995] Nielsen, J.: Hypertext and Hypermedia; Academic Press (1995)

Managing Editor's Column

Vol. 1, No. 12; December 28, 1995

Dear Readers:

This last issue of volume 1 of J.UCS consists of five high quality papers, most of them (contrasting to the previous issue) relating to more theoretical or fundamental results.

It is a pleasure to see how well J.UCS has developed within the first year, and how it has established itsself as one of the major electronic publications in computer science. Note that this volume 1 of J.UCS consisting of 12 issues will also appear on CD-ROM: indeed, 30,000 such CD-ROM's will be produced and distributed by Springer free of charge. If you want to be sure to get one you may want to drop me a note: hmaurer@iicm.tu-graz.ac.at! But volume 1 of J.UCS will also appear in printed form as rather impressive book with some 800 pages. Thus, contributions in J.UCS have and will continue to have high visibility.

I would like to take this opportunity to thank all contributors for choosing J.UCS as medium of publication, and particulalry all editors for their effort in reviewing papers. Most of all I want to thank the two other editors in chief, Cris Calude from the University of Auckland and Arto Salomaa from the University of Turku for their continued help, encouragement and support.

Let us now get started on the second volume of J.UCS!

Happy reading and all the best for 96, cordially

Hermann Maurer
email: hmaurer@iicm.tu-graz.ac.at

Journal of Universal Computer Science, vol. 1, no. 12 (1995), 752-761
submitted: 17/11/95, accepted: 21/12/95, appeared: 28/12/95 © *Springer Pub. Co.*

A Novel Type of Skeleton for Polygons

Oswin Aichholzer
Franz Aurenhammer
Institute for Theoretical Computer Science
Graz University of Technology
Klosterwiesgasse 32/2, A-8010 Graz, Austria
{oaich,auren}@igi.tu-graz.ac.at

David Alberts
Bernd Gärtner
Institut für Informatik
Freie Universität Berlin
Takustraße 9, D-14195 Berlin, Germany
{alberts,gaertner}@inf.fu-berlin.de

Abstract A new internal structure for simple polygons, the straight skeleton, is introduced and discussed. It is composed of pieces of angular bisectores which partition the interior of a given n-gon P in a tree-like fashion into n monotone polygons. Its straight-line structure and its lower combinatorial complexity may make the straight skeleton preferable to the widely used medial axis of a polygon. As a seemingly unrelated application, the straight skeleton provides a canonical way of constructing a polygonal roof above a general layout of ground walls.

Keywords: Simple polygon, angular bisectors, internal skeleton, roof construction

1 Introduction and basic properties

The purpose of this paper is to introduce and discuss a new and interesting internal structure for simple polygons in the plane. The new structure, called the *straight skeleton*, is solely made up of straight line segments which are pieces of angular bisectors of polygon edges. It uniquely partitions the interior of a given n-gon P into n monotone polygons, one for each edge of P.

The straight skeleton, in general, differs from the well-known *medial axis* of P which consists of all interior points whose closest point on P's boundary is not unique; see e.g. Lee [L]. If P is convex then both structures are identical. Otherwise, the medial axis contains parabolically curved segments in the neighborhood of reflex vertices of P which are avoided by the straight skeleton. If P is rectilinear then the straight skeleton is the medial axis of P for the L_∞-metric. Skeletons have numerous applications inside and outside computer science as is documented e.g. in Kirkpatrick [K].

While the medial axis is a Voronoi-diagram-like concept, the straight skeleton is not defined using a distance function but rather by an appropriate *shrinking process* for P. Imagine that the boundary of P is contracted towards P's interior, in a self-parallel manner and at the same speed for all edges. Lengths of edges might decrease or increase in this process. Each vertex of P moves along the angular bisector of its incident edges. This situation continues as long as the boundary does not change topologically. There are two possible types of changes:

(1) *Edge event*: An edge shrinks to zero, making its neighboring edges adjacent now.

(2) *Split event*: An edge is split, i.e., a reflex vertex runs into this edge, thus splitting the whole polygon. New adjacencies occur between the split edge and each of the two edges incident to the reflex vertex.

After either type of event, we are left with a new, or two new, polygons which are shrunk recursively if they have non-zero area. Note that certain events will occur simultaneously even if P is in general position, namely three edge events letting a triangle collapse to a point. The shrinking process gives a hierarchy of nested polygons; see Figure 1(a).

The straight skeleton, $S(P)$, is defined as the union of the pieces of angular bisectors traced out by polygon vertices during the shrinking process. $S(P)$ is a unique structure defining a polygonal partition of P. Each edge e of P sweeps out a certain area which we call the *face* of e. Bisector pieces are called *arcs*, and their endpoints which are not vertices of P are called *nodes*, of $S(P)$. See Figure 1(b).

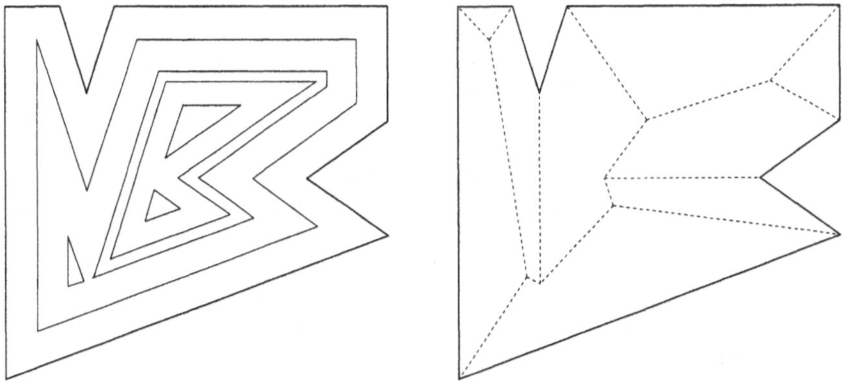

Figure 1: (a) Polygon hierarchy and (b) straight skeleton

As far as it is known to the authors, no attention has been paid to the straight skeleton in the literature. We show that $S(P)$ has several useful properties. For example, its tree structure implies that, if P is non-convex, $S(P)$ is of smaller combinatorial size than the medial axis of P. The latter, though also being a tree, has to distinguish between curved and straight parts of arcs. To be precise, if P is an n-gon with r reflex vertices then $S(P)$ realizes $2n-3$ arcs whereas the medial axis of P realizes $2n+r-3$ arcs, r of which are parabolically curved. As a particularly nice property, $S(P)$ partitions P into monotone polygons.

A three-dimensional interpretation of $S(P)$, the roof model, is discussed in Section 2 and Section 3. This leads us to the interesting and practically relevant question of constructing a roof of fixed slope above a given layout P of ground walls. The roof model allows us to gain more insight into the structure of straight skeletons and, in particular, gives a way to define $S(P)$ non-procedurally. On the other hand, $S(P)$ provides a canonical way of constructing a roof above P. We show that the roof corresponding to $S(P)$ exclusively has the property that rainwater runs off from each roof facet to its defining edge of P. We also disprove the obvious conjecture that roofs can be expressed as lower envelopes of simply-shaped linear functions. Hence $S(P)$ is no Voronoi-diagram-like structure, a fact that complicates its algorithmic construction. Section 4 offers a short discussion of the presented topic.

The rest of this section describes some basic properties of $S(P)$.

Lemma 1. *$S(P)$ is a tree and consists of exactly n connected faces, $n-2$ nodes and $2n-3$ arcs.*

Proof. The construction of a face $f(e)$ starts at its edge, e, of P. $f(e)$ cannot be split even if e happens to be. The construction of $f(e)$ is completed when (every part of) e has shrunk to zero. As e cannot reappear again, $f(e)$ is connected, and $S(P)$ is acyclic. That is, $S(P)$ is a tree with the n vertices of P as leaves, and has $n-2$ nodes and $2n-3$ arcs. □

Two types of arcs of $S(P)$ can be distinguished. Each arc is a piece of the angular bisector of two edges e and e' of P or, more precisely, of the lines $\ell(e)$ and $\ell(e')$ supporting these edges. Note that the angular bisector of $\ell(e)$ and $\ell(e')$ actually consists of two lines that intersect at $\ell(e) \cap \ell(e')$. We single out the one relevant for $S(P)$ as follows. Each line $\ell(e)$ defines a halfplane $h(e)$ that contains P near e. One of the bisector lines intersects the wedge $h(e) \cap h(e')$ while the other avoids it. We call the former the *bisector* of the edges e and e' and will ignore the latter in our considerations. An arc a defined by this bisector is called a *convex arc* or a *reflex arc* depending on whether its wedge contains e and e' in its boundary or not. We also consider a as labeled by the ordered pair (e, e'). The order reflects the side of a where $\ell(e)$ contributes to the boundary of the wedge.

Each convex (reflex) vertex of P obviously gives rise to a convex (reflex) arc of $S(P)$. While convex arcs can also connect two nodes of $S(P)$, this is impossible for reflex arcs.

Lemma 2. *Reflex arcs of $S(P)$ only emanate from reflex vertices of P.*

Proof. Let vu be an arc emanating from some vertex v of P. Then u is a node which corresponds either to an edge event or to a split event. It suffices to show that, after the event, $S(P)$ continues at u with convex arcs only.

In the former case, let vw be the vanishing edge. Since the arc wu meets vu at u, u is a convex vertex of the shrunk polygon at the moment the event takes place. In the latter case, the polygon splits at u. It is obvious that, at that moment, u is a convex vertex of both new polygons.

In conclusion, each new vertex generated during the shrinking process is convex. Hence the arcs continuing at u are convex, too. □

2 Graph model and roof model

It seems hard to give a non-procedural definition of the straight skeleton, as it is available for the medial axis using distances from the boundary. The shrinking model suggests to define the distance of a point $x \in P$ from an edge e as the normal distance from x to the supporting line $\ell(e)$. This definition fails as e might have vanished before $\ell(e)$ sweeps across x. Below we discuss two other approaches, the graph model and the roof model, that allow us to gain more insight into the structure of straight skeletons.

$S(P)$ can be seen as a geometric graph whose arcs are pieces of bisectors defined by the edges of P, each arc being labeled by an ordered pair of edges. Arcs are bounded by P's vertices, which have degree 1 in the graph, and by $S(P)$'s nodes which have degree 3. Each node is the intersection point of three bisectors. (To ease the discussion, we exclude degeneracies caused by special shapes of P.) Its three incident arcs have labels of the form (a, b), (b, c), (c, a), and the ordering of each label (a, b) indicates the position of the faces $f(a)$ and $f(b)$ relative to the arc. We call a graph with these properties a *bisector graph* for P.

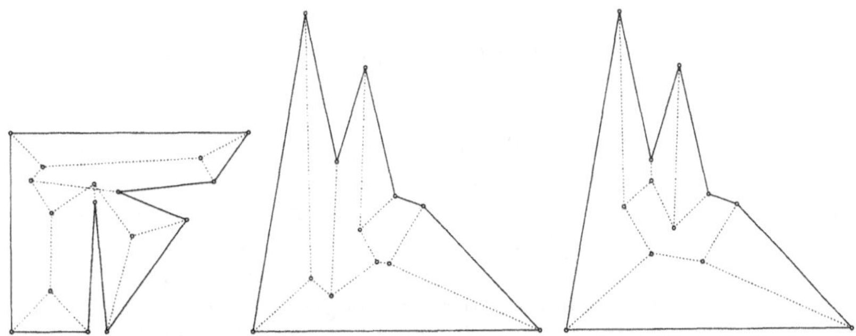

Figure 2: Bisector graphs; self-intersection and ambiguity

However, these properties are by far to weak to imply uniqueness. A bisector graph need not even define a partition of P (and thus a face structure) as long as we do not require it to be plane. Restriction to plane graphs, even to plane trees (as it is the case for $S(P)$, see Lemma 1) still gives no unique structure; see Figure 2.

Alternatively, and more intuitively appealing, a plane bisector graph for P can be viewed as the projection of a three-dimensional object.

Let P be contained in the horizontal plane Π_0, and associate each edge e of P with a halfplane $\Pi(e)$ in three-space. $\Pi(e)$ is bounded by $\ell(e)$, has a fixed slope (say 45 degrees) with respect to Π_0, and is inclined towards P. For any two distinct edges e and e' of P, the halfline $\Pi(e) \cap \Pi(e')$ projects vertically to the (relevant halfline of the) bisector of e and e'.

We now define a *roof* for P as a terrain (graph of a piecewise-linear continuous function) over P whose facets are from the halfplanes above and whose intersection with Π_0 is the boundary of P. Intuitively speaking, this is a 45-degree roof with P's edges as ground walls; see Figure 3.

Theorem 3. *Every roof for P corresponds to a unique plane bisector graph for P, and vice versa.*

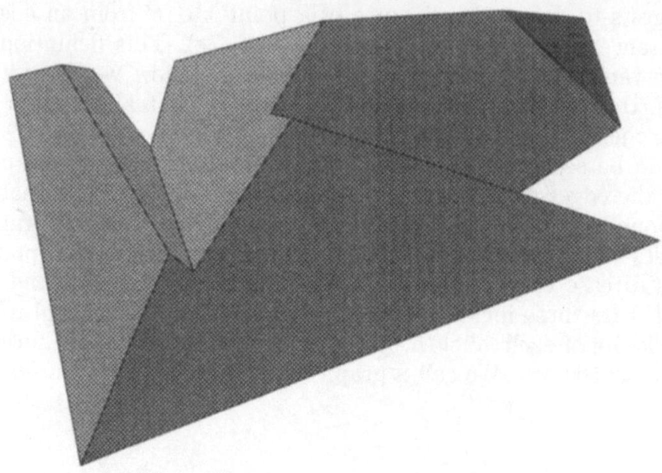

Figure 3: Roof model for straight skeleton in Figure 1

Proof. Let R be a roof for P. By the choice of the halfplanes supporting R's facets, the edges of R project vertically to pieces of edge bisectors. Bisectors are labeled correctly, as each node of the resulting graph is the projected intersection of three halfplanes. Finally, the graph is plane as R is a terrain.

Let G be a plane bisector graph for P. Each node u of G is the center of a circle that touches three lines supporting the three edges of P that define u. We lift up u vertically by the radius of this circle, getting a point $\lambda(u)$ in three-space. Note that, if u's arcs are labeled (a,b), (b,c), (c,a), then $\lambda(u) \in \Pi(a) \cap \Pi(b) \cap \Pi(c)$. Let now f be a face of G. Each arc bounding f has a label of the form (x,e), where e is a fixed edge of P , and x runs through the edges defining the faces of G adjacent to f. Hence $\lambda(u) \in \Pi(e)$ for all nodes u of f. Clearly, $e \in \Pi(e)$ by definition. (Note, however, that e does not necessarily bound f.) This shows that f is lifted up by λ to a planar facet. As G is a plane graph, we obtain a piecewise-linear function over P. This function is continuous as facets stemming from faces $f(e)$ and $f(e')$ touch along the lifted arc with label (e,e'). □

In the unique roof of a plane bisector graph, convex arcs of the graph give rise to *ridges* of the roof (both facets going downwards) and reflex arcs give rise to *valleys* (both facets going upwards). Note the impossibility of having one facet upwards and the other downwards, as all facets have the same slope. Endpoints of ridges or of valleys that are not polygon vertices are called *corners* of the roof. They lie above plane Π_0 and project to the nodes of the graph.

It is interesting – also from a practical point of view – to study which kind of roofs are legitimate by our definition. Surprisingly, a halfplane may contribute more than one facet to the roof. That is, an edge of P may yield several faces in the bisector graph. Even local minima may arise; see Figure 4. The first anomaly indicates that, in contrast to the straight skeleton, the size of general plane bisector graphs need not be linear. A trivial upper bound is $O(n^3)$, as each node of the graph comes from a different triple of edges of P. The second anomaly is particularly undesirable for real-world roofs as rain water cannot run off.

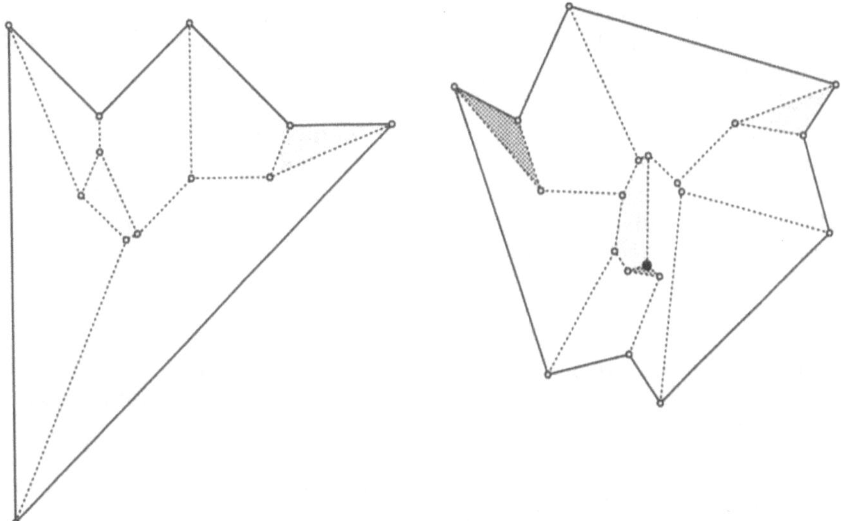

Figure 4: Disconnected faces and local minimum

Despite of the ambiguity of plane bisector graphs, their faces have a nice property which is easy to prove using the roof model.

Lemma 4. *Each face $f(e)$ of a plane bisector graph is monotone in direction of its defining edge e. That is, the intersection of $f(e)$ with every line normal to e is connected.*

Proof. Let F be the roof facet corresponding to $f(e)$. Recall $F \subset \Pi(e)$ and consider some line L in $\Pi(e)$ normal to e. Obviously, L has slope 1, which is the maximum possible on the roof. Assume now that $f(e)$ is not monotone in direction e. Then L can be chosen so as to leave F at some point x and to re-enter F at some higher point y. In between, the roof consists of facets contained in halfplanes different from $\Pi(e)$. Hence, when following the vertical projection of the segment xy on the roof, one traces segments of slope less than 1, thus ending up at a point vertically below y. This implies that the roof is not continuous – a contradiction. □

3 Islands

The concept of straight skeleton $S(P)$ offers a unique way of constructing a roof avoiding the anomalies mentioned above, for a general layout P of ground walls. When viewing $S(P)$ as a roof, the shrinking process defining $S(P)$ has a nice physical interpretation. The roof is interpreted as an island with P deliminating the coast. Water level stands at plane Π_0 and rises steadily during the shrinking process. Splits occur when the water surrounds local maxima of the island. The unique roof for P corresponding to $S(P)$ will be called the *island* of P, $I(P)$, in the sequel.

This *flooding process* gives sense for non-island roofs, too. In fact, each roof for P defines a particular flooding process which is uniquely determined by a sequence of events sorted by increasing height. This fact will allow us to characterize $I(P)$ among all possible roofs for P.

Let R be an arbitrary roof for P. In the flooding process for R, we now may encounter new types of events beside edge events and split events. For example, it is possible that the water level reaches a local minimum of a facet at a corner c of R. If c is no local minimum of R then – in the shrunk polygon – an edge parallel to some edge of P starts expanding there (inverse edge event). Else a triangular hole appears (three simultaneous inverse edge events). Compare Figure 4. This list of events is not complete.

Lemma 5. *If R is a roof for P different from $I(P)$ then R has a valley not incident to a (reflex) vertex of P. That is, R contains a valley that connects two corners of R.*

Proof. Note first that the flooding process starts in the same way for all possible roofs for P. That is, P starts to shrink in a unique manner. Now consider the first event that makes R differ from $I(P)$. This event must come from a corner of R. If it would come from a corner of $I(P)$ then an edge event or a split event would miss in the flooding process for R, contradicting its terrain property. Let now c be the corner of R that corresponds to this event. Immediately before reaching c, water surrounds the part of R containing c and defines a shrunk polygon P' whose boundary deliminates the local coast. Obviously, the part of $I(P)$ above P' is $I(P')$. As $I(P')$ continues with the next-higher edge event or split event, and c is no corner of $I(P')$, c corresponds to a non-island type of event. In particular, some edge that does not appear in P' must be involved in this event. That is, some new edge(s) start(s) expanding. An expansion of edges, however, can only take place at reflex arcs. Hence some valley of R starts at c, and the lemma is proved. □

Theorem 6. *Let R be a roof for P. Then $R = I(P)$ if and only if each valley of R is incident to P.*

Proof. Combine Lemma 2 and Lemma 5. □

It is easy to see that each roof for P has the same surface area. A natural question to ask is whether $I(P)$ optimizes some other parameter among all possible roofs for P. However, $I(P)$ achieves neither the maximum nor the minimum roof volume in general; see Figure 2 (shows $I(P)$ in the middle) and Figure 5, respectively. These examples also reveal that neither the maximum nor the minimum global roof height is guaranteed. Still, the facets of $I(P)$ obey a nice rule which is particular to $I(P)$.

Let R be any roof for P. For a point x on R, let $g(x)$ denote the path that starts from x and follows the steepest gradient on R. We say that a facet F of R has the *gradient property* if, for every $x \in F$, $g(x)$ reaches the edge e defining F either in its interior or at a vertex.

Theorem 7. *A roof R for P is the island of P if and only if each facet of R fulfills the gradient property.*

Proof. Assume $R = I(P)$. Let e be an edge of P, let F be its facet in R, and consider a point $x \in F$. By the monotonicity of faces stated in Lemma 4, $g(x)$ reaches the boundary of F exactly once, at point y, say. If $y \in e$ then we are done. Else y lies in a valley V of R. This is because valleys correspond to reflex arcs of the bisector graph, and only these arcs form an angle larger than 90 degree with e. It remains to be observed that $g(x)$ follows V to its lowest point which, by Lemma 2, is a vertex of e.

Now assume $R \neq I(P)$. By Lemma 5, R contains a valley V whose lowest point is a corner c of R. Let F be a facet of R which has c as a local minimum, and let e be its defining edge. Then we can choose a point $x \in F$ near V such that $g(x)$ reaches and follows V and ends at $c \notin e$. □

A physical interpretation of Theorem 7 is that on $I(P)$, and only there, every raindrop that hits a facet F runs off to the edge defining F.

Theorem 6 and Theorem 7 can be used as definitions for $I(P)$ and thus for $S(P)$. It would be elegant, however, to have a definition which does not resort to the explicite structure of $I(P)$. One approach that suggests itself is to try to express $I(P)$ as the lower envelope of partial linear functions, each function being defined locally by an edge of P and its appropriate neighborhood. However, the example in Figure 5 shows us that such functions do not exist.

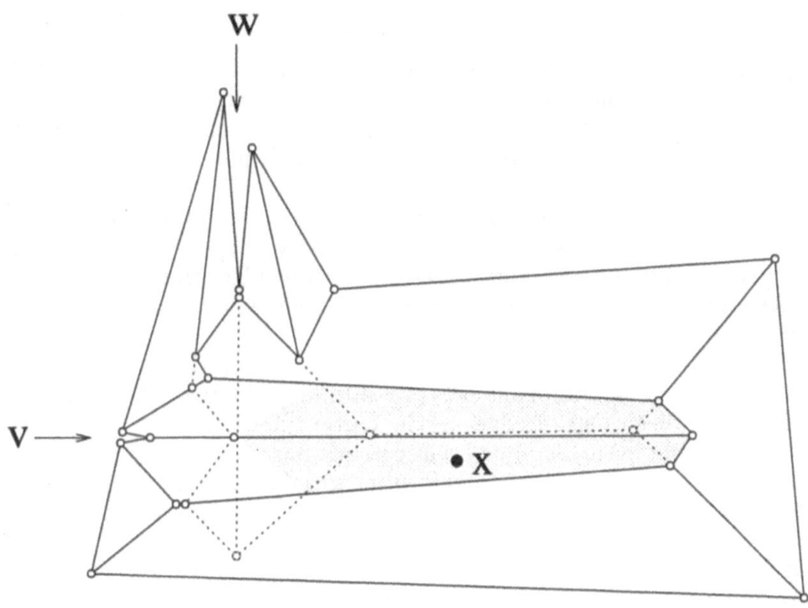

Figure 5: $I(P)$ (dotted) dominates another roof $R(P)$ (solid) at shaded area

Consider the reflex vertex v, and let e be the edge incident to v whose facet in $R(P)$ contains the point x. Let $\phi(e) \subset \Pi(e)$ be the graph of some partial linear function for e. The facet of e in $I(P)$ does not contain x, as $I(P)$ is above

$\Pi(e)$ at x. So, if $I(P)$ is the lower envelope of the functions ϕ, then $\phi(e)$ must not contain x. On the other hand, a change of P not in the neighborhood of e, namely moving the reflex vertex w slightly upwards, makes $R(P)$ the valid island of P. Now $\phi(e)$ has to contain x in order to ensure the envelope property for the modified polygon. This shows that $\phi(e)$ cannot be defined without knowledge of $I(P)$.

This undesirable property of $I(P)$ reveals that $S(P)$ is no Voronoi-diagram-like structure. To be more precise, $S(P)$ cannot be interpreted as some Voronoi diagram for the edges of P, if the underlying distance function is defined without prior knowledge of $S(P)$.

4 Discussion

The contributions of this paper are two-fold: The introduction of a new internal structure for simple polygons, and the first systematic treatment of the problem of constructing a roof above a polygonal layout of ground walls.

The general advantages of the straight skeleton over the medial axis are its straight-line structure and its lower combinatorial complexity. Both structures reflect the shape of a polygon in a compact manner. However, the straight skeleton is more sensible to changes of the shape. Adding a reflex vertex with very small exterior angle may alter the skeleton structure completly. If this effect is undesirable then such vertices may be cut locally, without much changing the polygon and achieving exterior angles of at least 90 degrees.

The straight skeleton provides a unique way of computing a polygonal roof, given a general placement of ground walls. We have shown that roofs are highly ambiguous objects, and that constructing a roof is a non-trivial task. To our knowledge, the roof construction method presented here is the first one in the literature.

A disadvantage of straight skeletons is the lack of a Voronoi diagram structure, which excludes the well-developed machinery of constructing Voronoi diagrams [A] from application, and makes tailor-made algorithms neccessary. Powerful techniques like divide-and-conquer or incremental insertion can be shown to fail.

The most promising approach, which might work sufficiently well in practical situations, is a simulation of the polygon shrinking process. The trivial method would consider each pair of edges of the current polygon(s) to detect the next edge event or split event. As each event corresponds to a node of $S(P)$, this leads to an $O(n^3)$ time and $O(n)$ space algorithm. Organizing the events in a priority queue brings down the construction time to $O(n^2 \log n)$, but at an expense of $O(n^2)$ storage.

Of course, the determination of the next edge event is easy as it can be done locally, but finding the next split event in low worst-case time is by no means trivial. A heuristic that can be expected to be fast on the average is tracing the reflex vertices through a suitable partition of the shrinking polygon. This would lead to an $O(n)$ space algorithm whose running time depends (more or less) on the number of reflex vertices. The challange is to find an algorithm with performance comparable to medial axis algorithms; for example, $O(n \log n)$ time. We do not further persue this matter here.

Acknowledgements: The second author would like to express thanks to G.L. Sicherman from AT&T Bell Labs. for drawing his attention to straight skeletons. Discussions on the presented topic with J.-D. Boissonnat, O. Devillers, M. Formann, R. Klein, D.T. Lee, G. Rote, and K. Varadarajan are gratefully acknowledged. Thanks also go to Th. Natschläger for implementing an algorithm for visualizing islands.

References

[A] F. Aurenhammer, *Voronoi diagrams – a survey of a fundamental geometric data structure*, ACM Computing Surveys 23, 3 (1991), 345 - 405.

[L] D.T. Lee, *Medial axis transformation of a planar shape*, IEEE Trans. Pattern Analysis and Machine Intelligence, PAMI-4 (1982), 363-369.

[K] D.G. Kirkpatrick, *Efficient computation of continuous skeletons*, Proc. 20th Ann. IEEE Symp. FOCS (1979), 18 - 27.

Journal of Universal Computer Science, vol. 1, no. 12 (1995), 762-789
submitted: 11/12/95, accepted: 27/12/95, appeared: 28/12/95 © Springer Pub. Co.

Constraint Agents for the Information Age

Jean-Marc Andreoli, Uwe M. Borghoff and Remo Pareschi
Rank Xerox Research Centre, Grenoble Laboratory
6, chemin de Maupertuis. F-38240 Meylan, France.
Email: {andreoli,borghoff,pareschi}@xerox.fr

Johann H. Schlichter
Institut für Informatik, Technische Universität München
D-80290 München, Germany.
Email: schlicht@informatik.tu-muenchen.de

Abstract: We propose constraints as the appropriate computational constructs for the design of agents with the task of selecting, merging and managing electronic information coming from such services as Internet access, digital libraries, E-mail, or on-line information repositories. Specifically, we introduce the framework of *Constraint-Based Knowledge Brokers*, which are concurrent agents that use so-called *signed feature constraints* to represent partially specified information and can flexibly cooperate in the management of distributed knowledge. We illustrate our approach by several examples, and we define application scenarios based on related technology such as Telescript and workflow management systems.

Key Words: multiagent coordination, agent-interaction, distributed problem solving, signed feature constraints, negotiation, cooperation strategies.
Category: H.3.3., I.2.

1 Introduction

New electronic sources of information, such as E-mail, Internet access and on-line information repositories flood the desktop environment of users with an evergrowing flow of information which, in order to be exploitable, demand efficient management. The inundation of electronic data coming from all kind of sources must convert into real knowledge in order to benefit the whole range of users from business people to casual surfers and shoppers on the Internet. Intelligent agents [CACM, 1994; Wooldridge and Jennings, 1995] interacting through multiagent systems have been proposed as the appropriate answer to this demand. Indeed, software processes of this kind may one day manage distributed knowledge by "living on the network" and manipulating electronic information on users' behalf.

A central question faces us in order to reach an effective deployment of such technology: How intelligent agents can be best designed and customized to meet users' individual information needs. The issue at stake concerns essentially one of adequate computational support. However, the motivations differ from those underlying linguistic frameworks for multiagent systems such as Actors [Agha, 1986] and Agent-oriented Programming (AOP) [Shoham, 1993] as well as of multiagent architectures, either "reactive" (see e.g. [Brooks, 1991]) or "deliberative" [Bratman et al., 1988] or "hybrid" [Kaelbling and Rosenschein, 1990]. In these cases the agents are assumed to be situated in an environment which they can modify while pursuing their own goals. These goals range from collecting empty cans, for simple robotic agents, or optimally solving scientific programming problems, for software agents in massively parallel multiprocessing architectures, to more complex types of activities for correspondingly more complex types of agents. Furthermore, the agents communicate either by passing messages (as in Actor languages) or by issuing, declining, or committing to requests, as well as performing other speech acts (as in the higher-level AOP languages). Thus, these agents explicitly communicate with their fellows and implicitly assume their situatedness in given environments. By contrast, agents primarily concerned with the elaboration and manipulation of information must have a more direct and explicit relationship with the environment since by its exploration they derive their very *raison d'etre*. Communication with fellow agents will at times be implicit and other times explicit: these agents effectively elaborate information and then communicate it, either to other agents or to humans. The recipients of information may be unknown to the senders – communication resembles more a radio broadcast or a conference presentation than a conversation between entities that know each other.

A computational model should satisfy a few precise requirements in order to support this notion of agency:

1. By definition these agents continually watch for information that meets preestablished criteria. For instance, in a given company, they can routinely scan news wires for breaking reports about the company's current customers, whoever they happen to be. Thus, it must be possible to express and implement agents' behavior in terms of a set of criteria through which information is filtered and selected. These criteria act as a partial specification of the information to come.
2. Electronic information domains are wide open lands where most of the times we do not know exactly what we are looking for, nor what we are going to find. In these conditions, a good way to guide our search is to explicitly exclude things we are not interested in. This can be conveniently expressed by freely mixing "positive" and "negative" requirements in the specification of the behavior of agents. Thus, users should be allowed to feed agents with such requests and criteria as "find me all books written by Umberto Eco which are not novels" or "I am not interested in reports on sales reps from Canada Customer Operations".
3. The scope of exploration of agents should be dynamically readjustable to optimize their work. As a minimal requirement, they should be capable of "focusing on targets," thus incrementally reducing their scope as they proceed. More intelligence could plausibly come from long-term memory, that is the remembrance of things past: They should be able to reuse the knowledge they have gained from executing a certain request in the context of other requests. Take for instance a request such as "find me all books by Umberto Eco which are not novels" and a subsequent request such as "find me all books by Umberto Eco which are literary essays."
4. We would also like to implement cooperative behavior of multiple agents on given tasks. Cooperation should arise naturally from handling queries involving the selection and composition of information from different knowledge repositories (often called backends) reachable through the Internet. Another example is the creation of compound documents on the fly from preexisting documents, according to some hierarchical description language

like SGML [ISO, 1986], with each part of the final document being assigned to a specific agent.

5. Finally, it should be possible to tune interagent communication in terms of different communication protocols according to such parameters as the nature of the problem to be solved, the underlying system architecture, etc.

In this paper we investigate these issues from the point of view of a computational construct that has already found widespread application in artificial intelligence and computer science, namely the notion of *constraint*. Constraints have been exploited mainly in the context of search and combinatorial optimization but their significance is more general and extends to the management and manipulation of information. In fact, constraints can be used to provide partial specifications on the possible values of variables. This paper illustrates how this capability can be exploited to implement predefined criteria for filtering and selecting information. The specific constraint framework we shall adopt is the Constraint-Based Knowledge Brokers (CBKBs) [Andreoli et al., 1994; Andreoli et al., to appear] model, which exploits constraints to support knowledge-intensive tasks executed by concurrent agents and views the management and manipulation of information in distributed environments as a form of distributed problem solving. A CBKB is capable of understanding and enacting both "requests" and "negations of requests," is self-sufficient in managing its own scope of exploration over a given information domain and is capable of knowledge reuse. Furthermore, different communication protocols for CBKBs have been defined that can be used to tune interagent communication and cooperation.

The remainder of this paper is organized as follows. In Sect. 2, we characterize the notion of multiagent interaction in the context of distributed problem solving. Agents are classified and given a set of general requirements. Agent cooperation is then illustrated in terms of CBKBs. Two different protocols for interagent communication are introduced and described, one supporting direct, explicit communication and the other supporting group-oriented communication. Sect. 3 introduces a specific type of constraints suitable for representing electronic information, namely signed feature constraints (SFC). In Sect. 4, SFCs are used to illustrate a number of specific issues of information management, such as interdependencies, thresholds, and reuse of information. Sect. 5 explains related scenarios. In particular we discuss negotiation in the contract-net protocol, Telescript as a promising agent infrastructure, and workflow management as an interesting application domain for remote programming. In Sect. 6, related work is discussed. Sect. 7 concludes the paper.

2 Multiagent Interaction

The area of Distributed Problem Solving (DPS) has led to various approaches which allow distributed (semi-)autonomous agents to cooperate in order to solve complex problems and accomplish tasks which might not be solvable by one individual system. From the problem solving point of view, distribution implies the decomposition of the problem into a set of subproblems and the dissemination of the subproblems to the appropriate agents which solve them autonomously and concurrently. The final solution of the global problem can be generated by composing the solutions of the subproblems. Thus, agents can be viewed as problem solvers which cooperate to generate the solution of the global problem.

2.1 Classification

We distinguish between passive and active agents. *Passive* agents act under direct user control. The user explicitly triggers the execution of agent functions, e.g. sorting and filing electronic messages in the user's mailbox. Unlike passive agents, *active* agents react to incoming messages, such as requests for information or the execution of functions, autonomously or semi-autonomously. *Autonomous* agents may perform actions without user involvement. They have enough knowledge about the problem domain and the contextual constraints to interpret received messages and react appropriately. During execution, the user has no direct control over the agent's behavior. On the other hand, *semi-autonomous* agents perform routine tasks for the user. Exceptional requests or situations are referred to the user who handles them personally. The behavior of semi-autonomous agents is directly controlled by the user who has read and write access to the rules which specify the agent's behavior.

Agents are used in a wide area of different application domains ranging from robotics, distributed sensoring to Computer-Supported Cooperative Work (CSCW) and information gathering [Wayner, 1994]. The emerging field of CSCW provides a demanding area for distributed problem solving. CSCW systems need to support the interaction of humans and overcome the difficulties of temporal and spatial distribution. For instance, agents may be used to support the scheduling of meetings (see [Sen and Durfee, 1991]). Another related application domain is that of workflow management and document processing where agents might be used to coordinate the tasks and information exchange between tasks and humans. The rapid growth of the Internet and the World-Wide Web have demonstrated the need for innovative and efficient ways of information gathering, and this provides the main focus for this paper. The World-Wide Web makes available an incredible amount of information; however, in many cases the user is unable to find and extract the desired information effectively. In this case agents may be used to collect relevant information, filter the search results according to contextual constraints, and present the resulting information to the user in an appropriate form. *Telescript* [White, 1994b] is an example of system providing infrastructural support for this type of agent application.

The *contract-net protocol* [Smith, 1980] was one of the first approaches to provide a general framework for DPS. It supports an application protocol for communication between problem solving agents and facilitates distributed control during the problem solving effort. Special emphasis is put on

- localizing those agents which are eligible for solving the created subproblems;
- the negotiation between agents for the information exchange with respect to subproblem descriptions, required agent capabilities and subproblem solutions [Davis and Smith, 1983].

The Rank Xerox Research Centre at Grenoble has developed the model of *Constraint-Based Knowledge Brokers* (CBKBs) which uses constraints to provide computational support for DPS. CBKBs explicitly separate aspects of local problem solving, based on computations specific to a single agent, from aspects of global problem solving, deriving from the interaction of different agents. CBKBs model active agents which act autonomously and concurrently. In the following sections some of the specific capabilities of the CBKB model will be discussed in more detail.

In order to effectively cooperate and participate in the problem solving effort, an agent must satisfy the following requirements:

- an agent must be able to communicate with other agents of the system (e.g. send and receive request/answer messages);
- an agent must be able to act upon receipt of messages.

2.2 Cooperation between Agents

The phenomenon of cooperation which is well-known in the human environment may also be applied to agent interaction. A number of different cooperation strategies between agents have been proposed, ranging from strongly hierarchical master-slave relationship, to the less hierarchical contract-net [Smith, 1980], to the sharing of common goals. In the latter case agents not only exchange information with respect to their individual tasks and problems, but they also communicate their goals. Thus, the agents follow shared goals when pursuing the problem solving activities.

In general, cooperation between agents is based on explicit communication, i.e. agents send messages to transfer knowledge and requests. The message content can range from values, formal and informal descriptions, to constraints. The CBKB model uses values and constraints to represent knowledge and requests for problem solving. The basic message types in the context of DPS are requests and answers. Usually messages are completely structured and are only intended for agent consumption; the messages are not in human-readable form. The message structures can be tailored to reduce network bandwidth and interpretation complexity by the agents. Both the contract-net protocol and the CBKB model apply structured messages to model agent interaction. An example for a system which uses semi-structured messages is *Object Lens* [Malone and Lai, 1988], which provides intelligent filtering and dissemination of electronic mail messages. Semi-structured messages are based on the notion of a semi-formal system [Malone, 1989] which:

- represents and interprets information that is formally specified,
- permits the human user to create and interpret formal information informally,
- allows the formal interpretation by the computer and the informal interpretation by the user to be easily changed.

Semi-formal systems are especially useful in heterogeneous environments where there is no clear separation between human tasks and agent tasks. They support the co-existence of humans and agents in the same environment. For example, some people use personal agents to cooperate in the distributed meeting scheduling process, while other people perform the required requests manually. Thus, semi-formal systems facilitate a smooth transition from a purely human-oriented environment to a completely agent-based environment. However, semi-formal systems use rather complex messages. This creates a significant network load and requires complex interpretation functionality by the agents.

2.3 CBKB Interaction Protocols

Within the CBKB model, two different agent interaction protocols have been designed:

- the request-subrequest protocol;
- the local caching protocol.

2.3.1 The Request-Subrequest Protocol

CBKB's request-subrequest protocol exploits dependencies between agents: the request carries an index that is added to all output information sent out as answers to the original request. In this way, requester and requestee are directly linked. Information is provided only if requested, and is sent only to the agents that have explicitly requested it.

The initial request carries an index which acts as an address for the requesting agents, as well as a description of the problem to be solved. A problem description in a request is instantiated as a constraint on the problem domain. Thus, a request is basically a constraint (with some additional information such as the index). An agent takes the problem description and simplifies it into subproblems. These descriptions of the subproblems are then submitted as subrequests in the same way as the initial request. The subrequests are individually indexed so that they can be collected into a solution by the requestee agents.

2.3.2 The Local-Caching Protocol

The local caching protocol does not link requesters with requestees. By contrast, as soon as a solution for a particular subproblem is available, it is broadcast to all existing agents. The initial request carries only a description of the problem to be solved; no index is associated with it. As before, an agent takes the problem description and simplifies it into subproblems. However, as a consequence of this protocol, for some of the subproblems solutions may already be known to the agents. The description of yet unsolved subproblems are then submitted as subrequests in the same way as the initial request, i.e. again without index. In this way, we obtain a situation of local *caching* of information for all existing agents, thus decreasing the overall amount of traffic, as we avoid the re-generation of the same requests from different requesters. On the other hand, we may end up storing information which never gets used.

2.3.3 Hybrid Schemes

Obviously, the two protocols above are at the very opposite ends of a spectrum of possible protocols and intermediate cases are possible, for instance, when automatic deliveries are done for subsets of agents. For many practical applications these cases seem to be the most useful, so we need techniques for assigning agents to appropriate "interest groups," and for allowing flexible tuning of group-based communication. Furthermore, there are cases where the best strategy for distributed problem solving may involve splitting the problem into subproblems which are optimally solved according to different protocols. Again, we need flexible ways for expressing such protocols, and for mixing them freely in the overall solution of a particular problem. Besides, we need ways of guessing the right protocol, or the right *melange* of protocols, for specific problems. This calls for contributions from such diverse fields as programming linguistics, learning and simulation.

3 Broker Agents and Constraints

In the CBKB model we formalize the problem-subproblem relationship which is at the basis of DPS via the notion of *generator*. Intuitively, a generator defines the decomposition of a given problem into subproblems and the composition of the subproblem solutions into the final solution of the problem. Operationally, generators are associated with a special kind of agents, the so-called *broker* agents. A broker incorporates the generator functionality together with the capability of dynamically spawning other agents (clones of the broker) for solving subproblems. The generator function g is implemented by applying input arguments to it and producing corresponding output information which represents the answers of the request to the broker.

3.1 Generator

Given an abstract domain of values $\mathcal{D}$, representing pieces of knowledge, a generator is a mapping $g : \mathcal{D}^n \mapsto \wp(\mathcal{D})$, which produces new pieces of knowledge from existing ones. The argument a_i, $i \in \{1, \ldots, n\}$ of the generator g represents a solution of the i-th subproblem. a_i may be either a value which was computed or retrieved from a database by the agent responsible for the subproblem, or a constraint. The number of arguments n of the generator g specifies the number of subproblems created by the broker out of the initial request; the broker has the arity n and is called *broker/n*. The arity n is only of local importance; it solely depends on the number of subproblems of the decomposed initial request. The sender of the initial request has no knowledge of the number of subproblems created by the broker/n. With respect to the decomposition of requests and composition of subanswers brokers act as autonomous agents. Thus, it is possible that a broker/n sends a subrequest to a broker/m where $n < m$. This approach to the hierarchical decomposition of requests and recomposition of answers exploits insights from deductive frameworks for parsing [Pereira and Warren, 1983] and database querying [Vielle, 1986].

In the current prototype implementation of the CBKB model the generator g needs solutions for all argument positions to apply its function, i.e. the appropriate agents must have provided solutions for the assigned subproblems. However, an extension of the current prototype is envisioned that incorporates more complex generators which also handle partial solutions, i.e. the solution of the global problem is generated from a subset of subproblem solutions. A simple example is the creation of a document which consists of several document parts. The generator g collects individual document parts and combines them into the final document. If document parts are not available g inserts automatically "missing subsection" into the final document.

As already mentioned earlier the generator g of a broker B composes answers to its request r out of the subanswers to subrequests. For an individual subrequest several contacted agents may provide multiple subanswers which return independently at broker B. Even multiple answers from a single agent may be received by the broker B at different times. At the receipt of a subanswer the generator g attempts to compose an answer to request r out of the newly received subanswer and the already previously received ones. The resulting answer will be checked by the broker B against the initial constraint of r in order to decide if it represents a valid answer. If there are multiple subanswers for certain subrequests available the generator g will construct all possible combinations to compose answers for the request r. Suppose the broker B decomposed the initial request r into two subrequests r_1 and r_2. For r_1 the broker B received two subanswers, and for r_2 three subanswers. The generator g will construct a solution space consisting of six potential solutions for r. By checking the initial constraints of r, only valid solutions are extracted from the solution space and propagated to the requester of r. In [Prasad et al., 1995], a related negotiation-driven multiagent retrieval approach is proposed where inconsistencies between different subanswers are dynamically resolved.

A set of generators identifies a class of subsets of the domain which are stable under these generators, that is, if the arguments a_i are within the subset, the knowledge generated by g is also within the same subset [Andreoli et al., 1994]. The class of stable sets is closed under intersection, so that it has a smallest element in the sense of inclusion, given by the intersection of all the stable sets. This minimal stable set, also called *minimal model*, represents the intended semantics of the set of generators.

3.2 Knowledge Representation

Brokers are agents which can process knowledge search requests. Knowledge is taken here to be any piece of electronic information intended to be publicly accessible. Different, possibly distributed, information sources are assumed to be available, from a simple file in a user's directory to a database local to a site, up to a wide area information service (WAIS) on the internet, for example.

When receiving a request, a broker may have sufficient knowledge to process it, or may need to retrieve more knowledge. For that purpose, it releases subrequests, aimed at other brokers. Thus, knowledge retrieval is achieved by the collaboration of all the brokers which are alternatively service providers processing requests and clients of these services generating subrequests. We are not concerned here by the infrastructure required to support such collaboration, nor by the way knowledge is stored locally within each broker, but rather by the knowledge manipulations occurring within each broker.

In order to collaborate, the brokers must at least understand each other. This means that all the requests must be formulated in a common language (and also all the answers to the requests), even if the brokers may perform local translations. Logic provides the adequate language for such a purpose. A request can be expressed by a pair $\langle x, P\rangle$ where x is a logical variable and P a logical formula involving x, meaning "*Retrieve* knowledge objects x such that the property expressed by formula P holds". Interestingly, an answer to such a request can be expressed in the same formalism, i.e. a pair $\langle x, Q\rangle$, meaning "*There exists* a knowledge object x satisfying the property expressed by formula Q". The requirement here is that P must be a logical consequence of Q, so that the answer contains at least as much knowledge as the request. Moreover, the same logical formalism can be used to capture the scope of a broker, i.e. the area of knowledge it is concerned with: a broker with scope $\langle x, R\rangle$ means "*I am not capable of retrieving* knowledge objects x which do not satisfy the property expressed by formula R". In many situations, the scope of a broker may vary, because it gets specialized or, on the contrary, expands its capacities, either externally or due to the knowledge retrieval process itself.

In other words, logic provides a common language where both requests, answers and scopes can be expressed. Brokers then perform logical operations on these three components. The most important logical operation, from which all the others can be reconstructed, is satisfiability checking, i.e. deciding whether some object could satisfy the property expressed by a formula, or, on the contrary, whether it is intrinsically contradictory. Unfortunately, it is well known that this operation, for *full* Classical Logic, is not algorithmic, i.e. it is provably impossible to write a program which implements it and always terminates. Given this limitation, a lot of research in knowledge representation has been focused on identifying *fragments* of Classical Logic in which satisfiability is algorithmically decidable. The trade-off here is between expressive power and tractability: the empty fragment, for example, is obviously tractable, but it is not very expressive! A very popular fragment which emerged from this research is known as "feature constraints". The satisfiability problem in this case is also known as "feature constraint solving".

Traditionally, feature constraints are built from atomic constraints which are either sorts or features. A sort is a unary relation, expressing a property of a single entity. For example, `P:person` expresses that an entity `P` is of sort `person`. A feature is a binary relation expressing a property linking two entities. For example, `P:employer->E` expresses that entity `P` has an employer, which is an entity `E`. Apart from sorts and features, most feature systems also allow built-in relations such as equality and disequality.

3.3 Constraints

The full fragment of feature constraints, where the atomic components mentioned above are allowed to be combined by all the logical connectives (conjunction, disjunction, negation and quantifiers), although very expressive, is hardly tractable. Therefore, we consider a subfragment, called "basic feature constraints" (BFC), where negation and disjunction are simply forbidden. Efficient constraint solving algorithms have been proposed for this subfragment. However, completely disallowing negation puts strong limitations on the kind of operations a knowledge broker may wish to perform.

In particular, we have identified a very common and powerful operation named "scope-splitting", which relies on the use of negation. Indeed, a broker may wish to split its scope, specified by a pair $\langle x, P\rangle$ according to a criterion expressed by a formula F, thus creating two brokers with scope $P \wedge F$ and $P \wedge \neg F$. Thus, a broker in charge of bibliographic information may wish to split its scope into two new scopes: "books written after 1950", which can be represented by the BFC

```
X
  X : book,
  X : year -> Y, Y > 1950
```

and its complement, i.e. "books written before 1950 *or* documents which are *not* books"; this latter scope cannot be expressed using BFC, because negation and disjunction cannot be dispensed with. We have found that the scope splitting operation is needed in many situations, for example to implement brokers capable of memorizing and reusing information gathered during their lifetime. Our approach presents on the one hand a fragment of feature constraints, called "signed feature constraints" (SFC), which allows limited use of negation, precisely capable of expressing the kind of scope splitting mentioned above, and on the other hand, an efficient constraint solving method for SFC.

3.3.1 Signed Feature Constraints

A signed feature constraint is composed of a positive part and a list of negative parts, both of them being basic feature constraints. For example, the following signed feature constraint

```
P
+ P : person,
  P : employer-> E, E : "Xerox"
- P : nationality-> N, N : "American"
- P : spouse-> P',
  P': person,
  P': employer-> E', E': "Xerox"
```

specifies a Xerox employee who is not American and is not married to another Xerox employee. We can represent this SFC graphically as in Fig. 1. The round boxes denote the entities (logical variables), the sort relations (unary) are represented by dashed arrows labeled by the name of the sort in a square box, the feature relations (binary) are represented by plain arrows labeled by the name of the feature in a square box. The built-in predicates (not present in the example) are represented by rhombuses. The positive part of the SFC is contained in the top box and marks the distinguished entity of the scope (P in the example) by a double round box. The negative parts of the SFC are contained in the lower boxes in grey.

The main interest of SFC comes from the following property:

> If the scope of a broker is represented by an SFC e_o, and this scope is split by a BFC e, then the two resulting split scopes e^+, e^- are both SFC.

Indeed, e^+ is obtained by merging the positive part of e_o with the BFC e; and e^- is obtained by extending e_o with a new negative part containing e alone. For example, assume a broker in charge of a bibliographical database containing various documents (books, videos etc.) about Art, but not authored by an American. It is represented by the SFC

```
X
+ X : topic-> T, T : "Art"
- X : author-> A,
  A : nationality-> N, N : "American"
```

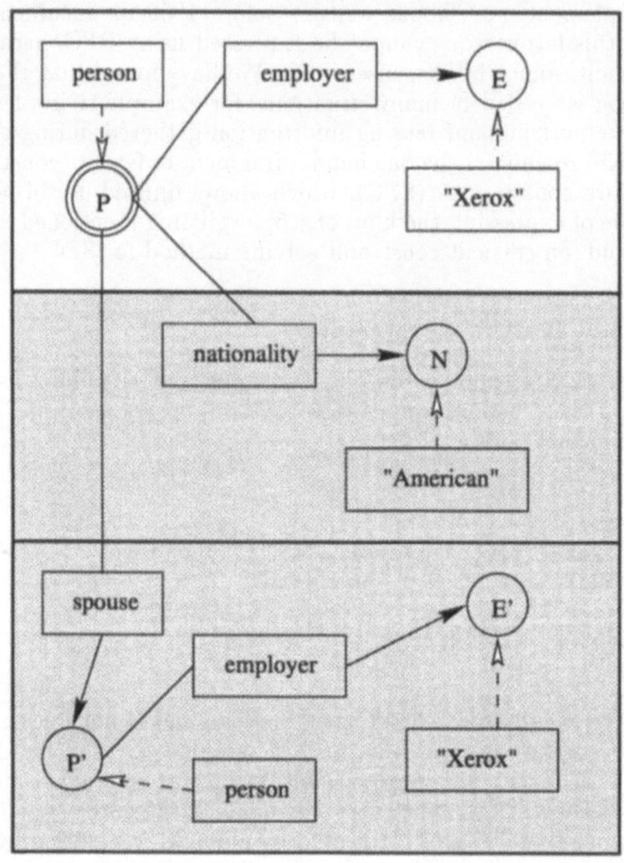

Figure 1: A signed feature constraint (the negative parts are in grey).

It may be split by the constraint "books written after 1950", expressed by the BFC

```
X
  X : book,
  X : year-> Y, Y > 1950
```

The resulting scopes are simply

```
X
+ X : book,
  X : topic-> T, T : "Art",
  X : year-> Y, Y > 1950
- X : author-> A,
  A : nationality-> N, N : "American"
```

i.e. "Art books written after 1950 but not by an American author" and

```
X
+ X : topic-> T, T : "Art"
- X : author-> A,
  A : nationality-> N, N : "American"
- X : book,
  X : year-> Y, Y > 1950
```

i.e. "Art documents not authored by an American but not books subsequent to 1950".

3.3.2 Solving Signed Feature Constraints

Most constraint systems make a number of assumptions on the nature of sorts and features, called the axioms of the systems. These axioms are crucial to the satisfiability algorithm, since they determine when a feature constraint is contradictory and when it is satisfiable.

3.3.2.1 Feature Axioms

For the purpose of simplicity, we make use here of a slight variant of the basic axiom system used in [Aït-Kaci et al., 1994], although the principles of the method apply to other sets of axioms as well.

1. Features are functional: this means that if two pairs of entities which are constrained by the same feature have the same first term, they also have the same second term. For example, we can consider that the feature **spouse** is functional (within a specific cultural setting), meaning that a person cannot have two spouses: if, for a person X, we have **X:spouse->Y** and **X:spouse->Z**, then the entities **Y** and **Z** coincide (i.e., denote the same person). Other systems allow multi-valued features.
2. Sorts are disjoint: this means that no entity can be of two distinct sorts. For example, a book is not a person: we cannot have an entity **X** with **X:book** and **X:person**. Other systems consider hierarchies of sorts where some entities can have multiple sorts as long as they have a common denominator in the hierarchy.
3. There is a distinguished subset of sorts, called "value" sorts, so that no two distinct entities can be of the same value sort. Traditional basic elements (strings, numbers, etc.) are typical value sorts: for example, the string **"Xerox"** or the number **1950** are value sorts. Value sorts are not allowed to have features: this is the only axiom connecting sorts and features. Other systems consider more refined connections between sorts and features.
4. There is a distinguished built-in binary predicate, equality, with the traditional congruence axioms (which involve sorts and features). The axioms describing all the other built-in predicates are assumed to contain no mention of sorts and features.

These axioms form a theory $\mathcal{T}$.

3.3.2.2 Constraint Satisfaction

First, we assume that satisfiability over built-in predicates is decidable. This means that there is an algorithm which, given a formula F using only built-in predicates (F is also called a built-in constraint), can decide whether F is a logical consequence of the theory $\mathcal{T}$ (written $\vdash_{\mathcal{T}} F$).

Constraint satisfaction over BFCs is defined by a set of conditional rewrite rules over BFCs which have the following properties

- *The system of rules is convergent and hence defines a "normal form" for BFCs.* This can be shown in a classical way by proving that the system is "Church-Rosser" (critical pairs converge) and "Noetherian" (the size of the terms strictly decrease by rewriting).
- *A BFC is satisfiable if and only if its normal form is not reduced to a contradiction.* One implication can be proved by showing that rewrite steps preserve satisfiability. The reverse implication can be proved by displaying a model which satisfies BFCs whose normal form is not reduced to a contradiction.

Thus the rewrite rules describe the steps of the constraint satisfaction algorithm. The algorithm always terminates because the system of rewrite rules is convergent. Notice that the definition of the rules rely on satisfiability tests of built-in constraints, which has been assumed decidable. This means that our algorithm is modular and can accommodate any kind of built-in constraints as long as a proper built-in constraint satisfaction algorithm is provided.

Using rewrite rules for constraint satisfaction algorithm is quite traditional. They can be implemented in a naive way is some symbolic language like Lisp or Prolog or be optimized, taking into account the properties of the specific built-in constraints which are used.

The algorithm for constraint satisfaction over SFCs can informally be described as follows. Given an SFC, its positive component is first normalized by the algorithm for BFCs. If the result is a contradiction, the whole SFC is unsatisfiable. Otherwise, the positive component (normalized) is inserted in each of the negative components, which are then normalized by the algorithm for BFCs. If a resulting negative component has a contradictory normal form, it is eliminated, and if it has a tautological normal form the whole SFC is unsatisfiable. The normal form for SFCs thus obtained has the following property:

> *An SFC is satisfiable if and only if its normal form is not reduced to a contradiction.*

As in the previous case, the difficult part of the implication can be proved using model theory.

3.4 Implementation

The prototype implementation of the SFC solver is written in Prolog.

SFC are handled in a data structure `sfc(CV,POSFL,NEGFLL)` where `CV` represents the constraint variable, `POSFL` represents a list containing the feature entries for the positive part of SFC, and `NEGFLL` represents a list of lists where each list contains the feature entries for a single negative part of SFC. `NEGFLL` may be empty; then it is specified as empty list. In general, the SFC solver is realized as a list-transforming algorithm with additional checks for constraint satisfaction.

The built-in predicate for equations is solved using the unification mechanism and the build-in test "==" of Prolog. The precedence constraints ($>, <, \geq$, and $\leq$) are added through Prolog-predicates explicitly.

3.5 Searching the Backends and Caching of Information

Typically, at system initialization a set of initial brokers is provided. Each of these brokers has a predefined scope covering a subset of the domain of some backends. The sizes of the predefined scopes are application dependent and they may range from very specialized constraints to general descriptions of a constraint space covering the minimal model. By processing requests new brokers and agent specialists are cloned. Each of the newly cloned agents handles only a subset of their parent scope. This results in a continuous refinement of the scopes until the requested subset of the domain is handled by an agent specialist.

The scope of a broker is represented by a single SFC. There are labels $a_1, \ldots, a_n$ for each argument of the broker's generator. The label a_0 corresponds to the expected result.

Example 1. Assume a broker that is in charge of answering requests concerning opera information. A requester has to submit the name of a composer, and will receive all operas written by this composer in return. Assume further that the broker need not generate subproblems to generate a solution, i.e. the labels for $a_1, \ldots, a_n$ are not needed. Instead, in order to generate a solution it searches a backend, in our case, an attached opera database.

The initial scope of this broker is

```
X
+ X : a0-> O,
  O : opera
```

meaning that the broker is in charge of all possible operas (covered by the backend). The expected result is an opera. If the broker receives a request "Find me all operas of Richard Wagner", written as a BFC

```
O
  O : opera,
  O : composer-> C, C : "Richard Wagner"
```

it spawns an agent specialist in charge of exploring "Richard Wagner", and, as in the book example before, continues with an reduced scope.

As schematically illustrated in Fig. 2, the agent specialist in charge of exploring "Richard Wagner" searches an underlying opera database (or many databases where appropriate) and answers the request. The answer is an element of the domain and is represented by a BFC, e.g.

```
O
  O : opera,
  O : composer-> C, C : "Richard Wagner",
  O : name-> T, T : "Parsifal",
  O : number_of_acts-> NA, NA : 3
```

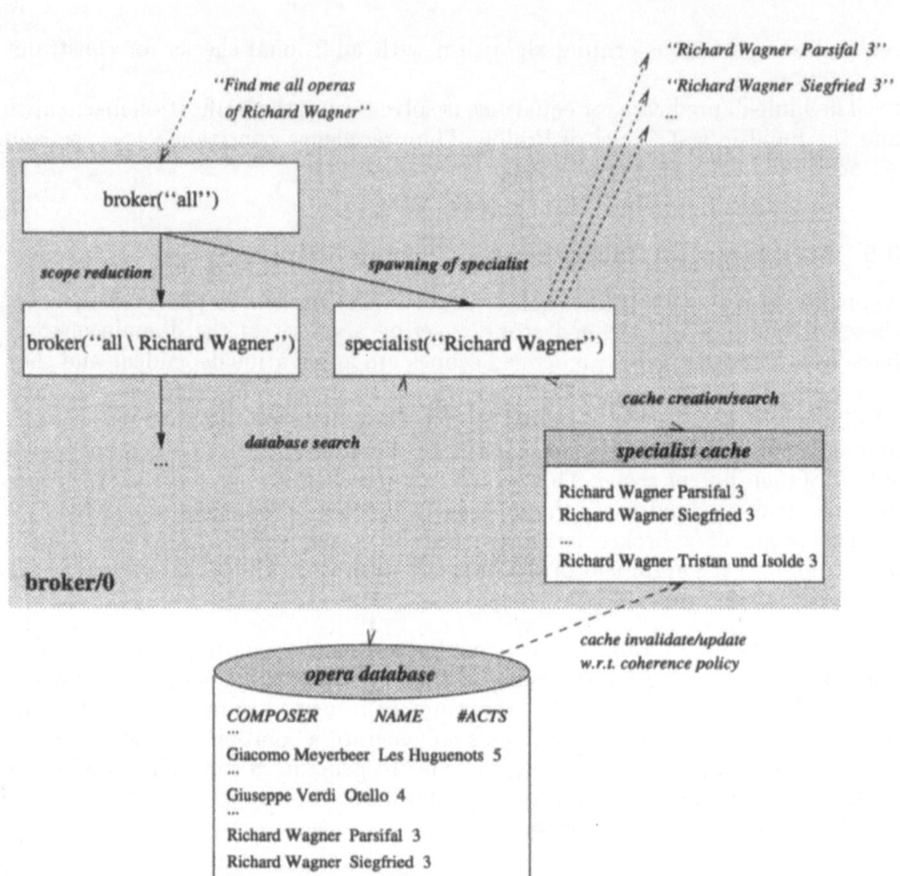

Figure 2: Specialist creation, caching and searching the backends.

The set of features "filled" by the answer depends on available information in the attached database.

This agent remains active as a specialist for Wagner operas, i.e., whenever another request for Wagner operas is sent, this specialist may simply return the results it has already collected. It is worth to point out that, due to its scope reduction, the parent broker will no longer react to requests concerning Wagner operas. On the other hand, a request "Find me all operas of Giuseppe Verdi with three acts" (provided the opera database has entries for act information), written as

```
O
  O : opera,
  O : composer-> C, C : "Giuseppe Verdi",
  O : number_of_acts-> NA, NA : 3
```

will lead to the spawning of a Verdi specialist for three-act-operas, and a corresponding (further) reduction of the broker's scope.

Now, we can show another characteristic of the approach: Imagine a follow-on request "Find me all operas of Giuseppe Verdi". This request will be answered by two specialists: First, the old Verdi specialists for three-act-operas will answer (typically, using already obtained information). Moreover, a newly created specialist for all Verdi operas not having three acts will answer. The requester will, due to earlier requests, get answers from two different specialists. Due to the scope splitting mechanism, redundant work is avoided. Already generated solutions for the overlapping part of the problem domain (three-act-operas of Verdi) are reused.

To make things complete, assume now a request "Find me all operas". This request will be answered by the three specialists already in existence. Moreover, a newly created, rather unconventional "specialist" for all operas but the ones by Wagner or Verdi (no matter whether three-acted or not) will answer. On the other hand, the scope reduction of the parent broker will lead to an empty scope. The parent broker will disappear.

The example raises some interesting questions. First, should a specialist send out its answers one by one, e.g. a single answer-message for each opera found, or should it collect all answers into a list, and send a single answer containing this list?

The second question concerns the valid reuse of information. The agent specialist remains active as a specialist for its subset of the constraint domain. Whenever, a request is sent concerning this domain, the specialist may reuse the already collected information, e.g. the list of Wagner operas. For Wagner or Verdi operas, this behavior seems appropriate. But assume a specialist for a living composer whose most important operas are still to be composed. We can see the specialist's domain as a cache, for which, of course, cache coherence policies are needed. As soon as cache-related information is updated in its original constraint store (e.g. updates in the underlying opera database concerning the specialist's composer), the cached information must either be invalidated or updated. Strategies concerning the valid reuse of information are discussed in Sect. 4.2.

4 Broker Processing

As we already discussed in previous sections the main tasks of an agent are the communication with other agents (e.g. sending and receiving of messages) and the reaction upon receipt of messages which may be either requests or answers to requests. The typical processing of a request submitted to a broker agent (broker/n) is – *cum grano salis* – accomplished through the following steps:

1. checking the problem description of the request with respect to the scope of the broker.
2. exploring the subset of the broker's scope that intersects with the constraint given in the problem description and spawning an agent specialist handling the subset currently under exploration. The broker itself continues to be in charge of the reduced scope which is derived from the "old" scope without the scope of the agent specialist.

3. applying back-dependencies to each of the broker's argument positions of the generator function g in order to simplify the problem description into subproblems.
4. checking the conditions to verify for which of the argument positions the simplified problem description can already be submitted as a subrequest (these conditions, which we call *threshold conditions*, will be discussed in more detail in Sect. 4.1).
5. submitting these subrequests in the same way as the initial request, i.e. with an index when using the request-subrequest protocol, or without when using local caching.
6. updating the (local) constraint store upon receipt of answers to these subrequests. Other argument positions of g may reach their threshold conditions and are submitted as in step 5.
   Once a combination of answers satisfies the initial request (after applying the broker's generator function), a solution is found. This solution is then sent to the initial requester, when using the request-subrequest protocol, or to all broker agents, when local caching is the protocol of choice. In addition to the scope splitting mechanisms where the creation of redundant agent specialists is avoided, local caching is of special interest when subproblems overlap. Redundant work is reduced by communicating relevant results in advance. As stated in [Oates et al., 1994], it is also interesting to see that a solution or even a partial solution generated by an agent might facilitate (by focusing or constraining) the problem solving of another agent. For instance, due to an "unsolicited" solution to a subproblem, a threshold could be satisfied and a (possibly more refined) subrequest could be launched.

Obviously, the steps described above simply illustrate a sort of upper-layer brokers providing solutions to a request. In another reading, we can see a broker/n as an agent that extends the functionality offered by lower-layer brokers. The solutions of a broker/n are higher-level, composite and tailored to the scopes of the lower-layer brokers. They reflect the assembled knowledge processed by the individual generators. However, someone has to provide real "basic" solutions. Synthesizing and combining answers is only possible when there are brokers in the CBKB model that need not further decompose the problem description into subproblems, but answer a request (immediately) by other means, e.g. by searching some backends. This is achieved by so-called brokers of an arity 0, written as *broker/0*. A typical example of a broker/0 might be an agent which handles queries to a database as shown in Example 1 or an agent that gets in contact with some service provider in the Internet.

A broker/0 reacts to an incoming request as in steps 1 and 2. However, instead of steps 3–6, the simplification of the problem description into subproblems, a broker/0

- searches/retrieves, e.g. by inspection of database files, or
- activates, e.g. by starting a calculation task within a spreadsheet application, or
- executes, e.g. by starting a process that evaluates some broker-internal sensoric data.

Of course, this is just a small fraction of possible activities a broker/0 may use to provide a solution to the request. It is clear that the set of all brokers having arity

0 forms the basis for searches over, most probably, heterogeneous data sources. A broker/0 also provides the interface to external tools and applications. Thus, the CBKB model can smoothly be integrated into an already existing application environment without changing legacy applications (see [Borghoff and Schlichter, 1995] for more details).

The following example illustrates the interaction of a broker/3 and some broker/0.

Example 2. Many people with an avocation for classic music may have asked the following question to extend their private library.

> "Find me all books, not written by a German author, where the title of the book is the name of a Wagner opera."

Writing this problem description as a feature constraint yields to the following BFC, constraining the request variable R:

```
R
  R : req_opera-> O,
  R : req_book-> B,
  R : req_person-> P,
  O : opera,
  O : name-> T,
  O : composer-> C, C : "Richard Wagner",
  B : book,
  B : title-> T,
  B : author-> PN,
  P : person,
  P : name-> PN,
  P : nationality-> N, N != N', N' : "German"
```

In order to answer the request, let a broker/3 compose results obtained from three different brokers, namely a broker/0 for operas, a broker/0 for books, and a broker/0 to verify the nationality of a person. The initial scope of broker/3 be

```
X
+ X : a0-> R,
  X : a1-> O,
  X : a2-> B,
  X : a3-> P,
  O : opera,
  B : book,
  P : person,
  R : req_opera-> O,
  R : req_book-> B,
  R : req_person-> P
```

The agent specialist cloned by broker/3 may decompose the problem domain into the following requests: First

> "Find me all operas of Richard Wagner".

This request may involve a first broker/0 that searches, for instance, a marketing server installed at Bayreuth. See Example 1 for more details.

Upon receipt of answers to this first request, the agent specialist extracts for every opera `O` the name `T` (e.g. Parsifal, Siegfried, Tristan und Isolde, etc.) and submits a second request of the form:

"Find me all books with title `T`."

This request may involve a second broker/0 that executes a script to get in contact with a relevant service provider that may reside within the World-Wide Web. For example, at http://lcmarc.dra.com a form is provided to allow searches of the DRA-LCMARC database containing millions of relevant entries. If Telescript's visions [White, 1994a] become real it should also be possible to attach a Telescript engine to such a broker/0.

Upon receipt of answers to this second request, the agent specialist extracts for every book `B` the author `P` (e.g. for title "Parsifal", book authors are Piotr Bednarski, Friedrich Oberkogler, Hans-Jürgen Syberberg, Peter Vansittart, etc.) and submits a third request of the form:

"Find me the nationality of the author `P`".

This request may involve a third *broker/0* that searches a commercial who's-who server to get the nationality of the author.

Upon receipt of an answer `N` (assuming that a person has only one nationality), the agent specialist feeds its generator with `O`, `B`, and `N` to generate a result that is sent back to the requester. The result generation is quite simple. If `N` is not German a solution is found, the answer `B`, i.e., the particular book, is provided.

Composed and/or verified using three different broker/0, the following would be a solution, and therefore be within the minimal model covered by CBKB:

Vansittart, Peter. Parsifal : a novel / Peter Vansittart. London : P. Owen; Chester Springs, PA : U.S. distributor, Dufour Editions, 1988.

The final important aspect of broker processing discussed here refers to the life span of agents. As already mentioned above a set of initial broker agents is provided at system startup. By processing requests the system creates new agent specialists and modifies the scopes of its broker agents. The agents' life span is application dependent and may range from one individual user query to one user session to persistent existence. In the first case, agents are only created for handling the initial query. After the final answer has been generated all agents are removed. The reuse of cached information will be low. In the second case, agents live until the session is explicitly ended. Requests within sessions may lead to an increasing number of agents. Within one session the results of previous requests are reused to generate the answers of new requests. In the third case agents are persistent. Agents exist until they are explicitly removed from the system (e.g. at system shutdown, or attaching expiration times to agents). Thus, agents are similar to daemons in operating system environments. Again, agents reuse cached results of previous requests. However, because of the extended agent life span the cached information might be not up-to-date. Section 4.2 will discuss that aspect in more detail.

4.1 Interdependencies and Thresholds

The support of several interdependencies among subproblems models the general case of distributed processing, as required by DPS. Constraints provide a powerful and declarative approach to prune the search space of agents. Interdependencies may be used to model the order of sending the subrequests and thus the order of handling the subproblems. For example, the interdependency might specify that the subrequests are handled in sequential order, i.e. the subrequest k (argument position k of g) may sent only after the answers for the subrequest $k-1$ (argument position $k-1$ of g) have been received. Thus, interdependencies provide a powerful mechanism for modeling causal and temporal relationships between subproblems.

What we need are interdependency constraints and information thresholds.

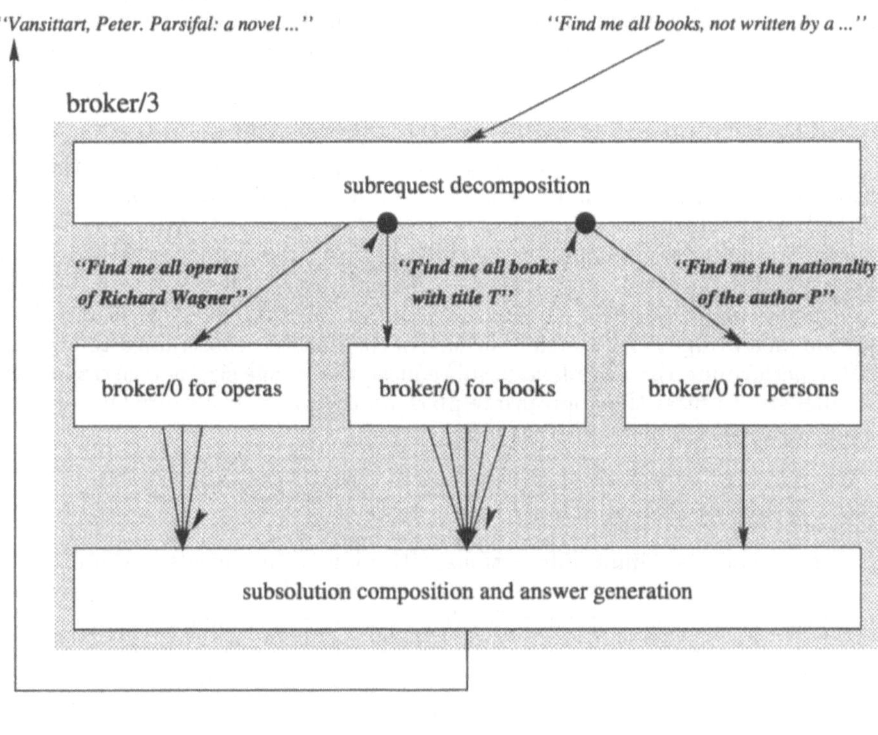

Figure 3: Broker interaction.

Interdependency constraints are quite simple. They are part of the constraint store. We have already used them in Example 2: Among other things, there is an interdependency constraint stating that the name of the opera and the title of the book must coincide, that is `O : name-> T` and `B : title-> T`, and another interdependency constraint forcing the coincidence of the author of the book and the person's name, that is `B : author-> PN` and `P : name-> PN`.

Information thresholds, on the other hand, are associated with each argument position. They are based on entailment tests, checking whether an argument entails a given (basic) feature constraint. Whenever a threshold condition of an argument position is satisfied the associated subrequest is triggered and sent to other brokers and agent specialists.

Example 3. In our example as illustrated in Fig. 3, it makes no sense to request a book without the knowledge of its title, or to query the nationality of someone who's name is not yet known.

Using the threshold mechanism and the interdependency constraint, broker/3 implements an argument ordering scheme, i.e., a request for argument position a_1 (Wagner operas) is sent first, a request for argument position a_2 (books with relevant title `T`) is sent whenever an answer for the first request arrives, i.e. whenever `nonvar(T)` (true if argument `T` is not a variable). Analogously, a request for argument position a_3 (nationality of a given author) depends on answers received for argument position a_2.

Thresholds may also be used to model repeated invocations of the same subrequest with refined input constraint values. Suppose the subrequest k was already sent and the associated answer has been received. After receiving the answer for another subrequest j the threshold for subrequest k is satisfied again; however, this time with new, refined constraint values. An example in document processing would be the following. Initially in the subrequest k an image of a person on a bridge is requested. The size of the image is constrained to one page. After performing the page layout subrequest the image size is constrained to a smaller size to fit at the appropriate place on the page. The subrequest k is sent again with the smaller size constraint.

4.2 Reuse of Information

Complex requests require interactions with many other agents and information stores in the network in order to gather the desired information. However, the execution of complex generator functions can be rather time consuming. Thus, in large information networks, such as the World-Wide Web the reuse of generated and already collected information is especially important. There are certain types of information which are quite stable. For example, the names and characteristics of known operas of Richard Wagner do not change; only the number of performances of them will change over time.

As a leitmotif, the interaction protocols of the CBKB model support the reuse of information and the avoidance of redundant generation of solutions. Actually, the constraint stores of agent specialists can be interpreted as caches of information. The cached information are values and constraints of already executed requests and subrequests to other agents. The quantity of reuse ranges from minimal to maximal. For minimal reuse all generated information is made potentially available, but it can be delivered only in response to specific requests (request-subrequest protocol). For maximal reuse all generated information is immediately broadcast to all agents (local caching protocol). The notion of quantity of reuse of information was formally introduced in [Arcelli et al., 1995]; it discusses heuristics in order to provide criterias for choosing between the two interaction protocols.

In static environments where knowledge does not change or is not extended, the information in the agent caches remains valid over time and can be reused by subsequent requests. On the other hand, in many applications the agents attached to a database have to deal with database entries that evolve over time due to updates. Older knowledge is replaced by newer knowledge or additional knowledge is defined and appended to existing database entries. These modifications must be propagated to the agent caches in order to provide reliable knowledge in the information network. Two different, basic cache coherence protocols are applicable:

- write-invalidate;
- write-update

In the first approach an information change invalidates all caches which utilize that information explicitly or implicitly, i.e. information derived from it by using generator functions. The constraint stores of the affected agents must be cleared. Thus, subsequent requests to an agent specialist with a cleared constraint store will require the renewed distribution of subrequests and the composition of all possible answers out of the newly received subanswers (see steps 5 and 6 for broker/n, or the activities of a broker/0 to interact with the external environment).

The write-update protocol propagates the modified information to all relevant agents which incorporate the new information into the already existing cache. The old cache entries must be identified and replaced. Additionally the execution of the generator function might be required and thus, new answers are generated which are sent to the requesters of the agents. The association between old and new cache entries might require an extension of the current CBKB model by assigning identifiers to constraints and values. It seems that the write-invalidate protocol fits better with the current architecture of the CBKB model.

The requirement of cache consistency is application dependent and we can identify three different application domains: First, domains where *no updates* occur at all and where *all processed information remains up-to-date*. Second, domains that are *update-tolerant*. For a given period of time, the application does not care about updates and reuses cached values even when already obsolete (e.g. statistics concerning the sales force where the latest sold disc player should not influence the results too much). In the World-Wide Web, location paths may be cached locally and cache entries are not updated automatically. If a user follows an invalid path then an error message is displayed (in some more user-friendly cases the path to the new web page location is displayed). Finally, there are the *update-critical* domain such as money brokering, tele-banking etc.

5 Related Technologies

In this section we try to explain how the proposed mechanisms of agent-based interaction can be applied to or be seen in related scenarios. In particular we focus on the contract-net protocol as a negotiation-based approach, Telescript as a promising agent infrastructure, and workflow management as an interesting application domain.

5.1 Contract-net

The contract-net protocol [Smith, 1980] can be seen as a particular instance of a CBKB-system with two broker roles, namely a manager and a set of bidders. The manager tries to localize a contractor among the bidders that solves a particular problem. Therefore the manager is equipped with a very specific generator for the bid selection.

The protocol is negotiation-based along five different phases: In the first phase, the manager announces the problem by sending a request for bids to the set of bidders, e.g. by sending a request constraining the problem domain and constraining the capabilities a potential contractor must have. In the next phase, the bidders check the problem constraints and propagate their bids, e.g. by tailoring the problem domain to the bidders' scope. The next phase comprises the selection of a contractor by the manager. Upon receipt of answers the manager invokes its generator. The result generation is quite simple. If the bid satisfies the initial constraint, a potential contractor is found. Among all potential contractors, a "best" (according to some problem dependent criteria) potential contractor is selected as contractor. In the fourth phase, the problem solving task is transmitted to the contractor. The final phase concludes with the problem solving itself.

5.2 Telescript

With General Magic's Telescript [White, 1994b] a promising technology is provided for the necessary infrastructure required to enable interacting autonomous agents in the so-called *electronic marketplace*. The electronic marketplace representing the Telescript world consists of a number of electronic places (e.g. a user's communicator, an electronic shopping center, etc.). Carrying a script to execute a particular task and permits that limit their capabilities, Telescript agents may migrate to perform transactions related to the visited places (e.g. a shopping order) or to simply search electronically provided information. The electronic places are homogeneous in the sense that they are able to interpret these scripts and to communicate with agents according to a defined protocol. In our proposed framework of CBKB, Telescript can play a vital role to fill the gap between the broker/n that synthesizes and combines answers received with respect to a complex request and the broker/0 that actually "gathers" information in the electronic marketplace. Obviously, a broker/0 could use a Telescript agent as its means to find and retrieve the information requested. On the other hand, a Telescript agent itself could internally implement CBKBs. In this case constraint handling, partial solution processing, and "agent specialist" creation would be added to the Telescript infrastructure. The latter issue corresponds to the Telescript ability the clone an agent (specialist) that does not migrate back to the requester in order to deliver the results but awaits further tasks within the place. One such task could be answering further requests using some locally cached information.

5.3 Workflow Management

The previous examples and application domains had a strong emphasis on information gathering as it is often integrated into the user environment. The user initiates a query by specifying the relevant feature constraints (e.g. in a form template); the query is transformed into a request which is then sent to brokers and agent specialists available in the system. However, the CBKB model may also be embedded in other application environments. Applications might directly communicate with brokers and agent specialists to gather and extract knowledge necessary for their internal functionality. In the following we will briefly discuss some of the possibilities how the CBKB model may be embedded into the workflow management domain.

In recent years there has been considerable work and publication related to workflow systems, models and studies. Also the growing interest in business process reengineering [Davenport, 1993] led to the development of commercial workflow systems [Abbott and Sarin, 1994] in order to support and improve business processes. McCarthy and Bluestein [McCarthy and Bluestein, 1991] define workflow management "as a proactive system which manages the flow of work among participants according to a defined procedure consisting of a number of tasks. It coordinates user and system participants, together with the appropriate data resources which may be accessible directly by the system or off-line, to achieve defined objectives by set deadlines." In the context of workflow management, agents and constraints may be used in a variety of different ways. Some of the possibilities are discussed below.

In general, a workflow consists of a task structure which models the tasks of the associated business process, and the temporal and causal interdependencies between tasks. Task structures are embedded into the organizational environment, and thus must incorporate organizational information. Examples for organizational information are the organizational structure (static information), information about people's work load or time schedules (dynamic information), information about organizational policies and strategies or other external and internal documents of organizational importance. During the specification and execution phase of task structures brokers and agent specialists might be used to gather the relevant organizational information and integrate it into task structures. For example, several brokers might access the static and dynamic information of the organization database and assign people to tasks according to their position in the organizational structure and their current work load. Additionally brokers could find and retrieve the relevant documents in the database in order to support the execution of individual tasks. In both examples, brokers and agent specialists are used for information gathering (see also example 2) to incorporate dynamically relevant information into task structures and thus support more efficient task execution.

Traditional workflow systems are inflexible with respect to exception handling and adapting to changing objectives. The goal-based workflow model [Ellis and Wainer, 1994] is an approach to improve that. In this model a workflow captures the goals of individual tasks and of the global business process in addition to the procedural steps. Goals and contextual information could be modeled as constraints. Brokers and agent specialists could be used during the planning phase to extract task structure templates and instantiate them appropriately to satisfy given goals and contextual constraints. Using the generator functionality, simple task structures could be composed into more complex tasks structures which incorporate interdependencies between tasks. The planning phase supported by brokers and the execution of tasks could take place intermittently to achieve a more reactive behavior with respect to changing goals and contextual constraints.

6 Related Work

Constraint-Based Knowledge Brokers (CBKBs) were first introduced in [Andreoli et al., 1994], where the request-subrequest protocol was also defined and described, together with such notions as reuse of information, recursion control, ordering of subrequest deliveries, and thresholds. In [Andreoli et al., to appear], the CBKB model is described in more detail. Complexity analysis are given concerning number of messages exchanged, number of agents cloned, and number of generations through the broker-attached generators. A simple example is provided in the domain of parsing of feature-based grammars.

In [Arcelli et al., 1995], the local caching protocol for CBKBs is introduced and compared with the request-subrequest protocol. Arguments are given, why, in many cases, it would be best to make use of both protocol schemes, or even devise hybrid schemes. Some examples, numerical values for the measure of reuse, and graphical illustrations of reuse potentials are provided.

For a conceptual characterization of Distributed Problem Solving see [Decker et al., 1989; Durfee et al., 1989]. However, so far DPS has been lacking a real computational model. Our contribution can be seen as step in the direction of providing a computational framework for DPS. More recently, a cooperative information gathering (IG) approach using a multiagent system based on DPS was illustrated in [Oates et al., 1994]. Additional relevant literature can be found in [Lander and Lesser, 1992].

We have mentioned Telescript [White, 1994b] as a possible solution for the infrastructural support of CBKBs on wide area networks. As for the implementation of the constraint solving aspects, a current prototype makes use of ForumTalk [Andreoli, 1995], a distributed language based on the *LO* model [Andreoli and Pareschi, 1991] for object-oriented rules-based computations. The built-in *LO* facilities for dynamic process spawning and broadcast communication are advantageously exploited in the definition of the agent interaction protocols. Other implementation choices are, however, possible [Borghoff, 1995]. A promising alternative is given by languages based on the Concurrent Constraint Programming model [Saraswat et al., 1991], such as Oz [Henz et al., 1995]. An advantage of these languages is that they have a built-in notion of constraint, and they come with *ask-tell* primitives for controlling the suspension/resumption of the activities of concurrent agents depending on the availability of relevant information. Thus, they provide a straightforward direction for the implementation of information thresholds for CBKBs.

7 Conclusion

In the course of this paper, we have shown how constraints can provide appropriate computational support for the management of electronic information, thus enabling a breed of intelligent agents that can help users to deal with the problem of "information overflow". The coming of age of a number of complementary technologies, e.g. programming languages for network navigation like Telescript, make this framework not just an elegant formal solution but also a promising practical approach.

References

[Abbott and Sarin, 1994] K. R. Abbott and S. K. Sarin. Experiences with workflow management: Issues for the next generation. In R. Furuta and C. Neuwirth, editors, Proc. 5th Int. Conf. on Computer-Supported Cooperative Work, pp. 113–120, Chapel Hill, NC, October 1994. New York: SIGCHI/SIGOIS ACM.

[Agha, 1986] G. A. Agha. Actors: A Model of Concurrent Computation in Distributed Systems. Cambridge, MA: MIT Press, 1986.

[Aït-Kaci et al., 1994] H. Aït-Kaci, A. Podelski, and G. Smolka. A feature-based constraint-system for logic programming with entailment. Theoretical Computer Science, 122, 263–283, 1994.

[Andreoli and Pareschi, 1991] J.-M. Andreoli and R. Pareschi. Communication as fair distribution of knowledge. In Proc. Conf. on Object-Oriented Programming Systems, Languages and Applications (OOPSLA '91), pp. 212–229, Phoenix, AZ, November 1991. ACM SIGPLAN Notices **26**:11.

[Andreoli et al., 1994] J.-M. Andreoli, U. M. Borghoff, and R. Pareschi. Constraint-based knowledge brokers. In H. Hong, editor, Proc. 1st Int. Symp. on Parallel Symbolic Computation (PASCO '94), pp. 1–11, Hagenberg/Linz, Austria, September 1994. Lecture Notes Series in Computing **5**, Singapore, New Jersey, London, Hong Kong: World Scientific.

[Andreoli et al., to appear] J.-M. Andreoli, U. M. Borghoff, and R. Pareschi. The constraint-based knowledge broker model: Semantics, implementation and analysis. J. Symbolic Computation, to appear.

[Andreoli, 1995] J-M. Andreoli. Programming in forumtalk. Technical Report CT–003, Rank Xerox Research Centre, Grenoble Lab., France, 1995.

[Arcelli et al., 1995] F. Arcelli, U. M. Borghoff, F. Formato, and R. Pareschi. Tuning constraint-based communication in distributed problem solving. In Proc. 1st Int. Workshop on Concurrent Constraint Programming (CCP '95), Venice, Italy, May 1995.

[Borghoff and Schlichter, 1995] U. M. Borghoff and J. H. Schlichter. On combining the knowledge of heterogeneous information repositories. Technical report, Rank Xerox Research Centre, Grenoble Lab., France, September 1995.

[Borghoff, 1995] U. M. Borghoff. A procedural specification of the constraint-based knowledge broker model with partial results. Technical Report CT–004, Rank Xerox Research Centre, Grenoble Lab., France, May 1995.

[Bratman et al., 1988] M. E. Bratman, D. J. Israel, and M. E. Pollack. Plans and resource-bounded practical reasoning. Computational Intelligence, 4, 349–355, 1988.

[Brooks, 1991] R. A. Brooks. Intelligence without representation. Artificial Intelligence, 47, 139–159, 1991.

[CACM, 1994] **37**:7 CACM. Special issue on intelligent agents. Communications of the ACM, July 1994.

[Davenport, 1993] T. H. Davenport. Process Innovation: Reengineering Work through Information Technology. Boston, MA: Harvard Business School Press, 1993.

[Davis and Smith, 1983] R. Davis and R. G. Smith. Negotiation as a metaphor for distributed problem solving. Artificial Intelligence, 20, 1, 63–109, 1983.

[Decker et al., 1989] K. S. Decker, E. H. Durfee, and V. R. Lesser. The evaluation of research in cooperative distributed problem solving. In M. N. Huhns and L. Gasser, editors, Distributed Artificial Intelligence. Research Notes in Artificial Intelligence **2**. San Mateo: Pitman/Morgan Kaufmann, 1989.

[Durfee et al., 1989] E. H. Durfee, V. R. Lesser, and D. D. Corkill. Trends in cooperative distributed problem solving. IEEE Transactions on Knowledge and Data Engineering, 1, 1, 63–83, March 1989.

[Ellis and Wainer, 1994] C. A. Ellis and J. Wainer. Goal-based models of collaboration. Collaborative Computing, 1, 1, 61–86, March 1994.

[Henz et al., 1995] M. Henz, G. Smolka, and J. Würtz. Object-oriented concurrent constraint programming in oz. In P. v. Hentenryck and V. Saraswat, editors, Principles and Practice of Constraint Programming, pp. 27–48. Cambridge, MA: MIT Press, 1995.

[ISO, 1986] 8879 ISO. Information Processing – Text and Office Systems – Standard Generalized Markup Language (SGML). Int. Organization for Standardization: ISO IS, October 1986.

[Kaelbling and Rosenschein, 1990] L. P. Kaelbling and S. J. Rosenschein. Action and planning in embedded agents. In P. Maes, editor, Designing Autonomous Agents, pp. 35–48. Cambridge, MA: MIT Press, 1990.

[Lander and Lesser, 1992] S. Lander and V. R. Lesser. Customizing distributed search among agents with heterogeneous knowledge. In T. W. Finin, C. K. Nicholas, and Y. Yesha, editors, Proc. 1st Int. Conf. on Information and Knowledge Management, Baltimore, MD, November 1992. Berlin, Heidelberg, New York: Springer-Verlag.

[Malone and Lai, 1988] T. W. Malone and K.-Y. Lai. Object lens: A spreadsheet for cooperative work. In Proc. 2nd Int. Conf. on Computer-Supported Cooperative Work, Portland, OR, September 1988. New York: SIGCHI/SIGOIS ACM.

[Malone, 1989] T. W. Malone. Semiformal systems and shared object spaces. In Proc. Groupware Technology Workshop, Palo Alto, CA, August 1989.

[McCarthy and Bluestein, 1991] J. C. McCarthy and W. M. Bluestein. The Computing Strategy Report: Workflow's Progress. Cambridge, MA: Forrester Research Inc., 1991.

[Oates et al., 1994] T. Oates, M. V. N. Prasad, and V. R. Lesser. Cooperative information gathering: A distributed problem solving approach. Technical Report TR-94-66, Dept. of Computer Science, Univ. of Massachusetts, Amherst, MA, 1994.

[Pereira and Warren, 1983] F. C. N. Pereira and D. H. D. Warren. Parsing as deduction. In Proc. 21st Annual Meeting of the Association for Computational Linguistics, MIT, Cambridge, MA, June 1983.

[Prasad et al., 1995] M. V. N. Prasad, V. R. Lesser, and S. Lander. Retrieval and reasoning in distributed case bases. Technical Report TR-95-27, Dept. of Computer Science, Univ. of Massachusetts, Amherst, MA, 1995.

[Saraswat et al., 1991] V. A. Saraswat, M. Rinard, and P. Panangaden. Semantic foundations of concurrent constraint programming. In Proc. 18th ACM SIGACT/SIGPLAN Annual Symp. on Principles of Programming Languages, pp. 333–352, Orlando, FL, January 1991. New York: ACM.

[Sen and Durfee, 1991] S. Sen and E. H. Durfee. A formal study of distributed meeting scheduling: Preliminary results. In Proc. Conf. on Organizational Computing Systems, pp. 55–68, Atlanta, GA, November 1991. New York: SIGOIS ACM.

[Shoham, 1993] Y. Shoham. Agent-oriented programming. Artificial Intelligence, 60, 1, 51–92, 1993.

[Smith, 1980] R. G. Smith. The contract net protocol: High-level communication and control in a distributed problem solver. IEEE Transactions on Computers, C–29, 12, 1104–1113, December 1980.

[Vielle, 1986] L. Vielle. Recursive axioms in deductive databases: The query-subquery approach. In L. Kerschberg, editor, Proc. 1st Conf. on Expert Database Systems, Menlo Park, CA, April 1986. Benjamin/Cummings Publ. Company.

[Wayner, 1994] P. Wayner. Agents away. Byte, pp. 113–118, May 1994.

[White, 1994a] J. E. White. Telescript technology: Scenes from the electronic marketplace. General Magic White Paper, 1994.
[White, 1994b] J. E. White. Telescript technology: The foundation for the electronic marketplace. General Magic White Paper, 1994.
[Wooldridge and Jennings, 1995] M. Wooldridge and N. R. Jennings. Intelligent agents: Theory and practice. Knowledge Engineering Review, 10, 2, 1995.

Acknowledgement

We like to thank Nathalie Glance for her careful reading of an earlier draft.

The work of the last author was done while visiting the Rank Xerox Research Centre at Grenoble on a sabbatical leave.

Journal of Universal Computer Science, vol. 1, no. 12 (1995), 790-810
submitted: 29/11/95, accepted: 7/12/95, appeared: 28/12/95 © *Springer Pub. Co.*

Parikh prime words and GO-like territories[1]

A. Mateescu
(Academy of Finland and University of Turku
Department of Mathematics, FI-20500 Turku, Finland)

Gh. Păun
(Institute of Mathematics of the Romanian Academy
PO Box 1 - 764, RO-70700 Bucharest, Romania)

G. Rozenberg
(Leiden University, Department of Computer Science
P.O. Box 9512, NL-2300 RA Leiden, the Netherlands)

A. Salomaa
(Academy of Finland and University of Turku
Department of Mathematics, FI-20500 Turku, Finland)

Abstract: An n-dimensional vector of natural numbers is said to be prime if the greatest common divisor of its components is one. A word is said to be Parikh prime if its Parikh vector is prime. The languages of Parikh prime and of Parikh non-prime words are investigated (they are neither semilinear nor slender, hence are not context-free or D0L languages; both of them can be generated by matrix grammars with appearance checking).
Marking in the plane the points identified by prime (2-dimensional) vectors, interesting patterns of non-marked ("free") points appear (they are similar to the territories in the game of GO). The shape of such possible territories is investigated (with an exhaustive analysis of tro-, tetro-, pento- and hexominoes). Some open problems are formulated (both concerning the mentioned languages and the "GO territories theory").

Key Words: formal languages, context free languages, L-systems, Parikh mapping, word problems
Category: F.4.2, F.4.3, G.2.1

1 Introduction

The investigation here starts from the already (in)famous open problem asking whether or not the set Q of all primitive words is context-free or not. (A word is primitive if it cannot be written as a power of a different word.) Many things are known about this language and about its complement (see [6], [9] and their references), but not the answer to the mentioned question. The conjecture is that Q is not context-free. The topic is part of a more general area of interest in language theory and combinatorics on words [10]: investigate languages consisting of words containing or not containing given patterns. The history of the problem goes back to Axel Thue [15], who considered words without adjacent repeats. From pumping lemmas, a language consisting of such words cannot be context-free. For a while the problem was open whether or not the language of

[1] Research supported by the Academy of Finland, project 11281, and the ESPRIT Basic Research Working Group ASMICS II.

repetitive words (words containing adjacent repeats, that is of the form $x_1x_2x_2x_3$, with non-empty x_2) is context-free. It was conjectured in [1] that the answer is negative and, indeed, this has been confirmed in [12].

In view of the difficulty of the context-freeness problem for the language Q, it is natural to look for variants of it. If w is a non-primitive word, $w = z^k, k \geq 2$, then its Parikh vector, $\Psi(w)$, will be of the form $\Psi(w) = k \cdot \Psi(z)$. Consequently, also $\Psi(w)$ is non-primitive, in the sense that all its components are multiples of an integer greater than or equal to 2. The converse is not true: $\Psi(aabb) = (2,2)$, but *aabb* is primitive. Anyway, this suggests to consider the language of all words having "primitive" Parikh vectors, in the sense that the greatest common divisor of their elements is one. We call them *prime vectors* and *Parikh prime words*, respectively.

The place of the languages of Parikh prime and of Parikh non-prime words in the Chomsky hierarchy and in the L hierarchy is investigated in the following section. Then, the patterns of points identified by non-prime 2-dimensional vectors are examined. Being surrounded by points identified by prime vectors, these patterns are reminiscant of the notion of a *territory* in the celebrated game of GO, definitely one of the most interesting games ever invented. (GO is probably the oldest significant logical game, and yet considered the ultimate challenge for artificial intelligence: although spectacular progresses were recently made concerning the mathematical theory of parts of a game – of the end games in [2] – the GO programs are still far from being competitive, a quite different situation compared to that in chess. We do not present here the rules of GO, every *real* scientist knows the game...) A series of surprising results are obtained about such territories (if a pattern appears once, then it appears infinitely many times, there are arbitrarily large territories, etc.), and a complete study of territories with less than seven free points is done. However, a series of challenging problems remains unsettled.

2 Parikh primality versus Chomsky and L hierarchy

As usual, for an alphabet V we denote by V^* the set of all words over V; the empty string is denoted by λ and $V^* - \{\lambda\}$ by V^+. The length of $x \in V^*$ is $|x|$ and $|x|_a$ is the number of occurrences of the symbol $a \in V$ in the string $x \in V^*$. The left derivative (of a string x with respect to a symbol a) is denoted by $\partial_a(x)$ and it is defined by $\partial_a(x) = x'$ iff $x = ax'$.

If $V = \{a_1, \ldots, a_n\}$, then the Parikh mapping $\Psi_V : V^* \longrightarrow \mathbf{N}^n$ is defined by $\Psi_V(w) = (|w|_{a_1}, \ldots, |w|_{a_n}), w \in V^*$, and it is extended to languages $L \subseteq V^*$ by $\Psi_V(L) = \{\Psi_V(w) \mid w \in L\}$.

For (other) basic elements of formal language theory (including L systems), we refer to [13], [14]. We denote by CF, CS the families of context-free and of context-sensitive languages, respectively; by $0L, D0L, E0L, ET0L$ we denote the families of languages generated by 0L systems, D0L, E0L, and ET0L systems, respectively.

We introduce now some new notions.

A vector $(v_1, \ldots, v_n) \in \mathbf{N}^n$ is said to be *prime* if $gcd(v_1, \ldots, v_n) = 1$.

A word $w \in V^*, V = \{a_1, \ldots, a_n\}$, is called *Parikh prime* if $\Psi_V(w)$ is prime. For an alphabet V, we denote by P_V the set of all Parikh prime words over V and by $\bar{P}_V$ its complement, $\bar{P}_V = V^* - P_V$.

Remark. By definition, $\lambda \in \bar{P}_V$. Considering that $gcd(n) = n$ for all $n \geq 1$, we get $P_{\{a\}} = \{a\}$ and $\bar{P}_{\{a\}} = \{\lambda\} \cup \{a^i \mid i \geq 2\}$, hence this case is trivial. From now on, we will assume that the alphabet we work with contains at least two letters.

It is a natural question to find the place of languages $P_V, \bar{P}_V$ in the Chomsky (and in the L) hierarchy. We shall do that using the notion of *semilinearity* (and of *slenderness*).

A set $M \subseteq \mathbf{N}^n$ is called *linear* if there are $v_0, v_1, \ldots, v_p \in \mathbf{N}^n$ such that $M = \{v_0 + \sum_{i=1}^{p} v_i r_i \mid r_i \in \mathbf{N}\}$. A set $M \subseteq \mathbf{N}^n$ is *semilinear* if it is the union of a finite number of linear sets. A language $L \subseteq V^*$ is *semilinear* if $\Psi_V(L)$ is semilinear.

The well-known *Parikh theorem* says that every context-free language is semilinear. However, we have

Theorem 1. *For all V with card(V) ≥ 2, the language P_V is not semilinear.*

Proof. Take the semilinear set $M = \{(v_1, v_2, 0, 0, \ldots, 0) \mid v_1, v_2 \in \mathbf{N}\}$. For each V with card$(V) \geq 2$, if $\Psi_V(P_V)$ is semilinear, then $\Psi_V(P_V) \cap M$ is semilinear (the class of semilinear sets of vectors is closed under intersection [7]). Therefore it is enough to prove that $\Psi_V(P_V) \cap M$ is not semilinear, hence it is enough to consider the case of two-letter alphabets. We denote simply by P the language P_V for $V = \{a, b\}$ (we also write a, b instead of a_1, a_2).

Assume that $\Psi_V(P)$ is semilinear, hence $\Psi_V(P) = \cup_{j=1}^{l} T_j$, for $T_j, 1 \leq j \leq l$, linear subsets of $\mathbf{N}^2$. Assume

$$T_j = \{v_{0j} + \sum_{i=1}^{k_j} v_{ij} r_i \mid r_i \in \mathbf{N}\} \qquad (*)$$

for given vectors $v_{0j}, v_{1j}, \ldots, v_{k_j j} \in \mathbf{N}^2, 1 \leq j \leq l$.

All strings of the form $a^p b^n$ for p a prime number and $n \in \mathbf{N} - p \cdot \mathbf{N}$ are in P, hence (p, n) are in $\Psi_V(P)$. For each such (p, n) there is $j, 1 \leq j \leq l$, such that $(p, n) \in T_j$. For each prime p, the number n as above can be arbitrarily large, hence $(p, n) \in T_j$ implies that there is v_{ij} with $i > 0$ and $r_j > 0$ in the expression $(*)$ for (p, n). More precisely, for a fixed prime p and arbitrarily large n, we need a vector $v_{i_0 j} = (0, m)$ with $m > 0$ used in the writing $(p, n) = v_{0,j} + \sum_{i=1}^{k_j} v_{ij} r_i$.

This implies that all vectors of the form

$$(p, n) + r(0, m) = (p, n + rm) \qquad (**)$$

for $r \in \mathbf{N}$ are in $\Psi_V(P)$.

The set of prime numbers is infinite, the set of vectors $(0, m)$ used in writing $\Psi_V(P)$ as above is finite. Consequently, there are such p and m with $p > m$. For such p and n we have $gcd(p, m) = 1$, hence there are $s, t \in \mathbf{Z}$ such that $sp + tm = 1$. Without loss of generality we may assume that $s > 0, t < 0$ (otherwise we replace s with $s - mq$ and t with $t + pq$, with negative q, large enough in absolute value to have $s - mq > 0$ and $t + pq < 0$). Write

$$1 + |t|m = sp$$

and multiply by n:

$$n + n|t|m = nsp.$$

For $r = n|t|$ in (**) we obtain

$$(p, n) + n|t|(0, m) = (p, n + n|t|m) = (p, nsp),$$

which must be in $\Psi_V(P)$, a contradiction with $gcd(p, nsp) = p$. In conclusion, $\Psi_V(P)$ cannot be semilinear. □

Also $\bar{P}_V$ is non-semilinear, and the proof for this language is much easier.

Theorem 2. *For all V with card$(V) \geq 2$, the language $\bar{P}_V$ is not semilinear.*

Proof. As above, it is enough to consider the case of V consisting of two letters. We denote by $\bar{P}$ the language $\bar{P}_V$ for $V = \{a, b\}$.

Assume that $\Psi_V(\bar{P})$ is semilinear and consider it as the union of finitely many linear sets T_j as in the previous proof. All vectors (p, pn), with prime p and $n \geq 1$, are in $\Psi_V(\bar{P})$. In order to write such vectors (p, pn) with given p and arbitrarily large n we need a vector $(0, m), m > 0$, in the writing of some set T_j. All vectors

$$(p, pn) + r(0, m) = (p, pn + rm),$$

$r \geq 0$, are in the corresponding set T_j. Because $gcd(p, pn + rm)$ must be greater than 1, we must have $gcd(p, pn + rm) = p$, which implies that m must be a multiple of p (n and r can be arbitrary). However, there are only finitely many vectors $(0, m)$ in the writing of sets T_j, they cannot contain as divisors all prime numbers, a contradiction. □

Corollary. *For all V with card$(V) \geq 2$, the languages P_V and $\bar{P}_V$ are not context-free, simple matrix, matrix of finite index, unordered vector languages.*

For definitions of the mentioned families, other than that of context-free languages, as well as for the proof that they contain only semilinear languages, the reader is referred to [4] and to its bibliography.

We recall now from [4] the definition of a matrix grammar.

A *matrix grammar* (with appearance checking) is a system

$$G = (N, T, S, M, F),$$

where N, T are disjoint alphabets (of nonterminal and terminal symbols, respectively), $S \in N$, M is a finite set of sequences $(A_1 \to u_1, \ldots, A_n \to u_n), n \geq 1$, of context-free rules over $N \cup T$ (called *matrices*), and F consists of some rules appearing in M.

For $x, y \in (N \cup T)^*$ we write $x \Longrightarrow y$ if there is $(A_1 \to u_1, \ldots, A_n \to u_n) \in M$ and $w_1, w_2, \ldots, w_{n+1} \in (N \cup T)^*$ such that $x = w_1, y = w_{n+1}$ and for each $i = 1, 2, \ldots, n$ either $w_i = w_i' A_i w_i'', w_{i+1} = w_i' u_i w_i''$ or $|w_i|_{A_i} = 0, w_i = w_{i+1}$ and $A_i \to u_i \in F$. (The rules of a matrix are used consecutively, in the order indicated, possibly skipping rules appearing in F, providing they cannot be applied to the current string.) Then $L(G) = \{x \in T^* \mid S \Longrightarrow^* x\}$.

We denote by MAT_{ac} the family of languages generated by matrix grammars as above, with λ-free rules. If $F = \emptyset$ (hence all rules must be effectively used), then we say that the grammar is without appearance checking. The corresponding family of languages is denoted by MAT (again λ-rules are not allowed).

It is known that $CF \subset MAT \subset MAT_{ac} \subset CS$, all inclusions being proper, and that MAT contains non-semilinear languages.

For saving space, in the following theorems we consider only the languages P and $\bar{P}$ (hence over $V = \{a, b\}$), but similar constructions can be obtained also for general alphabets.

Theorem 3. $P \in MAT_{ac}$.

Proof. We construct the matrix grammar

$$G = (N, \{a, b, c\}, S_0, M, F),$$

where

$$N = \{S_0, S, A, A', A'', \bar{A}, B, \bar{B}, X, Y, Z, Z', Z'', Z''', U, U', U'', V, \#\},$$

F contains all rules with the right-hand member equal with $\#$, and M contains the following matrices:

$$\begin{aligned} 1.\ & (S \to XS), \\ & (X \to X, S \to AS), \\ & (X \to X, S \to BS), \\ & (X \to Y, S \to A), \\ & (X \to Y, S \to B). \end{aligned}$$

(One produces a string $Yw, w \in \{A, B\}^+$.)

$$2.\ (Y \to Z, A \to A', A \to A').$$

(One introduces two occurrences of A'; we shall check whether or not 2 is a common divisor for $|w|_A$ and $|w|_B$. In general, the current number of A' occurrences will be checked as a possible common divisor of $|w|_A$ and $|w|_B$.)

$$\begin{aligned} 3.\ & (Z \to Z, A' \to A'', A \to \bar{A}), \\ & (Z \to Z', A' \to \#), \\ & (Z' \to Z', A'' \to A'), \\ & (Z' \to Z, A'' \to \#). \end{aligned}$$

(In the presence of Z one marks by a bar as many occurrences of A as there are occurrences of A' in the current string; the operation is iterated.)

$$4.\ (Z \to Z'', A' \to \#, A \to \#).$$

(One finishes at the same time both the A' occurrences and the A occurrences, hence $|w|_A$ is divisible by the number of A' occurrences.)

$$5.\ (Z \to Z''', A' \to A', A \to \#).$$

(The number $|w|_A$ is not a multiple of the number of A' occurrences.)

$$\begin{aligned}6.\ &(Z''' \to Z''', A'' \to A'),\\ &(Z''' \to Z''', \bar{A} \to A),\\ &(Z''' \to Z, A'' \to \#, \bar{A} \to \#, A \to A').\end{aligned}$$

(One returns to a string containing only symbols A' and A, with the number of A' occurrences increased by one. Matrices in groups 3 – 5 are now applied for the divisibility by the new number of A' symbols.)

$$\begin{aligned}7.\ &(Z'' \to Z'', A'' \to A'),\\ &(Z'' \to U, A'' \to \#),\\ &(U \to U, A' \to A'', B \to \bar{B}),\\ &(U \to U', A' \to \#),\\ &(U' \to U', A'' \to A'),\\ &(U' \to U, A'' \to \#).\end{aligned}$$

(Having concluded in 4 that the number of A occurrences is a multiple of the number of A' occurrences, one now checks whether the number of B occurrences is a multiple of the number of A' occurrences.)

$$8.\ (U \to U'', A' \to A', B \to \#).$$

(The number of B occurrences is not divisible by the number of A' occurrences. Only in this case we can continue, otherwise # is introduced.)

$$\begin{aligned}9.\ &(U'' \to U'', \bar{B} \to B),\\ &(U'' \to Z''', \bar{B} \to \#).\end{aligned}$$

(One returns to group 6, for continuing the process with an increased number of occurrences of A'.)

$$\begin{aligned}10.\ &(Z''' \to V, A'' \to \#, \bar{A} \to \#, A \to \#),\\ &(V \to V, A' \to a),\\ &(V \to V, B \to b),\\ &(V \to c).\end{aligned}$$

(When all occurrences of A were replaced by A' and still $|w|_B$ is not divisible by this number, the string is "accepted", the nonterminals are replaced by terminals.)

¿From the explanations above we have

$$P = \partial_c(L(G)) \cup b^*ab^*$$

(the grammar G produces all strings cw with $w \in P, |w|_a \geq 2$). As MAT_{ac} is closed under left derivative and union, we have $P \in MAT_{ac}$. □

Theorem 4. $\bar{P} \in MAT_{ac}$.

Proof. We construct the matrix grammar

$$G = (N, \{a, b, c\}, S_0, M, F),$$

with

$$N = \{S_0, S, A, B, A', A'', X, Y, Z, Z', U, U', V, \#\},$$

F containing all rules introducing the symbol #, and M consisting of the following matrices:

$$\begin{aligned} 1.\ & (S \to XS), \\ & (X \to X, S \to AS), \\ & (X \to X, S \to BS), \\ & (X \to Y, S \to A), \\ & (X \to Y, S \to B). \end{aligned}$$

(As above, one produces a string $Yw, w \in \{A, B\}^+$.)

$$\begin{aligned} 2.\ & (Y \to Y, A \to A'), \\ & (Y \to Z, A \to A', A \to A'). \end{aligned}$$

(At least two occurrences of A are replaced by A'. The derivation will end correctly if and only if $|w|_A$ and $|w|_B$ are both divisible by the number of A' occurrences.)

$$\begin{aligned} 3.\ & (Z \to Z, A' \to A'', A \to a), \\ & (Z \to Z', A' \to \#), \\ & (Z' \to Z', A'' \to A'), \\ & (Z' \to Z, A'' \to \#). \end{aligned}$$

(The number of A occurrences is checked for divisibility with the number of A'.)

$$4.\ (Z' \to U, A'' \to \#).$$

(After introducing U, the symbols A cannot be rewritten, hence their number must have been multiple of the number of A' occurrences.)

$$\begin{aligned} 5.\ & (U \to U, A' \to A'', B \to b), \\ & (U \to U', A' \to \#), \\ & (U' \to U', A'' \to A'), \\ & (U' \to U, A'' \to \#). \end{aligned}$$

(The symbols B are terminated, in blocks of size equal to the total number of occurrences of A'.)

$$6.\ (U' \to V, A'' \to \#).$$

(No further B will be rewritten, hence their number must have been a multiple of the number of A' occurrences.)

$$\begin{aligned} 7.\ & (V \to V, A' \to a), \\ & (V \to c). \end{aligned}$$

We have

$$\bar{P} = \partial_c(L(G)) \cup a^* \cup b^*,$$

hence $\bar{P} \in MAT_{ac}$. □

Consider now the place of languages $P, \bar{P}$ in the L hierarchy.

A language $L \subseteq V^*$ is called *slender* [11] iff there is a constant k such that $\text{card}(L \cap V^n) \leq k$ for all $n \in \mathbf{N}$ (the number of words in L of any given length is bounded).

In [5] it is proved that each D0L language is slender. Clearly, P and $\bar{P}$ are not slender: for any prime numbers p, q, all permutations of $a^p b^q$ are in P and all permutations of $a^p b^{2p}$ are in $\bar{P}$. Consequently, P and $\bar{P}$ are not D0L languages. Moreover, we have

Theorem 5. $P \notin 0L$.

Proof. Assume that $P = L(G)$ for some 0L system $G = (\{a,b\}, w, \sigma)$ (σ is a finite substitution, but we consider it as a set of rules of the form $c \to u$ for $u \in \sigma(c), c \in \{a,b\}$).

1. G must be propagating.

Assume that $a \to \lambda \in \sigma$. There is at least one rule $b \to x$. If $|x|_a \geq 1, |x|_b \geq 1$, then $aaabb \Longrightarrow xx$, which is not in P. If we have both $b \to a^i$ and $b \to b^j$ in σ, $i,j \geq 1$, then $abbbb \Longrightarrow b^{2i}b^{2j}$, again not in P. If we have $b \to a^i$ and $a \to b^j, i,j \geq 1$, or $b \to b^i$ and $a \to a^j, i,j \geq 1$, then $aaabb \Longrightarrow a^{2i}b^{2j}$ or $aaabb \Longrightarrow a^{2j}b^{2i}$, which are not in P. If the only b-rule is $b \to \lambda$, then we must have $a \to x$ in σ, with $|x|_a \geq 1, |x|_b \geq 1$ and then $aab \Longrightarrow xx$, not in P. In all cases (because we need rules introducing both a and b) we reach a contradiction.

Consequently, G is propagating, hence its axiom must be one of the shortest strings in P. These strings are

$$a, b, ab, ba, aab, aba, baa, abb, bab, bba.$$

Assume that the axiom is a. The case of $w = b$ is symmetric.

Then the rule $a \to b$ must be in σ (in order to obtain $b \in P$).

2. No rule $c \to d^i, c \in \{a,b\}, d \in \{a,b\}, i \geq 2$, is possible: take $e \neq c$ such that $\{e,c\} = \{a,b\}$ and a rule $e \to x$. Then $e^i c \Longrightarrow x^i d^i$, which is not in P.

3. Assume that we have the rule $a \to ab$ in σ. Then:
   - if $a \to a \in \sigma$, then $aaabb \Longrightarrow (ab)(a)(b)xx \notin P$,
   - if $b \to a \in \sigma$, then $aabbb \Longrightarrow (ab)(b)(a)(a)(a) \notin P$,
   - if $b \to b \in \sigma$, then $aaab \Longrightarrow (ab)(ab)(b)(b) \notin P$.

All cases are contradictory.

4. Examine now the case of the string aab. It cannot be produced starting from a string of length three, because, as we have seen above, we cannot use rules $a \to a, b \to a, b \to b$. Moreover, it cannot be produced from a string of length two: we need either $a \to a$ or $a \to aa$ in the case of $ab \Longrightarrow aab$, and either $b \to a$ or $b \to aa$ in the case of $ba \Longrightarrow aab$, and this is contradictory.

If $b \to aab \in \sigma$, then $aab \Longrightarrow (ab)(b)(aab) \notin P$. Consequently, we must have the rule $a \to aab$ in σ.

Consider now the case of the string abb. As above, it cannot be produced from strings of length three. If $ab \Longrightarrow abb$, then we need $b \to b$ or $b \to bb$, a contradiction. If $ba \Longrightarrow abb$, then we need $b \to ab$ and $aaab \Longrightarrow (ab)(ab)(ab)(ab) \notin P$.

They remain two cases:

$a \to abb \in \sigma$; then $a^4b^3 \Longrightarrow (a^2b)(a^2b)(ab^2)(ab^2)xxx \notin P$,

$b \to abb \in \sigma$; then $ab \Longrightarrow (a^2b)(ab^2) \notin P$.

All cases are contradictory, the assumption that $a \to ab \in \sigma$ cannot be true.

5. If $b \to ab \in \sigma$, then:
   - if $a \to a \in \sigma$, then $aabbb \Longrightarrow (a)(b)(ab)(ab)(ab) \notin P$,
   - if $b \to a \in \sigma$, then $aaabb \Longrightarrow (b)(b)(b)(a)(ab) \notin P$,
   - if $b \to b \in \sigma$, then $abbb \Longrightarrow (b)(ab)(ab)(b) \notin P$.

All cases are contradictory.

6. Examine the possibilities to produce the string aab. We cannot obtain it from strings of length three (we cannot use rules as above) and also not from strings ab, ba (in both cases we need rules already discussed: $a \to a, a \to aa, b \to a, b \to aa$).

If $a \to aab \in \sigma$, then $aab \Longrightarrow (aab)(b)(ab) \notin P$.

If $b \to aab \in \sigma$, then $abb \Longrightarrow (b)(ab)(aab) \notin P$.

The string aab cannot be generated, a contradiction with $L(G) = P$, hence $P \notin 0L$. □

Open problems. Is $\bar{P}$ a 0L language ? Which are the relationships between $P, \bar{P}$ and $E0L, ET0L$ and MAT ?

The syntactic monoid (of course, infinite) of the languages $\bar{P}_V$ has a nice property: it is isomorphic with $\mathbf{N}^k$, for $k = \text{card}(V)$.

Indeed, take $V = \{a_1, \ldots, a_k\}$. For $x, y \in V^*$ we define

$$x \approx y \text{ iff } (uxv \in \bar{P}_V \Leftrightarrow uyv \in \bar{P}_V), \text{ for all } u, v \in V^*.$$

Lemma 1. *For all $x, y \in V^*, x \approx y$ if and only if $\Psi_V(x) = \Psi_V(y)$.*

Proof. If $\Psi_V(x) = \Psi_V(y)$, then for all $u, v \in V^*$ we have $\Psi_V(uxv) = \Psi_V(uyv)$, therefore $uxv \in \bar{P}_V$ if and only if $uyv \in \bar{P}_V$.

Conversely, suppose that $x \approx y$, but $\Psi_V(x) \neq \Psi_V(y)$. Assume $\Psi_V(x) = (i_1, \ldots, i_k)$, and $\Psi_V(y) = (j_1, \ldots, j_k)$.

Without loss of generality, we may assume that there is $r, 1 \le r \le k$, such that $i_r < j_r$ (if necessary, we interchange x and y). Denote $D = j_r - i_r$.

Take two consecutive prime numbers p_1, p_2 such that $p_2 - p_1 > D$ and such that

$$\frac{p_1}{3} > \max\{i_h \mid 1 \le h \le k\}.$$

Denote $q = p_1 - i_r$. Because

$$p_1 = i_r + q < j_r + q = p_1 + (j_r - i_r) = p_1 + D < p_2,$$

it follows that $j_r + q$ is not a prime number. Therefore, $j_r + q = df$ for some numbers $d > 1, f > 1$ such that $d < \frac{p_1}{2}$.

Let $d_1, \ldots, d_k$ be such that $(j_h + d_h) \equiv 0 \pmod{d}$, $1 \le h \le k$. We can take these numbers such that $0 \le d_h < d, 1 \le h \le k$.

Consider the words

$$u = a_1^{d_1} a_2^{d_2} \ldots a_{r-1}^{d_{r-1}} a_r^q a_{r+1}^{d_{r+1}} \ldots a_k^{d_k},$$
$$v = \lambda.$$

We have

$$\Psi_V(uyv) = (j_1 + d_1, \ldots, j_{r-1} + d_{r-1}, j_r + q, j_{r+1} + d_{r+1}, \ldots, j_k + d_k).$$

¿From the previous construction, d divides all components of this vector, hence $uyv \in \bar{P}_V$.

On the other hand,

$$\begin{aligned}\Psi_V(uxv) &= (i_1 + d_1, \ldots, i_{r-1} + d_{r-1}, i_r + q, i_{r+1} + d_{r+1}, \ldots, i_k + d_k) = \\ &= (i_1 + d_1, \ldots, i_{r-1} + d_{r-1}, p_1, i_{r+1} + d_{r+1}, \ldots, i_k + d_k).\end{aligned}$$

For all $h, 1 \leq h \leq k, h \neq r$, we have

$$i_h + d_h < \frac{p_1}{3} + \frac{p_1}{2} < p_1.$$

Consequently, p_1 does not divide any of the components $i_h + d_h, h \neq k$, that is $gcd(i_1 + d_1, \ldots, i_{r-1} + d_{r-1}, p_1, i_{r+1} + d_{r+1}, \ldots, i_k + d_k) = 1$. This means that $uxv \notin \bar{P}_V$, a contradiction to $x \approx y$. □

Consequently, for each $x \in V^*$, the equivalence class of x, denoted by $\hat{x}$, consists of all permutations of x.

Theorem 6. *The monoid $M = V^*/_{\approx}$ is isomorphic with the monoid* $(\mathbf{N}^k, +, (0 \ldots, 0))$.

Proof. We define $\varphi : M \longrightarrow \mathbf{N}^k$ by $\varphi(\hat{x}) = \Psi_V(x)$ for all $x \in V^*$. From the previous lemma, if $x \approx y$, then $\Psi_V(x) = \Psi_V(y)$, hence φ is well defined.

Because for all $x, y \in V^*$ we have

$$\varphi(\hat{x}\hat{y}) = \varphi(\widehat{xy}) = \Psi_V(xy) = \Psi_V(x) + \Psi_V(y) = \varphi(\hat{x}) + \varphi(\hat{y}),$$

this is a morphism.

If $\varphi(\hat{x}) = \varphi(\hat{y})$, then $\Psi_V(x) = \Psi_V(y)$, and according to Lemma 1 we have $\hat{x} = \hat{y}$, hence φ is injective. The surjectivity is obvious: for each vector $t \in \mathbf{N}^k$ there is a word $w \in V^*$ such that $\Psi_V(w) = t$, hence $\varphi(\hat{w}) = t$. In conclusion, φ is an isomorphism of monoids. □

3 Prime vectors in the plane

Let us mark by a dot the points of coordinates (n, m) with $gcd(n, m) = 1$. We have done this in Figure 1 for n, m positive and with $n < m, 1 \leq n \leq 19, 1 \leq m \leq 23$. It is obvious that the arrangements of dots is symmetric with respect to the axes and with respect to the diagonals of the plane, hence it is enough to examine only the region of points $(n, m), n, m \in \mathbf{N}$, with $n < m$ (as in Figure 1).

If we interpret the dots as (say black) GO stones, we find in this figure a series of *territories*: regions of empty points, connected horizontally or vertically, and surrounded by occupied points.

Which shapes can these territories have ? Which is their relative distribution ? Are there territories of an arbitrarily large size (as regards the number of points) ?

These questions and other related ones can be formulated starting from Figure 1. We shall answer part of them, after introducing some more formal terminology.

Every vector $(n,m) \in \mathbf{Z}^2$ is called a *point*. Two points $(n_1,m_1),(n_2,m_2)$ are *neighbors* if $|n_1 - n_2| + |m_1 - m_2| = 1$ (two diagonally adjacent points are not considered neighbors). A point (n,m) with $gcd(n,m) = 1$ is called *marked/occupied* (the marked points correspond to Parikh prime strings over two letters). A point (n,m) with $gcd(n,m) > 1$ is called *free* (point of territory). A sequence of points $(n_1,m_1),(n_2,m_2),\ldots,(n_k,m_k)$ is called a *path* (from (n_1,m_1) to (n_k,m_k)) if for all $j = 1,2,\ldots,k-1$, the points $(n_j,m_j),(n_{j+1},m_{j+1})$ are neighbors. A set $M \subseteq \mathbf{Z}^2$ is said to be *connected* if for all two points $(n_1,m_1),(n_2,m_2)$ in M there is a path from (n_1,m_1) to (n_2,m_2) using only points of M. A maximal connected set of free points is a *territory* (maximality means that no further free point can be added without losing the connectedness). Of course, every one-point set is connected.

Before examining the possible territories, let us consider their size (the number of free points).

Obviously, the points on the plane axes are all free (by convention, $gcd(0,n) = n$ for all n), hence they form together an infinite territory. This is the only infinite territory:

Theorem 7. *Outside the axes, there are arbitrarily large territories, but no one of them is unbounded.*

Proof. For a given $n \in \mathbf{N}$, take n consecutive natural numbers, $m+1, m+2,\ldots,m+n, m \geq 1$. For $q = \prod_{i=1}^{n}(m+i)$, consider all points $(m+i,q), 1 \leq i \leq n$. They are clearly in the same territory: $gcd(q,m+i) = m+i, 1 \leq i \leq n$, and $(q,m+j),(q,m+j+1)$ are adjacent for each j. We have found a territory of at least n points, thus proving the first assertion.

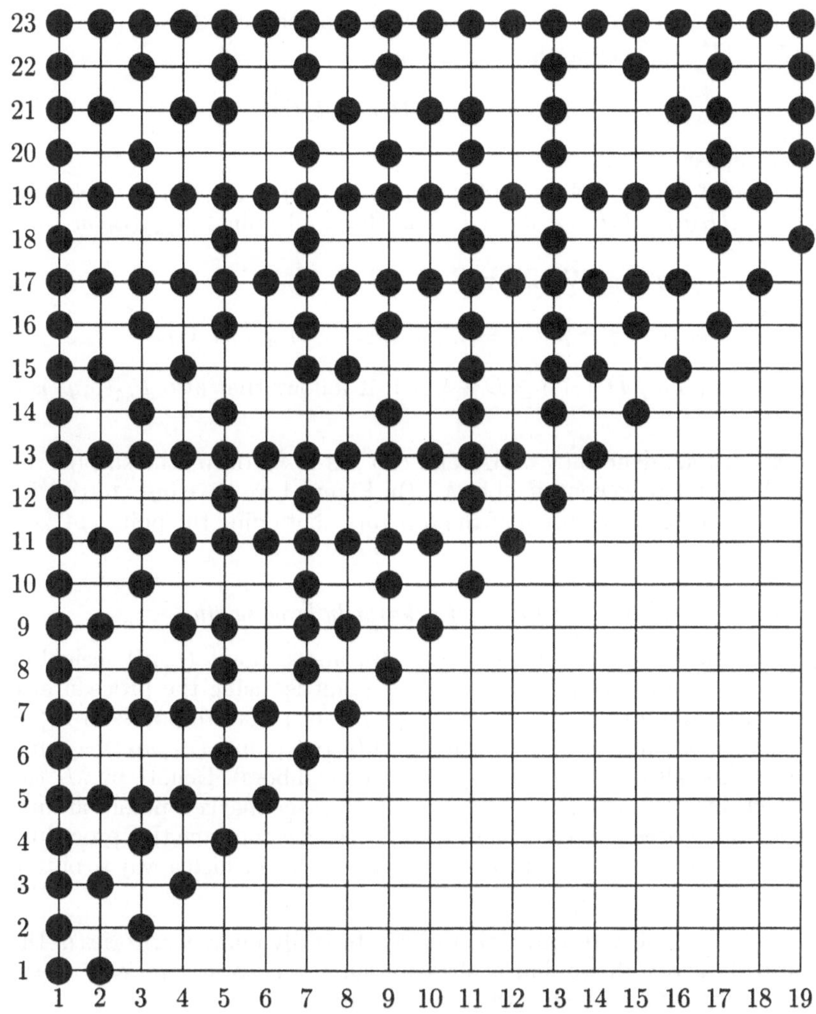

Figure 1

All points (n, m) with either $|n| = 1$ or $|m| = 1$ are marked. Moreover, all points (n, m) with $||n| - |m|| = 1$ are marked. Therefore, it is enough to prove that there is no unbounded territory in the region corresponding to Figure 1, of points (n, m) with $0 < n < m$. For every prime number p, all points $(n, p), 0 < n < p$, are marked ($gcd(n, p) = 1$). Consequently, each territory from this region is included in the horizontal stripe delimited by two consecutive primes, hence it cannot be unbounded. □

In fact, a stronger result is true.

Lemma 2. *If $M \subseteq \mathbf{Z}^2$ is a finite territory and (p, q) is an arbitrary point in $\mathbf{Z}^2 - \{(0,0)\}$, then there is a translation $f : \mathbf{Z}^2 \longrightarrow \mathbf{Z}^2$ such that all points $f(n, m)$ for $(n, m) \in M$, as well as $f(p, q)$ are free.*

Proof. Assume $M = \{(n_1, m_1), \ldots, (n_k, m_k)\}$ and denote $gcd(n_i, m_i) = d_i, 1 \leq i \leq k$. For $D = \prod_{i=1}^{k} d_i$, define the translation

$$f_{t_1,t_2}(n, m) = (n + t_1 D, m + t_2 D),$$

for any given integers t_1, t_2.

For every point (n_i, m_i) of M we have $f_{t_1,t_2}(n_i, m_i) = (n_i + t_1 D, m_i + t_2 D)$ and $gcd(n_i + t_1 D, m_i + t_2 D) \geq d_i > 1$. Therefore, all points $f_{t_1,t_2}(n_i, m_i)$ are free, for all t_1, t_2.

Take now $t_1 = p, t_2 = q$. We obtain

$$f_{p,q}(p, q) = (p + pD, q + qD) = (p(D + 1), q(D + 1)).$$

Because $gcd(p(D + 1), q(D + 1)) \geq D + 1 > 1$, it follows that also $f_{p,q}(p, q)$ is a free point. □

For a territory M, denote by $w(M)$ and call *the width* of M, the size (of the edge) of the largest square contained in M. (In Figure 1 we have only territories of width 1, with the only exception of the territory containing the point $(14, 20)$, whose width is 2.)

Theorem 8. *There are territories of arbitrarily large width.*

Proof. Take an arbitrary finite territory M_0 and a point (n, m), neighbor to a point in M_0 and marked. Whichever this point is, using the procedure in Lemma 2, we can find a translation $f : \mathbf{Z}^2 \longrightarrow \mathbf{Z}^2$ such that all points in $M_1' = f(M_0) \cup \{f(n, m)\}$ are free and M_1' is connected (if two points $(n_1, m_1), (n_2, m_2)$ are neighbors, then also $f(n_1, m_1), f(n_2, m_2)$ are neighbors). Denote by M_1 the territory which includes M_1' (it is possible that further marked points around M_0 are translated to free points around $f(M_0)$). We can continue this procedure arbitrarily many times, choosing the marked point (n, m) in such a way to obtain territories with larger and larger widths. □

Consequently, for every territory there are arbitrarily many territories of the same shape or larger. Can we find arbitrarily many territories precisely *of the same shape* ? Surprisingly, the answer is affirmative.

We say that two territories M_1, M_2 are (strongly) *congruent* if there is a translation $f : \mathbf{Z}^2 \longrightarrow \mathbf{Z}^2$ such that $f(M_1) = M_2$. Given a territory M, we denote by $F(M)$ the *frontier* of M, that is the set of all marked points (n, m) for which there is a free point (n', m') in M such that $(n, m), (n', m')$ are neighbors.

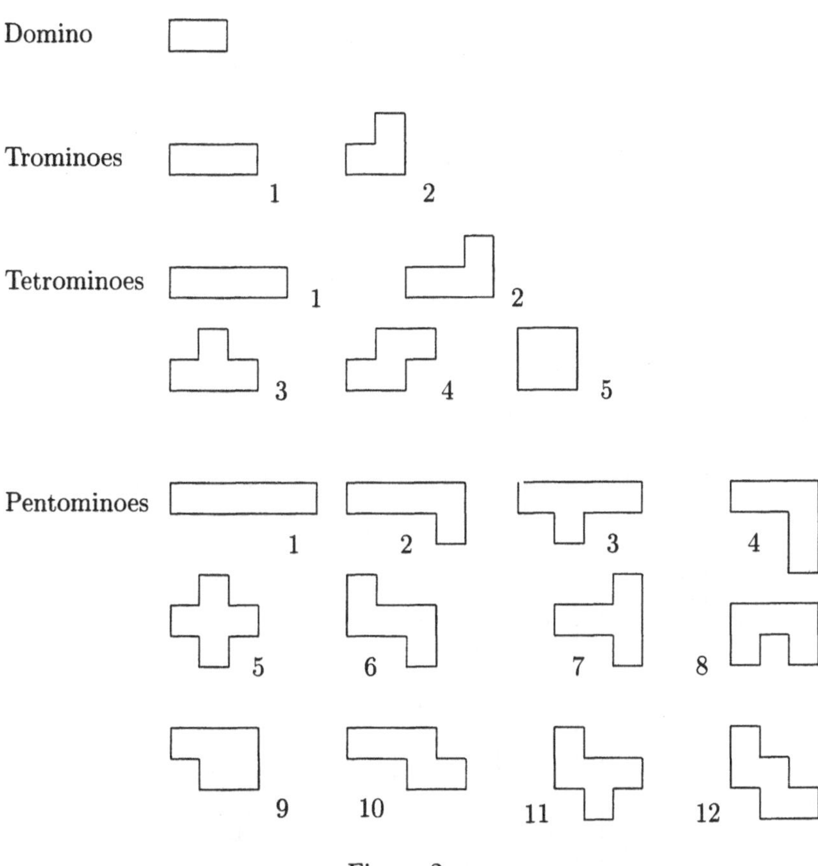

Figure 2

Theorem 9. *Given a finite territory, there are infinitely many territories congruent with it.*

Proof. Consider a territory $M = \{(n_1, m_1), \ldots, (n_k m_k)\}$, denote $d_i = gcd(n_i, m_i)$, $1 \leq i \leq k$, and $d = \prod_{i=1}^{k} d_i$. Assume that $F(M) = \{(p_1, q_1), \ldots, (p_s, q_s)\}$. Clearly, all p_i, q_i are non-zero numbers and we have $gcd(p_i, q_i) = 1$ for all $i, 1 \leq i \leq s$.

Consider the translation $f : \mathbf{Z}^2 \longrightarrow \mathbf{Z}^2$ defined by

$$f(n, m) = (n + pqd, m),$$

where

$$p = \prod_{i=1}^{s} p_i, \quad q = \prod_{i=1}^{s} q_i.$$

Because $gcd(n_i + pqd, m_i) \geq d_i > 1$, each point $f(n_i, m_i), 1 \leq i \leq k$, is a free point.

Moreover, for each $(p_i, q_i) \in F(M)$ we have

$$f(p_i, q_i) = (p_i + pqd, q_i) = (p_i(1 + \frac{p}{p_i} qd), q_i),$$

therefore $gcd(p_i + pqd, q_i) = 1$, hence $f(p_i, q_i)$ is a marked point.

Clearly, if two points $(n, m), (n', m')$ are neighbors, then also $f(n, m), f(n', m')$ are neighbors. Consequently, $M' = f(M)$ is a territory and $F(M') = f(F(M))$. The two territories M, M' are congruent (and different). Continuing the procedure (starting now from M', then from the currently constructed territory), we can find arbitrarily many congruent territories, all congruent with M. □

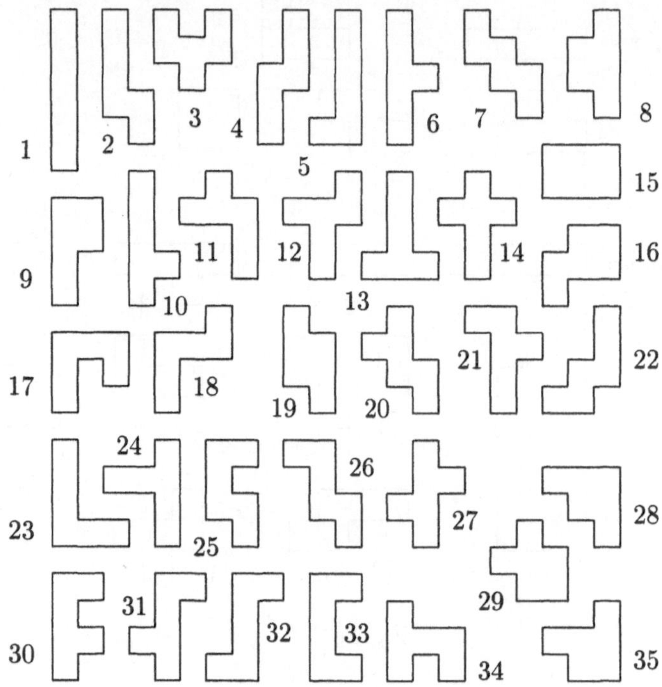

Figure 3

Observe that the previous Theorems 7 – 9 can be extended to the n-dimensional space.

Therefore, according to Theorem 9, if a pattern appears, then it appears infinitely many times. However, the question arises: which patterns actually appear ? For instance, Figure 1 contains a series of patterns, but no domino (a territory consisting of two points). As we shall see, only a few of the small polyominoes are possible. We shall complete the analysis for the domino, trominoes, tetrominoes, pentominoes (Figure 2), and hexominoes (Figure 3). We shall refer to these polyominoes with the number associated to them in these figures. (Lists of polyominoes can be found in many places; we refer here to the monumental book [3]. As usual, two polyominoes which can be obtained from one another by rotations and mirroring are considered identical.)

Before discussing particular polyominoes, we give a simple and useful general lemma.

Given a territory M, we say that a set E is a *horizontal edge* of M if

1. $E = \{(n, m), (n+1, m), \ldots, (n+k, m)\} \subseteq M$,
2. $(n-1, m)$ and $(n+k+1, m)$ are marked points,
3. either all points $(n, m-1), (n+1, m-1), \ldots, (n+k, m-1)$, or all points $(n, m+1), (n+1, m+1), \ldots, (n+k, m+1)$ are marked.

Similarly we can define a *vertical edge.*

Lemma 3. *There is no territory having an edge of even length.*

Proof. Assume that there is a territory M having a horizontal edge of length $2k, k \geq 1$; the case of vertical edges is similar. Assume that we have a situation as in Figure 4; the case when the marked neighboring points are above is similar.

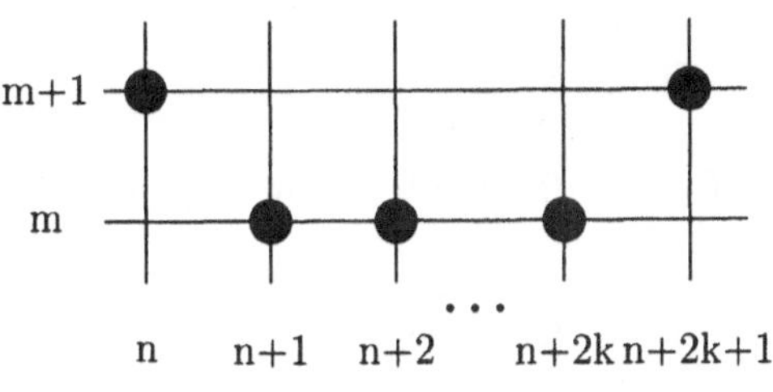

Figure 4

If m is even, because at least one of $n+1, n+2$ is even, one of the points $(n+1, m), (n+2, m)$ must belong to M, a contradiction.

If m is odd, then $m+1$ is even. One of $n, n+2k+1$ is even, hence either $(n, m+1)$ or $(n+2k+1, m+1)$ belongs to M, again a contradiction.

In conclusion, M cannot be a territory. □

Theorem 10. (i) *No straight, horizontal or vertical, line of even length can be a territory (hence the domino cannot appear).*

(ii) *Both trominoes appear as territories.*

(iii) *Only the tetromino 3 appears as a territory.*

Proof. All the negative assertions are proved by the previous lemma (all the mentioned patterns have an edge of even length). Both the trominoes and the tetromino 3 are present in Figure 1. □

Theorem 11. *From pentominoes, only those with numbers 1, 4 and 5 in Figure 2 appear as territories.*

Proof. The pentomino 4 appears in Figure 1. An example of territory of the form of pentomino 1 is $\{(2,30), (3,30), (4,30), (5,30), (6,30)\}$. Figure 5 indicates a place where the pentomino 5 appears. Because

$$\begin{aligned}
103 &= \text{prime}, & 214 &= 2 \cdot 107, \\
104 &= 2^3 \cdot 13, & 215 &= 5 \cdot 43, \\
105 &= 3 \cdot 5 \cdot 7, & 216 &= 2^3 \cdot 3^3, \\
106 &= 2 \cdot 53, & 217 &= 7 \cdot 31, \\
107 &= \text{prime}, & 218 &= 2 \cdot 109,
\end{aligned}$$

we have indeed a territory of the specified shape.

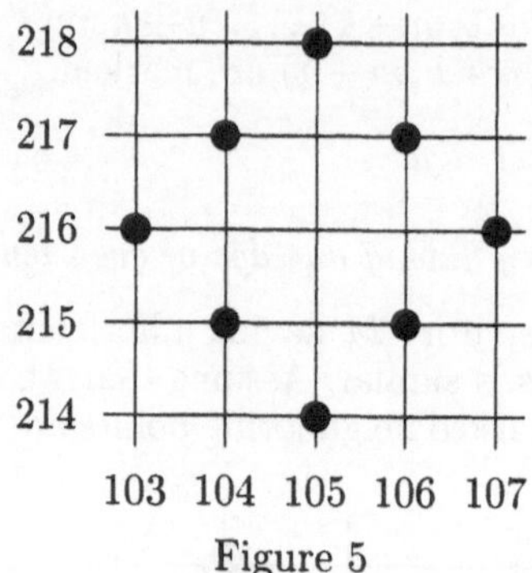

Figure 5

The pentominoes 2, 3, 6, 8, 9, 10, 11, 12 contain edges of even lengths, hence they cannot appear.

There remains the pentomino 7. It is also impossible as territory (but it cannot be refuted by Lemma 3). Consider the position in Figure 6; all other orientations can be handled in the same way.

If m is odd, then $m + 1$ is even; one of $n + 1$ and $n + 2$ is even, hence one of the points $(n + 1, m + 1)$, $(n + 2, m + 1)$ belongs to the territory, a contradiction.

If m is even, then also $m + 2$ is even. If n is even, then $(n, m + 2)$ must be in the territory, which is contradictory. If n is odd, then $n + 3$ is even, hence $(n+3, m)$ must be in the territory. In conclusion, the situation in Figure 6 cannot appear. □

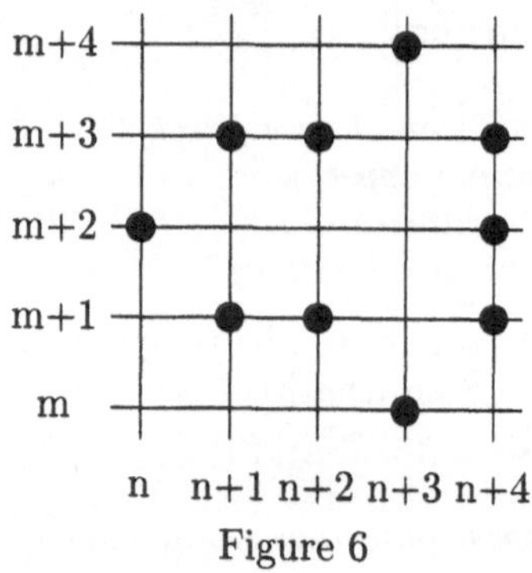

Figure 6

Theorem 12. *From hexominoes, only those with numbers 10, 11, and 28 in Figure 3 are possible.*

Proof. From Lemma 3 it immediately follows that the following hexominoes cannot appear as territories: 1, 2, 3, 5, 7, 8, 9, 12, 15, 16, 17, 18, 20, 21, 22, 23, 24, 25, 26, 29, 30, 31, 32, 33, 34, 35.

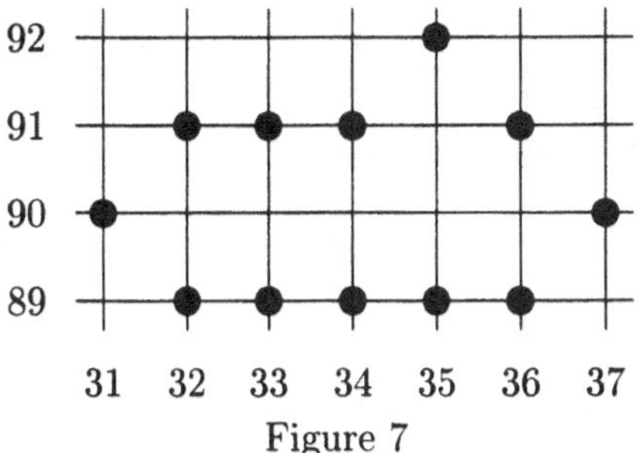

Figure 7

In Figure 1 the hexominoes 11 and 28 already appear. Also that with number 10 is possible, as indicated in Figure 7. We have

$$\begin{array}{ll} 89 = \text{prime}, & 31 = \text{prime}, \\ 90 = 2 \cdot 3^2 \cdot 5, & 32 = 2^5, \\ 91 = 7 \cdot 13, & 33 = 3 \cdot 11, \\ 92 = 2^2 \cdot 23, & 34 = 2 \cdot 17, \\ & 35 = 5 \cdot 7, \\ & 36 = 2^2 \cdot 3^2, \\ & 37 = \text{prime}, \end{array}$$

and this shows that we have, indeed, a territory of the desired form.

It remains to consider the hexominoes 4, 6, 13, 14, 19, 27. The impossibility of each of them to appear as a territory can be proved in the same way, by examining the parity of coordinates. We consider only two cases:

Figure 8 shows that the hexomino 4 cannot appear: if m is even, then one of $(n+1, m), (n+2, m)$ is free; if m is odd, then $m+1$ is even, hence one of $(n+4, m+1), (n+5, m+1)$ is free. A contradiction is obtained in each case.

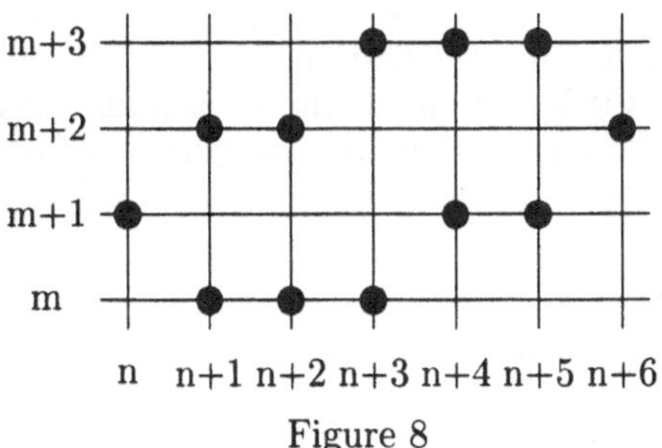

Figure 8

Figure 9 shows that the hexomino 6 is impossible, too: if m is even, then one of $(n+1, m), (n+2, m)$ must be in the territory. If m is odd, then both $m+1$ and $m+3$ are even. If n is even, then $(n, m+1)$ is free, if n is odd, then $n+3$ is even, hence $(n+3, m+3)$ is free. All cases are contradictory.

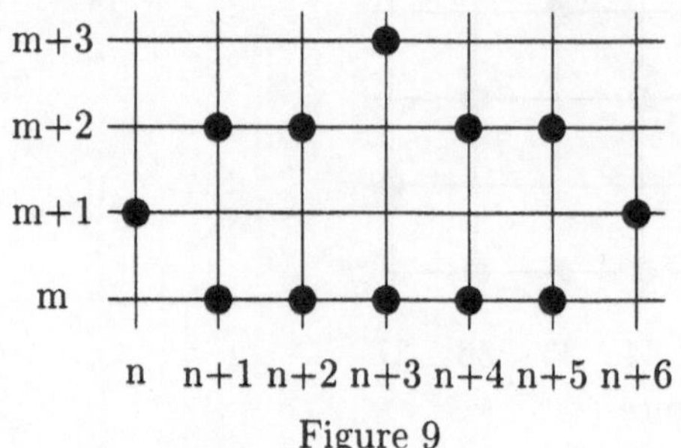

Figure 9

The reader can check in the same way the other cases. □

We can conclude that only a few polyominoes of the specified types can appear as territories. What about larger polyominoes ? What about squares, for instance ? (Of course, squares of even dimensions cannot appear.) Such problems remain to be investigated.

As a challenge for the reader, we remark that the 3×3 square appears as a territory. Indeed, consider the situation in Figure 10. We have

$$\begin{aligned} 103 &= \text{prime}, & 6203 &= \text{prime},\\ 104 &= 2^3 \cdot 13, & 6202 &= 2 \cdot 7 \cdot 443,\\ 105 &= 3 \cdot 5 \cdot 7, & 6201 &= 3^2 \cdot 13 \cdot 53,\\ 106 &= 2 \cdot 53, & 6200 &= 2^3 \cdot 5^2 \cdot 31,\\ 107 &= \text{prime}, & 6199 &= \text{prime}. \end{aligned}$$

It is easy to see that the situation in Figure 10 is correct, the 3×3 square is a territory. Other 3×3 squares can be found centered around the points of coordinates (105, 150891), (105, 295581), (105, 440271), (105,584961), etc. Of course, these examples have been found using a computer. Observe the places where the squares appear; it seems that the first one is one of the closest to the origin of the plane. (It is surely the lowest one on the vertical lines 104, 105, 106.

What about larger squares ? We *conjecture* that all squares $(2k+1) \times (2k+1)$ are possible.

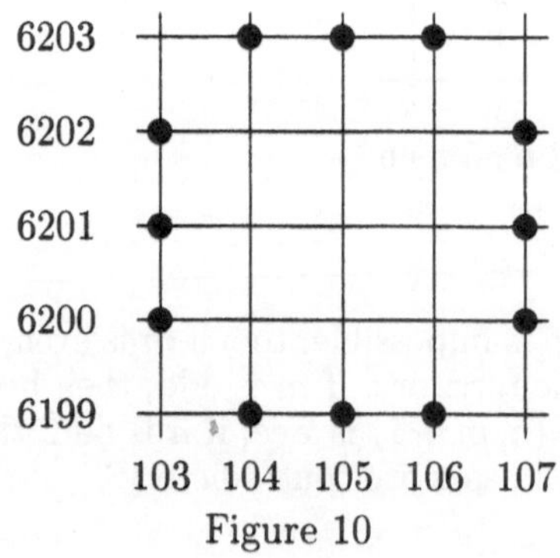

Figure 10

A series of number-theoretic (the geometry of numbers) questions can be formulated about the above free/marked points, starting with a problem similar to the famous Gauss' one (see problem F1 in [8], as well as the references of [8]): how many free/marked points there exist inside the circle with centre in the origin and radius r ? (In the case of Gauss' problem, all lattice points are counted.) What about the presumably easier problem concerning the number of free/marked points in a square centered in the origin and with a given size ? Which is the ratio of the number of free points over the number of marked points in such a square ? Is this ratio convergent ? If yes, which is the limit ?

4 References

1. J. M. Autebert, J. Beauquier, L. Boasson, M. Nivat, Quelques problèmes ouverts en théorie des langages algébriques, *RAIRO, Th. Informatics*, 13, 4 (1979), 363 - 378.
2. E. R. Berlekamp, D. Wolfe, *Mathematical GO: Chilling Gets the Last Point*, Ishi Press, 1994.
3. E. R. Berlekamp, J. H. Conway, R. K. Guy, *Winning Ways for Your Mathematical Plays*, Academic Press, New York, 1982.
4. J. Dassow, Gh. Păun, *Regulated Rewriting in Formal Language Theory*, Springer-Verlag, Berlin, Heidelberg, 1989.
5. J. Dassow, Gh. Păun, A. Salomaa, On thiness and slenderness of L languages, *Bulletin of EATCS*, 49 (1993), 152 - 158.
6. P. Dömösi, S. Horváth, M. Ito, L. Kászonyi, M. Katsura, Formal languages consisting of primitive words, *FCT Conf. 1993*, Szeged (Z. Esik, ed.), *LNCS* 710, Springer-Verlag, 1993, 194 - 203.
7. S. Ginsburg, *The Mathematical Theory of Context-Free Languages*, McGraw-Hill Book Comp., New York, 1966.
8. R. K. Guy, *Unsolved Problems in Number Theory*, Springer-Verlag, New York, 1981.
9. M. Ito, M. Katsura, Context-free languages consisting of non-primitive words, *Intern. J. Computer Math.*, 40 (1991), 157 - 167.
10. M. Lothaire, *Combinatorics on Words*, Addison-Wesley, Reading, Mass., 1983.
11. Gh. Păun, A. Salomaa, Thin and slender languages, *Discrete Appl. Math.*, 61 (1995), 257 - 270.
12. R. Ross, K. Winklmann, Repetitive strings are not context-free, *Report CS-81-070*, Computer Sci. Dept., Washington Univ., 1981.
13. G. Rozenberg, A. Salomaa, *The Mathematical Theory of L Systems*, Academic Press, New York, 1980.
14. A. Salomaa, *Formal Languages*, Academic Press, New York, London, 1973.
15. A. Thue, Über unendliche Zeichenreihen, *Norske Videns. Selsk. Skrifter Mat.-Nat. Kl.*, Kristiania, 7 (1906), 1 - 22.

Journal of Universal Computer Science, vol. 1, no. 12 (1995), 811-820
submitted: 5/4/95, accepted: 20/12/95, appeared: 28/12/95 © Springer Pub. Co.

Exploiting Parallelism in Constraint Satisfaction for Qualitative Simulation

Marco Platzner
(Graz University of Technology, Austria
marco@iti.tu-graz.ac.at)

Bernhard Rinner
(Graz University of Technology, Austria
rinner@iti.tu-graz.ac.at)

Reinhold Weiss
(Graz University of Technology, Austria
rweiss@iti.tu-graz.ac.at)

Abstract: Constraint satisfaction is very common in many artificial intelligence applications. This paper presents results from parallelizing constraint satisfaction in a special application — the algorithm for qualitative simulation QSim [Kuipers 94].
A parallel-agent based strategy (PAB) is used to solve the constraint satisfaction problem (CSP). Two essential steps of PAB are studied in more detail to achieve a good performance of the parallel algorithm. Partitioning heuristics to generate independent parts of the overall search space are investigated. Sequential CSP algorithms are compared in order to reveal the most efficient one for QSim. The evaluation of these heuristics and algorithms is based on runtime measurements using CSPs traced from QSim. These runtimes allow a best- and worst-case estimation of the expected speedup of the parallel algorithms. The comparison of sequential CSP algorithms leads to following strategy for solving partitioned problems. Less complex problems are solved with simple backtracking, and more complex models are solved with graph-directed backjumping (GBJ).
Key Words: Parallel constraint satisfaction, QSIM, distributed AI
Category: I.2.11, F.2.2, C.3

1 Introduction

Constraint satisfaction is very common in artificial intelligence applications, and it is also a basic operation in qualitative simulation. Constraint satisfaction problems (CSP) are often solved by backtracking algorithms, which find solutions with depth-first search. Many sequential and parallel algorithms have been developed to solve CSPs more efficiently. This paper presents results of our work in parallelizing and distributing constraint satisfaction for the special application QSIM.

QSIM, the widely-used algorithm for qualitative simulation, has been developed by Kuipers [Kuipers 94]. Qualitative simulation is a new and challenging simulation paradigm. Major areas of qualitative simulation applications are design, monitoring, and fault-diagnosis. A drawback of current QSIM implementations is poor execution speed. In our research project [Platzner, Rinner, Weiss 95] a special-purpose computer architecture for QSIM is developed to improve the performance. Better performance is achieved by SW/HW-migration of frequently

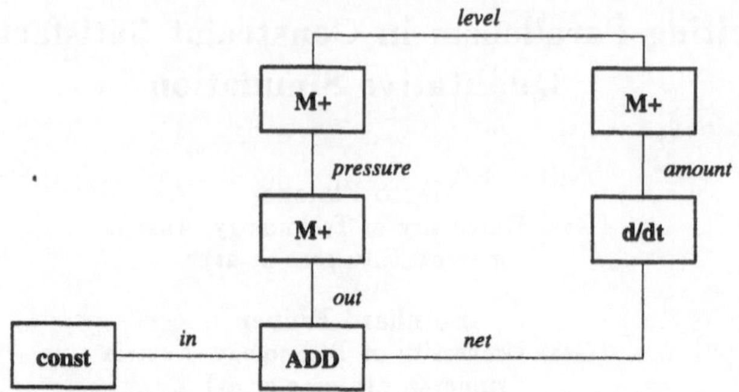

Figure 1: Constraint graph of the QSIM bathtub model. Constraints are represented by the nodes of the graph. The constraint arity ranges from 1 to 3. Edges between nodes correspond to shared variables. Sets of valid tuples are attached to all constraints after constraint-filtering.

used primitive functions, and mapping QSIM kernel functions onto a multiprocessor system. The overall application-specific computer architecture consists of digital signal processors TMS320C40 which are equipped with specialized FPGA-based coprocessors for executing the primitive functions.

2 Constraint Satisfaction in QSIM

A constraint satisfaction problem can be informally described as follows: Given a set of n variables each with an associated domain, and given a set of constraints each involving a subset of the variables, find an n-tuple such that this n-tuple is an instantiation of the n variables satisfying all constraints. A more formal description can be found in [Dechter 92].

Constraint satisfaction is a basic operation in the qualitative simulator QSIM. It is used to determine all possible successors of a given qualitative state — i.e. calculating all solutions of a CSP, specified by a *constraint network* (variables and constraints) and *possible values* of all variables (domains). In QSIM CSPs are represented dual to the representation in [Mackworth 77]. The nodes of the constraint graph correspond to constraints, and the edges between the nodes correspond to variables. A constraint graph of a QSIM example is shown in [Figure 1]. This dual representation is used because the arity of QSIM constraints is not limited by 2.

Since solving CSPs is NP-complete, preprocessing or filtering steps before backtracking can eliminate large parts of the overall search space [Mohr, Henderson 86]. These techniques are *node*, *arc*, and *path* consistency and are widely applied in constraint satisfaction. In QSIM node consistency is achieved by the constraint-filter. For each QSIM constraint all possible tuples of the attached variables are checked against the constraint conditions. Tuples violating these conditions are discarded. Arc consistency is achieved by the Waltz-filter, which eliminates inconsistencies between adjacent constraints. Each tuple associated with constraint C_i is discarded unless the same value of the shared variable is assigned in at least one tuple of each adjacent constraints. Path consistency is not currently used in QSIM. The final backtracking step generates all valid assignments of the remaining tuples and thus all solutions of the CSP. A simple backtracking algorithm is used for this depth-first search. Increased performance is achieved by interleaving node and arc consistency algorithms and by a heuristic ordering of the constraints for the backtracking step.

There are many techniques exploiting the parallelism of these filtering steps [Conrad, Agrawal, Bahler 92][Cooper, Swain 92]. We also parallelize the node and arc consistency algorithm of QSIM in our research project, but in this paper we present only the results in parallelizing and distributing the backtracking algorithm [Riedl 95].

CSPs in QSIM have special characteristics which are different from many other CSPs. These characteristics have to be considered in selecting appropriate algorithms and parallelizing techniques as presented in the next section.

number of solutions QSIM needs *all* solutions of the CSP for further processing. Searching cannot be finished after finding one solution. All parts of the search space have to be checked. This is different from many other applications, where just one solution is required. Efficiency considerations for these applications can be found in [Rao, Kumar 93].

variable domain Pure qualitative simulation uses *discrete* variables and the number of values is limited in most cases by 4.[1]

arity of the constraints QSIM describes the simulation model with different constraints. The arity of the most important constraints ranges from 1 to 3.

structure of the CSP In qualitative simulation CSPs with the same structure — CSPs with the same constraints and variables but different domains — often have to be solved successively. The description of such CSPs can be simplified, a representation of the domain of the variables is sufficient.

3 Parallel Constraint Satisfaction

3.1 Existing Algorithms

Many parallel algorithms for constraint satisfaction are known in literature. Luo, Hendry, and Buchanan [Luo, Hendry, Buchanan 94] have classified the most common algorithms as *distributed-agent-based (DAB)*, *parallel-agent-based (PAB)*, and *functional-agent-based (FAB)*. Different strategies involve different control structures, problem spaces, and communication methods. The FAB strategy can be excluded from further considerations, because it requires shared memory architectures. Important features of the remaining strategies can be summarized as follows.

DAB In the DAB strategy, the problem is distributed based on the variables. Each agent controls one or more variables and their domains. The search space is shared among the agents and the agents have to communicate because of the constraints between distributed variables.

PAB In the PAB strategy, the problem is distributed based on the domains of the variables. Each agent solves a part of the complete search space, which is independent from each other, because each search space involves all

[1] Calculating the initial states from an incomplete state description can lead to more than 4 values of individual variables.

variables. Therefore, all agents solve a unique CSP and no communication between agents is required.

Our application-specific computer architecture has to fulfill several requirements, which obviously influence the parallelization of the constraint satisfaction algorithm. The following requirements are of special interest.

scalability Our special-purpose computer architecture consists of several independent processors, each equipped with its own local memory. The number of processing elements is moderate but variable. Thus, the parallel constraint satisfaction algorithm should be scalable.

model independence The parallel algorithm should be applyable to all QSIM models — i.e. the application of the algorithm should not depend on the structure of the model (CSP graph).

There are several reasons for choosing a PAB strategy for our application. First, it is an excellent strategy for finding all solutions of a given CSP and it is an inherent scalable algorithm. Second, the PAB strategy can be applied to problems with arbitrary structure. Finally, the independent search spaces can be solved with any sequential (and optimized) algorithm. A detailed comparison between DAB and PAB strategies can be found in [Luo, Hendry, Buchanan 94].

In the next two subsections, we consider the essential steps of PAB in more detail — we investigate methods to achieve a *good* partitioning of the complete search space, and compare sequential algorithms to use the *best* one for QSIM-models and their partitioned subproblems.

3.2 Generating Independent Subproblems

3.2.1 Evaluation and Speedup Estimation

Partitioning of the complete search space is essential for an efficient parallel algorithm. The partitioning methods are evaluated using runtimes of the subproblems. The most interesting runtimes are the overall runtime t_o, which is the sum of the runtimes of all subproblems, the maximum runtime of all subproblems t_{max}, and the sequential runtime of the unpartitioned problem t_{seq}. Due to redundancies in the independent subproblems the overall runtime t_o can be longer than t_{seq}. An efficient partitioning method keeps the overall runtime small. If t_o gets smaller than t_{seq} a superlinear speedup is expected. The subproblem with the longest runtime restricts the maximum speedup. Thus, a balanced partitioning, where all subproblems have nearly the same runtime, should be achieved.

Using these runtimes (t_{seq}, t_{max}, and t_o), it is possible to estimate the speedup of the parallel algorithm. Communication times are not considered in this estimation, and simple *task attraction* is assumed to schedule tasks to free processors. We determine the limits of the speedup by worst- and best-case estimation. First of all, the speedup is defined as $S(n) = t_{seq}/t_{par}$, where t_{par} denotes the runtime using n processors.

The worst-case condition is satisfied if the longest task is scheduled last and all other tasks are equally distributed among the processors. The worst case runtime of the parallel algorithm can be given as

$$t_{par} = \frac{t_o - t_{max}}{n} + t_{max}$$

For best case estimation we have to consider two cases. If the number of processors is greater than $\lceil \frac{t_o}{t_{max}} \rceil$ the parallel runtime is limited by t_{max}, otherwise all tasks are equally divided among the processors. More formally, the best case parallel runtime can be estimated as

$$t_{par} = \begin{cases} \frac{t_o}{n} & if \;\; n \leq \lceil \frac{t_o}{t_{max}} \rceil \\ t_{max} & otherwise \end{cases}$$

3.2.2 Partitioning Methods

Two partitioning methods are investigated — *constraint-based partitioning* and *variable-based partitioning*.

constraint-based partitioning (CBP) This partitioning is based on the tuple sets of the constraints. The tuple set of an individual constraint is divided into two or more disjunct subsets. A subproblem is defined by one subset and the tuple sets of the remaining constraints. Thus, two or more subproblems are generated. To achieve more subproblems than elements of one tuple set partitioning is extended recursively.
Two variants of this method are studied. CBP-ALL divides the tuple set of the constraint in as many subsets as elements in the tuple set. CBP-ALL tries to generate tuple sets with just one tuple. All variables of such constraints can be instantiated before backtracking starts. CBP-HALF divides the tuple set into two parts. Hence, more tuple sets can be divided and the overall number of tuples in the subproblems is a little smaller.

variable-based partitioning (VBP) The tuple sets of adjacent constraints are not independent from each other. The tuple sets depend on the domain of the shared variables. This dependency is exploited by the VBP method. The domain of the variable is divided into two or more subdomains. This induces a partitioning of the tuple sets of all attached constraints. In an individual subset there are only the same values of the shared variable as in the corresponding subdomain. Combinations of subsets with different values of the shared variable are inconsistent and can be discarded. Hence, as many subproblems as subdomains are generated. To generate more subproblems than the ordinality of one domain, partitioning is extended to other variables. Four variants of VBP can be classified by the sequence of variables which domains are partitioned. VBP-INST uses the same order as the sequential algorithm. Variables which are shared by many constraints are partitioned first by VBP-CON. VBP-DOM divides the largest domains first. Finally, VBP-TUP takes variables with the largest number of *attached* tuples first — i.e. the order of the variables is given by the number of tuples of the attached constraints.

3.3 Solving the Subproblems

With the parallel CSP strategy PAB the individual subproblems can be solved with any sequential algorithm. QSIM uses a simple backtracking algorithm, extended by a constraint ordering scheme, for this task. There are many extensions and improvements of simple backtracking known in literature. [Prosser 93] presents an overview of possible improvements, other enhancement schemes are also presented in [Dechter 90]. Most of these improvements were evaluated with *standard CSP benchmarks* (ZEBRA problem, N-queens, randomly generated CSPs, etc.).

QSIM CSPs have different characteristics than those benchmark CSPs. Obviously we are interested in fast algorithms for QSIM CSPs. Therefore, we evaluate improved backtracking algorithms with CSPs traced from QSIM. These algorithms are: FC (forward checker), CBJ (conflict-directed backjumping), and GBJ (graph-directed backjumping). A simple backtracking algorithm (BT) is also executed as a reference. The implementation of these algorithms is based on [Kondrak 94] and the CSP-library of [Beck 94].

4 Experimental Results

4.1 QSIM CSPs

To obtain realistic results from our measurements, three different QSIM models have been simulated and the generated CSPs have been traced. Two simulation models were chosen from the QSIM-package. The *Starling* model (STLG) has 17 variables and 18 constraints, and the *Heart* model (HEART) consists of 28 variables and 21 constraints. The *Reaction-Control-System* (RCS) [Kay 92], which is not included in the QSIM-package, is the most complex model we have traced. It consists of 45 variables and 48 constraints.

8 to 16 CSPs with different complexity — different cardinality of the variables' domains — were chosen from the big number of CSPs generated during qsim runs. The CSPs were executed on a digital signal processor TMS320C40. The runtimes of all backtracking algorithms were measured with the internal hardware timer of this processor.

4.2 Partitioning Methods

The most interesting runtimes for evaluating the two partitioning methods (CBP and VBP) and its variants are presented in [Table 1] and [Table 2]. Only the runtime of the backtracking algorithm for solving the subproblems is shown in these tables. The overall runtime (t_o) and the maximum runtime (t_{max}) of all subproblems are summarized for all CSPs of an individual model. The sums are presented in the corresponding rows of the table. All subproblems were solved with the simple backtracking algorithm as used in QSIM.

A further interesting point is the influence of the number of generated subproblems to t_o and t_{max}. Three cases are considered — the CSP is partitioned into at most 16, at most 64, and at most 256 subproblems. The corresponding runtimes are also presented in the tables.

Due to the exploitation of the dependencies between adjacent constraints, the VBP method achieves better results than CBP. Especially, the big increase of the overall runtime t_o and the size of the maximum subtask t_{max} lead to poor parallel performance with CBP. VBP generates shorter maximum subtasks, and in some cases t_o is shorter than the runtime of the single-processor algorithm.

	Model	*16 Subtasks* t_o [ms]	*16 Subtasks* t_{max} [ms]	*64 Subtasks* t_o [ms]	*64 Subtasks* t_{max} [ms]	*256 Subtasks* t_o [ms]	*256 Subtasks* t_{max} [ms]
CBP-ALL	STLG	9.09	3.21	13.51	3.19	37.77	3.09
	HEART	28.70	7.97	34.57	5.01	60.07	4.94
	RCS	741.97	450.93	763.48	442.79	947.65	231.14
CBP-HALF	STLG	9.15	3.21	14.00	3.11	27.93	2.31
	HEART	35.04	8.26	53.48	7.89	83.64	7.76
	RCS	741.73	476.34	771.12	245.51	911.53	191.81

Table 1: CBP method. All runtimes of CSPs of an individual QSIM model are summarized and are presented in the corresponding row. The runtimes are measured on a digital signal processor TMS320C40. The runtimes for the single-processor algorithm are 6.12 ms for STLG, 25.72 ms for HEART, and 726 ms for RCS.

	Model	*16 Subtasks* t_o [ms]	*16 Subtasks* t_{max} [ms]	*64 Subtasks* t_o [ms]	*64 Subtasks* t_{max} [ms]	*256 Subtasks* t_o [ms]	*256 Subtasks* t_{max} [ms]
VBP-INST	STLG	6.96	3.49	6.55	3.28	6.34	3.18
	HEART	27.89	8.85	26.64	8.53	27.80	5.33
	RCS	739.48	497.93	746.44	495.45	865.42	259.95
VBP-CON	STLG	6.02	3.29	5.60	1.99	9.40	1.53
	HEART	25.23	5.48	45.49	4.71	58.05	4.55
	RCS	1370.53	104.29	826.66	67.86	825.96	30.71
VBP-DOM	STLG	34.96	3.15	24.73	1.99	18.12	1.70
	HEART	26.52	6.61	24.83	6.35	36.31	5.74
	RCS	3932.79	265.16	15119.29	252.02	4739.37	244.82
VBP-TUP	STLG	7.65	2.15	5.60	1.99	9.40	1.53
	HEART	65.85	12.11	52.62	6.31	73.83	5.94
	RCS	1401.59	103.31	779.47	51.08	780.95	44.95

Table 2: VBP method. All runtimes of CSPs of an individual QSIM model are summarized and are presented in the corresponding row. The runtimes for the single-processor algorithm are 6.83 ms for STLG, 28.77 ms for HEART, and 805.63 ms for RCS. The small increase compared to the single-processor runtimes of CBP is due to different memory mappings of the target system.

Speedup Estimation of VBP

A comparison of the speedup estimation for VBP-INST and VBP-CON is shown in [Figure 2]. In most cases VBP-CON outperforms VBP-INST — especially for complex CSPs (model RCS). VBP-CON results in a linear speedup for worst- and best-case estimation. It turns out that the length of the maximum task limits the expected speedup for VBP-INST.

Speedup increases with the number of generated tasks. However, the more tasks are generated the more overall communication time is required and the speedup of highly partitioned CSP can be lost. Best results are expected with VBP-CON and a medium number of tasks.

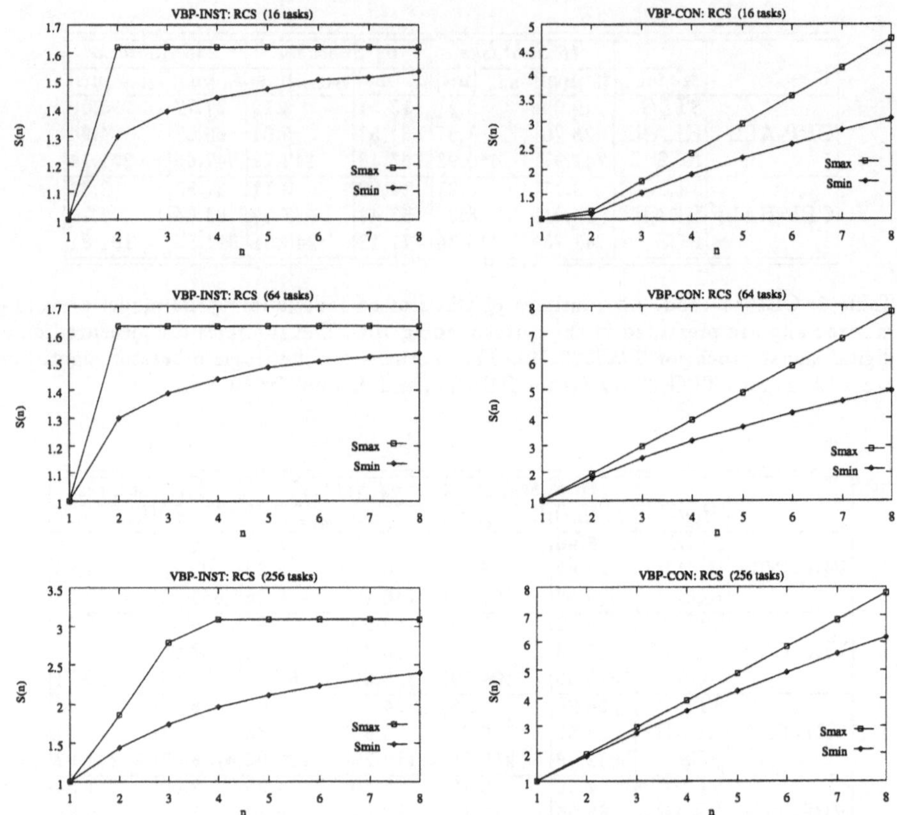

Figure 2: Speedup estimation of VBP for the RCS model. Worst- and best-case speedup for VBP-INST and VBP-CON are shown in the left and right column plots. Especially for complex models VBP-CON performs better than VBP-INST.

4.3 Comparison of Single-Processor CSP Algorithms

The CSPs of the three QSIM models have been solved with different sequential algorithms. We have tried to find a parameter to estimate the runtime of a given CSP. The average number of tuples per constraint (T/C) was chosen as such a parameter. A plot of the runtimes is presented in [Figure 3]. The CSPs are ordered corresponding to this parameter.

It turns out that simple backtracking is the fastest algorithm for simple QSIM models. For complex models sophisticated algorithms perform better. Graph-directed backjumping (GBJ) has the shortest runtime on almost all complex models. Thus, the parameter T/C can be used to divide QSIM CSPs into two parts. Simple CSPs (T/C is smaller than a given limit) should be solved with simple backtracking, the other CSPs should be solved with the GBJ algorithm.

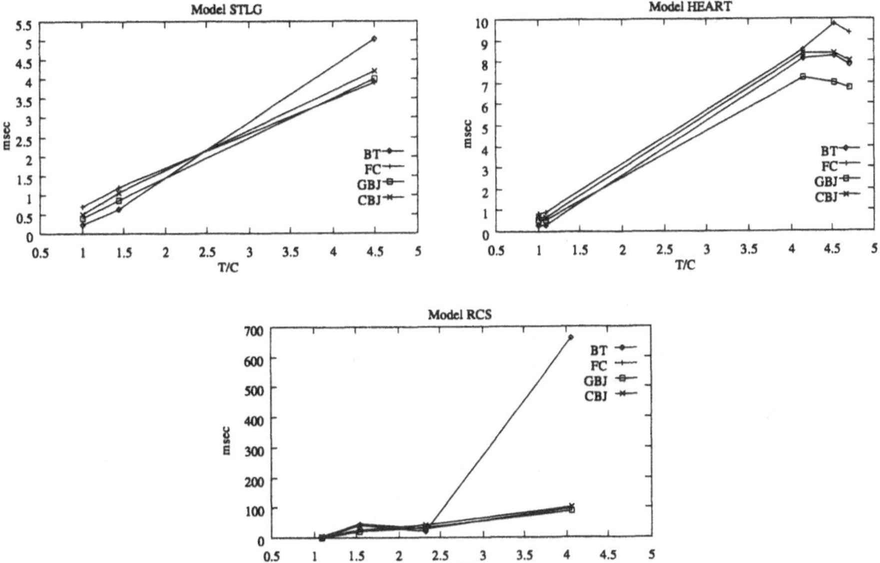

Figure 3: Comparison of sequential backtracking algorithms. The CSPs are ordered to the average number of tuples per constraint (T/C). For simple CSPs BT performs better than the other algorithms. On more complex CSPs the opposite is true — especially GBJ is up to 7 times faster than BT for RCS at $T/C = 4$.

5 Conclusions

In this paper we have presented a parallelizing strategy for constraint satisfaction in QSIM. Two important steps of the PAB strategy are studied in detail. First, partitioning methods for the CSP are introduced and evaluated. The evaluation of these methods is based on runtime measurements of the subproblems and a worst- and best-case speedup estimation. Second, different sequential backtracking algorithms are compared using QSIM CSPs. Results from this work can be summarized as follows.

VBP-CON partitioning method VBP-CON performs better than the other partitioning methods. A medium number of generated subproblem should be chosen to achieve a good tradeoff between communication times and length of the maximum subtask.

BT and GBJ for solving the subproblems Simple CSPs should be solved with simple backtracking, more complex CSP should be solved with graph-directed backjumping (GBJ). The complexity of a CSP can be estimated with the average number of tuples per constraint (T/C). The exact limit between BT and GBJ depends on the implementation of the algorithms and has to be determined experimentally.

Implementation of parallel constraint satisfaction based on the PAB strategy is in progress. The strategy is implemented on a multiprocessor system consisting of TMS320C40. The speedup estimations are compared with experimental results from this implementation.

6 References

References

[Beck 94] Peter van Beck.: "CSP Library"; Department of Computing Science, University of Alberta (1994), library of CSP algorithms.

[Conrad, Agrawal, Bahler 92] James M. Conrad, Dharma P. Agrawal, and Dennis R. Bahler.: "Scalable Parallel Arc Consistency Algorithms for Shared Memory Computers"; Proceedings 6th International Parallel Processing Symposium, IEEE, Los Alamitos, CA, (1992), 242–249.

[Cooper, Swain 92] Paul R. Cooper and Michael J. Swain.: "Arc consistency: parallelism and domain dependence"; Artificial Intelligence, 58 (1992), 207–235.

[Dechter 90] Rina Dechter.: "Enhancement Schemes for Constraint Processing: Backjumping, Learning, and Cutset Decomposition"; Artificial Intelligence, 41 (1990), 273–312.

[Dechter 92] Rina Dechter.: "Constraint Networks"; Stuart C. Shapiro, editor, Encyclopedia of Artificial Intelligence, John Wiley & Sons, 1 (1992), 276–285.

[Kay 92] Herbert Kay.: "A qualitative model of the space shuttle reaction control system"; Technical Report AI92-188, Artificial Intelligence Laboratory, University of Texas (1992).

[Kondrak 94] Grzegorz Kondrak.: "A Theoretical Evaluation of Selected Backtracking Algorithms"; Master's thesis, Department of Computing Science, University of Alberta (1994)

[Kuipers 94] Benjamin Kuipers.: "Qualitative Reasoning: Modeling and Simulation with Incomplete Knowledge"; Artificial Intelligence, MIT Press (1994)

[Luo, Hendry, Buchanan 94] Q.P. Luo, P.G. Hendry, and J.T. Buchanan.: "Strategies for Distributed Constraint Satisfaction Problems"; Proceedings 13th International DAI Workshop, DAI, Seattle, WA (1994)

[Mackworth 77] Alan K. Mackworth.: "Consistency in Networks of Relations"; Artificial Intelligence, 8 (1977), 99–118.

[Mohr, Henderson 86] Roger Mohr and Thomas C. Henderson.: "Arc and Path Consistency Revised"; Artificial Intelligence, 28 (1986), 225–233.

[Platzner, Rinner, Weiss 95] Marco Platzner, Bernhard Rinner, and Reinhold Weiss.: "A Distributed Computer Architecture for Qualitative Simulation Based on a Multi-DSP and FPGAs"; 3rd Euromicro Workshop on Parallel and Distributed Processing, IEEE Computer Society Press, San Remo (1995), 311–318.

[Prosser 93] Patrick Prosser.: "Hybrid Algorithms for the Constraint Satisfaction Problem"; Computational Intelligence, 9, 3 (1993) 268–299.

[Rao, Kumar 93] V. Nageshwara Rao and Vipin Kumar.: "On the Efficiency of Parallel Backtracking"; IEEE Transactions on Parallel and Distributed Systems, 4, 4 (1993), 427–437.

[Riedl 95] Johannes Riedl.: "Parallele Algorithmen und Laufzeitmessungen für Constraint Satisfaction im qualitativen Simulator QSim"; Master's thesis, Institute for Technical Informatics, Graz University of Technology (1995)

Acknowledgements

This project is partially supported by the Austrian National Science Foundation *Fonds zur Förderung der wissenschaftlichen Forschung* under grant number P10411-MAT.

Journal of Universal Computer Science, vol. 1, no. 12 (1995), 821-827
submitted: 13/12/95, accepted: 19/12/95, appeared: 28/12/95

A MARKOV PROCESS FOR SEQUENTIAL ALLOCATION

Cătălina Ştefănescu [1]

Abstract: We describe a Markov process which models the sequential allocation for two adjacent tables coexisting in memory by growing towards each other. The tables are expected to fill at the same rate; random deletions and insertions are allowed.

1 Introduction

A widespread technique for representing two variable-size sequential lists in memory is to store them in reverse order, so that list 1 expands to the right and list 2 expands to the left. Overflow occurs only when the total size of both lists exhausts the available space.

D. E. Knuth proposed in [4] the following mathematical model: fluctuations in the tables are represented by a finite sequence of insertion and deletion operations $a_1, a_2, \ldots, a_n$, where each $a_i \in \{1, 2\}$ is interpreted with probability p as a deletion and with probability $1-p$ as an insertion on top of stack a_i. A deletion from an empty list has no effect. Let l_1 and l_2 be the respective sizes of the tables during this process, k_1 and k_2 their sizes after the memory is full and m the number of memory locations available. The process continues until $l_1 + l_2 = m$. The purpose of this paper is to examine the dependence of $\max(k_1, k_2)$ on p and m and to determine formulæ for the probability distribution of (k_1, k_2).

2 A Mathematical Model

We introduce a finite state Markov process modelling the random fluctuations in the adjacent tables. The set of states is

$$S = \{\{a, b\} \mid 0 \leq a \leq b \leq m, 0 \leq a + b \leq m\}.$$

The system has n_m states, where

$$n_m = \sum_{k=0}^{m}([k/2] + 1) = \left(\left[\frac{m}{2}\right] + 1\right)\left(\left[\frac{m+1}{2}\right] + 1\right).$$

We label the states of the system in a manner similar to Cantor's diagonalization method; state $\{a, b\}$ comes before state $\{c, d\}$ if $a + b < c + d$ or $a + b = c + d$ and $a < c$. The system is in state $\{a, b\}$ if $l_1 = a$, $l_2 = b$ or $l_1 = b$, $l_2 = a$.

We denote by $\{a, b\} \to \{c, d\}$ a transition from state $\{a, b\}$ to state $\{c, d\}$ and define the transition probabilities according to the following deletion/insertion rules :

1991 *Mathematics Subject Classification.* Primary 60J20, Secondary 62M05, 68P05.

$P(\{0,0\} \to \{0,0\}) = p$ and $P(\{0,0\} \to \{0,1\}) = 1 - p$

$P(\{a,b\} \to \{c,d\}) = 0$ if $c \notin \{a-1, a, a+1\}$ or $d \notin \{b-1, b, b+1\}$.

$P(\{a,b\} \to \{a,b\}) = 1$ if $a + b = m$

$P(\{a,b\} \to \{a,b\}) = p/2$ if $a = 0,\ b \neq 0,\ b \neq m$

$P(\{a,b\} \to \{a-1,b\}) = p/2$ if $a \neq 0,\ a \neq b,\ a + b \neq m$

$P(\{a,b\} \to \{a-1,b\}) = p$ and $P(\{a,b\} \to \{a,b+1\}) = 1 - p$ if $a = b \neq 0$

$P(\{a,b\} \to \{a,b-1\}) = p/2$ and $P(\{a,b\} \to \{a+1,b\}) = P(\{a,b\} \to \{a,b+1\}) = \frac{1-p}{2}$ if $a \neq b,\ a + b \neq m$

Let $k_m = [m/2] + 1$. The process begins in the state $\{0,0\}$ when both lists are empty and continues until the memory is full, that is until one of the last k_m states with $l_1 + l_2 = m$ is reached. Therefore we may regard each of these states as an absorbing state; the states $1, 2, \ldots, n_m - k_m$ are transient because they certainly will not be occupied when the process stops (their limiting probability is null).

We are interested in the limiting state probability of absorbing states which represent the probability distribution of (k_1, k_2). They can be obtained from the theory of canonical decomposition of matrices using a procedure of approximation of characteristic roots outlined in [1]. Since our transition matrix is large and sparse we shall instead use the technique of the generating function described in [2] to determine the asymptotic behavior of transition probabilities.

Let $\pi(n)$ be the row vector with components $\pi_i(n)$, where $\pi_i(n)$ is the probability that the system will occupy state i after n transitions. Then

$$\pi_j(n+1) = \sum_{i=1}^{n_m} \pi_i(n) p_{ij}, \quad n = 0, 1, 2, \ldots$$

and

(1) $$\pi(n+1) = \pi(n)P, \quad n \in \mathbb{N}$$

where $P = (p_{i,j})_{1 \le i,j \le n_m}$ is the transition probability matrix.

Let $\Pi(z)$ denote the z-transform of the vector $\pi(n)$. From (1) we obtain

$$z^{-1}[\Pi(z) - \pi(0)] = \Pi(z)P$$

and through rearrangement

(2) $$\Pi(z) = \pi(0)(I - zP)^{-1}$$

where I is the identity matrix of order n_m. Let the matrix $H(n)$ be the inverse transform of $(I - zP)^{-1}$ and $H(n)[i,j]$ the element at the intersection of row i and column j in $H(n)$. Taking the inverse transform of (2) we obtain

$$\pi(n) = \pi(0)H(n)$$

Since the process begins in the first state the initial state probabilities are $\pi(0) = (1, 0, \ldots, 0)$, so that

(3) $$\pi_i(n) = H(n)[1, i], \quad 1 \le i \le n_m.$$

R. Howard shows in [3] that $H(n) = S + T(n)$, where the matrix $T(n)$ representing the transient behavior of the process tends to zero as n becomes very large. The stochastic matrix S is the steady-state component that arises from a term of $(I - zP)^{-1}$ of the form $1/(1-z)$. The i-th row of S represents the limiting state probability distribution that would exist if the system were started in the i-th state.

The last k_m rows of matrix P are the vectors $e_{n_m-k_m+1}, \ldots, e_{n_m}$ from the canonical base of $\mathbb{R}^{n_m}$, therefore we can express P as

$$P = \begin{pmatrix} A & B \\ 0 & I \end{pmatrix}$$

where the region 0 consists entirely of zeroes, I is the identity matrix of k_m dimension, $A \in \mathcal{M}_{n_m-k_m}(\mathbb{R}[p])$, $B \in \mathcal{M}_{n_m-k_m,k_m}(\mathbb{R}[p])$. (Here $\mathbb{R}[p]$ denotes the ring of real polynomials in the variable p.)
Hence we obtain

$$I - zP = \begin{pmatrix} I - zA & -zB \\ 0 & (1-z)I \end{pmatrix}.$$

From Laplace's rule we have

$$\det(I - zP) = \det(I - zA) \cdot \det((1-z)I) = (1-z)^{k_m} \widetilde{Q}(z,p)$$

where we have denoted $\det(I - zA) = \widetilde{Q}(z,p) \in \mathbb{R}[z,p]$, $\deg_p \widetilde{Q}(z,p) = n_m - k_m$.

Lemma 1. *The relation $\widetilde{Q}(1,p) \neq 0$ holds true.*

Proof. In any finite Markov chain the probability that after n steps the process is in an ergodic state tends to 1 as n tends to infinity. The $(n_m - k_m) \times (n_m - k_m)$ matrix A concerns the process as long as it stays in transient states, hence its powers tend to 0. We consider the identity

$$(I - A) \cdot (I + A + A^2 + \cdots + A^{n-1}) = I - A^n,$$

whose right side tends to I. Thus, for sufficiently large n, the determinant of the matrix $I - A^n$ must be non-zero, therefore the determinant of the matrix $I - A$ cannot be zero.
But $\widetilde{Q}(1,p) = \det(I - A)$, so that $\widetilde{Q}(1,p) \neq 0$, which completes the proof.

Let $R_i = \lim_{n\to\infty} \pi_i(n)$ be the probability of an absorption in the state i when the system has started from state 1. From (3) it follows that $R_i = \lim_{n\to\infty} H(n)[1,i]$. Now we are able to prove the following

Theorem 2.1 *There exist $Q(p) \in \mathbb{R}[p]$ and $Q_i(p) \in \mathbb{R}[p]$, $n_m - k_m \leq i \leq n_m$, with $\deg Q = n_m - k_m$, $\deg Q_i < n_m - k_m$ such that*

$$R_i = \frac{Q_i(p)}{Q(p)}, \quad i = n_m - k_m + 1, \ldots, n_m.$$

Proof. Let M_i be the matrix obtained from matrix $I - zP$ by deleting the first column and the i-th row. Therefore $\det(M_i) = (1-z)^{k_m-1}\widetilde{Q}_i(z,p)$ for $n_m - k_m \leq i \leq n_m$, where $\widetilde{Q}_i(z,p) \in \mathbb{R}[z,p]$, $\deg_p \widetilde{Q}_i(z,p) < n_m - k_m$. We have

$$(I-zP)^{-1}[1,i] = \frac{(-1)^{i+1}\det M_i}{\det(I-zP)} = \frac{(-1)^{i+1}(1-z)^{k_m-1}\widetilde{Q}_i(z,p)}{(1-z)^{k_m}\widetilde{Q}(z,p)} = \frac{(-1)^{i+1}\widetilde{Q}_i(z,p)}{(1-z)\widetilde{Q}(z,p)}$$

which is a function of z with a factorable denominator. By partial fraction expansion

$$\frac{(-1)^{1+i}\widetilde{Q}_i(z,p)}{(1-z)\widetilde{Q}(z,p)} = \frac{T_i(p)}{1-z} + \frac{S_i(z,p)}{\widetilde{Q}(z,p)}$$

where $T_i(p)$ is a rational fraction in the variable p. It follows that

$$T_i(p)\widetilde{Q}(z,p) + (1-z)S_i(z,p) = (-1)^{i+1}\widetilde{Q}_i(z,p).$$

For $z = 1$ we obtain $T_i(p)\widetilde{Q}(1,p) = (-1)^{i+1}\widetilde{Q}_i(1,p)$. Since by lemma (1) $\widetilde{Q}(1,p) \neq 0$, we have

$$T_i(p) = (-1)^{i+1}\frac{\widetilde{Q}_i(1,p)}{\widetilde{Q}(1,p)}, \quad n_m - k_m < i \leq n_m. \tag{4}$$

Let us make the notation $Q_i(p) = (-1)^{i+1}\widetilde{Q}_i(1,p)$ and $Q(p) = \widetilde{Q}(1,p)$. Since $H(n)$ is the inverse transform of $(I-zP)^{-1}$ and $R_i = \lim_{n\to\infty} H(n)[1,i]$, we have from [3] that R_i equals the coefficient of $\frac{1}{1-z}$ in the expansion of $(I-zP)^{-1}[1,i]$ and therefore $R_i = T_i(p)$. Now by (4) we have the desired representation of R_i.

In an absorbing chain the limiting probabilities of the transient states are zero, therefore the sum of the absorption probabilities is 1. Since the states $\{l_1, l_2\}$ with $l_1 + l_2$ are absorbing, it follows that $\sum_{i=n_m-k_m+1}^{n_m} R_i = 1$. But $R_i, n_m - k_m < i \leq n_m$ are the limiting probabilities of the states $\{k_1, k_2\}$, hence we have obtained a representation of the distribution of (k_1, k_2) depending on p.

3 Examples

In [4] Knuth mentions the probability distribution of (k_1, k_2) for $m = 4$ and notes that the difference between k_1 and k_2 tends to increase as p increases. We shall further analyze the case $m = 5$. The ordered set of states is $S = \{\{0,0\},\{0,1\},\{0,2\},\{1,1\},\{0,3\},\{1,2\},\{0,4\},\{1,3\},\{2,2\},\{0,5\},\{1,4\},\{2,3\}\}$. The transition probability matrix is

$$P = \begin{pmatrix}
p & 1-p & 0 & 0 & 0 & 0 & 0 & 0 & 0 & 0 & 0 & 0 \\
\frac{p}{2} & \frac{p}{2} & \frac{1-p}{2} & \frac{1-p}{2} & 0 & 0 & 0 & 0 & 0 & 0 & 0 & 0 \\
0 & \frac{p}{2} & \frac{p}{2} & 0 & \frac{1-p}{2} & \frac{1-p}{2} & 0 & 0 & 0 & 0 & 0 & 0 \\
0 & p & 0 & 0 & 0 & 1-p & 0 & 0 & 0 & 0 & 0 & 0 \\
0 & 0 & \frac{p}{2} & 0 & \frac{p}{2} & 0 & \frac{1-p}{2} & \frac{1-p}{2} & 0 & 0 & 0 & 0 \\
0 & 0 & \frac{p}{2} & \frac{p}{2} & 0 & 0 & 0 & \frac{1-p}{2} & \frac{1-p}{2} & 0 & 0 & 0 \\
0 & 0 & 0 & 0 & \frac{p}{2} & 0 & \frac{p}{2} & 0 & 0 & \frac{1-p}{2} & \frac{1-p}{2} & 0 \\
0 & 0 & 0 & 0 & \frac{p}{2} & \frac{p}{2} & 0 & 0 & 0 & 0 & \frac{1-p}{2} & \frac{1-p}{2} \\
0 & 0 & 0 & 0 & 0 & p & 0 & 0 & 0 & 0 & 0 & 1-p \\
0 & 0 & 0 & 0 & 0 & 0 & 0 & 0 & 0 & 1 & 0 & 0 \\
0 & 0 & 0 & 0 & 0 & 0 & 0 & 0 & 0 & 0 & 1 & 0 \\
0 & 0 & 0 & 0 & 0 & 0 & 0 & 0 & 0 & 0 & 0 & 1
\end{pmatrix}.$$

The quantities R_{10}, R_{11}, R_{12} are the limiting probability distribution of states $\{0,5\}, \{1,4\}, \{2,3\}$. We have

$$\widetilde{Q}(1,p) = -\frac{(p^4 - 17p^3 + 68p^2 - 96p + 64)(p-1)^5}{64},$$

$$\widetilde{Q}_{10}(1,p) = \begin{vmatrix}
p-1 & 0 & 0 & 0 & 0 & 0 & 0 & 0 & 0 \\
1-\frac{p}{2} & \frac{p-1}{2} & \frac{p-1}{2} & 0 & 0 & 0 & 0 & 0 & 0 \\
\frac{-p}{2} & 1-\frac{p}{2} & 0 & \frac{p-1}{2} & \frac{p-1}{2} & 0 & 0 & 0 & 0 \\
-p & 0 & 1 & 0 & p-1 & 0 & 0 & 0 & 0 \\
0 & \frac{-p}{2} & 0 & 1-\frac{p}{2} & 0 & \frac{p-1}{2} & \frac{p-1}{2} & 0 & 0 \\
0 & \frac{-p}{2} & \frac{-p}{2} & 0 & 1 & 0 & \frac{p-1}{2} & \frac{p-1}{2} & 0 \\
0 & 0 & 0 & \frac{-p}{2} & 0 & 1-\frac{p}{2} & 0 & 0 & \frac{p-1}{2} \\
0 & 0 & 0 & \frac{-p}{2} & \frac{-p}{2} & 0 & 1 & 0 & 0 \\
0 & 0 & 0 & 0 & -p & 0 & 0 & 1 & 0
\end{vmatrix}$$

$$= \frac{(p^3 - p^2 + 4)(p-1)^5}{64},$$

$$\widetilde{Q}_{11}(1,p) = \begin{vmatrix}
p-1 & 0 & 0 & 0 & 0 & 0 & 0 & 0 & 0 \\
1-\frac{p}{2} & \frac{p-1}{2} & \frac{p-1}{2} & 0 & 0 & 0 & 0 & 0 & 0 \\
\frac{-p}{2} & 1-\frac{p}{2} & 0 & \frac{p-1}{2} & \frac{p-1}{2} & 0 & 0 & 0 & 0 \\
-p & 0 & 1 & 0 & p-1 & 0 & 0 & 0 & 0 \\
0 & \frac{-p}{2} & 0 & 1-\frac{p}{2} & 0 & \frac{p-1}{2} & \frac{p-1}{2} & 0 & 0 \\
0 & \frac{-p}{2} & \frac{-p}{2} & 0 & 1 & 0 & \frac{p-1}{2} & \frac{p-1}{2} & 0 \\
0 & 0 & 0 & \frac{-p}{2} & 0 & 1-\frac{p}{2} & 0 & 0 & \frac{p-1}{2} \\
0 & 0 & 0 & \frac{-p}{2} & \frac{-p}{2} & 0 & 1 & 0 & \frac{p-1}{2} \\
0 & 0 & 0 & 0 & -p & 0 & 0 & 1 & 0
\end{vmatrix}$$

$$= -\frac{(3p^3 - 16p^2 + 25p - 20)(p-1)^5}{64},$$

$$\tilde{Q}_{12}(1,p) = \begin{vmatrix} p-1 & 0 & 0 & 0 & 0 & 0 & 0 & 0 & 0 \\ 1-\frac{p}{2} & \frac{p-1}{2} & \frac{p-1}{2} & 0 & 0 & 0 & 0 & 0 & 0 \\ \frac{-p}{2} & 1-\frac{p}{2} & 0 & \frac{p-1}{2} & \frac{p-1}{2} & 0 & 0 & 0 & 0 \\ -p & 0 & 1 & 0 & p-1 & 0 & 0 & 0 & 0 \\ 0 & \frac{-p}{2} & 0 & 1-\frac{p}{2} & 0 & \frac{p-1}{2} & \frac{p-1}{2} & 0 & 0 \\ 0 & \frac{-p}{2} & \frac{-p}{2} & 0 & 1 & 0 & \frac{p-1}{2} & \frac{p-1}{2} & 0 \\ 0 & 0 & 0 & \frac{-p}{2} & 0 & 1-\frac{p}{2} & 0 & 0 & 0 \\ 0 & 0 & 0 & \frac{-p}{2} & \frac{-p}{2} & 0 & 1 & 0 & \frac{p-1}{2} \\ 0 & 0 & 0 & 0 & -p & 0 & 0 & 1 & p-1 \end{vmatrix}$$

$$= \frac{(p^4 - 15p^3 + 53p^2 - 71p + 40)(p-1)^5}{64}.$$

Therefore

$$R_{10} = \frac{p^3 - p^2 + 4}{p^4 - 17p^3 + 68p^2 - 96p + 64},$$

$$R_{11} = -\frac{3p^3 - 16p^2 + 25p - 20}{p^4 - 17p^3 + 68p^2 - 96p + 64},$$

$$R_{12} = \frac{p^4 - 15p^3 + 53p^2 - 71p + 40}{p^4 - 17p^3 + 68p^2 - 96p + 64}.$$

For $m = 6$ the Markov chain has 16 states and the quantities $R_{13}, R_{14}, R_{15}, R_{16}$ represent the limiting probability distribution of the absorbing states $\{0,6\}$, $\{1,5\}$, $\{2,4\}$, $\{3,3\}$. Similar calculations lead to

$$R_{13} = -\frac{p^4 - 5p^3 + 4p^2 - 4}{2(p^6 - 9p^5 + 44p^4 - 120p^3 + 192p^2 - 160p + 64)},$$

$$R_{14} = \frac{3p^4 - 16p^3 + 41p^2 - 44p + 24}{2(p^6 - 9p^5 + 44p^4 - 120p^3 + 192p^2 - 160p + 64)},$$

$$R_{15} = \frac{p^6 - 9p^5 + 45p^4 - 125p^3 + 196p^2 - 160p + 60}{2(p^6 - 9p^5 + 44p^4 - 120p^3 + 192p^2 - 160p + 64)},$$

$$R_{16} = \frac{p^6 - 9p^5 + 41p^4 - 104p^3 + 151p^2 - 116p + 40}{2(p^6 - 9p^5 + 44p^4 - 120p^3 + 192p^2 - 160p + 64)}.$$

As $p \to 1$ we obtain $R_{10} = 1/5, R_{11} = R_{12} = 2/5$ for $m = 5$ and $R_{13} = R_{16} = 1/6, R_{14} = R_{15} = 2/6$ for $m = 6$, which shows that in both cases the distribution of k_1 becomes uniform when p approaches unity.

Acknowledgment

I am grateful to Professor Monica Dumitrescu who read and criticised a previous version of this paper.

References

1. A. Brauer: Limits for the characteristic roots of a matrix. IV : Applications to stochastic matrices, *Duke Math. J.* , **19**, 75–91 (1952).
2. W. Feller: *An Introduction to Probability Theory and Its Applications*, vol.I, Wiley& Sons (1960).
3. R. A. Howard: *Dynamic Programming and Markov Processes*, Wiley& Sons (1962).
4. D. E. Knuth: *The Art of Computer Programming*, Addison Wesley (1969).
5. J. G. Kemeny, J. L. Snell: *Finite Markov Chains*, Springer-Verlag (1976).

Author Index

A

Adolphe K. 195
Aichholzer O. 752
Alberts D. 752
Andreoli J. M. 762
Andrews K. 206
Anklesaria F. X. 235
Aranha R. F. M. 633
Asserrhine J. 454
Aurenhammer F. 752

B

Bacher C. 706
Bajard J.-C. 436
Balázs J. 339
Banach R. 339
Borghoff U. M. 762
Brackett P. 195
Bulitko V. 151

C

Cailliau R. 221
Calude C. 48
Carlson P. 156, 571
Chesneaux J. 454
Csuhaj-Varju E. 252
Culik II K. 675

D

Daumas M. 162
Doran R.W. 176
Duval E. 269, 687

F

Fenwick P. 2, 591
Flinn B. 35
Freund R. 105

G

Gärtner B. 752
Ganster H. 614
Götze D. 232
Gutwin C. 195

H

Honkala J. 131, 652

J

Jameson D. 269
Jézéquel F. 469
Jones M. 195

K

Kappe F. 84, 206
Kari J. 675
Klauser A. 399
Kornerup P. 484, 527
Kuich W. 131

L

Lamotte J. 454
Larralde V. 156
Lennon J. 410, 719
Leppänen V. 23
Lester D. 504
Lynch T. 439

M

Markov S. 514

Mateescu A. 292, 790
Matula D. 484
Maurer H. 35, 206, 719
Mayerwieser W. 728
Mazenc C. 162
McCahill M. P. 235
Merrheim X. 162
Michelucci D. 436
Moreau J.-M. 436
Mülner H. 247
Muller J.-M. 162, 436

N

Nielsen A. 527

O

Olivié H. 269, 687
Ottmann T. 706
O'Hanlon P. 269

P

Pam A. 744
Panaitopol L. 603
Pandu Rangan C. 633
Papadopoulos G. 339
Pareschi R. 762
Păun G. 67, 105, 252, 790
Pavec R. 548
Pinz A. 614
Platzner M. 811
Popova E. 560
Posch K.C. 728
Posch R. 399, 728
Prantl M. 614

R

Rinner B. 811
Rozenberg G. 67, 790

S

Salomaa A. 67, 252, 292, 790
Salomaa K. 292
Scherbakov N. 687
Schindler V. 728
Schlichter J. H. 762
Schulte M. 439
Seberry J. 136
Shearer J. 312
Stefănescu C. 821
Stefănescu D. 603
Svozil K. 201

T

Tomek I. 423

V

Vermeer A. 312, 410, 744

W

Wang D. 658
Weiss R. 811

Y

Yu S. 292

Z

Zhang X. 136, 320
Zheng Y. 136, 320

This CD-ROM contains the complete Volume 1 (1995) of J.UCS which is based on Hyper-G. The Hyper-G client "Amadeus" is also included on this CD-ROM and will be installed together with J.UCS. The files are stored in the directory `JUCS`. Windows is required.

Please refer to the `README` file in the `JUCS` directory for installation instructions.

Please note:

Amadeus is a native Win32 application. If you install it under Windows 3.1x, the setup will also copy Win32s and WinG extensions in your `WINDOWS/SYSTEM` directory. Older versions of Win32s will be overwritten. Problems with some versions of the Mosaic browser (if older than version 2.0) could occur.